LEARNING AND MEMORY: A COMPREHENSIVE REFERENCE

LEARNING AND MEMORY: A COMPREHENSIVE REFERENCE

Volume 1
LEARNING THEORY AND BEHAVIOUR

Volume Editor
Randolf Menzel
Institut für Biologie – Neurobiologie, Freie Universität Berlin, Berlin, Germany

Editor-in-Chief
John H. Byrne
Department of Neurobiology & Anatomy, The University of Texas Medical School at Houston, Houston, Texas, USA

ELSEVIER

AMSTERDAM BOSTON HEIDELBERG LONDON NEW YORK OXFORD
PARIS SAN DIEGO SAN FRANCISCO SINGAPORE SYDNEY TOKYO

Academic Press is an imprint of Elsevier
The Boulevard, Langford Lane, Kidlington, Oxford OX5 1GB, UK
525 B Street, Suite 1900, San Diego, CA 92101-4495, USA

First edition 2008

Notice
No responsibility is assumed by the publisher for any injury and/or damage to persons
or property as a matter of products liability, negligence or otherwise, or from any use
or operation of any methods, products, instructions or ideas contained in the material
herein, Because of rapid advances in the medical sciences, in particular, independent
verfication of diagnoses and drug dosages should be made

British Library Cataloguing in Publication Data
A catalogue record for this book is available from the British Library

Library of Congress Catalog Number: 2008922261

ISBN: 978-012-370504-4

For information on all Elsevier publications
visit our website at books.elsevier.com

Printed and bound in Slovenia

07 08 09 10 11 10 9 8 7 6 5 4 3 2 1

Working together to grow
libraries in developing countries

www.elsevier.com | www.bookaid.org | www.sabre.org

ELSEVIER   BOOK AID International   Sabre Foundation

Contents

Contributors to Volume 1

B. W. Balleine
University of California, Los Angeles, CA, USA

P. R. Benjamin
University of Sussex, East Sussex, UK

A. P. Blaisdell
University of California at Los Angeles, Los Angeles, CA, USA

L. Borrelli
Stazione Zoologica A. Dohrn, Naples, Italy

M. E. Bouton
University of Vermont, Burlington, VT, USA

C. Broglio
Universidad de Sevilla, Sevilla, Spain

E. J. Capaldi
Purdue University, West Lafayette, IN, USA

J.-P. Changeux
URACNRS 2182, Collège de France and Institut Pasteur, Paris, France

K. Cheng
Macquarie University, Sydney, NSW, Australia

N. S. Clayton
Cambridge University, Cambridge, UK

S. Corkin
Massachusetts Institute of Technology, Cambridge, MA, USA, and Massachusetts General Hospital, Boston, MA, USA

J. D. Crystal
University of Georgia, Athens, Georgia, USA

P. Dalton
Royal Holloway University of London, Egham, Surrey, UK

R. J. De Marco
Freie Universität Berlin, Berlin, Germany

S. Dehaene
Collège de France, Paris, France; and INSERM-CEA Cognitive Neuroimaging Unit, Neurospin Center, Gif-sur-Yvette, France

A. Dickinson
Cambridge University, Cambridge, UK

M. Domjan
University of Texas at Austin, Austin, TX, USA

A. S. Dunlap
University of Minnesota, St. Paul, MN, USA

E. Durán
Universidad de Sevilla, Sevilla, Spain

D. Eisenhardt
Freie Universität Berlin, Berlin, Germany

G. Fiorito
Stazione Zoologica A. Dohrn, Naples, Italy

J. Fischer
German Primate Center, Göttingen, Germany

N. Fortin
Boston University, Boston, MA, USA

C. R. Gallistel
Rutgers University, Piscataway, NJ, USA

B. Gerber
Universität Würzburg, Würzburg, Germany

A. C. Giles
University of British Columbia, Vancouver, BC, Canada

M. Giurfa
CNRS, Université Paul Sabatier, Toulouse, France

A. Gómez
Universidad de Sevilla, Sevilla, Spain

M. K. Goode
Washington University in St. Louis, St. Louis, MO, USA

K. L. Gould
Luther College, Decorah, IA, USA

G. Hall
University of York, York, UK

M. E. Hasselmo
Boston University, Boston, MA, USA

M. Heisenberg
Universität Würzburg, Würzburg, Germany

M. L. Howe
Lancaster University, Lancaster, UK

J. Jozefowiez
Duke University, Durham, NC, USA

A. C. Kamil
University of Nebraska-Lincoln, Lincoln, NE, USA

E. J. Kehoe
University of New South Wales, Sydney, NSW, Australia

G. Kemenes
University of Sussex, East Sussex, UK

E. A. Kensinger
Boston College, Chestnut Hill, MA, USA

R. A. Koene
Boston University, Boston, MA, USA

O. F. Lazareva
University of Iowa, Iowa City, IA, USA

P. Marler
University of California at Davis, Davis, CA, USA

A. Martins
Purdue University, West Lafayette, IN, USA

R. Menzel
Freie Universität Berlin, Berlin, Germany

R. R. Miller
State University of New York at Binghamton, Binghamton, NY, USA

S. B. Moldakarimov
Salk Institute for Biological Studies, La Jolla, CA, USA

L. Nadel
University of Arizona, Tuscon, AZ, USA

S. B. Ostlund
University of California, Los Angeles, CA, USA

C. H. Rankin
University of British Columbia, Vancouver, BC, Canada

F. Rodríguez
Universidad de Sevilla, Sevilla, Spain

H. L. Roediger, III
Washington University in St. Louis, St. Louis, MO, USA

E. T. Rolls
University of Oxford, Oxford, UK

C. Salas
Universidad de Sevilla, Sevilla, Spain

L. H. Salwiczek
Cambridge University, Cambridge, UK

S. J. Sara
Collège de France, Paris, France

T. J. Sejnowski
Salk Institute for Biological Studies and University of California at San Diego, La Jolla, CA, USA

W. Singer
Max Planck Institute for Brain Research, Frankfurt am Main, Germany

C. Spence
University of Oxford, Oxford, UK

J. E. R. Staddon
Duke University, Durham, NC, USA

D. W. Stephens
University of Minnesota, St. Paul, MN, USA

N. Stollhoff
Freie Universität Berlin, Berlin, Germany

G. P. Urcelay
State University of New York at Binghamton, Binghamton, NY, USA

E. A. Wasserman
University of Iowa, Iowa City, IA, USA

N. E. Winterbauer
University of California, Los Angeles, CA, USA

A. M. Woods
University of Vermont, Burlington, VT, USA

F. M. Zaromb
Washington University in St. Louis, St. Louis, MO, USA

Contents List of All Volumes

FOREWORD

A comprehensive reference work on learning and memory could not be better timed than this. During the second half of the twentieth century, the study of learning and memory moved from a descriptive science largely based on the pioneering behavioral analyses of Pavlov, Thorndike, Watson, Skinner, Kamin, Rescorla, and Wagner to a new mechanistic science of mind that combines these brilliant behavioral studies with an analysis of the underlying neural mechanisms, first in a regional manner by Milner, Tulving, Mishkin, Squire, Schachter, and Morris, then on the cellular level, and finally on the molecular level.

The challenges that now face the field are outlined by the five great pioneers in the study of memory – the editor-in-chief Jack Byrne and the editors of these four extraordinary volumes: *Learning Theory and Behavior*, edited by Randolf Menzel; *Cognitive Psychology of Memory*, edited by Henry Roediger; *Memory Systems*, edited by Howard Eichenbaum; and *Molecular Mechanisms of Memory*, edited by David Sweatt. The challenge faced by the contributors to these volumes was to combine the molecular mechanisms with the other three levels in order to provide a coherent, systematically and intellectually satisfying understanding of learning and memory. This is central to the new science of mind. Since memory is the glue that holds our mental life together, the topics covered by these four volumes are central to and paradigmatic for all aspects of the neurobiology of mental life, which has as its goal the understanding of all mental processes in neurobiological terms. Indeed, it is the plasticity of the brain that is the key to understanding the continuity of all mental function. The goal for each of these four volumes was to bridge the subdisciplines concerned with the various forms of memory into a coherent science. The chapters of each of these volumes succeed admirably in doing just that. As a result, this rich and rewarding reference work will serve as a superb framework for the decades ahead, a reference that will provide both the student and the working scientist with the intellectual background necessary to understand and function effectively in the study of learning and memory.

Eric R. Kandel, M.D.
University Professor, Fred Kavli Professor and Director, Kavli Institute for Brain Sciences
Senior Investigator, Howard Hughes Medical Institute, Center for Neurobiology and Behavior
Columbia University, New York, NY, USA

PREFACE

Learning and Memory: A Comprehensive Reference is the most authoritative set of volumes ever produced on learning and memory and represents the state of the science in the early 21st century. The study of learning (the process of acquiring new information) and memory (retention of that information for future use) has intrigued philosophers and writers for centuries because our memories and plans for the future consolidate who we are, and disruption of these processes dramatically interferes with our daily lives. The fascination with learning and memory is not limited to the humanities, but has been the subject of intense scientific research. Psychologists are concerned with elucidating the features of learning and memory processes and systems, neurobiologists seek to determine the neuronal mechanisms of learning and memory, and neurologists and psychiatrists focus on research and treatment of failures or disruptions in learning and memory.

The study of learning and memory represents a scientific field that has matured at all levels – from the discovery of the protein chemistry and molecular biology of the cellular events underlying learning and memory, through the delineations of the properties and functions of neuronal networks, to formulating and testing the psychological and behavioral neuroscientific theories of learning and memory. In addition, many basic research findings have applied implications on such diverse fronts as education, legal issues hinging on eyewitness testimony, learning disorders in children, memory disorders following brain damage, and declines in memory in older adults.

The volumes in this *Comprehensive Reference* are the result of a meeting in London in July of 2005 where the editors planned the massive work of consolidating all facets of the study of learning and memory. We collected nearly all the topics (albeit from many different disciplines and directions) that we considered constituted scientific approaches to learning and memory and proceeded to parcel the topics into four volumes, resulting in *Learning Theory and Behavior* edited by Randolf Menzel; *Cognitive Psychology of Memory* edited by Henry Roediger III; *Memory Systems* edited by Howard Eichenbaum; and *Molecular Mechanisms of Memory* edited by David Sweatt. This was a formidable task, not only because of the richness and diversity of the subject matter, but also because we needed to logically place topics in the appropriate volume. Although some of the decisions may seem arbitrary, and indeed there is overlap both within and between volumes, each editor ended up with a set of coherent topics that they could organize and introduce in a logical manner.

With approximately 40 chapters per volume, it is no surprise that the editors cover an unusually wide range of intellectual territory or that there is a difference in interpretation by some authors. The organization is a significant editorial challenge and investment in and of itself. However, it is the editor's selection of authors, and the ensuing scholarship on learning and memory from different perspectives, that make this series unique. Authors were identified and invited based on their expertise on a particular topic, and their contributions represent a marvelous compendium of research in learning and memory. The chapters in this series not only represent scientific strength and breadth, but also range from learning at the synaptic level to a systems level approach, and include studies of remarkable learning capabilities in a variety of invertebrates and vertebrates, including human beings.

The first volume in the series, *Learning Theory and Behavior* edited by Randolf Menzel, consists of 38 chapters and sets the tone for the interdisciplinary and comparative approach to the study of learning and memory. He introduces the volume by emphasizing both the value and the limitation of the comparative approach in natural and laboratory settings, stressing that we need information from the behaving animal as well as the neuronal structures in order to understand the processes involved in information storage and retrieval. Several chapters review progress from using animal models, including worms, molluscs, insects, rodents, birds, and nonhuman and human primates. In addition, concepts such as planning, decision-making, self-awareness and episodic-like memory, usually reserved for human beings, are discussed at several taxonomic levels. The final chapters take an engineering perspective and describe synthetic approaches, including modeling neuronal function and developing a concise theory of the brain.

The second volume, *Cognitive Psychology of Learning* edited by H. Roediger, is comprised of 48 chapters on various aspects of cognitive ability and the underlying neuroscience. The basics of attention, working memory, forgetting, false memories, remembering vs. knowing, the process of recognition, and episodic memory are covered. In addition, topics that are often not included in "memory" volumes deservedly receive attention here, e.g., learning of concepts and categories, learning of perceptual and motor skills, language learning, and implicit learning. This volume also covers memory processes throughout the human lifespan and includes chapters on individual differences in memory ability, both subnormal (learning disabilities) and supranormal (performance of mnemonists and experts in particular domains). Finally, chapters on applied aspects of memory research, dealing with such topics as eyewitness identification in the legal system and applications of research to educational issues, are included.

Volume 3, edited by H. Eichenbaum, consists of 29 chapters which represent a "progress report" on what we know about memory systems and their relationship to different parts of the brain. *Memory Systems* returns to a comparative approach of learning and memory. This volume introduces the concepts of multiple memory systems, and many chapters discuss in extensive detail the different features of declarative memory and their underlying brain structures. Procedural learning in humans and other animals is addressed, and a short section details the involvement of hormones and emotions on memory retention or loss. Finally, changes in memory systems associated with aging, disease processes, and drug use are addressed.

The final 42 chapters in Volume 4, *Molecular and Cellular Mechanisms of Memory* edited by J.D. Sweatt, represent a review of the state of the science of what we know at the systems, cell, and molecular levels on learning and memory formation, as well as providing a look at the emerging and future areas of investigation. Once again, this volume covers an impressive amount of information derived from studies at many taxonomic levels, from molecular associative learning mechanisms, through an array of studies on synaptic plasticity, to the cell level of fear conditioning.

The centrality of learning and memory to our daily lives has led to intense analysis by psychologists and neurobiologists for the past century, and it will undoubtedly remain at the forefront of research throughout this new century as well. It is our intention that this set of volumes will contribute significantly to the consolidation of this field, and it is meant as a resource for scientists and students interested in all facets of learning and memory. No other reference work covers so wide a territory and in so much depth.

Learning and Memory: A Comprehensive Reference would not have been possible without the tremendous work of the Editorial Board, who identified the topics and their authors, and reviewed each contribution. Special thanks also go to Johannes Menzel, Senior Acquisitions Editor at Elsevier, for supporting the project and Andrew Lowe and Laura Jackson, Production Project Managers, and Joanna De Souza, Developmental Editor, for ensuring that the production schedule was maintained.

John H. Byrne

1.01 Introduction and Overview

R. Menzel, Freie Universität Berlin, Berlin, Germany

1.01.1 Introduction

The central question of behavioral neuroscience is: What is the source of information that creates and controls perception, reaction, and action in animals and humans?

Since Plato and Aristotle, Western philosophy has found two opposing answers that still guide our thinking today. Idealism proposes preexisting information unfolding as the organism develops, whereas empiricism states that all information is gathered by the interaction of the organism with the environment. As behavioral science developed into its modern form in the second half of the nineteenth century, these two philosophical approaches provided the epistemological framework for two different experimental approaches to animal behavior. Ethology emphasized the preexisting information inherited from the evolution of the species, whereas behaviorism, including Pavlov's physiology-driven approach, focused on collecting information through perception and action. Reference to idealism and empiricism gave these two opposing approaches a strong theoretical backbone, turning anthropomorphic descriptions of behavior and pure collections of observations into hypothesis-driven science. Ethology benefited from Darwin's theory of evolution that provided a conceptual framework for the accumulation and transmission of information, while behaviorism gained from the strength of laboratory-based experimentation and suitability for formal descriptions (*See* Chapters 1.03, 1.06). Although the history of the two behavioral science disciplines is a success story, we also know of their limitations and their failure to capture the breadth of behavior. The dualistic (and initially exclusive) conceptualization of the two forms of information that drive behavior is not adequate to explain brain functions. Regardless of the source of the information stored in the brain, it is expressed in properties of the brain, the wiring of neurons, and the communication between them. The two historical disciplines in behavioral science also failed to develop concepts that included brain functions. Ethology relied too heavily on simple-minded models of brain function, whereas behaviorism eliminated any reference to the brain.

In the end, behavior needs to be explained by underlying body functions, with the brain as the most important player in this game. Where are we now in such an attempt? This volume deals with behavior, theory, and system functions of the brain. Although cognitive neuroscience and the "emergent new science of mind" (Kandel, 2006) offer novel levels of integration between behavioral science and neuroscience, we still have a long way to go. The chapters in this volume should contribute to this exciting endeavor.

1.01.2 Biology of Learning and Memory: The Value of a Comparative Approach

Learning from experience is a property embedded into the survival strategies of all animals living in natural surroundings. Animal species live in different ecological niches, are equipped with different sensory and motor capacities, and communicate differently with other individuals of the same species and with other species (*See* Chapters 1.17, 1.20, 1.21, 1.22, 1.26, 1.31). They also come with different nervous systems, which can be large or small, and some are highly centralized, while others have several rather separate ganglia. There is no one model animal for this research endeavor, and different animal species have different advantages. One species can be reared more easily in the lab, another has a better-worked-out toolbox of molecular genetics, another provides for large and identifiable neurons or allows recordings from multiple neurons simultaneously over long periods of time, while another has already been analyzed in a wide range of behavioral tests. The main goal of this research is to unravel the general rules and species-specific adaptations in selecting relevant information, adding it to existing knowledge, storing it such that passing time does not eliminate it, and making it available for better-adapted behavioral acts in the future. Comparative studies provide the tool for identifying generalities and specificities.

Observing animals in their natural habitat can suggest relevant research questions (*See* Chapters 1.17, 1.20, 1.21, 1.22, 1.23, 1.25, 1.26, 1.29). While we have ideas about what is worth observing and measuring, we need to be open-minded about unexpected outcomes, as these are often the discoveries that propel research. Food-storing behavior in birds and mammals (*See* Chapters 1.22, 1.23), communication via gestures and/or sound (*See* Chapters 1.16, 1.17) or by ritualized movements in bees (*See* Chapters 1.12, 1.25, 1.29), learning during courtship in *Drosophila* (*See* Chapter 1.28), and navigation (*See* Chapters 1.20, 1.21, 1.25, 1.26) are examples, and many more will be described in this volume. The animal species studied are varied: Worms (*Caenorhabditis elegans*; *See* Chapter 1.32), mollusks (*Aplysia, Limax, Lymnea, Hermissenda*; *See* Chapter 1.30), cephalopods (octopus, *Sepia, Loligo*; *See* Chapter 1.31), insects (*Drosophila*, *See* Chapter 1.28; the honeybee *Apis*, *See* Chapters 1.12, 1.25, 1.29), rodents (e.g., mice, rats, squirrels, chipmunks, deer mice, Merriam's kangaroo rats; *See* Chapter 1.22), birds (e.g., Clark's nutcrackers, Eurasian nutcracker, marsh tits, black-capped chickadees, pinyon jays, Mexican jays, Western scrub jays, willow tits, crested tits, many song-learning bird species, the oscines of the Passeriform birds; *See* Chapters 1.17, 1.22, 1.23), and primates (chimpanzees, orangutans, macaques, vervet monkeys, baboons, capuchin monkeys, and pygmy marmosets; *See* Chapter 1.16), including human beings. Each of these species provides us with the opportunity to discover novel ways of solving similar problems brought about by an ever-changing environment and to unravel general strategies by comparison.

The transition from the natural habitat to the laboratory is an essential step in hypothesis-driven behavioral research, but is by no means a simple step (*See* Chapter 1.11). We cannot expect to get full control over the animal, which is sometimes a misleading assumption in some of the behavioral studies (*See* Chapters 1.03, 1.06, 1.10, 1.18). However, the history of an individual's experience can be traced more accurately in the laboratory, and the proper control experiments can be established. The chapters in this volume provide ample evidence for successful transition from the natural environment to the laboratory.

Often an additional and more critical step is required. Animals need to be constrained for physiological measurements, or they are genetically manipulated to isolate cellular components of neural function. It is essential to remember that constrained animals or genetically manipulated animals are no longer the living creatures that we observed in their natural environment, and they are not even those seen in the laboratory behavioral tests. It might not matter so much whether a nutcracker caches a nut in the bark of a tree or in a plastic Lego building block, but it will make a great deal of difference whether a chimpanzee learns to move between tree branches or is sitting in a training chair connected to amplifiers while performing stereotypical arm movements. It is true that in most cases we do not yet have alternatives attempting to relate neural function with behavioral performance, but while presently there are no better experimental tools of neural recording, we must not forget the distance between the natural conditions and the experimental surroundings where we collect data.

Invertebrates such as the nematode *C. elegans* (*See* Chapter 1.32), the mollusks *Limax* or *Aplysia* (*See* Chapter 1.30), the fly *Drosophila* (*See* Chapter 1.28), and the bee *Apis* (*See* Chapters 1.25, 1.27, 1.29) are of particular value in laboratory settings since the transitions from natural to laboratory to experimentally interfering conditions presumably impact them less. Intermediate transition steps from natural to laboratory conditions can be made more easily, and the behavior of these invertebrates appears to be controlled more strongly by innate components. Nevertheless, transgenic nematodes and flies are not normal animals with just one isolated function that has been modified. It is, therefore, very advantageous that transgenes in *C. elegans* and *Drosophila* can be switched on and off rather quickly, and even more important, can be genetically rescued, which allows us to test the isolation of the targeted effect very carefully. Transgenic mice are by far more complicated to analyze, and special care must be taken in interpreting their behavioral alterations.

Many questions about learning and memory cannot be moved into the laboratory, and these may often be the particularly interesting questions (*See* Chapters 1.16, 1.22). This has two consequences: (1) The data are correlational in nature as control groups often cannot be studied or serve as partial controls and animal manipulations are very difficult or impossible, and (2) recording brain functions is difficult or impossible. These limitations should not reduce our efforts to collect data under natural conditions, as these data are essential for future laboratory studies and for comparative studies in humans.

A comparative approach should include human beings, and the motivation of many animal studies is to better understand humans. This is justified if appropriate caution is taken and the general limitations of a comparative approach are observed. Both ethology and behaviorism carry their historical burdens regarding inappropriate generalizations between animals and humans (*See* Chapters 1.03, 1.10), but cognitive neuroscience offers tools and strategies that help to guide such comparisons. If processes and mechanisms have been identified that apply across animal species, they are less likely to be species-specific adaptations and can safely be generalized to humans (e.g., cellular and molecular processes of neural plasticity as discussed elsewhere in this work, or basic rules of associative learning (*See* Chapters 1.05, 1.06, 1.09, 1.10, 1.11, 1.18)). The involvement of homolog brain structures for related forms of learning and/or memory formation are strong hints for homolog function. The hippocampus (e.g., in the case of spatial learning and episodic-like memory) and the amygdala (e.g., in fear learning) are two examples, and many more will be found in the chapters of this volume (*See* Chapters 1.14, 1.15, 1.21, 1.22, 1.23). Comparison between animals with very different brain structures (e.g., mammals and insects) is much more difficult, and often no more than analog functions can be assumed (e.g., navigation according to a geometric representation of space, different forms of memories according to their time course, and susceptibility to experimental interference).

One of the most important and controversial issues related to comparison between animals and humans relates to language and self-awareness (*See* Chapters 1.15, 1.16, 1.23, 1.37, 1.38). Although language acquisition has deep biological roots, the relation to nonverbal or acoustic communication in monkeys is not yet understood (*See* Chapter 1.16). The neural requirements of self-awareness exist in animals (*See* Chapters 1.37, 1.38), but it is not clear whether additional neural functions are required for the human form of self-awareness. The case of episodic memory, as discussed in several chapters (*See* Chapters 1.21, 1.22, 1.23), is a particularly interesting example because essential features of knowledge about what happened, when it happened, and where it happened exist at different degrees of complexity in many animal species (e.g., in the honeybee; *See* Chapters 1.12, 1.25, 1.29). Food-storing birds appear to relate these memories to themselves and appear to expect to find food at that location in the future (*See* Chapter 1.23), showing a capacity that is close to personal recollection in humans. Salwiczek et al. (*See* Chapter 1.23) call this memory episodic-like and see a gradual, rather than a principle, difference with the introspective experience of mental time travel in humans. This pragmatic approach might be exemplary in the sense that other human mental functions could also be broken down into additive features, which could then be tested for their existence in animals in various combinations and complexities. However, the demonstration of the existence of the components does not prove that the full function of a cognitive faculty as observed (or personally experienced) in humans exists in a particular animal species. Nevertheless, the strength of this approach lies in the assumption that there are no categorical differences between animals and humans, and gradual differences can be traced to different performances according to the complexity of the elements found. An example could be dance communication in honeybees (*See* Chapters 1.12, 1.25, 1.29). The bee communicates a location, and depending on the context, the dance might indicate a feeding place, a water or resin resource, or a new nest site. Although the communication process is symbolic and has a vocabulary (although a very reduced one) and a form of syntax (context-dependence), it does not qualify as a language because it lacks essential features, for example, semantics and grammar. One might call it language-like, as one might categorize other symbolic indexical forms of communications, but the point is that a research program can be set up by this decomposition strategy which allows scientists to search for the related neural processes of the components rather than the mental faculty as a whole. It appears to me that a similar research strategy is proposed by Changeux and Dehaene (*See* Chapter 1.38) in their attempt to decompose conscious processing and learning. They propose a unified or global workspace for the neural synthesis of past, present, and expected experiences. Such research approaches are promising because they avoid the epistemological deadlock connected with the preoccupation of a categorical separation between animals and humans (MacPhail, 1998) or the assumption of equality between the animal mind and the human mind (Griffin, 1984).

1.01.3 Theories, Processes, and Mechanisms

Animal learning theory has been a rich research area over the last 60 years or so, and we may ask whether some of its concepts might join with physiological studies for a better understanding of the underlying processes. Theories derived from associative forms of learning have been elaborated the most (*See* Chapters 1.03, 1.06, 1.09, 1.10, 1.18), and it appears that three concepts are most useful in a search for functional implementations: associative strengths, associability, and prediction error (Dickinson, 2007).

1. Associative strength between two elements (stimulus or response) depends on the history of experience and the stimuli/responses involved and controls both acquisition and retrieval of memory. Although different behavioral theories compete for the best way of capturing the essence of associative strengths (e.g., Rescorla and Wagner, 1972; Pearce and Hall, 1980; Bouton, 1994; *See* Chapters 1.03, 1.06, 1.09), it is not yet clear whether unidirectional or bidirectional associations predict the relations between the elements. Neuroscientists are more than prepared to absorb this concept and translate it into processes of neural plasticity. Donald Hebb (1949) proposed such a neural implementation, and it is widely accepted that synaptic strength is closely related to associative strength (*See* Vol. 4). Long-term potentiation and long-term depression are processes that are based on the accurate timing of neural activity in the pre- and postsynaptic elements of neural nets (*See* Chapter 1.34).

The coincidence of spike activity as a means of modulating synaptic efficiency appears to play a role not only between pairs of pre- and postsynaptic neurons, but also in networks of many neurons. Singer (*See* Chapter 1.37) points out that coherence of spike activity is an essential feature of cortical nets in up- and downregulation of learning-related neural plasticity. It will be important to show that spike synchrony in biological networks is an emergent property similar to artificial networks (*See* Chapter 1.34) and to establish the causal relationship between these global network characteristics and learning. Since small networks composed of identified neurons do not depend on spike coherence in a global sense to establish associative changes in synaptic efficacy (e.g., in mollusks; *See* Chapter 1.30), it will be interesting to search for additional qualities of synchronizing neurons. Such additional qualities could lie in the fact that the three components of memory (formation, retrieval, and consolidation) are so tightly connected that only under conditions of synchronized activity are all three memory components activated. New contents can only be stored in distributed brain regions which jointly reorganize the network according to the new information.

2. Associability is another concept developed in behavioral learning theory that promises to be useful in neural studies. The concept captures the properties of the stimuli and/or outcomes that determine associative strengths as they are reflected in the salience of the stimulus, the predictability or surprise value of a stimulus, or the outcome. Cognitive dimensions of operant learning (*See* Chapters 1.06, 1.10) or perceptual learning (*See* Chapter 1.07) involve attention as a critical parameter of learning (*See* Chapter 1.13), a parameter that can be traced to particular structures (e.g., cholinergic projections from basal ganglia, amygdala, and the septohippocampal system).

3. Prediction error: Learning theories state that learning occurs as long as the outcome of a behavior is not fully predicted, and thus the deviation of the expected from the experienced outcome changes the current associative strengths. Behavioral theories differ with respect to their assumption of whether the error affects associative strength directly (e.g., Rescorla and Wagner, 1972; Mackintosh, 1975) or indirectly (Pearce and Hall, 1980). The implementation of the prediction error into machine learning (Sutton and Barto, 1990) has been very successful (*See* Chapters 1.34, 1.36), and strong neural correlates exist: for example, the neural properties of reward neurons (dopamine neurons of the mammalian ventral tegmentum (Schultz, 2006) and octopamine VUMmx1 neurons in the honeybee brain (Hammer, 1992; Menzel and Giurfa, 2001)).

When dealing with learning, several chapters in this volume draw their underlying concepts from both behavioral and neural data to document that the strongest expectations for an understanding of processes and mechanisms come from collecting experimental data from both behavioral and neural studies (Dickinson, 2007). How far will such a hybrid theory and understanding lead us?

Forty years ago, Kandel and Spencer wrote a seminal paper entitled "Cellular neurophysiological approaches in the study of learning," calling for a novel approach in translating basic psychological concepts of learning into strategies for the search for their neural implementations (Kandel and Spencer, 1968). Less than 20 years later, Hawkins and Kandel (1984) presented a first review on their finding on *Aplysia* associative and nonassociative learning and derived neural components comprising a cellular alphabet of learning (*See* Chapters 4.01, 4.02). This strategy has turned out to be most successful in localizing in space and time neural events induced by learning. It appears that the associative events are distributed, multifaceted, and dependent both on innate predispositions and earlier learning. *Drosophila* provides a particularly carefully studied case (*See* Chapter 4.07). Different neural structures are involved in learning the same odor by reward or punishment, and short- and long-term memories of the same content reside in different neural nets. Localizing the memory trace is an important step in a functional analysis.

A major unresolved issue in both behavioral and neural studies is the relationship between learning with and without external reinforcing or evaluating stimulus. As pointed out above, concise behavioral theories have been developed for Pavlovian and instrumental conditioning, but perceptual learning (*See* Chapter 1.07), navigational learning (*See* Chapters 1.12, 1.20, 1.25), and interval learning (*See* Chapter 1.19) provide cases in which no obvious external reinforcer may be present. Is associative learning a special case of a more general form of learning (the learning of temporal sequences; *See* Chapter 1.12), or is every kind of learning associative? Does an internal reinforcer provide the evaluating function in the latter forms of learning? Learning theory has not settled the debate, and it might well be that functional analysis will show that internal reinforcing circuits are active at the proper time when animals learn by observation. An important component in such forms of learning is attention (*See* Chapters 1.13, 1.36), as is assumed in a modeling study of navigational learning in the honeybee (Montague et al., 1995).

Only selectively attended stimuli are learned. Most importantly, modulatory circuits that appear to be involved in coding evaluating stimuli also participate in selective attention. It will be necessary to build conceptual bridges between the concept of associability as developed in theories of associative

learning and the evaluating property of directed attention as described in observational learning. Further advances will only be made with the combination of behavioral and neural approaches.

1.01.4 What Is Memory and What Is a Memory Trace?

The many facets of memory are reflected in the many terms used to capture them (*See* Chapters 1.02, 1.04). Are there 256 different kinds of memory, as Tulving (1972) asked? Irrespective of whether we divide up memories according to time, cellular mechanisms, brain structures involved, categories of contents, type of learning, or type of retrieval, we always imply that memory directs behavior via the process of retrieving information. As pointed out at the beginning of this chapter, brains are equipped with information before, and independent of, acquired information. Thus the content of memory provides a knowledge base for behavioral guidance (including perception, planning, expecting, and thinking), and splitting it up may obscure the basic and unifying property of memory. One question that needs to be asked, then, is: How do we go about measuring the knowledge stored in memory? We do not know, and this ignorance might be one of the reasons why so much emphasis is placed on the need to define memory by retrieval processes (*See* Chapters 1.02, 1.04, 1.12, 1.14, 1.15, 1.24). As long as measurement of memory content is based only on retrieving it from memory, we will not be able to separate stored memory from used memory.

Nadel (*See* Chapter 1.04) quotes from Aristotle's *Ars Memoria*: "It has already been stated that those who have a good memory are not identical to those who are quick at recollecting. But the act of recollecting differs from that of remembering, not only chronologically, but also in this – that many of the other animals (as well as man) also have memory, but of all that we are acquainted with, none, we venture to say, except man, shares in the faculty of recollection." Indeed, the distinction between memory and recollection is multifaceted (*See* Chapters 1.02, 1.04, 1.05, 1.14, 1.15, 1.24), and one of the most important distinctions relates to memory formation versus memory retrieval. Behavioral measures, as well as human subjective introspection, reach memory via retrieval, but the postlearning reactivation process can work only if learning left traces in the form of an engram. Since the process of memory formation is not directly accessible to behavioral studies, it has been seriously questioned from a behavioral analytical perspective, in terms of whether it makes sense to distinguish between memory as an entity independent of retrieval (*See* Chapters 1.04, 1.05). The notion of a physical memory trace, independent of its use, however, is a central presumption in neuroscience. Indeed, only when neurologically related interference procedures were introduced into memory research did a clear separation between memory formation and memory retrieval become possible. The key discovery in this context was the consolidation process.

Does a memory exist if it is not retrieved? This question is addressed in several chapters in this volume, and rather diverse opinions are expressed. If the knowledge stored in memory does not guide behavior, a behavioral biologist cannot know whether memory exists (and may thus define memory by its retrievability). But a neuroscientist cannot help but assume that the knowledge stored in memory continues to exist during time periods when it is not retrieved, because the physiological measures of memory are independent of whether the animal performs the corresponding behavior. The concept of memory consolidation is essential in this debate. Hermann Ebbinghaus (1964) described a fast and a slow component in forgetting, and William James (1890) proposed that these may be related to two forms of sequential memories: Primary and secondary memory. The concept of consolidation as a time-dependent process following learning was introduced by Müller and Pilzecker (1900) on the basis of their finding that new learning interfered with the formation of recently acquired memory for short, but not for long intervals. At this stage of analysis, a separation between an internal, time-dependent, and self-organizing process of memory formation and retrieval of memory was not possible, but when experimental interference was introduced and neurological cases of retrograde amnesia were analyzed, strong arguments in favor of an independent engram-building process could be presented (*See* Chapters 1.14, 1.15). However, the situation is not as simple as was believed (*See* Chapters 1.04, 1.05). For example, amnesia-inducing procedures could have led to competing learning processes. Irrespective of the unresolved questions in separating memory formation and memory retrieval processes, the body of evidence is overwhelming, proving that neural traces are indeed induced by the learning process independent of retrieval, and consolidation has a physical basis in the structuring and restructuring processes of neural net properties.

Procedures interfering with ordered neural activity or cellular metabolism during periods of consolidation induce retrograde amnesia. Memory gets better over time, even when it is not used. Sleep phases strengthen the consolidation process (Born et al., 2006) and are related to repetition of content-specific patterns of neural activity (Wilson and McNaughton, 1994). It appears to me that the debate about the nature of the memory trace (*See* Chapter 1.04) will continue as long as we cannot read the encoding processes and directly measure knowledge stored in neural nets. Once we can show these in suitable animals such as *Drosophila*, we will probably discover that, in addition to the constructive processes of reactivating memory and using its content, there is an essential component that exists independent of the reactivation process. Whether we like to call this lasting component memory is a question of definition.

Reactivation of memory leads to new learning and its subsequent consolidation processes (*See* Chapter 1.09). Only recently has neuroscience become interested in the mechanistic aspects of extinction learning and memory formation. The phenomena subsumed under the term reconsolidation provide case studies (*See* Chapters 1.24, 1.27). Reconsolidation refers to the effect that retrieving memory may lead to cue-dependent amnesia if the retrieval process is followed by treatment with an amnestic agent. What are these learning and reconsolidation processes? Does reactivation indeed make the old memory trace vulnerable to amnestic interference, indicating that new learning overwrites old memory, or do the learning processes involved in memory reactivation induce parallel consolidation processes that reflect the addition of a new memory trace to the existing one? The ongoing debate reflects the same dilemma addressed above. Our inability to measure knowledge as stored information directly restricts our mechanistic analysis to global and indirect arguments. Once again, behavioral analysis needs to be combined with fine-grained neural analysis addressing the critical question much more directly at the level of the neural elements of the engram.

What might be a suitable strategy toward a direct reading of knowledge? A first step should be to develop criteria that allow us to identify and localize a memory trace. Heisenberg and Gerber (*See* Chapter 1.28) address this question by defining four essential requirements of a memory trace:

1. Neuronal plasticity occurs in particular neurons that are localized and identified, and these neurons are essential for a particular kind of memory.
2. The neuronal plasticity in these neurons is necessary for this particular memory context.
3. Memory cannot be expressed if these neurons cannot contribute during retrieval.
4. Memory cannot be established if these neurons do not receive the required input for the memory content to be stored.

Note that this checklist of experimental procedures does not yet provide us with access to information stored in the memory trace, but we can hope that in a next step a localized and thus-characterized memory trace will be accessible to the really important question of how neural circuits encode and store particular pieces of information. So far only one organism, *Drosophila*, offers the opportunity to localize and characterize a memory trace at the level of cellular resolution, and, indeed, in applying this strategy to rather small neural circuits it was found that traces for short-term memory of an olfactory discrimination task and long-term forms of the same memory content appear to be localized in different, probably partially overlapping neural circuits. Furthermore, it was found that memory traces of appetitively or aversively evaluated stimuli of the same kind occupy different but partially overlapping neural circuits (*See* Chapter 1.28).

A whole battery of highly sophisticated molecular–genetic tools are available to measure the spatial–temporal patterns of memory traces in selected neurons and neural nets of the *Drosophila* brain (Keene and Waddell, 2007). Reading the dynamics of the neural elements during the learning process (i.e., consolidation and retrieval under conditions in which the animal tells us via its behavior whether it perceives, attends, and retrieves) will help us understand at least part of the knowledge stored in memory. How close are we then to direct knowledge reading?

Localizing and characterizing the memory trace by applying correlation analysis is the mainstream of the neuroscience approach today (*See* the volumes edited by Sweatt and Eichenbaum). Correlating elemental with system properties is an important step in any mechanistic analysis. The next step will be to establish closer, possibly causal, links following the strategy outlined by Heisenberg and Gerber (*See* Chapter 1.28). The tools also exist for the worm *C. elegans* (*See* Chapter 1.32) and are becoming available step by step for other species (e.g., the mouse). The hunt

for direct knowledge reading will be embedded in a concerted approach to understanding the workings of neural nets and the brain as a whole.

1.01.5 The Engineer's Approach to Learning and Memory

Engineers compose and biologists de-compose, so a combination of these two strategies should be favorable to the study of a complex system such as the brain. Constructive thinking in theoretical neuroscientists is inspired by rules derived from behavioral studies (e.g., Hebb's rule), by the morphology of brains and the connectivity patterns of neurons (e.g., the matrix-like connectivity in the hippocampus), by the functional properties of neurons (e.g., synaptic plasticity), and by theoretical concepts developed independently from, but motivated by, thoughts about how the brain might work (e.g., autoassociative or attractor networks). Our volume contains chapters dealing with all of these aspects (*See* Chapters 1.33, 1.34, 1.35, 1.37, 1.38). Irrespective of the intellectual pleasure one experiences when thinking about theoretical neural nets, one might ask how the joint efforts propel our understanding. I see the following points that are also well-illustrated in the respective chapters:

1. Hypothesis-driven research like ours requires well-formulated concepts and hypotheses. Theories developed for neural nets shape these concepts and allow us to formulate predictions (*See* Chapters 1.33, 1.35).
2. The analysis of the vast amounts of data collected by anatomical, electrophysiological, optophysiological, and molecular studies requires the contribution of theoretical neuroscientists to extract relevant information and interpret it (*See* Chapters 1.34, 1.37).
3. There exists no concise theory of the brain. Global brain functions need to be constructed from elemental and network functions and implemented into a model (e.g., the neuronal workspace model of Changeux and Dehaene; *See* Chapter 1.38).

At any of these levels of a modeling approach, one has to decide what is considered an essential feature and which of the many characteristics of the neurons, their connectivity at the local and the global level, are implemented or not. Should one use simplified integrate-and-fire neurons or Hodgkin-Huxley-type neurons? Should the model care about the real gestalt of neurons or not? How seriously should one take the neuroanatomical data on local and global connectivity? These and many other decisions are hard to make, and different choices produce serious debates about the suitability of these models. There are many measures of suitability: Are experiments stimulated, predictions offered, and interpretations of data supported or rejected? Five chapters (*See* Chapters 1.33, 1.34, 1.35, 1.37, 1.38) provide a range of examples where strong arguments can be presented for the suitability of the respective models and experimental approaches are suggested. Other examples are given in Vol. 4 that deal with small neural nets partially composed of identified neurons (*See* Chapter 1.30). Indeed, small biological neural nets (e.g., the stomatogastric ganglion in the lobster) have been successfully modeled, and the models in the electronic version were directly hooked up with the biological neural net to analyze the contribution of certain cellular properties (Golowasch et al., 1999). These approaches have been applied in the search for the neural implementation of operant learning in the buccal ganglion of *Aplysia* (Brembs et al., 2002; Vol. 4; *See* Chapter 4.10).

Given the technological advances with the expression of light-driven conductances in specified neurons (e.g., channel rhodopsin), similar analyses will be possible (e.g., in *Drosophila*; *See* Chapter 1.28), which emphasizes the need for theoretical concepts and models of the respective networks.

Ultimately, models of neural function should also predict behavioral outcomes. Singer (*See* Chapter 1.37) makes the case for the role of spike synchrony and oscillatory spike patterns in memory formation. Koene and Hasselmo (*See* Chapter 1.35) formulate predictions for the role of theta rhythm in the hippocampus for memory formation and retrieval, and Rolls (*See* Chapter 1.33) explicitly characterizes the properties of the autoassociative network of the hippocampus for behavioral phenomena such as completion and graceful degradation. It is to be expected that the success of the combined theoretical and experimental approach will make modeling an indispensable part of the search for the memory trace.

1.01.6 Conclusion

Curiosity-driven behavioral studies, theory-guided laboratory behavioral experiments, and modeling of neural functions define a unique workspace in the search for the engram. Joining forces will help, and the chapters presented here will hopefully facilitate

communication between these disciplines. The task is indeed demanding, because the goal will not only be to localize and characterize the memory trace, but to measure the knowledge stored in the memory trace independent of and in addition to the behavioral read-out process.

References

Born J, Rasch B, and Gais S (2006) Sleep to remember. *Neuroscientist* 12: 410–424.
Bouton ME (1994) Context, ambiguity, and classical conditioning. *Curr. Dir. Psychol. Sci.* 3: 49–53.
Brembs B, Lorenzetti FD, Reyes FD, Baxter DA, and Byrne JH (2002) Operant reward learning in *Aplysia*: Neuronal correlates and mechanisms. *Science* 296: 1706–1709.
Dickinson A (2007) Learning: The need for a hybrid theory. In: Roediger HL, Dudai Y, and Fitzpatrick SM (eds.) *Science of Memory: Concepts*, pp. 41–44. Oxford: Oxford University Press.
Ebbinghaus H (1964) *Memory: A Contribution to Experimental Psychology*, Ruger HA and Bussenius CE (trans.). New York: Dover [originally published in German in 1885].
Golowasch J, Casey M, Abbott LF, and Marder E (1999) Network stability from activity-dependent regulation of neuronal conductances. *Neural Comput.* 11: 1079–1096.
Griffin DR (1984) *Animal Thinking*. Cambridge, MA: Harvard University Press.
Hammer M (1992) A single identified neuron contributes to associative learning of olfactory cues in honey bees. In: Elsner N and Richter DW (eds.) *Rhythmogenesis in Neurons and Networks*, pp. 81–82. Stuttgart: Thieme Verlag.
Hawkins RD and Kandel ER (1984) Is there a cell-biological alphabet for simple forms of learning? *Psychol. Rev.* 91(3): 375–391.
Hebb DO (1949) *The Organization of Behavior: A Neuro-psychological Theory*. New York: Wiley.
James W (1890) *The Principles of Psychology*. New York: Holt.
Kandel ER (2006) *In Search of Memory – The Emergence of a New Science of Mind*. New York: Norton.
Kandel ER and Spencer WA (1968) Cellular neurophysiological approaches in the study of learning. *Physiol. Rev.* 48: 65–134.
Keene AC and Waddell S (2007) Drosophila olfactory memory: Single genes to complex neural circuits. *Nat. Rev. Neurosci.* 8: 341–354.
Mackintosh NJ (1975) A theory of attention: Variations in the associability of stimuli with reinforcement. *Psychol. Rev.* 82: 276–298.
MacPhail E (1998) *The Evolution of Consciousness*. Oxford: Oxford University Press.
Menzel R and Giurfa M (2001) Cognitive architecture of a mini-brain: The honeybee. *Trends Cogn. Sci.* 5: 62–71.
Montague PR, Dayan P, Person C, and Sejnowski TJ (1995) Bee foraging in uncertain environments using predictive hebbian learning. *Nature* 377: 725–728.
Müller GE and Pilzecker A (1900) Experimentelle Beiträge zur Lehre vom Gedächtnis. *Z. Psychol.* 1: 1–288.
Pearce JM and Hall G (1980) A model for Pavlovian learning: Variations in the effectiveness of conditioned but not of unconditioned stimuli. *Psychol. Rev.* 87: 522–525.
Rescorla RA and Wagner AR (1972) A theory of classical conditioning: Variations in the effectiveness of reinforcement

and non-reinforcement. In: Black AH and Prokasy WF (eds.) *Classical Conditioning II: Current Research and Theory*, pp. 64–99. New York: Appleton-Century-Crofts.

Schultz W (2006) Behavioral theories and the neurophysiology of reward. *Annu. Rev. Psychol.* 57: 87–115.

Sutton RS and Barto AG (1990) Time-derivative models of pavlovian reinforcement. In: Gabriel A and Moore J (eds.) *Learning and Computational Neuroscience: Foundations and Adaptive Networks*, pp. 497–567. Cambridge, MA: MIT Press.

Tulving E (1972) Episodic and semantic memory. In: Tulving E and Donaldson W (eds.) *Organization of Memory*, pp. 381–403. New York: Academic Press.

Wilson MA and McNaughton BL (1994) Reactivation of hippocampal ensemble memories during sleep. *Science* 265: 676–679.

1.02 A Typology of Memory Terms

H. L. Roediger, III, F. M. Zaromb, and M. K. Goode, Washington University in St. Louis, St. Louis, MO, USA

1.02.1 Introduction

The English language provides us with the term memory to denote several interrelated ideas, such as 'the power of the mind to remember things' or 'something remembered from the past; a recollection' (both quotes are from the Oxford American Dictionary). These definitions of memory are fine for everyday conversation and communication, but scientists interested in studying the biochemical, neural, or psychological underpinnings of this topic have found the need to describe many distinctions about memory that laypeople do not use. Such a need is further underscored by a growing interest in interdisciplinary approaches

to the study of human memory (*See* Chapters 3.05, 3.06, 3.14) and in adapting cognitive research paradigms to the study of nonhuman animal learning, an area that has developed largely in isolation of the human memory research tradition (e.g., Wright, 1998; Wright and Roediger, 2003; *See* Chapters 1.04, 1.13, 1.14, 1.15, 1.21, 1.22, 1.23). This chapter is intended to explain the meaning of some of the most popular terms that have been contributed to the literature.

We aim to paint with a fairly broad brush and not to get involved in matters such as whether one term (say, implicit memory) is to be preferred to another term (indirect memory), although buckets of ink have been spilt on these matters. Rather, we intend to provide general definitions and meanings of terms without defending them as theoretically critical (or not). In this sense, the chapter is descriptive rather than theoretical, although we fully understand that by choosing one's terms and their definitions, one implicitly adopts a theory.

How many types of memory are there? In the early 1970s, Tulving wrote: "In a recent collection of essays edited by Norman (1970) one can count references to some 25 or so categories of memory, if one is willing to assume that any unique combination of an adjectival modifier with the main term refers to something other than any of the references of other such unique combinations" (Tulving, 1972: 382). Tulving added two more terms (episodic memory and semantic memory) in that chapter. Yet more important for present purposes, Tulving continued to keep a list of memory terms as he encountered them. Thirty-five years later, Tulving (2007) wrote another chapter entitled "Are there 256 different kinds of memory?" which was the number of combinations of the adjective + memory sort that he had collected by that time. The list goes from abnormal memory (at the beginning), through terms such as diencephalic memory and false memory, then on to rote memory and sensory memory, and finally, at the end of the list, to working memory. (There are 250 others.)

We hasten to add that we are not going to cover 256 kinds of memory in this chapter. We aim to provide a lexicon of some of the primary terms that readers will find in the four volumes of *Learning and Memory: A Comprehensive Reference*. We have tried to weave the terms together in a loose sort of story, so as not to provide just a glossary with a long list of terms and definitions. The story is one conception of the varieties of memory provided elsewhere (Roediger et al., 2002). We try to give a verbal definition of each type of memory we chose to include, as well as a practical example of how the type of memory might operate in a person or other animal, and we usually point to a paradigm by which this type of memory is studied, to provide kind of an operational definition.

The reader will notice that in some cases the same memory term (e.g., episodic memory) may refer to a process, entity (e.g., memory trace), system, mental state of awareness, or type of cognitive task, depending on the context. Such linguistic flexibility can easily lead to confusion, so we attempt to distinguish among different uses of each term where appropriate. The index of the book can be used to glean other uses of the term. In addition, semantic confusion can easily arise from

the types of metaphors employed to describe a memory concept. Most cognitive psychologists use a spatial metaphor in which memories are conceived as physical entities stored in a mind space, and the act of remembering involves searching through the mind's space in order to retrieve the objects of memory (e.g., Roediger, 1980; Tulving, 2000; *See* Chapters 1.04, 1.05). In contrast, others have proposed nonspatial metaphors that make analogies to concepts such as strength – memories are comparable to muscles whose strengths are directly related to performance on memory tasks (e.g., Hull, 1943); construction – the act of remembering involves constructing memories from available information (e.g., Bartlett, 1932); depth of processing – memory is a by-product of the level of perceptual analysis (Craik and Tulving, 1975; *See* Chapters 1.07, 1.08); or auditory resonance – memories are like notes played on piano keys or individual tuning forks resonating (e.g., Wechsler, 1963; Ratcliff, 1978), to list but a few. To reiterate, we do not mean to provide exhaustive coverage, but rather to paint with broad strokes and to represent the way memory terms are used by cognitive psychologists and others.

We begin with consideration of some general distinctions made among types of memory. We then turn to the idea that it is useful to catalog memories by their time course in the system (from brief sensory memories, to short-term conscious memories, to various sorts of long-term memory). Most work has been devoted to the various types of long-term memory that have been described, so this is the focus of the next section of the chapter. Inevitably, given our organization, there is a bit of repetition because we needed to cover the same term (say, episodic memory) in more than one context.

1.02.2   Broad Distinctions

This section of the chapter is devoted to consideration of several broad distinctions among forms of memory. We consider the issue of explicit and implicit memory, conscious and unconscious forms of memory, voluntary and involuntary retention, intentional and incidental learning and retrieval, declarative and procedural memory, and retrospective and prospective memory.

1.02.2.1   Explicit and Implicit Memory

Explicit memory refers to cases of conscious recollection. When we remember our trip to Paris or recognize that some words occurred in a recent list, these are instances of explicit memory. In cases of explicit retention, people respond to a direct request for information about their past, and such tests are called explicit memory tests. On the other hand, on tests of implicit memory, people are asked to perform some task, and the measure of interest is how some prior experience affects the task. For example, take the simple case of the word elephant appearing in a long list of words. If subjects are given a recognition test in which they are instructed to identify words studied in the list (and to reject nonstudied words), then their choice of elephant as a studied word would represent an instance of explicit retention. However, if a different group of subjects were given the same set of words to study and then were given a word stem completion test (with instructions to say the first word that comes to mind to the word stem ele_____), then this would constitute a test of implicit memory. The relevant measure on this test is priming, the greater probability of completing the stem with elephant rather than other plausible words (element, elegant, electricity, etc.) when the word has been studied than when it has not been studied. For example, the probability of producing elephant to the word stem might be 10% if the word had not been studied in the list and 40% when it had been studied, which would constitute a 30% priming effect. One reason for believing that these two measures represent different forms of memory is that they can be dissociated by many experimental (and subject) variables.

Graf and Schacter (1985) introduced the terms explicit and implicit memory to the field. Explicit retention refers to most typical measures of retention that psychologists have used over the years (recall, recognition, and their variations), whereas implicit memory refers to transfer measures when people may not be aware of using memory at all (Jacoby, 1984). Some writers prefer the terms direct and indirect memory for this contrast, because explicit tests measure memory directly, whereas implicit tests are indirect measures. Schacter (1987) offers a fine historical review of concepts related to implicit memory.

1.02.2.2 Conscious and Unconscious Forms of Memory

Conscious and unconscious forms of memory refer to the mental states of awareness associated with remembering the past. Attempts to describe human memory in relation to consciousness hearken back to the early introspective tradition of experimental psychology and the writings of Wilhelm Wundt, Edward Titchener, and William James (e.g., James, 1890/1950), as well as the psychoanalytic tradition and especially the well-known writings of Sigmund Freud (e.g., Freud, 1917/1982). Less well known is the fact that in the very first experiments on memory, Ebbinghaus (1885/1964) devised a relearning/savings technique for measuring memory that could detect unconscious knowledge. In fact, Ebbinghaus preferred savings measures over the merely introspective techniques of recall and recognition, because these latter tests cannot, almost by definition, measure memories that are not conscious (Slamecka, 1985).

In contemporary studies of memory, conscious recollection refers to the subjective awareness of remembering information encountered in the past, a process that is likened to the experience of mentally traveling back in time (Tulving, 1985). Tulving has also termed this state of awareness autonoetic (self-knowing) consciousness. In contrast, a noetic (knowing) state of consciousness is the type of awareness associated with retrieving previously learned information, such as a geographical, historical, or personal fact, without recollecting details about the place and time in which that information was originally acquired. For example, noetic consciousness might characterize the experience of a person being asked to name the capital of Canada and who, after thinking for a bit, responds "Ottawa" without remembering when he or she last encountered or originally learned this fact. Autonoetic consciousness, on the other hand, is reflected by the person's ability to think back to and re-experience an episode, such as a visit to Ottawa.

Conscious recollection may be intentional and effortful, or it may occur without the intent to explicitly remember information relevant to a given memory task, as is the case with involuntary conscious recollection (e.g., Richardson-Klavehn et al., 1996). This term refers to the fact that one may suddenly be remembering some event from the past without ever having tried to do so. In some cases of patients with damage to the frontal lobes, they may experience confabulation, or the experience of conscious recollection occurring for events that never occurred. The patients believe they are having memories, but in many cases the events are preposterous and could not have occurred. Such cases are extremely rare yet do occur.

Unconscious retention may be observed in performance on tests of implicit memory where individuals indirectly demonstrate their prior exposure to the test material under conditions in which they do not consciously recognize the material. Tulving has referred to the state of awareness associated with unconscious retention as anoetic consciousness. Unconscious retention also occurs when subjects show savings in retention without being able to recollect the experience that gave rise to the savings, as Ebbinghaus (1885/1964) first pointed out.

1.02.2.3   Voluntary and Involuntary Retention

Voluntary retention refers to deliberate, willful recollection, whereas involuntary or incidental retention refers to recollection that occurs without conscious effort. Involuntary retention, as the name implies, refers to memories that arise in consciousness unbidden, with no conscious effort to recollect. For example, in studies of autobiographical memory (memory for events in one's life), voluntary recollections may be assessed by asking individuals to remember personal events in response to queries (e.g., recall a memory from your past that is associated with an automobile). The naturalistic study of involuntary memories can be achieved by asking individuals to keep a diary and jotting down memories that seem to come out of the blue, as it were, wherever and whenever they occur (e.g., Berntsen and Rubin, 2002; Rubin and Berntsen, 2003).

It should be noted, though, that acts of voluntary or involuntary recollection may not be entirely pure, and one may influence the other. For instance, a person's attempt to remember the details of a baseball game that occurred years ago might be influenced by his inadvertently remembering details of a more recent game. Or when engaging in a test of implicit memory, such as completing word fragments, a person might become aware of the fact that some of the target words were encountered during the study phase and, therefore, might intentionally think back to the study phase to help complete the test word fragments (Jacoby, 1991). In addition, as previously mentioned, one might experience involuntary conscious recollection whereby thoughts of a past event come to mind automatically, and it might take further reflection to realize how the memory came to mind (Richardson-Klavehn et al., 1996).

1.02.2.4   Intentional and Incidental Learning and Retrieval

1.02.2.4.1   *Intentional and incidental learning*

Intentional and incidental learning refer to whether or not people intend to learn material to which they are exposed. Of course, as we go about the world watching TV, driving, or reading the paper, we rarely say to ourselves: I need to remember this commercial on TV. Educational systems provide the main form of relentless intentional learning, although of course we all sometimes try to remember the name of a new acquaintance or the name of a book or movie someone recommended. In the laboratory, intentional or incidental learning is manipulated by instructions to subjects. In an intentional learning situation, an individual studies certain materials with the express purpose of remembering them at some later point in time. In an incidental learning task, the same materials might be provided but with an orienting task to induce some sort of processing of the material but without any instructions concerning a later memory test. For example, in a standard levels-of-processing manipulation (e.g., Craik and Tulving, 1975), a person might be shown a list of words and asked to judge whether each word (e.g., BEAR) is presented in capital letters (graphemic or structural processing), whether it rhymes with a certain word like chair (phonemic processing), or whether it fits into a certain category such as animals (semantic processing). Subjects in incidental learning conditions would be told that the researchers are interested in studying the speed with which people can make such decisions. In the intentional learning conditions, they would be told the same rationale, but would also be told that their memory for the words will be tested later.

The natural expectation is that material studied under intentional learning conditions is better retained than under incidental learning conditions, and this outcome is sometimes obtained (Postman, 1964). However, at least when semantic orienting tasks are used, the differences between incidental and intentional learning conditions are surprisingly slight and often there is no difference at all (Craik and Tulving, 1975; Hyde and Jenkins, 1969).

1.02.2.4.2   *Intentional and incidental retrieval*

Just as intentionality can be manipulated during study of materials, so can it be manipulated during testing. In fact, the distinction already drawn between explicit and implicit memory tests can be cast in this light. Explicit tests require intentional retrieval, but implicit tests reveal incidental retrieval (Jacoby, 1984). Under intentional retrieval conditions, a person is asked to engage in conscious, deliberate recollection of a past event (e.g., recalling a word from a previously studied list that completes a word stem). By contrast, incidental retrieval involves giving people the same word stem with the instruction to write the first word that comes to mind. Incidental retrieval is indexed by priming, the better performance in completing the stem with the target word relative to a control condition in which the word had not been studied.

As noted, the comparison between intentional and incidental retrieval is not necessarily a pure one, because performance on explicit memory tests may be affected by incidental retrieval just as performance on implicit memory tests can be influenced by intentional retrieval (Jacoby, 1991). Several solutions exist for attempting to gain leverage on this issue. Schacter and his colleagues (1989) proposed the retrieval intentionality criterion to test for the contamination of incidental retrieval measures by conscious recollection. The basic idea is to compare incidental and intentional recollection, holding all other study and test conditions constant. If performance differs markedly between the two tests when all conditions are held constant except for instructions just prior to the test, then one can have greater confidence that they measure intentional (conscious) and incidental (automatic or unconscious) retrieval. Roediger et al. (1992) crossed intentional and incidental study and test conditions with other variables and showed that incidental tests reflected quite different patterns of performance from the intentional tests. Jacoby (1991) proposed a different method, the process dissociation procedure, to separate conscious from unconscious influences during retrieval. Although providing the details of his ingenious method is outside the scope of this chapter, his method has proved extraordinarily useful in separating conscious from unconscious (or automatic) cognitive processes.

1.02.2.5 Declarative and Nondeclarative Memory

Declarative memory and nondeclarative memory (sometimes referred to as procedural memory) are terms that have gained prominence following their use by Squire (1982), although the original distinction was proposed by Ryle (1949). Ryle distinguished between declarative knowledge (knowing that) and procedural knowledge (knowing how). For example, we know that Washington, D.C., is the capital of the United States, but we know how to tie our shoes.

More recently, Squire has proposed declarative memory as an overarching category that includes episodic memory (remembering specific events of the past) as well as semantic memory (general knowledge). Declarative memory processes rely upon the hippocampus and related structures in the medial-temporal lobe including the perirhinal, entorhinal, and parahippocampal cortices. As it has been extended, the term declarative memory has become a bit of a misnomer, because the concept is often applied to infrahuman species that are not prone to making declarations. (Ryle tied his distinction specifically to linguistic usage so that people would know that such and such occurred.)

Procedural memory was originally intended to cover motor skills, such as tying shoes, riding a bicycle, or typing (Ryle, 1949), but it was broadened to cover mental as well physical procedures. For example, the mental processes involved in multiplying 24×16 are examples of mental procedures that can be studied. As Squire (1992) developed his theory, the term procedural memory became broader and covered such topics as priming on implicit memory tests, classical conditioning of responses, and habituation. Because of these and other uses, the broader term nondeclarative memory came into use. It refers both to traditional procedural tasks and to others such as priming and skill learning. The distinction between declarative and nondeclarative types of memory rests partly on evidence that different brain structures are involved in various forms of memory. The evidence supporting the differences between the different forms of memory has come both from studies of human amnesic patients with damage to the medial-temporal lobes and in animals where such alterations can be achieved experimentally (e.g., Squire, 1992).

As noted, the term declarative memory originally referred to memories that could be verbally stated (Ryle, 1949). This term has also been broadened so that it now includes many other kinds of memory, including spatial memory, some types of long-term visual memory, and any other form of memory subserved by the hippocampal complex. Nondeclarative memories include all other types, whether they involve memories for physical movements and actions, priming, or skills.

Tulving (1985) has proposed a somewhat different schematic arrangement of episodic, semantic, and procedural memory systems. In Tulving's scheme, procedural memory is phylogenetically oldest and is shared among all organisms. Semantic memory grows out of (and depends upon) procedural memory. Episodic memory is evolutionarily most recent and, according to Tulving, only humans have this form of memory (see Tulving, 2005, for further elaboration). Different forms of consciousness are proposed for the three systems: anoetic (non-knowing) for procedural memory, noetic (knowing) for semantic memory, and autonoetic (self-knowing) for episodic memory. Tulving proposes that a critical function of autonoetic consciousness is planning for the future, which brings us to another critical distinction.

1.02.2.6   Retrospective and Prospective Memory

The vast majority of memory research deals with the ability to remember past events when given specific cues (as in explicit memory tests of recall or recognition) or with the effects of past experience on current behavior (priming on implicit memory tests). All tests that fall into these categories assess retrospective memory: memory for the past or effects of past experience on current behavior. In the past 2 decades, researchers have examined memory for intentions to be performed in the future, or prospective memory. Strictly speaking, prospective memory is retrospective in nature: it involves remembering a past intention. A prospective memory task differs from a retrospective memory tasks in that there is usually no explicit cue to elicit recall of the intention. Instead, a prospective memory task requires that subjects must use an environmental cue to know when to retrieve the intention, so it is a curious mix of incidental and intentional retrieval. We face prospective memory tasks all the time, whenever we need to remember to perform some act in the future. Prospective memory tasks can be classified as cue-based or event-based when some cue should remind us to perform an action (e.g., pass along a message to a friend when we see her) or time-based (e.g., remembering to take out the trash Tuesday evenings). Both cue-based and time-based prospective memory tasks have been investigated in naturalistic settings and in the laboratory. Retrieval of prospective memories may sometimes involve

monitoring and may sometimes be spontaneous and effortless (Einstein and McDaniel, 2005).

We turn next to categorizations of memory based on (roughly) the time they persist, starting with varieties of short-term memory.

1.02.3   Types of Short-Term Memory

Information from the external world is believed to be represented in various storage systems that, roughly speaking, hold information for fractions of a second, seconds, or much longer. Atkinson and Shiffrin's (1969, 1971) influential theory, shown in **Figure 1**, provides one conceptualization. Our treatment here provides some amendments to their original theory.

1.02.3.1   Sensory Memories

The border between perceiving and remembering is blurred. There is no good answer to the question: When does perception end and memory begin? Even the operations in the two types of experiments are similar. When stimuli are presented rapidly to the visual or auditory system and some report or judgment is made quickly afterward, the experiment is referred to as one of perception. If the report or judgment is delayed after presentation, the study is usually called a memory experiment. Sensory memories are the brief holding systems for information presented to the various sensory systems; the information is thought to be held briefly in each system as it undergoes further processing.

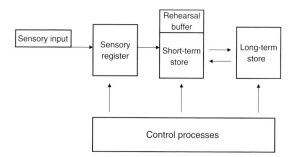

Figure 1   Simplified version of the original multi-store memory model of Shiffrin and Atkinson. Information is conceived as being transmitted through various memory stores. Adapted from Shiffrin RM and Atkinson RC (1969) Storage and retrieval processes in long-term memory. *Psychol. Rev.* 76: 179–193; used with permission of the American Psychological Association.

Sperling (1960) identified a rapidly fading store of visual information that he called precategorical visual storage. The term precategorical was in the title, because Sperling's evidence convinced him that the information was held in a relatively raw form, before linguistic categorizations had been applied. Somewhat later, other researchers proposed a system of precategorical acoustic storage, the auditory equivalent of Sperling's visual store (Crowder and Morton, 1969). These two sensory stores have been studied quite thoroughly by many researchers (*See* Chapter 2.03), but the names they are given in the literature today have been changed to iconic and echoic memory (following Neisser's (1967) suggested terminology). Iconic memory refers to the visual store, whereas echoic memory is used for auditory storage. Echoic storage seems to persist longer than iconic storage, although the decay characteristics of both systems have been debated and depend on such factors as stimulus intensity and the technique used to measure loss of information over time.

Researchers assume that similar storage systems exist for the other senses, but touch is the only sense that has been studied in this regard (and rather sporadically). The close association between smell and taste makes such studies difficult, although longer-term olfactory memory, in particular, has been well studied.

1.02.3.2 Short-Term Storage

Short-term memory (or short-term storage; the two are often used interchangeably) refers to retention of information in a system after information has been categorized and reached consciousness. In fact, contents of short-term memory are sometimes equated with the information of which a person is consciously aware. Information can be continually processed in short-term storage (e.g., via rehearsal or subvocal repetition). If a person is distracted, information is rapidly lost from this store.

Many different techniques have been developed to study aspects of short-term memory, but all have in common that subjects are given relatively brief numbers of items (often digits or words) and are asked to recall or recognize them later (often after some brief interfering task). Another term used for short-term memory is primary memory, owing to a distinction introduced by William James (1890/1950) between primary and secondary memory (reintroduced to the field much later by Waugh and Norman, 1965). Primary memory is what can be held

in mind at once, whereas secondary memory referred to all other kinds of long-term memory. The terms short-term memory and long-term memory seem to have become accepted today.

1.02.3.3 Working Memory

Working memory is a term for the type of memory used to hold information for short periods of time while it is being manipulated (Baddeley, 2001). Working memory encompasses short-term memory, which in Baddeley's theory refers only to the short-term passive storage of information. Working memory also adds the concept of a central executive that functions to manipulate information in working memory and three separate storage components: the phonological loop, visuospatial sketchpad, and episodic buffer (see **Figure 2**). To test the short-term memory of humans, tasks that require short-term storage of information (such as digits in a digit span task) are used. On the other hand, working memory tests use tasks that require both short-term storage and manipulation of information (such as the operation span task, in which

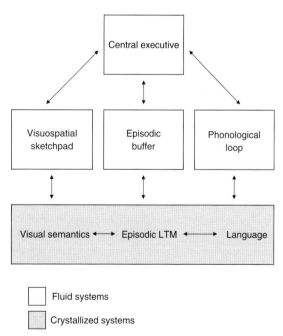

Figure 2 Baddeley's updated working memory model. Working memory is conceived as having separate storage components and a central executive process. LTM, long-term memory. Adapted from Baddeley A (2001) Is working memory still working? *Am. Psychol.* 56: 849–864; used with permission.

subjects solve simple arithmetic problems while also being given words to remember (*See* Chapter 2.04).

Three different storage systems are believed to constitute working memory. The phonological loop is involved in subvocal rehearsal and storage of auditory information (or written visual information) and is the most-studied component of working memory. The phonological loop is responsible for subvocal rehearsal and is used to account for many different empirical findings, such as the word length effect, or the finding that longer words are recalled less well than shorter words (because they take longer to rehearse).

The visuospatial sketchpad is similar to the phonological loop, except it maintains visual and spatial information, rather than acoustic information. The visual and spatial components of the sketchpad are at least partially separable, because one can observe dissociations between performance on visual working memory tasks and spatial working memory tasks (Baddeley, 2001). Most of the work on the visuospatial sketchpad up to now has focused on dissociating it from the other components of working memory.

The episodic buffer is the newest component of working memory, proposed only recently by Baddeley (2000) to explain several experimental findings. The episodic buffer is much like the phonological loop or the visuospatial sketchpad: It is a short-term store of information, although it is assumed to be able to store information of different modalities. Any information that is retrieved from long-term episodic memory (see section titled 'Episodic memory') is temporarily stored and manipulated in the episodic buffer.

The central executive component of working memory controls the subsystems. Some critics have complained that the concept is underspecified and that the concept is used to explain findings not well handled by the basic model. However, the executive component has much in common with other proposals of a central executive attention system that is used to explain how people can divide attention to different sources of information, switch attention among sources or tasks, or focus attention exclusively on one task.

1.02.3.4   Long-Term Working Memory

Long-term working memory extends the concept of working memory to account for a person's ability to readily access and utilize information stored in long-term memory. The concept of long-term working memory is particularly useful in explaining how

skilled readers have the ability to easily read and comprehend texts. Indeed, the act of reading seems to require much more capacity and flexibility than the proposal for short-term or working memory can offer. A skilled reader must keep in mind words from previous sentences, paragraphs, or pages of text and readily access prior background knowledge in order to quickly and fluently process upcoming words and understand the text as a whole (e.g., Ericsson and Kintsch, 1995).

The concept of long-term working memory is also used to describe the superior mnemonic skills of experts functioning within their domain of expertise. For instance, chess masters demonstrate a remarkable ability to quickly encode and accurately remember the positions of every piece on a chess board sampled from the middle of a game, or to readily call to mind moves played in thousands of previous games in order to decide how to make the next move in a game. While researchers have attempted to explain the superior memory capacity of experts in their domain within the limits of short-term memory (Chase and Simon, 1973), evidence suggests that expert memory performance is mediated by long-term memory (e.g., Chase and Ericsson, 1982; Charness, 1991).

In contrast to the limited, fixed capacity of short-term working memory, the capacity of long-term working memory is assumed to be flexible and may even be expanded through training. Thus, according to Ericsson and Kintsch (1995), long-term working memory is not a general cognitive ability, but rather a specialized ability that is acquired through the development of expertise for specific domains of knowledge. On the other hand, long-term working memory still depends upon the maintenance and utilization of a few retrieval cues in working memory that are, in turn, linked to retrieval structures stored in long-term memory.

1.02.4   Varieties of Long-Term Memory

Long-term memory is one of the most abused terms in psychology (and there is great competition for this honor). The reason is that the term is made to cover nearly every kind of memory not covered in the previous section. The term is used to refer to retention of words from the middle of a list presented 15 s previously to recollection of early childhood memories.

Not surprisingly, there exist various ways of carving up this huge subject. One is by type of material and mode of presentation, with the primary distinctions being among verbal memory, visual/spatial memory, and olfactory memory. Relatedly, learning of motor skills (sometimes called procedural memory, as discussed in the section 'Declarative and nondeclarative memory') is another critical and somewhat separate topic, sometimes called kinesthetic memory.

Another set of distinctions, which cut across those above, are among types of declarative (or perhaps explicit) memory: Episodic memory, autobiographical memory, semantic memory, and collective memory. We begin discussing specific codes thought to underlie long-term memory and then turn to the various types of explicit, declarative memory that have been proposed.

1.02.4.1 Code-Specific Forms of Retention

As humans possess multiple senses, there are multiple ways to sense new information and to encode that information. Raw sensory information comes in as visual, auditory, or olfactory information, as well as in other modalities. However, memories for tastes have not been much studied and because smell so greatly affects taste, separating these modalities would be difficult. Haptic memory, referring to memory for skin sensations, is also not much studied, although kinesthetic memory (for muscular movements) is a well-studied area. Studying memory for information presented in different sensory modalities has revealed both similarities and remarkable differences in how modality affects memory performance.

1.02.4.1.1 Visual–spatial memory
Memory for scenes and spatial relationships is often referred to as visual–spatial memory or just spatial memory (*See* Chapter 2.11). This type of memory is responsible for humans navigating around town in a car and for squirrels finding buried caches of acorns. Although spatial memory and episodic memory both rely on the hippocampus and surrounding areas, some theorists have argued that spatial memory is different from episodic memory and other relational (semantic) memory systems because it requires the formation of mental maps (O'Keefe and Nadel, 1978). On the other hand, Mackintosh (2002) argued that spatial learning is no different than other types of associative learning.

1.02.4.1.2 Imagery
Information presented either in events or pictures or words may be represented in the spatial system in imaginal form. One may see a butterfly and remember its appearance using this imaginal coding, or one may hear the word butterfly and be asked to form an image of the named insect. Converting verbal memories to images aids their memorability, either because the image is a deeply meaningful form (Nelson, 1979) or because coding information in verbal and imaginal codes provides additional retrieval routes to the information (Paivio, 1986).

1.02.4.1.3 Olfactory memory
Olfactory memory is more difficult to study than visual or auditory memory. Due to limitations of human olfaction, memory for odors has generally been tested with recognition tests, not with recall tests (see Herz and Engen, 1996, for a review). Olfactory memories seem to differ in some ways from other forms of memory, such as a tendency of smells to be particularly evocative of emotional memories. Indeed, the olfactory nerve is only two synapses away from the amygdala (responsible for certain types of emotions) and three synapses away from the hippocampus (which is critical for long-term memory). Olfactory memory is similar to auditory and visual memory in that performance on recognition tests decreases as the distracter set increases and as distracter similarity to targets increases. However, olfactory memory does differ from other kinds of memory in two respects. First, olfactory memory is highly resistant to forgetting: Multiple studies have shown that recognition performance for odors in a laboratory preparation is only about 5% less after 1 year than after a 30-s delay. Related to this remarkably flat forgetting curve is the finding that olfactory memory is highly resistant to retroactive interference. Proactive interference reduces olfactory memory performance greatly.

1.02.4.1.4 Skill learning
Perhaps the largest subset of different kinds of memory is the broad class of memories classified as types of kinesthetic memory or skill learning or procedural memory (the last of which was described earlier). Kinesthetic memories are those involved in motor skills: The swing of a baseball bat, how to keep a hula hoop going, and so on through hundreds of other examples (*See* Chapter 2.34). These are motor skills, the classic type of procedural memory. However, many other types of skill learning exist. There is verbal skill

learning, such as learning to read distorted or inverted text (Kolers and Roediger, 1984) – learning of grammars, both real ones and artificial ones (e.g., *See* Chapter 2.31) – and even the skillful learning of what items belong in what categories (*See* Chapter 2.47). Although a review of the various kinds of skill learning is beyond the scope of this article (see Gupta and Cohen, 2002), we can briefly point out one of the most consistent findings across the procedural learning literature: Skill learning is highly specific and transfer is often quite narrow, for example, learning to read inverted (upside down) text does not aid in learning to read backward text (Kolers and Roediger, 1984; Healy, 2007).

1.02.4.1.5   Verbal memory

Doubtless the greatest form of memory recoding and storage for human beings is based on language. People can remember events as verbal information even if they were originally presented in a different form (visual, auditory, or even olfactory or kinesthetic). Psychologists have long believed in the primacy of verbal coding, and Glanzer and Clark (1964) even proposed a verbal loop hypothesis, which theorized that all human experience is recoded into language. Subsequent research indicates that this hypothesis was a bit overstated and other forms of coding exist, but nonetheless verbal coding and verbal memories are critically important in human cognition. Verbal recoding can be impaired by instructing subjects to perform some irrelevant verbalization such as repeating nonsense words while being exposed to nonverbal information, a technique known as articulatory suppression.

1.02.4.2   Forms of Explicit Memory

We have covered these earlier in the 'Broad distinctions' section, but review them again here in more detail and provide more detailed examples of tasks used to study these forms of memory.

1.02.4.2.1   Episodic memory

Episodic memory refers to memory for particular events situated in space and time, as well as the underlying cognitive processes and neural mechanisms involved in remembering those events. A key ingredient of episodic memory that distinguishes it from other forms of memory is the retrieval of information regarding the spatial and/or temporal context in which the remembered event occurred. As previously mentioned, episodic memory is also associated with autonoetic consciousness, considered

by some researchers to be an evolutionarily advanced, unique human capacity (e.g., Wheeler, 2000; Tulving, 2002, 2005).

One can point to a wide variety of examples of episodic memory, ranging from remembering what a friend wore at a party the night before to individual words studied in a list moments ago. In most contexts, episodic memory is synonymous with explicit memory, although the former term is usually used to represent a memory system and the latter term to designate types of tests that are used. Many tests have been designed to measure certain aspects of episodic memory in the lab, including free recall (recall of a set of material in any order), serial recall (recall of events in order), cued recall (recall of events given specific cues), recognition judgments (recognizing studied material intermixed with nonstudied material), source judgments (recognizing the source of presented material, such as whether it was presented auditorily or visually). Subjects may also be asked to make judgments of the recency of an event, its frequency of occurrence, or of some other quality. In addition, subjects can be asked to make metamemory judgments, or judgments about their memories. For example, a student might be asked to rate how confident he or she is in the accuracy of his/her recollections. Similarly, individuals might be asked to judge whether they can remember the moment an event occurred or the context in which it occurred or whether they only just know that they were previously encountered but cannot remember the context (Tulving, 1985). These remember/know judgments (with remember judgments reflecting episodic recollection) have been much studied (*See* Chapter 2.17).

1.02.4.2.2   Autobiographical memory

Autobiographical memory refers to memory for one's personal history (Robinson, 1976). Examples might include memories for experiences that occurred in childhood, the first time learning to drive a car, or even one's Social Security number or home address. Brewer (1986) divided autobiographical memories into categories of personal memories, autobiographical facts, and generic personal memories. Personal memories are memories for specific events in one's life that are accompanied by imagery. As such, personal autobiographical memories are thought by some to be the real-world analog to episodic memories as studied in the lab, because they are the episodes of one's life as dated in space and time. On the other hand, autobiographical facts are facts about the person that are devoid of personally experienced temporal or spatial context information. For example, you know when and where you were born, but you cannot remember the event. Finally, generic personal memory refers to more abstract knowledge about oneself (what you are like) or to acquired procedural knowledge such as knowledge of how to ride a bicycle, ski, or play a musical instrument. Despite the conceptual overlap across classification schemes, a unique feature of autobiographical memory is that it must directly relate to oneself or one's sense of personal history.

A variety of techniques have been used to examine autobiographical memory. One approach is to simply ask people to report the most important personal events of their life (e.g., Fitzgerald, 1988; Berntsen and Rubin, 2002; Rubin and Berntsen, 2003) or to report self-defining memories (e.g., Conway et al., 2004). Another frequently used method is to ask people to describe for each of a given set of cue words the first personal memory that comes to mind, e.g., being given the word window and asked to retrieve a discrete event from your past involving a window. This task is known as the Galton-Crovitz cueing technique after its inventor (Galton, 1879) and its first modern proponent (Crovitz and Schiffman, 1974).

Many studies have plotted the temporal distribution of autobiographical memories across the life span, as described more fully by Conway (*See* Chapter 2.46). Briefly, such distributions usually exhibit three striking features (Rubin et al., 1986; Janssen et al., 2005). The first is that people tend to recall very little from the first few years of their life. This is referred to as childhood amnesia. Second, people tend to recall quite a few events from early adulthood, roughly the ages 15–25. This effect is called the reminiscence bump. Finally, most reported events are recalled from the last few years, which (like many other examples of good recall of recent information) is known as the recency effect.

Due to the personal nature of autobiographical memory, researchers have difficulty comparing what a person remembers to what actually occurred. Researchers overcome this challenge in one of several ways. One approach is to have subjects keep a diary for a length of time (e.g., days, months, years) and to record events that occurred to them at regular intervals or in response to specific cues. In addition to providing descriptions of the events that occurred, subjects might also record other accompanying details such as the exact time or location of the event and its emotional valence, salience, or distinctiveness. In turn, the diary entries are treated as the to-be-

remembered stimuli in subsequent tests of memory. Moreover, as previously mentioned, the diary method is also used to capture involuntary recollections of personal events that are extremely difficult to elicit in laboratory settings. Such involuntary recollections tend to come out of the blue in response to environmental cues such as specific smells, words, or objects (e.g., Berntsen, 1996).

Another method is to assess individuals' recollections for specific historical events (e.g., the German occupation and liberation of Denmark during World War II) and then to compare the recollections with objective records of what occurred at the time, such as weather reports, newspapers, or radio broadcasts (Berntsen and Thomsen, 2005). Numerous studies of flashbulb memories (vivid recollections that surround a salient personal experience) focus on personal recollections surrounding unexpected, momentous, or emotionally charged events of public or personal significance, such as the assassination of President John F. Kennedy, the explosion of the space shuttle Challenger, or the more recent terrorist attacks on New York's World Trade Center (Brown and Kulik, 1977; Neisser and Harsh, 1993; Talarico and Rubin, 2003). However, it still remains unclear how reliable such memories are, what types of events induce flashbulb memories, and whether they really differ from memories for emotionally charged stimuli or circumstances (*See* Chapter 2.09).

1.02.4.2.3   *Semantic memory*

Semantic memory broadly refers to a person's general knowledge of the world. Of course, this is a vast store of information. Examples of semantic memory range from knowledge of words and their meanings, all kinds of concepts, general schemas or scripts that organize knowledge, and also specific facts about the world, such as the capital of France or famous battles in World War II.

It is reasonable to assume that when information is first learned, it is accompanied by information regarding the time and place of the learning episode. Over time and with repeated presentations of the same information, the accompanying episodic information may be lost or detached, and what remains is semantic memory. Still the distinction between episodic and semantic memory can easily blur. If someone asks about what you learned during a recent lecture, your response will likely reflect the influence of both episodic and semantic memory: Your reliance on temporal or contextual cues to remember particular points made during the lecture would reflect episodic memory. In contrast, how you choose to reconstruct, organize, interpret, or paraphrase knowledge garnered from the lecture would reflect the influence of semantic memory.

In addition to tests of explicit and implicit memory, a variety of cognitive tests are designed to measure the contents and organization of semantic memory. These tasks might involve naming as many members of a category or words that start with a given letter that come to mind, providing word definitions, answering general knowledge questions. Other measures are designed to capture the psychological representations of word meanings by having individuals provide quantitative ratings of individual words along a variety of semantic dimensions (e.g., Osgood et al., 1957).

One of the most powerful tools for studying semantic memory is the word-priming technique in which individuals are asked to make lexical decisions (word–nonword decisions) for pairs of stimuli that might be semantically related or unrelated. For example, individuals are faster and more accurate at identifying a word (doctor) if it is was preceded by a related word (nurse) relative to an unrelated word (shoe). Indeed, comparisons in the response times for items that are semantically related versus unrelated to current or previously encountered stimuli have inspired and helped to distinguish among competing theories of how knowledge is mentally represented and accessed (e.g., Collins and Quillian, 1969; Meyer and Schvaneveldt, 1971; Collins and Loftus, 1975; Neely, 1977; *See* Chapter 2.28).

1.02.4.2.4   *Collective memory*

Collective memory is conceptualized in a variety of ways. In a literal sense, collective memory refers to remembering that occurs within any social context. When employees at a company meeting attempt to recall what was discussed during a previous meeting, they are engaging in a collaborative recall effort. In general, social situations can influence what individuals remember or choose to report of the past. A given social setting can dictate what sorts of recollections are most appropriate or commensurate with individual goals of communication. For instance, it is very tempting to highlight or embellish certain details of a remembered event in order tell a more entertaining story. And in turn, an individual can influence what other individuals of a group remember of the past. Studies of collaborative recall typically involve having a group of people study lists of words, pictures, or prose passages and then asking them to recall the previously studied materials either individually or in collaboration with the rest of the group (Weldon, 2000).

Work in this area has shown that collaborative recall can increase the amount of previously studied information recalled as compared to individual recall performance, but that collaborative recall tends to reduce or inhibit the amount of information recalled per individual within a group (e.g., Weldon and Bellinger, 1997). Furthermore, collaborative recall can induce recall errors, as erroneous information supplied by one member of a group is accepted and later remembered by other members of the group (e.g., Roediger et al., 2001; Meade and Roediger, 2002).

Collective memory also refers to a representation of the past that is shared by members of broader social groups defined by nationality, religion, ethnicity, or age cohort (*See* Chapter 2.48). Such a conception of collective memory is shared across the fields of psychology, anthropology, and sociology, as may be seen in the writings of Wilhelm Wundt (1910/1916), Sir Frederic Bartlett (1932), and the French sociologists Maurice Halbwachs (1950/1980) and Emile Durkheim (1915). Carl Jung (1953) used the notion of a collective unconscious in a similar sense. One commonly held assumption is that remembering is shaped by active participation within the life of a particular group. Thus, group characteristics may bias the recollections of individual group members. For instance, Russian and American high school students are likely to tell strikingly different versions of the history of World War II, with each group recalling and weaving together a different set of key events in their narratives (Wertsch, 2002). Despite the widespread use of the term collective memory, both in public discussions of how groups remember historical events such as the Vietnam War or the Holocaust and across academic disciplines, there is still little agreement as to its definition or methods of study (*See* Chapter 2.48).

In contemporary memory research, studies of collective memory bear resemblance to those of autobiographical memory in the sense that remembering one's personal history may be heavily influenced by one's cultural background. For instance, numerous studies of flashbulb memories have examined individual recollections for major historical events such as the assassinations of President John F. Kennedy, Martin Luther King, Jr., and the fall of the Berlin Wall in 1989. Some of these studies have shown striking differences in recollections across groups.

Berntsen and Thomsen (2005) examined Danes' memories for the German invasion of Denmark in 1940 and their liberation in 1945. Interestingly, they found that individuals who had ties to the Danish resistance had more vivid and accurate memories than those who did not. A key difference between autobiographical and collective memory might, therefore, lie in the impact of group identification on memory and the extent to which remembering in general is socially framed.

1.02.5   Conclusions

This chapter has surveyed some of the most common terms and distinctions among types of memory. Although we have considered only a fraction of the 256 types that Tulving (2007) identified in his (semi-serious) essay, we believe we have hit upon the great majority in contemporary use. Most of the terms used in this chapter were not used by researchers 50 years ago. We hazard the guess that someone examining the field in 50 more years might have an even greater variety of items to review, even if the serious contenders do not quite approach 256.

References

Atkinson RC and Shiffrin RM (1971) The control of short-term memory. *Sci. Am.* 225: 82–90.

Baddeley A (2000) The episodic buffer: A new component of working memory? *Trends Cogn. Sci.* 4: 417–423.

Baddeley A (2001) Is working memory still working? *Am. Psychol.* 56: 849–864.

Bartlett FC (1932) *Remembering: A Study in Experimental and Social Psychology*. Cambridge: Cambridge University Press.

Berntsen D (1996) Involuntary autobiographical memories. *Appl. Cogn. Psychol.* 10: 435–454.

Berntsen D and Rubin DC (2002) Emotionally charged autobiographical memories across the life span: The recall of happy, sad, traumatic, and involuntary memories. *Psychol. Aging* 17: 636–652.

Berntsen D and Thomsen DK (2005) Personal memories for remote historical events: Accuracy and clarity of flashbulb memories related to World War II. *J. Exp. Psychol. Gen.* 134: 242–257.

Brewer WF (1986) What is autobiographical memory? In: Rubin DC (ed.) *Autobiographical Memory*, pp. 25–49. Cambridge: Cambridge University Press.

Brown R and Kulik J (1977) Flashbulb memories. *Cognition* 5: 73–99.

Charness N (1991) Expertise in chess: The balance between knowledge and search. In: Ericsson KA and Smith J (eds.) *Toward a General Theory of Expertise: Prospects and Limits*, pp. 39–63. Cambridge: Cambridge University Press.

Chase WG and Ericsson KA (1982) Skill and working memory. In: Bower GH (ed.) *The Psychology of Learning and Motivation,* vol. 16, pp. 1–58. New York: Academic Press.

Chase WG and Simon HA (1973) The mind's eye in chess. In: Chase WG (ed.) *Visual Information Processing*, pp. 215–281. New York: Academic Press.

Collins AM and Loftus EF (1975) A spreading activation theory of semantic processing. *Psychol. Rev.* 82: 407–428.

Collins AM and Quillian MR (1969) Retrieval time from semantic memory. *J. Verb. Learn. Verb. Behav.* 8: 240–248.

Conway MA, Singer JA, and Tagini A (2004) The self and autobiographical memory: Correspondence and coherence. *Soc. Cogn.* 22: 491–529.

Craik FIM and Tulving E (1975) Depth of processing and the retention of words in episodic memory. *J. Exp. Psychol. Gen.* 104: 268–294.

Crovitz HF and Schiffman H (1974) Frequency of episodic memories as a function of their age. *Bull. Psychon. Soc.* 4: 517–518.

Crowder RG and Morton J (1969) Precategorical acoustic storage (PAS). *Percept. Psychophys.* 5: 365–373.

Durkheim E (1915) *Elementary Forms of the Religious Life*. New York: Macmillan.

Ebbinghaus H (1885/1964) *Memory: A Contribution to Experimental Psychology*. New York: Dover.

Einstein GO and McDaniel MA (2005) Prospective memory: Multiple retrieval processes. *Curr. Dir. Psychol. Sci.* 14: 286–290.

Ericsson KA and Kintsch W (1995) Long-term working memory. *Psychol. Rev.* 102: 211–245.

Fitzgerald JM (1988) Vivid memories and the reminiscence phenomenon: The role of a self narrative. *Hum. Dev.* 31: 261–273.

Freud S (1917/1982) An early memory from Goethe's autobiography. In: Neisser U (ed.) *Memory Observed: Remembering in Natural Contexts*, pp. 289–297. New York: Freeman.

Galton F (1879) Psychometric experiments. *Brain* 2: 149–162.

Glanzer M and Clark WH (1964) The verbal-loop hypothesis: Conventional figures. *Am. J. Psychol.* 77: 621–626.

Graf P and Schacter DL (1985) Implicit and explicit memory for new associations in normal and amnesic subjects. *J. Exp. Psychol. Learn. Mem. Cogn.* 11: 501–518.

Gupta P and Cohen NJ (2002) Theoretical and computational analysis of skill learning, repetition priming, and procedural memory. *Psychol. Rev.* 109: 401–448.

Halbwachs M (1950/1980) *The Collective Memory*, Ditter FJ Jr and Ditter VY (trans.) New York: Harper and Row.

Healy AF (2007) Transfer: Specificity and generality. In: Roediger HL, Dudai Y, and Fitzpatrick SM (eds.) *Science of Memory: Concepts*, pp. 271–282. New York: Oxford University Press.

Herz RS and Engen T (1996) Odor memory: Review and analysis. *Psychon. Bull. Rev.* 3: 300–313.

Hull CL (1943) *Principles of Behavior*. New York: Appleton-Century-Crofts.

Hyde TS and Jenkins JJ (1969) Differential effects of incidental tasks on the organization of recall of a list of highly associated words. *J. Exp. Psychol.* 82: 472–481.

Jacoby LL (1984) Incidental versus intentional retrieval: Remembering and awareness as separate issues. In: Squire LR and Butters N (eds.) *Neuropsychology of Memory*, pp. 145–156. New York: Guilford Press.

Jacoby LL (1991) A process dissociation framework: Separating automatic from intentional uses of memory. *J. Mem. Lang.* 30: 513–541.

James W (1890/1950) *The Principles of Psychology*, vol. 1. New York: Henry Holt and Co.

Janssen SMJ, Chessa AG, and Murre JMJ (2005) The reminiscence bump in autobiographical memory: Effects of age, gender, education, and culture. *Memory* 13: 658–668.

Jung CG (1953)Read H, Fordham M, and Adler G (eds.) *The Collected Works of CG Jung,* vol. 9, Part I. New York: Pantheon Books.

Kolers PA and Roediger HL (1984) Procedures of mind. *Jo. Verb. Learn. Verb. Behav.* 23: 425–449.

Mackintosh NJ (2002) Do not ask whether they have a cognitive map, but how they find their way about. *Psicologica* 23: 165–185.

Meade ML and Roediger HL (2002) Explorations in the social contagion of memory. *Mem. Cogn.* 30: 995–1009.

Meyer DE and Schvaneveldt RW (1971) Facilitation in recognizing pairs of words: Evidence of a dependence between retrieval operations. *J. Exp. Psychol.* 90: 227–234.

Neely JH (1977) Semantic priming and retrieval from lexical memory: Roles of inhibitionless spreading activation and limited-capacity attention. *J. Exp. Psychol. Gen.* 106: 226–254.

Neisser U and Harsh N (1993) Phantom flashbulbs: False recollections of hearing the news about Challenger. In: Winograd E and Neisser U (eds.) *Affect and Accuracy in Recall: Studies of "Flashbulb" Memories*, pp. 9–31. New York: Cambridge University Press.

Neisser U (1967) *Cognitive Psychology*. East Norwalk, CT: Appleton-Century-Crofts.

Nelson DL (1979) Remembering pictures and words: Appearance, significance, and name. In: Cermak LS and Craik FIM (eds.) *Levels of Processing in Human Memory*, pp. 45–76. Hillsdale, NJ: Erlbaum.

Norman DA (ed.) (1970) *Models of Human Memory*. New York: Academic Press.

O'Keefe J and Nadel L (1978) *The Hippocampus as a Cognitive Map*. New York: Oxford University Press.

Osgood CE, Suci GJ, and Tannenbaum PH (1957) *The Measurement of Meaning*. Urbana, IL: University of Illinois Press.

Paivio A (1986) *Mental Representations: A Dual Coding Approach*. New York: Oxford University Press.

Postman L (1964) Short-term memory and incidental learning. In: Melton AW (ed.) *Categories of Human Learning*, pp. 145–201. New York: Academic Press.

Ratcliff R (1978) A theory of memory retrieval. *Psychol. Rev.* 85: 59–108.

Richardson-Klavehn A, Gardiner JM, and Java RI (1996) Memory: Task dissociation, process dissociations and dissociations of consciousness. In: Underwood GDM (ed.) *Implicit Cognition*, pp. 85–158. Oxford: Oxford University Press.

Robinson JA (1976) Sampling autobiographical memory. *Cogn. Psychol.* 8: 578–595.

Roediger HL (1980) Memory metaphors in cognitive psychology. *Mem. Cogn.* 8: 231–246.

Roediger HL, Weldon MS, Stadler ML, and Riedgler GL (1992) Direct comparison of two implicit memory tests: Word fragment and word stem completion. *J. Exp. Psychol. Learn. Mem. Cogn.* 18: 1251–1269.

Roediger HL, Meade ML, and Bergman ET (2001) Social contagion of memory. *Psychon. Bull. Rev.* 8: 365–371.

Roediger HL, Marsh EJ, and Lee SC (2002) Varieties of memory. In: Pashler H and Medin D (eds.) *Steven's Handbook of Experimental Psychology,* 3rd edn. Hoboken, NJ: John Wiley and Sons.

Rubin DC and Berntsen D (2003) Life scripts help to maintain autobiographical memories of highly positive, but not highly negative, events. *Mem. Cogn.* 31: 1–14.

Rubin DC, Wetzler SE, and Nebes RD (1986) Autobiographical memory across the adult life span. In: Rubin DC (ed.) *Autobiographical Memory*, pp. 202–221. Cambridge: Cambridge University Press.

Ryle G (1949) *The Concept of Mind*. New York: Barnes and Noble.

Schacter DL (1987) Implicit memory: History and current status. *J. Exp. Psychol. Learn. Mem. Cogn.* 13: 501–518.

Schacter DL, Bowers J, and Booker J (1989) Intention, awareness, and implicit memory: The retrieval intentionality criterion. In: Lewandowsky S, Dunn J, and Kirsner K (eds.) *Implicit Memory: Theoretical Issues*, pp. 47–65. Hillsdale, NJ: Lawrence Erlbaum Associates.

Shiffrin RM and Atkinson RC (1969) Storage and retrieval processes in long-term memory. *Psychol. Rev.* 76: 179–193.

Slamecka NJ (1985) Ebbinghaus: Some associations. *J. Exp. Psychol. Learn. Mem. Cogn.* 11: 414–435.

Sperling G (1960) The information available in brief visual presentation. *Psychol. Monogr.* 11: 29.

Squire LR (1982) The neuropsychology of human memory. *Annu. Rev. Neurosci.* 5: 241–273.

Squire LR (1992) Declarative and nondeclarative memory: Multiple brain systems supporting learning and memory. *J. Cogn. Neurosci.* 4: 232–243.

Talarico JM and Rubin DC (2003) Confidence, not consistency, characterizes flashbulb memories. *Psychol. Sci.* 14: 455–461.

Tulving E (1972) Episodic and semantic memory. In: Tulving E and Donaldson W (eds.) *Organization of Memory*, pp. 381–403. New York: Academic Press.

Tulving E (1985) Memory and consciousness. *Can. J. Psychol.* 26: 1–12.

Tulving E (2000) Concepts of memory. In: Tulving E and Craik FIM (eds.) *The Oxford Handbook of Memory*, pp. 33–43. New York: Oxford University Press.

Tulving E (2002) Episodic memory: From mind to brain. *Annu. Rev. Psychol.* 54: 1–25.

Tulving E (2005) Episodic memory and autonoesis: Uniquely human? In: Terrace H and Metcalfe J (eds.) *The Missing Link in Cognition: Origins of Self-Reflective Consciousness*, pp. 3–56. New York: Oxford University Press.

Tulving E (2007) Are there 256 kinds of memory? In: Nairne J (ed.) *The Foundations of Remembering: Essays in Honor of Henry L Roediger III*, pp. 39–52. New York: Psychology Press.

Waugh NC and Norman DA (1965) Primary memory. *Psychol. Rev.* 72: 89–104.

Weldon MS (2000) Remembering as a social process. In: Medin DL (ed.) *The Psychology of Learning and Motivation,* vol. 40, pp. 67–120. San Diego: Academic Press.

Weldon MS and Bellinger KD (1997) Collective memory: Collaborative and individual processes in remembering. *J. Exp. Psychol. Learn. Mem. Cogn.* 23: 1160–1175.

Wechsler DB (1963) Engrams, memory storage, and mnemonic coding. *Am. Psychol.* 18: 149–153.

Wertsch JV (2002) *Voices of Collective Remembering*. Cambridge: Cambridge University Press.

Wheeler MA (2000) Episodic memory and autonoetic awareness. In: Tulving E and Craik FIM (eds.) *The Oxford Handbook of Memory*, pp. 597–608. New York: Oxford University Press.

Wright AA (1998) Auditory and visual serial position functions obey different laws. *Psychon. Bull. Rev.* 5: 564–584.

Wright AA and Roediger HL (2003) Interference processes in monkey auditory list memory. *Psychon. Bull. Rev.* 10: 696–702.

Wundt W (1910/1916) *Elements of Folk Psychology*, Schaub EL (trans.). New York: Macmillan.

1.03   History of Behavioral Learning Theories

E. J. Capaldi and A. Martins, Purdue University, West Lafayette, IN, USA

1.03.1   Instrumental Learning Historically and Today

One way to better understand a subject is to approach it historically – to contrast previous ideas, discarded or not, with contemporary ones. Another way is to examine current ideas in depth. The advantage of the historical method is that by contrasting older ideas with current ones, a better understanding is available of why one idea was rejected and another accepted. A disadvantage is that it requires time and effort and so may detract from an in-depth analysis of the evidence for and against contemporary ideas, which is the strength of the in-depth approach. So in examining some contemporary ideas, we would like to know if alternatives to it were raised in the past and, if so, the extent to which such alternatives are still seen as viable. Obviously a better understanding of a subject matter requires both approaches described earlier. Accordingly, both are used here to better understand instrumental learning.

In an attempt to provide historical perspectives, brief thumbnail examinations of selected views of significant figures who have theorized about instrumental learning are provided. This treatment by no means provides a complete discussion of the theorizing of the historical figures, nor is it meant to. Rather, we selected for examination only those views of historical figures that can help to illuminate current approaches to instrumental learning. Some of these earlier views provide illumination because they are still accepted, and some because they have been replaced by other, more adequate views. In either case, contrasting earlier views with current ones is intended to provide a broader context for a better understanding of where, theoretically speaking, we are today.

The framework that encompasses all matters treated here is provided by two major issues. The two issues are relevant to any attempt to understand acquisition processes, e.g., instrumental learning or not. One issue is: What conditions are necessary for learning to occur? For example, if Event A precedes Event B, will Event A become a signal for Event B merely because the two occur together in close temporal relation (contiguity principle), or must Event B be a motivationally significant event such as food for a hungry animal (reinforcement principle)? Or must some other condition or conditions prevail for learning to occur? The second major issue is: When learning occurs, precisely what changes occur? Consider a hungry animal that traverses a runway (a tunnel of sorts) at the end of which is food. Does the animal learn an S-R association, an S-S association, an R-O association, or some combination of these, or is learning encoded in some more cognitive propositional form? According to the S-R view, a stimulus (S, runway stimuli), elicits a response (R, in the presence of these runway stimuli, run down the runway). According to the S-S view, the animal learns that the initial runway cues (S_1) are followed by terminal runway cues (S_2). In runway situations, the hungry animal would tend to use S_1 to approach S_2 when S_2 signals the availability of food. The S-S view, unlike the S-R view, does not suggest that a specific response is learned, only that the animal may perform any number of different responses to get to the second stimulus and food. The R-O view suggests that an association is formed between the response (run down the runway) and the food reward or outcome (O). Learning, in propositional form, may be expressed as follows: If in the presence of these stimuli I traverse this runway, I will obtain a satisfying morsel of food appropriate to my state of hunger.

In any instrumental situation, a response in the presence of a discriminative stimulus produces a reinforcer. For example, a person who enters a building (response) when the sky darkens (discriminative stimulus) to avoid being rained on (reinforcer) is exhibiting a form of instrumental learning. In the laboratory, a rat might cross a barrier when a tone sounds to avoid a shock. In this form of instrumental learning, called avoidance learning, as in various other forms to be discussed, a response (entering a building, crossing a barrier) in the presence of a discriminative stimulus (dark sky, tone) produces a reinforcer (avoiding rain, avoiding shock). Clearly we engage in instrumental behavior under many conditions: when we go to the supermarket, work for a paycheck, study for a test, or do myriad other things. In a word, instrumental behavior is ubiquitous.

The three components of instrumental behavior (a discriminative stimulus, a response, and a reinforcer) will each be examined in some depth, comparing contemporary views on these topics with selected views of major figures, such as Thorndike and Hull. This approach should provide a sound introduction to some of the major findings and theoretical issues of the day (*See* Chapters 1.06 and 1.10).

Instrumental learning cannot be fully understood by focusing on instrumental behavior alone. Two related matters that cannot be completely ignored when considering instrumental behavior are biology and Pavlovian conditioning. By biology we refer to the innate capacities an animal brings to the instrumental situation. Procedurally, Pavlovian learning differs from instrumental learning in not requiring a response to obtain a reinforcer. For example, in the laboratory, food may be presented following a tone of a given duration, regardless of whether or not a rat responds. Over the years a variety of differences between instrumental and Pavlovian learning have been suggested (*See* Chapters 1.06 and 1.10). Although these are interesting for considering the relation between the two, they do not constitute the single greatest reason why some considerations must be given to Pavlovian learning when considering instrumental learning. The major reason is the wide acceptance of the proposition that instrumental learning involves, and to some extent is influenced by, Pavlovian learning. By considering what has been called misbehavior, and some of the research and theory it spawned, we can illustrate clearly why instrumental learning cannot be examined in any depth independent of biological factors and Pavlovian conditioning. Later we shall suggest that instrumental learning may be influenced by another form of learning in addition to Pavlovian learning.

1.03.1.1 Misbehavior

Keller and Marian Breland (Breland and Breland, 1961) trained a variety of animals ranging from birds to whales to make instrumental responses that might be amusing to people at zoos and other places. A very interesting finding in a variety of species was that the instrumental behavior, performed smoothly at first, began to deteriorate with further execution. For example, hungry pigs were required to deposit four or five coins in a piggy bank before food reinforcement was provided. Pigs learned this instrumental task rather easily. But with further execution, the pigs became slower and slower in depositing the coins. A major reason for the slow-down was that the pigs, instead of taking the coin to the bank straight away, would repeatedly drop it, root it, drop it again, toss it in the air, and so on. Of course these rooting behaviors with the coin are the sorts of behavior pigs perform to food itself. To explain this unexpected behavior in pigs (unexpected because it was thought at the time that with further execution instrumental responding would improve), which was called misbehavior, the Brelands suggested that the pigs were drifting back to the sort of instinctive behaviors they innately made to food, just as other species were exhibiting their own form of instinctive drift (Breland and Breland, 1961). In this view, innate responses an animal might have to, say, food were reinforced and strengthened and so came to interfere with "arbitrary" instrumental responses such as depositing a coin in a piggy bank. The idea that signals for food can cause animals to respond to those signals as they would, more or less, to the food itself has given rise to very surprising results under laboratory conditions. In a famous example, when a light signal for food was located some distance from the food itself, pigeons developed the tendency to peck the light before running back to the food hopper. Because food was available only for a rather short specified time this sign tracking behavior, as it is called, either reduced the quantity of reinforcement the animal received or caused the bird to miss reinforcement entirely. The 'rational' thing for the bird to do, of course, would have been

to simply wait near the food hopper, ingesting food when it appeared over the entire time it was available. We see that innate behaviors of the animal can interfere with the smooth performance of instrumental behavior.

Sometime later Boakes et al. (1978) produced misbehavior under controlled laboratory conditions. Rats had to press a flap to obtain a ball bearing to deposit in a chute for food reward. As training progressed, the rats became more and more reluctant to deposit the ball bearings. They developed the tendency to mouth and paw the balls before letting them go. Boakes et al. (1978) suggested a rather different view of misbehavior than did the Brelands. The instinctive drift hypothesis as indicated suggested that food reward was strengthening instinctive food-related behavior. Boakes et al. (1978) suggested that the ball bearings were conditioned stimuli (CSs) eliciting unconditioned Pavlovian responses (URs). Essentially, the ball bearing CSs were eliciting innate food-related behaviors. Further evidence that misbehavior was due to Pavlovian learning interfering with instrumental learning was supplied shortly after by Timberlake et al. (1982).

In the case of misbehavior, instrumental behavior was disrupted. A little reflection serves to show that the interaction of Pavlovian responses with instrumental ones may not always disrupt instrumental performance. To elaborate on a familiar example, the Pavlovian relation between a dark cloud signaling rain and unpleasant wetness may energize the instrumental response of entering a building. One of the oldest, broadest, and most well-developed approaches to instrumental learning assumes that Pavlovian learning interacts with instrumental learning either to facilitate it or disrupt it, an approach generally called two-factor theory. The two factors, of course, are Pavlovian learning and instrumental learning. There are many examples of two-factor theory applied to a variety of instrumental learning phenomena. For now let us examine two-factor theory in relation to two different types of instrumental learning, avoidance conditioning and the acquisition and extinction of an appetitive response.

According to Mowrer (1960), a dark cloud signaling rain is classically conditioned (i.e., is Pavlovian). It supplies motivation for entering the building (i.e., fear of getting wet). Entering the building is an instrumental response, reinforced by a reduction of the fear of getting wet.

Amsel (1958) suggested that when an instrumental response is consistently reinforced with food, stimuli that accompany the food, e.g., the stimuli in the feeding area, are classically conditioned to the feeding response that occurs. Once this Pavlovian conditioning occurs, stimuli prior to the feeding area may elicit a conditioned form of the eating response. This conditioned response itself produces stimuli that become conditioned to the instrumental response and energize it. This conditioning to the instrumental response of stimuli produced by classically conditioned eating responses is identified with expectancy of reward in the Hullian framework favored by Amsel. We shall hear more of Hull later. Amsel suggests that after expectancy of reward is established and the animal is subsequently nonrewarded, the discrepancy between the reward expected and the reward obtained will give rise to a frustrative response. This response will produce frustrative stimuli that, if introduced for the first time, will disrupt instrumental responding.

1.03.1.2   Guthrie

It will be helpful to begin with Guthrie's theory because his views, which are simple and easy to understand, provide a context for better illuminating a variety of other issues. Guthrie (1935) views instrumental learning as S-R associations established by contiguity. He suggests that a combination of stimuli that accompany some movement will on repetition tend to again produce that movement. A stimulus combination gains its full associative strength on its initial pairing with the response. One reason why repetition may be necessary to produce effective performance is that other stimuli may intervene between the movement made and a particular combination of stimuli. The effective association occurs only between simultaneous events.

In a famous experiment intended to demonstrate that behavior tends to repeat itself under highly similar conditions, Guthrie and Horton (1946) provided instead a good reason (like misbehavior much later) for being aware of an animal's natural behavior. In the Guthrie and Horton experiments, cats were photographed as they learned to escape from a small box. To escape, the cat had to make some response to a rod near the box. In responding to the rod, the cat's behavior was described as highly stereotyped behavior interpreted as providing evidence for S-R associations. The reader has probably had experience with hungry housecats brushing against his or her leg in a particular manner. If so, you have a pretty good idea of the response the cats made to the pole. They

are instinctive greeting reactions made by a variety of cats, wild and domestic, known as flank rubbing. In a series of experiments Moore and Stuttard (1979) demonstrated that domestic cats would make the responses observed by Guthrie and Horton even when they are not hungry and are not rewarded for responding. They are greeting responses elicited by the sight of human observers. In the Guthrie and Horton study, the cats were aware of being observed by people. Keep this behavior in mind for later, when the behavior systems approach to instrumental learning is considered.

1.03.1.3   Estes Stimulus Sampling Theory

Stimulus sampling theory began as an attempt to formalize certain of Guthrie's ideas. Various versions of stimulus sample theory are in vogue today, as will be briefly considered later, so in this sense Guthrie lives today. In the Estes (1950) version of stimulus sampling theory, the stimulus is represented as a population of elements. On a trial, only a sample of elements from the entire population is effective (i.e., sampled). Two sources affecting which elements are sampled are random events (noises, etc.) and changes in the participant (variable behavior over trials, etc.). One view of stimulus sampling suggests that each element has a particular probability of being sampled. Another is that a number of elements is drawn without replacement from the population elements. Still another view suggests other possibilities. Estes assumed that each element is connected to one response. In this manner different S-R associations would be formed.

1.03.1.4   Thorndike

Thorndike's (1898) experiments in which hungry cats had to make some response to escape from a puzzle box to obtain food essentially introduced a new way to study learning and, for that reason alone, were justly famous. Learning was seen by Thorndike as forming connections. According to Thorndike, most learning could be explained in terms of animals making responses to situations as they were perceived. In an earlier formulation Thorndike identified three laws of learning: readiness, exercise, and effect. For learning to occur (i.e., for connections to be made), an animal had to be ready to learn (e.g., ready to read), practice or exercise was required, and the consequences of an act would determine whether the connection would be strengthened or weakened, with satisfying consequences strengthening connections and annoying consequences weakening them.

Later on, the law of exercise was practically rejected, and the law of effect was modified. The famous finding that a blindfolded subject showed no improvement in drawing a line of a given length was among those that led to rejection of the law of exercise. The results of several experiments led Thorndike to believe that reward had a more powerful effect than punishment. For example, in certain choice experiments, Thorndike (1898) found that performance was much more affected by correct choice and reward than by incorrect choice and punishment. Punishment, according to Thorndike, caused animals to make other than the punished response. Something new introduced by Thorndike (1898) was the principle of belongingness. According to this principle, some stimuli are more easily associated with some responses than others. For example, taste cues are more easily associated with sickness than visual cues.

1.03.1.5 Hull

On considering Hull, we focus on his best-known single work, the *Principles of Behavior* (Hull, 1943). According to Hull, if in the presence of some stimuli a response was made, and the response was followed by a reinforcer, learning would occur in the form of strengthening a stimulus–response connection called a habit and symbolized as $_SH_R$. Reinforcement occurred when a need was reduced, as when a hungry animal obtained food. The bigger the need reduction, the greater the reinforcement. Greater reinforcement leads to stronger habits and more vigorous performance. But the expression of a habit in performance depends on several other factors, the most important for our purposes being drive (D), hunger drive produced by food deprivation, thirst drive being produced by water deprivation, and so on. Habit and drive interacted in multiplicative manner (i.e., $_SH_R \times D$). If D were zero, or near zero, as in the case of hunger drive in a recently fed animal, the product $_SH_R \times D$ would be near zero, and the animal would not respond, press a lever, run down a runway, and so on. Of course, if D and $_SH_R$ had high values, the product $_SH_R \times D$ would be large, and the animal would respond vigorously.

Responding produced inhibition, which opposed responding. The conditioned form of inhibition was symbolized as $_SI_R$. Reinforcement in this case was produced by the fading or diminution of inhibition with rest or not responding. Because in Hull's 1943 system $_SI_R$ was subtracted from $_SH_R$ (i.e., $_SH_R - _SI_R$), it may be seen that if the tendency to perform a response ($_SH_R$) was opposed by an equally strong tendency not to perform the response ($_SI_R$), responding would not occur. The failure of an acquired response to occur because of nonreinforcement is called extinction. It's important to note that extinction in Hull's 1943 system was due to competition between the tendency to respond ($_SH_R$) and the tendency not to respond ($_SI_R$). Although competing responses may play a role in extinction, as will become clear later, other mechanisms may play larger roles.

1.03.1.6 Skinner

Although few on the contemporary scene would claim to be, say, Hullians, many, it seems, would be happy to describe themselves as Skinnerians. Skinner's system may be classified as a descriptive one. Two examples may make clear what is meant by a descriptive system. A reinforcer is defined by its effects: Any stimulus that increases the probability of a response is a reinforcer. By drive Skinner (1938) means to point to a set of operations (say the number of hours since feeding) that have an effect on responding. Reinforcement does not arise from need reduction or a satisfying state of affairs. Drive does not arise from a state of need.

Thus Skinner is interested in functional relations between variables. He and his followers are not interested in explaining, for example, bar pressing as a habit arising from that response being followed by food that reduced a need, as Hull did. Sometimes Skinner's approach is classified as radical behaviorism. In our view it can be more correctly identified as a form of radical empiricism.

In Skinner's system the causes of behavior are not in the organism (its habits, drive, cognition, and so on) but are in the environment (reinforced behaviors are strengthened). This approach, among other things, has led Skinner to place much emphasis on schedules of reward – how, for example, ratio schedules (only some responses are reinforced), time schedules (reinforcement is available following a certain elapsed time), and other schedules influence behavior. So Skinner had little use for systems postulating hypothetic entities. He placed heavy emphasis on the practical implications of his system. In his book *Walden Two* (Skinner, 1948), he essentially designed a society in terms of reinforcement principles. In other ways, too, Skinner went beyond the laboratory. For example, he applied reinforcement principles to verbal behavior.

It is important to note that Skinner did not necessarily deny the existence of nonobservable concepts such as cognitions. What he did deny is that such unobservable concepts, if they exist, cause behavior.

1.03.1.7   Tolman

Tolman (1932) suggested that behavior is molar and purposeful. Molar behavior, Tolman suggested, has properties all its own and cannot be identified with muscular movement, glandular secretion, or neural processes. By purpose, Tolman suggested, behavior occurs with some end in mind. Mailing a letter, buying a car, or going to a movie are purposeful behaviors executed with an end in mind. Signal learning is a distinctive feature of Tolman's system. For example, in traversing a complex maze, the learner is guided by internal and external stimuli rather than by executing a series of muscular movements. Put slightly differently, the participant follows signs to a goal, learns, in effect, a route rather than movements without meaning. This may be illustrated by an early experiment from Tolman's laboratory: Rats that learned to run through a complex maze still performed correctly when later the maze was flooded and entirely different movement patterns were required (swimming rather than running). This sort of reasoning led to what is without doubt Tolman's best-known idea on the contemporary scene, cognitive maps. Although there is some disagreement as to the definition of a cognitive map, Tolman (1948) suggested that it is a representation of the environment that includes paths, routes, and environmental relationships that a participant may use in deciding where to move.

Experiments by Blodgett (1929) and later Tolman and Honzik (1930) indicated that hungry animals could learn their way through a maze even when not given food reward. Animals performing more or less at chance prior to being given food immediately reduced errors substantially when given food reward. Acquired learning in the absence of appropriate performance was called latent learning. In order for learning that is latent to manifest itself in performance, appropriate conditions of motivation and reinforcement must be present.

1.03.2   Types of Instrumental Behavior

Various types of instrumental learning that have been used are briefly described next.

1. *Appetitive.* In an appetitive situation a response produces an appetitive stimulus such as food. Example: Pressing a bar produces food. In secondary reward training, pressing a bar might produce a stimulus, called a secondary or learned reinforcer, that was initially paired with a primary reinforcer such as food. Secondary reinforcers may be effective in increasing performance.

2. *Punishment training.* In punishment training a response produces an aversive effect such as shock. Animals make punished responses because some appetitive stimulus is provided, such as food. Evidence suggests that when nonreinforced trials are given along with reinforced ones, called partial reward, the nonreinforced trials are aversive (Brown and Wagner, 1964). Partial reward then may be a variety of punishment training.

3. *Extinction.* Following acquisition training, all trials may be nonreinforced. This is called extinction. Typically, behavior declines in extinction.

4. *Discrimination training.* Responses may receive appetitive training in the presence of one stimulus and nonreinforcement in the presence of another stimulus. Such discrimination training has many variations. For example, both stimuli may receive appetitive training, but appetitive outcomes may occur more frequently in one alternative than in the other.

5. *Escape training.* In escape training, a response terminates an aversive stimulus – usually shock. For example, an animal that is shocked may learn to run to a place in which shock does not occur.

6. *Avoidance training.* In a signaled avoidance situation, if an animal makes some response when some stimulus occurs, it can avoid an aversive event, usually shock; otherwise it is shocked. In a popular version of avoidance training, running or jumping to the other side of a box when a tone sounds can avoid shock. In Sidman or operant avoidance, the animal can avoid shock for a certain time (the response–shock interval) by making a response. Shock occurs at a shorter interval if a response is not made (the shock–shock interval). For example, the response–shock interval may be 20 s and the shock–shock interval 10 s. Thus, it pays the animal to respond.

7. *Passive avoidance*. In the passive avoidance situation, the animal is shocked for making a response. It differs from punishment training in that only the aversive shock event occurs, and not the appetitive event. As might be expected, behavior is quickly modified in the laboratory by passive avoidance training.

Sometimes the instrumental procedures just described are explicitly combined with Pavlovian ones. A popular example is as follows: After learning to press a bar for food, a rat may be shocked when a tone sounds. The tendency of the tone to reduce bar pressing is used to index fear of the tone.

1.03.3 What Makes a Stimulus a Reinforcer?

The three elements of an instrumental response are a discriminative stimulus, a response, and a reinforcer. In this section we consider various theoretical positions on reinforcers.

1.03.3.1 Contiguity

According to Guthrie (1935), reinforcement is not necessary for learning, temporal contiguity between stimulus and response being sufficient. Or one may assume, along with Skinner, that explaining why a reinforcer is a reinforcer is not necessary. All that is required is the description of a functional relationship between some response and some stimulus. The latent learning studies of Blodgett (1929) and Tolman and Honzik (1930) suggest that the effect of reinforcement is not on learning but on the motivation to engage in behavior learned by other means. Hull, who changed his position on reinforcement between his 1943 book and his 1952 book, suggested an important role for incentive motivation in determining behavior. He added to $_SH_R \times D$ a role for incentive motivation (V), so that in his later statement, we have $_SH_R \times D \times V$. Like D, if V is zero, behavior will not occur.

1.03.3.2 Satisfying Needs

As to the various explanations of what makes a reinforcer a reinforcer, Thorndike's idea that satisfaction and discomfort were key to understanding the effectiveness of reinforcers has several drawbacks: It is subjective, and like Skinner's view, it suggests that one can determine what is or is not a reinforcer only after the fact, after observing its effects on responding.

1.03.3.3 Need Reduction

Hull's idea of need reduction provides a means for determining whether a stimulus is or is not a reinforcer that is independent of its effects on the behavior it follows. For example, food deprivation will increase the need for food, and thus eating food will reduce the need and become reinforcing. Two problems with this formulation are that learning has been shown to occur when rats are given sucrose, which has no calories and thus does not reduce a need or drive (Sheffield and Roby, 1950), and when drive is increased rather than decreased, as with learning responses that increase sex drive (Sheffield, 1966). Hull's 1943 position was that greater need reduction increased the limit of asymptote to which learning could occur, a popular position today, as we shall see. In 1952, Hull assumed that reinforcement was necessary for learning but did not affect the asymptote of learning. More vigorous performance for larger reinforcers was now suggested to be due to V or incentive motivation, as indicated earlier. A major reason Hull modified his position was a set of findings provided by Crespi (1942). Crespi reported that after rats had been trained to respond, shifting reinforcement from large to small or vice versa produced a rapid change in behavior – too rapid, Hull thought, to be explained in terms of changes in learning or $_SH_R$. Rapid behavior change was due to a change in incentive motivation, or V.

Hull's 1952 position suggested that reinforcers can exert an effect on responding that is independent of its effects on the S-R association itself. More recent theories accept this view, as we will see in greater depth when we take up the issue of what is learned (i.e., what changes occur when learning occurs). For now it is enough to say the following: If a response is followed by a reinforcer, the execution of the response can be affected by devaluing the reinforcer in the absence of the response itself. That is, if the reinforcer is associated with lithium chloride, a poison that makes the animal sick, the animal will avoid that reinforcer, and its tendency to make the response that produced the reinforcer will be reduced (Rescorla, 2001). Along similar lines is the finding that merely placing the animal in an empty goal box, in effect showing the animal that food may no longer be available, reduces the vigor of responding, an effect called latent extinction or nonresponse extinction (Young et al., 1960).

1.03.3.4 Premack Principle

Monkeys placed in a box by Butler and Harlow (1954) learned a response for the opportunity to look into a room. Rats will learn a maze simply by exploring it (Montgomery, 1951). These and other findings suggest that stimuli not necessary for physical survival can function as reinforcers. This view was forcefully put forward by David Premack (1965). According to Premack, activities are reinforcing to the extent that they are probable. For example, depriving a rat of food makes eating more probable, and thus reinforcing. Higher-probability responses reinforce lower-probability responses. Thus, higher-probability eating will reinforce lower-probability bar pressing. As another example, a teenager may be induced to clean his or her room, a low-probability behavior, for the opportunity to watch TV, a higher-probability behavior. This view, unlike the views of Skinner and Thorndike, allows us to determine, in advance of learning, the reinforcing capacity of particular behaviors. That is, before putting an animal in a learning situation, we can determine how probable it is that an animal would perform various behaviors under particular conditions. If the Premack principle is correct, it is possible to predict in advance which behavior will reinforce which.

1.03.3.5 The Response Deprivation Hypothesis

There is evidence that, contrary to the Premack principle, low-probability responses can reinforce higher-probability responses. It is a matter of depriving the animal of the less-probable response. For example, if ingesting X is less probable than ingesting Y, the tendency to ingest Y can be increased above its baseline by depriving the animal of X and making the availability of X contingent on ingesting Y (e.g., Timberlake and Allison, 1974; Allison, 1989). There are many interesting applications of the response deprivation hypothesis. For example, 3-year-old children who loved to run around and scream were induced in a fairly short time to sit still, a not highly probable activity for 3 year olds. Essentially, after the children sat quietly for a specified time period, they were allowed to run and scream for a few minutes (Homme et al., 1963).

The response deprivation hypothesis allows us, like the Premack principle, to determine in advance how reinforcing some activity might be. It also allows us to adjust reinforcers to particular animals or people. For example, a person who enjoys TV will perform other behaviors if those behaviors allow TV viewing, which is otherwise reduced. But if a person enjoys reading more than TV watching, let reading be contingent on TV watching.

A more subtle implication of the response deprivation hypothesis bears mention. Normally we think of instrumental behavior such as bar pressing as different from consummatory behavior such as eating. This distinction is violated by the response deprivation hypothesis. That is, any behavior can serve as a reinforcer if it is made to occur below its normal baseline. Animals deprived of food will run in order to eat, and an animal deprived of activity will eat in order to run.

1.03.3.6 Reinforcer Relativity

A popular view of reinforcement and its effects today is that it is determined by some state of the organism. For example, in Amsel's 1958 formulation of frustration theory, a given reward magnitude would tend to increase responding if it were larger than expected but would be frustrating and would tend to decrease responding it if were smaller than expected. The most recognizable form of this 'relativity' of reinforcement is contained perhaps in the Rescorla-Wagner model (Rescorla and Wagner, 1972). On a given trial, the learning actually accomplished might be lower or higher than that supported by the reinforcer employed. If it were lower, excitatory learning would occur, the change in excitation being greater the greater the difference between the learning accomplished and the learning supported by the reinforcer. However, if learning accomplished on a trial is greater than that supported by the reinforcer, inhibitory learning would occur, the inhibitory change being greater the greater the discrepancy between learning accomplished and learning supported by the reinforcer. It is probably the case that most learning psychologists accept some form of reinforcer relativity.

1.03.4 Discriminative Stimuli

Identifying the stimuli that give rise to instrumental responding is one of the most controversial types of learning at present. We treat the topic under seven headings.

1.03.4.1   Common Understanding

In many theories, particularly earlier ones such as those of Thorndike, Hull, and Guthrie, the stimuli that controlled instrumental responding were described in commonsense terms. For example, if the animal ran down a black runway to obtain food, the situation might be described as the black runway elicits the instrumental response (I) of running. Symbolically this may be expressed as $S_B \rightarrow I$. In Hull's 1943 formulation, for example, this S-R formulation was considered adequate to explain instrumental responding. Both earlier in his journal publications (see Amsel, 1958, for Hull's collected journal papers) and later in his 1952 book, Hull would consider other important stimuli in controlling responding, as will be considered in due course. But in his 1943 statement, Hull considered instrumental responding to be controlled by exteroceptive stimuli such as "black runway" and certain interoceptive cues such as drive stimuli (stimuli produced by, e.g., hunger) and proprioceptive cues such as feedback stimuli from overt responses such as turning left or right.

1.03.4.2   Contextual Cues

Both in Pavlovian and instrumental learning, the idea arose that various contextual cues controlled responding in ways other than merely eliciting them as the S-R formulation considered earlier suggests. An important thing to note about contextual cues is that they could arise from any source: from the apparatus, from the passage of time, to just name a few. In one manifestation of this approach, the contextual cues affect responding by competing with or supporting the cues of interest to the experimenters. In the Pavlovian situation, for example, contextual apparatus cues occur along with the CS when the US is presented. To the extent that the contextual cues signal the US, they would, for one reason or another, weaken responding to the CS (see, e.g., Miller and Matzel, 1989; Rescorla and Wagner, 1972). In the instrumental situation, the contextual cues might also reduce instrumental responding. For example, animals that learned a discrimination under a so-called irrelevant cue (degree of floor tilt) had that discrimination disrupted when the floor was titled differently (Thomas, 1985). So one effect of

considering context was to bring to our attention to the fact that the animal was responding to a greater range of stimuli than was previously recognized.

Another way of thinking about context is that it may function as a superordinate stimuli, informing the animal as to the specific relations that prevail under a given set of conditions. For example, in a wide variety of both instrumental and Pavlovian situations, it has been found that the extinction of responding in one context (e.g., white box) after acquisition in another context (e.g., black box) is 'renewed' when the animal is returned to the original black context. That is, responding extinguished in the black box reappears to some extent when the animal is returned to the original context, or even some novel context (see, e.g., Bouton, 1993, 2004).

Precisely how context regulates responding is a matter of some interest, which will be considered when reward produced memories are considered.

1.03.4.3   Configural Cues

When two or more cues are presented, they may be fused, so to speak, into a single representation that is perceived differently than the individual cues that comprise it. Such fused stimuli are called configural cues. In both the instrumental (e.g., Spence, 1952) and Pavlovian areas (e.g., Pearce, 1987), there are phenomena that, in the opinion of some, call for a configurational approach. We consider three examples of such phenomena. In a feature negative discrimination, the stimuli A and B are reinforced, while the combination of stimuli AB is nonreinforced (A+, B+, AB−). Animals will come to respond more strongly to the stimuli A and B than to the combination AB. It is perhaps clear that if the stimuli in a feature negative discrimination are conceptualized, as is commonly understood, then the feature negative discrimination could not be solved. That is, if the stimuli A and B are excitatory, then the compound AB must be even more excitatory. Other examples also difficult to understand are feature positive discriminations (A−, B−, AB+) and biconditional discriminations (e.g., AB+, CD+, AC−, BD−).

One way to deal with the learning of these complex discrimination problems is to assume that stimuli are configured. For example, in the negative patterning case, it may be assumed that the stimuli A and B differ from AB in that AB is a configuration. In this view, AB may be conceptualized as giving rise to a distinct stimulus X. In this way, excitation that generalizes from A and B will have less of an effect on X than on AB. One configural approach is to assume that stimuli such as AB are configured under some circumstances but not others (e.g., Rescorla and Wagner, 1972). Another (Pearce, 1987) is to assume that all stimuli are configured whether presented alone (A, B) or in compound (AB). The former view suggests that in, say, the negative patterning case, generalization and discrimination occur between A and X and B and X. In the Pearce view, generalization and discrimination occur between the configurations A, B, and AB. Still another view, considered in the next section, rejects configuration, attempting to solve problems like negative patterning by considering stimuli to be composed of a number of discrete elements that interact.

1.03.4.4 Stimulus Sampling Theory Revisited

As we saw, Estes's version of stimulus sampling theory was derived from Guthrie's theory. Several different, newer versions of stimulus sampling theory are designed to explain phenomena such as negative pattern. One such that eschews any type of configural cue, proposing to postulate stimulus elements only, is that of McLaren and Mackintosh (2002). Prominent assumptions of this view are as follows: Some elements of a stimulus may be more weakly activated than others; however, elements weakly activated in individual stimuli may be strongly activated when two stimuli are presented in compound. This view explains a conditional discrimination such as the negative patterning problem, suggesting that certain elements weakly activated in stimulus A and in stimulus B are strongly activated in the AB compound. In this way the AB compound is made discriminative from A and from B using an element model and not a configural model. Thus, the animal can learn to respond strongly to the reinforced A and B stimuli and weakly to the nonreinforced AB compound.

1.03.4.5 Behavior Systems

According to the behavior systems approach (Timberlake et al., 1982), animals possess instinctive behavior systems such as feeding, predation, defense, mating, and so on. Certain stimuli are effective in activating a particular behavior system (see Timberlake, 2001). Stimuli employed in the laboratory are effective in activating a behavior system according to their similarity with natural stimuli. For example, a moving object

will activate predator responses in a rat, which results in the responses such as chasing and biting.

1.03.4.6 Reinforcement-Produced Stimuli (Pavlovian Version)

Outcomes such as food reward, shock, nonreward, and so on, it is generally agreed, produce stimuli that may come to control instrumental responding. What mechanisms produce these stimuli? One approach, the Pavlovian one, is considered in this section. The other approach, the memory view, is considered later.

One version of the Pavlovian approach is associated with Hull and Spence and, in its most popular form perhaps, by Amsel (1958). Consider a rat that, having completed an instrumental response, is fed in the goalbox of the runway. Events in the goalbox can be seen as analogous to Pavlovian conditioning. Thus the goalbox cues (S_C) may be seen as the CS, the food as the US, and eating as the unconditioned response (R_G). The goalbox cues can be seen to elicit a conditioned eating response. This conditioned response is referred to as r_g, the conditioned form of the unconditioned eating response R_G. So we have $S_C \rightarrow r_g$. Runway cues prior to the goalbox (approach cues S_A) will elicit r_g to the extent that they are similar to S_C. Response in this formulation produces stimuli (i.e., $r_g \rightarrow s_g$). In the early portions of the runway, runway stimulus (S_A) elicits r_g, which produces s_g, and so s_g becomes conditioned to the instrumental response (I_R). This may be expressed as is shown in **Figure 1**.

This is a very powerful formulation. Earlier we indicated that merely placing the animal in the goalbox could lead to extinction. Such nonresponsive extinction is easily explained by the r_g mechanism. In the goalbox without food, the S_C-r_g association is extinguished as would any Pavlovian association. Thus, after goal placement, we would have $S_A \rightarrow I_R$. In the absence of the s_g-I_R association, instrumental responding would decline.

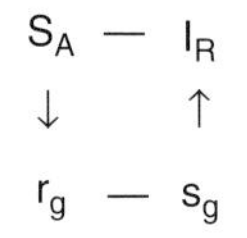

$$S_A - I_R$$
$$\downarrow \quad \uparrow$$
$$r_g - s_g$$

Figure 1 How stimuli produced by anticipatory responses come to control instrumental responses according to Hull, Spence, and Amsel.

$$r_f \ — \ s_f$$
$$\uparrow \qquad \downarrow$$
$$S_A \ — \ I_R$$
$$\downarrow \qquad \uparrow$$
$$r_g \ — \ s_g$$

Figure 2 Amsel's formulation slowing how stimuli produced by anticipatory consumatory responses and anticipatory frustration responses come to control instrumental responses.

A powerful assumption introduced by Amsel is that if obtained reward was smaller than expected reward (r_g), the animal would be frustrated (R_F). As with R_g, a conditioned form of R_F will be elicited by goalbox cues (r_f). By the same means used in connection with r_g, r_f will become conditioned to runway cues and would produce s_g, which will become conditioned to I_R. We would have what is shown in **Figure 2**.

Among the many phenomena this view explains, the most prominent is the partial reinforcement extinction effect or PREE. The PREE consists of greater resistance to extinction when responses are both nonreinforced and reinforced (partial reinforcement or PRF) than when all responses are reinforced (consistent reinforcement or CRF). The PREE was a problem for all the major earlier theories (Thorndike, Hull, Guthrie, Skinner, and so on). Amsel's frustration view explains the PREE as follows. Extinction following CRF results in the introduction of considerable unconditioned frustration (R_F), which produces stimuli that elicit responses incompatible with the instrumental responses or I_R. Following PRF, frustration is conditioned to I_R, and so the animal is able to respond over a considerable number of nonrewarded trials.

What is sometimes called modern two-process theory, like the Hull-Spence-Amsel traditional version of two-process theory, assumes that classical conditioning is important in guiding and motivating instrumental behavior (Rescorla and Solomon, 1967). Modern two-process theory, unlike the traditional version, does not assume that some particular response is learned. What classical conditioning does, according to modern two-process theory, is to elicit a particular type of motivation, called a central emotional state. The emotional state elicited by the CS corresponds to that produced by the US. The emotional states do not result in a particular response. A frown may produce fear, anger, or

indifference, for example – fear if the frowner is a stronger competitor, anger if the frowner is a weaker competitor, and indifference if the frowner is a stranger we likely will not encounter again. Instrumental behavior may be disrupted when, for example, a CS that is followed by shock elicits fear that disrupts bar pressing for food. A CS followed by food may, however, increase bar pressing for food by increasing hope. Traditional two-process theory with its emphasis on specific responses producing specific stimuli and modern two-process theory with its emphasis on motivational state affecting responding are not necessarily at odds with each other. For example, Rescorla, one of the authors of modern two-process theory, has recently found some of Amsel's assumptions useful for explaining extinction (Rescorla, 2001).

1.03.4.7 Stimulus Process Models

Earlier theories, on the whole, tended to assume a rather passive organism. For example, Spence (1936, 1937) suggested that all stimuli falling on the animal's receptors become associated with the instrumental response. Lashley (1951) put forward an attention view suggesting that animals actively and selectively attend to stimulus dimensions. Lashley's view did not gain general acceptance. At present a variety of proposals have been put forward suggesting that some stimuli may be more successful than others in gaining control over responding.

One suggestion, generally accepted, is that some stimuli are more salient than others and therefore will tend to be more successful in gaining control over responding. For example, brighter lights or louder tones may be more salient than less bright lights or less loud tones.

Another general type of suggestion is that over trials the organism may become more or less receptive to some stimuli than others. For example, Mackintosh (1975) assumed that stimuli will be attended to depending on the extent to which they predict reinforcement. Pearce and Hall (1980) made the rather different assumption that stimuli that predict reinforcement will not be attended to. Wagner (1978) assumed that stimuli will be processed to the extent that they are surprising. Each of these views can explain an important phenomenon that has been investigated in both instrumental and Pavlovian situations: blocking. In blocking, a given stimulus A is reinforced. Following this, stimulus A is presented along with stimulus B, and the compound is reinforced. A typical finding is that responding to B is weak when B is presented in isolation. Mackintosh (1975) suggested that the animal is attending to A and not B, and thus blocking occurs. Pearce and Hall (1980) assumed that the compound AB predicts reward, and thus B is not attended to. Wagner (1978) assumed that the compound is not surprising and thus is not processed, and so blocking occurs.

1.03.4.8   Reward-Produced Memories

The stimuli produced by reinforcement events may be conceptualized as memories rather than the feedback stimuli of Pavlovian responses. In some cases (e.g., the PREE), the memory view and the r_g view successfully explain the same phenomena. In other cases some phenomena are better explained by one view than the other. For example, faster running sometimes occurs under PRF relative to CRF, an effect that the frustration model explains well. In another example, the sequence in which larger and smaller reinforcement occur may have profound effects on responding. The sequential model is better equipped to explain such findings (see, e.g., Capaldi, 1967, 1994).

The sequential model assumes that discriminable stimuli (memories) are associated with a large and small magnitude of reinforcement, with nonreinforcement, with different numbers of these events (e.g., the memory of two nonrewards in succession differs from that of a single nonreward), and with different combinations of reinforcement (e.g., the memory associated with nonreinforcement following reinforcement differs from that associated with the successive non-reinforcement or a single nonreinforcement).

The sequential model has been applied to a variety of phenomena. To best understand the implications of the view with a minimal amount of data, it is well to recognize that two PRF schedules equated along many dimensions (e.g., percentage of reinforcement, number of trials, magnitude of reinforcement) but differing in terms of the sequence in which the reinforced and nonreinforced trials are presented may produce quite different responses in acquisition and extinction, both when the interval between trials is short and when it is long (e.g., Capaldi, 1994). This is explained in terms of different sequences of reinforcement giving rise to different stimuli (memories) that then exercise control over responding. The details of this approach are too complex to be fully elaborated here, but some idea of the process may be gleaned from the following example: If a reinforced trial follows a nonreinforced trial, the memory of nonreward will tend to become a signal for reward. But if the nonreinforced trial follows the reinforced trials, then the memory of reward will tend to become a signal for nonreinforcement. In this example, quite different things are learned when the same number and percentage of rewarded and nonrewarded trials are presented in different sequences.

Perhaps the best intuitive understanding of how memories control instrumental responding is provided by a schedule in which reinforced and nonreinforced trials are given in single alternation fashion (SA schedule). Under the SA schedule, rats will come to show pattern responding and faster running on reinforced than on nonreinforced trials even at intervals between trials of 20 min and 24 h (Capaldi and Stanley, 1963).

1.03.5   Response

Two somewhat different but related issues are considered in this section. One is concerned with how to characterize the instrumental response. The other is concerned with the role the response might exercise in relation to reinforcement outcome (R-O association).

1.03.5.1   Characterizing the Response

In the simple T maze shown in **Figure 3**, the animal starts at S and can gain food by making the correct response. One of the most divisive issues of early theories was with how to characterize the correct response. Is the rat learning a movement pattern associated with left turning, as Guthrie would say, or is the animal learning something more general, such as going to a place? In an attempt to resolve this issue, a variety of procedures have been employed.

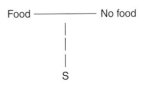

Figure 3 A simple T maze. The animal is placed in the maze at S and can respond by turning to the left or the right – a right turn produces food reward, a left turn no reward.

1.03.5.1.1 Extensive training

One procedure is to train the animal for a considerable number of trials to see whether the response becomes progressively more stereotyped with training. The idea here is that if the response is best characterized in terms of movements, it should show less and less variability as training progresses. But if the animal is learning something more general, such as obtaining food by approaching the windowed wall on the left, behavior could show considerable variability over trials. Muenzinger (1928) trained guinea pigs to approach a bar and to press it to obtain food. The animals were trained for 1000 trials; considerably more training was required for performance to improve. Muenzinger classified the animal's behavior into nine classes: press with left foot, press with right food, press with both feet, press with head, and so on. Behavior varied over trials, with one behavior rising and another falling. Tolman (1932) used results of this sort to support his idea that animals obtain goals and do not necessarily engage in movement patterns. For an alternative interpretation of these findings, see MacCorquodale and Meehl (1954).

1.03.5.1.2 Shift responses

Another approach is to allow an animal to obtain reinforcement by performing one response, then requiring another response to obtain the same reinforcement. For example, an animal might obtain reinforcement by running through a maze. Then after learning, as indicated, the maze might be flooded so that now a different series of movements (swimming) must be made to obtain food (Tolman, 1932). Lashley (1951) operated on animals so that a new response, rolling through the maze, rather than running, was required to obtain food. In both cases, considerable transfer was obtained from running to swimming and from running to rolling.

1.03.5.1.3 Blocked routes

A third way was to have animals obtain reinforcement by going to some particular place for food by a given route. After learning, the original path would be blocked and a variety of new alternative paths provided. The question was: Would the animal select an optimal path to the goal such as the shortest one? In a famous experiment of this sort, Tolman et al. (1946) obtained positive findings.

1.03.5.1.4 Cross maze

A related method involved the use of a cross maze of the sort shown in **Figure 4**. A trial would start by

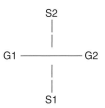

Figure 4 A cross maze. The animal may be placed at either S_1 or S_2. It may respond by turning either to G1 or to G2.

placing the animal at S1 or at S2. One group, the place group, was required to go to G1 to obtain food, both when started from S1 and when started from S2. The other group, the response group, was required to turn in a given direction, say left, for food. This means that when started from S1, the animal was required to go to G1, and when started from S2, the animal was required to go to G2. Better performance by the place group than by the response group would suggest that a more cognitive characterization of what was learned would be in order, according to Tolman et al. (1946). Better performance by the response group would indicate that more stereotyped responses were learned according to Tolman et al.

Considerable research was reported using the cross maze. The outcome of this research was that better place than response learning occurred under some conditions, the opposite being the case under other conditions (see Restle, 1957).

Restle suggested that animals may learn either stereotyped responses or broader responses, a conclusion that is not surprising, considering earlier research. For example, it was shown early on that rats that learned to run a certain distance for food would turn into an empty wall when the runway was lengthened, and they would fly out into empty space when the runway was shortened (Munn, 1950).

On the other hand, it is clear that animals can also obtain a reinforcer using other than the original response, such as swimming instead of running.

1.03.5.2 R-O Association

Classically, two sorts of associations have been posited by theorists such as Thorndike and Hull in instrumental learning, S-R associations and S-S associations (stimulus–outcome associations). In an S-S association, some stimulus (window on the right) elicits some response (turn left or approach the window). Recently several theorists have suggested that the reward outcome (O) may be anticipated on the basis of the response, an R-O association. This makes common sense: A person might say "I am pressing the bar (R) in order to obtain food (O)."

A major procedure for investigation of R-O association involves reinforcer devaluation. We will now describe in general terms how this is done. The animal might be trained to make two different responses such as bar pressing (R1) or chain pulling (R2) to obtain two different reinforcers, say plain pellets (O1) and sucrose pellets (O2) (e.g., R1-O1, R2-O2). Following this training, one of the outcomes may be devalued by poisoning it following its ingestion. Without further training, the animal is given access to both R1 and R2. A critical finding is that the response followed by the poisoned reinforcer is reduced relative to the other (see, e.g., Colwill and Rescorla, 1985). This indicates that the animal is able to anticipate which O follows which R.

1.03.6 Extinction

Every theory of learning has to deal not only with acquisition of responding but with its extinction as well. The theories of extinction embraced by Thorndike, Hull, Spence, Estes, and others have not fared well. For example, Hull (1943) suggested a theory of extinction in which the tendency to respond and the tendency to not respond at the end of extinction would be in balance. Essentially, according to the Hullian position, at the end of extinction, reacquisition of responding would be impossible. At the other extreme, the Rescorla-Wagner view of extinction (Rescorla and Wagner, 1972) suggests that original learning would be erased by extinction, and reacquisition would have to start from scratch and be no different from original acquisition.

Numerous phenomena indicate that whatever was learned in the acquisition phase survives in extinction to a considerable extent. One is so-called spontaneous recovery, in which responding recovers following the elapse of time since extinction. Rapid reacquisition following extinction is another example. In rapid reacquisition, three phases may occur: CRF, extinction, and CRF again. In the third phase, responding that was lost in extinction quickly recovers.

Over the years three views of extinction have been suggested. One is the sort of competing response view suggested by Hull (1943) – that the tendency to respond in extinction is opposed by the growth in extinction of the tendency not to respond. Another is

the unlearning view suggested, for example, by Rescorla and Wagner (1972) that whatever was learned in acquisition is unlearned in extinction. The third is that extinction is a variety of discrimination learning in which stimuli that are excitatory in acquisition are replaced in extinction by stimuli that are not excitatory (e.g., Capaldi, 1967, 1994). Some theories, Amsel (1958) for example, assumed all three. According to Amsel, in extinction r_g is extinguished, unconditioned frustration elicits responses incompatible with the instrumental reaction, and frustration may introduce entirely new nonexcitatory stimuli in extinction, particularly following CRF acquisition. Extinction, a highly popular area of investigation in the 1960s to about 1980, has recently become a fertile area of investigation again (see, e.g., Rescorla, 2001; Bouton, 2004).

References

Allison J (1989) The nature of reinforcement. In: Klein SB and Mowrer RR (eds.) *Contemporary Learning Theories: Instrumental Conditional Theory and the Impact of Biological Constraints in Learning*, pp. 13–39. Hillsdale, NJ: Erlbaum.
Amsel A (1958) The role frustrative nonreward in noncontinuous reward situations. *Psychol. Bull.* 55: 102–119.
Blodgett HC (1929) The effect of the introduction of reward upon the maze performance of rats. *Univ. Calif. Publ. Psychol.* 4: 113–134.
Boakes RA, Poli M, Lockwood MJ, and Goodall G (1978) A study of misbehavior: Token reinforcement in the rat. *J. Exp. Anal. Behav.* 29: 115–134.
Bouton ME (1993) Context, time, and memory retrieval in the interference paradigms of Pavlovian learning. *Psychol. Bull.* 114: 80–99.
Bouton ME (2004) Context and behavioral processes in extinction. *Learn. Mem.* 11: 485–494.
Breland K and Breland M (1961) The misbehavior of organisms. *Am. Psychol.* 16: 681–684.
Brown RT and Wagner AR (1964) Resistance of punishment and extinction following training with shock or nonreinforcement. *J. Exp. Psychol.* 68: 503–507.
Butler RA and Harlow HF (1954) Persistence of visual exploration in monkeys. *J. Comp. Physiol. Psychol.* 47: 257–263.
Capaldi EJ (1967) A sequential hypothesis of instrumental learning. In: Spence KS and Spence JT (eds.) *The Psychology of Learning and Motivation*, Vol. 1, pp. 67–156. New York: Academic Press.
Capaldi EJ (1994) The sequential view: From rapidly fading stimulus traces to the organization of memory and the abstract concept of number. *Psychol. Bull. Rev.* 1: 156–181.
Capaldi EJ and Stanley LR (1963) Temporal properties of reinforcement aftereffects. *J. Exp. Psychol.* 65: 169–175.
Colwill RC and Rescorla RA (1985) Instrumental conditioning remains sensitive to reinforcer devaluation after extensive training. *J. Exp. Psychol. Anim. Behav. Process.* 11: 520–536.
Crespi LP (1942) Quantitative variation of incentive and performance in the white rat. *Am. J. Psychol.* 55: 467–517.

Estes WK (1950) Toward a statistical theory of learning. *Psychol. Rev.* 57: 94–107.

Guthrie ER (1935) *The Psychology of Learning.* New York: Harper.

Guthrie ER and Horton GP (1946) *Cats in a Puzzle Box.* New York: Rinehart.

Homme LW, de Baca PC, Devine JV, Steinhorst R, and Rickert EJ (1963) Use of the Premack principle in controlling the behavior of nursery-school children. *J. Exp. Anal. Behav.* 6: 544.

Hull CL (1943) *Principles of Behavior.* New York: Appleton-Century.

Hull CL (1952) *A Behavior System.* New Haven, CT: Yale University Press.

Lashley KS (1951) The problem of serial order in behavior. In: Jeffress LS (ed.) *Cerebral Mechanisms in Behavior: The Hixon Symposium,* pp. 112–146. New York: Wiley.

MacCorquodale K and Meehl PE (1954) Edward C. Tolman. In: Estes WK, Koch S, MacCorquodale K, Meehl PE, Mueller CG, Jr., Schonefeld WN, and Verplank WS (eds.). *Modern Learning Theory: A Critical Analysis of Five Examples,* pp. 177–266. New York: Appleton-Century-Crofts.

Mackintosh NJ (1975) A theory of attention: Variations in the associability of stimuli with reinforcement. *Psychol. Rev.* 82: 276–298.

McLaren IPL and Mackintosh NJ (2002) An elemental model of associative learning: I. Latent inhibition and perceptual learning. *Anim. Learn. Behav.* 38: 211–246.

Miller RR and Matzel LD (1989) Contingency and relative associative strength. In: Klein SB and Mowrer RR (eds.) *Contemporary Learning Theories: Pavlovian Conditioning and the Status of Traditional Learning Theory,* pp. 61–84. Hillsdale, NJ: Erlbaum.

Montgomery KC (1951) The relation between exploratory behavior and spontaneous alternation in the white rat. *J. Comp. Physiol. Psychol.* 44: 582–589.

Moore BR and Stuttard S (1979) Dr. Guthrie and *Felis domesticus* or: Tripping over the cat. *Science* 205: 1031–1033.

Mowrer OH (1960) *Learning Theory and Behavior.* New York: Wiley.

Muenzinger KF (1928) Plasticity and mechanization of the problem box habit in guinea pigs. *J. Comp. Psychol.* 8: 45–69.

Munn NL (1950) *Handbook of Psychological Research on the Rat: An Introduction to Animal Psychology.* Boston: Houghton Mifflin.

Pearce JM (1987) A model for stimulus generalization in Pavlovian conditioning. *Psychol. Rev.* 94: 61–73.

Pearce JM and Hall G (1980) A model for Pavlovian learning: Variations in the effectiveness of conditioned but not unconditioned stimuli. *Psychol. Rev.* 87: 532–552.

Premack D (1965) Reinforcement theory. In: Levine D (ed.) *Nebraska Symposium on Motivation,* pp. 123–180. Lincoln: University of Nebraska.

Rescorla RA (2001) Experimental extinction. In: Mowrer RR and Klein SB (eds.) *Handbook of Contemporary Learning Theories,* pp. 119–154. Mahwah, NJ: Erlbaum.

Rescorla RA and Solomon RL (1967) Two-process learning theory: Relations between Pavlovian conditioning and instrumental learning. *Psychol. Rev.* 74: 151–182.

Rescorla RA and Wagner AR (1972) A theory of Pavlovian conditioning: Variations in the effectiveness of reinforcement and nonreinforcement. In: Black AH and Prokasy WF (eds.) *Classical Conditioning II: Current Research and Theory,* pp. 64–99. New York: Appleton-Century-Crofts.

Restle F (1957) Discrimination of cues in mazes: A resolution of the "place-vs.-response" question. *Psychol. Rev.* 64: 217–228.

Sheffield FD (1966) New evidence on the drive-induction theory of reinforcement. In: Haber RH (ed.) *Current Research in Motivation,* pp. 98–111. New York: Holt.

Sheffield FD and Roby TB (1950) Reward value of a nonnutritive sweet taste. *J. Comp. Physiol. Psychol.* 43: 471–481.

Skinner BF (1938) *The Behavior of Organisms: An Experimental Analysis.* New York: Appleton-Century-Crofts.

Skinner BF (1948) *Walden Two.* New York: Macmillan.

Spence KW (1936) The nature of discrimination learning in animals. *Psychol. Rev.* 43: 427–449.

Spence KW (1937) The differential response in animals to stimuli varying within a single dimension. *Psychol. Rev.* 44: 430–444.

Spence KW (1952) The nature of the response in discrimination learning. *Psychol. Rev.* 59: 89–93.

Thomas DR (1985) Contextual stimulus control of operant responding in pigeons. In: Balsam PD and Tomie A (eds.) *Context and Learning,* pp. 295–322. Hillsdale, NJ: Erlbaum.

Thorndike EL (1898) Animal intelligence: An experimental study of the associative process in animals. *Psychol. Rev.* 2: 1–109.

Timberlake W (2001) Motivational modes in behavior system. In: Mowrer RR and Klein SB (eds.) *Handbook of Contemporary Learning Theories,* pp. 155–209. Mahwah, NJ: Erlbaum.

Timberlake W and Allison J (1974) Response deprivation: An empirical approach to instrumental performance. *Psychol. Rev.* 81: 146–164.

Timberlake W, Wahl G, and King D (1982) Stimulus and response contingencies in the misbehavior of rats. *J. Exp. Psychol. Anim. Behav. Process.* 8: 62–85.

Tolman EC (1932) *Purposive Behavior in Animals and Men.* New York: Appleton-Century.

Tolman EC (1948) Cognitive maps in rats and men. *Psychol. Rev.* 55: 189–208.

Tolman EC and Honzik CH (1930) Introduction and removal of reward and maze performance of rats. *Univ. Calif. Publ. Psychol.* 4: 257–275.

Tolman EC, Ritchie BF, and Kalish D (1946) Studies in spatial learning. I. Orientation and the short-cut. *J. Exp. Psychol.* 36: 13–24.

Young RK, Mangum WP, and Capaldi EJ (1960) Temporal factors associated with nonresponse extinction. *J. Comp. Physiol. Psychol.* 53: 435–438.

Wagner AR (1978) Expectancies and the priming of STM. In: Hulse SH, Fowler H, and Honig WH (eds.) *Cognitive Processes in Animal Behavior,* pp. 177–209. Hillsdale, NJ: Erlbaum.

1.04 Multiple Memory Systems: A New View

L. Nadel, University of Arizona, Tuscon, AZ, USA

1.04.1 Introduction

It has been already stated that those who have a good memory are not identical with those who are quick at recollecting. But the act of recollecting differs from that of remembering, not only chronologically, but also in this, that many also of the other animals (as well as man) have memory, but, of all that we are acquainted with, none, we venture to say, except man, shares in the faculty of recollection. (Aristotle, *Ars Memoria*)

While Aristotle clearly recognized that memory comes in different forms, and pointed out that remembering and recollecting seem different, he left many questions open. Is there a single memory that can be accessed in different ways – by remembering or recollecting? Are there multiple memories, one of which supports remembering, the other recollecting? If so, how do these relate to one another, if at all? Questions like these, asked in a variety of ways, have dominated the memory literature in recent years. While it is beyond the scope of this chapter to represent all these approaches (see Schacter and Tulving, 1994; and a collection of papers in a special recent issue of *Neurobiology of Learning and Memory*

(Vol. 82) for a sampling of views; *See* Chapters 1.02, 1.05), I hope to illuminate some recent history and provide a new perspective on how one might think about memory and its various forms.

Memory is best conceived as a set of functions that serve specific adaptive purposes (cf., Klein et al., 2002). These functions all share the common property of enabling organisms to benefit from prior experience. Since these experiences are many and varied, and the needs of complex organisms are similarly diverse, it is hardly surprising that there would be many kinds of memory. This chapter considers the different types of memory and ask how they differ, how they are instantiated in the brain, and how they interact. It also speculates about the separate functions they serve and discusses implications of the fact that memory comes in multiple forms.

Before diving into this thicket, we need to clear some brush and ask what we mean by each of the terms in the phrase 'memory system'. What exactly is memory? What do we mean by a system? We'll start by briefly discussing what is meant by the term system and then address the nature of memory systems at some length. This will lead to the surprising proposal that we change the way we think about memory altogether.

1.04.2   What Is a System?

A standard definition of system goes something like this: A system is a group of interacting, interrelated, or interdependent elements forming a complex whole. There seem to be two critical parts to this definition. First, a system is composed of parts, and second, these parts interact in some way to form a whole whose properties are more than just the sum of the separate parts. As important as what the definition includes is what it does not. A system need not make up a coherent physical entity, and it need not always act in an interrelated fashion. The parts of a system can be distant from one another (an extended family for example), and they can sometimes act together and sometimes not. What is more, the parts of a system can be made up of similar things or of quite different things.

Complex biological systems come in a variety of forms, but one thing we can assume they all share is that they have achieved their present form through a process of selection, shaped by phylogeny, epigenetic needs, and their environmental niche. The brain is among the most complex of biological systems and is not one but many systems that must interact effectively to sustain life and maximize the potential for procreation. Memory, in this context, is but one of many neurobiological systems, the one that allows organisms to benefit from knowledge obtained during their individual lifetimes. Organisms also benefit from knowledge acquired in the course of phylogeny by virtue of the fact that fundamental aspects of the world we inhabit are built into the structure of the nervous system. Although this knowledge about the world may emerge over the course of individual development, it is in no sense learned or remembered: It is simply known. Basic facts about the physical world, such as the laws pertaining to gravity, space, time, and causality, are examples of this kind of knowledge. The associative rules that govern our understanding of how the things we experience relate to each other are another example (*See* Chapters 1.03, 1.06).

1.04.3   What Is a Memory, and a Memory System?

Memory is, by definition, a record created by an individual as a result of its past experience. But what is the nature of this record, and how long does it last? How is it accessed? It has long been understood that some memories are evanescent while others last a long time. A distinction between short-term and long-term memory has been part of the scholarly discussion of memory for more than a century, even though the boundaries between these two are not clearly worked out. In recent years, the notion of working memory has emerged to complicate matters. For some, short-term memory and working memory (which may or may not be the same thing) are memory systems, and given the generic definition of systems offered above, this seems indisputably true. However, these are not the systems of which memory researchers typically speak when they speak of multiple memory systems. The notion of multiple memory systems emerged well after the idea that memory could exist in different temporal forms was entrenched in the field.

For much of the past century, most memory researchers have adopted a particular framework that viewed memory as reflecting the presence of a coherent trace in the brain, an engram that could be identified if only we knew just what we were looking for. The difficulty inherent in this pursuit was forcefully expressed by Lashley, whose failed search for the engram led to the contrarian thought that:

> I sometimes feel, in reviewing the evidence on the localization of the memory trace, that the necessary conclusion is that learning just is not possible. It is difficult to conceive of a mechanism which can satisfy the conditions set for it. (Lashley, 1950: 501)

A possible solution to the problem raised by Lashley's work was provided by Hebb (1949) in his connectionist theory of synaptic change, cell assembly formation, and phase sequence activity. These postulated mechanisms presumed to show how an engram could be distributed within the brain and how the full pattern of the memory trace could be activated by many different paths, or cell assemblies (*See* Chapters 1.33, 1.34, 1.35). His theory showed how a memory trace could exist, could avoid total disruption when damage occurred, and could permit what we now call pattern completion. It seemed, in other words, that Lashley searched in vain because he was looking for the wrong thing, and that it still made sense to talk about a fixed memory trace.

In order to understand this debate, it is important to recognize that the term memory was at that time reserved for what we now call episodic memory (*See* Chapters 1.22, 1.23). The term was used to refer to the recollection, in Aristotle's terms, of specific events in one's past, such as what happened yesterday, or the week/month/year before. This usage persisted at least until the 1960s. Other forms of knowledge that reflected prior experience were not labeled as memory *per se*. Instead, terms such as habit were used. One result of this usage was the long-standing resistance to attributing memories to non-human animals (again reflecting Aristotle).

A major shift in terminology resulted from the emergence of neuroscience and attempts to understand the neural bases of learning and memory. Since the relevant studies were being done in rodents and various invertebrates, the notion of what constituted a memory had to be broadened. The term memory came to be applied to just about any change in the nervous system that resulted from prior experience, becoming interchangeable with the notion of plasticity. Given this much broader definition of memory, it was only a matter of time before the idea that there were qualitatively different kinds of memory emerged. I have sketched out my understanding of some of the historical forces at play here in earlier papers (Nadel, 1992, 1994), so I will be relatively brief here.

When the patient HM was first described (Scoville and Milner, 1957), memory was thought of in the univocal way described above. Milner (1966) described the deficit created by medial temporal excision in HM and several other patients as follows:

> The pattern of amnesia which emerges from the clinical observations of the patients with bilateral hippocampal damage is one in which long-term memories survive, as does the ability to attend normally to on-going events. The essential difficulty appears to be in adding any new information to the long-term store. (Milner, 1966: 124)

HM could show some learning of motor skills (cf. Corkin, 1968), suggesting to Milner that "the pattern of amnesia demonstrated by these patients is incompatible with a unitary-process theory of memory" (Milner, 1966: 131). However, this did not lead immediately to the notion that there were multiple memory systems, since such motor learning, after all, did not actually involve memory by the definitions of the time. Instead, the data from amnesia were taken to support then current models of memory involving separate short-term and long-term systems, with a memory consolidation process responsible for the transition from one system to another. Milner suggested "It is possible that in normal learning, the hippocampal region acts to prime activity in cortical areas where storage is taking place" (Milner, 1966: 130). From this notion the idea that the hippocampus was critical for what is now called systems consolidation emerged, and it has played a central role in thinking about the hippocampal role in memory ever since (see Nadel, 2007, for a brief history and update of this idea). Although the concept of multiple memory systems is implicit in this notion, it remained implicit for some years.

Research attention turned instead to the issue of which brain areas were critical to the amnesic deficit, and the attempt to establish an animal model of the syndrome observed in HM. The initial failure to replicate HM's memory deficit with what were assumed to be comparable lesions in primates (Orbach et al., 1960) left researchers confused. Had significant changes in the function of the relevant structures emerged during evolution? Did the medial temporal lobe do something very different in primates and humans, not to mention rats? These kinds of questions were very much in the air in the 1960s.

In a seminal series of papers in the late 1960s, Warrington and Weiskrantz (1968, 1970) showed that amnesic patients could indeed benefit from some forms of prior experience in addition to showing motor learning. Their early demonstrations included the use of fragmented pictures and words – amnesic patients exposed to such materials took less and less time to identify the materials with repetition. They noted that there are "two types of task, motor learning and retention by partial information, which are relatively well preserved in amnesic subjects," and they wondered "Is there a common factor linking performance on these apparently dissimilar tasks?" (Warrington and Weiskrantz, 1970: 630). They pointed out that the presence of spared memory capacity might allow one to explain the apparent discrepancy in the data from the clinic and from animal studies, but this would necessitate dropping the idea that the defect caused by hippocampal damage was one of impaired memory consolidation.

From a historical perspective, it is intriguing that both research programs, in Canada and the United Kingdom, had uncovered the fact that in the amnesic syndrome some forms of learning and memory were spared while others were impaired, but neither jumped to the idea that there were multiple memory systems.

This advance came instead from the domain of animal research, in particular several programs focused on the functions of the rat and monkey hippocampus. Three publications in 1974 proposed, in rather different ways, that there were multiple forms of memory and that the hippocampus was only responsible for one of them. Gaffan (1974) suggested that there were two forms of memory, one involving recognition, the other association, and that the hippocampal system was only critical for recognition. Hirsh (1974) suggested that memory could be either context bound or context free, and that the hippocampus was critical only for context-bound memory. Nadel and O'Keefe (1974), building on the discovery of place cells in the hippocampus of the rat (O'Keefe and Dostrovsky, 1971), suggested that the hippocampus was critical only for acquiring cognitive maps and that the place learning and episodic memories that depend upon them, whereas other forms of learning and memory depended on other brain circuits.

O'Keefe and Nadel (1978, 1979) laid out a comprehensive theory that rested squarely on the notion that there are multiple forms of memory.

> there are different types of memory … localized in many, possibly most, neural systems. …

> there is no such thing as the memory area … there are memory areas, each responsible for a different form of information storage. The hippocampus … both constructs and stores cognitive maps (O'Keefe and Nadel, 1978: 373–374).

The authors argued that the hippocampal system was concerned with knowing that, while other memory circuits were concerned with knowing how. This idea was taken up by Cohen and Squire (1980), who showed that amnesics could learn how to mirror read but could not remember that they had done so. Within a matter of a few years, the notion of multiple forms of memory was accepted in both the animal and human domains, and though there have been occasional attempts to argue against this view, the idea seems firmly rooted.

The answer to the question – what memory is – seems only to complicate matters, because memory is many things, not one. But how are these many things, these multiple forms of memory, to be distinguished from one another? Do they reflect the operation of different systems, in the sense described above? In order to answer this one question we need to ask, and answer, several others. Do the different forms of memory reflect different kinds of information? Do they differ in terms of the processes they instantiate? Do they differ in terms of the brain mechanisms and

structures they involve? Do these separate learning and memory systems obey different rules of operation? Most researchers would agree that there are different memory systems only if the answer to most of these questions is yes.

Because of the central role played by the hippocampal system in thinking about memory, the early tendency was to talk about two kinds of memory, one dependent upon hippocampal circuits and the other not. Thus, O'Keefe and Nadel (1978, 1979) talked about locale and taxon memory, Cohen (1984) and Squire (1987) talked about declarative and procedural systems, and others talked about explicit and implicit systems, to name but a few. There are many commonalities among these various ways of handling the multiplicity of memory, but they all share the fate that they are too simplistic. Current approaches suggest as many as 5 to 10 kinds of memory. As the number of putatively separable memory systems increases, it becomes important to step back and ask the fundamental questions again. What exactly do we mean by memory? How is prior experience incorporated into current behavior?

1.04.4   What Is Memory, Redux

Given the expanded view of memory forced upon us by neuroscientific exploration of memory's biological bases, it seems time to rethink the notion of memory itself. If there are 5, 6, or 10 different kinds of memory, does it make sense to call them all memory? My answer is that it does not. Instead, I propose to go back to using the term as it had been used before recent developments widened its application. That is, I believe we should use the term memory solely to refer to what happens when an organism recollects the past. All else would best be called knowledge (Nadel and Wexler, 1984). As a function of experience we acquire knowledge, which is represented in various brain systems. Knowledge is used to generate both memories and behaviors. What we call a memory is constructed from this knowledge as required. The hippocampal system, serving as a contextual binding device, a creator of cognitive maps, plays a critical role in this construction process.

This way of thinking has its roots in debates more than 60 years ago between adherents of different views of learning and behavior. Following Tolman (1932), we assumed that organisms always act with purpose, trying out one or another strategy or hypothesis to deal with their current situation (cf. O'Keefe and Nadel, 1978: chapter 2). We focused our attention on spatial behavior and spelled out a number of different hypotheses an animal could use to get around in the world, including place, guidance (or cue), and orientation (or response) hypotheses. Typically, hypotheses require complex interactions among different knowledge systems, only some of which reflect learning. That is, some of the knowledge an animal uses to act in the world comes from prewired circuits. For example, animals do not have to learn *de novo* that stimuli in close temporal contiguity are more likely to be causally linked to one another than stimuli widely separated in time.

By this analysis, we have multiple knowledge systems, which we use to generate various forms of behavior and to construct memories. Much the same set of questions applies to these multiple knowledge systems as applies to what have been called multiple memory systems. How do they differ, how do they interact, what rules of operation do they obey, how are they instantiated in the brain? If the reader prefers, she or he can continue to think about multiple memory systems as they read the words multiple knowledge systems.

One consequence of this proposed shift in terminology is that the idea of a brain system devoted purely to long-term memory no longer makes sense. This idea, stated perhaps most forcefully by Squire and his colleagues with reference to the medial temporal lobe (e.g., Squire, 1994), depended on the idea that damage to this part of the brain affected only memory but not short-term processing or perception. This idea has been criticized both in the past (Horel, 1978, 1994) and in recent writings (cf. Ranganath and Blumenfeld, 2005; Hannula et al., 2006), and in my view it should now be retired. It makes more sense to think about all neural systems as both processing and storing knowledge, with the differences between systems reflecting the nature of the knowledge being processed and stored, and the timescale of that storage.

1.04.5 Multiple Knowledge Systems

What kinds of knowledge does an organism need to acquire about its world in order to survive and even prosper? Bear in mind we are assuming that fundamental facts about how the world works are built into the organism's system by phylogeny and do not have to be relearned by each generation. What does have

to be learned are those things that cannot have been acquired in the course of phylogeny. What are they?

Quite a lot it turns out: who your mother, father, sister, or brother are; who, what, and where you should approach or avoid; what you should eat and drink, and when; who you should try to copulate with, and when (and where); how to do various things such as explore, play, fight, hunt, escape predation, find your way home again, and more. A special form of acquired knowledge concerns those accidental conjunctions that we call events, when actors, actions, and worldly objects come together in combinations that could never have been predicted in advance. What sorts of knowledge/memory systems would provide the best way of learning all this and solving all the problems life confronts us with?

As a first cut, it is useful to note that organisms appear to need knowledge systems concerned with two very different kinds of information – first is the need for knowledge accumulated over many similar events, and second is the need for knowledge about unique occurrences, and the limits these might put on the application of cumulative knowledge (cf., Klein et al., 2002). Tulving's (1972) discussion of semantic and episodic memory captured this distinction. I have tried to make the case that the term memory should be reserved for recollections of unique episodes, but there has lately been considerable interest in cumulative knowledge, which has been viewed as allowing organisms to extract reliable information about the statistical structure of the environment. A significant complication in thinking about knowledge systems is that the systems engaged in processing these two types of information are in constant interaction. Indeed, how to think about the relations between episodic and semantic knowledge, and the brain systems underlying these forms of information, constitutes one of the major challenges for the future. We return to this issue later, after addressing in more detail the question of what kinds of knowledge systems the brain must contain.

Before turning to a discussion of types of knowledge systems, it is worth pointing out that thinking in terms of knowledge rather than memory forces us to put the function of knowledge acquisition front and center. What propels an organism to gather knowledge in the first place? This is a question that bedeviled early psychologists focused on biological categories and drives. The existence of curiosity and exploration were an embarrassment since the mere acquisition of knowledge could not be simply related to any particular biological drive. Within a framework that emphasizes knowledge, curiosity and exploration become critical. Instead of being relegated to sidebar status, these behaviors deserve careful study in their own right. It remains a remarkable fact about modern cognitive neuroscience that so little attention has been paid to these core functions (cf. Avni et al., 2006; Whishaw et al., 2006; for two recent exceptions to this neglect).

1.04.5.1 Types of Knowledge Systems

One way to think about knowledge systems is in the following simplistic fashion – an organism needs knowledge about what it experiences, where and when things happened, who was involved, the value of the things experienced, and how to act in the future when confronted with similar experiences (*See* Chapters 1.21, 1.22, 1.23). One might imagine that organisms extract and store knowledge about each of these aspects of experience in separate systems, combining this knowledge when required to do so by the demands of a given situation, or an experimenter-defined laboratory task. As we consider each of these separately, it becomes clear that things are not as simple as they might seem. To start, these categories are not absolutely clear-cut – there is overlap between them in some instances, as we see later. Further, some kinds of knowledge are inferred rather than experienced. Perhaps the best example concerns why things happen. Organisms make inferences about causality, even though these are rarely backed up by direct experience, and these inferences become an important part of their knowledge base. Notwithstanding these problems, it still seems worthwhile thinking about knowledge systems along these lines. In what follows, I briefly discuss each of these kinds of knowledge. A serious analysis of this approach would require a substantial expansion of this discussion, one that is beyond the scope of this chapter.

1.04.5.1.1 *Knowing what*
It is best to start with the kind of knowledge that informs an organism about the stuff of which existence is made. All else is subservient to this kind of knowledge, since in the absence of what there is no where, when, why, or how. Or, as Kant put it, form in the absence of content is meaningless. What knowledge provides this content, the semantics of existence one might say.

The category of what knowledge is complex, comprising several different kinds of knowledge, including:

- What happened
- What entities were involved
- What properties these entities have

These three forms of knowledge are quite different in kind, and one might imagine that they are subserved by quite separate underlying neural and cognitive systems themselves.

Processing and storing information about what happened is central to memory for events, or episodes, and hence must incorporate the ability to capture sequence information. Every such sequence would consist of entities interacting in space and/or time. The entities themselves must be represented in a fashion that captures their properties, both structural and functional. The ventral visual stream (Ungerleider and Mishkin, 1982) is a well-known example of what I am here calling a what system, and indeed this is the name given to it by Ungerleider and Mishkin. It is reasonable to assume that similar what systems exist within each of the sensory/perceptual processing streams. These systems contain representations of entities in the world and their properties, representations that have been shaped by the experiences an organism has had with these entities in multiple event contexts. Each time an entity is encountered in the world, its "what" representation is activated, and as a function of this new experience, the representation altered. These representations are activated and hence mobilized in the act of memory retrieval.

1.04.5.1.2 *Knowing where*
This category is also complex, because animals need to know several things that could be referred to as where knowledge. They need to know where they are at any given moment. They need to know where important things, such as food, water, safety, and conspecifics, are located, both with respect to an environmental framework and with respect to where they are themselves located at any given moment. They need to know where events happened. They also need to know how to get from one place to another (*See* Chapters 1.20, 1.21, 1.25).

It seems clear that significant neural resources are devoted to processing and storing where knowledge. Extensive systems seem devoted to representing where things are relative to the current location of the organism. What is more, this information seems to be multiply represented, in that it is captured with respect to several frames of reference. That is, organisms simultaneously know where an object is with respect to the head, the eyes, the hands, and the body. This is important because action depends upon such knowledge. In addition to these various ego-centered spatial systems, there is a system, centered on the hippocampal formation, that represents an organism's location in absolute, or allocentric, space. This system makes use of inputs from multiple sources, and includes elements such as place cells in the hippocampus (e.g., O'Keefe, 1976), head-direction cells in the thalamus and postsubiculum (e.g., Taube et al., 1990), and the recently discovered grid-cells in the entorhinal cortex (Hafting et al., 2005).

In addition to providing specific information about an animal's location in space, this system is also central to knowledge about context, that is, the spatial setting within which events happen (cf., Nadel and Willner, 1980; Nadel et al., 1985). It is this role, we have argued, that makes the hippocampal cognitive mapping system central to episodic memory, which by definition incorporates information about where an event transpired. It is certainly one of the main challenges for the future to discover why and how spatial mapping and episodic memory utilize the same circuits (*See* Chapter 1.33).

1.04.5.1.3   Knowing when

There are at least two kinds of when knowledge that organisms might need. First, they might need to know when, over a long span of time, an event occurred. Was it yesterday, last week, last year? This kind of knowledge is integral to episodic memory, and there remain debates about whether animals other than humans actually represent it. Second, organisms need to know when within a particular event the various parts of that event occurred. This might seem a trivial matter, but if one argues, as we are arguing, that the various parts of an event are processed and represented in separable brain regions, then being able to assemble them in appropriate temporal order, to know when each of them occurred with respect to the others, is critical. The simplest example will suffice to make this point: it makes all the difference whether A comes before or after B, because the attribution of causality depends upon knowing which of these two entities or events came first. An organism that gets temporal order wrong is going to make the wrong attributions and is not going to survive very long.

1.04.5.1.4   Knowing who

This is a somewhat simpler category, and one that might be of importance only in species with the capacity to recognize individuals, itself a function of the sophistication of its what systems. In humans, it plays a critical role, of course. George is smarter than Dick leads to a very different conclusion than Dick is smarter than George, although both statements employ the same words.

1.04.5.1.5   Knowing how

This is a big category, comprising all the knowledge referred to as procedural by many authors. There are some important distinctions to be drawn, however, between some of these forms of how knowledge. For example, knowledge of how to carry out some kind of motor act, such as brushing your teeth or driving your car or playing squash, is rather different than knowledge about how to get from one place to another (e.g., which route to take, not how to move). It is not within the scope of this chapter to go into much detail on this category of knowledge, but current work on the functions of the caudate nucleus in particular, and the basal ganglia in general, are shedding light on how we know about how.

1.04.5.1.6   Knowing valence

In addition to storing knowledge about the kinds of entities they confront in the world, organisms represent the value of these entities, whether they are good or bad, exciting or frightening, and so on. This kind of knowledge plays a critical role in determining not only how an organism deals with such entities in the future but also how strongly the knowledge itself is committed to storage. In general, the greater the valence, the more robust the storage, at least within most of the brain's knowledge systems. As with all kinds of knowledge, the use of value information is highly dependent upon the context within which an organism is acting, including its internal motivational context. Knowing that something tastes good is much more useful when one is hungry than when sated, for example. Considerable evidence in recent decades suggests that the amygdala plays a central role in representing value knowledge, but it is by no means the only structure so engaged. Extensive midbrain circuits are devoted to assessing and presumably storing information about the reinforcing value of various stimuli an organism comes into contact with. Portions of the cingulate cortex and frontal cortex also contribute to this system.

1.04.5.1.7 *Implications of the existence of multiple systems*

There are many implications of assuming that the brain is organized into multiple knowledge systems. Consider the fact that the knowledge about an episode in one's life is dispersed within the brain, across multiple systems. What happened, who was involved, where and when it happened – these various aspects of a memory are widely distributed, which means that retrieving and reporting an episode memory must be a constructive act, much as Bartlett (1932) and others have argued. And being constructed, memory for episodes must be open to error in a way that engrams were not supposed to be.

Different knowledge systems, utilizing separable neural substrates, could operate by distinct rules. O'Keefe and Nadel (1978), for example, proposed that there were two quite different brain systems engaged in learning and remembering, which they called the locale and taxon systems. The locale system was associated with the hippocampal formation, and the various taxon systems were associated with neocortical and subcortical structures. It was suggested that learning within these two kinds of systems reflected different operating principles. The taxon systems obeyed standard laws of reinforcement and followed associative principles. Learning within the locale system, by contrast, was assumed to proceed independent of reinforcements such as food, water, safety, or access to a mate – animals formed cognitive maps whether rewarded or not. Further, O'Keefe and Nadel asserted that learning within the locale system did not follow associative rules. Consistent with these speculations, Hardt and Nadel have shown that learning within the locale system differs from learning within taxon systems in that the latter reflect the operation of standard associative phenomena such as overshadowing and blocking, whereas the former does not. Instead, knowledge acquisition in the locale system is automatic, such that new information updates previous representations, whether or not reward contingencies have changed. Behind the assertion that these two learning systems obey different rules is the assumption that the underlying neural architectures in the systems subserving these two forms of knowledge differ in critical ways that allow different learning rules to be implemented in each.

In addition to these system-level implications, there are a number of others that reflect the fact that by being separate, knowledge systems can be affected differentially by all that life has to offer. In what follows, I discuss several examples, including development, aging, and the reaction of different systems to stress. In each case it will be seen that knowledge systems vary in how they are affected, and that these variations help us to understand a number of phenomena of considerable importance.

1.04.6 The Development of Knowledge Systems

It is reasonable to assume that each neural system develops at its own rate, and that there are differences among neural systems in this regard. To the extent to which a particular form of knowledge depends upon a specific neural substrate, it is then likely that the various knowledge systems have different developmental trajectories. The very capacity to know certain things depends upon the development of the underlying neural system that processes and represents that kind of knowledge. Until that happens, such knowing should be impossible. It is a reasonable further assumption that still-developing systems are susceptible to alteration, induced either by experience or the unfolding of some genetic program. Such factors are less likely to act on already-developed systems. This means that ways of knowing can be more or less influenced by early life experience as a function of when they develop.

Neural systems responsible for processing knowledge about objects in the world seem largely functional early in life, as must be the case if organisms are to respond appropriately to those entities and events that are of critical survival value. However, large differences are seen within this category. Systems responsible for knowing about the smell or taste of things seem in general to develop before systems responsible for knowing about the sight or sound of things. The generalization here might be that systems concerned with knowledge about internal states, and stimuli related to those states, develop before systems concerned with external states.

In most mammals, several neural systems, and the knowledge systems that depend upon them, show prolonged maturation, much of it postnatal. This has significant implications for understanding how both our memory and performance capabilities change during early life. A prominent example is the hippocampal formation, portions of which undergo substantial postnatal maturation (cf. Nadel and Hupbach, in press). Evidence about the development of the hippocampus comes from studies of both structure and function. At present, the best evidence comes from studies with rodents, but we now know enough about primates and humans to state a general case. Across a wide range of species, it appears that the hippocampus first becomes functional at about the natural time of weaning. Unfortunately, we do not know when this is for humans, hence we must make guesses based on anatomical, physiological, and behavioral data to determine just when the hippocampus becomes functional in humans. Note that it is unlikely that this, or any other, brain structure suddenly becomes functional, as if by the flipping of a switch. It is more likely that hippocampal function emerges piecemeal, taking a considerable time to reach the adult state.

It has been known for several decades that the dentate gyrus of the rat is particularly subject to postnatal development (see Frotscher and Seress, 2006, for a recent review). Large numbers of dentate granule cells are created after birth in the rat in a special proliferative zone within the hippocampus itself. Initially it was thought that rodents were unique, and that postnatal maturation of hippocampus was either absent or less prominent in primates and humans. This, however, turns out not to be the case. Even in these species, the hippocampal system emerges into function after birth. Hippocampal pyramidal cells, unlike dentate granule cells, proliferate in the prenatal stage. But, two other critical components of any developed brain system – the integration of inhibitory neurons and the myelination of fibers – lag behind in hippocampus. Seress and his colleagues conclude that while cells are generally born early, further steps critical to normal function are quite prolonged.

In rodents, we can use the appearance of exploration and place learning as markers of the emergence of hippocampal function. Data from such studies in general support what was deduced from studies of structure – namely, that hippocampal function begins at about 3 weeks of life in the rat. Since the two major cognitive functions in humans that depend upon the hippocampus are episodic memory and memory for allocentric spatial location, delayed maturation should be reflected in the late emergence of these capacities.

Infants at quite a young age can learn about space as it relates to their body or its parts (eyes, hand, head). They can learn to crawl or walk to objects in space and readily solve simple spatial tasks such as 'go right' or 'go to the door and turn left.' These kinds of spatial learning do not, however, depend upon a functioning hippocampus. Instead they depend upon knowledge systems subserved by other, earlier-developing, neural systems. The capacity to know, and use, allocentric space, on the other hand, does depend upon the hippocampus, and data from a variety of studies suggest that this capacity emerges only between 18 and 24 months of age in humans (cf. Newcombe et al., 1998).

There are several major implications of the postnatal maturation of the hippocampus. The first concerns behavior. We assume adult behavior reflects the presence of both hippocampal and non-hippocampal systems, what they do and how they interact. Prior to hippocampal emergence, however, behavior reflects functions and behaviors dependent on brain systems operational at birth. The second major implication concerns development. A developing system is more susceptible to influence than an already developed one. This is presumably why environmental influences exert a particularly strong impact on the developing hippocampus.

1.04.6.1   The Delayed Emergence of Episodic Memory

In general, little evidence of episodic memory, as measured in standard recall and recognition tests, is observed until the age of 3 or 4 years. The absence of episode memories from the first 2 years of life resulting from the late maturation of the hippocampus can help us understand at least part of the syndrome of infantile amnesia (Nadel and Zola-Morgan, 1984; See Chapters 1.15, 2.37). It is a well-established fact that for most individuals, few if any early episode memories survive into adulthood. It is only after 2–3 years of age that significant numbers of episode memories appear to be formed and retained. Over the years, there has been considerable debate as to whether this syndrome, first discussed at length by Freud, reflects biological maturation or some other factors, such as the mismatch between the nonverbal coding of early memories and the verbal means used later in life to retrieve and report memories or the emergence of a sense of self at around 2–3 years of age. Arguments against the biological case depend on assertions that the hippocampus develops early in life, as noted above. These assertions, as we have seen, rested either on the use of inappropriate tasks or on incorrect interpretations of the nature of contextual coding and the hippocampal role in it. Now that a consensus has emerged to the effect that hippocampus is most likely to become functional between 18 and 24 months of age in children (Newcombe et al., 2007; Nadel and Hupbach, in press), we can conclude that a significant part of infantile amnesia reflects biological maturation.

Further support for this view comes from the study of the unique population of developmental amnesics, individuals with damage to the hippocampus caused, typically, by an early anoxic or ischemic event (cf. Vargha-Khadem et al., 1997). These individuals, mentioned earlier, went unrecognized for quite a while because they did reasonably well in educational settings. Only careful testing brought out the fact that they suffered from quite severe losses in the domain of episodic and spatial memory. Developmental amnesics have general difficulties orienting in space and time, remembering events, finding their way through any but the most familiar environments, and remembering where they placed objects. However, they are usually not impaired in their social and language development and score low to average on standard tests of intelligence. They have a relative preservation of semantic memory and often show normal scores on immediate or short-term episodic memory tests, but they are unable to retain episodic information over longer periods of time. Studies using structural magnetic resonance imaging suggest that the described symptoms of developmental amnesia are caused by bilateral hippocampal volume reduction of at least 20%–30%.

The increased susceptibility to influence following from postnatal development of the hippocampus manifests itself in two rather different ways. First, the hippocampus seems to be very sensitive to environmental perturbations. Careful studies of the neuropsychological impact of early exposure to lead, for example, suggest that impairment of hippocampal function contributes to the resulting cognitive deficit (e.g., Finkelstein et al., 1998). Second, genetic conditions that influence development in a general way seem to have their greatest impact on late-developing parts of the nervous system (and other organ systems as well). There is a kind of selection bias inherent here: Genetic conditions that affect structures formed early in development might have such devastating effects that they are inevitably lethal. Influences on late-developing structures might be prevalent simply because they are the only ones that can be survived.

Down syndrome presents such a case. This condition, resulting from an error in very early embryonic life, almost always reflects the existence of an extra copy of chromosome 21 (cf. Nadel, 2003). As a consequence, extra gene product results, and this in turn leads to a variety of problems in a host of biological systems. In almost all cases, these problems seem to impact the later-developing parts of the relevant system. Thus, in the nervous system, the hippocampus, cerebellum, and prefrontal cortex, all of which mature late, are disproportionately affected. How these effects translate into the mental retardation observed in Down syndrome remains to be determined, and the creation of appropriate mouse models is moving toward that goal. Williams syndrome might present another such case, as it has recently been shown that children with this syndrome, caused by deletion of a subset of the genes on chromosome 7, have significant abnormalities in hippocampal structure and function (Meyer-Lindenberg et al., 2005).

It seems clear from these various examples that some knowledge systems, and in particular those critical for what we are here calling memory, develop later than other knowledge systems critical for such things as what and how much knowledge. It is worth pointing out that at the other end of the age scale, aging also has an uneven impact on knowledge systems. Evidence suggests that as in development, it is the hippocampal system, central to episodic memory, that is most at risk (cf. Burke and Barnes, 2006).

1.04.6.2 The Impact of Stress

Another way in which the existence of multiple knowledge systems matters is that these systems can be differentially affected by experience. One very important example is offered by how knowledge systems are affected by arousal and stress. The literature in this area has been confusing, since evidence existed that arousal facilitates memory formation (Reisberg and Heuer, 2004), while at the same time acute stress, which is undoubtedly arousing, has been shown to impair memory in several studies (Jackson et al. 2006; Payne et al., 2006). The best way to understand this discrepancy is in terms of multiple knowledge systems and how they are differentially affected by stress. Payne et al., for example, showed that memory for neutral information is impaired by stress at the same time that memory for emotional information is facilitated. This result is best understood by assuming that emotional information (value knowledge) is handled by one system in the brain, the amygdala, while neutral detail, typically of the background context (where knowledge), is handled by another brain system, the hippocampus. It has been established that within much of the range of physiological stress, amygdala function is enhanced while hippocampal function is impaired. Thus, the same stress manipulation can simultaneously increase acquisition of one kind of knowledge while decreasing acquisition of another. The implications of this simple fact for various legal issues, such as the viability of eyewitness testimony, and the veracity of recovered memories, are immense (see Jacobs and Nadel, 1998; Payne et al., 2003, for some discussion of these matters; *See* Chapters 2.14, 2.44).

1.04.7 Conclusions

That there are multiple systems engaged in acquiring and deploying knowledge gained from experience seems clear. I have argued that it is better to think about these as knowledge systems rather than as memory systems. This difference is not a mere semantic quibble, since a number of consequences flow from this change in terminology. However one does refer to these systems, the fact that they exist as separable entities has a variety of implications that I have tried to briefly explore in this chapter.

One final implication that I have not explored concerns the fact that the existence of multiple, separate, systems opens up the possibility of competition between systems for control of behavioral output. Within the domain of spatial behavior there is strong evidence that such competition exists between, for example, strategies that depend upon the egocentric information subserved by caudate and other structures and the allocentric information subserved by hippocampus and related structures (cf. Nadel and Hardt, 2004). Similar findings have been reported recently for a nonspatial task involving probabilistic classification (Foerde et al., 2006). It remains for future research to explicate these competitive relations in greater detail, as they will ultimately turn out to be extremely important in understanding how organisms deploy optimal knowledge in various circumstances. Looked at in this way, all forms of behavior involve decision-making at some level, creating linkages between previously disconnected literatures on memory and choice.

Acknowledgments

Preparation of this chapter was supported by grants from the National Institute of Neurological Disorders and Stroke (NS044107) and the Department of Health Services, State of Arizona, HB2354.

References

Avni R, Zadicario P, and Eilam D (2006) Exploration in a dark open field: A shift from directional to positional progression and a proposed model of acquiring spatial information. *Behav. Brain Res.* 171: 313–323.

Bartlett FL (1932) *Remembering.* Cambridge: Cambridge University Press.

Burke SN and Barnes CA (2006) Neural plasticity in the ageing brain. *Nat. Rev. Neurosci.* 7: 30–40.

Cohen NJ (1984) Preserved learning capacity in amnesia: evidence for multiple memory systems. In: Squire LR and Butters N (eds.) *Neuropsychology of Memory*, vol. 1, New York: Guilford Press.

Cohen NJ and Squire LR (1980) Preserved learning and retention of pattern-analyzing skill in amnesia: Dissociation of knowing how and knowing that. *Science* 210: 207–210.

Corkin S (1968) Acquisition of motor skill after bilateral medial temporal-lobe excision. *Neuropsychologia* 6: 255–265.

Finkelstein Y, Markowitz ME, and Rosen JF (1998) Low-level lead-induced neurotoxicity in children: An update on central nervous system effects. *Brain Res. Rev.* 27: 168–176.

Foerde K, Knowlton BJ, and Poldrack RA (2006) Modulation of competing memory systems by distraction. *Proc. Natl. Acad. Sci. USA* 3: 11778–11783.

Frotscher M and Seress L (2006) Morphological development of the hippocampus. In: Andersen P, Morris RGM, Amaral D, Bliss T, and O'Keefe J (eds.) *The Hippocampus Book*. Oxford: Oxford University Press.

Gaffan D (1974) Recognition impaired and association intact in the memory of monkeys after transection of the fornix. *J. Comp. Physiol. Psychol.* 86: 1100–1109.

Hafting T, Fyhn M, Molden S, Moser MB, and Moser EI (2005) Microstructure of a spatial map in the entorhinal cortex. *Nature* 436: 801–806.

Hannula DE, Tranel D, and Cohen NJ (2006) The long and the short of it: Relational memory impairments in amnesia, even at short lags. *J. Neurosci.* 26: 8352–8359.

Hebb DO (1949) *The Organization of Behavior.* New York: Wiley-Interscience.

Hirsh R (1974) The hippocampus and contextual retrieval of information from memory: A theory. *Behav. Biol.* 12: 421–444.

Horel JA (1978) The neuroanatomy of amnesia. A critique of the hippocampal memory hypothesis. *Brain* 101: 403–445.

Horel JA (1994) Some comments on the special cognitive functions claimed for the hippocampus. *Cortex* 30: 269–280.

Jackson ED, Payne JD, Nadel L, and Jacobs WJ (2006) Stress differentially modulates fear conditioning in healthy men and women. *Biol. Psychiatry* 59: 516–522.

Jacobs WJ and Nadel L (1998) Neurobiology of reconstructed memory. *Psychol. Public Policy Law* 4: 1110–1134.

Klein SB, Cosmides L, Tooby J, and Chance S (2002) Decisions and the evolution of memory: Multiple systems, multiple functions. *Psychol. Rev.* 109: 306–329.

Lashley K (1950) In search of the engram. *Symposia of the Society for Experimental Biology*, No. 4, pp. 454–482. Cambridge: Cambridge University Press [reprinted in Beach FA, Hebb DO, Morgan CT, and Nissen HW (eds.) (1960) *The Neuropsychology of Lashley: Selected Papers of KS Lashley*, pp. 478–505. New York: McGraw-Hill].

Meyer-Lindenberg A, Mervis CB, Sarpal D, et al. (2005) Functional, structural and metabolic abnormalities of the hippocampal formation in Williams syndrome. *J. Clin. Invest.* 115: 1888–1895.

Milner B (1966) Amnesia following operation on the temporal lobes. In: Whitty CWM and Zangwill OL (eds) *Amnesia*, pp. 109–133. London: Butterworths.

Nadel L (1992) Multiple memory systems: What and why. *J. Cogn. Neurosci.* 4: 179–188.

Nadel L (1994) Multiple memory systems: What and why. An update. In: Schacter D and Tulving E (eds.) *Memory Systems 1994*, pp. 39–63. Cambridge, MA: MIT Press.

Nadel L (2003) Down's syndrome: A genetic disorder in biobehavioral perspective. *Genes Brain Behav.* 2: 156–166.

Nadel L (2007) Memory consolidation: In search of a paradigm. In: Roediger HL, Dudai Y, and Fitz Patrick S (eds.) *Science of Memory: Concepts*. Oxford University Press.

Nadel L and Hardt O (2004) The spatial brain. *Neuropsychology* 18: 473–476.

Nadel L and Hupbach A (in press) Brain and neuroscience: hippocampus. In: Haith M and Benson J (eds.) *Encyclopedia of Infant and Early Childhood Development*, Elsevier.

Nadel L and O'Keefe J (1974) The hippocampus in pieces and patches: An essay on modes of explanation in physiological psychology. In: Bellairs R and Gray EG (eds.) *Essays on the Nervous System. A Festschrift for Prof. JZ Young*, pp. 367–390. Oxford: Clarendon Press.

Nadel L and Wexler K (1984) Neurobiology, representations and memory. In: Lynch G, McGaugh JL and Weinberger N (eds.) *The Neurobiology of Learning and Memory*. New York: The Guilford Press.

Nadel L and Willner J (1980) Context and conditioning: A place for space. *Physiol. Psychol.* 8: 218–228.

Nadel L and Zola-Morgan S (1984) Infantile amnesia: A neurobiological perspective. In: Moscovitch M (ed.) *Infant Memory*, pp. 145–172. New York: Plenum Press.

Nadel L, Willner J, and Kurz EM (1985) Cognitive maps and environmental context. In: Balsam P and Tomie A (eds.) *Context and Learning*. Hillsdale, NJ: Lawrence Erlbaum Associates.

Newcombe N, Huttenlocher J, Drummey AB, and Wiley J (1998) The development of spatial location coding: Place learning and dead reckoning in the second and third years. *Cogn. Dev.* 13: 185–201.

Newcombe NS, Lloyd ME, and Ratliff KR (2007) Development of episodic and autobiographical memory: A cognitive neuroscience perspective. In: Kail R (ed.) *Advances in Child Development and Behavior*, vol. 35. New York: Elsevier.

O'Keefe J (1976) Place units in the hippocampus of the freely moving rat. *Exp. Neurol.* 51: 78–109.

O'Keefe J and Dostrovsky J (1971) The hippocampus as a spatial map. Preliminary evidence from unit activity in the freely-moving rat. *Brain Res.* 34: 171–175.

O'Keefe J and Nadel L (1978) *The Hippocampus as a Cognitive Map*. Oxford: Clarendon Press, Oxford.

O'Keefe J and Nadel L (1979) Précis of O'Keefe and Nadel's The hippocampus as a cognitive map, and Author's Response to Commentaries. *Behav. Brain Sci.* 2: 487–534.

Orbach J, Milner B, and Rasmussen T (1960) Learning and retention in monkeys after amygdala-hippocampus resection. *Arch. Neurol.* 3: 230–251.

Payne JD, Nadel L, Britton WB, and Jacobs WJ (2003) The biopsychology of trauma and memory in humans. In: Reisberg D and Hertel P (eds.) *Memory and Emotion*, pp. 76–128, Oxford: Oxford University Press.

Payne JD, Jackson ED, Ryan L, Hoscheidt S, Jacobs WJ, and Nadel L (2006) The impact of stress on neutral and emotional aspects of episodic memory. *Memory* 1: 1–16.

Ranganath C and Blumenfeld RS (2005) Doubts about double dissociations between short- and long-term memory. *Trends Cogn. Sci.* 9: 374–380.

Reisberg D and Heuer F (2004). Memory for emotional events. In: Reisberg D and Hertel P (eds.) *Memory and Emotion*, pp. 3–41. London: Oxford University Press.

Schacter DL and Tulving E (1994) *Memory Systems 1994* Cambridge, MA: MIT Press.

Scoville WB and Milner B (1957) Loss of recent memory after bilateral hippocampal lesion. *J. Neurol. Neurosurg. Psychiatry* 20: 11–21.

Special Issue on Multiple Memory Systems (2004) *Neurobiol. Learn. Mem.* 82: 169–351.

Squire LR (1987) *Memory and Brain.* New York: Oxford University Press.

Squire LR (1994) Declarative and nondeclarative memory: Multiple brain systems supporting learning and memory. In: Schacter DL and Tulving E (eds.) *Memory Systems 1994*, pp. 203–231, Cambridge, MA: MIT Press.

Taube JS, Muller RU, and Ranck JB (1990) Head direction cells recorded from the postsubiculum in freely moving rats: I. Description and quantitative analysis. *J. Neurosci.* 10: 420–435.

Tolman EC (1932) *Purposive Behavior in Animals and Men.* New York: Century.

Tulving E (1972) Episodic and semantic memory. In: Tulving E and Donaldson W (eds.) *Organisation and Memory*, pp. 382–403. New York: Academic Press.

Ungerleider LG and Mishkin M (1982) Two cortical visual systems. In: Ingle DJ, Goodale MA, and Mansfield RJ (eds.) *Analysis of Visual Behavior*, pp. 549–586, Cambridge, MA: MIT Press.

Vargha-Khadem F, Gadian DG, Watkins KE, Connelly A, Van Paesschen W, and Mishkin M (1997) Differential effects of early hippocampal pathology on episodic and semantic memory. *Science* 277: 376–380.

Warrington EK and Weiskrantz L (1968) A study of learning and retention in amnesic patients. *Neuropsychologia* 6: 283–291.

Warrington EK and Weiskrantz L (1970) Amnesic syndrome: consolidation or retrieval? *Nature* 228: 628–630.

Whishaw IQ, Gharbawie OA, Clark BJ, and Lehmann H (2006) The exploratory behavior of rats in an open environment optimizes security. *Behav. Brain Res.* 171: 230–239.

1.05 Retrieval from Memory

G. P. Urcelay and R. R. Miller, State University of New York at Binghamton, Binghamton, NY, USA

1.05.1 Retrieval from Memory

The field of learning and memory has traditionally emphasized acquisition and storage as the critical determinants of learned behavior (*See* Chapters 1.02, 1.04). In the field of associative learning, this orientation is clearly evident in Pavlov's work, which suggested that spreading activation between nodes was necessary for memory formation (Pavlov, 1927). Similarly, Hebb (1949) proposed that experiencing a learning event temporarily activates certain neural circuits that, while active, strengthen the synaptic connections that constitute the basis for that experience becoming permanently stored in memory. This emphasis on acquisition and storage can be seen at many different levels of analysis. For instance, in the human memory literature, Craik and Lockhart (1972) proposed that the acquisition and storage of new information would create a more durable memory trace if processing during the acquisition (i.e., study) phase occurred at a relatively deep level (i.e., more integrative semantic than superficial phonetic). As another example, the Rescorla–Wagner rule for the formation of associations assumes that competition between stimuli trained together in a Pavlovian conditioning preparation occurs exclusively during the training phase (Rescorla and Wagner, 1972). All these views share the common assumption that any disruptive manipulation that occurs during training will inevitably result in that learned information being permanently lost and unavailable in future encounters within a similar situations. The influence of this view is so pervasive that the term *learning* itself for some researchers represents the totality of information processing underlying stimulus-specific changes in behavior resulting from prior experience. This use of the term discourages consideration of any of the post-acquisition processing that may also be necessary to see learned behavior. By definition, learning is the process by which experience is encoded and results in stimulus-specific changes in behavior that can be observed later. By memory, we are referring to any stimulus-specific permanent change in the brain (structural and chemical) resulting from past experience that allows usage of that previous experience on future occasions. Finally, retrieval is the process of reactivating an established memory so it can influence ongoing behavior, and thus we will argue that retrieval is a key component of memory performance.

In the early 1960s, however, a number of studies showed that information thought to be lost or not encoded was still available, provided that the appropriate retrieval cues were presented at the time of testing (see Tulving and Thomson, 1973, for a review). In other words, these studies suggested that memory deficits typically thought to result from processing limitations during training could be recovered at the time of testing. These experiments, conducted primarily with human subjects, provided a strong rationale for investigating a critical stage in the information processing stream: retrieval from memory. In most of these experiments, subjects were presented with material to be learned (encoding) and subsequently evaluated to determine the conditions under which that information could be retrieved and brought to bear on response generation. As a result of this research, the emphasis on encoding that dominated the early stages of human memory research shifted to also encompass retrieval mechanisms. Interestingly, these observations with human subjects promoted changes in the study of animal memory. A vast amount of data concerning retrieval processes has been gathered from nonhumans since the late 1960s, and ever since, the notion of retrieval has proven to be a useful heuristic for the study of memory phenomena.

This chapter will focus on memory research with nonhuman animals. In the first section, we will review the empirical evidence suggesting that deficits in memory tasks do not necessarily reflect a deficit in acquisition or storage. Specifically, we will summarize representative experiments in which memory deficits are observed after changes in the internal state of the organism, or the administration of amnesic treatments such as electroconvulsive shock or protein synthesis inhibition. Moreover, we will review recent evidence suggesting that already consolidated memories, when reactivated, undergo a new period of vulnerability, so-called reconsolidation. Importantly, memory deficits can also be obtained by manipulating the amount of information presented either during training of the target memory (cue competition) or by presenting additional information at other points in the study (interference). Cue competition and memory interference experiments have also contributed evidence concerning the role of encoding and retrieval of memory and therefore will also be analyzed in this section. In the second part, we will summarize how these observations led to the development of memory models that account for a wide range of phenomena. As is the case in most scientific disciplines, there is no single approach that accounts for all the empirical evidence available. Therefore we will review three models that address the phenomena described in the first section. The first general framework is that proposed by Spear in the late 1970s that explains memory deficits induced by changes in the context or insufficient retrieval cues at the time of test. The second retrieval framework we will review is focused on associative phenomena originally thought to reflect learning deficits. As we will see, these deficits

are easily anticipated in a framework that emphasizes retrieval mechanisms. The third framework is that proposed by Bouton to explain several characteristics of extinction that are important to understand some anxiety disorders in human populations (*See* Chapter 1.09). Lastly, we will briefly review neurobehavioral studies in which the physiological substrates of memory retrieval have been investigated. The importance of these studies lies in the fact that inquiries into the neurobiological basis of memory are inspired by behavioral models, such as the ones we describe in the section titled 'Theories of memory retrieval.'

1.05.2 Empirical Evidence

Several key empirical observations suggest that numerous deficits in acquired behavior result from information processing that occurs when subjects are tested rather than when they acquire or store information. Critical here is the fact that, theoretically speaking, if information is inadequately acquired or is not retained, then that information will not be available to influence the animal's behavior in any test situation. In contrast, the following observations suggest that the target information has often been sufficiently encoded and stored, but a processing deficit occurs when the information is evoked, which translates into decreased performance at the time of testing. We will review decrements in retrieval that arise from natural changes in the organism's internal state and from changes in the state of the external environment between training and testing, as well as those that arise in the laboratory as a result of programmed invasive manipulations (i.e., experimentally induced amnesia). Moreover, we will review recent evidence suggesting that memories that are retrieved from an inactive state could be subject to new consolidation processes, so-called reconsolidation (*See* Chapter 1.24, 1.27). Finally, we will review demonstrations of recovery from performance deficits arising in situations in which multiple cues are simultaneously present during training (cue competition) and from exposing subjects to select nontarget information removed from target training (stimulus interference).

1.05.2.1 Changes in the Organism's Internal State

One of the earlier observations that suggested a deficit in retrieval was state-dependent learning. State-dependent learning refers to the observation that when the internal state of the organism is different at testing than it was at training, acquired performance is impaired (Overton, 1964). Operationally, state-dependent learning is observed when subjects experience training under one of two internal states (a state induced by the presence or absence of a drug in Overton's case) and tested under the opposite internal state. The common finding is that when subjects are trained in a nondrug state and tested in a nondrug state, behavior consistent with training is observed. Conversely, if subjects are trained while in a drug-induced state (e.g., amphetamine) and tested while not in a drug state, a decrement in performance is typically observed. This decrement could easily be accounted for by a deficit in learning, perhaps due to the drug-altering perceptual processes or the encoding of information. Similar decrements in performance are observed when subjects are trained while undrugged and tested while drugged. These decrements can be accounted for by perceptual processes at the time of testing. However, subjects trained under a drugged state and tested under the same drugged state do not always show a decrement in memory performance. This suggests that the observed performance decrements often result from retrieval deficits due to a change in the internal state of the organism (Spear, 1978). If the internal state of the subject during testing is the same as during training, regardless of whether it is a state induced by administration of a drug, performance consistent with training is observed. State-dependent learning has been observed in a wide range of memory tasks and with states induced by several different drugs, such as amphetamine, alcohol, and morphine (Overton, 1972, 1985), and also emotional states induced by various manipulations (for a review, see Overton, 1985). Obviously *state-dependent learning* is a misnomer; the phenomenon would more accurately be called *state-dependent retrieval.*

Another example of state-dependent learning that can be understood as a retrieval failure is the Kamin effect (Kamin, 1957, 1963). This effect typically has been observed in avoidance tasks in which subjects show poor retention of avoidance training when they are tested at intervals ranging from 1 to 6 h after training. The interesting observation is that such poor retention is not observed if subjects are tested a half hour after training or more than 24 h after training. In other words, subjects show a U-shaped retention function, with retention being good immediately after training and at later intervals, but not between 1 and 6 h after training. This U-shaped

function has been viewed as the result of memory retrieval being dependent on the internal state of the organism. A more specific hypothesis was based on the fact that most of these demonstrations of the Kamin effect used aversively motivated tasks, which are known for their capacity to induce a stressful internal state. Moreover, the release of a hormone closely correlated with stress, adrenocorticotropic hormone (ACTH), is inhibited relatively soon after a stressful experience (McEwen and Weiss, 1970). Researchers reasoned that, because of ACTH inhibition, the internal state of the subjects from 1 to 6 h after training was different from the internal state during training, leading to a failure to retrieve the appropriate information required to perform in the task. Consistent with this interpretation, exposing subjects to foot shocks immediately before testing overcame the deficient retention observed at intermediate test intervals (Klein and Spear, 1970). Moreover, exposure to other stressors, such as immersion in cold water for 2 min, also alleviated the intermediate interval deficit in retention (Klein, 1972). Note that this stressor was unrelated to the training situation in terms of external, sensory attributes of the memory (other than being stressful), but it apparently restored the internal state that was temporarily inhibited after the original stressful experience. Importantly, the cold water bath had no effect at other retention intervals, suggesting that the effects are not related to overall activation or motivational effects of the stressor (Klein, 1972). Presumably, exposure to either foot shock or cold water provided subjects with an internal state (ACTH release) that corresponded to that of training and consequently alleviated the deficit observed at intermediate intervals. Moreover, this deficit in retention was also alleviated if subjects were infused with ACTH into the lateral anterior hypothalamus or if the same structure was electrically stimulated (Klein, 1972). More recently, Gisquet-Verrier and colleagues observed an alleviation of the Kamin effect when they exposed subjects simultaneously to the conditioned stimulus (CS) and the training context in a brightness-discrimination avoidance task 7.5 min before an intermediate interval test (Gisquet-Verrier et al., 1989; Gisquet-Verrier and Alexinsky, 1990). Overall, all of these demonstrations suggest that the Kamin effect can be alleviated if (a) the subject's internal state is restored (either by administration of ACTH or exposure to a stressor), or (b) the appropriate retrieval cues (such as the CS and the training context) are presented before testing.

Similar recovery effects have been found when retention deficits were induced with hypothermia. Specifically, subjects showed impaired retention if they were immersed in cold water immediately after training (Vardaris et al., 1973). However, if they were recooled before testing, no impaired retention was observed (Hinderliter et al., 1976; Mactutus and Riccio, 1978). These results have been interpreted as arising from a retrieval failure if there is a mismatch between training and testing in the subject's internal state. Consistent with this explanation, administering the recooling treatment immediately before testing presumably alleviates the effects of the hypothermic treatment by providing contextual cues that were present close to the time of training.

1.05.2.2 Experimentally Induced Amnesias

The notion that deficits in acquired behavior result from a processing deficit at the time of retrieval has received additional support from experimental manipulations known to induce amnesia (*See* Chapter 1.14). It is important to note that the three examples from the previous section resulted from changes in the internal state of the subject. In contrast to state-dependent learning and the Kamin effect, in the studies reviewed later, a performance deficit was induced by the administration of an amnestic agent. For example, if soon after training subjects are administered an electroconvulsive shock (hereafter ECS; Duncan, 1949), hypothermia (described earlier; Vardaris et al., 1973), or protein synthesis inhibitors (e.g., Barraco and Stettner, 1976), little behavior indicative of retention is observed. These observations have been taken by many as evidence that amnestic treatments work by disrupting memory consolidation (Gold and King, 1974; McGaugh, 1966, 2000). Memory consolidation is defined as a time-dependent process by which recent learned experiences are transformed into long-term memory, presumably by structural and chemical changes in the nervous system (e.g., the strengthening of synaptic connections between neurons). Support for this explanation comes from the fact that the effects of amnestic treatments are retrograde in nature, with recent memories being more vulnerable than earlier memories to the amnestic treatment (e.g., Duncan, 1949). The temporally graded nature of amnesia is explained by the consolidation view in the following way: After a given learning experience, memories undergo a consolidation process that leaves the memory trace more stable as time passes. Following this logic, the shorter the interval between training and the administration of the amnestic treatment, the larger the impact of the amnestic agent on the formation of the memory trace.

Since the discovery of these amnestic treatments, however, a number of observations have suggested that, instead of disrupting the consolidation process, these treatments might alter the memory's retrievability, thereby rendering it inaccessible at the time of retrieval (*See* Chapter 1.14). Evidence supporting this notion comes from studies that reminded subjects of the original episode. For example, Lewis et al. (1968) trained rats in a passive avoidance task and immediately administered amnesia-inducing ECS. They tested their subjects 20 h later and observed that subjects that received the amnestic treatment showed no behavior indicative of the passive avoidance event; that is, the amnestic treatment was effective in inducing amnesia. However, 4 h after training, they placed other rats given the amnesic treatment immediately following training in a separate compartment (different from that of training) and administered a foot shock (unconditioned stimulus – US), similar to the reinforcer used in training. When these subjects were tested 20 h later in the training compartment, they showed recovery from the amnestic treatment, as evidenced by longer avoidance latencies. In other words, when they exposed rats to a reminder of the initial training experience, subjects' performance indicated that the memory trace was not altered by the amnestic treatment. Subjects lacking original training showed no effect of such reminder shocks. Because this recovery effect could have been specific to the avoidance tasks involving stressful situations, Miller et al. (1974) conducted a similar study, but instead of using an aversive preparation, they used an appetitively motivated task with sucrose as a reinforcer. Interestingly, they reported that, after the amnestic treatment, a foot shock did not affect a recovery of memory. Moreover, they showed that exposure to the sucrose solution following the amnestic treatment reversed the retention deficit induced by the amnestic treatment. Further experiments demonstrated that exposure to the training apparatus also recovered the memory rendered silent by the amnestic treatment. Thus, exposure to any of several elements from the training task restored access to the target memory, whereas exposure to task-irrelevant stimuli, even if they were of strong affective value, did not restore memory.

1.05.2.3 Reconsolidation

As part of the effort to understand and contrast approaches to memory, studies of experimentally induced amnesias gained popularity during the late 1960s and 1970s. This popularity was recently reinvigorated when new findings suggested that old memories when reactivated need new (*de novo*) protein synthesis to become once again stable and permanently stored in the brain (Przybyslawski and Sara, 1997; Nader et al., 2000; *See* Chapter 1.24). This phenomenon has been called reconsolidation. For example, a day after Nader et al. exposed their rats to simple CS → US pairings, they presented the CS alone (which presumably reactivated the memory trace for that association) and immediately infused anisomycin (a protein synthesis inhibitor) into the lateral and basal amygdala. When they tested subjects 1 day later, they observed decreased conditioned freezing to the CS relative to anisomycin-treated rats lacking the CS exposure on day 2, suggesting that the memory trace that was activated needed new protein synthesis to become stable again. These findings brought back the question extensively debated in the 1970s: Are memories destroyed or simply made inaccessible after a retrieval manipulation followed by an amnestic agent (e.g., Gold and King, 1974; Miller and Springer, 1973, 1974)? Several recent reports suggest an answer to this question. For example, Lattal and Abel (2004) observed that after reactivating a memory of contextual fear and administrating systemic anisomycin, subjects showed decreased conditioned freezing when tested 1 day later in the training context. However, if the test was delayed by 21 days (a standard retention interval used for spontaneous recovery from extinction of fear memories), no effect of protein synthesis inhibition was observed. In fact, Lattal and Abel observed that 21 days after anisomycin treatment, response to the context was larger than that observed during immediate retrieval (1 day after training). Other recent studies also cast doubt on the generality of the reconsolidation account because similar recovery from retrieval-induced reconsolidation has been observed (Anokhin et al., 2002; Fisher et al., 2004; Power et al., 2006; but see Debiec et al., 2002; Duvarci and Nader, 2004). Moreover, some studies did not observe any immediate effect of anisomycin after retrieval-induced reconsolidation (Lattal and Abel, 2001; Vianna et al., 2001; Biedenkapp and Rudy, 2004; Cammarota et al., 2004; Hernandez and Kelley, 2004). Overall, these contradictory findings,

together with demonstrations of recovery from retrieval-induced amnesia after inhibition of protein synthesis, show that further research is needed to determine whether anisomycin erases the reactivated memory or simply constrains future retrieval of the memory. More generally, it is still unclear if amnestic agents following initial training impair consolidation (storage) or subsequent retrieval (e.g., Gold and King, 1974; Miller and Matzel, 2006).

Two points deserve further discussion here. First, as recently pointed out by Rudy et al. (2006), anisomycin also has other effects beyond inhibition of protein synthesis, such as genetically programmed cell death (apoptosis). Moreover, the apoptotic cascade occurs at lower doses than those that are necessary for the inhibition of protein synthesis. Whether this is the main cause of the observed amnesia remains to be determined, but it is noteworthy that tests have not yet been conducted to determine the role of apoptosis in experimental amnesia. Second, a recent report from the same laboratory that sparked early interest in reconsolidation showed that memories activated indirectly by an associate of the target cue do not undergo reconsolidation (Debięc et al., 2006). They trained rats in a second-order conditioning preparation in which one cue was paired with the US in a first phase (CS$_1$ → US), and in a second phase another cue was paired with the cue trained in phase 1 (CS$_2$ → CS$_1$). This procedure ordinarily results in conditioned responding to CS$_2$, presumably because when presented at test it retrieves a neural representation of the US through an associative chain mediated by CS$_1$ (or a direct CS$_2$ → UR link; see Rescorla, 1980, for a discussion). Notably, Debięc et al. found that responding to CS$_1$ was not impaired after retrieval through presentation of CS$_2$ and subsequent administration of anisomycin. This suggests that the reactivation treatment, at most, leaves only part of the memory in a labile state, but alternatively the entire content of the memory might not be substantially altered.

In contrast to reconsolidation accounts of the reconsolidation phenomenon, there are retrieval-focused accounts of reconsolidation such as that proposed by Millin et al. (2001). In line with Spear's (1973, 1978; see following discussion) views concerning retrieval, Riccio and his collaborators have proposed that when previously stored memories are reactivated, reprocessing of the attributes of these memories will take place for some time after the reactivation episode. As a result, the internal context provided by an amnestic treatment becomes associated with the target memory. At test, the context provided by the amnestic treatment is not ordinarily present, and thus retrieval failure occurs. Consistent with this account, amnesia induced by the administration of anisomycin has been observed to be alleviated if subjects are administered anisomycin just prior to testing (Bradley and Galal, 1988). Another explanation of this phenomenon has been advanced by Miller and Matzel (2000; also see Nadel and Land, 2000), who proposed that the amnestic treatment produces a change in the memory representation that interferes with retrieval itself, leaving the memory trace silent after the administration of the amnestic treatment. Regardless of the specific version of the retrieval explanation for the reconsolidation phenomenon put forth, these alternative views can be contrasted with reconsolidation accounts by determining the extent to which amnestic treatments really erase the memory trace or simply render it inaccessible for future use. Based on the recovery data presented earlier, the latter alternative seems to be the more plausible at this time (Prado-Alcalá et al., 2006).

Four points are important to keep in mind. (1) Recovery from amnestic treatment is often observed when subjects are exposed to a portion of the event that had been presented during training. Such reminder treatments are most effective soon before testing, but sometimes have enduring effects even when presented 24 h before testing. (2) Control groups have demonstrated that the recovery is not purely the result of altering stress levels in the subject. (3) Recovery can be obtained by reminding subjects about the training situation not only with the US, but also with other cues (such as contextual cues or sometimes even the CS) that are part of the target memory. (4) The effect of the reminder does not result from new learning concerning the cue-outcome relationship, as long as learning is defined as receiving relevant new information from events in the environment. Subjects exposed to the reminder without any prior learning experience did not show any evidence of relevant learning after the reminder experience.

So far, we have argued that most impairments in memory retention result at least in part from a retrieval failure rather than an acquisition or storage failure. We have based our assertion on studies involving changes in the state of the organism (state-dependent learning and the Kamin effect), experimentally induced amnesia (ECS, hypothermia, and antimetabolites), or reconsolidation phenomena. Next, we review evidence suggesting that decrements in learning and memory that are thought to result from processing limitations (competition) at the time of training, or from deleterious effects on learning or retention due to learning additional information (interference), could instead result from a retrieval deficit at the time of testing.

1.05.2.4   Cue Competition and Outcome Competition

Cue competition refers to a decrement in behavioral control by a target CS (X), which results from the addition of a nontarget stimulus to a simple CS–US learning situation (*See* Chapters 1.03, 1.07, 1.08). This can be observed in a number of different circumstances. For example, one can add a second CS to training and train a compound of the target cue and the added CS instead of the target cue alone (i.e., $AX \rightarrow US$ as opposed to $X \rightarrow US$) and see less behavioral control to the target cue X (overshadowing; Pavlov, 1927). Alternatively, one can train a nontarget cue in a first phase and in a second phase train a compound of cues that contains the target cue as well as the previously trained nontarget cue ($A \rightarrow US$ in phase 1; $AX \rightarrow US$ in phase 2). This results in less behavioral control by X, the target cue, than in subjects lacking phase 1 (blocking; Kamin, 1969). A second rather different form of stimulus competition can be seen when, instead of adding a second CS, a second outcome is added. For example, one can train a cue followed by an outcome in a first phase and that same cue followed by the same outcome plus a new outcome in a second phase, and then later assess performance governed by the association between the cue and the second outcome ($X \rightarrow O_1$ in phase 1, $X \rightarrow O_1O_2$ in phase 2, test $X \rightarrow O_2$; Rescorla 1980; Esmoris-Arranz et al., 1997). This is called blocking between outcomes. Taking these examples together, one can see that the addition of nontarget stimuli (a cue or an outcome) attenuates behavioral control by the target cue X.

Phenomena like blocking between cues gave rise to a family of models of Pavlovian conditioning that emphasized critical differences in information processing during acquisition. These models assumed that limitations in processing (e.g., attention to the CS or US) during training impeded the normal establishment of associations and consequently resulted in the observed decrements in behavioral control (e.g., Rescorla and Wagner, 1972; Mackintosh, 1975;

Pearce and Hall, 1980). Similar to consolidation theory (e.g., McGaugh, 1966, 2000), these behavioral models predict that what has not been stored due to processing constraints during learning will not be reflected in behavior simply because the information was not initially acquired.

As previously mentioned, overshadowing is observed as a response decrement that results from training a target cue (X) in the presence of another, usually more salient, cue (A). Interestingly, Kauffman and Bolles (1981; see also Matzel et al., 1985) conducted overshadowing training (AX → US) and subsequently extinguished the overshadowing cue (A) by presenting it in the absence of reinforcement. After extinguishing the overshadowing cue, they observed a recovery from overshadowing, that is, strong behavioral control by the overshadowed cue X at test. Similarly, after blocking treatment (A → US followed by AX → US), extinguishing the blocking cue (A alone presentations) can result in recovery from blocking (Blaisdell et al., 1999). However, extinction of the competing cue is not the only manipulation known to affect overshadowing and blocking. Kraemer et al. (1988) found a recovery from overshadowing training when they interposed a long retention interval between overshadowing treatment and testing, which suggests that the association between the overshadowed cue and the outcome had been established during training but was not reflected in behavior soon after training. A similar recovery from blocking has been observed after interposing a long retention interval between training and testing (Batsell, 1997; Piñeno et al., 2005).

In the same way that recovery from experimentally induced amnesia has been observed after exposing subjects to some portions of the events presented during training (CS, US, or the training context), stimulus competition phenomena have been observed to be attenuated as a result of these manipulations. For example, Kasprow et al. (1982) observed a recovery from overshadowing after they exposed subjects to two brief presentations of the overshadowed cue (the target CS). In another series of experiments, a similar recovery from blocking was observed (Balaz et al., 1982). Specifically, Balaz et al. observed a recovery from blocking after reminding subjects of the training experience either by presenting the blocked CS, the US, or the context in which subjects were trained. Additional control groups demonstrated that this recovery was specific to the blocked association and was not due to nonspecific

increases in responding. All these demonstrations of recovery from cue competition are problematic for models that emphasize impaired acquisition (see earlier discussion) because, if the association between the overshadowed or blocked cue and the outcome was not learned during training, any manipulation that does not involve further training with that cue should not alter behavioral control by that cue.

Although little attention has been given to competition between outcomes, some recent studies have not only observed similar competition phenomena as those observed between cues (e.g., blocking between outcomes; Emoris-Arranz et al., 1998), but also observed that these deficits in behavioral control can be alleviated with the appropriate manipulations. For example, Wheeler and Miller (2005) observed reliable blocking between outcomes (X → O_1 during phase 1; X → O_1O_2 during phase 2), similar to the blocking between cues trained together originally observed by Kamin (1969). That is, responding based on the X → O_2 association was weaker than in subjects that had received X → O_3 in phase 1. Wheeler and Miller went on to extinguish the blocking outcome (O_1) and observed recovery from blocking between outcomes (i.e., behavioral consistent with the X → O_2 association). Moreover, they observed a similar recovery when they interposed a retention interval between training and testing, and when they briefly presented the blocked outcome before testing (i.e., a reminder treatment). Overall, the results of these experiments demonstrated that blocking between outcomes can be attenuated by several manipulations similar to those that often yield recovery from blocking between cues.

1.05.2.5 Interference between Cues and Outcomes Trained Apart

Earlier we distinguished between impairments in acquired behavior that arise from training stimuli together (competition) and from experiencing additional training apart from training of the target stimuli (provided that the additional training includes one of the target associates). The latter deficit is called interference. We have already described how impaired performance that arises from stimulus competition can be recovered, thus suggesting that retrieval mechanisms play a fundamental role in behavioral control influenced by stimulus competition. Next we will review the basic conditions under which interference is observed and the different manipulations that often result in recovery from interference. Interference in Pavlovian conditioning is evidenced as impaired behavioral control by a target cue when it is paired with a given outcome in one phase of training and paired with another outcome in an earlier or later phase of training (e.g., $X \rightarrow O_1$ in phase 1 and $X \rightarrow O_2$ in phase 2). But this is not the only situation in which interference is observed. Interference is also observed when a target cue (X) is trained with an outcome in one phase of training and in a separate phase of training another cue is trained with the same outcome (e.g., $X \rightarrow O$ in phase 1 and $Y \rightarrow O$ in phase 2). A common characteristic of these two forms of interference is that there is always a common element between the two phases of training (the cue X in the case of interference between outcomes (*See* Chapter 1.09), and the outcome O in the case of interference between cues). The critical feature of these decrements in otherwise anticipated behavioral control by X is that the interfering cues (or outcomes) are not trained together with the target cue (or outcome).

Extinction, latent inhibition, and counterconditioning (Pavlov, 1927; Lubow, 1973; Bouton and Peck, 1992; Brooks and Bouton, 1993) are three treatments that can be viewed as forms of interference between outcomes. In simple extinction, a cue is first paired with an outcome ($X \rightarrow US$), and in a second phase it is trained in the absence of the outcome (X-alone presentations; i.e., $X \rightarrow No\ US$). As a result of these nonreinforced presentations, the cue loses behavioral control, which used to be taken as evidence of unlearning the original $X \rightarrow US$ association (e.g., Rescorla and Wagner, 1972). However, overwhelming evidence has shown that the original $X \rightarrow US$ association is not destroyed during the second phase, but rather, new learning during phase 2 interferes with the expression of the phase 1 learning. Pavlov (1927) was the first to find a [partial] recovery effect from extinction. His observation (widely replicated since then; e.g., Brooks and Bouton, 1993; Rescorla and Cunningham, 1978) was that conditioned responding soon after extinction was minimal, but if a retention interval was interposed between extinction and the test, a recovery (which Pavlov termed *spontaneous recovery*) from extinction was observed. In other words, behavior after a retention interval was relatively similar in subjects who received extinction training and those who did not receive extinction training. What was puzzling at that time (and might have encouraged Pavlov to name the effect 'spontaneous recovery') was the fact that the extinguished response was recovered despite the fact that the subjects did not undergo any treatment other than interpolation of a long retention interval. Another manipulation that also leads to recovery from extinction is a shift in context between extinction and testing. This phenomenon is called renewal. For example, one might train subjects in a distinctive context A and conduct extinction training in a different context (B). The critical determinant of renewal is that testing be conducted outside the extinction context. If subjects are tested in a different context from the one used during extinction (ABC or ABA, where the first letter denotes the training context, the second the extinction context, and the third the test context), recovery from extinction is observed (Bouton and Bolles, 1979; Bouton and King, 1983; Bouton and Swartzentruber, 1989). If subjects are tested in the same context in which extinction took place (AAA or ABB), no such recovery is observed. A similar finding is observed when the context is defined to include the internal state of the organism, which can typically be altered by administering a drug that would change the internal state. For example, renewal has been observed when the extinction context is characterized by alcohol intoxication, and subjects are tested in a sober state, which creates a different internal context (Cunningham, 1979).

Latent inhibition is observed as a retarded emergence of behavioral control due to nonreinforced presentations of the target CS prior to conditioning (X-alone presentations in phase 1; $X \rightarrow US$ in phase 2), in comparison with subjects that experience the same phase 2 training without phase 1 treatment (Lubow, 1973). Similar to extinction, in a latent inhibition treatment subjects experience the target CS alone, but before the reinforced trials rather than after. One characteristic of latent inhibition that is suggestive of the response deficit being a retrieval effect is its context specificity. Specifically, it has been observed that if subjects experience phase 1 and phase 2 training in different contexts, latent inhibition is abolished (Channell and Hall, 1983). Presumably, during phase 1 nonreinforced presentations, the CS becomes associated with the context in which it is being presented, and these associations interfere with subsequent behavioral control after reinforcement in the same context. Thus, a context switch or massive extinction of the context (Grahame et al., 1993) between phases 1 and 2 attenuates the latent inhibition effect. A recent observation that has captured researchers' attention is the super latent inhibition effect (De la Casa and Lubow, 2000,

2002; Wheeler et al., 2004). This effect is typically observed when a retention interval is interposed between phase 2 reinforced training and testing. One critical condition necessary for this effect to be observed is that subjects have to spend the retention interval in a context different from that of conditioning. Thus, the superlatent inhibition effect might be seen as a shift from behavior based on recency (phase 2 training) to behavior based on primacy (phase 1 training) after interposing a long retention interval between phase 2 training and testing.

Counterconditioning is a phenomenon similar to extinction, but during the second phase of training, the target cue is associated with a qualitatively different outcome instead of being associated with the absence of an outcome, as is the case with extinction. The phase 2 treatment radically attenuates conditioned responding based on phase 1 training (Pavlov, 1927). What distinguishes extinction from counterconditioning is the motivational nature of the outcomes, in that in counterconditioning, the outcomes of phases 1 and 2 engage different motivational systems. For example, in a counterconditioning experiment, subjects might experience a CS followed by food in the first phase ($X \rightarrow$ food) and the same CS followed by foot shock in the second phase ($X \rightarrow$ shock; this is called appetitive-aversive transfer, but counterconditioning is also observed when the two phases are reversed, which is called aversive-appetitive transfer). After this training, the CS $\rightarrow$ shock association is thought to retroactively interfere with the CS $\rightarrow$ food associations. The question of interest is whether phase 2 learning destroys the memory of phase 1 training or if it simply interferes with the expression of that association. To address this question, Peck and Bouton (1990) trained phases 1 and 2 in two physically distinct contexts and tested subjects in the phase 1 context. Consistent with an explanation in terms of retrieval disruption rather than impaired retention, subjects tested in the phase 1 context showed responding appropriate to phase 1 training, indicating that the information had not been erased (or unlearned) but rather that behavior appropriate to each phase could be observed depending on the contextual cues present at the time of testing. Similarly, Brooks et al. (1995) trained rats with $X \rightarrow$ shock pairings in phase 1 and $X \rightarrow$ food pairings in phase 2. Before testing, they exposed the critical group to six unsignaled shocks and at test (relative to appropriate control groups) found that subjects froze to the CS, consistent with the shock US, rather than approached the food hopper,

which demonstrated reinstatement of original training after counterconditioning. Moreover, this reinstatement effect was dependent on the shocks being presented in the context in which testing would occur, because no reinstatement was observed when the shocks were presented in a context other than the test context.

As we mentioned earlier, interference is observed not only when a cue is associated with two outcomes (extinction and counterconditioning), but also when two cues are associated with the same outcome. For example, Escobar et al. (2001) paired a cue with an outcome ($X \rightarrow O$) in a first phase and subsequently paired a second cue with the same outcome ($A \rightarrow O$) and observed impaired responding to X (relative to subjects that received A and O explicitly unpaired in phase 2), thereby providing a demonstration of retroactive interference. In subsequent experiments, they showed that the retroactive interference effect could be alleviated if subjects experienced phase 1 ($X \rightarrow O$) and phase 2 ($A \rightarrow O$) training in different contexts and subsequently were tested in the context in which the $X \rightarrow O$ association was trained. That is, interference was affected by the context in which testing took place. Similarly, in another experiment, they presented priming stimuli (stimuli presented during phase 1 or during phase 2 sessions but far removed from presentations of the target cue or interfering cue) that distinctively signaled phase 1 or 2 of their procedure and observed retroactive interference to be dependent on which priming cue was presented immediately before the critical test. When they primed phase 2, robust retroactive interference was observed, but when they primed phase 1, an alleviation of retroactive interference was observed, relative to subjects that did not receive any priming treatment at the time of test. Similar findings were reported by Amundson et al. (2003) but in a proactive interference preparation (i.e., $A \rightarrow US$ training followed by $X \rightarrow US$ training). Specifically, they observed an attenuation of proactive interference with responding to X when they primed the second phase of their training procedure, presumably because this impaired retrieval of the competing (phase 1) association and facilitated retrieval of the second association. Moreover, they observed recovery from proactive interference when they extinguished the phase 1 association. In summary, based on these and similar findings, it is reasonable to conclude that interference is highly dependent on the cues provided at the time of testing, thus suggesting a strong role for retrieval mechanisms. Moreover, there are now several demonstrations of parallels in interference between cues and between outcomes in that both of these effects can be alleviated if the appropriate conditions prevail at the time of testing.

1.05.3 Theories of Memory Retrieval

There are several approaches to memory retrieval, each having been designed to explain different phenomena. However, the frameworks that we describe next point to several shared principles that have proven to be important and reliable tools for the study of retrieval from memory following learning. No single approach accounts for all the deficits in retention we have reviewed earlier. But each framework has provided an explanation of a number of observations and therefore deserves discussion.

1.05.3.1 Matching of Information as Critical for the Retrieval from Memory

Tulving and Thomson (1973) proposed the encoding specificity principle of retrieval that at the time accounted for many of the retrieval effects that were found with human participants. The principle states that subjects form a representation of events that encompasses not only the target events themselves but also many of the events surrounding the target event. Additionally, these episodic memories encode not only which events occurred, but where and when each event occurred relative to neighboring events. Moreover, the encoding specificity principle asserts that items (words, in the framework of the proposal) presented to aid retrieval will be effective only if they (or very similar items) were presented during training, consistent with the view that subjects encode a global representation of an item, its semantic meaning, and its content during training. Critical to this proposal is the notion that what enters into a memory representation (what it is encoded) is determined by the perceived functional meaning of an item, and this in turn determines which retrieval cues will be effective for memory retrieval.

Along similar lines, Spear (1973, 1978) has emphasized that similarity between retrieval cues and cues presented during training is critical for memory expression. He proposed the following principles as a conceptual framework for effective memory processing.

1. Attributes of memory function independently. In other words, an animal encodes a collection of separate but associated attributes that correspond to the events that form a memory episode. A constellation of attributes will be activated every time the subject experiences an event that has some similarity in attributes to the target memory. Moreover, an associated attribute might be activated when an event memory is activated. That is, some attributes might activate an event memory that in turn will activate attributes that need not have been presented but rather are associatively linked to retrieval cues presented. Additionally, attributes might activate memories of other attributes, regardless of whether they activate the full event memory representation.

2. The process of retrieval is determined by the number of retrieval cues that correspond to attributes of that memory. A memory failure is observed when an insufficient number of retrieval cues correspond at test to the memory of a given event, other things being equal. Moreover, events that are presented during testing but were not presented during training will lead to retrieval of nontarget memories that will interfere with retrieval of target memories (similar to the phenomenon of external inhibition that Pavlov, 1927, described).

3. A contextual cue is any event noticed by the organism, with the exclusion of the target stimuli that form the learning experience (e.g., the CS and US in a Pavlovian conditioning situation). Forgetting is caused in large part by a change between the context of acquisition and the context of retrieval. Context changes can result from different sources, and the differences in contextual information are more likely to increase as time passes (i.e., as the retention interval is increased; Bouton, 1993, views this as resulting from time actually being part of the context). Thus, in this framework sensory contexts from training will dissipate rapidly (soon after the stimuli are terminated), and neurochemical and hormonal states will dissipate somewhat more slowly. Importantly, contextual information here can be composed of internal stimuli (or states) and external stimuli, such as the physical attributes of the context where training or testing takes place. The internal context can also change due to preprogrammed factors such as aging or cyclical changes

in hormonal states (e.g., estrus). Contextual attributes learned during new experiences also might interfere with retrieval of the target memory if they share attributes in common.

This general framework has been one of the foundations for studying retrieval mechanisms in memory retention. For example, it easily explains state-dependent learning and the Kamin effect by assuming that the conditions at test are different than those during training. Consistent with this framework, several manipulations that recreate the training conditions at the time of testing have proven effective in restoring the deficient behavior observed due to changes in the organism's internal states or changes in the environment.

1.05.3.2 The Comparator Hypothesis: A Retrieval-Focused View of Cue Competition

As was mentioned in the introduction, models that emphasize processing during encoding and storage have been prevalent in the study of learned behavior in animals. One such example is the well-known Rescorla and Wagner (1972; also see Wagner and Rescorla, 1972) model. This model asserts that error correction at the time of training governs what information is acquired; that is, acquisition should be greatest when the discrepancy between the US that occurs and the US that is expected based on all cues present is largest. The model has been widely applied to Pavlovian conditioning situations in which one or more cues are concurrently paired with a given outcome. After repeated pairings, subjects emit a conditioned response when one (or more) of these cues are presented. One of the strengths of the model is that it elegantly anticipates the occurrence of cue competition (overshadowing, blocking, etc). In fact, the model was conceived in part to account for such phenomena after Kamin's (1969) demonstration of blocking. However, one of the weaknesses of the model is that it only emphasizes processing during training, with the additional vague assumption that associative strengths map monotonically onto behavior. Given all the aforementioned examples of recovery from cue competition (see prior section on empirical evidence), it is attractive to detail here a model that also explains cue-competition phenomena but appeals centrally to a retrieval mechanism.

One such model is the comparator hypothesis of conditioned responding (Miller and Matzel, 1988). The model assumes that all pairs of stimuli, including

cues, that are presented together gain associative strength with each of the other stimuli present, independent of the associative status of other cues present during training. In other words, in this model there is no competition between cues for associative strength during training – all information is stored. Associative strength between stimuli A and B depends only on their spatiotemporal contiguity and saliencies. The training context also gains associative strength, although at a much slower rate due to its lower salience than punctate stimuli. Thus, following Bush and Mosteller's (1951) error correction rule, the comparator hypothesis assumes noncompetitive learning of associations between cues and outcomes, of within-compound associations between cues trained together, and of associations between cues and the training context. What is critical in the comparator hypothesis is the process of retrieval of memories. According to this framework, responding to the presentation of a CS will be determined by a comparison between the representation of the US that is directly activated by the target CS → US association and the representation of the US that is indirectly activated conjointly by the associations between the target CS and any other cues presented during training (punctate cues or the training context) and the association between those cues and the US. In **Figure 1**, a depiction of the comparator hypothesis is provided. The

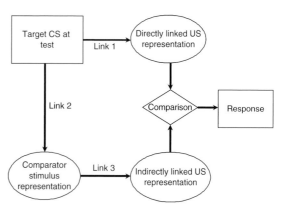

Figure 1 The original comparator hypothesis (after Miller RR and Matzel LD (1988) The comparator hypothesis: A response rule for the expression of associations. In: Bower GH (ed.) *The Psychology of Learning and Motivation, Vol. 22*, pp. 51–92. San Diego, CA: Academic Press). Rectangles represent physical events, and ovals correspond to internal representations of events that were previously associated with those physical events. The diamond represents the comparator process. Responding is directly related to the strength of link 1 and negatively related to the product of links 2 and 3.

boxes represent the external events observable in the test situation, that is, the target stimulus and the conditioned response. Ovals represent internal representations of events that were presented during training, and the diamond represents the comparator process (also internal). Direct activation of a US representation due to presentation of the target cue at test depends on the strength of the association between the target cue and the outcome, represented by link 1. Importantly, the target cue also activates a US representation mediated through other cues that were presented in the training situation, and this is represented by links 2 and 3. Responding is determined by a comparison between the directly activated representation of the US (the strength of which is determined by the target CS-US association, i.e., link 1) and the indirectly activated representation of the US (the strength of which is determined by the product of links 2 and 3). This comparison process is represented by the diamond. In an overshadowing situation (AX → US; with X being the target cue to be tested), the comparator hypothesis states that during training, subjects associate the target cue with the US (link 1 in **Figure 1**), the target cue with the overshadowing cue A (which is X's comparator cue; link 2), and A with the US (link 3). These associations are acquired independently of each other (i.e., cues do not compete during training for associative strength with the US). Critical for the comparator hypothesis is what happens when the target cue X is presented during testing. When X is presented, it directly activates a representation of the US, but it also indirectly activates a representation of the US, mediated by the overshadowing cue (which was associated during training with both the target cue and the US). This indirectly activated (competing) US representation is said to decrease (downmodulate) responding to the target cue, and thus overshadowing is observed relative to a group that experienced elemental training (X → US alone).

What differentiates the comparator hypothesis from acquisition-focused models (i.e., those that focus on limitations in processing during training) is not only the mechanism through which it explains cue competition phenomena, but also several novel predictions that have received empirical support in recent years. One such prediction is that after overshadowing training, extinguishing the overshadowing cue (that is, presenting A alone after training) should result in recovery from overshadowing. Specifically, by presenting A alone after overshadowing training, the links that mediate the indirectly activated

representation of the US decrease in associative strength, and consequently the overshadowing cue should no longer interfere with the representation of the US that is directly activated by X. Importantly, here we have an example of a change in behavioral control by X as a result of conducting a posttraining manipulation that does not involve further training of X (that is, subjects have no additional experience with X after the overshadowing treatment), and still a recovery from cue competition is observed. Most models that emphasize processing during acquisition (e.g., Rescorla and Wagner, 1972; Wagner 1981) cannot account for these results for two reasons: (1) they do not have a mechanism that allows learning about absent cues, and (2) these models state that overshadowing results from a deficit in the establishment of the X → US association during overshadowing training, so any manipulation that does not involve the presentation of X should not affect its behavioral control. In fact, recovery from overshadowing after extinguishing the overshadowing cue has been observed repeatedly (e.g., Kaufman and Bolles, 1981; Matzel et al., 1985; Urcelay and Miller, 2006), thereby lending support to a retrieval-failure account of cue competition.

A related example is recovery from blocking. After blocking treatment (A → US followed by AX → US), responding to X is usually diminished relative to a group that experienced an irrelevant cue during training of phase 1 (B → US; AX → US). According to the comparator hypothesis, acquisition of the X → US association proceeds without any competition between A and X. At the time of testing, the blocking cue is thought to decrease responding to the blocked cue through its associations with X and the US (links 2 and 3). Similar to overshadowing, the comparator hypothesis predicts that extinguishing the blocking cue should result in recovery from blocking, as has been empirically observed (e.g., Blaisdell et al., 1999).

For several years, the comparator hypothesis was unique in predicting these recovery effects that could not be explained by traditional models that emphasized acquisition processes (e.g., Rescorla and Wagner, 1972; Wagner, 1981). However, recent revision of the Rescorla–Wagner (1972) model by Van Hamme and Wasserman (1994) and of Wagner's (1981) SOP model by Dickinson and Burke (1996) introduced mechanisms that allow for learning about an absent cue provided an associate of the absent cue is present. Posttraining extinction of a companion cue (i.e., an overshadowing or blocking cue) constitutes a situation in which these models anticipate new learning about a target cue. Consequently, these two models are able to account for phenomena such as recovery from overshadowing and blocking as a result of extinction of an overshadowing or blocking cue. This prompted a revision of the comparator hypothesis, in part to differentiate this model from the revised versions of acquisition-focused models and also to account for data that were problematic for the original comparator hypothesis (Williams, 1996; Rauhut et al., 1999).

The extended comparator hypothesis (Denniston et al., 2001; also see Stout and Miller, in press, for a mathematical implementation of this model) carries the same assumptions as the original comparator hypothesis, but it further assumes that the links mediating the indirectly activated representation of the US (links 2 and 3) are also subject to a comparator process in which nontarget cues present during training can compete for roles as comparator stimuli for the target cue (see **Figure 2**). In other words, the extended version of the model is similar to the original version but allows more than one cue (comparator) to modulate conditioned responding to the target cue. If there's more than one comparator stimulus for the target, these comparator stimuli can in select situations cancel each other with respect to their capacity to modulate responding to the target cue. Thus, the extended comparator hypothesis makes a number of new predictions that allow for differentiating this retrieval-based account from models that emphasize processing during acquisition. For example, it makes the counterintuitive prediction that combining select pairs of treatments that

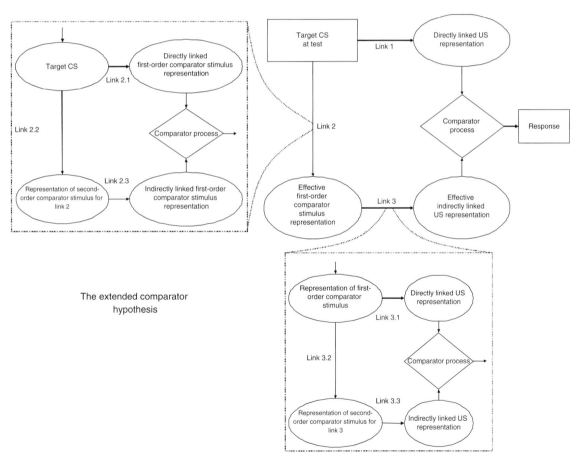

Figure 2 The extended comparator hypothesis (after Denniston JC, Savastano HI, and Miller RR (2001) The extended comparator hypothesis: Learning by contiguity, responding by relative strength. In: Mowrer RR and Klein SB (eds.) *Handbook of Contemporary Learning Theories*, pp. 65–117. Hillsdale, NJ: Erlbaum). Note principles similar to the original comparator hypothesis but with the inclusion of second-order comparator processes that operate over links 2 and 3. The magnitude of second-order comparator processes directly affects conditioned responding to the target CS, by decreasing the effectiveness of first-order comparator stimuli.

alone lead to a decrement in conditioned responding (e.g., overshadowing and the deficit seen in responding when trials are massed; see Barela, 1999, for a review of the trial massing effect) under certain circumstances can result in less (rather than more) of a decrement in behavioral control. In other words, the model predicts that the two response-degrading treatments can counteract each other, and thus less of a decrement in behavioral control should be observed during testing than with either treatment alone. How does the model anticipate this result? Because the extended comparator hypothesis allows for cues (other than the target cue) to compete with each other for comparator status provided they share a within-compound association, any treatment that establishes two comparator stimuli as potential competitors for comparator status with respect to the target cue can lead to a mutual reduction in the comparator roles of each of these stimuli and thus a reduced decrement in conditioned responding to the target cue.

As a test of this prediction, Stout et al. (2003) manipulated overshadowing and trial spacing, so that one group received elemental training with spaced trials (X → US spaced), one group received overshadowing training with spaced trials (AX → US spaced), and two more groups received identical training but with massed trials (X → US and AX → US massed). In this last group, presumably both the overshadowing cue (because of the compound training) and the training context (because of massed trials) should have been effective comparators for the target cue X, and they also should have served as comparators for each other (because A and the context should have been strongly associated). Interestingly, Stout et al. observed strong behavioral control by X in the group that experienced elemental training with spaced trials, less responding in the groups that experienced only one of the response-degrading treatments (either overshadowing or massed trials), and a recovery from these treatments (more responding) in the group that experienced both overshadowing treatment and massed trials. Similar counteractive effects have been observed when combining overshadowing with several other treatments that presumably establish the training context as a strong comparator for the target cue. These treatments include pretraining exposure to the CS alone (i.e., latent inhibition, Blaisdell et al., 1998), long CS duration during conditioning (Urushihara et al., 2004), unsignaled outcomes interspersed among the CS-outcome trials (i.e., degraded contingency,

Urcelay and Miller, 2006), and unsignaled outcome alone before or after the CS → US trials (Urushihara and Miller, 2006).

In summary, the comparator hypothesis (Miller and Matzel, 1988) and its extension (Denniston et al., 2001) have proven to be powerful alternatives to associative models that emphasize acquisition processes, as evidenced by their explanatory and predictive power. However, as we shall see next, there are several effects for which the comparator model cannot account. In the next section, we detail a model that accounts for interference effects outside the domain of models of associative learning designed to explain cue competition phenomena.

1.05.3.3 Bouton's Retrieval Model of Outcome Interference

Perhaps one of the most intriguing findings that Pavlov (1927) documented was the occurrence of a recovery in conditioned responding after a retention interval is interposed between extinction treatment and testing. Since Pavlov's time, there have been many theoretical frameworks proposed to explain extinction and its recovery under different circumstances. One old view of extinction is that nonreinforced presentations of an already trained CS will result in a loss of the CS's associative strength with the US, leading to an irreversible loss of behavioral control. For example, the Rescorla and Wagner (1972) model explains extinction in this manner. However, as we have mentioned before, if the associative strength of an extinguished CS is reduced, there is no reason to expect that responding to the CS will ever recover without further training with the CS, which is opposite to the spontaneous recovery effect observed when a long retention interval is interposed between extinction and testing.

After conducting extensive work on extinction, Bouton (1993) proposed an alternative to the models that view extinction as unlearning of the original association between the CS and US (*See* Chapter 1.09). This model emphasizes retrieval mechanisms that apply to a wide range of phenomena. Bouton's model has four principles.

1. Contextual stimuli influence memory retrieval. That is, analogous to Tulving and Thomson's (1973), Spear's (1978), and Riccio's (Riccio et al., 2002; Riccio et al., 2003) emphasis on the importance of similarity between the conditions of training and testing, Bouton proposed that

retrieval of a representation depends on the similarity between the conditions present at the time of testing with those that were present during training. Thus, as changes between the context of training and the context of testing are introduced, retrieval failure (i.e., forgetting) is more prone to occur. Furthermore, and perhaps in disagreement with Spear's elemental view, Bouton has proposed that CSs and contextual information are stored as interactive units containing information about the cues, the context, and the US. These interactive units function as an AND gate that requires activation of both the cue and the context for the activation of the representation of the US.

2. Time is part of the training context. As time elapses following training, the temporal component of the test context that is provided by external and internal cues is likely to change. In other words, the passage of time by itself will progressively result in a context change. Therefore, forgetting as a result of the passage of time is an instance of retrieval failure due to a change in the temporal context between training and testing.

3. Different memories depend differentially on the contextual information. In his 1993 seminal article, Bouton proposed that excitatory memories are relatively stable over time and do not depend on contextual information as much as do inhibitory memories (including those that represent extinction experience). Additionally he stated that a memory's sensitivity to contextual information depended on whether the training procedures promote subjects to encode and integrate contextual information with other features of the memory representation. One such procedure is when a CS takes a new meaning different from that of earlier training, as is the case when a CS is consistently followed by the US in one phase and it is no longer followed by the US (operationally, extinction) in a second phase. In this case, the second phase makes the CS an ambiguous signal for the US, and thus the model anticipates that the second-learned association will depend more on contextual information. In fact, Bouton (1997) later clarified this issue by stating that regardless of whether a memory is excitatory or inhibitory, each instance in which there is ambiguity with regard to the content of a memory (i.e., training in two sequential phases with opposing outcomes in the

different phases), the second-learned meaning will be more context dependent. This later assertion has received empirical support from Nelson (2002; also see De la Casa and Lubow, 2000, 2002).

4. Interference occurs at the time of testing rather than at the time of training. This principle captures all of the previously mentioned principles by stating that interference occurs at retrieval rather than during learning. With ambiguity in the meaning of the CS, the activation of an outcome representation occurs in direct relationship to the similarity between the context at test and those during the different phases of training. Additionally, information that is similar to, but incompatible with, the target memory will compete for a limited available space in working memory (i.e., currently active memory). That is, activation of a conflicting memory could reduce activation of the target memory. Thus, forgetting can result from two sources: retrieval failure (because of a change in context) and interference due to activation of conflicting information.

Bouton's model explains spontaneous recovery from extinction by assuming that the second-learned meaning of the CS (that is, CS → no outcome or an inhibitory association between the CS and the outcome) is context dependent, based on the principle of context dependency of the second-learned meaning of a cue. Moreover, the model states that a change in temporal context is analogous to a change in spatial context. As a result, when the temporal context of the second meaning of a cue is changed between phase 2 of treatment and testing (i.e., interposing a long retention interval after extinction), the memory representation of extinction treatment cannot be as readily retrieved. Thus, a recovery from extinction is observed with a long retention interval. A similar explanation is put forth by this model to explain all forms of renewal, spatial as well as temporal. In renewal, the second-learned meaning of the CS (CS → no US) should be context dependent, so any change in the spatial attributes of the context between extinction treatment and testing will result in interference in retrieving that memory. As a result of such a context shift, a recovery from extinction should be observed.

Another finding that is problematic for models that emphasize processing during acquisition is reinstatement, which is a recovery from extinction observed when subjects experience outcome-alone presentations in the test context prior to testing. In this case, Bouton's model assumes that the test context becomes associated with the outcome so that at test it biases retrieval in favor of the memory of reinforcement. Thus, a recovery from extinction is observed. Another way by which this model has been tested is by associating a neutral cue (a priming stimulus) with the phase of treatment in which extinction occurs. If the test is conducted in a context different from that of extinction treatment, renewal typically occurs. However, if during testing subjects are presented with this neutral cue from the extinction phase soon before being tested with the target cue, renewal is attenuated, presumably because this cue retrieves the memory of extinction treatment (Brooks and Bouton, 1994). A parallel attenuation of spontaneous recovery from extinction has been observed when the temporal context, as opposed to the spatial context, is altered between extinction training and testing (i.e., interpolation of a long retention interval). That is, reduced spontaneous recovery has been observed when a retrieval cue for the memory of extinction treatment is presented before testing following a long retention interval (Brooks and Bouton, 1993).

As we previously discussed, counterconditioning is another example of the context dependency of memory. If counterconditioning training is conducted with an appetitive reinforcer given in one context and an aversive reinforcer given in a different context, conditioned responding to the CS is guided by the context in which subjects are tested (Peck and Bouton, 1990). The retrieval model outlined earlier simply states that whichever memory representation is facilitated by contextual cues will be more prone to guide behavior.

In summary, we have reviewed general models of memory that emphasize retrieval mechanisms as critical for behavioral control. In general, Spear's (1978) model emphasizes the similarity between the total information presented during training and that presented at test and by this simple principle explains memory phenomena such as state-dependent learning and the Kamin effect. The comparator hypothesis (Miller and Matzel, 1988) is an associative model that emphasizes competition between representations and explains cue-competition phenomena and recovery from cue competition that does not involve further training with the target cue. Bouton's model (1993, 1997) emphasizes the role of retrieval cues in situations in which one cue has more than one meaning, as in the cases of extinction, latent inhibition, and

counterconditioning. One obvious conclusion is that each model has been designed to account for a family of phenomena at the expense of explaining other phenomena. For example, the comparator hypothesis (Miller and Matzel, 1988) accounts for cue competition phenomena and several other effects in classical conditioning, but it does not explain the recovery from extinction or counterconditioning effects that are consistently observed. Moreover, this model does not explain state-dependent learning. In contrast, Bouton's retrieval model (Bouton, 1993, 1997) accounts elegantly for interference effects, but it does not incorporate any mechanism that accounts for cue competition phenomena. Perhaps the biggest challenge these models face is to explain phenomena outside their current domain without necessarily increasing their complexity and thus losing predictive power. As we shall see in the next section, a few efforts have been made to integrate these behavioral models with the neurobiological evidence concerning the role of retrieval in memory performance.

1.05.4 Neurobiology of Retrieval

Recent technological advances have widened the possibilities of understanding learning and memory phenomena by studying their underlying neurophysiological basis. Interestingly, the focus on acquisition processes (e.g., Waelti et al., 2001) and memory consolidation (e.g., McGaugh, 2000) has dominated the field, perhaps because of the discovery of potential molecular mechanisms underlying long-term potentiation (Bliss and Lomo, 1973) that are thought to be the basis for the formation of memories (but see Shors and Matzel, 1997, for an alternative view). However, the neurobiological basis of retrieval mechanisms has also received some attention. But before we review some experiments that studied the role of different brain regions in retrieval, it is important that we clarify the general strategy underlying these studies. In any memory experiment, there are at least three identifiable phases amenable to study, namely acquisition, consolidation, and retrieval. As pointed out by Abel and Lattal (2001), one of the problems associated with different manipulations (pharmacological, genetic, and lesions) is that, with the exception of recently developed inactivation techniques that allow researchers to temporarily inactivate a specific anatomical area, they can affect more than one of the three stages. For example, a lesion soon after acquisition might impair not only consolidation but also retrieval. A lesion before any training might alter training, consolidation, and/or retrieval. Moreover, pharmacological manipulations might be temporary, but the effects of the mere exposure to the drug are not always completely known, as reflected earlier when we discussed the apoptotic effects of anisomycin (Rudy et al., 2006). Clearly all these considerations have to be taken into account to obtain valid information regarding the neurobiological underpinnings of memory.

Next, we briefly summarize the main findings regarding contextual determinants of memory retrieval. Notably, because of space limitations, we will only summarize a few studies that have the merit of integrating behavioral theories with neurobiological data. Studies such as these are few in number (but see, for example, Fanselow, 1999; Waelti et al., 2001; McNally and Westbrook, 2006; for notable exceptions focused on acquisition).

The hippocampus is one of the most extensively studied brain regions with regard to retrieval mechanisms (as well as acquisition processes). In general, the hippocampus has been implicated in both the coding and retrieval of spatial information and also in relations between events in the environment (e.g., Maren, 2001; but see Wiltgen et al., 2006). In fear conditioning, the hippocampus is thought to assemble contextual representations before they reach the amygdala, which is the site in which fear-motivated information is mainly processed. As we previously mentioned, contextual information is critical for the retrieval of associations. One of the questions researchers have recently asked concerns the role of the hippocampus in the retrieval as opposed to acquisition of contextual information. For example, behavior indicative of extinction is observed when contextual cues facilitate the retrieval of the extinction memory as opposed to the acquisition memory. Based on this finding, Wilson et al. (1995) investigated the effect on context-dependent extinction of fornix (one of the two primary inputs into the dorsal hippocampus) lesions made prior to training. It is important to recall that two of these context-dependent effects are renewal and reinstatement, and in terms of Bouton's theory of retrieval, they are mediated by different mechanisms. In the case of renewal, the context seems to disambiguate the two meanings a CS has after acquisition and extinction training. In the case of reinstatement, the test context-US association facilitates retrieval of the original CS → US association. Wilson et al. (1995) observed that fornix lesions attenuated reinstatement, which

depends on context-US associations, but not renewal nor spontaneous recovery which depend more on the properties of the context to disambiguate information. This outcome is surprising because it leaves no role for the hippocampus on the retrieval of ambiguous information. However, other studies using temporary reversible lesions have found that the hippocampus does in fact participate in the retrieval of information needed to disambiguate the meaning of an extinguished CS. Specifically, Corcoran and Maren (2001) used muscimol (a gamma-aminobutyric acid$_A$ (GABA$_A$) receptor agonist) infusions into the dorsal hippocampus just prior to testing (i.e., retrieval) to investigate the effect of the hippocampus on the retrieval of ambiguous memories (renewal). They found that the renewal effect was attenuated when they deactivated the dorsal hippocampus. Similar findings have been observed by Corcoran and Maren (2004; although the effect was not seen in ABA renewal). Overall, these findings raise several interesting points: (1) These results show that the hippocampus, a brain region known for its role in the encoding and retrieval of contextual information, is critical for the expression of extinction memories, which are context dependent. (2) Reversible lesions have the advantage of allowing dissection of the different processes (such as retrieval) involved in memory performance. (3) Behavioral theories (e.g., Bouton, 1993) can provide fertile grounds for research in the neurobiology of learning and memory and vice versa. Clearly, the key is to combine information from both approaches as a starting point for conducting further research.

Another recent study exemplifies context-dependent memories and the role of the hippocampus in such learning. As previously stated, latent inhibition refers to retarded emergence of behavioral control that results from CS-alone exposures prior to CS → US pairings (Lubow, 1973). A retrieval-based account such as the comparator hypothesis (Miller and Matzel, 1988) explains latent inhibition by positing that, during CS preexposure, subjects associate the CS with the context, which interferes during testing with the retrieval of the CS → US association. Consistent with this explanation, extinction of the training context abolished the latent inhibition effect (e.g., Grahame et al., 1994; Westbrook et al., 2000). Moreover, if CS preexposure is conducted in one context and reinforced training in a second context, latent inhibition is not observed (Channell and Hall, 1993). Consistent with these predictions, Talk et al. (2005) found that context extinction following the

CS-US pairings increased neural firing to the preexposed CS in the posterior cingulate cortex, a structure hypothesized to have a role in retrieval of learned behavior. Presumably, the hippocampal formation sends (through the fornix) contextual information to the posterior cingulate cortex. When the contextual information is decreased as a result of the context extinction treatment, an increase in neural responses to the CS is observed, and this is reflected in the diminished latent inhibition.

These examples have the merit of integrating retrieval-focused behavioral theories of memory and neurobiological evidence concerning the underlying mechanisms of retrieval. We believe that further understanding of the neurophysiology of learning and memory will be most fruitful when it has some relationship to behavioral models. As these examples demonstrate, research guided by knowledge obtained in behavioral experiments (and the theoretical developments that follow those results) seems to be a reliable foundation for investigation of the neural foundations of retrieval.

1.05.5 Concluding Remarks

In this review, we started with the premise that a vast majority of the research concerning mechanisms of learning and memory has been guided by the notion that memory depends uniquely on mechanisms of acquisition and storage. Although we should not underestimate the contribution of these processes, we pointed out numerous phenomena suggesting that retrieval mechanisms also play an important role in determining stimulus control of behavior. We reviewed various examples, ranging from forgetting due to natural changes in the environment or in the organism's internal state, through amnesia experimentally induced in the laboratory, to situations in which additional (sometimes conflicting) information decreases target behavior. In all of these examples, there was evidence that the information was not lost, but rather was present but not expressed at the time of testing. Providing conditions during testing similar to those during training strongly facilitates retrieval and, as a consequence, stimulus control of behavior. In a similar vein, facilitating retrieval by the aid of reminder cues has also proven effective for memory performance. These demonstrations imply that information was stored but not expressed at the time of testing, which suggests a strong role of retrieval mechanisms.

In the second section, we described several models that emphasize processing at the time of retrieval as being critical for memory expression. Perhaps the unsatisfying conclusion from this section is that there is not a single approach that accounts for all of the data available. Some models seem to fare well in accounting for some phenomena, but fail to explain fundamental aspects of other phenomena. As an example, we pointed out how well the comparator model accounts for cue competition phenomena, but also recognized its failure in addressing important aspects of extinction and competition between cues trained apart. Obviously, the ultimate goal of any science of behavior is not only to explain behavior but also to predict it. At least the models we reviewed provide strong foundations for future theoretical developments, and in some ways each proposal has proven its heuristic value as a tool to guide new research. Current behavioral models have stimulated research into the neurobiological underpinnings of memory. We see this avenue as perhaps the most fruitful in the future because bridging the gap that exists between behavior and its underlying neurobiological basis is an important step toward societal application.

Retrieval, the act of making stored information available for use, is as important as acquisition in terms of adaptive value. Consider, for example, what would happen if an organism faces a dangerous situation and is able to survive. If the animal does not retain that information by virtue of either acquisition failure or storage failure, memory of that experience will not be available for future use. On the contrary, if the animal stores the information, it will be available for later encounters with the dangerous situation. This brings us to the question: why does retrieval failure occur? Perhaps retrieval failures, as we have seen, arise from processing limitations. But more important, it seems plausible that retrieval failures arise from a strategy for organizing information based on how relevant this information is in the test situation. That is, leaving some information less accessible enables organisms to have access to other information that could be more important, depending on the demands imposed by the immediate environment.

Acknowledgments

Support for this research was provided by National Institute of Mental Health Grant 33881.

References

Abel T and Lattal KM (2001) Molecular mechanisms of memory acquisition, consolidation and retrieval. *Curr. Opin. Neurobiol.* 11: 180–187.

Amundson JC, Escobar M, and Miller RR (2003) Proactive interference in first-order Pavlovian conditioning. *J. Exp. Psychol. Anim. Behav. Process.* 29: 311–322.

Anokhin KV, Tiunova AA, and Rose SPR (2002) Reminder effects – reconsolidation or retrieval deficit? Pharmacological dissection with protein synthesis inhibitors following reminder for a passive-avoidance task in young chicks. *Eur. J. Neurosci.* 15: 1759–1765.

Balaz MA, Gutsin P, Cacheiro H, and Miller RR (1982) Blocking as a retrieval failure: Reactivation of associations to a blocked stimulus. *Q. J. Exp. Psychol.* 34B: 99–113.

Barela PB (1999) Theoretical mechanisms underlying the trial-spacing effect in pavlovian fear conditioning. *J. Exp. Psychol. Anim. Behav. Process.* 25: 177–193.

Barraco RA and Stettner LJ (1976) Antibiotics and memory. *Psychol. Bull.* 83: 242–302.

Batsell WR (1997) Retention of context blocking in taste-aversion learning. *Physiol. Behav.* 61: 437–446.

Biedenkapp JC and Rudy JW (2004) Context memories and reactivation: Constraints on the reconsolidation hypothesis. *Behav. Neurosci.* 118: 956–964.

Blaisdell AP, Bristol AS, Gunther LM, and Miller RR (1998) Overshadowing and latent inhibition counteract each other: Support for the comparator hypothesis. *J. Exp. Psychol. Anim. Behav. Process.* 24: 335–351.

Blaisdell AP, Gunther LM, and Miller RR (1999) Recovery from blocking achieved by extinguishing the blocking CS. *Anim. Learn. Behav.* 27: 63–76.

Bliss TV and Lomo T (1973) Long-lasting potentiation of synaptic transmission in the dentate area of the anaesthetized rabbit following stimulation of the perforant path. *J. Physiol.* 232: 331–356.

Bouton ME (1993) Context, time, and memory retrieval in the interference paradigms of Pavlovian learning. *Psychol. Bull.* 114: 80–99.

Bouton ME (1997) Signals for whether versus when an event will occur. In: Bouton ME and Fanselow MS (eds.) *Learning, Motivation and Cognition. The Functional Behaviorism of Robert C. Bolles*. Washington, DC: American Psychological Association.

Bouton ME and Bolles RC (1979) Contextual control of the extinction of conditioned fear. *Learn. Motiv.* 10: 445–466.

Bouton ME and King DA (1983) Contextual control of the extinction of conditioned fear: Tests for associative value of the context. *J. Exp. Psychol. Anim. Behav. Process.* 9: 248–265.

Bouton ME and Peck CA (1992) Spontaneous recovery in cross-motivational transfer (counterconditioning). *Anim. Learn. Behav.* 20: 313–321.

Bouton ME and Swartzentruber DE (1989) Slow reacquisition following extinction: Context, encoding, and retrieval mechanisms. *J. Exp. Psychol. Anim. Behav. Process.* 15: 43–53.

Bradley PM and Galal KM (1988) State-dependent recall can be induced by protein synthesis inhibition: Behavioural and morphological observations. *Brain Res.* 40: 243–251.

Brooks DC and Bouton ME (1993) A retrieval cue for extinction attenuates spontaneous recovery. *J. Exp. Psychol. Anim. Behav. Process.* 19: 77–89.

Brooks DC and Bouton ME (1994) A retrieval cue for extinction attenuates response recovery (renewal) caused by a return to the conditioning context. *J. Exp. Psychol. Anim. Behav. Process.* 20: 366–379.

Brooks DC, Hale B, Nelson JB, and Bouton ME (1995) Reinstatement after counterconditioning. *Anim. Learn. Behav.* 23: 383–390.

Bush RR and Mosteller F (1951) A mathematical model for simple learning. *Psychol. Rev.* 58: 313–323.

Cammarota M, Bevilaqua LRM, Medina JH, and Izquierdo I (2004) Retrieval does not induce reconsolidation of inhibitory avoidance memory. *Learn. Mem.* 11: 572–578.

Channell S and Hall G (1983) Contextual effects in latent inhibition with an appetitive conditioning procedure. *Anim. Learn. Behav.* 11: 67–74.

Corcoran KA and Maren S (2001) Hippocampal inactivation disrupts contextual retrieval of fear memory after extinction. *J. Neurosci.* 21: 1720–1726.

Corcoran KA and Maren S (2004) Factors regulating the effects of hippocampal inactivation on renewal of conditional fear after extinction. *Learn. Mem.* 11(5): 598–603.

Craik FI and Lockhart RS (1972) Levels of processing: A framework for memory research. *J. Verb. Learn. Verb. Behav.* 11: 671–684.

Cunningham CL (1979) Alcohol as a cue for extinction: State dependency produced by conditioned inhibition. *Anim. Learn. Behav.* 7: 45–52.

De la Casa LG and Lubow RE (2000) Super-latent inhibition with delayed conditioned taste aversion testing. *Anim. Learn. Behav.* 28: 389–399.

De la Casa LG and Lubow RE (2002) An empirical analysis of the super-latent inhibition effect. *Anim. Learn. Behav.* 30: 112–120.

Debięc L, LeDoux JE, and Nader K (2002) Cellular and systems reconsolidation in the hippocampus. *Neuron* 36: 527–538.

Debięc J, Doyère V, Nader K, and LeDoux JE (2006) Directly reactivated, but not indirectly reactivated, memories undergo reconsolidation in the amygdala. *Proc. Natl. Acad. Sci. USA* 103: 3428–3433.

Denniston JC, Savastano HI, and Miller RR (2001) The extended comparator hypothesis: Learning by contiguity, responding by relative strength. In: Mowrer RR and Klein SB (eds.) *Handbook of Contemporary Learning Theories*, pp. 65–117. Hillsdale, NJ: Erlbaum.

Dickinson A and Burke J (1996) Within-compound associations mediate the retrospective revaluation of causality judgments. *Q. J. Exp. Psychol.* 49B, 60–80.

Duncan CP (1949) The retroactive effect of electroshock on learning. *J. Comp. Physiol. Psychol.* 42: 32–44.

Duvarci S and Nader K (2004) Characterization of fear memory reconsolidation. *J. Neurosci.* 24: 9269–9275.

Escobar M, Matute H, and Miller RR (2001) Cues trained apart compete for behavioral control in rats: Convergence with the associative interference literature. *J. Exp. Psychol. Gen.* 130: 97–115.

Esmoris-Arranz FJ, Miller RR, and Matute H (1997) Blocking of subsequent and antecedent events: Implications for cue competition in causal judgment. *J. Exp. Psychol. Anim. Behav. Process.* 23: 145–156.

Fanselow MS (1999) Learning theory and neuropsychology: Configuring their disparate elements in the hippocampus. *J. Exp. Psychol. Anim. Behav. Process.* 25: 275–283.

Fisher A, Sananbenesi F, Schrick C, Speiss J, and Radulovic J (2004) Distinct roles of hippocampal de novo protein synthesis and actin rearrangement in extinction of contextual fear. *J. Neurosci.* 24: 1962–1966.

Gisquet-Verrier P and Alexinsky T (1990) Facilitative effect of a pretest exposure to the CS: Analysis and implications for the memory trace. *Anim. Learn. Behav.* 18: 323–331.

Gisquet-Verrier P, Dekeyne A, and Alexinsky T (1989) Differential effects of several retrieval cues over time:

Evidence for time-dependent reorganization of memory. *Anim. Learn. Behav.* 17: 394–408.

Gold PE and King RA (1974) Retrograde amnesia: Storage failure versus retrieval failure. *Psychol. Rev.* 81. 465–469.

Grahame NJ, Barnet RC, Gunther LM, and Miller RR (1994) Latent inhibition as a performance deficit resulting from CS-context associations. *Anim. Learn. Behav.* 22: 395–408.

Hebb DO (1949) *The Organization of Behavior: A Neuropsychological Theory.* Oxford, UK: Wiley.

Hernandez PJ and Kelley AE (2004) Long-term memory for instrumental responses does not undergo protein synthesis-dependent reconsolidation upon retrieval. *Learn. Mem.* 11: 748–754.

Hinderliter CF, Webster T, and Riccio DC (1976) Amnesia induced by hypothermia as a function of treatment-test interval and recooling in rats. *Anim. Learn. Behav.* 3: 257–263.

Kamin LJ (1957) The retention of an incompletely learned avoidance response. *J. Comp. Physiol. Psychol.* 50: 457–460.

Kamin LJ (1963) Retention of an incompletely learned avoidance response: Some further analyses. *J. Comp. Physiol. Psychol.* 56: 713–718.

Kamin LJ (1969) Predictability, surprise, attention, and conditioning. In: Campbell BA and Church MR (eds.) *Punishment and Aversive Behavior*, pp. 279–296. New York: Appleton-Century-Crofts.

Kasprow WJ, Cacheiro H, Balaz MA, and Miller RR (1982) Reminder induced recovery of associations to an overshadowed stimulus. *Learn. Motiv.* 13: 155–166.

Kaufman MA and Bolles RC (1981) A nonassociative aspect of overshadowing. *Bull. Psychonomic Soc.* 18: 318–320.

Klein SB (1972) Adrenal-pituitary influence in reactivation of avoidance-learning memory in the rat after intermediate intervals. *J. Comp. Physiol. Psychol.* 79: 341–359.

Klein SB and Spear NE (1970) Reactivation of avoidance-learning memory in the rat after intermediate retention intervals. *J. Comp. Physiol. Psychol.* 72: 498–504.

Kraemer PJ, Lariviere NA, and Spear NE (1988) Expression of a taste aversion conditioned with an odor taste compound: Overshadowing is relatively weak in weanlings and decreases over a retention interval in adults. *Anim. Learn. Behav.* 16: 164–168.

Lattal KM and Abel T (2001) Different requirements for protein synthesis in acquisition and extinction of spatial preferences and context-evoked fear. *J. Neurosci.* 21: 5773–5780.

Lattal KM and Abel T (2004) Behavioral impairments caused by injections of the protein synthesis inhibitor anisomycin after contextual retrieval reverse with time. *Proc. Natl. Acad. Sci. USA* 101: 4667–4672.

Lewis DJ, Misanin JR, and Miller RR (1968) Recovery of memory following amnesia. *Nature* 220: 704–705.

Lubow RE (1973) Latent inhibition. *Psychol. Bull.* 79: 398–407.

Mackintosh NJ (1975) A theory of attention: Variations in the associability of stimuli with reinforcement. *Psychol. Rev.* 82: 276–298.

Mactutus CF and Riccio DC (1978) Hypothermia-induced retrograde amnesia: Role of body temperature in memory retrieval. *Physiol. Psychol.* 6: 18–22.

Maren S (2001) Neurobiology of Pavlovian fear conditioning. *Annu. Rev. Neurosci.* 24: 897–931.

Matzel LD, Schachtman TR, and Miller RR (1985) Recovery of an overshadowed association achieved by extinction of the overshadowing stimulus. *Learn. Motiv.* 16: 398–412.

McEwen BS and Weiss JM (1970) The uptake and action of corticosterone: Regional and subcellular studies on rat brain. *Prog. Brain Res.* 32: 200–212.

McGaugh JL (1966) Time-dependent processes in memory storage. *Science* 153: 1351–1358.

McGaugh JL (2000) Memory: A century of consolidation. *Science* 287: 248–251.

McNally GP and Westbrook RF (2006) Predicting danger: The nature, consequences, and neural mechanisms of predictive fear learning. *Learn. Mem.* 13: 245–253.

Miller RR and Matute H (1998) Competition between outcomes. *Psychol. Sci.* 9: 146–149.

Miller RR and Matzel LD (1988) The comparator hypothesis: A response rule for the expression of associations. In: Bower GH (ed.) *The Psychology of Learning and Motivation, Vol. 22*, pp. 51–92. San Diego, CA: Academic Press.

Miller RR and Matzel LD (2000) Memory involves far more than 'consolidation'. *Nat. Rev. Neurosci.* 3: 214–216.

Miller RR and Matzel LD (2006) Retrieval failure vs. memory loss in experimental amnesia: Definitions and processes. *Learn. Mem.* 13: 491–497.

Miller RR, Ott CA, Berk AM, and Springer AD (1974) Appetitive memory restoration after electroconvulsive shock in the rat. *J. Comp. Physiol. Psychol.* 87: 717–723.

Miller RR and Springer AD (1973) Amnesia, consolidation, and retrieval. *Psychol. Rev.* 80: 69–79.

Miller RR and Springer AD (1974) Implications of recovery from experimental amnesia. *Psychol. Rev.* 81: 470–473.

Millin PM, Moody EW, and Riccio DC (2001) Interpretations of retrograde amnesia: Old problems redux. *Nat. Rev. Neurosci.* 2: 68–70.

Nadel L and Land C (2000) Memory traces revisited. *Nat. Rev. Neurosci.* 1: 209–212.

Nader K, Schafe GE, and Le Doux JE (2000) Fear memories require protein synthesis in the amygdala for reconsolidation after retrieval. *Nature* 406: 722–726.

Nelson JB (2002) Context specificity of excitation and inhibition in ambiguous stimuli. *Learn. Motiv.* 33: 284–310.

Overton DA (1964) State dependent or "dissociated" learning produced with pentobarbital. *J. Comp. Physiol. Psychol.* 57: 3–12.

Overton DA (1972) State-dependent learning produced by alcohol and its relevance to alcoholism. In: Kissin B and Begleiter H (eds.) *The Biology of Alcoholism.* New York: Plenum Press.

Overton DA (1985) Contextual stimulus effects of drugs and internal states. In: Balsam PD and Tomie A (eds.) *Context and Learning*, pp. 357–384. Hillsdale, NJ: Lawrence Erlbaum Associates.

Pavlov IP (1927) *Conditioned Reflexes*, Anrep GV (ed. and trans.). London: Oxford University Press.

Pearce JM and Hall G (1980) A model for Pavlovian learning: Variations in the effectiveness of conditioned but not unconditioned stimuli. *Psychol. Rev.* 82: 532–552.

Peck CA and Bouton ME (1990) Context and performance in aversive-to-appetitive and appetitive-to-aversive transfer. *Learn. Motiv.* 21: 1–31.

Power AE, Berlau DJ, McGaugh JL, and Steward O (2006) Anisomycin infused into the hippocampus fails to block "reconsolidation" but impairs extinction: The role of re-exposure duration. *Learn. Mem.* 13: 27–34.

Pineño O, Urushihara K, and Miller RR (2005) Spontaneous recovery from forward and backward blocking. *J. Exp. Psychol. Anim. Behav. Process.* 31: 172–183.

Prado-Alcalá RA, del Guante MA D, Garín-Aguilar ME, Díaz-Trujillo A, Quirarte GL, and McGaugh JL (2006) Amygdala or hippocampus inactivation after retrieval induces temporary memory deficit. *Neurobiol. Learn. Mem.* 86: 144–149.

Przybyslawski J and Sara SJ (1997) Reconsolidation of memory after its reactivation. *Behav. Brain Res.* 84: 241–246.

Rauhut AS, McPhee JE, and Ayres JB (1999) Blocked and overshadowed stimuli are weakened in their ability to serve as blockers and second-order reinforces in Pavlovian fear conditioning. *J. Exp. Psychol. Anim. Behav. Process.* 25: 45–67.

Rescorla RA (1980) *Pavlovian Second-Order Conditioning: Studies in Associative Learning.* Hillsdale, NJ: Erlbaum.

Rescorla RA and Cunningham CL (1978) Recovery of the US representation over time during extinction. *Learn. Motiv.* 9: 373–391.

Rescorla RA and Wagner AR (1972) A theory of Pavlovian conditioning: Variations in the effectiveness of reinforcement and nonreinforcement. In: Black AH and Prokasy WF (eds.) *Classical Conditioning II: Current Research and Theory,* pp. 64–99. New York: Appleton-Century-Crofts.

Riccio DC, Millin PM, and Gisquet-Verrier P (2003) Retrograde amnesia: Forgetting back. *Curr. Dir. Psychol. Sci.* 12: 41–44.

Riccio DC, Moody EW, and Millin PM (2002) Reconsolidation reconsidered. *Integr. Physiol. Behav. Sci.* 37: 245–253.

Rudy JW, Biedenkapp JC, Moineau J, and Bolding K (2006) Anisomycin and the reconsolidation hypothesis. *Learn. Mem.* 13: 1–3.

Shors TJ and Matzel LD (1997) Long-term potentiation: What's learning got to do with it? *Behav. Brain Sci.* 20: 597–655.

Spear NE (1973) Retrieval of memories in animals. *Psychol. Rev.* 80: 163–194.

Spear NE (1978) *The Processing of Memories: Forgetting and Retention.* Hillsdale, NJ: Erlbaum.

Stout SC, Chang R, and Miller RR (2003) Trial spacing is a determinant of cue interaction. *J. Exp. Psychol. Anim. Behav. Process.* 29: 23–38.

Stout SC and Miller RR (in press) Sometimes competing retrieval (SOCR): A formalization of the comparator hypothesis. *Psychol. Rev.*

Talk A, Stoll E, and Gabriel M (2005) Cingulate cortical coding of context-dependent latent inhibition. *Behav. Neurosci.* 119: 1524–1532.

Tulving E and Thomson DM (1973) Encoding specificity and retrieval processes in episodic memory. *Psychol. Rev.* 80: 352–73.

Urcelay GP and Miller RR (2006) Counteraction between overshadowing and degraded contingency treatments: Support for the extended comparator hypothesis. *J. Exp. Psychol. Anim. Behav. Process.* 32: 21–32.

Urushihara K and Miller RR (2006) Overshadowing and the outcome-alone exposure effect counteract each other. *J. Exp. Psychol. Anim. Behav. Process.* 32: 253–270.

Urushihara K, Stout SC, and Miller RR (2004) The basic laws of conditioning differ for elemental cues and cues trained in compound. *Psychol. Sci.* 15: 268–271.

Van Hamme LJ and Wasserman EA (1994) Cue competition in causality judgments: The role of nonpresentation of compound stimulus elements. *Learn. Motiv.* 25: 127–151.

Vardaris RM, Gaebelein C, and Riccio DC (1973) Retrograde amnesia from hypothermia-induced brain seizures. *Physiol. Psychol.* 1: 204–208.

Vianna MR, Szapiro G, McGaugh JL, Medina JH, and Izquierdo I (2001) Retrieval of memory for fear-motivated training initiates extinction requiring protein synthesis in the rat hippocampus. *Proc. Natl. Acad. Sci. USA* 98: 12251–12254.

Wagner AR (1981) SOP: A model of automatic memory processing in animal behavior. In: Spear NE and Miller RR (eds.) *Information Processing in Animals: Memory Mechanisms,* pp. 5–47. Hillsdale, NJ: Erlbaum.

Wagner AR and Rescorla RA (1972) Inhibition in Pavlovian conditioning: Application of a theory. In: Boakes RA and Halliday MS (eds.) *Inhibition and Learning,* pp. 301–336. London: Academic Press.

Waelti P, Dickinson A, and Schultz W (2001) Dopamine responses comply with basic assumptions of formal learning theory. *Nature* 412: 43–48.

Westbrook RF, Jones ML, Bailey GK, and Harris JA (2000) Contextual control over conditioned responding in a latent inhibition paradigm. *J. Exp. Psychol. Anim. Behav. Process.* 26: 157–173.

Wheeler DS and Miller RR (2005) Recovery from blocking between outcomes. *J. Exp. Psychol. Anim. Behav. Process.* 31: 467–476.

Wheeler DS, Stout SC, and Miller RR (2004) Interaction of retention interval with CS-preexposure and extinction treatments: Symmetry with respect to primacy. *Learn. Behav.* 32: 335–347.

Williams BA (1996) Evidence that blocking is due to associative deficit: Blocking history affects the degree of subsequent associative competition. *Psychon. Bull. Rev.* 3: 71–74.

Wilson A, Brooks DC, and Bouton ME (1995) The role of the rat hippocampal system in several effects of context in extinction. *Behav. Neurosci.* 109: 828–836.

Wiltgen BJ, Sanders MJ, Anagnostaras SG, Sage JR, and Fanselow MS (2006) Context fear learning in the absence of the hippocampus. *J. Neurosci.* 26: 5484–5491.

1.06 Operant Behavior

J. Jozefowiez and J. E. R. Staddon, Duke University, Durham, NC, USA

1.06.1 Introduction

1.06.1.1 Behavior as a Function of Its Consequences

In a famous experiment, Edward Thorndike (1898) trained cats to escape from puzzle boxes by activating various mechanisms. The time taken by the animals to escape the box on successive trials tended to decrease. During early trials, the cat tried various ineffective behaviors (pawing at the door, scratching the wall of the box, etc.) until by accident, it triggered the mechanism unlocking the latch. Starting from this point, trial times improved because ineffective acts gradually dropped out. This led Thorndike to formulate his famous law of effect according to which behaviors followed by positive consequences are strengthened, while behaviors followed by negative consequences are weakened. Later, the American psychologist B. F. Skinner (1938) coined the term operant behavior for activities that follow the law of effect.

Operant behaviors are behaviors guided by their consequences. In most cases, this requires that the animal first solve an assignment-of-credit problem by deciding which events are a consequence of a specific behavior. This is operant learning. Once this is done, the behavior and its consequence are linked in a feedback loop, and depending on the motivational properties of the consequence, the emission of operant behavior will be regulated by it.

In this chapter, we will first deal with operant learning and the question of how animals are able to detect the connection between a behavior and its consequences. Then we will deal with the maintenance and regulation of operant behavior by consequences. But first, we must say a word about the procedures used to study operant behavior in psychology.

1.06.1.2 Operant Conditioning

The main procedure for the study of operant behavior in psychology is operant conditioning, a term proposed by Skinner in the early 1930s (Skinner, 1938; *See* Chapters 1.03, 1.10). In operant conditioning, delivery of a biologically significant stimulus or a neutral stimulus signaling such a stimulus is made contingent on an easily repeatable response with low energy cost. The main dependent variable is the response rate (number of responses emitted per unit of time). The standard version uses either hungry rats or pigeons in an experimental cage called a Skinner box (**Figure 1**), which allows for automated delivery of stimuli and recording of responses without any intervention by the experimenter. Rats are usually trained to press a lever for food pellets, whereas pigeons peck at illuminated response keys to gain access to grain. Electric shocks are used if negatively valued consequences are required by the experiment.

Operant conditioning procedures are classified according to their effect on responding and whether the consequence is the presentation or removal of a stimulus. If the procedure leads to an increase in the response rate, it is a reinforcement procedure and the consequence a reinforcer; otherwise, if it leads to a decrease in responding, it is a punishment procedure, and the consequence is a punisher. A reinforcer can be either the delivery of an appetitive stimulus (positive reinforcement, such as a hungry rat pressing a lever for food) or the withdrawal of an aversive one (negative reinforcement, for example, a rat pressing a lever to stop electric shock). Similarly, a punisher can either be the delivery of an aversive stimulus (positive punishment, such as a rat pressing a lever that produces electric shock) or the withdrawal of an appetitive stimulus (negative punishment, for example, food withdrawn from a cage if a hungry rat presses a lever). As a practical matter, research has focused on positive-reinforcement procedures (to the point that the word positive is usually omitted).

Figure 1   Pigeon in a Skinner box. By pecking on the illuminated disks (response keys), the pigeon occasionally gains access to food delivered in the feeder (opening below the response keys).

The rule that describes how reinforcement depends on responding, whether number-based, time-based, or according to some other rule, is called the schedule of reinforcement (Ferster and Skinner, 1957). Simple schedules arrange reinforcement for only one response, whereas concurrent schedules arrange reinforcement for two or more simultaneously.

The basic schedules of reinforcement are ratio and interval schedules. In ratio schedules, a certain number of responses (the ratio of the schedule) must be emitted for reinforcement to occur. The ratio is fixed in fixed-ratio (FR) schedules while it varies after each reinforcement around a mean in variable-ratio (VR) schedules. The ideal case of a VR is a random-ratio (RR) schedule where each response has a constant probability of reinforcement equal to the inverse of the ratio. In interval schedules, a certain amount of time (the interval of the schedule) must have elapsed before a reinforcement is made available. The interval is fixed in fixed-interval (FI) schedule but varies randomly around a mean after each reinforcement in variable-interval (VI) schedules. The ideal case of a VI is a random-interval (RI) schedule where the probability of a reinforcer being scheduled each time step is equal to the inverse of the interval. VI schedules usually generate a steady rate of responding, whereas in FI schedules, animals typically pause after trial onset (reinforcement) before starting to respond (Ferster and Skinner, 1957).

Traditionally, when describing an operant procedure using schedules of reinforcement, the acronym of the schedule (i.e., FR, VI) is given followed by its relevant parameter (i.e., its ratio for a ratio schedule or its interval for an interval schedule). So, instead of saying that a rat had to press a lever 50 times before a reinforcer was delivered, we would say that lever pressing was reinforced according to an FR 50. In the same way, instead of saying that a peck on a response key was reinforced only if 15 s have elapsed since the last reinforcement, we would say that key pecking was reinforced according to an FI 15 s. Instead of saying that a rat had the choice between two levers (a concurrent schedule), one delivering reinforcement according to a VI 15 s, the other according to a VI 30 s, we would say that the rat was exposed to a concurrent VI 15 s VI 30 s.

Finally, schedules of reinforcement can deliver either primary reinforcers – stimuli having biological significance for the organism (e.g., food for an hungry animal) – or conditioned reinforcers – stimuli that are correlated with the delivery of a primary reinforcer. For instance, pecking on a red key for a pigeon could be reinforced according to a VI 15 s, but when reinforcement occurs, instead of food being delivered, the key turns green, and pecking it is reinforced with food according to an FR 15. The green key is considered a conditioned reinforcer because it signals the future delivery of food. Such a procedure is also an example of a chain schedule (a chain VI 15 s FR 15 in this case) where reinforcement for one schedule is access to another schedule, and the transition from one to the other is signaled by a change in some stimulus. Tandem schedules resemble chain schedules, except that the transition from one schedule to the other is unsignaled.

Concurrent chain schedules (**Figure 2**) combine chain schedules with concurrent schedules. They comprise two phases: the initial link and the terminal link. During the initial link, the animal has a choice between two schedules, usually VI or RI with the same interval. When a response is reinforced on one of the two schedules, this leads to the terminal link: The two schedules used during the initial link are deactivated, and the animal is left with only one response opportunity, reinforced with food according to its own schedule of reinforcement. Each initial link leads to a different terminal link schedule: for instance, one VI initial link could lead to an FI 15 s terminal link, whereas the other leads to an FI 30 s

terminal link. The allocation of behavior on the two schedules during the initial link is used as a measure of the relative preference of the animal for the two terminal-link schedules. In this example, the animal would respond more often on the (initial-link) VI leading to the FI 15 s than on the one leading to the FI 30 s.

1.06.2 Operant Learning

1.06.2.1 Nonoperant Effects in Operant Conditioning

Before trying to understand the condition in which operant learning takes place, it is important to realize that not all the effects observed in operant conditioning are due to the operant aspect (i.e., to the response-reinforcer contingency *per se*). Reinforcers are highly motivating stimuli, and their mere delivery has an effect on the organism: It arouses it, increasing its general level of activity. Killeen et al. (1978) showed that the arousing effect of a single reinforcer delivery (measured as general activity) decreases exponentially with the time elapsed since the reinforcer delivery; when reinforcements are repeated, arousal builds up to an asymptotic level. According to Killeen (1998), this model implies that response rate should be proportional to reinforcement rate.

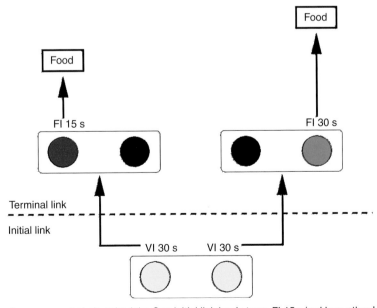

Figure 2 Example of a concurrent chain schedule: One initial link leads to an FI 15 s (red key; other key dark), whereas the other leads to an FI 30 s (green key, other key dark). The rate of entry in the initial link is determined by independent VI 30-s schedules (two yellow keys).

Functions relating response rate to reinforcement rate in VI are actually negatively accelerated (Catania and Reynolds, 1968; Herrnstein, 1970; Shull, 2005; **Figure 3**), but because rats are much more sensitive to reinforcement rate than pigeons, a linear approximation is reasonable for them. By contrast, pigeon functions quickly reach an asymptote (Shull, 2005; **Figure 3**). In this view, response rate in simple schedules is more determined by arousal than by the response-reinforcer contingency, although this might be masked by the fact that different response topographies might be selected by different schedules. For example, VR schedules lead to a higher rate of responding than VI schedules, even when matched for obtained reinforcement rates (i.e. Baum, 1993), presumably because VR schedules selectively reinforce shorter interresponse times than VI (Peele et al., 1984; Dawson and Dickinson, 1990).

Arousal is reinforcer-specific: Animals are more likely to engage in behavior related to the kind of reinforcers delivered. For instance, golden hamsters engage in activities directed at the environment (locomotion, active contact with the environment such as wall-scratching) when food deprived, more rarely in self-care activities such as grooming or scent-marking (Shettleworth, 1975). Similarly, rats receiving electric shocks will most likely freeze or flee (Bolles and Riley, 1973; Karpicke et al., 1977).

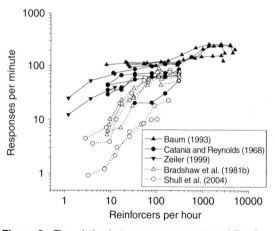

Figure 3 The relation between response rate and (food) reinforcement rate in simple VI schedules collected from various studies. Overall, it is hyperbolic, but rats (empty symbols) are much more sensitive to variations in the reinforcement rate than pigeons (filled symbols). From Shull RL (2005) The sensitivity of response rate to the rate of variable-interval reinforcement for pigeons and rats: A review. *J. Exp. Anal. Behav.* 84: 99–110, with permission from the Society for the Experimental Analysis of Behavior, Inc.

This provides the necessary behavioral variation from which the reinforcement contingency will select the appropriate response.

As a consequence, a behavior cannot be reinforced by a reinforcer if it is not naturally linked to that reinforcer in the repertoire of the animal (*See* Chapters 1.06, 1.18, 1.22). Hence, environment-related activities can be reinforced by food in hamsters but not self-care responses (Shettleworth, 1975), and rats will learn to press a lever for food (food consumption in rats involves manipulation) but not to avoid an electric shock, although they will quickly learn to freeze, run to another box, or jump over a barrier (all parts of the rat defensive repertoire) to achieve such a result (e.g., Biederman et al., 1964; Hineline and Rachlin, 1969). Although pigeons can learn to peck a key for both food and water, the topography of their responses differs depending on the kind of reinforcer used. They peck at the key the way they peck at food if food is used as the reinforcer (beak open until contact with the target), and the way they peck at water (beak closed until contact with the target) if water is used as the reinforcer (Jenkins and Moore, 1973).

The most spectacular example of the principle according to which only behaviors related to a specific reinforcer can be reinforced by it is instinctive drift (Breland and Breland, 1961), where, in procedures using food reinforcement, a species-specific food-related behavior will replace an operant response not naturally linked to food situations in the repertoire of the organism. For instance, a raccoon reinforced to put coins in a slot machine will learn the task, but then suddenly start washing the coins, while a pig trained in the same procedure will bury them instead (Breland and Breland, 1961).

Besides the reinforcement contingency, other variables contribute to the selection of the response, notably the Pavlovian stimulus–stimulus contingency that any operant procedure creates between the experimental context and the reinforcer. In some cases, this effect is so strong that there is nothing left for the response-reinforcer contingency to select for. This is notably the case of pigeon key pecking; simply illuminating the key briefly before intermittently delivered food is sufficient to trigger key pecking, a procedure known as autoshaping (Brown and Jenkins, 1968). This happens even if key pecking actually postpones food delivery (Williams and Williams, 1969). Other responses in other species, including lever pressing in rats, can be autoshaped. The exact nature of the autoshaped response depends on the relation between the reinforcer-predicting stimulus and the reinforcer-elicited behaviors. Pigeons peck at small circular objects (like grain), and this is probably why they will peck at a key, a small circular object, when that stimulus becomes a predictor of food: This behavior is compatible both with the kind of reinforcer delivered and with the stimuli present in the environment. Indeed, if a small dark dot is added to the center of the key, hence making it even more similar to the stimulus naturally supporting pecking, autoshaping is faster (Jenkins et al., 1981). In rats, if the stimulus predicting food is another rat instead of a lever, autoshaped responding will take the form of social behaviors directed at the stimulus rat (Timberlake and Grant, 1975).

Another aspect of the performance that seems to be determined by Pavlovian relations between the context and the reinforcer, at least in simple schedules, is the temporal regulation of behavior. If food is delivered at a specific time relative to trial onset (in an FI, for instance), animals adjust to this regularity, and their response rate is a function of time-to-reinforcement (Skinner, 1938), a phenomenon known as interval timing (more on this later). Wynne and Staddon (1988) exposed pigeons to a response-initiated schedule where the first peck on the key after trial onset started a fixed delay-to-food and measured the waiting time (the time between trial onset and the first response). This should have reinforced short waiting time, but instead, the pigeons waited an amount of time equal to a fixed proportion of the last time-to-food interval. On the same issue, Baum (1993) showed that if the reinforcement rate (which is the inverse of the average time of reinforcement) is equalized, wait times in VI and VR are identical (see also Jozefowiez et al., 2005, for additional experimental evidence). Note that, on the other hand, interval timing also occurs in concurrent schedules. For instance, Jozefowiez et al. (2005) exposed pigeons to a concurrent FI 20 s FI 60 s and observed temporally regulated choice: The pigeons started responding on the FI 20 s, then as time in a trial increased, switched to the FI 60 s. This is obviously operant timing, as it requires the animal to know with which response a specific time of reinforcement is associated. This argument has been used by Jozefowiez et al. (2005, 2006) to argue that different processes control responding in simple schedules versus concurrent schedules.

A corollary of interval timing is that if the animal is more likely to engage in reinforcer-related activity as the time of reinforcement grows nearer, it is less likely to engage in those activities when the time of reinforcement is far away and so more likely to engage in other activities at those times (See Chapters 1.12, 1.19). Staddon (1977) has divided the activities taking place during an interreinforcement interval into three classes. On one end of the interval, close to the time of reinforcement, is the terminal response – reinforcer-related activities such as key-pecking in pigeons or lever-pressing in rats. At the other end of the interreinforcement interval, close to trial onset, are interim activities (also termed adjunctive behavior). Interim activities, although unrelated to the reinforcer in the repertoire of the animal, are affected by the experimental parameters, their rate of emission being an inverted U-shaped function of the reinforcement rate (Staddon, 1977; Reid and Staddon, 1990). The classic example is polydipsia in rats (Falk, 1961): In any procedure where food is delivered at fixed intervals, rats will drink to excess just after food delivery – up to several times their daily water requirement – if given the opportunity. The excessive nature of polydipsia clearly indicates that it cannot be merely explained by efficient time allocation or homeostasis.

The type of adjunctive behavior observed depends on species-specific interaction between motivational systems and the connections existing between these systems and the stimuli present in the environment: If presented with another rat instead of water, rats will attack it (Thompson and Bloom, 1966; Gentry and Schaeffer, 1969), but on the other hand, if given access to both water and another member of their species, they will display schedule-induced polydipsia rather than schedule-induced aggression (Knutson and Schrader, 1975). In the same situation, pigeons only display schedule-induced aggression (Yoburn and Cohen, 1979). The motivation to engage in adjunctive behaviors is so strong that they can be used as reinforcers for other activities. For instance, a pigeon will learn to peck a key to be able to attack another pigeon (Cherek et al., 1973).

Finally, the time not filled by interim or terminal behavior is filled with facultative activities. In contrast to adjunctive behavior, they are not affected by the reinforcement rate and tend to be suppressed if more time is required by interim and terminal behavior (Staddon and Ayres, 1975).

So there is much more going in operant conditioning than simply operant learning. Yet there is clear evidence that the response-reinforcer contingency also plays a role. This is obviously the case in concurrent schedules, but it is also true for simple schedules. Even though pigeons will peck at a key and rats will press a lever anyway if these stimuli are signals for food, they are still more likely to do so if there is also a response-reinforcer contingency (Rescorla and Skucy, 1969; Woodruff et al., 1977), especially for rats (Lowe and Harzem, 1977). An omission procedure, where emission of the response postpones the delivery of the reinforcer, also has an effect on the behavior – on rats' approach behavior (Holland, 1977) or pigeons' key pecking (Schwartz and Williams, 1972).

There is also good evidence that animals can discriminate when a stimulus is a consequence of their behavior or not. In an experiment by Killeen (1978), pigeons were pecking on a key that turned black from time to time. If this change was the consequence of peck, reinforcement was scheduled on a second key; but if the change was spontaneously caused by a scheduling computer, they were reinforced for a peck on a third key. Pigeons had no problem mastering this task.

1.06.2.2   Determinants of Operant Learning

The operational distinction between Pavlovian and operant learning is clear: The animal learns a relation between a response and a stimulus in operant learning but a relation between two stimuli (the conditioned stimulus, CS, and the unconditioned stimulus, US) in Pavlovian learning. But are these two different forms of associative learning or does the same mechanism underlie both? The data favor the second hypothesis because the conditions leading to the learning of a CS–US relation in Pavlovian conditioning also lead to the reinforcement of a response in operant conditioning.

One important variable known to affect Pavlovian learning is the temporal contiguity between the CS and the US (Rescorla, 1988; *See* Chapter 1.03). Although testing to see if contiguity is also important in operant learning is a bit more complicated than it appears (for instance, if a response is emitted and scheduled for reinforcement D seconds later, do we allow more responses during the interval? If yes, the delay will be less than D. If no, we might artificially reduce responding), all studies that have looked at it have found that response rate is a decreasing function of the delay (Sizemore and Lattal, 1977; Lattal and Gleeson, 1990; Dickinson et al., 1992; Bruner et al., 1998; Stuphin et al., 1998). Also, even though it is commonly acknowledged that small delays have catastrophic consequences on the acquisition of operant

responding, recent studies have shown that after appropriate training, a substantial response rate can be sustained even with 30-s delays in rats, pigeons, and even Siamese fighting fish (Lattal and Gleeson, 1990; Lattal and Metzger, 1994; Bruner et al., 1998; Stuphin et al., 1998).

The other important determinant of Pavlovian learning is that the CS must be a good predictor of the US (Rescorla and Wagner, 1972). Once again, this seems also to be the case for operant learning, where the response has to be a reliable predictor of reinforcement. Responding is suppressed when the probabilities of response-dependent and response-independent reinforcement are equal, and it actually seems that the amount of responding is proportional to these two probabilities (Hammond, 1980; see also Lattal, 1974). In similar fashion, Pavlovian learning depends on the difference between the probability that the US is presented in the presence vs. absence of the CS; Rescorla and Wagner, 1972). This effect is reinforcer-specific: Response-independent food delivery reduces the rate of responding of a food-reinforced response but has no effect on a water-reinforced one (Dickinson and Mulatero, 1989). Moreover, response-independent food delivery has no effect if signaled by a stimulus, a manipulation that preserves the predictive value of the response (Hammond and Weinberg, 1984; Dickinson and Charnock, 1985).

Another line of evidence comes from a study by Williams (1999) that showed that operant learning does not occur if the reinforcer delivery is predicted by a stimulus. Naive rats were placed in a Skinner box, and lever-pressing led to food delivery 30 s later. There were three conditions. In the control condition, the delay of reinforcement was unsignaled. Consistent with earlier results of Lattal and Gleeson (1990), lever pressing increased in frequency despite the 30-s delay. In another condition, pressing of the lever turned on a house light that stayed on until food delivery. This kind of procedural arrangement is known to considerably aid delay conditioning because of the supposed conditioned-reinforcement properties of the food-predicting stimulus. Indeed, Williams (1999) found a higher response rate in that condition than in the unsignaled-delay-of-reinforcement one. But if the house light was turned on 5 s before reinforcement instead of just after response emission, responding was totally suppressed. According to Williams (1999), the higher reinforcement-predicting value of the light, which could not be compensated in this case by its conditioned reinforcement properties, blocked the learning of the response-reinforcer relation (see Williams, 1999, for additional experimental support for this hypothesis).

1.06.2.3 The Content of Operant Learning

Operant behaviors are emitted because of their consequences: A pigeon in a Skinner box is pecking at the key because it gives access to food. But does the pigeon 'know' that? In the framework of associative theory, this question is about whether operant learning leads to the formation of stimulus-response associations between the experimental context and the response or response-outcome associations between the response and its consequence.

Data seem to support the latter view. They come mainly from the reinforcer devaluation procedure where, after an operant behavior has been established, the value of the reinforcer to which it gives access is modified to see if this has any impact on the performance. For example, Colwill and Rescorla (1985) first trained a rat to press a lever for food. The rat was then given free access to food and made sick by injection of lithium, a procedure that creates a strong aversion for the food consumed prior to the poisoning (taste aversion learning; Garcia et al., 1966). When reintroduced into the Skinner box after that manipulation, response rate was massively depressed compared to baseline performance. At the same time, another operant response (chain pulling), which had been reinforced with water, was unaffected by the devaluation of the food reinforcer. The experiment by Dickinson and Charnock (1985) that we discussed previously, showing that response-independent food delivery had no effect on a water-reinforced response, points to the same conclusion. On the other hand, responding is not totally suppressed following reinforcer devaluation. That could be a clue that stimulus-response associations are also formed and partly control operant performance along with response-outcome associations (see Hall, 2004, for further discussion).

1.06.3 Interval Timing

Now that we have considered the conditions in which operant learning takes place, we can turn to the second issue regarding operant behavior – how it is regulated by its consequences. This is mainly the study of schedules of reinforcement, which has been heavily skewed toward interval schedules and

concurrent schedules, the former because they provide a way to study interval timing, whose influence seems pervasive in operant conditioning, and the latter because they are an experimental model of choice and decision making. We deal with interval timing in this section and with concurrent schedules and choice in the section titled 'Operant choice.'

1.06.3.1 Basic Facts

Interval timing is the ability of animals to perceive temporal relations between two events, ranging from seconds to several minutes (*See* Chapter 1.19) (based on neurological evidence, it seems that timing in the milliseconds range and circadian timing are different processes (e.g., Lewis and Miall, 2003; Lewis et al., 2003). In interval timing, the first event is termed the time marker because it starts the to-be-timed interval. On FI, where the time marker is trial onset and the interval is ended by reinforcement, interval timing leads to some temporal regulation of behavior. In most species, the animal pauses after trial onset and then, as time in a trial increases, starts responding at an increasing rate, reaching its maximum shortly before the time of reinforcement (Ferster and Skinner, 1957; Lejeune and Wearden, 1991). Some have argued (e.g., Gibbon, 1991; Cheng and Westwood, 1993) that this pattern of responding, called a scallop, is an artifact caused by averaging many trials together and that performance in individual trials actually follows a break-and-run pattern, with the animal moving abruptly, at a point varying from trial to trial (the break point), from a state of low responding to a state of high responding. But scallops were initially described based on the real-time performance of individual animals (Ferster and Skinner, 1957). Data from Schneider (1969), usually cited in support of the break-and-run hypothesis, actually show that although the break-and-run pattern dominates performance for short fixed intervals, scalloping is characteristic of longer intervals. Staddon (2001, Box 13.1) showed that this is what should be expected if the probability of responding increases monotonically during a trial.

For this reason, the pattern of local response rate across a trial, an estimate of the pattern of probability of responding across a trial, seems a better dependent variable than partial measures such as pause or break point. In FI, response rate increases during a trial, following a sigmoid, Gaussian function (Killeen et al., 1978; Lejeune and Wearden, 1991; **Figure 4**). What would happen if reinforcement was not delivered?

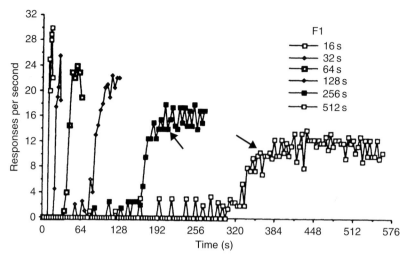

Figure 4 Proportional timing in FI: Response rate in FI is a sigmoid function of the time-to-reinforcement. Plotted in relative time, curves from FI with different intervals would superimpose. From Gibbon J (1991) Origin of scalar timing. *Learn. Mot.* 22: 3–38, with permission from Elsevier.

The peak procedure where, along with standard FI trials, empty trials lasting three or more times longer than the FI trials and ending without reinforcement are thrown in has been designed to answer this question (Catania, 1970; Roberts, 1981). After sufficient training with this procedure, response rate increases according to a sigmoid function up to the time of reinforcement and then decreases from that point, still according to a sigmoid function (**Figure 5**). The time of maximal responding (peak time) corresponds more or less to the time of reinforcement. It is not much affected by the number of peak trials, which mostly affect the absolute response rate, partly through their effect on arousal, because adding peak trials reduces the overall reinforcement rate.

Timed behavior, as observed in FI and the peak procedure, has two fundamental characteristics. The first is proportional timing: Performance is tuned to the time of reinforcement (**Figures 4** and **5**). Although this temporal adaptation of behavior was once believed to emerge only after extensive training with the procedure, recent research (Innis and Staddon, 1971; Wynne and Staddon, 1988; Higa et al., 1991; Higa and Staddon, 1997) has now shown that pigeons and rats can modify their behavior immediately following a change in the FI interval. Second is the scalar or timescale invariance property: Response curves superimpose when plotted in relative time (Dews, 1970; **Figure 5**). These properties have skewed theoretical thinking about interval timing toward a psychophysical framework.

In a psychophysical task, the subject is presented with two stimuli and asked if they are of similar intensity (or frequency, or color, etc.). The subject's responses are usually variable, assumed to be because of noise in sensory systems, but the probability that the two stimuli are judged identical is a function of their difference in intensity. If one stimulus is held constant, the curve showing how the probability that the subject judges the two stimuli identical as a function of the intensity of the second stimulus is called a psychometric function. A general property of many sensory systems is that they respect Weber's law: The higher the intensity of a stimulus, the more difficult it is for the subject to perceive differences when it is varied, an outcome that could result from a logarithmic encoding of stimulus intensity, a conjecture known as Fechner's law. One interesting consequence of Weber's law is that if psychometric functions are plotted on a relative stimulus scale, they superimpose (Falmagne, 1985).

This has led researchers to consider that the response rate curves obtained from animals in FI and peak procedures are indeed psychometric functions: The subject is comparing a representation of the current time in a trial to a representation of the time of reinforcement; the closer they are, the higher the probability of responding. Timescale invariance is observed because time perception follows Weber's law.

1.06.3.2 Scalar Expectancy Theory

Most theories of timing agree on this framework (Staddon, 2001) but differ about what is the basis for the representation of time. For many years, the most

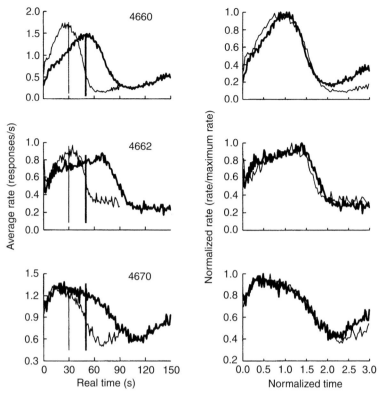

Figure 5 Proportional timing and timescale invariance in the peak procedure: Response rate in the peak procedure increases up to the time of reinforcement and then decreases, in both cases in a sigmoid fashion. Plotted in relative time, curves from peak procedures with different intervals superimpose. From Gallistel CR and Gibbon J (2000) Time, rate and conditioning. *Psych. Rev.* 107: 289–344. Copyright American Psychological Association. Reprinted with permission.

influential model was scalar expectancy theory (SET, Gibbon, 1977; Gibbon et al., 1984; **Figure 6**). SET assumes an internal pacemaker generating pulses at a more or less constant rate as soon as the time marker is presented (like most theories of timing, SET does not say how the animal identifies a time marker). These pulses accumulate in short-term memory, providing the basis for the representation of time which, as a consequence, is linear. When a reinforcer is delivered, the number of pulses currently accumulated is stored in long-term memory, but error is supposed to occur during the encoding process, leading to a Gaussian long-term memory distribution of time of reinforcement with a standard deviation proportional to the mean: This ensures that Weber's law is respected (Falmagne, 1985), even though Fechner's law is not (time is supposed to be encoded linearly, not logarithmically). At the beginning of a trial, the animal is supposed to sample one value from this distribution, which it will constantly compare to its representation of the elapsed time-in-trial to decide if it responds or not.

The empirical basis for SET is its ability to account for the basic data in timing procedures. But alternative theories of timing (i.e., the behavioral theory of timing, Killeen and Fetterman, 1988, and its neural network version, the learning-to-time model, Machado, 1997; the multiple timescale theory, Staddon, 2001, 2005; the packet theory of timing, Kirkpatrick, 2002) do just as well. Moreover, SET's achievement comes at the cost of parsimony. In adding to an already substantial number of free parameters, details of the models are usually modified to fit results from different procedures. For instance, the comparison rule between the representation of the current time in trial and the representation of the time of reinforcement is not the same depending on whether the data to be accounted for have been collected in an FI, a peak procedure, a bisection procedure, or a time-left procedure (Wearden, 1999; see the following paragraphs for a description of the latter two timing procedures).

In any event, it seems that the basic data about timing can be simulated by any model respecting

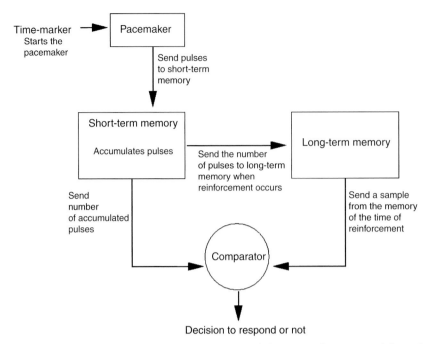

Figure 6   Scalar expectancy theory. When a time-marker is presented, the pacemaker starts emitting pulses at a more or less constant rate into short-term memory, where they are accumulated. When reinforcement occurs, the number of pulses currently in short-term memory is transferred to long-term memory. During a trial, the current number of pulses in short-term memory is continuously compared to a sample of the time of reinforcement retrieved from long-term memory to decide if a response should or should not be emitted.

Weber's law, and so it is not sufficient for a timing model to account just for those data. It must have additional empirical support for its assumptions. The behavioral theory of timing, for instance, is rooted in the data about adjunctive behavior we reviewed in the previous sections, considering that the sequence of behaviors an animal goes through a trial (from interim to facultative to terminal behavior) is the basis for interval timing instead of its consequence, as we have proposed. The multiple timescale theory is based on a model of memory developed to account for habituation data. What data support the existence of SET's internal pacemaker?

The best evidence is from the study of drug effects on timing performance. Meck (1996) proposed that dopamine agonists, such as amphetamine, accelerate the rate of the pacemaker. (Dopamine antagonists are supposed to have the reverse effect. Meck's (1996) model also has predictions concerning the effect of cholinergic drugs, but we will focus on dopamine antagonists in this review.) Then, in the peak procedure, chronic injection of a dopamine agonist should (1) immediately move the peak time to the left because the criterion number of pulses at which the animal starts responding is reached faster, but (2) the

peak time should gradually return to its original value as a new criterion is learned due to the fact that, with each reinforcement, the number of pulses in memory is transferred to long-term memory and a new representation of the time of reinforcement, generated by the drug-accelerated pacemaker, progressively overrides the previous one generated by the slower pacemaker. Once the dopamine agonist injection is discontinued, the same process takes place in reverse: The peak time shifts to the right and then progressively comes back to its original value. Similar effects should be observed for other measures of temporal control, such as the bisection point in the bisection procedure (see following paragraphs for a description of that procedure).

Although some studies have found the predicted effect of dopamine agonist on temporal dependent variables (i.e., Maricq et al., 1981; Maricq and Church, 1983; Spetch and Treit, 1984, with a bisection procedure; Maricq et al., 1981; Eckerman et al., 1987; Frederick and Allen, 1996; Kraemer et al., 1997, with a peak procedure), at least as many have failed to find such an effect (e.g., Lejeune et al., 1995; Chiang et al., 2000; Odum and Schaal, 2000, with a bisection procedure; Bayley et al., 1998; Knealing and

Schaal, 2002, with a peak procedure; see Odum et al., 2002, for a complete review). Moreover, studies using the peak procedure usually report only the peak time, whereas SET predictions are much broader and implicate the whole response function. It should be shifted to the left, and because of the scalar property, its variance should decrease. Saulsgiver et al. (2006) found that this is not what happens: Low responding early in a trial increases, while high responding before the time of reinforcement decreases; response rate after the time of reinforcement is mainly unaffected. As a consequence, the peak time shifts to the left, but the variance of the response-rate function increases, a result opposite to the SET interpretation.

In a critical review of the literature, Odum et al. (2002) argued that rate dependency provides a unifying account of drug effects in timing procedures, explaining results from experiments showing an effect and from those failing to find one. Rate dependency is a well-established and general empirical effect of drugs on operant behavior (Dews, 1958, 1981): High response rates are reduced by drug administration, whereas low response rates are increased. In an FI, for instance, this leads to a flattening of the whole response function. Odum et al.'s (2002) own studies, using a procedure borrowed from Catania and Reynolds (1968) that allowed them to differentiate timing from rate dependency (see Odum, 2002; Odum et al., 2002, for further details), seem to confirm that the dopamine-agonist effect in timing procedures is mainly due to rate dependency. (On the other hand, Odum (2002) found more support for an effect on timing of cholinergic drugs such as atropine or physostigmine, although the effect was small for physostigmine and the reverse of what is predicted by SET (Meck, 1996) for atropine.)

The results are just as problematic for other predictions of SET, like the progressive tolerance effect predicted if the dopamine agonist is injected chronically (Maricq et al., 1981, reported such an effect, but Frederick and Allen, 1996; Chiang et al., 2000; McClure et al., 2005; and Saulsgiver et al., 2006, failed to find it) or the rebound in peak time predicted after chronic injections of amphetamine cease (i.e., Saulsgiver et al., 2006). All in all, drug effects on timing performance provide no support for a pacemaker account of interval timing. The effects that are observed seem to be more a consequence of rate dependency than of a perturbation by the drug of an isolable temporal-information-processing mechanism.

An indirect way to prove the existence of an internal pacemaker would be to show that animals represent time linearly. Two experimental procedures have been designed to tackle this issue. The older one is the bisection procedure (Stubbs, 1968; Church and Deluty, 1977). It is a trial-based procedure where, following the presentation of one of two temporal stimuli, short or long, the animal is given a choice between two response alternatives. The animal is trained to make one response if the stimulus was short and another one if the stimulus was long. Then, on unreinforced probe trials, the animal is presented with stimuli having intermediate durations between the short and long stimuli used during training.

The closer the duration of the test stimulus to the duration of one of the stimuli used in training, the higher the probability the subject picks the response associated with that stimulus. Of special interest is the point of bisection, that is to say, the stimulus duration for which the animal picks each response with the same probability. On the animal's subjective timescale, the representation of that stimulus duration is supposed to be halfway between the representations of the duration of the two stimuli used during training. It usually falls around the geometric mean between these two durations. On a straightforward psychophysical interpretation, this result implies that time is represented logarithmically, rather than linearly, as the pacemaker approach implies. However, the linear assumption of SET can be made consistent with geometric-mean bisection by suitable modifications to other parts of the model (Gibbon, 1981).

In an attempt to resolve this issue, a more complex procedure, the time-left procedure (Gibbon and Church, 1981), was devised (**Figure 7**). Basically, it is a concurrent-chain procedure with VI initial links. At a random time T varying from trial to trial, the animal's response will commit it either to the time-left side, where food will be delivered C-T s later, or to the standard side, where food will be delivered S s later. According to Gibbon and Church (1981), the performance in this task is based on a series of mental computations. If we denote by f(x) the animal's representation of an interval of x s, and by t the time elapsed since trial onset, then at each time step, the animal is supposed to compute the difference f(C) − f(t) (time left to reinforcement on the time-left side) and compare it to f(S) (time to reinforcement on the standard side): if f(C) − f(t) > f(S) (which is more likely early in a trial since S < T), the animal

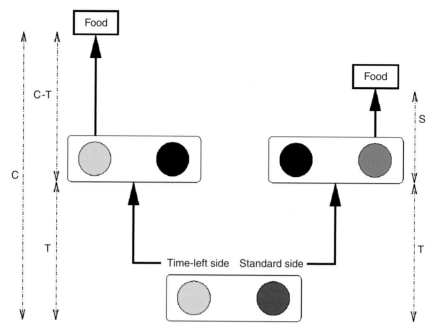

Figure 7   The time-left procedure for pigeons. The two keys are available to the pigeon for T s with T varying randomly from trial to trial. If, at time T s in a trial, the pigeon pecks on the time-left side, then (a) the standard side becomes unavailable and (b) reinforcement is delivered on the time-left side C–T s later so that time-to-reinforcement from trial onset on the time-left side is always fixed at C s. On the other hand, if at time T s in a trial, the pigeon pecks on the standard side, then (a) the time-left side becomes unavailable, (b) the standard side key color changes (by contrast, the time-left side key color remains the same), and (c) reinforcement is delivered on the standard side S s later.

picks the standard side; if $f(C) - f(t) < f(S)$ (more likely later in a trial when t is large enough), the animal should pick the standard side.

Because of noise, the animal's actual choice will be, of course, not as clear cut, but the preference of the animal for the time-left side should increase as a function of time in a trial, which is indeed what is observed (**Figure 8**). Moreover, when $f(C) - f(t) = f(S)$, the animal should be indifferent between the time-left and the standard side. $f(C) - f(t)$. Different hypotheses about the representation of time (linear vs. logarithmic) predict different locations of this point of subjective equality. Additionally, according to Gibbon and Church (1981), if the representation is logarithmic, the location of the point of subjective equality should be determined by the C/S ratio: if $C = 30$ s and $S = 20$ s, the point of subjective equality will be the same as if $C = 15$ s and $S = 10$ s. This highly counterintuitive prediction is, of course, not observed (Gibbon and Church, 1981), and although the point of subjective equality is not located precisely where it should be if time representation is linear (the animal switches to the time-left side well before it should), it is more compatible with this hypothesis than with

Gibbon and Church's version of the logarithmic one (**Figure 8**).

There are both philosophical and empirical problems with the Gibbon–Church analysis (Staddon and Higa, 1999). Their argument relies on the postulate that the animal's behavior is based on mental subtraction and comparison between the various durations involved in the procedure, but this assumption has no empirical basis. If different assumptions are made, notably concerning the way subjective time maps onto preference (see Cerutti and Staddon, 2004a, and Dehaene, 2001, for two examples), results from the time-left procedure can readily be reconciled with a logarithmic (or other monotonic) representation of time.

At an empirical level, puzzling results obtained in some other explorations of the time-left procedure (e.g., Preston, 1994; Cerutti and Staddon, 2004a; Machado and Vasconcelos, 2006) have shown that the processes involved in it are far from clear, a conclusion that should not surprise given its complexity. As **Figure 7** shows, in a standard time-left with pigeons, the color of the time-left side key is constant, whereas the standard side key color changes

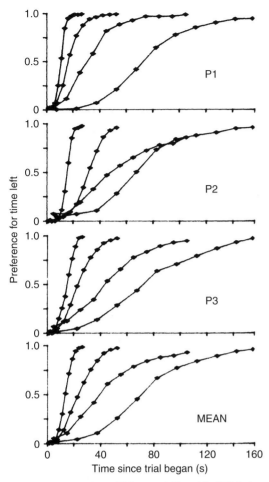

Figure 8 Results from Gibbon and Church's (1981) time-left procedure. The three top panels show individual subjects, whereas the bottom panel shows the group average. For each graph, the overall time-to-reinforcement on the time-left side (C) was (from the most leftward curves to the most rightward) 30, 60, 120, and 180 s. The duration of the standard side (S) was always half of the duration on the time-left side. Preference for the time-left side increases with time in a trial. From Gibbon J and Church R (1981) Time left: Linear versus logarithmic subjective time. *J. Exp. Psychol. Anim. Behav. Process* 22: 3–38. Copyright American Psychological Association. Reprinted with permission.

when the animal becomes committed to that side. Cerutti and Staddon (2004a) showed that this is the only configuration leading to an increase in the preference for the time-left side as time in a trial increases; every other variant (e.g., the color of the key changes on both sides or on the time-left side but not on the standard side or on neither side) leads to an exclusive preference for the time-left side – despite the fact that the temporal relations (the only

ingredient in the Gibbon–Church analysis) are the same for all arrangements.

Machado and Vasconcelos (2006) found that if the animals are trained separately with the time-left and standard sides, their performance changes when the two schedules are put together in a concurrent schedule, a result not expected if the animal was basing its behavior on the comparison of the temporal intervals involved in the experiment (the performance should be perfect from the start in this case).

Finally, in a simplified variant of the time-left procedure, Cerutti and Staddon (2004a) found that pigeon performance was strongly influenced by when the animal could be committed to a schedule. In their study, C = 60 s and S = 30 s. The pigeon could be committed to a schedule either anytime between 5 s and 55 s in a trial, anytime between 5 s and 30 s in a trial, or anytime between 30 s and 55 s in a trial. The pigeon's response allocation differed in each condition, a result that cannot be reconciled with the idea that the animal's behavior is controlled by a set of mental comparisons between the various intervals used in the experiment. Before we know more about the actual controlling variables in the time-left procedure, no definitive conclusion can be drawn from it regarding the shape of the representation of time.

1.06.3.3 Beyond Psychophysics

There is currently no proof that interval timing relies on an internal pacemaker. Actually, the whole framework for the study of interval timing may need some revision. First, the emphasis on Weber's law needs to be reevaluated, as many studies have now reported what look like violations of it (e.g., Dreyfus et al., 1988; Stubbs et al., 1994; Zeiler and Powell, 1994; Crystal, 1999; Bizo et al., 2006), although this needs to be considered carefully. A performance might appear to violate Weber's law, not because the underlying timing mechanism does not follow it but because processes other than timing influence the performance (e.g., Jozefowiez et al., 2006).

But beyond Weber's law, the whole psychophysical approach, the idea that interval timing relies on some kind of 'knowledge' the animal has of the intervals involved in the experiment, may need to be abandoned. In the peak procedure, the animal is usually first trained on an FI for several sessions before peak trials are thrown in. As we saw, during those peak trials, their response-rate pattern evolves according to a kind of bell-shaped function that peaks at the time of reinforcement. But this behavior is observed only after several sessions where the animal is exposed to a mix of reinforced FI trials and unreinforced peak trials. The first time a peak trial is introduced, the animal just keeps on responding until the end of the trial, apparently never noticing that the time of reinforcement has passed (an example of something studied many years ago as the reinforcement-omission effect, Staddon and Innis, 1969; Kello, 1972). This is a surprising result if we assume, as most theories of timing do, that the time of reinforcement is precisely what the animal learns when exposed to an FI.

Even more damaging evidence comes from a recent series of experiments by Machado and collaborators (Machado and Keen, 1999; Machado and Pata, 2005; Machado and Arantes, 2006). They trained pigeons in two bisection tasks simultaneously. In one task, response R1 (i.e., pecking on a red key) is reinforced after a 1-s stimulus while response R2 is reinforced after a 4-s one. In the other task, response R3 is reinforced after 4 s, whereas response R4 is reinforced after a 16-s one. Hence, both R2 and R3 are associated with a 4-s stimulus, so according to the psychophysical approach, they should be equivalent. But they are not. If given the choice between R2 and R3 after a test stimulus is presented, the pigeons are not indifferent as they should be according to the cognitive view. Instead, they switch their preference from R2 to R3 as the duration of the stimulus is increased (Machado and Keen, 1999; Machado and Pata, 2005). If these same animals are exposed to a new bisection procedure, performance is stable from the start if R3 is reinforced after a 1-s stimulus and R3 after a 16-s stimulus but is greatly disturbed in the reverse case (Machado and Arantes, 2006; **Figure 9**).

These data cannot be reconciled with the traditional psychophysical/cognitive account of interval timing and suggest the involvement of a simpler associative process, such as the one described in Machado's (1997) Learning-to-Time model. Instead of the time associated with each response, pigeons in a bisection task would learn through reinforcement and extinction to (1) approach the key associated with the short-duration stimulus and avoid the one associated with the longer-duration stimulus early in a trial and (2) do the reverse (i.e., avoid the key associated with the short-duration stimulus and approach the stimulus associated with the longer-duration stimulus) late in a trial (Machado and Arantes, 2006). Hence, when given the choice between R2 and R3 in Machado and Keen (1999) and Machado and Pata's (2005) studies, the pigeons

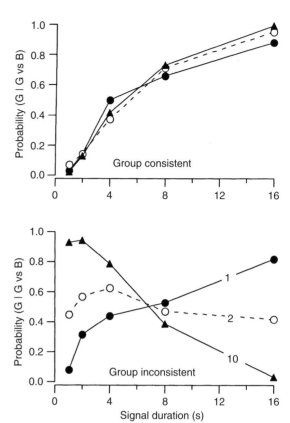

Figure 9 Group data from Machado and Arantes (2006). Pigeons were initially trained in two bisection procedures, one pitting a 1-s stimulus versus a 4-s one, the other pitting a 4-s stimulus versus a 16-s one. They were then trained in a third bisection task using the same two responses reinforced after a 4-s stimuli in the previous tasks. For the group whose data are shown in the top panel, the response previously reinforced after the 4-s stimulus pitted against a 1-s stimulus was now reinforced after a 16-s stimulus, whereas the response previously reinforced after the 4-s stimulus previously pitted against a 16-s stimulus was now reinforced after a 1-s duration. The y-axis of each graph shows the probability of emitting the response previously associated with a 4-s duration. For the second group, whose data are shown in the bottom panel, the reverse arrangement was used. Each curve in the graph represents the performance of the pigeons during the first (filled circles), second (empty circles), and tenth (filled triangles) sessions of the new bisection task. As can be seen, the pigeons' performance from the first group is stable from the first session. On the other hand, for the second group, performance takes several sessions to settle down. From Machado A and Arantes J (2006) Further tests of the Scalar Expectancy Theory (SET) and the Learning-to-Time model (LeT) in a temporal bisection task. *Behav. Processes* 72: 195–206, with permission from Elsevier.

would behave as they have learned previously, approaching R3 early in a trial while avoiding R2 and doing the reverse later. This pattern of approach/avoidance behavior is perfectly compatible with a new bisection procedure associating a 1-s stimulus with R3 and a 4-s stimulus with R2, and hence, the performance in this case is stable from the beginning. Otherwise, the pigeon has to relearn a new pattern of approach/avoidance behavior.

1.06.4 Operant Choice

1.06.4.1 The Matching Law

In a seminal experiment, Richard Herrnstein (1961) studied pigeons in concurrent VI VI schedules. He found that once behavior had stabilized, the ratio of response rates matched the ratio of reinforcement rates:

$$\frac{x}{y} = \frac{R(x)}{R(y)} \qquad [1]$$

where x and y are response rates on the two keys, and $R(x)$ and $R(y)$ are the reinforcement rates obtained.

The matching law is a fairly general phenomenon. It has been found with several species, including, of course, rats but also humans (e.g., Bradshaw et al., 1976). Instead of having a schedule associated with each response key, an alternative, called a Findley procedure (Findley, 1958), is to have both associated with the same key but signaled by different colors that are under the animal's control. The animal switches between the two schedules by pecking a second key, called a change-over key. Matching is still observed in this case. When different feeding schedules are associated with different places (e.g., the two ends of a long box), animals allocate the time spent in the two places to the relative rate of associated reinforcement (Baum and Rachlin, 1969). Matching is also observed in trial-based procedures where the animal is only allowed one response per trial, which leads either to reinforcement or to a blackout (Sugrue et al., 2004; Lau and Glimcher, 2005).

Matching behavior is consistent with reinforcement-rate maximization in concurrent VI schedules (Staddon and Motheral, 1978; Baum, 1981), but large deviations from matching lead to only a small reduction in the obtained reinforcement rate, so it is unlikely that matching is the result of any kind of explicit maximizing process. Moreover, Equation (1) rarely fits experimental data exactly, which has led to the proposal of a popular alternative termed the generalized matching law (Baum, 1974; see also Staddon, 1968):

$$\frac{x}{y} = b\left[\frac{R(x)}{R(y)}\right]^{a} \qquad [2]$$

where a and b are free parameters. Equation (2) can also be converted to logarithmic form, which has the advantage that the response-rate ratio remains a linear function of the reinforcement-rate ratio, allowing parameter b to be interpreted as bias and a as a measure of the sensitivity to the reinforcement rate ratio.

Violations of matching indicate that rather then being some kind of primary behavioral process (Herrnstein, 1970), matching is the outcome of more basic behavioral mechanisms. Unfortunately, determining these mechanisms can be difficult, as it seems that almost any model incorporating some form or the other of the law of effect predicts matching (Hinson and Staddon, 1983). Hence particular attention should be devoted to violations of the matching law as a way to limit the range of possible models.

Parameter b in the generalized matching law is a measure of any bias the animal might have toward one schedule. For instance, it can be systematically varied by using different kind of reinforcers for each schedule (e.g., wheat vs. buckwheat for pigeons; see Miller, 1976). The controlling variables for parameter a, on the other hand, remain more mysterious. Parameter a measures sensitivity to the reinforcement-rate ratio: When a is lower than 1, the animal is less sensitive to the reinforcement rate ratio than it should be according to the matching law (undermatching); when a is larger than 1, the animal is more sensitive to that ratio than it should be (overmatching). Reviews of the literature (e.g., Baum, 1979; Wearden and Burgess, 1982) have concluded that undermatching is more the rule than the exception, parameter a usually taking values between 0.8 and 0.9. Overmatching is seldom observed, except in very special situations (like concurrent VI FI schedules, Nevin, 1971; Trevett et al., 1972).

The causes of undermatching are not clear. The way the VI is scheduled (RI schedules lead to less undermatching, Taylor and Davison, 1983), the number of trials in a session (fewer trials lead to less undermatching; Todorov et al., 1983), and the number of conditions to which the subject has been exposed (more undermatching is obtained if the subject has been exposed to more conditions; Keller and Gollub, 1977) are a few of the variables that have an effect. The last two variables seem to indicate an effect of interference in memory. Animals seem also to be more sensitive to reinforcement-rate ratio when the overall reinforcement rate is high (Alsop and Elliffe, 1988; MacDonall, 2006), a problem for the matching law, which implies that animals should be sensitive only to the ratio of reinforcement rates, not to their absolute values.

The variable most often cited as having an effect on the sensitivity to the reinforcement rate ratio is the presence or absence of a procedural arrangement known as a changeover delay (COD). COD works like this: When the animal switches from one schedule to the other (called a changeover), there is a small period of time (the COD, typically between 0.5 and 2 s) during which no reinforcement can be delivered. The rationale for a COD is to avoid reinforcement for a third class of behavior, switching between schedules. In the limit, switching could predominate over 'stay' choice responses, leading to apparent indifference between the two choices – extreme undermatching. According to this analysis, the main cause of undermatching would be the occasional reinforcement of switching behavior; indeed, adding a COD generally reduces the amount of undermatching (Shull and Pliskoff, 1967). On the other hand, a COD is not essential to obtain matching (e.g., Shull and Pliskoff, 1967; Heyman, 1979; Hinson and Staddon, 1983).

1.06.4.2   The Structure of Choice

Moreover, other studies have shown that some reinforcement of switching behavior is necessary to obtain matching in concurrent schedules. If pigeons are trained separately on two simple VIs and then allowed to choose between them in the usual concurrent procedure, they will respond exclusively on the VI associated with the higher reinforcement rate (extreme overmatching; Crowley and Donahoe, 2004; Gallistel and Gibbon, 2000).

This result has potentially far-reaching implications for theories of operant choice. It suggests that switching is reinforced when a switch to a schedule is followed by reinforcement (switch reinforcers), whereas staying on a schedule is reinforced by reinforcers collected while responding on that schedule (stay reinforcers; Skinner, 1950; Houston and McNamara, 1981; MacDonall, 1999). The final performance is the outcome of both stay and switch reinforcement. Consider, for instance, a

concurrent VI 40 s VI 60 s. In this view, responding on the VI 40 s is reinforced according to a VI 40 s, but switching over from the VI 40 s is reinforced according to a VI 60 s.

This view is all the more plausible given that the tendency for an animal to switch between schedules is a function both of the probability that a switch is followed by reinforcement and the duration of the COD (e.g., Shull and Pliskoff, 1967; Pliskoff, 1971; Shull et al., 1981; Shahan and Lattal, 1998). Shull et al. (1981) also showed that a reinforcer delivered just after a changeover response has a massive impact on the rate of switching back and forth between the schedules. Also, in contrast to concurrent VI VI, concurrent VR VR schedules do not generate matching but exclusive preference for the schedule with the higher ratio (Herrnstein and Loveland, 1975); a reinforcer will not be scheduled on a VR until the animal works on it and hence, switching behavior will never be reinforced. If responses on a VR are counted not only for the schedule the animal is currently working on but also for the other one (hence leading to the reinforcement of switching behavior), matching is observed (MacDonall, 1988).

Another study by MacDonall (2005), in which he explicitly manipulated the reinforcement contingency for switching behaviors, provides additional support. Rats were exposed (for example) to a concurrent VI 36 s VI 360 s. In one condition, the schedule worked exactly as a traditional concurrent VI VI: Reinforcement for staying on the VI 36 s (respectively on the VI 360 s) was collected according to a VI 36 s (respectively VI 360 s), whereas reinforcement for switching away from the VI 36 s (respectively VI 360 s) was collected according to a VI 360 s (respectively VI 36 s). In the second condition, reinforcements for both staying and switching from the VI 36 s (respectively VI 360 s) were scheduled according to a VI 36 s (respectively 360 s). MacDonall (2005) reported that the latter condition yielded strong deviation from matching – unexpected by traditional views of operant choice but perfectly understandable in terms of the stay/switch framework.

From this view, the important empirical question is to understand how run length (number of responses emitted on a key between a changeover to that schedule and a changeover to the other schedule) and dwell time (time elapsing between a changeover to a schedule and a changeover to the other schedule) are determined by schedule parameters. The analysis is made easier by the fact that, in concurrent VI schedules, both of these dependent variables are distributed exponentially, indicating a constant probability through time of terminating a visit to a schedule (i.e., Heyman, 1979; Gibbon, 1995). Two contradictory accounts have been proposed.

The first one is by MacDonall (1998, 1999, 2000, 2005), who found that run length and dwell time on a schedule were power functions of the ratio of switch and stay reinforcers plus a bias, a kind of molecular generalized matching law. MacDonall (2006) also found some modulating effect of the overall reinforcement rate.

The second one can be inferred from an influential experiment on paradoxical choice by Belke (1992) in which pigeons were exposed to a concurrent VI 20 s VI 40 s and to a concurrent VI 40 s VI 80 s. Their behavior allocation conformed to matching in both conditions. On unreinforced probe trials, the pigeons were given the choice between the two VI 40 s, the one associated with the VI 20 s and the one associated with the VI 80 s. Even though both schedules signaled the same reinforcement rate, the pigeons preferred the VI 40 s associated with the VI 80 s in a proportion of 4 to 1. Even more surprising, Gibbon (1995) showed that, if given the choice between the VI 20 s and the VI 40 s usually presented along with the VI 80 s, they preferred the VI 40 s to the VI 20 s in a proportion of 2 to 1.

These results have a surprisingly simple explanation (Gallistel and Gibbon, 2000): They can be predicted if we simply assume that the probability to leave a schedule is a linear function of the reinforcement rate on the other schedule, that is to say, the rate of switch reinforcement. Indeed, in Gibbon's (1995) experiment, the dwell-time distribution on the VI 20 s is identical to the dwell-time distribution on the VI 80 s (Gallistel and Gibbon, 2000); both were pitted against a VI 40 s.

Further research is necessary to decide between MacDonall's account and the one that incorporates Belke's results. MacDonall did not directly measure run length and visit duration but deduced them from the number of responses made on a schedule and the number of changeovers to that schedule, which might not provide accurate estimates. On the other hand, it is surprising that stay reinforcers would have no effect on performance, although that could be explained by the fact that most of the reinforcers in concurrent VI schedules are collected just after a changeover (i.e., for switching) (Dreyfus et al., 1982). We also note the existence of a few other puzzling results (i.e., Williams and Bell, 1999;

McDevitt and Williams, 2003), which suggest that the determinants of performance in procedures such as Belke's (1992) are still not completely understood.

1.06.4.3 Local and Global Control of Behavior in Concurrent Schedules

Experiments on the matching law are typical of most studies of operant choice where the focus is on stable, asymptotic behavior obtained after many sessions in which the animal is continually exposed to the same condition. But recently, there has been more interest in the study of choice in transition.

Davison and Baum (2000) exposed pigeons to a concurrent VI schedule where, during a single session, the reinforcement-rate ratio changed after a fixed number of reinforcers (usually 10). The change was signaled by a 10-s blackout. Averaging across conditions and subjects, they were able to show that each reinforcer had an effect on choice, pushing the animal's preference toward the reinforced side. The effect of successive reinforcers on the same side had a diminishing effect on performance, whereas a 'disconfirming' reinforcer, for a switch response, on the other side had a stronger effect in pushing preference toward its side (**Figure 10**). This result has now been replicated in several studies, some using rats (Aparicio and Baum, 2006) or more traditional concurrent-schedule procedures where the reinforcement rate ratio does not change several times during the same session (Landon et al., 2002). This suggests some kind of surprise-driven learning mechanism similar to the one described in the Rescorla and Wagner (1972) model of Pavlovian conditioning: Behavioral change occurs when unexpected events take place in the environment.

Another interesting finding is that this local effect of reinforcement on behavior is modulated by more global variables. For instance, Davison and Baum (2000) reported that the change in behavior following reinforcement was larger when the overall reinforcement rate was high, leading to a more extreme preference for the schedule associated with the higher reinforcement rate (**Figure 10**). This is similar to Alsop and Elliffe's (1988) finding that sensitivity to the reinforcement rate ratio is higher when the overall reinforcement rate is higher. In other words, control of performance was more local with the higher reinforcement rate, with the last reinforcement delivered to the animal having a more important influence on performance in this case.

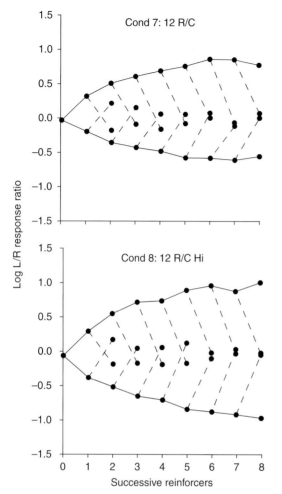

Figure 10 Effect of individual reinforcers on preference in concurrent VI schedules. Each reinforcer drives preference toward its schedule, although each successive reinforcer has a diminishing effect on behavior. The overall reinforcement rate was higher for the data presented in the bottom panel: The effect of individual reinforcers is more important in that condition than in the other. From Davison M and Baum WM (2000) Choice in a variable environment: Every reinforcer counts. *J. Exp. Anal. Behav.* 74: 1–24, with permission from the Society for the Quantitative Analysis of Behavior, Inc.

The best-documented global influence on the local control by reinforcement is the effect of overall environmental variability: When animals are submitted to the same experimental condition for many sessions, their behavior tends to change slowly when this condition is changed, whereas, on the other hand, when the environment is highly unstable, with experimental conditions changing often and unpredictably, they show more immediate behavioral change in response to a modification of the environment, with

less carryover effect from past conditions (e.g., Davis et al., 1993; Mazur, 1997; Schofield and Davison, 1997; Gallistel et al., 2001; see Staddon and Frank, 1974, for similar effects in multiple schedules). Other variables that have an influence on the local effect of reinforcement are the range of variation in the reinforcement-rate ratio (Landon and Davison, 2001; the more distinct the two schedules, the more local the control of behavior) and in the location of reinforcement (Krageloh et al., 2005). If reinforcement is alternating between the two schedules, behavioral control is more local than if several reinforcers are collected in a row on the same schedule.

1.06.5 Reinforcement Theory

Through operant learning, animals are able to learn about the consequences of their behavior. If these consequences have reinforcing value, they will be able to modulate the emission of the behavior that caused them. But not every event is a reinforcer. What, then, makes a reinforcer reinforcing? The answer depends on whether we are considering primary reinforcers (whose effect on behavior seems to be largely innate) or conditioned reinforcers (whose effect on behavior is due to the fact that they signal the delivery of a primary reinforcer; *See also* Chapter 1.03).

1.06.5.1 Primary Reinforcement

An accurate summary of our current knowledge of why primary reinforcers are reinforcing is still Skinner's (1953) definition of a reinforcer, which all in all boils down to "a reinforcer is something that reinforces behavior." In other words, we recognize a primary reinforcer through its effect on behavior, but we are hardly able to explain why it has such an effect. This is fine if your main interest is how a reinforcer modulates behavior, which indeed is the main topic of operant research, but is more problematic if you want to know why a reinforcer modulates behavior, a legitimate question, especially in an applied setting. The elaborate theories of primary reinforcement developed during the heyday of general learning theory in the 1950s (such as Hull's 1943 drive-reduction theory) have not stood the test of time but have not been replaced. Little more than commonsense generalities can be said about primary reinforcers. Primary reinforcers affect behavior presumably because they contribute to the Darwinian fitness of the organism (Skinner, 1966), but this is little help in identifying them. The fact that food, water, and sex are powerful primary reinforcers seems to indicate that they are linked to basic biological needs. But this is not very helpful either, as this kind of explanation becomes quickly circular. Wheel running is reinforcing in rats (i.e., Belke and Heyman, 1994; Belke, 1997) just like the opportunity to observe complex stimuli is in monkeys (Butler and Harlow, 1954; Butler and Alexander, 1955). Do we have to postulate a wheel-running drive in rats and an observation drive in monkeys? Does this add anything to our understanding of the reinforcing effect of wheel running or observation?

The most creative attempt to address the problem of primary reinforcement derives from Premack's (1962, 1965) proposal that behavior with a high probability of emission can be used as a reinforcer for behavior with a lower probability. Hence, feeding, a behavior with a high probability of emission in a hungry animal, can be used to reinforce lever pressing or key pecking, behaviors with a low probability of emission. Although the theory does not tell how the probability of emission of a behavior is set, it is an improvement over explanations of primary reinforcement in terms of biological needs because probabilities can be measured prior to conditioning.

In one experiment, Premack (1965) measured the preference of children for playing pinball versus eating candy. He then showed that making eating candy contingent on playing pinball reinforced this activity only in children preferring candy over playing pinball, whereas it had a punishing effect for the other children, and vice versa. In another study (Premack, 1962), rats had a restricted access to wheel running but unlimited access to water in one condition, whereas the reverse was true in another condition. Access to wheel running was an effective reinforcer for water drinking in the first condition, whereas water drinking was an effective reinforcer for wheel running in the second condition. As a last example, Chalop et al. (1990) found that echolalia and perseverative behavior, activities with a high probability of responding in autistic children, were very efficient reinforcers for these subjects, whereas food reinforcement had no effect.

Premack's view has been developed into behavioral-regulation models of operant performance (Timberlake and Allison, 1974; Rachlin, 1974; Allison, 1993; Staddon, 1979, 2001, 2003/1983). In these views, the animal has a preferred allocation of behavior, which works as a behavioral bliss point. By

making access to one behavior contingent on the omission of another, the animal is forced away from the bliss point. Behavior then adjusts to restore the system as close to the bliss point as possible. For instance, a hungry rat would prefer to spend most of its time eating and only a small portion of its time pressing a lever. By creating a contingency between pressing a lever and food delivery, an operant procedure does not allow the rat to settle on this preferred distribution of activity and forces it to increase its rate of lever-pressing to increase its rate of eating so that it is closer to the preferred allocation of behavior than it would be if it did not press the lever.

In contrast to Premack's theory, behavioral regulation makes the counterintuitive prediction that in some circumstances, a behavior with a low probability of responding may reinforce a behavior with a high probability of responding (e.g., Eisenberg et al., 1967; Mazur, 1975). Staddon (1979, 2003/1983) showed how basic data for simple schedules could be accounted by the bliss-point model. It can also be shown that this approach leads to a view of operant behavior equivalent to the classical microeconomic theory of consumer demand (i.e., Staddon, 2001, 2004/1983) and has favored the development of an economic approach to operant performance (Hursh, 1984).

Behavioral regulation is an original and elegant approach to the problem of primary reinforcement. It is radical in the sense that it denies what is implicit in most treatments of operant behavior — that there are special events (i.e. reinforcers and punishers) that have the power to modify behavior. This is actually a problem because it is hard to see how to integrate a behavioral regulation account of operant performance with the causal analysis we presented in the previous part of this chapter. How can we, for instance, interpret the effect of the delay of reinforcement and of the predictive value of the response, data that make a lot of sense within a more traditional associative account of operant learning, within the framework of behavioral regulation? The Irish mathematician Hamilton showed that the laws of Newtonian physics, the very model of causation, could be expressed as an optimality model. It is possible that this is the case also for operant behavior. Even though behavioral regulation looks like a model of the causality of operant behavior, the real mechanism would be the more traditional strengthening and weakening of behavior by reinforcement and punishment postulated since Thorndike's original formulation of the law of effect, even though the effects of this mechanism can often be predicted by an optimality model such as behavioral regulation. In this case, we should expect behavioral regulation to fail when animals are exposed to very unusual reinforcement schedules, which is exactly what was observed in a study by Ettinger et al. (1987), for instance.

1.06.5.2   Conditioned Reinforcement

In contrast to primary reinforcers, the question of why conditioned reinforcers affect behavior is less problematic: It is because they signal primary reinforcement. Learning with delayed reinforcement is much aided if a conditioned reinforcer is used to bridge the delay, as in the experiment by Williams (1999) discussed earlier. The question, then, is how do parameters of primary reinforcement determine the effectiveness of a conditioned reinforcer? The procedure usually used to address this question is the concurrent-chain schedule we described previously (**Figure 2**). The basic assumption is that response allocation during the initial link follows the matching law (i.e., the response-rate ratio during the initial link matches the conditioned reinforcement rate ratio). Hence, the response-rate ratio during the initial link is supposed to be a measure of the preference of the animal for one terminal link over the other.

When terminal links are both variable schedules (VI or VR), the response-rate ratio during the initial link sometimes matches the rate of primary reinforcement during the terminal links (Herrnstein, 1964b), suggesting that the value of a conditioned reinforcer could simply be equal to the rate of primary reinforcement in its presence. But, when given the choice between a variable schedule (VI or VR) or a fixed schedule (FI or FR), animals are strongly biased toward the variable alternative, even when they arrange identical reinforcement rates (Herrnstein, 1964a; Killeen, 1968; Davison, 1969, 1972; Mazur, 1986). They are indifferent between the two only when the reinforcement rate is computed using the harmonic mean of the various intervals used in the schedule instead of the arithmetic mean, as it is usually done. This is consistent with data collected in behavioral ecology showing preference for variable delay to food over fixed delay to food and relative indifference between variable and fixed amount of food (Staddon and Innis, 1966; Bateson and Kacelnik, 1995; Kacelnik and Bateson, 1996). This preference for VI over FI could be explained by assuming that the value of

a conditioned reinforcer is an amount-dependent hyperbolic function of the delay to primary reinforcement it signals (Mazur, 2001).

This would also account for data from self-control procedures where animals are given the choice between a small immediate reward and a larger delayed one. The classical result (Ainslie, 1974; Green et al., 1981; Laibson, 1997; Green and Estle, 2003 for data in rats, pigeons, and humans) is that, for short delays, the animal will pick the smaller reward (impulsive behavior) while, for long delays, it will pick the larger reward (self-controlled behavior). This choice pattern emerges automatically if we assume that choice between delayed reinforcers is based on their value and if these values are an amount-dependent hyperbolic function of the delay of reinforcement. As **Figure 11** shows, for long delays, the discounted value of the larger reward is higher than the value of the smaller reward, hence the animal displays self-control; on the other hand, for short delay of reinforcement, the value of the smaller reward is larger than the value of a larger reward, and the animal is impulsive (Rachlin, 1974; Ainslie, 1975; Herrnstein, 1981).

The best evidences for hyperbolic discounting come from studies using an adjusting procedure. The initial link is an FR 1 instead of an RI, so that the first response moves the animal to the terminal link. The delay and amount of reinforcement are held constant at one terminal link. If the subject chooses this link, either the delay (in the adjusting-delay procedure) or the amount (in the adjusting-amount procedure) of reinforcement available at the

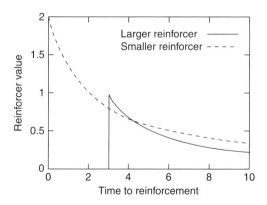

Figure 11   If a reinforcer value is an amount-dependent hyperbolic function of the time to reinforcement, the animal's preference for a large delayed reward over a smaller more immediate one will decrease and will eventually reverse as the time of the smaller reward delivery approaches.

other initial link is reduced (in the case of the delay) or increased (in the case of the amount). The reverse takes place if the subject chooses this terminal link. The goal is to determine a point of subjective equality where the animal is indifferent between the two terminal links. At this point, the values of the two conditioned reinforcers are supposed to be equal. If delay is manipulated, hyperbolic discounting predicts that, at indifference, the delay on the adjusting side will be a linear function of the delay on the constant side. The same way, if the amount is manipulated, hyperbolic discounting predicts that the amount on the adjusting side will be a hyperbolic function of the amount on the constant side. Both predictions have been confirmed empirically (Mazur, 1987, 2000; Rodriguez and Logue, 1988; Richards et al., 1997; Green et al., 2004).

All this research relies on the assumption that choice during the initial link is a function only of the values of the terminal links. But it is not; the longer the initial links, the less extreme the preference for the terminal links, reaching almost indifference with extremely long initial links (Fantino, 1969; Squire and Fantino, 1971; Fantino and Davison, 1983). This indicates that either choice is influenced by variables besides the values of the terminal links and/or that the value of a terminal link is context-dependent. Both kinds of influences have been incorporated in modern theories of conditioned reinforcement (i.e., delay reduction theory, Fantino, 1969; Squire and Fantino, 1971; hyperbolic value-added model, Mazur, 2001; contextual model of choice, Grace, 1994, 1996). All those models are equivalent in terms of their ability to fit the data.

Another interpretation of the surprising fact that a conditioned reinforcer value seems to depend on the context is to question the very notion of conditioned reinforcement and the usual assumption made about the control of behavior in concurrent chain schedules. This is exactly what Staddon and collaborators (Staddon and Ettinger, 1989; Staddon and Cerutti, 2003; Cerutti and Staddon, 2004a,b; Staddon, 2003/1983) have done by proposing that interval timing underlies most effects attributed to conditioned reinforcement. Their analysis is based on some results in simple chain schedules that are puzzling for a conditioned-reinforcement account. For example, no more than six FI or FR links can be linked together in a chained schedule without extreme pausing developing in the early links – leading to a dramatic drop in the obtained reinforcement rate (Kelleher and Gollub, 1962). Weak responding during the early links is sometimes observed with as few as three schedules chained together (Catania et al., 1980; Davison, 1974), and extreme pausing can develop even in a three-link chain schedule if the time from trial onset to primary reinforcement is long enough (Kelleher and Fry, 1962). On the other hand, if the change from one link to the other is not signaled by a stimulus change (tandem schedule) or if the stimuli used to signal such transitions change randomly after each trial (scrambled chain schedule), the animals have no difficulty mastering these tasks and achieve close to the maximum possible reinforcement rate (Kelleher and Gollub, 1962).

These results are surprising because stimulus changes in a chain schedule are supposed to act as conditioned reinforcers, so should aid performance, not disrupt it. Another surprising result is that it does not make any difference if the stimulus change from one link to the other is response-dependent or not (Catania et al., 1980), whereas we saw previously that an actual response-reinforcer contingency (as opposed to mere contiguity between the emission of the response and reinforcement) is critical to operant learning.

Based on these data, Staddon and collaborators proposed that stimuli in chain schedules work not as conditioned reinforcers but as time-markers. Hence, they lead the animal to pause an amount of time proportional to the time between the onset of the stimulus and primary reinforcement. This accounts for the excessive pausing observed in chain schedules (Staddon and Ettinger, 1989; Staddon and Cerutti, 2003). Supporting this view, Staddon and Cerutti (2003) showed that pause duration in the first link of a two-chain schedule was a linear function of time to primary reinforcement in data from Davison (1974). Innis et al. (1993) studied two-link chain schedules with one link of fixed duration and the other varying from reinforcer to reinforcer according to an ascending then descending sequence. Pauses in each link tracked their respective time to primary reinforcement with a lag of one interval.

Applied to concurrent chain schedules, this view considers preference for terminal links during the initial link to be an artifact of interval timing. Consider, for instance, a concurrent chain schedule with FI 15-s and FI 30-s terminal links (**Figure 12**). The animal will pause longer on the initial link leading to the FI 30 s because the time-to-reinforcement is longer on that side. Hence, the animal will respond more on the initial link leading to the FI 15 s,

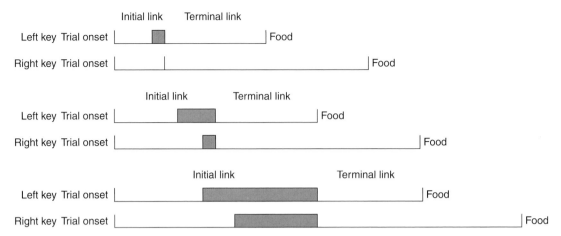

Figure 12   Interval timing account of concurrent chain performance. The animal pauses on an initial link for an amount of time proportional to the time between the onset and the initial link and primary reinforcement. As a consequence, it looks as if it prefers the initial link leading to the terminal link with the higher reinforcement rate. As the initial link duration is increased, the difference in pausing makes less and less of a contribution to the reinforcement rate ratio, and preference converges on indifference.

which will look like a preference for the FI 15-s initial link. Note that as the initial link duration is increased (while the terminal-link duration remains the same), pausing takes up a smaller fraction of the total first-link time so that the time available for responding becomes more equal on the two sides (**Figure 12**), eventually reaching indifference – as the data show. This analysis also explains the preference for variable over fixed terminal-link schedules because variable time-to-reinforcement leads to shorter pausing than fixed. Finally, Staddon and Ettinger (1989) and Staddon and Cerutti (2003) showed how this timing view of concurrent performance can account for hyperbolic discounting and data on self-control (the equations derived from the timing view turn out to be identical to those derivable from hyperbolic discounting).

More research will be needed to conclude if the timing approach of Staddon and collaborators is a better account of concurrent-chain performance than more traditional explanations in terms of conditioned reinforcement, but strong support for it can be found in a study by McDevitt and Williams (2001). They used terminal links associated with a 5-s and a 15-s delay-to-reinforcement. In one condition, each initial link was correlated with a different stimulus (as in standard concurrent-chain schedules), whereas the same stimulus was associated with both of them in another condition. A conditioned reinforcement approach would lead one to expect no differential responding during the initial link in the

single-stimulus terminal-link condition because the consequences of responding are identical for both choices. But McDevitt and Williams (2003) actually found the same strong preference for the 5-s terminal link in both conditions, concluding that time-to-reinforcement, not conditioned reinforcement, was the main controlling variable.

1.06.6   Conclusion

Operant behavior involves adaptation to the consequences of responding; it is the prototype of adaptive behavior during the life of the individual – the ontogenetic equivalent of Darwinian natural selection in phylogeny. Techniques for exploring operant behavior exploded with the invention of the Skinner box and the discovery of the orderly and powerful effects of schedules of reinforcement. In the 1950s and 1960s, much research addressed the limits of operant conditioning and in particular the intimate relationship between the processes underlying operant and classical conditioning. In recent decades, two research areas, interval timing and choice, have dominated the field. We have reviewed these topics and, in addition, discussed post-Skinner developments in the economics of operant behavior. We hope, with this chapter, to have aroused the interest of the reader for this fascinating and lively field of behavioral science.

Acknowledgments

This research was supported by grants from the National Institute of Mental Health to Duke University.

References

Ainslie G (1975) Specious reward: A behavioral theory of impulsiveness and impulse control. *Psychol. Bull.* 82: 275–281.

Ainslie GW (1974) Impulse control in pigeons. *J. Exp. Anal. Behav.* 21: 485–489.

Allison J (1993) Response deprivation, reinforcement and economics. *J. Exp. Anal. Behav.* 60: 129–140.

Alsop B and Elliffe D (1988) Concurrent schedule performance: Effects of relative and overall reinforcer rate. *J. Exp. Anal. Behav.* 49: 21–36.

Aparicio CF and Baum WM (2006) Fix and sample with rats in the dynamics of choice. *J. Exp. Anal. Behav.* 86: 43–63.

Bateson M and Kacelnik A (1995) Preferences for fixed and variable food sources: Variability in amount and delay. *J. Exp. Anal. Behav.* 63: 313–329.

Baum WM (1974) On two types of deviations from the matching law: Bias and undermatching. *J. Exp. Anal. Behav.* 22: 231–242.

Baum WM (1979) Matching, undermatching and overmatching in studies of choice. *J. Exp. Anal. Behav.* 32: 269–281.

Baum WM (1981) Optimization and the matching law as accounts of instrumental behavior. *J. Exp. Anal. Behav.* 36: 387–403.

Baum WM (1993) Performances on ratio and interval schedules of reinforcement: Data and theory. *J. Exp. Anal. Behav.* 59: 245–264.

Baum WM and Rachlin HC (1969) Choice as time allocation. *J. Exp. Anal. Behav.* 12: 861–874.

Bayley PJ, Bentley GD, and Dawson GR (1998) The effects of selected antidepressant drugs on timing behaviour in rats. *Psychopharmacology* 136: 114–122.

Belke TW (1992) Stimulus preference and the transitivity of preference. *Anim. Learn. Behav.* 20: 401–406.

Belke TW (1997) Running and responding reinforced by the opportunity to run: Effect of reinforcer duration. *J. Exp. Anal. Behav.* 67: 337–351.

Belke TW and Heyman GM (1994) A matching law analysis of the reinforcing efficacy of wheel running in rats. *Anim. Learn. Behav.* 22: 267–274.

Biederman GB, D'Amato MR, and Keller DM (1964) Facilitation of discriminated avoidance learning by dissociation of CS and manipulandum. *Psychon. Sci.* 1: 229–230.

Bizo LA, Chu JY M, Sanabria F, and Killeen PR (2006) The failure of Weber's law in time perception and production. *Behav. Processes* 71: 201–210.

Bolles RC and Riley AL (1973) Freezing as an avoidance response: Another look at the operant-respondent distinction. *Learn. Motiv.* 4: 268–275.

Bradshaw CM, Szabadi E, and Bevan P (1976) Behavior of humans in variable-interval schedules of reinforcement. *J. Exp. Anal. Behav.* 26: 135–141.

Breland K and Breland M (1961) The misbehavior of organisms. *Am. Psychol.* 16: 681–684.

Brown PL and Jenkins HM (1968) Autoshaping of the pigeon's key-peck. *J. Exp. Anal. Behav.* 11: 1–8.

Bruner CA, Avila SR, Acuna L, and Gallarno LM (1998) Effects of reinforcement rate and delay on the acquisition of lever pressing by rats. *J. Exp. Anal. Behav.* 69: 59–75.

Butler RA and Alexander HM (1955) Daily patterns of exploratory behavior in monkeys. *J. Comp. Physiol. Psychol.* 48: 247–249.

Butler RA and Harlow HF (1954) Persistence of visual exploration in monkeys. *J. Comp. Physiol. Psychol.* 47: 258–263.

Catania AC (1970) Reinforcement schedules and the psychophysical judgments: A study of some temporal properties of behavior. In: Schoenfeld WN (ed.) *The Theory of Reinforcement Schedules*, pp. 1–42. New York: Appleton-Century-Crofts.

Catania AC and Reynolds GS (1968) A quantitative analysis of the responding maintained by interval schedules of reinforcement. *J. Exp. Anal. Behav.* 11: 327–383.

Catania AC, Yohalem R, and Silverman PJ (1980) Contingency and stimulus change in chained schedules of reinforcement. *J. Exp. Anal. Behav.* 33: 213–219.

Cerutti DT and Staddon JER (2004a) Immediacy versus anticipated delay in the time-left experiment: A test of the cognitive hypothesis. *J. Exp. Psychol. Anim. Behav. Process.* 30: 45–57.

Cerutti DT and Staddon JER (2004b) Time and rate measures in choice transitions. *J. Exp. Anal. Behav.* 81: 135–154.

Chalop MH, Kurtz P, and Casey FG (1990) Using aberrant behaviors as reinforcers for autistic children. *J. Appl. Behav. Anal.* 23: 163–181.

Cheng K and Westwood R (1993) Analysis of single trials in pigeons' timing performance. *J. Exp. Psychol. Anim. Behav. Process* 19: 56–67.

Cherek DR, Thompson T, and Heistad GT (1973) Responding maintained by the opportunity to attack during an interval food reinforcement schedule. *J. Exp. Anal. Behav.* 11: 327–383.

Chiang TJ, Al-Ruwaitea ASA, Mobini S, Ho MY, Bradshaw CM, and Szabadi E (2000) The effect of d-amphetamine on performance in two operant timing schedules. *Psychopharmacology* 150: 170–184.

Church RM and Deluty MZ (1977) Bisection of temporal intervals. *J. Exp. Psychol. Anim. Behav. Process* 3: 216–128.

Colwill RM and Rescorla RA (1985) Post-conditioning devaluation of a reinforcer affects instrumental responding. *J. Exp. Psychol. Anim. Behav. Process* 11: 120–132.

Crowley MA and Donahoe JW (2004) Matching: its acquisition and generalization. *J. Exp. Anal. Behav.* 82: 143–159.

Crystal JD (1999) Systematic nonlinearities in the perception of temporal intervals. *J. Exp. Psychol. Anim. Behav. Process* 25: 3–17.

Davis DG, Staddon JER, Machado A, and Palmer RG (1993) The process of recurrent choice. *Psychol. Rev.* 100: 320–341.

Davison M (1974) A functional analysis of chained fixed-interval schedule performance. *J. Exp. Anal. Behav.* 21: 323–330.

Davison M and Baum WM (2000) Choice in a variable environment: Every reinforcer counts. *J. Exp. Anal. Behav.* 74: 1–24.

Davison MC (1969) Preference for mixed-interval versus fixed-interval schedules. *J. Exp. Anal. Behav.* 12: 247–252.

Davison MC (1972) Preference for mixed-interval versus fixed-interval schedules: Number of components intervals. *J. Exp. Anal. Behav.* 17: 169–176.

Dawson GR and Dickinson A (1990) Performance on ratio and interval schedules with matched reinforcement rates. *Q. J. Exp. Psychol.* 42B: 225–239.

Dehaene S (2001) Subtracting pigeons: Logarithmic or linear? *Psychol. Sci.* 12: 244–246.

Dews PB (1958) Studies on behavior. IV. Stimulant actions of methamphetamine. *J. Pharmacol. Exp. Ther.* 122: 137–147.

Dews PB (1970) The theory of fixed-interval responding. In: Schoenfeld WN (ed.) *The Theory of Reinforcement Schedules*, pp. 43–61. New York: Appleton-Century-Crofts.

Dews PB (1981) History and present status of the rate-dependency investigations. In: Thompson T, Dews PB, and Barrett JE (eds.) *Advances in Behavioral Pharmacology,* vol. 3, pp. 111–118. New York: Academic Press.

Dickinson A and Charnock DJ (1985) Contingency effect with maintained instrumental reinforcement. *Q. J. Exp. Psychol.* 37B: 397–416.

Dickinson A and Mulatero CW (1989) Reinforcer specificity of the suppression of the instrumental performance on a non-contingent schedule. *Behav. Processes* 19: 167–180.

Dickinson A, Watt A, and Griffiths JH (1992) Free-operant acquisition with delayed reinforcement. *Q. J. Exp. Psychol.* 45B: 241–258.

Dreyfus LR, Dorman LG, Fetterman JG, and Stubbs DA (1982) An invariant relation between changing over and reinforcement. *J. Exp. Anal. Behav.* 38: 335–347.

Dreyfus LR, Fetterman JG, Smith LD, and Stubbs DA (1988) Discrimination of temporal relations by pigeons. *J. Exp. Psychol. Anim. Behav. Process* 14: 349–367.

Eckerman DA, Segbefia D, Manning S, and Breese G (1987) Effect of methylphenidate and d-amphetamine on timing in the rat. *Pharmacol. Biochem. Behav.* 27: 513–515.

Eisenberg R, Karpman M, and Trattner J (1967) What is the necessary and sufficient condition for reinforcement in the contingency condition? *J. Exp. Psychol.* 74: 342–350.

Ettinger RH, Reid AK, and Staddon JER (1987) Sensitivity to molar feedback functions: A test of molar optimality theory. *J. Exp. Psychol. Anim. Behav. Process* 13: 366–375.

Falk JL (1961) The production of polydipsia in normal rats by an intermittent food schedule. *Science* 133: 195–196.

Falmagne JC (1985) *Elements of Psychophysical Theory.* Oxford: Oxford University Press.

Fantino E (1969) Choice and rate of reinforcement. *J. Exp. Anal. Behav.* 12: 723–730.

Fantino E and Davison M (1983) Choice: Some quantitative relations. *J. Exp. Anal. Behav.* 40: 1–13.

Ferster CB and Skinner BF (1957) *Schedules of Reinforcement.* New York: Appleton-Century-Crofts.

Findley JD (1958) Preference and switching under concurrent scheduling. *J. Exp. Anal. Behav.* 1: 123–144.

Frederick DL and Allen JD (1996) Effects of selective dopamine d1- and d2-agonists and antagonists on timing performance in rats. *Pharmacol. Biochem. Behav.* 53: 759–764.

Gallistel CR and Gibbon J (2000) Time, rate and conditioning. *Psychol. Rev.* 107: 289–344.

Gallistel CR, Mark TA, King A, and Latham PE (2001) The rat approximates an ideal detector of change in rates of reward: implications for the law of effect. *J. Exp. Psychol. Anim. Behav. Process* 27: 354–372.

Garcia J, Ervin FR, and Koelling RA (1966) Learning with prolonged delay of reinforcement. *Psychon. Sci.* 5: 121–122.

Gentry W and Schaeffer RW (1969) The effect of a FR response requirement on aggressive behavior. *Psychon. Sci.* 14: 236–238.

Gibbon J (1977) Scalar expectancy theory and Weber's law in animal timing. *Psychol. Rev.* 84: 279–325.

Gibbon J (1981) On the form and location of the psychometric bisection function for time. *J. Math. Psychol.* 24: 58–87.

Gibbon J (1991) Origin of scalar timing. *Learn. Mot.* 22: 3–38.

Gibbon J (1995) Dynamics of time matching: Arousal makes better seem worse. *Psychon. Bull. Rev.* 2: 208–215.

Gibbon J and Church R (1981) Time left: Linear versus logarithmic subjective time. *J. Exp. Psychol. Anim. Behav. Process* 22: 3–38.

Gibbon J, Church RM, and Meck WH (1984) Scalar timing in memory. *Ann. N. Y. Acad. Sci.* 423: 52–77.

Grace R (1994) A contextual model of concurrent-chains choice. *J. Exp. Anal. Behav.* 61: 113–129.

Grace R (1996) Choice between fixed and variable delays to reinforcement in the adjusting-delay procedure and concurrent chains. *J. Exp. Psychol. Anim. Behav. Process* 22: 362–383.

Green L and Estle SJ (2003) Preference reversals with food and water reinforcers in rats. *J. Exp. Anal. Behav.* 79: 233–242.

Green L, Fisher EBJ, Perlow S, and Sherman L (1981) Preference reversal and self-control: Choice as a function of reward amount and delay. *Behav. Anal. Lett.* 1: 43–51.

Green L, Myerson J, Holt DD, Slevin JR, and Estle SJ (2004) Discounting of delayed food rewards in pigeons and rats: Is there a magnitude effect? *J. Exp. Anal. Behav.* 81: 39–50.

Hall G (2004) Associative structures in Pavlovian and instrumental conditioning. In: Pashler H and Gallistel CR (eds.) *Stevens' Handbook of Experimental Psychology,* 3rd edn., vol. 3: *Learing, Motivation and Emotion,* pp. 1–44. New York: Wiley.

Hammond LJ (1980) The effect of contingency upon the appetitive conditioning of free-operant behavior. *J. Exp. Anal. Behav.* 34: 297–304.

Hammond LJ and Weinberg M (1984) Signaling unearned reinforcers removes suppression produced by zero correlation in an operant paradigm. *Anim. Learn. Behav.* 12: 371–374.

Herrnstein RJ (1961) Relative and absolute strength of a response as a function of frequency of reinforcement. *J. Exp. Anal. Behav.* 4: 267–272.

Herrnstein RJ (1964a) Aperiodicity as a factor in choice. *J. Exp. Anal. Behav.* 7: 179–182.

Herrnstein RJ (1964b) Secondary reinforcement and rate of primary reinforcement. *J. Exp. Anal. Behav.* 7: 27–36.

Herrnstein RJ (1970) On the law of effect. *J. Exp. Anal. Behav.* 13: 243–266.

Herrnstein RJ (1981) Self control as response strength. In: Bradshaw CM, Szabdadi E, and Lowe CF (eds.) *Quantification of Steady-State Operant Behavior,* pp. 3–20. New York: Elsevier.

Herrnstein RJ and Loveland DH (1975) Maximizing and matching on concurrent ratio schedules. *J. Exp. Anal. Behav.* 24: 107–116.

Heyman GM (1979) A Markov model description of changeover probabilities on concurrent variable-interval schedule. *J. Exp. Anal. Behav.* 31: 41–51.

Higa JJ and Staddon JER (1997) Dynamics of rapid temporal control in animals. In: Bradshaw CM and Szabadi E (eds.) *Time and Behavior: Psychological and Neurobiological Analyses,* pp. 1–40. Amsterdam: Elsevier.

Higa JJ, Wynne CDL, and Staddon JER (1991) Dynamics of time discrimination. *J. Exp. Psychol. Anim. Behav. Process* 17: 281–291.

Hineline PN and Rachlin H (1969) Escape and avoidance of shock by pigeons pecking a key. *J. Exp. Anal. Behav.* 12: 533–538.

Hinson JM and Staddon JER (1983) Matching, maximizing and hill climbing. *J. Exp. Anal. Behav.* 40: 321–331.

Holland PC (1977) Different effect of omission contingencies on various components of Pavlovian appetitive conditioned behavior in rats. *J. Exp. Psychol. Anim. Behav. Process* 5: 178–193.

Houston AL and McNamara J (1981) How to maximize reward rate on two variable-interval paradigms. *J. Exp. Anal. Behav.* 35: 367–396.

Hull CL (1943) *Principles of Behavior.* New York: Appleton-Century-Crofts.

Hursh SR (1984) Behavioral economics. *J. Exp. Anal. Behav.* 42: 435–452.

Innis NK and Staddon JER (1971) Temporal tracking on cyclic-interval reinforcement schedules. *J. Exp. Anal. Behav.* 16: 411–423.

Innis NK, Mitchell S, and Staddon JER (1993) Temporal control on interval schedules: What determines the postreinforcement pause? *J. Exp. Anal. Behav.* 60: 293–311.

Jenkins HM, Barnes RA, and Barrera FJ (1981) Why autoshaping depends on trial spacing. In: Locurto CM, Terrace HS, and Gibbon J (eds.) *Autoshaping and Conditioning Theory*, pp. 255–284. New York: Academic Press.

Jenkins HM and Moore BR (1973) The form of the autoshaped response with food or water reinforcers. *J. Exp. Anal. Behav.* 20: 163–181.

Jozefowiez J, Cerutti DT, and Staddon JER (2005) Timing in choice experiments. *J. Exp. Psychol. Anim. Behav. Process* 31: 213–225.

Jozefowiez J, Cerutti DT, and Staddon JER (2006) Timescale invariance and Weber's law in choice. *J. Exp. Psychol. Anim. Behav. Process* 32: 229–238.

Kacelnik A and Bateson M (1996) Risky theories: The effects of variance on foraging decisions. *Am. Zool.* 36: 293–311.

Karpicke J, Christoph G, Peterson G, and Hearst E (1977) Signal location and positive versus negative conditioned suppression in the rat. *J. Exp. Psychol. Anim. Behav. Process* 3: 105–118.

Kello JE (1972) The reinforcement-omission effect on fixed-interval schedules: Frustration or inhibition? *Learn. Motiv.* 3: 138–147.

Kelleher RT and Fry WT (1962) Stimulus functions in chained and fixed-interval schedules. *J. Exp. Anal. Behav.* 5: 167–173.

Kelleher RT and Gollub LR (1962) A review of positive conditioned reinforcement. *J. Exp. Anal. Behav.* 5: 543–597.

Keller JV and Gollub LR (1977) Duration and rate of responding as determinants of concurrent responding. *J. Exp. Anal. Behav.* 28: 145–153.

Killeen PR (1968) On the measure of reinforcement frequency in the study of preference. *J. Exp. Anal. Behav.* 14: 127–131.

Killeen PR (1978) Superstition: A matter of bias, not detectability. *Science* 199: 88–90.

Killeen PR (1998) The first principle of reinforcement. In: Wynne CDL and Staddon JER (eds.) *Models of Action: Mechanisms for Adaptive Behavior*, pp. 127–156. Mahwah, NJ: Lawrence Erlbaum Associates.

Killeen PR and Fetterman JG (1988) A behavioral theory of timing. *Psychol. Rev.* 95: 274–295.

Killeen PR, Hanson SJ, and Osborne SR (1978) Arousal: Its genesis and manifestation as response rate. *Psychol. Rev.* 85: 571–581.

Kirkpatrick K (2002) A packet theory of conditioning and timing. *Behav. Processes* 57: 89–106.

Knealing TW and Schaal DW (2002) Disruption of temporally organized behavior by morphine. *J. Exp. Anal. Behav.* 77: 157–169.

Knutson JF and Schrader SP (1975) A concurrent assessment of schedule-induced aggression and schedule-induced polydipsia in rats. *Anim. Learn. Behav.* 3: 16–20.

Kraemer PJ, Randall CK, Dose JM, and Brown RW (1997) Impacts of d-amphetamine on temporal estimation in pigeons tested with a production procedure. *Pharmacol. Biochem. Behav.* 58: 523–527.

Krageloh CU, Davison M, and Elliffe DM (2005) Local preference in concurrent schedules: The effect of reinforcer sequences. *J. Exp. Anal. Behav.* 84: 37–64.

Laibson D (1997) Golden eggs and hyperbolic discounting. *Q. J. Econom.* 112: 443–477.

Landon J and Davison M (2001) Reinforcer-ratio variation and its effect on rate of adaptation. *J. Exp. Anal. Behav.* 75: 207–234.

Landon J, Davison M, and Elliffe D (2002) Concurrent schedules: Short- and long-term effects of reinforcers. *J. Exp. Anal. Behav.* 77: 257–271.

Lattal KA (1974) Combinations of response-reinforcer dependence and independence. *J. Exp. Anal. Behav.* 22: 357–362.

Lattal KA and Gleeson S (1990) Response acquisition with delayed reinforcement. *J. Exp. Psychol. Anim. Behav. Process* 16: 27–39.

Lattal KA and Metzger B (1994) Response acquisition by Siamese fighting fish (Beta splendens) with delayed visual reinforcement. *J. Exp. Anal. Behav.* 16: 27–39.

Lau B and Glimcher PW (2005) Dynamic response-by-response models of matching behavior in rhesus monkeys. *J. Exp. Anal. Behav.* 84: 555–579.

Lejeune H, Hermans I, Mocaes E, Rettori MC, Poignant JC, and Richelle M (1995) Amineptine, response timing, and time discrimination in the albino rat. *Pharmacol. Biochem. Behav.* 51: 165–173.

Lejeune H and Wearden JH (1991) The comparative psychology of fixed-interval responding: Some quantitative analysis. *Learn. Motiv.* 22: 84–111.

Lewis PA and Miall RC (2003) Brain activation patterns during measurement of sub- and supra-second intervals. *Neuropsychologia* 41: 1583–1592.

Lewis PA, Miall RC, Daan S, and Kacelnik A (2003). Interval timing in mice does not rely upon the circadian pacemaker. *Neurosci. Lett.* 348: 131–134.

Lowe CF and Harzem P (1977) Species differences in temporal control of behavior. *J. Exp. Anal. Behav.* 28: 189–201.

MacDonall JS (1988) Concurrent variable-ratio schedules: Implication for the generalized matching law. *J. Exp. Anal. Behav.* 50: 55–64.

MacDonall JS (1998) Run length, visit duration and reinforcers per visit in concurrent performance. *J. Exp. Anal. Behav.* 69: 275–293.

MacDonall JS (1999) A local model of concurrent performance. *J. Exp. Anal. Behav.* 71: 57–74.

MacDonall JS (2000) Synthesizing concurrent interval performances. *J. Exp. Anal. Behav.* 84: 167–183.

MacDonall JS (2005) Earning and obtaining reinforcers under concurrent interval scheduling. *J. Exp. Anal. Behav.* 84: 167–183.

MacDonall JS (2006) Some effects of overall rate of earning reinforcers on run lengths and visit durations. *Behav. Processes* 73: 13–21.

Machado A (1997) Learning the temporal dynamics of behavior. *Psychol. Rev.* 104: 241–265.

Machado A and Arantes J (2006) Further tests of the Scalar Expectancy Theory (SET) and the Learning-to-Time model (LeT) in a temporal bisection task. *Behav. Processes* 72: 195–206.

Machado A and Keen R (1999) Learning to Time (LET) or Scalar Expectancy Theory? A critical test of two models of timing. *Psychol. Sci.* 10: 285–290.

Machado A and Pata P (2005) Testing the scalar expectancy theory (SET) and the Learning-to-Time model (LeT) in a double bisection task. *Learn. Behav.* 33: 111–122.

Machado A and Vasconcelos M (2006) Acquisition versus steady state in the time-left experiment. *Behav. Processes* 71: 172–187.

Maricq AV and Church RM (1983) The differential effects of haloperidol and methamphetamine on time estimation in the rat. *Psychopharmacology* 79: 10–15.

Maricq AV, Roberts S, and Church RM (1981) Methamphetamine and time estimation. *J. Exp. Psychol. Anim. Behav. Process.* 7: 18–30.

Mazur JE (1975) The matching law and quantifications related to Premack's principle. *J. Exp. Psychol. Anim. Behav. Process* 1: 374–386.

Mazur JE (1986) Fixed and variable ratios and delays: Further test of an equivalence rule. *J. Exp. Psychol. Anim. Behav. Process* 12: 116–124.

Mazur JE (1987) An adjusting procedure for studying delayed reinforcement. In: Commons ML, Mazur JE, Nevin JA, and Rachlin H (eds.) *Quantitative Analysis of Behavior, Vol. 5: The Effect of Delay and of Intervening Events on Reinforcement Value*, pp. 55–73. Hillsdale, NJ: Erlbaum.

Mazur JE (1997) Effects of rate of reinforcement and rate of change on choice behavior in transition. *Q. J. Exp. Psychol.* 50B: 111–128.

Mazur JE (2000) Tradeoffs among delays, rate and amount of reinforcement. *Behav. Processes* 49: 1–10.

Mazur JE (2001) Hyperbolic value addition and general models of animal choice. *Psychol. Rev.* 108: 96–112.

McClure EA, Saulsgiver KA, and Wynne CD L (2005) Effect of D-amphetamine on temporal discrimination in pigeons. *Behav. Pharmacol.* 16: 193–208.

McDevitt MA and Williams BA (2001) Effects of signaled versus unsignaled delay of reinforcement. *J. Exp. Anal. Behav.* 75: 165–182.

McDevitt MA and Williams BA (2003) Arousal, changeover responses and preference in concurrent schedules. *J. Exp. Anal. Behav.* 80: 261–272.

Meck WH (1996) Neuropsychology of timing and time perception. *Cogn. Brain. Res.* 3: 227–242.

Miller HL (1976) Matching-based hedonic scaling in the pigeon. *J. Exp. Anal. Behav.* 26: 335–347.

Nevin JA (1971) Rates and patterns of responding with concurrent fixed-interval and variable-interval reinforcement. *J. Exp. Anal. Behav.* 16: 241–247.

Odum AL (2002) Behavioral pharmacology and timing. *Behav. Processes* 57: 107–120.

Odum AL, Lieving LM, and Schaai DW (2002) Effects of D-amphetamine in a temporal discrimination procedure: Selective changes in timing or rate dependency? *J. Exp. Anal. Behav.* 78: 195–214.

Odum AL and Schaal DW (2000) The effects of morphine on fixed-interval patterning and temporal discrimination. *J. Exp. Anal. Behav.* 74: 229–243.

Peele DB, Casey J, and Silberberg A (1984) Primacy of interresponse-time reinforcement in accounting for rate differences under variable-ratio and variable-interval schedules. *J. Exp. Psychol. Anim. Behav. Process* 10: 149–167.

Pliskoff SS (1971) Effects of symmetrical and asymmetrical changeover delays on concurrent performance. *J. Exp. Anal. Behav.* 249–256.

Premack D (1962) Reversibility of the reinforcement relation. *Science* 136: 255–257.

Premack D (1965) Reinforcement theory. In: Levine D (ed.) *Nebraska Symposium on Motivation,* vol. 13, pp. 123–180. Lincoln: University of Nebraska Press.

Preston RA (1994) Choice in the time-left procedure and in concurrent chains with a time-left terminal link. *J. Exp. Anal. Behav.* 61: 349–373.

Rachlin H (1974) Self-control. *Behaviorism* 2: 94–107.

Reid AK and Staddon JER (1990) Mechanisms of schedule entrainment. In: Cooper SJ and Dourish CT (eds.) *Neurobiology of Stereotyped Behaviour*, pp. 200–231. Oxford: Clarendon Press.

Rescorla RA (1988) Behavioral studies of Pavlovian conditioning. *Annu. Rev. Neurosci.* 11: 329–352.

Rescorla RA and Skucy JC (1969) Effect of response-independent reinforcers during extinction. *J. Comp. Physiol. Psychol.* 67: 381–389.

Rescorla RW and Wagner AG (1972) A theory of Pavlovian conditioning: Variations in the effectiveness of reinforcement and nonreinforcement. In: Black AH and Prokazy WF (eds.)

Classical Conditioning II, pp. 64–99. New York: Appleton-Century-Crofts.

Richards JB, Mitchell SH, Witt H de, and Seiden L (1997) Determination of discount functions in rats with an adjusting-amount procedure. *J. Exp. Anal. Behav.* 67: 353–366.

Roberts S (1981) Isolation of an internal clock. *J. Exp. Psychol. Anim. Behav. Process* 7: 242–268.

Rodriguez ML and Logue AW (1988) Adjusting delay to reinforcement: Comparing choice in pigeons and humans. *J. Exp. Psychol. Anim. Behav. Process* 14: 105–117.

Saulsgiver KA, McClure EA, and Wynne CDL (2006) Effect of d-amphetamine on the behavior of pigeons exposed to the peak procedure. *Behav. Processes* 71: 268–285.

Schneider BA (1969) A two-state analysis of fixed-interval responding in pigeons. *J. Exp. Anal. Behav.* 12: 667–687.

Schofield G and Davison M (1997) Nonstable concurrent choice in pigeons. *J. Exp. Anal. Behav.* 68: 219–232.

Schwartz B and Williams DR (1972) The role of the response-reinforcer contingency in negative automaintenance. *J. Exp. Anal. Behav.* 17: 351–357.

Shahan TA and Lattal KA (1998) On the functions of changeover delay. *J. Exp. Anal. Behav.* 69: 141–160.

Shettleworth SJ (1975) Reinforcement and the organization of behavior in golden hamsters: Hunger, environment and food reinforcement. *J. Exp. Psychol. Anim. Behav. Process* 104: 56–87.

Shull RL (2005) The sensitivity of response rate to the rate of variable-interval reinforcement for pigeons and rats: A review. *J. Exp. Anal. Behav.* 84: 99–110.

Shull RL and Pliskoff SS (1967) Changeover delay and concurrent schedules: Some effects on relative performance measures. *J. Exp. Anal. Behav.* 10: 517–527.

Shull RL, Spear DJ, and Bryson AE (1981) Delay or rate of food delivery as a determiner of response rate. *J. Exp. Anal. Behav.* 35: 129–143.

Sizemore OJ and Lattal KA (1977) Dependency, contiguity and response-independent reinforcement. *J. Exp. Anal. Behav.* 27: 119–125.

Skinner BF (1938) *The Behavior of Organisms*. New York: Appleton-Century-Crofts.

Skinner BF (1950) Are theories of learning necessary? *Psychol. Rev.* 57: 193–216.

Skinner BF (1953) *Science and Human Behavior*. New York: Macmillan.

Skinner BF (1966) The phylogeny and ontogeny of behavior. *Science* 153: 1205–1213.

Spetch ML and Treit D (1984) The effects of d-amphetamine on short-term memory for time in pigeons. *Pharmacol. Biochem. Behav.* 21: 663–666.

Squire E and Fantino E (1971) A model for choice in simple concurrent and concurrent-chains schedules. *J. Exp. Anal. Behav.* 15: 27–38.

Staddon JER (1968) Spaced responding and choice: A preliminary analysis. *J. Exp. Anal. Behav.* 11: 669–682.

Staddon JER (1977) Schedule-induced behavior. In: Honig WK and Staddon JER (eds.) *Handbook of Operant Behavior*, pp. 125–152. Englewood Cliffs NJ: Prentice Hall.

Staddon JER (1979) Operant behavior as adaptation to constraint. *J. Exp. Psychol. Gen.* 108: 48–67.

Staddon JER (2001) *Adaptive Dynamics*. Cambridge, MA: MIT Press.

Staddon JER (2003/1983) *Adaptive Behavior and Learning*. Cambridge: Cambridge University Press. Available at: http://psychweb.psych.duke.edu/department/jers/abl/TableC.htm

Staddon JER (2005) Interval timing: Memory, not a clock. *Trends Cogn. Sci.* 9: 312–314.

Staddon JER and Ayres S (1975) Sequential and temporal properties of behavior induced by a schedule of periodic food delivery. *Behaviour* 54: 26–49.

Staddon JER and Cerutti DT (2003) Operant conditioning. *Annu. Rev. Psychol.* 54: 115–144.

Staddon JER and Ettinger RH (1989) *Learning: An Introduction to the Principle of Adaptive Behavior*. Orlando, FL: Harcourt Brace Jovanovich.

Staddon JER and Frank J (1974) Mechanisms of discrimination reversal. *Anim. Behav.* 22: 802–828.

Staddon JER and Higa JJ (1999) Time and memory: Towards a pacemaker-free theory of interval timing. *J. Exp. Anal. Behav.* 71: 215–251.

Staddon JER and Innis NK (1969) Reinforcement omission on fixed-interval schedules. *J. Exp. Anal. Behav.* 12: 689–700.

Staddon JER and Innis NK (1966) Preference for fixed vs. variable amounts of reward. *Psychon. Sci.* 4: 193–194.

Staddon JER and Motheral S (1978) On matching and maximizing in operant choice experiments. *Psychol. Rev.* 85: 436–444.

Stubbs DA (1968) The discrimination of stimulus duration by pigeons. *J. Exp. Anal. Behav.* 11: 223–238.

Stubbs DA, Dreyfus LR, Fetterman JG, Boynton DM, Locklin N, and Smith LD (1994) Duration comparison: Relative stimulus differences, stimulus age and stimulus predictiveness. *J. Exp. Anal. Behav.* 62: 15–32.

Stuphin G, Byrne T, and Poling A (1998) Response acquisition with delayed reinforcement: A comparison of two-lever procedure. *J. Exp. Anal. Behav.* 69: 17–28.

Sugrue LP, Corrado GS, and Newsome WT (2004) Matching behavior and the representation of value in the parietal cortex. *Science* 304: 1782–1787.

Taylor R and Davison M (1983) Sensitivity to reinforcement in concurrent arithmetic and exponential schedules. *J. Exp. Anal. Behav.* 39: 191–198.

Thompson T and Bloom W (1966) Aggressive behavior and extinction-induced response rate increase. *Psychon. Sci.* 5: 335–336.

Thorndike EL (1898) Animal intelligence: An experimental study of the associative processes in animals. *Psychol. Mono.* 2: 108.

Timberlake W and Allison J (1974) Response deprivation: An empirical approach to instrumental performance. *Psychol. Rev.* 81: 146–164.

Timberlake W and Grant GA (1975) Autoshaping in rats to the presentation of another rat predicting food. *Science* 190: 690–692.

Todorov JC, de Olivera Castro JM, Hanna ES, Bittencourt de Sa MC, and Barreto MQ (1983) Choice, experience and the generalized matching law. *J. Exp. Anal. Behav.* 40: 99–111.

Trevett AJ, Davison MC, and Williams RJ (1972) Performance in concurrent interval schedules. *J. Exp. Anal. Behav.* 17: 369–374.

Wearden JH (1999) "Beyond the fields we know...". Exploring and developing scalar timing theory. *Behav. Processes* 45: 3–21.

Wearden JH and Burgess LS (1982) Matching since Baum (1979). *J. Exp. Anal. Behav.* 38: 339–348.

Williams BA (1999) Associative competition in operant conditioning: Blocking the response-reinforcer association. *Psychon. Bull. Rev.* 6: 618–623.

Williams BA and Bell MC (1999) Preference after training with differential delays. *J. Exp. Anal. Behav.* 71: 45–55.

Williams DR and Williams H (1969) Automaintenance in the pigeon: Sustained pecking despite contingent non-reinforcement. *J. Exp. Anal. Behav.* 12: 511–520.

Woodruff G, Connor N, Gamzu E, and Williams DR (1977) Associative interaction: Joint control of key-pecking by stimulus-reinforcer and response-reinforcer relationships. *J. Exp. Anal. Behav.* 28: 133–144.

Wynne CDL and Staddon JER (1988) Typical delay determines waiting time on periodic food-schedules: Static and dynamic tests. *J. Exp. Anal. Behav.* 50: 197–210.

Yoburn BC and Cohen PS (1979) Assessment of attack and drinking in the White King pigeons on response-independent food schedules. *J. Exp. Anal. Behav.* 31: 91–101.

Zeiler MD and Powell DG (1994) Temporal control in fixed-interval schedules. *J. Exp. Anal. Behav.* 61: 1–9.

1.07 Perceptual Learning

G. Hall, University of York, York, UK

1.07.1 Introduction

It is not the aim of this chapter to provide a review of all the work that has been published in recent years under the heading of perceptual learning. The aim is more specific and is guided in part by theoretical considerations; it is to set perceptual learning in the context of what we know about learning more generally – to assess the extent to which the phenomena of perceptual learning can be explained in terms of known learning processes, to identify aspects of perceptual learning that cannot be explained in this way, and to attempt to outline the nature of any new learning process that may be required.

Nonetheless, the first major section of the chapter will offer a selective review of what may be considered to be the most important recent (and some not-so-recent) experimental findings. This is necessary not only to provide the grist for the explanatory mill of later sections, but also to allow us to define the field. As we shall see, the range of phenomena that have been studied under the heading of perceptual learning is exceedingly broad. However, it is possible to discern a set of important issues that is common to most of them and that constitute the core features of perceptual learning. The attempt to explain – to understand the psychological mechanisms responsible for – these core features is dealt with in the next two major sections of the chapter. The first of these deals with the application of the principles of associative learning theory to perceptual learning effects; the second is concerned with the role of nonassociative (principally attentional) learning processes.

1.07.2 Phenomena

All the studies to be described in this section have been regarded, by their authors or by later commentators, as involving perceptual learning. The variety is impressive. All major sensory systems have been subject to study; vision perhaps predominates, but there are also many studies of hearing, touch, olfaction, and taste. The stimuli used have varied, from the apparently simple (e.g., a touch with a pointer), to the undeniably complex (e.g., pictures of human faces). The stimuli used have often been difficult to discriminate from one another – for simple stimuli because they are chosen to lie close together on the dimension of difference; for complex stimuli, largely because of the presence of a host of irrelevant, nondistinguishing features in each of the displays. But perceptual learning has also been investigated in experiments using stimuli that, on the face of things, seem readily discriminable one from another – one of the earliest and most influential studies in nonhuman animals (Gibson and Walk, 1959) looked at the effects of training with two simple geometrical shapes, a triangle and a circle. This example serves to make the further point that relevant phenomena have been studied in a range of species – our own species is best fitted for psychophysics, but experiments on laboratory animals have some advantages when it comes to investigating basic mechanisms of learning. Finally, although all the work to be considered concerns the effect of experience with stimuli on the subject's subsequent response to them, the exact form of the experience given has been varied – notably some experimenters have been concerned with the effects produced by mere exposure to stimuli, whereas others have given explicit training with feedback (also called knowledge of results, or reinforcement).

In an attempt to impose some order on this apparent chaos, the sample of experimental work reviewed next is organized under a set of convenient headings. It will be evident, however, that these do not form exclusive categories and that many of the experiments described could legitimately be placed under more than one of the headings (*See* Chapters 1.08, 1.13).

1.07.2.1   Simple Sensory Thresholds

The study of perceptual learning appeared early in the history of experimental psychology. No sooner had psychophysics been established as a coherent enterprise than its proponents began to study the effects of experience on the sensory threshold measures that were one of its primary concerns. In 1859 A. W. Volkmann (Fechner's brother-in-law; Woodworth and Schlosberg, 1954) published a study of the effects of practice on the two-point tactile threshold (Volkmann, 1859). He found that with practice, the ability of a subject to make the discrimination – two points or one – was dramatically increased; that after a hundred or so trials, the minimum distance required for a judgment of two points was reduced by about half. The effect was limited to the general area of skin on which the stimuli had been applied, except that positive transfer was observed when the test was carried out on the equivalent region of the other hand or arm.

We can say straightaway, on the basis of these results, that the conventional title for studies of this sort is potentially misleading. Although the stimulus

may be simple, the mechanism responsible for the change in threshold is not. The fact that training failed to transfer to an adjacent patch of skin on the same arm indicates that the improvement is not a consequence of some general learning process (such as might result simply from familiarization with the procedure). But the fact that it did transfer to the other limb indicates that it is not a consequence of some change in the particular receptors that were stimulated in training – a more central mechanism must be involved.

Modern studies of difference thresholds have confirmed, for a range of stimuli, the essence of Volkmann's (1858) findings. Practice at the task (usually some version of a two-alternative forced-choice task in which the subject is presented briefly with two events, one after the other, and has to say whether they are the same or different) will produce a reduction in the magnitude of the difference that can be reliably detected. This is true for auditory frequency (e.g., Demany, 1985), for the orientation of visually presented lines (Shiu and Pashler, 1992), for hyperacuity (the ability to judge whether or not two line segments are colinear, e.g., McKee and Westheimer, 1978), for complex sinusoidal gratings (Fiorentini and Berardi, 1980), for the direction of motion of an array of moving dots (Ball and Sekuler, 1982; Liu and Weinshull, 2000), for the discrimination of visual texture (Karni and Sagi, 1991), and for many other tasks (see Fahle and Poggio, 2002). In most of these studies, the subjects were given feedback during training, but its role in producing the effect is unclear. Shiu and Pashler (1992) included subjects given no feedback, and these showed no within-session improvement, but this procedure was still capable of producing learning, as the subjects showed an improvement from one training session to the next.

As for Volkmann, the extent to which the effects of training transfer to other stimuli has been a focus of interest for modern experimenters. The intention has been to identify the stage in the perceptual system at which the training has had its effects – for instance, training that produces effects specific to the area of the visual field to which the stimuli were presented points to processes occurring at an early stage in the visual system, where retinotopic organization is still maintained. And, as was true for Volkmann's study, the pattern of transfer has turned out to be far from simple. For most of the visual tasks described, a degree of retinal specificity has been obtained, with performance falling to the starting level when the stimuli were presented in a different retinal location. But this does not mean that no transfer occurred – both Liu and Weinshull (2000) and Shiu and Pashler (1992) found that the new task was learned more rapidly than the original. And Ahissar and Hochstein (1997), using a version of the texture discrimination task of Karni and Sagi (1991), found transfer to a new retinal location when the initial training had been given on an easy version of the task (Liu and Weinshull, 2000, obtained a similar result for direction of motion). In other cases, the effect of training has proved specific to the particular stimuli used, but not to the receptors stimulated. Demany and Semal (2002) found that the effects of auditory training transferred readily to the other ear but not to a new discrimination involving a different frequency range (see also Amitay et al., 2005). And to return to the topic of tactile discrimination with which we began, Sathian and Zangaladze (1997) have demonstrated that the effects of training on a discrimination of the roughness of a pattern of ridges will transfer to a finger other than that used in training, but not to a new task in which the orientation of the pattern must be judged. The only conclusion justified by these observations at this stage is that although practice can facilitate performance on these simple discriminations, it would be foolish to conclude that these examples of a perceptual learning effect are to be explained solely in terms of processes occurring very early in the sensory/perceptual processing system.

1.07.2.2 More Complex Stimuli

In a study directly inspired by those described in the previous section, Furmanski and Engel (2000) looked for a perceptual learning effect with more complex visual stimuli. These were degraded pictures of everyday objects (e.g., a telephone, a pencil sharpener; see **Figure 1**) presented very briefly. The subjects had to name the object and were told if they were right or wrong. Initially performance was poor, but training (800 trials a day over several days) produced a sizable reduction in threshold (in the exposure duration necessary for correct identification). This effect was specific to the pictures presented in training, but not to retinal location – transfer was good when the size of the image was changed. Enhanced discrimination when the stimulus set is familiar appears to be a quite general phenomenon. An example for a very different procedure (and species) is provided by Todd and Mackintosh (1990). Their subjects, pigeons, were presented with 20 pictorial slides in a training

Figure 1 Two of the pictures of objects used by Furmanski and Engel (2000). To render discrimination difficult, the contrast was reduced to 12.5%, and each presentation was followed by the mask shown at the bottom of the figure. Used with permission.

session, each being presented twice, in random order. They were rewarded for pecking at the first but not at the second presentation. The pigeons learned this discrimination, but did so less well when a new set of pictures was used each session than when the same set was used throughout. This result – better performance on a judgment of relative recency than of absolute novelty – may seem surprising, but it makes sense if we accept that prolonged experience with a given set of pictures will enhance the subject's ability to discriminate among them.

Intriguing as the examples just cited may be, popular interest in the phenomenon of perceptual learning is most readily evoked by description of the special skills shown by experts in dealing with even more complex stimuli – the experienced radiographer who can detect a tumor on an x-ray where the rest of us see only a meaningless blur (Myles-Worsley et al., 1988) or the chicken sexer who can make a determination after inspecting the pinhead-sized genital eminence of the day-old chick for less than 0.5 s (Biederman and Shiffrar, 1987). These are abilities acquired through experience. Knowledge of results may play a role in this (if only because the chicken sexer will soon hear about it if a large proportion of the hens turn out to be cocks), and often there will be explicit training in which an established expert instructs the novice in what to look for (see Biederman and Shiffrar, 1987). And however exotic these specialized skills may seem, there are certain areas in which, even in the absence of explicit instruction, almost all of us have acquired the status of experts – we are all of us experts in dealing with the visual cues responsible for face recognition and the auditory cues underlying our native language.

Despite occasional embarrassing mistakes, our ability to discriminate among people, largely on the basis of their facial characteristics, is impressive. That this ability depends on experience is indicated by the fact that children are less good at it than adults (see Chung and Thomson, 1995). Further evidence comes from the so-called own-race effect – superior discrimination when the faces belong to individuals from our own racial group (Malpass and Kravitz, 1969). This effect depends on the fact that we have (usually) had much more experience of such faces – the magnitude of the effect is much reduced in people who have had extensive interaction with races other than their own (Chiroro and Valentine, 1995). What might be thought as a parallel, own-language effect describes our ability to discriminate the speech sounds of our native language. Native English speakers readily distinguish (on the basis of differences in the third formant) between the phonemes /r/ and /l/, a task that native speakers of Japanese find exceedingly difficult (e.g., Goto, 1971). Japanese speakers, on the other hand, can make distinctions (according to changes in the second formant) within the category of sounds that English speakers regard as all being examples of /r/ (Iverson et al., 2003). Explicit training, in which Japanese subjects were given feedback after being required to distinguish between word pairs such as *lock* and *rock*, has been shown to enhance their discriminative ability (Iverson et al., 2005).

The examples discussed so far in this section have involved training in which feedback has been given;

that is, the subjects have been told that their identification of a stimulus has been right or wrong. (This is explicitly arranged in most of the experimental studies, but something equivalent will occur in the natural environment as we learn the discriminations necessary for language or for the recognition of faces.) But perceptual learning effects can be obtained without such feedback, as a result of mere exposure to the stimuli (when this is arranged appropriately). Lavis and Mitchell (2006) required people to discriminate between pairs of checkerboards of the sort shown in **Figure 2**. When they are first presented with the one checkerboard followed, after a short interval, by another, people are poor at answering the question: Same or different? But performance was much enhanced by mere preexposure to the displays when this was organized such that the different stimuli were presented in alternation. Interestingly, preexposure, consisting of a block of trials with one stimulus followed by a block of trials with the other, was much less effective in enhancing subsequent discrimination. This outcome (to be discussed in detail later) is of interest as it accords with the influential analysis of perceptual learning offered by Gibson (1969), who emphasized the role of stimulus comparison in producing the effect (we may assume alternating preexposure is likely to foster the processes involved in comparison).

1.07.2.3 Categorization

The auditory discrimination described earlier is one that involves categorization; that is, faced with a range of different stimuli, the native English speaker learns to put instances of one set (which will differ

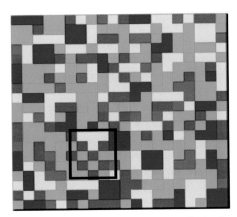 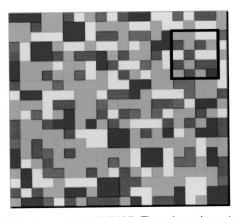

Figure 2 Examples of the colored checkerboard stimuli used by Lavis and Mitchell (2006). The unique elements are indicated (for the purposes of illustration only) by the black squares. Images courtesy of Y. Lavis.

among themselves in some respects) in one category (meriting /r/) and instances of another set in a different category (meriting /l/). The same is true of some of the visual tasks – one male chick will differ from another, but the experienced chicken sexer puts them all in the same category. An experimental demonstration of how such an ability can be acquired through experience comes from a study of face recognition by Quinn et al. (1999). In this experiment, the faces were pictures not of people, but of cats, and the participant's task was to sort them into two categories, male and female. The discrimination was difficult – initial performance was at chance level – but reinforced training with a subset of the pictures, those most easily identified as male or female, produced positive transfer to the ability to categorize other pictures.

Successful performance on a categorization task such as that used by Quinn et al. (1999) may seem to involve a reversal of the sort of perceptual learning effect that we have been concerned with so far – although discrimination between male and female is enhanced, the subjects appear to be less sensitive to differences among individuals that fall into a given category. But whether this is really the case requires explicit investigation. It is quite possible that the within-category discrimination was also enhanced – that, had they been asked, the trained subjects would have been better able to distinguish between Lucky and Widget, while still categorizing both as male. This is certainly true of human faces – we have no trouble in telling Ann from Zoe, and Andrew from Zach, while still distinguishing male from female.

The issue has been investigated experimentally, using complex artificial stimuli, by McLaren et al. (1994); see also McLaren, 1997). The stimuli used were based on the checkerboards shown in **Figure 3**.

Figure 3 Checkerboard stimuli used by McLaren et al. (1994). Those shown were the prototypes. Discrimination was between exemplars, produced by changing a proportion of the elements of each prototype from black to white, or vice versa. Image courtesy of I. McLaren.

Changing a proportion of the elements from black to white, or vice versa, produced two sets of exemplars of these prototypes. Training consisted of a categorization task in which subjects learned to assign exemplars to type 1 or to type 2. In the test, two stimuli were presented side by side, and the subjects were reinforced for reliably choosing one rather than the other. They proved to be very good at this discrimination when the two stimuli were the original prototypes and also when the test stimuli were novel exemplars of these prototypes not used in the original training. But although the effect of preexposure was less profound in this case, the participants were also at an advantage when required to discriminate between two exemplars drawn from the same category. These effects are not confined to our own species. Aitken et al. (1996), using similar stimuli, generated essentially the same pattern of result in an experiment that used pigeons as the subjects.

1.07.2.4 Taste and Smell

Unusually among psychologists, students of perceptual learning have paid almost as much attention to the chemical senses as to vision and hearing. Perhaps this derives in part from the fact that some of the most dramatic examples of acquired perceptual skills are found in these modalities. Foremost among these are the well-documented achievements of expert wine tasters (e.g., Soloman, 1990), but who can forget William James's description of "the blind-deaf mute ... Julia Brace [who] is said to have been employed in the Hartford Asylum to sort the linen of its multitudinous inmates, after it came from the wash, by her wonderfully educated sense of smell" (James, 1890, pp. 509–510).

These are obviously very special cases, but evidence that an approach to skills of this sort can be established in any of us comes from experimental studies. Thus, Peron and Allen (1988) found that novice beer drinkers, who were initially unable to tell one brand from another, became able to do so after training in which they simply sampled a range of beers and reflected on the flavor qualities that came to mind. (Training with the specialist vocabulary of master brewers conveyed no special advantage; see also Melcher and Schooler, 1996.) Rabin (1988), who asked subjects to make same/different judgments after sniffing two unusual odors, found that discrimination was enhanced when the subjects had been given prior exposure to the odors (and in this case, training in which a distinctive label was attached to each odor during preexposure was found to help). Preexposure is not always beneficial, however. Stevenson (2001) gave training in which his subjects sniffed two odor mixtures (call them AX and BY). Subsequent discrimination between components of separate pairs (e.g., A vs. B) was good, but discrimination between components of a compound (e.g., A vs. X) was poor.

Studies of perceptual learning using animal subjects have made extensive use of tastes – adding a flavor to the drinking water of a thirsty rat ensures that the animal receives full exposure to the relevant stimulus, and the flavor-aversion conditioning technique provides an effective way of assessing discrimination. **Figure 4** shows the results of one study (by Symonds and Hall, 1995, Experiment 1) that made use of this procedure. All the rats received a test phase consisting of aversion conditioning with flavor A, followed by a test with flavor B (A and B were solutions of salt and sugar, rendered more similar by the addition of the sour taste of acid to each). In rats given no previous experience of the flavors (group W in the figure), the aversion conditioned to A generalized readily to B; that is, they failed to discriminate between A and B. The same was true of rats given prior exposure either to A or to B. But rats given prior exposure consisting of alternating presentations of A and B (group A/B in the figure) showed poor generalization (i.e., an enhanced ability to discriminate). As in the experiments by Lavis and Mitchell (2006), described earlier, this alternating

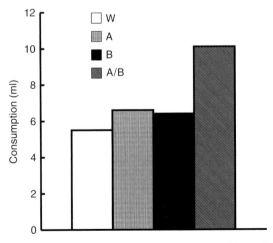

Figure 4 Group mean scores for consumption of flavor B, after aversion conditioning with flavor in the experiment by Symonds and Hall (1995). Before conditioning, different groups had received exposure to A, to B, to both (A/B), or just to plain water (W).

arrangement turned out to be critical. A subsequent study (Symonds and Hall, 1995, Experiment 3) showed that preexposure consisting of a block of A trials followed by a block of B trials (or vice versa) did not produce the same enhancement. It is interesting to note that closely parallel effects have been obtained with human subjects given initial training in which they tasted the compound flavors saline-lemon and sucrose-lemon either on alternating trials or on separate blocks of trials. Subsequent same/different judgments were found to be more accurate in those given the alternating schedule during preexposure (Dwyer et al., 2004).

1.07.2.5 Acquired Distinctiveness

The experiments discussed so far have commonly used a procedure in which the subjects received explicit discrimination training, with feedback or knowledge of results being given. But (as the authors of several of these studies have noted), it can often be difficult to be sure of the source of the improved discriminative performance that is obtained in these conditions. Is there a change in the way in which the stimuli are being perceived, or is the learning occurring at a later stage in the sequence of processes that connect input to response? Transfer studies in which the stimuli are presented to a different set of receptors (e.g., at a different retinal location) constitute one way of addressing this issue. It is usually assumed that effects that fail to transfer cannot be a consequence of some general learning process, but must be specific to the stimuli used in training. An alternative strategy is to retain the original stimuli, but to require the subjects to learn some new discrimination on the basis of them. In this case, we are looking for positive transfer. Such transfer could not be based on knowledge of general task requirements (these having been changed) but must be a consequence of some learned change in the properties of the stimuli.

This experimental design was first introduced in the classic study of animal discrimination learning reported by Lawrence (1949). In outline, rats were trained initially on a food-rewarded choice discrimination between black and white. They were then shifted to a new task involving the same cues but with a different response requirement – when given two black cues, they were required to choose the left (for example), and when given two white cues to choose the right. The responses acquired in the first stage (e.g., to approach black and avoid white) will be irrelevant in this new task; nonetheless, Lawrence found positive transfer from stage 1 to stage 2, transfer, he said, that must depend on something that has been learned about the stimuli. The effect has been called the acquired distinctiveness of cues, the implication being that the initial training in which black and white were associated with different responses and different outcomes had rendered those stimuli more distinguishable. The idea that training in which cues are associated with differing outcomes will enhance their subsequent discriminability goes back at least as far as James (1890).

Lawrence's (1949) study was followed by a rush of similar transfer-of-training experiments, some with animal subjects (reviewed by Sutherland and Mackintosh, 1971) and many with human participants. The latter, for the most part, concentrated on a procedure in which participants learned to apply verbal labels in the first stage of training followed by a discrimination involving overt motor responses to the same stimuli in the second stage. It was usually found (see Hall, 1991, for a review) that stage-1 training facilitated learning of the second task, although whether or not this effect was a consequence of changes in the distinctiveness of the cues is open to debate. In many of the classic experiments (e.g., Battig, 1956; Gagné and Baker, 1950; Holton and Goss, 1956), comparison was made with a control condition given no stage-1 training, raising the possibility that the advantage shown by the experimental condition simply reflected some general facilitatory effect produced by the first stage of training. What is needed is to compare the effects of initial discrimination training with those of some control stage-1 procedure that will be equally effective in producing general transfer effects but that does not involve the consistent stimulus-outcome associations characteristic of the experimental condition.

One strategy, illustrated in a study by Goldstone (1994), is to use compound stimuli. In Goldstone's experiment, the stimuli were squares, differing in size and brightness. One aspect of the stimuli (e.g., their size) was irrelevant to the discrimination (based, e.g., on brightness) trained in stage 1. Thus, when it came to the test phase (involving either a further brightness discrimination or one based on shape), all subjects were familiar with the stimuli and had received discriminative pretraining. It was found that the test task was performed more readily by those subjects for whom the same dimension (brightness, in this example) was relevant in both stages. Analogous effects, which have been interpreted as reflecting an acquired enhancement of the distinctiveness of an entire

dimension of stimulus variation, have been obtained in studies of animal discrimination learning (see, e.g., Mackintosh and Little, 1969).

An alternative strategy (also based on a design successfully used with animal subjects; see Bonardi et al., 1993) is presented schematically in **Table 1**. (At this point, we are concerned only with the first two stages shown in the table; the implications of Stage 3 will be taken up later). In this example, which comes from an experiment by Hall et al. (2003), people received stage-1 training with four different stimuli, four different geometrical shapes (A–D in the table). Two, A and B, were followed by one outcome (presentation of a red rectangle); two (C and D) by another outcome (a green rectangle). No overt response was required at this stage. Stage 2 consisted of a discrimination learning task in which the subjects had to learn to make one motor response rather than another to each of the shapes. Performance was good when the subjects were required to make different responses to stimuli that had been associated with different outcomes in Stage 1 (the consistent condition of the table) but was relatively poor in the inconsistent condition, when they had to make the same responses to shapes previously associated with different outcomes. Positive transfer in the consistent condition is what would be expected if cues associated with different outcomes had acquired distinctiveness.

It should be noted that with this experimental design (as with most others in this area; see Hall,

Table 1 Experimental design used by Hall et al. (2003)

Stage 1	Stage 2	Stage 3
Group Consistent		
A → red	A → left	
B → red	B → left	red → left/right?
C → green	C → right	green → left/right?
D → green	D → right	
Group Inconsistent		
A → red	A → left	
B → red	B → right	red → left/right?
C → green	C → left	green → left/right?
D → green	D → right	

Note: A, B, C, and D represent visual stimuli presented on a computer monitor; red and green refer to colored rectangles. Left and right refer to keyboard response required (left = backslash; right = forward slash). Feedback was given after responses in Stage 2. All subjects in a given group received all types of trial listed under a given stage of training. Source of data: Hall G, Mitchell C, Graham S, and Lavis Y (2003) Acquired equivalence and distinctiveness in human discrimination learning: Evidence for associative mediation. *J. Exp. Psychol. Gen.* 132: 266–276.

1991), it is possible that the effect derives, in whole or in part, from negative transfer in the inconsistent condition – that associating cues with the same outcome renders them less distinctive (an effect referred to as acquired equivalence; Miller and Dollard, 1941). But it should also be noted that acquired equivalence in itself constitutes an example of perceptual learning, one that is worth our attention. Our topic is how experience can change the way in which things are perceived. Although in almost all the examples given so far, the change has been for the better (that is, discriminability has been enhanced by experience) there is no reason why this should always be the case, and our analysis of the phenomenon would be incomplete if it failed to encompass acquired reductions in discriminability.

1.07.3 Theoretical Issues

In all the experiments described earlier, the test task requires the subject to discriminate between two similar stimuli. The situation is presented schematically in **Figure 5**. Each circle represents the set of features or elements that define or constitute a particular stimulus, A or B. Each stimulus will have a set of unique features that are not found in the other (and these are represented by the areas containing the elements labeled a and b). The fact that A and B are similar is represented by the overlap – the area marked containing the c elements designates a set of features that they hold in common. Successful discrimination is evident when the subject shows the ability to make one response to A (i.e., ac) and a different response to B (bc). It follows that the job of a theory of perceptual learning is that of explaining

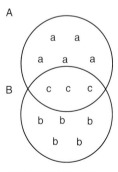

Figure 5 Each circle represents a stimulus (A or B) that is made up of a set of features (or elements). Some features are unique to a given stimulus (the a elements for A; the b elements for B); other features (c) are held in common and thus fall into the area of overlap of A and B.

how experience or training allows behavior to come to be controlled by the unique features (a and b), rather than by the common features (c). The behavior in question may be a gross overt movement, as when a rat approaches one stimulus object and avoids another; or it might be as minor as the verbal response of "higher" from a human participant presented with one of a pair of tones.

The scheme shown in **Figure 5** can be applied quite generally. It may need slight modification when the stimuli are drawn from a simple continuum, such as tonal frequency – here a given tone might be regarded as consisting of the elements a, b, c, d (say); its neighbor by the elements b, c, d, e; its neighbor by the elements c, d, e, f; and so on – but the principle remains the same; discrimination between adjacent (similar) tones requires control by the unique elements that distinguish between stimuli.

This characterization prompts an attempt at a definition of perceptual learning. It is the learning process (or processes) that increases the effectiveness of unique stimulus elements and/or reduces that of common stimulus elements, thus facilitating discrimination between similar stimuli. (Although this will serve for almost all the cases discussed in the previous section, we should note the possibility of instances in which training reduces discriminability. For these we must assume that the effectiveness of common elements is increased, that of the unique elements is reduced, or both; *See* Chapter 1.08 for configural processing).

This definition may allow us to rule out, as instances of true perceptual learning, some of the processes that result in improved performance during practice on a discrimination task. It is often found, for instance, that performance on even the simplest difference threshold task can show a dramatic improvement on the early trials, and this improvement could well be a consequence of the participant learning to deal with the requirements of the procedure. If, for example, the subject is initially a little unclear as to which button to press for the high tone and which for the low tone, practice will establish the relevant associations and remove one obstacle to accurate performance – but this improvement would not be a consequence of a change in the effectiveness of the unique or common features of the stimuli and thus would not count as perceptual learning.

This is not to say, however, that we would want to dismiss what some (e.g., Liu and Weinshull, 2000) have called 'cognitive' learning, as a possible mechanism of perceptual learning. For example, McLaren and Mackintosh (2000) suggest that we should exclude from consideration cases in which participants, instructed to look for differences between stimuli, learn to focus on aspects that enable them to solve the task required of them. But surely a strategy as simple as learning to attend to or fixate on a particular part of a visual display deserves to be regarded as a mechanism of perceptual learning if it serves to increase the effectiveness of unique features (which happen to be located at a particular point in space). Again, Bruce and Burton (2002), discussing the discrimination of faces, question the extent to which enhanced discrimination depends on the acquisition of verbal labels for the different faces as opposed to reflecting (true) perceptual learning. But the distinction may not be a useful one. It has long been thought (e.g., James, 1890) that the acquisition of associates, such as verbal labels, might be a way of increasing the range and number of distinctive features activated by the presentation of a given stimulus; if this is so, the consequent improvement in discrimination becomes an example of perceptual learning under our definition.

The general point is that our proposed definition is silent as to the nature of the learning processes involved. The approach taken here contrasts with that sometimes taken by other students of perceptual learning. For example, Fahle and Poggio (2002) began their survey of the topic by ruling out, by means of their definition of perceptual learning, a number of possibilities that we would want to consider. Perceptual learning, they say, is independent from conscious experience and leads to implicit memory; it is not declarative, as it does not consist of consciously memorized facts or events; it is not associative, as it does not bind things together, and does not rely on the mechanisms of classical and operant conditioning; it differs from other forms of learning in that it principally involves functional and anatomical changes in primary sensory cortex. It may well be that some of the examples of enhanced discrimination that were described earlier in this chapter are a consequence of the type of learning envisaged by Fahle and Poggio (and we will try to identify them in subsequent sections of the chapter). But declining to subscribe to such a restrictive definition leaves us free to consider a range of other possible mechanisms, including several (such as various cognitive, associative, and attentional learning processes) that have been well studied in other contexts. We begin by considering the extent

to which the associative analysis of learning can supply an explanation for perceptual learning phenomena.

1.07.4 The Role of Associative Processes

It may seem odd to give pride of place to a learning process that some have emphatically asserted is not responsible for perceptual learning effects; thus Gibson and Levin (1975, p. 23) wrote: "this simple and ancient notion does not work for perceptual learning, because what is learned [in perceptual learning] is not addition of something but rather extraction of something." There are, however, at least two good reasons for doing so. First, associative learning theory, in its modern form (see, e.g., Wagner, 1981; Mackintosh, 1983), provides by far the best worked out and most comprehensive account of basic learning mechanisms, and it seems a sensible first step to attempt to explain some (supposedly) new form of learning in terms of what we already know about learning more generally. Second, one of the earliest attempts to explain an instance of perceptual learning was, in fact, precisely in terms of the notion that it depended on the associative 'addition of something.'

1.07.4.1 Acquired Distinctiveness and Acquired Equivalence

Figure 6 (top part) presents a schematic version of the associative account offered by James (1890) for the acquired distinctiveness of cues. Recall that in this procedure, discrimination training, in which the cues are followed by different outcomes, enhances their subsequent discriminability. **Figure 6** shows the associations assumed to be formed when two similar cues (A and B) have been given training in which each has become linked to a different associate (X and Y); the associates are less similar (they share few common features) than are A and B. Discrimination between A and B prior to training will be difficult as they share many common elements. But the formation of the associative links means that presentation of A will produce associative activation of the representation of X, and presentation of B will associatively activate Y. As a result, discrimination between A and B will be enhanced because the proportion of common features present in the overall patterns of activation produced by these stimuli will

Acquired distinctiveness

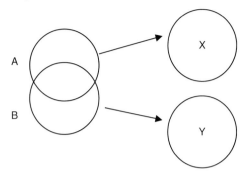

Acquired equivalence

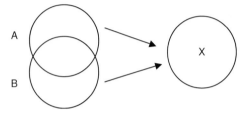

Figure 6 Associative structures in acquired distinctiveness and acquired equivalence. The overlapping circles represent two similar stimuli, A and B (see Figure 5); arrows represent associative links. In the acquired distinctiveness case, A and B have formed associations with quite different stimuli (X and Y). In the acquired equivalence case, both have become associated with the same stimulus.

be low, given the distinctiveness of their associates. The lower part of **Figure 6** shows the situation for the acquired equivalence procedure in which the two stimuli are given the same associate. Here the proportion of common elements is increased, and discriminability should go down. James focused on the case in which the associates were distinctive names, but the analysis applies (and the effect is found) when other events are used (as in experiments with animal subjects, or that presented in **Table 1**).

That stimuli can acquire new, and potentially distinctive, properties by associative means is nicely demonstrated by studies of odor perception. It has been noted that an odor such as vanilla is often described as smelling sweet, even though it is in itself tasteless. The suggestion that this quality is acquired as a result of associative learning (vanilla is often present in sweet foods) is supported by the results of a study by Stevenson et al. (1998), who gave subjects presentations of a novel odor (e.g., lychee) along with a sweet taste. Their subjects started to describe lychee as smelling sweet, a phenomenon that Stevenson et al. referred to as learned

synesthesia. (Parallel effects have also been found with sour and bitter tastes.)

Whether associations of this sort are actually responsible for acquired distinctiveness effects is another matter. Gibson (1969), in her influential discussion of the topic, argued that although associations might indeed be formed during training designed to establish acquired distinctiveness, they did not provide the mechanism for the effect. Rather, the role of discrimination training was simply to ensure that the subjects concentrated on the stimuli, noting their similarities and differences, with the result that there was an increase in the perceptual effectiveness of (and attention paid to) their intrinsic distinctive features. This is what was meant by the phrase 'extraction of something,' rather than 'addition of something.' The evidence that is currently available to us does not allow a clear choice between the alternatives, but suggests, rather, that both processes may play a role.

Evidence that the associations formed during initial training can influence subsequent discrimination performance comes from the experiment by Hall et al. (2003), outlined in **Table 1**. Why, in Stage 2, did subjects in the inconsistent condition find it difficult to assign different responses to cues (such as A and B) that had shared a common associate (red) in Stage 1? According to the associative theory, this is because the representation of red was activated by both A and B during Stage 2. When subjects learned to respond left to A, this response would come under the control both of the cue actually presented (A) and its associate (red). Small wonder, then, that they found it difficult to respond right to B, given that its associate already controlled a tendency to make a different response. For subjects in the consistent condition, on the other hand, the response tendency acquired by red on a trial with A would allow the correct response to emerge immediately when B was presented. In a final test (Stage 3 of the table), subjects were asked to choose left or right when presented with the colors used as associates in Stage 1. Those in the consistent condition made appropriate choices (choosing left for red and right for green, in our example), as would be expected if the associatively activated representations of these colors had been involved in the discrimination test of Stage 2.

A reason to think that associative processes are not wholly responsible for acquired distinctiveness effects comes from the observation that mere exposure to a pair of similar stimuli (if this is appropriately arranged – as we have seen, alternating presentations that give the opportunity for comparison to occur are particularly effective) can enhance subsequent discriminability. That is, distinctiveness can be acquired when the preexposure procedure seems to preclude the formation of links with distinctive associates. For humans, this argument may not be particularly convincing – members of this species may well provide their own associates (names or labels), no matter what the experimenter tries to arrange. But the effect is also seen with animal subjects (rats given alternating presentations of two flavors are better able subsequently to discriminate between them). If another, nonassociative, perceptual learning process is at work during mere exposure, might it not also be active when the exposure phase involves explicit discrimination training? Evidence in favor of this view comes from a study by Bonardi et al. (2005), who modified the procedure used by Hall et al. (2003) to rule out associative mediation and yet still found an acquired distinctiveness effect. Bonardi et al. concluded that the preexposure procedure had, in addition to establishing associations, modified the perceptual effectiveness of the various elements of the stimuli (specifically had enhanced the attention controlled by their distinctive features). The learning mechanisms that might be responsible for such an effect will be taken up in the final major section of this chapter, after we have considered the contribution of other associative mechanisms to perceptual learning effects.

1.07.4.2 Unitization

It has frequently been suggested (e.g., Goldstone, 2000; McLaren et al., 1989) that a process of unitization is, in part, responsible for perceptual learning effects. The idea has been expressed in a variety of different ways, but the central notion is that exposure to a complex and multifaceted stimulus will result in the formation of a unitary representation of that stimulus, in which the various features are somehow bound together. The concept has been much used in the study of complex visual perception (with its talk of object representations, face representations, and so on) but can readily be applied to other modalities (it forms the basis of the account of odor perception proposed by Stevenson and Boakes, 2003), and to seemingly simple stimuli (even a pure tone, for example, has many features – frequency, intensity, location, duration, etc).

When it comes to specifying the learning mechanism responsible for unitization, the only developed

proposal has been in terms of associative processes (see Goldstone, 1998). Presentation of a complex stimulus will, it is assumed, activate a set of units that correspond to its various constituent features. Concurrent activation of these units will lead to the formation of a network of excitatory links among them, and it is this network, in the simplest interpretation of the idea, that is taken to constitute the unitized representation. In terms of the diagram of **Figure 5**, experience of stimulus A will establish connections among all the a elements. (It will also, initially, allow the formation of a–c connections too; but because the c elements may also be activated in the absence of the a elements, when a stimulus such as B is presented, these will be weakened and eventually drop out of the picture.) A slightly more elaborate version of this analysis supposes that experience of the stimulus results in the formation of a separate configural unit (see, e.g., Pearce, 1994) that is not directly activated by any feature of the stimulus itself but that comes to receive its input from the units that correspond to those features.

The formation of a simple network of excitatory associations is enough in itself to explain a range of perceptual learning phenomena. As we have already seen, the learned synesthesia of Stevenson et al. (1998) depends on associations formed between two aspects of a compound stimulus (its taste and smell). And our difficulty in discriminating among the aspects of a previously experienced compound odor (Stevenson, 2001) can be explained in similar terms. When people have sniffed the AX compound, excitatory associations will form between A and X. Discrimination between A and X will be poor because the presentation of A will produce associative activation of the representation of X, and presentation of X will associatively activate A. It is usually assumed that the state produced by associative activation of a representation will be distinguishable from that produced by direct activation (if nothing else, the intensity of activation is likely to be less; see Hall, 1996), and accordingly, discrimination between A and X should still be possible. But the existence of association between A and X will increase the similarity of the overall patterns of activation elicited by A and X and render the task more difficult.

Further support for this interpretation of unitization comes from its ability to explain the finding that preexposure to a complex stimulus or event can enhance the ease with which that complex is subsequently learned about. An example from animal conditioning is supplied by Kiernan and Westbrook (1993), who gave rats a few minutes of exposure to a distinctive context prior to a session in which the context was paired with shock. On a subsequent test, these rats showed more evidence of learned fear in that context than did rats not given preexposure. (See also Fanselow, 1990; Bennett et al., 1996.) The only additional assumption needed to deal with this finding is that the animal's capacity to process all aspects of a complex stimulus will be limited, so that only a subset will be sampled at any one time. As the rat explores the context during preexposure, it will sample a range of contextual features, and connections will form among them. On the subsequent conditioning trial, only some of these features will be sampled, and only these will become associated with shock. A different set may be sampled on the test trial, but for animals given preexposure, the conditioned response should still be evoked, as those sampled on the test will be able to activate those that formed links with the shock during conditioning. Although presented in modern associative terminology, the central idea is essentially that popularized long ago as redintegration (by Hollingworth, 1928).

It will be apparent that the principle illustrated by this example from fear conditioning in the rat will be applicable to any case in which animals (including people) are given exposure to a stimulus containing more features than can be processed all at once. Appropriate response to a complex visual event (such as putting a name to a face) will be able to proceed more rapidly if inspection of one part of the display is able to activate representations of other features, or to activate a configural unit that is connected to the response-output mechanism. In the case of faces (and indeed other complex visual stimuli), it must be assumed that the configural unit is sensitive not just to the co-occurrence of various features but also to their spatial relationships. One of the classic findings from studies of face recognition is the inversion effect – the finding that faces are so much less well recognized when upside down; or, put another way, are especially well dealt with when they are the usual way up (Yin, 1969). This phenomenon is explained by assuming that experience of a face in the normal orientation establishes a configural unit that encodes the spatial relationships of the various features; when the face is inverted, these relationships are disrupted, and the unit will not be activated. Evidence for this interpretation comes from a study by Gauthier and Tarr (1997), who required people to learn the names of nonsense objects of the sort shown

Figure 7 Examples of the figures (referred to as Greebles) used by Gauthier and Tarr (1997) and of the names that subjects had to learn to apply to them. Used with permission.

in **Figure** 7. An inversion effect was found for these stimuli too – performance was poor when the stimuli were presented upside down – but only for people who had received extensive prior experience with the cues. The effect is specific not to faces but to complex familiar visual cues.

1.07.4.3   Associative Inhibition

McLaren et al. (1989; see also McLaren and Mackintosh, 2000) have pointed out that standard associative theory predicts that certain schedules of exposure to a pair of similar stimuli (such as A and B of **Figure** 5) will allow the formation of other associations, in addition to those considered so far. They were concerned in particular with a preexposure schedule in which A and B were presented in alternation. Gibson (1969) has argued that a process of comparison plays an important part in the enhancement of discrimination that follows exposure to similar stimuli. The exact nature of the comparison process was not specified, but it can be agreed that alternating presentations are likely to enhance its operation, making this schedule of special interest.

We have already discussed how exposure to the stimuli will allow unitization to occur, with the various elements of each stimulus becoming linked together. McLaren et al. (1989) noted that the within-stimulus links formed would include excitatory connections between common and unique elements (which we may summarize as c–a, for stimulus A, and c–b, for stimulus B). As a consequence, presentation of A would, by way of the c–a association, be able to activate the representation of the unique features of B (the b elements); similarly, presentation of B by way of the c–a link would activate the a elements. On the face of things, therefore, preexposure might be expected to hinder subsequent discrimination, as these excitatory links would render the patterns of activation produced by A and B more similar to one another. Such indeed would be the outcome but for another factor that comes into play when the alternating schedule is used – this schedule will allow the formation of inhibitory associative links. According to standard associative theory (e.g., Wagner, 1981; espoused by McLaren and Mackintosh, 2000) an inhibitory link will form between a directly activated stimulus representation and one that is activated associatively. The alternating schedule ensures that the subject experiences a sequence of trials in which a is associatively activated in the presence of b, and b is associatively activated in the presence of a. In these circumstances, inhibitory associations will form between a and b. Activation of an inhibitory link is assumed to oppose the effects of excitatory influences acting on a given representation, restricting the ability of that representation to be activated.

This analysis can supply an explanation for the results of the experiments described previously, in which discrimination was enhanced by intermixed preexposure (compared to a control condition in which the stimuli were presented in separate blocks of trials). Consider the experiment by Lavis and Mitchell (2006). When asked to make same–different judgments about stimuli like those shown in **Figure 2**, the excitatory links formed by subjects in the control condition mean that each stimulus would tend to activate, to some degree, the unique features of the other. Presentation of A would activate a and c directly and b associatively; presentation of B would activate b and c directly and a associatively. That is, all the same units would be activated in each case, and the judgment would therefore have to be made in terms of degree (or type) of activation. For subjects given intermixed exposure, on the other hand, inhibition between a and b would mean that A would activate only a and c, and B would activate only b and c, qualitatively different patterns of activation.

The difference between intermixed and blocked preexposure schedules has also been obtained in studies of animal conditioning (e.g., Symonds and Hall, 1995; see also Bennett and Mackintosh, 1999; Mondragón and Hall, 2002; Dwyer et al., 2004), and the associative inhibition analysis applies readily to this case too. In these experiments, subjects received conditioning with stimulus A followed by a generalization test with stimulus B. The poor discrimination (good generalization) produced by blocked exposure is explained in terms of the within-stimulus excitatory links formed during preexposure; specifically when tested with B, the c–a link will allow this cue to activate a stimulus representation (a) that had acquired associative strength during conditioning with A. For the intermixed condition, on the other

hand, the inhibitory association between b and a established during preexposure would prevent activation of a on the test trial, eliminating its contribution to responding and thus reducing the degree of generalization.

The role of associative inhibition as a mechanism of perceptual learning deserves our serious attention because it provides one of the few fully worked out accounts of the processes by which stimulus comparison might have its effects. It remains to be determined, however, whether or not this theoretical possibility is, in fact, responsible for the effects observed. There is some supportive evidence from a study by Dwyer et al. (2001; see also Dwyer and Mackintosh, 2002). Rats were exposed to intermixed presentations of the compound flavors, AX and BX, where A and B represent unique flavors, and X an explicitly added common element. According to the associative principles outlined earlier, alternating presentations of AX and BX should establish inhibition between A and B (just as alternating presentations of ac and bc establish inhibition between a and b). Dwyer et al. found that after extensive intermixed exposure, animals were retarded in learning an excitatory association between A and B – what would be expected if the prior training had established inhibitory associations between these cues. It seems likely that associative inhibition plays a role in the perceptual learning effect under these training conditions.

It should be noted, however, that this example of perceptual learning (better discrimination after intermixed than after blocked preexposure) can be obtained in the absence of associative inhibition. Inhibitory learning can take many trials to develop (Dwyer et al., 2001, gave extensive initial training), but the perceptual learning effect can be obtained after just a few preexposure trials, well before there is any evidence of inhibition between A and B (Artigas et al., 2006). What is more, the effect can be observed when the training procedure is modified so as to preclude the formation of inhibitory links. **Table 2** (Experiment 1) shows the design of an experiment (Blair and Hall, 2003, Experiment 1a) devised to demonstrate the basic effect using a within-subject design and a conditioning procedure. The subjects (rats) received intermixed preexposure to the compound stimuli AX and BX and a separate block of trials with CX. A response subsequently conditioned to AX was found to generalize less readily to BX (the stimulus presented intermixed with AX during preexposure) than to the control stimulus CX. This result in itself is compatible with the suggestion that the

Table 2   Experimental designs used to investigate the effects of preexposure on flavor discrimination in rats

	Preexposure	Conditioning	Test
Experiment 1	AX/BX _ CX	AX +	BX and CX
Experiment 2	AX/BX _ CX	X +	BX and CX
Experiment 3	X/BX _ CX	AX +	BX and CX
Experiment 4	AX/BX _ CX	—	B+ or C+

Note: A, B, C represent flavors that could be presented in compound with flavor X. In preexposure, AX (or X, in Experiment 3) was presented in alternation with BX. The CX compound was presented in a separate block of trials. In the conditioning phase of experiments 1–3 and the test phase of Experiment 4, flavors were presented along with (+) an aversive reinforcer. The test phase measured the extent of the aversion shown to the test stimuli (a generalized aversion in the case of experiments 1–3). Experiments 1 and 2 were fully reported by Blair CAJ and Hall G (2003) Perceptual learning in flavor aversion: Evidence for learned changes in stimulus effectiveness. *J. Exp. Psychol. Anim. B*. 29: 39–48; Experiment 3 by Hall G, Blair CAJ, and Artigas AA (2006) Associative activation of stimulus representations restores lost salience: Implications for perceptual learning. *J. Exp. Psychol. Anim. B*. 32: 145–155; and Experiment 4 by Blair CAJ, Wilkinson A, and Hall G (2004) Assessments of changes in the effective salience of stimulus elements as a result of stimulus preexposure. *J. Exp. Psychol. Anim. B*. 30: 317–324.

presence of B in the test inhibits activation of the representation of the (conditioned) A element. But this argument cannot apply to the modified design shown as Experiment 2 in the table (Blair and Hall, Experiment 5a). Here the same result was found (less generalization to BX than to CX) despite the fact that conditioning was given to the X element alone. If A has not been conditioned, then any ability that B might have to inhibit activation of the A representation would be irrelevant to the outcome of the procedure. The experiment presented as Experiment 3 in the table (Hall et al., 2006) makes the same point in a different way. Here the intermixed preexposure procedure involved alternation, not of AX and BX, but of BX and X alone. Obviously, inhibition between A and B cannot be established with this procedure. Nonetheless, conditioning to AX was still found to generalize less well to BX than to CX on the test (see also Rodriguez and Alonso, 2004).

The new results just described serve to support Gibson's (1969) suggestion that a preexposure procedure that allows comparison between two similar stimuli (such as alternating presentations of AX and BX) is particularly effective in enhancing discrimination between them. They also show that associative inhibition mechanism can supply only a partial explanation for these effects. Gibson's own interpretation was that comparison served to enhance the perceptual effectiveness of the distinguishing features of the

stimuli (A and B in this case). This notion can help explain the results produced by the experiments summarized in **Table 2**. In these experiments, performance on the generalization test will be largely determined by the response controlled by the X element, the response that was established during the conditioning phase. To the extent that the presence of another element (such as B or C) detracts from the ability of the animals to perceive stimulus X, the magnitude of the response will be reduced. It follows that if alternating preexposure enhances the perceptual effectiveness of the B element, this element will be better able to interfere with the ability of X to evoke its response on test and generalization will be restricted – the result obtained. What we need to consider now, therefore, is the mechanisms by which the perceptual effectiveness of stimuli might be modified; this issue is taken up in the next section of the chapter.

1.07.5 Attentional Learning Processes

The only learning process utilized so far has been one that results in the formation of links (excitatory or inhibitory) between the central representations of stimulus elements. Perhaps surprisingly, this notion has proved helpful in explaining some perceptual effects. But however powerful an explanatory tool this "simple and ancient notion" may be, it is not, on its own, enough to explain even simple associative learning. A number of learning theorists (e.g., Mackintosh, 1975; Pearce and Hall, 1980; McLaren and Mackintosh, 2000) have argued that the associative principle needs to be supplemented by another learning process, one that is capable of changing the properties of the stimulus representation, modulating its sensitivity to activation, for example, or modulating the readiness with which it will enter into association.

Because these theories are usually described as involving a process of attentional learning, it would be useful to clarify what is meant by attentional in his context, as the use of the term (which is really more of a chapter heading than a well-defined psychological construct) can vary widely. It is not meant to indicate a form of learning that occurs only when learners focus their attention on the task at hand (a characteristic that, in any case, would be difficult to identify in the experiments using animal subjects that will be considered shortly). Rather, it indicates a form of learning that modifies the processing that a stimulus will receive. As for the nature of the modification, two principal suggestions have been advanced. One is that experience might change the effective salience of a stimulus (making a dim light function as if it were bright or a loud noise as if it were soft) and thus modify the ability of the stimulus to command attention. The other, not necessarily alternative, suggestion is that experience might change the associability of a stimulus, the readiness with which it will be learned about. (A significant event might deserve attention, even if its salience is low.) Both of these possibilities merit the description attentional, but it will be noted that they have somewhat different implications, and where necessary, they will be distinguished in what follows.

1.07.5.1   Latent Inhibition and Associability Modulation

Prior exposure to an event that is to be used as the conditioned stimulus (CS) in a classical conditioning procedure produces a marked retardation in the subsequent rate of learning. The source of this phenomenon (known as latent inhibition; Lubow, 1989) is still a matter for debate (some possibilities will be considered shortly). For our present purposes, however, we may simply note that mere exposure to a stimulus can produce a reduction in the readiness with which it can be learned about, and then go on to explore the implications of this fact of perceptual learning.

McLaren et al. (1989) have proposed an interpretation of perceptual learning effects in which latent inhibition plays an important part. They point out that it is important to distinguish between the ease with which a stimulus can be learned about and the ease with which it can be discriminated from other similar stimuli (which is our major concern). A process that reduced the former might enhance the latter. Consider the stimuli of **Figure 5**. A response conditioned to A will generalize to B (i.e., a failure of discrimination will occur) because the common (c) elements acquire strength during conditioning with A (ac) and are present in the test stimulus B (bc). Prior exposure to A will reduce generalization (enhance discrimination) because the c elements will suffer latent inhibition and thus acquire little strength during conditioning. This effect will be most marked if the subjects are given preexposure to both A and B, as the c elements will be present in both types of exposure trial, thus having twice the opportunity to acquire latent inhibition. Generalization should,

therefore, be particularly weak after preexposure to both A and B – just the result obtained by Symonds and Hall (1995) and shown in **Figure 4**.

This simple notion generates an interesting prediction that has received experimental support. A perceptual learning effect (enhanced discrimination after preexposure) should only be found when the stimuli share a substantial number of common elements. When the stimuli are very different (as, in the limiting case, when A consists only of a elements and B only of b elements), latent inhibition of the c elements can play no part, and discrimination between A and B will be poor, as the latent inhibition suffered by the a and b elements will retard the acquisition of the (different) responses required to these stimuli. Trobalon et al. (1991; see also Prados et al., 1999) have demonstrated this result in a study of maze learning in rats. When the two maze arms that the rats had to choose from were very similar, preexposure to these arms facilitated discrimination learning; when the arms were made distinctively different, preexposure hindered learning.

Latent inhibition can provide an explanation for the result reported by McLaren et al. (1994) that people who had learned to assign checkerboard patterns (**Figure 2**) to different categories showed an enhanced ability to discriminate between new examples drawn from the same category. This result is unexpected, given that examples from the same category will have a common associate, in that both will elicit the same category label. Associative processes might be expected act to hinder discrimination between stimuli that have a common associate (the acquired equivalence effect). But this is to reckon without latent inhibition. McLaren et al. (1994) point out that during initial categorization training, the features common to all exemplars of that category occur on every trial. These features will therefore suffer extensive latent inhibition. Performance on the within-category discrimination will be facilitated, as this task requires precisely that the choice response should come under the control of features that distinguish the displays rather than features they hold in common.

The arguments just advanced hold whatever the mechanism of latent inhibition. Of the various possibilities (see Hall, 1991, for a review), perhaps the most widely accepted is that it reflects a loss of associability, this being expressed in formal terms as a reduction in the value of a stimulus-specific learning rate parameter (symbolized alpha in the influential learning model of Rescorla and Wagner,

1972; see Pearce and Hall, 1980). To adopt this interpretation raises a further interesting possibility. Latent inhibition itself involves only reduction in associability, but might it not be possible for the alpha-value of a stimulus to be increased under appropriate conditions? Mackintosh (1975) has adopted this proposal and devised a theory in which the associability of a stimulus is held to increase as a result of training in which it is a reliable predictor of its consequences (see also Kruschke, 2001). Direct tests of the validity of this proposal have generated mixed results (e.g., Hall and Pearce, 1979; Le Pelley, 2004). But if it could be confirmed, it would usefully extend the explanatory reach of the associability concept. In particular, it could supply an explanation for acquired distinctiveness effects. The acquired distinctiveness training procedure is one in which the subject experiences each of the critical stimuli in reliable association with another event (in **Table 1**, for example, A reliably predicts red, and B reliably predicts green). In addition to any associations that may be formed, Mackintosh's theory says that the associability of A and B will go up under these conditions. Subsequent discrimination between these cues would be enhanced, even in circumstances in which associative mechanisms do not seem to operate (Bonardi et al., 2005).

Whatever the fate of Mackintosh's (1975) theory of associability change, it will be evident that the basic latent inhibition process plays an important part in many perceptual learning effects. There is, however, one critical version of perceptual learning that defies explanation in terms of latent inhibition. This is the well-established, and already much-discussed, finding that discriminability is especially enhanced when the subject is able to compare the stimuli during preexposure. **Table 2** (Experiment 1) presents a simple experimental demonstration of the effect. In this experiment, the subjects can compare A and B during preexposure (they are presented on alternate trials), but will be less able to compare C with the others, as this stimulus is presented on a separate block of trials. But because the subjects experience the critical cues, A, B, and C, the same number of times, all three cues should acquire latent inhibition to the same extent. There are no grounds, therefore, for the latent inhibition account to predict the result obtained – poorer generalization from AX to BX than to CX. Further analysis of this finding is one of the topics of the final section of the chapter.

1.07.5.2 Habituation and Salience Modulation

Whatever other factors may play a part, there is no doubt that the effectiveness of a stimulus depends on its intensity. A strong stimulus will normally elicit a more vigorous response than a weak one (we show a bigger startle response to a loud noise than a soft one); associative learning occurs more rapidly when the events to be associated are intense. Formal theories of these phenomena (see, e.g., Hall, 1994) incorporate a notion of salience, a parameter associated with each stimulus and set by its intensity.

Stimulus salience will influence performance on the tests used in studies of perceptual learning. Subjects will be best able to discriminate (on a same-different test, say) between A and B when the unique features (a and b) are intense, and the common features (c) are not. And generalization between such stimuli will be poor, as the a element will dominate during conditioning with A, restricting the acquisition of control by the c element, and the b element will dominate on test with stimulus B, restricting the ability of c to influence performance. In most studies of the topic, we use stimuli with nonsalient unique features and salient common features; that is, we study the effects of experience on discriminations that are difficult. Perceptual learning effects would be obtained, then, if experience with stimuli was capable of boosting the effective salience of the unique features of stimuli (or of lowering that of common features, or both). What evidence is there that effective salience can change? We have discussed how simple exposure to repeated presentations of a stimulus can produce a loss of associability (latent inhibition), but there is reason to think that this procedure can also bring about a change in effective salience.

Repeated stimulus presentation results in habituation – the waning of the response unconditionally elicited by that stimulus. Explanation of this simple phenomenon turns out to be surprisingly complex (see Hall, 1991, for a review in the context of perceptual learning). But what we need to note for our present purposes is that the habituation procedure makes a salient stimulus behave like a less-salient one. After extensive habituation training, the startle response evoked by a loud noise will be much the same as the (weaker) response evoked by the first presentation of a softer noise. The habituation effect is most easily observed with motivationally significant events, as these evoke obvious responses; but the learning process responsible for it presumably operates for any stimulus, including those used as cues in experiments on perceptual learning. For a few of these, the effect can in fact be observed directly. Rats show neophobia to foods (that is, they are reluctant to consume a substance with a novel taste), and habituation of neophobia is commonly observed over the preexposure phase of perceptual learning experiments using flavor stimuli (Blair et al., 2004). Observations like these make it a reasonable presumption that the (unobservable) response evoked by presentation of a checkerboard, say, will also undergo habituation, or, in other words, that these stimuli too will lose effective salience with repeated exposure.

Blair et al. (2004) have investigated the role of salience modulation in perceptual learning, focusing on the differing effects of intermixed and blocked preexposure. Recall for the experiment shown as Experiment 1 in **Table 2** that rats consume more of BX than of CX on test, and that this difference is explained by the fact that at the end of preexposure, B has greater effective salience than C (the more salient a cue, the more it will interfere with expression of the response controlled by X). Blair et al. (2004, Experiment 3) tested the salience of B and C using the design shown in as Experiment 4 in **Table 2**. After preexposure, some rats received conditioning trials with B alone as the conditioned stimulus (CS); others received C alone as the CS. Acquisition occurred more rapidly to B than to C, as would be expected if B were higher in salience than C. In a further study, Blair et al. simply monitored the unconditioned response evoked by B and C at the end of preexposure. The neophobic reaction evoked by these flavors was found to have habituated to some extent over the course of preexposure, but it was still observable, particularly for flavor B. Thus the effective salience of both B and C was reduced by preexposure, but critically, the reduction was less for the cue presented in alternation with a similar cue in preexposure.

The conclusion that emerges from these and related studies (Hall, 2003; Hall et al., 2006) is that mere exposure to a stimulus will cause a loss of effective salience, but that with some schedules of preexposure, this loss can be attenuated or reversed. The critical arrangement appears to be one in which the cue in question is presented in alternation with another similar cue. Why this schedule should have the effects it does is not yet clear. There is some evidence from the experiments by Hall et al. (2006) to suggest that an important feature of this schedule is that on each trial the subject is likely to be (slightly) surprised at the omission of one of the unique features and at the occurrence of the other. (With the blocked schedule the same stimulus occurs trial after trial.) It seems plausible that an event that evokes surprise might also maintain its salience, but the precise learning mechanisms that might underlie such an effect remain to be specified.

1.07.6 Conclusions

The material reviewed in this chapter has covered a wide range; this is true both for the empirical phenomena considered in the first part and the theoretical analyses dealt with in the second part. The latter point might seem to be a cause for concern, given our customary aspiration to achieve parsimony in explanation. But the concern would probably be misplaced. There is every reason to think that perceptual learning effects are the product (usually the joint product) of several different processes. On the basis of the evidence reviewed in this chapter, a place should be found for associatively mediated acquired equivalence and distinctiveness, effects based on within-stimulus association (unitization) and between-stimulus associations (associative inhibition), latent inhibition (and possibly other learned changes in associability), habituation, and salience modulation.

It may have been noticed that the operation of these various learning mechanisms in perceptual learning has been demonstrated for only a subset of the phenomena described in the first section of the chapter. Analytic studies have, for the most part, made use of just a few well-established and tractable experimental procedures. This may raise the fear that detailed exploration of other paradigms would uncover a whole new set of explanatory principles, in addition to those already listed. But this fear is not justified. As was suggested earlier, the job of a theory of perceptual learning is to explain how experience of similar stimuli can enhance the perceptual effectiveness of features that distinguish them and reduce the perceptual effectiveness of features that they have in common. This description is valid generally – it applies equally, for example, to rats learning to discriminate between flavors and to people learning to distinguish between speech sounds. We have every reason to hope that explanatory principles established in one of these paradigms will also apply in the other.

References

Ahissar M and Hohstein S (1997) Task difficulty and the specificity of perceptual learning. *Nature* 387: 401–406.

Amitay S, Hawkey DJC, and Moore DR (2005) Auditory frequency discrimination learning is affected by stimulus variability. *Percept. Psychophys.* 67: 691–698.

Aitken MRF, Bennett CH, McLaren IPL, and Mackintosh NJ (1996) Perceptual differentiation during categorization learning by pigeons. *J. Exp. Psychol. Anim. B.* 22: 43–50.

Artigas AA, Sansa J, Blair CAJ, Hall G, and Prados J (2006) Enhanced discrimination between flavor stimuli: Roles of salience modulation and inhibition. *J. Exp. Psychol. Anim. Behav. Process* 32: 173–177.

Ball K and Sekuler R (1982) A specific and enduring improvement in visual motion discrimination. *Science* 218: 697–698.

Battig WF (1956) Transfer from verbal pretraining to motor performance as a function of motor task complexity. *J. Exp. Psychol.* 51: 371–378.

Bennett CH and Mackintosh NJ (1999) Comparison and contrast as a mechanism of perceptual learning? *Q. J. Exp. Psychol.* 52B: 253–272.

Bennett CH, Tremain M, and Mackintosh NJ (1996) Facilitation and retardation of flavour aversion conditioning following prior exposure to the CS. *Q. J. Exp. Psychol.* 49B: 220–230.

Biederman I and Shiffrar MM (1987) Sexing day-old chicks: A case study and expert systems analysis of a difficult perceptual-learning task. *J. Exp. Psychol. Learn.* 13: 640–645.

Blair CAJ and Hall G (2003) Perceptual learning in flavor aversion: Evidence for learned changes in stimulus effectiveness. *J. Exp. Psychol. Anim. Behav. Process* 29: 39–48.

Blair CAJ, Wilkinson A, and Hall G (2004) Assessments of changes in the effective salience of stimulus elements as a result of stimulus preexposure. *J. Exp. Psychol. Anim. Behav. Process* 30: 317–324.

Bonardi C, Graham S, Hall G, and Mitchell C (2005) Acquired distinctiveness and equivalence in human discrimination learning: Evidence for an attentional process. *Psychon. Bull. Rev.* 12: 88–92.

Bonardi C, Rey V, Richmond M, and Hall G (1993) Acquired equivalence of cues in pigeon autoshaping: Effects of training with common consequences and common antecedents. *Anim. Learn. Behav.* 21: 369–376.

Bruce V and Burton M (2002) Learning new faces. In: Fahle M and Poggio T (eds.) *Perceptual Learning*, pp. 317–334. Cambridge, MA: MIT Press,.

Chiroro P and Valentine T (1995) An investigation of the contact hypothesis of the own-race bias in face recognition. *Q. J. Exp. Psychol.* 48A: 879–894.

Chung MS and Thomson DM (1995) Development of face recognition. *Br. J. Psychol.* 86: 55–87.

Demany L (1985) Perceptual learning in frequency discrimination. *J. Acoust. Soc. Am.* 78: 1118–1120.

Demany L and Semal C (2002) Learning to perceive pitch differences. *J. Acoust. Soc. Am.* 111: 1377–1388.

Dwyer DM, Bennett CH, and Mackintosh NJ (2001) Evidence for inhibitory associations between the unique elements of two compound flavours. *Q. J. Exp. Psychol.* 54B: 97–107.

Dwyer DM and Mackintosh NJ (2002) Alternating exposure to two compound flavors creates inhibitory associations between their unique features. *Anim. Learn. Behav.* 30: 201–207.

Dwyer DM, Hodder KI, and Honey RC (2004) Perceptual learning in humans: Roles of preexposure schedule, feedback, and discrimination assay. *Q. J. Exp. Psychol.* 57B: 245–259.

Fanselow MS (1990) Factors governing one-trial contextual conditioning. *Anim. Learn. Behav.* 18: 264–270.

Fahle M and Poggio T (2002) *Perceptual Learning.* Cambridge, MA: MIT Press.

Fiorentini A and Berardi N (1980) Perceptual learning specific for orientation and spatial frequency. *Nature* 287: 43–44.

Furmanski CS and Engel SA (2000) Perceptual learning in object recognition: Object specificity and size invariance. *Vision Res.* 40: 473–484.

Gagné RM and Baker KE (1950) Stimulus predifferentiation as a factor in transfer of training. *J. Exp. Psychol.* 40: 439–451.

Gauthier I and Tarr MJ (1997) Becoming a "greeble" expert: Exploring mechanisms for face recognition. *Vision Res.* 37: 1673–1682.

Gibson EJ (1969) *Perceptual Learning and Development.* New York: Appleton-Century-Crofts.

Gibson EJ and Levin H (1975) *The Psychology of Reading.* Cambridge, MA: MIT Press.

Gibson EJ and Walk RD (1956) The effect of prolonged exposure to visually presented patterns on learning to discriminate them. *J. Comp. Physiol. Psychol.* 49: 239–242.

Goldstone RL (1994) Influences of categorization on perceptual discrimination. *J. Exp. Psychol. Gen.* 123: 178–200.

Goldstone RL (1998) Perceptual learning. *Annu. Rev. Psychol.* 49: 585–610.

Goldstone RL (2000) Unitization during category learning. *J. Exp. Psychol. Gen.* 26: 86–112.

Goto H (1971) Auditory perception by normal Japanese adults of the sounds "L" and "R". *Neuropsychologia* 9: 317–323.

Hall G (1991) *Perceptual and Associative Learning.* Oxford, UK: Clarendon Press.

Hall G (1994) Pavlovian conditioning: Laws of association. In: Mackintosh NJ (ed.) *Handbook of Perception and Cognition, Vol. 9: Animal Learning and Cognition*, pp. 15–43. San Diego, CA: Academic Press.

Hall G (1996) Learning about associatively activated representations: Implications for acquired equivalence and perceptual learning. *Anim. Learn. Behav.* 24: 233–255.

Hall G (2003) Learned changes in the sensitivity of stimulus representations: Associative and nonassociative mechanisms. *Q. J. Exp. Psychol.* 56B: 43–55.

Hall G, Blair CAJ, and Artigas AA (2006) Associative activation of stimulus representations restores lost salience: Implications for perceptual learning. *J. Exp. Psychol. Anim. Behav. Process* 32: 145–155.

Hall G, Mitchell C, Graham S, and Lavis Y (2003) Acquired equivalence and distinctiveness in human discrimination learning: Evidence for associative mediation. *J. Exp. Psychol. Gen.* 132: 266–276.

Hall G and Pearce JM (1979) Latent inhibition of a CS during CS-US pairings. *J. Exp. Psychol. Anim. Behav. Process* 5: 31–42.

Hollingworth HL (1928) *Psychology: Its Facts and Principles.* New York: Appleton-Century.

Holton RB and Goss AE (1956) Transfer to a discriminative motor task as a function of amount and type of preliminary verbalization. *J. Gen. Psychol.* 55: 117–126.

Iverson P, Kuhl PK, Akahane-Yamada R, et al. (2003) A perceptual interference account of acquisition difficulties for non-native phonemes. *Cognition* 87: B47–B57.

Iverson P, Hazan V, and Bannister K (2005) Phonetic training with acoustic cue manipulations: A comparison of methods for teaching English /r/-/l/ to Japanese adults. *J. Acoust. Soc. Am.* 118: 3267–3278.

James W (1890) *The Principles of Psychology.* New York: Holt.

Karni A and Sagi D (1991) Where practice makes perfect in texture discrimination: Evidence for primary visual cortex plasticity. *Proc. Natl. Acad. Sci. USA* 88: 4966–4970.

Ketermann A and Siebert C (2003) A perceptual interference account of acquisition difficulties for non-native phonemes. *Cognition* 87: B47–B57.

Kiernan MJ and Westbrook RF (1993) Effects of exposure to a to-be-shocked environment upon the rat's freezing response: Evidence for facilitation, latent inhibition, and perceptual learning. *Q. J. Exp. Psychol.* 46B: 271–288.

Kruschke JK (2001) Toward a unified model of attention in associative learning. *J. Math. Psychol.* 45: 812–863.

Lavis Y and Mitchell C (2006) Effects of preexposure on stimulus discrimination: An investigation of the mechanisms responsible for human perceptual learning. *Q. J. Exper. Psychol.* 59: 2083–2101.

Lawrence DH (1949) Acquired distinctiveness of cues: I. Transfer between discriminations on the basis of familiarity with the stimulus. *J. Exp. Psychol.* 39: 770–784.

Le Pelley ME (2004) The role of associative history in associative learning: A selective review and a hybrid model. *Q. J. Exp. Psychol.* 57B: 193–243.

Liu Z and Weinshall D (2000) Mechanisms of generalization in perceptual learning. *Vision Res.* 40: 97–109.

Lubow RE (1989) *Latent Inhibition and Conditioned Attention Theory.* New York: Cambridge University Press.

Mackintosh NJ (1975) A theory of attention: Variations in the associability of stimuli with reinforcement. *Psychol. Rev.* 82: 276–298.

Mackintosh NJ (1983) *Conditioning and Associative Learning.* Oxford, UK: Clarendon Press.

Mackintosh NJ and Little L (1969) Intradimensional and extradimensional shift learning by pigeons. *Psychon. Sci.* 14: 5–6.

Malpass RS and Kravitz J (1969) Recognition of faces of own or other race. *J. Pers. Soc. Psychol.* 13: 330–334.

McKee SP and Westheimer G (1978) Improvement in vernier acuity with practice. *Percept. Psychophys.* 24: 258–262.

McLaren IPL (1997) Categorization and perceptual learning: An analogue of the face inversion effect. *Q. J. Exp. Psychol.* 50A: 257–273.

McLaren IPL, Kaye H, and Mackintosh NJ (1989) An associative theory of the representation of stimuli: Applications to perceptual learning and latent inhibition. In: Morris RGM (ed.) *Parallel Distributed Processing: Implications for Psychology and Neurobiology*, pp. 102–130. Oxford, UK: Clarendon Press.

McLaren IPL, Leevers HJ, and Mackintosh NJ (1994) Recognition, categorization, and perceptual learning (or, how learning to classify things together helps one to tell them apart). In: Umilta C and Moscovitch M (eds.) *Attention and Performance XV: Conscious and Nonconscious Information Processing*, pp. 889–909. Cambridge, MA: MIT Press,.

McLaren IPL and Mackintosh NJ (2000) An elemental model of associative learning: I. Latent inhibition and perceptual learning. *Anim. Learn. Behav.* 28: 211–246.

Melcher JM and Schooler JW (1996) The misremembrance of wines past: Verbal and perceptual expertise differentially mediate verbal overshadowing of taste memory. *J. Mem. Lang.* 35: 231–245.

Miller NE and Dollard J (1941) *Social Learning and Imitation.* New Haven, CT: Yale University Press.

Mondragón E and Hall G (2002) Analysis of the perceptual learning effect in flavour aversion learning: Evidence for stimulus differentiation. *Q. J. Exp. Psychol.* 55B: 153–169.

Myles-Worsley M, Johnston WA, and Simons MA (1988) The influence of expertise on X-ray image processing. *J. Exp. Psychol. Learn.* 14: 553–557.

Pearce JM (1994) Similarity and discrimination: A selective review and a connectionist model. *Psychol. Rev.* 101: 587–607.

Pearce JM and Hall G (1980) A model for Pavlovian learning: Variations in the effectiveness of conditioned but not of unconditioned stimuli. *Psychol. Rev.* 87: 532–552.

Peron RM and Allen GL (1988) Attempts to train novices for beer flavor discrimination: A matter of taste. *J. Gen. Psychol.* 115: 403–418.

Prados J, Chamizo V, and Mackintosh NJ (1999) Latent inhibition and perceptual learning in a swimming pool task. *J. Exp. Psychol. Anim. B.* 25: 37–44.

Quinn PC, Palmer V, and Slater AM (1999) Identification of gender in domestic-cat faces with and without training: Perceptual learning of a natural categorization task. *Perception* 28: 749–763.

Rabin MD (1988) Experience facilitates olfactory quality discrimination. *Percept. Psychophys.* 44: 532–540.

Rescorla RA and Wagner AR (1972) A theory of Pavlovian conditioning: Variations in the effectiveness of reinforcement and nonreinforcement. In: Black AH and Prokasy WF (eds.) *Classical Conditioning II: Current Research and Theory*, pp. 64–99. New York: Appleton-Century-Crofts.

Rodriguez G and Alonso G (2004) Perceptual learning in flavor aversion learning: Alternating and blocked exposure to a compound of flavors and to an element of that compound. *Learn. Motiv.* 35: 208–220.

Sathian K and Zangaladze A (1997) Tactile learning is task specific but transfers between fingers. *Percept. Psychophys.* 59: 119–128.

Shiu L-P and Pashler H (1992) Improvement in line orientation discrimination is retinally local but dependent on cognitive set. *Percept. Psychophys.* 52: 582–588.

Soloman GEA (1990) Psychology of novice and expert wine talk. *Am. J. Psychol.* 103: 495–517.

Stevenson RJ (2001) Perceptual learning with odors: Implications for psychological accounts of odor quality perception. *Psychon. Bull. Rev.* 8: 708–712.

Stevenson RJ and Boakes RA (2003) A mnemonic theory of odor perception. *Psychol. Rev.* 110: 340–364.

Stevenson RJ, Boakes RA, and Prescott J (1998) Changes in odor sweetness resulting from implicit learning of a simultaneous odor-sweetness association: An example of learned synesthesia. *Learn. Motiv.* 29: 113–132.

Sutherland NS and Mackintosh NJ (1971) *Mechanisms of Animal Discrimination Learning.* New York: Academic Press.

Symonds M and Hall G (1995) Perceptual learning in flavor aversion learning: Roles of stimulus comparison and latent inhibition of common elements. *Learn. Motiv.* 26: 203–219.

Todd IA and Mackintosh NJ (1990) Evidence for perceptual learning in pigeon's recognition memory for pictures. *Q. J. Exp. Psychol.* 42B: 385–400.

Trobalon JB, Sansa J, Chamizo V, and Mackintosh NJ (1991) Perceptual learning in maze discriminations. *Q. J. Exp. Psychol.* 43B: 389–402.

Volkmann AW (1858) Über den Einfluss der Uebung auf das Erkennen räumlicher Distanzen. *Ber. Verh. Sachs. Ges. Wiss. Leipzig Math. Phys. Kl.* 10: 38–69.

Woodworth RS and Schlosberg H (1954) *Experimental Psychology.* London: Methuen.

Wagner AR (1981) SOP: A model of automatic memory processing in animal behavior. In: Spear NE and Miller RR (eds.) *Information Processing in Animals: Memory Mechanisms*, pp. 5–47. Hillsdale, NJ: Erlbaum.

Yin RK (1969) Looking at upside-down faces. *J. Exp. Psychol. Gen.* 81: 141–145.

1.08 Discrimination and Generalization

E. J. Kehoe, University of New South Wales, Sydney, NSW, Australia

1.08.1 Introduction

Studies using discrimination and generalization methods have been intimately intertwined with research and theory in learning and memory. All or nearly all the other articles in this volume will describe findings based on discrimination and generalization tasks (*See* Chapters 1.03, 1.05, 1.07, 1.11, 1.12, 1.22). From a biological perspective, learning to respond distinctively to different stimuli and transferring that learning to new situations are essential to survival in all but the most static of environments.

From a cognitive perspective, understanding distinctions and perceiving similarities underpins processes of attention, perception, recognition, categorization, and reasoning, all of which usually require learning and memory for developing their content and expression.

In brief, discrimination training tests how well a learner can distinguish among stimuli, while generalization procedures test how well training with one stimulus transfers to another stimulus. These two procedures have been used in three major ways. First, they provide psychophysical techniques for revealing the processes of stimulus encoding. Second, they have been used in delineating the roles of excitation and inhibition in learning. Third, they have contributed to the investigation of cognitive processes, particularly in nonverbal creatures. In the present article, key examples of each of these uses will be outlined after the basic methods have been described.

1.08.2 The Basics

This section describes the basic procedures and outcomes of discrimination training and generalization testing. In addition, this section treats generalization testing in the wider context of transfer of training.

1.08.2.1 Discrimination Learning

Basic discrimination training entails the presentation of two stimuli, one of which is associated with the reinforcer (S+), and one of which is not (S−). In classical conditioning, one conditioned stimulus (CS+) is consistently paired with the unconditioned stimulus (US), and the other conditioned stimulus (CS−) is not paired with US. Similarly, in operant conditioning, the target response is reinforced whenever one discriminative stimulus (SD) is present, and the target response is not reinforced whenever the other discriminative stimulus (SΔ) is present. Discrimination learning is said to occur when the level of responding is greater during S+ than S−. **Figure 1** shows discrimination learning curves obtained under different circumstances in different species.

Discrimination training using stimuli that differ along a single dimension is commonly called intradimensional training. When the S+ and S− differ along multiple dimensions, including their sensory modalities, the procedure is called either interdimensional or extradimensional training. Across investigators, there is no apparent convention for using these latter two terms.

Go/no-go discriminations. **Figures 1(a)** and **1(b)** illustrate differential classical conditioning of the eyeblink response in rabbits and humans (Gynther, 1957; Moore, 1972). For the rabbits, the stimuli were tones of different frequencies (400 Hz, 1600 Hz), and for the humans, red and white lights were used. The assignment of the two stimuli as CS+ and CS− was counterbalanced across subjects. In both cases, the

likelihood of a conditioned response (CR) to both CS+ and CS− increased during the early trials of training. Thereafter, respondes to CS+ continued to rise, while respondes to CS− either stabilized or declined to a lower level.

Figure 1(c) shows results of a free-operant discrimination procedure. Rats were initially trained to press a lever bar for intermittent reinforcement (Herrick et al., 1959). Discrimination training was conducted by switching between periods in which an indicator lamp was on (S+) and periods in which the lamp was off (S−). During the S+ periods, barpresses were intermittently reinforced. During the S− periods, barpresses were never reinforced. The rate of barpressing during S+ rose steadily and approached a level around 70 responses per minute. In contrast, responses during S− gradually disappeared.

Choice discriminations. The examples of discrimination learning shown in **Figures 1(a)–1(c)** are all based on procedures in which the S+ and S− stimuli are alternated in a successive fashion. Such successive discriminations are also labeled as *go/no-go discriminations*, because the subject's task is to either display or withhold the target response, depending on the stimulus. Operant conditioning procedures also allow for *choice discriminations*, in which S+ and S− are presented simultaneously in separate locations. Most commonly, visual stimuli are used. The subject is reinforced for responding toward S+, but not if it responds toward S−. Thus, responding entails choice behavior, in which both correct responses and errors can be observed. Learning is expressed as an increase in 'percent correct responses,' that is, the proportion of trials on which the subject responds toward S+.

Choice discrimination tasks have been investigated in a wide number of species, ranging from honeybees (Couvillon and Bitterman, 1985) to elephants (Nissani et al., 2005). **Figures 1(d)–1(f)** show examples of choice discrimination learning. Specifically, **Figure 1(d)** shows learning curves obtained using a T-maze. As the name implies, the apparatus consisted of three narrow boxes arranged in a T-shaped pattern. The subjects were mice from two strains, specifically, a control strain and a transgenic strain that mimics Huntington's Disease (Lione et al., 1999). On each trial, a mouse was placed in the central arm. The subject then moved of its own accord to the junction of the maze, where it encountered S+ in one arm and S− in the other arm. In this case, the stimuli were created by making

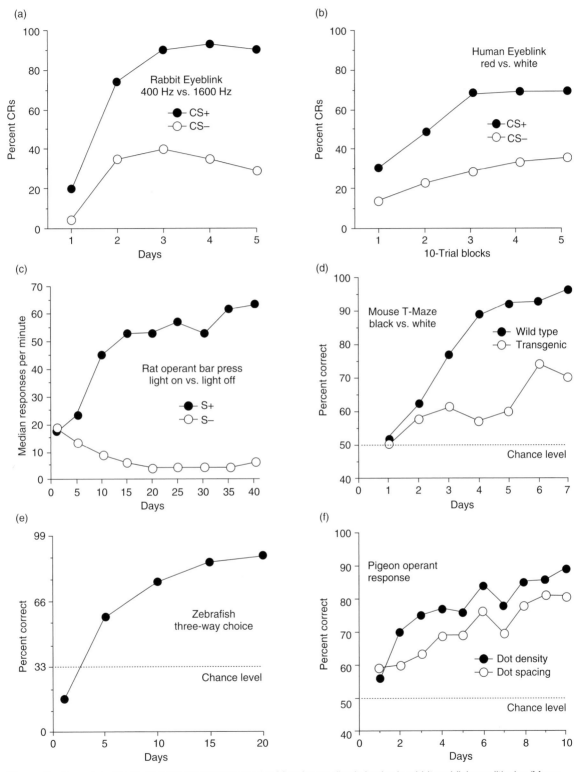

Figure 1 Examples of basic discrimination learning tasks: (a) go/no-go discrimination in rabbit eyeblink conditioning (Moore, 1972); (b) go/no-go discrimination in human eyeblink conditioning (Gynther, 1957); (c) go/no-go discrimination in operant barpress conditioning in rats (Herrick et al., 1959); (d) choice discrimination in two types of mice (Lione et al., 1999); (e) three-way choice in zebrafish (Bilotta et al., 2005); (f) visual on-screen choice in pigeons (Cook, 2001). All figures adapted with permission. CS, conditioned stimulus.

the ceiling of one arm black, and the ceiling of the other arm white. If the subject moved up the S+ arm, it would find a food pellet. If the subject moved up the other arm, there was no food pellet. As can be seen in **Figure 1(d)**, the likelihood of a correct response in the control strain gradually rose from a chance level of 50% correct to a level near 100%, while the transgenic mice only reached a level around 70%.

Figure 1(e) shows the results of a three-way choice discrimination in zebra fish (Bilotta et al., 2005). Each fish was presented with a choice between three windows, one of which was illuminated. The subject was reinforced for swimming through the illuminated window but not the other windows. The location of the illuminated window was randomly altered from trial to trial. Initially, performance was below chance level, because trials on which a subject failed to make any choice were counted. Across days of training, the likelihood of correct responding rose to 80%, at which point training was stopped.

Modern technology allows for the projection of complex visual stimuli on video screens. In some cases, the subject can indicate its choice by touching specific regions on the screen. **Figure 1(f)** shows an example of an on-screen discrimination in which pigeons were presented with a field of regularly spaced dots. The S+ was a square containing either more densely packed dots or irregularly spaced dots. The S+ was placed at a random location on the screen, and the pigeon was reinforced only if it pecked at the S+. As can be seen, the likelihood of pecking at the S+ region reached a level near 90% (Cook, 2001).

In choice discrimination tasks, subjects often display response patterns that prevent them from coming into contact with the discriminative contingencies among the stimuli, responses, and reinforcers. Subjects often adopt a position habit, such as always choosing the left-hand response. Because the S+ and S− appear equally often in left and right positions, a left-hand response will be reinforced 50% of the time. Although this rate of reinforcement is less than the maximum the subjects could obtain, it is sufficient to maintain a position habit. To ensure that the subjects do encounter all the contingencies, a correction procedure may be used. In this procedure, the choice of S− is followed by a *correction trial*, in which only S+ is presented and the subject can only make the correct response. For example, during a correction trial in a T-maze, only the arm associated with S+ will be open.

1.08.2.2 Generalization and Transfer of Training

1.08.2.2.1 Stimulus generalization: immediate, specific transfer

Basic generalization testing entails two stages. The first stage entails reinforced training in which a single stimulus (S+) is used. Once responding to S+ has reached a high level, the second stage begins. In this stage, the subject is presented with a set of test stimuli that differ systematically from S+.

Figure 2 shows three alternative plots for the results of generalization testing (Moore, 1972). In this experiment, three groups of rabbits received eyeblink conditioning in which a 1200-Hz tone was paired with the US (CS+). One group (T1) received single-stimulus training, in which only CS+ trials occurred. The second group (T1-T2) received discrimination training, in which CS+ trials were intermixed with CS− trials using another tone (2400 Hz). The third group (T-L) received training in which CS− was from a different modality, specifically, a brief illumination of the chamber. Following initial training, all three groups were tested with tones of 400 Hz, 800 Hz, 1200 Hz (CS+), 1600 Hz, and 2000 Hz.

Figure 2(a) shows the mean likelihood of a CR as a function of tone frequency. As can be seen, the highest level of responding in all three groups was elicited by the 1200-Hz CS+. As the frequencies of the test tones increasingly deviated from 1200 Hz, responding fell off in a graded fashion. However, the three groups showed some differences in both the absolute height and steepness of their gradients. To make it easier to compare the slopes of the gradients, **Figures 2(b)** and **2(c)** show two types of plots that depict *relative generalization gradients*, which adjust for differences in the level of responding to CS+.

In **Figure 2(b)**, the level of responding to each stimulus is plotted in proportion to the level of responding to CS+. Thus, responding to CS+ is always set to 1.00, and the slopes of the gradients can be readily seen. **Figure 2(c)** shows a method of plotting that emphasizes *stimulus control*, that is, how specific responding is to CS+ relative to the other test stimuli. In this method, the total amount of responding to all tested stimuli is added together, and responding to each stimulus is expressed as a proportion of that total. Thus, taller, sharper gradients indicate greater stimulus control but, conversely, less generalization. Inspection of **Figures 2(b)** and **2(c)** indicate that both discrimination groups showed less generalization, and hence greater stimulus control, than Group T1.

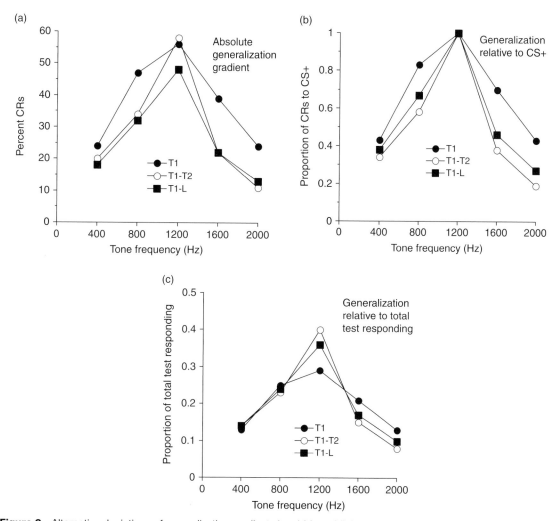

Figure 2 Alternative depictions of generalization gradients in rabbit eyeblink conditioning: (a) Absolute percentage conditioned response (CR) to each stimulus, (b) Responding to each test stimulus as a proportion of responding to CS+, (c) Proportion of total responding to each stimulus, including CS+ (Moore, 1972). All figures adapted with permission. CS, conditioned stimulus.

As shown in **Figure 2**, discrimination training tends to sharpen generalization gradients. Conversely, when efforts have been made to eliminate all potential sources of discrimination training, generalization gradients can be virtually flat. For example, **Figure 3** shows the results of generalization testing after two kinds of operant conditioning in which pigeons were reinforced for pecking a lighted keyswitch (Jenkins and Harrison, 1960). In *nondifferential training*, a 1000-Hz tone (S+) was present whenever the key was lit, which was for 33 s out of every 40 s. The 7-s period without the keylight precluded the pigeons from making the target response. In contrast, in *differential training*, the subjects received training with a go/ no-go discrimination, in which S+ trials with a tone

were alternated randomly with S− periods in which the keylight was on but the tone was off. The 7-s blackout periods also continued to occur in this latter condition.

In subsequent testing sessions, pecking at the keylight was tested during tones ranging from no tone (0 Hz) to 3500 Hz. As can be seen in **Figure 3**, the level of responding to the test stimuli after non-differential training was similar to that during S+. That is, there was nearly complete generalization to the test stimuli even though the birds had only ever been trained with a 1000-Hz tone. However, the pigeons were not tone deaf. After differential training, there was a sharp generalization gradient centered on S+.

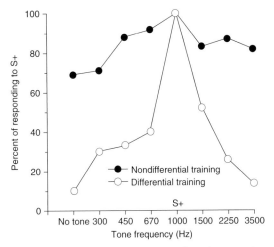

Figure 3   Relative generalization gradients in operant conditioning of pigeon's keypecking after nondifferential training with S+ only versus differential training S+ versus S− (Jenkins and Harrison, 1960). Figure adapted with permission. S, stimulus.

1.08.2.2.2   Other types of transfer

The instances of stimulus generalization described above represent only one of four basic types of transfer. Specifically, stimulus generalization testing reveals the ability of a subject to use its previous learning when it first encounters new stimuli that more or less physically resemble the stimulus used in initial training. This type of transfer can appear immediately on the first test and is specific to stimuli that differ from the training stimulus along one or more sensory dimensions (see Blough, 2001a, for an extensive discussion of the concept of *similarity*.) Provided the appropriate response is retrieved, such immediate specific transfer can be extraordinarily valuable to the survival of subjects when presented with fleeting opportunities and imminent threats. Likewise, human society highly prizes the abilities of paramedics confronted by an accident victim, pilots in an emergency, students in an examination, and even contestants in a quiz show to respond quickly and correctly to situations that are variations on their previous experience.

Despite the premium placed on immediate specific transfer, it is not the sole type of transfer. There are three other ways that transfer can appear. The second type of transfer is immediate but nonspecific. That is, previous learning is applied in situations that bear little similarity at a sensory level to the situations used in training. Instead, nonspecific transfer can be based on structural similarities between the training situation and test situation,

for example, analogical reasoning in humans (Gick and Holyoak, 1980; Novick and Holyoak, 1991; Reeves and Weisberg, 1994). The third and fourth types of transfer do not appear on the first encounter with a new situation. Rather, the effect of the previous training is latent and is detected as an increase in the rate of response acquisition during reinforced training in the new situation. A specific form of latent transfer is seen whenever original learning cannot be retrieved immediately but does reappear quickly during refresher training. This type of transfer is known as *savings*. Humans refer to savings whenever they say, "I can't remember how to do it, but I know I can pick it up again quickly." A nonspecific form of latent transfer can appear in situations that share some similarity in their underlying structure, but not in the sensory features of their stimuli. This latent, nonspecific transfer is labeled variously as *learning to learn, learning set,* or *general transfer* (Ellis, 1965, p. 32).

These distinctions among types of transfer are useful for exposition but should not be taken as strict dichotomies. The immediate-versus-latent distinction is relatively clear when the new situations are relatively brief and demand a rapid response. However, when a new situation has less urgent demands, latent transfer could appear during the first encounter if learning occurs as a result of false starts and tentative solutions. As for the specific-versus-nonspecific distinction, it is more accurately construed as a continuum. It is probably difficult, if not impossible, to create situations that differ in every sensory feature from those in original training. In laboratory experiments, however, the number and magnitude of changes can be systematically varied and described.

To ground these distinctions, the remainder of this section will describe examples of the different types of transfer. However, before doing so, a few sentences about the design of transfer experiments are needed. As previously described, the detection and quantification of stimulus generalization uses the level of responding to the training stimulus (S+) as the reference point for comparison to the level of responding to the test stimuli. Such within-subject comparisons are efficient, but one must be confident that there would be little or no responding to the test stimuli in the absence of prior training with S+. Otherwise, a between-subjects design is necessary. At a minimum, there are two groups. The experimental group receives the initial training with S+, and in the basic version, the other group – known as the *rest control* – receives no training with S+. That is, while the experimental group receives its initial training, the subjects in the rest control group sit either in their home cages or in the experimental chambers. Then, both the experimental and control groups receive the test stimuli for immediate transfer plus any subsequent training with the test stimuli to detect latent transfer. The level responding in the control group provides the reference point for the experimental group. If responding in the experimental group exceeds that of the control group, *positive transfer* or *facilitation* is said to occur. If responding in the experimental group is the lesser of the two, then *negative transfer, interference*, or *retardation* is said to have occurred.

1.08.2.2.2.(i) Immediate, nonspecific transfer

A textbook case of immediate, nonspecific transfer would be cross-modal generalization, in which the subjects are trained with a stimulus in one modality (e.g., tone) and then tested with a novel stimulus in another modality (e.g., light). Reports of successful cross-modal generalization are rare. It has been seen in eyeblink conditioning in humans (Marlatt et al., 1966) but not rabbits (e.g., Kehoe, 1992; Weidemann and Kehoe, 2005). Something like immediate, nonspecific transfer, however, has emerged when the test stimuli have previously undergone even a tiny bit of training. **Figure 4** shows the results of two such experiments.

Figure 4(a) shows an example of cross-modal transfer in rabbit eyeblink conditioning (Schreurs and Kehoe, 1987). One group of rabbits (Expt'l) received 15 pairings of the ultimate test stimulus (CSX; e.g., tone) with the US. These CSX-US pairings were too few to yield discernible CR acquisition. At the same time, a rest control group received only exposure to the experimental apparatus. Subsequently, both groups received 240 pairings of a stimulus from another sensory modality (CSA; e.g., light).

During CSA-US training, the subjects were periodically tested with presentations of CSX. As can be seen **Figure 4**, both groups showed CR acquisition to CSA. As CRs were acquired to CSA, Group Expt'l also showed progressive increases in responding on CSX test trials to a level of 34% CRs. In contrast, Group Rest showed no generalized responding to CSX.

Figure 4(b) shows an example of transfer across different visual dimensions (Rodgers and Thomas, 1982). In this experiment, pigeons were given training in which the response key contained a line tilted at either a 60-degree or a 30-degree angle. One group was given go/no-go discrimination training, in which the pigeons were reinforced for pecking at the one line (S+) and not the other line (S−). The other group received *pseudo-discrimination training*, in which pecking at each line was reinforced for a random half of their trials. After this initial training, both

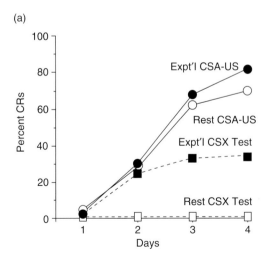

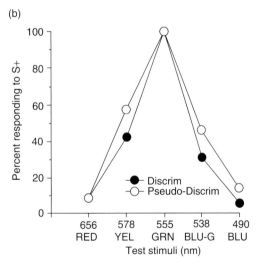

Figure 4 Examples of extradimensional transfer in rabbit eyeblink conditioning (a) and operant conditioning of the pigeon's keypeck (b). Panel (a) shows the results of testing a stimulus from one modality (CSX), while acquisition training was conducted with a stimulus from a different modality (CSA-US). The experimental group had previously received a small number of CSX-US pairings, while the control group had not (Schreurs and Kehoe, 1987). Panel (b) shows the results of generalization testing along the color dimension after pigeons had received either true discrimination training or randomized psuedo-discrimination training with two line-tilt stimuli (Rodgers and Thomas, 1982). All figures adapted with permission. CS, conditioned stimulus; US, unconditioned stimulus; YEL, yellow; GRN, green; BLU-G, blue-green; BLU, blue.

groups were given training in which they were reinforced for pecking at a green (555 nm) keylight. Finally, both groups received generalization tests along the color dimension.

Inspection of **Figure 4** reveals that the discrimination group showed a sharper gradient compared to pseudo-discrimination training. Thus, discrimination training on one dimension altered generalization along an orthogonal dimension.

1.08.2.2.2.(ii) Savings: latent, specific transfer

Figure 5 shows two examples of savings. **Figure 5(a)** shows percent CRs in four successive cycles of CS-US acquisition and CS-alone extinction in rabbit eyeblink conditioning (Kehoe, 2006). **Figure 5(b)** shows the percent correct response in successive reversals of a choice discrimination. Specifically, rats were trained in a T-maze, in which they were reinforced for choosing one arm but not the other. Within each training session, the same choice was always reinforced, but, in the next session, the opposite choice was reinforced (Watson et al., 2006). As can be seen, in both tasks, the successive acquisitions become progressively faster.

1.08.2.2.2.(iii) Learning to learn: latent, nonspecific transfer

Figure 6(a) shows the best known set of curves that demonstrate learning to learn (Harlow, 1949). Rhesus monkeys were trained with a series of 344 discrimination problems, each using a different pair of objects. In each problem, the monkeys were given six or more trials in which to choose between two objects presented on a tray; for example, two different-shaped blocks. If a subject chose the correct object (S+), there was a food reward underneath it. If the subject selected the other block (S−), there was no reward. From one trial to the next, the S+ and S− objects were randomly switched from one side to the other. After a minimum of six trials with one problem, the monkeys were then given another problem using completely different objects; for example, two small toys. Each of the learning curves shows the average percentage of correct choices for successive blocks of problems.

On Trial 1 of each problem, the choice between the two objects was necessarily random. Thus, the learning curve for each problem always starts at 50% correct for Trial 1. For the first set of problems (1–8), the rate of learning was slow. The monkeys' second choice was correct only 52% of the time, and their third choice was correct only 59% of the time. However, as the monkeys accumulated experience with the discrimination problems, the rate of learning progressively accelerated. By the final set (Problems 289–344), the monkeys made nearly 100% correct responses on Trial 2, regardless of their initial choice. In descriptive terms, the monkeys had learned a *win-stay/lose-shift strategy*. That is, if the monkeys won a reward on the Trial 1 by selecting S+, then the monkeys continued to select the same object on

(a)

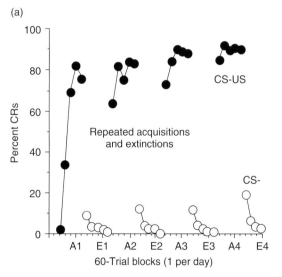

(b)

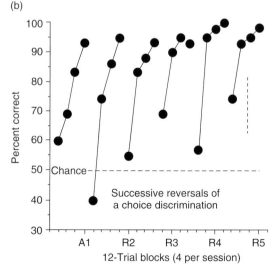

Figure 5 Examples of latent, specific transfer. (a) Repeated acquisitions (CS-US) and extinctions (CS−) in rabbit eyeblink conditioning (Kehoe, 2006). (b) Successive reversals of a choice discrimination in a T-maze by rats (Watson et al., 2006). All figures adapted with permission. CS, conditioned stimulus; US, unconditioned stimulus.

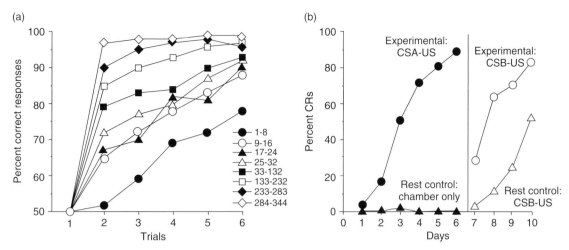

Figure 6 Examples of latent, nonspecific transfer. (a) Learning curves in successive blocks of choice discriminations in monkeys (Harlow, 1949). (b) Learning curves in two successive stages of training with one stimulus from one sensory modality (CSA-US) and a second stimulus from a different sensory modality (CSB-US)(Kehoe and Macrae, 2002). All figures adapted with permission. CS, conditioned stimulus; US, unconditioned stimulus.

subsequent trials. If, however, the monkeys lost by selecting S− on Trial 1, they shifted their choice to S+ on Trial 2 and thereafter.

Learning to learn has also been demonstrated in nonprimate species (Warren, 1960; Kamil et al., 1977). In rats, learning to learn has been obtained using visual patterns in choice discrimination (Wallace and Daniels, 1972), odors in a go/no-go discrimination (Slotnick and Hanford, 2000), and different locations of a platform in the Morris water escape task (Whishaw, 1985). Learning to learn has even been seen in classical conditioning (Kehoe and Holt, 1984; Holt and Kehoe, 1985; Kehoe and Macrae, 1997).

Figure 6(b) shows an example of learning to learn in rabbit eyeblink conditioning. In Stage 1, one group of rabbits (Experimental) received 6 days of CSA-US pairings. For half of this group, the A stimulus was a 1000-Hz tone, and for the other half, the A stimulus was a flashing light. Another group of rabbits (Rest Control) was restrained in the training apparatus without CS or US presentations. At the end of initial training, Group Experimental showed CRs on 90% of CSA-US trials, while Group Rest Control showed only a few, random blinks during blank periods corresponding to CSA.

Subsequently, both groups were tested with a new stimulus (CSB). For Group Experimental, the rabbits initially trained with the tone were tested with the light, and the rabbits initially trained with the light were tested with the tone. Correspondingly, Group Rest Control was also tested with either the light or the

tone. No immediate transfer was evident in these tests. However, once CSB-US pairings were started, learning to learn became evident. As can be seen in **Figure 6(b)**, Group Experimental showed rapid CR acquisition to CSB. Within the first day of Stage 2, Group Experimental showed CRs on 29% of its CSB-US trials, while Group Rest Control showed CRs on only 3% of its CSB-US trials.

Latent transfer, both in the form of savings and learning to learn, appears to be irreversible and separate from the specific contents of the original learning. **Figure 7** shows the results of two studies that illustrate this point. First, rats were initially reinforced for choosing the right arm of a T-maze (Bunch, 1939). After reaching a criterion of 10 consecutive correct responses, each rat was assigned to one of five groups. All these groups underwent reversal training in which they were reinforced for choosing the left arm of the T-maze. The groups differed in the amount of time that elapsed between initial training and reversal training. One group was immediately switched to reversal training, and the other groups waited in their home cages for 2, 7, 14, and 28 days, respectively. A sixth group was a rest control and only received training with the left-arm task.

Figure 7(a) plots the mean number of errors committed during reversal training by each group prior to achieving 10 consecutive correct responses. Relative to the rest control, Group 0, which received the immediate switch, showed negative transfer. That is, Group 0 showed more errors by persisting in

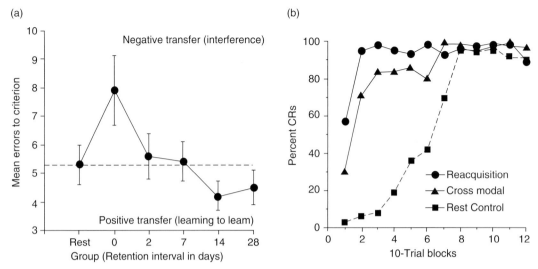

Figure 7 Examples of latent transfer after retention loss and extinction. (a) Reversal of a T-maze response in rats after a range of retention intervals (Bunch, 1939). (b) Reacquisition and cross-modal acquisition after extinction (Macrae and Kehoe, 1999). All figures adapted with permission.

performing the formerly correct response. However, as the retention interval increased, negative transfer progressively disappeared. More importantly, Groups 14 and 28 displayed positive transfer. Specifically, they showed fewer errors during the reversal than the Rest Control group. Thus, as retrieval of the original response faded, learning to learn appeared.

Figure 7(b) illustrates savings and learning to learn after an eyeblink CR was eliminated through extinction (Macrae and Kehoe, 1999). Two groups of rabbits were given initial training with either a tone or light CS. After CRs were established, both groups underwent extinction training using the same CS. After the CR had been thoroughly extinguished, one group (Reacquisition) was tested for savings by recommencing pairings of the original CS with the US. The other group (Cross Modal) was tested for learning to learn by starting pairings of the alternate CS with the US. A third group (Rest Control) was trained with either the tone or light CS. Relative to the rate of CR acquisition in the rest control group, the reacquisition group showed considerable savings. Furthermore, the cross-modal group showed strong learning to learn. In fact, acquisition to the cross-modal CS was nearly as rapid as reacquisition to the original CS.

1.08.3   Psychophysics

A central question in psychology is, "What is the stimulus for a behavior?" Psychophysical research

provides the basic methods, results, and theories for answering how a stimulus input is encoded and transformed in the nervous system to eventuate in a behavioral output. In investigating the psychophysics of animals, discrimination learning and generalization testing have played a central role.

1.08.3.1   Sensory Thresholds

There are two kinds of thresholds: absolute and difference. An absolute threshold is the level of intensity of a stimulus at which a subject is able to detect the presence of the stimulus some proportion of the time, usually 50%. A difference threshold is the magnitude of the difference between two stimuli that a subject is able to detect; again, a 50% criterion is common. **Figure 8** shows four examples of psychophysical curves using a combination of discrimination training and generalization testing.

1.08.3.1.1   Absolute thresholds
Figure 8(a) shows generalization tests for detecting a sinusoidal modulation in the amplitude of background noise (Kelly et al., 2006). Rats were trained on a lick suppression task, in which a mild shock to the tongue was signaled by a 3-s modulation of the background noise. Training and testing were then conducted by using combinations of modulation depths and modulation rates. The figure shows the mean percent correct as a function of modulation depths for modulation rates of 10 Hz, 100 Hz, and

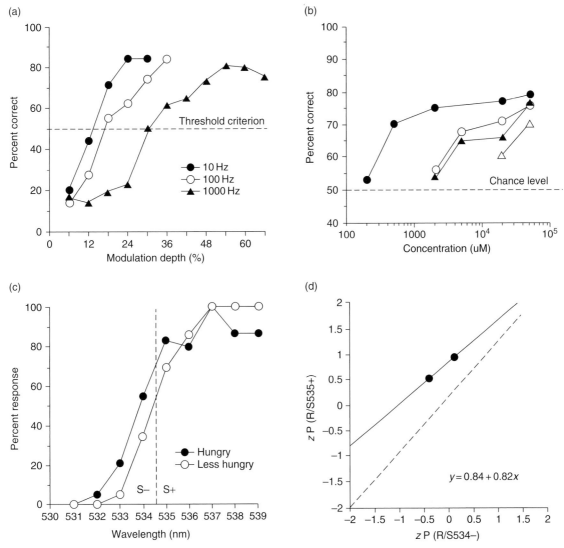

Figure 8 Examples of psychophysical curves. (a) Generalization tests for detection of a sinusoidal modulation in the amplitude of a broadband, background noise by rats (Kelly et al., 2006). (b) Curves of four squirrel monkeys tested for discrimination between increasing dilutions of an androgen-based odorant versus an odorless solvent (Laska et al., 2006). (c) Percent response in pigeons reinforced for pecking at keys of wavelengths of 535 nm and greater (Boneau and Cole, 1967). (d) The relative operating characteristic (ROC) plot for the probability of responding to the 535-nm S+ versus the 534-nm S− (Boneau and Cole, 1967). All figures adapted with permission.

1000 Hz. The absolute threshold for detecting modulation was designated as the point at which the curve for each modulation rate crossed the 50% criterion line. For example, the threshold for detecting a 100-Hz modulation was a 17% depth.

Figure 8(b) shows the individual psychophysical curves of four squirrel monkeys in a choice discrimination task. Specifically, the monkeys were tested for their ability to detect an androgen-based odorant (Laska et al., 2006). On each trial, the monkeys sniffed two strips mounted on two closed food

cups. One strip was impregnated with the odorant (S+), and the other with the odorless solvent (S−). The monkeys were then allowed to open one of the cups to discover whether or not it contained the reinforcer. After the initial discrimination was established, training was continued, in which the S+ odorant was progressively diluted until a monkey failed to discriminate it from the solvent. The left-hand point in each curve represents the dilution at which the monkey's choices failed to differ significantly from the 50% chance level.

1.08.3.1.2 Difference thresholds, sensitivity, and criterion

Figures 8(c) and **8(d)** show the results of an experiment aimed at identifying the difference threshold along the color dimension in a pigeon (Boneau and Cole, 1967). The procedure was a combination of discrimination training and generalization testing. A pigeon was reinforced for pecking at wavelengths of 535 nm and above, but not for shorter wavelengths. Two levels of hunger were used on different days. **Figure 8(c)** shows the resulting psychophysical curves, which indicate that the pigeon could detect a difference as small as 1 nm. The pigeon responded more when it was hungrier, displacing the function to the left. However, the slope of the function appeared the same, suggesting that the pigeon's sensitivity to stimulus differences was unaltered. Thus, the hunger is said to bias responding but not sensitivity.

These concepts of sensitivity and bias originate in signal detection theory (SDT) (Suboski, 1967; Blough, 2001b). According to SDT, observed responding results from the joint operation of the subject's ability to detect the stimulus (sensitivity) and their bias to respond (criterion). For a given sensitivity, a change in bias will cause the psychometric function to shift, as seen in **Figure 8(c)** with the effects of hunger. However, a clearer picture of the joint effect of sensitivity and criterion appears in a different type of plot, the relative operating characteristic (ROC). The ROC plots the probability of the target response to S+ against the probability of the response to S−. **Figure 8(d)** shows the ROC for the 535-nm S+ and the 534-nm S− under the two hunger conditions. The two points are plotted on axes scaled in z scores. The two points fall on a line that lies above the diagonal. The distance of the line above the diagonal is a measure of the sensitivity, while the position of the points along the line indicates the criterion. A slope of 1.00 indicates that the sensitivity is constant across the factors that influence the criterion. Conversely, deviations in the slope indicate that a manipulation influences sensitivity. In this case, a slope less than one suggests that, in fact, sensitivity declined as hunger increased.

1.08.3.2 Psychophysics of Memory

Discrimination training and generalization testing have been extended to the study of memory, often using a type of choice discrimination. In the basic version, called delayed matching to sample (DMTS), the subject is presented with one stimulus called the sample. Then, the subject is presented with pair of target stimuli. Choosing the stimulus that matches the sample results in reinforcement (S+), while choosing the other stimulus (S−) does not yield reinforcement. By manipulating the interval between the sample stimulus and target stimuli across trials, short-term memory for the sample stimulus can be mapped.

Figure 9 plots the results of two recent DMTS studies using rats and a single monkey, respectively. The rat study entailed a two-way spatial discrimination (Harper et al., 2006). On each trial, the sample stimulus was a presentation of a retractable bar on one side or the other of a wall in the test chamber. To ensure the sample bar was attended to, the rats were trained to press the bar three times before it was withdrawn. A delay interval of 0.1, 3.0, 9.0, or 18.0 s was then imposed. To prevent the rats from simply facing the location of the sample bar during this interval, they were trained to turn around and press another bar behind them. On completion of the delay, both the left and right bars were inserted into the chamber. As soon as either bar was pressed, the bars were retracted, and if the rat had pressed the previous sample bar, the reinforcer was delivered. As can be seen in **Figure 9**, accuracy in the choice response gradually declined when the delay interval exceeded 3 s, but even after 18 s, the level of performance still exceeded the chance level (50%).

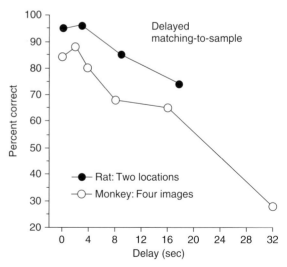

Figure 9 Percent correct choices in delayed-matching-to-sample tasks in rats (Harper et al., 2006) and a monkey (Hampton and Hampstead, 2006) as a function of delay interval between presentation of the sample and choice stimuli. All figures adapted with permission.

The other curve in **Figure 9** shows the results obtained from a monkey in a four-way visual discrimination, for which the sample and test stimuli were images of 'clip art' (Hampton and Hampstead, 2006). On each trial, the sample stimulus appeared in the center of a touchscreen. After the monkey contacted this image, one of six delay intervals (0, 2, 4, 8, 16, or 32 s) was imposed. Then, four test stimuli appeared, one in each corner of the screen. Only one of the test stimuli matched the sample stimulus. A large set of images was used such that each image was seen only once in each session, which contained 48 trials. The monkey's performance showed a progressive decline but only sank to its chance level (25%) after a 32-s delay.

1.08.3.3 Psychophysics of Time

Timing is everything, and not just in comedy. Predators must pounce at just the right moment to catch their next meal, suitors must pick the right moment to make their advance, and prey must pick the right moment to dash for cover. Even a widespread, basic protective response like the eyeblink has demands on its timing. A blink that is too early or too late will not protect the eye from injury, and a blink that is too long may effectively blind an individual at a crucial moment.

Figure 10 shows a psychophysical function for stimulus duration (Church and Deluty, 1977). Rats were first trained in a choice discrimination. A press on one bar was reinforced after a 2-s light stimulus, and a press on another bar was reinforced after an 8-s light stimulus. After this training, the rats were tested with stimuli of intermediate durations. The curve in **Figure 10** shows the mean percentage of tests in which the rats pressed the bar for the longer, 8-s signal. Under these conditions, the difference threshold was slightly greater than 4 s, a point approximately equal to the geometric mean of the 2-s and 8-s durations used in training.

A wide variety of studies have tracked the time course of responding based on the interval between a stimulus and a reinforcer. These studies have yielded two reliable results that are illustrated in **Figure 11**. **Figure 11(a)** shows the time course of an eyeblink CR in four groups of rabbits that were trained with four different intervals between CS onset and US onset, specifically, 125, 250, 500, and 1000 ms (Smith, 1968). The results are based on sporadic test trials in which the CS was presented without the US, and hence without any intrusion from the unconditioned

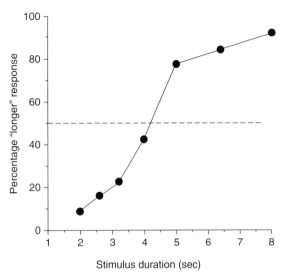

Figure 10 Psychophysical function in for stimulus duration after choice discrimination training in which rats were reinforced for pressing one lever when signaled by a 2-s stimulus and for pressing another lever when signaled by an 8-s stimulus (Church and Deluty, 1977). Figure adapted with permission.

response (UR). Similarly, **Figure 11(b)** shows the time course of barpress responding in a group of rats that had been trained in a temporal discrimination using a noise and a light (Roberts, 1981). For one stimulus, the first barpress after 20 s elapsed was reinforced by food. For the other stimulus, the first barpress after 40 s was reinforced. The results are based on test trials in which each stimulus was presented for 80 s without the reinforcer. Finally, **Figure 11(c)** shows the results of a study in which human participants were trained with stimuli of either 8, 12, or 21 s (Rakitin et al., 1998). After exposure to the target stimulus, the participants were asked to press a key when they thought that the appropriate time had passed.

Despite the large differences in the time scales, procedures, and species used in these three studies, responding showed similar temporal patterns. In each case, the peak of responding was well aligned to the interval used in training. Moreover, the variability in the placement of responding increased proportionally as the interval increased. Together, these proportional increases in the time and variability of peak placement are known as the 'scalar property' of timing. The theoretical and neural mechanisms responsible for the acquisition of response timing and its scalar property have been a matter of intensive research and theorizing in recent

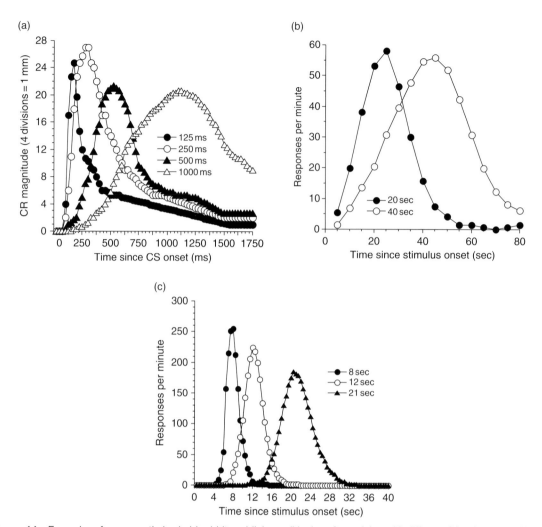

Figure 11   Examples of response timing in (a) rabbit eyeblink conditioning after training with different CS-US intervals (Smith, 1968), (b) barpressing by rats after training with two fixed intervals signaled by different discriminative stimuli (Roberts, 1981), and (c) reproduction of different stimulus intervals by humans (Rakitin et al., 1998). All figures adapted with permission. CS, conditioned stimulus; US, unconditioned stimulus.

years (e.g., Gallistel and Gibbon, 2000; McGann and Brown, 2000; Medina et al., 2000; Buhusi and Meck, 2005).

1.08.4   Excitatory and Inhibitory Learning Processes

Pavlov (1927) borrowed the terms of *excitation* and *inhibition* from neurophysiology to describe the processes underlying rises and falls in conditioned responding. Among other things, he proposed that discrimination learning could entail both excitatory learning for CS+ and inhibitory learning for CS−. Later, Spence (1936, 1937) extended these ideas to

generalization testing after discrimination training. He proposed that responding to test stimuli would be influenced jointly by generalization from both S+ and S−. That is, the level of responding to each test stimulus would reflect an algebraic sum of generalized excitation from S+ and generalized inhibition from S−.

1.08.4.1   Transfer Tests of Inhibition

The measurement of inhibitory associative strength has not been a simple matter for two reasons. First, the absence of responding to a CS− may reflect a lack of excitatory learning rather than a negative association. Hence, the level of inhibitory learning can only be inferred from the ability of the CS− to disrupt excitatory learning in a transfer test. Second, identifying transfer tests that isolate the effect of inhibitory learning from other possible disruptive factors has been difficult (Williams et al., 1992; Papini and Bitterman, 1993).

Two transfer tests have been used in tandem to determine whether a CS has acquired an inhibitory association (Brown and Jenkins, 1967; Rescorla, 1969; Cole et al., 1997). These two tests are known as the *summation* test and the *retardation* test. A candidate CS passes the summation test if it reduces CRs to another excitatory stimulus presented at the same time. Second, the candidate CS passes the retardation test if it shows a slow rate of CR acquisition when paired with the US.

Figure 12 illustrates the results of summation and retardation tests in fear conditioning in rats (Cole et al., 1997). The subjects were first given a discrimination learning task originated by Pavlov (1927), known as the *conditioned inhibition* procedure. Specifically, one stimulus was paired with an aversive US (A+), while a compound of two stimuli was presented alone (AX−). In addition, another stimulus was established as an excitatory stimulus by pairing it with the US (B+). Acquisition of excitatory fear conditioning was indexed by an appetitive response, specifically, licking water from a drinking tube. Thus, the greater the fear, the longer the time needed to complete a specified number of licks.

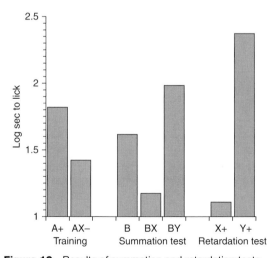

Figure 12 Results of summation and retardation tests after rats were given conditioned inhibition training, in which one stimulus was paired with an aversive US (A+), while a compound of two stimuli was presented alone (AX−). A third stimulus had also been paired with the US (B+), and a fourth stimulus was novel at the time of testing (Y) (Cole et al., 1997). Figure adapted with permission.

As can be seen in the left-hand portion of **Figure 12**, moderate discriminative responding to A+ versus AX− was achieved during initial training. Summation and retardation tests were conducted by splitting the subjects into five groups. For the summation test, one group was tested with the conditioned excitatory stimulus (B), another group was tested with a compound of the B stimulus plus the candidate inhibitor (BX), and a third group was tested with a compound of the B stimulus plus another stimulus (Y) that had not undergone any training (BY). This latter group was included to test whether compounding a neutral stimulus with B would disrupt the fear response. For the retardation test, the fourth group received pairings of the candidate inhibitor with the US (X+), and the fifth group received pairings of the untrained stimulus with the US (Y+).

Examination of **Figure 12** reveals that the candidate inhibitor (X) passed the summation test. That is, the BX compound yielded a lower level of responding than B stimulus alone. This reduction could not be attributed to unlearned effect of another stimulus, because the BY compound elicited a greater response than the B stimulus. Furthermore, the X stimulus also passed the retardation test. After X+ and Y+ pairings, the X stimulus produced a negligible response, while the Y stimulus produced a substantial response.

The two tests for associative inhibition are complementary (Rescorla, 1969). Together, they rule out different sources of response interference that do not reflect associative inhibition. The summation test reveals that the candidate CS has an antagonistic effect on responding to an excitatory stimulus. However, this antagonistic effect could have also occurred through either a division of attention between the two stimuli or a perceptual interaction between the two stimuli that would obscure the excitatory CS. The retardation test rules out these possibilities, because training with a single candidate CS is not subject to such influences from another stimulus. However, the retardation test by itself is not sufficient to demonstrate an inhibitory association, because slow CR acquisition may result from inattention to the CS (Lubow and Moore, 1959; Reiss and Wagner, 1972; Lubow, 1989; Schmajuk et al., 1996) In turn, the summation test guards against inattention, because attention to the candidate CS is needed for it to reduce responding to the excitatory CS.

The expense of conducting a thorough assay for conditioned inhibition like that of Cole et al. (1997) might seem prohibitive. However, more compact designs are possible, albeit with some risk that multiple tests of the same subjects will alter the results. If four distinctive stimuli can be found, then a single group can be used. The subjects would first receive training identical to that used in Cole et al. (1997), specifically, A+, AX−, and B+. Subsequently, the summation test would be conducted using tests of BX versus B. If the testing, which is usually done without the US, reduces overall responding, refresher training can be conducted. Then, retardation can be assessed by pairing the candidate stimulus X with the US (X+) while a novel stimulus Y is also paired with the US (Y+). If there is mutual generalization between X+ and Y+ trials, this test will be conservative and reduce the differences in acquisition to the stimuli. If only three distinctive stimuli can be identified, then a rest control group or something like it would be needed to conduct the retardation test.

1.08.4.2 Generalization after Discrimination Training

Generalization testing has been used to infer whether or not S− has acquired inhibitory associative strength. Spence (1937) himself conducted experiments aimed at testing whether his theory could explain demonstrations of *transposition* in generalization tests after choice discrimination training. For example, chimpanzees were initially rewarded for selecting the larger of two squares, e.g., $160\,cm^2$ (S+) versus $100\,cm^2$ (S−). The subjects were then tested with other pairs of squares. Of particular interest was the pair that contained the S+ ($160\,cm^2$) versus a larger square ($256\,cm^2$). For this pair, the subjects selected the original S+ on only 22% of trials and, conversely, selected the larger square on 88% of the trials. Findings like this suggested that the subjects were learning a relational property of *larger than*.

Spence (1937) argued that the transposition results could be explained by the net amount of excitation and inhibition activated by each stimulus. **Figure 13** illustrates this hypothesis. In the figure, associative strength is plotted as a function of the value of stimuli along a dimension, e.g., size. There is a gradient of generalized excitation around S+ and a gradient of generalized inhibition around S−. The net amount of associative strength activated by any one stimulus is represented by the third gradient, which is the point-by-point algebraic sum of the excitatory and inhibitory strengths. As may be apparent, there is a region of stimulus values that have a larger

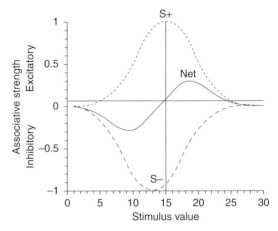

Figure 13   Theoretical net gradient based on hypothetical excitatory and inhibitory generalization gradients established during discrimination training with an S+ and S− along a stimulus dimension.

net associative strength than the S+ (Alberts and Ehrenfreund, 1951; Ehrenfreund, 1952).

This hypothesis has also been used to explain the results of generalization testing after go/no-go discrimination training. After training with an S+ and S− along a stimulus dimension, generalization testing can produce asymmetric gradients (Ghirlanda and Enquist, 2003). In some cases, the peak of the gradient is shifted away from S+ (Hanson, 1959). In other cases, the peak of the gradient remains at S+, but the subjects respond more to test stimuli on the S+ side of the dimension than to stimuli on the S− side. This type of result is called an area shift.

Figure 14 shows an example of peak shift in a single horse (Dougherty and Lewis, 1991). Initially, the subject was reinforced with food for pressing a bar during a 60-s S+, which was a 2.5-in (63 mm) circle. After this single-stimulus training, generalization testing was conducted with a series of circles ranging in diameter from 0.5 in (13 mm) to 4.5 in (114 mm). As can be seen in **Figure 14**, the generalization gradient was more or less symmetric and centered on S+. Then, discrimination training was conducted, in which a 1.5-in (38 mm) circle was introduced as S−. After discriminative responding was established, further generalization testing occurred. The resulting gradient was shifted away from S+ and S−, and its peak was located at the 3.0-in (76 mm) circle.

The peak-shift and area-shift phenomena are consistent with the excitation-inhibition hypothesis (Spence, 1937). However, there are well-developed alternative theories that can explain these phenomena without resorting to associative inhibition (Blough,

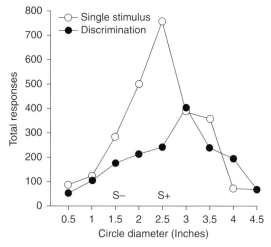

Figure 14 Peak shift after discrimination training. Generalization gradients of an operant response shown by a horse after single stimulus training and subsequent discrimination training along a size dimension (Dougherty and Lewis, 1991). Figure adapted with permission.

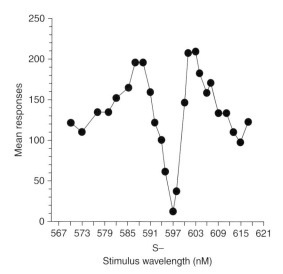

Figure 15 Generalization gradient obtained in pigeons during discrimination training in which keypecking to all stimuli along the wavelength dimension, except one (597 nm), was reinforced (Blough, 1975). Figure adapted with permission.

1975; Ghirlanda and Enquist, 2003). Furthermore, attempts to study generalization gradients during sustained operant training have yielded results contrary to the excitation-inhibition hypothesis (Blough, 1975; Hinson and Termison, 1997).

In these latter studies, discrimination training and generalization testing are conducted simultaneously, much like the psychophysical procedures described previously. Specifically, the subjects, often pigeons, are initially given reinforced training with multiple stimuli along a sensory dimension (e.g., visual wavelength). Once responding has been established to all the stimuli, discrimination training is begun. In positive discrimination training, responding to one stimulus (S+) continues to receive reinforcement, but responding to all the other stimuli along the dimension do not receive reinforcement. In the negative procedure, responding to all of the stimuli, bar one (S−), is reinforced.

Both procedures yield generalization gradients on a sustained basis. The positive discrimination yields a generalization gradient centered on S+. Conversely, the negative discrimination yields what has been described as an inhibitory gradient, in which responding is reduced at the S− value and also at nearby stimulus values (Jenkins and Harrison, 1962). An example of such an inhibitory gradient is shown in **Figure 15**.

The problem for the excitation-inhibition hypothesis arises from the shoulders that appear in the gradients at stimulus values that are at an intermediate distance from S+ or S−. In **Figure 15**, these shoulders appear for the stimulus values around 587 and 603 nm. According to the excitation-inhibition hypothesis, the negative impact of generalized inhibition from S− on responding to the excitatory stimuli should diminish in a smooth fashion. Instead, these contrast effects have been explained by models that do not use the construct of inhibition (Blough, 1975; Hinson and Termison, 1997).

1.08.4.3 Inhibition and Nonassociative Contributions to Responding

Revival of interest in learned inhibition has complicated the methodology of classical conditioning (Rescorla, 1967; Gormezano and Kehoe, 1975). In measuring excitatory conditioning, it would be ideal if each observed response were based entirely on the subject's history with the training manipulations, for example, the number of prior CS-US pairings. Not surprisingly, this ideal has never been achieved. The target response can and does occur during the CS in the absence of any CS-US pairings. The sources of this *nonassociative* responding include spontaneous occurrences of the target response, any innate tendency for the CS to evoke the target response, and pseudoconditioning, which is a sensitization-like effect arising from presentations of the US (Grant, 1943; Gormezano, 1966; Sheafor, 1975). Furthermore, in classical and also operant conditioning, performance of the learned response can be elevated or depressed by a variety of third factors, e.g., fatigue, satiation, drugs, and individual differences in responsiveness.

In classical conditioning, a suite of control conditions has evolved for determining what proportion of responding during the CS arises from CS-US contiguity versus nonassociative sources. These control conditions traditionally include CS-alone presentations, US-alone presentations, and explicit unpairings of the CS and US. If one's goal is to obtain a pure measure of the excitatory associative strength of CS, then be prepared to be frustrated. None of these control groups provides an unbiased estimate of nonassociative responding. In particular, explicitly unpaired presentations of the CS and US, in which they are well separated in time, can foster inhibitory learning (Rescorla, 1967; Siegel and Domjan, 1971; Napier et al., 1992). Rescorla (1967) advocated a control in which the presentations of the CS and US were randomized in time. However, this truly random control itself can be biased. In particular, CS-US pairings can randomly occur. When they do, they produce excitatory conditioning and thus yield an overestimate of the nonassociative contributions (Ayres et al., 1975). Despite the possible biases, together these controls do guard against a gross overestimation of the excitatory associative effects of CS-US pairings (Kehoe and Macrae, 2002).

The implementation of the full suite of controls in separate groups of subjects dramatically increases the size of an experiment. Each subject, however, can serve as its own nonassociative control by using a discrimination procedure (Schneiderman, 1972; Schneiderman et al., 1987). Specifically, responding to CS+ reflects the total contribution of excitatory associative effects plus any nonassociative contributions. In contrast, responding to CS− would ideally reflect only nonassociative contributions. However, just as with the separate control conditions, this estimate is probably biased in two opposing ways. On the one hand, responding to CS− may be elevated by excitatory generalization from CS+. On the other hand, the explicit unpairing of CS− and the US may promote inhibitory learning that will reduce responding to CS−, and through generalization, it may also reduce responding to CS+. In summary, the difference in responding to CS+ versus CS− will be a conservative estimate of the net associative effect of excitatory and inhibitory associative learning.

1.08.4.4   Commentary

The concept of learned inhibition has been a powerful but elusive concept. Whether a form of negative association is needed to explain any or all of the phenomena remains an open question. Even the results of the conditioned inhibition procedure may be explained without assuming a negative association (Miller and Matzel, 1988). Regardless of the fate of inhibition as a theoretical construct, the empirical phenomena suggestive of inhibition provide a valuable means for investigating the ability of learning mechanisms to regulate responding downward as well upward.

1.08.5   Perception, Attention, and Cognition

Research using discrimination learning and generalization testing has progressively revealed a variety of phenomena that come under the headings of perception, attention, and cognition. There has been – and undoubtedly will continue to be – vigorous debate concerning the value of top-down versus bottom-up explanations. The transposition effect is an early example of a phenomenon that seems to require a top-down explanation, but as seen in excitation-inhibition theory (Spence, 1937), the effect may be explained by an imaginative extension of bottom-up, associative mechanisms. Other chapters in this volume describe in greater detail the theory and research surrounding the increasing number of higher-order phenomena that have been identified. The remainder of this chapter describes some key phenomena that illustrate the application of discrimination and generalization methods in these areas.

1.08.5.1   Compound Stimulus Paradigms

A compound stimulus in its simplest form consists of two elements, often a tone and a light, presented together. By varying the conditions of training for the compound and its elements in relatively small ways, a startling, diverse set of phenomena has appeared. In turn, these phenomena have driven key developments in conditioning theory since the late 1960s (Kamin, 1968; Wagner et al., 1968).

1.08.5.1.1   Compound versus element discriminations

There are four basic discrimination procedures entailing a compound and its elements, which are denoted the *feature-negative, feature-positive, negative patterning*, and *positive patterning* procedures. With the exception of the feature-positive procedure (Jenkins and Sainsbury 1969; Jenkins, 1973), they originated with Pavlov, who used them to demonstrate both conditioned inhibition (Pavlov, 1927, pp. 68–87) and the perceptual synthesis of stimuli (Pavlov, 1927, p. 144). **Figure 16** depicts examples of the outcomes from these four procedures as seen in rabbit eyeblink conditioning, using a compound of tone and light elements (Kehoe, 1988).

1.08.5.1.1.(i)   Feature-negative and feature-positive discriminations   Figures **16(a)** and **16(b)** show the acquisition of feature-negative and feature-positive discriminations between a compound versus one of its elements. The feature-negative discrimination is, in fact, the same as used in the conditioned inhibition task. That is, the compound is presented alone (AX−), while one element is paired with the US (A+). Conversely, in the feature-positive procedure, the compound is paired with the US (AX+), and one element is presented alone (A−). The A stimulus is labeled as the *feature cue*, because it is the distinguishing element on AX versus X trials. The X

stimulus is labeled as the *target stimulus*. In the experiments described here, the X stimulus was presented sporadically (X test) to determine the level of responding it alone would elicit.

As can be seen, discriminative responding was acquired in both tasks. The feature-negative task yielded a high level of responding on A+ trials, a low level of responding on AX− trials, and virtually no responding on X tests (Marchant et al., 1972; Solomon, 1977). In the feature-positive task, CRs were quickly acquired on AX+ trials, while responding on A− trials grew only slightly (Kehoe and Schreurs, 1986). Tests with the X stimulus revealed that it elicited nearly as much responding as did the AX+ trials.

Both these results have suggested that the level of responding to the compound reflects a summation of the separate associative strengths of the separate elements. Thus, the low level of responding on AX− trials in the feature-negative task can be attributed to the algebraic sum of A's positive strength and

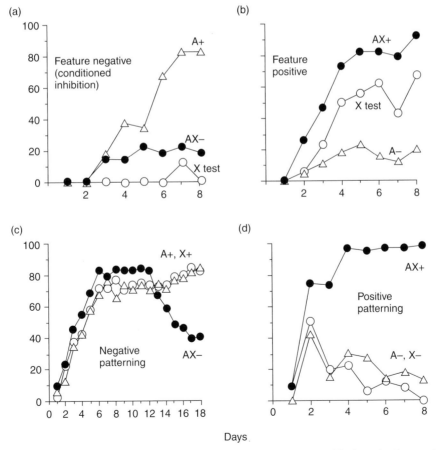

Figure 16   Compound-versus-element discrimination learning in rabbit eyeblink conditioning using tone and light elements (Kehoe, 1988). Figure adapted with permission.

X's unseen negative strength. In the feature-positive case, the high-level responding on AX+ trials can be explained as the sum of the high positive strength of the X stimulus and the low positive strength of the A stimulus. However, this elemental summation seems at most to be true only for cases like these. As will be described below, different processes appear to be engaged when these circumstances are varied (Kehoe and Gormezano, 1980).

1.08.5.1.1.(ii) Negative and positive patterning

Figures 16(c) and **16(d)** show the results of discrimination training using a compound and both its elements. In these patterning tasks, no element is strictly a feature cue or target stimulus, but for the sake of consistency in exposition, the elements remain labeled as A and X. **Figure 16(c)** shows the results of negative patterning. The early training sessions contained a mixture of trials in which the individual elements were each repeatedly paired with the US (A+, X+). The compound without the US (AX−) was presented only occasionally. Once the CR was established on A+ and X+ trials, more AX− trials were added. By the end of the experiment, each session contained 40 AX− trials, 10 A+ trials, and 10 X+ trials. Responding on AX− trials gradually declined, while responding on A+ and X+ trials was maintained. In contrast to the slow acquisition of negative patterning, discriminative responding (**Figure 16(c)**) emerged rapidly in the positive patterning procedure, in which the compound was paired with the US (AX+), and the elements were not (A−, X−).

Patterning has attracted considerable theoretical interest. In particular, the low level of responding on AX− trials in negative patterning cannot be explained by the summation of the elements' positive associative strengths. Since the first demonstrations of patterning (Pavlov, 1927, p. 144), it has been widely supposed that there is a perceptual synthesis of the elements to form an additional configural stimulus that can acquire its own associative strength, either alongside the elemental associations (Rescorla, 1973; Kehoe, 1988) or in place of them (Bellingham et al., 1985; Pearce, 1987, 1994). As an alternative to configural theories, other theories postulate that elements and compounds have distinctive and shared features. By the appropriate assignment of excitatory and inhibitory strengths to these features, patterning can be explained (Estes and Burke, 1953; Kehoe and Gormezano, 1980; Harris, 2006). Apart from these theoretical debates, patterning procedures have been used in distinguishing the neural substrates for "simple" conditioning for single CSs from the substrates of more complex processes engaged by compound stimuli (Sutherland and Rudy, 1989; Rudy and Sutherland, 1995; O'Reilly and Rudy, 2001).

1.08.5.1.1.(iii) Serial conditional discriminations

The discriminations described above all entailed compounds in which the elements were presented simultaneously. There are corresponding tasks that use stimuli presented in a serial fashion to form conditional discriminations. The delayed matching-to-sample task, previously described, is one form of a serial conditional discrimination. **Figure 17** shows the acquisition of discriminative behavior to a target stimulus (X) in three serial procedures, which are denoted, respectively, the *serial feature positive*, the *serial*

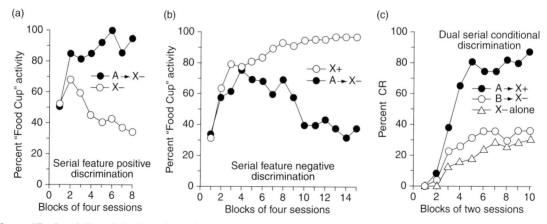

Figure 17 Acquisition of discriminative behavior to a target stimulus (X) in serial conditional discriminations, specifically a feature-positive procedure (a) and a feature-negative procedure (b) in appetitive conditioning of rats (Holland et al., 1999), plus a dual-feature procedure in rabbit eyeblink conditioning (Kehoe et al., 1987). All figures adapted with permission.

feature negative, and the *dual serial conditional* procedures. In the first two cases, the appetitive behaviors of rats for a food reinforcer were measured during the target stimulus (Holland et al., 1999). In the third case, conditioned eyeblinks in rabbits were measured during the target stimulus (Kehoe et al., 1987).

In all three cases, the feature cues (A, B) were presented before the target stimulus (X). This sequencing permits responding during the target stimulus to be measured under the influence of the prior feature cues. To denote this arrangement, the serial feature positive procedure is described as A→X+ versus X−, and the serial feature negative procedure is denoted as A→X− versus X+. For the discriminations shown here, the feature cue was a 5-s light (A) followed by a 5-s gap before the target stimulus (X), which was a 5-s tone. In the third case, both the reinforced and nonreinforced presentations of the X stimulus are preceded by a different feature cue (A→X+ vs. B→X−). In the example shown here, the feature cues were an 800-ms tone and an 800-ms noise. Each feature cue was followed by a gap of 3400 ms, and the target stimulus was a 100-ms light. On reinforced trials, the US was presented 300 ms after the light.

The discriminations shown in **Figure 17** were based on serial compounds in which there was a gap between the feature cue and target stimulus. However, similar discriminations have been established when the feature cues were extended to overlap and even extend past the target stimulus. In rabbit eyeblink conditioning, serial conditional discriminations have been reliably obtained with feature cues up to a minute in length (e.g., Brandon and Wagner, 1991; Macrae and Kehoe, 1995; Weidemann and Kehoe, 1997; Rogers and Steinmetz, 1998).

Serial conditional discriminations have been of interest in addressing several theoretical questions. The control of the feature cue over responding during the target stimulus has been thought to reveal a special type of learning. The feature cues may act indirectly on the ability of the X stimulus to elicit the CR by either (1) exercising superordinate control over memory retrieval, so-called *occasion-setting* (Holland, 1992; Schmajuk and Holland, 1998), (2) evoking an appropriate motivational state for responding (Konorski, 1967; Brandon and Wagner, 1991), or (3) perceptually fusing with the target stimulus in working memory to form a configural stimulus (Kehoe et al., 1987; Brandon and Wagner, 1998; Schmajuk et al., 1998). Finally, like delayed matching to sample, manipulations of the interval between the feature cue and target stimulus have been used to investigate working

memory (Holland et al., 1997; Holland, 1998; Weidemann, 1999; Kehoe et al., 2000).

1.08.5.1.2 Compound and element testing

In investigations using compound stimuli, there are two counterparts to generalization testing after single-stimulus training. First, in *compound conditioning*, training is conducted with a compound of stimuli, and these elements are then tested separately. Second, in *stimulus compounding*, two stimuli receive separate training and are then tested by presenting them simultaneously. Since the late 1960s, investigations using compound conditioning have played a key role in the development of associative theories in which the stimuli in a compound compete for attention and/or associative strength (Kamin, 1968; Rescorla and Wagner, 1972; Mackintosh, 1975). Since then, both procedures have been used in a now-massive body of research stimulated by these contending theories, as well as newer ones (Kehoe and Gormezano, 1980; Miller et al., 1995; Wasserman and Miller, 1997; Kehoe, 1998; Blaisdell and Miller, 2001; Pearce and Bouton, 2001; Pearce, 2002).

Compound conditioning and stimulus compounding can be viewed as the endpoints of a continuum in which AX+ trials are intermixed with element trials (A+, X+) in varying proportions. For example, **Figure 18** shows conditioned eyeblink responding in

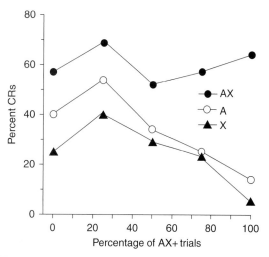

Figure 18 Conditioned eyeblink responding in rabbits to a tone+light compound (AX+) and its elements (A+, X+) as a function of the proportion of AX+ trials relative to A+ and X+ trials (Kehoe, 1986). All figures adapted with permission.

five groups of rabbits, in which the proportion of AX+ trials relative to A+ and X+ trials was varied from 0% (stimulus compounding) to 100% (compound conditioning). The A and X elements were a tone and a light. As shown in **Figure 18**, responding on AX test trials was at a high level across groups. In contrast, responding on A and X test trials was generally lower and progressively declined to negligible levels as the proportion of AX+ trials increased. These results suggest that there was summation of the associative strengths of the elements on AX trials when A+ and X+ pairs predominated. However, as the proportion of AX+ trials increased, a configural stimulus appeared to capture most of the associative strength, thus reducing the level of associative strength possessed by the A and X elements (Kehoe, 1986).

1.08.5.2   Multiple Discrimination Procedures

Multiple discrimination tasks, often presented in succession, have been used to illuminate the perceptual, memorial, navigational, and cognitive abilities of rats and pigeons in the laboratory, as well as other species in more natural environments (Roitblat et al., 1984; Bekoff et al., 2002; Spetch et al., 2003; Blaisdell et al., 2006; Hurley and Nudds, 2006). In the section on basic methods, two examples of multiple discriminations were described. One is the discrimination reversal procedure, in which two stimuli are repeatedly switched in their assignment as S+ and S−. The other is the learning set procedure, in which different pairs of stimuli are successively used as S+ and S−. This section will describe two relatively simple extensions of these procedures used to investigate higher-order processes in learning and memory in animals.

1.08.5.2.1   *Overtraining reversal effect*

Animals given extended discrimination training can, under many circumstances, acquire reverse discrimination more rapidly than animals given only moderate training (Reid, 1953; Sutherland and Mackintosh, 1971; Orona et al., 1982; Weiner et al., 1986; Van Golf Racht-Delatour and Massioui, 2000). This effect has seemed paradoxical, because basic learning rules predict that extra training should make the original discriminative responding more resistant, not less resistant, to reversal. This paradox has stimulated diverse theoretical accounts (e.g., Lovejoy, 1966; Siegel, 1967; Denny, 1970; Hall, 1974; Mackintosh, 1974). Among them, attentional

accounts have been prominent. For example, the additional training may more firmly fix the subject's attention on the relevant stimulus dimension, which would make the reversal a relatively easy matter of switching the specific stimulus-response assignments (Sutherland and Mackintosh, 1971).

1.08.5.2.2   *Oddity learning sets*

Harlow (1949) argues that learning to learn "transforms the organism from a creature that adapts to a changing environment by trial and error to one that adapts by seeming hypothesis and in-sight." In this respect, learning set research foreshadows more recent investigations of the cognitive abilities of animals (Kamil, 1987). Research using the learning set procedure has, among other things, produced evidence that animals can acquire what appear to be abstract concepts (Delius, 1994; Thomas, 1996).

One example of such concept acquisition is found in oddity learning. In oddity learning, each problem involves a choice between three stimuli, two alike and one different. Selecting the different stimulus is reinforced. As is the case in the more familiar two-stimulus problems, the subjects initially show gradual improvement over trials in their ability to select the correct stimulus. The subject is said to have acquired an oddity concept when it selects the correct stimulus on the first trial of each problem, prior to any reward or nonreward for that set of stimuli. In fact, after extensive experience with oddity problems, correct choices of the odd stimulus on the first encounter with a new set of stimuli do emerge in primates (e.g., Thomas and Frost, 1983). Among nonprimate species, there has been a recent demonstration of above-chance performance on the first trial of visual oddity problems in a seal (Hille et al., 2006). However, for rats, first-trial selections of the odd stimulus have not as yet proved reliable using either visual or olfactory stimuli (Thomas and Noble, 1988; Bailey and Thomas, 1998).

1.08.5.3   Reinforcer-Related Discriminations

1.08.5.3.1   *Sequential effects*

Reinforcers are sensory events and thus can serve as cues in learning tasks just as well as tones and lights. In operant fixed-interval training, for example, the delivery of a reinforcer is often the only external cue for timing the next interval. Similarly, in other forms of conditioning, food has been used to signal food (Goddard, 1997), shock has been used to signal shock

(Schreurs and Alkon, 1990), water has been used to signal shock (Gormezano and Tait, 1976), and shock has been used to signal water (Gormezano and Tait, 1976).

Reinforcers have also been used extensively as feature cues in serial conditional discriminations (Capaldi, 1994). The most well-developed examples of this use may be found in investigations of the sequential features of reinforcement schedules in instrumental runway tasks using rats. These studies have revealed that the episodic memory of a reinforcer on one trial can control responding on succeeding trials. The simplest sequential effect is seen in the single alternation schedule, in which reinforced trials (R) are strictly alternated with nonreinforced trials (N). From trial to trial, the external events remain the same. If the apparatus is considered the target stimulus (X), then the single alternation schedule can be viewed as a serial conditional discrimination involving N→X+ versus R→X− trials. Through studies using variations on this basic discrimination task, the qualitative and quantitative features of reinforcers on one or more trials have been found to be effective conditional cues (Capaldi, 1994; Fountain and Benson, 2006).

1.08.5.3.2   Differential outcomes effect

The use of different reinforcers can aid discrimination learning. In the original demonstration of this effect (Trapold, 1970), two groups of rats were trained using a conditional choice discrimination. On each trial, both groups were presented with two bars to press. On half the trials, a tone (A) was presented, and presses on the right bar were reinforced. On the other half of the trials, a clicking sound (B) was presented, and presses on the left bar were reinforced. In the experimental group, different reinforcers – a food pellet and sucrose solution – were used on the A and B trials. For half the rats in this group, the two reinforced sequences were A→Right→Food and B→Left→Sucrose. The other half of the rats received sucrose on A trials, and food on B trials. In contrast, the control group received the same reinforcer on both A and B trials. Thus, half the rats in this group received the reinforced sequences of A→Right→Food and B→Left→Food. The other half of the control group received sucrose as the reinforcer.

As can be seen in **Figure 19**, the experimental group showed both faster acquisition of the correct responses and a higher asymptote of correct responding than the control group. This facilitation of

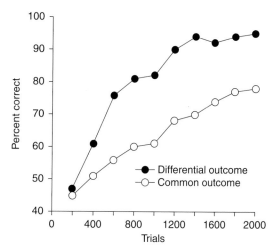

Figure 19 Acquisition of a choice discrimination in rats trained with different reinforcers (differential outcome) or the same reinforcer (common outcome) for the two responses (Trapold and Overmier, 1972). Figure adapted with permission.

discrimination learning and its terminal accuracy by using differential outcomes has been widely replicated in birds (Jones and White, 1994; Poling et al., 1996), horses (Miyashita et al., 2000), and humans (Overmier et al., 1999; Estevez et al., 2001). As well as using qualitatively different reinforcers, the effect has been obtained using different probabilities of food presentation, durations of food presentation, and locations of the food dispenser (see Jones and White, 1994, for a brief review).

The differential outcome effect and similar results have been variously attributed to 'expectancy learning,' 'prospective memory,' and 'response-outcome associations' (Rescorla, 1992; Overmier et al., 1999; Donahoe and Burgos, 2000). To objectify these notions, it has been noted that, during the reinforced sequences, the feature cue is effectively paired with the reinforcer just as in classical conditioning (Trapold and Overmier, 1972). Subsequently, like CR acquisition, the feature cue could elicit a central state describable as an expectancy or prospective memory of the reinforcer. If these central states are at all salient, they could act as additional cues that aid discriminative responding in the experimental group but interfere with discriminative responding in the control group. For example, a food-related state can be denoted X, and a sucrose-related state can be denoted Y. In subjects receiving differential outcomes, these central cues would be distinctive for each reinforced sequence, specifically, AX→Right→Food versus BY→Left→Sucrose. In contrast, for the control group, the reinforced sequences have a common element, for example, AX→Right→Food and BX→Left→Food.

In one demonstration that expectancies acquired through classical conditioning may be responsible for the differential outcome effect, rats were first trained in a differential outcomes procedure using, once again, tone and clicker cues (A, B), plus food and sucrose as the reinforcers (Kruse et al., 1983). Second, in a different box without the operant bars, the same rats were given pairings of a white noise stimulus (C) with either food or sucrose. Third, the rats were returned to the choice discrimination task, but on test trials, the C stimulus was substituted for the A and B cues. In line with expectancy theory (Trapold and Overmier, 1972), a C stimulus that had been paired with the food caused the rats to press the bar that had been reinforced with food. Likewise, the C stimulus that had been paired with sucrose caused the rats to press the bar that had been reinforced with sucrose.

1.08.6   Conclusion

The uses of discrimination learning and generalization testing are limited only by the imagination of the investigator. This article is only a sampler of the methods that have been used and their major results. Although this article was intended to be atheoretical, it was necessary to delve into some theoretical issues in order to place particular methods in their wider context. The reader should not make any inferences about the relative merits of any particular theory and should consult wider literature cited here to understand the fully range of research and theory surrounding a specific topic. In conclusion, this article should serve as a point of departure for investigators who wish to adapt these methods to address their interests.

Acknowledgment

Preparation of this manuscript was supported by Australian Research Council Grant DP0344082.

References

Alberts E and Ehrenfreund D (1951) Transposition in children as a function of age. *J. Exp. Psychol.* 41: 30–38.
Ayres JB, Benedict JO, and Witcher E (1975) Systematic manipulation of individual events in a truly random control in rats. *J. Comp. Physiol. Psychol.* 88: 97–103.

Bailey AM and Thomas RK (1998) An investigation of oddity concept learning by rats. *Psychol. Rec.* 48: 333–344.
Bekoff M, Allen C, and Burghardt MG (eds.) (2002). *The Cognitive Animal: Empirical and Theoretical Perspectives on Animal Cognition.* Cambridge, MA: MIT Press.
Bellingham WP, Gillette-Bellingham K, and Kehoe EJ (1985) Summation and configuration in patterning schedules with the rat and rabbit. *Anim. Learn. Behav.* 13: 152–164.
Bilotta J, Risner ML, Davis EC, and Haggbloom SJ (2005) Assessing appetitive choice discrimination learning in zebrafish. *Zebrafish* 2: 259–268.
Blaisdell AP and Miller RR (2001) Conditioned inhibition produced by extinction-mediated recovery from the relative stimulus validity effect: A test of acquisition and performance models of empirical retrospective revaluation. *J. Exp. Psychol. Anim. Behav. Process.* 27: 48–58.
Blaisdell AP, Sawa K, Leising KJ, and Waldmann MR (2006) Causal reasoning in rats. *Science* 311: 1020–1022.
Blough DS (1975) Steady state data and a quantitative model of operant generalization and discrimination. *J. Exp. Psychol. Anim. Behav. Process.* 104: 3–21.
Blough DS (2001a) Theperception of similarity.. In: Cook RG (ed.) *Avian Visual Cognition.* http://www.pigeon.psy.tufts.edu/avc/dblough/. (accessed January 2007)
Blough DS (2001b) Some contributions of signal detection theory to the analysis of stimulus control in animals. *Behav. Process.* 54: 127–136.
Boneau CA and Cole JL (1967) Decision theory, the pigeon, and the psychophysical function. *Psychol. Rev.* 74: 123–135.
Brandon SE and Wagner AR (1991) Modulation of a discrete Pavlovian conditioned reflex by a putative emotive Pavlovian conditioned stimulus. *J. Exp. Psychol. Anim. Behav. Process.* 17: 299–311.
Brandon SE and Wagner AR (1998) Occasion setting: Influences of conditioned emotional response and configural cues. In: Schmajuk NA and Holland PC (eds.) *Occasion Setting: Associative Learning and Cognition in Animals,* pp. 343–382. Washington, DC: American Psychological Association.
Brown PL and Jenkins HM (1967) Conditioned inhibition and excitation in operant discrimination learning. *J. Exp. Psychol.* 75: 255–266.
Buhusi CV and Meck WH (2005) What makes us tick? Functional and neural mechanisms of interval timing. *Nat. Rev. Neurosci.* 6: 755–765.
Bunch ME (1939) Transfer of training in the mastery of an antagonistic habit after varying intervals of time. *J. Comp. Psycho.* 28: 189–200.
Capaldi EJ (1994) The sequential view: From rapidly fading stimulus traces to the organization of memory and the abstract concept of number. *Psychon. Bull. Rev.* 1: 156–181.
Church RM and Deluty MZ (1977) Bisection of temporal intervals. *J. Exp. Psychol. Anim. Behav. Process.* 3: 216–228.
Cole RP, Barnet RC, and Miller RR (1997) An evaluation of conditioned inhibition as defined by Rescorla's two-test strategy. *Learn. Motiv.* 28: 323–341.
Cook RG (2001) Hierarchical stimulus processing by pigeons. In: Cook RG (ed.) *Avian Visual Cognition.* http://www.pigeon.psy.tufts.edu/avc/dblough/. (accessed January 2007)
Couvillon PA and Bitterman ME (1985) Analysis of choice in honeybees. *Anim. Learn. Behav.* 13: 246–252.
Delius JD (1994) Comparative cognition of identity. In: Bertelson P, Eelen P, and d'Ydewalle G (eds.) *International Perspectives on Psychological Science,* vol. 1, Leading Themes, pp. 25–40. Hillsdale, NJ: Lawrence Erlbaum.
Denny MR (1970) Elicitation theory applied to an analysis of the overlearning reversal effect. In: Reynierse JH (ed.) *Current Issues in Animal Learning.* New York: Academic Press.

Donahoe JW and Burgos JE (2000) Behavior analysis and revaluation. *J. Exp. Anal. Behav.* 74: 331–346.

Dougherty DM and Lewis P (1991) Stimulus generalization, discrimination learning, and peak shift in horses. *J. Exp. Anal. Behav.* 56: 97–104.

Ehrenfreund D (1952) A study of the transposition gradient. *J. Exp. Psychol.* 43: 81–87.

Ellis H (1965) *The Transfer of Learning*, New York: Macmillan.

Estes WK and Burke CJ (1953) A theory of stimulus variability in learning. *Psychol. Rev.* 60: 276–286.

Estevez AF, Fuentes LJ, Mari-Beffa P, Gonzalez C, and Alvarez D (2001) The differential outcome effect as a useful tool to improve conditional discrimination learning in children. *Learn. Motiv.* 32: 48–64.

Fountain SB and Benson DM (2006) Chunking, rule learning, and multiple item memory in rat interleaved serial pattern learning. *Learn. Motiv.* 37: 95–112.

Gallistel CR and Gibbon J (2000) Time, rate, and conditioning. *Psychol. Rev.* 107: 289–344.

Ghirlanda S and Enquist M (2003) A century of generalization. *Anim. Behav.* 66: 15–36.

Gick ML and Holyoak KJ (1980) Analogical problem solving. *Cogn. Psychol.* 12: 306–355.

Goddard MJ (1997) Spontaneous recovery in US extinction. *Learn. Motiv.* 28: 118–128.

Gormezano I (1966) Classical conditioning. In: Sidowski JB (ed.) *Experimental Methods and Instrumentation in Psychology*, pp. 385–420. New York: McGraw-Hill.

Gormezano I and Kehoe EJ (1975) Classical conditioning: Some methodological-conceptual issues. In: Estes WK (ed.) *Handbook of Learning and Cognitive Processes*, pp 143–179. Hillsdale, NJ: Lawrence Erlbaum.

Gormezano I and Tait RW (1976) The Pavlovian analysis of instrumental conditioning. *Pavlov. J. Biol. Sci.* 11: 37–55.

Grant DA (1943) Sensitization and association in eyelid conditioning. *J. Exp. Psychol.* 32: 201–212.

Gynther MD (1957) Differential eyelid conditioning as a function of stimulus similarity and strength of response to the CS. *J. Exp. Psychol.* 53: 408–416.

Hall G (1974) Transfer effects produced by overtraining in the rat. *J. Comp. Physiol. Psychol.* 87: 993–994.

Hampton RR and Hampstead BM (2006) Spontaneous behavior of a rhesus monkey (*Macaca mulatta*) during memory tests suggests memory awareness. *Behav. Process.* 72: 184–189.

Hanson HM (1959) Effects of discrimination training on stimulus generalization. *J. Exp. Psychol.* 58: 321–334.

Harlow HF (1949) The formation of learning sets. *Psychol. Rev.* 56: 51–65.

Harper DN, Hunt M, and Schenk S (2006) Attenuation of the disruptive effects of (+/−) 3:4-methylene dioxymethamphe-tamine (MDMA) on delayed matching-to-sample performance in the rat. *Behav. Neurosci.* 120: 201–205.

Harris JA (2006) Elemental representations of stimuli in associative learning. *Psychol. Rev.* 113: 584–605.

Herrick RM, Myers JL, and Korotkin AL (1959) Changes in SD and Sd Rates during the development of an operant discrimination. *J. Comp. Physiol. Psychol.* 52: 359–363.

Hille P, Dehnhardt G, and Mauck B (2006) An analysis of visual oddity concept learning in a California sea lion (*Zalophus Californianus*). *Learn. Behav.* 34: 144–153.

Hinson JM, and Termison LR (1997) An attentional model of dimensional contrast. *J. Exp. Psychol. Anim. Behav. Process.* 23: 295–311.

Holland PC (1992) Occasion setting in Pavlovian conditioning. In: Medlin, DL (ed.) *The Psychology of Learning and Motivation*, pp. 69–125. New York: Academic Press.

Holland PC (1998) Temporal control in Pavlovian occasion setting. *Behav. Process.* 44: 225–235.

Holland PC, Hamlin PA, and Parsons JP (1997) Temporal specificity in serial feature-positive discrimination learning. *J. Exp. Psychol. Anim. Behav. Process.* 23: 95–109.

Holland PC, Lamoureux JA, Han J-S, and Gallagher M (1999) Hippocampal lesions interfere with Pavlovian negative occasion setting. *Hippocampus* 9: 143–157.

Holt PE and Kehoe EJ (1985) Cross-modal transfer as a function of similarities between training tasks in classical conditioning of the rabbit. *Anim. Learn. Behav.* 13: 51–59.

Hurley S and Nudds M (eds.) (2006). *Rational Animals?* Oxford: Oxford University Press.

Jenkins HM (1973) Noticing and responding in a discrimination based on a distinguishing element. *Learn. Motiv.* 4: 115–137.

Jenkins HM and Harrison RH (1960) Effect of discrimination training in auditory generalization. *J. Exp. Psychol.* 59: 246–253.

Jenkins HM and Harrison RH (1962) Generalization gradients of inhibition following auditory discrimination learning. *J. Exp. Anal. Behav.* 5: 435–441.

Jenkins HM and Sainsbury RS (1969) The development of stimulus control through differential reinforcement. In: Mackintosh NJ and Honig WK (eds.) *Fundamental Issues in Associative Learning*, pp. 123–161. Halifax: Dalhousie University Press.

Jones BM and White KG (1994) An investigation of the differential-outcomes effect within sessions. *J. Exp. Anal. Behav.* 61: 389–406.

Kamil AC (1987) A synthetic approach to the study of animal intelligence. *Nebr. Symp. Motiv.* 35: 257–308.

Kamil AC, Jones TB, Pietrewicz A, and Mauldin JE (1977) Positive transfer from successive reversal training to learning set in blue jays (*cyanocitta cristata*). *J. Comp. Physiol. Psychol.* 91: 79–86.

Kamin LJ (1968) "Attention-like" processes in classical conditioning. In: Jones MR (ed.) *Miami Symposium on the Prediction of Behavior: Aversive Stimulation*, pp. 9–31. Coral Gables FL: University of Miami Press.

Kehoe EJ (1986) Summation and configuration in conditioning of the rabbit's nictitating membrane response to compound stimuli. *J. Exp. Psychol. Anim. Behav. Process.* 12: 186–195.

Kehoe EJ (1988) A layered network model of associative learning: Learning-to-learn and configuration. *Psychol. Rev.* 95: 411–433.

Kehoe EJ (1992) Versatility in conditioning: A layered network model. In: Levine DS and Levin SJ (eds.) *Motivation, Emotion and Goal Direction in Neural Networks*, pp. 63–90. Hillsdale, NJ: Lawrence Erlbaum.

Kehoe EJ (1998) Can the whole be something other than the sum of its parts? In: Wynne CDL and Staddon JER (eds.) *Models of Action: Mechanisms for Adaptive Behavior*, pp. 87–126. Hillsdale, NJ: Lawrence Erlbaum.

Kehoe EJ (2006) Repeated acquisitions and extinctions in classical conditioning of the rabbit nictitating membrane responses. *Learn. Mem.* 13: 366–375.

Kehoe EJ and Gormezano I (1980) Configuration and combination laws in conditioning with compound stimuli. *Psychol. Bull.* 87: 351–378.

Kehoe EJ and Holt PE (1984) Transfer across CS-US intervals and sensory modalities in classical conditioning in the rabbit. *Anim. Learn. Behav.* 12: 122–128.

Kehoe EJ and Macrae M (1997) Savings in animal learning: Implications for relapse and maintenance after therapy. *Behav. Ther.* 28: 141–155.

Kehoe EJ and Macrae M (2002) Fundamental behavioral methods and findings in classical conditioning. In: Moore JW (ed.) *A Neuroscientist's Guide to Classical Conditioning*, pp. 171–231. New York: Springer.

Kehoe EJ and Schreurs BG (1986) Compound-component differentiation as a function of CS-US interval and CS duration in the rabbit's nictitating membrane response. *Anim. Learn. Behav.* 14: 144–154.

Kehoe EJ, Marshall-Goodell B, and Gormezano I (1987) Differential conditioning of the rabbit's nictitating membrane response to serial compound stimuli. *J. Exp. Psychol. Anim. Behav. Process.* 13: 17–30.

Kehoe EJ, Palmer N, Weidemann G, and Macrae M (2000) The effect of feature-target intervals in conditional discriminations on acquisition and expression of conditioned nictitating membrane and heart-rate responsed in the rabbit. *Anim. Learn. Behav.* 28: 80–91.

Kelly JB, Cooke JE, Gilbride PC, Mitchell C, and Zhang H (2006) Behavioral limits of auditory temporal resolution in the rat: Amplitude modulation and duration discrimination. *J. Comp. Psycho.* 120: 95–105.

Konorski J (1967) *Integrative Activity of the Brain: An Interdisciplinary Approach.* Chicago: University of Chicago Press.

Kruse JM, Overmier JB, Konz WA, and Rokke E (1983) Pavlovian CS effects upon instrumental choice behavior are reinforcer specific. *Learn. Motiv.* 14: 165–181.

Laska M, Wieser A, and Salazar LTH (2006) Sex-specific differences in olfactory sensitivity for putative human pheromones in nonhuman primates. *J. Comp. Psycho.* 120: 106–112.

Lione LA, Carter RJ, Hunt MJ, Bates GP, Morton J, and Dunnett SB (1999) Selective discrimination learning impairments in mice expressing the human Huntington's disease mutation. *J. Neurosci.* 19: 10428–10437.

Lovejoy E (1966) Analysis of the overlearning reversal effect. *Psychol. Rev.* 73: 87–103.

Lubow RE (1989) *Latent Inhibition and Conditioned Attention Theory.* Cambridge: Cambridge University Press.

Lubow RE and Moore AU (1959) Latent inhibition: The effect of non-reinforced preexposure to the conditioned stimulus. *J. Comp. Physiol. Psychol.* 52: 415–419.

Mackintosh NJ (1974) *The Psychology of Animal Learning*, New York: Academic Press.

Mackintosh NJ (1975) A theory of attention: Variation in the associability of stimuli with reinforcement. *Psychol. Rev.* 82: 276–298.

Macrae M and Kehoe EJ (1995) Transfer between conditional and discrete discriminations in conditioning of the rabbit nictitating membrane response. *Learn. Motiv.* 26: 380–402.

Macrae M and Kehoe EJ (1999) Savings after extinction in conditioning of the rabbit's nictitating membrane response. *Psychobiology* 27: 85–94.

Marchant HG, Mis FW, and Moore JW (1972) Conditioned inhibition of the rabbit's nictitating membrane response. *J. Exp. Psychol.* 95: 408–411.

Marlatt GA, Lilie D, Selvidge BD, Sipes MD, and Gormezano I (1966) Cross-modal generalization to tone and light in human eyelid conditioning. *Psychon. Sci.* 5: 59–60.

McGann JP and Brown TH (2000) Fear conditioning model predicts key temporal aspects of conditioned response production. *Psychobiology* 28: 303–313.

Medina JF, Garcia KS, Nores WL, Taylor NM, and Mauk MD (2000) Timing mechanism in the cerebellum: Testing predictions of a large-scale computer simulation. *J. Neurosci.* 20: 5516–5525.

Miller RR and Matzel LD (1988) The comparator hypothesis: A response rule for the expression of associations. In: Bower GH (ed.) *The psychology of learning and motivation*, vol. 22, pp. 51–92. San Diego: Academic Press.

Miller RR, Barnet RC, and Grahame NJ (1995) Assessment of the Rescorla-Wagner model. *Psychol. Bull.* 117: 363–386.

Miyashita Y, Nakajima S, and Imada H (2000) Differential outcome effect in the horse. *J. Exp. Anal. Behav.* 74: 245–253.

Moore JW (1972) Stimulus control: Studies of auditory generalization in rabbits. In: Black AH and Prokasy WF (eds.) *Classical Conditioning II: Current Research and Theory*, pp. 206–230. New York: Appleton-Century-Crofts.

Napier RM, Macrae M, and Kehoe EJ (1992) Rapid reacquisition in conditioning of the rabbit's nictitating membrane response. *J. Exp. Psychol. Anim. Behav. Process.* 18: 182–192.

Nissani M, Hoefler-Nissani D, Lay UT, and Htun UW (2005) Simultaneous visual discrimination in Asian elephants. *J. Exp. Anal. Behav.* 83: 15–29.

Novick LR and Holyoak KJ (1991) Mathematical problem solving by analogy. *J. Exp. Psychol. Learn. Mem. Cogn.* 17: 398–415.

O'Reilly RC and Rudy JW (2001) Conjunctive representations in learning and memory: Principles of cortical and hippocampal function. *Psychol. Rev.* 108: 311–345.

Orona E, Foster K, Lambert RW, and Gabriel M (1982) Cingulate cortical and anterior thalamic neuronal correlates of the overtraining reversal effect in rabbits. *Behav. Brain Res.* 4: 133–154.

Overmier JB, Savage LM, and Sweeney WA (1999) Behavioral and pharmacological analyses of memory: New behavioral options for remediation. In: Haug M and Whalen RE (eds.) *Animal Models of Human Emotion and Cognition*, pp. 231–245. Washington, DC: American Psychological Association.

Papini MR and Bitterman ME (1993) The two-test strategy in the study of inhibitory conditioning. *J. Exp. Psychol. Anim. Behav. Process.* 19: 342–352.

Pavlov IP (1927) *Conditioned Reflexes: An Investigation of the Physiological Activity of the Cerebral Cortex*. London: Oxford University Press.

Pearce JM (1987) A model for stimulus generalization in Pavlovian conditioning. *Psychol. Rev.* 94: 61–73.

Pearce JM (1994) Similarity and discrimination: A selective review and a connectionist model. *Psychol. Rev.* 101: 587–607.

Pearce JM (2002) Evaluation and development of a connectionist theory of configural learning. *Anim. Learn. Behav.* 30: 73–95.

Pearce JM and Bouton ME (2001) Theories of associative learning in animals. *Annu. Rev. Psychol.* 52: 111–139.

Poling A, Temple W, and Foster TM (1996) The differential outcomes effect: A demonstration in domestic chickens responding under a titrating-delayed-matching-to-sample procedure. *Behav. Process.* 36: 109–115.

Rakitin BC, Gibbon J, Penney TB, Chara M, Hinton SC, and Meck WH (1998) Scalar expectancy theory and peak-interval timing in humans. *J. Exp. Psychol. Anim. Behav. Process.* 24: 15–33.

Reeves L and Weisberg RW (1994) The role of content and abstract information in analogical transfer. *Psychol. Bull.* 115: 381–440.

Reid LS (1953) The development of non-continuity behavior through continuity learning. *J. Exp. Psychol.* 46: 107–112.

Reiss S and Wagner AR (1972) CS habituation produces a "latent inhibition effect" but no active "conditioned inhibition." *Learn. Motiv.* 3: 237–245.

Rescorla RA (1967) Pavlovian conditioning and its proper control procedures. *Psychol. Rev.* 74: 71–80.

Rescorla RA (1969) Pavlovian conditioned inhibition. *Psychol. Bull.* 72: 77–94.

Rescorla RA (1973) Evidence for "unique stimulus" account of configural conditioning. *J. Comp. Physiol. Psychol.* 85: 331–338.

Rescorla RA (1992) Response-outcome versus outcome-response associations in instrumental learning. *Anim. Learn. Behav.* 20: 223–232.

Rescorla RA and Wagner AR (1972) A theory of Pavlovian conditioning: Variations in the effectiveness of reinforcement and nonreinforcement. In: Black AH and Prokasy WF (eds.) *Classical Conditioning II: Current Research and Theory*, pp. 64–99. New York: Appleton-Century-Crofts.

Roberts S (1981) Isolation of an internal clock. *J. Exp. Psychol. Anim. Behav. Process.* 7: 242–268.

Rodgers JP and Thomas DR (1982) Task specificity in nonspecific transfer and in extradimensional stimulus generalization in pigeons. *J. Exp. Psychol. Anim. Behav. Process.* 8: 301–312.

Rogers RF and Steinmetz JE (1998) Contextually based conditional discrimination of the rabbit eyeblink response. *Neurobiol. Learn. Mem.* 69: 307–319.

Roitblat HL, Bever L, and Terrace H (1984) *Animal Cognition*. Hillsdale, NJ: Lawrence Erlbaum.

Rudy JW and Sutherland RJ (1995) Configural association theory and the hippocampal formation: An appraisal and reconfiguration. *Hippocampus* 5: 375–389.

Schmajuk NA and Holland PC (1998) *Occasion Setting: Associative Learning and Cognition in Animals*. Washington, DC: American Psychological Association.

Schmajuk NA, Lam Y-W, and Gray JA (1996) Latent inhibition: A neural network approach. *J. Exp. Psychol. Anim. Behav. Process.* 22: 321–349.

Schmajuk NA, Lamoureux JA, and Holland PC (1998) Occasion setting: A neural network approach. *Psychol. Rev.* 105: 3–32.

Schneiderman N (1972) Response system divergencies in aversive classical conditioning. In: Black AH and Prokasy WF (eds.) *Classical Conditioning II: Current Theory and Research*, pp. 341–376. New York: Appleton-Century-Crofts.

Schneiderman N, McCabe PM, Haselton JR, Ellenberger HH, Jarrell TW, and Gentile CG (1987) Neurobiological bases of conditioned bradycardia in rabbits. In: Gormezano I, Prokasy WF, and Thompson RF (eds.) *Classical Conditioning III*, pp. 37–63. Hillsdale, NJ: Lawrence Erlbaum.

Schreurs BG and Kehoe EJ (1987) Cross-modal transfer as a function of initial training level in classical conditioning with the rabbit. *J. Exp. Psychol. Anim. Learn. Behav.* 15: 47–54.

Schreurs BG and Alkon DL (1990) US-US conditioning of the rabbit's nictitating membrane response: Emergence of a conditioned response without alpha conditioning. *Psychobiology* 18: 312–320.

Sheafor PJ (1975) "Pseudoconditioned" jaw movements of the rabbit reflect associations conditioned to contextual background cues. *J. Exp. Psychol Anim. Behav. Process.* 104: 245–260.

Siegel S (1967) Overtraining and transfer processes. *J. Comp. Physiol. Psychol.* 64: 471–477.

Siegel S and Domjan M (1971) Backward conditioning as an inhibitory procedure. *Learn. Motiv.* 2: 1–11.

Slotnick B and Hanford L (2000) Can rats acquire an olfactory learning set? *J. Exp. Psychol. Anim. Behav. Process.* 26: 399–415.

Smith MC (1968) CS-US interval and US intensity in classical conditioning of the rabbit's nictitating membrane response. *J. Comp. Physiol. Psychol.* 66: 679–687.

Solomon PR (1977) Role of hippocampus in blocking and conditioned inhibition of the rabbit's nictitating membrane response. *J. Comp. Physiol. Psychol.* 91: 407–417.

Spence KW (1936) The nature of discrimination learning in animals. *Psychol. Rev.* 43: 427–449.

Spence KW (1937) The differential response in animals to stimuli varying within a single dimension. *Psychol. Rev.* 44: 430–444.

Spetch ML, Rust TB, Kamil AC, and Jones JE (2003) Searching by rules: Pigeons' (*Columba livia*) landmark-based search according to constant bearing or constant distance. *J. Comp. Psycho.* 117: 123–132.

Suboski MD (1967) The analysis of classical discrimination conditioning experiments. *Psychol. Bull.* 68: 235–242.

Sutherland NS and Mackintosh NJ (1971) *Mechanisms of Animal Discrimination Learning*. New York: Academic Press.

Sutherland RJ and Rudy JW (1989) Configural association theory: The role of the hippocampal formation in learning, memory, and amnesia. *Psychobiology* 17: 129–144.

Thomas RK (1996) Investigating cognitive abilities in animals: Unrealized potential. *Cogn. Brain Res.* 3: 157–166.

Thomas RK and Frost T (1983) Oddity and dimension-abstracted oddity (DAO) in squirrel monkeys. *Am. J. Psychol.* 96: 51–64.

Thomas RK and Noble LM (1988) Visual and olfactory oddity learning in rats: What evidence is necessary to show conceptual behavior? *Anim. Learn. Behav.* 16: 157–163.

Trapold MA (1970) Are expectancies based upon different positive reinforcing events discriminably different? *Learn. Motiv.* 1: 129–140.

Trapold MA and Overmier JB (1972) The second learning process in instrumental learning. In: Black AH and Prokasy WF (eds.) *Classical Conditioning II: Current Research and Theory*, pp. 427–452. New York: Appleton-Century-Crofts.

Van Golf Racht-Delatour B and Massioui NE (2000) Alleviation of overtraining reversal effect by transient inactivation of the dorsal striatum. *Eur. J. Neurosci.* 12: 3343–3350.

Wagner AR, Logan FA, Haberlandt K, and Price T (1968) Stimulus selection in animal discrimination learning. *J. Exp. Psychol.* 76: 171–180.

Wallace RB and Daniels CE (1972) An analysis of learning set formation in the albino rat. *J. Gen. Psychol.* 86: 141–147.

Warren JM (1960) Oddity learning set in a cat. *J. Comp. Physiol. Psychol.* 53: 433–434.

Wasserman EA and Miller RR (1997) What's elementary about associative learning? *Annu. Rev. Psychol.* 48: 573–607.

Watson DJ, Sullivan JR, Frank JG, and Stanton ME (2006) Serial reversal learning of position discrimination in developing rats. *Dev. Psychobiol.* 48: 79–94.

Weidemann G, Georgilas A, and Kehoe EJ (1999) Temporal specificity in patterning of the rabbit's conditioned nictitating membrane response. *Anim. Learn. Behav.* 27: 99–187.

Weidemann G and Kehoe EJ (1997) Transfer and counterconditioning of conditional control in the rabbit nictitating membrane response. *Q. J. Exp. Psychol.* 50B, 295–316.

Weidemann G and Kehoe EJ (2005) Stimulus specificity of concurrent recovery in the rabbit nictitating membrane response. *Learn. Behav.* 33: 343–362.

Weiner I, Ben Horin E, and Feldon J (1986) Amphetamine and the overtraining reversal effect. *Pharmacol. Biochem. Behav.* 24: 1539–1542.

Whishaw IQ (1985) Formation of a place learning-set by the rat: A new paradigm for neurobehavioral studies. *Physiol. Behav.* 35: 139–143.

Williams DA, Overmier JB, and LoLordo VM (1992) A reevaluation of Rescorla's early dictums about Pavlovian conditioned inhibition. *Psycholog. Bull.* 111: 275–290.

1.09 Extinction: Behavioral Mechanisms and Their Implications

M. E. Bouton and A. M. Woods, University of Vermont, Burlington, VT, USA

Extinction is one of the best-known phenomena in all of learning theory. In Pavlovian learning, extinction occurs when the conditioned stimulus (CS) that has been associated with a biologically significant event (unconditioned stimulus, US) is now presented repeatedly without the US. In operant or instrumental learning, extinction occurs when an action or behavior that has been associated with a reinforcer is no longer reinforced. In either case, the learned performance declines. Extinction is important because it allows behavior to change and adapt as the environment also changes. Despite its fame and importance, however, it is not necessarily obvious how extinction works. One surprisingly common idea is that extinction involves the destruction of what was originally learned. Although this idea is built into several models of learning and memory (e.g., Rescorla and Wagner, 1972; McClelland and Rumelhart, 1985; see also McCloskey and Cohen, 1989), there is ample evidence that much of the original learning survives extinction (e.g., see Rescorla, 2001; Bouton, 2002, 2004; Myers and Davis, 2002; Delamater, 2004). This chapter selectively reviews results and theory from the behavioral literature in an effort to understand what is learned in extinction, what causes extinction, and how we can use our understanding of extinction to address certain clinical issues outside the laboratory.

There has been renewed interest in extinction in recent years. One reason is that as neuroscientists have made progress in understanding the brain mechanisms behind acquisition processes in learning (e.g., *See* Chapters 1.36, 3.23, 4.11), they have naturally turned their attention to extinction and inhibition too. A detailed review of the biological work is beyond the scope of this chapter, although we consider some of its implications in the final sections. Another reason for renewed interest in extinction is that it is now clearly understood to be part of cognitive behavioral therapy. That is, in clinical settings, extinction is often the basis of treatment that is used to effectively eliminate maladaptive behaviors, thoughts, or emotions (e.g., Bouton, 1988; Conklin and Tiffany, 2002). However, as this chapter highlights, extinction does not result in a permanent removal of the behavior but instead leaves the organism vulnerable to relapse. This conclusion provides one illustration of how basic research on extinction provides information that is practically important.

The first part of this chapter introduces several extinction phenomena that any adequate theory of extinction will need to explain and accommodate. These phenomena suggest that extinction does not destroy the original learning, but instead involves new learning that is at least partly modulated by the context. They also potentially contribute to lapse and relapse effects that may occur after extinction therapies. The second part of the chapter then asks: if extinction is an example of new learning, what events reinforce or cause it? We come to the conclusion that extinction is mainly caused by generalization decrement and by new learning caused by the violation of an expectancy of reinforcement. The third part of the chapter takes knowledge from the first two sections and asks what can be done to optimize extinction learning in a way that eliminates the possibility of relapse. Our discussion in the first two sections expands and updates discussions in Bouton (2004); the last section updates a discussion in Bouton et al. (2006b).

1.09.1 Six Recovery Effects after Extinction

A number of experimental manipulations can be conducted after extinction that cause the extinguished response to return to performance. All of them are consistent with the idea that extinction involves new learning, and it therefore leaves the CS with two available meanings or associations with the US. As is true for an ambiguous word, the context is crucial in selecting between them.

1.09.1.1 Renewal

The renewal effect is perhaps the most fundamental postextinction phenomenon. In this effect (e.g., Bouton and Bolles, 1979a; Bouton and King, 1983), a change of context after extinction can cause a robust return of conditioned responding. Several versions of the renewal effect have been studied, but all cases of it support the idea that (1) extinction does not destroy the original learning and (2) the response triggered by the extinguished CS depends on the current context. In the most widely studied version, ABA renewal, conditioning is conducted in one context (Context A) and extinction is then conducted in

a second one (Context B). (The contexts are typically separate and counterbalanced apparatuses housed in different rooms of the laboratory that differ in their tactile, olfactory, and visual respects.) When the CS is returned to the original conditioning context (Context A), responding to the CS returns (e.g., Bouton and Bolles, 1979a; Bouton and King, 1983; Bouton and Peck, 1989). In a second version, ABC renewal, conditioning is conducted in Context A, extinction is conducted in Context B, and then testing is conducted in a third, "neutral" context – Context C. Here again, a renewal of responding is observed (e.g., Bouton and Bolles, 1979a; Bouton and Brooks, 1993; Harris et al., 2000; Duvarci and Nader, 2004). In a final version, AAB renewal, conditioning and extinction are both conducted in the same context (Context A) and then the CS is tested in a second context (Context B). Here again, conditioned responding returns (e.g., Bouton and Ricker, 1994; Tamai and Nakajima, 2000), although there is currently less evidence of this type of renewal in operant than in Pavlovian conditioning (e.g., Nakajima et al., 2000; Crombag and Shaham, 2002).

Research on the renewal effect has helped us understand how contexts control behavior—in addition to understanding extinction itself. Several facts about the renewal effect are worth noting. First, it has been observed in virtually every conditioning preparation in which it has been investigated (see, e.g., Bouton, 2002, for a review). Second, it can occur after very extensive extinction training. In fear conditioning (conditioned suppression) in rats, Bouton and Swartzentruber (1989) observed it when 84 extinction trials followed eight conditioning trials. Other evidence suggests that it can occur after as many as 160 extinction trials (Gunther et al., 1998; Rauhut et al., 2001; Denniston et al., 2003), although at least one report suggests that it might not survive an especially massive extinction treatment (800 extinction trials after eight conditioning trials; Denniston et al., 2003). Third, the role of the context is different from the one anticipated by standard models of classical conditioning (e.g., Rescorla and Wagner, 1972; Pearce and Hall, 1980; Wagner, 1981; Wagner and Brandon, 1989, 2001). Those models accept the view that the context is merely another CS that is presented in compound with the target CS during reinforcement or nonreinforcement. It therefore enters into simple excitatory or inhibitory associations with the US. In the ABA renewal effect, for example, Context A might acquire excitatory associations with the US, and Context B might acquire inhibitory associations. Either kind of association would summate with the CS to produce the renewal effect (inhibition in B would reduce responding to the CS, whereas excitation in A would enhance it). However, a number of experiments have shown that the renewal effect can occur in the absence of demonstrable excitation in Context A or inhibition in Context B (e.g., Bouton and King, 1983; Bouton and Swartzentruber, 1986, 1989). These findings, coupled with others showing that strong excitation in a context does not influence performance to a CS unless the CS is under the influence of extinction (described later; Bouton, 1984; Bouton and King, 1986), suggest that direct associations in a context are neither necessary nor sufficient for a context to influence responding to a CS. The implication (e.g., Bouton, 1991b; Bouton and Swartzentruber, 1986) is that the contexts modulate or set the occasion for the current CS–US or CS–no US association (e.g., Holland, 1992; Swartzentruber, 1995; Schmajuk and Holland, 1998). Put another way, they activate or retrieve the CS's current relation with the US (*See* Chapter 1.05).

Another fact about renewal is that it appears to be supported by many kinds of contexts, including physical, temporal, emotional, and physiological ones (e.g., Bouton, 2000). For example, when fear extinction is conducted in the interoceptive context provided by benzodiazepine tranquilizers chlordiazepoxide and diazepam, renewed fear was observed when the rat was tested in the original nondrug state (Bouton et al., 1990). Cunningham (1979) had reported compatible evidence with alcohol, and we have recently collected similar observations with the benzodiazepine midazolam. State-dependent learning or retention can be conceptualized as the drug playing the role of context (e.g., Overton, 1985).

A further important characteristic of the renewal effect is that it implies that extinction learning is more context specific than original conditioning. This asymmetry in context dependence between conditioning and extinction must be true if one observes ABC and AAB renewal; in either case, conditioning transfers better to the final test context than extinction does. There is typically no measurable effect of switching the context after conditioning on responding to the CS in either fear or appetitive conditioning paradigms (e.g., Bouton and King, 1983; Bouton and Peck, 1989). This is also true of taste aversion learning (e.g., Rosas and Bouton, 1998) and human causal learning, in which humans are asked to judge the causal relationship between cues and outcomes presented over a series of trials (e.g.,

Rosas et al., 2001). The presence of the renewal effect indicates that extinction, on the other hand, is especially context specific. Some research suggests that both conditioning and extinction become somewhat context specific after extinction has occurred (Harris et al., 2000). However, there is little question that extinction comes under relatively more contextual control than original conditioning.

The reason for the difference in the context dependence of conditioning and extinction has been the subject of recent research. Given the similarities between extinction and inhibition, Bouton and Nelson (1994) and Nelson and Bouton (1997) asked whether pure inhibition (as acquired in the feature-negative paradigm, in which a CS is paired with the US when it is presented alone, but not when it is combined with an inhibitory CS) was context specific. Inhibition acquired by the inhibitory CS transferred without disruption to a new context; thus, extinction is not context specific merely because it is a form of inhibition. A second reason why extinction might be context specific is that it is the second thing the organism learns about the CS. Nelson (2002) confirmed that excitatory conditioning (tone–food pairings) transferred undisturbed across contexts, unless the tone had first been trained as a conditioned inhibitor, as discussed earlier, in the feature-negative paradigm. Conversely, inhibition to a conditioned inhibitor also transferred across contexts unless the CS had first been trained as a conditioned excitor (through tone–food pairings). Thus, regardless of whether the association was excitatory or inhibitory, the second thing learned was more context specific than the first (cf. Rescorla, 2005). Compatible data had been shown by Swartzentruber and Bouton (1992), who found that excitatory conditioning was context specific if it had been preceded by nonreinforced preexposure to the CS.

The evidence therefore suggests that the learning and memory system treats the first association as context free, but the second association as a kind of context-specific exception to the rule. (The main exception to the second-association rule is latent inhibition, in which the first phase can be shown to exert a context-dependent influence on the second phase (e.g., Hall and Channell, 1985), despite the fact that it is arguably the first thing learned. Latent inhibition is unique, however, in that the CS is not paired with anything significant in the first phase. One possibility, therefore, is that the CS is in part encoded as a feature of the context, making it difficult to extract it from that context when it is paired with the US in Phase 2 (cf. Gluck and Myers, 1993).)

There may be functional reasons for this (Bouton, 1994). A conditioning trial provides a sample from which an animal may make inferences about the state of the world (e.g., Staddon, 1988). Statistically, if the world is composed of two types of trials (CS–US and CS–no US), then the probability of sampling a particular type of trial will reflect its true prevalence in the world. Therefore, an early run of conditioning trials would reflect its high incidence in the population; a subsequent trial of another type might reflect an exception to the rule. Learning and memory may thus be designed to treat second-learned information as conditional and context-specific. At a more mechanistic level, recent research in human predictive learning (Rosas and Callejas-Aguilera, 2006) and in taste-aversion learning with rats (Rosas and Callejas-Aguilera, 2007) suggests that ambiguity introduced by conflicting information in Phase 2 leads the participants to pay attention to the context. The key finding is that after conflicting information about one CS or predictor is introduced, other subsequently learned associations are context dependent, even if they are entirely new or learned in a separate context. Thus, the introduction of a competing, conflicting association appears to encourage the participant to pay attention to all contexts.

It is worth concluding this section by noting the direct relevance of the renewal effect to exposure therapy in humans. Several studies have now shown that an exposure treatment that diminishes fear of spiders in one context (a room or a patio outdoors) can still allow a renewal of the fear when exposure to the spider was tested in the other context (Mystkowski et al., 2002; see also, e.g., Mineka et al., 1999; Vansteenwegen et al., 2005). Similar renewal has also been reported in the study of cue exposure therapy with both alcohol (Collins and Brandon, 2002) and cigarette users (Thewissen et al., 2006). Both types of participants reported a renewed urge to use the drug when tested in a context that was different from the one in which exposure to drug-related cues (e.g., visual and/or olfactory cues associated with the drug) had taken place; the alcohol participants also demonstrated renewal of a salivation response. All such results suggest limits to the effectiveness of cue exposure therapy (see also Conklin, 2006). However, renewal effects can be attenuated if the participant is reminded of extinction just prior to the renewal test. Collins and Brandon (2002) found that presenting explicit cues (a unique pencil, eraser, and clipboard) that had been a feature of the extinction context reduced renewal of the aforementioned

reactivity to alcohol cues. Mystkowski et al. (2006) reported that renewal of spider fear could be decreased if human participants mentally reinstated (imagined) stimuli from the treatment context before being tested in a different context. Both studies extended earlier findings that the renewal effect can be reduced in rats if cues that were part of the extinction context were later presented before the test (Brooks and Bouton, 1994). Renewal can be viewed as due to a failure to retrieve extinction outside the extinction context (*See* Chapter 1.05). Retrieval cues can provide a "bridge" between the extinction context and possible relapse contexts which allows for the generalization of extinction learning between the contexts (see Bouton et al., 2006b).

1.09.1.2 Spontaneous Recovery

Pavlov (1927) first observed spontaneous recovery, another well-known postextinction effect that involves recovery of the conditioned response as time passes following extinction. There are several available explanations of spontaneous recovery (for a discussion, see Brooks and Bouton, 1993; Devenport et al., 1997; Robbins, 1990; Rescorla, 2004a), and it seems likely to be multiply determined. However, we have argued (e.g., Bouton, 1988, 1993) that just as extinction is relatively specific to its physical context, it may also be specific to its temporal context. The passage of time might also bring about changes in internal and external stimulation that provide a gradually changing context. Spontaneous recovery can be seen as the renewal effect that occurs when the CS is tested outside its temporal context. Both are due to a failure to retrieve memories of extinction outside the extinction context. Consistent with this perspective, a cue that is presented intermittently during the extinction session and again just before the final test (an 'extinction cue') can attenuate both spontaneous recovery and renewal by reminding the subjects of extinction (Brooks and Bouton, 1993, 1994; Brooks, 2000). Interestingly, changing the physical and temporal contexts together can have a bigger effect than changing either context alone, as if their combination creates an even larger context change (Rosas and Bouton, 1997, 1998).

A series of experiments in appetitive conditioning with rats further suggests that temporal context can include the intertrial interval (ITI), the time between successive extinction trials (Bouton and García-Gutiérrez, 2006). Previous experiments had shown that rats that received extinction trials spaced by either 4-min or 16-min ITIs showed equivalent spontaneous recovery when tested 72 h later (Moody et al., 2006). However, when the retention interval was 16 min rather than 72 h (Bouton and García-Guiterrez, 2006), rats that had received extinction trials separated by the 4-min interval showed spontaneous recovery, whereas rats that had received the extinction trials separated by the 16-min interval did not. These results are consistent with the possibility that the ITI was coded as part of the extinction context. Thus, analogous to a renewal effect, conditioned responding returned when the animals were tested after an interval between trials that differed from the ITI that was used in extinction. However, a mismatch between the extinction ITI and the retention interval is not always sufficient to produce renewal; rats that received extinction trials spaced by 16 min and then received a short retention interval of 4 min failed to show spontaneous recovery. This anomaly is consistent with results that emerged in discrimination experiments in which the different ITIs were used as signals about whether or not the next CS presentation would be reinforced (see Bouton and García-Gutiérrez, 2006). Specifically, rats readily learned that a 16-min ITI signaled reinforcement of a CS, whereas a 4-min ITI did not. In contrast, they had considerably more difficulty learning that a 4-min ITI signaled reinforcement and a 16-min ITI did not. The results suggest that there are interesting constraints on how the interval between trials may be coded and/or used as a context.

1.09.1.3 Rapid Reacquisition

A third effect further indicates that conditioning is not destroyed in extinction. In rapid reacquisition, when CS–US pairings are reintroduced after extinction, the reacquisition of responding can be more rapid than initial acquisition with a novel CS (e.g., Napier et al., 1992; Ricker and Bouton, 1996; Weidemann and Kehoe, 2003). Although such an effect again suggests that the original learning has been 'saved' through extinction, the early literature was often difficult to interpret because many early designs were not equipped to rule out less interesting explanations (see Bouton, 1986, for a review). To add to the complexity, studies of fear conditioning (conditioned suppression) (Bouton, 1986; Bouton and Swartzentruber, 1989) and flavor aversion learning (Danguir and Nicolaidis, 1977; Hart et al., 1995) have shown that reacquisition can be slower than

acquisition with a new CS. (It is more rapid than initial acquisition with a CS that has received the same number of nonreinforced trials without conditioning (Bouton and Swartzentruber, 1989).) In fear conditioning, slow reacquisition requires extensive extinction training; more limited extinction training yields reacquisition that is neither fast nor slow (Bouton, 1986). At least part of the reason these preparations support slow reacquisition is that both typically involve very few initial conditioning trials. In contrast, procedures in which rapid reacquisition has been shown (conditioning of the rabbit nictitating membrane response (NMR) and rat appetitive conditioning) have usually involved a relatively large number of initial conditioning trials. Consistent with a role for number of trials, Ricker and Bouton (1996) demonstrated that slow reacquisition occurred in an appetitive conditioning preparation when the procedure used the number of conditioning and extinction trials that had been used in previous fear conditioning experiments. In rabbit NMR and heart rate conditioning, extensive extinction training has abolished rapid reacquisition, although slow reacquisition has yet to be observed (Weidemann and Kehoe, 2003).

Ricker and Bouton (1996) suggested that rapid reacquisition may partly be an ABA renewal effect that occurs when the animal has learned that previous USs or conditioning trials are part of the original context of conditioning. That is, when CS–US pairings are resumed after extinction (a series of CS–no US trials), they return the animal to the original conditioning context. The hypothesis is compatible with Capaldi's (1967, 1994) sequential analysis of extinction, which has made excellent use of the idea that responding on a particular trial is determined by how the animal has learned to respond in the presence of similar memories of previous trials. Presumably, conditioning preparations that employ a relatively large number of conditioning trials (e.g., rabbit NMR) allow many opportunities for the animal to learn that previous reinforced trials are part of the context of conditioning. Furthermore, Ricker and Bouton (1996) reported evidence that high responding during the reacquisition phase was more likely after a reinforced than a nonreinforced trial, which had signaled conditioning and extinction, respectively.

Bouton et al. (2004) reasoned that if rapid reacquisition is caused by recent reinforced trials generating ABA renewal, then an extinction procedure that includes occasional reinforced trials among many nonreinforced trials should slow down rapid reacquisition by making recent reinforced trials part of the context of both conditioning and extinction. Consistent with this hypothesis, a very sparse partial reinforcement procedure in extinction slowed reacquisition compared to a group that had received simple extinction. Evidence of a similar slowed reacquisition effect has also been obtained in instrumental conditioning (Woods and Bouton, 2007) when a lever-press response was sparsely reinforced during extinction and then paired again more consistently with the reinforcer. Such a result is consistent with the idea that rapid reacquisition is at least partly an ABA renewal effect. Because the partial reinforcement treatment involved many more CS–US (or response–reinforcer) pairings than simple extinction, it is difficult to reconcile with the view that rapid reacquisition is a simple function of the strength of an association that remains after extinction (e.g., Kehoe, 1988; Kehoe and Macrae, 1997). Slowing rapid reacquisition of an instrumental response may be especially relevant from a clinical perspective, because instrumental learning is often involved in maladaptive behaviors such as substance abuse (e.g., Bouton, 2000). The evidence suggests that extinction (i.e., strict abstinence) might not be the most effective treatment to prevent relapse in all situations (cf. Alessi et al., 2004). A more successful technique might be one that permits occasional reinforcers during treatment (e.g., see Sobell and Sobell, 1973; Marlatt and Gordon, 1985) and therefore provides a bridge between the extinction and testing contexts (see also Bouton et al., 2006b).

1.09.1.4   Reinstatement

A fourth context-dependent postextinction phenomenon is reinstatement. In this effect, the extinguished response returns after extinction if the animal is merely reexposed to the US alone (e.g., Pavlov, 1927; Rescorla and Heth, 1975; Bouton and Bolles, 1979b). If testing of the CS is contemporaneous with US delivery, then the USs may cause a return of responding because they were encoded as part of the conditioning context (as earlier; see Reid, 1958; Baker et al., 1991; Bouton et al., 1993). On the other hand, in many studies of reinstatement, testing is conducted at an interval of at least 24 h after US reexposure; here one still observes reinstatement compared to controls that were not reexposed to the US (e.g., Rescorla and Heth, 1975; Bouton and Bolles, 1979b). In this case, evidence strongly suggests that the effect is due to conditioning of the

context. When the US is presented after extinction, the organism associates it with the context; this contextual conditioning then creates reinstatement. For example, if the reinstating USs are presented in an irrelevant context, there is no reinstatement when the CS is tested again (e.g., Bouton and Bolles, 1979b; Bouton and King, 1983; Bouton, 1984; Baker et al., 1991; Wilson et al., 1995; Frohardt et al., 2000). Independent measures of contextual conditioning also correlate with the strength of reinstatement (Bouton and King, 1983; Bouton, 1984). Recent evidence that the effect in fear conditioning is abolished by excitotoxic lesions of the bed nucleus of the stria terminalis (Waddell et al., 2006), a brain area thought to control anxiety (e.g., Walker et al., 2003), suggests that in the fear-conditioning situation, at least, the effect may be mediated by anxiety conditioned in the context. Also, if the animal receives extensive extinction exposure to the context after the reinstatement shocks are presented, reinstatement is not observed (Bouton and Bolles, 1979b; Baker et al., 1991). These results indicate that mere reexposure to the US is not sufficient to generate reinstatement. It is necessary to test the CS in the context in which the US has been reexposed.

This effect of context conditioning is especially potent with an extinguished CS. For example, Bouton (1984) compared the effects of US exposure in the same or a different context on fear of a partially extinguished CS or another CS that had reached the same low level of fear through simple CS–US pairings (and no extinction). Although contextual conditioning enhanced fear of the extinguished CS, it had no impact on the nonextinguished CS (see also Bouton and King, 1986). This result is consistent with the effects of context switches mentioned earlier: An extinguished CS is especially sensitive to manipulations of the context. One reason is that contextual conditioning may be another feature of the conditioning context; its presence during a test may cause a return of responding after extinction because of another ABA renewal effect (Bouton et al., 1993).

1.09.1.5   Resurgence

Another recovery phenomenon has been studied exclusively in operant conditioning. In resurgence, a new behavior is reinforced at the same time the target behavior is extinguished. When reinforcement of the new behavior is discontinued, the original response can resurge. Resurgence can occur in two different forms. In one, a response (R1) is first trained and then extinguished. After R1 is extinguished, a new response (R2) is trained and subsequently extinguished. Recovery, or resurgence, of R1 happens during the extinction of R2 (Epstein, 1983; Lieving and Lattal, 2003, Experiment 1). The other version of the procedure, which can be called the ALT-R procedure (for reinforcement of an alternative response), involves first training R1 and then reinforcing R2 during the extinction of R1. When R2 then undergoes extinction, recovery of R1 occurs (Leitenberg et al., 1970, 1975; Rawson et al., 1977; Epstein, 1985; Lieving and Lattal, 2003). Like the other recovery phenomena described earlier, both forms of resurgence support the idea that extinction does not produce unlearning.

There has been little research designed to uncover the actual mechanisms behind resurgence. One possibility is that extinction of R2 could cause an increase in behavioral variability, or frustration, that might result in an increase in any alternative behavior, not just R1 (e.g., Neuringer et al., 2001). Few studies have included a control response to show that resurgence is unique to an extinguished response. The sole exception is a study by Epstein (1983), who reported that pigeons rarely pecked an alternative, previously nonreinforced response key. An explanation with specific regard to the ALT-R procedure is that reinforcement of R2 during extinction of R1 physically prevents the animal from emitting R1 and thus prevents exposure to the R1–no reinforcer contingency (Leitenberg et al., 1975; Rawson et al., 1977). It is also possible, however, that resurgence follows from the mechanisms implicated in the other recovery effects described earlier. In particular, resurgence observed in the ALT-R procedure could be due to the fact that extinction of R1 occurs in the context of R2 responding. Then, given that extinction is context-specific, R1 would return when extinction of R2 occurs and the frequency of R2 decreases. That is, little R2 responding would return the animal to the context in which R1 had been reinforced, and thus recovery of R1 in the ALT-R procedure would be analogous to an ABA renewal effect.

A somewhat different explanation would be required to explain the form of resurgence in which R1 is extinguished before R2 training begins. In this case, testing of R1 occurs after extinction of R2, and thus responding on R2 would be minimal in both the extinction and testing conditions and thus no renewal effect should result. For this scenario, we might suggest the following explanation. The reinforcer is consistently presented during training of R2, which occurs simultaneously with extinction of R1, and thus

this would continuously reinstate responding to R1 (e.g., Rescorla and Skucy, 1969; Baker et al., 1991). Reinstatement of R1 is possible due to conditioning of background context or due to the fact that the reinforcer is a discriminative stimulus signaling to make the response (e.g., Baker et al., 1991). While R2 is being reinforced, the response will interfere with the reinstated performance of R1. However, when R2 then undergoes extinction, the reinstated R1 responding (i.e., resurgence) can then be revealed. In this case, then, resurgence may be an example of the basic reinstatement effect.

1.09.1.6   Concurrent Recovery

Concurrent recovery is another effect indicating that extinction does not destroy original learning. To date, the phenomenon has been studied exclusively in rabbit NMR conditioning: In that preparation, extinguished responding to a target CS can return if a completely different CS is separately paired with the US (e.g., Weidemann and Kehoe, 2004, 2005). One interesting fact about concurrent recovery is that the effect does not necessarily depend on extinction. Rather, similar to a "learning to learn" effect in which conditioning with one CS increases the subsequent rate of conditioning with other CSs (e.g., Kehoe and Holt, 1984), responding to a weakly conditioned target CS can be increased as a result of conditioning with a different CS (Schreurs and Kehoe, 1987). Kehoe (1988) has interpreted these phenomena from a connectionist perspective. He has suggested that the effects occur because inputs from different CSs might converge on a common hidden unit. When a nontarget CS is paired with the US, it strengthens the association of the common hidden unit with the US and thereby allows more responding when the target CS is again presented. This account suggests that extinction plays no special role in enabling concurrent recovery, although the effects that reinforcing one CS has on responding to extinguished and nonextinguished target CSs have not been compared.

A different account of concurrent recovery is that it might merely be a reinstatement effect that occurs due to presentation of the US (with another CS) after extinction of the target CS. Thus, rather than depending on new CS–US pairings, the mere presence of the US alone might be enough to produce concurrent recovery and would suggest that it is similar to a basic reinstatement effect. This possibility appears unlikely in the case of NMR conditioning, because exposure to the US on its own after extinction does not cause much reinstatement in that preparation (e.g., Napier et al., 1992). However, in the many other preparations where reinstatement does occur (e.g., fear conditioning or appetitive conditioning), a demonstration of concurrent recovery might merely be a reinstatement effect – exposure to CS–US pairings simply involves reexposure to the US (see Rescorla and Heth, 1975; Bouton and Bolles, 1979b, for evidence of reinstatement when the US is presented with or without a CS). Additional work on concurrent recovery is required to determine whether it differentially influences an extinguished CS and, importantly, whether it (like reinstatement) is context specific. Perhaps reinforcing a CS in the same context where a target CS was previously extinguished could remove the contextual inhibition that had accrued there or allow excitation to generalize to the target CS via common associations between the CSs and the context (cf. Honey and Hall, 1989).

1.09.1.7 Summary

A great deal of research thus indicates that responding to an extinguished CS is susceptible to any of a number of recovery effects, suggesting that extinction is not unlearning. Indeed, based on the results of a number of tests that allow a specific comparison of the strength of the CS–US association before and after extinction (e.g., Delamater, 1996; Rescorla, 1996a), Rescorla (2001) has suggested that extinction involves no unlearning whatsoever; the original CS–US association seems to survive essentially intact. Extinction must thus depend on other mechanisms. The renewal effect, and the fact that extinction leaves the CS so especially sensitive to manipulations of context, is consistent with the idea that extinction involves new learning that is especially context-dependent. We have therefore suggested that extinction leaves the CS under a contextually modulated form of inhibition (e.g., Bouton, 1993): The presence of the extinction context retrieves or sets the occasion for a CS–no US association.

1.09.2 What Causes Extinction?

A theoretically and clinically significant question in the field of learning and memory is what event or behavioral process actually causes the loss of responding during extinction? Several ideas have been examined and are discussed next.

1.09.2.1 Discrimination of Reinforcement Rate

One possibility is that the animal eventually learns that the rate of reinforcement in the CS is lower in extinction than it was during conditioning. Gallistel and Gibbon (2000) have argued that the animal continually decides whether or not to respond in extinction by comparing the current rate of reinforcement in the CS with its memory of the rate that prevailed in conditioning. Because rate is the reciprocal of time, the animal computes a ratio between the amount of time accumulated in the CS during extinction and the amount of time accumulated in the CS between USs during conditioning. When the ratio exceeds a threshold, the animal stops responding.

This approach has been tested in several experiments. Haselgrove and Pearce (2003) examined the impact of varying the duration of the CS during extinction; when longer CSs are used in extinction, time in the CS accumulates more quickly, and the animal should stop responding after fewer trials. In some experiments, rats were given appetitive conditioning with a 10-s CS and then given extinction exposures to a series of 10-s or 270-s presentations of the CS. When responding was examined at the start of each CS, there was an occasionally significant, but surprisingly small, effect of increasing the duration of the CS during extinction. For instance, by the 12th two-trial block, the 10-s and 270-s CS groups had similar nonzero levels of responding, even though they had accumulated a total of 4 and 108 min of exposure in the CS, respectively. On the other hand, responding did decline as a function of time within a single presentation of the 270-s CS, perhaps reflecting generalization decrement resulting from the increasing difference between the current CS and the 10-s CS employed in conditioning. Consistent with that view, when conditioning first occurred with a 60-s CS, extinction of responding occurred more rapidly with a 10-s CS than with a 60-s CS. Thus, either an increase or a decrease in the duration of the CS relative to conditioning accelerated the loss of responding. This effect of time was not anticipated by the rate-discrimination view (Gallistel and Gibbon, 2000).

Drew et al. (2004) reported compatible results in experiments on autoshaping in ring doves. Doubling or halving the duration of the CS from the 8-s value used in conditioning did not affect the number of trials required to stop responding. The fact that extinction was thus largely controlled by the number of CS presentations is consistent with experiments that have examined the effects of the number and duration of nonreinforced trials added to conditioning schedules (Bouton and Sunsay, 2003). On the other hand, Drew et al. found that a more extreme increase in CS duration (from 8 to 32 s) increased the rate of extinction. This was attributed to the animal learning to discriminate the longer nonreinforced CS presentations from the shorter reinforced CS presentations: When 8-s CSs were presented again after extinction, birds extinguished with 4-s and 32-s CSs responded again. Animals are sensitive to time in the CS, but the number of extinction trials appears to be an important factor.

As noted by Gallistel and Gibbon (2000), the rate discrimination theory seems especially consistent with a well-known extinction phenomenon, the partial reinforcement effect (PRE; see Mackintosh, 1974, for a review). In this phenomenon, conditioning with partial reinforcement schedules (in which nonreinforced trials are intermixed with reinforced trials) creates a slower loss of responding in extinction than does conditioning with a continuous reinforcement schedule (in which every trial is reinforced). According to a rate-discrimination hypothesis (Gallistel and Gibbon, 2000), the partially reinforced subjects have learned to expect the US after more accumulated time in the CS, and it thus takes more CS time in extinction to exceed the threshold of accumulated extinction time/expected time to each US. The more traditional approach, in contrast, has been to think that partially reinforced subjects have learned to expect the US after more trials than continuously reinforced subjects have. It therefore takes more trials to stop generalizing from conditioning to extinction (e.g., Mowrer and Jones, 1945; Capaldi, 1967, 1994).

Contrary to the rate discrimination hypothesis, Haselgrove et al. (2004) and Bouton and Woods (2004) have shown that a PRE still occurs when partially and continuously reinforced subjects expect the reinforcer after the same amount of CS time. For example, both sets of investigators showed that a group that received a 10-s CS reinforced on half its presentations (accumulated CS time of 20 s) extinguished more slowly than a continuously reinforced group that received every 20-s CS presentation reinforced. Bouton and Woods (2004) further distinguished the time-discrimination account from the traditional trial-discrimination account (e.g., Mowrer and Jones, 1945; Capaldi, 1967, 1994). Rats that had every fourth 10-s CS reinforced extinguished more slowly over a series of alternating 10-s and 30-s extinction trials than

rats that had received every 10-s CS reinforced. This PRE was still observed when extinction responding was plotted as a function of time units over which the US should have been expected (every 40 s for the partially reinforced group but every 10 s for the continuously reinforced group). In contrast, the PRE disappeared when extinction responding was plotted as a function of the trials over which the US should have been expected (every fourth trial for the partially reinforced group and every trial for the continuously reinforced group). Ultimately, the PRE is better captured by trial-based theories (e.g., Capaldi, 1967, 1994; see Mackintosh, 1974, for a review of the older literature).

We have already seen that responding on a particular trial occurs in the context of memories of the outcomes of previous trials – that was the explanation provided earlier of rapid reacquisition as an ABA renewal effect (Ricker and Bouton, 1996; Bouton et al., 2004). Interestingly, the recent finding that occasional reinforced trials in extinction (partial reinforcement) can slow down the rate of reacquisition (Bouton et al., 2004; Woods and Bouton, 2007) is really just the inverse of the PRE: In the PRE, nonreinforced trials in conditioning allow more generalization from conditioning to extinction, whereas Bouton et al.'s finding suggests that reinforced trials in extinction allowed for more generalization of extinction to reconditioning. Either finding suggests the importance of considering recent trials as part of the context that controls performance in extinction.

In summary, there is little support for the idea that responding extinguishes when the US is omitted because the organism detects a lower rate of reinforcement in the CS. The number of extinction trials, rather than merely the accumulating time in the CS across trials, appears to be important to the extinction process. Time in the CS can have an effect: It appears to be another dimension over which animals generalize and discriminate (Drew et al., 2004; Haselgrove and Pearce, 2003). Explanation of the PRE, however, appears to be most consistent with a view that animals utilize their memories of the outcomes of preceding trials as a dimension over which they generalize and respond (see also Mackintosh, 1974, for an extended review).

1.09.2.2 Generalization Decrement

It is possible that the animal stops responding in extinction from the point at which it stops generalizing between the stimuli that prevailed in conditioning and those that prevail in extinction (e.g., Capaldi, 1967, 1994). This idea has had a long history in research on extinction, especially in research on the PRE. It is interesting to note that a generalization decrement theory of extinction does not imply destruction of the original learning in extinction, or indeed any new learning at all. However, there is still good reason to think that extinction also involves new learning. For instance, nonreinforcement of a food CS elicits measurable frustration, and this can be associated with stimuli present in the environment (Daly, 1974). Nonreinforcement of the CS in the related conditioned inhibition paradigm (in which a CS is nonreinforced in the presence of a second stimulus and that second stimulus acquires purely inhibitory properties) also generates measurable new learning in the form of conditioned inhibition. There is also evidence for new learning in the renewal effect. For example, either ABC renewal or AAB renewal (see earlier discussion) implies that the extinction context acquires an ability to modulate (suppress) performance to the CS. Such observations suggest that the animal has not merely stopped responding in extinction because of a failure to generalize. Instead, it appears to have learned that the CS means no US in the extinction context (see earlier).

1.09.2.3 Inhibition of the Response

Rescorla (2001) suggested that extinction might involve learning to inhibit the conditioned response. He summarized evidence from instrumental (operant) conditioning experiments indicating that the effects of extinction can be specific to the response that undergoes extinction. For example, Rescorla (1993) reinforced two operant behaviors (lever pressing and chain pulling) with food pellets and then extinguished each response in combination with a new stimulus (a light or a noise). Subsequent tests of the two responses with both light and noise indicated that each response was more depressed when it was tested in combination with the cue in which it had been extinguished (see also Rescorla, 1997a). There is thus good reason to think that the animal learns something specific about the response itself during operant extinction: It learns not to perform a particular response in a particular stimulus. One possibility is that the animal learns a simple inhibitory S–R association (Colwill, 1991). Another possibility, perhaps more consistent with the context-modulation account of extinction emphasized earlier, is that the animal learns that S sets the

occasion for a response – no reinforcer relationship. Rescorla (1993: 335; 1997a: 249) has observed that the experiments do not separate the two possibilities. To our knowledge, no analogous experiments have been performed in the Pavlovian conditioning situation.

The main implication examined in Pavlovian conditioning is that extinction procedures should be especially successful at causing inhibitory S–R learning if they generate high levels of responding in extinction. This prediction may provide a reasonable rule of thumb (Rescorla, 2001). For example, when a CS is compounded with another excitatory CS and the compound is extinguished, there may be especially strong responding in extinction (due to summation between the CSs), and especially effective extinction as evidenced when the CS is tested alone (Wagner, 1969; Rescorla, 2000; Thomas and Ayres, 2004). Conversely, when the target CS is compounded with an inhibitory CS, there is relatively little responding to the compound (excitation and inhibition negatively summate), and there is also less evidence of extinction when the target is tested alone (Soltysik et al., 1983; Rescorla, 2003; Thomas and Ayres, 2004). However, although these findings are consistent with the hypothesis that the effectiveness of extinction correlates with the degree of responding, either treatment also affects the degree to which the animal's expectation of the reinforcer is violated: The stimulus compound influences the size of the error term in the Rescorla-Wagner model, and in more cognitive terms the extent to which the expectation of the US created by the compound is violated when the US does not occur. The results do not separate the response-inhibition hypothesis from an expectancy-violation hypothesis, which will be covered in the next section.

An eyeblink experiment by Krupa and Thompson (2003) manipulated the level of responding another way. During extinction, rabbits were given microinjections of the gamma-aminobutyric acid (GABA) agonist muscimol adjacent to the motor nuclei that control the conditioned response (the facial nucleus and the accessory abducens). The injection therefore eliminated the CR during extinction. However, when the subjects were then tested without muscimol, the CS evoked considerable responding, suggesting that evocation of the CR was necessary for extinction learning. Unfortunately, the muscimol microinjections also had robust stimulus effects. They caused complete inactivation of the ipsilateral facial musculature: "the external eyelids were flaccid, the left ear hung down unsupported, and no vibrissae movements were observed on the side of the infusion" (Krupa and Thompson, 2003: 10579). In effect, the rabbits received extinction in a context that was different from the one in which conditioning and testing occurred (the ordinary state without partial facial paralysis). There are thus strong grounds for expecting a renewal effect. The hypothesis that elicitation of the CR is necessary for extinction must await further tests.

There are also data suggesting that the number of responses or level of responding in extinction does not correlate with effective extinction learning. For example, Drew et al. (2004) noted that although animals given long CSs in extinction responded many more times in extinction than animals given shorter CSs, extinction was mainly a function of the number of extinction trials. In fear conditioning experiments with mice, Cain et al. (2003) reported that extinction trials that were spaced in time produced a slower loss of freezing than extinction trials that were massed in time. Nevertheless, there was less spontaneous recovery after the massed treatment, suggesting that extinction was more effective when the treatment involved less overall responding. Experiments in our own laboratory with rat appetitive conditioning (Moody et al., 2006) suggest a similar conclusion, even though the results were different. Spaced extinction trials again yielded more responding in extinction than massed trials, but the treatments caused indistinguishable amounts of extinction learning as assessed in spontaneous recovery and reinstatement tests.

In related conditioned suppression experiments, Bouton et al. (2006a) compared the effects of extinction in multiple contexts on the strength of ABA and ABC renewal effects (discussed more in the section titled 'Other behavioral techniques to optimize extinction learning'). Rats received fear conditioning with a tone CS in Context A, and then extinction of the tone for three sessions in Context B, or a session in B, then C, and then D, before final renewal tests in the original context (Context A) or a neutral fifth context (Context E). Although the successive context switches in the BCD group caused more fear responding during extinction (due to renewal effects with each context switch), the groups showed strikingly similar renewal in either Context A or Context E. Thus, higher responding in extinction does not indicate better extinction learning; in fact, the level of responding on extinction trials was positively, rather than negatively, correlated with the level of renewal (see also Moody et al., 2006). The results seem inconsistent with a response-inhibition hypothesis. Their

impact on the expectancy violation hypothesis is perhaps less clear.

Rescorla (2006, Experiment 5) provided perhaps the most direct test of whether enhanced responding or enhanced associative strength is responsible for the increased extinction (loss of responding) that typically follows compound presentation of two extinguished stimuli (see also Reberg, 1972; Hendry, 1982). He studied the effects of a diffuse excitor (e.g., a noise paired with food) and a diffuse positive occasion setter (e.g., a houselight that signaled the reinforcement of a keylight CS) on extinction of autoshaped key pecking in pigeons. When combined with a target keylight CS that was undergoing extinction, the diffuse excitor failed to increase the amount of pecking at the keylight, although it theoretically increased the animal's expectation of the US. In contrast, when combined with the target keylight CS, the diffuse occasion setter increased the amount of pecking at the CS without theoretically increasing the direct expectancy of the US. Contrary to Rescorla's (2001) rule of thumb about more responding resulting in more extinction, extinction in combination with the excitor caused a more durable extinction effect (assessed in reacquisition) than did extinction in combination with the occasion setter. The occasion setter caused no more effective extinction than extinction of the target alone. This finding suggests that the actual level of responding in extinction is not as important in determining the success of extinction as the extent to which the US is predicted and thus nonreinforcement is surprising.

In summary, although animals that receive extinction after operant conditioning may in fact learn to refrain from performing a particular response in a particular context (e.g., Rescorla, 1993, 1997a), the importance of response inhibition in Pavlovian extinction is not unequivocally supported at the present time. High responding in extinction does not guarantee more effective extinction learning, and a better explanation of the results of stimulus-compounding experiments (where the level of responding does appear to predict the success of extinction) may be the violation-of-expectation hypothesis, to which we now turn.

1.09.2.4 Violation of Reinforcer Expectation

It is commonly thought that each CS presentation arouses a sort of expectation of the US that is disconfirmed on each extinction trial. For example, in the error-correction rule provided by Rescorla and Wagner (1972), the degree of unlearning (which we have seen can create inhibition) is provided by the difference in the overall associative strength present on a trial and the actual US that occurs on the trial. In the Pearce-Hall model (Pearce and Hall, 1980), the discrepancy was conceptualized as an event that reinforced new inhibitory learning that is overlaid on the original excitatory learning (see also Daly and Daly, 1982). Wagner's SOP ("sometimes opponent process") model (1981) accepts a similar idea. One piece of evidence that seems especially consistent with the expectation-violation view is the "overexpectation experiment," in which two CSs are separately associated with the US and then presented together in a compound that is then paired with the US. Despite the fact that the compound is paired with a US that can clearly generate excitatory learning, the two CSs undergo some extinction (e.g., Kremer, 1978; Lattal and Nakajima, 1998). The idea is that summation of the strengths of the two CSs causes a discrepancy between what the animal expects and what actually occurs, and some extinction is therefore observed. As mentioned earlier, the expectation-violation view is also consistent with the effects of compounding excitors and inhibitors with the target CS during no-US (extinction) trials (Wagner, 1969; Soltysik et al., 1983; Rescorla, 2000, 2003, 2006; Thomas and Ayres, 2004).

One theoretical challenge has been to capture the expectancy violation in real time. Gallistel and Gibbon (2000) have emphasized the fact that traditional trial-based models like the Rescorla–Wagner model have been vague about the precise point in time in a trial when the violation of expectation actually occurs. The issue is especially clear when trial-based models explain the extinction that occurs with a single extended presentation of the CS, as is the case for the context or background in conditioning protocols with very widely spaced conditioning trials. (Spaced trials are held to facilitate conditioning of the CS because long intertrial intervals allow more context extinction and thus less blocking by context.) There is good evidence that widely spaced trials do create less contextual conditioning than massed trials (e.g., Barela, 1999). To account for contextual extinction over long intertrial intervals, many trial-based models arbitrarily assume that the single long-context exposure is carved into many imaginary trials, and that more imaginary trials occur and create more extinction in longer-context exposures.

It is worth noting, however, that Wagner's SOP model (e.g., Wagner, 1981; Wagner and Brandon, 1989, 2001) is relatively specific about where in time the process that generates extinction occurs. According to that model, CS and US are represented as memory nodes that can become associated during conditioning. For the association between them to be strengthened, both nodes must be activated from inactivity to an active state, "A1," at the same time. Once the association has been formed, the presentation of the CS activates the US node to a secondarily active state, "A2." This in turn generates the CR. An inhibitory connection is formed between a CS and a US when the CS is activated to the A1 state and the US is activated to A2 rather than A1. This happens in simple extinction because the CS activates the US into A2. This process occurs in real time; thus, during any nonreinforced trial, inhibition will accrue to the CS from the point in time at which the US node is first activated to A2 until the CS leaves the A1 state, which may not occur until the CS is turned off at the end of the trial. Thus, extinction learning will proceed continuously as long as the CS is on and no US occurs on any extinction trial. A limiting factor, however, is the extent to which the CS itself is in the A2 state: The longer it remains on, the more likely the elements in the CS node will be in A2 rather than A1, making new learning about the CS more difficult. Nonetheless, extensions of the CS in extinction will have an effect, because elements in A2 eventually return to the inactive state, from where they will return to A1 because of the continued presence of the CS. SOP thus accounts for extinction in extended CSs without recourse to imaginary trials, and a recent extension of the model (Vogel et al., 2003) may also account for generalization decrement as a function of CS time (Haselgrove and Pearce, 2003; Drew et al., 2004). Although a complete analysis of SOP requires computer simulations that are beyond the scope of the present chapter, the principles contained in the model are consistent with many of the facts of extinction reviewed here. From the current point of view, its most significant problem is that it underestimates the role of context in extinction, and might not account for the negative occasion-setting function of context (e.g., Bouton and King, 1983; Bouton and Swartzentruber, 1986, 1989; Bouton and Nelson, 1998) that arguably provides the key to understanding the renewal, spontaneous recovery, rapid reacquisition, and reinstatement phenomena (for a start at addressing occasion-setting phenomena in terms of SOP, see Brandon and Wagner, 1998; Wagner and Brandon, 2001).

In fear extinction, at the physiological level, expectation violation may be mediated by activation of opioid receptors (see McNally and Westbrook, 2003). Fear conditioning is typically impaired by opioid receptor agonists (e.g., Fanselow, 1998) but facilitated by antagonists, such as naloxone. Extinction, in contrast, is facilitated by opioid receptor agonists and impaired by antagonists (McNally and Westbrook, 2003). According to McNally and Westbrook, opioid receptors may be involved in fear extinction because the omission of the expected US leads to a feeling of relief (Konorski, 1967; Dickinson and Dearing, 1978) that is mediated by opioid peptides; the relief associated with the absence of the US might countercondition fear responses. The idea is also captured in SOP theory's sometimes opponent process, A2. That is, activation of the US node in A2 reduces the effectiveness of the US and also constitutes the crucial event that leads to extinction. Activation of opioid receptors may thus play the physiological role of A2 in fear conditioning. A similar physiological mechanism has not yet been specified for appetitive conditioning, although the underlying basis of frustration is an obvious candidate.

1.09.3 Can Extinction Be Made More Permanent?

Recent research on extinction has explored several methods that might enhance extinction learning. These methods are discussed here because they provide further insight into the causes of extinction and how extinction therapies might be enhanced.

1.09.3.1 Counterconditioning

One way to optimize extinction learning might be to actually pair the CS with another US that evokes a qualitatively different (or opposite) response. In counterconditioning, a CS that has been associated with one US is associated with a second US, often incompatible with the first, in a second phase. Not surprisingly, performance corresponding to the second association replaces performance corresponding to the first. Clinical psychologists have incorporated this idea into therapies, such as in systematic desensitization, which involves the training of relaxation responses in the presence of a CS while fear to that CS extinguishes (e.g., Wolpe, 1958). Although

counterconditioning may result in a quicker loss of phase-1 performance than simple extinction does (e.g., Scavio, 1974), it is another paradigm that, like extinction, involves a form of retroactive interference. Similar principles may therefore apply (Bouton, 1993). As with extinction, the original association remains intact despite training with a second outcome. This is true in both Pavlovian (Delamater, 1996; Rescorla, 1996a) and instrumental conditioning (Rescorla, 1991, 1995).

Equally important, counterconditioning procedures do not necessarily guarantee protection against relapse effects (the postextinction phenomena discussed earlier) (see also Rosas et al., 2001; García-Gutiérrez and Rosas, 2003, for compatible results in human causal learning). Renewal of fear occurs when rats receive CS–shock pairings in one context, then CS–food pairings in another, and are finally returned to the original context (Peck and Bouton, 1990). Complementary results were obtained when CS–food preceded CS–shock pairings. Spontaneous recovery occurs if time elapses between phase 2 and testing (Bouton and Peck, 1992; Rescorla, 1996b, 1997b). Finally, reinstatement has also been observed (Brooks et al., 1995): When CS–food follows CS–shock, noncontingent shocks delivered in the same context (but not in a different context) can reinstate the original fear performance. Counterconditioning thus supports at least three of the recovery effects suggesting that extinction involves context-dependent new learning.

1.09.3.2 Other Behavioral Techniques to Optimize Extinction Learning

If extinction involves new learning, then procedures that generally promote learning might also facilitate extinction. This idea has motivated recent research in several laboratories. For example, one idea is that conducting extinction in multiple contexts might connect extinction with a wider array of contextual elements and thereby increase the transfer of extinction learning to other contexts and potentially reduce the renewal effect (e.g., Bouton, 1991a). The results, however, have been mixed. Experiments in conditioned lick suppression (Gunther et al., 1998) and flavor-aversion learning with rats (Chelonis et al., 1999) have shown that extinction in multiple contexts can attenuate (but not abolish) instances of both ABC and ABA renewal relative to that observed after extinction in a single context (see also Vansteenwegen et al., 2006, for a related example). In contrast, as discussed earlier, our own experiments using a fear conditioning method (conditioned lever-press suppression) with rats found that extinction in multiple contexts had no discernible influence on either ABA or ABC renewal (Bouton et al., 2006a). Null results (in ABA renewal) have also been reported with a fear conditioning (shock expectancy) procedure in humans (Neumann et al., 2007). All results together suggest that there are important variables that modulate the positive impact of extinction in multiple contexts on the renewal effect (see Bouton et al., 2006a, for a discussion).

Another approach to optimizing extinction learning is to space extinction trials in time. This idea has been inspired by the fact that spaced trials often yield better excitatory learning than massed trials (e.g., Spence and Norris, 1950). It is worth noting, though, that the behavioral mechanisms behind trial-spacing effects on conditioning are multiple and complex (e.g., see Bouton et al., 2006b), and that many of them focus on the facilitating effects of spacing US presentations, which obviously are not involved in extinction. Nonetheless, there are still some grounds for expecting trial spacing effects in extinction, and these have been tested in several experiments. Spaced trials often cause a slower loss of responding in extinction (e.g., Cain et al., 2003; Morris et al., 2005; Moody et al., 2006), as one might expect, for example, if long intervals between successive CS presentations allow some spontaneous recovery. However, the long-term effects of spacing extinction trials have been variable and much less clear. When responding is tested after a long retention interval, spaced extinction trials have been shown to reduce responding (e.g., Westbrook et al., 1985; Morris et al., 2005), have no effect on responding (Moody et al., 2006), and create more responding than massed extinction trials (Cain et al., 2003; Rescorla and Durlach, 1987). Another complication is the results mentioned earlier, which suggest that extinction ITI can also be part of the context that controls extinction performance (Bouton and García-Gutierrez, 2006). More work will be necessary to untangle these various effects.

Another temporal manipulation has attracted recent interest. In the fear-potentiated startle paradigm in rats, extinction conducted immediately after fear acquisition leads to seemingly more durable extinction (Myers et al., 2006). In particular, rats that received extinction 10 min or 1 h (and in some cases 24 h) after a single acquisition session later failed to exhibit reinstatement, renewal, or spontaneous recovery, whereas rats tested after a longer 72-h acquisition-to-extinction interval showed all these postextinction recovery effects. Immediate extinction thus seemed to produce a more permanent form of extinction that potentially corresponds to biological depotentiation (i.e., reversal) of potentiated synapses (e.g., see Lin et al., 2003). However, once again there are complications and boundary conditions. For example, humans that have received extinction within a few minutes of fear acquisition still show reinstatement (LaBar and Phelps, 2005) and renewal (Milad et al., 2005) when these phenomena are tested later. In rat experiments that measured freezing rather than potentiated startle, Maren and Chang (2006) found that immediate fear extinction may be less effective than delayed extinction under some conditions; immediate extinction never produced a more durable loss of freezing after delayed extinction. And in several appetitive conditioning preparations, Rescorla (2004b) independently found more spontaneous recovery (less-effective extinction) in rats when extinction occurred 1 day, rather than 8 days, after acquisition. Rescorla's methods differed substantially from those in the aforementioned studies, and it is worth noting that his extinction after a 1-day interval might already be outside the temporal window in which depotentiation is possible (e.g., see Staubli and Chun, 1996; Huang et al., 2001). But it seems clear that additional research will be required to fully understand the effects of the interval between conditioning and extinction on the long-term effects of extinction.

1.09.3.3 Chemical Adjuncts

Research on the neurobiology of conditioning and extinction suggests that certain pharmacological agents may also be used to optimize extinction learning. For example, there has been a great deal of recent interest in D-cycloserine (DCS), a compound that is a partial agonist of the N-methyl-D-aspartate (NMDA) glutamate receptor. The NMDA receptor is involved in long-term potentiation, a synaptic model of learning (e.g., Fanselow, 1993), and has now been shown to be involved in several examples of learning including fear conditioning (e.g., Miserendino et al., 1990; Campeau et al., 1992, see Davis and Myers, 2002; Walker and Davis, 2002). The discovery that NMDA receptor antagonists interfere with fear extinction (e.g., Falls et al., 1992; Cox and Westbrook, 1994; Baker and Azorlosa, 1996; Lee and Kim, 1998; Santini et al., 2001) supported the idea that the NMDA receptor was also involved in extinction learning. The next step was to ask whether an NMDA agonist like DCS might correspondingly facilitate extinction. And it does; there is now evidence that administration of DCS facilitates extinction of conditioned fear in rats (Walker et al., 2002; Ledgerwood et al., 2003). And importantly, it also enhances exposure therapy in humans with acrophobia (Ressler et al., 2004) and social phobia (Hofmann et al., 2006). In each of these cases, when DCS was combined with a number of extinction trials that only partially reduced fear in a control group, it yielded more complete fear extinction as revealed during tests that were conducted without the drug.

The fact that DCS can facilitate extinction needs to be interpreted cautiously. For example, there is little in the description of how DCS works to suggest that it would do more than merely strengthen ordinary extinction learning, which, as we have shown, is relatively context specific and subject to relapse. Consistent with this possibility, although DCS facilitates the rate of fear extinction, it does not decrease the strength of the ABA renewal effect (Woods and Bouton, 2006). That is, rats for whom DCS had facilitated extinction still showed a robust return of fear when they were tested with the CS in the original conditioning context. This result indicates that DCS combined with extinction does not abolish the original learning. Woods and Bouton (2006) actually suggested that DCS might facilitate inhibitory conditioning of the context in which extinction occurs. Such a possibility is consistent with rapid extinction (enhanced contextual inhibition would decrease fear of the CS presented in it) and intact renewal (context inhibition would be gone when the CS is tested in another context). It is also consistent with other DCS effects reported in the literature. For example, DCS given during extinction can later reduce reinstatement (Ledgerwood et al., 2004); enhanced inhibition in the context would interfere with reinstatement by disrupting the development of context conditioning during US-alone presentations. DCS combined with extinction of one CS also causes less fear of a second CS tested in the same context (Ledgerwood et al., 2005); if the context were an inhibitor, it would inhibit fear of any CS tested in that context. Although DCS can have positive effects on fear extinction, it does not create unlearning.

Another compound that has been of interest is yohimbine, an alpha-2 adrenergic antagonist. This substance may cause paniclike responding when it is injected in animals or panic patients (Davis et al., 1979; Pellow et al., 1985; Johnston and File, 1989; see Stanford, 1995, for review). For that reason, it might increase the level of fear during extinction, and by

thus enabling either increased response inhibition or a higher violation of reinforcer expectation (see earlier discussion), allow for better extinction learning. Consistent with this possibility, yohimbine administered before a fear extinction session can lead to better extinction learning in mice (i.e., less freezing in a subsequent test session conducted 24 hours later; Cain et al., 2003). We have replicated this effect in rats (Morris and Bouton, 2007). However, the facilitated extinction was highly context specific; rats tested in a new context or back in the original conditioning context after extinction with yohimbine still showed a strong renewal of fear. Thus, as we saw with DCS, yohimbine facilitates the rate of extinction learning without necessarily abolishing relapse. Further results suggested that presenting yohimbine on its own in a context allows that context to suppress subsequent extinguished fear performance – as if it was conditioning a form of context-specific fear inhibition. Although the exact mechanism is unclear, it seems apparent that as an adjunct to extinction, yohimbine once again may not prevent the occurrence of future relapse.

Behavioral neuroscientists have recently also become interested in memory "reconsolidation" effects (*See* Chapter 1.24) that might suggest a new way to modify previously learned memories. It has long been known that freshly learned memories may be labile and easily disrupted before they are consolidated into a stable long-term form (e.g., McGaugh, 2000; Dudai, 2004). The consolidation process requires synthesis of new proteins in the brain (e.g., Davis and Squire, 1984; Goelet et al., 1986) and can therefore be blocked by administration of a protein synthesis inhibitor, such as anisomycin (e.g., Schafe and LeDoux, 2000). In the case of fear memories, whose consolidation can be modulated by stress hormones, consolidation can also be hindered by administration of a β-adrenergic receptor blocker such as propranolol (Pitman et al., 2002; Vaiva et al., 2003; McGaugh, 2004; see also Pitman, 1989). Recent research suggests that an older memory that has recently been reactivated (for example) by a single exposure to the CS likewise temporarily returns to a labile state from which it needs to be reconsolidated (e.g., Nader et al., 2000; Sara, 2000; Walker et al., 2003; Lee et al., 2004; Suzuki et al., 2004; Alberini, 2005). Like consolidation, reconsolidation can be blocked by anisomycin (e.g., Nader et al., 2000), and in the case of a fear memory, by administration of propranolol (Przybyslawski et al., 1999; Debiec and LeDoux, 2004). In these experiments, memory is returned to a labile state by presenting the CS on a very small number of occasions that are insufficient to produce extinction on their own (e.g., Suzuki et al., 2004). The crucial new result is that administration of anisomycin or propranolol while the memory is in this state can reduce evidence of conditioned responding when the CS is tested later. A therapeutic implication may be that one of these drugs in combination with one or two presentations of a CS may weaken an aversive fear memory. However, more basic research is needed. For example, it is not necessarily clear that a behavioral reconsolidation result involves actual modification of the original memory or mere difficulty in retrieving it (see Duvarci and Nader, 2004, for a critical analysis of these possibilities as induced by anisomycin). It seems clear that caution is necessary in interpreting the results of any effect of a drug or chemical on learning, extinction, and therapy.

1.09.3.4   Summary

A variety of manipulations have been thought to hold promise in optimizing extinction learning, but their effects have been mixed and (at this point in time) are not well understood. When investigators have specifically tested their effects on the relapse effects we reviewed in the first part of this chapter, they have often provided surprisingly little protection (see Bouton et al., 2006b, for a review). In contrast, one of the most effective and durable ways to optimize extinction learning and protect against relapse seems to be with the use of techniques that bridge the extinction and testing contexts, such as retrieval cues and presentation of occasional reinforced trials during extinction (discussed earlier). Bridging treatments accept the inherent context-specificity of extinction and work by increasing the similarity between the extinction context and test contexts where lapse and relapse may be a problem.

1.09.4   Conclusions

Extinction is a highly complex phenomenon, even when analyzed at a purely behavioral level. It is probably multiply determined. But, according to the results reviewed here, it usually does not involve destruction of the original learning. Instead, the main behavioral factors that cause the loss of responding appear to be generalization decrement and new learning that may be initiated by the violation of an expectation of the US. In SOP (e.g., Wagner,

1981; Wagner and Brandon, 2001), perhaps the most powerful and comprehensive model of associative learning that is currently available, that expectation violation takes the form of the CS activating the US node into a secondarily active (A2) state that potentially enables new inhibitory learning as long as the CS remains on and no US is presented. Importantly, this new inhibitory learning leaves the original CS–US association intact.

Bouton (1993) has argued that the fact that extinction might leave the original learning intact means that the CS emerges from extinction with two available associations with the US. It therefore has properties analogous to those of an ambiguous word, and the current performance depends on which of two associations is retrieved. Consistent with this idea, another fact that emerges from behavioral research on extinction is that it is relatively context dependent. Given this, the CS's second (inhibitory) association is especially dependent on the context for its activation or retrieval. The role of the context is usually modulatory; it activates or retrieves the CS's second (inhibitory) association, much as a negative occasion setter might (e.g., Holland, 1992). This hypothesis begins to integrate several facts about extinction and brings relapse effects like the renewal effect, spontaneous recovery, rapid reacquisition, reinstatement, and perhaps resurgence to center stage.

The major implication of behavioral research on extinction is thus that lapse and relapse are always possibilities after exposure therapy. As just reviewed, there is substantial interest among basic researchers in discovering new ways to make extinction more permanent. To date, behavioral and pharmacological methods of enhancing or optimizing extinction learning have produced lawful effects on the rate of extinction, but their effectiveness in the long term is less clear. Treatments that increase the rate at which fear is lost in therapy may not change extinction learning's inherent context specificity. At the current time, the best way to combat the various relapse phenomena reviewed here may be to consider their behavioral causes and develop techniques that might defeat them. This perspective has led to certain bridging treatments, such as the use of reminder cues or strategies or conducting extinction in the presence of the contextual cues that can lead to particular examples of relapse, which do appear to hold some promise in maintaining extinction performance in the presence of conditions that might otherwise initiate relapse.

Acknowledgments

Preparation of this chapter was supported by Grant RO1 MH64847 from the National Institute of Mental Health.

References

Alberini CM (2005) Mechanisms of memory stabilization: Are consolidation and reconsolidation similar or distinct processes? *Trends Neurosci.* 28: 51–56.

Alessi SM, Badger GJ, and Higgins ST (2004) An experimental examination of the initial weeks of abstinence in cigarette smokers. *Exp. Clin. Psychopharmacol.* 12: 276–287.

Baker JD and Azorlosa JL (1996) The NMDA antagonist MK-801 blocks the extinction of Pavlovian fear conditioning. *Behav. Neurosci.* 110: 618–620.

Baker AG, Steinwald H, and Bouton ME (1991) Contextual conditioning and reinstatement of extinguished instrumental responding. *Q. J. Exp. Psychol.* 43B: 199–218.

Barela PB (1999) Theoretical mechanisms underlying the trial spacing effect in Pavlovian conditioning. *J. Exp. Psychol. Anim. Behav. Process* 25: 177–193.

Bouton ME (1984) Differential control by context in the inflation and reinstatement paradigms. *J. Exp. Psychol. Anim. Behav. Process* 10: 56–74.

Bouton ME (1986) Slow reacquisition following the extinction of conditioned suppression. *Learn. Motivation* 17: 1–15.

Bouton ME (1988) Context and ambiguity in the extinction of emotional learning: Implications for exposure therapy. *Behav. Res. Ther.* 26: 137–149.

Bouton ME (1991a) A contextual analysis of fear extinction. In: Martin PR (ed.) *Handbook of Behavior Therapy and Psychological Science: An Integrative Approach*, pp. 435–453. Elmsford, NY: Pergamon Press.

Bouton ME (1991b) Context and retrieval in extinction and in other examples of interference in simple associative learning. In: Dachowski L and Flaherty CF (eds.) *Current Topics in Animal Learning: Brain, Emotion, and Cognition*, pp. 25–53. Hillsdale, NJ: Erlbaum.

Bouton ME (1993) Context, time, and memory retrieval in the interference paradigms of Pavlovian learning. *Psychol. Bull.* 114: 80–99.

Bouton ME (1994) Conditioning, remembering, and forgetting. *J. Exp. Psychol. Anim. Behav. Process* 20: 219–231.

Bouton ME (2000) A learning-theory perspective on lapse, relapse, and the maintenance of behavior change. *Health Psychol.* 19: 57–63.

Bouton ME (2002) Context, ambiguity, and unlearning: Sources of relapse after behavioral extinction. *Biol. Psychiatry* 52: 976–986.

Bouton ME (2004) Context and behavioral processes in extinction. *Learn. Mem.* 11: 485–494.

Bouton ME and Bolles RC (1979) Contextual control of the extinction of conditioned fear. *Learn. Motivation* 10: 445–466.

Bouton ME and Bolles RC (1979) Role of conditioned contextual stimuli in reinstatement of extinguished fear. *J. Exp. Psychol. Anim. Behav. Process* 5: 368–378.

Bouton ME and Brooks DC (1993) Time and context effects on performance in a Pavlovian discrimination reversal. *J. Exp. Psychol. Anim. Behav. Process* 19: 165–179.

Bouton ME, García-Gutiérrez A, Zilski J, and Moody EW (2006a) Extinction in multiple contexts does not necessarily make

extinction less vulnerable to relapse. *Behav. Res. Ther.* 44: 983–994.

Bouton ME and García-Gutiérrez A (2006) Intertrial interval as a contextual stimulus. *Behav. Processes* 71: 307–317.

Bouton ME, Kenney FA, and Rosengard C (1990) State-dependent fear extinction with two benzodiazepine tranquilizers. *Behav. Neurosci.* 104: 44–55.

Bouton ME and King DA (1983) Contextual control of the extinction of conditioned fear: Tests for the associative value of the context. *J. Exp. Psychol. Anim. Behav. Process* 9: 248–265.

Bouton ME and King DA (1986) Effect of context on performance to conditioned stimuli with mixed histories of reinforcement and nonreinforcement. *J. Exp. Psychol. Anim. Behav. Process* 12: 4–15.

Bouton ME and Nelson JB (1994) Context-specificity of target versus feature inhibition in a feature-negative discrimination. *J. Exp. Psychol. Anim. Behav. Process* 20: 51–65.

Bouton ME and Nelson JB (1998) Mechanisms of feature-positive and feature-negative discrimination learning in an appetitive conditioning paradigm. In: Schmajuk N and Holland PC (eds.) *Occasion Setting: Associative Learning and Cognition in Animals*, pp. 69–112. Washington, DC: American Psychological Association.

Bouton ME and Peck CA (1989) Context effects on conditioning, extinction, and reinstatement in an appetitive conditioning preparation. *Anim. Learn. Behav.* 17: 188–198.

Bouton ME and Peck CA (1992) Spontaneous recovery in cross-motivational transfer (counterconditioning). *Anim. Learn. Behav.* 20: 313–321.

Bouton ME and Ricker ST (1994) Renewal of extinguished responding in a second context. *Anim. Learn. Behav.* 22: 317–324.

Bouton ME, Rosengard C, Achenbach GG, Peck CA, and Brooks DC (1993) Effects of contextual conditioning and unconditional stimulus presentation on performance in appetitive conditioning. *Q. J. Exp. Psychol.* 46B: 63–95.

Bouton ME and Sunsay C (2003) Importance of trials versus accumulating time across trials in partially-reinforced appetitive conditioning. *J. Exp. Psychol. Anim. Behav. Process* 29: 62–77.

Bouton ME and Swartzentruber D (1986) Analysis of the associative and occasion-setting properties of contexts participating in a Pavlovian discrimination. *J. Exp. Psychol. Anim. Behav. Process* 12: 333–350.

Bouton ME and Swartzentruber D (1989) Slow reacquisition following extinction: Context, encoding, and retrieval mechanisms. *J. Exp. Psychol. Anim. Behav. Process* 15: 43–53.

Bouton ME and Woods AM (2004) Separating time-based and trial-based accounts of the partial reinforcement extinction effect. Presented at the meeting of the Eastern Psychological Association, Washington, DC.

Bouton ME, Woods AM, Moody EW, Sunsay C, and García-Gutiérrez A (2006b) Counteracting the context-dependence of extinction: Relapse and some tests of possible methods of relapse prevention. In: Craske MG, Hermans D, and Vansteenwegen D (eds.) *Fear and Learning: Basic Science to Clinical Application*. Washington, DC: American Psychological Association.

Bouton ME, Woods AM, and Pineño O (2004) Occasional reinforced trials during extinction can slow the rate of rapid reacquisition. *Learn. Motivation* 35: 371–390.

Brandon SE and Wagner AR (1998) Occasion setting: Influences of conditioned emotional responses and configural cues. In: Schmajuk NA and Holland PC (eds.) *Occasion Setting: Associative Learning and Cognition in Animals*, pp. 343–382. Washington, DC: American Psychological Association.

Brooks DC (2000) Recent and remote extinction cues reduce spontaneous recovery. *Q. J. Exp. Psychol.* 53B: 25–58.

Brooks DC and Bouton ME (1993) A retrieval cue for extinction attenuates spontaneous recovery. *J. Exp. Psychol. Anim. Behav. Process* 19: 77–89.

Brooks DC and Bouton ME (1994) A retrieval cue for extinction attenuates response recovery (renewal) caused by a return to the conditioning context. *J. Exp. Psychol. Anim. Behav. Process* 20: 366–379.

Brooks DC, Hale B, Nelson JB, and Bouton ME (1995) Reinstatement after counterconditioning. *Anim. Learn. Behav.* 23: 383–390.

Cain CK, Blouin AM, and Barad M (2003) Temporally massed CS presentations generate more fear extinction than spaced presentations. *J. Exp. Psychol. Anim. Behav. Process* 29: 323–333.

Campeau S, Miserendino MJD, and Davis M (1992) Intra-amygdala infusion of the N-methyl-D-aspartate receptor antagonist AP5 blocks acquisition but not expression of fear-potentiated startle to an auditory conditioned stimulus. *Behav. Neurosci.* 106: 569–574.

Capaldi EJ (1967) A sequential hypothesis of instrumental learning. In: Spence KW and Spence JT (eds.) *Psychology of Learning and Motivation,* vol. 1, pp. 67–156. New York: Academic Press.

Capaldi EJ (1994) The sequential view: From rapidly fading stimulus traces to the organization of memory and the abstract concept of number. *Psychon. Bull. Rev.* 1: 156–181.

Chelonis JJ, Calton JL, Hart JA, and Schachtman TR (1999) Attenuation of the renewal effect by extinction in multiple contexts. *Learn. Motivation* 30: 1–14.

Collins BN and Brandon TH (2002) Effects of extinction context and retrieval cues on alcohol cue reactivity among nonalcoholic drinkers. *J. Consult. Clin. Psychol.* 70: 390–397.

Colwill RW (1991) Negative discriminative stimuli provide information about the identity of omitted response-contingent outcomes. *Anim. Learn. Behav.* 19: 326–336.

Conklin C (2006) Environments as cues to smoke: Implications for human extinction-based research and treatment. *Exp. Clin. Psychopharmacol.* 14: 12–19.

Conklin CA and Tiffany ST (2002) Applying extinction research and theory to cue-exposure addiction treatments. *Addiction* 97: 155–167.

Cox J and Westbrook RF (1994) The NMDA receptor antagonist MK-801 blocks acquisition and extinction of conditioned hypoalgesia responses in the rat. *Q. J. Exp. Psychol.* 47B: 187–210.

Crombag HS and Shaham Y (2002) Renewal of drug seeking by contextual cues after prolonged extinction in rats. *Behav. Neurosci.* 116: 169–173.

Cunningham CL (1979) Alcohol as a cue for extinction: State dependency produced by conditioned inhibition. *Anim. Learn. Behav.* 7: 45–52.

Daly HB (1974) Reinforcing properties of escape from frustration aroused in various learning situations. In: Bower GH (ed.) *The Psychology of Learning and Motivation,* vol. 8, pp. 187–232. New York: Academic Press.

Daly HB and Daly JT (1982) A mathematical model of reward and aversive nonreward: Its application in over 30 appetitive learning situations. *J. Exp. Psychol. Gen.* 111: 441–480.

Danguir J and Nicolaidis S (1977) Lack of reacquisition in learned taste aversions. *Anim. Learn. Behav.* 5: 395–397.

Davis HP and Squire LR (1984) Protein synthesis and memory. *Psychol. Bull.* 96: 518–559.

Davis M, Redmund DE, and Baraban JM (1979) Noradrenergic agonists and antagonists: Effects on conditioned fear as measured by the potentiated startle paradigm. *Psychopharmacology* 65: 111–118.

Davis M and Myers KM (2002) The role of glutamate and gamma-aminobutyric acid in fear extinction: Clinical implications for exposure therapy. *Biol. Psychiatry* 52: 998–1007.

Debiec J and LeDoux JE (2004) Disruption of reconsolidation but not consolidation of auditory fear conditioning by noradrenergic blockade in the amygdala. *Neuroscience* 129: 267–272.

Delamater AR (1996) Effects of several extinction treatments upon the integrity of Pavlovian stimulus-outcome associations. *Anim. Learn. Behav.* 24: 437–449.

Delamater AR (2004) Experimental extinction in Pavlovian conditioning: Behavioural and neuroscience perspectives. *Q. J. Exp. Psychol.* 57B: 97–132.

Denniston JC, Chang RC, and Miller RR (2003) Massive extinction treatment attenuates the renewal effect. *Learn. Motivation* 34: 68–86.

Devenport L, Hill T, Wilson M, and Ogden E (1997) Tracking and averaging in variable environments: A transition rule. *J. Exp. Psychol. Anim. Behav. Process* 23: 450–460.

Dickinson A and Dearing MF (1978) Appetitive-aversion interactions and inhibitory processes. In: Dickinson A and Boakes RA (eds.) *Mechanisms of Learning and Motivation: A Memorial Volume to Jerzy Konorski,* pp. 203–231. Hillsdale, NJ: Erlbaum.

Drew MR, Yang C, Ohyama T, and Balsam PD (2004) Temporal specificity of extinction in autoshaping. *J. Exp. Psychol. Anim. Behav. Process* 30: 163–176.

Dudai Y (2004) The neurobiology of consolidations, or how stable is the engram? *Annu. Rev. Psychol.* 55: 51–86.

Duvarci S and Nader K (2004) Characterization of fear memory reconsolidation. *J. Neurosci.* 24: 9269–9275.

Epstein R (1983) Resurgence of previously reinforced behavior during extinction. *Behav. Anal. Lett.* 3: 391–397.

Epstein R (1985) Extinction-induced resurgence: Preliminary investigations and possible applications. *Psychol. Rec.* 35: 143–153.

Falls WA, Miserendino MJD, and Davis M (1992) Extinction of fear-potentiated startle: Blockade by infusion of an NMDA antagonist into the amygdale. *J. Neurosci.* 12: 854–863.

Fanselow MS (1993) Associations and memories: The role of NMDA receptors and long-term potentiation. *Curr. Dir. Psychol. Sci.* 2: 152–156.

Fanselow MS (1998) Pavlovian conditioning, negative feedback, and blocking: Mechanisms that regulate association formation. *Neuron* 20: 625–627.

Frohardt RJ, Guarraci FA, and Bouton ME (2000) The effects of neurotoxic hippocampal lesions on two effects of context after fear extinction. *Behav. Neurosci.* 114: 227–240.

Gallistel CR and Gibbon J (2000) Time, rate, and conditioning. *Psychol. Rev.* 107: 289–344.

García-Gutiérrez A and Rosas JM (2003) Context change as the mechanism of reinstatement in causal learning. *J. Exp. Psychol. Anim. Behav. Process* 29: 292–310.

Gluck M and Myers CE (1993) Hippocampal mediation of stimulus representation: A computational theory. *Hippocampus* 3: 492–516.

Goelet P, Castellucci VF, Schacher S, and Kandel ER (1986) The long and short of long-term memory – A molecular framework. *Nature* 322: 419–422.

Gunther LM, Denniston JC, and Miller RR (1998) Conducting exposure treatment in multiple contexts can prevent relapse. *Behav. Res. Ther.* 36: 75–91.

Hall G and Channell S (1985) Differential effects of contextual change on latent inhibition and on the habituation of an orienting response. *J. Exp. Psychol. Anim. Behav. Process* 11: 470–481.

Harris JA, Jones ML, Bailey GK, and Westbrook RF (2000) Contextual control over conditioned responding in an extinction paradigm. *J. Exp. Psychol. Anim. Behav. Process* 26: 174–185.

Hart JA, Bourne MJ, and Schachtman TR (1995) Slow reacquisition of a conditioned taste aversion. *Anim. Learn. Behav.* 23: 297–303.

Haselgrove M and Pearce JM (2003) Facilitation of extinction by an increase or a decrease in trial duration. *J. Exp. Psychol. Anim. Behav. Process* 29: 153–166.

Haselgrove M, Aydin A, and Pearce JM (2004) A partial reinforcement extinction effect despite equal rates of reinforcement during Pavlovian conditioning. *J. Exp. Psychol. Anim. Behav. Process* 30: 240–250.

Hendry JS (1982) Summation of undetected excitation following extinction of the CER. *Anim. Learn. Behav.* 10: 476–482.

Hofmann SG, Meuret AE, Smits JAJ, et al. (2006) Augmentation of exposure therapy with D-cycloserine for social anxiety disorder. *Arch. Gen. Psychiatry* 63: 298–304.

Holland PC (1992) Occasion setting in Pavlovian conditioning. In: Medin DL (ed.) *The Psychology of Learning and Motivation*, vol. 28, pp. 69–125. San Diego, CA: Academic Press.

Honey RC and Hall G (1989) Acquired equivalence and distinctiveness of cues. *J. Exp. Psychol. Anim. Behav. Process* 15: 338–346.

Huang CC, Liang YC, and Hsu KS (2001) Characterization of the mechanism underlying the reversal of long-term potentiation by low frequency stimulation at hippocampal CA1 synapses. *J. Biol. Chem.* 276: 48108–48117.

Johnston AL and File SE (1989) Yohimbine's anxiogenic action: Evidence for noradrenergic and dopaminergic sites. *Pharmacol. Biochem. Behav.* 32: 151–156.

Kehoe EJ (1988) A layered network model of associative learning: Learning to learn and configuration. *Psychol. Rev.* 95: 411–433.

Kehoe EJ and Holt PE (1984) Transfer across CS-US intervals and sensory modalities in classical conditioning in the rabbit. *Anim. Learn. Behav.* 122–128.

Kehoe EJ and Macrae M (1997) Savings in animal learning: Implications for relapse and maintenance after therapy. *Behav. Ther.* 28: 141–155.

Konorski J (1967) *Integrative Activity of the Brain*. Chicago: University of Chicago Press.

Kremer EF (1978) The Rescorla-Wagner model: Losses in associative strength in compound conditioned stimuli. *J. Exp. Psychol. Anim. Behav. Process* 4: 22–36.

Krupa DJ and Thompson RF (2003) Inhibiting the expression of a classically conditioned behavior prevents its extinction. *J. Neurosci.* 23: 10577–10584.

LaBar KS and Phelps EA (2005) Reinstatement of conditioned fear in humans is context dependent and impaired in amnesia. *Behav. Neurosci.* 119: 677–686.

Lattal KM and Nakajima S (1998) Overexpectation in appetitive Pavlovian and instrumental conditioning. *Anim. Learn. Behav.* 26: 351–360.

Ledgerwood L, Richardson R, and Cranney J (2003) Effects of D-cycloserine on extinction of conditioned freezing. *Behav. Neurosci.* 117: 341–349.

Ledgerwood L, Richardson R, and Cranney J (2004) D-cycloserine and the facilitation of extinction of conditioned fear: Consequences for reinstatement. *Behav. Neurosci.* 118: 505–513.

Ledgerwood L, Richardson R, and Cranney J (2005) D-cycloserine facilitates extinction of learned fear: Effects on reacquisition and generalized extinction. *Biol. Psychiatry* 57: 841–847.

Lee JL, Everitt BJ, and Thomas KL (2004) Independent cellular processes for hippocampal memory consolidation and reconsolidation. *Science* 304: 839–843.

Lee H and Kim JJ (1998) Amygdalar NMDA receptors are critical for new fear learning in previously fear-conditioned rats. *J. Neurosci.* 18: 8444–8454.

Leitenberg H, Rawson RA, and Bath K (1970) Reinforcement of competing behavior during extinction. *Science* 169: 301–303.

Leitenberg H, Rawson RA, and Mulick JA (1975) Extinction and reinforcement of alternative behavior. *J. Comp. Physiol. Psychol.* 88: 640–652.

Lieving GA and Lattal KA (2003) Recency, repeatability, and reinforcer retrenchment: An experimental analysis of resurgence. *J. Exp. Anal. Behav.* 80: 217–233.

Lin C-H, Yeh SH, Lu H-S, and Gean P-W (2003) The similarities and diversities of signal pathways leading to consolidation of conditioning and consolidation of extinction of fear memory. *J. Neurosci.* 23: 8310–8317.

Mackintosh NJ (1974) *The Psychology of Animal Learning*. New York: Academic Press.

Maren S and Chang C (2006) Recent fear is resistant to extinction. *Proc. Natl. Acad. Sci. USA* 103: 18020–18025.

Marlatt GA and Gordon JR (1985) *Relapse Prevention: Maintenance Strategies in the Treatment of Addictive Behaviors*. New York: Guilford Press.

McClelland JL and Rumelhart DE (1985) Distributed memory and the representation of general and specific information. *J. Exp. Psychol. Gen.* 114: 159–188.

McCloskey M and Cohen NJ (1989) Catastrophic interference in connectionist networks: The sequential learning problem. In: Bower GH (ed.) *The Psychology of Learning and Motivation*, vol. 24, pp. 109–165. San Diego, CA: Academic Press.

McGaugh JL (2000) Memory – A century of consolidation. *Science* 287: 248–251.

McGaugh JL (2004) The amygdala modulates the consolidation of memories of emotionally arousing experiences. *Annu. Rev. Neurosci.* 27: 1–28.

McNally GP and Westbrook RF (2003) Opioid receptors regulate the extinction of Pavlovian fear conditioning. *Behav. Neurosci.* 117: 1292–1301.

Milad MR, Orr SP, Pitman RK, and Rauch SL (2005) Context modulation of memory for fear extinction in humans. *Psychophysiology* 42: 456–464.

Mineka S, Mystkowski JL, Hladek D, and Rodriguez BI (1999) The effects of changing contexts on return of fear following exposure therapy for spider fear. *J. Consult. Clin. Psychol.* 67: 599–604.

Miserendino MJD, Sananes CB, Melia KR, and Davis M (1990) Blocking of acquisition but not expression of conditioned fear-potentiated startle by NMDA antagonists in the amygdala. *Nature* 345: 716–718.

Moody EW, Sunsay C, and Bouton ME (2006) Priming and trial spacing in extinction: Effects on extinction performance, spontaneous recovery, and reinstatement in appetitive conditioning. *Q. J. Exp. Psychol.* 59: 809–829.

Morris RW and Bouton ME (2007) The effect of yohimbine on the extinction of conditioned fear: A role for context. *Behav. Neurosci.* 121: 501–514.

Morris RW, Furlong TM, and Westbrook RF (2005) Recent exposure to a dangerous context impairs extinction and reinstates lost fear reactions. *J. Exp. Psychol. Anim. Behav. Process* 31: 40–55.

Mowrer OH and Jones HM (1945) Habit strength as a function of the pattern of reinforcement. *J. Exp. Psychol.* 35: 293–311.

Myers KM and Davis M (2002) Behavioral and neural analysis of extinction. *Neuron* 36: 567–584.

Myers KM, Ressler KJ, and Davis M (2006) Different mechanisms of fear extinction dependent on length of time since fear acquisition. *Learn. Mem.* 13: 216–223.

Mystkowski JL, Craske MG, and Echiverri AM (2002) Treatment context and return of fear in spider phobia. *Behav. Ther.* 33: 399–416.

Mystkowski JL, Craske MG, Echiverri AM, and Labus JS (2006) Mental reinstatement of context and return of fear in spider-fearful participants. *Behav. Ther.* 37: 49–60.

Nader K, Schafe GE, and LeDoux JE (2000) Fear memories require protein synthesis in the amygdala for reconsolidation after retrieval. *Nature* 406: 722–726.

Nakajima S, Tanaka S, Urushihara K, and Imada H (2000) Renewal of extinguished lever-press responses upon return to the training context. *Learn. Motivation* 31: 416–431.

Napier RM, Macrae M, and Kehoe EJ (1992) Rapid reacquisition in conditioning of the rabbit's nictitating membrane response. *J. Exp. Psychol. Anim. Behav. Process* 18: 182–192.

Nelson JB (2002) Context specificity of excitation and inhibition in ambiguous stimuli. *Learn. Motivation* 33: 284–310.

Nelson JB and Bouton ME (1997) The effects of a context switch following serial and simultaneous feature-negative discriminations. *Learn. Motivation* 28: 56–84.

Neumann DL, Lipp OV, and Cory SE (2007) Conducting extinction in multiple contexts does not necessarily attenuate the renewal of shock expectancy in a fear-conditioning procedure with humans. *Behav. Res. Ther.* 45: 385–394.

Neuringer A, Kornell N, and Olufs M (2001) Stability and variability in extinction. *J. Exp. Psychol. Anim. Behav. Process* 27: 79–84.

Overton DA (1985) Contextual stimulus effects of drugs and internal states. In: Balsam PD and Tomie A (eds.) *Context and Learning*, pp. 357–384. Hillsdale, NJ: Erlbaum.

Pavlov IP (1927) *Conditioned Reflexes*. Oxford, UK: Oxford University Press.

Pearce JM and Hall G (1980) A model for Pavlovian conditioning: Variations in the effectiveness of conditioned but not unconditioned stimuli. *Psychol. Rev.* 87: 332–352.

Peck CA and Bouton ME (1990) Context and performance in aversive-to-appetitive and appetitive-to-aversive transfer. *Learn. Motivation* 21: 1–31.

Pellow S, Chopin P, File SE, and Briley M (1985) Validation of open:closed arm entries in an elevated plus-maze as a measure of anxiety in the rat. *J. Neurosci. Methods* 14: 149–167.

Pitman RK (1989) Post-traumatic stress disorder, hormones, and memory. *Biol. Psychiatry* 44: 221–223.

Pitman RK, Sanders KM, Zusman RM, et al. (2002) Pilot study of secondary prevention of posttraumatic stress disorder with propranolol. *Biol. Psychiatry* 51: 189–192.

Przybyslawski J, Roullet P, and Sara SJ (1999) Attenuation of emotional and nonemotional memories after their reactivation: Role of beta adrenergic receptors. *J. Neurosci.* 19: 6623–6628.

Rauhut AS, Thomas BL, and Ayres JJB (2001) Treatments that weaken Pavlovian conditioned fear and thwart its renewal in rats: Implications for treating human phobias. *J. Exp. Psychol. Anim. Behav. Process* 27: 99–114.

Rawson RA, Leitenberg H, Mulick JA, and Lefebvre MF (1977) Recovery of extinction responding in rats following discontinuation of reinforcement of alternative behavior: A test of two explanations. *Anim. Learn. Behav.* 5: 415–420.

Reberg D (1972) Compound tests for excitation in early acquisition and after prolonged extinction of conditioned suppression. *Learn. Motivation* 3: 246–258.

Reid RL (1958) The role of the reinforcer as a stimulus. *Br. J. Psychol.* 49: 202–209.

Rescorla RA (1991) Associations of multiple outcomes with an instrumental response. *J. Exp. Psychol. Anim. Behav. Process* 17: 465–474.

Rescorla RA (1993) Inhibitory associations between S and R in extinction. *Anim. Learn. Behav.* 21: 327–336.

Rescorla RA (1995) Full preservation of a response-outcome association through training with a second outcome. *Q. J. Exp. Psychol.* 48B: 235–251.

Rescorla RA (1996a) Preservation of Pavlovian associations through extinction. *Q. J. Exp. Psychol.* 49B: 245–258.

Rescorla RA (1996b) Spontaneous recovery after training with multiple outcomes. *Anim. Learn. Behav.* 24: 11–18.

Rescorla RA (1997a) Response inhibition in extinction. *Q. J. Exp. Psychol.* 50B: 238–252.

Rescorla RA (1997b) Spontaneous recovery after Pavlovian conditioning with multiple outcomes. *Anim. Learn. Behav.* 25: 99–107.

Rescorla RA (2000) Extinction can be enhanced by a concurrent exciter. *J. Exp. Psychol. Anim. Behav. Process* 26: 251–260.

Rescorla RA (2001) Experimental extinction. In: Mowrer RR and Klein SB (eds.) *Handbook of Contemporary Learning Theories*, pp. 119–154. Mahwah, NJ: Erlbaum.

Rescorla RA (2003) Protection from extinction. *Learn. Behav.* 31: 124–132.

Rescorla RA (2004a) Spontaneous recovery. *Learn. Mem.* 11: 501–509.

Rescorla RA (2004b) Spontaneous recovery varies inversely with the training-extinction interval. *Learn. Behav.* 32: 401–408.

Rescorla RA (2005) Spontaneous recovery of excitation but not inhibition. *J. Exp. Psychol. Anim. Behav. Process* 31: 277–288.

Rescorla RA (2006) Deepened extinction from compound stimulus presentation. *J. Exp. Psychol. Anim. Behav. Process* 32: 135–144.

Rescorla RA and Durlach PJ (1987) The role of context in intertrial interval effects in autoshaping. *Q. J. Exp. Psychol.* 39B: 35–48.

Rescorla RA and Heth CD (1975) Reinstatement of fear to an extinguished conditioned stimulus. *J. Exp. Psychol. Anim. Behav. Process* 1: 88–96.

Rescorla RA and Skucy JC (1969) Effect of response-independent reinforcers during extinction. *J. Comp. Physiol. Psychol.* 67: 381–389.

Rescorla RA and Wagner AR (1972) A theory of Pavlovian conditioning: Variations in the effectiveness of reinforcement and nonreinforcement. In: Black AH and Prokasy WK (eds.) *Classical Conditioning II: Current Research and Theory*, pp. 64–99. New York: Appleton-Century-Crofts.

Ressler KJ, Rothbaum BO, Tannenbaum L, et al. (2004) Cognitive enhances as adjuncts to psychotherapy: Use of D-cycloserine in phobics to facilitate extinction of fear. *Arch. Gen. Psychiatry* 61: 1136–1144.

Ricker ST and Bouton ME (1996) Reacquisition following extinction in appetitive conditioning. *Anim. Learn. Behav.* 24: 423–436.

Robbins SJ (1990) Mechanisms underlying spontaneous recovery in autoshaping. *J. Exp. Psychol. Anim. Behav. Process* 16: 235–249.

Rosas JM and Bouton ME (1997) Additivity of the effects of retention interval and context change on latent inhibition: Toward resolution of the context forgetting paradox. *J. Exp. Psychol. Anim. Behav. Process* 23: 283–294.

Rosas JM and Bouton ME (1998) Context change and retention interval can have additive, rather than interactive, effects after taste aversion extinction. *Psychon. Bull. Rev.* 5: 79–83.

Rosas JM and Callejas-Aguilera JE (2006) Context switch effects on acquisition and extinction in human predictive learning. *J. Exp. Psychol. Learn. Mem. Cogn.* 32: 461–474.

Rosas JM and Callejas-Aguilera JE (2007) Acquisition of a conditioned taste aversion becomes context dependent when it is learning after extinction. *Q. J. Exp. Psychol.* 60: 9–15.

Rosas JM, Vila NJ, Lugo M, and Lopez L (2001) Combined effect of context change and retention interval on interference in causality judgments. *J. Exp. Psychol. Anim. Behav. Process* 27: 153–164.

Santini E, Muller RU, and Quirk GJ (2001) Consolidation of extinction learning involves transfer from NMDA-independent to NMDA-dependent memory. *J. Neurosci.* 21: 9009–9017.

Sara SJ (2000) Retrieval and reconsolidation: Toward a neurobiology of remembering. *Learn. Mem.* 7: 73–84.

Scavio MJ (1974) Classical-classical transfer: Effects of prior aversive conditions upon appetitive conditioning in rabbits (*Oryctolagus cuniculus*). *J. Comp. Physiol. Psychol.* 86: 107–115.

Schafe GE and LeDoux JE (2000) Memory consolidation of auditory Pavlovian fear conditioning requires protein synthesis and protein kinase A in the amygdala. *J. Neurosci.* 20: RC96 (1–5).

Schmajuk NA and Holland PC (eds.) (1998) *Occasion-Setting: Associative Learning and Cognition in Animals*. Washington, DC: American Psychological Association.

Schreurs BG and Kehoe EJ (1987) Cross-modal transfer as a function of initial training level in classical condition with rabbit. *Anim. Learn. Behav.* 15: 47–54.

Sobell MB and Sobell LC (1973) Individualized behavior therapy for alcoholics. *Behav. Ther.* 4: 49–72.

Soltysik SS, Wolfe GE, Nicholas T, Wilson J, and Garcia-Sanchez JL (1983) Blocking of inhibitory conditioning within a serial conditioned stimulus-conditioned inhibitor compound: Maintenance of acquired behavior without an unconditioned stimulus. *Learn. Motivation* 14: 1–29.

Spence KW and Norris EB (1950) Eyelid conditioning as a function of the inter-trial interval. *J. Exp. Psychol.* 40: 716–720.

Staddon JER (1988) Learning as inference. In: Bolles RC and Beecher MD (eds.) *Evolution and Learning*, pp. 59–78. Hillsdale, NJ: Erlbaum.

Stanford SC (1995) Central noradrenergic neurones and stress. *Pharmacol. Ther.* 68: 297–342.

Staubli U and Chun D (1996) Factors regulating the reversibility of long-term potentiation. *J. Neurosci.* 16: 853–860.

Suzuki A, Josselyn SA, Frankland PW, Masushige S, Silva AJ, and Kida S (2004) Memory reconsolidation and extinction have distinct temporal and biochemical signatures. *J. Neurosci.* 24: 4787–4795.

Swartzentruber D (1995) Modulatory mechanisms in Pavlovian conditioning. *Anim. Learn. Behav.* 23: 123–143.

Swartzentruber D and Bouton ME (1992) Context sensitivity of conditioned suppression following preexposure to the conditioned stimulus. *Anim. Learn. Behav.* 20: 97–103.

Tamai N and Nakajima S (2000) Renewal of formerly conditioned fear in rats after extensive extinction training. *Int. J. Comp. Psychol.* 13: 137–147.

Thewissen R, Snijders S, Havermans RC, van den Hout M, and Jansen A (2006) Renewal of cue-elicited urge to smoke: Implications for cue exposure treatment. *Behav. Res. Ther.* 44: 1441–1449.

Thomas BL and Ayres JJB (2004) Use of the ABA fear renewal paradigm to assess the effects of extinction with co-present fear inhibitors or excitors: Implications for theories of extinction and for treating human fears and phobias. *Learn. Motivation* 35: 22–51.

Vaiva G, Ducrocq F, Jezequel K, et al. (2003) Immediate treatment with propranolol decreases posttraumatic stress disorder two months after trauma. *Biol. Psychiatry* 54: 947–949.

Vansteenwegen D, Dirikx T, Hermans D, Vervliet B, and Eelen P (2006) Renewal and reinstatement of fear: Evidence from human conditioning research. In: Craske MG, Hermans D, and Vansteenwegen D (eds.) *Fear and Learning: Basic Science to Clinical Application*, pp. 197–215. Washington, DC: American Psychological Association.

Vansteenwegen D, Hermans D, Vervliet B, et al. (2005) Return of fear in a human differential conditioning paradigm caused by a return to the original acquisition context. *Behav. Res. Ther.* 43: 323–336.

Vogel EH, Brandon SE, and Wagner AR (2003) Stimulus representation in SOP: II. An application to inhibition of delay. *Behav. Processes* 62: 27–48.

Waddell J, Morris RW, and Bouton ME (2006) Effects of bed nucleus of the stria terminalis lesions on conditioned anxiety: Aversive conditioning with long-duration conditional stimuli and reinstatement of extinguished fear. *Behav. Neurosci.* 120: 324–336.

Wagner AR (1969) Stimulus selection and a 'modified continuity theory.' In: Bower GH and Spence JT (eds.) *The Psychology of Learning and Motivation,* vol. 3, pp. 1–41. New York: Academic Press.

Wagner AR (1981) SOP: A model of automatic memory processing in animal behavior. In: Spear NE and Miller RR (eds.) *Information Processing in Animals: Memory Mechanisms*, pp. 5–47. Hillsdale, NJ: Erlbaum.

Wagner AR and Brandon SE (1989) Evolution of a structured connectionist model of Pavlovian conditioning (AESOP). In: Klein SB and Mowrer RR (eds.) *Contemporary Learning Theories: Pavlovian Conditioning and the Status of Traditional Learning Theory*, pp. 149–189. Hillsdale, NJ: Erlbaum.

Wagner AR and Brandon SE (2001) A componential theory of Pavlovian conditioning. In: Mowrer RR and Klein SB (Eds.) *Handbook of Contemporary Learning Theories*, pp. 23–64. Mahwah, NJ: Erlbaum.

Walker DL and Davis M (2002) The role of amygdala glutamate receptors in fear learning, fear-potentiated startle, and extinction. *Pharmacol. Biochem. Behav.* 71: 379–392.

Walker DL, Ressler KJ, Lu, K-T, and Davis M (2002) Facilitation of conditioned fear extinction by systemic administration or intra-amygdala infusions of D-cycloserine as assessed with fear-potentiated startle in rats. *J. Neurosci.* 15: 2343–2351.

Walker DL, Toufexis DJ, and Davis M (2003) Role of the bed nucleus of the stria terminalis versus the amygdala in fear, stress, and anxiety. *Eur. J. Pharmacol.* 463: 199–216.

Walker MP, Brakefield T, Hobson JA, and Stickgold R (2003) Dissociable stages of human memory consolidation and reconsolidation. *Nature* 425: 616–620.

Westbrook RF, Smith FJ, and Charnock DJ (1985) The extinction of an aversion: Role of the interval between non-reinforced presentations of the averted stimulus. *Q. J. Exp. Psychol.* 37B: 255–273.

Wilson A, Brooks DC, and Bouton ME (1995) The role of the rat hippocampal system in several effects of context in extinction. *Behav. Neurosci.* 109: 828–836.

Weidemann G and Kehoe EJ (2003) Savings in classical conditioning in the rabbit as a function of extended extinction. *Learn. Behav.* 31: 49–68.

Weidemann G and Kehoe EJ (2004) Recovery of the rabbit's conditioned nictitating membrane response without direct reinforcement after extinction. *Learn. Behav.* 32: 409–426.

Weidemann G and Kehoe EJ (2005) Stimulus specificity of concurrent recovery in the rabbit nictitating membrane response. *Learn. Behav.* 33: 343–362.

Wolpe J (1958) *Psychotherapy by Reciprocal Inhibition*. Stanford, CA: Stanford University Press.

Woods AM and Bouton ME (2006) D-cycloserine facilitates extinction but does not eliminate renewal of the conditioned emotional response. *Behav. Neurosci.* 120: 1159–1162.

Woods AM and Bouton ME (2007) Occasional reinforced responses during extinction can slow the rate of reacquisition of an operant response. *Learn. Motivation* 38: 56–74.

1.10 Cognitive Dimension of Operant Learning

A. P. Blaisdell, University of California at Los Angeles, Los Angeles, CA, USA

1.10.1 Introduction

1.10.1.1 Thorndike and the Law of Effect

A rat presses a lever and quickly scurries to the feeding niche to collect its meal. A crow picks up a piece of newspaper – uncovering a morsel of food dropped by a passerby. A child lifts the lid off of a cookie jar and takes a cookie. These are the types of acquired behaviors that a theory of instrumental learning seeks to explain. Instrumental learning is the acquisition of a new response through reinforcing feedback. Thorndike (1898, 1911) provided the first general theory of instrumental learning with his Law of Effect. The Law of Effect is a simple trial-and-error learning model in which the actions an individual makes in the presence of a particular stimulus or context are strengthened or weakened depending on the consequences of those actions. Actions followed by desirable consequences – such as attainment of food rewards or escape from aversive situations – become strengthened in that stimulus context, while actions followed by undesirable consequences – such as a loss of food or attainment of an aversive stimulus – become weakened in that

context. His theory grew out of experiments on escape learning in animals – most famously cats. In these experiments he studied the acquisition of a new behavior in a controlled manner. A cat was placed in a cage that Thorndike called a puzzle box (**Figure 1**), with food located in view just outside. The cat could escape the box by manipulating a device.

Various puzzle boxes were rigged so that each one required a different manner of escape, such as pushing the door aside, pressing a lever, pulling a string, or a series of these behaviors. Thorndike repeatedly placed the cat inside a puzzle box and observed the latency to escape. As the cat learned which responses led to its release from the box, the latency to escape would diminish (**Figure 2**).

What struck Thorndike was that the cat initially tried all manners of escape – trying to squeeze through the bars, pawing at the door, clawing and biting and things in the box. The cat would

> strive instinctively to escape from confinement. The vigor with which it struggles is extraordinary. For eight or ten minutes it will claw and bite and squeeze incessantly. (Thorndike, 1898: 13)

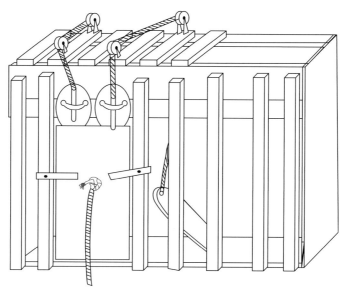

Figure 1 One of the puzzle boxes used by Thorndike to study the acquisition of new behaviors in cats. From Thorndike EL (1911) *Animal Intelligence: Experimental Studies.* New York: Macmillan.

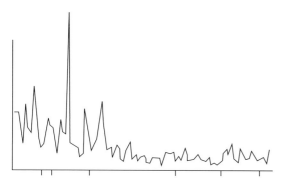

Figure 2 Escape times as a function of trials for one cat in a puzzle box experiment. From Thorndike EL (1911) *Animal Intelligence: Experimental Studies.* New York: Macmillan.

These strivings, however, diminished upon repeated exposures to the box as the cat learned which actions led to escape and which did not. The cat become more successful over repeated trials – successful escape responses that at first had been unleashed fortuitously in the random fury of its strivings became more systematically employed, while those behaviors that led to no release died away. It was this transformation from seemingly random behaviors to successfully organized ones that led Thorndike to formulate the Law of Effect.

Importantly, observations of the behavior of the cat during and after learning an escape response led Thorndike to conclude that the cat did not understand the relationship between its behavior and the

consequence. Rather, the cat appeared to blindly engage in the trained action whenever it was placed in the box. Thus, in Thorndike's framework the consequences of action play an important role in the strengthening or weakening of behavior, but those consequences do not themselves enter into an association with the action or with the prevailing stimulus conditions. Rather, the subject only learns an association between the stimulus context (S) and the response (R) (**Figure 3**).

Many other behaviorists, perhaps Watson being the most famous, had their own take on S-R psychology. The behaviorist ideology eschewed references to mental terms, such as expectations, wants, and desires, and attempted to describe all acquired behavior through the objective lens of stimulus input and response output, with outcomes and consequences of behavior serving only to solidify S-R

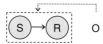

Figure 3 Theoretical associative structure underlying instrumental conditioning. S = stimulus representation, R = response representation, O = outcome. Solid arrow indicates hypothetical unidirectional excitatory association between the S and R representations. The dashed-line box envelopes the content of learning. The dotted arrow indicates that O only plays a role in reinforcing the strength of the S-R association but does not enter into an association with either S or R.

relationships (*See also* Chapters 1.03, 1.06, 1.07). Thus, to characterize the learning of a cat in a puzzle box or of a rat in a maze, the cat (or rat) is said to engage in a series of conditioned responses (muscle twitches) when they are in a certain context. The fact that these muscle twitches typically bring about a consequence is irrelevant from the cat's (or rat's) point of view. That is, the behavior of the cat or the rat is not goal directed. If one were to ask the behaviorists, "Why did the chicken cross the road?" their reply would be "Because the chicken had crossed the road a number of times in the past, and each time the crossing was followed by a satisfying outcome; whereas each failure to cross the road was followed by an unsatisfying outcome. Thus, when in the presence of the road, the experienced chicken will cross to the other side." Likewise, a child learns to lift the lid off of a cookie jar because doing so in the past has repeatedly been followed by a satisfying outcome. If the child were to be asked why they are lifting the lid off of the cookie jar, the behaviorist would expect a reply of "I dunno."

1.10.1.2 Tolman's Purposive Psychology

But doesn't it strike us as being exceedingly odd to interpret the child's act of lifting the lid off the cookie jar as NOT being due to the child's desire for a cookie – as the behaviorist would have it? Tolman agreed, and suggested that actions are performed for some purpose, that is, they are driven by expectations of an outcome (Tolman, 1932). Experiments conducted in Tolman's lab led to this conclusion. In one example, rats were given nine trials on which they learned to run down a maze and collect a desirable food reward – bran mash – in the goal box. On the tenth trial, the rats found a less desirable sunflower seed in the goal box rather than the bran mash. On the eleventh trial, the rats ran down the maze more slowly than they had on the preceding ten trials. In contrast with behaviorist theory, the rats appeared to have learned during the first nine trials to expect bran mash when they reached the goal box. The violation of this expectation on the tenth trial caused a dramatic and immediate shift in their behavior. Tolman used the behaviorist's controlled methodology and strict adherence to empirical validation to support cognitive processes as variables that intervene between stimulus and response. As a result, cognitive theories of animal learning and behavior have again become fashionable.

1.10.2 Operant Behavior: Goal Directed versus Habitual

In the past few decades, there has been a resurgence in the analysis of goal-directed behavior in psychology according to which an individual's actions are motivated by the outcome representation with which they are associated. Beyond being merely a catalyst for learning, the consequence of a response can become part of what is learned. The response–outcome (R-O) association allows the outcome to motivate the response. That is, the subject *expects* to receive O if it engages in R. A more contemporary view holds that all three elements of an instrumental learning association, S, R, and O, can be bound by associations (**Figure 4**; see also Balleine and Ostlund, 2007, for a review).

The claim that instrumental behavior can be goal-directed should not be taken to deny the existence of non-goal-directed, habitual behavior. Much of our behavior is clearly produced without the aid of any explicit representation, such as when we walk from our car to our doorstep. We may carry out such a task almost perfectly in complete darkness, or if we are otherwise distracted – such as when we are engaged in conversation with a visitor. Likewise, it is said that one way to catch a sleepwalker in the act is by rearranging the furniture in their dwelling. Presumably they will wake up when they bump into furniture that is now blocking a previously unobstructed pathway. Even when we are aware that we have rearranged the furniture in a room, it usually takes time to stop going to the corner where the easy chair used to be to have a seat. Discovering the empty corner quickly reminds us of our error. Old habits die hard, as the saying goes.

To be theoretically useful, there must be a way to empirically distinguish habitual (S-R) from goal-directed (R-O) behavior. According to several theorists (Colwill and Rescorla, 1986; Dickinson and Balleine, 1994), behavior is said to be goal directed

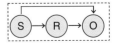

Figure 4 Theoretical associative structure underlying instrumental conditioning. S = stimulus representation, R = response representation, O = outcome representation. Arrows indicate hypothetical unidirectional excitatory associations between representations. The dashed-line box envelopes the contents of learning. Associations are hypothesized to form between S and R, between S and O, and between R and O.

if it is mediated by the instrumental contingency between the action and the outcome and by the value of the outcome (*See also* Chapters 1.03, 1.06). This operational definition is consistent with the two lines of evidence in support of R-O associations: posttraining changes in the value of the outcome and manipulations of the response–outcome contingency.

1.10.2.1 Behavioral Dissociations

1.10.2.1.1 Outcome devaluation
Perhaps the simplest way to demonstrate that the instrumental response is motivated by the expectation of the outcome is to change the value of the outcome after instrumental learning. The logic is straightforward: If desire for the outcome is motivating the instrumental response, then rendering the outcome less desirable should reduce the motivation to acquire it. Thus, reducing the value of the instrumental reinforcer after training should render it less desirable and weaken the instrumental response that had previously earned that reinforcer. Likewise, increasing the value of a reinforcer should increase the motivation to work toward obtaining that reinforcer.

Tolman and Honzik (1930) provided early empirical support for the role of the outcome expectancy in motivating the instrumental response (see also Tinklepaugh, 1928). Their study involved three groups of rats placed in a complex alley maze (**Figure 5**).

Each rat was placed into a start box at one end of the maze and removed from a goal box at the other end. Only one sequence of arms of the maze led from the start box to the goal box, and a number of other arms led to dead ends. Tolman and Honzik scored the number of dead-end arms rats entered ('errors') during each trip from start to goal box. One group of rats was rewarded with food when they reached the goal box, and the number of errors decreased dramatically as a function of the number of trips they made (**Figure 6**).

The second and third groups of rats received no food in the goal box for the first 10 trials in the maze. One of these groups, however, did find food in the goal box on the eleventh and subsequent trials. **Figure 6** reveals that after finding food in the goal box for the first time on the eleventh trial, the number of errors this group of rats made dramatically decreased on the twelfth and subsequent trials. This result is perhaps the most famous demonstration of latent learning in the literature, showing that rats had learned to traverse the maze efficiently (i.e., with few turns into dead ends) even in the absence of explicit food reinforcement. In fact, this learning was just as strong in the group that was not rewarded during the first 10 trials as it was for the group for which food was available from the very beginning of training. More important for our purposes, this study also demonstrates that an increase in the motivational significance of a goal (in this case the contents of the goal box) has a dramatic and immediate effect on performance. The rats in the latent group must have changed their representation of the outcome on the eleventh trial, which motivated their performance on the twelfth trial. More recent

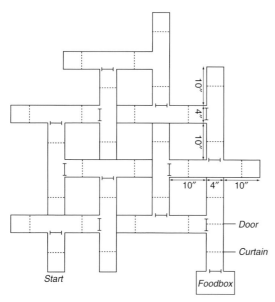

Figure 5 Maze used by Tolman and Honzik (1930) to study latent learning in rats. From Tolman EC (1948) Cognitive maps in rats and men. *Psychol. Rev.* 55: 189–208.

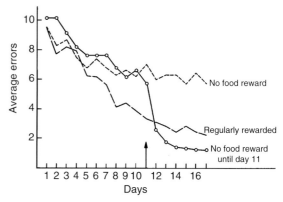

Figure 6 Acquisition performance from Tolman and Honzik (1930). From Tolman EC (1948) Cognitive maps in rats and men. *Psychol. Rev.* 55: 189–208.

demonstrations of positive behavioral contrast effects like this provide further support for the role of outcome representations in mediating the strength of instrumental behavior (for a review see Flaherty, 1996).

Tolman and Gleitman (1949) also showed that a downshift in the cues surrounding the reinforcer can affect instrumental performance. Rats first learned to find food at either end of a T-maze. The goal box at the end of one arm was always dark, and that at the end of the other arm was always lit. Both goal boxes, however, always contained the same amount of food, and thus had equal value. Following training, the rats were taken to a separate room that was dark, in which they received foot shocks. After this experience, the rats were returned to the T-maze. Not surprisingly, the rats avoided the dark goal box in favor of the lit goal box, despite both boxes containing the same amount of food and having no shocks. This preference suggests that the rats had encoded the illumination properties of the two goal boxes and avoided the dark box in which they expected the possibility of receiving another shock.

One problem with the above studies is that they involve a change in the quality of the reinforcer, such as from no food to food in the goal box, or from food to food + shock in the dark part of the box. Perhaps the new outcome itself caused rapid changes in the instrumental response through the normal S-R mechanisms, rather than affecting the representation of the outcome mediating the response. That is, the added or altered outcome reinforces a new S-R association. This problem can be avoided by directly manipulating the value of the reinforcer itself without affecting its qualities or attributes. Adams and Dickinson (1981) demonstrated in an operant lever-pressing preparation that a downward shift in the value of the reinforcer immediately affects instrumental performance (but see Adams, 1980, 1982). Rats first learned to press a lever by reinforcing lever pressing with a food reward. After subjects had acquired the task, the reinforcer was devalued through pairings with a mild toxin that produced gastric malaise. After being paired with the toxin, rats were highly reluctant to consume the food, showing that they had acquired an aversion to it. When placed back into the conditioning chamber with the lever available that had earned the food during initial training, rats were now reluctant to press the lever as well. Importantly, the devaluation procedure was conducted away from the conditioning situation, which rules out effects of the manipulation

on learning of the response and on context-illness associations. Moreover, the devaluation procedure had an immediate effect on instrumental responding when the rat was returned to the operant chamber.

More compelling evidence for the role of outcome representations in the mediation of an instrumental response comes from work by Colwill and Rescorla (1985). They demonstrated the specificity of the devaluation manipulation to the instrumental response that had earned that outcome using a choice procedure. In their study, rats were trained on two action–outcome contingencies involving two actions (lever pressing and chain pulling) and two outcomes (a sugar solution and food pellets). For each subject, one of the actions was always reinforced with one of the outcomes (e.g., lever press → sugar solution), and the other action was always reinforced with the other outcome (e.g., chain pull → food pellet). Following instrumental training of the two action → outcome sequences, one of the outcomes was devalued through pairings with a mild toxin. The effect of this devaluation procedure was to depress instrumental responding of the action that had previously earned that outcome, but not of the action that had earned the other outcome (**Figure 7**).

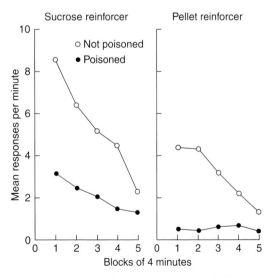

Figure 7 Experiment 1 of Colwill and Rescorla (1985). Mean response rate on the levers that had earned the poisoned (filled symbols) and nonpoisoned (open symbols) actions, for both sucrose reinforcer (left panel) and pellet reinforcer (right panel). Reprinted from Colwill RM and Rescorla RA (1985) Postconditioning devaluation of a reinforcer affects instrumental responding. *J. Exp. Psychol. Anim. Behav. Process.* 11: 120–132, with permission from the authors.

Similar results are obtained if the animal is satiated on one of the outcomes prior to the choice test session. Balleine and Dickinson (1998b) trained rats to make two instrumental responses (right and left lever presses), one for a salt-flavored and one for a lemon-flavored polycose solution. Following instrumental training, rats were given one hour to feed freely on one of the foods immediately prior to an extinction choice test in which both responses were available (but no reinforcement was delivered during the test session). Response rates were significantly lower on the lever that had earned the food reward to which they had been sated than on the lever that had earned the nonsated reward. The results of these experiments reveal the selective nature of the devaluation procedure and provide strong evidence that two separate R-O associations motivated instrumental responding. The selective nature of the devaluation treatments further show that the qualitative features of each outcome were specifically associated with the instrumental response that earned that outcome. One important caveat needs to be mentioned. In most cases, the suppressive effects of outcome devaluation on instrumental responding require the subject to reexperience the devalued food during the extinction choice test (i.e., incentive learning; Balleine, 1992; Balleine and Dickinson, 1998a,b). Initial failures to find outcome devaluation effects on instrumental responding stemmed from failures to expose the subject to the devalued outcome after devaluation treatment (Adams, 1980, 1982).

1.10.2.1.2 Manipulations of the R-O contingency

A second line of evidence for R-O associations comes from manipulations of the R-O contingency. If an instrumental response is goal directed, then by definition it should be sensitive to the relation between the action and the outcome. If the outcome is made freely available, for example, then there is no need for the individual to go through the extra effort involved in making the instrumental response to earn that outcome. Evidence showing the necessity of the R-O contingency on instrumental behavior comes from experiments using the omission procedure. In an omission procedure, a behavior is initially conditioned through pairings with reinforcement. After conditioning is established, the reinforcer is scheduled to be omitted if the subject makes a response. The reinforcer will be delivered, however, if the subject withholds responding. This procedure was developed for the purpose of dissociating

instrumental from Pavlovian conditioned responding. The logic of the procedure is that Pavlovian conditioned responses (CRs) are not sensitive to the response–reinforcer contingency, and thus should not be affected by the omission of the reinforcer, whereas while instrumental responses, which by definition are sensitive to their own consequences, should be affected by the omission of the reinforcer. This procedure has been useful in discriminating acquired responses that are Pavlovian or instrumental in nature. For example, Holland (1979) showed that the acquisition of magazine approach during a tone that was paired with food developed despite the fact that food was withheld if the animal approached the food magazine during the tone. Although magazine approach appeared goal directed, it was actually shown to be insensitive to the negative response–reinforcer contingency. Rather, magazine approach appears to be a Pavlovian response (see Dickinson, 1988, for a fuller discussion of the omission procedure).

More recently, demonstrations that animals are sensitive to the response–outcome contingency have been pursued for the explicit aim of showing the goal-directedness of instrumental behavior. A simple method that demonstrates the goal-directed nature of instrumental responding is to deliver free (i.e., noncontingent) reinforcers during an instrumental session. Delivery of noncontingent food pellets during a session in which a rat is engaged in pressing a lever for food suppresses instrumental lever pressing. Moreover, if a rat has two manipulanda available, each delivering a different outcome, the suppressive effects of noncontingent delivery of one outcome is selective to the manipulandum that earns that outcome (Hammond, 1980; Dickinson and Charnock, 1985; Colwill and Rescorla, 1986; Dickinson and Mulatero, 1989). For example, Colwill and Rescorla trained rats on two instrumental responses (lever press and chain pull), each for a particular outcome (sucrose solution and food pellet). After response rates had stabilized, one of the outcomes was freely delivered in addition to being earned by the response. The rate of responding on the manipulandum that earned the noncontingent outcome decreased, while the rate of responding on the other manipulandum was unaffected. In some cases, noncontingent presentations of one outcome can depress both responses that earn that outcome and those that earn a different outcome, but the response that earns the same outcome that is made freely available shows significantly greater suppression (**Figure 8**; Balleine and Dickinson, 1998a).

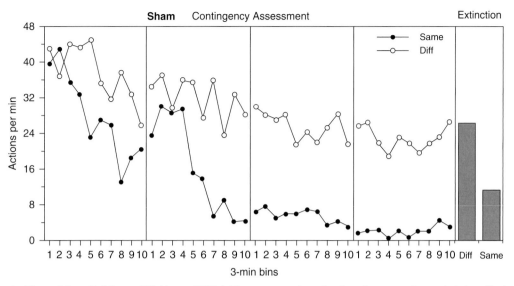

Figure 8 Figure 1 from Balleine and Dickinson (1998a). The mean number of actions (lever pressing and chain pulling) per minute during the four sessions of training under the noncontingent training and during the final extinction test (right-hand panel). The response rates are shown separately for the actions paired with the reward that was same as and different from the unpaired reward. Reprinted from Balleine BW and Dickinson A (1998) Goal-directed instrumental action: Contingency and incentive learning and their cortical substrates. *Neuropharmacology* 37: 407–419, copyright (1998), with permission from Elsevier.

1.10.2.2 Neurobiological Dissociations

The distinction between habitual and goal-directed behavior can also be made at the level of neural circuitry. Vertebrates and invertebrates both show parallel circuitry for reflexive behavior – including unconditional reflexes and species-typical fixed-action patterns on the one hand, and conditioned reflexes on the other – and voluntary behavior. For example, there are two circuits that mediate tail-flick escape behavior in the crayfish (*Procambarus clarkii*): one that mediates rapid and automatic escape responses and one that mediates slower and more flexibly controlled responses (Wine and Krasne, 1972; Edwards et al., 1999; see **Figure 9**).

The rapid escape reflex in response to abrupt stimulation, such as a sharp tap to the side of the abdomen, is a fixed-action pattern that is mediated by medial giant (MG) command neurons. Intracellular recordings from the MGs detect electrical responses in as little as 10 ms after the tap stimulus is applied. The nongiant system, which is excited by gentle prodding and pinching, mediates longer-latency responses that are under a much greater degree of control by the animal than are the immediate escape behaviors. The nongiant neural circuitry innervates and controls the same muscle systems as do the MGs, but it is much more complex (**Figure 9**) in both the interconnections and the number of layers between the sensory and

motor neurons. Although much less is known about the functional control by the nongiant system, presumably it allows for a finer degree of control over the timing and direction of the movement and may even monitor actions as they are planned to allow for corrective feedback prior to execution of the action (see Section 1.10.4.1).

The distinction between the neural basis of the habit system and the voluntary or goal-directed action system can be made in vertebrates as well. There is not sufficient space here to adequately review the extensive literature on this dissociation, but it appears that, in mammals at least, S-R habit learning can be mediated at many locations within the nervous system, including the spinal cord (Chen and Wolpaw, 1995), the basal ganglia (White, 1989), and the striatum (Yin et al., 2004), whereas goal-directed R-O learning is mediated by cortical structures, such as the prelimbic area and the insular cortex (Balleine and Dickinson, 1998a).

1.10.3 Agency

1.10.3.1 Intentional Psychology: Beliefs and Desires

Now that we have established the veracity of the goal-directedness of some acquired behaviors, we can speak with some assurance about the role of

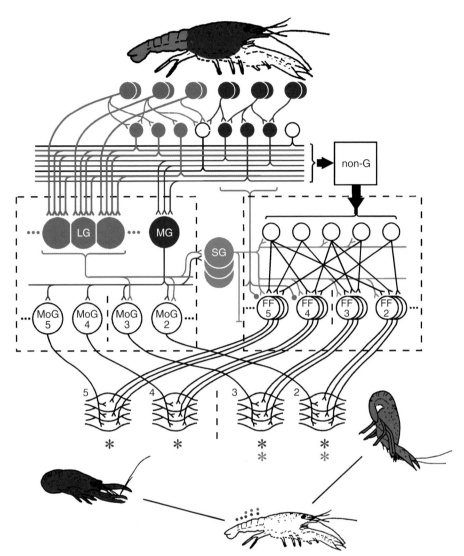

Figure 9 Neural circuitry mediating the escape reflex and volitional tail flipping in the crayfish. Giant-fiber (GF)-mediated reactions are portrayed in the drawings at the bottom of the left side of the figure: the red crayfish represents a lateral giant-axon (LG)-mediated response, and the blue crayfish represents a medial giant-axon (MG)-mediated response. The segmental joints at which bending occurs to produce these reactions are indicated by small colored circles above the white crayfish. LG-associated elements and MG-associated elements are colored in red and blue, respectively. The sensory fields (mechanosensory for LG and mechanosensory and visual for MG) for the two types of GF-mediated reactions are indicated at the top of the figure. Circuitry for GF-mediated responses is shown on the left with primary afferents, sensory interneurons, LG and MG, and giant motor neurons (MoGs) arranged from top to bottom. The multisegmental nature of the LG, which is an electrically well-coupled chain of segmental neurons, each with its own dendrites, is indicated. Colored asterisks mark phasic flexor muscles of segments 2–5 that are used in each type of GF reaction. Circuitry for responses that do not use giant neurons (non-G responses) is shown on the right. A separate population of fast flexor (FF) motor neurons generates non-G responses; uncharted circuitry (box marked non-G) and a set of partially identified premotor interneurons (open circles) mediate between sensory neurons and FF motor neurons. The segmental giant neuron (SG; green), with its blind-ending axon, allows the LG and MG to recruit non-G motor and premotor units. Lateral giant-neuron-associated sensory circuitry provides inhibitory input to caudal FFs (red) so that the SG will not cause bending at caudal joints during LG-type tail flips. Curly brackets show that multiple neurons of the population innervate the indicated target. Reprinted from Edwards DH, Heitler WJ, and Krasne FB (1999) Fifty years of a command neuron: The neurobiology of escape behavior in the crayfish. *Trends Neurosci.* 22: 153–161, copyright (1999), with permission from Elsevier.

beliefs and desires in an intentional psychology (Dickinson, 1988). Intentionality is notoriously difficult to establish in a system because so much behavior can be described using intentional language. We readily slip into intentional language to describe the behavior of our pets (Rover is barking to warn the stranger at the doorstep), computers (My laptop is searching its memory for the file), and the weather (Political leaders escaped Katrina's wrath). The language of intentional folk psychology provides a convenient shorthand to describe and explain behavior, even when we fully recognize that the behavior itself is not intentional at all (Dennett, 1987). Learning theorists themselves find it difficult not to slip into intentional language when describing the behavior of their subjects. In fact, we frequently apologize to our peers for slipping into teleological or anthropomorphic language when we catch ourselves doing so or diffuse the affront by placing the offending material in scare quotes. The rampant misuse of intentional language, however, is for the most part benign and should not devalue the scientific investigation of behavior that is truly intentional in nature. In fact, describing nonintentional behavior using intentional language may assist humankind's ability to predict and control nonintentional systems.

Given the evidence for goal-directed, intentional behavior in the animal kingdom, what is its function? That is, why would it have evolved? Couldn't a creature that lacked goal-directed behavior function just as well in its world as one that had it? Perhaps not. Explicit representation of a goal may serve to motivate behavior to bring the animal into contact with the goal. Furthermore, an animal that believes that an action produces (or prevents) a goal, and that desires (or dislikes) that goal, can be more flexible in when and how it goes about seeking and obtaining (or avoiding) the goal. For example, an omnivorous species – such as a rat, a pig, or a human – must learn which foods are good to eat and which should be avoided. A food previously discovered to be safe for consumption, however, may become spoiled or otherwise unpalatable. The animal that is capable of learning about the devalued food should be able to refrain from seeking out and consuming that food more rapidly than an animal that depended on trial-and-error learning alone. A rat is much more likely to live after one poisoning event than after many. Likewise, an animal that learns of another source where food can be obtained with much reduced effort should be able to immediately curtail exertions to acquire that food from its previous source. Such an

animal can plan for the future. So far, these suppositions are no better than Kipling's (1912) *Just So Stories*. There may, however, be a more important and defensible role for intentional behavior that led to its evolution. This has to do with the concept of agency – a term that often arises in discussions of goal-directed action and intentional behavior.

1.10.3.2 Animals as Free Agents

Leslie (1995) defines an agent as an object that has three properties that distinguish it from other physical objects: mechanical, actional, and cognitive properties. The mechanical property that distinguishes agents from other types of objects is that they have an internal and renewable source of energy (or FORCE in Leslie's terminology) that allows them to *cause* things to happen in the world without themselves having to rely on external sources of energy and force (although we must acknowledge the fact that even agents must refuel). Premack (1990) has made the same distinction, invoking the term 'self-propelledness.' This property allows the agent to be a source of causation (though perhaps not the ultimate source according to adherents of philosophical determinism). To be classified as agents, objects also need to exhibit actional properties, which consist of the object's ability to act and react to events or circumstances in the world that are spatially and/or temporally distant. This property is what characterizes the agent's behavior as goal directed or intentional – at least by appearance. Note, this property of agenthood can be ascribed to an object that only appears to have intentional, purposeful, goal-directed behavior, even if the internal control mechanism itself is not goal directed. For example, a moth's suicidal plunge into a burning flame appears goal directed (the moth sought the flame) even though the control mechanism is a simple, innate (i.e., 'blind') phototaxic reflex. The third property of agency is the cognitive property. An agent's behavior is determined by its beliefs about the world (propositional knowledge). Beliefs are not only about static, coherent states of the world (semantic knowledge) but, more important, are about the causal texture of the world. To believe that A causes B asserts the belief that certain values of A (a1, a2, a3...) are determinants of certain values of B (b1, b2, b3...), and that changes in the state of A (e.g., a1 → a2) should bring about a complimentary change in the state of B (i.e., b1 → b2) (see Woodward, 2003, for a discussion of causal explanation).

1.10.4 Interventions and Causal Reasoning

1.10.4.1 Making Things Happen

What advantages does an agent gain with its ability to represent causal relationships in this manner and hold desires for particular outcomes? One obvious advantage is that such an agent could test its belief system – that is, to fact check. More important, an agent could check facts systematically (cf. Dennett's [1995] Popperian creatures) rather than through blind or random trial and error (cf. Dennett's Skinnerian creatures). The intersection of causal beliefs with desires for goals provides a creature with the ability to manipulate its environment to achieve its goals. This feature of agency provides a creature with a powerful tool – instrumental manipulation of its world. A purely Pavlovian creature can merely passively learn about the causal texture of the world through observation; such a creature is stuck in its world and can merely predict effects based on their cues and respond in anticipation. A creature with both Pavlovian and instrumental learning processes available to it could both passively learn about the causal texture of the world through observation and actively manipulate the world to directly discover its causal texture. Goal-directed instrumental learning allows the agent to actively explore its world through direct intervention. This exploration will uncover many cause–effect relationships that would have remained hidden to a purely passive observer.

Another important feature of agency is that goal-directed behaviors impart a sense of agency to the individual's intentional behaviors. That is, in contrast to reflexive habits, goal-directed behavior is accompanied by unique sensory feedback that is responsible for the sense that 'I' (the agent) control events in the outside world (Haggard, 2005). This distinction is supported by experimental (Libet, 1985) and neurobiological (Sirigu et al., 2004) evidence. These internal sensory markers of intentional behavior should be important, if not critical, to the ability to reason from causal interventions (see discussion below). That is, without the ability to distinguish effects resulting from self-generated, intentional actions from effects resulting from other causal sources (including the agent's nonvoluntary or reflexive behavior), the agent would be incapable of interventional reasoning. This suggestion is supported by imaging studies that use transcranial magnetic stimulation to temporarily inactivate a particular brain area. These studies suggest that the presupplementary motor area – which tracks the neural pathways responsible for intentional action – acts as an internal monitor of intentional action (Haggard et al., 2002; Haggard and Clark, 2003). This predicting signal allows the agent to correct errors in the execution of the action before the action itself occurs. Moreover, this predictive signal can be used to enhance the perception of non-self-generated sensations. For example, the tactile sensation that results from one finger touching the adjacent one is perceived as weaker than the same stimulus imposed from an external source. Attenuated self-generated sensations can more readily be ignored, freeing up attentional resources to focus on the external world. This attenuation of self-generated sensory experience may result from a predictive process that anticipates self-generated sensations, or a postdictive process that judges the source of the perception to be self-generated or externally generated after the sensation has been experienced.

A recent study suggests that the process is predictive (Bays et al., 2006). Participants were required to judge whether a second (comparison) tap was stronger or weaker than a first (sample) tap to their left index finger. The first tap was always the same magnitude, while the strength of the second tap was varied across trials. On most trials, the second tap followed the first by a short interval and was produced by the subject tapping with their right hand onto a button positioned above the left-hand index finger (Contact Trials, **Figure 10(a)**, top panel). This produced a sensation of tapping on one's finger through a solid object. Occasionally, subjects would receive a trial on which the second tap was artificially delayed by 500 ms after they tapped the button with their right hand. On Delay trials, the second tap was perceived as being much stronger than a tap of the same magnitude on Contact trials (**Figure 10(b)**, Group A). The increased magnitude of the perceived tap on Delay trials was not, however, a result of the absence of a right-index finger press at the time the tap was felt. Of primary importance, however, were the occasional No-Contact trials that were conducted to test whether subjects were predicting a self-generated sensation when they attempted to press the button. On No-Contact trials, the button was removed so that when the subject attempted to make a button press they failed to actually press the button (**Figure 10(a)**, bottom panel). Despite the absence of a button press, the subjects reported these No-Contact taps to be much weaker than the

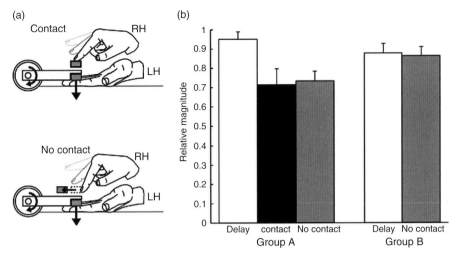

Figure 10   (a) Schematic of the apparatus and task used by Bays et al. (2006). On contact trials (top), in response to an auditory go signal, participants produced a brief force pulse with their right index finger on a force sensor fixed above their left index finger. A similar force pulse was delivered to the left index finger by a torque motor. On no-contact trials (bottom), the force sensor was moved at the start of the trial so that participants made a tapping movement with their right index finger but did not make contact. (b) Mean relative magnitude of the comparison tap to the test tap at the point of perceptual equality as a function of trial type and participant group. Error bars represent ±1 SE. Reprinted from Bays PM, Flanagan JR, and Wolpert DM (2006) Attenuation of self-generated tactile sensations is predictive, not postdictive. *PLoS Biol.* 4: e28.

taps felt on Delay trials. In fact, No-Contact taps were perceived as being the same magnitude as Contact taps (**Figure 10(b)**, Group A). These results show that the subjects anticipated the sensation of a self-generated tap, even when they were prevented from physically engaging the tap. It therefore appears that the process that monitors intentional actions is predictive and attempts to attenuate sensations arising from self-generated actions. This in turn can enhance the perception of sensations caused by an external source.

1.10.4.2   Seeing versus Doing

A burgeoning literature exploring the theoretical mechanisms of causal interventions is developing in the fields of computer science, statistical theory, philosophy, and psychology (Spirtes et al., 1993; Pearl, 2000; Steyvers et al., 2003; Woodward, 2003; Sloman, 2005; Waldmann and Hagmayer, 2005; Waldmann et al., 2006). A resulting achievement is a clear and precise language, taxonomy, and formalization of the difference between observing the cause–effect relationships among a set of variables (Seeing) and intervening on one variable to determine its causal status in relation to the other variables (Doing). These analyses describe the special status interventions have on our (human) ability to determine cause–effect

relationships in the world. "If I flick this switch, the light turns on. If I don't flick the switch, the light remains dark." Such a simple cause–effect relationship can only be determined through intervention. (Note that the agent does not have to actively intervene; the agent can merely observe another agent intervening or observe a fortuitous intervention, such as a book that falls off the shelf and accidentally flicks the switch on its journey to the floor. Theoretical treatment of causal interventions does not treat these scenarios as being different in any significant way.) The ability to reason about cause–effect relationships through the intervention on a single variable is the basis for the scientific method, which gives humankind an incredible analytical power over the world. "If I put reagent X into a beaker filled with reagent Y, the mixture ignites, otherwise the mixture remains inert." "If I look at a blue-filled circle for 60 seconds, I then see a yellow, circular afterimage when I look at a white wall."

A simple example will serve to clarify the fundamental difference between Seeing and Doing and the powerful role interventions (Doing) play in causal reasoning processes. Consider the workings of a barometer (**Figure 11**).

The barometer's reading may vary upward or downward, and this variation correlates strongly with changes in the weather. If we observe an

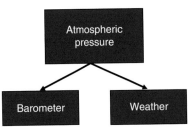

Figure 11 Causal model for how a barometer and the weather are both effects of a common cause, atmospheric pressure. Arrows indicate causal relationship directed from the cause to the effect.

increase in the barometer's reading, we can expect to see sunny skies when we look out the window. If we observe a decrease in the barometer's reading, however, we can expect to see rain clouds gathering. This tight correlation between the barometer and the weather is not the result of a direct causal relationship between the two events. Rather, changes in both the reading of the barometer and the weather are caused by a third event – changes in atmospheric pressure. If we understand the actual causal relationship among these three variables, then we would predict that tampering with the barometer (an intervention) should not affect the weather (or air pressure for that matter; Waldmann and Hagmayer, 2005). Imagine a child observing a barometer for the first time. Without prior schooling on its operation, she might at first entertain the notion – because of temporal priority – that changes in the barometer's reading cause changes in the weather. If she set the barometer to a higher reading, however, she would soon discover that she did not bring about sunny skies. Through intervention on the barometer she was able to test her hypothesis and discover a more accurate underlying causal structure. She would never have been able to discover the underlying causal relationship without access to interventional knowledge (her own or someone else's). Gopnik et al. (2004) provide another telling example:

> smoking is correlated both with having yellow fingers and with getting cancer, so having yellow fingers is correlated with getting cancer, but cleaning your hands will not keep you from getting cancer, and quitting smoking will. Knowing the right causal structure may not be essential for predicting one thing from another, but it is essential for predicting the effects of interventions that deliberately manipulate events. (Gopnik et al., 2004: 8)

Goal-directed behavior provides an important foundation for interventional reasoning. The ability to use interventions to examine causal relationships within a system is predicated on three assumptions (adapted from Gopnik and Schulz, 2004): (1) that interventions are exogenous to the system being studied and not caused by other variables within the system, (2) the intervention directly fixes one variable within the system to a specific value (e.g., a switch is moved from OFF to ON), and (3) the intervention does not affect the values of other variables within the system except through its influence on the variable that is the target of the intervention. The second and third assumptions necessarily depend on goal-directed behavior. If an individual can not represent the contingent relationship between their actions and goals, then they would not profitably use their actions – via the effects their actions have on the world – to investigate cause–effect relationships.

1.10.4.2.1   *Seeing versus doing in children*
Children, it turns out, do appreciate the special role of interventions in diagnosing cause–effect relationships from an early age (Gopnik et al., 2004). In one experiment, 4-year-old children were shown two or three colored rubber balls attached to sticks (hereafter referred to as 'puppets') and placed on top of a box. The children observed the puppets move up and down simultaneously. The puppets could be attached to each other – though the children could not see the attaching mechanisms – so that the experimenter could arrange for the simultaneous movement of the puppets (**Figure 12**). This enabled the children to observe the correlation of movement without observing the intervention by the experimenter. In other conditions, the experimenter could move one puppet at a time, independently of the others. In the pretraining phase of the experiment, the children watched the puppets move together simultaneously. They were then told that one of the puppets was 'special' in that it always made the other puppet(s) move.

The children were then presented with two types of tasks. In the common-effects task, the children observed two puppets (X and Y) move and then stop together simultaneously a number of times, followed by a demonstration that one of the puppets (Y) could be moved without affecting the movement of the other puppet (X). This was accomplished by the experimenter visibly moving puppet Y by moving the top of the stick to which it was attached. Finally, the children watched both puppets move

Front view   Back view

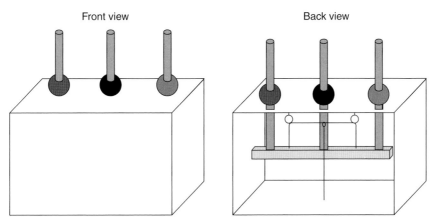

Figure 12 The puppet machine used by Gopnik et al. (2004). Reprinted from Gopnik A, Glymour C, Sobel DM, Schulz LE, Kushnir T, and Danks D (2004) A theory of causal learning in children: Causal maps and Bayes nets. *Psychol. Rev.* 111: 3–32, with permission from A. Gopnik.

together again by the experimenter invisibly moving the connecting mechanism behind the box. The children were asked "Which is the special puppet?" The children chose puppet X a majority (78%) of the time. This suggest that they drew the 'correct' causal interpretation of the relationship between the puppets; that is, that movement of Y is a common effect of both the experimenter's intervention (I) and of the movement of X. I use quotes because the movement of puppet Y was always the result of intervention by the experimenter; however, the children could not see this intervention when it was hidden by the box. Thus, given their sensory data, they observed two conditions: puppets X and Y moving without an apparent intervention by the experimenter, and puppet Y moving in the absence of the movement of puppet X when the experimenter intervened on it. The children's selection of puppet X as special indicates that they represented the causal relationships in the following way: $I \rightarrow Y \leftarrow X$, where the letters represent the events (I = intervention, Y and X = puppets) and the arrows indicate causal directionality. In causal graphs, arrows always point from the cause to the effect. Thus, in the causal graph the children inferred, Y was a common effect of both intervention by the experimenter (I) and of the movement of puppet X.

The second task involved a common-cause relationship among events. In this task, children observed three new colored puppets (X, Y, and Z) move and stop together a number of times. Then they observed the experimenter intervene to move Y independently of the other two puppets and then intervene to move Z independently of the other two puppets. The causal relationships the children should have drawn from this pattern of observations can be graphed as follows: $I \rightarrow Z \leftarrow X \rightarrow Y \leftarrow I$. This causal graph follows from the observations that puppets Z and Y could be moved independently through intervention (I) or moved simultaneously with puppet X. Thus, the children should have inferred that X was a common cause (i.e., a special puppet) of the movements of the other two puppets. This is exactly what the children reported, choosing X as the special puppet 84% of the time.

These experiments reveal how important information from interventions is for young children to reason about the causal texture of their world. If the children only had access to observations of the puppets moving together, then it would have been completely ambiguous which puppet or puppets caused the others to move, if indeed any of them were causally related to the others. It would also have been just as likely that some other, hidden force caused all of the puppets to move together (cf. changes in a barometer and the weather being driven by the unobservable air pressure). Observing that direct interventions on some of the puppets caused only those puppets to move allowed the children to select out the unlikely causal relationships among them and zero in on the most likely interpretation. That is, interventions allowed them to test their hypotheses.

1.10.4.2.2 *Seeing versus doing in rats*

If children can reason about cause–effect relationships from interventions, what about other animals? What is the evidence that nonhuman animals can reason about their causal interventions? Blaisdell et al. (2006) recently investigated this question in rats using conventional conditioning procedures. In a training phase, rats observed a light followed by a tone (L → T) in one session and a light followed by food (L → F) in a second session (Blaisdell et al., 2006, Experiment 2).

One possible causal representation the rats could derive from this observational learning is that the light was a common cause of both the tone and food. No levers were present during the training phase, but during the test phase a lever was inserted into the conditioning chamber for the first time. Note that the rats had never seen this lever before and had certainly not received any training to press the lever. Nevertheless, the following contingency was put in place for half of the rats in the study: if the rat pressed the lever, the tone would come on. In contrast to this Intervention condition, the remaining rats were allocated to an Observation condition. Rats in the Observation condition also had the lever available, but pressing the lever had no effect. That is, the rats in the Observation condition had an inactive lever. The Intervention condition allowed Blaisdell et al. to assess what the rat inferred when it intervened via the lever press to turn on the tone. The Observation condition measured whether the rats expected food when they heard the tone. If rats had formed the causal model T ← L → F, then by observing the tone (Group Observe) they should diagnostically predict the light and thus also predict that food should be available (**Figure 13**, top panel, left-hand graph). By intervening on the tone, however, the rats should infer that they – and not the light – had caused

the tone. Therefore, they should neither predict the light nor the food (**Figure 13**, top panel, right-hand graph). This pattern of data was exactly what Blaisdell et al. observed (**Figure 14**, left-hand bars).

If the rats were reasoning correctly about their interventions, then lever-pressing should not invariably disrupt all causal relationships between the tone and other events but only between other causes of the tone. For example, interventions on the tone should not disrupt expectations of the tone's effects. To show this, Blaisdell et al. (2006) tested another group of rats that had similar training as described above but for one key difference. Rather than receiving Light → Tone pairings in the first phase of training, they received Tone → Light pairings. This treatment, when combined with the following phase of Light → Food pairings should have taught the rats a Tone → Light → Food causal chain (**Figure 13**, bottom panels). Again the rats were divided into two test groups after receiving causal-chain training, with half the rats receiving the Intervention condition (lever pressing turned on the tone) and the remaining rats receiving the Observation condition (tones were presented independent of lever pressing). If rats had learned to treat the light as an effect of the tone, then interventions on the tone at test should still activate an expectation of the light that should then generate the expectation of food (**Figure 13**, bottom panel, right-hand graph). Thus, equivalent amounts of magazine entries should be observed in both the Intervention and Observation conditions. This is exactly what was observed (**Figure 14** central

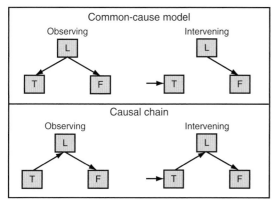

Figure 13 Causal models of the relationships among events in Experiment 2 of Blaisdell et al. (2006). Reprinted from Blaisdell AP, Sawa K, Leising KJ, and Waldmann MR (2006) Causal reasoning in rats. *Science* 311(5763): 1020–1022, with permission.

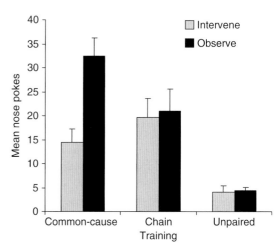

Figure 14 Data from Blaisdell et al (2006) Experiments 2a and 2b. Adapted from Blaisdell AP, Sawa K, Leising KJ, and Waldmann MR (2006) Causal reasoning in rats. *Science* 311(5763): 1020–1022, with permission. See text.

bars). It was furthermore established that magazine entries evoked by the tone depended on the tone having an indirect causal relationship to the food. This was shown through the inclusion of a third group of rats that had received unpaired presentations of the tone and light, so that the two could not enter into any kind of causal relationship, which prevented the tone from eliciting magazine entries at test (**Figure 14**, right-hand bars).

These results show that even rats can reason in a sophisticated manner about their goal-directed interventions by using them to infer the causal structure of the world. I am pitching this description of reasoning processes in rats at the computational level of analysis (Marr, 1982), which is described in terms of representations. The distinction should be made between a causal representation and the learning process though which the representation is acquired (Dickinson, 1980; Heyes and Dickinson, 1990). The learning process might take the form of an entirely algorithmic level associative process. The rats for which a lever press produced a tone did not expect food as strongly as did rats that received tones unconnected to their lever pressing behavior. A plausible explanation for this difference at the algorithmic level of description lies in the rat's knowledge about what instrumental actions do. That is, the rats in our study (and rats in general) have had lots of experience learning about the effects of their actions on the world. This learning starts in infancy (if not earlier) and continues throughout the lifetime of the rat. In fact, both 1-day-old rat pups (Johanson and Hall, 1979) and newborn human infants (DeCasper and Fifer, 1980) can learn instrumental responses. Thus, throughout their lifetimes, rats acquire a large number of action–outcome associations. This learning is typically accompanied by unique feedback cues associated with self-generated, volitional behavior (see Section 1.10.4.1). These feedback cues are presumably present while the rat is engaged in lever pressing in the study phase of the test by Blaisdell et al. (2006). If the associations between these feedback cues and prior outcomes of self-generated, goal-directed action generalize to the current test situation, then the rats that experience the tone following their lever press should discriminate the tone as being the outcome of a self-generated cause rather than the outcome of a non-self-generated cause. Therefore, the tone in the intervention condition should be treated as being caused by the rat itself, and not by the light. The light should not be expected (at a higher rate than its baseline rate of occurrence), and hence neither should the food. In other words,

there are strong grounds for believing that rats can distinguish between self-generated and non-self-generated events, allowing them to learn that they can produce effects through their actions. Rats that received a tone when they pressed the lever may have generalized from their vast instrumental experience and treated the tone as the effect of their own action. This is a likely psychological mechanism candidate for reasoning about causal interventions in both nonhuman and human animals.

The analysis above suggests that, while the rats in the study by Blaisdell et al. (2006) used causal beliefs or models to reason about the source cause of the tone at test, these beliefs or models could have been acquired through conventional associative learning processes (Dickinson, 1980). Dickinson has argued that, in both animals and humans, associative learning processes can support the acquisition of causal beliefs (as distinct from associations) that then control performance through a process of practical inference (see also Heyes and Dickinson, 1990). Of course, humans also have other routes to causal knowledge available, such as verbal and instructional, but the associative (statistical) process is clearly of great importance to humans, as it is to other species.

1.10.5   Tool Use: From Crow to Cro-Magnon

The intentional, goal-directed dissection of cause–effect relationships in the world depends on two abilities: (1) the ability to discriminate self-generated intentional acts from those elicited reflexively by the environment and (2) the ability to discriminate changes in the environment resulting from one's own actions from those changes produced by other means (e.g., environmentally caused). Hence, it is only through the intentional and systematic probing and manipulation of an object that one can build a representation of its causal features. Our knowledge of everyday folk physics – that unsupported objects fall toward the ground, that pushing or pulling on an object usually moves it in the direction of the push or pull, and so on – derives from our vast lifetime experience of manipulating objects and observing the dynamic world (Gopnik et al., 2004). The ability to construct causal maps of the world through observation and planned intervention (what Gopnik et al. refer to as egocentric causal navigation) is not confined only to the human animal but is likely present in many other species as well. I already presented above evidence that rats in a conventional laboratory setting are capable of deriving causal inferences from observational and interventional data. Below I review some of the recent literature investigating what type of causal understanding underlies tool use in nonhuman primates and in Corvids – a family of birds.

1.10.5.1 Tool Use in Primates

Tool use provides an interesting case in which to study causal knowledge and reasoning. Tools are objects with properties and affordances that convey functional value to achieving a particular goal. For example, chimpanzees (*Pan troglodytes*) in West Africa learn to use hammer-anvil stone tools to crack open palm nuts and extract the meat inside (**Figure 15**).

This behavior is transmitted culturally from one generation to the next. The full act, which takes many years to master, involves placing a round palm nut on a large, flat anvil stone and striking it hard enough with a hammer stone without causing the nut to fly off of the anvil. The learning process is motivated by many hours spent observing a proficient adult perform the act and is shaped during many hours of practice of the individual steps involved (Matsuzawa, 1994; Inoue-Nakamura and Matsuzawa, 1997; Hayashi et al., 2005). The final functional sequence eventually develops, and the skill can be usefully employed to extract the rich and nutritious meat inside the nuts.

For a tool to be functional, the user must learn about its properties and about how the user can manipulate the tool to achieve a goal. This learning might involve only a superficial understanding of the tool. For example, the animal might learn how to use the tool through procedural or habit learning without representing the underlying causal structure of the tool. The tool user may, however, acquire a deeper understanding of how the tool works. They may represent both the tool's physical properties, the rules by which those properties can be put to use (i.e., functional properties and affordances), the goal motivating the use of the tool, and the interrelationships among these domains of knowledge. This is a more complex set of relationships than what the rat was faced with in the experiment by Blaisdell et al. (2006). Perhaps this is why it has been difficult to empirically demonstrate that a tool-using animal understands the causal properties of tools and their effects.

The trap-tube task was first developed to study causal reasoning processes involved in tool use in capuchin monkeys and chimpanzees and has become a standard test for assessing causal understanding involved in tool use in nonhuman animals (Visalberghi and Limongelli, 1994; Limongelli et al., 1995; Povinelli, 2000). The trap-tube task involves the placement of a piece of food inside of a clear tube with two open ends (**Figure 16**). The subject is provided with a stick that can be used to retrieve

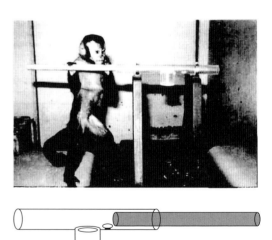

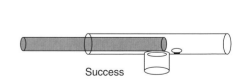

Failure

Success

Figure 16 Trap-tube task for capuchin monkeys See text. Reprinted from Visalberghi E and Limongelli L (1994) Lack of comprehension of cause–effect relations in tool-using capuchin monkeys (*Cebus apella*). *J. Comp. Psychol.* 108: 15–22, with permission from E. Visalberghi.

Figure 15 Chimpanzee using hammer and anvil stones as tools to crack open palm nuts. (Photo courtesy of Etsuko Nogami.)

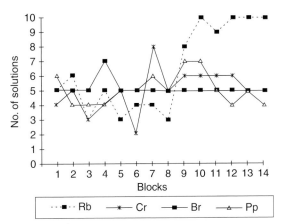

Figure 17 Number of solutions in each 10-trial block of Experiment 1 of Visalberghi and Limongelli (1994). See text. Reprinted from Visalberghi E and Limongelli L (1994) Lack of comprehension of cause–effect relations in tool-using capuchin monkeys (*Cebus apella*). *J. Comp. Psychol.* 108: 15–22, with permission from E. Visalberghi.

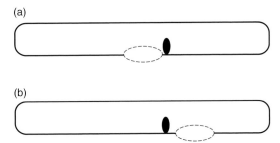

Figure 18 Trap-tube task for capuchin monkeys (Visalberghi and Limongelli, 1994) and chimpanzees (Limongelli et al., 1995). Trap Tube A is the training configuration with the trap located in the center of the tube and the food placed to one side of the trap. Trap Tube B is the transfer configuration with the trap located closer to one side of the tube and food placed in the same location within the trap that it appeared in the training tube. Whereas Trap Tube A required placing the stick in the side of the tube farthest from the reward to prevent the food from becoming trapped, Trap Tube B required changing this distance-based solution to one of inserting the stick into the side of the tube closest to the food. Reprinted from Limongelli L, Boysen ST, and Visalberghi E (1995) Comprehension of cause–effect relations in a tool-using task by chimpanzees (*Pan troglodytes*). *J. Comp. Psychol.* 109: 18–26, with permission from E. Visalberghi.

the food by pushing the food out of one end of the tube. On one side of the tube there is a hole that can trap the food if it is pushed across it. If the subject understands the nature of the trap, it should push the food out of the opposite end from the side with the trap.

In an initial study, three of four capuchins failed to learn to push the food out of the side of the tube away from the trap (see **Figure 17**), and even the successful subject only learned after about 60 trials.

Further tests revealed, however, that the successful subject did not understand how the action of the stick affected the displacement of the reward. Rather, it appeared to solve the task using a simple distance-based associative rule of placing the stick into the side of the tube farthest from the reward. A new trap tube was constructed with the trap placed closer to one end of the tube (**Figure 18(b)**). To prevent food from falling into the trap in Trap Tube B, the subject had to insert the stick into the side of the tube closest to the food rather than the side of the trap furthest from the food as was the correct solution for Trap Tube A. The successful subject, however, continued to insert the stick into the side furthest from the reward in Trap Tube B, hence causing the reward to fall into the trap. This clearly indicates that the successful monkey did not understand the relationship between the trap and the direction the food had to be moved to be successfully retrieved.

Five chimpanzees were also tested on the trap tube problem, and like the capuchins, only some of the chimpanzees learned to solve the task successfully

(Limongelli et al., 1995). Unlike the capuchins, however, the two chimps that learned to solve the task did not appear to be using a simple distance-based strategy. When presented with Trap Tube B (**Figure 18(b)**), the chimps that were successful with Tube A correctly inserted the stick into the side of the trap closest to the food, thereby allowing them to push the food out of the other end of the tube (**Figure 19**).

Although the interpretation of how the chimpanzees solved the trap tube problem has been challenged with scrutiny (Tomasello and Call, 1997; Povinelli, 2000), more recent demonstrations that avoid some of the methodological problems of the earlier studies tend to support the existence of some form of appreciation of the causal nature of the task, at least by small samples of apes (Mulcahy and Call, 2006).

1.10.5.2 Tool Use in Corvids

Despite the extensive research on primates engaged in the trap tube task, some of the strongest evidence that animals can represent the causal structure underlying the tools they use comes from rooks (*Corvus frugilegus*), a member of the Corvid family, which includes crows, ravens, and jays (**Figure 20**). Although rooks are not known to use tools habitually in the wild, they will readily do so in a laboratory

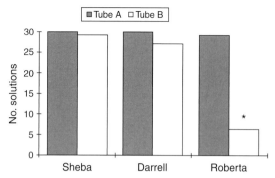

Figure 19 Performance of chimpanzees (Sheba and Darrell) and a capuchin monkey (Roberta) on Trap Tube B after having successfully learning to retrieve food from Trap Tube A. Both chimpanzees correctly inserted the stick into the side of the tube closest to the reward, allowing the successful retrieval of the food. The capuchin did not consistently insert the stick into the correct side of Tube B, and hence the food was trapped on most trials. Reprinted from Limongelli L, Boysen ST, and Visalberghi E (1995) Comprehension of cause–effect relations in a tool-using task by chimpanzees (*Pan troglodytes*). *J. Comp. Psychol.* 109: 18–26, with permission from E. Visalberghi.

Figure 20 A rook. Photo courtesy of Raven J. Brown, used with permission.

setting. In a recent study rooks were presented with a modified trap-tube task (Seed et al., 2006).

Rooks were presented with Task A, shown in **Figure 21(a)**, whereas others were presented with Task B, shown in **Figure 21(b)**. Each task involved a tube with a small piece of food located in its center. A stick was already inserted into the tube at the start of the trial, and the food was enclosed by two plastic discs. Pushing the stick forward or pulling it backward would cause the food to move in the direction of the push or pull. A 'trap' was located below the floor of both sides of the tube. One of the traps was effective in that if the food was dragged across the top

it would drop inside and become trapped – preventing the subject from retrieving the food. The other trap was ineffective and could not trap the food. For the tube in **Figure 21(a)**, the trap on the right side was functional and could trap the food, and the tube on the left was ineffective. Hence, to solve the tube-trap task shown in **Figure 21(a)**, the subject should move the food over the nonfunctional trap on the left, thereby allowing the food to be retrieved. (Note, the side of the functional trap was left–right counterbalanced across trials to prevent the subject from learning a simple side-bias to solve the task.) The tube shown in **Figure 21(b)** contained a similar functional trap to that shown in **Figure 21(a)**, but the nonfunctional trap was different. Rather than pulling the food entirely across the surface of the ineffective trap, the trap was completely open so that food would fall through and out of the tube, where the subject could retrieve it.

Seven out of eight rooks learned to solve the task they were given (**Figure 22**). Task B was learned more quickly than Task A. Furthermore, transfer was almost perfect to the other task (i.e., from A to B or from B to A). This excellent performance suggests that the rooks acquired a deeper causal understanding of the task. There is, however, a simpler alternative explanation for the superb transfer between tasks. Because both tubes have the same functional trap, it is possible that the birds had simply learned to avoid moving the food in the direction of the functional trap. To test this alternative hypothesis, the birds were presented with the trap tubes shown in **Figures 21(c)** and **21(d)**. These tubes lacked the functional trap present in both Tubes A and B, and both tubes contained the nonfunctional traps from Tubes A and B. One of the originally nonfunctional traps from the initial tasks was now made functional in the new tasks. For Tube C, the nonfunctional trap from Tube A was made functional by placing bungs at the ends of the tube. Thus, the food could only be retrieved by dragging it across the trap with the opening in the bottom. For Tube D, the nonfunctional trap from Tube B was made functional by lowering the entire tube onto the floor. Thus, food dragged across the trap from Tube B would trap the food inside, while dragging the food across the trap from Tube A would allow the bird to retrieve food.

Figure 23 shows the performance on Tubes C and D. Only one bird (open squares) consistently performed well above chance on these tubes, suggesting that this bird had acquired a deep understanding of

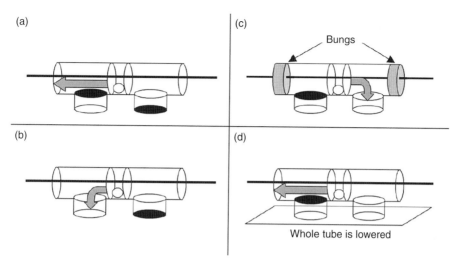

(a)

(b)

(c)

Bungs

(d)

Whole tube is lowered

Figure 21   Trap tube problems used by Seed et al. (2006). See text. Reprinted from Seed AM, Tebbich S, Emery NJ, and Clayton NS (2006) Investigating physical cognition in rooks, *Corvus frugilegus*. *Curr. Biol.* 16: 697–701, with permission from Elsevier.

the causal structure of the trap tubes. None of the other birds were consistently above chance, and thus they likely had learned to solve Tubes A and B by avoiding the functional trap. Thus, although a majority of the birds appeared not to understand the causal properties of the tasks, one bird demonstrated knowledge of the causal properties of objects, such as that objects fall toward the earth when unsupported and that objects cannot move through physical barriers. The generalization of the knowledge about the properties of objects, and of the functional properties of the trap tube itself (i.e., how the food in the tube can be moved by moving the stick), allowed this bird to solve Tasks C and D.

The New Caledonian crow (*Corvus moneduloides*), another species of Corvid, has shown the ability to develop novel techniques to bend aluminum strips in order to use them as hook tools to retrieve food (**Figure 24**). The rapidity with which the crow achieved success not only shows that the behavior is goal directed but also conveys a deeper understanding of some of the properties of the tools and the materials and a representation of the kinds of solutions that are likely to work (Weir et al., 2002; Kenward et al., 2005). In fact, simple generalization of learned rules could not explain the excellent performance, because in most cases the solution required manipulating the tool in a way that was inconsistent or that conflicted with prior successful solutions. For example, one crow named Betty was able to correctly anticipate on four out of five trials whether bending or unbending pieces of novel

materials was required to retrieve food (Weir and Kacelnik, 2007). Even this adept crow, however, often probed the recess containing the out-of-reach food with unmodified tools before modifying them or attempted to use the unmodified end of a modified tool. Though suggestive, the details of Betty's performance prevent us from determining whether she understood the physical causality underlying these tools.

1.10.5.3   Tool Use by Humankind

Although some animal species, in particular among the corvids and primates, have shown remarkable tool use abilities in the laboratory and the wild, these abilities pale in comparison to that shown by humankind. The earliest evidence for tool use among the hominids dates back by at least 2 million years, from which time modified stone tools consisting of struck flakes of volcanic rock have been found among the remains of our ancestor *Homo habilis* (**Figure 25**; Klein, 1989).

There is more extensive evidence of stone tool use by *Homo erectus* throughout Africa, Asia, and Europe dating from about 1.8 to 0.5 million years ago. By 40,000 years ago, when anatomically modern *Homo sapiens* – historically called Cro-Magnon but more appropriately referred to as *Homo sapiens sapiens* – first arrived at Europe, tool use had become quite sophisticated compared to earlier species of Homo. Furthermore, after 40,000 years ago, the evolution of tools and other technologies advanced at a very

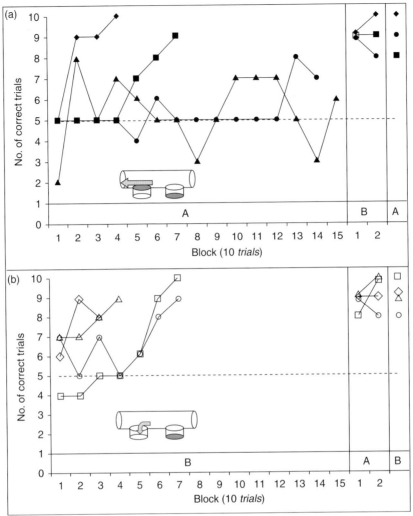

Figure 22 Results of Experiment 1 from Seed et al. (2006). See text. Reprinted from Seed AM, Tebbich S, Emery NJ, and Clayton NS (2006) Investigating physical cognition in rooks, *Corvus frugilegus*. *Curr. Biol.* 16: 697–701, with permission from Elsevier.

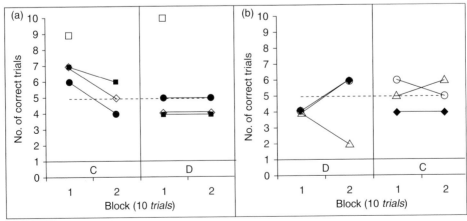

Figure 23 Results from Experiment 3 of Seed et al. (2006). See text. Reprinted from Seed AM, Tebbich S, Emery NJ, and Clayton NS (2006) Investigating physical cognition in rooks, *Corvus frugilegus*. *Curr. Biol.* 16: 697–701, with permission from Elsevier.

Figure 24 Left panel: Betty, a New Caledonian Crow, using a modified hook to retrieve a food reward. Right panel: Examples of hook tools modified by Betty in an experiment involving the retrieval of food. Photo courtesy of Alex Weir, used with permission.

Figure 25 Oldowan flake tools. Olduvai Gorge, Tanzania, Africa. Reproduced from University of California, Berkeley, Department of Anthropology Collection, with permission from Peter A. Bostrom.

rapid pace and showed major geographic diversification (Klein, 1989). Archeological sites throughout Europe show evidence of painting, engraving, sculpture, body ornamentation, and music. There is even indirect evidence for the weaving of wool into cloth, such as is used for clothing. Remains of dwellings, sculpture, and weapons are plentiful at many archeological sites, but perhaps Cro-Magnons are most famous for their cave paintings.

Humankind's extensive, habitual tool use, along with the evolution of language, contributes to our unique ability to adapt ourselves to life in almost every niche of the globe and to exploit a wide range of natural resources from engineered crops to nuclear energy and even allows for our occasional forays into space. This would not have been possible without our ability to represent the goals of our actions.

Acknowledgment

Support for the production of this chapter was provided by National Institute of Mental Health Grant MH 070633 (A.P. Blaisdell).

References

Adams CD (1980) Postconditioning devaluation of an instrumental reinforcer has no effect on extinction performance. *Q. J. Exp. Psychol.* 32: 447–458.

Adams CD (1982) Variations in the sensitivity of instrumental responding to reinforcer devaluation. *Q. J. Exp. Psychol.* 34B: 77–98.

Adams CD and Dickinson A (1981) Instrumental responding following reinforcer devaluation. *Q. J. Exp. Psychol.* 33B: 109–121.

Balleine B (1992) Instrumental performance following a shift in primary motivation depends on incentive learning. *J. Exp. Psychol. Anim. Behav. Process.* 18: 236–250.

Balleine BW and Dickinson A (1998a) Goal-directed instrumental action: Contingency and incentive learning and their cortical substrates. *Neuropharmacology* 37: 407–419.

Balleine BW and Dickinson A (1998b) The role of incentive learning in instrumental outcome revaluation by sensory-specific satiety. *Anim. Learn. Behav.* 26: 46–59.

Balleine BW and Ostlund SB (2007) Still at the choice-point: Action selection and initiation in instrumental conditioning. *Ann. N. Y. Acad. Sci.* 1104: 147–171.

Bays PM, Flanagan JR, and Wolpert DM (2006) Attenuation of self-generated tactile sensations is predictive, not postdictive. *PLoS Biol.* 4: e28.

Blaisdell AP, Sawa K, Leising KJ, and Waldmann MR (2006) Causal reasoning in rats. *Science* 311(5763): 1020–1022.

Chen XY and Wolpaw JR (1995) Operant conditioning of H-reflex in freely moving rats. *J. Neurophysiol.* 73: 411–415.

Colwill RM and Rescorla RA (1985) Postconditioning devaluation of a reinforcer affects instrumental responding. *J. Exp. Psychol. Anim. Behav. Process.* 11: 120–132.

Colwill RM and Rescorla RA (1986) Associative structures in instrumental learning. In: Bower GH (ed.) *The Psychology of Learning and Motivation*, vol. 20, pp. 55–104. San Diego, CA: Academic Press.

DeCasper AJ and Fifer WP (1980) Of human bonding: Newborns prefer their mothers' voices. *Science* 208(4448): 1174–1176.

Dennett DC (1987) *The Intentional Stance*. Cambridge, MA: MIT Press/A Bradford Book.

Dennett DC (1995) *Darwin's Dangerous Idea: Evolution and the Meanings of Life*. New York: Simon and Schuster.

Dickinson A (1980) *Contemporary Animal Learning Theory*. Cambridge: Cambridge University Press.

Dickinson A (1988) Intentionality in animal conditioning. In: Weiskrantz L (ed.) *Thought without Language*, pp. 305–325. New York: Clarendon Press/Oxford University Press.

Dickinson A and Balleine B (1994) Motivational control of goal-directed action. *Anim. Learn. Behav.* 22: 1–18.

Dickinson A and Charnock DJ (1985) Contingency effects with maintained instrumental reinforcement. *Q. J. Exp. Psychol.* 37B: 397–416.

Dickinson A and Mulatero CW (1989) Reinforcer specificity of the suppression of instrumental performance on a non-contingent schedule. *Behav. Process.* 19(1–3): 167–180.

Edwards DH, Heitler WJ, and Krasne FB (1999) Fifty years of a command neuron: The neurobiology of escape behavior in the crayfish. *Trends Neurosci.* 22: 153–161.

Flaherty CF (1996) *Incentive Relativity*. New York: Cambridge University Press.

Gopnik A, Glymour C, Sobel DM, Schulz LE, Kushnir T, and Danks D (2004) A theory of causal learning in children: Causal maps and Bayes nets. *Psychol. Rev.* 111: 3–32.

Gopnik A and Schulz L (2004) Mechanisms of theory formation in young children. *Trends Cogn. Sci.* 8(8): 371–377.

Haggard P (2005) Conscious intention and motor cognition. *Trends Cogn. Sci.* 9: 290–295.

Haggard P and Clark S (2003) Intentional action: Conscious experience and neural prediction. *Conscious Cogn.* 12: 695–707.

Haggard P, Clark S, and Kalogeras J (2002) Voluntary action and conscious awareness. *Nat. Neurosci.* 5: 382–385.

Hammond LJ (1980) The effect of contingency upon the appetitive conditioning of free-operant behavior. *J. Exp. Anim. Behav.* 34: 297–304.

Hayashi M, Mizuno Y, and Matsuzawa T (2005) How does stone-tool use emerge? Introduction of stones and nuts to naive chimpanzees in captivity. *Primates,* 46: 91–102.

Heyes C and Dickinson A (1990) The intentionality of animal action. *Mind Lang.* 5: 87–104.

Holland PC (1979) Differential effects of omission contingencies on various components of pavlovian appetitive conditioned responding in rats. *J. Exp. Psychol. Anim. Behav. Process.* 5: 178–193.

Inoue-Nakamura N and Matsuzawa T (1997) Development of stone tool use by wild chimpanzees (*Pan troglodytes*). *J. Comp. Psychol.* 111: 159–173.

Johanson IB and Hall WG (1979) Appetitive learning in 1-day-old rat pups. *Science* 205(4404): 419–421.

Kenward B, Weir AA, Rutz C, and Kacelnik A (2005) Behavioural ecology: Tool manufacture by naive juvenile crows. *Nature* 433(7022): 121.

Kipling R (1912) *Just So Stories* (Reprint ed.). Garden City, NY: Doubleday.

Klein RG (1989) *The Human Career: Human Biological and Cultural Origins*. Chicago: The University of Chicago Press.

Leslie AM (1995) A theory of agency. In: Sperber D, Premack D, and Premack AJ (eds.) *Causal Cognition: A Multidisciplinary Debate*, pp. 121–149. New York: Clarendon Press/Oxford University Press.

Libet B (1985) Unconscious cerebral initiative and the role of conscious will in voluntary action. *Behav. Brain Sci.* 8: 529–566.

Limongelli L, Boysen ST, and Visalberghi E (1995) Comprehension of cause–effect relations in a tool-using task by chimpanzees (*Pan troglodytes*). *J. Comp. Psychol.* 109: 18–26.

Marr D (1982) *Vision: A Computational Investigation into the Human Representation and Processing of Visual Information*. San Francisco: W.H. Freeman.

Matsuzawa T (1994) Field experiments on use of stone tools by chimpanzees in the wild. In: Wrangham RW, McGrew WC, de Waal FBM, and Heltne PG (eds.) *Chimpanzee Cultures*, pp. 351–370. Cambridge, MA: Harvard University Press.

Mulcahy NJ and Call J (2006) How great apes perform on a modified trap-tube task. *Anim. Cogn.* 9: 193–199.

Pearl J (2000) *Causality: Models, Reasoning, and Inference*. Cambridge: Cambridge University Press.

Povinelli DJ (2000) *Folk Physics for Apes: The Chimpanzee's Theory of How the World Works*. Oxford/New York: Oxford University Press.

Premack D (1990) The infant's theory of self-propelled objects. *Cognition* 36: 1–16.

Seed AM, Tebbich S, Emery NJ, and Clayton NS (2006) Investigating physical cognition in rooks, *Corvus frugilegus*. *Curr. Biol.* 16: 697–701.

Sirigu A, Daprati E, Ciancia S, et al. (2004) Altered awareness of voluntary action after damage to the parietal cortex. *Nat. Neurosci.* 7: 80–84.

Sloman S (2005) *Causal Models: How People Think About the World and Its Alternatives*. Oxford: Oxford University Press.

Spirtes P, Glymour C, and Scheines R (1993) *Causation, Prediction, and Search*. New York: Springer-Verlag.

Steyvers M, Tenenbaum JB, Wagenmakers E, and Blum B (2003) Inferring causal networks from observations and interventions. *Cogn. Sci.* 27: 453–489.

Thorndike EL (1898) Animal intelligence: An experimental study of the association processes in animals. *Psychol. Rev. Monogr. 2* (Whole No. 8).

Thorndike EL (1911) *Animal Intelligence: Experimental Studies*. New York: Macmillan.

Tinklepaugh OL (1928) An experimental study of representative factors in monkeys. *J. Comp. Psychol.* 8: 197–236.

Tolman EC (1932) *Purposive Behavior in Animals and Men*. New York: The Century Co.

Tolman EC (1948) Cognitive maps in rats and men. *Psychol. Rev.* 55: 189–208.

Tolman EC and Gleitman H (1949) Studies in learning and motivation: I. Equal reinforcements in both end-boxes, followed by shock in one end-box. *J. Exp. Psychol.* 39: 810–819.

Tolman EC and Honzik CH (1930) Introduction and removal of reward, and maze performance in rats. *Univ. Calif. Publ. Psychol.* 4: 257–275.

Tomasello M and Call J (1997) *Primate Cognition*. New York: Oxford University Press.

Visalberghi E and Limongelli L (1994) Lack of comprehension of cause–effect relations in tool-using capuchin monkeys (*Cebus apella*). *J. Comp. Psychol.* 108: 15–22.

Waldmann MR and Hagmayer Y (2005) Seeing versus doing: Two modes of accessing causal knowledge. *J. Exp. Psychol. Learn. Mem. Cogn.* 31: 216–227.

Waldmann MR, Hagmayer Y, and Blaisdell AP (2006) Beyond the information given: Causal models in learning and reasoning. *Curr. Dir. Psychol. Sci.* 15: 307–311.

Weir AA, Chappell J, and Kacelnik A (2002) Shaping of hooks in New Caledonian crows. *Science* 297(5583): 981.

Weir AA and Kacelnik A (2007) A New Caledonian crow (*Corvus moneduloides*) creatively re-designs tools by bending or unbending aluminium strips. *Anim. Cogn.* 9: 317–334.

White NM (1989) Reward or reinforcement: What's the difference? *Neurosci. Biobehav. Rev.* 13: 181–186.

Wine JJ and Krasne FB (1972) The organization of escape behavior in the crayfish. *J. Exp. Biol.* 56: 1–18.

Woodward J (2003) *Making Things Happen: A Theory of Causal Explanation*. Oxford: Oxford University Press.

Yin HH, Knowlton BJ, and Balleine BW (2004) Lesions of dorsolateral striatum preserve outcome expectancy but disrupt habit formation in instrumental learning. *Eur. J. Neurosci.* 19: 181–189.

1.11 Categories and Concepts in Animals

O. F. Lazareva and E. A. Wasserman, University of Iowa, Iowa City, IA, USA

1.11.1 Introduction and Theoretical Distinctions

Concepts . . . give our world stability. They capture the notion that many objects or events are alike in some important respects, and hence can be thought about and responded to in ways we have already mastered. Concepts also allow us to go beyond the information given. . . . In short, concepts are critical for perceiving, remembering, talking, and thinking about objects and events in the world. (Smith and Medin, 1981: p. 1)

The ability to categorize objects and events and to extend this categorization behavior to new instances is fundamental to many human activities. We sort the objects and events around us into categories, while still being able to recognize some or all of the individual members of each category. For example, we categorize a Ferrari, a Cadillac, and a Toyota as cars, even though they do not look identical, have different engines, and are manufactured in different countries. This ability is undoubtedly beneficial.

When we encounter a new model of car, we immediately recognize it as a car and engage in appropriate behavior (e.g., driving).

We also construct higher-level categories – such as clothing, tools, or furniture – whose members are perceptually disparate, but functionally similar. A violin, a piano, a flute, and a cymbal may not look alike, but we nevertheless classify them as orchestral instruments because they play music. Furthermore, we create abstract concepts that go beyond any perceptual similarities or functional interconnections; such abstract concepts entail relations between or among objects. For example, in poker, a flush entails five cards from the same suit, regardless of the values of the cards. Our everyday life contains many examples of such abstract, relational concepts: Things can be faster or slower, larger or smaller, inside or outside, same or different.

The ability to form concepts is surely adaptive, because concepts allow us to respond appropriately to novel stimuli after having experience with only a few instances from a given category. The same ability should also be beneficial for animals. One can often observe a red-tailed hawk attacking pigeons in downtown Iowa City; undoubtedly, those downtown pigeons should soon learn to flee when they spot members of this hawk species. But, there are other, albeit rarer, hawk species which prey on pigeons, such as Cooper's Hawk or the Northern Goshawk. Clearly, the ability to recognize these less frequent predators as a threat should be advantageous for the birds, just as is our ability to recognize a Toyota as a car is advantageous for us. Charles Darwin himself in *The Descent of Man* proposed that "the senses and intuitions, the various emotions and faculties, such as … memory, attention, … reason, etc., of which man boasts, may be found in an incipient, or even sometimes in a well-developed condition, in the lower animals" (Darwin, 1896, p. 126). In our chapter, we review empirical studies that strongly suggest that categories and concepts are not unique to the human brain (*See* Chapters 1.07, 1.08, 1.29). Before we begin, however, we attempt to define some relevant terms.

1.11.2   Operational Definitions of Category and Concept

Since C. Lloyd Morgan (1894/1977), comparative psychologists have struggled with the following question: Do animals exhibit conceptual behavior? As is often the case with controversial questions in animal cognition, providing an operational definition of the behavior in question is the first critical step.

Cognitive psychologists often define categorization as the process of grouping objects or events into categories and responding to these categories in a similar manner (e.g., Medin and Aguilar, 2001). Concepts, on the other hand, are thought to be the elements of knowledge that assist categorization (e.g., Smith and Medin, 1981; Hampton, 2001). Many authors suggest that the term 'category' should be used to refer to classes of items, whereas the term 'concept' should be used to refer to the mental representation of those classes (Laurence and Margolis, 1999). Still others propose that the term 'concept' should be used to refer to well-defined classes characterized by a set of necessary and sufficient features and the term 'category' should be reserved for ill-defined or fuzzy classes with gradual membership (Medin, 1998). In any case, concepts and categories are treated as entities: Things to be found either in the environment or in one's mind.

Keller and Schoenfeld (1950) were first to develop an operational definition of concepts that could be made suitable for animal research. These authors began by noting that "one does not *have* a concept, just as one does not *have* extinction – rather, one demonstrates conceptual behavior, by acting in a certain way" (Keller and Schoenfeld , 1950, p. 154). What behavior, then, do we call conceptual? Keller and Schoenfeld proposed that organisms exhibit conceptual behavior when they respond similarly to members of one class of stimuli and differently to members of other classes of stimuli: "Generalization *within* classes and discrimination *between* classes – this is the essence of concepts" (Keller and Schoenfeld, 1950: p. 155). In other words, when a child says 'doggie' if she sees any dog but not if she sees a cat, or when a pigeon pecks the screen if a human being is displayed but refrains from pecking otherwise, we could say that the child and the pigeon have behaved conceptually.

The Keller-Schoenfeld definition also suggests a useful distinction between categorization and discrimination: We speak of categorization when the organism discriminates among classes of multiple stimuli rather than among individual instances of each class. So, if an organism has been trained to make one response to a single photograph of a car and to make a second response to a single photograph of a chair, then we say that the organism discriminates the car from the chair. But, if an organism has been trained to make one response to multiple exemplars of cars and to make a second response to multiple exemplars of chairs, then we say that the organism categorizes the cars and chairs. In essence, categorization entails a subset of discrimination problems in which multiple stimuli are associated with a common response.

Suppose, however, that we trained an organism to associate ten photographs of cars with one response and to associate ten photographs of chairs with a second response. Is successful learning enough to claim that conceptual behavior has been exhibited? No. Because the organism might master this task by memorizing all 20 photographs, it is obvious that we need to expand our definition: Conceptual behavior ought to be transferable to novel instances from the familiar categories. Only if the organism can produce the correct response in the presence of novel cars and novel chairs should we speak of conceptual behavior.

Indeed, even this additional requirement may not be sufficient to define conceptual behavior. What if the novel cars and novel chairs were indistinguishable from the familiar cars and the familiar chairs seen in training? Then, the organisms' performing the correct responses in the presence of the novel testing stimuli would be a trivial failure to discriminate. A revised Keller-Schoenfeld definition of conceptual behavior should now say that an organism exhibits conceptual behavior if it can learn to respond similarly to members of one class and to respond differently to members of another class, as well as to transfer these differential report responses to novel, discriminably different members of these classes (Wasserman et al., 1988).

1.11.2.1   Types of Concepts

Humans use concepts in an extremely broad and flexible manner, classifying objects and events because they look alike, because they perform the same function, or because they entail the same relationship. For example, people may classify an object as a Ferrari (subordinate level based on subgroups within basic-level categories), a car (basic level), or a vehicle (superordinate level based on aggregation of several basic-level categories). Consequently, many researchers place concepts into three broad types (e.g., Zentall et al., 2002). Perceptual concepts (e.g., German Shepard, tree, or airplane) entail categories based on physical similarities among their members; these concepts are reviewed in the sections titled 'Perceptual concepts as basic-level categories' and 'Perceptual concepts as subordinate-level categories.' In contrast, nonsimilarity-based concepts (e.g., tools or furniture) include perceptually diverse stimuli that are grouped on the basis of common function or association; these concepts are reviewed in the section titled 'Nonsimilarity-based concepts.' Finally, abstract concepts (e.g., above or different) are based on relations between or among stimuli instead of their physical properties; these concepts are reviewed in the section titled 'Abstract concepts.'

1.11.3   Perceptual Concepts as Basic-Level Categories

Perceptual concepts have often been studied in the context of human basic-level and subordinate-level categorizations. Categorization at the basic level is generally believed to be based on high perceptual similarity among members of the same category and low perceptual similarity among members of different categories (Rosch and Mervis, 1975). In contrast, categorization at the subordinate level distinguishes subgroups within basic-level categories. So, subordinate categorization entails high within- and between-category similarity, rendering this level of categorization less preferred by humans than the basic level (Rosch and Mervis, 1975; Rosch et al., 1976; but see Tanaka and Taylor, 1991).

In this section, we review studies exploring animals' sensitivity to basic-level categories based on perceptual similarity; categorization at the subordinate level is considered in the section titled 'Perceptual concepts as subordinate-level categories.'

1.11.3.1   History of Animal Categorization Research: Herrnstein's Studies

Studies of visual categorization in animals date back to the pioneering work of Herrnstein and Loveland (1964). Using the familiar go/no-go procedure, Herrnstein and Loveland reinforced pigeons for pecking at the response plate if the photograph projected on it contained a person, but they did not reinforce the pigeons' pecks otherwise. The researchers collected 1,200 color slides, some of which contained people and some of which did not. **Figure 1** shows examples of the photographic slides used in the study.

The photographs varied in coloration and lightning. Some of them contained a group of people, whereas others depicted a single person. The depicted person or people could be partially obscured by other objects, such as trees or window frames, or could appear off center and at a distance. Nevertheless, the pigeons learned the discrimination: That is, they predominantly pecked at the photographs containing people, in spite of the great variation in content of the photographs. Moreover, the pigeons successfully categorized previously unseen photographs, thereby demonstrating an important hallmark of conceptual behavior: transfer to new exemplars from the category.

In later experiments, Herrnstein and his colleagues demonstrated that pigeons could learn tree/nontree, fish/nonfish, and even water/nonwater categories, as well as transfer their discriminative performance to novel exemplars from each category (Herrnstein et al., 1976; Herrnstein and de Villiers, 1980). Although pigeons' long-term memory can retain over 800 associations between a specific picture and a correct response (Vaughan and Greene, 1984; Cook et al., 2005), successful transfer to novel

Figure 1   Representative stimuli from Herrnstein's early experiments on pigeon categorization. The left column depicts reinforced stimuli with people, and the right column depicts nonreinforced stimuli without people. Images courtesy of Will Vaughan.

members of the categories precludes simple memorization as an explanation for the pigeons' behavior.

Careful scrutiny of the slides on **Figure** 1, however, reveals a potential alternative explanation of the pigeons' performance. The backgrounds of the images in the person and nonperson categories were not matched; hence, if some features of the background (e.g., man-made objects) correlated with the presence of people, then those features might have come to control the pigeons' behavior, instead of the target object. In fact, later research has shown that, when presented with nonmatched photographs, pigeons might memorize category-relevant features, background features, or both (Greene, 1983), but when the photographs are matched, pigeons are more likely to learn category-relevant features (Edwards and Honig, 1987). Note that transfer to new exemplars can also be explained by background features being correlated with the presence or absence of the category member; such correlated features are likely to be present in the testing photographs, just as they were in the training photographs.

One could nevertheless argue that using background features together with (or instead of) the presence or absence of the target object does not mean that the pigeon cannot form the concepts of person or tree; rather, the concept formed by the pigeons may simply differ from that expected by the experimenter. Being nonverbal animals, pigeons have to discern the rules of the game from the stimulus material with which they are presented during the experiment: If the stimulus material permits an alternative strategy (e.g., trees are always located near shrubs), then the pigeons might learn to attend to such 'incorrect' cues.

Would we then conclude that pigeons' performance in these experiments fits the definition of conceptual behavior that we developed earlier? Yes. A more important and challenging question is: What features of the stimuli actually control the pigeons' behavior? The very strength of Herrnstein's approach, the use of highly varied, rich, and lifelike photographs, makes it problematic for researchers to answer this question. As we see in the next section, later studies have struggled with this problem with varying degrees of success.

1.11.3.2 Further Research on Basic-Level Categorization

Much of research that followed Herrnstein's pioneering studies continued to use the go/no-go procedure, in which one class of pictures is associated with some schedule of positive reinforcement and another class is associated with experimental extinction. Additionally, these studies generally used a single category (e.g., person) together with its complementary category (e.g., nonperson); we term this design mutually exclusive categorization. Most human language categories, however, are not of the presence/absence sort; instead, people partition the world around them into multiple clusters, such as cars, chairs, rocks, and flowers. Indeed, some authors have suggested that, although many animals can learn dichotomous presence/absence classifications, "only primates may sort the world, i.e. divide it into its indeterminately many classes" (Premack, 1976, p. 215). Although the go/no-go design can be used to study such noncomplementary categories as cats versus dogs (e.g., Ghosh et al., 2004; see also Roberts and Mazmanian, 1988), this categorization is still restricted to only two categories.

Another experimental design involves the multiple-alternative forced-choice procedure (**Figure** 2), which provides an effective means of studying categorization among multiple noncomplementary categories, such as cars, chairs, people, flowers, or cats. Using this multiple categorization scheme, pigeons have been found to be able to learn at least four noncomplementary categories of stimuli by pecking at four distinctively different choice keys and to transfer their discriminative responses to novel exemplars from those categories (Bhatt et al., 1988; Lazareva et al., 2004). Moreover, ongoing research in our laboratory suggests that pigeons' categorization is not limited to only four classes of stimuli: The birds can learn to discriminate 16 noncomplementary categories, such as ducks, bottles, trees, hats, and so on.

More than four decades of research on basic-level categorization in animals have made it clear that many animals, including primates and pigeons, can discriminate a great number of categories, including non-complementary categories (**Table** 1). Although some early reports suggested that pigeons may be unable to categorize human-made stimuli, such as cars or bottles (Herrnstein, 1985), later research has not supported this claim: Several studies have since found that pigeons can easily discriminate cars and chairs from flowers and people (Bhatt et al., 1988; Lazareva et al., 2004), and even Picasso's paintings from Monet's (Watanabe et al., 1995; Watanabe, 2001). Still, pinpointing the stimulus properties used for categorization has been elusive.

Go/No-Go

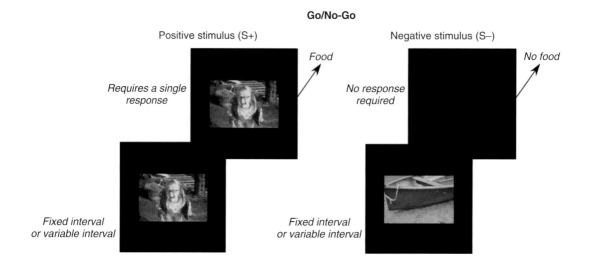

Multiple-alternative forced-choice task

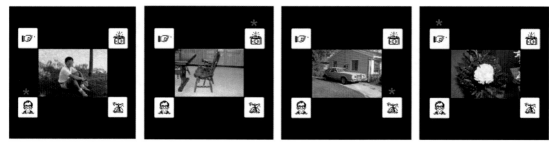

Correct response always followed by food

Figure 2   Comparison of go/no-go and multiple-alternative forced-choice procedures. The go/no-go procedure associates one class of stimuli (positive stimuli, or S + s) with reinforcement and the other class of stimuli (negative stimuli, or S − s) with experimental extinction. With a few exceptions, this procedure has been used with mutually exclusive categories, such as *tree/no-tree*. The multiple-alternative forced-choice procedure requires a subject to select one of the choice responses associated with a given class of stimuli (the red asterisks indicate the correct choices). This procedure has been used to study noncomplementary categories, such as people, flowers, cars, and chairs.

Table 1   Animal studies of categorization at basic level

Category	Species	References
Fish	Pigeons, rhesus monkeys	Herrnstein and de Villiers, 1980; Vogels, 1999
Trees	Pigeons, rhesus monkeys	Herrnstein et al., 1976; Vogels, 1999
Cars	Pigeons	Bhatt et al., 1988; Wasserman et al., 1988; Astley and Wasserman, 1992; Lazareva et al., 2004, 2006
Chairs	Pigeons	Bhatt et al., 1988; Wasserman et al., 1988; Astley and Wasserman, 1992; Lazareva et al., 2004;, 2006
Flowers	Pigeons	Bhatt et al., 1988; Wasserman et al., 1988; Astley and Wasserman, 1992; Lazareva et al., 2004, 2006
Humans	Pigeons, capuchin monkeys, rhesus monkeys, gorilla, baboons, chimpanzee	Fujita and Matsuzawa, 1986; Schrier and Brady, 1987; Bhatt et al., 1988; D'Amato and Van Sant, 1988; Wasserman et al., 1988; Astley and Wasserman, 1992; Watanabe, 2000; Aust and Huber, 2001, 2002; Vonk and McDonald, 2002; Aust and Huber, 2003; Lazareva et al., 2004; Matsukawa et al., 2004; Lazareva et al., 2006; Martin-Malivel et al., 2006

Studies attempting to disclose the stimulus properties controlling discriminative behavior in categorization tasks have generally used two different approaches. The first group of studies have used a *post hoc* analysis of already collected data concerning the presence or absence of some feature(s) on the target object (Schrier and Brady, 1987; D'Amato and Van Sant, 1988; Roberts and Mazmanian, 1988; Vonk and McDonald, 2004). For example, Schrier and Brady (1987) trained rhesus monkeys to discriminate photographs that contained people from photographs that did not. The photographs were rated from good (where people comprised at least 50% of the scene) to intermediate (25%–50%) to poor (less than 25%); monkeys' discrimination accuracy proved to be positively correlated with these ratings. However, other researchers using this method have often experienced difficulties in finding significant or meaningful correlations between the stimulus properties and the subjects' discriminative behavior (e.g., Roberts and Mazmanian, 1988; Vonk and McDonald, 2004).

The second and more successful group of studies has used different modifications of the training images or novel testing images varying along specific dimensions to discern the features controlling subjects' behavior (Herrnstein and Loveland, 1964; Schrier and Brady, 1987; Wasserman et al., 1988; Cook et al., 1990; Vogels, 1999; Watanabe, 2000, 2001; Aust and Huber, 2002; 2003; Ghosh et al., 2004; Lazareva et al., 2006). In a representative study, Aust and Huber (2002) trained pigeons to discriminate photographs based on the presence or absence of a person. **Figure 3** depicts some of

Figure 3 Examples of images used for training the *person/no-person* discrimination and for subsequent testing of features controlling pigeons' performance. Modified from Aust U and Huber L (2002) Target-defining features in a "people-present/people-absent" discrimination task by pigeons. *Anim. Learn. Behav.* 30: 165–176.

the images used in this study. As in earlier reports, pigeons successfully learned this discrimination. To find out which visual features controlled the pigeons' behavior, the birds were later presented with several sets of novel, nonreinforced probe stimuli that depicted some parts of the human body (hands, head, legs, and trunk) or patches of human skin of various sizes and shapes. The pigeons responded to images containing hands as if they were members of the person category, whereas images containing feet or skin patches generated the nonperson response. Aust and Huber (2002) also found that, as the similarity of the testing stimuli to the target category 'person' increased, the pigeons were more likely to classify the testing stimuli as members of the person category. Thus, artifacts imitating people (e.g., dolls or scarecrows) were more likely to produce the person response than were primates, mammals, or birds. Similarly, photographs of animals wearing clothes were more likely to be classified as members

of the person category than either clothes in isolation or animals without clothes. Overall, these results suggest that pigeons' classification behavior was based on category-relevant features that were combined in an additive fashion: Exemplars with more category-relevant features were more likely to be classified as members of the person category than were exemplars with few such features.

Although some studies have been successful in identifying specific features controlling animal behavior in categorization experiments, many attempts have raised more questions than answers. For example, in our own recent study (Lazareva et al., 2006), we trained pigeons to discriminate cars, chairs, flowers, and people using a four-alternative forced-choice task. We then explored whether the pigeons' categorization behavior depended on the overall shape of the object or on its local details by using two stimulus manipulations: blurring and scrambling (**Figure 4**). Blurring

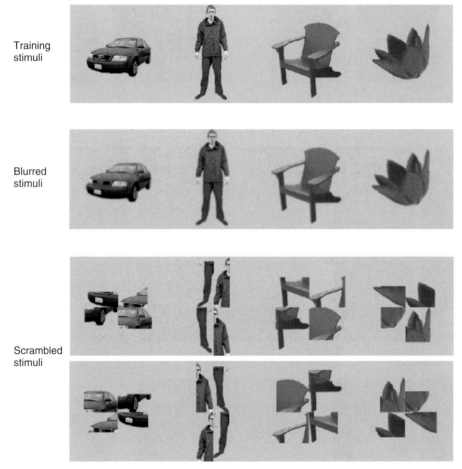

Training stimuli

Blurred stimuli

Scrambled stimuli

Figure 4   Examples of blurred and scrambled testing stimuli, together with the training stimuli from which they were derived. From Lazareva OF, Freiburger KL, and Wasserman EA (2006) Effects of stimulus manipulations on visual categorization in pigeons. *Behav. Process.* 72: 224–233.

distorts the fine details of the image while leaving the overall shape of the target object relatively intact, whereas four-part sectioning and scrambling leaves most of the fine details of the image unmodified but distorts the overall shape of the target object. Surprisingly, these two manipulations had decidedly different effects depending on the category of the target stimulus: Blurring impaired the discrimination of cars (and, to some extent, chairs), but it had no effect on the discrimination of flowers and people, whereas scrambling impaired the discrimination of flowers and people, but it had no effect on the discrimination of cars and chairs. These results suggest that the birds may have discriminated photographs of cars and, perhaps, chairs by using some local feature(s) and relied on the overall shape of the object when discriminating photographs of flowers and people.

But, what does it mean to say that cars and chairs were discriminated by pigeons' using some local feature? Just what might this local feature be? Similarly, what does it mean to say that pigeons relied on the overall shape of the object when discriminating flowers and people? In order to pinpoint these controlling features more precisely, additional tests, analogous to those used by Aust and Huber (Aust and Huber, 2002) are necessary. Given the large number of potential local and global features that can work alone or in combination with each other, conducting such tests for four categories would be impractical. This limitation of complex naturalistic stimuli has prompted researchers to use simpler stimuli that permit more precise analysis and manipulation to study stimulus control in categorization (see the section titled 'Artificial polymorphous categories as models of basic-level categories').

As well, innovative experimental procedures now allow researchers to efficiently isolate features of complex visual stimuli that control subjects' behavior. Martin-Malivel et al. (2006) have recently applied the reverse correlation method to disclose features controlling the categorization of human and baboon faces by humans and baboons. These researchers first trained participants to discriminate human and baboon faces at high levels of accuracy. Next, the training stimuli were warped so that the overall shape of all images was identical, a procedure that permitted the construction of a human–baboon morph. Finally, random visual noise was superimposed on the warped and morphed images to create the testing images (see top panel of **Figure** 5). The trials of interest were the morphed human–baboon images with superimposed random noise that could render the image more similar to the human face or more similar to the baboon face. The patterns of noise were then correlated with the subject's responses on a trial-by-trial basis, allowing the researchers to determine the areas of the image that were critical for categorization (see Mangini and Biederman, 2004, for procedural details).

This analysis revealed intriguing differences in the visual information utilized by people and baboons. Baboons' discrimination performance was controlled by the contrast between the eyes and the surrounding region: Lighter eye areas prompted human responses, whereas darker eye areas prompted baboon responses. People's discrimination performance, on the other hand, was controlled by this contrast information as well as by a number of other facial features, such as nose, mouth, and facial contour.

In another study deploying a different innovative technique (Gibson et al., 2005), some pigeons were trained to discriminate whether the depicted face was a man's or a woman's, whereas other pigeons were trained to discriminate whether the face had a happy or a neutral expression (see bottom panel of **Figure** 5). After pigeons' performance reached high levels of accuracy, the training stimuli were covered by a gray mask containing several openings or bubbles. The bubbles were presented at random locations on the screen, and their position determined trial difficulty. For example, the specific configuration of the mask on a 20-bubble face (**Figure** 5, bottom panel) makes it easy to determine gender, but not emotion. Thus, by correlating the locations of the bubbles with a subject's categorization responses, we can again determine the features that support reliable discrimination behavior (see Gosselin and Schyns, 2001, 2005, for details). Here, both pigeons and people were found to utilize similar pictorial information. When discriminating happy from neutral faces, both pigeons and people relied heavily on the bottom part of the face including the mouth. When discriminating male from female faces, both pigeons and people relied on regions near the eyes and the chin.

Clearly, both reverse correlation and bubbles procedures have great potential for elucidating the perceptual bases of categorization in animals (see Gosselin and Schyns, 2002, and Gosselin and Schyns, 2004, for a comparison of the techniques). Note especially that the conventional methods of modifying or deleting parts of the images to divulge which features might control performance requires some notion as to the identity of those features. In contrast, neither reverse correlation nor bubbles make such assumptions; instead, these techniques sample all of the information that is available in the images. We expect

Reverse correlation method

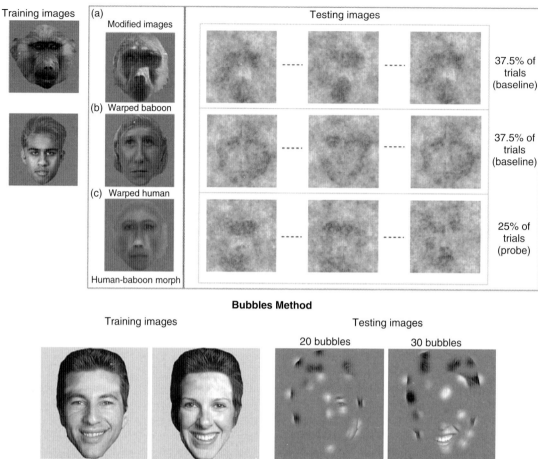

Bubbles Method

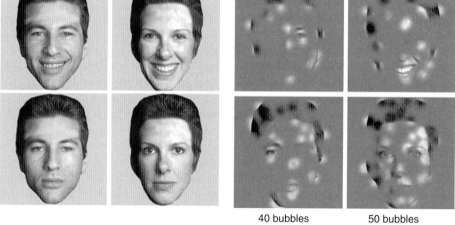

Figure 5 Illustration of training and testing stimuli for the reverse correlation method (top) and for the Bubbles method (bottom). Top: After subjects learned to discriminate human faces from baboon faces (training images), the training images were warped (modified images) or superimposed with random visual noise to obtain the testing images. Note that the human–baboon morph stimulus superimposed with random noise can look more similar to the human face on some trials and more similar to the baboon face on other trials. Modified from Martin-Malivel J, Mangini MC, Fagot J, and Biederman I (2006) Do humans and baboons use the same information when categorizing human and baboon faces? *Psychol. Sci.* 17: 599–607. Bottom: After training to report whether a face is happy or neutral or whether it belongs to a male or a female, the training stimuli were covered with a mask revealing only a portion of the stimuli through the openings or 'bubbles.' Note that the position of the bubbles randomly varied across trials so that different areas of the faces could be revealed on different trials. Modified from Gibson BM, Wasserman EA, Gosselin F, and Schyns PG (2005) Applying Bubbles to localize features that control pigeons' visual discrimination behavior. *J. Exp. Psychol. Anim. Behav. Process.* 31: 376–382.

that deploying these and other new methods will greatly advance our understanding of how animals categorize complex visual stimuli.

1.11.3.3 Do Animals Perceive the Cohesiveness of Basic-Level Categories?

Extensive experimental evidence suggests that animals can be assiduously trained to sort stimuli into different basic-level categories, including noncomplementary categories (cf. **Table 2**). But, do animals view the members of these categories as being perceptually coherent before such categorization training, as do people? In other words, do animals directly perceive the members of a basic-level category to be more similar to one another than to the members of other categories?

Several studies suggest that primates may indeed perceive basic-level categories to be perceptually cohesive clusters of stimuli. Fujita and Matsuzawa (1986) used a sensory reinforcement procedure to find out whether a chimpanzee can form the category 'person' without explicit reinforcement. The chimpanzee was shown a picture on a screen and was required to touch a response key repeatedly to keep viewing the same picture. If the response key was not touched within 10 s, a new picture was presented. Analysis of the intervals between responses and the duration of responses revealed that the chimpanzee preferred to view photographs containing people; it rarely pressed the key to repeat photographs that did not contain people. This nonpreferred, no-person category also included some ambiguous photographs in which the target object was very small as well as entirely white or entirely black photographs.

Table 2   Animal studies of artificial polymorphous categories

Species	Technique	Reference
Pigeons	Go/no-go	Lea and Harrison, 1978; von Fersen and Lea, 1990; Huber and Lenz, 1993; Jitsumori, 1993; Huber and Lenz, 1996; Jitsumori, 1996
	Two-alternative forced-choice	Lea et al., 1993
Rhesus monkeys	Go/no-go	Jitsumori, 1994
Baboons	Two-alternative forced-choice	Depy et al., 1997

In another experiment (Sands et al., 1982), rhesus monkeys were trained to move a lever in one direction if two successively shown pictures were identical and to move the lever in a different direction if the pictures were nonidentical. The set of pictures included six different exemplars of human faces, monkey faces, trees, flowers, and fruits. If the monkeys perceived members of the same category (e.g., fruit) to be more similar to each other, then they should have been more likely to erroneously respond same when a picture of an apple was followed by a picture of an orange than when it was followed by a picture from another category (e.g., an oak). Analysis of confusion errors found this to be the case: All pictures of fruit fell into the same region of multidimensional space. Interestingly, pictures of monkey faces and human faces were clustered together, as were pictures of trees and flowers, suggesting that rhesus monkeys viewed monkey faces as being similar to human faces and that they viewed trees as being similar to flowers.

What about pigeons? Several reports suggest that pigeons too perceive similarity among the members of basic-level categories (Wasserman et al., 1988; Astley and Wasserman, 1992). For example, Astley and Wasserman (1992) evaluated the perceptual coherence of basic-level categories using a go/no-go method. For some pigeons, 12 photographs of cars could serve as positive discriminative stimuli: The birds were reinforced for pecking these stimuli when they were shown. For other pigeons, 12 photographs of chairs, flowers, or people could serve as the positive discriminative stimuli. The set of negative discriminative stimuli was common to all of the pigeons and consisted of 12 photographs each of cars, chairs, flowers, and people that were different from the 12 photographs that were used as the positive discriminative stimuli. As pigeons learn this discrimination, their rate of responding to all of the negative discriminative stimuli is expected to fall. However, if pigeons see categories as collections of perceptually similar items, then the rate of responding to the negative stimuli from the same category as the positive discriminative stimuli should have fallen more slowly than to the stimuli from the other categories. Astley and Wasserman (1992) again found that the data supported such perceptual coherence: Pigeons committed most errors to the negative discriminative stimuli from the same category as the positive discriminative stimuli.

In sum, most researchers have found that, just like people, animals perceive basic-level categories to be perceptually cohesive clusters of stimuli (but see Sutton and Roberts, 2002). Recent research in our own laboratory has also begun to explore similarities across different basic-level categories, specifically natural categories, like 'flower' or 'person,' and artificial or human-made categories, like 'chair' or 'car'. Studies of certain cerebral pathologies in humans have found an intriguing dissociation between impaired recognition and the naming of living objects and nonliving objects, suggesting that these types of categories could be represented in a qualitatively different manner (see Farah, 1999, and Martin and Caramazza, 2003, for a review). Some researchers have proposed that the categorization of artificial objects is based on their functional specifications or on the kinesthetic representation of the movements performed in using them, whereas the categorization of natural objects is based solely on their perceptual properties (Warrington and McCarthy, 1987; Damasio, 1990). Other researchers have suggested that the difference is one of degree and not of kind: The members of natural categories may be more similar to each other than are the members of artificial categories (Humphreys et al., 1988; Gaffan and Heywood, 1993; Lamberts and Shapiro, 2002; McRae and Cree, 2002).

Of course, when nonverbal animals are trained to sort photographs of cars, chairs, flowers, and people, this categorization ought to be based only on perceptual similarity. Thus, finding a natural–artificial dissociation in pigeons' categorization behavior suggests that people's categorization behavior may also be based on the perceptual coherence of the given categories. So far, our data suggest that pigeons perceive two natural categories, flowers and people, to be more similar to each other than to either cars or chairs, but they perceive cars and chairs as being just as similar to one another as they are to either flowers or people (Lazareva et al., 2004). Similarly, rhesus monkeys appear to perceive living objects as more similar to each other than to nonliving objects (Gaffan and Heywood, 1993). Although more research is needed, current data point to many potential similarities in how animals and humans perceive similarities within and between basic-level categories. The neural mechanisms of such classification behavior may be especially informed by comparative studies of the sort reviewed here.

1.11.3.4   Artificial Polymorphous Categories as Models of Basic-Level Categories

Although considerable research has demonstrated that animals can classify pictures of objects such as trees or cars, the stimulus features controlling such

discriminative behavior have been much more difficult to determine (see the section titled 'Further research on basic-level categorization'). Consequently, some researchers have adopted a different approach: Instead of trying to deal with already-existing categories, they have constructed *m*-out-of-*n* artificial polymorphous categories, where a specific instance is a member of a category if it contains *m* out of *n* relevant features. Natural basic-level categories are often believed to be polymorphous; that is, there is no single feature that is necessary or sufficient for category membership. Thus, artificial polymorphous categories constructed in a similar manner might to be an effective way to model basic-level categories.

Figure 6 depicts one example of such an artificial polymorphous category studied by Jitsumori (1993). The relevant dimensions are the shape of the elements (circles or triangles), the color of the elements (white or black), and the color of the background (red or green). Here, as well as in many other similar studies, the dimensions are selected to be orthogonal, so that the contribution of each feature can be independently

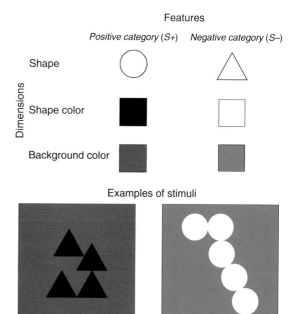

Figure 6   Construction of a two-out-of-three polymorphous category (Jitsumori, 1993). The stimuli were created by changing features from three dimensions: shape (circle or triangle), shape color (black or white), and background color (red or green). The features were randomly assigned to represent the positive and negative categories. The top panel depicts one such assignment. Stimuli with two positive and one negative feature belonged to the positive category, whereas stimuli with two negative and one positive feature belonged to the negative category.

assessed. The features are then randomly assigned to represent either a positive or a negative category. In Jitsumori's study, a stimulus with two positive and one negative features was assigned to the positive category, whereas a stimulus with two negative and one positive features was assigned to the negative category. Pigeons were then trained to respond when a member of the positive category was shown and to refrain from responding when a member of the negative category was shown, a standard go/no-go procedure. This experiment, and others listed in **Table 2**, has found that animals can learn such artificial polymorphous categories.

Despite such successful learning, other experimental data cast doubt on the similarity of artificial polymorphous categories to natural basic-level categories. Lea et al. (2006) observed that, although the discrimination of basic-level categories is easily learned, artificial polymorphous categories are often difficult to master for both animals and people. For example, pigeons took an average of 5400 trials to master the two categories depicted in **Figure 6** (Jitsumori, 1993). For comparison, pigeons trained to discriminate cars, chairs, flowers, and people in a four-alternative forced-choice task required fewer than 1000 trials to master all four categories (Bhatt et al., 1988; Wasserman et al., 1988).

Lea et al. (2006) proposed several factors that may affect the rate of learning artificial polymorphous categories. For example, in artificial polymorphous categories, each feature is equally valid: So, in the task presented in **Figure 6**, the color of the shape is as good a predictor of a category membership as is the shape itself. In contrast, the predictive value of different features identifying members of natural categories can vary. Therefore, if a subject is trained to discriminate cars from chairs, then the presence of tires on car images or the presence of thin elongated parts, such as chair legs, on chair images may be sufficient features for discrimination. Further research is needed to elucidate to what extent research on artificial polymorphous categories can be used as an effective model of basic-level categorization.

1.11.4 Perceptual Concepts as Subordinate-Level Categories

Subordinate categories are nested within basic-level categories. For example, the category monkey includes Japanese monkeys, rhesus monkeys, and capuchin monkeys. Subordinate categories have high within-

category similarity, but unlike basic-level categories, they also have high between-category similarity; after all, most monkey species look quite similar to each other. Consequently, categorization at the basic level is preferred to categorization at the subordinate level (Rosch and Mervis, 1975). Nevertheless, the less-privileged status of subordinate categories can be moderated by expertise: Dog experts and bird experts identified objects at the subordinate level just as fast as at the basic level within their domain of expertise (Tanaka and Taylor, 1991; Johnson and Mervis, 1997).

Can animals learn to categorize at the subordinate level? Although categorization at the subordinate level has received far less attention than categorization at the basic or superordinate levels, several species have been successfully trained to categorize at the subordinate level (**Table 3**). Curiously, several animal studies suggest that some subordinate levels, namely, the level of species, may be a preferred level of categorization. For example, pigeons and rhesus monkeys readily learned and transferred the subordinate-level kingfisher/nonkingfisher discrimination, but they were unable to master the basic-level bird/nonbird discrimination (Roberts and Mazmanian, 1988). In another experiment (Yoshikubo, 1985), rhesus monkeys were trained to respond to photographs containing rhesus monkeys and to refrain from responding to photographs that did not contain rhesus monkeys or any other animals. In later testing, photos of Japanese monkeys were shown as probe trials. If, during initial training, rhesus monkeys formed the basic-level category 'monkey', then they should have responded to these photographs. However, they refrained from responding, suggesting that the subordinate category 'rhesus monkey' had instead been acquired. Similar data were obtained for other monkey species (Fujita, 1987).

Of course, rhesus monkeys, as well as other monkey species, have extensive experience recognizing and categorizing members of their own species. It can, thus, be argued that the shift in preferred level of categorization may be the result of high proficiency, just as in humans (Tanaka and Taylor, 1991; Johnson and Mervis, 1997). The Roberts and Mazmanian (1988) data seem to argue against this hypothesis, because both pigeons and monkeys preferred the subordinate-level category kingfisher; presumably, rhesus monkeys do not have extensive expertise with different bird species. However, other reports suggest that pigeons can, in fact, successfully master the bird/mammal discrimination (Cook et al., 1990), casting doubt on their failure to master the

Table 3   Animal studies of categorization at subordinate level

Category	Species	References
Style of painting	Pigeons	Watanabe et al., 1995; Watanabe, 2001
Oak leaves	Pigeons	Cerella, 1979
Facial expressions or gender of conspecifics	Chimpanzees, Japanese monkeys	Parr et al., 1998; Koba and Izumi, 2006
Human facial expressions or gender	Pigeons, Japanese monkeys	Jitsumori and Yoshihara, 1997; Kanazawa, 1998; Troje et al., 1999; Huber et al., 2000; Gibson et al., 2005
Conspecifics	Pigeons, chimpanzees, rhesus monkeys, Japanese monkeys, stumptailed monkeys, bonnet monkeys, pigtail monkeys, baboons	Poole and Lander, 1971; Yoshikubo, 1985; Fujita, 1987; Brown and Boysen, 2000; Watanabe, 2000; Vonk and McDonald, 2004; Martin-Malivel et al., 2006
Animal species (other than the subject's own species)	Pigeons, chimpanzees, orangutans, gorilla	Roberts and Mazmanian, 1988; Cook et al., 1990; Brown and Boysen, 2000; Vonk and McDonald, 2002; Ghosh et al., 2004;

bird/nonbird discrimination reported by Roberts and Mazmanian (1988). Future research systematically examining the preferred level of categorization across different species is needed to disclose potential differences and similarities in subordinate-level categorization in animals and humans.

1.11.5 Nonsimilarity-Based Concepts

Nonsimilarity-based concepts have often been studied in the context of human-language superordinate categories, constructed from several basic-level categories. For example, the category animal may include birds, frogs, and fish (e.g., Wasserman et al., 1992); this approach is reviewed in the section titled 'Nonsimilarity-based concepts as superordinate-level categories'. Another approach to nonsimilarity-

based concepts involving equivalence class formation is reviewed in the section titled 'Nonsimilarity-based concepts as equivalence classes.'

1.11.5.1 Nonsimilarity-Based Concepts as Superordinate-Level Categories

Can animals learn to respond differentially to superordinate human-language categories? Starting with Herrnstein's studies, many animals have been found to be able to sort objects into various superordinate categories, such as bodies of water, vehicles, or food (**Table 4**). In one instance, Roberts and Mazmanian (1988) used a go/no-go task to train pigeons and squirrel monkeys to discriminate color photographs at three different levels: kingfisher versus other birds, birds versus other animals, and animals versus various outdoor scenes containing trees, furniture, houses, and other inanimate objects.

Table 4   Animal studies of categorization at the superordinate level

Category	Species	References
Bodies of water	Pigeons	Herrnstein et al., 1976
Vehicles	Chimpanzees, Japanese monkeys	Murai et al., 2004; Murai et al., 2005
Furniture	Chimpanzees, Japanese monkeys	Murai et al., 2004, 2005
Mammals, birds, or animals	Pigeons, chimpanzees, Japanese monkeys, orangutans, gorilla, rhesus monkeys	Roberts and Mazmanian, 1988; Delorme et al., 2000; Vonk and McDonald, 2002; Povinelli and Vonk, 2003; Murai et al., 2004, 2005
Man-made vs. natural, or living vs. nonliving	Pigeons, rhesus monkeys	Lubow, 1974; Roberts and Mazmanian, 1988; Gaffan and Heywood, 1993; Lazareva et al., 2004, 2006
Food	Mangabeys, gorilla, rhesus monkeys	Delorme et al., 2000; Deputte et al., 2001; Vonk and McDonald, 2002

Both pigeons and squirrel monkeys readily learned the kingfisher/nonkingfisher discrimination, and both species transferred their performance to novel exemplars. The animal/nonanimal discrimination required additional training, but it was eventually mastered. In contrast, neither monkeys nor pigeons could correctly classify novel pictures in the bird/nonbird discrimination. Similar results were obtained for a juvenile gorilla that learned the orangutan versus human, primate versus nonprimate, and animal versus food discriminations, but that animal only showed reliable transfer to novel exemplars for the orangutan versus human and the animal versus food discriminations (Vonk and McDonald, 2002). In a replication of this study, Vonk and McDonald (2004) found that, unlike the gorilla, adult orangutans readily learned all three discriminations, and they transferred their discriminative performance to novel exemplars from all three categories. It is not clear why some animals appear to have difficulty with some of the superordinate categories (e.g., birds/nonbirds) but not with others (e.g., animals/nonanimals).

Most published studies have explored animals' categorization at different levels in different experiments and usually with different visual stimuli. Yet, flexible classification of objects and events at different levels is thought to be one of the most important and perhaps the unique features of human categorization (Markman, 1989): Humans can refer to the same object as a Toyota, a car, or a vehicle, depending on context. Recently, work in our laboratory has explored whether pigeons can flexibly classify the same photographs at the basic level or at the superordinate level, depending on task demands (Lazareva et al., 2004).

As **Figure 7** illustrates, our experiment used four basic-level categories (cars, chairs, flowers, and humans) that were arranged into two superordinate-level categories (artificial: cars and chairs, natural: flowers and humans). During training, the same photograph randomly required basic-level discrimination if four choice keys were presented and superordinate-level discrimination if two different choice keys were presented. Our pigeons readily mastered both discriminations, attesting to their ability to flexibly categorize the photos; as well,

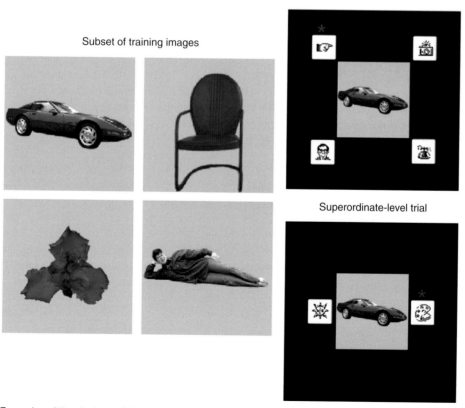

Figure 7 Examples of the photographic stimuli and the schematic layout of a basic-level trial and a superordinate-level trial used in Lazareva et al. (2004). The choice response assignments varied across birds.

our pigeons demonstrated reliable transfer to novel exemplars at both basic and superordinate levels. Flexible categorization therefore appears not to be a uniquely human ability.

1.11.5.2 Nonsimilarity-Based Concepts as Equivalence Classes

Instead of training animals to sort objects according to superordinate human-language categories, other experiments have studied how superordinate categories are created in the first place. If, by definition, superordinate categories are not based on perceptual similarity, then how and why are they formed?

One possibility (Astley et al., 2001) concerns learned or acquired equivalence: Perceptually distinct stimuli may be grouped together if all of them have been associated with the same outcome or with the same behavior. We know that the perceptually distinctive stimuli have formed a functional equivalence class if a change in response tendencies to some members of the class generalize spontaneously to other members of the class, when members of the class become interchangeable, or both (Schusterman et al., 2000; Sidman, 2000; Zentall, 2000).

Some theorists believe that functional equivalence classes need to be distinguished from stimulus equivalence classes, which represent a higher level of complexity and are empirically documented by reflexivity, symmetry, and transitivity (Hayes et al., 2001). Others argue that functional equivalence classes do not differ from stimulus equivalence classes (Sidman, 2000). Regardless of how this debate is resolved, functional equivalence classes appear to be quite close to superordinate human-language categories.

For example, we use both cars and motorcycles to travel; as cars and motorcycles each produce a common outcome (moving us from one place to another), we combine these two classes of objects into a single superordinate category, vehicle. Likewise, we call any organism that preys on other organisms (i.e., exhibits a common behavior) a predator, grouping together such diverse organisms as flatworms, ant lions, and killer whales. Is this aggregative ability uniquely human? Can animals also construct categories based on their functional, rather than perceptual, properties?

In the representative experiment depicted in **Figure 8** (Wasserman et al., 1992), pigeons were trained to peck one button when photographs of two basic-level categories (e.g., flowers and chairs) were presented and to peck a second button when photographs of other two basic-level categories (e.g., cars and people) were

presented. Then, with the first two buttons unavailable, the pigeons were trained to peck a third button to photographs of flowers and to peck a fourth button to photographs of people, a procedure called reassignment training (Lea, 1984). No photographs of cars or chairs were shown during reassignment training. Finally, the researchers showed the pigeons photographs of cars and chairs with only the third and fourth buttons available. If, during original training, the pigeons grouped the two basic-level categories associated with a common response into a higher-order category, then they should have been able to select the response associated with the complementary basic-level category during reassignment training. In the testing phase, the pigeons did predominately peck the button that had been associated with the complementary basic-level category during reassignment training, thus documenting functional stimulus equivalence.

Later research in our laboratory has revealed that pigeons can form functional equivalence classes via associations with a common delay, a common probability, and a common quantity of reinforcement (Astley and Wasserman, 1999; Astley et al., 2001; see also Frank and Wasserman, 2005). For example, when cars and flowers were associated with a 15-s delay to reinforcement, or were reinforced on one out of ten trials, or were reinforced by five pellets, pigeons grouped these two basic-level categories together into a functional equivalence class.

Many other reports have documented the formation of functional equivalence classes via a many-to-one mapping procedure (e.g., Grant and Kelly, 2001; Neiman and Zentall, 2001; Urcuioli et al., 2006; see Zentall, 1998, for a review). In a typical many-to-one matching experiment, organisms are trained to make a common response after two or more entirely arbitrary stimuli. For example, pigeons could be presented with a red hue or a vertical line as an initial (or sample) stimulus; in this case, the choice of a vertical line (a comparison stimulus) is reinforced. Alternatively, a pigeon could be presented with a green hue or a horizontal line as a sample, and in this case the choice of a horizontal line is reinforced (Urcuioli et al., 1989). After that, one sample from each class is associated with a novel response: The red hue sample with the choice of a black circle and the green hue sample with the choice of a white circle. Finally, the second sample from each class, the vertical line and the horizontal line, was presented with the novel comparison stimuli, the black circle and the white circle. The pigeons selected the black circle when the vertical line was presented, and they selected the white circle when the horizontal

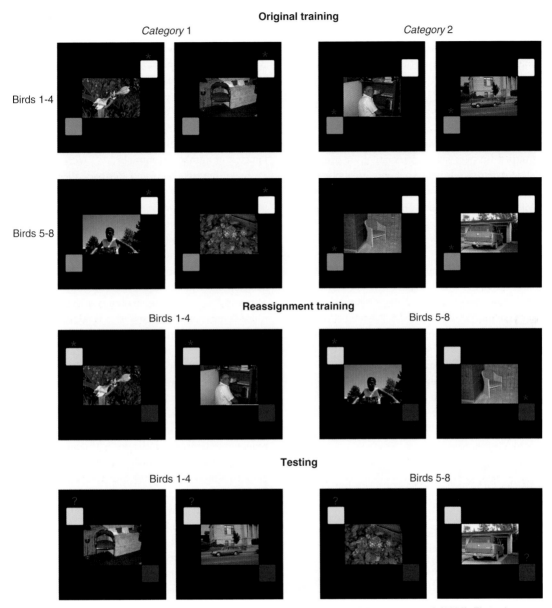

Figure 8 Schematic depiction of the training and testing procedures used in Wasserman et al. (1992). First, pigeons were trained to associate two basic-level categories with one response and two other basic-level categories with a different response (original training), creating two higher-level, superordinate categories. Later, one of the basic-level categories from each superordinate category was associated with a different response (reassignment training). Finally, the withheld basic-level categories were presented with the novel choice responses (testing). If the birds were forming superordinate-level categories during original training, then they should be able to select the correct response associated with the other class of stimuli during reassignment training. Different assignments were given to two subsets of birds in the experiment.

line was presented, divulging an emergent relation between the stimuli associated with the same event, quite similar to the experiments described earlier.

Note, however, that the functional equivalence classes in this design do not comprise several basic-level categories. Therefore, although research on many-to-one matching may have important implications for understanding superordinate categorization in animals, it does not entail many of the important features of superordinate categories, such as their hierarchical structure. To our knowledge, no research has explicitly explored to what extent superordinate-level categorization is comparable to many-to-one matching.

1.11.6   Abstract Concepts

Many theorists have drawn a distinction between natural concepts, such as tree or furniture, and abstract or relational concepts, such as above/below or same/different (Premack, 1983a; Lea, 1984; Herrnstein, 1990; Pearce, 1994; Thompson, 1995; Wasserman, 1995; Mackintosh, 2000; Wright et al., 2003; Cook and Wasserman, 2006). Members of natural concepts are grouped by perceptual, associative, or functional similarity, whereas abstract concepts are believed to go beyond the specific features of the stimuli. Instead, abstract concepts are based on relations between or among those stimuli. As C. Lloyd Morgan (1894/1977) stated in his *Introduction to Comparative Psychology*:

> Two particular objects, billiard balls for example, are perceived to be a span asunder. The balls are removed, and pieces of chalk being substituted they too are seen to be a span asunder. All sorts of small objects may be substituted for the chalk, and ... the space relationship remains unchanged. [...] We do not merely perceive those two billiard balls to be related in such a way, but we conceive the relationship in its abstract and general form. ... [T]his conception is not concrete, particular, and individual, but abstract, general, and of universal application. (Lloyd Morgan, 1894/1977, pp. 262–263)

Lloyd Morgan (1894/1977) considered whether animals can form such abstract concepts, but he later rejected this intriguing possibility, "in no dogmatic spirit, and not in support of any preconceived theory or opinion, but because the evidence now before us is not ... sufficient to justify the hypothesis" (Lloyd Morgan, 1894/1977, p. 377). Morgan's conservative assessment persists today (Premack, 1983a; Pearce, 1994; Mackintosh, 2000). Nevertheless, substantial experimental evidence now suggests that animals can, in fact, form concepts that transcend specific properties of the stimuli, such as symmetrical or same/different (see **Table 5** for more examples). We review the evidence relevant to the most extensively studied concepts in this section.

1.11.6.1   Concept of Number

Can animals count? One of the difficulties in answering this question lies in the enormous variety of behaviors that can be controlled by numerical attributes of stimuli. An organism may be trained to select the larger (or the smaller) of two arrays of items, with the experimenter controlling the nonnumerical attributes of the stimuli (e.g., area or density), so that only the number of items in the array can reliably predict reinforcement (e.g., Thompson and Chase, 1980; Zorina and Smirnova, 1996; Anderson et al., 2005). Is this evidence of counting? What about an experiment in which an organism is trained to select an array of three items, irrespective of the items' identity or configuration (e.g., Davis, 1984)? Do any of these studies represent clear evidence for the concept of number in animals?

According to Davis and Perusse (1988), who have proposed one of the most extensive theoretical analyses of numerical competence in animals, the concept of number is an abstract or modality-free numerical ability. As such, this ability ought to be revealed by means of transfer across different modalities (e.g., from visual to auditory) or across different procedures (e.g., from simultaneous to successive presentation). The concept of number is one of the attributes of true counting, "a formal enumerative process" that requires "the application of reliably ordered cardinal tags in one-to-one correspondence to the items in the array" (Davis and Perusse, 1988, p. 562). In other words, true counting requires the presence of cardinality, the one-to-one assignment of a numerical tag to an array, and the presence of ordinality, the ability to order these numerical tags. Finally, some authors have proposed transfer to new numbers as an indicator of the number concept. For example, a rat trained to press a lever two times after two light flashes and four times after four light flashes ought to be able to spontaneously press a lever three times after three light flashes with no additional training (Davis and Perusse, 1988; see also Boysen and Capaldi, 1993, and Brannon, 2005, for more recent discussion of numerical competence in animals).

To our knowledge, only one study has successfully obtained evidence for cross-modal transfer of a numerical discrimination. In this study (Church and Meck, 1984), rats were trained to press the right lever when two sounds were presented and to press the left lever when four sounds were presented. The nonnumerical features of the stimuli – such as the duration of each sound, the interval between sounds, and the total duration of the sound sequence – was controlled, so that a reliable discrimination could be based only on the number of the sounds in a sequence. After rats learned this discrimination, the sounds were replaced with light flashes; for half of the rats the response rule remained unchanged, whereas for the other half of the rats the response rule was reversed. As **Figure 9** illustrates, the rats in the nonreversal group continued to make the correct responses when sounds were

Table 5 Animal studies of abstract or relational concept learning

Concept	Species	References
Symmetry	Honeybees, pigeons, starlings	Delius and Habers, 1978; Delius and Novak, 1982; Giurfa et al., 1996; Horridge, 1996; Swaddle and Pruett-Jones, 2001
Direction or type of movement	Pigeons	Dittrich et al., 1998; Cook et al., 2002
Above/below	Baboons, capuchin monkeys	Depy et al., 1999; Spinozzi et al., 2006
Number: Cross-modal transfer	Rats	Church and Meck, 1984
Number: Cardinality	African Grey parrot, pigeons, chimpanzees	Matsuzawa, 1985; Boysen and Berntson, 1989; Rumbaugh and Washburn, 1993; Pepperberg, 1994, Biro and Matsuzawa, 2001;; Xia et al., 2000, 2001; Pepperberg, 2006
Number: Ordinality	Squirrel monkeys, rhesus monkeys	Brannon and Terrace, 1998; Brannon and Terrace, 2000; Cantlon and Brannon, 2006; Olthof et al., 1997; Washburn and Rumbaugh, 1991
Relational learning: Transposition	Pigeons, rats, chimpanzees	Gonzales et al., 1954; Lawrence and DeRivera, 1954; Riley et al., 1960; Marsh, 1967; Lazareva et al., 2005
Identity: Matching-to-sample	Honeybees, pigeons, crows, rats, harbor seal, sea lions, capuchin monkeys, orangutans, gorilla, chimpanzees	Zentall and Hogan, 1974; Fujita, 1983; Wright et al., 1988; Oden et al., 1990; Kastak and Schusterman, 1994; Smirnova et al., 2000; Giurfa et al., 2001; Barros et al., 2002; Vonk, 2003; Mauk and Dehnhardt, 2005; Pena et al., 2006
Identity: Same-different	Pigeons, African grey parrot, baboons, capuchin monkeys, rhesus monkeys	Pepperberg, 1987; Cook et al., 1995; Young et al., 1997; Wasserman et al., 2001; Young and Wasserman, 2001; Cook, 2002; Blaisdell and Cook, 2005; Gibson et al., 2006
Relation among relations	Pigeons, gorilla, orangutan, chimpanzees	Gillan et al., 1981; Premack, 1983b; Thompson et al., 1997; Fagot et al., 2001; Vonk, 2003; Cook and Wasserman, 2007

Because of the extremely large number of studies devoted to some of the concepts (e.g., the concept of number), only selected studies are listed.

replaced by flashes, although at a lower level of accuracy than in training. Moreover, the rats in the reversal group followed the previously learned rule: They continued to press the right lever in the presence of two light flashes and to press the left lever in the presence of four light flashes, even though the opposite response was now reinforced. Together, these results show that the rats' numerical discrimination was modality-free. More comparative research is needed to further explore this important competence.

Several studies provide evidence for cardinality: numerical tags that animals can use to identify arrays of items (see **Table 5**). For example, Boysen and Berntson (1989) trained the chimpanzee Sheba to select an Arabic numeral corresponding to the number of candies on a tray. Once Sheba mastered this task, she was presented with the Arabic numerals displayed on a computer monitor and was required to select the placard with the correct number of metal disks attached to it. After this training, Sheba could select the correct Arabic numeral for arrays consisting of novel, nonedible items, thereby demonstrating that she indeed learned the one-to-one correspondence between Arabic numerals and arrays of items. Similar evidence was obtained for other primates, for an African Gray parrot, and even for pigeons (see **Table 5**).

Evidence for ordinality – the ability to order numerical tags – was considerably more difficult to obtain. In order to conclude that animals are ordering numerical tags, one must eliminate the possibility that the ordering is based on other stimulus dimensions, such as density or surface area or the hedonic value of reinforcement. The latter possibility is particularly important because many studies have used

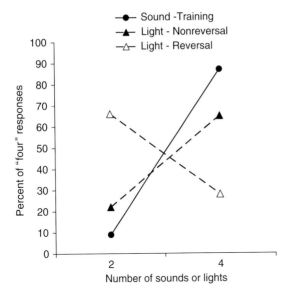

Figure 9 Transfer of the 'two' vs. 'four' discrimination from the number of sounds to the number of light flashes. For half of the rats, the response rule remained the same (Light – Nonreversal), whereas for the other half of the rats, the response rule was reversed (Light – Reversal). Data compiled from Church RM and Meck WH (1984) The numerical attribute of the stimuli. In: Roitblat HL, Bever TG, and Terrace HS (eds.) *Animal Cognition*, pp. 445–46. Hillsdale, NJ: Erlbaum.

the number of food items to establish a one-to-one correspondence between the number of items and the numerical tags (e.g., Washburn and Rumbaugh, 1991; Boyson et al., 1993; Olthof et al., 1997). In this case, the animals could have used the hedonic value of reinforcement to order the numerical tags instead of the number of items in the corresponding array.

Recently, Brannon, Terrace, and colleagues (Brannon and Terrace, 1998, 2000; Cantlon and Brannon, 2006) adopted a new approach for studying ordinality. Instead of training animals to use numerical tags, the researchers focused on the extent to which a nonverbal system for representing numbers in animals is similar to a nonverbal system for representing numbers in humans. When humans compare single-digit numbers or random-dot arrays, they exhibit a numerical distance effect (e.g., 1 vs. 7 is easier than 1 vs. 2) and a numerical magnitude effect (e.g., 1 vs. 2 is easier than 6 vs. 7), suggesting that number discriminability conforms to the Weber-Fechner Law (Dehaene et al., 1990). Does the discriminative behavior of rhesus monkeys exhibit the same regularities?

To find out, Brannon and Terrace (1998, 2000) trained monkeys to touch simultaneously presented arrays of one, two, three, and four items on a computer screen in ascending order to receive juice reinforcement. As **Figure 10** illustrates, the non-numerical attributes of the stimuli (e.g., area, density, or shape of the items) were carefully controlled, so that successful discrimination could be based only on the number of items in the array. Monkeys successfully learned the task and transferred their discriminative performance to novel arrays of five to nine items, providing strong evidence for ordinality. In a follow-up experiment, Cantlon and Brannon (2006) slightly modified the task, so that only two arrays were simultaneously presented; in addition, the number of items in the array varied from 1 to 30. The monkeys were still required to touch the arrays in ascending order. For comparison, human participants were trained to

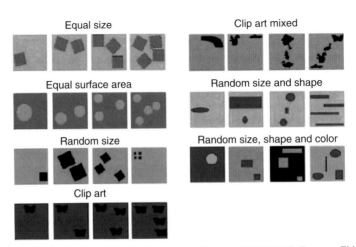

Figure 10 Examples of stimuli used during training in Bannon and Terrace (1998, 2000). Brannon EM and Terrace HS (2000) Representation of the numerosities 1–9 by rhesus macaques (*Macaca mulatta*). *J. Exp. Psychol. Anim. Behav. Process.* 26: 31–49.

perform a similar task. Cantlon and Brannon (2006) found that monkeys' performance exhibited both the numerical distance effect and the numerical magnitude effect. Moreover, monkeys' performance and humans' performance was similar not only qualitatively but also quantitatively, suggesting that monkeys and humans share the same nonverbal system for representing number. More comparative research is needed to establish whether this nonverbal system for number representation is shared by other animal species.

1.11.6.2 Relational Concepts in the Transposition Paradigm

Can animals respond to the relations between or among stimuli, rather than to the absolute properties of the stimuli? Perhaps the most famous attempt to experimentally examine this possibility comes from the case of transposition, first explored by Köhler (1918/1938). Suppose that an organism is given a simultaneous discrimination task in which the positive discriminative stimulus (S+) is a 2-cm-diameter circle and the negative discriminative stimulus (S−) is a 3-cm-diameter circle. When the organism masters the visual discrimination, just what has it learned? Has it learned that only the 2-cm circle signals food? Or has it learned the concept of smaller?

A possible answer to this question comes by considering how the organism ought to respond to new pairs of stimuli that are presented during a postdiscrimination test. If the former S+ is presented along with the even smaller 1-cm-diameter circle, then having learned to respond to the relation between the circles, the organism may actually choose the untrained stimulus over the former S+. In his pioneering studies, Köhler (1929, 1918/1938) found that chickens and chimpanzees did indeed respond in this relational manner, a result that led him to propose that stimuli are not judged in absolute terms but as relative to one another.

Does choice of the untrained stimulus over the former S+ necessarily indicate control by the relation between the stimuli rather than by specific features of these stimuli? Kenneth W. Spence (1937) famously demonstrated that relational responding in the transposition paradigm can be explained as the result of the interaction of learned tendencies to make responses to S+ and to withhold responses to S−.

If both training stimuli are located on the same dimension, then the algebraic summation of those learned tendencies leads to two peak shifts: The

peak of maximal associative strength shifts away from the former S−, and the peak of minimal associative strength shifts away from the former S+. In other words, the organism may prefer the 1-cm circle because the associative strength of this stimulus is actually higher than associative strength of the formerly reinforced 2-cm circle. So, according to Spence's generalization theory, the preference for the novel stimulus over the former S+ found by Köhler was no more relational than was the tendency to approach S+ and the tendency to avoid S− after standard discrimination training. Spence's stimulus generalization theory yielded several important predictions that have been confirmed in different species, including humans, and in different experimental situations (e.g., Ehrenfreund, 1952; Honig, 1962; Cheng, 1999; Cheng and Spetch, 2002; reviewed by Reese, 1968; Riley, 1968; Purtle, 1973).

Several reports have provided data that have challenged generalization theory as the sole account of an organism's behavior in transposition tasks (**Table 5**). Consider the intermediate stimulus problem, in which an animal is presented with 1-cm, 2-cm, and 3-cm circles and is required to select the 2-cm circle to obtain reinforcement. In the test, the animal is presented with 2-cm, 3-cm, and 4-cm circles; if the animal had previously learned to respond according to the relation among the stimuli, then it ought to select the previously nonreinforced 3-cm circle. Generalization theory predicts that the animal ought to select the previously reinforced (2-cm circle) stimulus instead of the middle value. Nonetheless, chimpanzees have been found to transpose the solution of the intermediate-size problem (Gonzales et al., 1954).

Other studies have compared transposition after simultaneous and successive discrimination training. Unlike successive discrimination training, simultaneous discrimination training affords the subject the opportunity to compare the training stimuli at the same time; therefore, relational responding ought to be enhanced. Yet, stimulus generalization theory makes no distinction between simultaneous and successive modes of presentation. Several studies have indeed reported higher transposition after simultaneous training than after successive training (Riley et al., 1960; Marsh, 1967), suggesting that direct comparison does enhance relational learning (but see Hebert and Krantz, 1965; Wills and Mackintosh, 1999).

Finally, several reports, including our own, have found presentation of multiple pairs of discriminative stimuli instead of a single pair enhances relational responding in pigeons, even when such responding is contrary to the predictions of stimulus generalization theory (Marsh, 1967; Lazareva et al., 2005). It is well known that increasing the number of exemplars leads to better acquisition of a concept in many species of animals, including pigeons (Wright et al., 1988; Wright, 1997; Cook, 2002; Katz et al., 2002). Similarly, pigeons may need to encounter multiple instances of a rule in order to exhibit strong relational responding. Unfortunately, we do not yet know whether the same is true for other animal species. (*See* Chapter 1.29 for a corresponding experiment with honeybees).

1.11.6.3   Concept of Identity

The concept of identity, or sameness and difference, is perhaps the most extensively studied concept in animals. The most frequently used experimental procedures are matching-to-sample and same-different discrimination (**Figure 11**). In the standard matching-to-sample task, an animal first views a single stimulus, or sample, and performs several observing responses to it (e.g., touching or pecking the sample). After that, the animal is shown two comparison stimuli and is required to select the comparison that matches the sample (identity matching) or that does not match the sample (oddity matching). The simultaneous same-different discrimination task requires the choice of one response if the two presented stimuli are identical and a second response if the two stimuli are different.

Regardless of training procedure, evidence of successful transfer to novel stimuli is necessary to demonstrate the identity concept. The term full-concept learning is used when an animal discriminates the novel stimuli as accurately as the training stimuli, most strongly documenting the abstract nature of the acquired behavior. Partial concept learning refers to cases in which the novel stimuli are discriminated less accurately than the training stimuli, signifying the stimulus-dependent nature of the acquired behavior, even when discriminative performance is reliably above chance. Early research suggested that some species may only be capable of partial concept learning (e.g., Premack, 1983a). However, recent reports have shown that the number of stimuli used during training is an important parameter affecting identity concept learning, a sensible finding, as an increase in the number of training stimuli makes memorizing individual stimulus associations a more costly strategy. Different species, though, may require different numbers of training stimuli to achieve full identity concept learning, with as few as 16 stimuli for great apes and as many as 512 stimuli for pigeons (**Figure 12**; Wright et al., 2003).

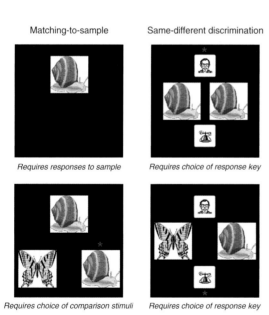

Matching-to-sample   Same-different discrimination

Requires responses to sample   *Requires choice of response key*

Requires choice of comparison stimuli   *Requires choice of response key*

Figure 11 Comparison of matching-to-sample and same-different discrimination. In the (identity) matching-to-sample paradigm, the animal is required to select the correct (identical) comparison stimulus (the red asterisks indicate the correct choices). In the same-different discrimination, the animal is required to select one response key if the items are the same and the other response key of the items are different.

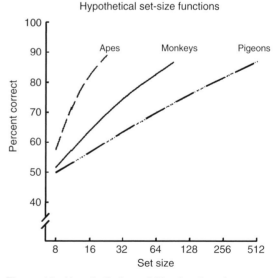

Figure 12 Hypothetical acquisition functions for apes, monkeys, and pigeons, showing low abstract-concept learning might vary as a function of training set size. From Wright AA, Rivera JU, Katz JS, and Bachevalier J (2003) Abstract-concept learning and list-memory processing by capuchin and rhesus monkeys. *J. Exp. Psychol. Anim. Behav. Process.* 29: 184–198.

Another important parameter affecting identity concept learning is the type of training procedure. Pigeons trained using simultaneous same-different discrimination or matching-to-sample procedures require hundreds of training stimuli to achieve full identity concept learning (Wright et al., 1988; Wright et al., 2003), but pigeons can also attain full identity concept learning when only two training stimuli are used (Cook et al., 2003).

What was the secret in successfully training pigeons with a small number of stimuli? In this experiment, pigeons were presented with stimuli that were alternated several times within a single trial, so that the birds had multiple opportunities to compare them. It is possible that these extended sequences were critical for the initial acquisition of the abstract concept, although the available experimental data are insufficient for substantiating this conclusion.

Interestingly, another experiment that used a similar procedure found only partial concept acquisition in pigeons (Young et al., 1997). In this experiment, pigeons were shown 16 computer icons, one at a time; either all 16 icons were nonidentical or all 16 icons were identical. Just as in the previous experiment, this procedure allowed for multiple opportunities to discern the relationship among the items. Nonetheless, pigeons' transfer to new icons, although well above chance, was below performance with the icons used in training. Clearly, additional research is needed to elucidate the factors affecting acquisition of the abstract same-different concept.

Another important consideration is the nature of the concept learned in different types of experimental procedures. Given the variety of stimuli and experimental approaches that have thus far been used, it is important to establish whether the same processes control animals' behavior in different tasks. In a representative study (Cook, 2002), pigeons were trained using a simultaneous same-different discrimination task with different types of stimuli (**Figure 13**). For some birds, all same displays and all different displays were associated with consistent report responses, regardless of the display type. For example, both different texture and different photo displays required the choice of the left key. This group was called the consistent group. In the inconsistent group, response assignment differed by display type; for example, all different texture displays required the choice of the left key, whereas all different photo displays required the choice of the right key. If pigeons learned a set of specific rules for each type of display, then they should have learned the inconsistent task just as easily as the consistent task. In fact, the consistent group learned the task faster and reached higher levels of accuracy by the end of the training than the inconsistent group. Moreover, only the consistent group demonstrated significant transfer to novel stimuli, indicative of concept formation. These results suggest that, despite dramatic perceptual differences among the types of displays, pigeons' discriminative performance was based on a single general rule that was abstract enough to be applicable to a wide variety of visual stimuli.

On the other hand, seemingly minor changes in experimental procedure may lead to dramatically different strategies employed for task solution as Gibson et al. (2006) demonstrated. In their study, pigeons were again trained to perform a simultaneous same-different discrimination. In the 16S versus 16D condition (**Figure 14**), the birds had to select one choice key if all 16 items in the display were the same and to select the other choice key if all 16 items in the display were different. In the 16S versus 15S:1D condition, different displays contained 15 identical items and 1 odd item, thus resembling previously described task (Cook, 2002; **Figure 14**). Although pigeons readily mastered the 16S versus 16D discrimination, they were unable to learn the 16S versus 15S:1D discrimination unless they were required to peck the odd item prior to making a choice response.

In a follow-up project, pigeons were trained to concurrently perform the already learned 16S versus 16D discrimination plus the newly introduced 16S versus 15S:1D discrimination. If the birds were using the same strategy in both tasks, then they should begin to make many more errors on same trials in the 16S versus 16D task, as the 16S displays are quite similar to the 15S:1D displays. On the contrary, the birds should make many fewer errors on different trials, as the 16D displays should appear even more different than the 16S display when the 15S:1D displays are introduced. Yet, none of these changes were observed. Acquisition of the 16S versus 15S:1D task did not come at the expense of 16S versus 16D task performance, suggesting that the pigeons may have used different strategies to solve these tasks. Other evidence also points to the conclusion that these two tasks are qualitatively different (reviewed by Cook and Wasserman, 2006).

1.11.6.4 Relations Among Relations

Can animals discriminate higher-order relations between multiple first-order relations? Suppose that an animal is shown a sample stimulus with two equal-size circles and comparison stimuli with two equal-size

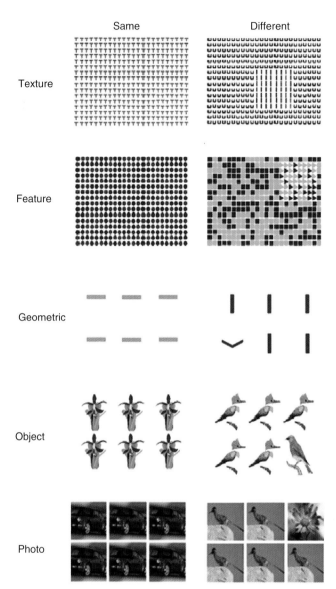

Figure 13 Examples of displays used by Cook (2002). The left column shows examples of same displays, and the right column shows examples of different displays for each display type. From Cook RG (2002) The structure of pigeon multiple-class same-different learning. *J. Exp. Anal. Behav.* 78: 345–364.

triangles and two unequal-size squares (**Figure 15**). Can the animal learn to select the comparison stimulus that entails the same relation (equal size), even though none of the shapes is identical? The ability to detect such higher-order relations is similar to human analogical reasoning, which is believed to be one of the central components of human cognition (Gentner et al., 2001).

Early research suggested that only language-trained chimpanzees can process second-order relations, whereas non-language-trained chimpanzees perform first-order same-different discriminations

only on the basis of physical similarities (Premack, 1983b). Later research has found, however, that this conclusion was premature. Using a two-item display (**Figure 15**, left panel) task, several ape species have been found to respond in accord with second-order relations (Thompson et al., 1997; Vonk, 2003).

Two other studies have used a multiple-item display task (**Figure 15**, right panel) in which a sample contains an array of 16 items that are either identical or nonidentical. The comparison stimuli also contain arrays of 16 identical or nonidentical items; however, none of the items used for the sample display are

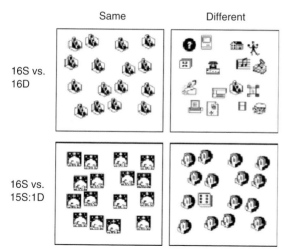

Figure 14 Examples of displays used in the 16S vs. 16D task and in the 16S vs. 15S:1D task. Modified from Gibson BM, Wasserman EA, and Cook RG (2006) Not all same-different discriminations are created equal: Evidence contrary to a unidimensional account of same-different learning. *Learn. Motiv.* 37: 189–208.

repeated in the comparison displays. Therefore, the correct response is only possible if the animal is able to detect the higher-order relations between the sample and comparison arrays. Both baboons (Fagot et al., 2001) and pigeons (Cook and Wasserman, 2006) have successfully learned this task and transferred their discriminations to arrays of novel items. It remains to be seen whether the mastery of two-item display tasks and multiple-item display tasks is based on the same cognitive mechanisms. In any case, these data suggest that the perceptual and cognitive foundations for analogical reasoning may exist not only in the mammalian brain but also in the avian brain.

1.11.7 Conclusion: What Does It All Mean?

Early in this chapter, we offered a definition of conceptual behavior that involves two key components: (1) the ability to respond similarly to members of one class of stimuli and to respond differently to members of other classes of stimuli and (2) the ability to transfer these differential responses to novel, discriminably different members of these classes of stimuli. The extensive evidence that we have reviewed here strongly supports the conclusion that concepts are not unique to human beings. Animals too form concepts based on perceptual similarity among their members, classifying objects into basic-level categories and subordinate-level categories. Moreover, animals appear to sense the perceptual structure of their environment, viewing members of basic-level categories (such as humans or trees) as being more similar to one another than to members of other categories. Animals can sort objects into non-similarity-based, superordinate categories, flexibly switching from basic-level categorization to super-ordinate-level categorization. Even the ability to form abstract concepts based on the relation between or among stimuli is not exclusively human; animals can respond to first-order and even to second-order relations between or among stimuli.

What does it mean to say that we share cognitive abilities with many animal species, from honeybees to chimpanzees? We are still far from answering that question. Most of the research until now has focused on whether a particular species is able to form a specific concept. Although such studies are an important first step in our understanding of categorization and conceptualization in animals, they do not tell us

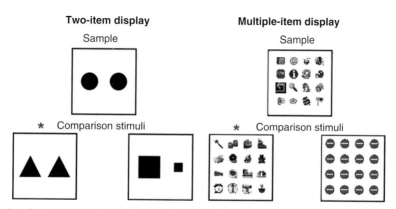

Figure 15 Examples of displays used for testing relational matching. For both types of displays, the correct choice is the comparison stimulus that involves the same relation as the sample stimulus (the red asterisks indicate the correct choices).

how the species attains concept mastery. With a few possible exceptions (e.g., Cantlon and Brannon, 2006), the mechanisms of concept formation in humans and animals remain mysterious.

Why do we need to understand the mechanisms of concept formation in animals? At least two reasons, one theoretical and one applied, can be suggested. The theoretical rationale centers on the relationship between the human mind and the minds of other animals. One exciting possibility is that the cognitive abilities of humans and animals have a common origin; that is, they may be based on some primitive trait shared by many species. For example, it is possible that conceptualization is based at least in part on fundamental laws of associative learning (Wasserman, 1995; Wasserman and Miller, 1997; Mackintosh, 2000), laws that apply to many species which are widely separated in evolutionary history. On the over hand, we may be witnessing another spectacular example of convergent evolution, similar to the bird's wing, the bat's wing, and the insect's wing. Although an adaptation for a similar function, flight, induced similar overall structures of those wings, there are enough differences in details (e.g., the absence of fused fingers in the bat's wings) that help us recognize it as an analogy (a gross similarity caused by similarity in function) rather than a homology (a detailed similarity in organization caused by common origin).

Perhaps conceptualization in humans and animals is similar only at the gross level but is dramatically different in details. Indeed, there may be dramatic differences between different animal species: Maybe the acquisition of the concept of sameness in honeybees with their compound eyes has nothing in common with the acquisition of the concept of sameness in pigeons with their lens eyes. Until we learn much more about the mechanisms of cognition in different species, we will not be able to answer this intriguing question.

From the applied perspective, sound knowledge of the mechanisms of cognition in different species may provide fresh insights for applied researchers. Indeed, research with animals may be of particular interest to applied mental health researchers, because that work usually explores the conditions under which concept formation is or is not likely to occur. For example, learning that the simultaneous presentation of stimuli and multiple instantiations of the relationship among stimuli each strengthen relational responding in pigeons may help applied mental health workers develop better techniques for teaching relational learning in humans, especially individuals who are otherwise inclined to respond to the absolute properties of stimuli instead of the relations between or among them (Carlin et al., 2003; Happe and Frith, 2006).

Fortunately, the focus of recent research has begun to shift to the mechanisms underlying the conceptual abilities of different species (Wasserman et al., 2004). Some remarkable similarities, as well as some remarkable differences, have already been revealed (e.g., Cook and Wasserman, 2006; Wright et al., 2003), and undoubtedly more await discovery. Such future research should provide essential information for elucidating the evolutionary origins of cognition. Together with Stewart Hulse (2006), we hope for "less and less research on existence proof, that is, whether or not a given species has the same cognitive capacity as we, or some other species, do" (Hulse, 2006, p. 674) and for more and more research on how these cognitive capacities operate.

Acknowledgments

The authors' research was supported by research grant IBN 99-04569 from the National Science Foundation and by research grant MH 47313 from the National Institute of Mental Health.

References

Anderson US, Stoinski TS, Bloomsmith MA, Marr MJ, Smith AD, and Maple TL (2005) Relative numerousness judgment and summation in young and old Western lowland gorillas. *J. Comp. Psychol.* 119: 285–295.

Astley SL and Wasserman EA (1992) Categorical discrimination and generalization in pigeons: All negative stimuli are not created equal. *J. Exp. Psychol. Anim. Behav. Process.* 18: 193–207.

Astley SL and Wasserman EA (1999) Superordinate category formation in pigeons: Association with a common delay or probability of food reinforcement makes perceptually dissimilar stimuli functionally equivalent. *J. Exp. Psychol. Anim. Behav. Process.* 25: 415–432.

Astley SL, Peissig JJ, and Wasserman EA (2001) Superordinate categorization via learned stimulus equivalence: Quantity of reinforcement, hedonic value, and the nature of the mediator. *J. Exp. Psychol. Anim. Behav. Process.* 27: 252–268.

Aust U and Huber L (2001) The role of item- and category-specific information in the discrimination of people versus nonpeople images by pigeons. *Anim. Learn. Behav.* 29: 107–119.

Aust U and Huber L (2002) Target-defining features in a "people-present/people-absent" discrimination task by pigeons. *Anim. Learn. Behav.* 30: 165–176.

Aust U and Huber L (2003) Elemental versus configural perception in a people-present/people-absent discrimination task by pigeons. *Learn. Behav.* 31: 213–224.

Barros RDS, Galvao ODF, and McIlvane WJ (2002) Generalized identity matching-to-sample. *Cebus apella. Psychol. Rec.* 52: 441–460.

Bhatt RS, Wasserman EA, Reynolds WF, and Knauss KS (1988) Conceptual behavior in pigeons: Categorization of both familiar and novel examples from four classes of natural and artifical stimuli. *J. Exp. Psychol. Anim. Behav. Process.* 14: 219–234.

Biro D and Matsuzawa T (2001) Use of numerical symbols by the chimpanzee (*Pan troglodytes)*: Cardinals, ordinals, and the introduction of zero. *Anim. Cogn.* 4: 193–199.

Blaisdell AP and Cook RG (2005) Two-item same-different concept learning in pigeons. *Learn. Behav.* 33: 67–77.

Boysen ST and Berntson GG (1989) Numerical competence in a chimpanzee (*Pan troglodytes). J. Comp. Psychol.* 103: 23–31.

Boysen ST and Capaldi EJ (1993) *The Development of Numerical Competence: Animal and Human Models.* Hillsdale, NJ: Erlbaum.

Boysen ST, Berntson GG, Shreyer TA, and Quigley KS (1993) Processing of ordinality and transitivity by chimpanzees *(Pan troglodytes). J. Comp. Psychol.* 107: 208–215.

Brannon EM (2005) What animals know about numbers. In: Campbell JID (ed.) *Handbook of Mathematical Cognition*, pp. 87–107. New York: Psychology Press.

Brannon EM and Terrace HS (1998) Ordering of the numerosities 1 to 9 by monkeys. *Science* 282: 746–749.

Brannon EM and Terrace HS (2000) Representation of the numerosities 1–9 by rhesus macaques. *Macaca mulatta). J. Exp. Psychol. Anim. Behav. Process.* 26: 31–49.

Brown DA and Boysen ST (2000) Spontaneous discrimination of natural stimuli by chimpanzees (*Pan troglodytes). J. Comp. Psychol.* 114: 392–400.

Cantlon JF and Brannon EM (2006) Shared system for ordering small and large numbers in monkeys and humans. *Psychol. Sci.* 17: 401–406.

Carlin MT, Soraci S Jr., and Strawbridge C (2003) Enhancing performances of individuals with mental retardation: Manipulations for visual structure. In: Soraci S Jr. and Murata-Soraci K (eds.) *Visual Information Processing*, pp. 81–108. Westport, CT: Praeger.

Cerella J (1979) Visual classes and natural categories in the pigeon. *J. Exp. Psychol. Hum. Percept. Perform.* 5: 68–77.

Cheng K (1999) Spatial generalization in honeybees confirms Shepard's law. *Behav. Process.* 44: 309–316.

Cheng K and Spetch ML (2002) Spatial generalization and peak shift in humans. *Learn. Motiv.* 33: 358–389.

Church RM and Meck WH (1984) The numerical attribute of the stimuli. In: Roitblat HL, Bever TG, and Terrace HS (eds.) *Animal Cognition*, pp. 445–446. Hillsdale, NJ: Erlbaum.

Cook RG (2002) The structure of pigeon multiple-class same-different learning. *J. Exp. Anal. Behav.* 78: 345–364.

Cook RG and Wasserman EA (2006) Relational discrimination learning in pigeons. In: Wasserman EA and Zentall TR (eds.) *Comparative Cognition: Experimental Explorations of Animal Intelligence*, pp. 307–324. Oxford: Oxford University Press.

Cook RG, Wright AA, and Kendrick DF (1990) Visual categorization by pigeons. In: Commons ML and Herrnstein RJ (eds.) *Behavioral Approaches to Pattern Recognition and Concept Formation*, pp. 187–214. Hillsdale, NJ: Erlbaum.

Cook RG, Cavoto KK, and Cavoto BR (1995) Same-different texture discrimination and concept learning by pigeons. *J. Exp. Psychol. Anim. Behav. Process.* 21: 253–260.

Cook RG, Shaw R, and Blaisdell AP (2002) Dynamic object perception by pigeons: Discrimination of action in video presentation. *Anim. Cogn.* 4: 137–146.

Cook RG, Kelly DM, and Katz JS (2003) Successive two-item same-different discrimination and concept learning by pigeons. *Behav. Process.* 62: 125–144.

Cook RG, Levison DG, Gillet SR, and Blaisdell AP (2005) Capacity and limits of associative memory in pigeons. *Psychon. Bull. Rev.* 12: 350–358.

D'Amato MR and Van Sant P (1988) The person concept in monkeys (*Cebus apella). J. Exp. Psychol. Anim. Behav. Process.* 14: 43–55.

Damasio AR (1990) Category-related recognition defects as a clue to the neural substrates of knowledge. *Trends Neurosci.* 13: 95–98.

Darwin C (1896) *The Descent of Man, and Selection in Relation to Sex.* New York: Appleton.

Davis H (1984) Discrimination of the number three by a raccoon (*Procyon lotor). Anim. Learn. Behav.* 12: 409–413.

Davis H and Perusse R (1988) Numerical competence in animals: Definitional issues, current evidence, and a new research agenda. *Behav. Brain Sci.* 11: 561–615.

Dehaene S, Dupoux E, and Mehler L (1990) Is numerical comparison digital? Analogical and symbolic effects in two-digit number comparisons. *J. Exp. Psychol. Hum. Percept. Perform.* 16: 626–641.

Delius JD and Habers G (1978) Symmetry: Can pigeons conceptualize it? *Behav. Neural Biol.* 22: 336–342.

Delius JD and Novak B (1982) Visual symmetry recognition by pigeons. *Psychol. Res.* 44: 199–212.

Delorme A, Richard G, and Fabre-Thorpe M (2000) Ultra-rapid categorisation of natural scenes does not rely on colour cues: A study in monkeys and humans. *Vision Res.* 40: 2187–2200.

Deputte BL, Pelletier S, and Barbe S (2001) Visual categorization of natural and abstract items in forest monkeys and humans. *Behav. Process.* 55: 51–64.

Depy D, Fagot J, and Vauclair J (1997) Categorisation of three-dimensional stimuli by humans and baboons: Search for prototype effects. *Behav. Process.* 39: 299–306.

Depy D, Fagot J, and Vauclair J (1999) Processing of above/below categorical spatial relations by baboons (*Papio papio). Behav. Process.* 48: 1–9.

Dittrich WH, Lea SEG, Barrett J, and Gurr PR (1998) Categorization of natural movements by pigeons: Visual concept discrimination and biological motion. *J. Exp. Anal. Behav.* 70: 281–299.

Edwards CA and Honig WK (1987) Memorization and "feature selection" in the acquisition of natural concepts in pigeons. *Learn. Motiv.* 18: 235–260.

Ehrenfreund D (1952) A study of the transposition gradient. *J. Exp. Psychol.* 43: 81–87.

Fagot J, Wasserman EA, and Young ME (2001) Discriminating the relation between relations: The role of entropy in abstract conceptualization by baboons (*Papio papio*) and humans (*Homo sapiens). J. Exp. Psychol. Anim. Behav. Process.* 27: 316–328.

Farah MJ (1999) Relations among the agnosias. In: Humphreys GW (ed.) *Case Studies in the Neuropsychology of Vision*, pp. 181–200. Hove: Psychology Press.

Frank A and Wasserman EA (2005) Response rate is not an effective mediator of learned stimulus equivalence in pigeons. *Learn. Behav.* 33: 287–295.

Fujita K (1983) Formation of the sameness-difference concept by Japanese monkeys from a small number of color stimuli. *J. Exp. Anal. Behav.* 40: 289–300.

Fujita K (1987) Species recognition by five macaque monkeys. *Primates* 28: 353–366.

Fujita K and Matsuzawa T (1986) A new procedure to study the perceptual world of animals with sensory reinforcement: Recognition of humans by a chimpanzee. *Primates* 27: 283–291.

Gaffan D and Heywood CA (1993) A spurious category-specific visual agnosia for living things in normal human and nonhuman primates. *J. Cogn. Neurosci.* 5: 118–128.

Gentner D, Holyoak KJ, and Kokinov BN (2001) *The Analogical Mind: Perspectives from Cognitive Science*. Cambridge, MA: MIT Press.

Ghosh N, Lea SEG, and Noury M (2004) Transfer to intermediate forms following concept discrimination by pigeons: Chimeras and morphs. *J. Exp. Anal. Behav.* 82: 125–141.

Gibson BM, Wasserman EA, Gosselin F, and Schyns PG (2005) Applying Bubbles to localize features that control pigeons' visual discrimination behavior. *J. Exp. Psychol. Anim. Behav. Process.* 31: 376–382.

Gibson BM, Wasserman EA, and Cook RG (2006) Not all same-different discriminations are created equal: Evidence contrary to a unidimensional account of same-different learning. *Learn. Motiv.* 37: 189–208.

Gillan DJ, Premack D, and Woodruff G (1981) Reasoning in the chimpanzee: I. Analogical reasoning. *J. Exp. Psychol. Anim. Behav. Process.* 7: 1–17.

Giurfa M, Eichmann B, and Menzel R (1996) Symmetry perception in an insect. *Nature* 382: 458–461.

Giurfa M, Zhang S, Jenett A, Menzel R, and Srinivasan MV (2001) The concepts of 'sameness' and 'difference' in an insect. *Nature* 410: 930–933.

Gonzales RC, Gentry GV, and Bitterman ME (1954) Relational discrimination of intermediate size in the chimpanzee. *J. Comp. Physiol. Psychol.* 47: 385–388.

Gosselin F and Schyns PG (2001) Bubbles: A technique to reveal the use of information in recognition tasks. *Vision Res.* 41: 2261–2271.

Gosselin F and Schyns PG (2002) RAP: A new framework for visual categorization. *Trends Cogn. Sci.* 6: 70–77.

Gosselin F and Schyns PG (2004) A picture is worth thousands of trials: Rendering the use of visual information from spiking neurons to recognition. *Cogn. Sci.* 28: 141–146.

Gosselin F and Schyns PG (2005) Bubbles: A User's Guide. In: Gershkoff-Stove Land Rakison DH (eds.) *Building Object Categories in Developmental Time*, pp. 91–106. Mahwah, NJ: Erlbaum.

Grant DS and Kelly R (2001) Many-to-one matching with temporal and hedonic samples in pigeons. *Learn. Motiv.* 32: 477–498.

Greene SL (1983) Feature memorization in pigeon concept formation. In: Commons ML, Herrnstein RJ, and Wagner AR (eds.) *Quantitative Analyses of Behavior: Discrimination Processes,* vol. 4, pp. 209–229. Cambridge, MA: Ballinger.

Hampton JA (2001) Concepts. In: Wilson RA and Keil FC (eds.) *The MIT Encyclopedia of the Cognitive Sciences*, pp. 176–179. Cambridge MA: MIT Press.

Happe F and Frith U (2006) The weak coherence account: Detail-focused cognitive style in autism spectrum disorders. *J. Autism Dev. Disord.* 36: 5–25.

Hayes S, Barnes-Holmes D, and Roche B (2001) *Relational Frame Theory: A Post-Skinnerian Account of Human Language and Cognition*. New York: Kluwer Academic.

Hebert JA and Krantz DL (1965) Transposition: A reevaluation. *Psychol. Bull.* 63: 244–257.

Herrnstein RJ (1985) Riddles of natural categorization. *Philos. Trans. R. Soc. Lond. B Biol. Sci.* 308: 129–143.

Herrnstein RJ (1990) Levels of stimulus control: A functional approach. *Cognition* 37: 133–166.

Herrnstein RJ and de Villiers PA (1980) Fish as natural category for people and pigeons. In: Bower GH (ed.) *The Psychology of Learning and Motivation: Advances in Research and Theory,* vol. 14, pp. 59–95. New York: Academic Press.

Herrnstein RJ and Loveland DH (1964) Complex visual concept in the pigeon. *Science* 146: 549–551.

Herrnstein RJ, Loveland DH, and Cable C (1976) Natural concepts in pigeons. *J. Exp. Psychol. Anim. Behav. Process.* 2: 285–302.

Honig WK (1962) Prediction of preference, transposition, transposition-reversal from the generalization gradient. *J. Exp. Psychol.* 64: 239–248.

Horridge GA (1996) The honeybee (*Apis mellifera*) detects bilateral symmetry and discriminates its axis. *J. Insect Physiol.* 42: 755–764.

Huber L and Lenz R (1993) A test of the linear feature model of polymorphic concept discrimination with pigeons. *Q. J. Exp. Psychol.* 46B: 1–18.

Huber L and Lenz R (1996) Categorization of prototypical stimulus classes by pigeons. *Q. J. Exp. Psychol.* 49B: 111–133.

Huber L, Troje NF, Loidolt M, Aust U, and Grass D (2000) Natural categorization through multiple feature learning in pigeons. *Q. J. Exp. Psychol.* 53B: 341–357.

Hulse SH (2006) Postscript: An essay on the study of cognition in animals. In: Wasserman EA and Zentall TR (eds.) *Comparative Cognition: Experimental Explorations of Animal Intelligence*, pp. 668–678. New York: Oxford University Press.

Humphreys GW, Riddoch MJ, and Quinlan PT (1988) Cascade processes in picture identification. *Cogn. Neuropsychol.* 5: 67–103.

Jitsumori M (1993) Category discrimination of artificial polymorphous stimuli based on feature learning. *J. Exp. Psychol. Anim. Behav. Process.* 19: 244–254.

Jitsumori M (1994) Discrimination of artificial polymorphous categories by rhesus monkeys (*Macaca mulatta*). *Q. J. Exp. Psychol.* 47B: 371–386.

Jitsumori M (1996) A prototype effect and categorization of artificial polymorphous stimuli in pigeons. *J. Exp. Psychol. Anim. Behav. Process.* 22: 405–419.

Jitsumori M and Yoshihara M (1997) Categorical discrimination of human facial expressions by pigeons: A test of the linear feature model. *Q. J. Exp. Psychol.* 50B: 253–268.

Johnson KE and Mervis CB (1997) Effects of varying levels of expertise on the basic level of categorization. *J. Exp. Psychol. Gen.* 126: 248–277.

Kanazawa S (1998) What facial part is important for Japanese monkeys (*Macaca fuscata)* in recognition of smiling and sad faces of humans (*Homo sapiens)*? *J. Comp. Psychol.* 112: 363–370.

Kastak D and Schusterman RJ (1994) Transfer of visual identity matching-to-sample in two California sea lions (*Zalophus californianus*). *Anim. Learn. Behav.* 22: 427–435.

Katz JS, Wright AA, and Bachevalier J (2002) Mechanisms of same/different abstract-concept learning by rhesus monkeys (*Macaca mulatta*). *J. Exp. Psychol. Anim. Behav. Process.* 28: 358–368.

Keller FS and Schoenfeld WN (1950) *Principles of Psychology: A Systematic Text in the Science of Behavior*. New York: Appleton-Century-Crofts.

Koba R and Izumi A (2006) Sex categorization of conspecific pictures in Japanese monkeys (*Macaca fuscata*). *Anim. Cogn.* 9: 183–191.

Köhler W (1929) *Gestalt Psychology*. New York: H. Liveright.

Köhler W (1918/1938) Simple structural functions in the chimpanzee and in the chicken. In: Ellis WD (ed.) *A Source Book of Gestalt Psychology*, pp. 217–227. London: Routledge and Kegan Paul.

Lamberts K and Shapiro L (2002) Exemplar models and category-specific deficits. In: Forde EME and Humphreys GW (eds.) *Category Specificity in Brain and Mind*, pp. 291–314. New York: Psychology Press.

Laurence S and Margolis E (1999) Concepts and cognitive science. In: Margolis E and Laurence S (eds.) *Concepts*, pp. 3–81. Cambridge, MA: MIT Press.

Lawrence DH and DeRivera D (1954) Evidence for relational transposition. *J. Comp. Physiol. Psychol.* 47: 465–471.

Lazareva OF, Freiburger KL, and Wasserman EA (2004) Pigeons concurrently categorize photographs at both basic and superordinate levels. *Psychon. Bull. Rev.* 11: 1111–1117.

Lazareva OF, Wasserman EA, and Young ME (2005) Transposition in pigeons: Reassessing Spence (1937) with multiple discrimination training. *Learn. Behav.* 33: 22–46.

Lazareva OF, Freiburger KL, and Wasserman EA (2006) Effects of stimulus manipulations on visual categorization in pigeons. *Behav. Process.* 72: 224–233.

Lea SEG (1984) In what sense do pigeons learn concepts? In: Roitblat HL, Bever TG, and Terrace HS (eds.) *Animal Cognition*, pp. 263–277. Hillsdale, NJ: Erlbaum.

Lea SEG and Harrison SN (1978) Discrimination of polymorphous stimulus sets by pigeons. *Q. J. Exp. Psychol.* 30: 521–537.

Lea SEG, Lohman AE, and Ryan CM (1993) Discrimination of five-dimensional stimuli by pigeons: Limitations of feature analysis. *Q. J. Exp. Psychol.* 46B: 19–42.

Lea SEG, Wills AJ, and Ryan CM (2006) Why are artificial polymorphous concepts so hard for birds to learn? *Q. J. Exp. Psychol.* 59: 251–267.

Lloyd Morgan C (1894/1977) *An Introduction to Comparative Psychology*. Washington, DC: University Publications of America.

Lubow RE (1974) High-order concept formation in the pigeon. *J. Exp. Anal. Behav.* 21: 475–483.

Mackintosh NJ (2000) Abstraction and discrimination. In: Heyes C and Huber L (eds.) *The Evolution of Cognition*, pp. 123–142. Cambridge, MA: MIT Press.

Mangini MC and Biederman I (2004) Making the ineffable explicit: Estimating the information employed for face classifications. *Cogn. Sci.* 28: 209–226.

Markman EM (1989) *Categorization and Naming in Children: Problems of Induction*. Cambridge, MA: MIT Press.

Marsh G (1967) Relational learning in the pigeon. *J. Comp. Physiol. Psychol.* 64: 519–521.

Martin A and Caramazza A (2003) Neuropsychological and neuroimaging perspectives on conceptual knowledge: An introduction. *Cogn. Neuropsychol.* 20: 195–212.

Martin-Malivel J, Mangini MC, Fagot J, and Biederman I (2006) Do humans and baboons use the same information when categorizing human and baboon faces? *Psychol. Sci.* 17: 599–607.

Matsukawa A, Inoue S, and Jitsumori M (2004) Pigeon's recognition of cartoons: Effect of fragmentation, scrambling, and deletion of elements. *Behav. Process.* 65: 23–34.

Matsuzawa T (1985) Use of numbers by a chimpanzee. *Nature* 315: 57–59.

Mauk B and Dehnhardt G (2005) Identity concept formation during visual multiple-choice matching in a harbor seal (*Phoca vitulina*). *Learn. Behav.* 33: 428–436.

McRae K and Cree GS (2002) Factors underlying category-specific semantic deficits. In: Forde EME and Humphreys GW (eds.) *Category Specificity in Brain and Mind*, pp. 211–249. New York: Psychology Press.

Medin DL (1998) Concepts and conceptual structure. In: Thagard P (ed.) *Mind Readings: Introductory Selections on Cognitive Science*, pp. 93–125. Cambridge, MA: The MIT Press.

Medin DL and Aguilar C (2001) Categorization. In: Wilson RA and Keil FC (eds.) *The MIT Encyclopedia of the Cognitive Sciences*, pp. 104–106. Cambridge, MA: MIT Press.

Murai C, Tomonaga M, Kamegai K, Terazawa N, and Yamaguchi MK (2004) Do infant Japanese macaques (*Macaca fuscata*) categorize objects without specific training? *Primates* 45: 1–6.

Murai C, Kosugi D, Tomonaga M, Tanaka M, Matsuzawa T, and Itakura S (2005) Can chimpanzee infants (*Pan troglodytes*) form categorical representations in the same manner as human infants (*Homo sapiens*)? *Dev. Sci.* 8: 240–254.

Neiman ER and Zentall TR (2001) Common coding of samples associated with the same comparison: The nature of the common representation. *Learn. Motiv.* 32: 367–382.

Oden DL, Thompson RKR, and Premack D (1990) Infant chimpanzees spontaneously perceive both concrete and abstract same/different relations. *Child Dev.* 61: 621–631.

Olthof A, Iden CM, and Roberts WA (1997) Judgments of ordinality and summation of number symbols by squirrel monkeys (*Saimiri sciureus*). *J. Exp. Psychol. Anim. Behav. Process.* 23: 325–339.

Parr LA, Hopkins WD, and de Waal FBM (1998) The perception of facial expression by chimpanzees. *Pan troglodytes. Evol. Comm.* 2: 1–23.

Pearce JM (1994) Discrimination and categorization. In: Mackintosh NJ (ed.) *Animal Learning and Cognition. Handbook of Perception and Cognition Series.* 2nd ed., pp. 109–134. New York: Academic Press.

Pena T, Ritts RC, and Galizio M (2006) Identity matching-to-sample with olfactory stimuli in rats. *J. Exp. Anal. Behav.* 85: 203–221.

Pepperberg IM (1987) Acquisition of the same/different concept by an African Grey parrot (*Psittacus erithacus*): Learning with respect to categories of color, shape, and material. *Anim. Learn. Behav.* 15: 423–432.

Pepperberg IM (1994) Numerical competence in an African gray parrot (*Psittacus erithacus*). *J. Comp. Psychol.* 108: 36–44.

Pepperberg IM (2006) Grey parrot (*Psittacus erithacus*) numerical abilities: Addition and further experiments on a zero-like concept. *J. Comp. Psychol.* 120: 1–11.

Poole J and Lander DG (1971) The pigeon's concept of pigeon. *Psychon. Sci.* 25: 157–158.

Povinelli DJ and Vonk J (2003) Chimpanzee minds: Suspiciously human? *Trends Cogn Sci* 7: 157–160.

Premack D (1976) *Intelligence in Ape and Man*. Hillsdale, NJ: Wiley.

Premack D (1983a) Animal cognition. *Annu. Rev. Psychol.* 34: 351–362.

Premack D (1983b) The codes of man and beasts. *Behav. Brain Sci.* 6: 125–167.

Purtle RB (1973) Peak shift: A review. *Psychol. Bull.* 80: 408–421.

Reese HW (1968) *The Perception of Stimulus Relation: Discrimination Learning and Transposition*. New York: Academic Press.

Riley DA (1968) *Discrimination Learning*. Boston: Allyn and Bacon.

Riley DA, Ring K, and James T (1960) The effect of stimulus comparison on discrimination learning and transposition. *J. Comp. Physiol. Psychol.* 53: 415–421.

Roberts WA and Mazmanian DS (1988) Concept learning at different levels of abstraction by pigeons, monkeys, and people. *J. Exp. Psychol. Anim. Behav. Process.* 14: 247–260.

Rosch E and Mervis CB (1975) Family resemblances: Studies in the internal structure of categories. *Cogn. Psychol.* 7: 573–605.

Rosch E, Mervis KB, Gray WD, Johnson DM, and Boyes-Braem P (1976) Basic objects in natural categories. *Cogn. Psychol.* 8: 382–439.

Rumbaugh DM and Washburn DA (1993) Counting by chimpanzees and ordinality judgements by macaques in video-formatted tasks. In: Boysen ST and Capaldi EJ (eds.) *The Development of Numerical Competence: Animal and Human Models*, pp. 87–106. Hillsdale, NJ: Erlbaum.

Sands SF, Lincoln CE, and Wright AA (1982) Pictorial similarity judgments and the organization of visual memory in the rhesus monkey. *J. Exp. Psychol. Gen.* 111: 369–389.

Schrier AM and Brady PM (1987) Categorization of natural stimuli by monkeys (*Macaca mulatta*): Effects of stimulus set size and modification of exemplars. *J. Exp. Psychol. Anim. Behav. Process.* 13: 136–143.

Schusterman RJ, Reichmuth CJ, and Kastak D (2000) How animals classify friends and foes. *Curr. Dir. Psychol. Sci.* 9: 1–6.

Sidman M (2000) Equivalence relations and the reinforcement contingency. *J. Exp. Anal. Behav.* 74: 127–146.

Smirnova AA, Lazareva OF, and Zorina ZA (2000) Use of number by crows: Investigation by matching and oddity learning. *J. Exp. Anal. Behav.* 73: 163–176.

Smith EE and Medin DL (1981) *Categories and Concepts.* Cambridge, MA: Harvard University Press.

Spence KW (1937) The differential response in animals to stimuli varying within a single dimension. *Psychol. Bull.* 44: 440–444.

Spinozzi G, Lubrano G, and Truppa V (2006) Categorization of above and below spatial relations by tufted capuchin monkeys (*Cebus apella*). *J. Comp. Psychol.* 118: 403–412.

Sutton JE and Roberts WA (2002) Failure to find evidence of stimulus generalization within pictorial categories in pigeons. *J. Exp. Anal. Behav.* 78: 333–343.

Swaddle JP and Pruett-Jones S (2001) Starlings can categorize symmetry differences in dot displays. *Am. Natural.* 158: 300–307.

Tanaka JW and Taylor M (1991) Object categories and expertise: Is the basic level in the eye of the beholder? *Cogn. Psychol.* 23: 457–482.

Thompson RKR (1995) Natural and relational concepts in animals. In: Roitblatt HL and Meyer J-A (eds.) *Comparative Approaches to Cognitive Science*, pp. 176–224. Cambridge, MA: MIT Press.

Thompson RKR and Chase L (1980) Relative numerousness judgments by squirrel monkeys. *Bull. Psychon. Soc.* 16: 79–82.

Thompson RKR, Oden DL, and Boysen ST (1997) Language-naive chimpanzees (*Pan troglodytes)* judge relations between relations in a conceptual matching-to-sample task. *J. Exp. Psychol. Anim. Behav. Process.* 23: 31–43.

Troje NF, Huber L, Loidolt M, Aust U, and Fieder M (1999) Categorical learning in pigeons: The role of texture and shape in complex static stimuli. *Vision Res.* 39: 353–366.

Urcuioli P, Zentall TR, Jackson-Smith P, and Steirn JN (1989) Evidence for common coding in many-to-one matching: Retention, intertrial interference, and transfer. *J. Exp. Anal. Behav.* 15: 264–273.

Urcuioli P, Lionello-DeNolf K, Michalek S, and Vasconcelos M (2006) Some tests of response membership in acquired equivalence classes. *J. Exp. Anal. Behav.* 86: 81–107.

Vaughan W and Greene SL (1984) Pigeon visual memory capacity. *J. Exp. Psychol. Anim. Behav. Process.* 10: 256–271.

Vogels R (1999) Categorization of complex visual images by rhesus monkeys. Part 1: Behavioural study. *Eur. J. Neurosci.* 11: 1223–1238.

Von Fersen L and Lea SEG (1990) Category discrimination by pigeons using five polymorphous features. *J. Exp. Anal. Behav.* 54: 69–84.

Vonk J (2003) Gorilla (*Gorilla gorilla gorilla)* and orangutan (*Pongo abelii*) understanding of first- and second-order relations. *Anim. Cogn.* 6: 77–86.

Vonk J and McDonald SE (2002) Natural concepts in a juvenile gorilla (*Gorilla gorilla gorilla*) at three levels of abstraction. *J. Exp. Anal. Behav.* 78: 315–332.

Vonk J and McDonald SE (2004) Levels of abstraction in orangutan (*Pongo abelii*) categorization. *J. Comp. Psychol.* 118: 3–13.

Warrington EK and McCarthy RA (1987) Categories and knowledge: Further fractionations and an attempted integration. *Brain* 110: 1273–1296.

Washburn DA and Rumbaugh DM (1991) Ordinal judgments of numerical symbols by macaques (*Macaca mulatta*). *Psychol. Sci.* 2: 190–193.

Wasserman EA (1995) The conceptual abilities in pigeons. *Am. Sci.* 83: 246–255.

Wasserman EA and Miller RR (1997) What's elementary about associative learning? *Annu. Rev. Psychol.* 48: 573–607.

Wasserman EA, Kiedinger RE, and Bhatt RS (1988) Conceptual behavior in pigeons: Categories, subcategories, and pseudocategories. *J. Exp. Psychol. Anim. Behav. Process.* 14: 235–246.

Wasserman EA, DeVolder CL, and Coppage DJ (1992) Nonsimilarity-based conceptualization in pigeons via secondary or mediated generalization. *Psychol. Sci.* 3: 374–378.

Wasserman EA, Fagot J, and Young ME (2001) Same-different conceptualization by baboons (*Papio papio*): The role of entropy. *J. Comp. Psychol.* 115: 45–142.

Wasserman EA, Young ME, and Cook RG (2004) Variability discrimination in humans and animals: Implications for adaptive action. *Am. Psychol.* 59: 879–880.

Watanabe S (2000) Discrimination of cartoons and photographs in pigeons: Effects of scrambling of elements. *Behav. Process.* 53: 3–9.

Watanabe S (2001) Van Gogh Chagall and pigeons: Picture discrimination in pigeons and humans. *Anim. Cogn.* 4: 147–151.

Watanabe S, Sakamoto J, and Wakita M (1995) Pigeons' discrimination of painting by Monet and Picasso. *J. Exp. Anal. Behav.* 63: 165–174.

Wills S and Mackintosh NJ (1999) Relational learning in pigeons? *Q. J. Exp. Psychol.* 52(B): 31–52.

Wright AA (1997) Concept learning and learning strategies. *Psychol. Sci.* 8: 119–123.

Wright AA, Cook RG, Rivera JU, Sands SF, and Delius JD (1988) Concept learning by pigeon: Matching-to-sample with trial-unique video picture stimuli. *Anim. Learn. Behav.* 16: 236–244.

Wright AA, Rivera JU, Katz JS, and Bachevalier J (2003) Abstract-concept learning and list-memory processing by capuchin and rhesus monkeys. *J. Exp. Psychol. Anim. Behav. Process.* 29: 184–198.

Xia L, Siemann M, and Delius JD (2000) Matching of numerical symbols with number of responses by pigeons. *Anim. Cogn.* 3: 35–43.

Xia L, Emmerton J, Siemann M, and Delius JD (2001) Pigeons (*Columba livia*) learn to link numerosities with symbols. *J. Comp. Psychol.* 115: 83–91.

Yoshikubo S (1985) Species discrimination and concept formation by rhesus monkeys (*Macaca mulatta*). *Primates* 26: 285–299.

Young ME and Wasserman EA (2001) Evidence for a conceptual account of same-different discrimination learning in the pigeon. *Psychon. Bull. Rev.* 8: 677–684.

Young ME, Wasserman EA, and Dalrymple RM (1997) Memory-based same-different conceptualization by pigeons. *Psychon. Bull. Rev.* 4: 552–558.

Young ME, Wasserman EA, and Garner KL (1997) Effects of number of items on the pigeon's discrimination of same from different visual displays. *J. Exp. Psychol. Anim. Behav. Process.* 23: 491–501.

Zentall TR (1998) Symbolic representation in animals: Emergent stimulus relations in conditional discrimination learning. *Anim. Learn. Behav.* 26: 363–377.

Zentall TR (2000) Symbolic representation by pigeons. *Curr. Dir. Psychol. Sci.* 9: 118–123.

Zentall TR and Hogan D (1974) Abstract concept learning in the pigeon. *J. Exp. Psychol.* 102: 393–398.

Zentall TR, Galizio M, and Critchfield TS (2002) Categorization, concept learning, and behavioral analysis: An introduction. *J. Exp. Anal. Behav.* 78: 248.

Zorina ZA and Smirnova AA (1996) Quantitative evaluations in gray crows: Generalization of the relative attribute. *Neurosci. Behav. Physiol.* 26: 357–364.

1.12 Learning and Representation

C. R. Gallistel, Rutgers University, Piscataway, NJ, USA

In a representational theory of learning, the brain computes a representation of the experienced world, and behavior is informed by that representation. By contrast, in associative theories of learning, which dominate neurobiological thinking, experience causes a plastic brain to rewire itself to make behavior better adapted to the experienced world, without the brain's computing a representation of that world (Pavlov, 1928; Hull, 1952; Hawkins and Kandel, 1984; Rumelhart and McClelland, 1986; Smolensky, 1986). The computation of a representation seems to require a functional architecture that is not transparently consistent with our current understanding of neurobiological mechanisms (Gallistel, 2006), which is why representational theories of learning have not found favor among neurobiologists. Associative theories, in contrast, have been strongly influenced by neurobiological considerations for more than a century. For them, consistency with the current understanding of neurobiology is a major consideration (e.g., Gluck et al., 2005), which is why they predominate in neurobiological thinking about learning.

The results of behavioral experiments on nonhuman animals have increasingly implied that much learned behavior is informed by enduring temporal and spatial representations (e.g., Menzel et al., 2005), as even some prominent advocates of associative theories have recently acknowledged (Clayton et al., 2006a). Moreover, direct electrophysiological observation of neural activity has shown that the nervous system represents where the animal is and has been within the environment (O'Keefe and Nadel, 1978; Muller, 1996; Lee et al., 2004; Hafting et al., 2005; Foster and Wilson, 2006; See Chapter 1.21), how it is oriented (Ranck, 1984; Golob et al.,

2001; Sargolini et al., 2006; Yoganarasimha et al., 2006), where objects are in relation to it (Muller et al., 2005; Campos et al., 2006; Goossens and Van Opstal, 2006), and the timing of repetitive or predictable events (Schultz and Dickinson, 2000; Leon and Shadlen, 2003; Meck, 2003; Ivry and Spencer, 2004; Penney, 2004; See Chapter 1.19). Thus, there is a conceptual tension between the behavioral and electrophysiological findings that seem to imply a computational–representational architecture, on the one hand, and on the other hand, current conceptions of neural structure and mechanism, in which seemingly essential elements of the requisite functional architecture appear to be absent.

The extent to which one believes that consistency with currently understood neurobiological mechanisms should be a constraint on models of learning depends on whether one believes that those mechanisms provide, or could provide, satisfactory accounts of the behaviorally well-documented phenomena that are the focus of this chapter – dead reckoning in insect navigation, the capacity of insects to record landmark 'snapshots,' and the capacity of food-caching jays to remember and make versatile use of a large number of episode-specific facts about each cache. They also depend on whether one believes that computation in the brain must be consistent with the principles that computer scientists believe constrain physically realizable computations. Perhaps, as many neuroscientists believe, the brain escapes the limitations and requirements that computer scientists believe are imposed by mathematics, logic, and physics.

Instructive instances can be found in the history of science where findings and analyses at a higher level of inquiry seemed to require mechanisms at a more basic level for which there was then no explanation. Throughout the latter part of the nineteenth century, the eminent physicists William Thompson (Lord Kelvin) and P. G. Tait argued that Darwin and the geologists must be grossly in error in their estimates of the age of the earth, because no heat-generation process known to physics was consistent with a solar age of more than 100 million years. (Tait thought the upper limit imposed by physical considerations was 10 million years – see Lindley (2004) for an account.) Thompson (1862) wrote, for example, "It is impossible that hypotheses assuming an equibility of sun and storms for 1,000,000 years can be wholly true." Importantly, Kelvin did not have a satisfactory theory of where the sun's heat came from – he worked on the problem off and on throughout his career – but he was confident that a satisfactory explanation could be based on physical principles and phenomena that were then understood. Radioactivity was not discovered until 1896, and it was only in 1903 that the Curies showed that it was accompanied by the liberation of heat. The following contemporary quote gives an idea of just how revolutionary this discovery was:

> [this phenomenon] can barely be distinguished from the discovery of perpetual motion, which it is an axiom of science to call impossible, [and] has left every chemist and physicist in a state of bewilderment. (Lindley, 2004: 302)

This discovery of something that Kelvin and Tait literally could not imagine bore tellingly on their argument with Darwin and the geologists.

Whether we are in such a situation now remains, of course, to be seen. However, I argue in this chapter that the behavioral evidence for representation and computation, together with basic insights in computer science about the centrality of a read-write memory mechanism in physically realized computation, implies the existence of a neurobiological read-write memory mechanism. Given the centrality of such a mechanism to computation, as computer scientists understand it, the discovery of such a mechanism may someday have an impact on neuroscience comparable to the impact of the discovery of radioactivity on physics.

1.12.1 Representations: Definition and Explication

From the perspective of cognitive science, the brain is an organ of computation (Newell and Simon, 1975; Marr, 1982). What it computes are representations of selected aspects of the world and the animal's relations to it (the distal stimuli). It computes these representations from the signals engendered in sensory organs by the stimuli that impinge on them (the proximal stimuli) and from signals generated by the motor system, which carry information about how the animal is moving (efference copy signals; Holst and Mittelstaedt, 1950).

A representation consists of signals, symbols, and the operations on them (see **Figure 1**). The signals and symbols carry information about properties of the experienced world. The operations on those signals and symbols enable the brain to compute explicit

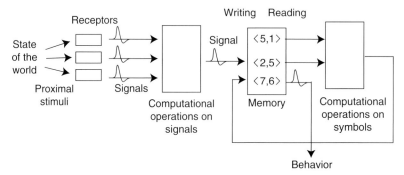

Figure 1 Schematic representation of the flow of information in a neurobiologically realized representational system. Proximal stimuli deriving from a state of the world (distal stimulus) act on sensory receptors to generate sensory signals, from which a perceptual signal specifying that state of the world is computed. The perceptual signal conveys the information to memory, where it is written into a symbol, which carries the information forward in time. Computational operations combine that symbol with other symbols to create further symbols and symbol strings in memory. The information contained in a symbol is read from memory and converted to signals in the motor system that give form to behavior.

representations from implicit ones and to anticipate behaviorally relevant states of the world.

Information is an abstract quantity carried by any signal or symbol that can reduce the brain's uncertainty about the present state of some aspect of the world (Shannon, 1948; Rieke et al., 1997). Information cannot be communicated to a device that has no representation of the world because the measure of the amount of information communicated is the reduction in the receiver's uncertainty about the state of the world. A receiver that has no representation of states of the world cannot have uncertainty about those states; more technically, it cannot have a probability distribution defined on those states. Thus, a receiver incapable of representing at least some states of the world is not something to which information can be communicated; it cannot extract from information-bearing signals the information that they carry.

Signals carry information from one place to another (from one spatial location to another). In a computer, the signals are current pulses. In the nervous system, they are action potentials, synaptic transmitters, and hormones. Symbols carry information forward in time (from one temporal location to a later one). In a computer, the symbols are bit patterns in a memory register. We do not know the physical realization of symbols in the nervous system. One school of thought doubts that they exist (Rumelhart and McClelland, 1986; Wallace and Fountain, 2003; Hay and Baayen, 2005).

The essential features of a physically realized symbol are that it encodes information about something else (to which it refers) and that it enters into symbol processing operations appropriate to the information that it encodes. Base-pair sequences in DNA are biological examples of physically realized symbols. The sequence of exon codons (base-pair triplets) between a start codon and a stop codon encodes the sequence of amino acids that compose a protein. These codon sequences carry forward in time evolutionarily accumulated information about functional amino acid sequences. They enter into combinatorial operations that recreate the sequences they encode. Base-pair sequences also encode promoters. The binding and unbinding of translation factors (themselves usually proteins) to one another and to promoters control the timing and amounts of protein synthesis. The base-pair sequences in promoters carry forward in time evolutionarily accumulated information about functional patterns of protein synthesis (when and where it is functional

to synthesize which proteins). The two kinds of information carried by base-pair sequences in DNA – exon information and promoter information – are roughly analogous to the two kinds of information carried in computer memory – data and program information.

In order to refer, the signals and symbols in a representational system must be causally connected to the things or states of the world to which they refer. In a process-control computer, the causal connection is effected by means of the transducers that generate signals proportional to critical variables, such as temperature, torque, concentration, velocity, and force. Often these signals are analog signals (voltages), but these are usually converted almost immediately to symbols (bit patterns stored in memory buffers) by analog-to-digital converters. The bit patterns are then converted to digital signals (current pulses) that are transmitted over signal lines to the input registers (memory buffers) of the computer, where they write the bit patterns into memory registers. This chain of causes and effects causally connects the bit pattern in a memory register that represents the current temperature to the temperature to which it refers. The function of the memory register is to carry that bit pattern (hence, the information about temperature that it encodes) forward indefinitely in time for use in later computations. When it is to be used in a computation, the pattern is read from the register. In short, a symbolic memory register is written to by impinging information-conveying signals and read from by computational processes.

In the nervous system, inputs acting on, for example, the retina of the eye or the basilar membrane of the ear are converted first into analog signals (receptor potentials) and then into digital action potentials, which carry the information into the central nervous system. The behavioral evidence implies that the nervous system possesses a read-write memory mechanism that performs the same essential function performed by the memory registers in a computer, but we do not yet know what that mechanism is.

Because a symbolic memory mechanism has not so far been identified, it is often assumed not to exist. It is assumed that "memory [elements in the brain take the] form of modifiable interconnections within the computational substrate" so that "no separate 'fetch' [read] and 'store' [write] cycles are necessary" (Koch and Hepp, 2006). These modifiable interconnections (synaptic conductances) are thought to be the physical realization of the associations in associative learning theory (Fanselow, 1993; *See* Chapters 1.33, 1.34, 1.35). There are, however, no proposals about how either associations in the abstract or experientially modified synaptic conductances (physically realized associations) can encode acquired information in a computationally accessible form. There are, for example, no proposals about how associations could specify the coordinates of a remembered location. Generally speaking, for associative theories of learning, this is not a problem. Because they are nonrepresentational theories, they do not require a symbolic memory mechanism.

For representational theories of learning, however, the absence of a symbolic memory mechanism is a problem, because a mechanism functionally equivalent to the tape in Turing's abstract conception of a general purpose computing machine (Turing, 1936, 1950) is essential to computation and representation (Gallistel, 2006). Representations are computed by combining information that arrives in dribs and drabs spread out in time, as is illustrated shortly with the example of the dead reckoning process. For new information to be combined with old information, a mechanism must carry the old information forward in time in a computationally accessible form.

Symbols and the processes that operate on them create functioning homomorphisms between the symbol system and the aspects of the world to which the symbols refer (Gallistel, 1990). A homomorphism between two systems is a (partial) sameness in their abstract, mathematical form. Symbolic processes and relations in the representing system formally parallel nonsymbolic processes and relations in the represented system. A functioning homomorphism is one in which the representing system exploits this parallelism to inform its interactions with the represented system.

1.12.2 Behavioral Evidence for Representations in Learning

1.12.2.1 Dead Reckoning

The position of an animal in its environment, as a function of time, is the integral of its velocity with respect to time. This is a mathematical fact about the relation between these vector variables (velocity and position). In mobile animals, a representation of their position relative to places of behavioral importance (nest or resting area, food sources, hiding places, landmarks with reference to which these other places can be located, and so on) informs their

behavior in many fundamental ways. The animal brain computes a representation of the animal's position by integrating with respect to time signals that convey information about its velocity. This symbolic integration process is called path integration in mathematical work and dead reckoning in traditional texts on marine navigation. It is a foundation of animal navigation (Mittelstaedt and Mittelstaedt, 1973; Wehner and Srinivasan, 1981; Gallistel, 1990; Wehner and Srinivasan, 2003; Collett and Graham, 2004; Etienne and Jeffery, 2004; Kimchi et al., 2004; Grah et al., 2005; *See* Chapter 1.20).

Dead reckoning is a particularly simple example of representational learning – if by 'learning' we understand the process of acquiring knowledge from experience. The animal acquires knowledge of its current position (and of past positions of behavioral interest) by means of a neurobiological process that integrates experienced velocity, as conveyed by signals from sensory and motor mechanisms sensitive to correlates of velocity. The process of neurobiological integration in the brain, which is the representing system, parallels the physical integration of velocity that occurs as the animal moves within its environment. The animal's location in its environment is the represented system. In technical jargon, the symbolic processes in the brain are homomorphic to the displacement process in the system that the brain is representing, because there is a partial correspondence in the abstract (mathematical) form of the processes going on in the two systems. The resulting symbolic specification of position enables the brain to, for example, set the animal on the course for home. Insofar as the courses the brain sets actually bring the animal to its home, the symbolic representation of position informs functional behavior. This makes the neurobiological integration of velocity signals to obtain position symbols an example of a functioning homomorphism, that is, a representation.

Dead reckoning provides a particularly clear and simple example of the need for a symbolic memory in computation. The essence of dead reckoning is the adding of the current displacement to the sum of the previous displacements. For this to be possible, there must be a mechanism that carries the sum of the previous displacements forward in time in a form that makes it possible to add to it. The mechanism that carries the sum forward in time must not leak; the sum must not get smaller simply from the passage of time. It must not get smaller because it is the physical realization of the symbol that specifies the subject's displacement from the origin of the reference frame, typically the nest. If the sum gets smaller simply with the passage of time, then the brain represents the animal as getting closer to home just by sitting still.

1.12.2.2 Learning the Solar Ephemeris

The integration of the velocity vector in dead reckoning is meaningless unless the velocity vector is represented in a stable geocentric coordinate framework. The velocity vector specifies the subject's rate of displacement in two orthogonal directions (for example, latitudinal displacement and longitudinal displacement or radial displacement and tangential displacement – see Gallistel, 1990, Chapter 4, for a detailed explication of path integration computations in different coordinate frameworks). Thus, a consistent directional reference must be maintained. In navigational jargon, this is called carrying the parallel, because lines of direction at different locations (e.g., lines running north–south) are parallel. The line from the observer to any nearby landmark changes its direction as the observer moves. This is called parallax. The farther away the landmark is, the less the parallax, and hence the better it functions as a directional referent. Extraterrestrial landmarks like the sun and the stars are, for practical purposes, infinitely far away, so they have negligible parallax. These extraterrestrial landmarks are strongly preferred as directional referents by animals of many different species (Gallistel, 1990). However, they have one drawback: Because of the earth's rotation about its own axis, their terrestrial direction changes continuously.

The solar ephemeris is the direction of the sun in a terrestrial frame of reference as a function of the time of day (that is, as a function of the angular position of the earth in its daily rotational cycle; *See* Chapter 1.25). To use the sun as a directional referent in dead reckoning, the brain must learn the azimuthal component of the solar ephemeris (Schmidt-Koenig, 1960). This function (solar compass direction versus time of day, see **Figure 2**) varies greatly, depending on which hemisphere the observer is in (northern or southern), its latitude (angular distance from the equator), and the season of the year. Thus, it is a highly contingent fact about the animal's environment, the sort of thing that must be learned from experience.

There is an experimental literature on the learning of the solar ephemeris by homing pigeons and

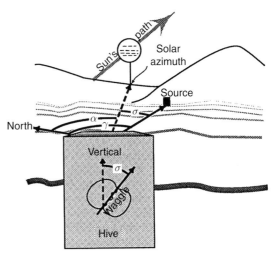

Figure 2 In the waggle dance, the returned forager circles in alternate directions from one waggle run to the next, forming a figure 8. The angle of the repeated waggle runs, relative to vertical, indicates the solar bearing of the source from which the forager has returned. The number of waggles indicates its distance. α = the solar azimuth, its compass direction; σ = the solar bearing of the source, its direction relative to the direction of the sun; γ = the compass direction of the source. Note that the compass direction of the source is the sum of the solar azimuth and the solar bearing: $\gamma = \alpha + \sigma$. (Reproduced by permission of the author and publisher from Gallistel CR (1998) Symbolic processes in the brain: The case of insect navigation. In: Scarborough D and Sternberg S (eds.) *An Invitation to Cognitive Science*, vol. 4, pp. 1–51. Cambridge, MA: MIT Press.)

foraging bees (e.g., Budzynski et al., 2000; Dyer, 2002; Towne et al., 2005). To learn the solar ephemeris is to learn, for some point of view (e.g., the hive entrance or the nest), what parts of the local horizon profile the sun is over as a function of the time of day (see **Figure 2**). To learn that, the brain must represent the horizon profile, the position of the sun relative to this horizon profile, and the time of day. The time-of-day signal is provided by the animal's circadian clock (Mouritsen and Frost, 2002; Giunchi et al., 2003; Homberg, 2004; Stalleicken et al., 2005). The universally valid parameter of the circadian clock, its period, is genetically specified. The clock parameter that must be adjusted based on local experience is the phase. The entrainment mechanism adjusts the phase of the clock in response to the rapid changes in photon flux that occur at dawn and dusk (Takahashi et al., 1984; Foster et al., 2003; Bertolucci and Foa, 2004; Foster and Bellingham, 2004).

The learning of the relation between the time-of-day signal provided by the circadian clock and the position of the sun relative to the horizon profile at the chosen point of view appears to be a curve-fitting process (Dyer and Dickinson, 1994, 1996; Dickinson and Dyer, 1996). Built into the learning mechanism is a parameterized dynamic process – the physical realization of an equation (function) specifying the relation between two circular variables: time of day and position on the horizon. This built-in equation specifies what is universally true about the solar ephemeris, namely, that the sun is somewhere to the east all morning and somewhere to the west all afternoon. Incubator-raised bees that have seen the sun only in the late afternoon when it is declining in the west nonetheless represent it as being due east all morning long, stepping abruptly to due west around noon (Dyer and Dickinson, 1994). This default form for the ephemeris function is in fact valid only near the equator.

Notice that the information about where the sun is in the morning cannot have come from these incubator-raised bees' experience, because they never saw it in the morning. It is carried forward in time from the remote evolutionary past by the genes that code for the built-in dynamic process relating the horizon position cycle to the circadian clock's cycle, just as the information specifying the period of the circadian clock is carried forward in time by the genes that specify its molecular structure. In experienced bees, which have observed the sun at the hive at several different times of day, the parameters of the built-in function are adjusted so that the function specifies locally appropriate horizon positions for the sun throughout the day. In the summer at midlatitudes in the northern hemisphere, where the Dyer and Dickinson (1994) experiments were conducted, the sun rises north of east, moves continuously along the horizon in the clockwise direction to reach due south at noon and then on through west to north of west in the late afternoon. (By contrast, in winter at midsouthern latitudes, it rises north of east and moves continuously counterclockwise along the horizon to due north at noon and then on to north of west in the late afternoon.)

What bees learn from their experience of the sun's position over the horizon at different times of day is the locally appropriate values for the parameters of their built-in solar ephemeris function. These parameter settings are not explicitly specified by the bees' experiences of the sun's position above the horizon profile. There is no first-order sensory signal generated by any aspect of the bees' experiences that directly specifies appropriate parameter values in

the way in which, for example, the signal from a photoreceptor explicitly specifies the number of photons captured by that receptor. Even the positional data – where the sun is over the profile – are only implicitly present in the spatiotemporal distribution of action potentials from the retina. The sun's profile-position coordinate must be computed from this pattern. And even then, the appropriate values for the parameters of the ephemeris equation are only implicit in data specifying several different profile positions at several different times of day. Thus, the explicit parameter values, the actual settings of the parameters, must be computed from these positional data. Moreover, the positional data are not given all at once. Experience provides different data points at different times of day. When it has extracted from the incoming retinal signals an explicit representation of the sun's profile position, the brain requires a symbolic memory to carry that information forward in time, so that it may be computationally combined with the positional data obtained later in the day to determine the appropriate values of the ephemeris parameters.

The symbolic information provided by the learned ephemeris informs not only the dead reckoning process but other behaviors as well. When a foraging bee returns from a rich source, it does a waggle dance on the vertical surface of the hive, which symbolically specifies the direction and distance of the source (**Figure 2**). The direction is specified by the angle of the waggle run relative to vertical in the solar bearing of the source, the angle at which an outbound forager must hold the sun to fly toward the source. The solar bearing communicated by the dance is not the bearing that the returning forager has just flown; rather, it is the inverse of that bearing. If the returning forager flew with the sun at its back to reach the hive, then its dance tells the other bees to fly toward the sun. This information about the relation between the direction of the source from the hive and the direction of the sun from the hive was acquired many minutes earlier. A symbolic memory is required to carry this direction vector forward in time until it is used to inform the waggle dance (cf. Menzel et al., 2006; *See* Chapter 1.25).

The information communicated by the dance is carried forward in the nervous systems of both the dancer and the observers of the dance in a computationally accessible form. If the hive is closed for several hours and then opened, outward-bound foragers do not fly the solar bearing indicated by the dance they witnessed hours earlier; rather, they fly a time-compensated solar bearing, a bearing that takes into account the intervening change in the sun's compass direction (Frisch, 1967). This implies that either (1) a recruited bee remembers the danced solar bearing and uses its solar ephemeris to compute the expected change in solar bearing over the interval since the dance, or (2) the remembered solar ephemeris was used at the time of the dance to compute a compass bearing or the indicated location on the cognitive map (map coordinates). The remembered compass bearing (or remembered map coordinates) must then be combined with the solar ephemeris function at the time of the outward-bound flight to compute an appropriate solar bearing (how to fly relative to the sun to fly a remembered direction relative to the earth).

The learning and use of the solar ephemeris illustrates the manner in which different bits of information, gathered from experience at widely different times in the past, are computationally combined to obtain the explicit information (the current solar bearing of the food source) that informs current behavior.

1.12.2.3   The Cognitive Map

A map is a record of two or more locations in a common coordinate framework. It gives access to other (nonpositional) information about those locations (for example, information that enables the navigator to recognize surrounding landmarks and information about the food to be found there or the dangers to be wary of). A cognitive map is a map of experienced terrain computed by a brain and recorded in its (presumed) symbolic memory. Dead reckoning and the construction and use of a cognitive map are intimately interrelated (Gallistel, 1990, 1998; Collett et al., 1999; McNaughton et al., 2006; *See* Chapter 1.25).

The information that dead reckoning provides about the animal's current position becomes more valuable as the number of locations on the cognitive map increases. It also becomes more valuable as the brain records more information that will enable it to recognize those places on subsequent occasions (for example, 'snapshots' of surrounding landmarks, together with their direction and distance from the point of interest; Cartwright and Collett, 1979, 1983, 1987; Collett et al., 1986). The information about current position becomes more valuable as the map becomes richer in information, because a major function of the cognitive map is to enable the brain to

compute the range (distance from the animal) and bearing (direction from the animal) of points of behavioral importance like food and the nest (Collett et al., 1999). The directional information extracted by this vector computation is critical to the setting of a course toward or away from those points. The distance information is critical to the making of decisions based on estimates of the time it will take to reach a point.

Often, dead reckoning itself provides the estimate of the animal's position on its map, but sometimes either natural circumstances (gusts of wind) or experimental intervention renders the dead reckoning position useless, in which cases the brain must rely on landmark recognition to reestablish its position on its cognitive map and compute the course back to home or to the destination it had before it was displaced (Fukushi and Wehner, 2004; Menzel et al., 2005, 2006).

Conversely, the better the positional information supplied by the dead reckoning process, the more accurate a cognitive map becomes and the easier it is to recognize relevant landmarks (Cartwright and Collett, 1979, 1983, 1987; Durier et al., 2003; Graham et al., 2004). The map becomes more accurate as dead reckoning improves because it is likely that dead reckoning is the principal determinant of the position vectors recorded on the map. When the animal finds a point of behavioral interest, such as a food source, the position vector that represents that location on the brain's cognitive map is the dead reckoning position vector (the symbol that specifies where it is in the frame of reference used for dead reckoning, for example, 50 m south and 22 m east of the nest) plus the egocentric position vector for the point of interest (the symbol that specifies the location in the egocentric frame of reference, for example, 30° left and 2 m away). Combining these two symbols is an exercise in coordinate transformation. The computation is spelled out in Gallistel (1990: 106ff; see also Gallistel, 1999). Thus, errors in the dead reckoning become errors in recorded locations. This is a major reason for the inaccuracies in early marine charts; in those charts, too, estimates of longitude were largely based on dead reckoning.

It becomes easier to recognize landmarks as dead reckoning becomes more accurate because estimates of one's location play a major role in the process. To recognize a landmark is to identify what is now perceived with something recorded on the chart. In both human and animal navigation, position confers identity (Gallistel, 1990: 140, 168ff). That is, for a navigator to recognize a landmark, the navigator's estimate of its location must be within his uncertainty about where he is in relation to it on his cognitive map (Cartwright and Collett, 1983; Collett et al., 2002; Dale et al., 2005). A sailor on Long Island Sound seeing to her east something that looks exactly like Mount Vesuvius will not conclude that she is in Italy. She will ponder either why she never knew there was any part of Long Island that looked anything like Mount Vesuvius or, more likely, how remarkable it is that a cloud formation could look exactly like Mount Vesuvius. Thus, contrary to the common assumption, a major factor in the recognition of a landmark is that it be roughly where it is supposed to be. Being where it is supposed to be is an essential aspect of its identity. If it is not where it is supposed to be, it is not that landmark.

In short, dead reckoning provides major input to the computations that determine the recorded locations (position vectors) of points on the cognitive map. The recognition of landmarks along familiar routes (these are called waypoints in traditional navigation) is a substantial aid to dead reckoning (Kohler and Wehner, 2005). However, the animal's estimate of its position and orientation on the cognitive map is a major determinant of whether it looks for a given landmark and whether it accepts a possible landmark as the one it is looking for. Finding a looked-for landmark helps to correct error in the dead reckoning (Etienne et al., 2004) and get the animal back onto a familiar route (Kohler and Wehner, 2005).

All of this — all of our understanding of animal navigation — presupposes a symbolic memory, a memory capable of encoding information about the world and the animal's relation to it and carrying that information forward in time in a computationally accessible form. The physical realization of the geocentric position vector in the dead reckoning machinery must be such that it can be computationally combined with the physical realization of the egocentric position vector in the machinery that assigns egocentric positions to perceived landmarks (see Gallistel, 1999, for a review of the neurobiology of coordinate transformations). The resulting vector symbol (the physical realization of the geocentric coordinates of a perceived landmark) must preserve the information about the location of the landmark on the cognitive map. It must do so in a form that makes it possible to add and subtract that position vector from other position vectors, because that is what is required in computing the range and bearing

of one location from another location (cf. Collett et al., 1999).

In order to recognize a landmark, the brain must previously have made a record of what that landmark looks like (a 'snapshot,' cf. Collett and Collett, 2002; Graham et al., 2004). The record must contain enough information to distinguish between that landmark and other landmarks the animal has encountered in that vicinity. The number of distinguishable snapshots that the brain of an ant or bee might make is for all practical purposes infinite — larger than the number of elementary particles in the universe. Thus, there cannot be for every possible snapshot a genetically specified neural circuit excited by that snapshot and only that snapshot. There cannot be a "gnostic neuron" (Konorski, 1967) for every possible visual scene the ant or bee may need to record. This is derisively known as the grandmother-neuron theory of perceptual encoding.

When applied to, for example, a digital camera, the grandmother-neuron theory is that the factory builds into each camera all possible pictures that might ever be taken. When you press the shutter release, the camera detects the correspondence between the image on the camera's retina and one of the images built into it at that factory, so the 'neuron' for that picture is activated. In this way, the camera (or the brain) 'recognizes' the picture that you are taking.

Clearly this will not do; the possible snapshots cannot be genetically specified and prewired into the nervous system of the ant or the bee. There must be some decompositional encoding scheme that permits finite representational resources to encode the finite number of actual snapshots taken in any one lifetime. No matter how enthusiastic a photographer you are, the pictures you actually take are a negligible fraction of all the possible pictures! A digital camera decomposes images into pixels. It uses symbolic memory to record the image values for each pixel. Thus, it encodes in memory only the pictures actually encountered, not all the pictures that might ever be encountered.

There are much more efficient encodings, as we learn when we compress image files. The use of basis functions, as in Fourier decomposition, is an example of a less obvious and potentially much more efficient encoding. Efficient encodings reduce complex inputs to vectors (in the loose sense of ordered strings of numbers) that specify parameter values for the functions that form a basis of the encoded space. Another example of the use of finite resources to encode an infinite range of possibilities is the encoding of to-be-printed pages of drawings and text using Postscript. The number of distinguishable pages that may be printed is infinite. However, the file for any actual page is surprisingly short, which is a tribute to the efficiency of the encoding scheme.

This approach to understanding how the decidedly finite nervous system of an ant might preserve the information in a snapshot presupposes that there is a symbolic memory mechanism capable of preserving the decomposition of a snapshot (a visual scene) for later computational use. The decomposition made when the landmark was first encountered must be available when the animal encounters that landmark again, and it must be available in a form that allows it to be compared to the decomposition of the currently viewed landmark. The computational architecture should allow for the generation of a measure of similarity between the two encodings being compared (the encoding of the old image in memory and the encoding of the image now on the retina). Moreover, the making of a snapshot, as the term implies, cannot require repeated presentation of the image to be recorded; it must be a one-off process, like the process in a digital camera, which makes fundamental use of a symbolic memory mechanism (but *See* Chapter 1.33).

Recognition is, of course, what attractor networks do (*See* Chapters 1.33, 1.34, 1.35) and they do not have a symbolic memory. (The lack of a symbolic memory is what distinguishes a neural net from a conventional computing machine.) However, because it lacks a symbolic memory, a neural net cannot compute measures of similarity or relative probability. Thus, a neural net recognizer cannot provide information about two different possible matches at the same time. Activity in the net must migrate to one attractor state or another. The net cannot be in two different activity states at the same time. When it is not in one attractor state or another, its activity state does not specify anything about the input. Activity states intermediate between two attractor states do not specify, for example, the relative probabilities of two different possible matches (two different attractor states that the net might be in but is not).

The net's inability to specify a probability distribution over possible states of the world (possible matches between the current image and previous images) makes it difficult to combine the evidence from different computational procedures. For example, it makes it difficult to combine the evidence from image comparison (the probability distribution on the possible matching images, considering only the information in the images themselves) with the evidence from dead reckoning (the prior probability distribution over the possible matching images in memory, given the probability distribution on the animal's position and orientation on its cognitive map).

This last point is important because it relates to recent findings demonstrating that (1) the cognitive map gives access to other information about the world, and (2) even insects engage in what looks like Bayesian inference, combining probabilistic information acquired at different times from different sources. In these experiments (Gould and Gould, 1988; Tautz et al., 2004), foraging bees return from a food source on a rowboat in the middle of a pond or small lake. The returning foragers do the waggle dance, indicating the range and bearing of the food source, but the dance fails to recruit other foragers. This implies that (1) what the dance really communicates is not flying instructions (range and solar bearing) but rather map coordinates, and (2) the bees that observe the dance consult their cognitive maps before deciding whether to act on it (*See* Chapter 1.25). If their own past experience, as recorded on their map of where they have found food, indicates that no food is to be found anywhere near the location indicated by the dance, they decide not to go. Most interestingly, when the boat with the food source is moved close to an island, then the dance of the returning foragers does recruit new foragers. However, the recruits do not come to the boat but rather to the shore near the boat (Tautz et al., 2004). This implies that they have combined the probability distribution for the source location indicated by the dance (the approximate location of the source implied by the dance) with the prior probability distribution (based on their experience, as recorded on their map) to arrive at a posterior distribution, whose modal point is the nearby shore (the most probable location, all considered).

These findings suggest how grossly we may have underestimated the representational and computational capacities of even very small brains. Our gross underestimation of the representational capacity of brains as small as the head of a pin has allowed us to suppose that brains can get along without the symbolic memory mechanism that makes representation possible.

1.12.2.4 The Representation of Past Episodes

Our memory for episodes is another example of one-off memory for specific occurrences, where the number of possible episodes is infinite. Episodes by definition happen only once. We often recall them, however, long after they were encoded and committed to memory (albeit not as accurately as we like to think). More importantly, we combine the information from one episode with the information from another to draw conclusions not justified by any single episode: The fourth time you see a man dining with an attractive woman not his wife, you begin to think he might be a philanderer. When this conclusion becomes a fixed belief, it is an example of a declarative memory ("The man's a philanderer") inferred from a sequence of episodic memories. This does not, of course, imply that the episodic memories are forgotten. Indeed, we may call on them to justify our inference to others. Recent ingeniously constructed experiments with food-caching jays show that we are not alone in our ability to remember episodes, nor to draw behaviorally informing inferences and declarative memories from them.

In times of plenty, many birds gather food and store it in caches (*See* Chapters 1.22, 1.23). Western scrub-jays are particularly remarkable cachers. They make more than 30 000 different caches spread over square miles of the landscape (Vander Wall, 1990). Weeks and months later, during the winter when food is scarce, they retrieve food from these caches, one by one. This is another illustration of the vast demands on memory made by a cognitive map. It also emphasizes the critical importance of a computational architecture that can effect the same computation (vector subtraction) on many different symbol combinations (pairs of vectors) without having a different neural circuit for each possible symbol combination. If we suppose that the jay can set a course toward the remembered location of any one cache while at the location of any other, then, given 30 000 locations, there are on the order of 10^{10} possible course computations (vector subtractions with distinct pairs of vectors formed from the 30 000 vectors in memory). Whatever the computational architecture of the nervous system, it cannot be such as to require 10^{10} different genetically specified neural circuits to effect these 10^{10} different computations.

A long series of ingenious experiments by Clayton and Dickinson and their collaborators have shown that jays remember much more than simply the locations of their caches (Clayton and Dickinson, 1998, 1999; Emery and Clayton, 2001; Clayton et al., 2003a,b; Emery et al., 2004; Dally et al., 2005a,b; de Kort et al., 2005; Clayton et al., 2006b). They remember what kind of prey they hid in each cache, when they made each cache, which other jay, if any, was watching when they made that cache, and whether they have subsequently emptied that cache. They also remember whether they themselves have pilfered the caches of another bird. They remember the intervals that have elapsed in the past between the hiding and retrieval of a given kind of food and whether the food, when retrieved, had or had not rotted. All of this remembered information combines to determine the order in which they will visit caches they have made. The information drawn from memory that is combined to inform current behavior comes from a mixture of episodic memories ("Three days ago, I hid meal worms there, there and there, and 5 days ago, I hid peanuts there, there and there") and declarative memories ("Meal worms rot in 2 days; peanuts don't rot").

These experiments demonstrate a rich representation of the jay's past experience and the ability to compute with the symbols that carry the information gained from that experience forward in time. For example, the birds compute from the current date-time and the remembered date-time at which they made a particular cache the time elapsed since they made that cache. They compare the time elapsed since that cache was made with the remembered time that it takes the contents of that cache to rot. If the computed time elapsed is greater than the remembered rotting time, they visit first the caches where they put the peanuts, even though they prefer (unrotted) meal worms to peanuts, and even though they made the meal worm caches more recently.

When their caching is observed by another jay, they combine the memory of which particular jay it was with a memory of their own much earlier thieving (from which they appear to infer the existence of evil) and their memory for the social status of that jay. If it was a dominant jay and if their experience of their own behavior (their own pilfering) has made them believe in the evil nature of jays, then they are likely to return to the cache when no one is looking, retrieve the food, and hide it elsewhere.

The rich representation of past episodes implied by these results again implies a decompositional scheme of some kind, because the number of possible caching episodes is infinite. Indeed, it suggests the kind of representation of our experience that appears in our linguistic descriptions of episodes (agents, actions, objects of actions, locations, markers of temporal position relative to the present and to other events, and so on). Perhaps we should not be surprised to find evidence for such representations in nonverbal animals. Our ability to use language to communicate to others the information we have extracted from our own experience of the world is itself astonishing. It would be far more astonishing if we assumed that our nonverbal ancestors had no high-level decompositional representation of the world prior to the emergence of language.

1.12.3 Implications for Neurobiology

As mentioned at the outset, the hypothesis that learning depends on the brain's computing representations of selected aspects of the experienced world is controversial because we do not know what the neurobiological realization of key components of the requisite machinery is. Indeed, we do not even have a clear notion of what this realization might be, let alone persuasive evidence that a hypothesized realization is in fact the realization. The keystone in any symbolic computation is a symbolic read-write memory mechanism. That is a mechanism to which information conveyed in signals can be written and that will carry this information forward into the more or less indefinite future, until such time as it is needed in further computation. From a neurobiological perspective (that is, from a material reduction perspective), symbols are the enduring physical changes in the nervous system that carry the information forward in time.

The behavioral evidence implies that a vast amount of acquired information is carried forward by this mechanism, even in the brains of birds and insects. This constrains physically plausible mechanisms (Gallistel, 2002). Whatever the mechanism is, it must realize a very high density of information storage; it must pack gigabytes into cubic microns. It must be thermodynamically stable, so that the preservation of the information has little or no metabolic cost. One cannot pack a great deal of information into a very small volume using a mechanism that depends on the expenditure of metabolic energy to preserve the information, because (1) there is no way to supply the requisite amount of energy within the small volume, and (2) if there were, there would be no way to dissipate the heat generated.

In short, we must remember that the laws of thermodynamics apply to whatever symbolic memory mechanism we may imagine. These thermodynamic considerations make reverberating circuits an implausible physical realization of a mechanism whose essential function is to store large amounts of information for long periods of time. This is important because reverberating activity is the mechanism for storing previously computed information in recurrent neural net models, for example, in moving-activity-bump models for dead reckoning (Samsonovich and McNaughton, 1997; Stringer et al., 2002; Conklin and Eliasmith, 2005; Song and Wang, 2005).

Another constraint on the physical realization of the symbolic memory is that it must both be capable of encoding information and be in a readable form. That is, it must be possible to envision how the enduring physical change hypothesized to be the physical realization of a symbol could in principle specify a fact about the world and how that fact could be recovered (read) from it. It is this consideration that makes Hebbian synapses implausible as the physical realization of symbolic memory. Hebbian synapses are synapses that enduringly change their conductance as the result of the pairing of pre- and postsynaptic activity. The conductance of a synapse is the amplitude and duration of the transient change in the postsynaptic membrane potential when a spike arrives at the presynaptic terminal.

The first thing to be noted in this connection is that there are few if any published suggestions that it is the synaptic conductances themselves that encode information about the world (as opposed to the gnostic neurons that are connected through those conductances). As already noted, changes in synaptic conductances are the hypothesized physical realization of changes in the strengths of associative bonds. Associative theories of learning have traditionally not been representational theories, for the simple reason that it is hard to make a symbol out of an association.

Traditionally, associative strengths have been assumed to change slowly and in a manner dependent on many different aspects of a repeated experience: how close two stimuli are in time, how strong each of them is, how often they have occurred in close temporal conjunction, and so on. Thus, the strength of an association, that is, the conductance of a modifiable synapse, is the product of many different aspects of experience. This means that it cannot encode any one of those aspects. Mathematically speaking, the mapping from experience to an associative strength is a many-one function, and many-one functions are not invertible; you cannot recover the many from the one.

Even if the process of modifying a synaptic conductance were somehow constrained in such a manner that the conductance of a memory synapse could be made, for example, proportional to a to-be-remembered distance, the architecture of the nervous system, as currently understood, would not permit the conductance of that synapse to be read. The postsynaptic signal is a product (or joint function) of the presynaptic signal and the synaptic conductance The synaptic conductance is usually called the synaptic weight, because it is a multiplicative constant that weights or scales the presynaptic signal to determine what is seen by the postsynaptic integration process. Unless the postsynaptic mechanism has independent access to the presynaptic signal (unless it has information about that signal by a pathway other than the presynaptic pathway), it cannot estimate from the postsynaptic signal what the conductance of the synapse is. Thus, even if experience had made the strength of a synaptic conductance proportional to the distance to the food, it is hard to see how that information could be recovered by the postsynaptic integration process.

The mathematical impossibility of recovering the conductance of a synapse from the postsynaptic effect of an unknown presynaptic signal does not go away when one considers instead the problem of recovering the synaptic conductances (weights) in a neural network from the activity in its output neurons. If the postsynaptic effects are linear in the presynaptic signal strengths, then the activities of the output neurons may be regarded as the known values in a linear algebra problem, in which the input signal strengths and the intervening synaptic conductances are the unknown values. Unless there are as many knowns (output signals) as there are unknowns (input signals and synaptic conductances), it is a basic algebraic truth that the values of the unknowns cannot be recovered.

If the network is a richly connected one, with more synapses than inputs and outputs combined, then the conductances of the synapses cannot be recovered, even when both the output and the input signals are known. If postsynaptic effects are nonlinear in the inputs, the problem is still worse, because there is loss of information in nonlinear operations. Intuitively, this is because when there are thresholds, one cannot estimate from the signal on the other side of the threshold what is going on below the threshold. Thus, recognizing that the

synapses whose alteration is supposed to carry information forward in time are embedded in complex networks does not on the face of it make the problem of readability less of a problem; it makes it more of a problem.

This is not to say that some particular network architecture may not solve the problem. A particular architecture dictated by the logic of the problem is just what we see in the read-write memory of a computer. One might imagine, for example, that modifiable synapses only had two states, conducting and nonconducting, and that information about facts like distance and direction was encoded in banks of such synapses, using the same binary code by which distance and direction information is encoded in the memory registers of conventional computers. However, this, too, would require revising our conception of the functional architecture of the nervous system to enable write and read operations. As indicated by the quotation from Koch (Koch and Hepp, 2006), the current understanding of the nervous system has led to the conclusion that this is precisely what its architecture does not support. Moreover, as the Koch quotation indicates, this is taken to be an advantage of the architecture, not a deficiency. Thus, within our current understanding of the functional architecture of the nervous system, there does not appear to be a way to make modifiable synaptic conductances be the mechanism of symbolic memory. This accounts in some measure for the strong strain of antirepresentational theorizing in neurobiologically inspired models of learning.

The presence of a read-write memory mechanism has far-reaching architectural implications. There is no point in writing information to memory if you cannot find it later. Thus, the existence of a read-write mechanism implies or presupposes that the architecture of the system supports memory addressing. It makes no functional sense to have a read-write memory in a machine whose architecture does not support memory addressing.

It is memory addressing that makes possible (1) the distinction between a variable and the value of that variable, (2) the ability to bind a value to a variable, and therefore, (3) the creation of symbolic structures (data structures). Memory addressing makes all this possible because the address in memory at which a given piece of information (a symbol) is to be found is itself information that may be written to memory at another address. This leads to indirect addressing in which the value to be operated on is specified not by its address but, rather, by the address where its address is stored. The bit pattern specifying

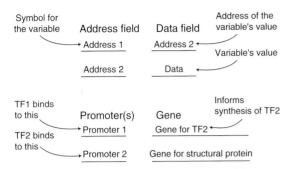

Figure 3 Indirect addressing in computers and the genome. TF = transcription factor. In both examples, the entry in the bottom right field ('Data' or 'Gene for structural protein') may be yet another address (another gene for a TF). This recursive addressing logic makes possible hierarchical data structures with a (potentially) unlimited number of levels.

the first address (Address 1 in **Figure 3**) is the symbol for the variable itself (e.g., the distance to the food source), not for the value that the variable happens to have at any one time (e.g., 10 m). The symbol for the variable gives access to the value of the variable by means of the bit pattern stored in the data field at the address specified by the symbol for the variable. The datum stored in that field is the address of the value (Address 2 in **Figure 3**). The bit pattern (symbol) that specifies the value is in the data field at the second address. To change the value of the variable, the computer changes the bit pattern stored at the second address, not the bit pattern for the first address (the symbol for the variable) nor the bit pattern stored at the first address (the address of the variable's value).

This sounds far removed from biological reality, but, as shown in **Figure 3**, the information stored in DNA is retrieved by the same functional architecture, implemented now at the molecular level, which is to say more compactly than in current computer memory. The address at which a datum (the codon sequence specifying a protein) is stored is the promoter for that gene. Transcription factors initiate the reading of that information (transcription) by binding to the promoter. When a transcription factor binds to the promoter for a gene, the amino acid sequence coded for by that gene is used by the molecular machinery that synthesizes proteins to control the synthesis of the protein defined by that sequence. The protein thereby synthesized may be either a structural protein (a building block of cellular structure, analogous to the actual value of variable) or a transcription factor (an address). Addressing the promoter of a transcription factor (synthesizing a protein

that binds to its address) gives access to the addresses (promoters) of the genes to which that transcription factor binds. As that transcription factor is synthesized, it binds to those promoters, leading to the synthesis of the proteins coded by their genes, many of which proteins may themselves be yet further transcription factors. This indirect addressing makes possible the hierarchical structure of the genome. It makes it possible to have an 'eye' gene that, when activated (addressed by the transcription factor for its promoter), leads to the development of an entire eye (Halder et al., 1995). The eye gene codes only for one protein, but that protein does not itself appear anywhere in the structure of the eye. It is a transcription factor. It gives access to the addresses of other transcription factors and, eventually, through them, to the addresses of the proteins from which the special tissues of the eye are built and to the transcription factors whose concentration gradients govern how those tissues are arranged to make an organ.

What is needed for a brain to have learned representations is a similar architecture for accessing the information acquired from experience, an architecture in which it is possible to write information into biochemically realized symbols as well as read it from them.

The other critical components of a machine capable of representation that is missing from our current conception of the nervous system are the machines that operate on symbols. Needed are mechanisms that perform unary operations, such as negation, and binary operations, such as the arithmetic operations, string-building operations (e.g., concatenation), and logical operations (e.g., AND and OR). The existence of mechanisms operating on symbols would be implied by the existence of a symbolic memory mechanism, because it does not make functional sense to have a read-write memory if there are no mechanisms for operating on the symbols in it. (It's like having chromosomes without ribosomes, which are the machines that put the amino acids together to form a protein.) What makes a representation are the symbols, together with the operations on them. The operations enable the extraction of explicit representations from information that is only implicitly present in the symbols already computed. A representation, that is, a functioning homomorphism, exists only when a machine can operate on its symbols to construct new symbols, symbol strings, and data structures.

A constraint on the mechanisms that operate on symbols is that there not be as many different mechanisms as there are distinct variables. As noted earlier in connection with the 30 000 cache locations that a jay can remember, it is not plausible to imagine an architecture in which there is a separate neural circuit dedicated *a priori* to each different vector subtraction that might ever have to be performed. The reason is once again the infinitude of the possible; there are too many possibilities.

This last constraint may seem almost too obvious to mention. However, in many neural net models of even simple computations, such as those involved in dead reckoning, the combinatorial operations are implemented by a table-look-up architecture (e.g., Samsonovich and McNaughton, 1997). There is a separate look-up table for each instance of a given kind of operation – a different table for each different case in which two variables must be added. A given table can effect the multiplication of all possible values of two variables, but it can operate only on those two variables. Moreover, each such table is composed of tens of thousands of neurons because each different combination of values for the two variables is effected by the neurons that compose the corresponding cell in the table. In short, there are as many different look-up tables as there are pairs of variables whose values may have to be combined, and within each such table, there are as many different neural subcircuits as there are pairs of values for the two variables. Such an architecture is prodigally wasteful of material resources. It is nakedly exposed to combinatorial explosions that lurk behind every tree in the computational forest. That appears to be the price that must be paid for doing without a symbolic memory.

These considerations suggest that the nervous system may in fact contain a yet-to-be discovered read-write memory mechanism. They suggest, moreover, that the mechanism is likely to be found at the level of molecular structure, rather than at the level of cellular structure. Finally, they suggest that the discovery of such a mechanism and the functional architecture that is required to make it effective would change our conception of how the brain works in fundamental ways.

References

Bertolucci C and Foa A (2004) Extraocular photoreception and circadian entrainment in nonmammalian vertebrates. *Chronobiol. Int.* 21(4–5): 501–519.

Budzynski CA, Dyer FC, and Bingman VP (2000) Partial experience with the arc of the sun is sufficient for all-day sun compass orientation in homing pigeons, *Columba livia*. *J. Exp. Biol.* 203: 2341–2348.

Campos M, Cherian A, and Segraves MA (2006) Effects of eye position upon activity of neurons in macaque superior colliculus. *J. Neurophysiol.* 95(1): 505–526.

Cartwright BA and Collett TS (1979) How honey bees know their distance from a nearby visual landmark. *J. Exp. Biol.* 82: 367–372.

Cartwright BA and Collett TS (1983) Landmark learning in bees: Experiments and models. *J. Comp. Physiol.* 151: 521–543.

Cartwright BA and Collett TS (1987) Landmark maps for honey bees. *Biol. Cybern.* 57: 85–93.

Clayton NS, Bussey TJ, and Dickinson A (2003a) Can animals recall the past and plan for the future? *Nat. Rev. Neurosci.* 4: 685–691.

Clayton NS and Dickinson A (1998) Episodic-like memory during cache recovery by scrub jays. *Nature* 395: 272–274.

Clayton NS and Dickinson A (1999) Memory for the content of caches by scrub jays (*Aphelocoma coerulescens*). *J. Exp. Psychol. Anim. Behav. Process.* 25(1): 82–91.

Clayton NS, Emery NJ, and Dickinson A (2006a) The rationality of animal memory: Complex caching strategies of western scrub jays. In: Hurley S and Nudds M (eds.) *Rational Animals?* pp. 197–207. Oxford: Oxford University Press.

Clayton NS, Emery NJ, and Dickinson A (2006b) The prospective cognition of food caching and recovery by western scrub-jays (*Aphelocoma californica*). *Comp. Cog. Behav. Rev.* 1(1): 1–11.

Clayton NS., Yu KS, and Dickinson A (2003b) Interacting cache memories: Evidence of flexible memory use by scrub jays. *J. Exp. Psychol. Anim. Behav. Process.* 29: 14–22.

Collett M, Collett TS, and Wehner R (1999) Calibration of vector navigation in desert ants. *Curr. Biol.* 9(18): 1031–1034.

Collett M, Harland D, and Collett TS (2002) The use of landmarks and panoramic context in the performance of local vectors by navigating bees. *J. Exp. Biol.* 205: 807–814.

Collett TS, Cartwright BA, and Smith BA (1986) Landmark learning and visuo-spatial memories in gerbils. *J. Comp. Physiol. A* 158: 835–851.

Collett TS and Collett M (2002) Memory use in insect visual navigation. *Nat. Rev. Neurosci.* 3: 542–552.

Collett TS and Graham P (2004) Animal navigation: Path integration, visual landmarks and cognitive maps. *Curr. Biol.* 14(12): R475–477.

Conklin J and Eliasmith C (2005) A controlled attractor network model of path integration in the rat. *J. Comput. Neurosci.* 18(2): 183–203.

Dale K, Harland DP, Manning-Jones A, and Collett TS (2005) Weak and strong priming cues in bumblebee contextual learning. *J. Exp. Biol.* 208(Pt 1): 65–74.

Dally JM, Emery NJ, and Clayton NS (2005a) Cache protection strategies by western scrub-jays, *Aphelocoma californica*: Implications for social cognition. *Anim. Behav.* 70(6): 1251–1263.

Dally JM, Emery NJ, and Clayton NS (2005b) The social suppression of caching in western scrub-jays (*Aphelocoma californica*). *Behaviour* 142(7): 961–977.

de Kort SR, Dickinson A, and Clayton NS (2005) Retrospective cognition by food-caching western scrub-jays. *Learn. Motiv.* 36(2): 159–176.

Dickinson J and Dyer F (1996) How insects learn about the sun's course: Alternative modeling approaches. In: Maes P, Mataric MJ, Meyer J-A, Pollack J, and Wilson SW (eds.) *From Animals to Animats*, vol. 4, pp. 193–203. Cambridge, MA: MIT Press.

Durier V, Graham P, and Collett TS (2003) Snapshot memories and landmark guidance in wood ants. *Curr. Biol.* 13(18): 1614–1618.

Dyer FC (2002) The biology of the dance language. *Annu. Rev. Entomol.* 47: 917–949.

Dyer FC and Dickinson JA (1994) Development of sun compensation by honeybees: How partially experienced bees estimate the sun's course. *Proc. Natl. Acad. Sci. USA* 91: 4471–4474.

Dyer FC and Dickinson JA (1996) Sun-compass learning in insects: Representation in a simple mind. *Current Direction in Psychological Science* 5(3): 67–72.

Emery NJ and Clayton NS (2001) It takes a thief to know a thief: Effects of social context on prospective caching strategies in scrub jays. *Nature* 414: 443–446.

Emery NJ, Dally J, and Clayton NS (2004) Western scrub-jays (*Aphelocoma californica*) use cognitive strategies to protect their caches from thieving conspecifics. *Anim. Cogn.* 7: 37–43.

Etienne AS and Jeffery KJ (2004) Path integration in mammals. *Hippocampus* 14(2): 180–192.

Etienne AS, Maurer R, Boulens V, Levy A, and Rowe T (2004) Resetting the path integrator: A basic condition for route-based navigation. *J. Exp. Biol.* 207: 1491–1508.

Fanselow MS (1993) Associations and memories: The role of NMDA receptors and long-term potentiation. *Curr. Dir. Psychol. Sci.* 2(5): 152–156.

Foster DJ and Wilson MA (2006) Reverse replay of behavioural sequences in hippocampal place cells during the awake state. *Nature* 440(7084): 680–683.

Foster RG and Bellingham J (2004) Inner retinal photoreceptors (IRPs) in mammals and teleost fish. *Photochem. Photobiol. Sci.* 3(6): 617–627.

Foster RG, Hankins M, Lucas RJ, et al. (2003) Non-rod, non-cone photoreception in rodents and teleost fish. *Novartis Found. Symp.* 253: 3–23; discussion 23–30, 52–25, 102–109.

Frisch K (1967) *The Dance-Language and Orientation of Bees.* Cambridge, MA: Harvard University Press.

Fukushi T and Wehner R (2004) Navigation in wood ants *Formica japonica*: Context dependent use of landmarks. *J. Exp. Biol.* 207: 3431–3439.

Gallistel CR (1990) *The Organization of Learning.* Cambridge, MA: Bradford Books/MIT Press.

Gallistel CR (1998) Symbolic processes in the brain: The case of insect navigation. In: Scarborough D and Sternberg S (eds.) *An Invitation to Cognitive Science,* vol. 4, pp. 1–51. Cambridge, MA: MIT Press.

Gallistel CR (1999) Coordinate transformations in the genesis of directed action. In: Bly BM and Rumelhart D (eds.) *Cognitive Science (A Volume in Handbook of Perception and Cognition),* 2nd edn., pp. 1–42. San Diego: Academic Press.

Gallistel CR (2002) The principle of adaptive specialization as it applies to learning and memory. In: Kluwe RH, Lüer G, and Rösler F (eds.) *Principles of Human Learning and Memory,* pp. 250–280. Berlin: Birkenaeuser.

Gallistel CR (2006) The nature of learning and the functional architecture of the brain. In: Jing Q, Rosenzweig MR, Ydewalle G, Zhang H, Chen HC, and Zhang K (eds.) *Psychological Science around the World: Proceedings of the 28th International Congress of Psychology, Vol. 1: Neural, Cognitive and Developmental Issues,* pp. 63–71. Sussex, UK: Psychology Press.

Giunchi D, Mongini E, Pollonara E, and Baldaccini NE (2003) The effect of clock-shift on the initial orientation of wild rock doves (*Columba l. livia*). *Naturwissenschaften* 90(6): 261–264.

Gluck MA, Myers C, and Meeter M (2005) Cortico-hippocampal interaction and adaptive stimulus representation: A neurocomputational theory of associative learning and memory. *Neural Netw.* 18(9): 1265–1279.

Golob EJ, Stackman RW, Wong AC, and Taube JS (2001) On the behavioral significance of head direction cells: Neural and behavioral dynamics during spatial memory tasks. *Behav. Neurosci.* 115: 285–304.

Goossens HH and Van Opstal AJ (2006) Dynamic ensemble coding of saccades in the monkey superior colliculus. *J. Neurophysiol.* 95(4): 2326–2341.

Gould J and Gould CG (1988) *The Honey Bee.* New York: Freeman.

Grah G, Wehner R, and Ronacher B (2005) Path integration in a three-dimensional maze: Ground distance estimation keeps desert ants *Cataglyphis fortis* on course. *J. Exp. Biol.* 208: 4005–4011.

Graham P, Durier V, and Collett TS (2004) The binding and recall of snapshot memories in wood ants (*Formica rufa l.*). *J. Exp. Biol.* 207(Pt 3): 393–398.

Hafting T, Fyhn M, Molden S, Moser M-B., and Moser EI (2005) Microstructure of a spatial map in the entorhinal cortex. *Nature* 436: 802–806.

Halder G, Callaerts P, and Gehring WJ (1995) Induction of ectopic eyes by target expression of the eyeless gene in *Drosophila. Science* 267: 1788–1792.

Hawkins RD and Kandel ER (1984) Is there a cell-biological alphabet for simple forms of learning? *Psychol. Rev.* 91: 375–391.

Hay JB and Baayen RH (2005) Shifting paradigms: Gradient structure in morphology. *Trends in Cogn. Sci.* 9(7): 342–348.

Holst E and Mittelstaedt H (1950) The reafference principle (interaction between the central nervous system and the periphery) (English translation). In: *The Behavioral Physiology of Animals and Man. Selected Papers of E. von Holst,* vol. 1. Coral Gables, FL: University of Miami Press. 1973.

Homberg U (2004) In search of the sky compass in the insect brain. *Naturwissenschaften* 91(5): 199–208.

Hull CL (1952) *A Behavior System.* New Haven, CT: Yale University Press.

Ivry RB and Spencer RMC (2004) The neural representation of time. *Curr. Opin. Neurobiol.* 14: 225–232.

Kimchi T, Etienne AS, and Terkel J (2004) A subterranean mammal uses the magnetic compass for path integration. *Proc. Natl. Acad. Sci. USA* 101(4): 1105–1109.

Koch C and Hepp K (2006) Quantum mechanics in the brain. *Nature* 440: 611–612.

Kohler M and Wehner R (2005) Idiosyncratic route-based memories in desert ants, *Melophorus bagoti*: How do they interact with path-integration vectors? *Neurobiol. Learn. Mem.* 83(1): 1–12.

Konorski J (1967) *Integrative Activity of the Brain: An Interdisciplinary Approach.* Chicago: Chicago University Press.

Lee I, Yoganarasimha D, Rao G, and Knierim JJ (2004) Comparison of population coherence of place cells in hippocampal subfields Ca1 and Ca3. *Nature* 430(6998): 456–460.

Leon MI and Shadlen MN (2003) Representation of time by neurons in the posterior parietal cortex of the macaque. *Neuron* 38(2): 317–327.

Lindley D (2004) *Degrees Kelvin: A Tale of Genius, Invention and Tragedy.* Washington, DC: Joseph Henry Press.

Marr D (1982) *Vision.* San Francisco: W. H. Freeman.

McNaughton BL, Battaglia FP, Jensen O, Moser EI, and Moser M-B. (2006) Path integration and the neural basis of the 'cognitive map.' *Nat. Rev. Neurosci.* 7: 663–678.

Meck WH (ed.) (2003) *Functional and Neural Mechanisms of Interval Timing.* New York: CRC Press.

Menzel R, DeMarco RJ, and Greggers U (2006) Spatial memory, navigation and dance behaviour in *Apis mellifera. J. Comp. Physiol.* 192: 889–903.

Menzel R, Greggers U, Smith A, et al. (2005) Honey bees navigate according to a map-like spatial memory. *Proc. Natl. Acad. Sci. USA* 102(8): 3040–3045.

Mittelstaedt H and Mittelstaedt ML (1973) Mechanismen der Orientierung ohne richtende Aussenreize. *Fortschr. Zool.* 21: 46–58.

Mouritsen H and Frost BJ (2002) Virtual migration in tethered flying monarch butterflies reveals their orientation mechanisms. *Proc. Natl. Acad. Sci. USA* 99(15): 10162–10166.

Muller JR, Philiastides MG, and Newsome WT (2005) Microstimulation of the superior colliculus focuses attention without moving the eyes. *Proc. Natl. Acad. Sci. USA* 102(3): 524–529.

Muller RU (1996) A quarter of a century of place cells. *Neuron* 17: 813–822.

Newell A and Simon HA (1975) Computer science as empirical inquiry: Symbols and search. *Comm. Assoc. Comput. Mach.* 19: 113–136.

O'Keefe J and Nadel L (1978) *The Hippocampus as a Cognitive Map.* Oxford: Oxford University Press.

Pavlov IV (1928) *Lectures on Conditioned Reflexes: The Higher Nervous Activity of Animals* (H. Gantt, Trans.). London: Lawrence and Wishart.

Penney TB (2004) Electrophysiological correlates of interval timing in the stop RT task. *Cogn. Brain Res.* 21: 234–249.

Ranck JB Jr (1984) Head direction cells in the deep layer of dorsal presubiculum in freely moving rats. *Soc. Neurosci. Abstr.* 10(1): 599.

Rieke F, Warland D, de Ruyter van Steveninck R, and Bialek W (1997) *Spikes: Exploring the Neural Code.* Cambridge, MA: MIT Press.

Rumelhart DE and McClelland JL (1986) *Parallel Distributed Processing.* Cambridge, MA: MIT Press.

Samsonovich A and McNaughton BL (1997) Path integration and cognitive mapping in a continuous attractor neural network model. *J. Neurosci.* 17: 5900–5920.

Sargolini F, Fyhn M, Hafting T, et al. (2006) Conjunctive representation of position, direction, and velocity in entorhinal cortex. *Science* 312(5774): 758–762.

Schmidt-Koenig K (1960) The sun azimuth compass: One factor in the orientation of homing pigeons. *Science* 131: 826–827.

Schultz W and Dickinson A (2000) Neuronal coding of prediction errors. *Annu. Rev. Neurosci.* 23: 473–501.

Shannon CE (1948) A mathematical theory of communication. *Bell Syst. Tech. J.* 27: 379–423, 623–656.

Smolensky P (1986) Information processing in dynamical systems: Foundations of harmony theory. In: Rumelhart DE and McClelland JL (eds.) *Parallel Distributed Processing: Foundations*, vol. 1, pp. 194–281. Cambridge, MA: MIT Press.

Song P and Wang XJ (2005) Angular path integration by moving 'hill of activity': A spiking neuron model without recurrent excitation of the head-direction system. *J. Neurosci.* 25(4): 1002–1014.

Stalleicken J, Mukhida M, Labhart T, Wehner R, Frost B, and Mouritsen H (2005) Do monarch butterflies use polarized skylight for migratory orientation? *J. Exp. Biol.* 208(Pt 12): 2399–2408.

Stringer SM, Rolls ET, Trappenberg TP, and de Araujo IE (2002) Self-organizing continuous attractor networks and path integration: Two-dimensional models of place cells. *Network* 13(4): 429–446.

Takahashi JS, De Coursey PJ, Bauman L, and Menaker M (1984) Spectral sensitivity of a novel photoreceptive system mediating entrainment of mammalian circadian rhythms. *Nature* 308: 186–188.

Tautz J, Zhang SW, Spaethe J, Brockmann A, Si A, and Srinivasan MV (2004) Honeybee odometry: Performance in varying natural terrain. *PLoS Biol.* 2: 915–923.

Thompson W (1862) On the secular cooling of the earth. Paper read to the Royal Society of Edinburgh, April 28, 1862. In: *Mathematical and Physical Papers*, vol. 3, pp. 295–311 London: C. J. Clay and Sons.

Towne WF, Baer CM, Fabiny SJ, and Shinn LM (2005) Does swarming cause honey bees to update their solar ephemerides? *J. Exp. Biol.* 208(21): 4049–4061.

Turing AM (1936) On computable numbers, with an application to the Entscheidungsproblem. *Proc. Lond. Math. Soc.* 2nd ser. 42: 230–265.

Turing AM. (1950) Computing machinery and intelligence. *Mind* 59: 433–460.

Vander Wall SB (1990) *Food Hoarding in Animals.* Chicago: University of Chicago Press.

Wallace DG and Fountain SB (2003) An associative model of rat serial pattern learning in three-element sequences. *Q. J. Exp. Psychol. B* 56(3): 301–320.

Wehner J and Srinivasan MV (2003) Path integration in insects. In: Jeffery KJ (ed.) *The Neurobiology of Spatial Behaviour*, pp. 9–30. Oxford: Oxford University Press.

Wehner R and Srinivasan MV (1981) Searching behavior of desert ants, genus *Cataglyphis* (*formicidae*, hymenoptera). *J. Comp. Physiol.* 142: 315–338.

Yoganarasimha D, Yu X, and Knierim JJ (2006) Head direction cell representations maintain internal coherence during conflicting proximal and distal cue rotations: Comparison with hippocampal place cells. *J. Neurosci.* 26(2): 622–631.

1.13 Attention and Memory in Mammals and Primates

P. Dalton, Royal Holloway University of London, Egham, Surrey, UK

C. Spence, University of Oxford, Oxford, UK

1.13.1 Introduction

Our brains continuously receive huge amounts of sensory information concerning the busy and complicated world in which we live. In fact, Koch and Tsuchiya (2007) recently estimated that primates receive on the order of 1 megabyte of raw information per second through their eyes alone. In order to make sense of all of this sensory input, and to act upon it appropriately, it is essential that we are able to focus our attention selectively on certain stimuli at the expense of others (*See also* Chapters 1.07, 1.08). For example, as you read this sentence, you will probably be ignoring the feeling of the clothes on your body (see Graziano et al., 2002) and any number of background sounds from the world outside. In this chapter, we consider the extent to which our brains can achieve such selectivity of information processing in the visual, auditory, and tactile modalities and the means by which they might do so.

Empirical evidence from many different experimental methodologies now supports the claim that unattended sensory information is processed less thoroughly by the brain than is attended information. The results of many behavioral studies have demonstrated that unattended sensory information is perceived and/or remembered less successfully than attended information. From a neurophysiological viewpoint, attentional modulation of neural activity has now been observed both in humans and in other animals. Here, we review the evidence from both of these lines of research, integrating the findings that have emerged from studies examining the cognitive constraints on information processing in audition, vision, and touch – the sensory modalities where attention has, to date, been most widely studied. We also draw out a number of the parallels in the mechanisms of selective attention as they affect the processing of information in the different senses.

Our focus for this chapter relates to what has perhaps been one of the most enduring questions in the study of selective attention, namely, the stage of processing at which unattended information is excluded. It is generally agreed that all information must be processed to some level, so that it can, at the very least, be designated as being either potentially relevant or irrelevant. However, estimates of the extent to which unattended information is processed in the brain have varied widely. The lively debate over this issue has continued apace for more than 50 years and is still a topic of interest for many attention researchers today. Below, we describe the origins of the debate and highlight some of the most important experimental evidence that has emerged over the years from studies of this issue in audition, vision, and touch.

1.13.2 Behavioral Evidence for Early Selection

Many of the earliest studies of attention focused on the selection taking place within the auditory modality. This research began in the early 1950s with the development of the dichotic listening paradigm (Cherry, 1953, 1954). The participants in these early studies were typically presented with two different auditory messages, one to either ear. They had to repeat out loud (i.e., 'shadow') the message presented to a specified ear while trying to ignore the message presented simultaneously to the other (unattended) ear. The typical finding reported in many different studies was that following the shadowing task, participants were unable to remember anything of the unattended message apart from its most basic physical characteristics. For example, participants failed to notice (or at least to recall) changes to the language being spoken but were often able to recall changes in the pitch of the speaker's voice (e.g., Cherry, 1953). Indeed, Moray (1959) reported that participants often failed to recognize words that had been repeated as many as 35 times in the unattended channel. In the light of such evidence, researchers argued that attentional selection must occur at a relatively early stage of information processing, such that unattended stimuli were rejected as soon as their simple physical characteristics (such as their location, frequency, etc.) had been determined, and were not subject to any significant further processing (Broadbent, 1958). We note, however, that the definition of a "simple, physical characteristic" may not be as straightforward as it might at first seem (Allport, 1992). For example, properties that are coded early in processing in one sensory modality (such as location in vision) may only be derived much later in other sensory modalities (e.g., location is derived comparatively late in auditory processing; see Spence and Driver, 1994).

It is important to emphasize that these demonstrations of early selection assessed the extent of processing of the unattended information in terms of participants' subsequent memory for the content of the unattended stream. This approach was soon criticized on the grounds that, by the time the participants were asked about the contents of the unattended stream, they may simply have forgotten the information, rather than never having perceived it in the first place (see Wolfe, 1999, for a discussion of this critical distinction between inattentional amnesia and genuine inattentional blindness).

Nevertheless, the proposal that unattended stimuli were ruled out at a relatively early stage of information processing was also supported by subsequent studies examining the effectiveness of selective attention within the visual modality. At first, these visual studies drew inspiration from the auditory studies described above and were therefore typically designed to create a more or less direct visual analogue of the dichotic listening task. For example, in one of the earliest studies of visual selective attention, reported by Neisser and Becklen (1975), participants were presented with two superimposed video streams, one showing two people playing a hand-slapping game and the other showing three people passing a basketball between one another. The participants in this study had to attend to one of the two video streams in order to carry out a task on this attended information (such as counting the number of ball passes or hand slaps) while ignoring the other stream (in which unexpected events, such as the appearance of a new person carrying an umbrella, occasionally occurred). Just as had been found in previous auditory studies, the participants in Neisser and Becklen's study were unable to recall any of the unusual events in the unattended visual stream, despite the fact that this stream had been presented from the same location as the attended stream.

However, one might argue that the failure to remember the unattended information in Neisser and Becklen's (1975) seminal study could reflect the fact that participants would have been focusing their overt attention on the attended stream and hence may have been making eye movements to keep track of the action occurring in that stream. Any such eye movements may simply have reduced the visibility of the unattended stream (due to retinal smearing). Note that this criticism also applies to a number of the more recent demonstrations of inattentional blindness, in which participants have typically been asked to carry out a task based on the events contained within a single video (in contrast to earlier studies involving superimposed videos). The striking finding to have emerged from this type of research is that participants can remain seemingly unaware of apparently salient visual events (e.g., the appearance of a person in a gorilla outfit) occurring in the same video as the visual task (e.g., counting the number of ball passes occurring in a basketball game) (Simons and Chabris, 1999). However, because the unexpected visual event never completely coincides spatially with the attended events, these findings are also open to alternative explanations in terms of participants' eye movements.

We note that early studies of selective attention may have used auditory stimuli (at least in part) in an attempt to rule out potential alternative explanations of any attentional effects obtained in terms of overt orienting involving eye movements. However, subsequent research has now demonstrated that eye movements can in fact influence auditory attentional allocation during dichotic listening tasks (Gopher, 1973; Hynd et al., 1986), so this assumption may not, after all, have been valid.

Nevertheless, results in favor of early selection have also been found in studies that have controlled for the potential influence of eye movements. For example, Rock and Gutman (1981) presented the participants in their study with pairs of superimposed outline drawings (either familiar or nonsense shapes) in different colors. The participants had to focus their attention on the line drawings that were presented in a particular color (with the dummy task of rating each drawing's pleasantness) while attempting to ignore the drawings presented in the other color. In a subsequent surprise memory test, the participants were often unable to recognize any of the unattended shapes, even if the test occurred no more than a second after the presentation of the shape in question (see Rock and Gutman's Experiment 4). By contrast, participants' performance on a similar memory test for the attended shapes was fairly good. The use of static presentation in this experimental design helped to reduce the likelihood that eye movements played any role in determining the pattern of results obtained (an assertion that was confirmed by the monitoring of the eye position of a subset of the participants in Rock and Gutman's Experiment 1).

However, all of the above findings of early visual selection (along with any research that attempted to assess the processing of unattended information in terms of the participants' memories for that information) are open to the criticism, already mentioned in relation to the research on auditory selective attention, that the unattended information may have been perceived but then rapidly forgotten, rather than not having been perceived at all (Wolfe, 1999). Nevertheless, the recent development of brain imaging techniques has allowed researchers to assess the neural processing of unattended information more directly, thereby removing the need to rely on participants' memory for the information. The neuroimaging approach has also provided evidence in favor of early selection. For example, Rees et al. (1999) presented the participants in their study with a series of pictures, each one superimposed with a string of letters (which formed a familiar word on certain trials but consisted of a meaningless string of letters on others). Note that the use of superimposed

visual stimuli in this experimental design is similar to that of Rock and Gutman (1981) described earlier. The participants in Rees et al.'s study had to detect immediate stimulus repetitions, either in the picture stream or in the letter stream. When the participants attended to the stream of letter stimuli, the neural activity elicited by the words differed from that elicited by the nonwords (i.e., the random letter strings). However, when the participants were attending to the pictures, the neural activity elicited by the words and nonwords did not differ significantly. This result suggests that the unattended words were not even being processed to the level at which they would have been differentiated from nonwords, despite the fact that the participants were looking directly at them (because they were presented at fixation). Thus it seems that unattended visual stimuli can be eliminated from processing at a relatively early stage, at least under the particular experimental conditions used by Rees et al.

It should, however, be noted that a more recent event-related potential (ERP) study by Ruz et al. (2005), based closely on the experimental design reported by Rees et al. (1999) in their functional magnetic resonance imaging (fMRI) study, found a somewhat different pattern of results. Specifically, they observed that the patterns of ERP components elicited by words and nonwords differed significantly, even when the letter stimuli were not attended. This result would appear to suggest that unattended stimuli can be processed to a semantic (and therefore relatively 'late') level after all. Given that the experimental designs used in the two studies were so similar, this difference in the pattern of results seems likely to be due to the differences in the relative sensitivity of fMRI and ERP techniques. Note, however, that Ruz et al. found that the nature of the word processing (as indicated by the differences in patterns of ERP components elicited by words and by nonwords) was different in the unattended and attended conditions. Thus, even though Ruz et al.'s results suggest that semantic processing of unattended stimuli can occur to some extent, they nevertheless suggest that unattended stimuli are processed differently (and presumably less thoroughly) than attended stimuli. The suggestion that unattended stimuli might in fact be processed to a semantic level of information processing is supported by a large amount of behavioral evidence, as described in the following section.

1.13.3   Behavioral Evidence for Late Selection

Despite the above evidence in favor of early selection, behavioral research has also provided much evidence to suggest that supposedly 'unattended' stimuli can in fact be processed to a degree beyond that of the simple registration of their physical characteristics. As with the evidence for early selection, these observations began with research on the dichotic listening paradigm. For example, Moray (1959) reported that many of the participants in his now classic study remembered hearing their own name when it was presented unexpectedly in the unattended channel (along with some instructions that followed the name in that channel). By contrast, the participants could not remember those same unattended instructions if they were not preceded by the participant's name (indeed, Moray demonstrated that participants could not even remember words that had actually been presented 35 times in the unattended stream).

In addition, other researchers found that participants could often be influenced implicitly by the information being presented in the unattended stream, even if they could not later recall it explicitly. For example, Mackay (1973) presented ambiguous sentences to the participant's attended ear (e.g., "they threw stones toward the bank yesterday"), along with disambiguating information to the unattended ear (e.g., 'river' or 'money'). A subsequent memory test (based this time on recognition of the attended information) suggested that the participants had resolved the meaning of the ambiguous sentences in line with the information presented to the unattended ear, despite being unable to recall the content of this stream explicitly.

Corteen and Dunn (1974; see also Corteen and Wood, 1972) also reported an elegant study in which they showed that people could process unattended stimuli to the level at which semantic information became available, without any explicit awareness of having done so. In particular, they conditioned their participants to expect a small electric shock upon hearing a city name. Then, during dichotic listening, they presented city names to the participant's unattended ear, with the additional instruction that participants should press a button every time they heard a city name. Less than 1% of the city names were explicitly detected by the participants. However more than 30% of the city

names elicited a galvanic skin response (GSR), consistent with the sound of the city name triggering a small psychophysiological fear response, presumably linked with the expectation of the electric shock. This finding suggests that the information in the unattended ear had been processed to a semantic level. Importantly, GSRs were even found for city names that had not been presented during the training phase of the experiment, thus demonstrating that the unattended names had been processed to a level at which semantic generalization had become possible. Based on findings such as these, late selection theorists (e.g., Deutsch and Deutsch, 1963) proposed that information was processed to a semantic level before being filtered out of the processing stream.

This proposal soon received support from studies of visual selective attention, as significant behavioral evidence emerged to suggest that, in many cases, unattended visual stimuli could be processed to a deeper level than had at first been thought. For example, many studies have now shown that participants' responses can be primed by the semantic content of apparently ignored visual stimuli. For instance, Tipper (1985) presented participants with superimposed line drawings and asked them to attend to the drawing in one color and to ignore the drawing presented in the other color. The participants had to try and name the object represented by each of the attended pictures. Tipper reported that participants' responses to a particular attended stimulus were affected by the identity of the stimulus presented on the immediately preceding trial, whether or not that previous stimulus had been attended. For example, the participants were able to name a picture of a dog more rapidly if they had named a dog (or a semantically related item, such as a cat) on the preceding trial than if they had previously named a neutral stimulus (such as a chair). This effect is often referred to as positive priming. In contrast, if participants had previously ignored a picture of a dog (or a semantically related item), they were found to be slower to name the picture of the dog on a subsequent trial (as compared with having previously ignored a neutral stimulus) – a result that is now commonly referred to as negative priming. Thus, even though participants were unable to recall the unattended stimuli explicitly (as shown on occasional catch trials in which they were asked to report the unattended stimulus but frequently failed to do so), their performance was nevertheless influenced by these stimuli at a semantic level. This result suggests that unattended visual stimuli can often be processed to a relatively advanced stage. In fact, Tipper (1985) suggested that the relatively poor subsequent recall of the unattended items in his study reflected the fact that the representation of these stimuli had been inhibited, following the relatively extensive processing necessary for producing priming effects (see also Tipper and Cranton, 1985; Tipper and Driver, 1988). Tipper went on to suggest that this inhibitory process might have been responsible for people's failures to remember the unattended information when subsequently tested (e.g., as found in the early dichotic listening studies). This view would appear to support an account of the early selection findings in terms of inattentional amnesia (aided by the inhibition of the representation of unattended stimuli), rather than inattentional blindness.

Another very popular task developed by cognitive psychologists in the attempt to determine the extent to which irrelevant distractors are processed has become known as the flanker task (Eriksen and Eriksen, 1974). Participants in a typical study are asked to respond to a central target letter, which is flanked by one or more distractor letters (which participants have to try and ignore). The distractor letters can be associated with responses that are congruent, incongruent, or neutral with respect to the target response. If the unattended distractors received no processing whatsoever, one would expect there to be no difference in target responses (in terms of participants' speeded response latencies or accuracy) as a function of the type of distractor that has been presented. If, however, the distractors are processed to some extent, then target performance would be expected to be better on congruent trials and worse on incongruent trials, as compared with performance on neutral trials. Thus, cognitive psychologists can infer the extent to which distractor stimuli are processed from the magnitude of any congruency effects observed in the target discrimination task (where congruency effects are usually calculated in terms of the impairment of performance seen on incongruent trials relative to that seen on the neutral or congruent trials). Eriksen and Eriksen's original study (along with many subsequent studies) demonstrated significant congruency effects due to the visual distractors, implying that, at least under certain conditions, the distractors could be processed to the level at which responses are programmed despite being irrelevant to the task.

The flanker paradigm has recently been extended to the auditory modality. Chan et al. (2005) presented participants with three simultaneous voices, each saying a different word from a different spatial location. On each trial, the participants had to make a speeded discrimination response regarding the identity of the word spoken by the central speaker, while trying to ignore the distracting words being spoken by the speakers situated to either side of the central speaker (at spatial separations varying between 30 and 90 degrees). Just as shown previously in the visual modality, the participants responded significantly more slowly (and less accurately) on the incongruent trials than on the congruent distractor trials, thus showing interference by task-irrelevant distractors in the auditory modality.

Generally speaking, there has been much less research on selective attention within the tactile modality than there has been in either vision or audition. However, this area of research has begun to grow over the last few years and is now attracting considerable empirical interest (see Johansen-Berg and Lloyd, 2000; Spence, 2002; Gallace and Spence, 2007) related, at least in part, to the very real practical implications that are now emerging in the area of tactile interface design (see Gallace et al., in press, for a recent review). For example, laboratory-based research has established tactile analogues of the Eriksen flanker paradigm already described. In one such study, Evans and Craig (1992) asked their participants to discriminate the direction of a moving tactile stimulus on one finger while ignoring a moving distractor presented to another finger. The participants responded more rapidly and more accurately when the direction of the distractor stimulus was congruent (vs. incongruent) with that of the target stimulus, suggesting that the tactile distractor was processed to a level at which it was able to influence responses, despite being clearly irrelevant to the task.

More recently, Soto-Faraco et al. (2004) developed a tactile response competition paradigm using static (rather than moving) tactile stimuli. The participants in their study had to discriminate the elevation of a series of continuous target vibrations (presented to either the top or bottom of a foam cube held in one hand) whilst trying to ignore pulsed distractor vibrations (presented to the other hand at an elevation that was either congruent or incongruent with that of the target stimulus). In line with the results of Evans and Craig's (1992) earlier study, Soto-Faraco et al. observed significantly better performance when the elevation of the vibrotactile distractor was congruent (vs. incongruent) with that of the tactile target, suggesting that the distractors were processed despite being entirely irrelevant to the participants' task (see also Driver and Grossenbacher, 1996). Note that, although these distractor congruency effects were most pronounced when the target hand was unpredictable, the same pattern of results (although somewhat reduced in magnitude) was also found when the target hand was made predictable throughout a block of trials. Thus tactile distractors can interfere with the processing of tactile targets, even when targets and distractors are made clearly distinguishable from one another spatially (thus allowing for the focusing of a participant's selective attention on the target hand). This might be taken as preliminary evidence that attentional selection within the tactile modality occurs relatively late in information processing. Indeed, subsequent research by Soto-Faraco et al. found that the magnitude of the tactile interference effect was modulated both by actual changes in the separation between the participant's hands (implying a role for proprioception in guiding selection) and by illusory changes in hand separation, induced by a mirror illusion (implying a role for visual information prior to tactile selection). This suggests that tactile selective attention was operating upon a representation of the tactile stimuli that was derived subsequent to the multisensory integration of tactile, proprioceptive, and visual information. This finding supports the idea that tactile selection occurs relatively late in information processing. However, it should be noted that little of the research on tactile selective attention has been designed specifically to address questions of early versus late selection. More research on this question might therefore be useful in the future.

Taken together, there is now a considerable body of evidence from research in audition, vision, and touch to suggest that supposedly unattended information can in fact be processed beyond the level of the simple registration of its physical features. However, as was the case with the research taken to support early selection, these findings have been subject to several alternative interpretations. For example, one particularly important criticism relating to all of the experiments that have provided evidence in favor of late selection is that although participants are asked to ignore the irrelevant information (and presumably attempt to do as they have been instructed), they may nevertheless fail to ignore this information completely, despite their best intentions. Any observations of semantic processing of the unattended information could therefore reflect failures in attentional focus, rather than necessarily indicating extensive processing of truly unattended material (e.g., Holender, 1986).

Indeed, there is some evidence to suggest that, under certain conditions, the apparent processing of unattended information can be prevented when controls are taken to ensure that the unattended information remains genuinely unattended. For example, Lachter et al. (2004) asked the participants in their study to decide on each trial whether a target stimulus constituted a word or a nonword (this is often referred to as a lexical decision task). Each target was preceded by a prime word, which was presented very briefly and then 'masked' (i.e., replaced by other visual stimuli to ensure that no trace of the original visual stimulus remained). The prime word was either identical to the target word or unrelated to it. Participants in this type of experiment are typically faster and more accurate on the lexical decision task when the target and prime are identical, as compared with when they are unrelated (an effect known as repetition priming). However, Lachter et al. (2004) demonstrated that this effect could be eliminated if the participants were prevented from paying any attention to the prime stimuli (e.g., by presenting the primes at an unattended location and for a duration that was too short to allow a shift of attention to that location). This suggests, in line with earlier results (e.g., Rees et al., 1999), that genuinely unattended words can be eliminated from information processing at a reasonably early stage. Indeed, Lachter et al. put forward a robust defense of Broadbent's (1958) original model of early selection based on their data and on the argument (mentioned above) that all evidence in favor of late selection can actually be explained in terms of a process they term slippage, in which attention is inadvertently paid to task-irrelevant items (see also Wood and Cowan (1995a,b) for evidence to suggest that hearing one's own name in the unattended stream during dichotic listening might reflect the consequences of a temporary failure of selective attention, rather than the semantic processing of unattended information). It should be noted that to date, the findings to support Lachter et al.'s claims relate only to very specific experimental paradigms and conditions. It will be interesting to see whether the finding that late selection results can be eliminated by preventing slips of attention can be generalized more widely.

1.13.4 Neural Mechanisms of Selective Attention

The behavioral evidence outlined in the previous two sections suggests that, under some circumstances, unattended information can be eliminated from information processing at a very early stage (see also Driver, 2001, for a review). This idea has been supported by neuroscientific findings suggesting that spatial attention can modulate even the very early stages of neural information processing in the auditory, visual, and tactile modalities.

One important advantage of the neuroscientific approach (as compared to the cognitive psychological approach described earlier) is that it has allowed researchers to examine whether the activation of specific brain areas at identifiable points in particular hierarchies of information processing can be modulated by attention. This approach might therefore appear to be able to provide more concrete definitions of early and late selection effects than those provided by the cognitive approach (see Allport (1992) for a discussion of some of the problems faced by cognitive researchers in this regard). However, it is important to emphasize that the notion that information passes sequentially through strict neural processing hierarchies has little support these days. For example, it is now generally agreed that visual information processing involves feedback (or 'recurrent') processing, in which later areas feed information back to earlier areas (Lamme et al., 1998). Indeed, some researchers have argued that such recurrent processing is essential for visual awareness (Lamme, 2003). In addition, there is reliable evidence to suggest that different aspects of incoming information can be processed in parallel by the brain, as demonstrated in vision (e.g., see Goodale and Milner (1992) for a review of evidence to support the existence of two parallel processing streams – known as the 'ventral' and 'dorsal' streams – in the neural processing of visual information), in hearing (see Rauschecker and Tian (2000) and Alain et al. (2001) for suggestions that a similar distinction may also apply to the processing of auditory stimuli), and in touch (see Pons et al. (1992) for early work on the possible parallel processing of different aspects of tactile information).

Nevertheless, the mounting evidence that even primary sensory areas (through which it is agreed that all incoming information from that particular sensory modality must pass) can be subject to attentional modulation is often taken to support an early selection view. In addition, researchers have sought to demonstrate that attentional modulations can occur soon after stimulus onset, providing a definition of early selection in terms of processing time rather than brain region. Below we discuss the evidence for attentional modulations of visual, auditory, and tactile information processing at stages that are defined as early either in terms of brain area or in terms of processing time, or both. We then examine the contribution that these findings have made to the question of the extent to which unattended information is processed. Note that our discussion here is focused on the neural mechanisms of spatially selective attention (rather than attention to other, nonspatial stimulus attributes) simply because this is the area in which the majority of the research has been carried out.

1.13.4.1 Audition

There is now considerable evidence to suggest that spatial attention can affect the early stages of auditory information processing (see Giard et al. (2000) for a review). One fruitful line of research has used ERP recording to assess neural processing of auditory information. In a typical design, participants are asked to attend to auditory stimuli presented at a particular location while attempting to ignore task-irrelevant stimuli at another spatial location. ERPs elicited by stimuli presented at the attended location are then compared with the ERPs elicited by the same stimuli when that location is unattended. Although there is no physical difference between the stimuli, they typically elicit different ERP patterns even at relatively short latencies after stimulus presentation, thus suggesting that auditory selective attention can have an important effect even on early perceptual processes. Specifically, the amplitudes of certain early, sensory-related ERP components elicited by attended stimuli have been shown to be greater than those elicited by unattended stimuli, with these differences starting as early as 60–80 ms after stimulus presentation (Hillyard et al., 1973; Näätänen et al., 1978; Hansen and Hillyard, 1983). There is now even some evidence to suggest that, under certain conditions, these differences can occur as early as 20–50 ms after stimulus presentation (Hoormann et al., 2000).

Neuroimaging studies of spatially selective auditory attention have also demonstrated that paying attention to the location of auditory stimuli (as compared with ignoring those very same stimuli) can activate areas of primary auditory cortex as well as temporal lobe auditory association areas (O'Leary et al., 1997; Alho et al., 1999). In line with the ERP research described above, this research implies that selective attention can have effects on relatively early stages of auditory information processing.

This assertion is further strengthened by studies using single-cell recording techniques in nonhuman primates, in which researchers have been able to measure the responses of individual neurons while an animal performs a particular task. This type of research has also demonstrated an attentional modulation of neuronal responses in auditory cortex (Benson and Hienz, 1978). Thus, overall, the neuroscientific research appears to agree that attentional modulations can occur very soon after stimulus onset and in brain areas that are involved in the early processing of auditory information.

1.13.4.2 Vision

There is also a consensus in the neuroscience community that spatial attention can modulate the early stages of processing of visual information. For example, O'Connor et al. (2002) carried out an fMRI study in which the participants either had to attend to a checkerboard stimulus or else attend to the other side of the screen (while the checkerboard remained present but was relatively unattended). Activity levels in the visual cortex (pooled in this case across several early visual processing areas, including primary visual cortex) were found to be higher in the attended condition than in the unattended condition. This result has been replicated frequently throughout the literature (see Kastner (2004) for a review). However, O'Connor et al. extended previous findings by demonstrating that this attentional modulation effect could also be found in the lateral geniculate nucleus (LGN) of the thalamus – a brain area that is known to be involved in the very early processing of visual information.

The finding that spatial attention can modulate brain areas that are involved in the early processing of visual information has been accompanied by findings of attentional modulations of certain visual ERP components soon after stimulus onset (for reviews see Mangun, 1995; Hillyard et al., 1998). Several studies have also combined brain imaging with ERP recording in order to exploit the high temporal resolution of ERP techniques as well as the relatively

high spatial resolution of PET or fMRI. For example, Heinze et al. (1994) used positron emission tomography (PET) and ERP recording to demonstrate an attentional modulation of responses in certain areas of visual cortex within 80–130 ms of stimulus onset.

Similar findings have also emerged from studies of attentional function at the neuronal level using single-cell recording techniques in nonhuman primates. In fact, there is now reliable evidence to suggest that spatial attention can modulate the responses of individual neurons throughout the macaque visual system (see Treue (2001) for a review). However, findings relating to the issue of whether or not neural responses in primary visual cortex (V1) are subject to attentional modulation have, until fairly recently, been rather mixed (see Posner and Gilbert (1999) for a review). For example, Moran and Desimone (1985) and Luck et al. (1997) both failed to find any attentional modulation of the activity of V1 neurons, despite finding clear evidence for attentional effects occurring in other early visual areas (e.g., in V2 and V4). Nevertheless, there is now an increasing body of evidence that V1 neurons can be subject to attentional modulation, at least under certain conditions (see Treue (2001) for a review). For example, Roelfsema et al. (1998) devised a task in which their monkeys had to fixate a dot, which was then joined to one of two curves, each leading to another dot. The monkey's task was to make an eye movement to the dot that was joined by the curve originating from the fixation dot. Using this task, a curve passing through a particular area of the visual field could either be made a target (by connecting it to the fixation dot) or a distractor (by not connecting it). Thus, the same cell's receptive field (RF) could fall on the target curve in one trial and on the distractor curve in another trial. Recordings were taken from 45 neurons in the primary visual cortex of two monkeys. Overall, firing rates were higher when the RF fell on a target curve than when it fell on a distractor curve, indicating that neuronal responses in primary visual cortex could be modulated by the attentional demands of the monkey's task.

Given the variability of the results concerning the attentional modulation of V1, it is perhaps not so surprising that studies looking at the possible attentional modulation of LGN neurons have also reported mixed results. Although there is some limited evidence to suggest that the activity of neurons within the LGN can be modulated by attention (Vanduffel et al., 2000), the few single-cell recording studies in this area have usually failed to find attentional effects at this very early level of information processing (e.g., Mehta et al., 2000; Bender and Youakim, 2001). Nevertheless, taken together, the findings from visual neuroscience studies in humans and nonhuman primates appear to agree that the attentional modulation of neural processing can occur in brain areas involved in the early stages of visual information processing and within around 100 ms of stimulus onset.

1.13.4.3 Touch

Just as we have seen to be the case for both audition and vision, the neuroscientific evidence also suggests that attention can affect the early stages of the neural processing of tactile information (see Johansen-Berg and Lloyd (2000) for a review). For example, researchers have demonstrated attentional modulations of ERP components relating to tactile perception as early as 80 ms after the onset of a tactile stimulus (Eimer and Forster, 2003).

Similarly, attentional effects in primary somatosensory cortex (S1) have been demonstrated in humans using fMRI (Johansen-Berg et al., 2000) and PET (Meyer et al., 1991). Note, however, that these results might depend on the exact parameters of the experimental design used, as other studies have failed to demonstrate clear attentional effects on activity in S1 (Mima et al., 1998; Burton et al., 1999), although these studies have nevertheless often demonstrated attentional modulation of other (later) somatosensory areas (e.g., S2).

This overall pattern of results is supported by a small number of single-cell recording studies demonstrating a significant attentional modulation of neuronal responses in primary somatosensory cortex (Hyvarinen et al., 1980; Hsiao et al., 1993). Thus, although there has been less research performed on the neural mechanisms of tactile selective attention than there has been on the mechanisms of visual and auditory attention, the available research appears to agree that attention can modulate the early stages of tactile information processing.

1.13.4.4 Implications for the Early versus Late Debate

Overall, there is a significant body of evidence to suggest that attentional modulation of visual, auditory, and tactile information can occur in brain areas

involved with early information processing and at times very soon after stimulus onset (see also Driver and Frackowiak (2001) for a review). However, the fact that the brain differentiates between attended and unattended inputs at an early stage of processing does not necessarily mean that unattended information is ruled out of processing altogether at that stage. Instead, these results simply demonstrate that attended and unattended stimuli are differentiated from this stage of processing onward. In fact, most of the studies described above demonstrated an attenuated response to unattended stimuli, rather than no response at all. Nevertheless, the research might suggest that unattended stimuli become less and less well represented as processing proceeds. For example, the extent to which attention can modulate neuronal activity has been seen to increase throughout the visual system, such that the attentional modulations of activity in V1 are typically smaller in magnitude than those elicited by the same experimental manipulation to activity in a higher visual area such as, for example, V4 (Kastner et al., 1998; Martinez et al., 1999; Mehta et al., 2000; O'Connor et al., 2002; Vibell et al., 2007). Recall that the research looking at possible attentional modulations of the neural processing of tactile information also found more reliable modulations in secondary somatosensory cortex than in primary somatosensory cortex (Mima et al., 1998). Such results might be taken to suggest that the neural representation of unattended stimuli is gradually reduced as processing progresses, rather than unattended stimuli necessarily being completely eliminated at one fixed point in information processing.

This suggestion would fit with the biased competition model of visual selective attention put forward by Desimone and Duncan (1995; reviewed in Duncan, 2006). According to this model, neuronal activity can be biased in favor of those neurons that respond to a particular attended stimulus. This initial prioritization of selected neurons gives them an advantage in their subsequent interactions with neurons that are not preferentially activated (because they do not respond to the attended stimulus). Thus, according to this model, unattended information would not be ruled out of processing at a particular point but would instead be subject to a continued bias against it throughout processing. This intermediate position is echoed in recent proposals for a resolution to the early versus late selection debate, as outlined here.

1.13.5   Possible Resolutions to the Debate

The studies reviewed so far all agree that, at some stage, attended information is processed with a higher priority than is unattended information. However, many of these studies differ in their estimates of the effects that this process of prioritization might have on the level to which the unattended information is processed. In contrast to the extreme positions espoused by the early selection theorists (e.g., Broadbent, 1958) and the late selection theorists (e.g., Deutsch and Deutsch, 1963), several researchers noted the variability of the findings and proposed compromise positions (see Shulman (1990) for a discussion of the dangers of failing to acknowledge the extent of the variability of the results in this research area). For example, Treisman (1960) proposed that unattended information was attenuated early in processing, rather than being filtered out completely. Her model accommodated the findings concerning the limited processing of unattended stimuli but also allowed for the possibility of further processing of this information if it were sufficiently salient (in which case, according to the model, it would be able to reach consciousness despite having been attenuated, because the thresholds for activating salient information were lower than for other information). This proposal of variable thresholds for triggering the processing of incoming information allowed for different participants to have different threshold levels for different types of information. Treisman's model was therefore capable of accounting for the observations of individual differences in the efficiency of selective attention, as described earlier (recall, for example, that Moray (1959) found that, although a subset of his participants noticed their own names when they were presented in the unattended ear, a significant number of participants did not). However, whereas these ideas relate mainly to the nature of the irrelevant information, subsequent research has indicated that the nature of the relevant information can also play a part in determining the amount of processing that unattended stimuli receive.

For example, Lavie (1995) reinvigorated the early/late selection debate by putting forward the suggestion that selection could occur either early or late in information processing, depending on the perceptual load of the relevant task (i.e., the demands placed on the perceptual system by that task; see Johnston and Heinz (1978) for an earlier hybrid model of selection). Lavie argued that the perceptual system has a limited capacity, but that all stimuli are automatically processed unless that capacity is exceeded. According to this view, selection can only occur at an early stage of information processing if the relevant task uses up all of the available processing capacity (i.e., under conditions of high perceptual load). If the perceptual load of the task is insufficient to exhaust the processing capacity, then distractors will be processed automatically, and selection will be seen to occur at a later stage of information processing.

In order to provide a direct test of this theory, Lavie (1995) assessed the performance of participants on a response competition task similar to that designed by Eriksen and Eriksen (1974; and described in the section titled 'Behavioral evidence for late selection'). Distractor interference was measured in terms of distractor congruency effects (in which responses are typically shown to be slower when distractors are associated with responses that are incongruent, vs. congruent, with the target response). Lavie also manipulated the demands of the target task, such that the perceptual load was either high (e.g., searching for an N among several other letters) or low (e.g., searching for an N among Os). Lavie reported that the participants were able to ignore the distractors more effectively (implying early selection) under conditions of high perceptual load than under conditions of low perceptual load (implying later selection in this case).

The idea that the stage of processing at which selection occurs can vary depending on the perceptual load of the relevant task has now been supported by a number of subsequent studies (Lavie, 2000; 2005). For example, Rees et al. (1997) carried out an fMRI study in which the participants viewed a peripheral display of moving dots that was irrelevant to a word-based task presented at fixation. Neural activity in motion areas MT/MST was reduced when the word-based task was highly demanding (i.e., identifying words containing two syllables) as compared to when it was less demanding (i.e., identifying words written in uppercase vs. in lowercase letters). This suggests, in line with perceptual load theory, that the neural processing of the irrelevant information was modulated by the perceptual demands of the relevant task. Similar effects have now been shown as early in visual processing as the LGN (O'Connor et al., 2002).

Given the wide range of experimental evidence now supporting perceptual load theory, it is often considered to have provided something of a resolution to the long-running early/late selection debate (although see Eltiti et al. (2005) for a possible alternative account of certain findings in terms of distractor salience). However, it is important to note that, as yet, no independent measure of perceptual load has been provided. Instead, researchers have had to rely on operational definitions, based on observations that a given manipulation of perceptual load worked in a given experimental setting. (Note that this raises particular problems when trying to interpret the results of studies where a manipulation of perceptual load is found to have no effect on distractor processing.)

Another possible limitation of the research in this area so far is that it has concentrated almost exclusively on perceptual load within the visual modality (although see Alain and Izenberg (2003) for evidence that ERP components elicited by deviant – yet task-irrelevant – auditory stimuli can be reduced under a high (vs. low) perceptual load in a relevant auditory task). Given that this line of investigation began with experiments looking at audition (with the dichotic listening paradigm) and has since expanded to look at attentional processes within the somatosensory modality, it would seem important to test the predictions of the perceptual load theory within those sensory modalities, as well as between combinations of different sensory modalities.

Despite a relative lack of unimodal studies of perceptual load effects in audition and touch, there have been a small number of recent studies that have investigated the possibility of crossmodal perceptual load effects. One possible advantage of this line of investigation is that it might provide a test of whether the limited perceptual capacity described within the perceptual load theory is modality specific (Wickens, 1984, 1992) or whether instead it consists of a common pool of processing resources that is shared between the different sensory modalities.

There is some variability in the results of the small amount of research published on this question so far, with some studies having failed to find reliable crossmodal effects of perceptual load (Rees et al., 2001; Tellinghuisen and Nowak, 2003), while others have found some suggestion of crossmodal effects (e.g., Otten et al., 2000). This variation in the results of the studies of crossmodal perceptual load might be related to the lack of an independent measure of the extent of the load imposed on the perceptual system

by a particular task. It could, for example, be argued that any failures to demonstrate significant crossmodal perceptual load effects may have been due to the studies in question simply using too weak a manipulation of perceptual load. For example, the auditory discrimination of the number of syllables, used in a crossmodal study by Rees et al. (2001), is likely to have been much easier than the discrimination of the number of syllables in words presented visually, which was used in their successful intramodal study of perceptual load in vision (Rees et al., 1997). Given these limitations of the research to date, it would seem premature to draw firm conclusions at the present time, especially given the general variability in the literature on the question of whether or not attentional resources are shared between the different sensory modalities (e.g., see Treisman and Davies, 1973; Martin, 1980; Spence et al., 2001; Soto-Faraco et al., 2002; Arnell, 2006, for successful demonstrations of crossmodal competition for attention; but see Duncan et al., 1997; Soto-Faraco and Spence, 2002; and Alais et al, 2006, for a failure to find any such crossmodal competition under slightly different experimental conditions).

Earlier, we outlined how the neuroscientific evidence appears to support a compromise position, suggesting that unattended stimuli might be gradually filtered out throughout information processing, rather than being completely eliminated from processing at one fixed point in the system. This suggestion from neuroscience, along with the behavioral evidence that unattended information receives more or less processing depending on the specific perceptual demands of the attended task (e.g., Lavie, 1995), would appear to agree that there is no fixed point at which unattended information is excluded from processing, but rather that the prioritization of processing is flexible, depending on the salience of the stimuli involved, the particular demands of the task at hand, and the current goals of the observer.

1.13.6 Working Memory and the Locus of Selection

There is also evidence to suggest that the extent to which unattended information is processed can vary from participant to participant. Recall, for example, that only one in three of Moray's (1959) participants noticed their own names being presented in the unattended stream. There is now evidence to suggest that this interparticipant variability might be related to individual differences in working memory capacity. For example, Conway et al. (2001) have shown that participants with lower working memory capacities, as assessed by their performance on the operation span task, in which participants are asked to remember short lists of words while carrying out mathematical operations (Turner and Engle, 1989), are more likely to notice their own name in the unattended stream in a dichotic listening experiment than participants with higher working memory capabilities. This finding suggests that working memory plays a key role in controlling attentional allocation, such that people with lower working memory capacities find it harder to control the deployment of their attentional resources. Note that such an interpretation might also imply, in line with the proposals of Holender (1986) and Lachter et al. (2004) mentioned earlier, that the semantic processing necessary to recognize one's own name in the unattended stream occurs as a result of the unintentional allocation of attention toward that stream (because if it simply reflected true semantic processing of all unattended information, there would have been no effect of individual working memory capacity on the likelihood of noticing the name). We note, however, that because Conway et al.'s study is correlational in nature, it cannot demonstrate a causal role for working memory in successful auditory selective attention (as it is also possible that participants' attentional abilities determined their performance on both tasks).

Nevertheless, further evidence has recently begun to emerge to support the suggestion of a causal role for working memory in control of selective attention, at least in the visual modality (De Fockert et al., 2001; Lavie et al., 2004). For example, Lavie et al. (2004) asked the participants in their study to respond to the identity of a target letter (X or Z) while ignoring a concurrently presented distractor letter, which could either be congruent with respect to the target letter (e.g., an X when the target was also an X) or incongruent (e.g., a Z when the target was an X). The participants carried out this task under conditions of either high working memory load (where they were asked to remember six randomly chosen digits) or low working memory load (where they only had to remember one digit). Incongruent distractors produced greater interference (by comparison with congruent distractors) under conditions of high working memory load than under low load conditions, suggesting that working memory availability is

important for minimizing interference by irrelevant stimuli, presumably through the active maintenance of current stimulus-processing priorities (see Lavie, 2005).

The latest research to emerge from our laboratory has suggested that working memory availability might also be important for the successful control of tactile selective attention. Dalton et al. (2006) asked the participants in their study to carry out a tactile response competition task similar to that used by Soto-Faraco et al. (2004), described earlier, under conditions of either high working memory load (in which the participants were asked to remember six randomly chosen digits) or low working memory load (in which the memory set always consisted of the digits 1–6 presented in ascending numerical order). In line with the results of the visual studies carried out by Lavie et al. (2004), Dalton et al. found that distractor congruency effects within the tactile modality were significantly larger under high working memory load than under low load, suggesting that working memory is also important for the control of tactile selective attention. Similar results have also emerged from a very recent study of the role of working memory in auditory selective attention (Dalton, Santangelo, and Spence, in preparation).

1.13.7 Summary

We have considered visual, auditory, and tactile research that has addressed the question of the extent to which unattended information is processed. While certain studies reported that participants are able to recall very little about information they had ignored (e.g., Cherry, 1953; Rees et al., 1999), other studies found evidence suggesting that supposedly ignored information had in fact been processed to a relatively late stage, involving semantic processing and/or response selection (e.g., Corteen and Dunn, 1974; Ruz et al., 2005). The emergence of these conflicting findings has led to a long-lasting debate in the literature over the exact stage of processing at which unattended information is excluded.

Proponents of early selection (e.g., Broadbent, 1958; Lachter et al., 2004) have argued that unattended information is filtered out early on in information processing, on the basis of simple physical characteristics. By contrast, late selection theorists (e.g., Deutsch and Deutsch, 1963) proposed that information was processed to a much deeper level before being excluded from the processing stream.

More recently, many researchers have converged on a more flexible position, in which the locus of selection can vary according to the task demands (Lavie, 2005), the salience of the stimuli (Eltiti et al., 2004), and the individual characteristics of the participant (Conway et al., 2001). When deeper processing of unattended stimuli is observed, it seems likely that it results from some level of attentional allocation toward the unattended stimuli, either due to inadvertent slips of attentional focus (e.g., Holender, 1986; Lachter et al., 2004) or due to automatic processing of irrelevant information under conditions of low perceptual load (e.g., Lavie, 2005). Research in recent years has also identified a key role for working memory in the control of selective attention, such that selection is more effective when working memory resources are available for the attention task than when they are not (e.g., Lavie et al., 2004).

References

Alain C, Arnott SR, Hevenor S, Graham S, and Grady CL (2001) "What" and "where" in the human auditory system. *Proc. Natl. Acad. Sci. USA* 98: 12301–12306.

Alain C and Izenberg A (2003) Effects of attentional load on auditory scene analysis. *J. Cogn. Neurosci.* 15: 1063–1073.

Alais D, Morrone C, and Burr D (2006) Separate attentional resources for vision and audition. *Proc. Biol. Sci.* 273: 1339–1345.

Alho K, Medvedev SV, Pakhomov SV, et al. (1999) Selective tuning of the left and right auditory cortices during spatially directed attention. *Brain Res. Cogn. Brain Res.* 7: 335–341.

Allport DA (1992) Selection and control: A critical review of 25 years. In: Meyer DE and Kornblum S (eds.), *Attention and Performance: Synergies in Experimental Psychology, Artificial Intelligence, and Cognitive Neuroscience,* vol. 14, pp. 183–218. Hillsdale, NJ: Erlbaum.

Arnell KM (2006) Visual, auditory, and cross-modality dual-task costs: Electrophysiological evidence for an amodal bottleneck on working memory consolidation. *Percept. Psychophys.* 68: 447–557.

Bender DB and Youakim M (2001) The effect of attentive fixation in macaque thalamus and cortex. *J. Neurophysiol.* 85: 219–234.

Benson DA and Hienz RD (1978) Single-unit activity in the auditory cortex of monkeys selectively attending left vs. right ear stimuli. *Brain Res.* 159: 307–320.

Broadbent DE (1958) *Perception and Communication.* Elmsford, NJ: Pergamon.

Burton H, Abend NS, MacLeod A-MK, Sinclair RJ, Snyder AZ, and Raichle ME (1999) Tactile attention tasks enhance activation in somatosensory regions of parietal cortex: A positron emission tomography study. *Cereb. Cortex* 9: 662–74.

Chan JS, Merrifield K, and Spence C (2005) Auditory spatial attention assessed in a flanker interference task. *Acta Acustica* 91: 554–563.

Cherry EC (1953) Some experiments upon the recognition of speech with one and two ears. *J. Acoust. Soc. Am.* 25: 975–979.

Cherry EC (1954) Some further experiments upon the recognition of speech, with one and with two ears. *J. Acoust. Soc. Am.* 26: 554–559.

Conway ARA, Cowan N, and Bunting MF (2001) The cocktail party phenomenon revisited: The importance of working memory capacity. *Psychon. Bull. Rev.* 8: 331–335.

Corteen RA and Dunn D (1974) Shock-associated words in an unattended message: A test for momentary awareness. *J. Exp. Psychol.* 102: 1143–1144.

Corteen RS and Wood B (1972) Autonomic responses to shock associated words in an unattended channel. *J. Exp. Psychol.* 94: 308–313.

Dalton P, Lavie N, and Spence C (2006) A visual working memory task interferes with tactile selective attention. Poster presented at the 2006 meeting of the International Multisensory Research Forum, Dublin, Ireland.

De Fockert J, Rees G, Frith C, and Lavie N (2001) The role of working memory load in selective attention. *Science* 291: 1803–1806.

Desimone R and Duncan J (1995) Neural mechanisms of selective visual attention. *Annu. Rev. Neurosci.* 18: 193–222.

Deutsch JA and Deutsch D (1963) Attention: Some theoretical considerations. *Psychol. Rev.* 70: 80–90.

Driver J (2001) A selective review of selective attention research from the past century. *Br. J. Psychol.* 92: 53–78.

Driver J and Frackowiak RSJ (2001) Neurobiological measures of human selective attention. *Neuropsychologia* 39: 1257–1262.

Driver J and Grossenbacher PG (1996) Multimodal spatial constraints on tactile selective attention. In: Inui T and McClelland JL (eds.) *Attention and Performance XVI: Information Integration in Perception and Communication,* pp. 209–235. Cambridge, MA: MIT Press.

Duncan J (2006) Brain mechanisms of attention. *Q. J. Exp. Psychol.* 59: 2–27.

Duncan J, Martens S, and Ward R (1997) Restricted attentional capacity within but not between sensory modalities. *Nature* 387: 808–810.

Eimer M and Forster B (2003) Modulations of early somatosensory ERP components by transient and sustained spatial attention. *Exp. Brain Res.* 151: 24–31.

Eltiti S, Wallace D, and Fox E (2005) Selective target processing: Perceptual load or distractor salience? *Percept. Psychophys.* 67: 876–885.

Eriksen BA and Eriksen CW (1974) Effects of noise letters upon the identification of a target letter in a nonsearch task. *Percept. Psychophys.* 16: 143–149.

Evans PM and Craig JC (1992) Response competition: A major source of interference in a tactile identification task. *Percept. Psychophys.* 51: 199–206.

Gallace A and Spence C (2007). The cognitive and neural correlates of "tactile consciousness": A multisensory perspective. *Conscious. Cogn.* [Epub ahead of print.].

Gallace A, Tan HZ, and Spence C (in press). The body surface as a communication system: The state of the art after 50 years. *Presence.*

Giard M-H, Fort A, Mouchetant-Rostaing Y, and Pernier J (2000) Neurophysiological mechanisms of auditory selective attention in humans. *Front. Biosci.* 5: 84–94.

Goodale MA and Milner AD (1992) Separate visual pathways for perception and action. *Trends Neurosci.* 15: 20–25.

Gopher D (1973) Eye-movement patterns in selective listening tasks of focused attention. *Percept. Psychophys.* 14: 259–264.

Graziano MSA, Alisharan SE, Hu X, and Gross CG (2002) The clothing effect: Tactile neurons in the precentral gyrus do not respond to the touch of the familiar primate chair. *Proc. Natl. Acad. Sci. USA* 99: 11930–11933.

Hansen JC and Hillyard SA (1983) Selective attention to multidimensional auditory stimuli. *J. Exp. Psychol. Hum. Percept. Perform.* 9: 1–19.

Heinze HJ, Mangun GR, Burchert W, et al. (1994) Combined spatial and temporal imaging of spatial selective attention in humans. *Nature* 392: 543–546.

Hillyard SA, Hink RF, Schwent VL, and Picton TW (1973) Electrical signs of selective attention in the human brain. *Science* 182: 177–179.

Hillyard SA, Vogel EK, and Luck SJ (1998) Sensory gain control (amplification) as a mechanism of selective attention: Electrophysiological and neuroimaging evidence. *Philos. Trans. R. Soc. Lond. B Biol. Sci.* 353: 1257–1270.

Holender D (1986) Semantic activation without conscious identification in dichotic listening, parafoveal vision, and visual masking: A survey and appraisal. *Behav. Brain Sci.* 9: 1–66.

Hoormann J, Falkenstein M, and Hohnsbein J (2000) Early attention effects in human auditory-evoked potentials. *Psychophysiology* 37: 29–42.

Horner DT (1997) The effect of shape and location on temporal masking of spatial vibrotactile patterns. *Percept. Psychophys.* 59: 1255–1265.

Hsiao SS, O'Shaughnessy DM, and Johnson KO (1993) Effects of selective attention of spatial form processing in monkey primary and secondary somatosensory cortex. *J. Neurophysiol.* 70: 444–447.

Hynd GW, Snow J, and Willis WG (1986) Visual-spatial orientation, gaze direction and dichotic listening asymmetries. *Cortex* 22: 313–317.

Hyvarinen J, Poranen A, and Jokinen Y (1980) Influence of attentive behavior on neuronal responses to vibration in primary somatosensory cortex of the monkey. *J. Neurophysiol.* 43: 870–882.

Johansen-Berg H, Christensen V, Woolrich M, and Matthews PM (2000) Attention to touch modulates activity in both primary and secondary somatosensory areas. *Neuroreport* 11: 1–5.

Johansen-Berg H and Lloyd DM (2000) The physiology and psychology of selective attention to touch. *Front. Biosci.* 5: D894-D904.

Johnston W and Heinz S (1978) Flexibility and capacity demands of attention. *J. Exp. Psychol. Gen.* 107: 420–435.

Kastner S (2004) Attentional response modulation in the human visual system. In: Posner MI (ed.) *Cognitive Neuroscience of Attention*, pp. 144–156. New York, NY: Guilford Press.

Kastner S, De Weerd P, Desimone R, and Ungerleider LG (1998) Mechanisms of directed attention in the human extrastriate cortex as revealed by functional MRI. *Science* 282: 108–111.

Koch C and Tsuchiya N (2007) Attention and consciousness: Two distinct brain processes. *Trends Cogn. Sci.* 11: 16–22.

Lachter J, Forster KI, and Ruthruff E (2004) Forty-five years after Broadbent (1958): Still no identification without attention. *Psychol. Rev.* 111: 880–913.

Lamme VAF (2003) Why visual attention and awareness are different. *Trends Cogn. Sci.* 7: 12–18.

Lamme VA, Super H, and Spekreijse H (1998) Feedforward, horizontal, and feedback processing in the visual cortex. *Curr. Opin. Neurobiol.* 8: 529–535.

Lavie N (1995) Perceptual load as a necessary condition for selective attention. *J. Exp. Psychol. Hum. Percept. Perform.* 21: 451–468.

Lavie N (2000) Selective attention and cognitive control: Dissociating attentional functions through different types of load. In: Monsell S and Driver J (eds.) *Attention and Performance: Vol. VXIII. Control of Cognitive Processes*, pp. 175–197. Cambridge, MA: MIT Press.

Lavie N (2005) Distracted and confused?: Selective attention under load. *Trends Cogn. Sci.* 9: 75–82.

Lavie N, Hirst A, De Fockert J, and Viding E (2004) Load theory of selective attention. *J. Exp. Psychol. Gen.* 133: 339–354.

Luck SJ, Chelazzi L, Hillyard SA, and Desimone R (1997) Neural mechanisms of spatial attention in areas V1, V2 and V4 of macaque visual cortex. *J. Neurophysiol.* 77: 24–42.

Mackay DG (1973) Aspects of the theory of comprehension, memory and attention. *Q. J. Exp. Psychol.* 25: 22–40.

Mangun GR (1995) Neural mechanisms of visual selective attention. *Psychophysiology* 32: 4–18.

Martin M (1980) Attention to words in different modalities: Four-channel presentation with physical and semantic selection. *Acta Psychol. (Amst.)* 44: 99–115.

Martinez A, Anllo-Vento L, Sereno MI, et al. (1999) Involvement of striate and extrastriate visual cortical areas in spatial attention. *Nat. Neurosci.* 2: 364–369.

Mehta AD, Ulbert I, and Schroeder CE (2000) Intermodal selective attention in monkeys II: Physiological mechanisms of modulation. *Cereb. Cortex* 10: 359–370.

Meyer E, Ferguson S, Zatorre RJ, et al. (1991) Attention modulates somatosensory CBF response to vibrotactile stimulation as measured by PET. *Ann. Neurol.* 29: 440–443.

Mima T, Nagamine T, Nakamura K, and Shibasaki H (1998) Attention modulates both primary and second somatosensory cortical activities in humans: A magnetoencephalographic study. *J. Neurophysiol.* 80: 2215–2221.

Moran J and Desimone R (1985) Selective attention gates visual processing in the extrastriate cortex. *Science* 229: 782–784.

Moray N (1959) Attention in dichotic listening: Affective cues and the influence of instructions. *Q. J. Exp. Psychol.* 11: 56–60.

Näätänen R, Gaillard AWK, and Mäntysalo S (1978) Early selective attention effect on evoked potential reinterpreted. *Acta Psychol. (Amst.)* 42: 313–329.

Neisser U and Becklen R (1975) Selective looking: Attending to visually specified events. *Cogn. Psychol.* 7: 480–494.

O'Connor DH, Fukui MM, Pinsk MA, and Kastner S (2002) Attention modulates responses in the human lateral geniculate nucleus. *Nat. Neurosci.* 5: 1203–1209.

O'Leary DS, Andreasen NC, Hurtig RR, et al. (1997) Auditory and visual attention assessed with PET. *Hum. Brain Mapp.* 5: 422–436.

Otten LJ, Alain C, and Picton TW (2000) Effects of visual attentional load on auditory processing. *Neuroreport* 11: 875–880.

Pons TP, Garraghty PE, and Mishkin M (1992) Serial and parallel processing of tactual information in somatosensory cortex of rhesus monkeys. *J. Neurophysiol.* 68: 518–527.

Posner MI and Gilbert CD (1999) Attention and primary visual cortex. *Proc. Natl. Acad. Sci. USA* 96: 2585–2587.

Rauschecker JP and Tian B (2000) Mechanisms and streams for processing of "what" and "where" in auditory cortex. *Proc. Natl. Acad. Sci. USA* 97: 11800–11806.

Rees G, Frith CD, and Lavie N (1997) Modulating irrelevant motion perception by varying attentional load in an unrelated task. *Science* 278: 1616–1619.

Rees G, Frith C, and Lavie N (2001) Processing of irrelevant visual motion during performance of an auditory attention task. *Neuropsychologia* 39: 937–949.

Rees G, Russell C, Frith CD, and Driver J (1999) Inattentional blindness versus inattentional amnesia for fixated but ignored words. *Science* 286: 2504–2507.

Rock I and Gutman D (1981) The effect of inattention on form perception. *J. Exp. Psychol. Hum. Percept. Perform.* 7: 275–285.

Roelfsema PR, Lamme VAF, and Spekreijse H (1998) Object-based attention in the primary visual cortex of the macaque monkey. *Nature* 395: 376–381.

Ruz M, Worden MS, Tudela P, and McCandliss BD (2005) Inattentional amnesia to words in a high attention load task. *J. Cogn. Neurosci.* 17: 768–776.

Shulman GL (1990) Relating attention to visual mechanisms. *Percept. Psychophys.* 47: 199–203.

Simons DJ and Chabris CF (1999) Gorillas in our midst: Sustained inattentional blindness for dynamic events. *Perception* 28: 1059–1074.

Soto-Faraco S, Ronald A, and Spence C (2004) Tactile selective attention and body posture: Assessing the contribution of vision and proprioception. *Percept. Psychophys.* 66: 1077–1094.

Soto-Faraco S, and Spence C (2002) Modality specific auditory and visual temporal processing deficits. *Q. J. Exp. Psychol.* 55A: 23–40.

Soto-Faraco S, Spence C, Fairbank K, Kingstone A, Hillstrom AP, and Shapiro K (2002) A crossmodal attentional blink between vision and touch. *Psychon. Bull. Rev.* 9: 731–738.

Spence C (2002) Multimodal attention and tactile information-processing. *Behav. Brain Res.* 135: 57–64.

Spence C and Driver J (1994) Covert spatial orienting in audition: Exogenous and endogenous mechanisms. *J. Exp. Psychol. Hum. Percept. Perform.* 20: 555–574.

Spence C, Nicholls MER, and Driver J (2001) The cost of expecting events in the wrong sensory modality. *Percept. Psychophys.* 63: 330–336.

Tellinghuisen DJ and Nowak EJ (2003) The inability to ignore auditory distractors as a function of visual task perceptual load. *Percept. Psychophys.* 65: 817–828.

Tipper SP (1985) The negative priming effect: Inhibitory priming by ignored objects. *Q. J. Exp. Psychol.* 37A: 571–590.

Tipper SP and Cranton M (1985) Selective attention and priming: Inhibitory and facilitatory effects of ignored primes. *Q. J. Exp. Psychol.* 37A: 591–611.

Tipper SP and Driver J (1988) Negative priming between pictures and words in a selective attention task: Evidence for semantic processing of ignored stimuli. *Mem. Cogn.* 16: 64–70.

Treisman A (1960) Contextual cues in selective listening. *Q. J. Exp. Psychol.* 12: 242–248.

Treisman AM and Davies A (1973) Divided attention to ear and eye. In: Kornblum S (ed.) *Attention and Performance,* vol. 4, pp. 101–117. New York: Academic Press.

Treue S (2001) Neural correlates of attention in primate visual cortex. *Trends Neurosci.* 24: 295–300.

Turner ML and Engle RW (1989) Is working memory capacity task dependent? *J. Mem. Lang.* 28: 127–154.

Vanduffel W, Tootell RB, and Orban GA (2000) Attention-dependent suppression of metabolic activity in the early stages of the macaque visual system. *Cereb. Cortex* 10: 109–126.

Vibell J, Klinge C, Zampini M, Spence C, and Nobre AC (2007) Temporal order is coded temporally in the brain: Early ERP latency shifts underlying prior entry in a crossmodal temporal order judgment task. *J. Cogn. Neurosci.* 19: 109–120.

Wickens CD (1984) Processing resources in attention. In: Parasuraman R and Davies DR (eds.) *Varieties of Attention*, pp. 63–102. San Diego, CA: Academic Press.

Wickens CD (1992) *Engineering Psychology and Human Performance,* 2nd edn. New York: HarperCollins.

Wolfe JM (1999) Inattentional amnesia. In: Coltheart V (ed.) *Fleeting Memories*, pp. 71–94. Cambridge, MA: MIT Press.

Wood NL and Cowan N (1995a) The cocktail party phenomenon revisited: Attention and memory in the classic selective listening procedure of Cherry (1953) *J. Exp. Psychol. Gen.* 124: 243–262.

Wood NL and Cowan N (1995b) The cocktail party phenomenon revisited: How frequent are attention shifts to one's name in an irrelevant auditory channel? *J. Exp. Psychol. Learn. Mem. Cogn.* 21: 255–260.

1.14 Amnesia: Point and Counterpoint

E. A. Kensinger, Boston College, Chestnut Hill, MA, USA

S. Corkin, Massachusetts Institute of Technology, Cambridge, MA, USA, and Massachusetts General Hospital, Boston, MA, USA

1.14.1 Introduction

In 1953, a man known by his initials, H.M., underwent an experimental brain operation to relieve his intractable epilepsy. This bilateral removal of medial temporal lobe (MTL) structures (see Corkin et al., 1997, for detailed report of his lesion location) was successful in lessening the frequency and severity of his epileptic seizures; however, it left him with a profound anterograde amnesia and an extensive retrograde amnesia extending to at least a decade before his surgery (Corkin, 1984; Scoville and Milner, 1957). Although H.M.'s intellectual abilities remained intact after the operation, and he was able to acquire new skills, he has not been able to consciously record any new experiences (see **Figure 1**; Corkin, 2002 for review).

H.M.'s pattern of spared and impaired abilities indicated not only that declarative (explicit, conscious) memory is dissociable from other forms of memory (e.g., implicit, unconscious) and from other perceptual and cognitive processes but also that the hippocampus and other MTL structures play a role in declarative, but not nondeclarative, memory formation (Scoville and Milner, 1957; Milner, 1962; Corkin, 1968, 1984, 2002). These realizations have spurred decades of research focusing on the role of MTL structures in learning and memory. Although initial studies focused primarily on the importance of the hippocampus in episodic memory, subsequent research has demonstrated that the surrounding cortical regions also are essential for normal declarative memory performance. Thus, patients with damage limited to the hippocampus tend not to show the magnitude of amnesia demonstrated in patients with more extensive MTL damage (e.g., Mishkin, 1978; Zola-Morgan and Squire, 1986; Meunier et al., 1993; Zola-Morgan et al., 1993; Barense et al., 2005). While these findings suggest that regions outside of the hippocampus proper contribute to declarative memory, the extent to which the different MTL structures make divergent contributions to learning and memory – and the nature of those regional specializations is hotly debated.

This chapter begins with a description of the anatomy of the MTL. We then discuss three ongoing debates concerning the role of different MTL

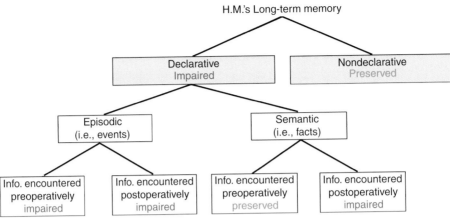

Figure 1 Pattern of spared and impaired learning following MTL resection in the amnesic patient H.M. Nondeclarative (implicit) learning is preserved in H.M., whereas declarative learning is markedly impaired. He does, however, show evidence of residual declarative learning. For example, he sometimes has demonstrated normal recognition memory performance (Freed et al., 1987; Freed and Corkin, 1988) and also has provided some evidence of new semantic learning following his operation (Corkin, 2002; O'Kane et al., 2004; Skotko et al., 2004).

structures in episodic memory. We focus on debates that have arisen from studies of patients with amnesia and from animal models of amnesia, but we also incorporate broader evidence from neuropsychology and neuroimaging.

In the first section, we describe a controversy regarding the extent to which MTL structures function together as an inseparable network that guides learning and memory versus the extent to which dissociations exist among the functioning of the different regions. At the heart of this debate is the question of whether the hippocampus performs specialized memory functions, or whether it carries out mnemonic functions redundant with those of the surrounding MTL cortices. Although some research has focused on examining whether the hippocampus plays a specialized role in spatial memory (e.g., Jarrard, 1995; O'Keefe, 1999; Aggleton and Brown, 2005; Eacott and Gaffan, 2005; O'Keefe and Burgess, 2005; *See also* Chapters 1.23, 1.33), we focus here on a controversy over the extent to which memory for interitem associations and individual items are differentially supported by the hippocampus proper and the surrounding medial temporal cortices, respectively.

In the second section, we outline a debate as to whether the perirhinal cortex plays a circumscribed role in object memory or a broader role in object perception and discrimination. According to some authors, perirhinal cortex is dedicated to memory and does not contribute to stimulus perception (e.g., Buffalo et al., 1999). In this view, stimulus perception

is dependent entirely on earlier cortical areas that make up the ventral processing stream. In contrast, other researchers have provided evidence that the perirhinal cortex may not be dedicated exclusively to mnemonic processing but, rather, may support performance on some perceptual discrimination tasks as well (e.g., Eacott et al., 1994; Buckley and Gaffan, 1997; *See* Chapter 1.08).

In the third section, we discuss the pattern of retrograde amnesia following MTL damage. According to one account of memory consolidation (often referred to as the standard model; Alvarez and Squire, 1994; Squire and Alvarez, 1995; Squire and Zola, 1998; Squire et al., 2004), MTL structures play a time-limited role in declarative memory: They are essential for the initial storage and retrieval of semantic and episodic memory traces, but they become unnecessary once memory traces are established permanently in the neocortex. According to this model, following MTL lesions, semantic and episodic memory will be affected equally, and each will show a temporal gradient, with remote memories relatively preserved.

An alternative model of consolidation (termed the multiple trace model; Nadel and Moscovitch, 1997; Moscovitch and Nadel, 1998; Nadel et al., 2000; *See* Chapter 1.04) proposes that the MTL serves as a mnemonic index, or as a pointer, to the neocortical areas that store the sensory and affective qualities associated with episodic events. Each time a memory is retrieved, a new mnemonic index, or pointer, is created. According to this model, a pointer always is needed for retrieval of episodic detail; thus, MTL structures provide lasting support during the retrieval of episodic memories. A temporal gradient could occur with partial MTL lesions, however, because remote memories tend to have more pointers than recent ones (because, on average, remote memories have been retrieved more often than recent memories). Thus, a partial MTL lesion is more likely to damage all pointers for a recent memory than for a remote memory. The multiple trace theory postulates that retrieval of semantic memories, unlike episodic memories, can occur without the MTL pointer. Because these memories are void of episodic detail, they may become consolidated and independent of the MTL.

Both models, therefore, make the same prediction for retrieval of semantic memories in amnesia: Semantic retrieval should show a temporal gradient, with better memory for remote than for recent facts. In contrast, the models make divergent predictions for the retrieval of autobiographical information. The standard model predicts that retrieval of remote memories should be preserved, whereas the multiple trace model predicts that all autobiographical retrieval should be impaired. We focus on the questions of whether amnesic patients are able to recall autobiographical memories from time periods prior to the onset of their MTL injury and, if so, whether the remote memories retrieved by amnesic patients are qualitatively the same as those retrieved by healthy individuals.

In each of these sections, we present key evidence supporting each viewpoint. We also speculate on the methodological considerations that may allow future research to help resolve these controversies. Although a consensus concerning these issues is still far in the future, the following sections highlight the contribution that studies of amnesia have made to conceptualizations of memory processes and MTL function.

1.14.2 Anatomy of the Medial Temporal Lobe

The MTL is composed of multiple structures: the amygdaloid complex, hippocampal formation (composed of the dentate gyrus, hippocampus, subicular complex, and entorhinal cortex), perirhinal cortex, and parahippocampal cortex (Suzuki and Amaral, 2003, 2004; **Figure 2**). The amygdala, an almond-shaped collection of nuclei, sits at the most anterior portion of the MTL, with direct connections to the hippocampus and surrounding cortices (Stefanacci

et al., 1996). The hippocampus (so-named for its sea horse shape) is located posterior to the amygdala. Information flow through the hippocampal formation proceeds from the entorhinal cortex to the dentate gyrus through the CA fields of the hippocampus proper and then to the subiculum. The entorhinal cortex (Brodmann's areas 28 and 34), located in the anterior and medial portion of the temporal lobe (medial to the rhinal fissure), serves as the principal source of input into the hippocampus, via the perforant path (Amaral et al., 1984; Amaral and Insausti, 1990). Information from unimodal and polymodal association cortices enters the MTL mainly through the perirhinal and parahippocampal cortices. The perirhinal cortex (Brodmann's areas 35 and 36) is located in the anterior and medial portion of the ventral temporal lobe, lateral to the entorhinal cortex. Posterior to the perirhinal cortex lies the parahippocampal cortex (von Economo's areas TH and TF), lining the banks of the collateral sulcus (which separates the fusiform and parahippocampal gyri) (Van Hoesen, 1995; Amaral, 1999; Pruessner et al., 2002; Suzuki and Amaral, 2003). The perirhinal cortex receives prominent input from lateral inferotemporal cortex (unimodal visual areas) and from the polymodal parahippocampal cortex (for a detailed review of the anatomical connectivity of perirhinal cortex, see Lavenex and Amaral, 2000). The parahippocampal cortex, caudal to the perirhinal cortex, receives its strongest input from the polymodal dorsal visuospatial processing stream (Goldman-Rakic et al., 1984; Selemon and Goldman-Rakic, 1988; Cavada and Goldman-Rakic, 1989; Suzuki and Amaral, 1994). Both the perirhinal and parahippocampal cortices send strong projections to the entorhinal cortex (**Figure 2**).

1.14.3 Do Medial Temporal Lobe Structures Have Dissociable Roles?

Although H.M.'s MTL lesion is large, his resultant amnesia originally was believed to be the result of damage to the amygdala and the hippocampus (e.g., Mishkin, 1978). For this reason, early animal models of amnesia focused primarily on the role of these structures in declarative memory. Early work, using aspiration lesions, indicated that damage to the hippocampus alone was sufficient to produce severe deficits in declarative memory (e.g., Zola-Morgan et al., 1982; Zola-Morgan and Squire, 1986), lending credence to the idea that these structures were

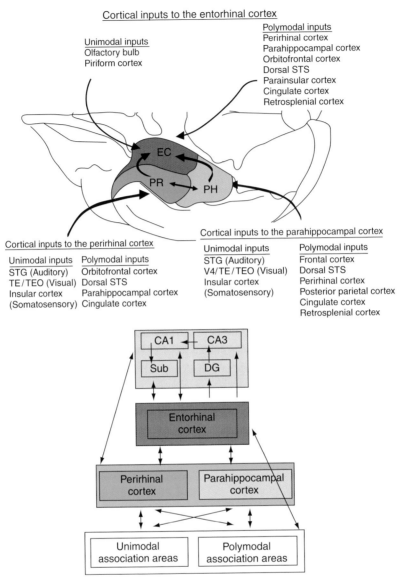

Cortical inputs to the entorhinal cortex

Unimodal inputs
Olfactory bulb
Piriform cortex

Polymodal inputs
Perirhinal cortex
Parahippocampal cortex
Orbitofrontal cortex
Dorsal STS
Parainsular cortex
Cingulate cortex
Retrosplenial cortex

Cortical inputs to the perirhinal cortex

Unimodal inputs   Polymodal inputs
STG (Auditory)   Orbitofrontal cortex
TE/TEO (Visual)   Dorsal STS
Insular cortex   Parahippocampal cortex
(Somatosensory)   Cingulate cortex

Cortical inputs to the parahippocampal cortex

Unimodal inputs   Polymodal inputs
STG (Auditory)   Frontal cortex
V4/TE/TEO (Visual)   Dorsal STS
Insular cortex   Perirhinal cortex
(Somatosensory)   Posterior parietal cortex
                       Cingulate cortex
                       Retrosplenial cortex

Figure 2   A schematic of MTL anatomy (top panel) and of projections within the medial temporal lobe (bottom panel). Colors reflect levels of integration within the MTL (bottom panel; green = first level of integration, pink = second level, blue = third level). Adapted from Lavenex P and Amaral DG (2000) Hippocampal-neocortical interaction: A hierarchy of associativity. *Hippocampus* 10: 420–430.

critical for declarative learning. It soon became apparent, however, that this view was too simplified: Several studies reported that recognition memory was impaired in animals with lesions that spared the amygdala or the hippocampus (e.g., Mahut et al., 1982; Murray and Mishkin, 1986; Zola-Morgan and Squire, 1986; Zola-Morgan et al., 1989). Researchers soon realized that part of the reason for the extensive declarative memory deficits following simultaneous aspiration lesions to the amygdala and hippocampus stemmed not from direct damage to those regions

but, rather, from the resultant damage to the underlying rhinal cortex and to the efferents to the hippocampus. Subsequent animal research using selective lesioning techniques and electrophysiological methods has confirmed that other regions, including the perirhinal and parahippocampal cortices, also play an important role in declarative memory formation (Zola-Morgan et al., 1989; Otto and Eichenbaum, 1992; Meunier et al., 1993; Mumby and Pinel, 1994; Squire et al., 2004). Studies in monkeys and rats have shown that damage limited to perirhinal cortex, or including perirhinal and entorhinal cortices, can lead to severe memory impairment on recognition memory tasks (Meunier et al., 1993; Eacott et al., 1994; Buffalo et al., 1999), and that such lesions also can exacerbate the memory deficits seen following lesions restricted to the hippocampus (Zola-Morgan et al., 1993; Wiig and Bilkey, 1995).

These results emphasize that MTL regions beyond the hippocampus play an essential role in declarative learning and memory. They do not, however, clarify the extent to which the different MTL structures make specialized contributions to learning and memory. It is clear that not all MTL structures support the same mnemonic functions. For example, although debate occurred for decades regarding the amygdala's role in memory, its focal role in emotion-related modulation of memory now has been well-established (Kensinger, 2004; Phelps, 2004; Phelps and LeDoux, 2005). In contrast, less consensus exists on the specialized contributions of other MTL structures to declarative memory.

In this section, we focus on a debate regarding the extent to which the hippocampus proper supports mnemonic functions that are independent of those mediated by surrounding neocortical regions. At the core of this debate is the question of whether recognition memory for individual items is dependent on the integrity of the hippocampus, or whether the hippocampus plays a specialized role in the recollection of interitem associations (relational memory), while memory for individual items (and intraitem features) can be mediated by adjacent cortical regions, such as perirhinal cortex.

1.14.3.1 Point: The Hippocampus Supports Mnemonic Functions That Are Independent of Those Mediated by Adjacent Neocortical Regions

If all MTL structures contribute equally to all forms of declarative learning, then it should follow that amnesic patients with MTL lesions should show similar magnitudes of impairment across a range of declarative memory tasks. Under certain encoding and retrieval conditions, however, amnesic patients show surprisingly good recognition memory coupled with poor recall ability (e.g., Johnson and Kim, 1985; Freed et al., 1987; Freed and Corkin, 1988; Green and Kopelman, 2002). For example, after studying a series of indoor and outdoor scenes, H.M. showed normal forced-choice recognition at delay intervals ranging from 10 min to 6 months (Freed et al., 1987; Freed and Corkin, 1988; **Figure 3**). In contrast, H.M.'s ability to recall items (or item locations) is at chance (e.g., Smith, 1988; reviewed in Corkin, 2002). Amnesic patients' rate of forgetting also differs based on the

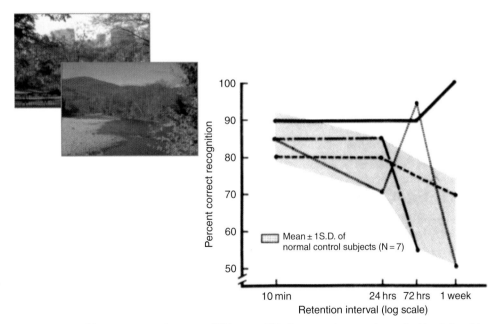

Figure 3 H.M.'s recognition memory performance. H.M. was within the normal range when asked to distinguish presented from nonpresented visual scenes. These results provide evidence of preserved learning despite his large MTL lesion. Modified from Freed DM, Corkin S, and Cohen NJ (1987) Forgetting in HM: A second look. *Neuropsychologia* 25: 461–471.

retrieval demands of the task. Recognition tasks often reveal normal rates of forgetting (Freed et al., 1987; Green and Kopelman, 2002), whereas recall tasks elicit accelerated forgetting (Green and Kopelman, 2002).

Direct comparisons between recall and recognition performance can be difficult to make, however. The two memory measures often are not matched in difficulty (recognition tasks typically are easier than recall tasks), and they always differ in their scales of measurement (with recognition tasks measuring percentage correct and recall assessing the number of items generated). To circumvent these problems, researchers often try to equate amnesic patients and control participants on recognition memory performance (e.g., by giving amnesic patients additional repetitions of studied stimuli, or by lengthening the delay after which the control participants' memory is tested), and then to assess whether, under these conditions of equated recognition, recall performance also is matched.

The initial reports using this approach revealed inconsistent results. Some investigations showed that when recognition was equated between amnesic patients and control participants, the patients' recall remained impaired (Hirst et al., 1986, 1988). Other studies, however, found that once patients' recognition memory was matched to that of control participants, recall memory was equated as well (Shimamura and Squire, 1988; Haist et al., 1992; MacAndrew et al.,

1994; Kopelman and Stanhope, 1998). A study by Giovanello and Verfaellie (2001) has shed light on at least part of the reason for these inconsistencies: The relation between amnesic patients' recall and recognition performance depends, at least in part, on the method by which their recognition performance is matched to that of controls. In one experiment, Giovanello and Verfaellie (2001) tested amnesic and control participants after the same delay, but they provided amnesic patients with additional study exposures to equate their recognition memory. In a second experiment, amnesic patients' memory performance was matched with control participants' performance by testing the amnesic patients after a short delay and the control participants after a 24-h delay. These two methods for equating performance led to different patterns of results. In the first experiment, amnesic patients' recall remained impaired, even though their recognition memory was equated. In the second experiment, recall and recognition both were equated across the amnesic and control groups.

At first blush, these findings are perplexing: Why would changing the method used to match amnesic and control participants' memory performance alter the pattern of memory preservation in amnesic patients? To understand this pattern of results, consider that different processes can contribute to a correct endorsement on a recognition memory task (Mandler, 1980; Tulving, 1985; **Figure 4**). On the one hand, a participant can recollect information from the

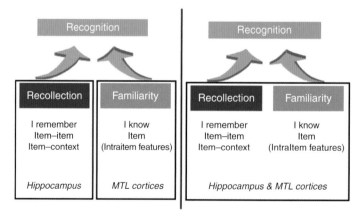

Figure 4 Processes contributing to recognition performance. When presented with an item on a recognition task, participants can use recollection to make their decision (i.e., they can determine that an item was studied because they remember something particular about the encoding episode for that item). Participants also can rely on stimulus familiarity: If a particular item seems more familiar than some other items on the list, it is likely that the enhanced familiarity stems from the fact that the item was presented on a recent study list. Debate exists as to whether these two processes are supported by different MTL circuits (with the hippocampus playing a critical role in recollection and the surrounding perirhinal and parahippocampal cortices being sufficient to support familiarity – left panel) or by the same MTL processes (with all regions of the MTL contributing to both recollection and familiarity – right panel).

study episode: Upon seeing a picture of a meadow on the recognition task, she may remember thinking about how peaceful the scene made her feel, she may recall sneezing while the picture was on the screen, or she may remember that she thought the picture of the meadow was juxtaposed with the prior picture of a crowded city street. Memory for any of this contextual information would allow the participant to confidently endorse the meadow as previously studied. On the other hand, a participant also can correctly endorse the meadow in the absence of any recollection, so long as she has a feeling of stimulus familiarity: If the meadow seems more familiar than other items that have appeared on the recognition task, it is likely that the enhanced familiarity has resulted from a recent encounter with the stimulus (i.e., that the meadow was present on the study list). In contrast, on a recall task, participants cannot rely on stimulus familiarity; they must generate the information themselves, and they therefore must be able to recollect the information and to attribute it to the study episode.

Keeping in mind that these two different processes can contribute to recognition performance, but that only recollective processes support accurate recall, let us return to the two different methods used to equate amnesic patients' performance. In the first experiment, Giovanello and Verfaellie (2001) equated recognition memory by altering the number of study repetitions (one for controls and many for amnesic patients) and by testing memory after a short delay. The fact that the two groups could be equated on recognition, but not on recall, can be explained by considering that control participants' recognition performance was likely to be supported primarily by recollective processes. The multiple item repetitions for the amnesic patients, in contrast, may have primarily boosted familiarity-based processes. Thus, while amnesic and control participants showed comparable recognition memory performance, that performance was supported by different processes in the two groups (more reliance on recollection in controls, and more reliance on familiarity in the amnesic patients). On a recall task, however, in which only recollection and not familiarity can support accurate retrieval, control participants performed better. In contrast, in the second experiment, in which Giovanello and Verfaellie (2001) equated amnesic and control participants' recognition performance by increasing the retention interval for the control participants, it is likely that the manipulation served primarily to decrease control participants' ability to rely on recollection. This reduction in recollection is probable because

recollection is believed to fade quickly over a delay, while familiarity is more stable over time (Tulving, 1985; Gardiner and Java, 1991). Because control participants' reliance on recollection was reduced, the equated performance on the recognition task probably resulted from a true equating of processes (e.g., similar reliance on recollection and familiarity in the control participants and the amnesic patients). Because control participants' reliance on recollection was reduced to a level comparable to that of the amnesic patients, performance was equated not only on a recognition memory task but also on a recall task.

These results emphasize the importance of analyzing amnesic patients' performance not just in terms of the type of task used to assess memory (e.g., recall or recognition) but by considering the underlying processes as well. The evidence for a disproportionate impairment in recollection in the study by Giovanello and Verfaellie (2001) was indirect (i.e., the authors did not directly measure the contribution of recollection and familiarity to recognition task performance), but more recent investigations have tackled this question head-on.

In many of these experiments, researchers have relied on participants' self-reports as to what types of information contributed to their recognition response. With this type of assessment (referred to as the remember-know procedure; *See* Chapter 2.17), participants are asked to not only decide whether information was presented in a study list but also to indicate whether they believe the information was presented because they remember something about the context in which the item was presented (i.e., they recollect details from the study episode) or because they simply know that they studied the item (i.e., the item is familiar but they are unable to recollect any information about its presentation; Mandler, 1980; Tulving, 1985; Rajaram, 1993). Evidence using the remember–know paradigm and other dual-process procedures suggests that the familiarity-based contribution to recognition memory performance is preserved in amnesic patients, whereas the recollective-based component is drastically impaired (e.g., Bastin et al., 2004; King et al., 2004; Aggleton et al., 2005; but see Medved and Hirst, 2006, for evidence of vivid recollection in amnesic patients). Amnesic patients often give far fewer remember responses than control participants, and their distribution of remember responses across different conditions differs from that of control participants. In contrast, the distribution of know responses for amnesic patients tends to be more in line with that of control participants (e.g., Rajaram et al., 2002).

The remember–know paradigm, however, has limitations. The first is that it relies on participants' subjective reports. It is likely that amnesic patients' subjective sense of remembering may not be qualitatively similar to the sense of remembering experienced by control participants (see Maguire et al., 2001b; Rajaram et al., 2002, for further discussion). The second is that, when a participant endorses an item as remembered, it is not clear what types of information the participant has retrieved. Depending on instructions used by investigators, a remember response can signify retrieval of information ranging from a wide variety of contextual elements (e.g., remembering a feeling elicited by the stimulus, or remembering the item that preceded the stimulus) to memory for the exact features of the presented stimulus (e.g., remembering the font in which the word was written). It is likely that memory for these different types of information (e.g., item–context associations, item–item associations, and memory for intraitem features) is supported by different processes; the remember–know procedure does not provide an easy way in which to parse their distinct contributions.

To circumvent these issues, researchers have adopted paradigms that more directly compare memory for associations or relations with memory for isolated items. One commonly used paradigm asks participants to distinguish between studied associations (e.g., fork–bench, pig–limousine, often referred to as intact pairs), novel associations between previously studied items (e.g., fork–limousine, recombined pairs), and novel associations between unstudied items (e.g., canary–tool, novel pairs). The ability to distinguish intact from recombined pairs (a measure of associative memory) has been compared with the ability to distinguish either of those pairs from novel pairs (a measure of item memory). Cognitive studies in young adults have provided empirical support for a dissociation between these two types of memory measures, with associative recognition being tied to recollective processes and item memory more reliant on familiarity signals (e.g., Hockley and Consoli, 1999).

Amnesic patients often show profound impairment on associative memory measures, even under conditions in which memory for items is equated (e.g., Giovanello et al., 2003; Turriziani et al., 2004). Not only are these associative memory deficits apparent on tasks that directly ask participants whether items were studied together but they also are apparent using eye tracking measures to indirectly assess memory for item relations. Cohen and colleagues (Ryan et al., 2000; Ryan and Cohen, 2004)

have found that control participants tend to look longer at components of scenes that have been moved, whereas amnesic patients do not show these effects. These data provide further evidence that amnesia may result in a fundamental deficit in processing the relations or associations among different stimuli.

The results discussed so far have suggested that amnesia does not always result in a declarative memory deficit that is equally pervasive across all memory measures. Rather, patients with amnesia are typically disproportionately impaired on recall tasks compared to recognition tasks, on tasks that require recollection as compared to those that can be supported by familiarity, and on tasks that rely on memory for associations as compared to those that can be supported by memory for items void of their context. Although these findings provide evidence for dissociations in the magnitude of mnemonic impairment based on the type of information retrieved, they do not speak to the precise regions within the MTL that may contribute differentially to different types of mnemonic functions.

Initial evidence for dissociations of function between the hippocampus proper and the surrounding MTL cortices came from animal models of amnesia. In a number of investigations, complete hippocampal removal had little to no effect on object recognition memory, even when memory was assessed after relatively long delays (Orbach et al., 1960; Stepien et al., 1960; Correll and Scoville, 1965; Meunier et al., 1993; Murray and Mishkin, 1998; Winters et al., 2004; Forwood et al., 2005). In fact, one study reported an inverse correlation between the amount of hippocampal damage and the magnitude of recognition memory impairment (Baxter and Murray, 2001). In contrast, lesions in perirhinal cortex can result in large decrements in object recognition memory (Mumby and Pinel, 1994; Brown and Aggleton, 2001; Mumby, 2001). Similar dissociations of function between the hippocampus and perirhinal cortex have been revealed in rats (Aggleton and Brown, 2005) by examining the expression of the immediate early gene *c-fos* as a marker of neural activity.

The advent of functional magnetic resonance imaging (fMRI) has made it possible to delineate the neural circuits that contribute to distinct memory processes in humans, and to examine the extent to which dissociations between the function of the hippocampus and perirhinal cortex explain dissociations in recollective and familiarity-based performance in amnesic patients. A number of studies employing the remember–know procedure and associative learning paradigms have now provided evidence that the hippocampus proper supports the encoding and retrieval of recollective information, whereas perirhinal cortex mediates the encoding and retrieval of familiarity-based memory traces (Wan et al., 1999; Davachi and Wagner, 2002; Davachi et al., 2003; Giovanello et al., 2004; Ranganath et al., 2004; Kensinger and Schacter, 2006).

Although these studies suggest a dissociation in the contribution of the hippocampus and surrounding cortical regions in recollection- and familiarity-based processing, respectively, these neuroimaging studies cannot speak to the necessity of particular regions for these memory functions. To fill this void, several studies have investigated the degree to which lesion locus or extent affects the likelihood that amnesic patients are impaired specifically on the recollective or associative components of a memory task. If the hippocampal formation is disproportionately engaged during recollective or associative processing, compared to familiarity-based item processing, then amnesic patients with damage limited to the hippocampus should show sparing of item recognition relative to associative recognition. In fact, patients with damage limited to the hippocampus sometimes slow preserved familiarity-based responding (Aggleton et al., 2005) and relatively normal item recognition performance (Vargha-Khadem et al., 1997; Holdstock et al., 2002; Mayes et al., 2002), despite impaired free recall (Henke et al., 1999; Duzel et al., 2001; Holdstock et al., 2005). These findings are consistent with the hypothesis that familiarity-based item memory can be supported by cortical regions outside of the hippocampus proper (e.g., perirhinal and parahippocampal cortices), while the hippocampus is critical for recollective and associative-memory performance.

Even this associative/item dichotomy may be too broad, however. Evidence suggests that the hippocampus is not equally engaged in all forms of recollective or associative memory. Rather, it may play a selective role in the learning of arbitrary associations between stimuli (O'Reilly and Rudy, 2001; Ryan and Cohen, 2004). Meaningful and preestablished relations between stimuli, in contrast, may be processed more as intraitem features, and memory for those associations may be mediated by regions outside of the hippocampus proper (Aggleton and Brown, 1999). Thus, amnesic patients with extensive hippocampal damage are able to learn

some stimulus pairings when those pairing are logical and build from preexisting knowledge (e.g., learning word pairs such as baby–cries or rose–red; Skotko et al., 2004). They show dramatic deficits, however, when attempting to learn stimulus associations that cannot build on such prior knowledge (e.g., apple–tent, balloon–fork; see Gilbert and Kesner, 2004, for similar results in rats with hippocampal lesions).

Evidence to support this conclusion comes from a study assessing memory for compound stimuli (e.g., pinpoint), which can be thought of as a class of non-arbitrary stimulus pairings. All amnesic patients showed a recognition advantage for these compound stimuli as compared to stimuli with no preexisting associations (Giovanello et al., 2006). Moreover, the advantage for the compound words was numerically greater for patients with lesions limited to the hippocampus than for patients with more widespread MTL damage. In other words, patients with circumscribed hippocampal lesions were able to take advantage of the preexisting associations of the compound stimuli to a greater degree than were patients whose lesions included the surrounding MTL cortices. This pattern of results is consistent with the hypothesis that regions outside of the hippocampus proper contribute to memory for nonarbitrary stimulus associations, whereas the hippocampus itself is essential for binding arbitrarily related stimuli together.

In summary, these findings provide strong evidence for dissociations of function between the hippocampus and surrounding cortical regions. In particular, they highlight instances in which the hippocampus proper plays a particular role in memory for recollective and associative information, allowing memory for an item to be bound to its context or to other items present during the encoding episode. This role of the hippocampus may be particularly critical when associations among items, or between an item and its context, do not hold preexisting significance but, rather, represent the arbitrary merging of previously unrelated stimuli.

1.14.3.2 Counterpoint: The Hippocampus and Surrounding Cortices Support Both Item and Relational Memory

Although the research described above provides compelling evidence for a dissociation of function between the hippocampus and surrounding cortical regions, other researchers argue that the hippocampus and surrounding cortices are broadly important for all forms of declarative learning, ranging from those that can rely on judgments of stimulus familiarity to those that depend on forming associations between previously unrelated stimuli (e.g., Reed and Squire, 1999; Stark and Squire, 2001). According to this view, any single dichotomy (e.g., recollection vs. familiarity or associative vs. item memory) is too simplistic to capture the division of labor between the hippocampus and the adjacent cortical structures in the MTL, although dissociations in function between different MTL structures may exist (e.g., Stark and Squire, 2003). In this section, we describe some of the neuroimaging and neuropsychological evidence suggesting that the dichotomies described above may not always hold.

If the hippocampus performs separable functions from the surrounding MTL cortices, then it should be difficult, if not impossible, to find patients with lesions limited to the hippocampus who do not show disproportionate deficits on tasks that assess the types of memory that the hippocampus mediates. In other words, patients with circumscribed hippocampal damage always should be disproportionately impaired on tasks that assess recall compared to recognition memory, recollection compared to familiarity, and memory for associations compared to isolated items. While these dissociations often occur in patients with focal hippocampal lesions (Henke et al., 1999; Holdstock et al., 2002, 2005; Mayes et al., 2002), they are not always present: Such patients can be equally impaired on measures of recall and recognition (Reed and Squire, 1997; Manns and Squire, 1999; Cipolotti et al., 2001; Manns, et al., 2003), and they can show comparable deficits on memory assessments for single items and for item conjunctions (Stark et al., 2002; Stark and Squire, 2003). For example, Stark et al. (2002) equated item recognition between patients with discrete hippocampal damage and control participants and then examined whether associative recognition was matched as well. When item recognition was equated between groups by providing hippocampal patients with eight study exposures, no impairment in associative recognition was observed for the patient group (although ceiling effects in patients' item recognition may have masked a disproportionate impairment in associative recognition; see Kensinger and Giovanello, 2005, for further discussion).

Moreover, if the hippocampus plays little to no role in familiarity-based processing of single items, then lesions limited to the hippocampus proper should largely spare performance on tasks that can be supported by these familiarity-based processes. As discussed in the preceding section, familiarity-based processing often is spared in amnesic patients with focal hippocampal damage. Some reports, however, indicate that damage circumscribed to the hippocampus can lead to marked deficits in recognizing factual knowledge about events that occurred after the amnesia onset (Manns et al., 2003; see also Reed and Squire 1998; Kapur and Brooks 1999; Holdstock et al. 2002) and in endorsing items as previously encountered (Beason-Held et al., 1999; Zola et al., 2000; Stark and Squire, 2003). These findings violate the prediction that performance on tasks that can be supported by familiarity alone should be intact after hippocampal lesions.

The reason for the discrepant findings across studies is a topic of heated discussion. Although any number of factors may contribute (e.g., differences in the tasks used, differences in lesion location, reorganization of function, deafferentation of regions due to fiber tract damage; see Mayes et al., 2002, 2004; Holdstock et al., 2005 for further discussion), we focus here on a few possibilities that we believe are particularly viable.

One feasible contributor to the conflicting findings is that patients' lesions likely are not circumscribed to functionally monolithic regions. Rather, the lesions probably encroach on multiple subregions that subserve distinct processes. For example, considering the entire hippocampus as a single functional entity, and expecting damage to any location within the hippocampus to result in similar mnemonic deficits, is probably an oversimplification. In fact, recent neuroimaging evidence has suggested that not all regions of the hippocampus play equivalent roles in associative memory (e.g., Giovanello et al., 2004; Kohler et al., 2005). For example, Kohler and colleagues (2005) found that while a middle hippocampal region responded more to novel associations than to novel objects, the same was not true of all hippocampal regions (and see Henson, 2005, for discussion of whether there is an anterior–posterior gradient within the hippocampus).

Similarly, it is likely that collapsing all extrahippocampal medial temporal-lobe cortical regions into one functional category overlooks critical divisions of labor. For example, patient and neuroimaging studies have suggested that the parahippocampal cortex plays an important role in memory for spatial and topographical information (e.g., Bohbot et al., 1998; Epstein and Kanwisher, 1998; Kohler et al., 1998; Maguire et al., 1998; Epstein et al., 1999; Ploner et al., 1999, 2000; Barrash et al., 2000), whereas the perirhinal cortex may play a more dominant role in the processing of object information (e.g., Aggleton and Brown, 2005; Buckley, 2005). Moreover, functional neuroimaging evidence suggests that the perirhinal cortex and parahippocampal gyrus may serve functionally distinct roles in familiarity-based and recollective-based retrieval, respectively. Thus, while perirhinal activity often corresponds with familiarity-based memory for isolated items or for intraitem features (Davachi et al. 2003; Dobbins et al. 2003; Henson et al. 2003; Kirwan and Stark 2004; Ranganath et al., 2004), activity in the posterior parahippocampal cortex often appears to relate to recollection and to memory for item context or item associations (Henke et al., 1999; Yonelinas et al., 2001; Davachi et al., 2003; Dobbins et al., 2003; Duzel et al., 2003; Kirwan and Stark, 2004; Ranganath et al., 2004).

It is also probable that differences between the role of the hippocampus proper and that of the surrounding cortices reflect gradations of specialization rather than complete dissociations. In other words, the function of adjacent MTL structures may overlap somewhat: Differences may exist in the proportion of particular neural networks within regions that subserve mnemonic functions, rather than absolute differences in the functions supported by the different structures. Electrophysiological studies back this interpretation. Although evidence indicates that neuronal activity in the hippocampus often provides a signal for conjunctive coding of items in a context (e.g., Wood et al., 2000), whereas perirhinal cortex neurons tend to respond in a stimulus-specific fashion (e.g., Suzuki et al., 1997; Young et al., 1997; Suzuki and Eichenbaum, 2000), one can find exceptions to these generalizations. For example, although most hippocampal cells respond based on stimulus-context conjunctions, stimulus-specific representations (i.e., responses to the stimulus regardless of its context) occasionally evoke hippocampal activity (e.g., Fried et al., 1997). Conversely, evidence suggests that at least in some instances, neural activity throughout the MTL cortices can correspond with memory for item associations (e.g., Buckmaster et al., 2004).

A study by Cipolotti et al. (2006) provided a strong warning that ignoring the types of stimuli for which memory is assessed leads to discrepant results regarding the role of the hippocampus in memory. These authors tested a patient with a focal hippocampal lesion on tasks assessing memory for a range of verbal, visual, and topographical information. Their results suggested that the hippocampus plays

a role in both recollective- and familiarity-based processing of verbal and topographical stimuli but is not necessary for recollection and familiarity-based memory of human faces. Although future studies will be needed to confirm the generality of these findings, and to clarify whether they extend to patients with damage located anywhere in the hippocampus or whether they may have arisen due to the precise location of this patient's hippocampal lesion, the data urge caution in trying to compare results across multiple studies using different stimulus types.

In summary, the results presented here caution against adopting too simplistic a division of labor between the hippocampus and the MTL cortices. While it is likely that these regions do make independent contributions to declarative learning and memory, a consensus has yet to be reached regarding the nature of those contributions.

1.14.4 The Role of the Perirhinal Cortex in Object Memory and Object Perception

In addition to debates regarding the distribution of mnemonic function across MTL structures, disagreement exists regarding the extent to which MTL structures play an isolated role in memory. In this section, we focus on a controversy regarding the role of the perirhinal cortex in memory vs. perception. As discussed earlier in this chapter, in order for animal models of amnesia to recreate the dense anterograde memory loss demonstrated in patients such as H.M., damage has often extended outside of the hippocampus proper and into the perirhinal cortex (e.g., Orbach et al., 1960; Mishkin, 1978; Zola-Morgan and Squire, 1985; Zola-Morgan et al., 1993; Murray and Mishkin, 1998). These studies emphasize that the perirhinal cortex must play an influential role in memory.

An ongoing debate, however, regards the extent to which the perirhinal cortex is important specifically for visual memory and the extent to which the perirhinal cortex plays a broader role in visual discrimination and object perception. Perirhinal cortex has the characteristics, in terms of anatomical connections, to support memory and perception side by side (e.g., Suzuki, 1996). Although perirhinal cortex is often considered part of the hippocampal-based memory system, with strong connections to the hippocampus via the entorhinal cortex (Suzuki, 1996), perirhinal cortex is a polymodal area with strong connections to regions within the ventral visual processing stream that are specialized for object identification (e.g., Burwell et al., 1995; Murray and Bussey, 1999; Goulet and Murray, 2001). Neurons in perirhinal cortex also have properties that could support both object memory and perception (e.g., large receptive fields that respond selectively to complex visual stimuli; Logothetis, 1998; Jagadeesh et al., 2001). In this section, we present evidence for each side of the debate: According to one view, the perirhinal cortex plays a role encompassing memory and perception (e.g., Eacott et al., 1994; Eacott and Heywood, 1995; Murray and Bussey, 1999; Buckley and Gaffan, 2000; Murray and Richmond, 2001; Bussey and Saksida, 2002); according to another view, the contribution of perirhinal cortex is limited to memory, with stimulus perception dependent entirely upon cortical areas earlier in the ventral visual processing stream (e.g., Squire and Zola-Morgan, 1991; Zola-Morgan et al., 1994; Buffalo et al., 1998; **Table 1**).

1.14.4.1 Point: The Perirhinal Cortex Supports Visual Perception

Perception refers to the process of acquiring, interpreting, and representing incoming sensory information. Memory, in contrast, refers to the retention and retrieval of these representations in the absence of the sensory information. A deficit restricted to memory, therefore, should be observed only when an individual is required to distinguish alternatives after they have been withdrawn from view. In contrast, a deficit in perception should be apparent when an individual is asked to distinguish objects in plain sight.

Some of the first evidence that perirhinal cortex may have a role in perception came from Eacott et al. (1994). They tested macaque monkeys on a matching-to-sample task. In this task, monkeys first learn that a particular object (e.g., a red square) is associated with a reward (the sample phase). They then are shown the rewarded object and a second object (e.g., a red square and a green circle), and the

monkeys must choose the initially rewarded object (the match phase). Critically, Eacott et al. (1994) included simultaneous match-to-sample and delayed match-to-sample conditions. While deficits in the delayed condition could result either from perceptual or mnemonic impairments, deficits in the simultaneous condition should reflect perceptual difficulties (because the objects remain in view). They found that when there was a large perceptual load in the task (i.e., when they used many different types of stimuli across all of the trials), the monkeys with perirhinal lesions showed impairments even in the simultaneous condition. These results support the interpretation that perirhinal cortex mediates visual perception.

Further delineating the exact role of perirhinal cortex in visual perception, however, has proved challenging. For example, Eacott and colleagues' (1994) study further showed that perirhinal cortex is not needed for all forms of object perception. When perceptual load was relatively low (i.e., when only a small set of items was used across all of the trials), monkeys with perirhinal lesions showed a delay-dependent deficit: They were impaired relative to control monkeys at the long delay but performed normally at the shortest delay. This pattern of performance is consistent with a mnemonic, and not a perceptual, deficit.

Several additional studies, using discrimination of pairs of visual stimuli, showed inconsistent results. Damage to the perirhinal cortex can lead to impairments in visual discrimination under some conditions, but it does not lead to a pervasive deficit across all assessments of visual discrimination. Thus, Buckley and Gaffan (1997), like Eacott et al. (1994), reported that monkeys with perirhinal cortex lesions performed as well as control monkeys when learning a small number of concurrent visual discriminations (see also Aggleton et al., 1997; Thornton et al., 1997; Buffalo et al., 1999; Baxter and Murray, 2001) but

Table 1 Predictions made by the perception-and-memory view of perirhinal cortex, compared to the mnemonic-only view, based on the stimulus characteristics and delay interval used on tasks such as matching-to-sample or visual discrimination learning

		Perirhinal cortex necessary?	
Stimulus characteristics	*Delay*	*Perception view*	*Mnemonic-only view*
Few stimuli, distinguishable by single object features	No	No	No
	Yes	Yes	Yes
Stimuli distinguishable only by conjunctions of intra-object features	No	Yes	No
	Yes	Yes	Yes

were impaired when required to learn a large number of discriminations (see also Buckley and Gaffan, 1998).

At a broad level, these results suggest that activity in perirhinal cortex may enhance the specificity of an object's representation (i.e., the level or amount of visual detail). When the task includes relatively few stimuli, the representation for each stimulus does not have to be precise or specific for discrimination to be successful. In contrast, when the stimuli are numerous and potentially confusable, each one must be represented precisely to avoid stimulus confusion (see Murray and Bussey, 1999; Bussey and Saksida, 2002, for further discussion). By this view, perirhinal lesions selectively impair object discrimination on tasks that employ large stimulus sets.

A study by Eacott et al. (2001), however, suggested that the perirhinal cortex is not critical for representing all fine-grained discriminations between objects. In their study, Eacott and colleagues required rats to distinguish between squares and rectangles, and they modulated the difference in side length between the two shapes such that the rats had to maintain a precise representation of the shapes to distinguish the square from the rectangle. Even with perirhinal cortex lesions, the rats were able to perform the task successfully. Critically, successful performance of this task could be based on representation of a single object feature: edge length. It is likely that this single-feature representation can be supported by areas earlier in the visual processing stream, such as inferotemporal cortex (see Buckley et al., 1997), and does not require engagement of perirhinal cortex (see also Buckley et al., 1997, 2001). Rather, perirhinal cortex may become necessary only when the representation of feature conjunctions is required.

In an influential model (the perceptual-mnemonic/feature-conjunction model), Bussey, Murray, and Saksida (e.g., Murray and Bussey, 1999; Bussey and Saksida, 2002) have proposed that perirhinal cortex serves as the final processor in the ventral visual processing stream (Desimone and Ungerleider, 1986; Ungerleider and Haxby, 1994), coding for complex visual representations. Within this framework, the results described above can be understood by considering the degree of feature ambiguity present across the different stimuli. The greater the number of object pairs to be discriminated, the greater the likelihood that a particular object feature will be rewarded when it is part of one object but not when it is part of another object (i.e., the greater the feature ambiguity). Because of the increased probability that a feature will be present among multiple stimuli, the representation of conjunctions of complex features in perirhinal cortex will be critical for successful task performance. The preservation of function in the study by Eacott et al. (2001) can be explained by reliance on a precise representation of a single feature (edge length) rather than on a need to integrate multiple intraitem features. Thus, the role of perirhinal cortex may be best described as representing configural relations among features, or conjunctions of intraobject features.

To test this hypothesis directly, Eacott et al. (2001) designed a visual discrimination task in which combinations of features, rather than any single object feature, signaled the rewarded object. Performance on this task was compared to performance on a task in which visual discrimination among stimuli could occur based on single features. Rats with perirhinal cortex lesions were impaired only when successful performance required discrimination based on the configuration of features; when performance could rely on representation of single features, the perirhinal-lesioned rats performed normally. Bussey et al. (2002, 2003) have found similar results when assessing visual discrimination in nonhuman primates: Monkeys with perirhinal lesions were impaired on tasks that required disambiguating shared features, but not on tasks that could be solved by discrimination of single object features. These results are consistent with the conclusion that perirhinal cortex functions as part of the ventral visual processing stream and plays a critical role in feature integration (see Bussey et al., 2005).

Further corroborating evidence has come from a study demonstrating that the requirement for feature integration can exacerbate the mnemonic deficits demonstrated after perirhinal damage. In a spontaneous recognition task, Norman and Eacott (2004) used rats' natural tendencies to explore novel items as a means to assess their ability to remember which objects had been encountered previously. The features of the novel objects were manipulated so that some differed from familiar objects in single features, whereas others differed from familiar objects in the conjunction of features. The critical finding was that perirhinal-lesioned animals showed an exaggerated memory deficit for the feature-ambiguous stimuli compared to the feature-unique stimuli. In fact, even after relatively short delays, the perirhinal-lesioned animals were at chance in distinguishing between the novel and familiar feature-ambiguous objects (Norman and Eacott, 2004).

These findings have led to the proposal that peri-rhinal cortex represents the association between intraitem features (Gaffan, 1994) or the gestalt representation of a whole object (Murray and Bussey, 1999). These putative functions of perirhinal cortex are consistent with its location among high-order processing regions in the ventral visual stream. These regions tend to respond to the whole object rather than to the individual features that comprise the object (Baker et al., 2002). Two open questions are whether perirhinal cortex plays a role in configural learning of all intraitem features and whether its role is limited to intraitem feature integration or also extends to the association of features that are spatially or temporally separable (see Alvarado and Bachevalier, 2005, for evidence of dissociable roles of the perirhinal and parahippocampal cortices in object vs. temporal configural memory; see Lee et al., 2005a,b, for evidence of dissociable roles of the hippocampus and MTL cortices in spatial vs. object perception; see Shaw et al., 1990, for evidence that perirhinal cortex may be important for cross-modal object processing). These questions are closely tied to the debate, discussed in the first section of this chapter, regarding the extent to which the roles of perirhinal cortex and hippocampus can be dissociated (e.g., with perirhinal cortex representing intraitem feature integration and the hippocampus representing item–item and item–context relations).

1.14.4.2 Counterpoint: The Perirhinal Cortex Supports Memory but Not Perception

As already discussed, perirhinal cortex is not required for all object perception. Patients with MTL lesions that include perirhinal cortex are not impaired on simultaneous visual recognition memory tasks (Milner et al., 1968; Buffalo et al., 1998; Holdstock et al., 2000) or on a wide variety of visual perception tasks (Lee et al., 2005b). Where debate arises, however, is in whether perirhinal cortex serves any role in visual perception. Although the evidence described in the preceding section suggests that this area does play a fundamental role in perception, at least for some classes of stimuli, other researchers have questioned the validity of these claims.

One concern relates to the way in which researchers analyzed their data to arrive at the conclusion that perirhinal cortex is critical for visual perception. For example, in a reanalysis of the data presented by Buckley and Gaffan (1997), Hampton (2005) demonstrated that the conclusions reached differ depending on whether the measure of assessment is considered to be errors made per problem or total number of errors. Animals with perirhinal lesions appear disproportionately impaired on tasks with larger stimulus sets when performance is measured by the total number of errors. The number of errors per problem, however, remains stable across different set sizes. Although extensive discussion has probed the extent to which these differences in analyses can account for all of the discrepant findings (Buckley, 2005; Lee et al., 2005b), at the least, the debate emphasizes the difficulty inherent in comparing perceptual ability across tasks with differently sized stimulus sets.

Another complaint has been that the studies described in the prior section have not always cleanly teased apart the perceptual and mnemonic demands of the task (Levy et al., 2005). Part of this conflation has stemmed from the fact that most of the studies have assessed the role of perirhinal cortex in rats or in monkeys. Teasing apart perception from memory is difficult in these animals. For example, failure to correctly identify a rewarded target could stem not only from difficulties perceiving the target but also from difficulties remembering which item is rewarded (e.g., whether the novel object or the familiar object is rewarded). It is much easier to dissociate perceptual and mnemonic processes in humans because explicit reminders about the task instructions can be given (e.g., "which of these stimuli matches this target object?"), thereby eliminating any mnemonic load.

A number of studies, therefore, have assessed the performance of amnesic patients with damage to perirhinal cortex on perceptual discrimination tasks. Buffalo et al. (1998) and Holdstock et al. (2000) used a matching-to-sample paradigm to assess object perception and recognition memory in amnesic patients, including those with focal damage to the perirhinal cortex. In the study by Buffalo et al. (1998), participants viewed four visual designs and then, following a variable delay, indicated whether an image presented alone had been one of the four previously seen. The results revealed that at short delays (0–2 s), patients with perirhinal lesions performed well on the task, whereas they were impaired at longer delays (6 s or more).

Similar results were revealed in the study by Holdstock et al. (2000), in which performance was compared in simultaneous and delayed matching-to-sample tasks. In the simultaneous matching condition, participants viewed a probe (an abstract pattern) along with possible targets and were asked to indicate which target matched the probe. In the delay conditions, the probe was shown and then removed from the screen. Following a delay (ranging from 0 to 30 s), participants saw the possible targets and were asked to select the one that matched the probe image. Holdstock and colleagues found that the patients with perirhinal lesions were impaired only at long delays (10 s or longer) and performed within the normal range with shorter delays (less than 5 s) and in the simultaneous matching condition. The fact that performance was impaired at longer delays but not at shorter ones suggests that perirhinal lesions primarily caused mnemonic deficits and not perceptual ones.

Further evidence in support of the conclusion that perirhinal damage does not impair perceptual ability comes from studies by Squire and colleagues. Stark and Squire (2000) tested three patients with MTL lesions that included all of the perirhinal cortex on the oddity task developed by Buckley and colleagues (Buckley and Gaffan, 1998, p. 15; Buckley et al., 2001). In this task, participants are shown five different views of the same object, and one view of a different object. Participants must indicate which object is the odd one. Obscuring the objects with a white-noise mask makes the object discrimination task quite difficult. Stark and Squire (2000) tested the amnesic participants on seven versions of the oddity task. Across each version, the patients performed as well as control participants.

Levy et al. (2005) also reported results suggesting that perirhinal lesions do not lead to perceptual deficits in humans. The authors tested two of the amnesic patients who had been assessed on the oddity tasks on a task that required discrimination of complex feature-ambiguous stimuli (using the stimulus manipulations of Bussey et al., 2003). Just as with the oddity task, these patients performed normally on similarity judgment tasks (indicating whether pairs of images were the same or different) and on simultaneous matching-to-sample tasks (indicating which of two blended images was closest to a target image). These results suggest that complex visual discrimination performance and discrimination between images that have high feature ambiguity can occur even in the absence of perirhinal cortex function.

One potential difficulty in interpreting the results of Levy et al. (2005) is that the scores obtained by the control participants were very close to ceiling. It is possible, therefore, that a mild deficit would be revealed in the patients if their perceptual abilities were assessed using tasks that resulted in poorer performance by everyone (see Lee et al., 2005, for further discussion). In the task used by Stark and Squire (2000), however,

the control participants' performance was well below ceiling, providing suggestive evidence that ceiling effects may not fully explain the findings.

Taken together, these results indicate that on a range of tasks, monkeys with perirhinal lesions fail, but humans with perirhinal lesions succeed. A few viable explanations for these contrary findings come to mind. First, the monkeys may have had damage to regions outside of perirhinal cortex. Damage to lateral visual areas is known to produce visual perception deficits (e.g., Mishkin, 1982; Miyashita, 1993; Buffalo et al., 1999), and it is possible that, in at least some of the studies in nonhuman primates, the lesions encroached on these lateral visual areas (Buffalo et al., 1999). Previous studies showed that the extent of inadvertent damage to lateral temporal areas can correlate more strongly with a monkey's ability to learn concurrent object discriminations than the extent of intentional damage to perirhinal cortex (Buffalo et al., 1998). Second, the function of perirhinal cortex with regard to visual perception may be distinct in humans and in nonhuman primates, or other regions within the human ventral processing stream may serve redundant functions with the perirhinal cortex in terms of processing feature conjunctions. Third, even stronger demands for processing high-level feature conjunctions may be required to witness impairments in humans with perirhinal damage; perhaps, on the tasks used to date, engagement of other types of strategies by human participants (i.e., other than discrimination based on feature conjunctions) has increased the likelihood that regions beyond perirhinal cortex can support successful task performance. Related to this last point, human perirhinal cortex may subserve visual perception only for a subset of object stimuli. For example, Lee et al. (2005c) demonstrated that patients with MTL damage were impaired at discriminating scenes and faces, but were less impaired at discriminating single objects, and were unimpaired at discriminating art (see also Lee et al., 2005a, for importance of stimulus type). A challenge for future studies is to determine whether any of these explanations can account for the conflicting results.

1.14.5 Retrieval of Autobiographical Memories in Amnesia

So far in this chapter, we have focused on the role of MTL structures in acquiring new declarative memories. In addition, considerable debate exists regarding their roles in retrieving remote memories. While the hallmark of bilateral MTL lesions is anterograde amnesia, this inability to form new memories typically is accompanied by difficulty retrieving memories from some time period prior to the onset of the amnesia (i.e., retrograde memory loss). As was first noted by the French psychologist Théodule Ribot in 1881 (Ribot, 1881), the retrograde memory loss often follows a temporal gradient: It is more pronounced for recently formed memories and is less pervasive for older memories (now referred to as Ribot's Law). Consistent with Ribot's law, initial studies reported that, following MTL damage, retrograde amnesia often was limited to only the few years prior to the injury, with more remote memories relatively preserved (e.g., Milner et al., 1968; Corkin, 1984).

These findings suggested that MTL structures were not required for permanent storage and retrieval of memories. Rather, the region seemed to play a time-limited role in memory storage and retrieval. Based on this evidence, the presence of consolidation processes were proposed: physiological changes that take place in the brain to stabilize memories and to make them resilient to disruption. Memory consolidation can be described on two levels. The first is a rapid, molecular-level consolidation during which the long-term conductivity of synapses is affected by experience with particular stimuli or pairings of stimuli and responses. The existence of this phase of consolidation is widely accepted and will not be considered further in this chapter (for more on molecular consolidation see McGaugh, 2000; Kandel, 2001; Lee et al., 2004). Memory consolidation can also be described at the system or network level. Broadly, this level of consolidation is believed to take place over the long term (days to decades), with MTL structures critical for mnemonic storage and retrieval only until the consolidation process is complete (e.g., Squire, 1992). Two primary models for this level of consolidation have been proposed: the standard model and the multiple trace model.

According to the standard model of consolidation, a prolonged process of system consolidation may last for a decade or more (e.g., Squire and Alvarez, 1995; Dudai, 2004). During the initial phases of this consolidation process, the MTL is required for the storage and recovery of a memory trace. Over time, however, these structures become unnecessary as neocortical activity becomes sufficient to support storage and retrieval of memory traces. This standard model, therefore, provides a mechanism to account for the temporal gradient of retrograde amnesia.

Retrieval of recent events is impaired because the MTL is still required for their retrieval, whereas retrieval of remote events is preserved because the MTL is not essential for their retrieval.

According to this standard model of consolidation, the MTL is required during the consolidation period for all declarative memories (i.e., both episodic and semantic) and becomes unnecessary after consolidation processes have terminated. Thus, this model predicts that retrograde memory loss should show the same temporal gradient regardless of whether the retrieved memories are semantic or episodic in nature (Squire, 1992; Squire and Alvarez, 1995).

In contrast to the standard model of consolidation, the multiple trace model (Nadel and Moscovitch, 1997) proposes that the MTL serves as a pointer, or index, to the neocortical areas that store the representations of information present during an encoding episode (see also Teyler and DiScenna, 1986). Thus, activity in a network of MTL neurons provides a means to bind together the different pieces of information that were attended to during a particular experience. Each time a memory trace is activated (e.g., through reminiscence), another pointer is created. These new pointers bind together many of the same representations as the original pointer, but they also may include some additional representations (reflecting new associations made during the reminiscence) and may neglect others (those not activated during the reminiscence). Because the exact content retrieved about an episodic memory varies somewhat in the representations retrieved, over time each autobiographical event will become represented by multiple, distinct neuronal networks distributed throughout the MTL. Because remote autobiographical memories tend to be activated a greater number of times than more recent ones, the number of neuronal networks representing a remote autobiographical memory usually will be greater than the number of neural networks representing a recent autobiographical memory. Probabilistically, damage to a subset of MTL neurons, therefore, will be more likely to eliminate all of the networks associated with recent memories than to erase all traces of remote memories. The multiple trace model, in contrast to the standard model, explains the temporal gradient of retrograde memory loss not in terms of a change in the necessity of the MTL for retrieval of the memories but, rather, in terms of a change in the likelihood that all of the MTL traces representing a memory would be damaged as a result of brain injury. The multiple trace model does, however, postulate that over time, semantic memories (factual knowledge void of context) can become represented solely in the neocortex. This shift can occur because, although these facts initially were acquired in specific contexts (e.g., we learned that the Eiffel Tower is in Paris by listening to our second grade teacher, we were reminded of it by reading a tour book, etc.), over time, the factual knowledge becomes extracted from the context in which it was learned. At the point where retrieval of this factual knowledge can occur without retrieval of its encoding context, MTL structures are no longer needed.

The standard model and the multiple trace model both predict that retrieval of remote semantic memories can occur in the absence of functional MTL structures. Indeed, abundant evidence shows that retrograde amnesia for semantic information tends to follow a temporal gradient (e.g., Kapur and Brooks, 1999; Fuji et al., 2000) and that retrieval of remote semantic knowledge often is preserved following extensive MTL damage (e.g., Kensinger et al., 2001; Schmolck et al., 2002). The two models, however, diverge in their predictions for whether MTL structures are always required for the retrieval of autobiographical memories (as proposed by the multiple trace model) or whether, over time, the role of those structures is eliminated such that retrieval of remote autobiographical memories can be supported by activity in other neocortical regions (as postulated by the standard model; **Figure 5**). In this section, we examine the evidence for and against the conclusion that retrieval of remote autobiographical memories requires the MTL.

1.14.5.1 Point: Retrieval of Remote Autobiographical Memories Does Not Require the Medial Temporal Lobe

If the retrieval of remote autobiographical memories can proceed in the absence of MTL function, then amnesic patients should show a temporal gradient in autobiographical memory (i.e., better memory for remote events than for recent events, in contrast to the pattern of results typically displayed by control participants) and relatively preserved memory for remote events. Both of these predictions have been upheld in a number of studies. Often, amnesic patients show a temporally graded retrograde amnesia for autobiographical memory, similar to the gradation shown for semantic knowledge (e.g., Reed and Squire, 1998; Kapur and Brooks, 1999). Particularly in individuals with damage limited to the

hippocampus, memory for events sometimes is affected only for recent time points, within a decade of amnesia onset (Reed and Squire, 1998). In contrast, patients with more extensive temporal lobe damage (including the temporal neocortex) often show more extensive retrograde memory loss (Reed and Squire, 1998).

Further, amnesic patients can also show a preserved ability to retrieve remote autobiographical experiences. Several studies have reported that amnesic patients recollect detailed, autobiographical experiences from time points removed from their amnesia onset (e.g., Schnider et al., 1995; Rempel-Clower et al., 1996; Reed and Squire, 1998; Fujii et al., 1999; Kapur and Brooks, 1999; Bayley et al., 2003, 2005). Particularly in patients with damage limited to the hippocampus, the level of detail recalled about these remote life events has been reported to be indistinguishable from that recalled by healthy individuals (Reed and Squire, 1998). In contrast, patients with larger lesions extending into the temporal neocortex often show pervasive impairments in retrieving autobiographical memories from remote time periods (Bayley et al., 2005).

The fact that hippocampal damage disproportionately affects memory for recent events, while relatively sparing memory for remote events, is consistent with the standard model's proposal that the hippocampus plays a time-limited role in memory retrieval. The correspondence of more extensive damage of the temporal neocortex to disruption of retrieval of remote autobiographical memories is consistent with the proposal that retrieval of these remote events is dependent on networks distributed throughout the neocortex.

Additional support for these claims comes from comparing the performance of patients with progressive MTL damage (e.g., patients with mild Alzheimer's disease) to the performance of patients with progressive damage to neocortical regions (e.g., patients with semantic dementia). Patients with Alzheimer's disease tend to show a temporally graded retrograde amnesia, with memory for recent events more impaired than memory for remote events (Piolino et al., 2003). In fact, a deficit in retrieval of remote memories typically occurs only later in the disease process, once the neuropathological changes have begun to appear in the neocortex. In semantic dementia, the opposite pattern of results has been demonstrated: a relative preservation of memories for recent events and a disruption in memories for remote events. Because semantic dementia causes

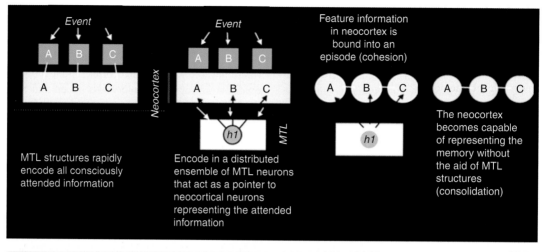

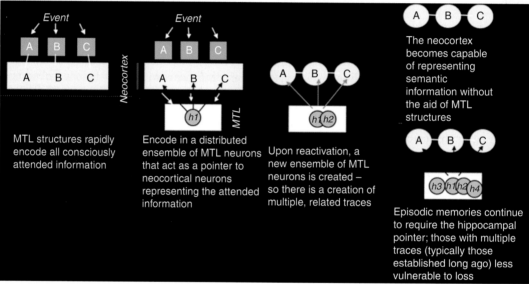

Figure 5   Phases of the consolidation process according to the standard model (top panel) and the multiple trace model (bottom panel). Adapted from Nadel L and Moscovitch M (1998) Hippocampal contributions to cortical plasticity. *Neuropharmacology* 37: 431–439.

progressive atrophy to the temporal neocortex, this pattern is consistent with the standard model's tenet that the hippocampus is needed for retrieval of recent memories but not for remote memories, while the temporal neocortex is critical for retrieval of remote memories (Murre et al., 2001; Nestor et al., 2002).

A study by Kopelman et al. (2003) reached a similar conclusion after assessing the correspondence between regional brain volume and autobiographical recall in 40 individuals with brain damage. They found that frontal lobe volume, and not MTL volume, accounted for individual differences in the retrieval of remote autobiographical memories. Corroborating evidence was revealed in a study by Eustache et al.

(2004), in which resting-state glucose utilization in the hippocampus correlated with amnesic patients' ability to remember autobiographical events from recent time periods, while their ability to retrieve remote memories corresponded with glucose utilization in frontal cortex. Similar findings were reported in two functional neuroimaging studies of healthy volunteers. Piefke et al. (2003) found greater hippocampal activity during retrieval of recent autobiographical memories than during retrieval of remote memories; Takashima et al. (2006) found decreasing hippocampal activity (but increasing prefrontal activity) as a function of a memory's age (ranging from 0 to 3 months). These data are consistent with the standard model's postulate that the hippocampus becomes less important as the age of a memory increases.

These findings all converge on the conclusion that MTL structures may not be required for retrieval of all autobiographical memories. While the function of MTL structures seems to be essential for retrieval of recently experienced events, remote memories appear to be retrieved in the absence of hippocampal function. Instead, retrieval of these events from one's past may rely on networks distributed throughout the neocortex.

1.14.5.2 Counterpoint: Medial Temporal Lobe Structures Are Required for Retrieval of Autobiographical Memories from All Time Periods

The story is not as straightforward as outlined above, however. A number of findings go against the claim that the MTL plays only a time-limited role in retrieval of autobiographical memories. For one, retrieval of remote autobiographical memories is not always spared in amnesia (e.g., Nadel and Moscovitch, 1997; Kopelman et al., 1999; Westmacott et al., 2001). For example, using family photos, Westmacott et al. (2001) found that the amnesic patient K.C. demonstrated a complete loss of memory for autobiographical episodes, even from remote time points (and see Rosenbaum et al., 2005, for similar findings). Steinvorth et al. (2005) similarly found that two amnesic patients (H.M. and W.R.) were severely impaired in retrieving remote autobiographical memories.

Second, amnesic patients often do not show a temporal gradient with regard to their autobiographical memories. This observation was made early on by Kinsbourne and Wood (1975), who suggested that amnesia affects autobiographical memories from recent and remote time points equally. This conclusion was corroborated in a series of studies by Warrington and colleagues, who demonstrated that amnesic patients often show a shallow temporal gradient (e.g., Warrington and McCarthy, 1988; Warrington, 1996). A few recent studies also have provided evidence of a flat temporal gradient for retrieval of autobiographical experiences (e.g., Cipolotti et al., 2001; Steinvorth et al., 2005).

How can one account for the discrepant findings in the amnesia literature, with some studies showing steep temporal gradients for autobiographical memory retrieval (with retrieval of remote memories relatively spared) and others showing shallower gradients (with retrieval of remote memories impaired)?

One point of reconciliation relates to the specific locus of the amnesic patients' lesions. It is possible that some of the autobiographical retrieval deficits stem not from damage to the MTL but from damage to neocortical regions (see Squire et al., 2004, for more discussion). While extra-MTL damage should be considered, it does not appear to account for all discrepant findings. In at least some instances, damage specifically done to the MTL seems to correspond with difficulty retrieving remote autobiographical memories. Thus, even a patient with a lesion restricted to the hippocampal formation showed a flat temporal gradient and impaired retrieval of remote autobiographical memories (Cipolotti et al., 2001). This result suggests that flat temporal gradients cannot be ascribed merely to damage beyond the MTL. Further evidence suggesting a role of the MTL in retrieval of remote autobiographical memories came from a study examining whether the extent of MTL damage, as compared to damage to anterior and lateral temporal cortex, corresponded with the ability of Alzheimer's patients to retrieve autobiographical and semantic memories. Gilboa et al. (2005) found that while memory for semantic information was associated with damage to temporal neocortex, retrieval of autobiographical episodes was associated with the degree of MTL atrophy. Further, the strength of the association between MTL pathology and autobiographical memory retrieval was strong, even for childhood memories. These findings provide converging evidence that MTL regions remain important for autobiographical memory retrieval, regardless of the age of the memories being retrieved.

It is doubtful, therefore, that extra-MTL damage alone can account for all of the inconsistencies in the literature. Another possibility is that all regions within the MTL may not be equally important for retrieval of remote autobiographical memories. Squire and colleagues have argued that the hippocampus proper plays a critical time-limited role in retrieval of autobiographical memories (e.g., Squire, 1975, 1992; Squire et al., 1984). In their view, the surrounding MTL cortices may continue to be important for retrieval even of remote memories.

Because of the difficulties confirming that damage is circumscribed to the hippocampus and does not result in any functional damage to surrounding regions (e.g., through disruption of white matter fiber tracts), this hypothesis is difficult to address through testing of amnesic patients. Some evidence suggests that patients with damage limited to the hippocampus show preserved retrieval of remote autobiographical memories (Levy et al., 2005), consistent with the claim that regions beyond the hippocampus are critical for retrieval of remote autobiographical experiences. Other studies, however, have reported impaired performance in patients with damage limited to the hippocampus (Cipolotti et al., 2001).

Neuroimaging studies in healthy individuals have provided one means to assess whether regions within the MTL are disproportionately active during retrieval of recent as compared to remote memories. As described in the previous section, some studies show that hippocampal activity is modulated by the age of the memory being retrieved (greater for recent than for remote memories; Piefke et al., 2003; Takashima et al., 2006). Increasing evidence, however, shows that hippocampal activity often is unrelated to the age of the retrieved memories. A number of studies have shown equivalent hippocampal activity during the retrieval of recent and remote autobiographical memories (Nadel et al., 2000; Maguire et al., 2001b; Ryan et al., 2001; Gilboa et al., 2004). One criticism of some of these studies is that the memories tested in the scanner were identified during a prescan interview; it is possible, therefore, that the true age of the memories was altered during this interview process. An fMRI study by Steinvorth et al. (2006) circumvented this problem. By assessing participants' memories for events written about in their diaries, or related by family members, these investigators measured brain activity associated with retrieval of memories that participants likely had not rehearsed recently. Although they found a large network of regions selective to autobiographical retrieval, the critical finding was that no MTL regions were more active during retrieval of recent autobiographical memories compared to remote ones. Although these studies cannot speak to the necessity of the regions, the fact that no MTL regions were less active during the retrieval of remote memories than during the retrieval of recent memories is inconsistent with the theory that the hippocampus plays a time-limited role in retrieval of autobiographical memories.

These results, therefore, suggest that differences in lesion location are unlikely to explain all of the contrary results within the amnesia literature. A more viable resolution may relate to a blurring of the contributions of semantic and episodic memory to autobiographical memory retrieval. Many of the studies that have assessed amnesic patients' ability to retrieve autobiographical memories have used procedures that do not differentiate memories that are semantic, or based on general knowledge about one's life, from those that are rich in contextual and temporal detail. Either of these types of information can allow one to recreate an autobiographical experience. For example, it is possible to remember one's sixth birthday party by reliving the tastes, sounds, and event locations. It also is possible to recall information about one's sixth birthday party by remembering the people present in a repeatedly viewed photograph, by repeating information often included in stories about the event, or by relying on general knowledge about the types of events that took place at most grade-school birthday parties.

Researchers have proposed that the ability to recall autobiographical information based on general knowledge relies on neocortical structures, just as do other forms of semantic memory (Nadel et al., 2000; Moscovitch et al., 2005). Thus, it is plausible that in studies that did not distinguish semantic from episodic contributions to autobiographical retrieval, amnesic patients appeared to have a preserved ability to retrieve autobiographical memories from remote time periods because those events had been rehearsed sufficiently to create a semantic memory, or because participants were able to rely on general knowledge about the event (Moscovitch et al., 2005).

The contribution of semantic and episodic memory to autobiographical retrieval has been assessed directly in studies that have asked participants to distinguish whether they vividly recollect a prior experience or simply know that the event has occurred. These studies have provided evidence that damage to MTL structures disrupts the ability to recall episodic details from events. A study with a patient with developmental damage to the hippocampus has clearly shown that such patients can retrieve autobiographical memories based not on episodic details but on semantic knowledge: The patient reported that there were some events from his life that he knew had happened, but that he could not recollect (Maguire et al., 2001a). Similar findings have been reported in a study of a patient who acquired MTL damage later in life (Hirano et al., 2002). In addition, Steinvorth and colleagues (2005) elicited memories for autobiographical events from two amnesic patients and from a number of age- and education-matched control participants. The investigators carefully scored the information generated by participants to distinguish recall of details based on semantic knowledge (e.g., the couch faced the television) from recall of details based on episodic knowledge (e.g., I felt the heat of the stove).

Neither patient could recall autobiographical memories with the same level of episodic detail as control participants. Their memories appeared to be constructed from semantic knowledge and were not associated with the feeling of being transported back in time (Steinvorth et al., 2005).

Further evidence to support the conclusion that many of the discrepancies in the literature relate to the amount of episodic detail remembered comes from comparing the findings of neuroimaging studies that reported greater hippocampal activity for recent than for remote memories with the findings from studies that found equivalent MTL activity regardless of a memory's age. In one study that demonstrated increased hippocampal activity for recent memories, those memories were associated with more episodic detail than were the remote memories (Piefke et al., 2003). The enhanced hippocampal activity, therefore, may relate not to the memory's age per se but, rather, to the amount of episodic detail retrieved. This hypothesis is consistent with studies that demonstrated greater hippocampal activity for memories retrieved with more episodic detail, both in patients with MTL damage (Maguire et al., 2001a) and in healthy individuals (e.g., Fink et al., 1996). In addition, a study by Addis et al. (2004) provided strong evidence that level of detail retrieved, rather than a memory's age, may be the strongest predictor of hippocampal engagement. Like Piefke et al. (2003), Addis and colleagues found that hippocampal activity was greater for recent memories than for remote ones. This finding, however, held only when the amount of episodic details recalled was not considered. Once level of detail was controlled, hippocampal activity no longer varied based on the age of the memories.

In another study that found greater hippocampal activation for recent than for remote memories, recognition memory was assessed over intervals ranging from 0 to 3 months (Takashima et al., 2006). As discussed earlier, two processes can contribute to recognition performance: episodic recollection or stimulus familiarity (Mandler, 1980; Tulving, 1985). Because recollection tends to decay over a delay faster than familiarity (Gardiner and Java, 1991), it is plausible that the decreasing hippocampal activity over time corresponded not with its reduced role in episodic recollection but with participants' increased reliance on stimulus familiarity (rather than on detailed recollection) after the delay. Support for this hypothesis is garnered from the fact that participants' performance after the delay

was poor (corrected recognition performance was around 16%; Takashima et al., 2006).

These findings emphasize the need to assess not only the age of a memory but also the amount and quality of episodic detail retrieved about the memory. Future research will be needed to examine whether contradictions regarding amnesic patients' performance can be explained by considering the level of episodic (vs. semantic) detail retrieved. Recently developed interview techniques have emphasized the distinction between episodic and semantic details and have encouraged participants to generate as much information as possible about the event (e.g., to recall the sounds, colors, etc., that were present; Levine et al., 2002). These careful interview techniques make it possible to investigate the extent to which MTL damage (and damage to specific MTL regions, such as the hippocampus) disrupts the ability to recall episodic details from remote as well as recent time periods.

1.14.6 Conclusions

Since Scoville and Milner's landmark report on the amnesic patient H.M., a great deal has been learned about the types of memories that are preserved and impaired following MTL damage. As this chapter has highlighted, however, many open questions remain to be answered. Although resolution of the debates described here is a distant goal, this chapter has raised plausible hypotheses for the contradictions in the current literature and has provided a few pointers for further investigation. A common theme has been the need to examine structure–function correlations at a more fine-grained level than has been done to date. Future research will make great strides in elucidating the contribution of different MTL structures to human learning and memory if investigators examine the roles of distinct MTL structures, parse memory function into different categories based on retrieval demands and stimulus characteristics, and document the strategies that participants use for task performance.

References

Addis DR, Moscovitch M, Crawley AP, and McAndrews MP (2004) Recollective qualities modulate hippocampal activation during autobiographical memory retrieval. *Hippocampus* 14: 752–762.

Aggleton JP and Brown MW (1999) Episodic memory, amnesia, and the hippocampal-anterior thalamic axis. *Behav. Brain Sci.* 22: 425–444.

Aggleton JP and Brown MW (2005) Contrasting hippocampal and perirhinal cortex function using immediate early gene imaging. *Q. J. Exp. Psychol. B* 58: 218–233.

Aggleton JP, Keen S, Warburton EC, and Bussey TJ (1997) Extensive cytotoxic lesions involving both the rhinal cortices and area TE impair recognition but spare spatial alternation in the rat. *Brain Res. Bull.* 43: 279–287.

Aggleton JP, Vann SD, Denby C, et al. (2005) Sparing of the familiarity component of recognition memory in a patient with hippocampal pathology. *Neuropsychologia* 43: 1810–1823.

Alvarado MC and Bachevalier J (2005) Selective neurotoxic damage to the hippocampal formation impairs performance of the transverse patterning and location memory tasks in rhesus macaques. *Hippocampus* 15: 118–131.

Alvarez P and Squire LR (1994) Memory consolidation and the medial temporal lobe: A simple network model. *Proc. Natl. Acad. Sci. USA* 91: 7041–7045.

Amaral DG (1999) Introduction: What is where in the medial temporal lobe? *Hippocampus* 9: 1–6.

Amaral DG and Insausti R (1990) The hippocampal formation. In: Paxinos G (ed.) *The Human Nervous System*, pp. 711–755. San Diego: Academic Press.

Amaral DG, Insausti R, and Cowan WM (1984) The commissural connections of the monkey hippocampal formation. *J. Comp. Neurol.* 224: 307–336.

Baker CI, Behrmann M, and Olson CR (2002) Impact of learning on representation of parts and wholes in monkey inferotemporal cortex. *Nat. Neurosci.* 5: 1210–1216.

Barense MD, Bussey TJ, Lee AC, et al. (2005) Functional specialization in the human medial temporal lobe. *J. Neurosci.* 25: 10239–10246.

Barrash J, Damasio H, Adolphs R, and Tranel D (2000) The neuroanatomical correlates of route learning impairment. *Neuropsychologia* 38: 820–836.

Bastin C, Linden M, Charnallet A, et al. (2004) Dissociation between recall and recognition memory performance in an amnesic patient with hippocampal damage following carbon monoxide poisoning. *Neurocase* 10: 330–344.

Baxter MG and Murray EA (2001) Opposite relationship of hippocampal and rhinal cortex damage to delayed nonmatching-to-sample deficits in monkeys. *Hippocampus* 11: 61–71.

Bayley P, Hopkins RO, and Squire LR (2003) Successful recollection of remote autobiographical memories by amnesic patients with medial temporal lobe lesions. *Neuron* 38: 135–144.

Bayley PJ, Gold JJ, Hopkins RO, and Squire LR (2005) The neuroanatomy of remote memory. *Neuron* 46: 799–810.

Beason-Held LL, Rosene DL, Killiany RJ, and Moss MB (1999) Hippocampal formation lesions produce memory impairment in the rhesus monkey. *Hippocampus* 9: 562–574.

Bohbot VD, Kalina M, Stepankova K, Petrides M, and Nadel L (1998) Spatial memory deficits in patients with lesions to the right hippocampus and to the right parahippocampal cortex. *Neuropsychologia* 36: 1217–1238.

Brown MW and Aggleton JP (2001) Recognition memory: What are the roles of the perirhinal cortex and hippocampus? *Nat Rev Neurosci* 2: 51–61.

Buckley MJ (2005) The role of the perirhinal cortex and hippocampus in learning, memory, and perception. *Q. J. Exp. Psychol. B* 58: 246–268.

Buckley MJ, Booth MC, Rolls ET, and Gaffan D (2001) Selective perceptual impairments after perirhinal cortex ablation. *J. Neurosci.* 21: 9824–9836.

Buckley MJ and Gaffan D (1997) Impairment of visual object-discrimination learning after perirhinal cortex ablation. *Behav. Neurosci.* 111: 467–475.

Buckley MJ and Gaffan D (1998) Perirhinal cortex ablation impairs visual object identification. *J. Neurosci.* 18: 2268–2275.

Buckley MJ and Gaffan D (2000) The hippocampus, perirhinal cortex and memory in the monkey. In: Bolhuis JJ (ed.) *Brain, Perception, Memory: Advances in Cognitive Neuroscience*, pp. 279–298. Oxford: Oxford University Press.

Buckley MJ, Gaffan D, and Murray EA (1997) Functional double dissociation between two inferior temporal cortical areas: Perirhinal cortex versus middle temporal gyrus. *J. Neurophysiol.* 77: 587–598.

Buckmaster CA, Eichenbaum H, Amaral DG, Suzuki WA, and Rapp PR (2004) Entorhinal cortex lesions disrupt the relational organization of memory in monkeys. *J. Neurosci.* 24: 9811–9825.

Buffalo EA, Ramus SJ, Clark RE, Teng E, Squire LR, and Zola SM (1999) Dissociation between the effects of damage to perirhinal cortex and area TE. *Learn. Mem.* 6: 572–599.

Buffalo EA, Reber PJ, and Squire LR (1998) The human perirhinal cortex and recognition memory. *Hippocampus* 8: 330–339.

Burwell RD, Witter MP, and Amaral DG (1995) Perirhinal and postrhinal cortices of the rat: A review of the neuroanatomical literature and comparison with findings from the monkey brain. *Hippocampus* 5: 390–408.

Bussey TJ and Saksida LM (2002) The organization of visual object representations: A connectionist model of effects of lesions in perirhinal cortex. *Eur. J. Neurosci.* 15: 355–364.

Bussey TJ, Saksida LM, and Murray EA (2002) Perirhinal cortex resolves feature ambiguity in complex visual discriminations. *Eur. J. Neurosci.* 15: 365–374.

Bussey TJ, Saksida LM, and Murray EA (2003) Impairments in visual discrimination after perirhinal cortex lesions: Testing "declarative" vs. "perceptual-mnemonic" views of perirhinal cortex function. *Eur. J. Neurosci.* 17: 649–660.

Bussey TJ, Saksida LM, and Murray EA (2005) The perceptual-mnemonic/feature conjunction model of perirhinal cortex function. *Q. J. Exp. Psychol. B* 58: 269–282.

Cavada C and Goldman-Rakic PS (1989) Posterior parietal cortex in rhesus monkey: I. Parcellation of areas based on distinctive limbic and sensory corticocortical connections. *J. Comp. Neurol.* 287: 393–421.

Cipolotti L, Bird C, Good T, Macmanus D, Rudge P, and Shallice T (2006) Recollection and familiarity in dense hippocampal amnesia: A case study. *Neuropsychologia* 44: 489–506.

Cipolotti L, Shallice T, Chan D, et al. (2001) Long-term retrograde amnesia ... the crucial role of the hippocampus. *Neuropsychologia* 39: 151–172.

Corkin S (1968) Acquisition of motor skill after bilateral medial temporal-lobe excision. *Neuropsychologia* 6: 255–265.

Corkin S (1984) Lasting consequences of bilateral medial temporal lobectomy: Clinical course and experimental findings in HM. *Semin. Neurol.* 4: 252–262.

Corkin S (2002) What's new with the amnesic patient HM? *Nat. Rev. Neurosci.* 3: 153–160.

Corkin S, Amaral DG, Gonzalez RG, Johnson KA, and Hyman BT (1997) HM's medial temporal lobe lesion: Findings from magnetic resonance imaging. *J. Neurosci.* 17: 3964–3979.

Correll RE and Scoville WB (1965) Performance on delayed match following lesions of medial temporal lobe structures. *J. Comp. Physiol. Psychol.* 60: 360–367.

Davachi L, Mitchell JP, and Wagner AD (2003) Multiple routes to memory: distinct medial temporal lobe processes build item and source memories. *Proc. Natl. Acad. Sci. USA* 100: 2157–2162.

Davachi L and Wagner AD (2002) Hippocampal contributions to episodic encoding: Insights from relational and item-based learning. *J. Neurophysiol.* 88: 982–990.

Desimone R and Ungerleider LG (1986) Multiple visual areas in the caudal superior temporal sulcus of the macaque. *J. Comp. Neurol.* 248: 164–189.

Dobbins IG, Rice HJ, Wagner AD, and Schacter DL (2003) Memory orientation and success: Separable neurocognitive components underlying episodic recognition. *Neuropsychologia* 41: 318–333.

Dudai Y (2004) The neurobiology of consolidations, or, how stable is the engram? *Annu. Rev. Psychol.* 55: 51–86.

Duzel E, Vargha-Khadem F, Heinze HJ, and Mishkin M (2001) Brain activity evidence for recognition without recollection after early hippocampal damage. *Proc. Natl. Acad. Sci. USA* 98: 8101–8106.

Duzel E, Habib R, Rotte M, Guderian S, Tulving E, and Heinze HJ (2003) Human hippocampal and parahippocampal activity during visual associative recognition memory for spatial and nonspatial stimulus configurations. *J. Neurosci.* 23: 9439–9444.

Eacott MJ and Gaffan EA (2005) The roles of perirhinal cortex, postrhinal cortex, and the fornix in memory for objects, contexts, and events in the rat. *Q. J. Exp. Psychol. B* 58: 202–217.

Eacott MJ, Gaffan D, and Murray EA (1994) Preserved recognition memory for small sets, and impaired stimulus identification for large sets, following rhinal cortex ablations in monkeys. *Eur. J. Neurosci.* 6: 1466–1478.

Eacott MJ and Heywood CA (1995) Perception and memory: Action and interaction. *Crit. Rev. Neurobiol.* 9: 311–320.

Eacott MJ, Machin PE, and Gaffan EA (2001) Elemental and configural visual discrimination learning following lesions to perirhinal cortex in the rat. *Behav. Brain Res.* 124: 55–70.

Epstein R, Harris A, Stanley D, and Kanwisher N (1999) The parahippocampal place area: Recognition, navigation, or encodings. *Neuron* 23: 115–125.

Epstein R and Kanwisher N (1998) A cortical representation of the local visual environment. *Nature* 392: 598–601.

Eustache F, Piolino P, Giffard B, et al. (2004) "In the course of time": A PET study of the cerebral substrates of autobiographical amnesia in Alzheimer's disease. *Brain* 127: 1549–1560.

Fink R, Gereon J, Markowitsch H, et al. (1996) Cerebral representation of one's own past: Neural networks involved in autobiographical memory. *J. Neurosci.* 16: 4275–4282.

Forwood SE, Winters BD, and Bussey TJ (2005) Hippocampal lesions that abolish spatial maze performance spare object recognition memory at delays of up to 48 hours. *Hippocampus* 15: 347–355.

Freed DM and Corkin S (1988) Rate of forgetting in HM: 6-month recognition. *Behav. Neurosci.* 102: 823–827.

Freed DM, Corkin S, and Cohen NJ (1987) Forgetting in HM: A second look. *Neuropsychologia* 25: 461–471.

Fried I, MacDonald KA, and Wilson CL (1997) Single neuron activity in human hippocampus and amygdala during recognition of faces and objects. *Neuron* 18: 753–765.

Fujii T, Yamadori A, Endo K, Suzuki K, and Fukatsu R (1999) Disproportionate retrograde amnesia in a patient with herpes simplex encephalitis. *Cortex* 35: 599–614.

Gaffan D (1994) Dissociated effects of perirhinal cortex ablation, fornix transection and amygdalectomy: Evidence for multiple memory systems in the primate temporal lobe. *Exp. Brain Res.* 99: 411–422.

Gardiner JM and Java RJ (1991) Forgetting in recognition memory with and without recollective experience. *Mem. Cogn.* 19: 617–623.

Gilbert PE and Kesner RP (2004) Memory for objects and their locations: the role of the hippocampus in retention of object-place associations. *Neurobiol. Learn. Mem.* 81: 39–45.

Gilboa A, Ramirez J, Kohler S, Westmacott R, Black SE, and Moscovitch M (2005) Retrieval of autobiographical memory in Alzheimer's disease: Relation to volumes of medial temporal lobe and other structures. *Hippocampus* 15: 535–550.

Gilboa A, Winocur G, Grady CL, Hevenor SJ, and Moscovitch M (2004) Remembering our past: Functional neuroanatomy of recollection of recent and very remote personal events. *Cereb. Cortex* 14: 1214–1225.

Giovanello KS, Keane MM, and Verfaellie M (2006) The contribution of familiarity to associative memory in amnesia. *Neuropsychologia.* 44: 1859–1865.

Giovanello KS, Schnyer DM, and Verfaellie M (2004) A critical role for the anterior hippocampus in relational memory: Evidence from an fMRI study comparing associative and item recognition. *Hippocampus* 14: 5–8.

Giovanello KS and Verfaellie M (2001) The relationship between recall and recognition in amnesia: Effects of matching recognition between amnesic patients and controls. *Neuropsychology* 15: 444–451.

Giovanello KS, Verfaellie M, and Keane MM (2003) Disproportionate deficit in associative recognition relative to item recognition in global amnesia. *Cogn. Affect. Behav. Neurosci.* 3: 186–194.

Goldman-Rakic PS, Selemon LD, and Schwartz ML (1984) Dual pathways connecting the dorsolateral prefrontal cortex with the hippocampal formation and parahippocampal cortex in the rhesus monkey. *Neuroscience* 12: 719–743.

Goulet S and Murray EA (2001) Neural substrates of crossmodal association memory in monkeys: The amygdala versus the anterior rhinal cortex. *Behav. Neurosci.* 115: 271–284.

Green RE and Kopelman MD (2002) Contribution of recollection and familiarity judgements to rate of forgetting in organic amnesia. *Cortex* 38: 161–178.

Haist F, Shimamura AP, and Squire LR (1992) On the relationship between recall and recognition memory. *J. Exp. Psychol. Learn. Mem. Cogn.* 18: 691–702.

Hampton RR (2005) Monkey perirhinal cortex is critical for visual memory, but not for visual perception: Reexamination of the behavioural evidence from monkeys. *Q. J. Exp. Psychol. B* 58: 283–299.

Henke K, Kroll NE, Behniea H, et al. (1999) Memory lost and regained following bilateral hippocampal damage. *J. Cogn. Neurosci.* 11: 682–697.

Henson RN (2005) A mini-review of fMRI studies of human medial temporal lobe activity associated with recognition memory. *Q. J. Exp. Psychol. B* 58: 340–360.

Henson RN, Cansino S, Herron JE, Robb WG, and Rugg MD (2003) A familiarity signal in human anterior medial temporal cortex? *Hippocampus* 13: 301–304.

Hirst W, Johnson MK, Kim JK, Phelps EA, Risse G, and Volpe BT (1986) Recognition and recall in amnesics. *J. Exp. Psychol. Learn. Mem. Cogn.* 12: 445–451.

Hirst W, Johnson MK, Phelps EA, and Volpe BT (1988) More on recognition and recall in amnesics. *J. Exp. Psychol. Learn. Mem. Cogn.* 14: 758–762.

Hockley WE and Consoli A (1999) Familiarity and recollection in item and associative recognition. *Mem. Cogn.* 27: 657–664.

Holdstock JS, Gutnikov SA, Gaffan D, and Mayes AR (2000) Perceptual and mnemonic matching-to-sample in humans: Contributions of the hippocampus, perirhinal and other medial temporal lobe cortices. *Cortex* 36: 301–322.

Holdstock JS, Mayes AR, Gong QY, Roberts N, and Kapur N (2005) Item recognition is less impaired than recall and associative recognition in a patient with selective hippocampal damage. *Hippocampus* 15: 203–215.

Holdstock JS, Mayes AR, Roberts N, et al. (2002) Under what conditions is recognition spared relative to recall after selective hippocampal damage in humans? *Hippocampus* 12: 341–351.

Jagadeesh B, Chelazzi L, Mishkin M, and Desimone R (2001) Learning increases stimulus salience in anterior inferior temporal cortex of the macaque. *J. Neurophysiol.* 86: 290–303.

Jarrard LE (1995) What does the hippocampus really do? *Behav. Brain Res.* 71: 1–10.

Johnson MK and Kim JK (1985) Recognition of pictures by alcoholic Korsakoff patients. *Bull. Psychonomic Soc.* 23: 456–458.

Kandel ER (2001) The molecular biology of memory storage: A dialogue between genes and synapses. *Science* 294: 1030–1038.

Kapur N and Brooks DJ (1999) Temporally-specific retrograde amnesia in two cases of discrete bilateral hippocampal pathology. *Hippocampus* 9: 247–254.

Kensinger EA (2004) Remembering emotional experiences: The contribution of valence and arousal. *Rev. Neurosci.* 15: 241–251.

Kensinger EA and Giovanello KS (2005) The status of semantic and episodic memory in amnesia. In: Chen FJ (ed.) *Brain Mapping and Language.* Hauppauge, NY: Nova Science.

Kensinger EA and Schacter DL (2006) Amygdala activity is associated with the successful encoding of item, but not source, information for positive and negative stimuli. *J. Neurosci.* 26: 2564–2570.

Kensinger EA, Ullman MT, and Corkin S (2001) Bilateral medial temporal lobe damage does not prevent the retrieval and use of grammatical or lexical information: Evidence from the amnesic patient HM. *Hippocampus* 11: 347–360.

King JA, Trinkler I, Hartley T, Vargha-Khadem F, and Burgess N (2004) The hippocampal role in spatial memory and the familiarity-recollection distinction: A case study. *Neuropsychology* 18: 405–417.

Kinsbourne M and Wood F (1975) Short-term memory processes and the amnesic syndrome. In: Deutsch D and Deutsch AJ (eds.) *Short-Term Memory*, pp. 258–291. New York: Academic Press.

Kirwan CB and Stark CE (2004) Medial temporal lobe activation during encoding and retrieval of novel face-name pairs. *Hippocampus* 14: 919–930.

Kohler S, Black SE, Sinden M, et al. (1998) Memory impairments associated with hippocampal versus parahippocampal-gyrus atrophy: An MR volumetry study in Alzheimer's disease. *Neuropsychologia* 36: 901–914.

Kohler S, Danckert S, Gati JS, and Menon RS (2005) Novelty responses to relational and non-relational information in the hippocampus and the parahippocampal region: A comparison based on event-related fMRI. *Hippocampus* 15: 763–774.

Kopelman MD, Lasserson D, Kingsley DR, et al. (2003) Retrograde amnesia and the volume of critical brain structures. *Hippocampus* 13: 879–891.

Kopelman MD and Stanhope N (1998) Recall and recognition memory in patients with focal frontal, temporal lobe and diencephalic lesions. *Neuropsychologia* 36: 785–796.

Kopelman MD, Stanhope N, and Kingsley D (1999) Retrograde amnesia in patients with diencephalic, temporal lobe or frontal lesions. *Neuropsychologia* 37: 939–958.

Lavenex P and Amaral DG (2000) Hippocampal-neocortical interaction: A hierarchy of associativity. *Hippocampus* 10: 420–430.

Lee AC, Barense MD, and Graham KS (2005b) The contribution of the human medial temporal lobe to perception: Bridging the gap between animal and human studies. *Q. J. Exp. Psychol. B* 58: 300–325.

Lee AC, Buckley MJ, Pegman SJ, et al. (2005a) Specialization in the medial temporal lobe for processing of objects and scenes. *Hippocampus* 15: 782–797.

Lee AC, Bussey TJ, Murray EA, et al. (2005c) Perceptual deficits in amnesia: Challenging the medial temporal lobe "mnemonic" view. *Neuropsychologia* 43: 1–11.

Lee JL, Everitt BJ, and Thomas KL (2004) Independent cellular processes for hippocampal memory consolidation and reconsolidation. *Science* 304: 839–843.

Levine B, Svoboda E, Hay JF, Winocur G, and Moscovitch M (2002) Aging and autobiographical memory: Dissociating episodic from semantic retrieval. *Psychol. Aging* 17: 677–689.

Levy DA, Shrager Y, and Squire LR (2005) Intact visual discrimination of complex and feature-ambiguous stimuli in the absence of perirhinal cortex. *Learn. Mem.* 12: 61–66.

Logothetis NK (1998) Single units and conscious vision. *Philos. Trans. R. Soc. Lond. B Biol. Sci.* 353: 1801–1818.

MacAndrew SBG, Jones GV, and Mayes AR (1994) No selective deficit in recall in amnesia. *Memory* 2: 241–254.

Maguire EA, Burgess N, Donnett JG, et al. (1998) Knowing where and getting there, a human navigation network. *Science* 280: 921–924.

Maguire EA, Henson RNA, Mummery CJ, and Frith CD (2001a) Activity in prefrontal cortex, not hippocampus, varies parametrically with the increasing remoteness of memories. *Cogn. Neurosci. Neuropsychol.* 12: 441–444.

Maguire EA, Vargha-Khadem F, and Mishkin M (2001b) The effects of bilateral hippocampal damage on fMRI regional activations and interactions during memory retrieval. *Brain* 124: 1156–1170.

Mahut H, Zola-Morgan S, and Moss M (1982) Hippocampal resections impair associative learning and recognition memory in the monkey. *J. Neurosci.* 2: 1214–1220.

Mandler G (1980) Recognizing the judgment of previous occurrence. *Psychol. Rev.* 87: 252–271.

Manns JR, Hopkins RO, Reed JM, Kitchener EG, and Squire LR (2003) Recognition memory and the human hippocampus. *Neuron* 37: 171–180.

Manns JR and Squire LR (1999) Impaired recognition memory on the Doors and People Test after damage limited to the hippocampal region. *Hippocampus* 9: 495–499.

Mayes AR, Holdstock JS, Isaac CL, Hunkin NM, and Roberts N (2002) Relative sparing of item recognition memory in a patient with adult-onset damage limited to the hippocampus. *Hippocampus* 12: 325–340.

Mayes AR, Holdstock JS, Isaac CL, et al. (2004) Associative recognition in a patient with selective hippocampal lesions and relatively normal item recognition. *Hippocampus* 14: 763–784.

McGaugh JL (2000) Memory – A century of consolidation. *Science* 287: 248–251.

Medved MI and Hirst W (2006) Islands of memory: Autobiographical remembering in amnestics. *Memory* 14: 276–288.

Meunier M, Bachevalier J, Mishkin M, and Murray EA (1993) Effects on visual recognition of combined and separate ablations of the entorhinal and perirhinal cortex in rhesus monkeys. *J. Neurosci.* 13: 5418–5432.

Milner B (1962) Les troubles de la mémoire accompagnants des lésions hippocampiques bilatérales. In: *Physiologie de l'hippocampe*, pp. 257–272 Paris: Centre National de la Recherche Scientifique.

Milner B, Corkin S, and Teuber H-L (1968) Further analysis of the hippocampal amnesia syndrome: 14-year follow-up study of HM. *Neuropsychologia* 6: 215–234.

Mishkin M (1978) Memory in monkeys severely impaired by combined but not by separate removal of amygdala and hippocampus. *Nature* 273: 297–298.

Mishkin M (1982) A memory system in the monkey. *Philos. Trans. R. Soc. Lond. B Biol. Sci.* 298: 83–95.

Miyashita Y (1993) Inferior temporal cortex: Where visual perception meets memory. *Annu. Rev. Neurosci.* 16: 245–263.

Moscovitch M and Nadel L (1998) Consolidation and the hippocampal complex revisited: In defense of the multiple-trace model. *Curr. Opin. Neurobiol.* 8(2): 297–300.

Moscovitch M, Rosenbaum RS, Gilboa A, et al. (2005) Functional neuroanatomy of remote episodic, semantic and spatial memory: A unified account based on multiple trace theory. *J. Anat.* 207: 35–66.

Mumby DG (2001) Perspectives on object-recognition memory following hippocampal damage: Lessons from studies in rats. *Behav. Brain Rev.* 127: 159–181.

Murray EA and Bussey TJ (1999) Perceptual-mnemonic functions of perirhinal cortex. *Trends Cogn. Sci.* 3: 142–151.

Murray EA and Mishkin M (1986) Visual recognition in monkeys following rhinal cortical ablations combined with either amygdalectomy or hippocampectomy. *J. Neurosci.* 6: 1991–2003.

Murray EA and Mishkin M (1998) Object recognition and location memory in monkeys with excitotoxic lesions of the amygdala and hippocampus. *J. Neurosci.* 18: 6568–6582.

Mumby DG and Pinel JP (1994) Rhinal cortex lesions and object recognition in rats. *Behav. Neurosci.* 108: 11–18.

Murray EA and Richmond BJ (2001) Role of perirhinal cortex in object perception, memory, and associations. *Curr. Opin. Neurobiol.* 11: 188–193.

Murre JM, Graham KS, and Hodges JR (2001) Semantic dementia: relevance to connectionist models of long-term memory. *Brain* 124: 647–675.

Nadel L and Moscovitch M (1997) Memory consolidation, retrograde amnesia and the hippocampal complex. *Curr. Opin. Neurobiol.* 7: 217–227.

Nadel L and Moscovitch M (1998) Hippocampal contributions to cortical plasticity. *Neuropharmacology* 37: 431–439.

Nadel L, Samsonovich A, Ryan L, and Moscovitch M (2000) Multiple trace theory of human memory: Computational, neuroimaging, and neuropsychological results. *Hippocampus* 10: 352–368.

Nestor PJ, Graham KS, Bozeat S, Simons JS, and Hodges JR (2002) Memory consolidation and the hippocampus: Further evidence from the study of autobiographical memory in semantic dementia and the frontal variant of frontotemporal dementia. *Neuropsychologia* 40: 633–654.

Norman G and Eacott MJ (2004) Impaired object recognition with increasing levels of feature ambiguity in rats with perirhinal cortex lesions. *Behav. Brain Res.* 148: 79–91.

O'Kane G, Kensinger EA, and Corkin S (2004) Evidence for semantic learning in amnesia: A study with the amnesic patient HM. *Hippocampus* 14: 417–425.

O'Keefe J (1999) Do hippocampal pyramidal cells signal non-spatial as well as spatial information? *Hippocampus* 9: 352–364.

O'Keefe J and Burgess N (2005) Dual phase and rate coding in hippocampal place cells: theoretical significance and relationship to entorhinal grid cells. *Hippocampus* 15: 853–866.

O'Reilly RC and Rudy JW (2001) Conjunctive representations in learning and memory: principles of cortical and hippocampal function. *Psychol. Rev.* 108: 311–345.

Orbach J, Milner B, and Rasmussen T (1960) Learning and retention in monkeys after amygdala-hippocampus resection. *Arch. Neurol.* 3: 230–251.

Otto T and Eichenbaum H (1992) Complementary roles of the orbital prefrontal cortex and the pirhinal-entorhinal cortices in an odor-guided delayed-nonmatching-to-sample task. *Behav. Neurosci.* 106: 762–775.

Phelps EA (2004) Human emotion and memory: Interactions of the amygdala and hippocampal complex. *Curr. Opin. Neurobiol.* 14: 198–202.

Phelps EA and LeDoux JE (2005) Contributions of the amygdala to emotion processing: From animal models to human behavior. *Neuron* 48: 175–187.

Piefke M, Weiss HP, Zilles K, Markowitsch JH, and Fink RG (2003) Differential remoteness and emotional tone modulate the neural correlates of autobiographical memory. *Brain* 126: 650–668.

Piolino P, Desgranges B, Belliard S, et al. (2003) Autobiographical memory and autonoetic consciousness: Triple dissociation in neurodegenerative diseases. *Brain* 126: 2203–2219.

Ploner CJ, Gaymard BM, Ehrle N, et al. (1999) Spatial memory deficits in patients with lesions affecting the medial temporal neocortex. *Ann. Neurol.* 45: 312–319.

Ploner CJ, Gaymard BM, Rivaud-Pechoux S, et al. (2000) Lesions affecting the parahippocampal cortex yield spatial memory deficits in humans. *Cereb. Cortex* 10: 1211–1216.

Pruessner JC, Kohler S, Crane J, et al. (2002) Volumetry of temporopolar, perirhinal, entorhinal and parahippocampal cortex from high-resolution MR images: Considering the variability of the collateral sulcus. *Cereb. Cortex* 12: 1342–1353.

Rajaram S (1993) Remembering and knowing: Two means of access to the personal past. *Mem. Cogn.* 21: 89–102.

Rajaram S, Hamilton M, and Bolton A (2002) Distinguishing states of awareness from confidence during retrieval: Evidence from amnesia. *Cogn. Affect. Behav. Neurosci.* 2: 227–235.

Ranganath C, Yonelinas AP, Cohen MX, Dy CJ, Tom SM, and D'Esposito M (2004) Dissociable correlates of recollection and familiarity within the medial temporal lobes. *Neuropsychologia* 42: 2–13.

Reed JM and Squire LR (1997) Impaired recognition memory in patients with lesions limited to the hippocampal formation. *Behav. Neurosci.* 111: 667–675.

Reed JM and Squire LR (1998) Retrograde amnesia for facts and events: Findings from four new cases. *J. Neurosci.* 18: 3943–3954.

Reed JM and Squire LR (1999) Impaired transverse patterning in human amnesia is a special case of impaired memory for two-choice discrimination tasks. *Behav. Neurosci.* 113: 3–9.

Rempel-Clower NL, Zola SM, Squire LR, and Amaral DG (1996) Three cases of enduring memory impairment after bilateral damage limited to the hippocampal formation. *J. Neurosci.* 16: 5233–5255.

Ribot T (1881) *Les Maladies de la Mémoire [Diseases of Memory]*. Paris: Germer Baillere.

Rosenbaum RS, Köhler S, Schacter DL, et al. (2005) The case of KC: Contributions of a memory-impaired person to memory theory. *Neuropsychologia* 43: 989–1021.

Ryan JD, Althoff RR, Whitlow S, and Cohen NJ (2000) Amnesia is a deficit in relational memory. *Psychol. Sci.* 11: 454–461.

Ryan JD and Cohen NJ (2004) Processing and short-term retention of relational information in amnesia. *Neuropsychologia* 42: 497–511.

Ryan L, Nadel L, Keil K, et al. (2001) Hippocampal complex and retrieval of recent and very remote autobiographical memories: Evidence from functional magnetic resonance imaging in neurologically intact people. *Hippocampus* 11: 707–714.

Schmolck H, Kensinger EA, Corkin S, and Squire LR (2002) Semantic knowledge in patient HM and other patients with bilateral medial and lateral temporal lobe lesions. *Hippocampus* 12: 520–533.

Schnider A, Bassetti C, Schnider A, Gutbrod K, and Ozdoba C (1995) Very severe amnesia with acute onset after isolated hippocampal damage due to systemic lupus erythematosus. *J. Neurol. Neurosurg. Psychiatry* 59: 644–666.

Scoville WB and Milner B (1957) Loss of recent memory after bilateral hippocampal lesions. *J. Neurol. Neurosurg. Psychiatry* 20: 11–21.

Selemon LD and Goldman-Rakic PS (1988) Common cortical and subcortical targets of the dorsolateral prefrontal and posterior parietal cortices in the rhesus monkey: Evidence for a distributed neural network subserving spatially guided behavior. *J. Neurosci.* 8: 4049–4068.

Shaw C, Kentridge RW, and Aggleton JP (1990) Cross-modal matching by amnesic subjects. *Neuropsychologia* 28: 665–671.

Shimamura AP and Squire LR (1988) Long-term memory in amnesia: Cued recall, recognition memory and confidence ratings. *J. Exp. Psychol. Learn. Mem. Cogn.* 14: 763–770.

Skotko B, Kensinger EA, Locascio JJ, et al. (2004) Puzzling thoughts for HM: Can new semantic memories be anchored to old semantic memories? *Neuropsychology* 18: 756–776.

Smith ML (1988) Recall of spatial location by the amnesic patient HM. *Brain Cogn.* 7: 178–183.

Squire LR (1975) A stable impairment in remote memory following electroconvulsive therapy. *Neuropsychologia* 13: 51–58.

Squire LR (1992) Memory and the hippocampus: A synthesis from findings with rats, monkeys and humans. *Psychol. Rev.* 99: 195–231.

Squire LR and Alvarez P (1995) Retrograde amnesia and memory consolidation: A neurobiological perspective. *Curr. Opin. Neurobiol.* 5: 169–177.

Squire LR, Cohen NJ, and Nadel L (1984) The medial temporal region and memory consolidation: A new hypothesis. In: Weingartner H, Parker E (eds.) *Memory Consolidation*, pp. 185–210. Hillsdale NJ: Lawrence Erlbaum.

Squire LR, Stark CE, and Clark RE (2004) The medial temporal lobe. *Annu. Rev. Neurosci.* 27: 279–306.

Squire LR and Zola SM (1998) Episodic memory, semantic memory, and amnesia. *Hippocampus* 8: 205–211.

Squire LR and Zola-Morgan S (1991) The medial temporal lobe memory system. *Science* 253: 1380–1386.

Stark CE, Bayley PJ, and Squire LR (2002) Recognition memory for single items and for associations is similarly impaired following damage to the hippocampal region. *Learn. Mem.* 9: 238–242.

Stark CEL and Squire LR (2000) Intact visual perceptual discrimination in humans in the absence of perirhinal cortex. *Learn. Mem.* 7: 273–278.

Stark CE and Squire LR (2001) Simple and associative recognition memory in the hippocampal region. *Learn. Mem.* 8: 190–197.

Stark CE and Squire LR (2003) Hippocampal damage equally impairs memory for single items and memory for conjunctions. *Hippocampus* 13: 281–292.

Stefanacci L, Suzuki WA, and Amaral DG (1996) Organization of connections between the amygdaloid complex and the perirhinal and parahippocampal cortices in macaque monkeys. *J. Comp. Neurol.* 375: 552–582.

Steinvorth S, Corkin S, and Halgren E (2006) Ecphory of autobiographical memories: An fMRI study of recent and remote memory retrieval. *Neuroimage* 30: 285–298.

Steinvorth S, Levine B, and Corkin S (2005) Medial temporal lobe structures are needed to re-experience remote autobiographical memories: Evidence from HM and WR. *Neuropsychologia* 43: 479–496.

Stepien LS, Cordeau JP, and Rasmussen T (1960) The effect of temporal lobe and hippocampal lesions on auditory and verbal recent memory. *Brain* 83: 470–489.

Suzuki WA (1996) The anatomy, physiology and functions of the perirhinal cortex. *Curr. Opin. Neurobiol.* 6: 179–186.

Suzuki WA and Amaral DG (1994) Perirhinal and parahippocampal cortices of the macaque monkey: Cortical afferents. *J. Comp. Neurol.* 350: 497–533.

Suzuki WA and Amaral DG (2003) Where are the perirhinal and parahippocampal cortices? A historical overview of the nomenclature and boundaries applied to the primate medial temporal lobe. *Neuroscience* 120: 893–906.

Suzuki WA and Amaral DG (2004) Functional neuroanatomy of the medial temporal lobe memory system. *Cortex* 40: 220–222.

Suzuki WA and Eichenbaum H (2000) The neurophysiology of memory. *Ann. NY Acad. Sci.* 911: 175–191.

Suzuki WA, Miller EK, and Desimone R (1997) Object and place memory in the macaque entorhinal cortex. *J. Neurophysiol.* 78: 1062–1081.

Takashima A, Petersson KM, Rutters F, et al. (2006) Declarative memory consolidation in humans: A prospective functional magnetic resonance imaging study. *Proc. Natl. Acad. Sci. USA* 103: 756–761.

Teyler TJ and DiScenna P (1986) The hippocampal memory indexing theory. *Behav. Neurosci.* 100: 147–154.

Thornton JA, Rothblat LA, and Murray EA (1997) Rhinal cortex removal produces amnesia for preoperatively learned discrimination problems but fails to disrupt postoperative acquisition and retention in rhesus monkeys. *J. Neurosci.* 17: 8536–8549.

Tulving E (1985) Memory and consciousness. *Can. Psychol.* 26: 1–12.

Turriziani P, Fadda L, Caltagirone C, and Carlesimo GA (2004) Recognition memory for single items and for associations in amnesic patients. *Neuropsychologia* 42: 426–433.

Ungerleider LG and Haxby JV (1994) "What" and "where" in the human brain. *Curr. Opin. Neurobiol.* 4: 157–165.

Van Hoesen GW (1995) Anatomy of the medial temporal lobe. *Magn. Reson. Imaging* 13: 1047–1055.

Vargha-Khadem F, Gadian DG, Watkins KE, et al. (1997) Differential effects of early hippocampal pathology on episodic and semantic memory. *Science* 277: 376–380.

Wan H, Aggleton JP, and Brown MW (1999) Different contributions of the hippocampus and perirhinal cortex to recognition memory. *J. Neurosci.* 19: 1142–1148.

Warrington EK (1996) Studies of retrograde memory: A long-term view. *Proc. Natl. Acad. Sci. USA* 93: 13523–13526.

Warrington EK and McCarthy RA (1988) The fractionation of retrograde amnesia. *Brain Cogn.* 7: 184–200.

Westmacott R, Leach L, Freedman M, and Moscovitch M (2001) Different patterns of autobiographical memory loss in semantic dementia and medial temporal lobe amnesia: A challenge to consolidation theory. *Neurocase* 7: 37–55.

Wiig KA and Bilkey DK (1995) Lesions of rat perirhinal cortex exacerbate the memory deficit observed following damage to the fimbria-fornix. *Behav. Neurosci.* 109(4): 620–630.

Winters BD, Forwood SE, Cowell RA, Saksida LM, and Bussey TJ (2004) Double dissociation between the effects of peri-postrhinal cortex and hippocampal lesions on tests of object recognition and spatial memory: Heterogeneity of function within the temporal lobe. *J. Neurosci.* 24: 5901–5908.

Wood ER, Dudchenko PA, Robitsek RJ, and Eichenbaum H (2000) Hippocampal neurons encode information about different types of memory episodes occurring in the same location. *Neuron* 27(3): 623–633.

Yonelinas AP, Hopfinger JB, Buonocore MH, Kroll NE, and Baynes K (2001) Hippocampal, parahippocampal and occipital-temporal contributions to associative and item recognition memory: An fMRI study. *Neuroreport* 12: 359–363.

Young BJ, Otto T, Fox GD, and Eichenbaum H (1997) Memory representation within the parahippocampal region. *J. Neurosci.* 17: 5183–5195.

Zola SM, Squire LR, Teng E, Stefanacci L, Buffalo EA, and Clark RE (2000) Impaired recognition memory in monkeys after damage limited to the hippocampal region. *J. Neurosci.* 20: 451–463.

Zola-Morgan S and Squire LR (1985) Medial temporal lesions in monkeys impair memory on a variety of tasks sensitive to human amnesia. *Behav. Neurosci.* 99: 22–34.

Zola-Morgan S and Squire LR (1986) Memory impairment in monkeys following lesions limited to the hippocampus. *Behav. Neurosci.* 100: 155–160.

Zola-Morgan S, Squire LR, Amaral DG, and Suzuki WA (1989) Lesions of perirhinal and parahippocampal cortex that spare the amygdala and hippocampal formation produce severe memory impairment. *J. Neurosci.* 9: 4355–4370.

Zola-Morgan S, Squire LR, Clower RP, and Rempel NL (1993) Damage to the perirhinal cortex exacerbates memory impairment following lesions to the hippocampal formation. *J. Neurosci.* 13: 251–265.

Zola-Morgan S, Squire LR, and Mishkin M (1982) The neuroanatomy of amnesia: amygdala-hippocampus versus temporal stem. *Science* 218: 1337–1339.

Zola-Morgan S, Squire LR, and Ramus SJ (1994) Severity of memory impairment in monkeys as a function of locus and extent of damage within the medial temporal lobe memory system. *Hippocampus* 4: 483–495.

1.15 The Nature of Infantile Amnesia

M. L. Howe, Lancaster University, Lancaster, UK

1.15.1 Introduction

Infantile amnesia, a term first used by Freud (1905/1953) over 100 years ago, refers to a unique memory phenomenon that occurs in humans and nonhumans alike. Essentially, infantile amnesia refers to a period very early in an organism's life when memories that are formed tend to be short-lived or inaccessible after a relatively short time frame. Historically, explanations have tended to fall into two camps. The first, or retrieval, camp holds that information that is stored early in life remains intact in storage and that infantile amnesia is the result of fluctuations in the retrievability of that information (Hoffding, 1891; Freud, 1914, 1938). The alternative, or storage, camp holds that memory storage is fragile early in life and that infantile amnesia is the direct result of this labile storage system (Kohler, 1929, 1941).

Modern theorists echo similar storage-failure and retrieval-failure conjectures about the nature of infantile amnesia. Proponents of this latter view argue that if storage is permanent and the inability to recall early experiences is simply a matter of retrieval failure, then such failures of remembering should be alleviated, given the appropriate reinstatement of retrieval cues (e.g., see Nash's (1987) discussion of the hypnotic age regression literature). This argument is fundamentally an encoding specificity one in which contextually dependent memories survive intact and can be recovered once the encoding context (internal and external) is reinstated. Of course it is difficult, if not impossible, to reinstate the context of infancy, and other data (reviewed later in this chapter) rule out a pure retrieval-based explanation in any event. Storage-based explanations have faired somewhat better. There is considerable evidence that although memory is much

better in infancy than originally thought, storage in the immature organism is relatively fragile (Rovee-Collier et al., 2001). If storage is not permanent, particularly in the immature organism, then no matter what retrieval remedies are brought to bear, recall of early experiences may be impossible. Indeed, the general volatility of memory storage has been well documented over the years (e.g., Loftus and Loftus, 1980) and that it is somehow fundamentally different in infancy is equally well known (Hayne, 2004).

The issue concerning the fate of early memories is central to many theories of development, as most theories place special formative emphasis on experiences that occur early in life. This particular relevance of early experience was pivotal in Freudian theory as well as many subsequent theories of social, emotional, and personality development (e.g., see Ainsworth and Bowlby, 1991). Indeed, some early research demonstrated the profound effects of early experience (in this case, social isolation) on subsequent development (Skeels, 1966; Harlow et al., 1971). The question is whether memories of very early experiences that are alleged to result in aberrant adult outcomes are still available to consciousness or are lost to infantile amnesia, potentially exerting their effects without the person's awareness (also see Kagan, 1996).

In the nonhuman animal literature, infantile amnesia refers to the faster forgetting that is associated with immature organisms than with more mature members of the species. This more rapid forgetting in younger than older animals occurs even when levels of initial learning have been equated (see Campbell and Spear, 1972; Arnold and Spear, 1997). Much of the animal research on accelerated forgetting during infancy has been conducted on the rat, with the early consensus being that young pups were more susceptible to interference effects in memory (Smith and Spear, 1981), a condition also thought to pertain to young humans (Kail, 2002).

Although increased susceptibility to interference effects is certainly one possible contributor to the frailty of early memory, it is by no means the sole factor. Indeed, depending upon encoding and testing conditions, young humans may be no more susceptible to interference than older children and adults (e.g., Howe, 2000; Rovee-Collier et al., 2001). As we will see, the waning of infantile amnesia is the result of changes to a number of basic memory processes, ones that emerge from correlated changes in cognitive structures. To see how, I review the latest research concerning neurobiological and behavioral underpinnings of infantile amnesia in human and nonhuman animal populations.

1.15.2 Neurobiological Factors

To begin, consider how neural maturation impacts memory. Because of the high degree of overlap between human and nonhuman animal species in the development, anatomy, and function of the hippocampus (and parahippocampal regions; e.g., Ferbinteanu et al., 2006; Manns and Eichenbaum, 2006), the results of this research will be considered together. Given space limitations, I present only a brief overview of the basics of the neural underpinnings of memory development and will touch on more specific aspects as needed (more detailed reviews can be found in Serres, 2001; Gogtay et al., 2006).

Nelson (1997, 2000) has argued that there are at least two memory systems that have different developmental trajectories. The earliest to emerge is implicit (or procedural) memory, a system that is capable of performing recognition tasks such as novelty preference, habituation, classical and operant conditioning, and visual expectancy tasks. The neurological substrates that are involved in implicit memory (e.g., the hippocampus, striatum, cerebellum, and olivary–cerebellar complex) are sufficiently developed very early in postnatal life to support this form of memory basically from birth (and perhaps before).

Explicit (or declarative) memory not only depends on hippocampal structures but is also thought to depend on inputs from elaborate networks of neocortex

that converge on parahippocampal structures (e.g., entorhinal cortex; Serres, 2001). These diverse inputs are then organized into a cohesive memory trace in the hippocampus. Although some of the neural structures related to explicit or declarative memory develop early, others have a more protracted developmental course, with significant changes occurring at the end of the first postnatal year and the beginning of the second year (Serres, 2001). Of particular interest is the dentate gyrus of the hippocampus, because this serves as a critical link in the circuitry that connects the parahippocampal structures to the hippocampus (specifically to the CA3 and CA1 regions). Developments are also occurring in the frontal cortex and in the reciprocal connections between the neocortex and the hippocampus (Serres, 2001). Although neurogenesis in the dentate gyrus continues throughout life (e.g., Aimone et al., 2006), the network necessary to sustain explicit memory reaches functional maturity (in humans) late in the first year of life (Nelson, 1997, 2000; Serres, 2001). Although additional refinements occur throughout development, by the beginning of the second year of postnatal life, humans are capable of sustaining explicit or declarative recollection.

From this brief review, it would seem that the timing of these neurological changes (at least in humans) is at odds with the oft-cited empirical finding that the earliest autobiographical memories begin around the end of the second year of life (see Howe and Courage, 1993, 1997). As will become clear in later sections, neurobiological constraints may not be at the source of infantile amnesia at all. Although there are clear advances in neocortical structures that continue during early maturation, some of which might contribute, albeit indirectly, to the demise of infantile amnesia (see later discussion; Levine, 2004), I have argued previously (Howe and Courage, 1993, 1997; Howe, 2000, 2004), as has Bauer (2004), that neither age nor neurological developments control memory longevity after the basic neural 'hardware' has been laid down. Instead, the termination of infantile amnesia, like changes in other areas of memory, is controlled by alterations in the basic processes of encoding, storage, retention, and retrieval that drive memory across development and perhaps species. Although such changes may have obvious neurobiological correlates, their origins may have more to do with the development of an organism's knowledge (cognitive) structures than with additional neurobiological change by itself.

1.15.3   Behavioral and Cognitive Factors

1.15.3.1   Nonhuman Animal Populations

Research on behavioral and cognitive manifestations of infantile amnesia has focused on both faster forgetting in immature organisms and whether non-human animals possess autobiographical (or even episodic) memory in the first place. This latter question asks whether animals are 'stuck in time' (for a review, see Roberts, 2002). If so, then they cannot travel cognitively into the past and hence do not have what Tulving (1985, 1989, 1993) refers to as episodic memory. Tulving contrasts episodic memory and its concomitant autonoetic consciousness (personal awareness of remembering) with semantic memory and noetic consciousness in which organisms possess general information but do not experience a specific awareness of experiencing it in time. This distinction has also been linked to remember–know judgments, where remember judgments involve episodic memory because the organism remembers a particular experience having occurred in a past context, whereas know judgments involve a sense of familiarity but not a sense of personal, past experience. Although this sense of time also refers to planning for the future, the main point is whether nonhuman animals do possess the what, where, when, and perhaps who of past events. Tulving argues that, although nonhuman animals do have a well-developed knowledge of the world (e.g., general relationships between stimuli and events) derived from specific episodes, they do not code temporal information that allows them to travel back and reexperience the past episodes – that is, they have semantic memory but not episodic memory.

Clearly, it is unlikely that we will ever establish whether nonhuman animals (or preverbal humans) have autonoetic consciousness. This is because there are no agreed-upon behavioral markers of conscious experience (Griffiths et al., 1999). Hence, any model of episodic memory that requires conscious awareness must apply solely to language-using organisms. As Clayton et al. (2003a) point out, with the exception of putatively language-savvy apes and parrots, there is no litmus test that would establish that an organism was reexperiencing the past when remembering an episode.

Recognizing the futility of using phenomenological criteria in language-challenged organisms, researchers have focused on behavioral criteria in an attempt to establish that nonhuman animals (and preverbal humans) do have episodic-like memory.

Specifically, there are three behavioral criteria that are consistent with Tulving's definition of episodic memory: (1) memory content, recollecting what happened where and when; (2) memory structure, having an integrated what-where-when representation; and (3) memory flexibility, deploying information in a flexible fashion (e.g., see Clayton et al., 2003a). Concerning the first criteria, the when of what-where-when seems to be particularly important in establishing that the memory is episodic. That is, a number of different episodes can all share what and where, but they cannot share when. Concerning the second criteria, what, where, and when cannot simply be linearly connected, but rather all three need to be in an integrated representation, so that retrieving any one retrieves the others. The third criteria simply states that, because episodic memories are declarative, they are by definition flexible (unlike nondeclarative memories, which are inflexible and inaccessible to consciousness). Therefore, animals should be able to flexibly deploy memories in new situations.

To date, episodic-like memories have been demonstrated in birds (e.g., western scrub jays, *Aphelocoma californica*; Clayton and Dickinson, 1998, 1999; Clayton et al., 2001, 2003c, 2005; Dally et al., 2006), rats (*Ratus norvegicus*; Eacott et al., 2005; Norman and Eacott, 2005), and gorillas (*Gorilla gorilla gorilla*; Schwartz et al., 2005). In this latter study, King, an adult male western lowland gorilla, remembered the order of past events as well as where the events occurred. Dally et al. (2006) have recently shown that western scrub jays remember not only the what-where-when of specific food caching episodes but also who (which other scrub jay) was watching them while they were hiding food, altering their recaching behavior accordingly. Episodic-like memories have also been demonstrated in pigeons (*Columba livia*; Zentall et al., 2001) and dolphins (*Tursiops truncates*; Mercado et al., 1998). Indeed, pigeons exhibited trace flexibility by accurately reporting whether they had recently been pecking when such reports were not anticipated, and dolphins too showed this flexibility by correctly reproducing actions recently performed (for a review, see Hampton and Schwartz, 2004).

Although some remain skeptical about whether these memories are episodic or even episodic-like (e.g., Roberts, 2002; Suddendorf and Busby, 2003a,b; but see Clayton et al., 2003b), questions concerning nonhuman animals' potential for autobiographical memory, at least as measured by behavioral criteria, remain an area of intense scientific debate and research. Indeed, there are those who suggest that the anatomical details of the hippocampus and parahippocampal regions of the brain are conserved across (human and nonhuman) mammals (Manns and Eichenbaum, 2006). Moreover, these authors also claim that the functional role of these neural regions in declarative memory is also conserved across species. To the extent that the hippocampus and parahippocampal regions are critical for declarative, episodic memory (e.g., Tulving and Markowitsch, 1998; de Hoz and Wood, 2006), these across-species similarities are consistent with the claim that episodic (and perhaps autobiographical) memory may exist in a variety of mammalian species and is not special to humans. Perhaps the autonoetic component of human conscious recollection is epiphenomenal and is not a requirement of the memory itself. Indeed, Ferbinteanu et al. (2006) argue that autonoetic experience is a feature of human consciousness and not an aspect of episodic memory per se. Hence, episodic memory may exist in many species and can be measured behaviorally in human and nonhuman species alike. Certainly, as Manns and Eichenbaum (2006) point out, there are differences across species in the psychological properties of episodic memories (perhaps including autonoetic experiences), but these may be due to other differences in neocortical inputs to the hippocampus and parahippocampal regions, as well as the neocortical circuitry that mediates their outputs, determining their behavioral expression, rather than to differences between species in the hippocampal and parahippocampal regions themselves.

Although there may be some additional research needed before we can close the book on episodic memory in nonhuman animals, that these same organisms experience infantile amnesia is not contentious, although like episodic memory itself, the cause of this amnesia may not be the same across human and nonhuman animal species. Research by Richardson and colleagues (Richardson et al., 1983, 1986; Westbrook et al., 2002; Yap et al., 2005; Kim et al., 2006; Weber et al., 2006) with rat pups has shown more rapid forgetting in younger rats than older rats. More important, this research has shown that many of the behavioral markers indexing infantile amnesia in human infants are similar to those observed in nonhuman animals. For example, both human and nonhuman infants show faster forgetting than older members of the species and increased recollection following reinstatement treatments. This latter phenomenon was thought to rule out

storage-failure hypotheses of infantile amnesia and instead favor retrieval failure mechanisms, because memories cannot be reactivated if they are not somehow present in storage. For example, the effects of infantile amnesia have been mitigated by injecting naloxone prior to training a fear response (Weber et al., 2006), indicating that central opioid receptors regulate retrieval of fear memories in rat pups. Similarly, in a recent article, Kim et al. (2006) have shown that, although younger rat pups retain fear conditioning for relatively short periods of time, administration of the gamma-aminobutyric acid$_A$ (GABA$_A$) receptor partial inverse agonist FG7142 alleviated infantile amnesia. It appears as though FG7142 facilitated the retrieval of a forgotten memory, showing for the first time that GABA receptors play a central role in the forgetting of fear memories from infancy.

Theoretically, these findings are critical to our thinking about infantile amnesia and memory continuity. Specifically, because GABA receptors play a role more generally in forgetting regardless of the age of the organism, perhaps forgetting early in life (infantile amnesia) and forgetting in adulthood simply represent quantitative variation rather than qualitative differences in forgetting mechanisms. Although certainly not conclusive, the fact that the same treatment that facilitates retrieval in adults also facilitates infant memory is more consistent with the memory-continuity hypothesis.

Of course, there is considerable evidence that storage factors play a role as well, because of the more rapid forgetting of information by more immature organisms. The longer an early memory has been in storage without reminders, the more likely it is to have decayed. Indeed, early memories that have been forgotten for longer periods of time are more difficult to recover than memories stored for shorter periods of time (e.g., Joh et al., 2002). Moreover, there is evidence that posttraining injections of pharmacological agents (glucose, epinephrine, norepinephrine) known to facilitate storage and consolidation in adult rats (Gold et al., 1982; Flint and Riccio, 1999) also mitigate the effects of infantile amnesia in rat pups. Thus, both storage and retrieval play roles in infantile amnesia, at least in nonhuman animals.

Finally, Richardson and his colleagues have shown that despite infantile amnesia, induction of fear responses in rat pups remains time-locked in memory. Specifically, for rats, fear is expressed in age-appropriate ways, ones that unfold with development (Yap et al., 2005). As it turns out, learned fear is expressed in terms of the age at which the animal was trained (time of encoding), not at the age at which it was tested (Richardson et al., 2000; Richardson and Fan, 2002). Interestingly, these memories can be updated by subsequent experience. That is, memory updating can occur, and the expression of fear can be recalibrated to a more mature response, if a similar fear experience occurs at an older age (Yap et al., 2005). These results have implications for whether and how single versus multiple fear events (including acute versus chronic adverse experiences) occurring early in life may be remembered and expressed. Moreover, for language-using organisms, these results raise the question of whether experiences that have occurred before the vocabulary (receptive or productive) necessary to communicate those experiences can ever be expressed linguistically. If responses are truly time-locked at encoding, and language is not available at that time, then the answer to this question is no. I return to this point in the next section, when I consider behavioral and cognitive factors relevant to infantile amnesia human populations.

1.15.3.2 Human Populations

Like their nonhuman counterparts, studies of memory with preverbal human infants are difficult at the best of times. This is because memory tasks must be nonverbal in nature, in terms of both the task instructions and also the types of responses indexing remembering. Moreover, like nonhuman animals, preverbal human infants cannot provide us with an unambiguous indication of their conscious state during recollection. Despite these difficulties, like studies with nonhuman animals, experiments using a wide range of tasks have established beyond a reasonable doubt that human infants do possess declarative, episodic memory if not before the end of the first year of life, shortly thereafter.

Although a complete review of techniques and outcomes from infant memory research is beyond the scope of this chapter, comprehensive overviews are readily accessible (Rovee-Collier et al., 2001; Howe et al., 2003; Courage and Howe, 2004; Hayne, 2004). Instead, I will focus on several key paradigms and outcomes that illustrate the precocity of infant memory and auger well for our discussion of infantile amnesia. To begin, there are a variety of reports concerning memory for operantly conditioned events very early in life, including memory for *in utero* conditioning. For example, DeCasper and his associates have shown that newborn infants can recognize the prosodic characteristics of a story heard

in the last trimester of their prenatal life and have determined the factors that affect this recognition memory (DeCasper and Fifer, 1980; Decasper and Prescott, 1984; DeCasper and Spence, 1986, 1991; Spence, 1996; Spence and Freeman, 1996).

Infants are also willing to imitate motor activities performed by an adult or peer. For example, Meltzoff and colleagues demonstrated that 6-week-olds reproduce various facial expressions and head movements modeled by an adult over a 24-h retention interval (Meltzoff and Moore, 1994). As infants mature, they can model more and more complex sequences over longer and longer delays (for a review, see Meltzoff, 1995). A strength of Meltzoff's work is that the activities performed were novel, were modeled without instruction, and were not performed by infants prior to the retention test. Thus, imitation was likely based on stored representations of previous experience and as such indexes recall (declarative memory) not recognition.

In all, experiments using conjugate reinforcement (Rovee-Collier et al., 2001), novelty preference (Courage and Howe, 1998; Courage et al., 2004), deferred imitation (Meltzoff, 1995; Hayne, 2004), elicited imitation (Bauer, 2004), and behavioral reenactment (McDonough and Mandler, 1994; Sheffield and Hudson, 1994) indicate that, like the findings for nonhuman animals: (1) when initial learning is equated, infant age and longevity of memory are positively correlated; (2) length of retention is affected by factors such as distribution of practice (spaced better than massed) and the match between proximal and distal cues at encoding and test; and (3) retention can be prolonged given appropriate reinstatement treatments. Thus, although fragile and short lasting, even very young infants can demonstrate declarative memory. As the neural structures that subserve declarative memory mature (see earlier sections in this chapter), declarative memories become longer lasting and less susceptible to decay and interference.

Although impressive, infants' encoding, storage, retention, and retrieval feats are still not as robust as those of children who have matured beyond the infantile amnesia threshold. Indeed, experiences before the age of 2 years appear to remain mysteriously 'time-locked' and inaccessible to conscious recall. Recollection, if any, is disjointed and fragmentary at best (Bruce et al., 2005) and may not be verbalizable (Simcock and Hayne, 2002). However, as has been known for a long time, at around the age of 2 years, memories become more stable and can be retrieved later in childhood and adulthood (Dudycha and

Dudycha, 1933; Kihlstrom and Harackiewicz, 1982; Usher and Neisser, 1993; Eacott and Crawley, 1998; Newcombe et al., 2000; Crawley and Eacott, 2006). Although often researchers will probe memories for specific, ostensibly significant events (e.g., birth of a sibling, death, traumatic experience), there does not appear to be any specific trend in the content of earliest memories. That is, although such recollections are not of mundane, everyday events (e.g., what one had for breakfast on the third day of December when one was 2 years old), neither do they have to be particularly traumatic (e.g., Bruce et al., 2005). Indeed, the recollections we have from around the age of two are often decontextualized segments of the past that are simple recollections of sensory experiences, behaviors and actions, or a feeling (Bruce et al., 2005).

As seen earlier in the neurobiological section, neurological changes can certainly drive many of the developments in memory that occur during the first postnatal year, but they cannot, by themselves, explain the changes in memory longevity observed in human episodic memory. Instead, we have to examine corresponding changes in cognitive development. Although many such changes exist around this transitional period (see Courage and Howe, 2002), the key development driving autobiographical memory is the onset of the cognitive self (Howe and Courage, 1993, 1997).

Briefly, consistent with trace-integrity theory (Howe, 2000), storage and retrieval lie on a single continuum, where traces consist of collections of primitive elements (e.g., features, nodes) that are integrated into a single cohesive (neural) structure in memory. The better integrated a trace is, the better it is retained over time and the less susceptible it is to interference. The less integrated a trace is, the more likely it is to recede into the background noise of other faded memories, losing its distinctiveness and hence its inherent memorability. Although these assumptions are consistent with most models of memory, it does organize a rather large literature on children's memory development more broadly and accounts for the offset of infantile amnesia and the onset of autobiographical memory, at least in humans. More specifically, as our proficiency with organizing information increases with changes in our knowledge structures, we are better able to group information in memory into cohesive structures that are more stable and relatively permanent. The key event relevant to autobiographical memory is the self – that is, you cannot have an autobiography until you have a self. As it turns out, there is considerable research that indicates that there is a dramatic shift in

the development of the self that occurs around 18 to 24 months, one that results in the advent of the cognitive self (for a recent review, see Howe et al., in press). Although the specific details are not critical here, the main point is that, because a recognizable self contributes features that increase the cohesion of a memory trace, such traces are no longer event memories but memories of events that happened to me. That is, they are autobiographical.

Interestingly, it may be no coincidence that there exist corresponding neurological developments relevant to this expanding knowledge base of the self. Indeed, prefrontal areas related to autobiographical recall and the self are undergoing developmental change – for example, cortical gray matter volume increases until age four and then declines (synatogenesis followed by pruning; see Pfefferbaum et al., 1994). Functional neuroimaging studies have shown that portions of the anteromedial prefrontal cortex are involved in processing self-related information and autobiographical recall (see Levine, 2004). Although I would not argue that there is any direct link between these neurobiological changes and the offset of infantile amnesia, given that the mind is somehow a function of the brain (Levine, 2004), the cognitive advances that drive the onset of autobiographical memory may have their neural correlates in early changes in the prefrontal cortex.

Behavioral evidence has been accumulating over the past decade or so that also indicates that the self plays a key role in the onset of human autobiographical memory. For example, Harley and Reese (1999) found that the critical event related to the onset of autobiographical memory was the advent of the cognitive self (as measured by mirror self-recognition) and not performance on language measures, deferred imitation tests, or sociolinguistic measures (e.g., style of maternal reminiscing). More recently, Howe et al. (2003) reported that long-term retention of a unique event was also contingent on children having a cognitive self and not on other, related measures (e.g., language). Most recently, Prudhomme (2005) found that the cognitive self was essential for early declarative, autobiographical memory. Indeed, Prudhomme found that children with a cognitive self were not only better than those without a cognitive self on an elicited memory task, but they were also much more flexible when retrieving information.

Consistent with the theoretical approach advocated by Howe and Courage (Howe and Courage 1993, 1997; Howe et al., in press), this research makes clear that early autobiographical memory in humans is contingent on cognitive advances, specifically the advent of the cognitive self. As children mature, the number of autobiographical events that can be retained increases due to a whole host of reasons related to memory development more generally, a discussion of which is beyond the mandate of this chapter (but see Howe, 2004; Howe et al., in press). However, an important question remains, namely what happens to memories from the infantile amnesia period. Although already acknowledged as being fragmentary at best, do they remain time-locked, or can they be later retrieved and recoded using newly acquired language skills? For humans, the period of infantile amnesia is also one in which language skills are relatively impoverished. Language acquisition was thought by many to herald the end of infantile amnesia (see Allport, 1937; Schachtel, 1947). Some current theories of infantile amnesia also emphasize the importance of language (see Harley and Reese, 1999). However, to the extent that infantile amnesia is similar in human and nonhuman animals, the role of language in the offset of infantile amnesia may be epiphenomenal. Indeed, the current evidence indicates that language does not play a causative role in the offset of infantile amnesia. However, language is one way in which humans rehearse, elaborate, preserve, and communicate memories, including autobiographical ones. So although it may not be germane to our nonhuman counterparts, it may be one of those neocortical inputs and outputs to the hippocampal and parahippocampal areas that varies across species and is important to later developments in autobiographical memory.

Curiously, although infants can recall past events behaviorally, there is little evidence that their memories are accessible to verbal report if they were laid down prior to the offset of infantile amnesia. Some studies that have shown verbal reports of early memories tested recall under conditions of high contextual support (e.g., Bauer and Wewerka, 1995, 1997). Other studies in which the degree of contextual support was much less have failed to produce verbal reports of early memories (Simcock and Hayne, 2002, 2003). Interestingly, in these latter studies, although children clearly had acquired the vocabulary to report the prior events, verbal ability was not related to memory performance. That is, children's sparse verbal reports of previous events were not due to poor memory per se, as these same children were able to accurately recognize photographs of the previous event as well as reproduce them behaviorally.

Simcock and Hayne's (2002, 2003) research provided considerably less contextual support than Bauer and Wewerka's (1995, 1997) studies. Could it be that contextual support is the key to 'helping' memories make the transition across the infantile amnesia barrier? More recent studies suggest this might be the case. For example, Bauer et al. (2004) found evidence of verbal reports of early memories only when event-related props, but not color photographs (as in the Simcock and Hayne studies), were provided as cues. Interestingly, verbal reports were not obtained from children who only experienced the events once. What this might indicate is that multiple exposures are necessary for events to cross the infantile amnesia threshold. Of course rehearsal is important in memory generally, and events that are repeated are better remembered than those that are not repeated.

More importantly, verbal evidence of memory was seen only in those children who were 20 months old at the time of the original experience and not those who were 13 or 16 months old at that time. Similar findings have been reported in other studies (e.g., Bauer et al., 1998, 2002) and are critical to the argument presented here concerning the importance of the cognitive self. Although language measures have been obtained in each of these studies (to insure adequate vocabulary to express the events), measures of the cognitive self have not been secured. However, it is clear from the vast literature on the development of the cognitive self (for a review, see Courage et al., 2004; Howe et al., in press) that the 13- and 16-month-olds who failed to exhibit later verbal recall were below this cutoff at the time the event was first experienced, whereas those who did evince verbal recall, the 20-month-olds, were above this cognitive self threshold. A similar finding has been reported by Morris and Baker-Ward (2007) using physical props (e.g., a bubble-making machine) to reinstate the encoding context in 2-year-olds; however, again, a test of the children's cognitive self was not administered.

1.15.4   Conclusions

Several conclusions emerge from this review of infantile amnesia. First, the recent literature on neural structures related to memory (particularly the hippocampus and parahippocampal regions) makes it clear that we share certain anatomical, functional, and developmental similarities with nonhuman animal species. Although there is clearly room for across-species variation in performance and the manner in which memories are expressed, due to well-documented and substantial differences in neocortical inputs and outputs, the marked similarity in hippocampal (and parahippocampal) anatomy, function, and development is unmistakable.

Second, perhaps because of our common hippocampal (and parahippocampal) neuroanatomy, functionality, and developmental trajectory, we share with our nonhuman animal counterparts episodic or episodic-like memory, a memory like others that develops with maturation. Regardless of species, human and nonhuman animals alike can code the what, where, when, and even who of past events and use that information to guide behavior. Although the conscious, autonoetic component of recollecting autobiographical memories may be uniquely human, something that may arise given the considerable across-species differences in neocortical structures, that we share episodic memory with other species is not in doubt.

Third, and perhaps because of our common episodic memory capabilities, we also share with other species one of the limitations of early episodic memory, infantile amnesia. That is, there is faster forgetting of information than in more mature organisms, memories that are laid down are more susceptible to interference in younger than older members of the species, and for those species that recall past events, memories for early events are less accessible later in life than memories for events that occur when we are older. For humans, this infantile amnesia abates at around 2 years of age and is aided by the advent of the cognitive self. This perhaps uniquely human construct may have its roots in additional neural development in the prefrontal cortex. This is consistent with the neurobiological evidence reviewed in this chapter, as well as with the idea that across-species variation in memory (and infantile amnesia) is due to across-species variation in neocortical structures.

Because of this across-species similarity in episodic memory and infantile amnesia, it would seem to be intellectual folly to explain the end of infantile amnesia in uniquely human terms. For example, Hayne (2004) has argued that such similarities force a basic process explanation. That is, the waning of infantile amnesia must occur at the level of changes to encoding, storage, consolidation, or retrieval from episodic memory. To the extent that species-unique capacities play a role in the ebbing of infantile amnesia, they do so only inasmuch as they affect these basic processes.

This memory-continuity view has been favored by a number of early memory researchers (see Howe and Courage, 1993, 1997; Howe, 2000, 2004; Bauer, 2004,

2005; Howe et al., in press). For humans, the capacity to better organize information in memory is the key to most, if not all, memory advances in childhood. Advances in children's knowledge structures, whether they have to do with the self or other constructs (e.g., animals, vehicles), aid children's organization and storage of incoming information, making memory traces more integrated and hence more resistant to forgetting. As we have seen in this chapter, the neurological components necessary for declarative/episodic memory are in place and operating by the end of the first year of life if not before. What drives memory development are changes in knowledge (cognitive) structures that subserve encoding, storage, retention, and retrieval, making these basic processes more robust. For the offset of infantile amnesia and the onset of autobiographical memory, this knowledge structure is the cognitive self.

It is perhaps of more than passing interest to note that the cognitive self may be present in species other than humans. The quintessential test for the cognitive self is mirror self-recognition. Results of this test have been reported for a number of nonhuman species of fish, birds, and mammals (for a review, see Gallup, 1979). Although most creatures respond toward the image as if they were viewing a conspecific, nonhuman primates (given a period of exposure to mirrors) will respond to the contingent movement cues and use the reflective properties to locate objects. However, chimpanzees and orangutans demonstrate self-recognition like humans. Although speculative, it may be that the end of infantile amnesia in some other species is also heralded by the acquisition of the cognitive self. Regardless, the common ingredient that brings about the end of infantile amnesia is some change in the organisms' ability to encode, store, consolidate, retain, or retrieve event memories. Whether that is through the advent of new knowledge (cognitive) structures or some other (cognitive) mechanism is unknown. That the various species possess different neocortical structures that moderate hippocampal (and parahippocampal) functions may provide some insight as to what those mechanisms are that modulate basic episodic memory processing and end infantile amnesia. This is the grist for future research.

To close, I refer to another unresolved issue that needs further research, and that is: what is the fate of early memories? As we saw earlier, events that were experienced once were not subsequently recollected (at least not verbally) in Bauer et al.'s (2004) study, nor were events that took place earlier than 20 months of age. Of course, these were not traumatic or life-changing experiences, but rather, innocuous laboratory-contrived events. However, there is converging evidence from adult participants that was also reviewed here that showed that recall of events, traumatic and otherwise, was limited by infantile amnesia across the first 2 years of life (e.g., Usher and Neisser, 1993; Eacott and Crawley, 1998). So the question remains, do memories for early events remain in storage despite our inability to bring them to consciousness during later childhood or adulthood?

Recall Kagan's (1996) discussion of the fate of early experience and how many theorists believe that, despite our inability to recollect early life events, they remain with us and shape our future behaviors. It is clear that early experience, by itself, does not determine future outcomes, as subsequent experience can alter that path. Even the bizarre behavior of 6-month-old isolated macaques was altered by placing them with younger female monkeys over a 4- to 5-month period (Suomi and Harlow, 1972). Indeed, there is a vast literature that shows that a strong form of early experiential determinism is not tenable (also see Howe, 2000). In light of this, there may be little reason to believe that these early experiences still exist in memory and have not been updated by more recent (and perhaps relevant) experiences.

However, recall from the discussion about neural development that in humans, at least, implicit memory precedes the development of explicit or declarative memory. Is it possible that implicit memories that have not been altered by subsequent experience (should such a thing exist) are still accessible implicitly and form the basis of our adult responses? Although there is some evidence that early implicit memories may still exist in humans (Newcombe et al., 2000), stronger evidence was presented earlier in this chapter for early fear responses in rats (e.g., Yap et al., 2005). If early postnatal fear responses are not altered by subsequent experience, then it is likely that earlier, immature conditioned responses might still predominate in the more mature organism. Because these response patterns are implicit, the organism would not be aware of the early experience, nor would it know why a particular response was occurring, something that may be akin to the apparent, sudden emergence of a phobic response. More importantly, implicit (as well as explicit) memories of early adverse experiences might be one source for later psychopathology in adulthood.

Unfortunately, here again, the evidence is wanting – however 'pleasing' such ideas may be, the literature is replete with examples that infirm rather than confirm such intuitions (for reviews, see Hardt and Rutter, 2004; Howe et al., 2006). What is not clear is how such memories are altered by subsequent experience and what the parameters are that drive such dynamic change in memory, regardless of species. Only subsequent research will clarify the fate of these early memories, particularly the ones that are laid down during the period of infantile amnesia. I suspect their fate is similar to that of early explicit memories and that they are as malleable and updatable as all memories throughout an organism's development.

References

Aimone JB, Wiles J, and Gage FH (2006) Potential role for adult neurogenesis in the encoding of time in new memories. *Nat. Neurosci.* 9: 723–727.

Ainsworth MS and Bowlby J (1991) An ethological approach to personality development. *Am. Psychol.* 46: 333–341.

Allport GW (1937) *Personality: A Psychological Interpretation.* New York: Holt.

Arnold HM and Spear NE (1997) Infantile amnesia: Using animal models to understand forgetting. In: Slater PJB, Rosenblatt JS, Snowden CT, and Milinski M (eds.) *Advances in the Study of Behavior*, vol. 26, pp. 251–284. New York: Academic Press.

Bauer PJ (2004) Getting explicit memory off the ground: Steps toward construction of a neuro-developmental account of changes in the first two years of life. *Dev. Rev.* 24: 347–373.

Bauer PJ (2005) Developments in declarative memory: Decreasing susceptibility to storage failure over the second year of life. *Psychol. Sci.* 16: 41–47.

Bauer PJ, Kroupina MG, Schwade JA, Dropik PL, and Wewerka SS (1998) If memory serves, will language? Later verbal accessibility of early memories. *Dev. Psychopathol.* 10: 655–679.

Bauer PJ, van Abbema DL, Wiebe SA, Cary MS, Phill C, and Burch MM (2004) Props, not picture, are worth a thousand words: Verbal accessibility of early memories under different conditions of contextual support. *Appl. Cogn. Psychol.* 18: 373–392.

Bauer PJ, Wenner JA, and Kroupina MG (2002) Making the past present: Verbal reports of preverbal memories. *J. Cogn. Dev.* 3: 21–47.

Bauer PJ and Wewerka SS (1995) One- to two-year-olds' recall of events: The more expressed, the more impressed. *J. Exp. Child Psychol.* 59: 475–496.

Bauer PJ and Wewerka SS (1997) Saying is revealing: Verbal expression of event memory in the transition from infancy to early childhood. In: van den Broek P, Bauer PJ, and Bourg T (eds.) *Developmental Spans in Event Comprehension and Representation: Bridging Fictional and Actual Events*, pp. 139–168. Mahwah, NJ: Erlbaum.

Bruce D, Wilcox-O'Hearn LA, Robinson JA, Phillips-Grant K, Francis L, and Smith MC (2005) Fragment memories mark the end of childhood amnesia. *Mem. Cogn.* 33: 567–576.

Campbell BA and Spear NE (1972) Ontogeny of memory. *Psychol. Rev.* 79: 215–236.

Clayton NS, Bussey TJ, and Dickinson A (2003a) Can animals recall the past and plan for the future? *Nat. Rev. Neurosci.* 4: 685–691.

Clayton NS, Bussey TJ, Emery NJ, and Dickinson A (2003b) Prometheus to Proust: The case for behavioral criteria for 'mental time travel.' *Trends Cogn. Sci.* 7: 436–437.

Clayton NS, Dally J, Gilbert J, and Dickinson A (2005) Food caching by western scrub-jays (*Aphelocoma californica*) is sensitive to the conditions at recovery. *J. Exp. Psychol. Anim. Behav. Process.* 31: 115–124.

Clayton NS and Dickinson A (1998) What, where, and when: Episodic-like memory during cache recovery by scrub jays. *Nature* 395: 272–274.

Clayton NS and Dickinson A (1999) Scrub-jays (*Aphelocoma coerulescens)* remember the relative time of caching as well as the location and content of their caches. *J. Comp. Psychol.* 113: 403–416.

Clayton NS, Yu KS, and Dickinson A (2001) Scrub jays (*Aphelocoma coerulescens*) form integrated memories of the multiple features of caching episodes. *J. Exp. Psychol. Anim. Behav. Process.* 27: 17–29.

Clayton NS, Yu KS, and Dickinson A (2003c) Interacting cache memories: Evidence for flexible memory use by western scrub-jays (*Aphelolcoma californica). J. Exp. Psychol. Anim. Behav. Process.* 29: 14–22.

Courage ML, Edison SE, and Howe ML (2004) Variability in the early development of visual self-recognition. *Infant Behav. Dev.* 27: 509–532.

Courage ML and Howe ML (1998) The ebb and flow of infant attentional preferences: Evidence for long-term recognition memory in 3-month-olds. *J. Exp. Child Psychol.* 70: 26–53.

Courage ML and Howe ML (2002) From infant to child: The dynamics of cognitive change in the second year of life. *Psychol. Bull.* 128: 250–277.

Courage ML and Howe ML (2004) Advances in early memory development: Insights about the dark side of the moon. *Dev. Rev.* 24: 6–32.

Courage ML, Howe ML, and Squires SE (2004) Individual differences in 3.5-month-olds' visual attention: What do they predict at 1 year? *Infant Behav. Dev.* 27: 19–30.

Crawley RA and Eacott MJ (2006) Memories of early childhood: Qualities of the experience of recollection. *Mem. Cogn.* 34: 287–294.

Dally JM, Emery NJ, and Clayton NS (2006) Food-caching western scrub-jays keep track of who was watching when. *Science* 312: 1662–1665.

DeCasper AJ and Fifer WP (1980) Of human bonding: Newborns prefer their mothers' voices. *Science* 208: 1174–1176.

DeCasper AJ and Prescott PA (1984) Human newborns' perception of male voices: Preference, discrimination, and reinforcing value. *Dev. Psychol.* 17: 481–491.

DeCasper AJ and Spence MJ (1986) Prenatal maternal speech influences newborns' perception of speech sounds. *Infant Behav. Dev.* 9: 133–150.

DeCasper AJ and Spence MJ (1991) Auditory mediated behavior during the prenatal period: A cognitive view. In: Weiss M and Zelazo P (eds.) *Newborn Attention: Biological Constraints and the Influence of Experience*, pp. 142–176. Norwood, NJ: Ablex.

de Hoz L and Wood ER (2006) Dissociating the past from the present in the activity of place cells. *Hippocampus* 16: 704–715.

Dudycha GJ and Dudycha MM (1933) Some factors and characteristics of childhood memories. *Child Dev.* 4: 265–278.

Eacott MJ and Crawley RA (1998) The offset of childhood amnesia: Memory for events that occurred before age 3. *J. Exp. Psychol. Gen.* 127: 22–33.

Eacott MJ, Easton A, and Zinkivskay A (2005) Recollection in an episodic-like memory task in the rat. *Learn. Mem.* 12: 221–223.

Ferbinteanu J, Kennedy PJ, and Shapiro ML (2006) Episodic memory – From brain to mind. *Hippocampus* 16: 691–703.

Flint RW Jr. and Riccio DC (1999) Posttraining glucose administration attenuates forgetting of passive-avoidance conditioning in 18-day-old rats. *Neurobiol. Learn. Mem.* 72: 62–67.

Freud S (1938) The psychopathology of everyday life. In: Brill AA (ed.) *The Writings of Sigmund Freud*, pp. 35–178. New York: Modern Library. (Original work published 1914.)

Freud S (1953) Three essays on the theory of sexuality. In: Strachey J (ed.) *The Standard Edition of the Complete Psychological Works of Sigmund Freud*, vol. 7, pp. 135–243. London: Hogarth Press. (Original work published 1905).

Gallup GG (1979) Self-recognition in chimpanzees and man: A developmental and comparative perspective. In: Lewis M and Rosenblum L (eds.) *The Child and Its Family: The Genesis of Behavior*, vol. 2, pp. 107–126. New York: Plenum.

Gogtay N, Nugent TF III, Herman DH, et al. (2006) Dynamic mapping of normal human hippocampal development. *Hippocampus* 16: 664–672.

Gold PE, Murphy JM, and Cooley S (1982) Neuroendocrine modulation of memory during development. *Behav. Neural Biol.* 35: 277–293.

Griffiths DP, Dickinson A, and Clayton NS (1999) Declarative and episodic memory: What can animals remember about their past? *Trends Cogn. Sci.* 3: 74–80.

Hampton RR and Schwartz BL (2004) Episodic memory in nonhumans: What, and where, is when? *Curr. Opin. Neurobiol.* 14: 192–197.

Hardt J and Rutter M (2004) Validity of adult retrospective reports of adverse childhood experiences: Review of the evidence. *J. Child Psychol. Psychiatry* 45: 260–273.

Harlow HF, Harlow MK, and Suomi SJ (1971) From thought to therapy: Lessons from a primate laboratory. *Am. Sci.* 59: 538–549.

Harley K and Reese E (1999) Origins of autobiographical memory. *Dev. Psychol.* 35: 1338–1348.

Hayne H (2004) Infant memory development: Implications for childhood amnesia. *Dev. Rev.* 24: 33–73.

Hoffding H (1891) *Outlines of Psychology*. New York: Macmillan.

Howe ML (2000) *The Fate of Early Memories: Developmental Science and the Retention of Childhood Experiences*. Washington, DC: American Psychological Association.

Howe ML (2004) Early memory, early self, and the emergence of autobiographical memory. In: Beike D, Lampinen JM, and Behrend DA (eds.) *The Self and Memory*, pp. 45–72. New York: Psychology Press.

Howe ML and Courage ML (1993) On resolving the enigma of infantile amnesia. *Psychol. Bull.* 113: 305–326.

Howe ML and Courage ML (1997) The emergence and early development of autobiographical memory. *Psychol. Rev.* 104: 499–523.

Howe ML, Courage ML, and Edison SE (2003) When autobiographical memory begins. *Dev. Rev.* 23: 471–494.

Howe ML, Courage ML, and Rooksby M (in press). The development of autobiographical memory. In Courage ML and Cowan N (eds.) *The Development of Memory in Childhood*. London, UK: Psychology Press.

Howe ML, Toth SL, and Cicchetti D (2006) Memory and developmental psychopathology. In: Cicchetti D and Cohen S (eds.) *Developmental Psychopathology, Developmental Neuroscience*, 2nd edn., vol. 2, pp. 629–655. New York: Wiley.

Joh A, Sweeny B, and Rovee-Collier C (2002) Minimum duration of reactivation at 3 months of age. *Dev. Psychol.* 40: 23–32.

Kagan J (1996) Three pleasing ideas. *Am. Psychol.* 51: 901–908.

Kail R (2002) Developmental change in proactive interference. *Child Dev.* 73: 1703–1714.

Kihlstrom JF and Harackiewicz JM (1982) The earliest recollection: A new survey. *J. Pers.* 50: 134–148.

Kim JH, McNally GP, and Richardson R (2006) Recovery of fear memories in rats: Role of gamma-amino butyric acid (GABA) in infantile amnesia. *Behav. Neurosci.* 120: 40–48.

Kohler W (1929) *Gestalt Psychology.* New York: Liveright.

Kohler W (1941) On the nature of associations. *Proc. Am. Philos. Soc.* 84: 489–502.

Levine B (2004) Autobiographical memory and the self in time: Brain lesion effects, functional neuroanatomy, and lifespan development. *Brain Cogn.* 55: 54–68.

Loftus EF and Loftus GR (1980) On the permanence of stored information in the human brain. *Am. Psychol.* 35: 409–420.

Manns JR and Eichenbaum H (2006) Evolution of declarative memory. *Hippocampus* 16: 795–808.

McDonough L and Mandler JM (1994) Very long-term recall in infants: Infantile amnesia reconsidered. *Memory* 2: 339–352.

Meltzoff AN (1995) What infant memory tells us about infantile amnesia: Long-term recall and deferred imitation. *J. Exp. Child Psychol.* 59: 497–515.

Meltzoff AN and Moore K (1994) Imitation, memory, and the representation of persons. *Infant Behav. Dev.* 17: 83–100.

Mercado E, Murray SO, Uyeyama RK, Pack AA, and Herman LM (1998) Memory for recent actions in the bottlenosed dolphin (*Tursiops truncates*): Repetition of arbitrary behaviors using an abstract rule. *Anim. Learn. Behav.* 26: 210–218.

Morris G and Baker-Ward L (2007). Fragile but real: Children's capacity to use newly acquired words to convey preverbal memories. *Child Dev.* 78: 448–458.

Nash M (1987) What, if anything, is regressed about hypnotic age regression? A review of the empirical literature. *Psychol. Bull.* 102: 42–52.

Nelson CA (1997) The neurobiological basis of early memory development. In: Cowan N (ed.) *The Development of Memory in Early Childhood*, pp. 41–82. Hove East Sussex, UK: Psychology Press.

Nelson CA (2000) Neural plasticity in human development: The role of early experience in sculpting memory systems. *Dev. Sci.* 3: 115–130.

Newcombe NS, Drummey AB, Fox NA, Lie E, and Ottinger-Alberts W (2000) Remembering early childhood: How much, how, and why (or why not). *Curr. Dir. Psychol. Sci.* 9: 55–58.

Norman G and Eacott MJ (2005) Dissociable effects of lesions to the perirhinal cortex and the postrhinal cortex on memory for context and objects in rats. *Behav. Neurosci.* 119: 557–566.

Pfefferbaum A, Mathalon DH, Sullivan EV, Rawles JM, Zipursky RB, and Lim KO (1994) A quantitative magnetic resonance imaging study of changes in brain morphology from infancy to late adulthood. *Arch. Neurol.* 51: 874–887.

Prudhomme N (2005) Early declarative memory and self-concept. *Infant Behav. Dev.* 28: 132–144.

Richardson R and Fan M (2002) Behavioral expression of learned fear in rats is appropriate to their age at training, not their age at testing. *Anim. Learn. Behav.* 30: 394–404.

Richardson R, Paxinos G, and Lee J (2000) The ontogeny of conditioned odor potentiation of startle. *Behav. Neurosci.* 114: 1167–1173.

Richardson R, Riccio DC, and Axiotis R (1986) Alleviation of infantile amnesia in rats by internal and external contextual cues. *Dev. Psychol.* 19: 453–462.

Richardson R, Riccio DC, and Jonke T (1983) Alleviation of infantile amnesia in rats by means of pharmacological contextual state. *Dev. Psychol.* 16: 511–518.

Roberts WA (2002) Are animals stuck in time? *Psychol. Bull.* 128: 473–489.

Rovee-Collier C, Hayne H, and Colombo M (2001) *The Development of Implicit and Explicit Memory.* Amsterdam: John Benjamins Publishing Company.

Schachtel EG (1947) On memory and childhood amnesia. *Psychiatry* 10: 1–26.

Schwartz BL, Hoffman ML, and Evans S (2005) Episodic-like memory in a gorilla: A review and new findings. *Learn. Motiv.* 36: 226–244.

Serres L (2001) Morphological changes of the human hippocampal formation from midgestation to early childhood. In: Nelson CA and Luciana M (eds.) *Handbook of Developmental Cognitive Neuroscience*, pp. 45–58. Cambridge, MA: MIT Press.

Sheffield EG and Hudson JA (1994) Reactivation of toddlers' event memory. *Memory* 2: 447–465.

Simcock G and Hayne H (2002) Breaking the barrier? Children fail to translate their preverbal memories into language. *Psychol. Sci.* 13: 225–231.

Simcock G and Hayne H (2003) Age-related changes in verbal and nonverbal memory during early childhood. *Dev. Psychol.* 39: 805–814.

Skeels HM (1966) Adult status of children with contrasting early life experiences. *Monogr. Soc. Res. Child Dev.* 31: 1–65.

Smith GJ and Spear NE (1981) Role of proactive interference in infantile forgetting. *Anim. Learn. Behav.* 9: 371–380.

Spence MJ (1996) Young infants' long-term auditory memory: Evidence for changes in preferences as a function of delay. *Dev. Psychol.* 29: 685–695.

Spence MJ and Freeman MS (1996) Newborn infants prefer the maternal low-pass filtered voice but not the maternal whispered voice. *Infant Behav. Dev.* 19: 199–212.

Suddendorf T and Busby J (2003a). Mental travel in animals? *Trends Cogn. Sci.* 7: 391–396.

Suddendorf T and Busby J (2003b). Like it or not? The mental time travel debate: Reply to Clayton et al. *Trends Cogn. Sci.* 7: 437–438.

Suomi SJ and Harlow HH (1972) Social rehabilitation of isolate reared monkeys. *Dev. Psychol.* 6: 487–496.

Tulving E (1985) How many memory systems are there? *Am. Psychol.* 40: 385–398.

Tulving E (1989) Remembering and knowing the past. *Am. Sci.* 77: 361–367.

Tulving E (1993) What is episodic memory? *Curr. Dir. Psychol. Sci.* 2: 67–70.

Tulving E and Markowitsch HJ (1998) Episodic and declarative memory: Role of the hippocampus. *Hippocampus* 8: 198–204.

Usher JN and Neisser U (1993) Childhood amnesia and the beginnings of memory for four early life events. *J. Exp. Psychol. Gen.* 122: 155–165.

Weber M, McNally GP, and Richardson R (2006) Opioid receptors regulate retrieval of infant fear memories: Effects of naloxone on infantile amnesia. *Behav. Neurosci.* 120: 702–709.

Westbrook RF, Iordanova M, Harris JA, McNally G, and Richardson R (2002) Reinstatement of fear to an extinguished conditioned stimulus: Two roles for context. *J. Exp. Psychol. Anim. Behav. Process.* 28: 97–110.

Yap CSL, Stapinski L, and Richardson R (2005) Behavioral expression of learned fear: Updating of early memories. *Behav. Neurosci.* 119: 1467–1476.

Zental TR, Clement TS, Bhatt RS, and Allen J (2001) Episodic-like memory in pigeons. *Psychon. Bull. Rev.* 8: 685–690.

1.16 Transmission of Acquired Information in Nonhuman Primates

J. Fischer, German Primate Center, Göttingen, Germany

1.16.1 Introduction

The development of human culture and technology largely rests on our ability to accumulate information about past experiences, store it, and transmit it to others, thus enabling a cumulative cultural evolution where innovations are based on previous innovations. Literally speaking, the ability to transmit acquired information spares us having to reinvent the wheel over and over again. What is the biological basis for this ability? Are any of these abilities shared with other species? Is there evidence for 'teaching' among animals? Do animals possess different cultures, and if so, how do they come about? Are animals informing each other about past experiences or events? These are the questions that I will address in the present article. My overview will focus on nonhuman primates because they are our closest living relatives, and thus, any comparative study will have to ask which of our abilities are shared with them; in addition, most of the evidence has indeed been collected on this taxon. To maintain a broad perspective, I will draw from studies on other animals whenever feasible.

The first part of this article will be devoted to the question of animal culture. I will begin with a discussion of the terminology used in this field and then review the evidence accumulated over the last five decades. The second part charts the communicative abilities of nonhuman primates, particularly in the vocal domain – one of the most important modes of information transmission in humans. This section will begin with the question of whether nonhuman primate signals refer to objects or events in the animals' environment, discuss the issue of vocal learning as well as the importance of auditory feedback, and then review studies that addressed the issue of whether monkeys or apes intentionally provide information to others. The third part of this article turns to the mechanisms that give rise to the observed variations in behavior, including the question of teaching among animals. My review will conclude with a discussion of how communicative skills and the development of culture are intertwined. I will argue that, in both animal communication and animal culture, there is a fundamental difference between the sender (or actor) on the one hand, and the listener (or observer) on the other. It appears that animals are good at seeking information, processing it, and adjusting their behavior accordingly, but what they apparently do not do is to provide information with the intention to alter the knowledge state of others. To get cumulative cultural evolution off the ground, more is needed than social learning; among other things, an understanding of other individuals' knowledge states and intentions, as well as a symbol system to represent and transmit accumulated knowledge. To date, this appears to be found only in our own species.

1.16.2 Animal Culture

1.16.2.1 Definition

How one approaches the question of the evolution of culture depends very much on the framework used. An anthropocentric research program might begin with a definition of human culture and then go on to ask which aspects of this phenomenon are shared with animals. An ecological research program instead might begin with charting behavioral diversity and then go on to identify the factors that give rise to this variation. Both approaches would greatly benefit from a clear definition of the phenomenon under study; however, there is no single agreed definition to work with. One frequently cited definition (e.g., Goodall, 1973; Van Schaik et al., 2003; McGrew, 2004) is that by Edward Tylor, who described culture as "that complex whole which includes knowledge, belief, art, law, morals, custom, and any other capabilities and habits acquired by man as a member of society" (Tylor, 1871, p. 1). Early on, it became clear that this definition was of little use to people who studied animal behavioral diversity. In the 1950s, the Japanese primatologist Kinji Imanishi proposed a broader definition in which he described as cultural behaviors all flexible behavior patterns that were socially transmitted (cf. Jolly, 2001). Hans Kummer, one of the pioneers of primatological research,

followed a similar line of argument. He suggested considering all behaviors as cultural that were socially transmitted and which remained in the populations ("If such social modification spreads and perpetuates a particular behavioral variant over many generations, then we have 'culture' in the broad sense in which a student of animals can use the term"; Kummer, 1971, p. 13). This view still resonates today, for instance in the definition by Laland and Janik, who describe as cultural all "group-typical behavior patterns, shared by members of animal communities, that are to some degree reliant on socially learned and transmitted information" (Laland and Janik, 2006, p. 542). The eminent cultural primatologist Bill McGrew took a somewhat different stance and defined culture as "the way we do things" (McGrew, 2004, p. 25), specifically referring to forms of behavior or artifacts that are standardized, or even stylized, and socially significant.

Not surprisingly, these broad definitions were later contested (Tomasello, 1994), and there is an ongoing and sometimes fierce debate about the terminology used when people chart and discuss behavioral diversity (Fragaszy and Perry, 2003). Andy Whiten argued that it is just an issue of definition whether or not we label the outcome of social learning as culture, while Kevin Laland and Vincent Janik find a broad definition simply more stimulating (Laland and Janik, 2006). The problem with a broad definition begins when people aim to study the evolution of human culture and implicitly operate with the same terminology for two possibly quite different phenomena. While some earlier researchers used the terms protoculture or preculture when they referred to animal behavioral diversity, this specification was at some point dropped. As a result, even proponents of a broad definition struggle with the distinction of their findings for animals versus for humans, and not surprisingly, our own species has recently been described as 'super-cultural' (Whiten, 2005, p. 54).

In addition, it is obviously logically flawed to herald observations of animal culture as signs for sharing the trait 'culture' with humans, as long as two different definitions are applied. For want of a better definition, I will in the following use the term animal culture to refer to behavioral variation among animals that appears to be socially mediated. I do not assume that animal culture and human culture are homologous, and I may note here that, in my view, human culture as a phenomenon is too complex and elusive to lend itself to a meaningful phylogenetic reconstruction. Instead, it seems more productive to investigate the mechanisms that give rise to animal culture or human culture. In a second step, one may then identify which of these traits are shared among taxa, constituting either homologies or convergences that may have arisen to similar ecological pressures. This eventually leads to an understanding of which aspects constitute derived traits of the human lineage.

1.16.2.2   History

The interest in animal culture was sparked when Japanese researchers reported that Japanese macaques, *Macaca fuscata*, on the island of Koshima had begun to wash the sweet potatoes that had been fed to them to habituate them to the presence of human observers and lure them to the beach, where they could be more easily observed. One day, a young female named Imo waded into the water and dipped the potato into the water to get rid of the sand. This habit slowly spread through the group – 2 years later, four more monkeys were regularly washing their potatoes, and 1 additional year on, 11 out of the 30 group members had been observed to clean their food that way (Kawamura, 1959). At the end of the 1950s, the researchers observed another food processing technique that slowly spread trough the study group. Again, it was Imo who first threw wheat that had been spread on the beach into the water. The sticky sand was thus washed off, and she could scoop the clean grains out of the water. Both habits did not spread randomly within the group; subjects that interacted more frequently with one another tended to adopt this new behavior earlier than subjects with only infrequent contacts (Kawai, 1965). Kawai was the first to introduce the term 'precultural behavior' into the debate. In the Western world, the question of animal culture became a hot topic in the 1970s. At the fourth conference of the International Primatological Society in Nairobi in 1971, a workshop was devoted to the topic of "Precultural Primate Behavior." Jane Goodall, who had begun her studies of the Gombe chimpanzees, *Pan troglodytes*, in 1960, presented a paper entitled "Cultural Elements in a Chimpanzee Community" (Goodall, 1973), thus advancing this great ape species to center stage.

1.16.2.3   Recent Advances

In the last 15 years, the field of primatology has experienced an explosion of publications on the topic of cultural behavior among nonhuman primates. In his 1992 book, *Chimpanzee Material Culture*,

Bill McGrew gave an overview on the differences in tool use in different chimpanzee populations (McGrew, 1992). West African chimpanzees, for instance, crack nuts using stones as hammers and other stones or roots as anvils (**Figure 1**). East African chimpanzees, in contrast, have never been observed to crack nuts, despite the fact that nuts occur in their habitat. Another behavior pattern is the so-called 'grooming hand clasp,' which was routinely observed at Mahale but absent at Gombe. There are also different variations of termite fishing. For instance, subjects at Taï use rather short sticks and insert them into termite mounds, and they pull the sticks through the mouth to harvest the termites, while subjects at Gombe pick up the termites with their hands (reviewed in McGrew, 2004). A comprehensive survey of the different variants of tool use and social behavior was initiated by Andy Whiten from the University of St. Andrews. Researchers who had observed wild chimpanzees for decades in seven different areas compiled a catalogue of behavioral patterns. They identified 39 different behavioral patterns which were either observed in only one or a few of the sites taken into account in this study and – importantly – could apparently not be related to the ecological conditions or genetic variation among subjects. Thus, the observation of behavioral variation could be well substantiated (Whiten et al., 1999). In the meantime, the interest in the so-called cultural variation has been extended to other species such as orangutans, *Pongo pygmaeus* (Van Schaik et al., 2003), and capuchin monkeys, *Cebus spp.* (Perry et al.,

Figure 1   Nut cracking in West African chimpanzees. Drawing by JF from a photograph taken by Roman Wittig, with permission.

2003; Fragaszy et al., 2004). However, the so-called 'ethnographic record' has recently been criticized by Laland and Janik (2006), who argue that it is logically impossible to rule out that some unknown ecological or genetic factor may account for the observed variation.

Cultural behavior (in the broad sense) is not restricted to the primate order. New Caledonian crows, *Corvus moneduloides*, for instance, manufacture tools from pandanus leaves (Hunt, 1996). With astonishing precision, the crows cut and tear the edges of barbed leaves to produce flat tools that are broad at one end and thin at the other, where they can be used for probing holes to harvest food. In addition, they make tools from a range of materials like tree twigs, small stems, and vines (Hunt, 1996). Hunt and Gray (2003) found that crows from different areas of New Caledonia produced leaf tools of different complexity. The authors concluded that different subpopulations apparently had developed varying degrees of expertise, indicative of a cumulative cultural transmission of the techniques used to manufacture these tools (Hunt and Gray, 2003). The crows' manufacturing skills were recently tested experimentally by Kacelnik and colleagues at Oxford University. Their studies indicate that social learning is not necessarily a prerequisite to develop the skill to manufacture hooks or choose the appropriate tool (Kenward et al., 2005; Weir et al., 2002, reviewed in Kacelnik et al., 2006), casting some doubt whether the observed variation in leaf production is indeed a sign of cumulative cultural evolution.

1.16.2.4 Dialects

Depending on the definition employed, dialects or regional variations in vocal behavior may be subsumed under the label of cultural variation. Several studies have suggested the existence of group-specific call characteristics in nonhuman primates that apparently could not be attributed to ecological or genetic variation (but see Laland and Janik, 2006). One of the earliest such reports came from Green (1975), who observed that three different populations of Japanese macaques produced acoustically different calls. Pygmy marmosets, *Cebuella pygmaea*, modified their trill vocalizations when placed with a new partner in such a way that the calls of both partners became more similar to each other than before pairing (Snowdon and Elowson, 1999). The alarm calls given by members of two populations of Barbary macaques, *M. sylvanus*, revealed significant variation between

sites. Playback experiments in which calls from their own or the other population were broadcast suggested that this observed variation was perceptually salient (Fischer et al., 1998). Chimpanzees also reveal differences in the acoustic structure of their pant-hoots (e.g., Mitani et al., 1992; Crockford et al., 2004).

Since learning is not a prerequisite to develop the species-specific repertoire, it is not quite clear how group-specific calls come about. Possible mechanisms will be discussed below. In contrast, whenever learning from models is mandatory, such as in the acquisition of bird song, local variation is almost inevitable. Songbirds (of the temperate regions) learn their songs as nestlings, either from their father or other singing males in the neighborhood (*See* Chapter 1.17), and hence, specific local variation, which may initially occur as a result of a copying error, can be transmitted to subsequent generations. In addition, song elements copied from other species may be incorporated into the vocal repertoire of a species (Catchpole and Slater, 1995). Another example for a regional dialect is the song of killer whales or orcas. Orcas live in groups or pods of several matrilines, and their vocalizations reveal group-specific as well as population-specific signatures (Deecke et al., 2000; Riesch et al., 2006).

1.16.3 Primate Communication

1.16.3.1 Referential Signaling

Do monkeys or apes talk about things? Are there any indications that they refer to objects and events in the external world? Does their communication have a semantic quality? These questions experienced a boost when Tom Struhsaker reported that vervet monkeys, *Chlorocebus aethiops*, living in the Amboseli National Park in Kenya produce three acoustically distinct alarm calls and three different adaptive escape strategies in response to their three main predators: leopards, eagles, and snakes (Struhsaker, 1967). This led to the question of whether the vervets denote the predator type when they give a predator-specific alarm call. Playback experiments revealed that upon hearing an alarm call, the monkeys selected the appropriate response, even when there was no predator around. The authors concluded that the vervets denoted the predator type, or that they encoded the required response (Seyfarth et al., 1980). Either way, the alarm calls were deemed to be referential, because they apparently referred to either objects or escape strategies external to the signaler herself. In due course, the question of semantic communication became a hot topic, and numerous studies were initiated that addressed the question of the meaning of animal signals (Zuberbühler, 2006).

While general theoretical accounts of communication (e.g., Shannon and Weaver, 1949) explicitly abstained from addressing the issue of signal meaning, such analyses as well as the work by John Smith (1977) stressed the importance of distinguishing between the role of the sender who generates the message and the recipient who interprets the signal. Accordingly, the problem with the initial conclusion (that callers may have denoted the predator type) was that the information provided in the signal was inferred from listeners' responses. The early studies on semantic or referential communication failed to differentiate between these two roles, and traces of this confusion can still be found today. Subsequent analyses, however, pointed out that, for such a seemingly referential communication system to function, signals simply have to be sufficiently specific (Macedonia and Evans, 1993). If this is the case, recipients can use these signals to predict subsequent events and choose their responses accordingly (Macedonia and Evans, 1993; Seyfarth and Cheney, 2003). Two sets of questions follow from this insight: first, how much control do primates have over their vocal production to produce specific sounds in specific situations; and second, how do primates (or other animals) attach meaning to sounds?

1.16.3.2 Learning

1.16.3.2.1 Vocal Production
Studies of the ontogeny of vocal production as well as the neurobiological foundations of vocal control in nonhuman primates suggest that the structure of primate vocalizations is largely innate. Unlike in most songbirds (*See* Chapter 1.17), exposure to species-specific calls is not a prerequisite for the proper development of the vocal repertoire (reviewed in Fischer, 2002). Nevertheless, developmental modifications occur. These can be mainly related to growth in body size. For instance, from the first week of life, rhesus macaque, *M. mulatta*, infants produced coo calls with a largely adult-like structure. With increasing age, however, the fundamental frequency dropped in pitch and the modulation of the fundamental frequency and the call amplitude decreased, while call duration slightly increased. Weight was the best predictor for almost all of the observed age-related changes (Hammerschmidt et al., 2000). Using a larger age range of subjects, Ey and colleagues analyzed the changes in the structure of contact barks in a cross-sectional study of 58 free-ranging Chacma baboons, *Papio hamadryas ursinus*. Baboon clear calls are tonal and harmonically rich (**Figure 2**). An acoustic analysis revealed that the duration of the calls and the mean fundamental frequency varied significantly with age. With increasing age, animals uttered longer calls with a lower fundamental frequency. These two variables also showed a significant interaction between age and sex, indicating that the profiles of age-related variations differed between the sexes (Ey et al., in press). The emergence of sexual differences corresponds to the onset of sexual dimorphism in body size and mass, suggesting that testosterone levels may play a role in driving changes in acoustic structure. In sum, there is ample evidence that primate vocalizations experience only minor structural changes during ontogeny. Most changes can be attributed to growth, and some also to hormonal changes during puberty, which may affect the usage and structure of certain signals.

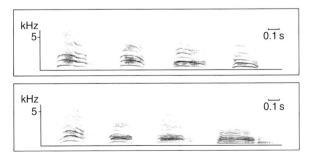

Figure 2   Spectrograms of Chacma baboon contact barks (frequency on the y-axis, time on the x-axis). The top row shows examples of calls recorded from females of different age classes (from left to right: infant, juvenile, adolescent, adult). The bottom row shows examples of male calls from the corresponding age classes.

1.16.3.2.2 Comprehension

The previous sections on modifications in the production and/or usage of calls showed that nonhuman primates apparently exhibit only little plasticity in their calls. In contrast, studies that examined the development of the comprehension of and correct responses to calls, indicated that subjects undergo pronounced changes in development. Most of the earlier work has focused on the development of vervet infants' responses to different alarm calls given to the main predators. Playback experiments showed that infants gradually develop the appropriate responses to alarm calls, and at an age of about 6 months, young vervets behaved like adults. Further evidence for a gradual development of responses comes from a study of infant baboons. Subjects developed the ability to discriminate between calls that fall along a graded acoustic continuum, as evidenced by the time spent looking toward the concealed speaker. At 2.5 months of age, infants did not respond at all to the playback of alarm or contact barks. At 4 months of age, they sometimes responded, but irrespective of the call type presented. By 6 months of age, infants reliably discriminated between typical variants of alarm and contact barks (Fischer et al., 2000). Further experiments showed that infants of 6 months and older exhibited a graded series of responses to intermediate call variants. They responded most strongly to typical alarm barks, less strongly to intermediate alarm calls, less strongly still to intermediate contact barks, and hardly at all to typical contact barks (Fischer et al., 2000). There appears to be some flexibility, because vervet infants who are exposed to specific alarm calls frequently develop the appropriate response earlier than infants who were rarely exposed to it (Hauser, 1988). Furthermore, a study of the development of maternal recognition showed that, from as early as 10 weeks of age, Barbary macaque infants responded significantly more strongly to playbacks of their mothers' calls than to playbacks of unrelated females from the same social group (Fischer, 2004). Apparently, infants are able to recognize their mothers by voice from this early age onward. Taken together, these findings corroborate the assumption that the structure of the vocalizations is largely innate, whereas call comprehension is based on learning (Seyfarth and Cheney, 1997). This asymmetry is shared with most other terrestrial mammals and taken to some extreme in the example of Rico, the domestic dog who was shown to be able to remember the names of over 200 toys. In addition, Rico was able to identify the referent of a new word by exclusion learning (Fischer et al., 2004; Kaminski et al., 2004).

How do infants learn to attach the correct meaning to sounds in their environment? To date, there is only indirect and partly contradictory evidence to what degree infant responses to calls are influenced by adult behavior. For instance, Seyfarth and Cheney (1986) reported that vervet infants were more likely to respond correctly to the different alarm calls when they had first looked at an adult. In contrast, infant baboons responded to intermediate alarm and contact barks which were typically ignored by adults, suggesting that in these situations, infants did not simply copy adult behavior (Fischer et al., 2000). In Barbary macaques, infant responses – looking toward the speaker – were not influenced by the behavior of their alloparental caretakers, that is, whether or not he or she looked toward the speaker (Fischer, 2004). Similarly, after playback of conspecific alarm calls, infant and juvenile Barbary macaques more frequently ran away or climbed into trees than did adults (Fischer et al., 1995; Fischer and Hammerschmidt, 2001). Apparently, social learning is not a prerequisite for the development of appropriate responses.

1.16.3.3 Neural Control of Vocalizations

The acoustic structure of nonhuman primate calls is determined by oscillation of the vocal folds and sometimes the vocal lip, articulatory gestures that influence the filtering characteristics of the vocal tract, and respiration (reviewed in Fitch and Hauser, 1995). Vocal behavior requires a coordination of all of these components, while vocal adjustment may take place at the level of laryngeal sound production, at the level of articulation, or both. Current evidence suggests that, in nonhuman primates, the anterior cingulate cortex serves to control the initiation of vocalizations, facilitating voluntary control over call emission and onset (Jürgens, 2002, for a review; Hammerschmidt and Fischer, in press). The periaqueductal grey (PAG) appears to serve as a relay station (Jürgens, 1998). Electrical stimulation of the PAG yields natural sounding, species-specific vocalizations. In a study with squirrel monkeys, most of the neurons in the PAG fired only before the start of vocalizations and did not show any vocalization-correlated activity (Düsterhöft et al., 2000). Recent retrograde tracing studies (Dujardin and Jürgens, 2005, 2006) revealed that vocalization-eliciting sites of the PAG receive widespread input from cortical and subcortical areas of the forebrain, large parts of the midbrain, as well as the pons and medulla oblongata. The actual motor patterns appear to be generated in a discrete area in the reticular formation just before the olivary complex. Neurons in this area increased their activity just before and during vocalizations and showed significant correlations with the syllable structure of these vocalizations (Hage and Jürgens, 2006a,b).

1.16.3.4 Auditory Feedback

While the structure of primate vocalizations appears strongly genetically determined, some experimental studies suggest an influence of auditory feedback on vocal output. For instance, Japanese macaques' coo calls produced in response to a playback coo were more similar to the playback coo than to spontaneous coos (Sugiura, 1998). Common marmosets, *Callithrix jacchus*, increase their sound level as well as their call duration in response to increased levels of white noise in their environment (Brumm et al., 2004). Cotton-top tamarins, *Saguinus oedipus*, uttered shorter combination long calls with fewer pulses when they were exposed to white noise. In contrast, when they were exposed to modified real-time versions of their own vocal output, their calls became louder and had longer interpulse intervals (Egnor et al., 2006). It seems likely that most of these adjustments are mediated in the lower brainstem (Hage et al., 2006).

A study by Eliades and Wang (2003) on common marmosets showed that self-initiated vocalizations led to the suppression of the majority of auditory cortical neurons, while a smaller population showed an increased firing rate after the onset of the call, probably as a result of auditory feedback. Furthermore, exposure to modified self-generated vocalizations over longer periods of time may alter the response properties of neurons in the primary auditory cortex of common marmosets (Cheung et al., 2005). Whether the modulation of the auditory system is achieved via forward or inverse control, or a combination of both, needs to be investigated. In any case, this line of research eventually may help us to understand how vocal production and perception are integrated and how response priming or other related mechanisms may account for the emergence of group-specific calls.

In conclusion, there are apparently two sources that contribute to the adjustment of vocal output: one socially mediated and probably effective over longer periods, leading to group-specific calls, and the other an immediate adjustment to perturbations of auditory feedback. Whatever the details of small-scale

adjustments of vocal output, learning is not a prerequisite for the development of the species-specific acoustic structure. To date, there is no reliable evidence that nonhuman primates incorporate novel sounds into their repertoire. In contrast, marine mammals such as bottlenose dolphins, *Tursiops truncatus*, were found to be able to imitate the whistles of other conspecifics (Janik, 2000); parrots, *Psittacus erithacus*, can be taught to imitate human speech sounds (Pepperberg, 2000); mocking birds mimic all sorts of sounds in their environment; and there is even an odd anecdote of Hoover, the harbor seal who was reported to be talking, albeit with a heavy Bostonian accent (cf. Fitch, 2000). That is, flexible vocal production has evolved several times independently, but we do not appear to share it with our closest living relatives (Fischer, 2003; Egnor and Hauser, 2004).

1.16.3.5 Gestures

Possibly as a consequence of the frustration with the lack of elaboration in the vocal production of nonhuman primates, researchers have become more interested in the gestural communication of apes, and recently also monkeys. The reasoning is that, while primates lack voluntary control over their vocal output, they do have excellent voluntary control over their hands. Therefore, it has been hypothesized that human speech possibly evolved via a proto-sign language (Corballis, 2002; Arbib, 2005). In addition, the brain area in monkeys (area F5) that controls manual movements is supposed to be homologous to Broca's area, which is involved in speech production, further fueling the interest in this modality of communication.

In this context, it is important to distinguish between enculturated subjects raised by humans, captive animals, and wild animals. One enculturated ape, the chimpanzee Lana, was taught to use certain gestures like 'open' and 'more,' which she used in a range of different contexts (Kellogg, 1968). Detailed studies of the signaling behavior of chimpanzees, bonobos, *Pan paniscus*, gorillas, *Gorilla gorilla*, and siamangs, *Symphalangus syndactylus*, in captivity, in contrast, did not provide any evidence that gestures referred to certain objects or events in the subjects' environment (see chapters in Call and Tomasello, in press). The majority of flexibly used gestures occurred in the play context – a context that by its definition is characterized by highly variable behaviors. The evidence for gestural communication among wild subjects is still somewhat sketchy. Recently, a study of the gesturing behavior of wild chimpanzees indicated that subjects used one specific gesture referentially (Pika and Mitani, 2006). Specifically, during grooming, groomees frequently used a "loud and exaggerated scratching movement" (Pika and Mitani, 2006, R191) on a part of their bodies. In 64% of all observed cases, the groomer then groomed that particular spot. The authors concluded that the exaggerated scratch constitutes a communicative signal. It seems equally likely, however, that the sequence of events is an example of either local enhancement (see following) and/or 'ontogenetic ritualization' (Tomasello, 2004), where both parties of the dyad learn about the consequences of certain actions.

1.16.3.6   Intentional Signaling

One important issue for the present purpose is the question of whether the usage of nonhuman primate vocal or gestural signals can be considered as intentional. In the domain of animal communication, researchers frequently invoke the definition of Daniel Dennett (1971). Dennett described different stages of intentionality, where zero-order intentionality would apply to simple expressions of emotion or fixed action patterns given in response to sign stimuli. First-order intentionality describes communicative acts employed in order to alter the behavior of the recipient. This does not necessarily imply that the signaler is conscious of her own behavior or mental state (Bruner, 1981), in the sense that the sender knows that she does have such an intention. Second-order intentionality would apply to cases where the sender intends to alter the knowledge state of the other, and not necessarily his or her immediate behavior. For second-order intentionality to apply, the sender must know that the receiver's mental state can be different from her own mental state. So far, there is no convincing evidence for second (or higher) order intentional communication in the animal realm (Seyfarth and Cheney, 2003), so most of the studies simply ask whether primates use signals with the intention to alter their group mates' behavior. Tomasello et al. (1997) listed a set of diagnostics of intentionality: (1) 'means-end dissociation' (Bruner, 1981), i.e., different signals are used to achieve the same goal while the same signal may be used to accomplish different goals; (2) 'persistence of the goal,' i.e., the sender continues to use the same signal or enhances his signaling behavior if the desired behavior cannot be achieved; (3) sensitivity to the social context, i.e., intentional signals should not only be addressed to a recipient, but the sender

should also take into account his attentional state; (4) flexibility, i.e., signals may be combined (relatively) freely. While these criteria appear all quite straightforward, it is not a trivial task to operationalize them. How, for instance, does one determine the 'goal' of the sender? The goal must be inferred from the recipients' response, opening up the same problem as mentioned for the identification of message content in the vocal domain. Hesler and Fischer (2007) used an alternative approach and aimed to identify the function of a signal by examining the contingency between signal use and responses in others. However, this approach does not give any insight into the sender's intention either. Despite its intuitive appeal, therefore, the identification of the signaler's goal remains rather elusive. This aside, it appears that apes choose appropriate signal modalities according to the state of the receiver (see chapters in Call and Tomasello, in press). Moreover, they meet the criterion of means–end dissociation in the sense that they use different signals to achieve the same 'goal' or may use the same signal to achieve different 'goals.' This ability is not restricted to apes. Despite the fact that great and small apes produce a larger diversity of manual postures than monkeys, Barbary macaques also fulfill the above-mentioned criteria (Hesler and Fischer, 2007). One difference between apes and monkeys may be that, while there is some flexibility in signal usage in monkeys, it is nevertheless quite predictable. In other words, certain patterns are frequently combined with certain other patterns (e.g., rounded open mouth threat with head bob and ground slap, but not with 'present hindquarters'). Tomasello (in press) maintains that nonhuman primate gestural communication shows much more flexibility than primate vocal communication. He supposes that this might be the case because gestures are used in "less evolutionarily urgent activities." However, except for alarm calls, the immediate survival value of most vocalizations is not very obvious either. In addition, gestural signals may be simply more variable and flexible because they have more degrees of freedom: movements can be described in terms of space and time (i.e., four dimensions), while vocalizations vary – depending on the definition – in two (amplitude and time) or three (amplitude, frequency, and time) dimensions only.

Moreover, the Barbary macaques' vocal communication also fulfills the criteria for intentional signaling listed earlier: the monkeys use the same call type in different contexts, while in one context, different call types may be uttered; if a pant is not sufficient to threaten a group member, subjects may begin to scream; when they approach another group member, they use vocal signals if the recipient is not looking at them, while they tend to use facial expressions if they do, and they may combine different call types in one call bout (Hesler and Fischer, 2007). To summarize, at least for Barbary macaques there seems to be no substantial difference between the vocal and nonvocal domain in terms of the criteria listed. In light of the view that most communicative acts serve to either decrease or increase the distance between social partners, this may not be so surprising. In conclusion, despite a high degree of voluntary control over their hands, there is no convincing evidence that manual gestures or other nonverbal signals are used (by wild apes or monkeys) to communicate about things or provide information to others (*See* Chapter 1.15 for nonverbal communication in humans). This finding suggests that a lack of voluntary control over the vocal apparatus is only one of the constraints that prevent a more elaborate communication among our closest living relatives.

1.16.4 Social Learning

So far we have seen that a variety of animal species have developed a certain degree of behavioral traditions. Apparently, vocal or gestural communication plays no particular role when such traditions are established or maintained (except when these traditions consider the signal repertoire itself). Nevertheless, the information transmission is socially mediated. Research during the last two decades has identified different social learning mechanisms that encompass a wide range of different forms with varying degrees of cognitive complexity. The common denominator is that the behavior of one subject facilitates or influences the behavior of another subject (see Heyes and Galef, 1996; Perry and Fragaszy, 2003, for comprehensive reviews). Note that the terminology is not always used consistently (Hurley and Chater, 2005).

1.16.4.1 Social Facilitation, Stimulus, and Local Enhancement

Social facilitation is invoked when an individual's learning is affected by the activity of another animal. Animals typically pay a lot of attention to what others, particularly their group mates, are doing. This may lead to stimulus enhancement, i.e., an

increase in salience of stimuli others are paying attention to, as well as local enhancement, i.e., the subject learns something about the contingencies of a specific local situation simply because it is near an individual who does something particular (Heyes, 2001). Therefore, the potato-washing behavior of Japanese macaques can be viewed as a consequence of local enhancement: subjects who were closely associated with Imo also spent more time near water and near potatoes. Hence, they may simply have individually learned how delicious potatoes tasted that had been dipped in seawater.

1.16.4.2 Emulation

Emulation has been defined as a form of social learning when the subject learns – through observation – something about the consequences of a certain action. It does not imply an understanding of the causal relationship underlying action and outcome, nor does it require an understanding of the agent's intention (Hurley and Chater, 2005). For instance, if an animal observes another subject that is manipulating a bolt at a box and then sees that the box can be opened, they associate the action (manipulating) with the outcome (opening). In other words, the animal may understand that manipulating the bolt leads to opening (the end of the action). Emulation does not require that the animal understands or follows the exact procedure (the means) of the action, nor does it entail an understanding of the other subject's intention.

1.16.4.3 Copying

Within the framework of the means–ends structure, copying would be the rendition of some other individuals' behavior with no understanding of what it is good for. In this sense, one follows the exact procedure of the model, but also follows any dysfunctional (or accidental) aspects of it. Copying has been invoked in a large array of situations, including mate choice where females may prefer males that have already mated successfully, bird song learning where songsters dutifully produce exact renditions of song models heard earlier, or the acquisition of food preferences (see Dugatkin, 1996; Zentall, 1996).

1.16.4.4 Imitation

Edward Thorndike was the first to note that most animals learn by trial and error, and not by imitation (*See* Chapters 1.06 and 1.10 for operant learning).

Indeed, thorough analyses of imitation led to the view that this capacity should be viewed as a relatively complex ability that requires an understanding of the means as well as the end of an action (Hurley and Chater, 2005). Researchers interested in imitation distinguish between perceptually opaque and perceptually transparent imitation. The former, for instance, applies to imitating someone else's facial expression, where one cannot see one's own face. Most phenomena discussed earlier, in contrast, should be viewed as perceptually transparent, because they involve hand movements and vocalizations (Heyes and Ray, 2000). For the present purposes, I will therefore not discuss models put forward to address the opacity problem.

Horner and Whiten initiated a series of experimental tests to assess the transmission of acquired knowledge in captive chimpanzees and human children. Subjects watched a human demonstrator first stab a stick into a hole at the top of an opaque box, then remove the stick and insert it into a second hole at the front panel to obtain a food reward (**Figure 3**). Both the chimpanzees (aged 2–6 years) and the children (aged about 4 years) followed this sequence of actions. However, when presented with a transparent box which revealed that sticking the tool into the top hole was inefficient, the chimpanzees switched from copying to a more goal-oriented emulation and simply used the stick to gather the reward. In contrast, the children continued to follow the demonstrated procedure of first inserting the stick into the top and then into the front hole. The authors viewed this result as evidence for the strong conformity bias of our own species (Horner and Whiten, 2005).

In a second set of experiments, Whiten and colleagues examined whether a novel technique would spread in a group of chimpanzees (Whiten et al., 2005). They first trained two female chimpanzees, each from a different social group, to use one of two different techniques (poke vs. lift) to obtain a food reward (**Figure 4**). After reintroducing the females into their groups, all but two of their group members adopted the specific strategy used by the model. Interestingly, some chimps in the lift group accidentally discovered the other technique as well. However, when retested, these chimps continued to use the originally seeded technique nevertheless, which led the authors to the conclusion that chimps show a conformity bias as well (Whiten et al., 2005).

What are the requirements to achieve the somewhat simpler case of transparent imitation? Associationist models propose that the capacity to imitate derives from the experience of simultaneously observing and executing that action in the past. Transformational theories, in contrast, suggest that an observed action is transformed into a sensory representation that is then used as an internal model for the motor program (see Heyes and Ray, 2000; Brass and Heyes, 2005, for detailed discussions). At a somewhat different level, two competing frameworks have been put forward to explain how imitation may be achieved: the sensorimotor and the ideomotor frameworks (see Prinz, 2005, for a review). In the sensorimotor model, perception and action are subserved by two distinct representational structures. Rule-based mappings connect the two. According to this model, an observer who perceives a given action needs some way of translating this into

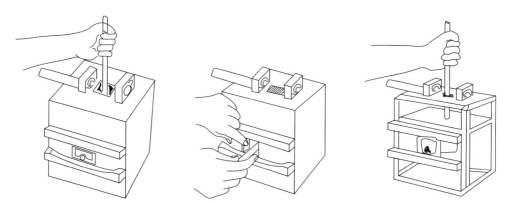

Figure 3 Opaque and transparent boxes used in the experiments with chimpanzees and children. Subjects first saw a familiar human stab a stick tool into the top and then into the front hole to recover food. In a second condition, the transparent box revealed that the first move (stabbing from the top) had no effect. In this second condition, chimpanzees switched from copying the sequence to emulation, while children continued to follow the human model. Adapted from Whiten A (2005) The second inheritance system of chimpanzees and humans. *Nature* 437: 52–55, with permission from Macmillan Publishers Ltd: NATURE.

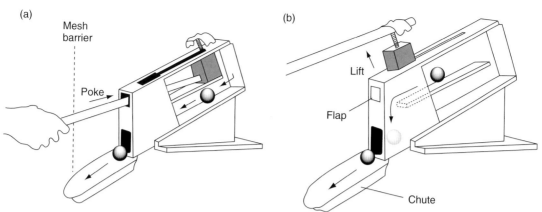

Figure 4 Two techniques for gaining food: (a) in the poke method, the stick tool is inserted into the apparatus and used to push (an invisible) blockage back along a ramp so that the food falls down and rolls forward underneath; (b) in the lift method, the stick tool is passed under hooks, allowing the blockage to be lifted and the food to roll forward. Redrawn version, adapted from Whiten A, Horner V, and De Waal FBM (2005) Conformity to cultural norms of tool use in chimpanzees. *Nature* 437: 737–740, with permission from Macmillan Publishers Ltd: NATURE.

her own motor planning. Feedback on the consequences of one's own movements can be used to correct the execution of that plan. This is generally compatible with the transformational model mentioned earlier. According to the ideomotor (common coding) framework, in contrast, perception and action are represented by the same system. This has two effects: first, to predict an ongoing action's perceivable consequences; second, to select a certain act in order to achieve certain effects (Prinz, 2005). Thus, both forward (predicting the outcome) and inverse models (using feedback) may play a role in imitation. Effectively, an understanding of imitation is part of understanding motor control and simulation and also bears on the issue of how mental state attribution is conceptualized.

While there is now some evidence that chimpanzees may be able to imitate, human children are 'imitation machines' (Tomasello, 1999, p. 159), and they have a strong tendency to imitate inefficient actions like pushing a light switch with the head instead of with the hand, or using rakes the wrong way around if the demonstrator did so. Thus, it appears that, to human children, imitation is rewarding per se. While imitation is difficult to distinguish phenomenologically from copying, true imitation requires an understanding of someone else's intention. That is, not only does the observer need to understand the goal (turning on the light) but also needs to assume that it matters to the demonstrator how the light is turned on. Thus, a certain form of perspective taking seems to be required to achieve full-fledged imitation (Tomasello, 1999).

1.16.4.5 Gaze Following

There are several studies showing that nonhuman primates follow the gaze of others regularly (reviewed in Tomasello and Call, 2006), while fewer studies systematically examined the ontogeny of gaze following in nonhuman primates. Tomasello and colleagues (2001) investigated the age at which rhesus macaque and chimpanzee infants began to follow the gaze of the human experimenter. In rhesus macaques, subjects followed the gaze of the experimenter at 5.5 months of age. Barbary macaque infants up to an age of 10 weeks did not follow the gaze of others (Fischer, 2004), but a more systematic study of the development of gaze following among nonhuman primates is still lacking.

1.16.4.6 Teaching

An assessment of teaching entails a change in perspective; all of the aforementioned social learning mechanisms tried to explain the behavior of observer or information seeker. An investigation of teaching, in contrast, focuses on the subject that provides the information. In an influential article, Caro and Hauser (1992) formulated the following criteria for the occurrence of teaching:

An individual actor A can be said to teach if it modifies its behavior only in the presence of a naïve observer, B, at some cost or at least without obtaining an immediate benefit for itself. A's behavior thereby encourages or punishes B's behavior, or provides B with experience, or sets an example for B. As a result, B acquires knowledge or learns a skill earlier in life or more rapidly or efficiently than it might otherwise do, or that it would not learn at all. (Caro and Hauser, 1992, p. 153)

This rather broad definition does not assume instruction; instead the authors argue that teaching does not depend on higher-order intentionality or attribution of mental states. Nevertheless, evidence for teaching in animals remains equivocal. In a recent study, Thornton and McAuliffe (2006) investigated the transfer of skills in free-ranging meerkats, *Suricata suricatta*. After emerging from the burrow, meerkat pups spend much of their time following helpers who capture and process prey for them. Helpers killed or disabled prey more frequently when pups were young, while they fed mostly intact prey to older pups. The authors also conducted an experiment where they presented live scorpions to helpers who then removed the sting and fed the pup (all of which then also bit into the scorpion). In contrast, only half of the pups bit into the prey when no helper was around (Thornton and McAuliffe, 2006). While the helpers' behavior conforms with the criteria listed above and, thus, can be defined as a form of teaching, it is questionable whether it helps us to understand different forms of information transmission. For instance, helpers may have learned that young pups cannot handle intact prey, so they have to disable or kill it. In addition, the outcome of the experiment can easily be explained by social facilitation. To date, there is no convincing evidence for active punishment or encouragement. Obviously, however, socially living animals do provide each other with experiences that they might not have if they lived alone, so this criterion does not help much to distinguish teaching from other forms of social learning, such as social facilitation. In other words, despite some superficial similarity of the observed meerkat helper behavior and the expected outcome of teaching (in the more canonical sense of the word), it is probably a good idea to consider the form of information transmission (active or passive) when teaching is investigated.

The same needs to be said about the acquisition of the diverse cultural behavior of chimpanzees or other primates. There is to date no indication that older animals correct or help youngsters to acquire a certain skill, e.g., nut cracking. Observations of the ontogenetic development of nut cracking in chimpanzees indicated that youngsters had a strong interest in their mothers' nut cracking activities. Nevertheless,

they needed to develop that ability through trial-and-error learning (Matsuzawa et al., 2001). The young chimpanzees' attention was drawn to hammer, anvil, and nut, but they could not acquire the appropriate technique through observation alone. There is no record that mothers ever corrected or punished youngsters' incorrect behavior. Therefore, it seems more plausible that the acquisition of nut cracking can be explained through a combination of social facilitation, emulation, and trial-and-error learning.

1.16.5 Conclusions

There is now convergent evidence to support the notion of a strong asymmetry between animals' intentional abilities to transmit versus to acquire information, and this is true for communication as well as social learning. Despite the fact that the structure of primate vocalizations appears fixed from birth, primate calls nevertheless provide rich information about sender attributes such as size, age, sex, hormonal levels, and also motivational state. Specific relations between motivational state and certain contextual situations allow listeners to use signals as predictors of upcoming events. There is, however, no conclusive evidence that signalers have the intention to provide this information to others. While nonvocal signals such as gestures and postures show a higher degree of variability (particularly in apes), there is no convincing evidence that gestures are used to intentionally communicate about objects or events, either. Similarly, the behavioral diversity observed among nonhuman primates can largely be attributed to social learning mechanisms where observers pay attention to and are influenced by the actors' behavior (social facilitation and goal emulation), but there is no evidence for teaching or instruction. Apparently, nonhuman primates lack the ability to attribute knowledge states to each other.

Social learning is clearly a prerequisite for the development of human culture, but it does not explain its complexity. One of the hallmarks of human culture is its rich symbolic structure (Jablonka and Lamb, 2005; *See also* Chapter 1.38). Moreover, cumulative cultural evolution (Boyd and Richerson, 2005) requires a system to represent and transmit knowledge. One such system is human speech: speech encompasses external reference as well as temporal and spatial transcendence. Once such a symbolic communication system is in place, it is possible to transmit information and knowledge without forcing the individuals to reenact each action every time information needs to be conveyed. Speech generally and writing in particular can be used to compress information transmission, store acquired knowledge, and drive technological development. In addition, the symbolic nature of speech allows for an increasing complexity of other human symbol systems. In conclusion, while both animals and humans share a number of social learning mechanisms, humans in addition are apt imitators, attribute knowledge to others, and are in command of a complex communication system. All of these contribute to the rich symbolic structure that characterizes human cultures. Future research should be devoted to the question of how mental state attribution and information transfer are linked, and how both of these are related to the formation of a symbol system.

References

Arbib M (2005) From monkey-like action recognition to human language: An evolutionary framework for neurolinguistics. *Behav. Brain Sci.* 28: 105–167.

Boyd R and Richerson PJ (2005) *The Origin and Evolution of Cultures.* New York: Oxford Unversity Press.

Brass M and Heyes C (2005) Imitation: Is cognitive neuroscience solving the correspondence problem? *Trends. Cogn. Sci.* 9: 489–495.

Brumm H, Voss K, Koellmer I, and Todt D (2004) Acoustic communication in noise: Regulation of call characteristics in a New World monkey. *J. Exp. Biol.* 207: 443–448.

Bruner JS (1981) Intention in the structure of action and interaction. *Adv. Infancy Res.* 1: 41–56.

Call J and Tomasello M (2007) *The Gestural Communication of Apes and Monkeys.* Mahwah, NJ: Lawrence Erlbaum Associates.

Caro TM and Hauser MD (1992) Is there teaching in nonhuman animals? *Q. Rev. Biol.* 67: 151–174.

Catchpole CK and Slater PJB (1995) *Bird Song. Biological Themes and Variations.* Cambridge: Cambridge University Press.

Cheung SW, Nagarajan SS, Schreiner CE, Bedenbaugh PH, and Wong A (2005) Plasticity in primary auditory cortex of monkeys with altered vocal production. *J. Neurosci.* 25: 2490–2503.

Corballis MC (2002) *From Hand to Mouth.* Princeton, NJ: Princeton University Press.

Crockford C, Herbinger I, Vigilant L, and Boesch C (2004) Wild chimpanzees produce group-specific calls: A case for vocal learning? *Ethology.* 110: 221–243.

Deecke VB, Ford JKB, and Spong P (2000) Dialect change in resident killer whales: Implications for vocal learning and cultural transmission. *Anim. Behav.* 60: 629–638.

Dennett DC (1971) Intentional systems. *J. Philos.* 68: 68–87.

Dugatkin LA (1996) Copying and mate choice. In: Heyes C and Galef BG (eds.) *Social Learning in Animals,* pp. 85–105. New York: Academic Press.

Dujardin E and Jürgens U (2005) Afferents of vocalization-controlling periaqueductal regions in the squirrel monkey. *Brain Res.* 1034: 114–131.

Dujardin E and Jürgens U (2006) Call type-specific differences in vocalization-related afferents to the periaqueductal gray of squirrel monkeys (*Saimiri sciureus*). *Behav. Brain Res.* 168: 23–36.

Düsterhöft F, Häusler U, and Jürgens U (2000) On the search for the vocal pattern generator. A single-unit recording study. *Neuroethology* 11: 2031–2034.

Egnor SER and Hauser MD (2004) A paradox in the evolution of primate vocal learning. *Trends Neurosci.* 27: 649–654.

Egnor SER, Iguina CG, and Hauser MD (2006) Perturbation of auditory feedback causes systematic perturbation in vocal structure in adult cotton-top tamarins. *J. Exp. Biol.* 209: 3652–3663.

Eliades SJ and Wang XQ (2003) Sensory-motor interaction in the primate auditory cortex during self-initiated vocalizations. *J. Neurophysiol.* 89: 2194–2207.

Ey E, Pfefferle D, and Fischer J (in press) Do age- and sex-related variations reliably reflect body size in non-human primate vocalizations? A review. *Primates.*

Fischer J (2002) Developmental modifications in the vocal behaviour of nonhuman primates. In: Ghazanfar AA (ed.) *Primate Audition,* pp. 109–125. Boca Raton, FL: CRC Press.

Fischer J (2003) *Vokale Kommunikation bei nichtmenschlichen Primaten: Einsichten in die Ursprünge der menschlichen Sprache?* PhD Thesis, Universität Leipzig.

Fischer J (2004) Emergence of individual recognition in young macaques. *Anim. Behav.* 67: 655–661.

Fischer J, Call J, and Kaminski J (2004) A pluralistic account of word learning. *Trends Cogn. Sci.* 8: 481.

Fischer J, Cheney DL, and Seyfarth RM (2000) Development of infant baboons' responses to graded bark variants. *Proc. Roy. Soc. London B Biol. Sci.* 267: 2317–2321.

Fischer J and Hammerschmidt K (2001) Functional referents and acoustic similarity revisited: The case of Barbary macaque alarm calls. *Anim. Cog.* 4: 29–35.

Fischer J, Hammerschmidt K, and Todt D (1995) Factors affecting acoustic variation in Barbary macaque *(Macaca sylvanus)* disturbance calls. *Ethology* 101: 51–66.

Fischer J, Hammerschmidt K, and Todt D (1998) Local variation in Barbary macaque shrill barks. *Anim. Behav.* 56: 623–629.

Fitch WT (2000) The evolution of speech: A comparative review. *Trends. Cogn. Sci.* 4: 258–266.

Fitch WT and Hauser MD (1995) Vocal production in nonhuman primates – acoustics, physiology, and functional constraints on honest advertisement. *Am. J. Primatol.* 37: 191–219.

Fragaszy D, Izar P, Visalberghi E, Ottoni EB, and De Oliveira MG (2004) Wild capuchin monkeys (*Cebus libidinosus*) use anvils and stone pounding tools. *Am. J. Primatol.* 64: 359–366.

Fragaszy DM and Perry S (2003) Towards a biology of traditions. In: Fragaszy DM and Perry S (eds.) *The Biology of Traditions,* pp. 1–32. Cambridge: Cambridge University Press.

Goodall J (1973) Cultural elements in a chimpanzee community. In: Menzel EW (ed.) *Precultural Primate Behaviour,* pp. 144–184. Basel: Karger.

Green S (1975) Variation of vocal pattern with social situation in the Japanese monkey (*Macaca fuscata*): A field study. In: Rosenblum LA (ed.) *Primate Behavior,* vol. 4, pp. 1–102. New York: Academic Press.

Hage SR and Jürgens U (2006a) Localization of a vocal pattern generator in the pontine brainstem of the squirrel monkey. *Eur. J. Neurosci.* 23: 840–844.

Hage SR and Jürgens U (2006b) On the role of the pontine brainstem in vocal pattern generation: A telemetric single-unit recording study in the squirrel monkey. *J. Neurosci.* 26: 7105–7115.

Hage SR, Jürgens U, and Ehret G (2006) Audio-vocal interaction in the pontine brainstem during self-initiated vocalization in the squirrel monkey. *Eur. J. Neurosci.* 23: 3297–3308.

Hammerschmidt K and Fischer J (in press) Constraints in primate vocal production. In: Griebel U and Oller K (eds.) *The Evolution of Communicative Creativity: From Fixed Signals to Contextual Flexibility.* Cambridge, MA: MIT Press.

Hammerschmidt K, Newman JD, Champoux M, and Suomi SJ (2000) Changes in rhesus macaque 'coo' vocalizations during early development. *Ethology* 106: 873–886.

Hauser MD (1988) How infant vervet monkeys learn to recognize starling alarm calls: The role of experience. *Behaviour* 105: 187–201.

Hesler N and Fischer J (2007) Gestures in Barbary macaques. In: Tomasello M and Call J (eds.) *Gestural Communication of Apes and Monkeys*, pp. 159–195. Mahwah, NJ: Lawrence Erlbaum Associates.

Heyes C (2001) Causes and consequences of imitation. *Trends Cogn. Sci.* 5: 253–261.

Heyes C and Galef BG (1996) *Social Learning: The Roots of Culture.* New York: Academic Press.

Heyes C and Ray ED (2000) What is the significance of imitation in animals? *Adv. Stud. Behav.* 29: 215–245.

Horner V and Whiten A (2005) Causal knowledge and imitation/emulation switching in chimpanzees (*Pan troglodytes*) and children (*Homo sapiens*). *Anim. Cog.* 8: 164–181.

Hunt GR (1996) Manufacture and use of hook-tools by New Caledonian crows. *Nature* 379: 249–251.

Hunt GR and Gray RD (2003) Diversification and cumulative evolution in New Caledonian crow tool manufacture. *Proc. Roy. Soc. London B Biol. Sci.* 270: 867–874.

Hurley S and Chater N (2005) The importance of imitation. In: Hurley S and Chater N (eds.) *Perspectives on Imitation: From Neuroscience to Social Science, Vol. 1: Mechanisms of Imitation and Imitation in Animals*, pp. 1–52. Cambridge, MA: MIT Press.

Jablonka E and Lamb MJ (2005) *Evolution in Four Dimensions.* Cambridge, MA: MIT Press.

Janik VM (2000) Whistle matching in wild bottlenose dolphins (*Tursiops truncatus*). *Science* 289: 1355.

Jolly A (2001) That, there, is me. *London Rev. Books* 23.

Jürgens U (1998) Neuronal control of mammalian vocalization, with special reference to the squirrel monkey. *Naturwiss.* 85: 376–388.

Jürgens U (2002) Neural pathways underlying vocal control. *Neurosci. Biobehav. Rev.* 26: 235–258.

Kacelnik A, Chappell J, Kenward B, and Weir AAS (2006) Cognitive adaptations for tool-related behavior in New Caledonian crows. In: Wasserman EA and Zentall TR (eds.) *Comparative Cognition*, pp. 515–528. Oxford: Oxford University Press.

Kaminski J, Call J, and Fischer J (2004) Word learning in a domestic dog: Evidence for "fast mapping." *Science* 304: 1682–1683.

Kawai M (1965) Newly-acquired pre-cultural behavior of the natural troop of Japanese monkeys on Koshima Islet. *Primates* 6: 1–30.

Kawamura S (1959) The process of sub-culture propagation among Japanese macaques. *Primates* 2: 43–60.

Kellogg WN (1968) Communication and language in home-raised chimpanzee – gestures, words, and behavioral signals of home-raised apes are critically examined. *Science* 162: 423–427.

Kenward B, Weir AAS, Rutz C, and Kacelnik A (2005) Tool manufacture by naive juvenile crows. *Nature* 433: 121.

Kummer H (1971) *Primate Societies.* New York: Aldine-Atherton.

Laland KN and Janik VM (2006) The animal culture debate. *Trends Ecol. Evol.* 21: 542–547.

Macedonia JM and Evans CS (1993) Variation among mammalian alarm call systems and the problem of meaning in animal signals. *Ethology* 93: 177–197.

Matsuzawa T, Biro D, Humle T, Inoue-Nakamura N, Tonooka R, and Yamakoshi G (2001) Emergence or culture in wild chimpanzees: Education by master-apprenticeship. In: Matsuzawa T (ed.) *Primate Origins of Human Cognition and Behavior*, pp. 557–574. Heidelberg: Springer-Verlag.

McGrew WC (1992) *Chimpanzee Material Culture. Implications for Human Evolution.* Cambridge: Cambridge University Press.

McGrew WC (2004) *The Cultured Chimpanzee.* Cambridge: Cambridge University Press.

Mitani JC, Hasegawa T, Gros-Louis J, Marler P, and Byrne RW (1992) Dialects in wild chimpanzees? *Am. J. Primatol.* 27: 233–243.

Pepperberg IM (2000) *The Alex Studies: Cognitive and Communicative Abilities of Grey Parrots.* Cambridge, MA: Harvard University Press.

Perry S and Fragaszy DM (eds.) (2003) *The Biology of Traditions.* Cambridge: Cambridge University Press.

Perry S, Panger M, Rose LM, et al. (2003) Traditions in wild white-faced capuchin monkeys. In: Fragaszy DM and Perry S (eds) *The Biology of Traditions*, pp. 391–425. Cambridge: Cambridge University Press.

Pika S and Mitani JC (2006) Referential gestural communication in wild chimpanzees (*Pan troglodytes*). *Curr. Biol.* 16: R191–R192.

Prinz W (2005) An ideomotor approach to imitation. In: Hurley S and Chater N (eds.) *Perspectives on Imitation: From Neuroscience to Social Science, Vol. 2: Imitation, Human Development, and Culture*, pp. 141–156. Cambridge, MA: MIT Press.

Riesch R, Ford JKB, and Thomsen F (2006) Stability and group specificity of stereotyped whistles in resident killer whales, *Orcinus orca*, off British Columbia. *Anim. Behav.* 71: 79–91.

Seyfarth RM and Cheney DL (1986) Vocal development in vervet monkeys. *Anim. Behav.* 34: 1640–1658.

Seyfarth RM and Cheney DL (1997) Some features of vocal development in nonhuman primates. In: Snowdon CT and Hausberger M (eds.) *Social Influences on Vocal Development*, pp. 249–273. Cambridge: Cambridge University Press.

Seyfarth RM and Cheney DL (2003) Meaning and emotion in animal vocalizations. *Ann. N. Y. Acad. Sci.* 1000: 32–55.

Seyfarth RM, Cheney DL, and Marler P (1980) Monkey responses to three different alarm calls: Evidence of predator classification and semantic communication. *Science* 210: 801–803.

Shannon CE and Weaver W (1949) *The Mathematical Theory of Communication.* Urbana, IL: University of Illinois Press.

Smith WJ (1977) *The Behavior of Communicating: An Ethological Approach.* Cambridge, MA: Harvard University Press.

Snowdon CT and Elowson AM (1999) Pygmy marmosets modify call structure when paired. *Ethology* 105: 893–908.

Struhsaker TT (1967) Auditory communication among vervet monkeys (*Cercopithecus aethiops*). In: Altmann SA (ed.) *Social Communication among Primates*, pp. 281–324. Chicago, IL: University of Chicago Press.

Sugiura H (1998) Matching of acoustic features during the vocal exchange of coo calls by Japanese macaques. *Anim. Behav.* 55: 673–687.

Thornton A and McAuliffe K (2006) Teaching in wild meerkats. *Science* 313: 227–229.

Tomasello M (1994) The question of chimpanzee culture. In: Wrangham RT, et al. (eds.) *Chimpanzee Cultures.* Cambridge, MA: Harvard University Press.

Tomasello M (1999) *The Cultural Origins of Human Cognition.* Cambridge, MA: Harvard University Press.

Tomasello M (2004) Learning through others. *Daedalus* Winter: 51–58.

Tomasello M (in press) If they're so good at grammar, then why don't they talk? Hints from apes' and humans' use of gestures. *Lang. Learn. Dev.*

Tomasello M and Call J (2006) Do chimpanzees know what others see – or only what they are looking at? In: Nudds M and Hurley S (eds.) *Rational Animals?* pp. 371–383. Oxford: Oxford University Press.

Tomasello M, Call J, Warren J, Frost GT, Carpenter M, and Nagell K (1997) The ontogeny of chimpanzee gestural signals: A comparison across groups and generations. *Evol. Comm.* 1: 223–259.

Tomasello M, Hare B, and Fogleman T (2001) The ontogeny of gaze following in chimpanzees, *Pan troglodytes*, and rhesus macaques, *Macaca mulatta. Anim. Behav.* 61: 335–343.

Tylor EB (1871) *Primitive Culture: Researches into the Development of Mythology, Philosophy, Religion, Language, Art, and Custom.* London: John Murray.

Van Schaik CP, Ancrenaz M, Borgen G, et al. (2003) Orangutan cultures and the evolution of material culture. *Science* 299: 102–105.

Weir AAS, Chappell J, and Kacelnik A (2002) Shaping of hooks in New Caledonian crows. *Science* 297: 981.

Whiten A (2005) The second inheritance system of chimpanzees and humans. *Nature* 437: 52–55.

Whiten A, Goodall J, McGrew WC, et al. (1999) Cultures in chimpanzees. *Nature* 399: 682–685.

Whiten A, Horner V, and De Waal FBM (2005) Conformity to cultural norms of tool use in chimpanzees. *Nature* 437: 737–740.

Zentall TR (1996) An analysis of imitative learning in animals. In: Heyes C and Galef BG (eds.) *Social Learning in Animals*, pp. 221–243. New York: Academic Press.

Zuberbühler K (2006) Alarm calls. In: Brown K (ed.) *Encyclopedia of Language and Linguistics*, pp. 143–155. New York: Elsevier.

1.17 Bird Song Learning

P. Marler, University of California at Davis, Davis, CA, USA

1.17.1 Introduction

All birds have a repertoire of calls for communication about danger, food, sex, and group movements, and their calls are used for many other purposes as well. Within this repertoire of a dozen or more sound signals, a distinction can be made between calls, which are usually brief and often monosyllabic, and song, which is a more extended pattern of sound, sometimes raucous, often tonal and melodic, and not infrequently a source of pleasure for human listeners (Catchpole and Slater, 1995). Defined in this way, virtually all birds have something that we can call a song, whether it be the crow of the cock or the music of nightingales. In close to half of all 9000 species of birds, the song is learned. Most of the 4000 or so probable learner species come from just one of the 27 orders into which taxonomists classify living birds. Excluded are waders, chicken-like birds, woodpeckers, cuckoos, doves, hawks, owls, and all marine and freshwater birds. The only groups that qualify are parrots, hummingbirds, and above all the very populous suborder of the Passeriforms known as the oscines, characterized by the complexity of their vocal organs and by their distinctive forebrain circuitry expressly evolved to sustain song learning. Parrots and perhaps hummingbirds seem to have independently achieved the same end with equivalent but neuroanatomically distinct brain circuitry (e.g., Striedter, 1994).

Songs are usually, though not always, a male, androgen-dependent prerogative. In species that are learners, the associated brain circuitry is often sexually dimorphic, and there is an extensive literature on the extent and functional significance of this dimorphism and its developmental basis (Nottebohm and Arnold, 1976; DeVoogd, 1991; Arnold, 1990; Vicario, 1991; Brenowitz and Kroodsma, 1996). A larger song system in male brains clearly implies a greater commitment to song learning, and the correlation between the size of song system nuclei, the presence of song, and song repertoire size extends not only to comparisons between the sexes but also between species, subspecies, and even individuals (Nottebohm et al., 1981; Canady et al., 1984; DeVoogd et al., 1993).

Unlike calls, which are occasionally learned but are typically innate, oscine songs always develop abnormally if a young male is reared out of hearing of adults. A common consequence of dependence on learning is the emergence of local song dialects, often varying on much the same geographic scale as dialects in human speech (Baker and Cunningham, 1985). Their distinctiveness depends on such factors as patterns of dispersal from the birthplace and the timing of song learning. When dialects are well defined, it seems to be a general rule that songs like a bird's own dialect are especially potent as vocal signals, both to territorial males and to females ready to mate. A bird's dialect may or may not correspond to that which prevails in the natal area.

Many analogies can be struck between song learning and the acquisition of human speech (Doupe and Kuhl, 1999). There is no nonhuman primate in which vocal patterns are culturally transmitted from generation to generation. Aside from cetaceans, which also engage in vocal learning, birds provide the most valuable animal model we have for studying the behavioral, hormonal, and neural basis of vocal plasticity (Konishi, 1985; Arnold, 1990; Marler, 1991; Nottebohm, 1993; Zeigler and Marler, 2004).

1.17.2 The Physiology of Song Learning

1.17.2.1 Special Brain Mechanisms

Although many important issues remain unexplored, much has been learned over the past 30 years about the specialized neural mechanisms that mediate avian vocal plasticity since the song system was discovered in the canary brain (Nottebohm et al., 1976; *See also* Chapter 3.23). There are two main functional requirements for controlling song production. Appropriate configurations of the articulators must be set up, primarily the syrinx and the

postsyringeal vocal tract. Also, the required pattern of air flow must be generated to set the articulators vibrating. These controls are required whether a song is learned or innate, and as might be predicted, some of the circuitry responsible is relatively conservative, located in the midbrain and the brain stem (Wild, 1994). The added requirements for songs to be learned are met by two major circuits in the forebrain, one to sustain the actual learning process, the so-called anterior forebrain pathway, and the other, the motor pathway, for control of the production of learned songs (Nottebohm, 1993; **Figure 1**). Disruption of the motor pathway always results in the distortion and even the elimination of learned songs, whereas the anterior forebrain pathway seems to be redundant except during actual song development. As with innate songs, the motor pathway must have access both to the vocal tract and the syringeal musculature, mapped in one part of the motor pathway and also to the respiratory system, mapped in another part, both in the robust nucleus of the archistriatum, or RA (Vicario, 1991). Demands on the motor pathway circuit are complicated by the existence of two semiindependent vibrators in the songbird syrinx, requiring precise coordination, since both participate in the production of learned songs (Greenewalt, 1968; Suthers, 1990).

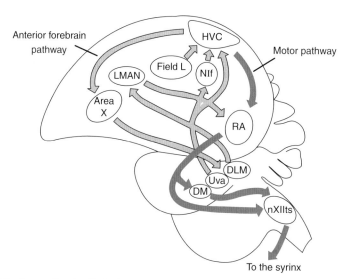

Figure 1 A diagram of the two major circuits in the song system of the oscine brain. One is for control of movements of the vocal apparatus in learned songs (motor pathway), the other for song learning (anterior forebrain pathway). There is a fork in the motor pathway from RA (robust nucleus of the arcopallium) to the hypoglossal nucleus in the brainstem, and to the vocal apparatus (nXIIts). One branch goes directly, the other passes through DM (dorsal medial nucleus) in the midbrain, thought to be involved in the control of respiration. A different circuit for the production of innate songs, involving the midbrain nucleus ICO (intercollicular complex), is not shown. Inputs to the higher vocal center (HVC, no formal name) include field L, the primary auditory forebrain area. Another auditory projection area close by that also projects to HVC. NCM (caudal medial mesopallium) is not shown (see text). Also labeled is LMAN (lateral magnocellular nucleus of the anterior nidopallium).

The hearing of birds has been extensively studied in relation to their vocal behavior (Dooling, 1982). Many parts of the song system are responsive to song stimulation. Strangely, one of the strongest stimuli, especially in the higher vocal center (HVC) of adult males, but also elsewhere, is the bird's own individually distinctive crystallized song (Margoliash, 1986). This finding has promoted the plausible speculation that adult males of some species use auditory feedback from their own song as a yardstick to calibrate the potency of songs of others when they hear them, especially those of conspecific neighbors and strangers.

Attunement of a male's song system to his own individual song, including all of its personal quirks, only emerges as songs crystallize (Doupe, 1993). Unfortunately, little attention has been paid to responsiveness of the brain of young birds to song stimuli prior to the production of plastic and crystallized song. Patterns of auditory responsiveness of the song bird brain during the earliest memorization phase of song learning remain almost unexplored (but see Whaling et al., 1995). Behavioral tests at this age demonstrate innate responsiveness to many features of song, especially those of the bird's own species (Nelson and Marler, 1993; Whaling et al., 1997). Details of the process of song memorization are consistent with involvement of the set of innate auditory predispositions that each species deploys, serving as a guide to the process of selective song learning. The neural mechanisms responsible still await neurophysiological investigation, and until they are elucidated, a full understanding of the physiological basis of song learning will continue to elude us. At present we do not know how songs are memorized by a young male, nor where they are stored in the brain in preparation for the guidance of song production.

One remarkable feature of the bird brain is the continuing development of new neurons in many parts of the brain, both in infancy and in adulthood, including the song system (Goldman and Nottebohm, 1983). Although it is not clear what relevance neurogenesis has to song learning, there are many fascinating hints, including the demonstration, in something of a technical tour de force, that some new neurons are actually inserted into the song system and become active there (Paton and Nottebohm, 1984; Alvarez-Buylla et al., 1990). It may be that neuronal turnover in the motor pathway prepares the way for the song plasticity that some birds such as the canary (Nottebohm and Nottebohm, 1978) display in adulthood.

Another place to look for song-related activity is in the forebrain auditory circuits concerned with the perceptual processing of song stimuli. One of these (caudal medial mesopallium, NCM) has been identified as the site of gene activation in response to conspecific stimulation and as a location where experience-dependent changes in electrophysiological responsiveness to song stimuli are occurring (Mello et al., 1992; Mello and Clayton, 1994). Circuits extrinsic to the song system may prove to be more involved in song learning than has been thought.

1.17.3 Sensitive Periods for Learning

In song development, as in the ontogeny of other kinds of behavior, the rapidity and precision with which learning takes place varies from one stage of the life cycle to another. All song birds seem to share a similar sequence of stages in the process of learning to sing. First is the acquisition phase often restricted to a short period, when a bird hears songs and commits some of them to memory. After storage for a period that ranges in duration from days to months, depending on the species, songs are recalled from memory, and imitations begin to emerge. Renditions are relatively faithful to the original model in some species, but others depart from it quite radically, with vocal inventiveness playing a significant role.

The separation in time between the acquisition or sensory phase and the production or sensorimotor phase, ending with the production of crystallized, adult song, is a significant one. In many birds, the sequence occurs just once, often in early adolescence. In such cases, adult song patterns remain fixed thereafter, their production waxing and waning with the passing of each breeding season. In other species, the sequence recurs repeatedly during adulthood, so that song patterns may continue to change. Even close relatives, such as canaries and sparrows, can differ in this respect.

Several species of sparrows have a sensitive period for song acquisition beginning at about 2 weeks of age, soon after they leave the nest, and ending 6–8 weeks later (Nelson et al., 1995). The precise duration varies, even in different populations of the same species (**Figure 2**). Sensitive periods for learning are not fixed but are changeable, within limits, depending on such things as the strength of song stimulation; access to a live, interactive tutor (Baptista and Petrinovich, 1986); and physiological factors, such as hormonal states, that vary with the season.

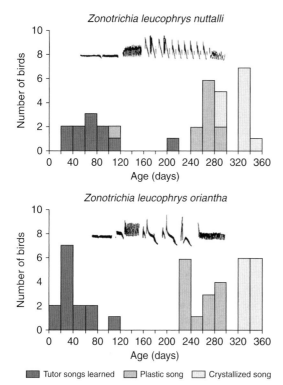

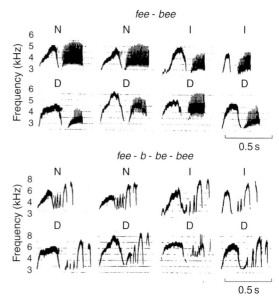

Figure 3 Within the passeriform perching birds, the oscine songbirds all have learned songs, but the suboscines, which lack the special song-system brain circuitry, do not. Here are examples of the innate song of a suboscine passerine, the eastern phoebe. Some developed normally in the wild (N), some in isolation (I), and some after deafening (D). Two song types are represented, the fee-bee and the fee-b-be-bee. Unlike oscines, whose songs are drastically modified by isolation or deafening, both isolated and deafened phoebes developed normal songs. From Kroodsma DE and Konishi M (1991) A suboscine bird (Eastern phoebe, *Sayornis phoebe*) develops normal song without auditory feedback. *Anim. Behav.* 42: 477–487.

Figure 2 The timing of song production and song acquisition from constantly changing programs of tape recordings throughout the first year of life in male white-crowned sparrows raised in the laboratory. The birds represent two populations: one resident year-round on the coast (subspecies nuttalli), the other migratory in the high Sierras (oriantha). The migratory birds began acquiring song earlier (peaking at 33 days vs. 52 days), and the acquisition period was significantly shorter. A representative song of each is shown. Both are about 2 s in duration. From: Nelson DA, Marler P, and Palleroni A (1995) A comparative approach to vocal learning: Intra-specific variation in the learning process. *Anim. Behav.* 50: 83–97.

Closure of the acquisition period can sometimes be delayed if songs of the bird's own species are withheld (Kroodsma and Pickert, 1980), as though termination of the sensory phase is delayed until adequate song stimulation has been experienced. If young are hatched late in the season and singing has already ceased for that year, the sensitive period may be extended until the following spring in some species, though this delay does not occur in all cases.

1.17.4 Vocal Development

1.17.4.1 The Ontogeny of Learned Song

In contrast with song learners, nonlearners develop normal song when raised in isolation, even after

deafening (Kroodsma, 1984; Kroodsma and Konishi, 1991). This is true of a male dove, a cockerel, and even of those passerines that are nonoscines, such as the New World flycatchers (**Figure 3**). In such cases, when a young bird starts to sing, its very first efforts are clearly identifiable as immature versions of what will ultimately be normal adult song. Early attempts may be noisy and fragmented, but there is a clear linear progression in the development of innate songs.

In birds that learn their songs, the developmental progression is quite different. They begin with the unique vocal pattern called subsong, a quiet, variable warbling that can begin as early as 3 or 4 weeks of age. It is reminiscent of the early babbling stage of speech development (Locke, 1993). Typically it seems to bear no resemblance to mature song, although we know less about its structure and function than any other aspect of song development. As defined, there are no imitations in subsong. In song learners, there is a kind of vocal metamorphosis between subsong and later stages of song development. The amorphous structure and noisy spectral organization of subsong are consistent with a role in the acquisition of the general motor skills of singing, in coping with the complexities of the oscine syrinx, and also in honing the ability to guide the voice by the ear, a prerequisite for vocal imitation (Thorpe, 1961; Nottebohm, 1972; Marler and Peters, 1982b). Duration of the subsong period varies greatly, even within a species, depending on individual histories. In deaf birds and social isolates, it may last for weeks, but a bird with adequate tutoring in youth may progress rapidly from subsong to the next phase, plastic song, in a few days.

In plastic song, signs of mature song structure first appear. Previously memorized song patterns emerge and begin to stabilize, first gradually, then rapidly, until adult, crystallized song is achieved, and the young male is ready to launch a full season of mature singing (**Figure 4**).

1.17.4.2 Overproduction, Attrition, and Action-Based Learning

Song learning has been traditionally viewed as memory based. Songs are acquired and memorized and then used later to guide motor development by auditory feedback, with no practice at the time of memorization. Another kind of vocal plasticity, involving only working memory, and with a key role for motor practice, occurs during the plastic song phase.

Several learner species overproduce during plastic song, generating more than they need for mature song, and discarding excess plastic songs as the time for song crystallization approaches (**Figure 5**). Some overproduced songs are invented, but many are imitated, and the richness of early song experience is one factor in determining the extent of the overproduced repertoire (Nelson et al., 1996). However, overproduction and attrition also occur in birds tutored and raised in individual isolation in the laboratory (Marler and Peters, 1982a). In this case, the decision about which songs to discard seems to be random, whereas in nature it is guided by social experience.

The attrition phase in which overproduced songs are discarded from the repertoire coincides with the efforts of young male sparrows to establish their first territory. As it competes with adults, those songs of the young bird that match song types of older rivals, even if only approximately, are most effective in eliciting counter singing and perhaps in territorial defense (Beecher, 1996). Young males tend to retain and crystallize those plastic songs that are the closest match to those of their rivals, and to discard the rest.

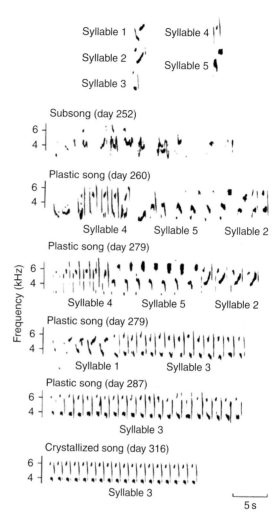

Figure 4 Development of the song of a male swamp sparrow raised in the laboratory and tutored with tape recordings of song from 20–60 days of age. Some of his training song syllables are shown at the bottom right. The first emergence of imitations can be seen in his plastic song from day 260, 200 days after the end of tutoring. His mature song crystallized around 300 days of age (see **Figure 5**).

Effects of male-to-male territorial interactions, either real or simulated, on song attrition have been described in several species of sparrows (Nelson, 1992; Nelson and Marler, 1994). In another species, the brown-headed cowbird, responses of females serve to shape male decisions about which overproduced songs to retain (West and King, 1988). The process by which a repertoire of varied motor patterns is selectively winnowed, with the selection process based on social feedback, has been termed action-based learning (Marler and Nelson, 1993). There are probably parallels with the development of other kinds of motor behavior, including play.

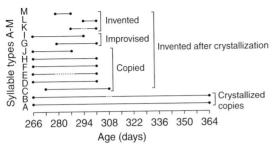

Figure 5 A diagram of song development in the same male swamp sparrow shown in **Figure 4**. In addition to the eight tape-recorded songs he imitated, he invented three more and modified two by improvisation. His crystallized adult repertoire of two song types is typical for this species.

Use-dependent processes of selective attrition may be widespread in the development of many kinds of behavioral activities. The actions that are discarded from the repertoire may themselves have functional significance. For example, songs that are practiced in youth and then rejected may provide a potential memory bank for the future, perhaps consulted in assessing the songs of others. In species that retain vocal plasticity into adulthood, discarded songs may be redeployed as the basis for producing new songs later in life.

The life-cycle timetable for action-based learning is different from that for memory-based learning. Action-based learning has the potential to recur whenever, for whatever reason; progression through a phase of variable action patterns is then followed by use-dependent winnowing of the variants. A mechanism is required for selective reinforcement of certain motor variants over others. Unlike memory-based learning, highly specialized brain mechanisms such as the oscine song system are not required. As a consequence, action-based learning is likely to have a wide phylogenetic distribution. For example, although nonhuman primates seem to be incapable of memory-based vocal learning, they do have a limited degree of vocal plasticity, possibly mediated by action-based learning.

1.17.4.3 Effects of Isolation and Deafness

Regardless of the opportunity to learn, certain aspects of the normal singing behavior of the species will always develop in oscines. When sparrows are raised in isolation, for example, the note structure and tonal quality of their songs is aberrant, but aspects of basic song syntax develop normally (**Figure 6**). Certain song features of the species are produced despite their absence from the tutoring songs a male has experienced, but with the important proviso that hearing must be intact.

The singing patterns of a hearing male oscine raised in isolation and of a male deafened early in life and raised in isolation are quite different. Typically, deaf male songs are highly degraded and variable, lacking most of the few normal features that an intact male can develop in isolation (Konishi, 1965). Songs of early-deafened males are not completely amorphous. This is true even when the critical step has been taken to be sure that there has been no song practice prior to deafening. This step

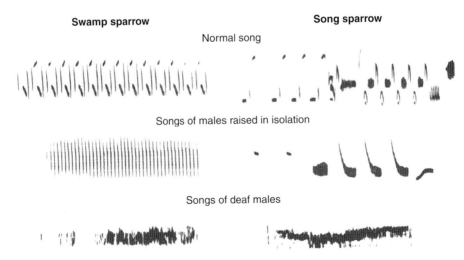

Figure 6 Normal songs of swamp and song sparrows compared with those developed by males raised in social isolation and by males deafened early in life. The simplicity of the note structure of the isolate songs is typical for sparrows. The high degree of species specificity, so evident in normal song, is largely erased from the songs of deaf males.

was lacking in some of the earliest studies. The emergence of some elements of species-specific song syntax in males deafened very early in life seems to implicate innate motor programs in song development. The highly abnormal song patterns characteristic of deaf birds develop both if a male becomes deaf before tutoring and if he is deafened after the tutoring but before singing has developed. There seems to be no internal brain circuitry that makes memorized songs directly available to guide vocal development. To transform a memorized song into a produced song, the bird must be able to hear its own voice. We can infer that some aspects of song production are guided by auditory templates for song, located in the brain, with specifications that vary from species to species (Konishi, 1965; Marler and Sherman, 1983). Neurobiologists have yet to demonstrate where these templates are located and how they operate (but see Whaling et al., 1997).

Like ornithologists, wild birds rely heavily on song for species identification. Each bird has its own distinctive way of singing, and this is recognized by other species members. Songs of early-deafened song birds, on the other hand, are often indistinguishable between species and are largely, though as noted not entirely, lacking in species specificity (**Figure 6**). Songs of males raised in isolation but with hearing intact fall somewhere between. They retain some species-typical features, and they lack others.

When tape-recorded songs are played to wild territorial males or to females in hormonally induced estrus, experienced birds of both sexes respond strongly to normal song of their species but completely disregard deaf songs as social signals (Searcy et al., 1985; Searcy and Marler, 1987). Similarly, songs of other species elicit none of the strong aggressive responses of territorial males, or the courtship of estradiol-primed females, that conspecific song evokes. But those of social isolates do retain a minimal level of effectiveness. Thus the efficacy of bird song as a social signal is augmented during development both by learning and by ontogenetic involvement of innate auditory templates that encode certain species-specific features of normal song.

1.17.4.4 Learning Preferences

Learning theorists once believed that any stimulus could be learned, given appropriate conditions; differences in stimulus potency, although present, were regarded as unimportant enough to be ignored in theorizing about the mechanisms underlying learning. We now know that innate predispositions play crucial roles in the adaptiveness of natural learning processes, and song learning in birds provides many illustrations of this principle. While birds are capable of learning a multiplicity of different sounds, including those of many other species (**Figure 7**), other-species mimicry is relatively rare in the wild (Kroodsma and Baylis, 1982). Leaving aside mimics, which only account for about 15% of songbirds, it is adaptive for most song birds to avoid other-species songs as models for learning.

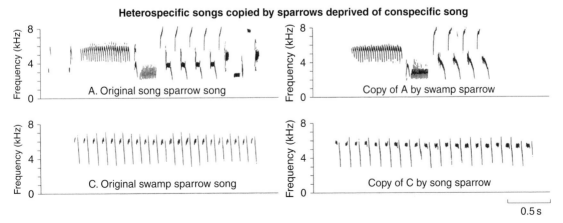

Figure 7 Although sparrows typically reject each other's songs as models for learning, they will sometimes accept them if given no other choice. Here male swamp and song sparrows learned a tape-recorded song of the other species when given no conspecific songs to listen to. Evidently the vocal apparatus is able to articulate the sounds of the other species song.

If males of two different species, such as swamp and song sparrows, are brought into the laboratory and exposed to identical tape recordings that include both species' songs, each displays a clear preference for song of its own kind, even if it has never been heard before (Marler and Peters, 1988, 1989). This preference does not arise from an inability to produce the other species song. An alien song that a male rejects, when given a choice, may become acceptable if it is the only option (**Figure 7**), especially when it is presented in a highly interactive situation by a live tutor caged nearby (Baptista and Petrinovich, 1986). But given a choice, there is typically a preference for conspecific song.

1.17.5   The Role of Innate Knowledge in Song Development

The view of the brain as a *tabula rasa*, a blank slate, all too long a basis for the thinking of learning theorists, is patently absurd. Whatever the task, every brain brings to bear a set of neurally based predispositions, each with its own evolutionary and experiential history, about how to proceed most efficiently in dealing with a given set of learning problems. Some of these predispositions are generic and pan-specific, and others are highly singular and even species specific, as with the innate processes that the human infant brings to bear on the development of speech behavior and language. Such is the case with birdsong.

The young bird embarks on the process of developing song armed with innate predispositions about how best to proceed. Some are generic, such as the widely shared tendency of songbirds to sing tonal sounds, evident even when they render imitations of sounds that were not originally strictly tonal (Nowicki et al., 1992). Others are species specific. When sparrows learn to sing, they favor conspecific song. They do so on the basis of not a single ethological sign stimulus but a range of song features. Naive young birds, recently fledged, are highly discriminating with regard to the song stimuli they find most potent, as revealed by their tendency to give more begging calls to them in response to playback (Nelson and Marler, 1993). By playing experimentally modified songs to young birds, innate responsiveness has been demonstrated to a range of conspecific song attributes. It is clear from their behavior that young birds possess extensive foreknowledge about the song of their species before they embark on the process of learning to sing. The

evidence indicates that they know much more than you might guess solely on the basis of the songs that a male produces when raised in social isolation. They behave as though auditory experience that matches their innate knowledge is required before that knowledge can be fully brought to bear on song development (Marler, 1984).

One way to view song learning is as a process of validation by use of a subset of innate knowledge, drawn from a more extensive library encoded in the brain that details the rules for the singing behavior for each species (Marler and Nelson, 1992). This innate library is shared by all species members. The species-universal rules encoded there are sufficiently flexible to provide almost infinite opportunities for differences in individual behavior as a function of personal experience, and yet firm enough to restrict the development of excessive divergence between individuals.

There are analogies with the rules for orderly musical composition that each human culture possesses, encompassing the potential for an infinite number of different melodies (Jackendoff, 1994). The genetic underpinnings of the immune system provide another parallel, with the major histocompatibility complex providing enough alleles for a vast number of possible combinations. The imposition of limitations is important because it ensures that, however individualistic a bird's singing behavior may be, it still conforms closely enough to species-universal rules that obstacles to communication with others are minimized.

In addition to predispositions evident in the sensory phase of song memorization, others are manifest during motor development. The emergence of some species-specific basics in the song syntax of early-deafened males has already been noted. A bird tricked into learning heterospecific songs may only reject them in late stages of plastic song as species-specific syntax emerges (Marler and Peters, 1989). When young sparrows were tutored using experimentally modified songs with abnormally high syllable repetition rates, they imitated the songs but reorganized them in invented patterns that conformed more closely to the temporal organization of their normal species song (Podos, 1996). Again there is great flexibility in these motor predispositions, but even though songs with abnormal temporal organization can be taught, there is an underlying tendency to conform to species-specific norms. The individual and population differences that characterize learned birdsongs are all-pervasive, but they rarely confuse experienced bird watchers in identifying the species responsible. With their genetic fitness at stake, the birds themselves are hardly likely to be any less perceptive.

1.17.6 Reinforcement and the Speed of Vocal Learning

Some of the distinctive features of song learning recur in other cases of developmental plasticity. It is not uncommon for developing behavioral and neural systems to exhibit sensitive phases, when the potential for plasticity is unusually great. Completion of one developmental stage is often a necessary precursor for embarking on the next.

Unlike some other widely studied forms of learning, no external reinforcement is required in song learning, even though social stimulation may augment the acquisition process. It suffices that the bird be exposed to an appropriate set of stimuli at the appointed stage of development for acquisition to occur. At the height of the sensitive period, learning can take place with great rapidity. Sometimes remarkably few exposures to a bird's own species song are sufficient. In sparrows, some acquisition can occur from 30 repetitions of a conspecific song. European blackbirds have learned from 15–20 song presentations on a single day.

The virtuoso performer in this regard is the nightingale, which can learn a sequence of song types accurately after 20 presentations – some males with as few as five. The virtuosity of nightingales is such that they can learn strings of up to 60 different songs and reproduce them in the original order. The sequencing is only retained in subsets of three to seven songs, however. After producing such a matched sequence, birds in one experiment then switched to another subset, beginning at a different point. These birds behaved as though they divide a string of many songs into manageable subsets of up to seven songs, using a strategy for memorizing long sequences reminiscent of that used by humans in memorizing strings of words (Hultsch and Todt, 1989, 1992, 2004). This is one of many avian accomplishments reminiscent of aspects of human speech behavior.

1.17.7 Song Development as a Creative Process

Perhaps most mysterious and intriguing of all is the ability of songbirds to invent new sounds. They achieve this in several different ways. Some birds first imitate the components of songs they have heard and then, as plastic song progresses, recombine them to create new sequences. In this way, parts can be exchanged within a song, between different songs, and even between songs that have been acquired many months apart (**Figure 8**). Rather than remaining faithful to the structure of imitated sounds, some birds find the temptation to improvise irresistible, especially during plastic song, so that songs originally imitated eventually become so changed as to be unrecognizable.

Not uncommonly, birds invent new sound patterns that they themselves have never heard. This is frequent in birds raised in isolation, with the result that, although the songs of isolates are abnormally simple in some respects, they are also extremely diverse. The act of producing novel and distinctively patterned sound seems to be itself reinforcing, attesting to the strong and deep-rooted commitment of many song birds to vocal inventiveness.

The drive to invention is stronger in some species than others. Certain birds remain quite rigidly faithful to their tutors, adding just sufficient individuality to personalize their song, and no more. Adherence to their models makes them especially tractable as subjects for laboratory investigation of song learning. Perhaps for this reason, the more imaginative songsters tend to be underrepresented in the roster of favored subjects for scientific study. The huge individual repertoires that males of some bird species possess, sometime with hundreds of song types,

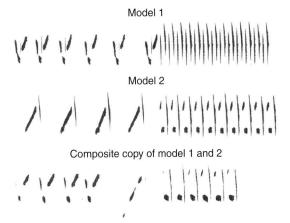

Figure 8 An example of a bird that created a new song by recombination. A captive male song sparrow was given only artificial songs to learn made up of two-parted swamp sparrow songs. He created a three-part song, approximating normal song sparrow syntax by combining parts of two different models.

built up by reiteration of these processes of imitation, segmentation, recombination, improvisation, and invention are barely manageable as subjects for scientific study. But for anyone interested in esthetic theory, the birds with large repertoires that give human listeners so much pleasure, such as mockingbirds and their relatives, the Australian lyre-bird, and certain thrushes, are unrivaled as subjects of choice. Utilitarian concerns are only one aspect of our fascination with birdsongs. If we are looking for animal models of the creative impulse, birdsong is one of the few that comes close to human standards.

1.17.8 Conclusions

As more bird species are studied, we find that each has achieved its own special solutions to the problems of developing a song. Songsters participate in a system of social communication that relies upon signals learned from others. Some species learn readily from song stimulation alone, and often remarkably few song stimuli are necessary, as though the brain is primed to be especially responsive to songs of a bird's own kind. Other species take longer to learn and require social stimulation.

Despite the possession of extensive innate foreknowledge about songs of their species, and a strong inclination to favor them if given a choice, they can be persuaded under special circumstances to learn songs of others. Certain species engage in the process of between-species mimicry naturally and create a species-specific song by imposing distinctive temporal patterning on the imitations as they are rendered. Some birds are faithful to the song they imitate, and others use imitations as a basis for improvisation, retaining certain features of the tutor and changing others.

The diversity of these patterns of behavioral development is made possible because, along with the oscine song system, the brain of each bird species brings to bear its own distinctive set of properties and predispositions to the task of learning to sing. The challenge for the neurobiologist is to understand not only the basic brain mechanisms that underlie the generic learning abilities of all song birds but also the more subtle, singular means by which a given species adds its own unique flavor to the process of developing a song, adapted to a particular set of social, ecological, and phylogenetic circumstances.

References

Alvarez-Buylla A, Kirn JR, and Nottebohm F (1990) Birth of projection neurons in adult avian brain may be related to perceptual or motor learning. *Science* 224: 901–903.

Arnold AP (1990) The Passerine bird song system as a model in neuroendocrine research. *J. Exp. Zool. Suppl.* 4: 22–30.

Baker MC and Cunningham MA (1985) The biology of bird-song dialects. *Behav. Brain Sci.* 8: 85–133.

Baptista LF and Petrinovich L (1986) Song development in the white-crowned sparrow: Social factors and sex differences. *Anim. Behav.* 34: 1359–1371.

Beecher MD (1996) Birdsong learning in the laboratory and field. In: Kroodsma DE and Miller EH (eds.) *Ecology and Evolution of Acoustic Communication in Birds*. Ithaca, NY: Cornell University Press.

Brenowitz E and Kroodsma DE (1996) The neuroethology of birdsong. In: Kroodsma DE and Miller EH (eds.) *Ecology and Evolution of Acoustic Communication in Birds*. Ithaca, NY: Cornell University.

Canady RA, Kroodsma DE, and Nottebohm F (1984) Population differences in complexity of a learned skill are correlated with the brain space involved. *Proc. Natl. Acad. Sci. USA* 81: 6232–6234.

Catchpole CK and Slater PJB (1995) *Bird Song*. Cambridge: Cambridge University Press.

DeVoogd TJ (1991) Endocrine modulation of the development and adult function of the avian song system. *Psychoneuroendocrinology* 16: 41–66.

DeVoogd TJ, Krebs JR, Healy SD, and Purvis A (1993) Relations between song repertoire size and the volume of brain nuclei related to song: comparative evolutionary analyses amongst oscine birds. *Proc. R. Soc. Lond. Ser. B* 254: 75–82.

Dooling RJ (1982) Auditory perception in birds. In: Kroodsma DE and Miller EH (eds.) *Acoustic Communication in Birds*, vol. 1, pp. 95–130. New York: Academic Press.

Doupe AJ (1993) A neural circuit specialized for vocal learning. *Curr. Opin. Neurobiol.* 3: 104–111.

Doupe AJ and Kuhl PK (1999) Birdsong and human speech: Common themes and mechanisms. *Ann. Rev. Neurosci.* 22: 567–631.

Goldman SA and Nottebohm F (1983) Neuronal production, migration, and differentiation in the vocal control nucleus of the adult female canary brain. *Proc. Natl. Acad. Sci. USA* 80: 2390–2394.

Greenewalt CH (1968) *Bird Song: Acoustics and Physiology*. Washington DC: Smithsonian Institution Press.

Hultsch H and Todt D (1989) Memorization and reproduction of songs in nightingales: evidence for package formation. *J. Comp. Physiol. A* 165: 197–203.

Hultsch H and Todt D (1992) The serial order effect in the song acquisition of birds: relevance of exposure frequency to song models. *Anim. Behav.* 44: 590–592.

Hultsch H and Todt D (2004) Learning to sing. In: Marler P and Slabbekoorn H (eds.) *Nature's Music*, pp. 80–107. San Diego: Elsevier Academic Press.

Jackendoff R (1994) *Patterns in the Mind: Language and Human Nature*. New York: Basic Books.

Konishi M (1965) The role of auditory feedback in the control of vocalization in the white-crowned sparrow. *Z. Tierpsychol.* 22: 770–778.

Konishi M (1985) Birdsong: from behavior to neuron. *Annu. Rev. Neurosci.* 8: 125–170.

Kroodsma DE (1984) Songs of the alder flycatcher (*Empidonax alnorum*) and willow flycatcher (*Empidonax traillii*) are innate. *Auk* 101: 13–24.

Kroodsma DE and Baylis JR (1982) A world survey of evidence for vocal learning in birds. In: Kroodsma DE and Miller EH (eds.) *Acoustic Communication in Birds*, pp. 311–337. New York: Academic Press.

Kroodsma DE and Konishi M (1991) A suboscine bird (Eastern phoebe, *Sayornis phoebe*) develops normal song without auditory feedback. *Anim. Behav.* 42: 477–487.

Kroodsma DE and Pickert R (1980) Environmentally dependent sensitive periods for avian vocal learning. *Nature* 288: 477–479.

Locke JL (1993) *The Path to Spoken Language*. Cambridge, MA: Harvard University Press.

Margoliash D (1986) Preference for autogenous song by auditory neurons in a song system nucleus of the white-crowned sparrow. *J. Neurosci.* 69: 1643–1661.

Marler P (1984) Song learning: Innate species differences in the learning process. In: Marler P and Terrace HS (eds.) *The Biology of Learning*, pp. 289–309. Berlin: Springer Verlag.

Marler P (1991) Song learning behavior: The interface with neuroethology. *Trends Neurosci.* 14: 199–206.

Marler P and Nelson D (1992) Neuroselection and song learning in birds: Species universals in a culturally transmitted behavior. In: Marler P (ed.) *Communication: Behavior and Neurobiology, vol. 4: Seminars in the Neurosciences*, pp. 415–423. London: Saunders Scientific Publications.

Marler P and Nelson DA (1993) Action-based learning: A new form of developmental plasticity in bird song. *Neth. J. Zool.* 43(1–2): 91–103.

Marler P and Peters S (1982a) Developmental overproduction and selective attrition: New processes in the epigenesis of bird song. *Dev. Psychobiol.* 15: 369–378.

Marler P and Peters S (1982b) Subsong and plastic song: Their role in the vocal learning process. In: Kroodsma DE and Miller EH (eds.) *Song Learning and Its Consequences, vol. 2: Acoustic Communication in Birds*, pp. 25–50. New York: Academic Press.

Marler P and Peters S (1988) The role of song phonology and syntax in vocal learning preferences in the song sparrow, *Melospiza melodia*. *Ethology* 77: 125–149.

Marler P and Peters S (1989) Species differences in auditory responsiveness in early vocal learning. In: Dooling RJ and Hulse HS (eds.) *The Comparative Psychology of Audition: Perceiving Complex Sounds*, pp. 243–273. Hillsdale, NJ: Lawrence Erlbaum.

Marler P and Sherman V (1983) Song structure without auditory feedback: Emendations of the auditory template hypothesis. *J. Neurosci.* 3: 517–531.

Mello CV and Clayton DF (1994) Song-induced ZENK gene expression in auditory pathways of songbird brain and its relation to the song control system. *J. Neurosci.* 14: 6652–6666.

Mello CV, Vicario DS, and Clayton DF (1992) Song presentation induces gene expression in the songbird's forebrain. *Proc. Natl. Acad. Sci. USA* 89: 6818–6822.

Nelson DA (1992) Song overproduction and selective attrition lead to song sharing in the field sparrow (*Spizella pusilla*) *Behav. Ecol. Sociobiol.* 30: 415–424.

Nelson DA and Marler P (1993) Innate recognition of song in white-crowned sparrows: A role in selective vocal learning? *Anim. Behav.* 46: 806–808.

Nelson DA and Marler P (1994) Selection-based learning in bird song development. *Proc. Natl. Acad. Sci. USA* 91: 10498–10501.

Nelson DA, Marler P, and Palleroni A (1995) A comparative approach to vocal learning: intra-specific variation in the learning process. *Anim. Behav.* 50: 83–97.

Nelson DA, Whaling C, and Marler P (1996) The capacity for song memorization varies in populations of the same species. *Anim. Behav.* 52: 379–387.

Nottebohm F (1972) Neural lateralization of vocal control in a passerine bird II. Subsong, calls and a theory of learning. *J. Exp. Zool.* 179: 35–49.

Nottebohm F (1993) The search for neural mechanisms that define the sensitive period for song learning in birds. *Neth. J. Zool.* 43: 193–234.

Nottebohm F and Arnold AP (1976) Sexual dimorphism in vocal control areas of the songbird brain. *Science* 194: 211–213.

Nottebohm F and Nottebohm ME (1978) Relationship between song repertoire and age in the canary *Serinus canaria*. *Z. Tierpsychol.* 46: 298–305.

Nottebohm F, Stokes TM, and Leonard CM (1976) Central control of song in the canary. *J. Comp. Neurol.* 165: 457–486.

Nottebohm F, Kasparian S, and Pandazis C (1981) Brain space for a learned task. *Brain Res.* 213: 99–109.

Nowicki S, Marler P, Maynard A, and Peters S (1992) Is the tonal quality of birdsong learned? Evidence from song sparrows. *Ethology* 90: 225–235.

Paton GA and Nottebohm F (1984) Neurons generated in the adult brain are recruited into functional circuits. *Science* 225: 1046–1048.

Podos J (1996) Motor constraints on vocal development in a songbird. *Anim. Behav.* 51: 1061–1070.

Searcy WA and Marler P (1987) Response of sparrows to songs of deaf and isolation-reared males: Further evidence for innate auditory templates. *Dev. Psychobiol.* 20: 509–520.

Searcy WA, Marler P, and Peters S (1985) Song of isolation-reared sparrows function in communication, but are significantly less effective than learned songs. *Behav. Ecol. Sociobiol.* 17: 223–229.

Striedter GF (1994) The vocal control pathways in budgerigars differ from those in songbirds. *J. Comp. Neurol.* 343: 35–56.

Suthers RA (1990) Contributions to birdsong from the left and right sides of the intact syrinx. *Nature* 347: 473–477.

Thorpe WH (1961) *Bird Song*. Cambridge, MA: Cambridge University Press.

Vicario DS (1991) Neural mechanisms of song production in songbirds. *Curr. Opin. Neurobiol.* 1: 595–600.

West MJ and King AP (1988) Female visual displays affect the development of male song in the cowbird. *Nature* 334: 244–246.

Whaling CS, Solis M, Carrillo G, Soha JA, Marler P, and Doupe AJ (1995) Song learning in sparrows: From behavior to brain. *Soc. Neurosci.* 21(2): 958.

Whaling CS, Solis MM, Doupe AJ, Soha JA, and Marler P (1997) Acoustic and neural bases for innate recognition of song. *Proc. Natl. Acad. Sci. USA* 94: 12694–12698.

Wild JM (1994) The auditory-vocal-respiratory axis in birds. *Brain Behav. Evol.* 44: 192–209.

Zeigler HP and Marler P (eds.) (2004) *Special Issue: Behavioral Neurobiology of Birdsong. Ann. NY Acad. Sci.* 1016: 1–788.

1.18 Adaptive Specializations and Generality of the Laws of Classical and Instrumental Conditioning

M. Domjan, University of Texas at Austin, Austin, TX, USA

1.18.1 Introduction

How general are the laws of classical and instrumental conditioning? Empirical observations invariably involve a particular species and responses and stimuli arranged in a particular fashion. But the findings would be of little interest if they were only applicable to the specific circumstances of their discovery. Scientists strive for generality. A specific experiment is of import only because we assume that it illustrates truths about the world that go beyond the circumstances of that experiment.

Early investigators of classical and instrumental conditioning were quick to assume that the behavior changes they were discovering in the laboratory represented general laws or principles of learning applicable to a variety of species and circumstances. Thorndike, for example, formulated the Law of Effect to characterize how instrumental behavior is acquired (Thorndike, 1898, 1911). Pavlov provided principles of classical conditioning, including delayed conditioning, inhibition of delay, extinction, and spontaneous recovery (Pavlov, 1927). Skinner characterized general

principles of shaping and schedules of reinforcement for operant conditioning. Hull, Guthrie, and Tolman followed suit in formulating general theories of learning which were not restricted to a particular species, response, or stimulus (Bower and Hilgard, 1981).

Formulations that ignore the species and the particular stimuli or responses that are involved in a conditioning experiment have continued to dominate learning theory in the latter part of the twentieth century. These include theories offered by Rescorla and Wagner (1972), Mackintosh (1975), and Pearce and Hall (1980), and more recently the sometimes opponent processes (SOP) theory and affective emotional SOP (AESOP) (Wagner, 1981; Wagner and Brandon, 1989), the comparator hypothesis (Miller and Matzel, 1988), the temporal coding hypothesis (Savastano and Miller, 1998), and Rate Expectancy Theory (Gallistel and Gibbon, 2000). (*See also* Chapters 1.06, 1.10, 1.12.)

The assumption of generality has shaped not only our theories but also the range of experimental preparations that we use to study classical and instrumental conditioning. If conditioning is in fact a general process, then we should be able to discover the laws of conditioning regardless of what species or situation we examine. This rationale, explicitly stated by Skinner, encouraged investigators to select experimental preparations based primarily on convenience. At the behavioral level, investigators have settled on a small number of experimental paradigms that have gained wide usage. These include pigeons key pecking for food as the reinforcer, rats pressing a lever for food or water, and the conditioned suppression or conditioned freezing procedure for studying classical conditioning.

The assumption that the laws of learning are general and widely applicable has also provided the fundamental justification for studies of the neurobiology of learning. Although such studies may be conducted in a hippocampal slice preparation or in a marine mollusk, the experiments are assumed to reveal general principles of neural plasticity that can be extended to intact vertebrates. The present chapter will review challenges to the generality of Pavlovian and instrumental conditioning at the behavioral level and discuss theoretical efforts to incorporate these challenges into a revised general theory of conditioning (*See also* Chapters 1.17, 1.20, 1.22). The exposition will focus on studies of conditioning in vertebrate species. However, the issues raised are also relevant to studies of learning in nonvertebrate species such as the honey bee (e.g., Menzel, 1990, 1999) (*See also* Chapters 1.27, 1.29).

1.18.2 Biological Constraints on Learning

Although the general-process perspective predominated theories of conditioning through much of the twentieth century, there were serious kinks in its armor. The first prominent challenges were actually provided by Thorndike, who studied learning in 15 different puzzle boxes and found some significant differences among them. In most of the puzzle boxes, the instrumental response was manipulating a latch or pulling a string to escape and get a piece of food. However, in some of the boxes, the required response was a self care behavior (e.g., grooming or yawning). Learning did not proceed smoothly in these boxes. The instrumental response initially increased, but the gain was not sustained. The

yawn or scratch became perfunctory and not as genuine as spontaneous occurrences of these behaviors. Thorndike proposed the concept of *belongingness* to characterize these failed instances of the Law of Effect. According to this concept, an instrumental response has to 'belong with' the reinforcer to show robust acquisition.

It is to Thorndike's great credit that he reported failures in instrumental conditioning and violations of his Law of Effect, along with the successes. However, the failures did not attract much attention for nearly half a century. That is not to say that learning psychologists were always successful in designing instrumental conditioning procedures. Rather, the number of common experimental paradigms quickly narrowed to three that investigators could rely on to produce orderly data (lever-pressing in rats, key pecking in pigeons, and running in a runway in rats), and the importance of 'belongingness' effects took a back seat to efficient data collection. Subsequent analyses suggested that the development of these standard conditioning paradigms required considerable tuning that helped to match the procedure to the animal's behavioral predilections (Timberlake, 1990, 2001b).

Potential problems with general principles of shaping and instrumental reinforcement only became evident when investigators stepped outside the scope of conventional procedures. Two of Skinner's graduate students ventured far from standard laboratory procedures in their efforts to create displays for amusement parks and shopping malls showing ducks, chickens, raccoons, rabbits, and pigs doing various entertaining things for food reinforcement (Breland and Breland, 1961). If the instrumental response was releasing an object or token for food (e.g., having a pig put a coin in a piggy bank), initial acquisition was followed by a serious deterioration in performance. The pig, for example, would root the coin on the ground, and the raccoon would rub the coins together or 'dunk' it into the coin slot instead of releasing it. These responses resembled the natural behavior of these animals in situations involving feeding. Therefore, Breland and Breland characterized these as instances of 'instinctive drift.'

The failures of the Law of Effect and the shortcomings of Skinnerian principles that were highlighted by the Brelands were soon followed by analogous examples in avoidance conditioning. Bolles (1970) reported that freezing and running were much easier to condition as avoidance responses than rearing, lever-pressing, or pecking a response key. Unexpected failures of learning also appeared in the area of stimulus control. Foree and LoLordo (1973) found that pigeons were less likely to use visual cues than auditory cues as discriminative stimuli for avoidance behavior. Garcia and Koelling (1966) found that rats could not associate audiovisual cues with illness or taste cues with foot shock.

These dramatic failures or constraints on learning were obtained at the same time that investigators discovered examples of remarkably rapid learning. Tastes could be associated with illness in a single trial, even if there was a long delay between the two events (Garcia et al., 1966). Pigeons could learn to peck a key-light paired with food (Brown and Jenkins, 1968), even if the pecking behavior was not required to obtain the food (Williams and Williams, 1969). Freezing and running were readily acquired as avoidance responses (Bolles, 1970), and audiovisual cues were readily associated with foot-shock even though they could not be associated with poisoning (Garcia and Koelling, 1966).

1.18.2.1 Empirical Analyses

Although initial theoretical efforts to explain biological constraints and adaptive specializations in classical and instrumental conditioning did not provide much insight into these phenomena, empirical analyses were more informative. In general, these served to confirm the validity of the initial findings and suggested ways in which problematic phenomena might be incorporated into general process theory (Domjan, 1983).

1.18.2.1.1 Constraints on the conditioning of token-release behavior

As noted earlier, one of the major problematic findings was that animals required to deposit a token for food or water reinforcement often refused to release the token (Breland and Breland, 1961). This behavior was initially puzzling because holding onto the token was not required for reinforcement and actually negated reinforcer delivery. Although the finding was puzzling from the perspective of instrumental conditioning, it could be easily explained once investigators considered the role of Pavlovian contingencies in the procedure. Requiring contact with the token before the delivery of food resulted in pairings of the token with the food reinforcer. Such stimulus–reinforcer pairings served to condition appetitive properties to the token stimulus, and the

subsequent reluctance of the animal to relinquish the token was a reflection of this Pavlovian conditioned appetitive behavior (Boakes et al., 1978). Consistent with this interpretation, Pavlovian pairings of a token stimulus with food are sufficient to generate contact and handling of the token (Timberlake et al., 1982; see also Timberlake and Washburne, 1989).

1.18.2.1.2 Constraints on the conditioning of self-care responses

Thorndike (1911) was the first of several investigators who noted that grooming responses such as scratching and yawning are difficult to increase with instrumental conditioning. Subsequent experiments with the golden hamster suggested that this constraint on learning was also due to the Pavlovian conditioning that inevitably accompanies an instrumental training procedure. Hamsters show a suppression of grooming in anticipation of daily feedings (Shettlesworth, 1975), and grooming occurs as an interim rather than a terminal response with periodic food deliveries (Anderson and Shettlesworth, 1977). Thus, Pavlovian processes tend to suppress rather than facilitate grooming. Another factor that might be responsible for constraints on the conditioning of grooming responses is lack of necessary support stimulation. Pearce et al. (1978) found that scratching in rats can be conditioned more easily as an instrumental response if the rats wear a collar that provides tactile stimulation. Scratching appears to be easier to condition in primates (Anderson et al., 1990), perhaps because primates are better able to discriminate instances of scratching (Morgan and Nicholas, 1979).

1.18.2.1.3 Constraints on the conditioning of avoidance learning

Avoidance behavior appears to be even more heavily constrained than positively reinforced behavior. The limitations operate both on the types of responses that can be learned to prevent aversive stimulation and the types of stimuli that can serve as cues for avoidance behavior. Rats readily learn to avoid aversive stimulation if the instrumental response is running in a wheel, jumping out of a shock box, or remaining still (Maatsch, 1959; Bolles, 1969; Brener and Goesling, 1970). However, they have difficultly learning to rear or press a lever to avoid shock (D'Amato and Schiff, 1964; Bolles, 1969). Pigeons have a much harder time learning to peck a response key to avoid shock (Schwartz, 1974) than they have learning to press a treadle (Foree and LoLordo, 1970).

Avoidance procedures typically provide a signal for the impending aversive stimulus, and responding during the signal cancels the scheduled shock and turns off the signal. Auditory cues tend to become conditioned more readily as warning signals than visual cues (Foree and LoLordo, 1973; Jacobs and LoLordo, 1977), whereas visual cues are more easily conditioned as signals for food. Subsequent research has shown that selective association effects can also be obtained with a single reinforcer (food or shock). In these studies, the stimulus control acquired by the auditory or visual element of a compound stimulus depended on whether the compound signaled the presence or absence of the reinforcer (Weiss et al., 1993; Panlilio and Weiss, 2005).

Initial efforts to understand biological constraints on avoidance learning emphasized the concept of species-specific defense reactions (SSDRs). Bolles (1970, 1971) proposed that, in an aversive situation, the organism's repertoire is severely limited to a set of instinctive defensive behaviors (SSDRs) that include freezing, fleeing, and aggression. Which of these responses predominates was assumed to depend on environmental factors. In the absence of an escape route, freezing was presumed to predominate. If there is a potential escape route, fleeing may be the predominant SSDR. Responses such as lever-pressing or key-pecking are never likely to be acquired as avoidance behaviors because they are not related to an SSDR.

The SSDR hypothesis was important because it emphasized for the first time that to understand avoidance behavior we first have to consider the instinctive defensive behavioral repertoire of the organism. However, the details of the SSDR hypothesis turned out to be incorrect. Studies showed that the predominant SSDR for rats was freezing whether or not a prominent escape route was available (see Fanselow and Lester, 1988). These observations led to a reformulation of the SSDR hypothesis that introduced the concept of predatory imminence (Fanselow and Lester, 1988). This revised theory assumes that which of a range of possible defensive behaviors occurs depends on the perceived imminence of danger or predation. A low level of perceived danger (or predatory imminence) may reduce the amount of time a rat spends foraging but does not generate a targeted defensive action. In contrast, a high level of perceived danger elicits freezing. When the danger (or predator) is actually encountered, a defensive circa strike response is elicited. Differences in how rapidly subjects learn various avoidance responses are explained by

reference to timing of expected danger and the instinctive responses that are elicited by a particular level of predatory imminence.

1.18.2.1.4   Long-delay taste-aversion learning

Another prominent phenomenon that encouraged consideration of adaptive specializations of learning is long-delay taste-aversion learning. This effect was originally discovered during the course of research on the biological effects of exposure to X-rays. Garcia and colleagues found that rats exposed to irradiation after drinking a saccharin solution subsequently showed a strong aversion to the saccharin flavor (Garcia et al., 1966; see also Smith and Roll, 1967). This type of learning was considered to be an exception to general process learning theory because it occurred in a single trial even if the irradiation (unconditioned stimulus, US) was presented several hours after the taste (conditioned stimulus, CS) exposure. Since this type of learning occurred rapidly over a long CS–US interval, it could hardly be considered a 'constraint' or limitation on learning. Furthermore, one could hardly argue that rats evolved to learn about exposure to irradiation. However, long-delay aversion learning helped explain how animals avoid nutritionally inadequate and poisonous foods and thereby end up eating a healthy diet. Therefore, taste-aversion learning became treated as an example of an adaptive specialization of learning that plays an important role in food selection (Rozin and Kalat, 1971).

Taste-aversion learning remains unique in permitting a delay of several hours between the CS and the US. Nevertheless, efforts to understand the basis for long-delay taste-aversion learning have identified a number of important factors. One factor concerns the nature of the taste stimulus and how it is encountered. In traditional classical conditioning procedures, the subject does not have to do anything to obtain either the CS or the US. In fact, the lack of a response contingency is considered to be a defining feature of classical conditioning. In contrast, taste stimuli are usually encountered as a result of licking a drinking tube. The licking behavior controls exposure to the CS and also provides nongustatory orosensory stimulation. The licking contingency and orosensory stimulation are important for taste-aversion learning. If a flavored solution is passed over the tongue without licking (through a cannula or while the subject is paralyzed with curare), the strength of the taste aversion is significantly attenuated (Domjan and Wilson, 1972a; Domjan, 1973).

Another factor that contributes to long-delay taste-aversion learning is that the stimuli that subjects are likely to encounter during the delay period are not readily associable with illness and therefore do not provide concurrent interference (Revusky, 1977). In the typical long-delay taste-aversion experiment, subjects are given a novel flavor to drink and are then injected with a toxin several hours later. During the interval between the taste and illness, the subjects inevitably encounter various visual, auditory, and tactile cues. However, these are not likely to interfere with conditioning of the target flavor because nongustatory stimuli are less likely to become associated with toxicosis (see following section). Consistent with this idea, introduction of other flavors during the delay interval disrupts learning an aversion to the target flavor (Kalat and Rozin, 1971; Revusky, 1977). The concurrent interference hypothesis is challenged in explaining long-delay aversion learning to the tactile or other nongustatory aspects of ingested food (e.g., Revusky and Parker, 1976; Domjan and Hanlon, 1982; Domjan et al., 1982), since these should be disrupted by other tactile stimuli encountered during the delay interval. However, these other tactile cues are not accompanied by orosensory stimuli related to eating and drinking, and therefore they may not be as available for association with illness.

1.18.2.1.5 *Selective associations*
Although novel tastes readily become associated with illness, novel auditory or visual cues do not. In contrast, auditory and visual cues readily become associated with foot-shock, whereas taste cues do not. These cue-consequence specificity effects were first clearly demonstrated by Garcia and Koelling (1966) and attracted a great deal of attention because they were entirely contrary to general-process learning theory as it was known at the time. Initial efforts to analyze the effect focused on various methodological issues to rule out potential artifacts. To properly compare learning about taste and audiovisual cues, the two types of stimuli have to be presented in the same manner. Garcia and Koelling (1966) equated the method of CS presentation by having rats lick a drinking tube that produced both the taste and the audiovisual stimuli. In a subsequent study, Domjan and Wilson (1972b) equated the method of stimulus presentation by having both types of CSs presented independent of behavior. Similar results were obtained with both approaches.

Another methodological concern was that shock and illness may have different nonassociative effects, and those might be responsible for cue-consequence specificity effects. That possibility was ruled out in a study in which rats were given both shock and illness unconditioned stimuli, but only one of the USs was paired with a CS (Miller and Domjan, 1981). Despite exposure to both USs, when taste and a visual cue were paired with illness only a taste aversion developed, and when the CSs were paired with shock, an aversion only to the visual cue occurred.

In all of the initial experiments, aversions were measured in terms of suppression of drinking, and some critics were concerned that this response measure was differentially sensitive to certain CS-US combinations. To evaluate that possibility, Miller (1984) recorded a variety of responses in a cue-consequence specificity experiment (freezing, rearing, grooming, chin-wiping, head shaking, gaping, and drinking). He found that a taste paired with illness elicited increased gaping, head-shaking, and chin-wiping, and an auditory cue that had been paired with shock elicited increased freezing and decreased rearing and grooming. No evidence of learning in any response measure was found if the taste had been paired with shock or the auditory cue had been paired with shock.

The aforementioned studies served to substantiate the cue-consequence specificity effect but did not prove that the phenomenon was due to adaptive specializations resulting from evolutionary selection. Because the experiments were conducted with adult rats, one could argue that their previous experiences resulted in selective associations in adulthood. During normal ontogenetic experience, tastes are correlated with interoceptive malaise, and telereceptive cues are correlated with cutaneous pain. Perhaps these historical experiences produce the cue-consequence specificity effect. This experiential hypothesis was evaluated by conducting conditioning 1 day after birth. Despite the young age of these subjects, the cue-consequence specificity effect was replicated (Gemberling and Domjan, 1982).

1.18.3 Theoretical Analyses
1.18.3.1 Biological Constraints
The examples of conditioning that were unexpected on the basis of general learning processes were initially characterized as *biological constraints* on learning (Shettlesworth, 1972; Hinde and Stevenson-Hinde,

1973). The term 'biological' was intended to capture the notion that these examples were the result of natural selection. The term 'constraint' was used because investigators found limitations on what animals could learn particularly noteworthy. However, beyond pointing out the relevance of the subject's evolutionary history, the concept of a biological constraint does little to further our understanding of these unusual learning phenomena and does little to help us discover new ones (Domjan and Galef, 1983). The various forms of learning that were identified as biologically constrained had little in common other than the fact that they were unexpected on the basis of extant general process theory. Thus, considering them in a single category did not help to identify their underlying processes. Furthermore, it is unlikely that these constraints on learning were specifically selected for. Rather, they were probably the consequence of the selection of other forms of conditioning that were especially useful for the organism and increased its reproductive fitness. Thus, constraints on learning may be epiphenomena that result from the selection of forms of conditioning that are especially effective in foraging for food or avoiding predation.

1.18.3.2   Adaptive Specializations

Characterizations of special forms of Pavlovian and instrumental conditioning as adaptive specializations also emphasized the evolutionary origins of these learning phenomena. But in this case the focus was on instances of more rapid or robust conditioning than on slow and laborious learning (Rozin and Kalat, 1971). Taste-aversion learning was frequently discussed as an adaptive specialization, since it occurs with long delays between taste and illness, can be acquired in just one trial, and is specific to taste cues. One could easily imagine how this kind of learning might have evolved, since it seems ideally suited to solve many of the challenges that omnivores face in selecting a healthy diet (Rozin and Kalat, 1971). Rapid acquisition of freezing behavior in aversive conditioning probably also evolved as a specialization of the defensive behavior system.

Although the adaptive specialization approach is more promising than the constraints approach, labeling something as an adaptive specialization is just a promissory note that requires demonstrating exactly how the conditioning process increases reproductive fitness. The promissory note has not been paid in the case of taste-aversion learning. The justification

is more convincing with conditioned freezing, since animals that freeze are less likely to be detected by a predator (Arduino and Gould, 1984; Suarez and Gallup, 1981). The only direct evidence of learning increasing reproductive fitness comes from studies of sexual conditioning (Hollis et al., 1997; Adkins-Regan and MacKillop, 2003; Mahometa and Domjan, 2005; Matthews et al., in press). However, those experiments employed conventional CSs, and the authors did not argue that the increase in reproductive fitness reflected an adaptive specialization in learning. Other examples of sexual conditioning (to be described later) involved species-typical CSs and may be more accurately characterized as representing adaptive specializations.

1.18.3.3   Preparedness

Biological constraints and adaptive specializations were proposed as alternatives to a general process account of conditioning phenomena. However, they did not dissuade investigators from looking for ways to incorporate unusual forms of learning into a more general conception. The first serious proposal along those lines was the concept of preparedness proposed by Seligman (1970; see also Seligman and Hager, 1972).

According to the concept of preparedness, tasks were considered to differ in the extent to which they were compatible or incompatible with the evolutionary history of the organism. Preparedness was defined as "the degree of input necessary to produce a specified output" in a learning procedure (Seligman, 1970, p. 407). Forms of learning that occurred quickly with relatively little input were said to be highly prepared. In contrast, forms of learning that required extensive training and input were said to be unprepared or contraprepared. Thus, the concept of preparedness enabled ordering various examples of learning along a continuum of preparedness. This continuum in turn served to integrate examples of biological constraints and adaptive specializations of learning without treating either category as an exception to general principles of learning. The proposal was to supplement general process theory with the continuum of preparedness that would then help characterize all forms of learning.

The concept of preparedness provided a convenient way to talk about instances of learning that were particularly easy or difficult to learn. However, the concept did little to advance our understanding or learning processes (Domjan and Galef, 1983). As first proposed, the concept was basically circular. Measures of the rate of learning were used to identify different levels of preparedness, at the same that preparedness was intended to explain differences in learning rate (Schwartz, 1974). Second, a common metric was not available to measure input or training across widely disparate learning tasks such as taste-aversion learning and language acquisition. Third, even if a common metric could be found, behaviors that are learned at similar rates may not share other characteristics, such as rates of extinction or sensitivity to temporal contiguity. Despite these shortcomings, the goal of defining a continuum of learning effects that differ in biological preparedness remains laudable.

1.18.3.4   Behavior Systems and Learning

One of the most systematic efforts to integrate specialized forms of learning into a general theory is the behavior systems approach. This approach provides a general framework for characterizing how evolutionary influences determine the specific behavioral outcomes of laboratory conditioning procedures. Its starting point is that behavior is organized into functional systems that evolved to deal with specific tasks.

Functional systems of behavior have been entertained by a variety of investigators. Garcia and colleagues, for example, invoked functional systems in their efforts to explain differences between taste-aversion learning and fear conditioning (Garcia et al., 1974). According to them, organisms evolved specialized behavioral and neural mechanisms to deal with interoceptive information provided by the taste of food and its postingestive consequences. The interoceptive system operates on a time scale that facilitates the association of interoceptive CSs and USs, and this is responsible for long-delayed taste-aversion learning. In contrast, different behavioral and neural mechanisms, operating on shorter time scales, are involved in organizing responses to external cues and their consequences, such distal visual and auditory input that may lead to cutaneous pain. According to Garcia et al. (1974), selective associations reflect differences in the systems that are designed to deal with the *milieu interne* as contrasted with the *milieu externe*.

The behavior systems approach is also consistent with how Bolles (1970, 1971) characterized constraints on avoidance conditioning. As was noted earlier, Bolles proposed that aversive situations activate the defensive behavior system, which constrains the response repertoire of the organism to species-specific defense reactions. This idea was subsequently fleshed out with the suggestion that the defensive behavior system is also characterized by differential sensitivity to auditory cues (Foree and LoLordo, 1973) and is organized along a temporal dimension dictated by perceptions of the imminence of danger (Fanselow and Lester, 1988).

The concept of behavior systems and how they shape the behavioral outcomes of conditioning were spelled out in greatest detail by Timberlake and his associates (e.g., Timberlake, 2001a; Timberlake and Lucas, 1989). Although Timberlake focused on the feeding system in his empirical and theoretical work, he proposed a general framework for conceptualizing behavior systems and their role in learning. According to this framework, behavior is organized into functional systems, each designed to accomplish a major biological goal (feeding, predatory defense, reproduction). Within each system, behavior is organized in terms of a hierarchy of control mechanisms. The first level consists of response modes, each of which contains a number of response modules.

Response modes have a linear temporal organization, with one mode reliably following another. For example, in the feeding system, the general search mode is followed by the focal search mode, which in turn is followed by the food/handling/consumption mode. The same linear order holds whether the sequence moves forward to ingestion of food or backward in the event that food is not found. That is, if the food/handling/consumption mode is not successful, the organism returns to the focal search mode rather than the general search mode. Most importantly for predictions of learning effects, each response mode and module is characterized by unique stimulus sensitivities and response propensities. In the focal search mode, for example, animals are more attuned to details of their environment as they look for food in a particular location. Once the food has been obtained, the response repertoire shifts to food handling behaviors, controlled by features of the food object itself.

The behavior systems approach helps us understand biological constraints on conditioning because it assumes that the ease of learning a particular task depends on the extent to which the task is consistent with the behavior system that is activated by that conditioning procedure. Food deprivation and periodic deliveries of food, for example, strongly activate the feeding system, increasing the probability of responses and stimulus sensitivities associated with that system. If a conditioning procedure requires an instrumental response, such as grooming, that is incompatible with the feeding modes and modules, that response will be difficult to reinforce with food. Responses more relevant to the feeding behavior system will emerge with food deprivation and food reinforcement, whether these are specifically reinforced or not. The emergence of these relevant behaviors is what Breland and Breland (1961) characterized as 'instinctive drift.'

1.18.4 Natural Learning Paradigms

All approaches to studying adaptive specializations in learning assume that specialized learning effects are the products of evolution. It is important to keep in mind that evolutionary selection is an interaction between selection processes and the ecology of the organism. Adaptation is not a progression to an ideal and does not occur in a vacuum. Rather, it occurs in the particular ecology and microenvironment inhabited by the species. Natural learning paradigms focus on that microenvironment.

General theories of conditioning are invariably couched in terms of abstract stimulus and response elements (conditioned and unconditioned stimuli or instrumental responses and reinforcers). An important assumption of general process theory is that these elements are unrelated before a conditioning procedure is introduced. In fact, this initial independence has been incorporated into the definitions of the stimulus and response elements. For example, a CS is defined as being 'arbitrary' or 'neutral' before its pairings with a US (Bower and Hilgard, 1981; Staddon, 1983; Shettleworth, 1998; Papini, 2002). These terms are used to signify that the CS has no inherent relation to a US prior to the introduction of a conditioning procedure.

The lack of an initial relation between CS and US may accurately characterize laboratory procedures for Pavlovian conditioning, but such independence cannot be true for naturally occurring instances of conditioning. If a CS and US were truly unrelated to each other in nature, they would not coincide with sufficient regularity to become associated. An arbitrary or neutral CS may be paired with a US once in a while by chance, but even if such pairings occurred, they would be preceded and followed by individual encounters with the stimuli, which would undermine their subsequent association (Benedict and Ayres,

1971; Rescorla, 2000). For a CS to be reliably paired with a US outside the laboratory, the CS has to be a natural precursor of the US or a stimulus that reliably occurs in the causal chain of events that leads to the US. Thus, in natural learning paradigms, the CS has to have an inherent or preexisting relation to the US before the onset of learning. Such an inherent relation is required for the CS to be reliably paired with the US so that an association can develop.

The fact that learning outside the laboratory depends on preexisting relations between events has been recognized for some time (Dickinson, 1980; Staddon, 1988). Being able to predict events of biological significance enables organisms to cope with those events more successfully (Domjan, 2005), and the best predictors of biologically significant events are "the causes of these events, or at least detectable indices of these causes" (Dickinson, 1980) – not arbitrary or neutral stimuli.

Interestingly, the first demonstrations of classical conditioning in Pavlov's laboratory involved a procedure that could readily occur in nature (Boakes, 1984). Studying how salivation may be elicited by various substances such as dry food, Stephan Vul'fson, one of Pavlov's students, observed that the dry food elicited salivation the first time it was placed in a dog's mouth. After several tests with the dry food, the sight of the food also started to elicit salivation. In this initial demonstration, the CS was the sight of the food and the US was the food in the mouth. Notice, that the CS was not arbitrary or initially unrelated to the US. Rather, the CS was a telereceptive feature of the food object.

Much of the early literature on adaptive specializations and biological constraints on learning involved learning situations that resembled natural learning paradigms. Long-delay taste-aversion learning is a prime example. Such learning probably evolved to discourage the ingestion of poisonous foods or substances with little nutritional value (Rozin and Kalat, 1971; Rzoska, 1953). An omnivore, such as a rat, that eats a varied diet has to learn to avoid eating foods that make it sick. Given that illness is usually a delayed consequence of eating something poisonous, the learning mechanism has to operate with a long delay between the taste and the consequent malaise. Note that the CS flavor is not arbitrary, neutral, or unrelated to the consequent poisoning. Rather, the taste is a feature of the poisonous food itself. Thus, it is inevitably encountered during the chain of events that results in food-induced illness.

Learning can occur to natural precursors of the US in a variety of response systems. In interacting with a sexually receptive female, for example, a male rat first encounters the odors of the female. Sexually naive males do not have a preference for the odor of estrous females. However, a preference develops with copulatory experience (Carr et al., 1965; Ågmo, 1999), presumably because of the pairings of the odor with sexual reinforcement.

Naturalistic learning can also occur in nursing situations, where tactile cues provided to an infant by the mother typically precede nursing and can come to elicit conditioned orientation and suckling responses (Blass, 1990). Cues that precede a nursing episode are also reliable precursors of the suckling stimulation that elicits oxytocin release and the milk let-down reflex on the part of the mother. Oxytocin release and the milk let-down reflex are initially unconditioned responses to suckling. However, they can also come to be elicited as anticipatory conditioned responses to prenursing tactile and olfactory cues provided by the nursing infant (Fuchs et al., 1987; Tancin et al., 2001).

Learning no doubt also occurs to stimuli that are encountered during the course of territorial and predator–prey interactions. Although predators have evolved strategies for surprising their prey, these improvements in offense have been accompanied by the evolution of detection and defensive tactics on the part of potential prey species. Cues that precede predatory attack are not arbitrary but are related to the visual, olfactory, or auditory features of a predator that can be detected at a distance before the attack. Learning to associate these cues with the subsequent predatory encounter can improve the effectiveness of defensive behavior (Hollis, 1990). Furthermore, fear is acquired more readily to ecologically relevant cues, such as the sight of a snake, than to ecologically irrelevant cues, such as the sight of flowers (Öhman and Mineka, 2001).

Repeated drug administration by drug addicts has also been described as a natural learning paradigm in which cues related to drug administration come to be associated with the drug effects and come to elicit conditioned physiological responses in anticipation of the impending drug delivery (Siegel et al., 2000). Consistent with this model, one approach to alleviating the symptoms of drug-addiction involves repeated presentations of the drug administration cues without the drug, so as to extinguish the drug-conditioned responses (Siegel and Ramos, 2002).

Siegel and his associates have extended the conditioning analysis of drug addition to learning about different components of a drug effect (Kim et al., 1999). This analysis focuses on the fact that drug effects are typically long lasting and have distinct onset properties. One cannot experience the enduring effects of a drug without first encountering its onset properties. Therefore, the early physiological effects of a drug can serve as a CS for later drug effects and can come to control conditioned anticipatory physiological adjustments, in a manner analogous to the effects of exteroceptive drug administration cues. In this paradigm the CS is clearly not arbitrary or neutral with respect to the US.

1.18.4.1 Special Properties of Naturalistic Learning

The provided examples illustrate that conditioned stimuli that are natural precursors of the US are excellent candidates for conditioning. However, these examples do not prove that learning with naturalistic CSs occurs more rapidly or is more evolutionarily prepared than learning with arbitrary CSs. Evaluation of that hypothesis requires direct comparisons of learning with naturalistic versus arbitrary cues. Such comparisons have been conducted in the context of taste-aversion learning (see reviews by Logue, 1979; Domjan, 1980) and fear conditioning (e.g., Öhman and Mineka, 2001). More recently, Domjan and associates have examined this issue in detail in studies of the sexual conditioning of male Japanese quail, *Coturnix japonica* (see review by Domjan et al., 2004).

Japanese quail are ground birds that live in the Far East and in Hawaii in areas with tall grass (Schwartz and Schwartz, 1949). Although not much is known about their natural history, when a male initially sees a female, he is likely to see only her head and some of her neck feathers. As the two get closer and closer to one another, they get to see more of each other, and that permits more proximal social interactions. Thus, the natural sequence of events that results in an intimate social interaction and copulation begins with limited visual (and perhaps auditory) contact. This sequence of events can be replicated in the laboratory in a special application of a sexual conditioning procedure.

In a sexual conditioning procedure, a signal or CS is presented shortly before a male (or female) is permitted to interact with and copulate with a sexual partner (Pfaus et al., 2001; Woodson, 2002; Krause, 2003). For basic demonstrations, the CS may be a light or an odor. However, the procedure can be also designed to model the sequence of events that potential sexual partners encounter in their natural habitat. In the case of the *Coturnix* quail, this has been done by using a three-dimensional object as the CS that included a taxidermically prepared female head with partial neck feathers. To determine how learning with such a naturalistic CS differs from learning with a more conventional arbitrary CS, an alternative CS object was constructed that was similar in size and general shape to the naturalistic CS but lacked the taxidermic head+neck component.

A basic question that has to be answered at the outset with a naturalistic CS is whether such a CS elicits behavior unconditionally, without pairings with a US. Several studies have examined the responding that develops in male *Coturnix* quail to a head+neck object that is either paired with sexual reinforcement or presented in an unpaired fashion (e.g., Köksal et al., 1994; Cusato and Domjan, 1998; Hilliard et al., 1998). These studies have shown that a head+neck CS elicits a low level of approach responding if it is unpaired with copulation, but this approach behavior is substantially enhanced if the head+neck CS is paired with the sexual reinforcer. Interestingly, this pattern of results is similar to what is typically observed in taste-aversion learning. Unpaired presentation of a novel taste with toxicosis results in a mild aversion or neophobia to the taste solution. Pairing of the taste with illness produces a much more profound aversion. In both of these naturalistic learning situations, conditioning enhances a preexisting response to the CS.

If substantial responding to a naturalistic CS requires pairings with a sexual US, how does such learning differ from learning with an arbitrary CS? The first examination of this question was conducted by Köksal et al. (1994) who compared the extent to which the blocking effect occurs if the blocked CS includes (or does not include) female head+neck cues. All of the male quail that served in the experiment were initially conditioned with an audiovisual CS as a cue for sexual reinforcement. The preconditioned audiovisual cue blocked conditioning of an arbitrary CS object but did not block conditioning if the CS object included head+neck cues. Thus, the naturalistic CS was resistant to the blocking effect.

Subsequent studies have identified a cluster of learning phenomena that serve to differentiate how sexual conditioning proceeds with naturalistic versus arbitrary CS objects. In general, conditioned responding develops more rapidly with the naturalistic CS, and a greater range of conditioned responses come to be elicited (Cusato and Domjan, 1998). In particular, whereas the arbitrary CS object only elicits conditioned approach behavior after modest levels of training (e.g., 10–15 conditioning trials), the naturalistic CS also comes to elicit vigorous copulatory attempts (grabs, mounts, and cloacal contact responses) directed at the CS. Including naturalistic features in a CS object also increases the effectiveness of that CS in producing second-order conditioning (Cusato and Domjan, 2001; also described in Domjan et al., 2004).

Another phenomenon that shows the more robust nature of learning with a naturalistic CS is that such learning is not easily disrupted by increasing the CS-US interval (Akins, 2000). Long-delay learning is one of the signature features of taste-aversion learning. Although learning in the sexual behavior system does not occur with delays on the order of several hours, the use of a naturalistic CS significantly extends the range of effective CS-US intervals in sexual conditioning. Akins found that with a 1-min CS-US interval, conditioned sexual approach behavior develops whether or not the CS includes naturalistic features. However, if the CS-US interval is increased to 20 min, conditioned approach responding develops only if the CS includes female head+neck cues.

Rate of acquisition, blocking, second-order conditioning, and manipulations of the CS-US interval are familiar ways to test the robustness of a learning phenomenon. A more recently developed manipulation involves the I/T ratio, where 'I' refers to the duration of time spent in the experimental context between trials (or the intertrial interval), and 'T' refers to the duration of the CS (or trial time). In general, CS-directed conditioned responding is less likely to develop with small I/T ratios (Gallistel and Gibbon, 2000). However, an I/T ratio that is too low to support conditioned sexual responding to an arbitrary CS will nevertheless support vigorous responding directed towards a naturalistic CS (Gean, 2006).

The original formulation of the concept of preparedness linked acquisition and extinction effects. Instances of evolutionarily prepared learning were assumed to show more rapid and robust acquisition effects as well as slower extinction effects. This linkage of acquisition and extinction has rarely been examined empirically. In one of the few examples of such linkage, Krause et al. (2003) found that once vigorous sexual conditioned responding develops to a naturalistic CS, the responding is much more resistant to extinction than is conditioned responding to an arbitrary CS. In this experiment, responding to the no-head CS declined to near-zero levels by the 14th day of extinction, but responding to the head+neck CS remained high through the end of the experiment on day 42. This effect may have been due to the fact that the subjects directed copulatory responses toward the naturalistic CS object. Even though this copulation occurred with an inanimate object, it might have provided some sexual reinforcement, which served to maintain responding during the extended extinction procedure (Köksal et al., 2004).

1.18.4.2 A Continuum of Learning Effects

The evidence reviewed suggests that learning in natural learning paradigms is more robust in a variety of respects as compared with learning with arbitrary cues. At least in the sexual behavior system, naturalistic learning takes place more quickly, recruits a broader range of conditioned responses, motivates stronger second-order conditioning, is resistant to blocking and extinction, and occurs with longer CS-US intervals and lower I/T ratios. This broad range of learning effects has not been examined with naturalistic and arbitrary conditioned stimuli in other response systems. Therefore, the generality of these findings remains to be evaluated. However, since evolutionary selection operates within the ecological niche of a species, it is reasonable to assume that selection for robust learning involves reactivity to naturalistic rather than arbitrary cues. Therefore, the phenomena that were observed in the sexual behavior system probably represent differences that occur more generally.

The naturalistic and arbitrary CS objects that were compared in the sexual conditioning studies represent two points along a continuum. One end of that continuum consists of stimulus objects that are entirely unrelated to a potential sexual partner. At this end of the continuum the CS has no features in common with the US. The other end consists of CS objects that have many features related to a sexual partner or the US. Such a continuum is reminiscent of the continuum of preparedness proposed by Seligman (1970). However, unlike the original preparedness concept, the continuum described here is not circular. Different points along the continuum are characterized in terms of the extent to which the CS is a natural precursor of the US, which can be determined independently of learning. Differences in learning effects can then be predicted based on positions along the continuum.

Many naturalistic learning paradigms fit the model of a CS that has some features in common with the US because unconditioned stimuli are typically complex sensory objects or events with multiple features. For example, food (whether it is inanimate or a potential prey) has visual, olfactory, and sometimes auditory features that are evident to the forager at a distance. These can act as conditioned stimuli that are predictive of other features (taste, texture, and postingestional properties) that are encountered only when the forager contacts and eats the food. The multifaceted nature of a potential food object provides opportunities to learn to predict the location, taste, and other features of the food. How this learning takes place is organized by the microecology of the foraging species. The spatial separation of the foraging animal from the food object determines the temporal order of exposure to different features of the food and determines the nature of the CS-US pairings.

Aversive conditioning during the course of predator defense can be analyzed in a similar fashion. The predator that attacks a prey species also provides a variety of telereceptive and more proximal cues. The sight, smell, or sounds of the predator can be detected at a distance and are predictive of attack and cutaneous pain if the predator manages to catch and bite its prey.

1.18.5 Conclusion

Investigators have always assumed that learning processes evolved because they provide an adaptive advantage. However, the full implications of this claim have been rarely appreciated. One important implication is that how learning occurs will depend on the details of the ecosystem in which it evolved. The generality of conditioning phenomena and processes cannot be established by proclamation or by studying arbitrary stimuli or responses. Rather, the generality of learning has to be established empirically. Furthermore, general learning effects are only apt to be evident to the extent that the demands of diverse ecosystems have common elements. In the case of Pavlovian conditioning, such generality exists in the causal and temporal structure of the experiences that lead to encounters with biologically significant events or unconditioned stimuli. However, in these natural sequences, the antecedent or signaling events are not arbitrary or unrelated to the US. Instead they have an inherent relation to the US that is determined by the details of the organism's ecosystem. Since learning evolves in the microecology of individual organisms, stimuli and responses that are a part of that ecology will activate the learning process more effectively. Thus, learning with ecologically relevant stimuli and reposes will be more robust than learning with arbitrary cues.

Acknowledgment

Preparation of this chapter was supported by grant MH39940 from the National Institute of Mental Health to M. Domjan.

References

Adkins-Regan E and MacKillop EA (2003) Japanese quail (*Coturnix japonica*) inseminations are more likely to fertilize eggs in a context predicting mating opportunities. *Proc. Biol. Sci.* 270: 1685–1689.

Ågmo A (1999) Sexual motivation – an inquiry into events determining the occurrence of sexual behavior. *Behav. Brain Res.* 105: 129–150.

Akins CK (2000) Effects of species-specific cues and the CS-US interval on the topography of the sexually conditioned response. *Learn. Motiv.* 31: 211–235.

Anderson JR (1995) *Learning and Memory*. New York: Wiley.

Anderson JR, Fritsch C, and Favre B (1990) Operant conditioning of scratching in lemurs. *Primates* 31: 611–615.

Anderson MC and Shettlesworth SJ (1977) Behavioral adaptation to fixed-interval and fixed-time food delivery in golden hamsters. *J. Exp. Anal. Behav.* 25: 33–49.

Arduino P and Gould JL (1984) Is tonic immobility adaptive? *Anim. Behav.* 32: 921–922.

Benedict JO and Ayres JJB (1971) Factors affecting conditioning in the truly random control procedure in the rat. *J. Comp. Physiol. Psychol.* 78: 323–330.

Blass EM (1990) Suckling: Determinants, changes, mechanisms, and lasting impressions. *Dev. Psychol.* 26: 520–533.

Boakes RA (1984) *From Darwin to Behaviorism*. London: Cambridge University Press.

Boakes RA, Poli M, Lockwood MJ, and Goodall G (1978) A study of misbehavior: Token reinforcement in the rat. *J. Exp. Anal. Behav.* 29: 115–134.

Bolles RC (1969) Avoidance and escape learning: Simultaneous acquisition of different responses. *J. Comp. Physiol. Psychol.* 68: 355–358.

Bolles RC (1970) Species-specific defense reactions and avoidance learning. *Psychol. Rev.* 71: 32–48.

Bolles RC (1971) Species-specific defense reaction. In: Brush FR (ed.) *Aversive Conditioning and Learning*, pp. 183–233. New York: Academic Press.

Bower GH and Hilgard ER (1981) *Theories of Learning*, 5th edn. Englewood Cliffs, NJ: Prentice Hall.

Breland K and Breland M (1961) The misbehavior of organisms. *Am. Psychol.* 16: 681–684.

Brener J and Goesling WJ (1970) Avoidance conditioning of activity and immobility in rats. *J. Comp. Physiol. Psychol.* 70: 276–280.

Brown PL and Jenkins HM (1968) Auto-shaping the pigeon's key peck. *J. Exp. Anal. Behav.* 11: 1–8.

Carr WJ, Loeb LS, and Dissinger ME (1965) Responses of rats to sex odors. *J. Comp. Physiol. Psychol.* 59: 370–377.

Cusato B and Domjan M (1998) Special efficacy of sexual conditioned stimuli that include species typical cues: Tests with a CS preexposure design. *Learn. Motiv.* 29: 152–167.

Cusato B and Domjan M (2001) Second-order sexual conditioning in male domesticated quail. Paper presented at meetings of the Southwest Psychological Association, Houston, TX.

D'Amato MR and Schiff D (1964) Long-term discriminated avoidance performance in the rat. *J. Comp. Physiol. Psychol.* 57: 123–126.

Dickinson A (1980) *Contemporary Animal Learning Theory*. London: Cambridge University Press.

Domjan M (1973) Role of ingestion in odor-toxicosis learning in the rat. *J. Comp. Physiol. Psychol.* 84: 507–521.

Domjan M (1980) Ingestional aversion learning: Unique and general processes. In: Rosenblatt JS, Hinde RA, Beer C, and Busnel M (eds.) *Advances in the Study of Behavior,* vol. 11, pp. 275–336. New York: Academic Press.

Domjan M (1983) Biological constraints on instrumental and classical conditioning: Implications for general process theory. In: Bower GH (ed.) *The Psychology of Learning and Motivation,* vol. 17, pp. 215–277. New York: Academic Press.

Domjan M (2005) Pavlovian conditioning: A functional perspective. *Annu. Rev. Psychol.* 56: 179–206.

Domjan M, Cusato B, and Krause M (2004) Learning with arbitrary vs. ecological conditioned stimuli: Evidence from sexual conditioning. *Psychon. Bull. Rev.* 11: 232–246.

Domjan M and Galef BG Jr (1983) Biological constraints on instrumental and classical conditioning: Retrospect and prospect. *Anim. Learn. Behav.* 11: 151–161.

Domjan M and Hanlon MJ (1982) Poison-avoidance learning to food-related tactile stimuli: Avoidance of texture cues by rats. *Anim. Learn. Behav.* 10: 293–300.

Domjan M, Miller V, and Gemberling GA (1982) Note on aversion learning to the shape of food by monkeys. *J. Exp. Anal. Behav.* 38: 87–91.

Domjan M and Wilson NE (1972a) Contribution of ingestive behaviors to taste-aversion learning in the rat. *J. Comp. Physiol. Psychol.* 80: 403–412.

Domjan M and Wilson NE (1972b) Specificity of cue to consequence in aversion learning in the rat. *Psychon. Sci.* 26: 143–145.

Fanselow MS and Lester LS (1988) A functional behavioristic approach to aversively motivated behavior: Predatory imminence as a determinant of the topography of defensive behavior. In: Bolles RC and Beecher MD (eds.) *Evolution and Behavior*, pp. 185–212. Hillsdale, NJ: Erlbaum.

Foree DD and Lolordo VM (1970) Signalled and unsignalled free-operant avoidance in the pigeons. *J. Exp. Anal. Behav.* 13: 283–290.

Foree DD and LoLordo VM (1973) Attention in the pigeon: The differential effects of food-getting vs. shock avoidance procedures. *J. Comp. Physiol. Psychol.* 85: 551–558.

Fuchs A-R, Ayromlooi J, and Rasmussen AB (1987) Oxytocin response to conditioned and nonconditioned stimuli in lactating ewes. *Biol. Repro.* 37: 301–305.

Gallistel CR and Gibbon J (2000) Time, rate, and conditioning. *Psychol. Rev.* 107: 289–344.

Garcia J, Ervin ER, and Koelling RA (1966) Learning with prolonged delay of reinforcement. *Psychon. Sci.* 5: 121–122.

Garcia J, Hankins WG, and Rusiniak KW (1974) Behavioral regulation of the milieu interne in man and rat. *Sci.* 185: 824–831.

Garcia J and Koelling RA (1966) Relation of cue to consequence in aversion learning. *Psychon. Sci.* 4: 123–124.

Gean E (2006) *Testing the Validity of a Non-Associative Theory of Pavlovian Learning, Rate Estimation Theory (RET)*. PhD Thesis, University of Texas at Austin.

Gemberling GA and Domjan M (1982) Selective association in one-day-old rats: Taste-toxicosis and texture-shock aversion learning. *J. Comp. Physiol. Psychol.* 96: 105–113.

Hilliard S, Domjan M, Nguyen M, and Cusato B (1998) Dissociation of conditioned appetitive and consummatory sexual behavior: Satiation and extinction tests. *Anim. Learn. Behav.* 26: 20–33.

Hinde RA and Stevenson-Hinde J (eds.) (1973) *Constraints on Learning*. Academic Press, New York.

Hollis KL (1990) The role of Pavlovian conditioning in territorial aggression and reproduction. In: Dewsbury DA (ed.) *Contemporary Issues in Comparative Psychology*, pp. 197–219. Sunderland, MA: Sinauer.

Hollis KL, Pharr VL, Dumas MJ, Britton GB, and Field J (1997) Classical conditioning provides paternity advantage for territorial male blue gouramis (*Trichogaster trichopterus*). *J. Comp. Psychol.* 111: 219–225.

Jacobs WJ and LoLordo VM (1977) The sensory basis of avoidance learning in the rat. *Learn. Motiv.* 8: 448–466.

Kalat JW and Rozin P (1971) Role of interference in taste-aversion learning. *J. Comp. Physiol. Psychol.* 77: 53–58.

Kim JA, Siegel S, and Patenall VRA (1999) Drug-onset cues as signals: Intra-administration associations and tolerance. *J. Exp. Psychol. Anim. Behav. Process.* 25: 491–504.

Köksal F, Domjan M, Kurt A, et al. (2004) An animal model of fetishism. *Behav. Res. Ther.* 42: 1421–1434.

Köksal F, Domjan M, and Weisman G (1994) Blocking of the sexual conditioning of differentially effective conditioned stimulus objects. *Anim. Learn. Behav.* 22: 103–111.

Krause M (2003) Behavioral mechanisms and the neurobiology of conditioned sexual responding. *Int. Rev. Neurobiol.* 56: 1–34.

Krause MA, Cusato B, and Domjan M (2003) Extinction of conditioned sexual responses in male Japanese quail (*Coturnix japonica*): Role of species typical cues. *J. Comp. Psychol.* 117: 76–86.

Logue AW (1979) Taste aversion learning and the generality of the laws of learning. *Psychol. Bull.* 86: 276–296.

Maatsch JL (1959) Learning and fixation after a single shock trial. *J. Comp. Physiol. Psychol.* 52: 408–410.

Mackintosh NJ (1975) A theory of attention: Variations in the associability of stimuli with reinforcement. *Psychol. Rev.* 82: 276–298.

Mahometa MJ and Domjan M (2005) Classical conditioning increases reproductive success in Japanese quail (*Coturnix japonica*). *Anim. Behav.* 69: 983–989.

Matthews RN, Domjan M, Ramsey M, and Crews D (in press) Learning effects on sperm competition and reproductive fitness. *Psychol. Sci.*

Menzel R (1990) Learning, memory, and "cognition" in honey bees. In: Kesner RP and Olton DS (eds.) *Neurobiology of Comparative Cognition*, pp. 237–292. Hillsdale, NJ: Erlbaum.

Menzel R (1999) Memory dynamics in the honeybee. *J. Comp. Physiol. A* 185: 323–340.

Miller RR and Matzel LD (1988) The comparator hypothesis: A response rule for the expression of associations. In: Bower GH (ed.) *The Psychology of Learning and Motivation*, pp. 51–92. Orlando, FL: Academic Press.

Miller V (1984) Selective association learning in the rat: Generality of response system. *Learn. Motiv.* 15: 58–84.

Miller V and Domjan M (1981) Specificity of cue to consequence in aversion learning in the rat: Control for US-induced differential orientations. *Anim. Learn. Behav.* 9: 339–345.

Morgan MJ and Nicholas DJ (1979) Discrimination between reinforced action patterns in the rat. *Learn. Motiv.* 10: 1–22.

Öhman A and Mineka S (2001) Fear, phobias and preparedness: Toward an evolved module of fear and fear learning. *Psychol. Rev.* 108: 483–522.

Panlilio LV and Weiss SJ (2005) Sensory modality and stimulus control in the pigeon: Cross-species generality of single-incentive selective-association effects. *Learn. Motiv.* 36: 408–424.

Papini MR (2002) *Comparative Psychology*. Upper Saddle River, NJ: Prentice Hall.

Pavlov IP (1927) *Conditioned Reflexes,* Anrep GV (trans.). London: Oxford University Press [Reprinted 1960, New York: Dover.]

Pearce JM, Colwill RM, and Hall G (1978) Instrumental conditioning of scratching in the laboratory rat. *Learn. Motiv.* 9: 255–271.

Pearce JM and Hall G (1980) A model for Pavlovian learning: Variations in the effectiveness of conditioned but not of unconditioned stimuli. *Psychol. Rev.* 87: 532–552.

Pfaus JG, Kippin TE, and Centeno S (2001) Conditioning and sexual behavior: A review. *Horm. Behav.* 40: 291–321.

Rescorla RA (2000) Associative changes with a random CS-US relationship. *Q. J. Exp. Psychol.* 53B: 325–340.

Rescorla RA and Wagner AR (1972) A theory of Pavlovian conditioning: Variations in the effectiveness of reinforcement and nonreinforcement. In: Black AH and Prokasy WF (eds.) *Classical Conditioning II: Current Research and Theory*, pp. 64–99. New York: Appleton-Century-Crofts.

Revusky SH (1977) The concurrent interference approach to delayed learning. In: Barker LM, Best MR, and Domjan M (eds.) *Learning Mechanisms in Food Selection*, pp. 319–366. Waco, TX: Baylor University Press.

Revusky SH and Parker L (1976) Aversions to unflavored water and cup drinking produced by delayed sickness. *J. Exp. Psychol. Anim. Behav. Proc.* 2: 342–355.

Rozin P and Kalat JW (1971) Specific hungers and poison avoidance as adaptive specializations of learning. *Psychol. Rev.* 78: 459–486.

Rzoska J (1953) Bait shyness, a study in rat behaviour. *Br. J. Anim. Behav.* 1: 128–135.

Savastano HI and Miller RR (1998) Time as content in Pavlovian conditioning. *Behav. Proc.* 44: 147–162.

Schwartz B (1973) Maintenance of key pecking in pigeons by a food avoidance but not a shock avoidance contingency. *Anim. Learn. Behav.* 1: 164–166.

Schwartz B (1974) On going back to nature: A review of Seligman and Hager's *Biological Boundaries of Learning*. *J. Exp. Anal. Behav.* 21: 183–198.

Schwartz CW and Schwartz ER (1949) *A Reconnaissance of the Game Birds in Hawaii*. Hilo, HI: Hawaii Board of Commissioners of Agriculture and Forestry.

Seligman MEP (1970) On the generality of the laws of learning. *Psychol. Rev.* 77: 406–418.

Seligman MEP and Hager JL (eds.) (1972) *Biological Boundaries of Learning*. New York: Appleton-Century-Crofts.

Shettleworth SJ (1972) Constraints on learning. In: Lehrman DS, Hinde RA, and Shaw E (eds.) *Advances in the Study of Behavior*, vol. 4, pp. 1–68. New York: Academic Press.

Shettleworth SJ (1975) Reinforcement and the organization of behavior in golden hamsters: Hunger, environment, and food reinforcement. *J. Exp. Psychol. Anim. Behav. Process.* 1: 56–87.

Shettleworth SJ (1998) *Cognition, Evolution, and Behavior*. New York: Oxford University Press.

Siegel S, Baptista MAS, Kim JA, McDonald RV, and Weise-Kelly L (2000) Pavlovian psychopharmacology: The associative basis of tolerance. *Exp. Clin. Psychopharmacol.* 8: 276–293.

Siegel S and Ramos BMC. (2002) Applying laboratory research: Drug anticipation and the treatment of drug addiction. *Exp. Clin. Psychopharmacol.* 10: 162–183.

Smith JC and Roll DL (1967) Trace conditioning with X-rays as an aversive stimulus. *Psychon. Sci.* 9: 11–12.

Staddon JER (1983) *Adaptive Behavior and Learning*. London: Cambridge University Press.

Staddon JER (1988) Learning as inference. In: Bolles RC and Beecher MD (eds.) *Evolution and Learning*, pp. 59–77. Hillsdale, NJ: Erlbaum.

Suarez SD and Gallup GG (1981) An ethological analysis of open-field behavior in rats and mice. *Learn. Motiv.* 12: 342–363.

Tancin V, Kraetzl W-D, Schams D, and Bruckmaier RM (2001) The effect of conditioning to suckling, milking and of calf presence on the release of oxytocin in dairy cows. *Appl. Anim. Behav. Sci.* 72: 235–246.

Thorndike EL (1898) *Animal Intelligence: An Experimental Study of the Association Processes in Animals*. New York: Macmillan.

Thorndike EL (1911) *Animal Intelligence: Experimental Studies*. New York: Macmillan.

Timberlake W (1990) Natural learning in laboratory paradigms. In: Dewsbury DA (ed.) *Contemporary Issues in Comparative Psychology*, pp. 31–54. Sunderland, MA: Sinauer.

Timberlake W (2001a) Motivational modes in behavior systems. In: Mowrer RR and Klein SB (eds.) *Handbook of Contemporary Learning Theories*, pp. 155–209. Mahwah, NJ: Erlbaum.

Timberlake W (2001b) Integrating niche-related and general process approaches in the study of learning. *Behav. Proc.* 54: 79–94.

Timberlake W and Lucas GA (1989) Behavior systems and learning: From misbehavior to general principles. In: Klein SB and Mowrer RR (eds.) *Contemporary Learning Theories: Instrumental Conditioning and the Impact of Biological Constraints on Learning*, pp. 237–275. Hillsdale, NJ: Erlbaum.

Timberlake W, Wahl G, and King D (1982) Stimulus and response contingencies in the misbehavior of rats. *J. Exp. Psychol. Anim. Behav. Process.* 8: 62–85.

Timberlake W and Washburne DL (1989) Feeding ecology and laboratory predatory behavior toward live and artificial moving prey in seven rodent species. *Anim. Learn. Behav.* 17: 2–11.

Wagner AR (1981) SOP: A model of automatic memory processing in animal behavior. In: Spear NE and Miller RR (eds.) *Information Processing in Animals: Memory Mechanisms*, pp. 5–47. Hillsdale, NJ: Erlbaum.

Wagner AR and Brandon SE (1989) Evolution of a structured connectionist model of Pavlovian conditioning (AESOP). In: Klein SB and Mowrer RR (eds.) *Contemporary Learning Theories: Pavlovian Conditioning and the Status of Learning Theory*, pp. 149–189. Hillsdale, NJ: Lawrence Erlbaum Associates.

Weiss SJ, Panlilio LV, and Schindler CW (1993) Single-incentive selective associations produced solely as a function of compound-stimulus conditioning context. *J. Exp. Psychol. Anim. Behav. Proc.* 19: 284–294.

Williams DR and Williams H (1969) Automaintenance in the pigeon: Sustained pecking despite contingent non-reinforcement. *J. Exp. Anal. Behav.* 12: 511–520.

Woodson JC (2002) Including "learned sexuality" in the organization of sexual behavior. *Neurosci. Biobehav. Rev.* 26: 69–80.

1.19   Learning to Time Intervals

K. Cheng, Macquarie University, Sydney, NSW, Australia

J. D. Crystal, University of Georgia, Athens, Georgia, USA

1.19.1   Introduction

Time is a fundamental dimension of life. Many animals have evolved the ability to time intervals lasting from a fraction of a second to hours. Traditionally, it is thought that a distinction must be made between circadian timing and interval timing (Gibbon et al., 1997a). Circadian timing concerns the ability to adjust to the daily cycle caused by the rotation of the Earth around its axis, which has a period of 24 h. Circadian clocks 'tick over' every 24 h or so when running 'free' (without external input about night and day), and the period is set to 24 h by external cues such as daylight. In vertebrate animals a neurological structure known as the suprachiasmatic nucleus is taken to be the 'master clock.' This chapter concerns interval timing, which is the ability to time shorter intervals, typically in the range of seconds to minutes.

We examine three experimental paradigms used to study interval timing and illustrate them with some characteristic results. Three theories of interval timing are discussed briefly. Then we turn to examining the differences between interval timing and circadian timing more closely, to show that the distinction is not so clear cut. We begin with three cases of the use of interval timing in the natural lives of animals.

1.19.2   Interval Timing in Everyday Life

The rat, normally a highly social animal, varies its eating behavior according to the size of the chunk of food it is eating. The motor patterns are so ingrained that it even does them when alone in an experimental arena, a standard operant chamber (Whishaw and Tomie, 1989; **Figure 1**). If a tiny pellet is delivered into the food magazine, the rat picks it up and eats it right at the magazine, without lowering its forepaws. With larger pellets, the rat lowers itself to the floor before eating. With still larger pellets, the rat takes the pellet and turns away from the magazine before

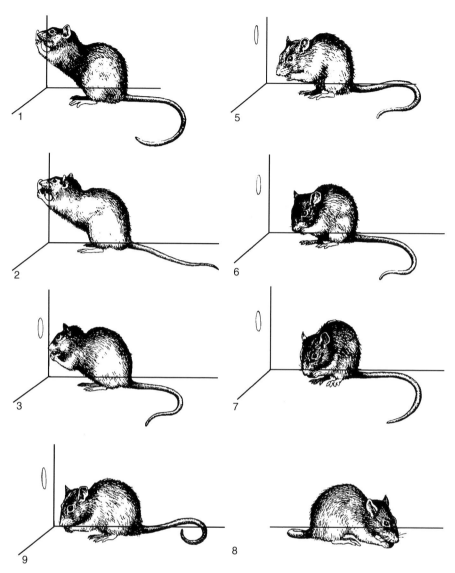

Figure 1 Illustration of what a rat does with a pellet of food of different sizes. Increasing numbers on the panels correspond to increasing food size. At the smallest sizes, the rat eats the food right at the hopper. At bigger sizes, it brings the food to ground level before eating it. At still larger food sizes, it turns away from the hopper before eating. At very large sizes (not shown), the rat hoards the food to an adjacent chamber. Reproduced with permission from Whishaw IQ and Tomie J (1989) Food-pellet size modifies the hoarding behavior of foraging rats. *Psychobiology* 17: 93–101.

eating. At the largest sizes, the rat hoards the pellet to an adjacent chamber. A further study showed that food handling time rather than food size was the determining factor in the rat's eating behavior (Whishaw, 1990). The rat varies what it does with food according to how long it takes to eat the pellet.

A foraging honeybee also needs to time short intervals regularly. Foragers rate the quality of pollen or nectar that they bring back relative to what others bring back (Seeley, 1995). This is achieved because foragers unload their booty to food storers in the hive.

The length of time it takes to unload the forage thus indicates how good it is relative to what others bring back. This in turn influences other behaviors, such as whether to recruit other foragers by 'dancing' and how long to do the waggle dance (*See* Chapters 1.25, 1.29). Timing abilities in bees have also been addressed in formal experiments (Greggers and Menzel, 1993; Boisvert and Sherry, 2006).

Another example of timing in everyday life comes from a study of Rufous hummingbirds (Henderson et al., 2006). Hummingbirds adjust their visits to flowers based on the rate at which the flowers replenish. Henderson and colleagues refilled multiple artificial flowers with sucrose solution 10 min after the bird emptied it; they refilled other flowers 20 min after the bird emptied these flowers. Throughout the day, the birds revisited the 10-min flowers sooner than they revisited the 20-min flowers. To revisit each flower at the right time throughout the day, the birds had to update their memories of when and where food was encountered for each flower and how long it has been since the last visit (Crystal, 2006a; Henderson et al., 2006).

1.19.3 Experimental Paradigms

The examples of timing just described involve learning about the temporal constraints of environmental resources. In the sections that follow, we discuss timing experiments; animals are required to learn to time target intervals in each preparation. In subsequent sections, alternative theories are discussed that make different predictions about the mechanism by which this temporal learning occurs (*See also* Chapter 1.12).

Most of the experimental work on interval timing has been done with three vertebrate species in highly controlled settings: laboratory rats, laboratory pigeons, and adult humans. Three kinds of experimental paradigms have been staples in research, and we describe them here and show some representative results.

1.19.3.1 Bisection Task

In the bisection task, also called the estimation or choice task, the subject is presented with two choices for responding, such as two levers to press for rats, two keys to peck for pigeons, or two keys to press on a keyboard for humans. During training, a single interval of time is presented on each trial. The interval is commonly signalled by the duration of a key that lights up or a tone that sounds. The interval might be one of two durations, a short duration S (e.g., 2 s) or a long duration L (e.g., 8 s). When the interval is over, the subject gets to make a choice. One of the choices is arbitrarily designated the 'short' choice and is correct for the short duration. The other choice, the 'long' choice, is correct for a long duration.

After sufficient training, subjects typically perform very well on the training intervals. Occasional tests are then given using intervals not used in training. These test intervals typically span the range of

durations between the short and the long training durations. In the example, durations of 2, 3, 4, 5, 6, 7, or 8 s might be presented on test trials. Typical data from rats and humans are shown in **Figure 2**. In general, a smooth psychophysical curve is obtained, with the probability of choosing 'long' increasing in a sigmoidal fashion with the test duration presented.

Of some concern in bisection studies is the point of subjective equality (PSE) or bisection point, from which the task obtains its name. This is the stimulus duration at which a subject is equally likely to choose 'long' and 'short,' or 50% of each. The bisection point is estimated by various curve-fitting techniques from the psychophysical function that is obtained on tests. For rats and humans, the bisection point is at the geometric mean when the ratio of long to short duration is small (Church and Deluty, 1977; Allan and Gibbon, 1991). The geometric mean of two numbers, **a** and **b**, is defined as:

$$M_{geom}(\mathbf{a}, \mathbf{b}) = \sqrt{(\mathbf{a} * \mathbf{b})}, \text{ the square root of } \mathbf{a} \text{ times } \mathbf{b}.$$

This is a midpoint by ratios rather than arithmetic differences, that is:

$$\mathbf{b}/M_{geom} = M_{geom}/\mathbf{a}, \quad \text{for } \mathbf{b} > \mathbf{a}.$$

In contrast, the familiar arithmetic mean (M_{arith}) of **a** and **b**, $(\mathbf{a} + \mathbf{b})/2$, is the midpoint by arithmetic differences:

$$\mathbf{b} - M_{arith} = M_{arith} - \mathbf{a}.$$

A bisection point at the geometric mean, then, suggests a comparison of ratios between the remembered reference durations and the duration presented on the test trial (more on this later).

What size ratio is small enough for a bisection point at the geometric mean differs between humans and rats. Church and Deluty (1977) found rats bisecting at the geometric mean with a L:S ratio of 4:1, as did others (Chiang et al., 2000; Santi et al., 2001; Crystal, 2002). For humans, Allan and Gibbon (1991) used L:S ratios of 2:1 or smaller and also used short durations (≤ 4 s). With larger L:S ratios, the bisection point is no longer at the geometric mean and is often closer to the arithmetic mean. In rats, an L:S ratio larger than 4:1 led to a bisection point that differed from the geometric mean (Raslear, 1983; Siegel, 1986; Shurtleff et al., 1990; Shurtleff et al., 1992). Unfortunately, the bisection point differed between the studies. In humans bisecting short durations (<1 s), Wearden

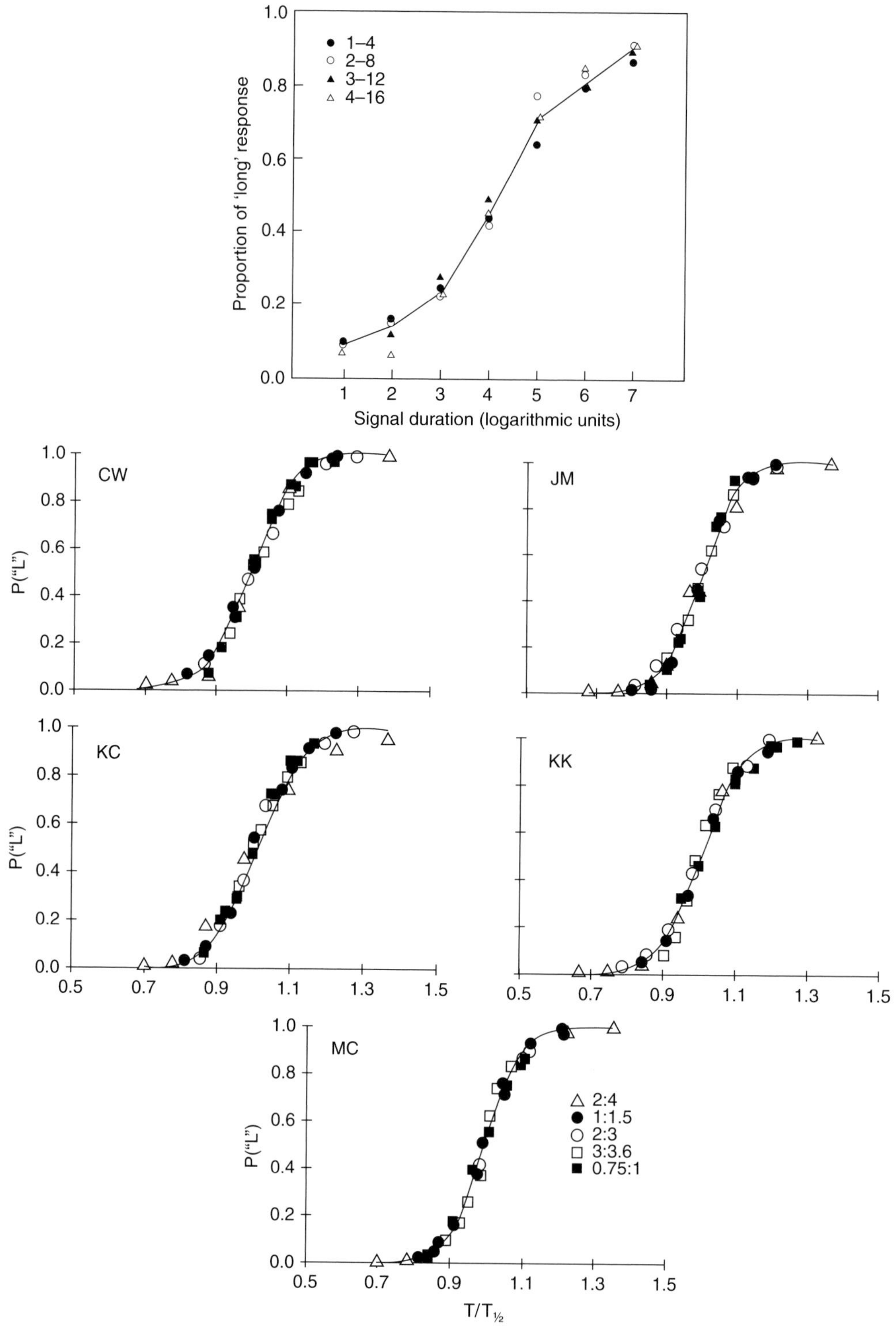

Figure 2   Representative data on the bisection task from rats (top) and individual humans (bottom). Tasks with different reference durations to be discriminated have been pooled together. Data are from unrewarded tests (for rats) and tests without feedback (for humans). Note that data from different conditions superimpose when plotted in this proportional fashion. Top, reproduced with permission from Church RM and Deluty MZ (1977) Bisection of temporal intervals. *J. Exp. Psychol. Anim. Behav. Process.* 3: 216–228; bottom, reproduced with permission from Allan LG and Gibbon J (1991) Human bisection at the geometric mean. *Learn. Motiv.* 22: 39–58.

and Ferrara (1996) found bisection at the geometric mean with an L:S ratio of 2:1, but with larger ratios, the bisection point was closer to the arithmetic mean. With longer durations in the seconds range, bisection was not at the geometric mean with any L:S ratio, including 2:1 (Wearden et al., 1997). The bisection points were closer to the arithmetic mean.

An interpretation for the variable results obtained with larger L:S ratios is that intermediate points are perceptibly different from both the L and the S durations to the subjects. A subject then in effect judges neither, and some strategic rule needs to be invoked as a basis for responding. The strategic rule is likely to vary from subject to subject, thus causing variablility in the data.

1.19.3.2   Peak Procedure

The peak procedure is an adaptation of the fixed interval schedule (**Figure 3**; *See also* Chapter 1.06). It is a production task in that the animal gets to emit responses over a stretch of time signaled by some event. Two types of trials are given to subjects. On training trials, a signal marks the start of an interval to be timed. Typically, this is a light or a tone that stays on. After a set interval has elapsed, a reward is delivered for a response (press a bar, peck a key, push a button), that is, the first response after a fixed interval from signal onset is rewarded. Responses before the fixed interval elapsed have no effect. On test trials, the signal also marks the start of a trial, but no rewards are dispensed. The signal stays on for much

longer than the fixed interval on training trials. We illustrate the paradigm and typical results with some examples.

Roberts (1981) presented rats the peak procedure using fixed intervals of 20 s and 40 s. A light and a tone signaled the two fixed intervals. For example, when the tone sounded on a trial, reward was given for the first bar press after 20 s; when a light lit up on a trial, reward was given for the first bar press after 40 s. Occasionally, unrewarded tests lasting 80 s were given using the light or the tone. On these trials, the light or tone stayed on for 80 s, but no reward was dispensed. **Figure 4** shows the results on tests from the last five sessions of Roberts' (1981) experiment, averaged across rats and trials. It can be seen that the rats started responding before the fixed interval elapsed, but the probability of responding peaks at around the fixed interval assigned to each signal.

Pigeons show a similar pattern of behavior on the peak procedure (Roberts et al., 1989). In **Figure 5**, the group of pigeons was also trained with two signals, a light and a tone. When the light signaled the start of a trial, a key peck was rewarded after 15 s; when a tone signaled the start of a trial, a key peck was rewarded after 30 s. The data came from unrewarded tests with each signal that lasted 90 s. Other than peaking at around the expected time of reward on training trials, two other features are noticeable. The response distribution curves are not perfectly symmetrical. The slope is steeper on the rise to the peak on the left side than the fall from the peak on the right side. In addition, the response distribution curve for the tone shows a rise toward the end of the test trial.

In a third example, humans were tested on the peak procedure (Rakitin et al., 1998). Training fixed intervals of 8, 12, and 21 s were presented using a

Training

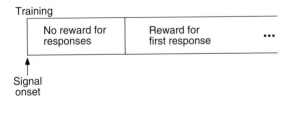

Test

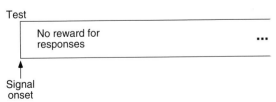

Figure 3   Schematic illustration of the peak procedure. On a training trial (top), a signal indicates the start of a trial. The first response after a fixed duration (FI) has elapsed is rewarded. On a test trial (bottom) the signal stays on for a duration much longer than the FI, and reward is withheld.

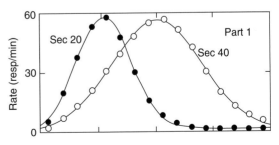

Figure 4   Representative data from rats on the peak procedure. On the *x*-axis is time elapsed because the of start of an unrewarded test trial lasting 80 s. Each tick mark represents 20 s. The peak rate of responding when averaged across trials occurs near the fixed duration. Reproduced with permission from Roberts S (1981) Isolation of an internal clock. *J. Exp. Psychol. Anim. Behav. Process.* 7: 242–268.

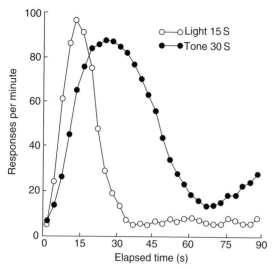

Figure 5 Representative data from pigeons on the peak procedure. These birds were trained with two different fixed intervals. A light was associated with fixed duration (FI) 15 s, whereas a tone was associated with FI 30 s. Data are from unrewarded test trials lasting 90 s. Reproduced with permission from Roberts WA, Cheng K, and Cohen JS (1989) Timing light and tone signals in pigeons. *J. Exp. Psychol. Anim. Behav. Process.* 15: 23–35.

computer. Subjects participated in multiple sessions, with the fixed interval constant in each session. Test trials were slightly different from those given to pigeons and rats. A subject could terminate a trial

by pressing the enter key on the keyboard, or the tests ended automatically after the fixed interval for the session had elapsed three times. Results showed orderly near-Gaussian distributions resembling those found for rats (**Figure 6**).

1.19.3.3 Generalization

In generalization, the subject gets to answer yes or no to the 'question' of whether a presented duration is the standard or rewarded duration. For example, Church and Gibbon (1982) presented rats with a house light that stayed on for different durations. A lever was inserted after (but not before) the house light went off. A standard duration was the positive duration, for example, 4 s if the house light lasted 4 s, and a bar press would be rewarded. For other durations, bar presses went unrewarded. Results showed an orderly generalization function peaking at the positive duration and dropping off nearly symmetrically in a Gaussian fashion (**Figure 7**). The response rate did not drop to zero; at all durations, the rats responded on a proportion of the trials.

The generalization paradigm has also been used on humans (Wearden, 1992; Wearden and Towse, 1994; Wearden et al., 1997). One standard duration was presented as the positive duration. Subjects' task was to answer YES or NO according to whether the

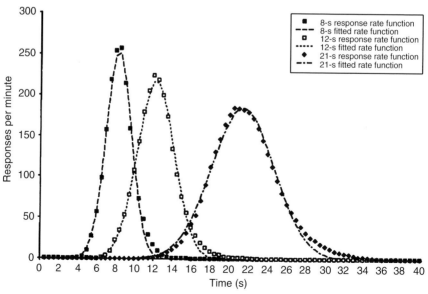

Figure 6 Representative data from humans on the peak procedure. Humans were instructed to hold down a key to 'bracket' a target fixed interval. They were to start before the interval had elapsed and stop after the interval had elapsed. Reproduced with permission from Rakitin BC, Gibbon J, Penney TB, Malapani C, Hinton SC, and Meck WH (1998) Scalar expectancy theory and peak-interval timing in humans. *J. Exp. Psychol. Anim. Behav. Process.* 24: 15–33.

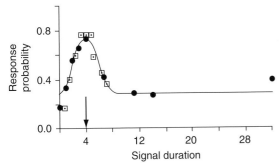

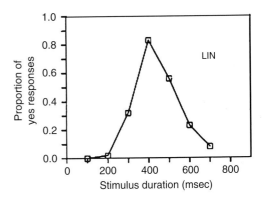

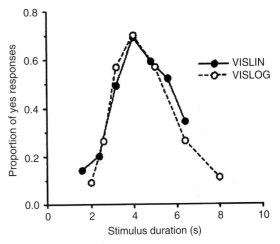

Figure 7 Representative data from rats on the generalization task. A duration of tone was presented to the rat, and then a lever was inserted. Lever presses were rewarded if the tone duration was 4 s, but not if it was any other duration. The data show a symmetric generalization gradient around the reinforced duration of 4 s. Reproduced with permission from Church RM and Gibbon J (1982) Temporal generalization. *J. Exp. Psychol. Anim. Behav. Process.* 8: 165–186.

duration presented on a trial was or was not the standard duration. Wearden (1992) and Wearden and Towse (1994) used very short durations that precluded counting. Longer durations in the seconds range were used by Wearden et al. (1997); subjects were prevented from counting by having to shadow (repeat back) an irregular list of numbers. For both short and long durations, orderly generalization gradients were obtained (**Figure 8**). A difference from those found with rats is that the gradients were asymmetric: More YES responses were given to durations longer than the standard (on the right side) than to durations shorter than the standard (on the left side).

1.19.4 Scalar Property

A property found in all the data examples that we have shown is the scalar property. Most of the data graphs are in absolute units of time. The scalar property emerges when data are plotted in units of time relative to the standard duration being measured (for the peak procedure and generalization) or the subjective middle (for the bisection task). When data are plotted in this fashion, graphs having different absolute standards superimpose, as shown in **Figure 9** for humans on the peak procedure and **Figure 2** (bottom) for humans in the bisection task. For this reason, the scalar property is also called superimposition.

Put more formally, some measure of spread, such as the standard deviation of a response distribution or the distance between the quartiles, is a constant proportion of the duration being measured in the peak procedure or generalization paradigms:

Figure 8 Representative data from humans on the generalization task with very short intervals (top) and intervals in the seconds range (bottom). Humans answered "yes" or "no" to the question of whether a presented duration matched a reference duration (400 ms in the top panel, 4 s in the bottom panel). Unlike rats, the generalization gradients are asymmetric, dropping more slowly to the right (corresponding to durations longer than the standard). Top, reproduced with permission from Wearden JH (1992) Temporal generalization in humans. *J. Exp. Psychol. Anim. Behav. Process.* 18: 134–144; bottom, reproduced with permission from Wearden JH, Denovan L, Fakhri M, and Haworth R (1997) Scalar timing in temporal generalization in humans with longer stimulus durations. *J. Exp. Psychol. Anim. Behav. Process.* 23: 502–511.

Spread $= \mathrm{k}X$, where X is the duration being measured.

This is also known as Weber's law. The constant k, which is Spread$/X$, is known as the coefficient of variation or Weber fraction.

1.19.5 Theories of Interval Timing

We examine briefly three different theories of interval timing; each theory makes different assumptions

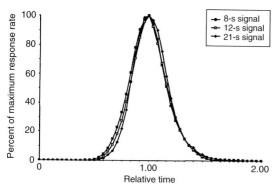

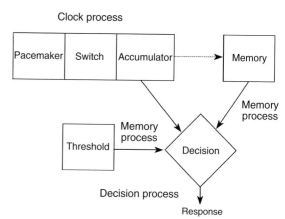

Figure 9 Superimposition in data from humans on the peak procedure. The data in Figure 6 have been replotted in relative terms, with the *x*-axis expressed as a proportion of the fixed duration. Reproduced with permission from Rakitin BC, Gibbon J, Penney TB, Malapani C, Hinton SC, and Meck WH (1998) Scalar expectancy theory and peak-interval timing in humans. *J. Exp. Psychol. Anim. Behav. Process.* 24: 15–33.

Figure 10 The Scalar Expectancy Theory (SET), consisting of three processes: a clock process, a memory process, and a decision process. The clock consists of a pacemaker that sends out regular pulses. The pulses may be gated by a switch into an accumulator for the purposes of timing a current duration. The elapsed time is compared to a standard duration retrieved from memory. If the ratio of the elapsed time to the reference time exceeds a threshold (which is also retrieved from memory for the trial), then the animal responds at a high rate (in the peak procedure) or answers "yes" in generalization. For the bisection task, two reference durations need to be retrieved, one for the long duration and one for the short duration. Ratio comparison is again made: elapsed time/S is compared with L/elapsed time. The subject chooses the reference (S or L) that generated a smaller ratio. Adapted with permission from Church RM (2003) A concise introduction to scalar timing theory. In: Meck WH (ed.) *Functional and Neural Mechanisms of Interval Timing*, pp. 3–22. Boca Raton, FL: CRC Press.

about the mechanism(s) of learning about the temporal constraints of the environment. A good number of other theories have been developed as well, but the chosen ones give some idea of the range of extant theories. At this stage, the field is far from agreeing to a single theory.

1.19.5.1   Scalar Expectancy Theory

A widely used explanation for interval timing is the Information Processing (IP) model (Gibbon et al., 1984; Church, 2003), also known as Scalar Expectancy Theory (SET; **Figure 10**). According to the IP model, timing is based on three stages of information processing: clock, memory, and decision. The clock stage of information processing consists of a pacemaker that sends pulses to an accumulator. A switch gate pulses from the pacemaker to the accumulator (or, alternatively, diverts these pulses away from the accumulator). The memory stage of information processing consists of working and reference memory storage systems. Working memory contains the current estimate of elapsed time, as indexed by the number of pulses accumulated at a particular point in time. Reference memory contains examples of previously rewarded elapsed durations that were previously transferred from working memory to reference memory. The decision stage of information processing compares a randomly selected example from reference memory to the currently elapsing duration. The decision to respond (or

not) is based on the relative similarity of the estimate of current and remembered times.

The scalar property or Weber's law suggests a ratio comparison process. Consider, for example, the peak procedure. The animal is said to switch to a high rate of responding after a ratio of elapsed time (from the clock process) to the reference duration (from the memory process) has been passed. If the *average* ratio threshold is the same at different fixed durations (FIs), this would produce the scalar property. Variations from trial to trial in the thresholds and reference durations used would produce the shape of the response distribution found when many test trials are pooled.

Many timing studies have interpreted results in terms of SET. Consider, for example, the generalization results shown in **Figures 7** and **8**. Results such as those from the rat in **Figure 7** can be modeled by a decision process that compares a ratio of two durations to a threshold ratio. The numerator is the absolute difference between the duration presented on the trial (clock process feeding working memory) and a reference duration from memory. The denominator is the reference duration. Thus, the comparison can be represented as

$$|t - T|/T < b?$$

In the inequality, T represents a reference duration from memory, whereas t represents the duration on the current trial. Such a process produces a symmetric generalization gradient. Wearden (1992) found that a modification of the comparison rule accounted for the asymmetric generalization gradients found in humans:

$$|t - T|/t < b?$$

The difference is that the denominator is the duration perceived on the current trial rather than a reference duration from memory. This shows that small modifications of SET can sometimes account for different patterns of data.

Another example of the application of SET concerns the role of attention in timing. Attention is thought to be required for the proper functioning of the clock process. We can use the analogy of filling a bucket with a hose, the bucket representing the accumulator. The hose is a pacemaker that drips constantly. The idea is that if attention is diverted, the hose will sometimes miss the bucket. One predicted result is that a longer actual duration of time must elapse under attentional demand before a subject judges that a particular reference duration has elapsed. This idea was tested on human subjects (Fortin and Massé, 2000; Fortin, 2003). Subjects had

to stop a tone after 2500 ms had passed (**Figure 11**). As an added complication, the tone had a break in it at some unpredictable point, and the break was not to be timed. That is, subjects had to time 2500 ms excluding the break. The authors reasoned that anticipating the break requires attention. This led to the prediction that the later the arrival of the break, the more subjects should overestimate. It was as if the bucket were likely to be missed by the hose before the arrival of the break. The duration of the break should not make a difference, as the timing process was hypothesized to stop during the break. This was precisely the pattern of results found (**Figure 11**).

1.19.5.2 Timing Without a Clock

One might imagine that to do interval timing, one would need a clock. Models without a clock, however, have been proposed. One such model adapts a neural network to do what a clock does (Hopson, 2003). The network has an input layer, a hidden layer, and an output layer, with weights between the input layer and the hidden layer and between the hidden layer and the output layer. It is different from a standard neural network in that the hidden layer takes time to build up activation. Different units in the hidden layer build up at different rates.

The idea is to have the system build up to a maximal activation level at the predicted time of reward. Activation should come to predict probability of reward. The system learns by a back-propagation-learning algorithm that adjusts the weights. The model can account for a good number of patterns of results in the literature.

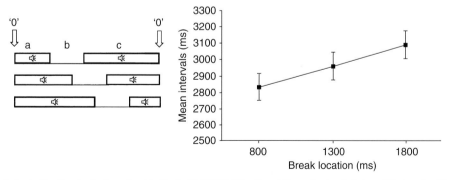

Figure 11 A dual-attention task described in Fortin C (2003) Attentional time-sharing in interval timing. In: Meck WH (ed.) *Functional and neural mechanisms of interval timing*, pp. 235–260. Boca Raton, FL: CRC Press. Reproduced with permission. Left: Humans have the task of holding down a key that produces a tone in order to produce a tone of 2500 ms duration. At some unpredictable time, the tone is interrupted by the experimenter, and the break is not to be timed. The data show that humans overproduce on this task, and the amount of overproduction varies directly with time elapsed before the break appears. The interpretation is that anticipating the break requires attention, which detracts from the task of timing. The result is that more actual time has to elapse before a perceived duration is judged to have elapsed.

1.19.5.3　Packet Theory

A recent information processing theory that makes detailed predictions is Packet Theory (Kirkpatrick, 2002; Kirkpatrick and Church, 2003; Church and Guilhardi, 2005; Guilhardi et al., 2005). It has four component processes (**Figure 12**). As an example, we consider a rat on a FI 30-s schedule of reinforcement for head entries into a food hopper. This means that 30 s after a pellet of food is delivered, the next pellet will be primed. The first head entry after the FI of 30 s results in food delivery.

The perception process is akin to the clock process in SET. It tracks the perceived time to the expected reward, about 30 s in this case. The memory in SET is a collection of reference durations from which the subject picks one for the current trial. In Packet Theory, the memory is the average expected time to reward, averaged over the reward times of the past. In the FI 30 example, this is also about 30 s. The memory process also has a threshold, in parallel with the threshold in SET. The threshold has a normal distribution about some mean proportion of time to expected reward. The decision process is based on the threshold. When the threshold has been passed, the animal switches from a low rate of response packets to a high rate of response packets.

Packets are theoretical entities that generate bouts of responding. This is signified in the response process, which turns packets into bouts of responses with particular characteristics, such as a distribution of interresponse times. The theory is thus explicit in producing an actual stream of response times in a simulated trial. Other theories are typically not quite as explicit about responses. For example, it is not clear how the activation level of the neural net in Hopson's (2003) model translates to actual responses in time.

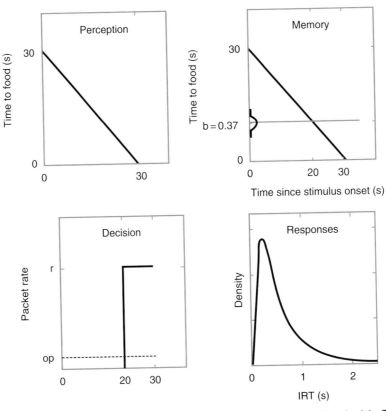

Figure 12　A schematic illustration of Packet Theory in explaining performance on a FI 30 schedule. The theory has four components. A perception unit parallels the clock process in Scalar Expectancy Theory and times the expected time to reward on the current trial. The memory process is a representation of the expected time to reward, derived from an average of past durations to reward. A variable threshold is retrieved for the current trial. The decision process switches to a high rate of production of Packets when the threshold has been crossed. Packets are theoretical underlying units that generate bouts of behavior, according to a function described in the response production unit on the right. Reproduced with permission from Church RM and Guilhardi P (2005) A Turing test of a timing theory. *Behav. Processes* 69: 45–58.

This explicit translation into responses in time means that the model can be compared against empirical data on numerous fronts, including response distributions, response rates, and interresponse times. On these multiple fronts, the model does a reasonable job of simulating the actual data obtained. Because the memory process is said to come up with an average expected time to reward, it does so even when durations to reward varied in the past, as in some random distribution about a mean. This means that the model can predict the behavior of rats in such seemingly 'nontiming' conditioning procedures. One of the strengths of the model is that it can encompass a range of conditioning procedures, and in fact, it is a new theory of conditioning (see other chapters on theories of conditioning in this volume).

A further contribution from the development of Packet Theory is an explicit recommendation for evaluating how well the model accounts for obtained data in the form of a Turing test (Church and Guilhardi, 2005). It is called a Turing test after the mathematician Alan Turing, who devised a similar test to examine whether a human can distinguish the responses of a computer-generated program from those of another human. In the case of Packet Theory, a set procedure such as FI 30 is given to rats and produces a sizeable set of trials at asymptote. The model is given the same procedure, parameters are chosen, and the model generates a set of trials. The data generated are responses in time. To test the 'fit,' one picks one trial from the rat and one trial from the model. A third trial is then picked from either the model or the rat. This trial is formally compared to the two reference trials (one from the model and one from the rat). The comparison process 'decides' whether the sample trial is more similar to the model's trial or to the rat's trial. This process can be repeated many times.

If the model generates data indistinguishable from a rat, the Turing comparison process should be at chance and be correct 50% of the time. In fact, it is correct about 60% of the time, which shows that the model, while having considerable success, may be improved by further development.

1.19.6 Connections Between Interval Timing and Circadian Timing

The examples of timing discussed earlier are referred to as interval timing (sometimes short-interval timing) to denote that the target duration is an elapsing interval. The basic idea is that an interval elapses with respect to the occurrence of some event (e.g., the onset of a light or a sound). A helpful metaphor is the familiar features of a stopwatch (Church, 1978). For example, a stopwatch may be used to time runners in a race. As the runners line up for the race, the stopwatch would be *reset* to zero. When the race begins, the stopwatch is *started*. When the runner crosses the finish line, the stopwatch is *ended*. The reading of the stopwatch provides an estimate of time to complete the event (running the race in this example). Implicit in the stopwatch metaphor is that timing an elapsed interval is quite flexible; the start and stop events are arbitrary.

One mechanism that may be used to instantiate a stopwatch mechanism is a pacemaker-accumulator. A pacemaker emits pulses as a function of time, and an accumulator integrates (i.e., counts) the number of pulses emitted. An hourglass is a familiar example of a pacemaker-accumulator; the amount of sand in the bottom chamber of an hourglass is an index of the elapsed duration since the hourglass was turned over (i.e., reset).

By contrast, circadian timing is based on the completion of a periodic process. As the name circadian implies, the periodic process is approximately a day. Therefore, time of day is indexed by the phase of a circadian periodic process. Circadian timing is widespread (Aschoff, 1981; Takahashi et al., 2001).

Unlike the pacemaker-accumulator and hourglass mechanism described for interval timing, circadian timing is based on an oscillator. The system is referred to as a circadian oscillator because the natural period of the oscillator is approximately 24 h.

1.19.6.1 Formal Properties of Interval and Circadian Timing

Gibbon et al. (1997a) described operating characteristics for interval and circadian timing systems, which is summarized in **Table 1** (the table is reproduced from Gibbon et al., 1997a). The circadian system is based on an endogenous oscillation. An oscillation is endogenous if it does not require continued periodic input to produce ongoing periodic output. For example, activity patterns occur at species-typical times of day when an animal is exposed to daily periodic light cycles (e.g., 12 h of light followed by 12 h of darkness). After the periodic light cycle is terminated (e.g., constant dim illumination), behavior 'free runs,' usually with a period that departs slightly from 24 h.

Table 1 Properties of circadian and interval timing systems

Circadian	Interval
Timing properties	
Endogenous oscillation: free run	Requires reset: one shot
Entrainment range: Limited	Training range: Broad
Approximately 8 h maximum	Approx. 3–4 orders of magnitude – seconds to hours
Phase shift adjustment: Slow	Phase shift immediate
Several cycles usually required	Arbitrary onset phase
Variance properties	
High level of precision:	Low level of precision:
$\sigma/\mu = 0.01 - 0.05$	$\sigma/\mu = 0.10 - 0.35$
Relationship to entrainment period (?)	Scalar property:
	Superposition in relative time $f_r(rt) = (1/r)f(t)$, $\sigma/\mu = \gamma$.

Reproduced from Gibbon J, Fairhurst S, and Goldberg B (1997a) Cooperation, conflict and compromise between circadian and interval clocks in pigeons. In: Bradshaw CM and Szabadi E (eds.) *Time and Behaviour: Psychological and Neurobehavioural Analyses*, pp. 329–384. New York: Elsevier. © 1997 Elsevier Science B.V.

Free-running behavior after the termination of periodic stimuli provides evidence that the timing system is an endogenous oscillator. In contrast, Gibbon et al. (1997a) described the interval timing system as requiring resetting. The timing system is presumed to time with respect to the occurrence of some stimulus; a single presentation of the stimulus is required to reset the interval timing system (i.e., one shot reset).

The circadian system is subject to a limited range of entrainment. For example, presentation of a periodic input is thought to entrain the endogenous oscillator only if the periodic input is within a limited range of periods near 24 h. By contrast, Gibbon et al. (1997a) described the interval timing system as having a broad training range covering 3-4 orders of magnitude from seconds to hours.

The circadian system adjusts slowly to a phase shift. A phase shift is an abrupt change in the initiation of a periodic process. A familiar example of a phase shift is the unusual wake-up times that people are exposed to after flying to a destination across several time zones. It usually requires several cycles (i.e., days) before one's activities are synchronized to the new time zone. By contrast, Gibbon et al. (1997a) stated that the interval timing system is characterized by immediate phase shift; because interval timing is not based on the phase of a periodic process, the response to a single shift in a cycle is complete adjustment or complete resetting of the timing processes (i.e., one-shot reset in Gibbon et al.'s terminology).

Temporal performance based on a circadian oscillator is highly precise as measured by cycle-to-cycle variation. For example, Gibbon et al. (1997a) summarize the coefficient of variation (CV; standard deviation of time estimates divided by the mean of time estimates) of circadian-mediated performance as approximately 1%–5%. By contrast, interval timing performance is characterized by a relatively low level of precision (coefficient of variation of 10%–35%). Therefore, it appears that a characteristic of a circadian oscillator is relatively high timing precision. In particular, a consequence of having an endogenous oscillator dedicated to timing select values within a limited range appears to be relatively high sensitivity to timing these target durations.

The variance properties of timing have played an important role in understanding interval timing (as noted in the section above about the scalar property). By contrast, the analysis of variance properties has had less impact in the study of circadian timing.

With some notable exceptions (Aschoff, 1984, 1985, 1989, 1993, 1998; Silver and Bittman, 1984; Terman et al., 1984; Aschoff and Daan, 1997; Gibbon et al., 1997a), the interaction of interval and circadian mechanisms has been largely neglected in the literature. In the sections that follow, we describe a series of empirical tests that were designed to evaluate the hypothesis that interval timing is based, at least in part, on oscillatory processes as described in **Table 1** from Gibbon et al. (1997a).

1.19.6.2 Resetting Properties of Short-Interval Timing

Figure 13 shows an example of a phase-shift manipulation applied to short-interval timing. Rats were

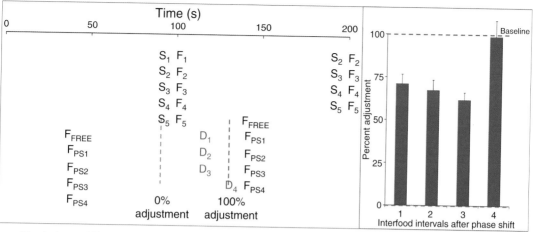

Figure 13 A phase shift produces gradual adjustment in short-interval timing. Left panel: Schematic representation of training, phase-shift manipulation, predictions, and data (double plotted to facilitate inspection of transitions across successive intervals; consecutive 100-s fixed intervals are plotted left to right and top to bottom). Rats ($n = 14$) timed 100-s intervals, and the last 5 intervals before the phase shift are shown (F = food pellet, S = start time of response burst). A 62-s phase advance (i.e., early pellet) on average was produced by the delivery of a response-independent food (F_{FREE}). All other food-to-food intervals were 100 s (F_{PS} = food post phase shift). Dashed lines indicate predictions if rats are insensitive (0% adjustment, purple) or completely sensitive (100% adjustment, pink) to the most recently delivered food pellet. A pacemaker-accumulator mechanism predicts 100% adjustment on the initial interval after the phase shift on the assumption of complete reset (Gibbon et al., 1997a). An oscillator mechanism predicts initial incomplete adjustment. Data (D) indicate incomplete adjustment on the first three trials. Right panel: Start times on the initial three trials were earlier than in preshift baseline ($t(13)$'s > 2, p's < .05). Resetting was achieved on the fourth trial ($t < 1$). Each 45-mg food pellet was contingent on a lever press after 100 s in 12-h sessions. The start of a response burst was identified on individual trials by selecting the response that maximized the goodness of fit of individual responses to a model with a low rate followed by a high rate (analysis as in Crystal et al., 1997). The same conclusions were reached by measuring the latency to the first response after food. Baseline was the average start time on the five trials before the phase shift. Left panel: Zero on the y-axis (purple dashed line) corresponds to complete failure to adjust to the phase shift; 100% (pink dashed line) corresponds to complete resetting. Error bars represent 1 SEM. Adapted from Crystal JD (2006c) Sensitivity to time: Implications for the representation of time. In: Wasserman EA and Zentall TR (eds.) *Comparative cognition: Experimental explorations of animal intelligence*, 270–284. New York: Oxford University Press. Reproduced from Crystal JD (2006d) Time, place, and content. *Comp. Cogn. Behav. Rev.* 1: 53–76. with permission.

trained to time 100 s; a food pellet was dispensed for the first response after the fixed interval of 100 s had elapsed. To implement the phase shift, an early, response-independent pellet was delivered (i.e., free food). Four food cycles were required before adjustment was complete, which is consistent with the hypothesis that short-interval timing of 100 s is based on an oscillator mechanism (Crystal, 2006c, 2006d). The prediction in the third row of **Table 1** is not supported by the data in **Figure 13**.

1.19.6.3 Endogenous Oscillations in Short-Interval Timing

The hypothesis that the timing of an interval is based on a pacemaker-accumulator or oscillator mechanism can be assessed by discontinuing periodic input (i.e., extinction) and assessing subsequent anticipatory behavior. A defining feature of an oscillator is that periodic output from the oscillator continues after the termination of periodic input. By contrast, a defining feature of a pacemaker-accumulator system is that elapsed time is measured with respect to the presentation of a stimulus, according to the classic description of this system (**Table 1**). Therefore, output of a short-interval system is periodic if presented with periodic input, but periodic output can be expected to cease if periodic input is discontinued. Groups of rats were trained to time short intervals (48, 96, and 192 s). The data from a representative individual rat in this experiment are shown in **Figure 14**, and group data are shown in **Figure 15**. As expected, periodic delivery of food produced periodic behavior during training (**Figure 15**, left column). Next, delivery of food was suspended. Behavior was periodic after termination

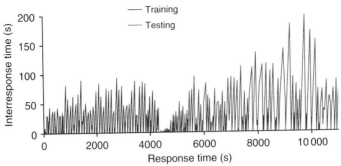

Figure 14 Many small interresponse times in short-interval timing are punctuated by much longer interresponse times, and punctuation by relatively long interresponse times continued after termination of periodic food delivery. Interresponse time (i.e., times of responses $R_{n+1} - R_n$) is plotted as a function of response time for a representative rat. During training, food was delivered on a fixed-interval 96-s schedule. During testing, food was not delivered (i.e., extinction). Extinction began at a randomly selected point in the session. The response measure was the time of occurrence of photobeam interruptions in the food trough. Reproduced from Crystal JD and Baramidze GT (2007) Endogenous oscillations in short-interval timing. *Behav. Processes*. 74: 152–158. © 2007, with permission from Elsevier.

of periodic input (**Figure 15**, right column). Importantly, the period in extinction increased as a function of the period in training, documenting that the periodic behavior in extinction was based on entrainment to the periodic feeding in training. These data suggest that short-interval timing is, at least in part, based on a self-sustaining, endogenous oscillator (Crystal and Baramidze, 2007). The prediction in the first row of **Table 1** is not supported by the data in **Figures 14** and **15**.

1.19.6.4 Timing Long Intervals

It is generally accepted that animals *cannot* anticipate intermeal intervals outside a limited range near 24 h (e.g., Stephan et al., 1979a,b; Boulos et al., 1980; Stephan, 1981; Aschoff et al., 1983; Mistlberger and Marchant, 1995; Madrid et al., 1998; White and Timberlake, 1999). However, this conclusion is based on a relatively limited data set. Indeed, caution is generally warranted when confronted with evidence for the absence of some ability (as in this case with the absence of temporal performance). An alternative explanation for the lack of evidence for timing noncircadian intervals is that timing is relatively superior near 24 h; by contrast, poorer temporal performance farther away from 24 h may make it more difficult to detect temporal performance. A major insight from interval timing in the range of seconds to minutes (Dews, 1970) is that temporal performance may be best compared across ranges if performance is expressed in relative time (elapsed time divided by the target interval, rather

than absolute time in seconds; and response rates expressed as a proportion of maximal rates). The power of this data analytic approach was documented in the section titled "Scalar property."

A series of experiments investigating meal anticipation was undertaken to test the hypothesis that a circadian oscillator is characterized by a local maximum in sensitivity to time (Crystal, 2001a); according to this prediction, temporal performance is superior near 24 h, relative to intermeal intervals outside the circadian range. Food was restricted to 3-h meals, which rats earned by breaking a photobeam in the food trough. The rats inspected the food trough before meals started, thereby providing a temporal anticipation function for each intermeal interval condition. **Figure 16** shows anticipation functions for intermeal intervals near the circadian range (22 to 26 h) and outside this range (14 and 34 h). The data are plotted in relative time on the horizontal axis and proportional response rate on the vertical axis (as described by Dews, 1970). Response rates increased later into the intermeal interval for intervals near the circadian range than for intervals outside this range. Sensitivity to time was estimated by the spread of the response distributions. The spread was smaller (i.e., lower variability) for intermeal intervals near the circadian range than for interval outside this range, as shown in **Figure 17**. Note that the data in **Figure 17** document a local maximum in sensitivity to time near 24 h, consistent with the hypothesis that a property of a circadian oscillator is improved sensitivity to time (Crystal, 2001a).

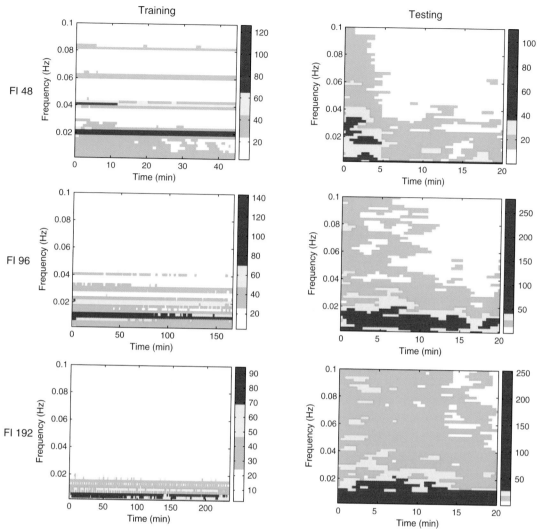

Figure 15 Endogenous oscillations in short-interval timing continue after the termination of periodic input. Short-time Fourier transforms are shown for training (left panels) and testing (right panels) conditions using fixed interval 48-, 96-, and 192-s procedures. The three-dimensional images show frequency (period = 1/frequncy) on the vertical axis as a function of time within the session along the horizontal axis; the color scheme represents the amount of power from the Fourier analysis. Concentrations of high power occur at a frequency of approximately 0.02, 0.01, and .0005, which correspond to periods of approximately 50, 100, and 200 s in top, middle, and bottom panels, respectively. Adapted from Crystal JD and Baramidze GT (2007) Endogenous oscillations in short-interval timing. *Behav. Processes.* 74: 152–158. © 2007, with permission from Elsevier.

Figure 18 shows a reanalysis of earlier published data on this problem. In particular, experiments were selected that used behaviors that are instrumental in producing food (e.g., approaching the food source or pressing a lever). Long intermeal intervals that are substantially less than 24-h are compared with a 24-h condition from each experiment. The critical part of the reanalysis was that the data were expressed in proportional time and rate. The reanalysis reveals that intervals below the circadian range (14, 18, and 19 h) are timed, but these temporal functions are less

steep and have lower terminal response rates than do functions for timing 24 h. The reanalysis of published data is consistent with the hypothesis that a property of a circadian oscillator is improved sensitivity to time, as was suggested by **Figures 16** and **17**.

1.19.6.5 Endogenous Oscillations in Long-Interval Timing

The examples of timing noncircadian long intervals in the section titled "Timing long intervals" document

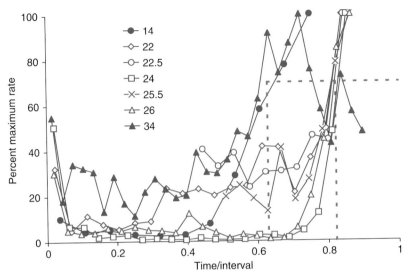

Figure 16 Response rate increased later into the interval for intermeal intervals near the circadian range (unfilled red symbols) relative to intervals outside this range (filled blue symbols); dashed lines indicate width of response rate functions. Anticipatory responses increase immediately prior to the meal for all intermeal intervals except 34 h. Each 45-mg food pellet was contingent on a photobeam break after a variable interval during 3-h meals. Intermeal intervals were tested in separate groups of rats ($n = 3-5$ per group). The end of the meal corresponds to 1 on the x-axis. Testing was conducted in constant darkness. Adapted from Crystal JD (2001a) Circadian time perception. *J. Exp. Psychol. Anim. Behav. Process.* 27: 68–78. Reproduced from Crystal JD (2006d) Time, place, and content. *Comp. Cogn. Behav. Rev.* 1: 53–76 with permission.

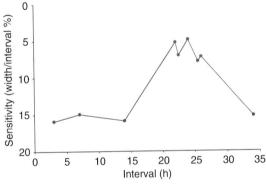

Figure 17 Intervals near the circadian range (red symbols) are characterized by higher sensitivity than intervals outside this range (blue symbols). Variability in anticipating a meal was measured as the width of the response distribution prior to the meal at 70% of the maximum rate, expressed as a percentage of the interval ($N = 29$). The interval is the time between light offset and meal onset in a 12–12 light–dark cycle (leftmost two circles) or the intermeal interval in constant darkness (all other data). The percentage width was smaller in the circadian range than outside this range ($F(1,20) = 22.65$, $p < .001$). The width/interval did not differ within the circadian ($F(4,12) = 1$) or noncircadian ($F(3,8) < 1$) ranges. The same conclusions were reached when the width was measured as 25%, 50%, and 75% of the maximum rate. The data are plotted on a reversed-order y-axis so that local maxima in the data correspond to high sensitivity, which facilitates comparison with other measures of sensitivity (e.g., Figure 20). Mean SEM = 2.4. Adapted from Crystal JD (2001a) Circadian time perception. *J. Exp. Psychol. Anim. Behav. Process.* 27: 68–78. Reproduced from Crystal JD (2006d) Time, place, and content. *Comp. Cogn. Behav. Rev.* 1: 53–76 with permission.

that rats can time intervals below the circadian range, but they do not identify the mechanism. In particular, the data stated earlier do not require an oscillator mechanism; an alternative is that the rats used a pacemaker-accumulator mechanism to time the long intervals. By contrast, the examples in the section titled Endogenous oscillations in short-interval timing document endogenous oscillations in timing short intervals (1–3 min) by demonstrating that timing continues after the termination of periodic input. The data described in this section document examples of endogenous oscillations in long-interval timing (16 h) by using the same experimental approach.

Rats earned food by interrupting a photobeam in a food trough during 3-h meals. The intermeal interval was 16 h. After approximately a month of experience with the intermeal interval, the meals were discontinued (Crystal, 2006b). **Figure 19** (top panel) shows that response rate increased as a function of time prior to the meals, documenting that the rats could time 16 h. To dissociate alternative timing mechanisms, it is diagnostic to consider the first two nonfood cycles. If the timing documented in the top panel of **Figure 19** is based on a pacemaker-accumulator mechanism reset by the meal, then response rate should increase as a function of time in the first nonfood cycle (as in training) because elapsed time since the last meal corresponds to the training interval. However, an

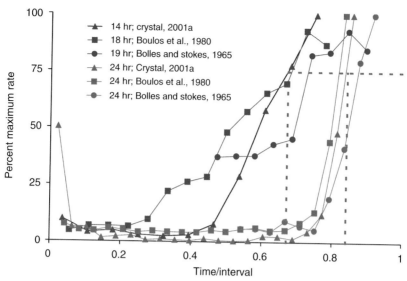

Figure 18 Rats anticipate intermeal intervals of 14, 18, and 19 h (blue symbols) with less precision (i.e., higher variability) than 24 h (red symbols); dashed lines indicate width of response rate functions. Data from Bolles and Stokes (1965) and Boulos Z, Rosenwasser AM, and Terman M (1980) Feeding schedules and the circadian organization of behavior in the rat. *Behav. Brain Res.* 1: 39–65, in which meals were earned by pressing a lever, were obtained by enlarging published figures by 200% and measuring each datum at 0.5-mm resolution. Adapted from Bolles RC and Stokes LW (1965), Rat's anticipation of diurnal and a-diurnal feeding. *J. Comp. Physiol. Psychol.* 60: 290–294 and Terman M (1980) Feeding schedules and the circadian organization of behavior in the rat. *Behav. Brain Res.* 1: 39–65, and Crystal JD (2001a) Circadian time perception. *J. Exp. Psychol. Anim. Behav. Process.* 27: 68–78. Reproduced from Crystal JD (2006b) Long-interval timing is based on a self sustaining endogenous oscillator. *Behav. Processes* 72: 149–160, © 2006, with permission from Elsevier.

estimate of the elapsed time with respect to the last meal continues to increase during the second nonfood cycle according to this proposal. Therefore, a pacemaker-accumulator does not predict an increase in response rate prior to the second skipped meal because elapsed time since the last meal is larger than the intermeal interval during the second nonfood cycle. In contrast, if the timing documented in the top panel of **Figure 19** is based on an endogenous oscillator, then response rate should increase as a function of time in both the first and second nonfood cycles because an endogenous oscillator is self-sustaining (i.e., periodic output from an oscillator is expected to continue after termination of periodic input).

The first two nonfood cycles are also shown in **Figure 19** (middle and bottom panels). Note that response rate increased as a function of time in the first and second nonfood cycles. In particular, response rate was significantly higher in the 3 h during the omitted meal relative to the 13 h prior to this point for both first and second nonfood cycles.

To characterize the period of behavior after termination of the meals, response rates were subjected to a periodogram analysis, which assesses the reliability of a periodic trend and estimates the

observed period. A significant periodic trend was detected for each rat. The mean period in extinction was $20.4 \pm 0.9\,\mathrm{h}$ (mean $\pm$ SEM), which was significantly different from 16 and 24 hr (Crystal, 2006b).

These data are consistent with the hypothesis that the natural period of the oscillator that drove behavior was 20.4 h, which is distinct from the circadian oscillator; according to this hypothesis, the two oscillatory systems are dissociated by their different characteristic periods. However, the data are also consistent with an alternative hypothesis, according to which the circadian oscillator's free-running period is modified by the periodic input to which it was previously exposed. Note that according to both of these hypotheses, long interval timing is based on a self-sustaining, endogenous oscillator; the hypotheses differ in specifying the characteristic period of the oscillator(s). Taken together, the data presented in the sections titled "Timing long intervals" and "Endogenous oscillations in long-interval timing" imply that long-interval timing is based on a self-sustaining, endogenous oscillator, which is not consistent with the prediction in the second row of **Table 1**.

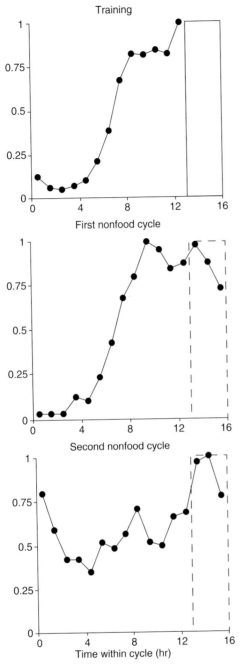

Figure 19 Endogenous oscillations in long-interval timing continue after the termination of periodic input. Response rate increased as a function of time within the 16-h intermeal interval cycle during the first and second nonfood cycle. Response rate (frequency of responses expressed as a proportion of the maximum frequency within the cycle) is plotted as a function of time within the cycle. The cycle included meals (indicated by the solid rectangle) during training (top panel). The meals were omitted (indicated by the dashed rectangles) in the first (middle panel) and second (bottom panel) nonfood cycles. Reproduced from Crystal JD (2006b) Long-interval timing is based on a self sustaining endogenous oscillator. *Behav. Processes* 72: 149–160, © 2006, with permission from Elsevier.

1.19.6.6   Variance Properties in Circadian and Short-Interval Timing

As noted in the section "Formal properties of interval and circadian timing," the study of variance properties has historically played a significant role in the development of theories of short-interval, but not circadian, timing. However, the data summarized in **Figure 17** suggest that a property of the well-established circadian oscillator is the relative improvement in sensitivity to time circadian intervals relative to noncircadian intervals. These data suggest that other putative oscillators may be identified by documenting other local maxima in sensitivity to time. Moreover, the observation that short-interval timing in the range of 1–3 min exhibits endogenous, self-sustaining patterns of behavior after the termination of periodic input reinforces the expectation that short-interval timing may be, at least in part, based on an endogenous oscillatory mechanism.

   Figure 20 shows a measure of sensitivity to time plotted as a function of stimulus duration from a series of experiments that evaluated many closely spaced target intervals (Crystal, 1999, 2001b). The data suggest that sensitivity to time short intervals is characterized by multiple local maxima. The procedure involved presenting a short or long stimulus followed by the insertion of two response levers. Left or right lever presses were designated as correct after short or long stimuli. For each short duration, accuracy was maintained at approximately 75% correct by adjusting the duration of the long stimulus after blocks of discrimination trials. Sensitivity to time (as measured by signal detection theory; Macmillan and Creelman, 1991) was approximately constant for short durations from 0.1 to 34 s. However, local peaks in sensitivity to time were observed at approximately 0.3, 1.2, 12, and 24 s.

   Figure 21 shows multiple local maxima in sensitivity to time across 7 orders of magnitude. The local maximum in sensitivity to time on the right side of the figure is replotted from **Figure 17**, which shows a local maximum in sensitivity to time of approximately 24 h. The local maxima in sensitivity to time on the left side of the figure are replotted from **Figure 20**. **Figure 21** documents that multiple local maxima in sensitivity to time are observed in the discrimination of time across several orders of magnitude.

   To provide an independent, converging line of evidence regarding local maxima in sensitivity to time, **Figure 22** replots coefficients of variability

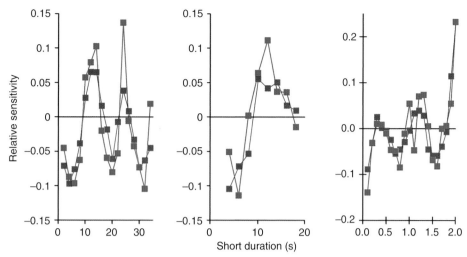

Figure 20 Sensitivity to time is characterized by local maxima at 12 and 24 s (left panel), 12 s (middle panel), and 0.3 and 1.2 s (right panel). Green symbols: average across rats. Red symbols: a running median was performed on each rat's data, and the smoothed data were averaged across rats to identify the most representative local maxima in sensitivity. Left panel: Rats discriminated short and long noise durations with the duration adjusted to maintain accuracy at approximately 75% correct. Short durations were tested in ascending order with a step size of 1 s ($n = 5$) and 2 s ($n = 5$). Sensitivity was similar across step sizes ($r(15) = .701$, $p < 01$), departed from zero based on a binomial test ($p < .001$), and was nonrandom ($r(14)_{lag1} = .710$, $p < .01$). Mean SEM = 0.03. Middle panel: Methods are the same as described in left panel, except short durations were tested in random order ($n = 7$) or with each rat receiving a single-interval condition ($n = 13$); results from these conditions did not differ. Sensitivity departed from zero based on a binomial test ($p < .001$) and was nonrandom ($r(7)_{lag1} = .860$, $p < .01$). Mean SEM = 0.02. Right panel: Methods are the same as described in left panel, except intervals were defined by gaps between 50-ms noise pulses, and short durations were tested in descending order with a step size of 0.1 s ($n = 6$). Sensitivity departed from zero based on a binomial test ($p < .001$) and was nonrandom ($r(18)_{lag1} = 0.736$, $p < .001$). Mean SEM = 0.04. Sensitivity was measured using d' from signal detection theory. $d' = z[p(\text{short response} \mid \text{short stimulus})] - z[p(\text{short response} \mid \text{long stimulus})]$. Relative sensitivity is d' – mean d'. Adapted from Crystal JD (1999) Systematic nonlinearities in the perception of temporal intervals. *J. Exp. Psychol. Anim. Behav. Process.* 25: 3–17; Crystal JD (2001b) Nonlinear time perception. *Behav. Processes* 55: 35–49; Crystal JD (2003) Nonlinearities in sensitivity to time: Implications for oscillator-based representations of interval and circadian clocks. In: Meck WH (ed.) *Functional and neural mechanisms of interval timing*, pp. 61–75. Boca Raton, FL: CRC Press. Reproduced from Crystal JD (2006d) Time, place, and content. *Comp. Cogn. Behav. Rev.* 1: 53–76 with permission.

(CV; ratio of standard deviation to the mean) as a function of the target intervals using 43 data sets from the literature selected by Gibbon et al. (1997b). The data from Gibbon and colleagues' scatter plot are replotted in the top panel of **Figure 22**, using a reverse-order vertical axis so that high points in the figure correspond to high sensitivity to time. To examine the shape of the sensitivity function, the data from Gibbon et al. were averaged in two-point blocks and subjected to a 3-point running median, which appears in the bottom panel of **Figure 22**. Sensitivity to time using Gibbon and colleagues' selection of data from the literature is characterized by multiple local maxima. The middle of the local maxima in the bottom panel of **Figure 22** occurs at approximately 0.2, 0.3, 1.2, 10, and 20 s. The top panel of **Figure 22** also shows clusters of high points near these intervals. The values of local maxima derived from Gibbon et al.'s selection of data are markedly

similar to local maxima that were observed in **Figure 20**: 0.3, 1.2, 12, and 24 s (Crystal, 1999, 2001b, 2003, 2006d). Although the shapes of the sensitivity functions in **Figures 20** and **22** differ, the similarity in the locations of local maxima is significant given that the data in **Figure 22** come from 43 different data sets. Moreover, the data that appear in **Figure 22** were independently selected by Gibbon and colleagues.

1.19.6.7 Integration of Interval and Circadian Timing

The data in **Figures 20, 21,** and **22** suggest that the psychological representation of time is nonlinearly related to physical estimates of time. The existence of a local maximum near a circadian oscillator (**Figure 21**, peak on right side) and local maxima in the short-interval range (**Figure 21**, peaks on left

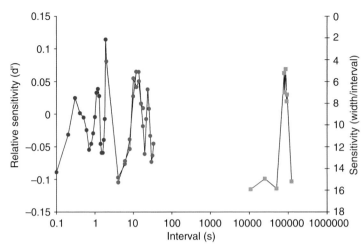

Figure 21 Multiple local maxima in sensitivity to time are observed in the discrimination of time across seven orders of magnitude. The existence of a local maximum near a circadian oscillator (peak on right side; purple squares) and other local maxima in the short-interval range (peaks on left side; blue, red, and green circles) are consistent with the hypothesis that timing is mediated by multiple oscillators. Intervals in the blank region in the center of the figure have not been tested. Left side: Rats discriminated short and long durations, with the long duration adjusted to maintain accuracy at 75% correct. Short durations were tested in sequential order (blue and red circles; $N = 26$) or independent order (green circles; $N = 20$). Circles represent relative sensitivity using d' from signal detection theory and are plotted using the y-axis on the left side of the figure. Right side: Rats received food in 3-h meals with fixed intermeal intervals by breaking a photobeam inside the food trough. The rate of photobeam interruption increased before the meal. Squares represent sensitivity, which was measured as the width of the anticipatory function at 70% of the maximum rate prior to the meal, expressed as a percentage of the interval ($N = 29$). The interval is the time between light offset and meal onset in a 12–12 light–dark cycle (leftmost two squares) or the intermeal interval in constant darkness (all other squares). Squares are plotted with respect to the reversed-order y-axis on the right side of the figure. Y-axes use different scales, and the x-axis uses a log scale. Adapted from Crystal JD (1999) Systematic nonlinearities in the perception of temporal intervals. *J. Exp. Psychol. Anim. Behav. Process.* 25: 3–17; Crystal JD (2001a) Circadian time perception. *J. Exp. Psychol. Anim. Behav. Process.* 27: 68–78; Crystal JD (2001b) Nonlinear time perception. *Behav. Processes* 55: 35–49. Reproduced from Crystal JD (2006d) Time, place, and content. *Comp. Cogn. Behav. Rev.* 1: 53–76, with permission.

side; **Figure 22**) is consistent with timing based on multiple oscillators (Church and Broadbent, 1990; Gallistel, 1990; Crystal, 1999, 2001b, 2003, 2006d). According to multiple-oscillator proposals, each oscillator is a periodic process that cycles within a fixed amount of time; an oscillator is characterized by its period (i.e., cycle duration) and phase (i.e., current point with the cycle). Each unit within a multiple oscillator system has its own period and phase. Therefore, a multiple-oscillator system includes several distinct periods. Sensitivity to time of an interval near an oscillator is expected to be higher than timing an interval farther away from the oscillator. Therefore, the multiple local maxima in sensitivity to time shown in **Figures 17, 20, 21**, and **22** suggest the existence of multiple short-period oscillators.

The data reviewed in this section conflict with the predictions of **Table 1**. The first row of **Table 1** focuses on the defining feature that distinguishes oscillator and pacemaker-accumulator mechanisms. Oscillators are endogenous and self-sustaining, meaning that they continue to cycle after the

termination of periodic input. By contrast, a pacemaker-accumulator requires resetting by an exogenous stimulus, and the timing system is presumed to be reset by a single event (i.e., one-shot reset). The data in **Figures 14** and **15** suggest that short-interval timing is endogenous and self-sustaining, thereby exhibiting a property of an oscillator rather than a pacemaker-accumulator.

The second row of **Table 1** focuses on the susceptibility of oscillator and pacemaker-accumulator mechanisms to time different ranges of target intervals; the former is described as subject to a limited training range, whereas the latter is subject to a broad training range. The data in **Figures 16** and **18** suggest that many long, but noncircadian, intervals can be timed, and the data in **Figure 19** suggest that long-interval timing is endogenous and self sustaining, consistent with an oscillator mechanism.

The third row of **Table 1** focuses on the responsiveness to abrupt changes in the phase of an input signal. A hallmark feature of an oscillator is gradual adjustment in phase responsiveness – meaning that

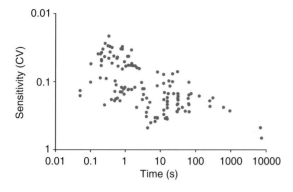

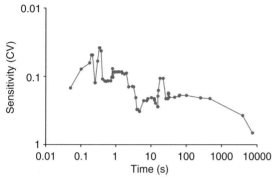

Figure 22 Top panel: Sensitivity is plotted as a function of time across six orders of magnitude. The scatter plot reveals that sensitivity to time declines as a function of increasing intervals. The data are from Figure 3 in Gibbon J, Malapani C, Dale CL, and Gallistel C (1997b) Toward a neurobiology of temporal cognition: Advances and challenges. *Curr. Opin. Neurobiol.* 7: 170–184. The published figure was enlarged by 375%, and each datum was measured at 0.5-mm resolution. The residuals from linear regression (not shown) were not random $(r(128)_{lag1} = .454, p < .001)$. The data are plotted on a reversed-order *y*-axis to facilitate comparison with other measures of sensitivity. Bottom panel: Sensitivity is plotted as a function of time across six orders of magnitude. The data from Gibbon et al. (1997b) shown in the top panel were averaged in two-point blocks and subjected to a three-point running median. Note that sensitivity to time is characterized by local maxima at approximately 0.2-0.3, 1.2, 10, and 20 s. Note that these values are similar to the local maxima that were observed by Crystal (1999, 2001b): 0.3, 1.2, 12, and 24 s (cf. Figure 21). The residuals from linear regression (not shown) were not random $(r(63)_{lag1} = .869, p < .001)$. The data are plotted on a reversed-order *y*-axis to facilitate comparison with other measures of sensitivity. Adapted from Gibbon J, Malapani C, Dale CL, and Gallistel C (1997b) Toward a neurobiology of temporal cognition: Advances and challenges. *Curr. Opin. Neurobiol.* 7: 170–184; and Crystal JD (2006c) Sensitivity to time: Implications for the representation of time. In: Wasserman EA and Zentall TR (eds.) *Comparative cognition: Experimental explorations of animal intelligence,* 270–284. New York: Oxford University Press. Reproduced from Crystal JD (2006d) Time, place, and content. *Comp. Cogn. Behav. Rev.* 1: 53–76. with permission.

multiple cycles under the new phase regime are required to produce complete adjustment. By contrast, a hallmark feature of a pacemaker-accumulator is immediate adjustment to a resetting stimulus — meaning that complete adjustment requires presentation of a single shifted cycle. The data in **Figure 13** suggest that short-interval timing is subject to gradual phase adjustment, consistent with an oscillator mechanism.

The fourth, and final, row in **Table 1** focuses on the variance properties of oscillator and pacemaker-accumulator timing systems. Circadian timing appears to be characterized by greater precision (i.e., lower relative variability) compared to short-interval timing. The data in **Figures 17, 20, 21,** and **22** suggest that both short-interval and circadian timing are characterized by local peaks in sensitivity to time.

The data suggest substantial continuity between short-interval and circadian timing systems. Indeed, in many situations, the predictions of multiple timing mechanisms are confounded, and specific empirical tests are required to dissociate these mechanisms (e.g., Pizzo and Crystal, 2002, 2004a,b; Babb and Crystal, 2006). The data reviewed in this chapter may prompt the development of a theory of timing that encompasses the discrimination of temporal intervals across several orders of magnitude, from milliseconds to days. The proposal to integrate ideas in short-interval and circadian timing is not unprecedented given the shared genetic makeup of some behaviors over both long and short time horizons (e.g., courtship behavior and circadian period in *Drosophila melanogaster,* Roche et al., 1998).

1.19.7   Conclusions

Time is a fundamental dimension of human and animal experience, affecting behaviors that span from milliseconds to days. Indeed, timing is ubiquitous in such familiar behaviors as speech, music, and motor control in the range of milliseconds, foraging, decision making, and time perception in the seconds-to-minutes range, and sleep–wake cycles and appetite in the range of a day (Buhusi and Meck, 2005). This review has focused on (1) methods of assessing temporal performance and (2) evaluating theoretical proposals about the mechanisms responsible for temporal performance. We draw some conclusions for each of these lines of focus.

The review of experimental methods illustrates the remarkable quantitative precision that may be obtained in studying temporal performance. One of the unifying principles is the scalar property; seemingly different patterns of performance that unfold in real time may be seen as representing cases from a single process when the data are rescaled in proportional units of time. We reviewed some of the many experiments that have demonstrated the ubiquity of this feature of temporal performance.

Nevertheless, the review of theoretical proposals suggests that the observation of superimposition does not, by itself, identify the mechanism(s) responsible for temporal performance. Although superimposition of data in relative units of time is consistent with SET (a classic pacemaker-accumulator theory of timing), other timing theories are also compatible with this feature of timing data (e.g., Hopson, 2003; Killeen and Fetterman, 1988). Moreover, we reviewed a series of experiments that sought to identify data diagnostic of pacemaker-accumulator or oscillator mechanisms. The conclusion that emerges from these lines of research is that short- and long-interval timing are characterized by oscillator-like properties.

Perhaps the greatest challenge for applying an oscillator mechanism to short-interval timing is the need to have an oscillator mechanism that is flexible enough to time intervals that span several orders of magnitude. Although this has traditionally been assumed to be compatible with a pacemaker-accumulator (but not an oscillator) mechanism, the observation of oscillator-like properties in timing intervals across several orders of magnitude encourages the view that multiple oscillators may be deployed to time a broad range of intervals (Church and Broadbent, 1990; Gallistel, 1990; Crystal, 2006d). Moreover, the data reviewed in this chapter may prompt the development of a unified theory of timing that encompasses the discrimination of time across several orders of magnitude – from milliseconds to days.

References

Allan LG and Gibbon J (1991) Human bisection at the geometric mean. *Learn. Motiv.* 22: 39–58.

Aschoff J (1981) *Handbook of Behavioral Neurobiology: Biological Rhythms* (Vol. 4). New York: Plenum.

Aschoff J (1984) Circadian timing. *Ann. N. Y. Acad. Sci.* 423: 442–468.

Aschoff J (1985) On the perception of time during prolonged temporal isolation. *Hum. Neurobiol.* 4: 41–52.

Aschoff J (1989) Temporal orientation: Circadian clocks in animals and humans. *Anim. Behav.* 37: 881–896.

Aschoff J (1993) On the passage of subjective time in temporal isolation. *Psychologica Belgica* 33: 147–157.

Aschoff J (1998) Human perception of short and long time intervals: Its correlation with body temperature and the duration of wake time. *J. Biol. Rhythms* 13: 437–442.

Aschoff J and Daan S (1997) Human time perception in temporal isolation: Effects of illumination intensity. *Chronobiol. Int.* 14: 585–596.

Aschoff J, von Goetz C, and Honma K (1983) Restricted feeding in rats: Effects of varying feeding cycles. *Zeitschrift für Tierpsychologie* 63: 91–111.

Babb SJ and Crystal JD (2006) Discrimination of what, when, and where is not based on time of day. *Learn. Behav.* 34: 124–130.

Boisvert MJ and Sherry DF (2006) Interval timing by an invertebrate, the bumble bee *Bombus impatiens. Curr. Biol.* 16: 1636–1640.

Bolles RC and Stokes LW (1965) Rat's anticipation of diurnal and a-diurnal feeding. *J. Comp. Physiol. Psychol.* 60: 290–294.

Boulos Z, Rosenwasser AM, and Terman M (1980) Feeding schedules and the circadian organization of behavior in the rat. *Behav. Brain Res.* 1: 39–65.

Buhusi CV and Meck WH (2005) What makes us tick? Functional and neural mechanisms of interval timing. *Nat. Rev. Neurosci.* 6: 755–765.

Chiang T, Al-Ruwaitea A, Mobini S, Ho M, Bradshaw C, and Szabadi E (2000) The effect of d-amphetamine on performance on two operant timing schedules. *Psychopharmacology* 150: 170–184.

Church RM (1978) The internal clock. In: Hulse SH, Fowler H, and Honig WK (eds.) *Cognitive Processes in Animal Behavior*, pp. 277–310. Hillsdale, NJ: Erlbaum.

Church RM (2003) A concise introduction to scalar timing theory. In: Meck WH (ed.) *Functional and Neural Mechanisms of Interval Timing*, pp. 3–22. Boca Raton, FL: CRC Press.

Church RM and Broadbent HA (1990) Alternative representations of time, number, and rate. *Cognition* 37: 55–81.

Church RM and Deluty MZ (1977) Bisection of temporal intervals. *J. Exp. Psychol. Anim. Behav. Process.* 3: 216–228.

Church RM and Gibbon J (1982) Temporal generalization. *J. Exp. Psychol. Anim. Behav. Process.* 8: 165–186.

Church RM and Guilhardi P (2005) A Turing test of a timing theory. *Behav. Processes* 69: 45–58.

Crystal JD (1999) Systematic nonlinearities in the perception of temporal intervals. *J. Exp. Psychol. Anim. Behav. Process.* 25: 3–17.

Crystal JD (2001a) Circadian time perception. *J. Exp. Psychol. Anim. Behav. Process.* 27: 68–78.

Crystal JD (2001b) Nonlinear time perception. *Behav. Processes* 55: 35–49.

Crystal JD (2002) Timing inter-reward intervals. *Learn. Motiv.* 311–326.

Crystal JD (2003) Nonlinearities in sensitivity to time: Implications for oscillator-based representations of interval and circadian clocks. In: Meck WH (ed.) *Functional and Neural Mechanisms of Interval Timing*, pp. 61–75. Boca Raton, FL: CRC Press.

Crystal JD (2006a) Animal behavior: Timing in the wild. *Curr. Biol.* 16: R252–253.

Crystal JD (2006b) Long-interval timing is based on a self sustaining endogenous oscillator. *Behav. Processes* 72: 149–160.

Crystal JD (2006c) Sensitivity to time: Implications for the representation of time. In: Wasserman EA and Zentall TR (eds.) *Comparative Cognition: Experimental Explorations of Animal Intelligence*, pp. 270–284. New York: Oxford University Press.

Crystal JD (2006d) Time, place, and content. *Comp. Cogn. Behav. Rev.* 1: 53–76.

Crystal JD, Church RM, and Broadbent HA (1997) Systematic nonlinearities in the memory representation of time. *J. Exp. Psychol. Anim. Behav. Process.* 23: 267–282.

Crystal JD and Baramidze GT (2007) Endogenous oscillations in short-interval timing. *Behav. Processes* 74: 152–158.

Dews PB (1970) The theory of fixed-interval responding. In: Schoenfeld WN (ed.) *The Theory of Reinforcement Schedules*, pp. 43–61. New York: Appleton-Century-Crofts.

Fortin C (2003) Attentional time-sharing in interval timing. In: Meck WH (ed.) *Functional and Neural Mechanisms of Interval Timing*, pp. 235–260. Boca Raton, FL: CRC Press.

Fortin C and Massé N (2000) Expecting a break in time estimation: Attentional time-sharing without concurrent processing. *J. Exp. Psychol. Hum. Percept. Perform.* 26: 1788–1796.

Gallistel CR (1990) *The Organization of Learning*. Cambridge, MA: MIT Press.

Gibbon J, Church RM, and Meck WH (1984) Scalar timing in memory. In: Gibbon J and Allan L (eds.) *Annals of the New York Academy of Sciences: Timing and Time Perception*, Vol. 423, pp. 52–77. New York: New York Academy of Sciences.

Gibbon J, Fairhurst S, and Goldberg B (1997a) Cooperation, conflict and compromise between circadian and interval clocks in pigeons. In: Bradshaw CM and Szabadi E (eds.) *Time and Behaviour: Psychological and Neurobehavioural Analyses*, pp. 329–384. New York: Elsevier.

Gibbon J, Malapani C, Dale CL, and Gallistel C (1997b) Toward a neurobiology of temporal cognition: Advances and challenges. *Curr. Opin. Neurobiol.* 7: 170–184.

Greggers U and Menzel R (1993) Memory dynamics and foraging strategies of honeybees. *Behav. Ecol. Sociobiol.* 32: 17–29.

Guilhardi P, Keen R, MacInnis MLM, and Church RM (2005) How rats combine temporal cues. *Behav. Processes* 69: 189–205.

Henderson J, Hurly TA, Bateson M, and Healy SD (2006) Timing in free-living rufous hummingbirds, *Selasphorus rufus. Curr. Biol.* 16: 512–515.

Hopson JW (2003) General learning models: Timing without a clock. In: Meck WH (ed.) *Functional and Neural Mechanisms of Interval Timing*, pp. 23–60. Boca Raton, FL: CRC Press.

Killeen PR and Fetterman JG (1988) A behavioral theory of timing. *Psychol. Rev.* 95: 274–295.

Kirkpatrick K (2002) Packet theory of conditioning and timing. *Behav. Processes* 57: 89–106.

Kirkpatrick K and Church RM (2003) Tracking of the expected time to reinforcement in temporal conditioning procedures. *Learn. Behav.* 31: 3–21.

Macmillan NA and Creelman CD (1991) *Detection Theory: A User's Guide*. New York: Cambridge University Press.

Madrid JA, Sanchez-Vazquez FJ, Lax P, Matas P, Cuenca EM, and Zamora S (1998) Feeding behavior and entrainment limits in the circadian system of the rat. *Am. J. Physiol. Regul. Integr. Comp. Physiol.* 275: R372–R383.

Mistlberger RE and Marchant EG (1995) Computational and entrainment models of circadian food-anticipatory activity: Evidence from non-24-hr feeding schedules. *Behav. Neurosci.* 109: 790–798.

Pizzo MJ and Crystal JD (2002) Representation of time in time-place learning. *Anim. Learn. Behavr.* 30: 387–393.

Pizzo MJ and Crystal JD (2004a) Evidence for an alternation strategy in time-place learning. *Behav. Processes* 67: 533–537.

Pizzo MJ and Crystal JD (2004b) Time-place learning in the eight-arm radial maze. *Learn. Behav.* 32: 240–255.

Rakitin BC, Gibbon J, Penney TB, Malapani C, Hinton SC, and Meck WH (1998) Scalar expectancy theory and peak-interval timing in humans. *J. Exp. Psychol. Anim. Behav. Process.* 24: 15–33.

Raslear TG (1983) A test of the Pfanzagl bisection model in rats. *J. Exp. Psychol. Anim. Behav. Process.* 9: 49–62.

Roberts S (1981) Isolation of an internal clock. *J. Exp. Psychol. Anim. Behav. Process.* 7: 242–268.

Roberts WA, Cheng K, and Cohen JS (1989) Timing light and tone signals in pigeons. *J. Exp. Psychol. Anim. Behav. Process.* 15: 23–35.

Roche JP, Talyn BCP, and Dowse HB (1998) Courtship bout duration in per circadian period mutants in *Drosophila melanogaster. Behav. Genet.* 28: 391–394.

Santi A, Coppa R, and Ross L (2001) Effects of the dopamine D2 agonist, quinpirole, on time and number processing in rats. *Pharmacol. Biochem. Behav.* 68: 147–155.

Seeley TD (1995) *The Wisdom of the Hive: The Social Physiology of Honey Bee Colonies*. Cambridge, MA: Harvard University Press.

Shurtleff D, Raslear TG, Genovese RF, and Simmons L (1992) Perceptual bisection in rats: Effects of physostigmine, scopalamine and pirenzepine. *Physiol. Behav.* 51: 381–390.

Shurtleff D, Raslear TG, and Simmons L (1990) Circadian variation in time perception in rats. *Physiol. Behav.* 47: 931–939.

Siegel SF (1986) A test of the similarity model of temporal bisection. *Learn. Motiv.* 17: 59–75.

Silver R and Bittman EL (1984) Reproductive mechanisms: Interaction of circadian and interval timing. *Ann. N. Y. Acad. Sci.* 423: 488–514.

Stephan FK (1981) Limits of entrainment to periodic feeding in rats with suprachiasmatic lesions. *J. Comp. Physiol. [A]* 143: 401–410.

Stephan FK, Swann JM, and Sisk CL (1979a) Anticipation of 24-hr feeding schedules in rats with lesions of the suprachiasmatic nucleus. *Behav. Neural Biol.* 25: 346–363.

Stephan FK, Swann JM, and Sisk CL (1979b) Entrainment of circadian rhythms by feeding schedules in rats with suprachiasmatic lesions. *Behav. Neural Biol.* 25: 545–554.

Takahashi JS, Turek FW, and Moore RY (2001) *Handbook of Behavioral Neurobiology: Circadian Clocks,* Vol. 12. New York: Plenum.

Terman M, Gibbon J, Fairhurst S, and Waring A (1984) Daily meal anticipation: Interaction of circadian and interval timing. *Ann. N. Y. Acad. Sci.* 423: 470–487.

Wearden JH (1992) Temporal generalization in humans. *J. Exp. Psychol. Anim. Behav. Process.* 18: 134–144.

Wearden JH, Denovan L, Fakhri M, and Haworth R (1997) Scalar timing in temporal generalization in humans with longer stimulus durations. *J. Exp. Psychol. Anim. Behav. Process.* 23: 502–511.

Wearden JH and Ferrara A (1996) Stimulus range effects in temporal bisection by humans. *Q. J. Exp. Psychol.* 49B: 24–44.

Wearden JH, Rogers P, and Thomas R (1997) Temporal bisection in humans with longer stimulus durations. *Q. J. Exp. Psychol.* 50B: 79–94.

Wearden JH and Towse JN (1994) Temporal generalization in humans: Three further studies. *Behav. Processes* 32: 247–264.

Whishaw IQ (1990) Time estimates contribute to food handling decisions by rats: Implications for neural control of hoarding. *Psychobiology* 18: 460–466.

Whishaw IQ and Tomie J (1989) Food-pellet size modifies the hoarding behavior of foraging rats. *Psychobiology* 17: 93–101.

White W and Timberlake W (1999) Meal-engendered circadian-ensuing activity in rats. *Physiol. Behav.* 65: 625–642.

1.20 Foraging

D. W. Stephens and A. S. Dunlap, University of Minnesota, St. Paul, MN, USA

1.20.1 Introduction

The oldest organisms on earth live on isolated peaks in the Great Basin. These bristlecone pines look like giant bonsai trees, twisted against the harsh conditions of the high, cold desert. The oldest of these trees are over 4500 years old. They have lived through most of recorded human history, but they do not remember. Indeed, students of learning and memory seldom give plants – whether old or young – a passing thought. It is, however, instructive to recall the differences between plants and animals and to ask whether these differences can tell us something about why one group comes equipped to learn and remember while the other does not. Nearly any introductory biology book will direct your attention to three key differences: animals move, animals have nervous systems, and animals consume living things. These three elements represent a deeply intertwined syndrome of animal features. A plant living in a flux of photons and a sea of CO_2 does not need to move. In contrast, living tissues do not flow into an animal's mouth. For animals, pastures are always greener elsewhere (often quite literally!), so animals need to move to find a fresh supply of living resources. And, of course, animals need nervous systems, and ultimately the ability to learn and remember, to control and refine these movements.

The business of acquiring and consuming living resources ranges from the spectacular – a spider swinging a bola of sticky silk to ensnare prey – to the mundane – cows eating grass. Whatever form it takes, it is a basic feature of the animal way of life. It follows that an understanding of foraging behavior is fundamental to our understanding of animal behavior and the mechanisms that control it, including learning and memory. To begin, we consider a concrete example that illustrates the role of learning and memory in foraging.

On summer mornings from July to September masses of tiny mayflies (genus *Tricorythyodes*) emerge from cold water streams in North America. The emergence occurs in the early morning. In the hour after dawn, clouds of these tiny flies hover over every riffle in the river. These clouds are mating swarms. As the mating swarms develop, fish in the stream below move into positions downstream of the swarming flies in the workman like manner of commuters arriving at their jobs. An hour and 30 minutes after dawn the mating swarms begin to break up as the mated adults die. Their bodies cover the surface of the stream and create a feeding bonanza for the waiting fish. Although the mayflies fall indiscriminately, the currents and properties of the streambed concentrate the food. The waiting fish are clearly sensitive to these hotspots, because as the mayflies continue to cover the water, one can see patches of the stream where the surface boils with the activity of feeding fish. The ecological drama ends as suddenly as it began. A few hours after dawn the mayflies will have been swept away by the current, and the fish will have dispersed to stations throughout the river.

This predictable daily drama is typical of the situations in which learning abilities guide animal feeding behavior. Like our feeding trout, honeybees and other nectar feeders are, for example, famous for learning the temporal availability and spatial pattern of food sources (*See* Chapters 1.25, 1.29). Feeding blue jays, to take another example, learn that monarch butterflies taste bad due to cardiac glycosides that the butterflies obtain as caterpillars. Broadly speaking, foraging animals clearly learn many basic properties of their prey: how to handle them (e.g., remove spines, avoid stinging parts), where they can be found (under leaves? on tree bark?), and so on. Similarly, foraging animals use memory to guide their decisions about which patches to exploit and when to exploit them. Animals that store food for later retrieval offer an especially compelling example. Clearly, the ability to relocate hidden food items is a basic feature of animal food-caching behavior. Over the last 20 years investigators have exploited

this behavior to produce new insights in how memory serves animals in naturally occurring resource gathering (*See* Chapter 1.22). Recently, for example, Clayton and Dickinson (1998) have exploited this aspect of foraging behavior to provide the first evidence that nonhumans can form 'episodic-like' memories (*See* Chapter 1.23).

As these remarks show, learning and memory play key roles in the day-to-day business of resource acquisition. In contrast, many of the classical methods for studying learning and memory seem abstract and somewhat contrived. Yet, there are deep connections between the two. One connection is procedural; food acquisition serves as a useful context with which to study learning and memory. Pavlov's dogs salivate in anticipation of food, Skinner's pigeons peck for access to food, and Olton's rats run down the arms of a radial arm maze to obtain food. It behooves students of learning and memory, therefore, to understand how the components of foraging behavior they study fit within the larger context of animal foraging. The second connection is more conceptual; a complete understanding of learning and memory will require analyses at all levels of biological organization from the molecular to the ecological, and foraging behavior stands out as one of the simplest situations in which to seek an understanding of the ecological significance of learning and memory.

1.20.1.1 Foraging Basics

Foraging refers to the business of food acquisition. Although we restrict the definition to food acquisition, ecologists commonly apply similar principles to other forms of resource acquisition (e.g., 'foraging' for mates). As a broad generalization, foraging is a relatively common and easily observed aspect of animal behavior (*See* Chapters 1.12, 1.21). As explained earlier, foraging is a fundamental component of animal existence both because it is a defining property of animals, and because it provides the fuel for the remainder of an animal's activities. Students of foraging behavior (Stephens and Krebs, 1986; Stephens et al., 2007) typically envision a three-level hierarchy of resources. At the highest level, animals forage within *habitats*. For example, a hummingbird may choose to feed in an alpine meadow or along a stream bank. Choosing a habitat determines the mix of resources that a forager will encounter at a fairly large spatial and temporal scale. Typically, we imagine that it is time consuming or costly to switch habitats. Food is virtually never spread evenly throughout a habitat, so it is useful to imagine that food occurs in discrete *patches* within habitats. So our hummingbird would encounter clumps of flowers within the alpine meadow. In practice, of course, the 'edges' of food patches are often fuzzy, but foraging models typically ignore this. In contrast with habitats, we imagine that a forager encounters many patches during any given foraging bout, and that it may choose to exploit or ignore any given patch it encounters. However, a forager must also choose how thoroughly a given patch should be exploited. Finally, within patches we commonly imagine that the forager finds *prey* items such as seeds or insects. For our hummingbird, the flower within an inflorescence would serve as prey. While the distinction between patches and prey is usually clear-cut, it can also be subtle. Economically, the key point is that a forager can choose how to exploit a patch, but it can only choose whether to exploit a prey item. Notice finally that we call discrete food items *prey* regardless of whether they are animals or plants.

1.20.2 Basic Foraging Models

Over the last 20 years, behavioral ecologists have developed a basic set of models that make predictions about foraging behavior in a wide range of 'standard' foraging situations (Stephens and Krebs, 1986; Stephens et al., 2007). In the next few paragraphs, we present these models following the hierarchy discussed in the previous section. We begin by discussing prey choice (the lowest level), then we discuss patch exploitation, and finally we discuss habitat choice. All of these models follow the premise of rate maximization. Crudely speaking, we know both from empirical studies of food choice behavior and from first principles that both time and amount matter to foraging animals, and rate represents a simple and natural way to combine time and amount. More formally, the hypothesis of rate maximization holds that natural selection favors behaviors that lead to high rates of food intake, because animals that obtain food at a high rate will have more time and more resources to pursue other important activities (like mating, or territorial defense). One can, of course, imagine situations in which rate maximization would be inappropriate (for example, if the habitat that provides the higher rate of food intake also has the most predators). As one might expect, many papers focus on situations in which this 'standard' assumption does not hold. Nonetheless, the premise of rate maximizing

represents a useful way to begin our analysis of how economic forces shape foraging behavior.

1.20.2.1 Prey Choice

Consider a bird searching for moths – prey items – along a tree trunk. We think of these items as particles dispersed through the environment that the animal 'bumps into' as it moves. Of course, there are different types of prey items. Our bird may encounter some small grey moths and some large white moths. The prey types vary in three ways. First, prey types provide different amounts of energy when consumed. To continue our example, small grey moths may provide 1.8 J when consumed, while large white moths provide 6.0 J. Second, prey take different amounts of time to pursue, handle, and consume – collectively we call this handling time. Small grey moths may require 10 s to handle, while the larger white moths take 25 s to handle. Finally, prey types have different abundances. Some types are common so the forager encounters them relatively frequently, while others are rare. This may seem like an odd way to introduce the simple idea of relative abundance, but to simplify our rate calculations we think of the average time between encounters with a particular prey type rather than using direct measures of abundance. The inverse of the time between encounters is the encounter rate, and generally speaking, abundant prey have high encounter rates. To summarize, we characterize prey items by their energy values, their handling times, and their encounter rates.

So, we have our bird hopping along a tree trunk encountering grey and white moths; now we need to think how the bird can express a choice. We will assume that the bird can decide whether to attack or ignore a given type when it is encountered. Mathematically, we represent this as a probability of attack upon encounter, and we have two such probabilities, one for the small gray moths and one for the large white moths. Now our mathematical problem is to find the attack probabilities that give the highest rate of energy intake. To do this, we need to express the intake in terms of the variables outlined here – encounter rates, handling times, energy value, and attack probabilities. This is fairly easy with one final trick. We recognize that our animal spends its time doing two things: searching and handling. By definition, if the λ_1 is the encounter rate of prey type 1, then an animal that searches for T_s units will encounter (not eat but encounter) $\lambda_1 T_s$ type 1 items, and similarly it will encounter $\lambda_2 T_s$ type 2 items.

Since our forager accepts type 1 items it encounters with probability p_1, the number it accepts in T_s units of searching is $p_1\lambda_1 T_s$; similarly the number of type 2s it accepts is $p_2\lambda_2 T_s$. Now we know each type 1 prey item requires h_1 time units to handle and provides e_1 calories; while each type 2 prey item takes h_2 time units to handle and provides e_2 calories. So, the rate we want to calculate is just the energy gain $(e_1 p_1\lambda_1 T_s + e_2 p_2\lambda_2 T_s)$ divided by the total time $(T_s + h_1 p_1\lambda_1 T_s + h_2 p_2\lambda_2 T_s)$. The rate of intake is

$$\frac{p_1\lambda_1 T_s e_1 + p_2\lambda_2 T_s e_2}{T_s + p_1\lambda_1 T_s h_1 + p_2\lambda_2 T_s h_2} \qquad [1]$$

Since T_s is a common factor in every term in both the numerator and denominator, it cancels out to leave us with

$$\frac{p_1\lambda_1 e_1 + p_2 T_s e_2}{1 + p_1\lambda_1 h_1 + p_2\lambda_2 h_2} \qquad [2]$$

More generally we have

$$\frac{\sum_i p_i\lambda_i e_i}{1 + \sum_i p_i\lambda_i h_i} \qquad [3]$$

This final form is commonly called 'Holling's disc equation' (Holling, 1959) and is the conventional expression for intake rate used in foraging models. The development we followed in the preceding paragraphs shows the central assumption of Holling's disc equation; specifically, it assumes that foraging animals are either searching or handling, and that these are mutually exclusive activities. In broad overview this is a useful assumption that describes the way in which many animals feed; however, there are some important situations in which animals can handle and search simultaneously. Notably, grazing animals can often 'search for the next blade of grass' while they handle (chew) previously encountered grass blades (Spalinger and Hobbs, 1992; Illius et al., 2000).

Now that we have an expression for rate, our problem is to find the probabilities of attack that maximize this rate. This is a straightforward mathematical operation that we can solve via calculus, and which we will not pursue here. We can understand the results without working through the calculus. First, we find that the rate-maximizing value of p_i should be either zero or one; that is, our forager should always attack or always ignore the ith prey type upon encounter. Once we know this, we can ask which types should be ignored and which should be attacked. Suppose, for example, that a hypothetical

forager is attacking types A and B; should it also attack type C? If we use Holling's disc equation to compare the rates of intake for a 'diet' of A and B alone to a diet of A, B, and C, then we find the effect of adding C depends on the type C's ratio of energy to handling time (e_c/h_c). We call these energy-to-handling-time ratios 'profitabilities,' and these are key variables to understanding the economics of prey choice. The basic algebraic result is that adding item C to the diet increases the overall rate of intake if C's profitability is greater than the intake rate obtained from a diet of A and B alone. This leads to the idea that foragers should rank prey types by their profitabilities. So we assign the prey type with the highest profitability rank 1, and second highest rank 2, and so on. Then, we can find the diet that maximizes intake rate by working through the prey types in rank order until we reach a situation where the rate obtained from attacking types 1 through N exceeds the profitability of the type $N+1$.

This economically derived, rate-maximizing 'diet' has several intriguing properties. First, it predicts, rather surprisingly, that animals should always take a given type upon encounter or always ignore it. This claim may surprise the casual observer, because people think of mixed-diets or 'well-balanced' diets as good diets. But this model only considers a single dimension of prey value (typically energy content), and so it cannot consider well-balanced diets. However, the idea of a 'single dimension of value' is often appropriate. In experimental studies, we often create prey types (or their logical equivalents) that value only in magnitude (e.g., big vs. small), and in nature many foragers eat a range of food items with similar nutrient contents (e.g., from the perspective of an insectivorous bird most insects have about the same balance of proteins and carbohydrates). Empirically, however, this so-called 'zero-one' rule seldom holds. Second, and most importantly, the model predicts that the better-ranked prey types control whether lower-ranked items should be attacked. When the good prey types are plentiful, foragers should ignore poorer prey types regardless of the abundance of these poorer prey types. Indeed, it is now a widely accepted principle that, in a rich environment (where foragers can easily obtain high-quality prey), animals will feed more selectively.

1.20.2.2 Patch Exploitation

At the next higher level of organization, we imagine that foragers encounter clumps of resources or patches. Our forager finds food inside well-defined and easily recognized patches but travels between patches by crossing 'empty' space to reach the next patch. In practice, a foraging patch for a small insectivorous bird might be pine cones in which insects hide, or for an aquatic snail it might be the sunlit top of a rock on which algae grow. When we think of prey items, we think of entities that provide a given amount of food in a given amount of time, but animals exploit patches more flexibly. Our insectivorous bird might 'skim the cream' from a patch by quickly extracting the obvious and easily captured prey and then moving to another fresher patch. Alternatively, it might exploit the patch thoroughly by meticulously peering behind every scale of the pine cone before traveling to the next patch. To represent this flexibility, we plot a gain function that represents the relationship between time spent exploiting a patch and amount of food extracted from a patch. **Figure 1** shows a typical gain function.

Patches deplete, of course, so as the figure shows, we expect that gains within a patch will increase at a declining rate, so the gain functions usually bend down as the example in the figure shows. A 'cream skimmer' will leave the patch early, when the gain function is still increasing relatively steeply; while a 'thorough exploiter' will stay much longer, until the curve flattens out. Both strategies have risks, of course. The 'cream skimmer' risks spending too much time unproductively traveling between patches, while the 'thorough exploiter' risks wasting time in the current patch when there are richer fresh patches to be had.

Foraging theory's models of patch exploitation address the balance between cream skimming and thorough exploitation directly. Again, we begin by

expressing the rate of food acquisition (again using eqn [3], Holling's disc equation). Let τ be the mean travel time, that is, the time it takes our forager to move from one patch to the next. Let t be the patch residence time. The variable t is the variable of interest here, because a small t corresponds with a cream-skimming strategy, while a large t implies thorough exploitation. Finally, let $g(t)$ be the gain function. Specifically, $g(t)$ gives the energy gains obtained when our forager exploits a patch for t units of time. So

$$\frac{g(t)}{\tau + t} \qquad [4]$$

gives the rate of energy intake for single patch type. Although one can solve this problem via calculus (find the t value that maximizes intake rate), there is an elegant and informative graphical solution.

Figure 2 shows the graphical solution.

We draw the gain function in the right-hand panel, so that patch residence time (t) is on the x-axis and energy gain is on the y-axis. Next we do something a bit unconventional. We let the negative part of the x-axis represent travel time (τ), with travel time increasing as we move away from the origin. Now for a given patch residence time, the intake rate (eqn [4]) is the slope of line drawn from travel time on the (usually) negative part of the x-axis to the point (t, $g(t)$) on the gain curve. If you imagine this point on the gain curve sliding up and down along the curve as we simultaneously maintain the straight line connecting our point to the travel time on the left side of the x-axis, then it is easy to see that the highest slope (and hence the highest rate) occurs when the line is just tangent to the gain curve.

Now that we know how to find the patch residence time that gives the highest rate, we can ask how the properties of the model determine the best patch residence time. There are two things within this simplified version of the model that we can consider: the gain function ($g(t)$) and the travel time (τ). The effects of travel time on patch exploitation have attracted the most attention. Broadly speaking, if the habitat is poor, then travel times will be long, but if the habitat is rich, then travel times will be short. If travel times are short, our tangent-construction solution predicts shorter exploitation times. Intuitively, in rich habitats foragers should adopt a cream-skimming strategy. In contrast, when travel times are long, the tangent-construction method shows that we should expect longer exploitation times. In poor habitats, then, we expect foragers to

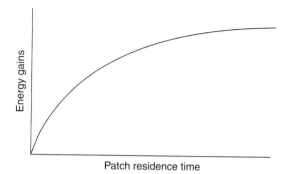

Figure 1 A typical patch gain curve. The x-axis shows the time spent exploiting a patch, and the y-axis shows the energy extracted from the patch. The forager extracts more energy as it spends more time in the patch, but this relationship tends to bend down because the patch depletes.

(a)

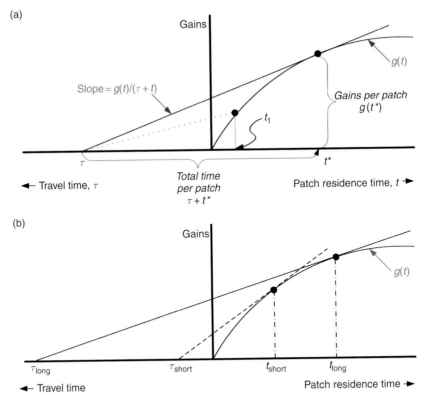

Figure 2 The graphical solution of the rate-maximizing patch exploitation time, sometimes called a Cowie plot or a rooted-tangent plot. Panel (a) shows the graphical method of find the patch residence time (t) that maximizes the forager's intake rate. On the x-axis we plot patch residence time (t) increasing to the right of the origin and travel time (τ) increasing to the left of the origin. The y-axis shows the energy gains as in **Figure 1**. The slope of a line drawn from a given travel time on the left side of the x-axis to a point on the gain curve on the right gives the intake rate associated with the corresponding patch residence time (t). Algebraically the slope of this line is $g(t)/(\tau + t)$, the quantity that our model seeks to maximize. One can readily see that the highest slope corresponds to a line that is just tangent to the gain function. The solid diagonal line illustrates this. Note that a line drawn to any other point on the gain curve will give a lower slope, as the dotted diagonal line shows. Panel (b) shows the main prediction of the model. When the travel time is long (τ_{long}), our tangent construction solution gives a long patch residence time (t_{long}), but when the travel time is short (τ_{short}), we predict a shorter patch residence time (t_{short}).

follow a 'thorough exploiter' strategy. The data provide strong support for the qualitative claim of cream-skimming in rich habitats and thorough exploiting in poor habitats. Indeed, this simple observation may be the single best-supported theoretical prediction from behavioral ecology. An appealing feature of this result is that we can understand it by comparing the value of continuing to exploit the present patch to the value of leaving to find a new patch. Short travel times increase the value of 'leaving,' and so we predict leaving earlier. The simplicity of this value of staying versus value of leaving comparison is important because, as we will see, it is the key to generalizing the model to more complex situations.

Gain functions can vary in a virtually unlimited number of ways, but our simple tangent construction method quickly shows the effects of different shapes.

For example, if foragers can search systematically, their gains will follow a simple straight line up to some maximum. The gain function for systematic search will be a straight line from zero to the maximum, and then it will kink and become a flat line at the maximum food obtainable from the patch. Our tangent construction method shows the highest obtainable corresponds to a line intersecting the 'kink' (predicting that foragers should stay until they have extracted the maximum amount, but no longer) in this special case. Obviously, we would predict no travel time effect in this situation. Again, this makes sense when we consider the value of staying versus the value of leaving. There is no point in leaving until you have extracted the maximum amount of food, because the very best thing that could happen if you leave is to encounter a new patch with the same linear rate of gain.

The behaviors associated with patch exploitation have not been widely used in studies of learning and memory, and this is unfortunate, because patch exploitation is an important and well-documented aspect of natural foraging behavior. In addition, the successful family of models described here provides useful insights into the economic forces that have shaped patch exploitation.

1.20.2.3 Ideal-Free Distribution

Now consider a simple and somewhat artificial situation in which each of two sites provide food, say site 1 and site 2. Some distance separates the two sources, so that a forager cannot feed at both sites simultaneously, but must choose whether to feed at site 1 or site 2. Now, suppose that site 1 provides food at a rate of 10 J per hour (call this r_1), while site 2 delivers food at a rate of 5 J per hour (call this r_2). Economically, this is a trivial problem. Any sensible economic agent would stick with the site that delivers resources at the highest rate. This situation is not terribly interesting as it stands, but it becomes much more interesting when we imagine several foragers exploiting the same pair of feeding sites.

If several foragers all move to the single best site, they will have to share the food available there, and this raises the possibility that some of the members of the group could do better by moving to the other, less desirable site. The simplest model that addresses this question is called the ideal-free distribution. Like the two models discussed above, a review of this model provides significant insight into the economic logic of group foraging. To begin, imagine a group of six fish, with two at site 1 and four at site 2. Now if we assume that the fish at site 1 roughly share the food arriving there, then each expects to gain 10 J per hour divided by 2, or by 5 J per hour; using the same reasoning the four fish at site 2 expect to gain 1.25 J per hour per fish (i.e., 5/4). In this situation, we would expect that at least one of the fish at site 2 would be tempted to move to site 1 where it can do better, so we would have 3 fish at site 1 and 3 fish at site 2. But now the per-fish rate at site 1 would be 3.3 J per hour (10/3), while the per-fish rate at site 2 is 1.67 J per hour (5/3). So fish at site 2 are still doing worse, and at least one of them should be tempted to move to site 1, making the distribution four fish at site 1 and two fish at site 2. Now, the per-fish rate at site 1 is $10/4 = 2.5$ J h^{-1}, and the per-fish rate at site 2 is $5/2 = 2.5$ J h^{-1}. In this situation, no individuals are tempted to move to the opposite site. So we conclude that this four and two arrangement is stable, and we would expect this pattern to persist. Notice that, in our

imaginary scenario, the fish have arranged themselves in a way that matches the inputs to the two sites. This 'input matching' result is the basic prediction of the ideal-free distribution model. This input-matching prediction holds reasonably well in experimental studies of animal feeding groups, even though the idealized assumptions of the model seldom hold. For example, the assumption that individuals share equally at feeding sites almost never holds, because some animals compete more effectively than others. Typically, this does not affect the input-matching result too much, because good competitors tend to occur at all feeding sites.

Logically, the ideal-free distribution's prediction of the input matching is quite similar to Herrnstein's matching law (Herrnstein, 1974), which predicts that individuals should distribute responses across two options in a way that matches the rates of food delivery associated with those responses. The matching law, however, focuses on the behavior of individuals, while the ideal-free model considers how the actions of individuals determine the properties of groups. While one derives the ideal-free model from very simple economic considerations, input matching for individuals (as the matching law predicts) only makes economic sense when rewards wait to be collected, as they commonly do in variable interval schedules.

1.20.2.4 General Principles and Conclusions

The central idea in the described models is the economics of lost opportunity. In prey selection a forager may reject a mediocre item, because to accept it means that the forager may miss an opportunity to obtain a better item. A forager exploiting patches in a rich environment leaves early, because it will lose opportunities to exploit new patches if it stays too long. A forager, feeding in a group, may choose to feed at a less productive site because competitors at the more productive site reduce the opportunities for success there. One should view these three basic models as starting points which, taken together, identify many fundamental variables in foraging behavior and draw our attention to the fundamental role of opportunity costs in foraging behavior.

Behavioral ecologists have extended these models in several significant ways. For example, these models tacitly assume that we can use averages to characterize the properties of resources (patches, prey, foraging sites). Models of risk-sensitive foraging consider the economic consequences of variability, predicting, for example, that foragers may prefer to take risks when their energy supply is very low, even though they should avoid risks when they are well-off (Bateson and Kacelnik, 1998). Another important theme has been the effects of predation. While the described models only consider energy and time, it is often the case that the best places to forage (sites or patches) are also the most dangerous. Predators, after all, readily learn where prey are concentrated. The threat of predation can have dramatic effects on the behavior of foragers (see the section titled 'Foraging and predator avoidance').

1.20.2.5 Connections to Learning and Memory

Virtually all experimental tests of foraging models rely on learning. For example, in a now classic test of the diet model, Krebs et al. (1977) allowed foraging great tits (a small European bird) to watch prey items passing by on a small conveyor belt. They used the conveyor belt to manipulate encounter rate, and they found that the encounter rate with the highest quality items determined selectivity as the prey model predicted. Obviously great tits did not evolve collecting meal worms from conveyor belts, so their experience must have determined their choice behavior in Krebs et al.'s experiment. In light of experiments like Krebs et al.'s, behavioral ecologists – a group stolidly committed to the idea that muddy boots are required equipment for behavioral studies – came to the realization that they could design better experiments and build more testable models by attending to the large extant literature of animal learning and memory.

Some students of foraging have taken the connection with learning a step further by directly considering the fitness value of learning in foraging situations. Imagine, for example, that the quality of a foraging site changes unpredictably according to some mathematically well-defined process. One can then ask whether a forager should use its experience with this variable resource to determine whether to exploit or ignore this resource (see, for example, Krebs et al., 1978; Lima, 1985; Stephens, 1987, 1989, 1991; Tamm, 1987; Shettleworth et al., 1988). The next section discusses this approach in more detail.

1.20.3 Behavioral Ecology of Learning and Memory

Foragers live in a changing world. In the morning, the best feeding sites may be below riffles, while deep pools provide the best foraging in the evening.

Competitors and predators may appear unpredictably. Foragers may encounter new prey types as the seasons progress or as the forager moves through its environment. Foragers need mechanisms that help them adjust to these changes, and surely learning and memory are a central part of this toolkit. In stark contrast to the world of change and the subsequent need for adjustment that real foragers face, the basic models of foraging (discussed in the previous section) assume that foragers can act with complete information about their options. Behavioral ecologists have used the machinery of statistical decision theory (Dall et al, 2005) to relax this complete information assumption. The family of models derived from these efforts considers the economics of adjusting to change. These 'incomplete information' models ask when and if it pays to learn about changing resources. The results, we argue, provide the foundation for an evolutionary approach to learning and memory and illustrate how an understanding of foraging can contribute to an enlarged view of the biology of learning and memory.

We will outline three basic approaches to the problems faced by an incompletely informed forager. To begin, we develop a simple model that calculates the value of information. This introduces the idea of environmental uncertainty and focuses our attention on the connection between information and action. Second, we move toward a model of learning by considering the economics of tracking a varying resource. In tracking models we explicitly consider how change generates uncertainty, and how animals may be sensitive to the properties of environmental change. Finally, we briefly discuss how environmental changes and the reliability of experience should influence memory.

1.20.3.1 The Value of Information

The working assumption of behavioral ecologists interested in learning and memory is that animals learn and remember things because acquiring and retaining particular kinds of information produces fitness benefits. Behavioral ecologists generally expect, therefore, that animals should learn and remember more valuable information more readily. But what makes information valuable and why would some types of information be more valuable than others?

To answer this question, imagine a simple situation in which some relevant state of the world (a prey type, a feeding site, . . .) can be any of several states. To be concrete, consider a squirrel foraging from pinecones.

Some pinecones are good feeding sites, others are mediocre, and still others are poor feeding sites. Our hypothetical squirrel cannot tell which is which. So when is information about pinecone type valuable? To find the value of information, we imagine two situations. First, suppose that the squirrel can recognize pinecone types perfectly. If this is true, then it should able to adopt an exploitation strategy that is appropriate for each pinecone type: aggressively exploiting good pinecones, skimming the cream from mediocre pine cones, and completely ignoring poor pinecones. Given the mix of pinecone types in the environment and our knowledge of how a 'knowledgeable' squirrel would treat them, we can – in theory – calculate the expected benefits of being completely informed about pinecone quality. Now, imagine the other extreme. Suppose that our squirrel cannot recognize pinecone quality, so it must treat all pinecones in the same way. Specifically, the best an ignorant squirrel can do is to adopt some average exploitation strategy that represents a compromise between the three types. Again, we can – in theory – calculate the expected benefit that an ignorant squirrel can achieve. The value of information about pinecone type is the difference between the expected benefits that a completely informed forager can obtain and the benefits expected by an 'ignorant' forager who must choose a single compromise tactic to suit all situations.

The general lesson here derives from the focus on action. The difference between informed and uninformed foragers is that the informed forager can treat different states differently, while the uninformed forager must adopt a single one-size-fits-all strategy. It follows that the value of information flows, in a very fundamental way, from information's potential to guide actions. Consider, for example, a situation in which the best way to exploit our hypothetical pinecones is the same regardless of type. What is the value of information then? Clearly, it must be zero. Because if the best action for all three types is the same, then an ignorant forager can adopt this single best action and do just as well as an informed forager. So, if a source of information cannot reveal something that will change the forager's action, then according to this definition it is not valuable. Valuable sources of information have the potential to change behavior.

1.20.3.2 Tracking

The value of information approach imagines a static but uncertain world – pinecones may be good or bad – and we ask whether a forager should make an effort to find out. In many important natural situations the properties of resources change: pinecones are bad now, but they might improve in the future. This is the problem of environmental tracking. It represents an important next step in models of uncertainty, because it considers the effects of environmental change. By considering change, tracking models make a more direct connection to studies of learning, because we think of learning as a mechanism that helps animals adjust to changing environments.

Tracking models usually assume that some aspect of the environment, say the quality of a feeding site, changes according to some stochastic process. A typical 'tracking' analysis might model the process of environmental change by assuming that the state stays the same from one time period to the next with a constant probability. If this persistence probability is high, the forager experiences relatively long runs of the same state (e.g., the varying site stays in the good state for a long time), but if the persistence probability is low, the state changes frequently. Finally, we imagine that the forager has some alternative but mediocre resource to exploit. So the varying site is the best choice when it is in the good state, but the mediocre alternative is best when the varying site is in the bad state. These assumptions create a basic tracking problem. The forager must somehow use its experience to decide whether to exploit the varying resource or the constant but mediocre resource. Specifically, we can ask how frequently the forager should check the state of the varying resource, given that its last observation showed that the varying resource was in the bad state. The optimal sampling frequency depends on how frequently the environment changes and on the underlying payoffs (i.e., the value of the varying resource when it is good, the value of the varying resource when it is bad, and the value of the constant-mediocre resource). A striking feature of the optimal solution is that it does not make economic sense to sample in many situations. The region which it makes economic sense to sample increases with environmental persistence. When there is no environmental persistence, the varying resource changes randomly from one time to the next, so the forager has no option but to use the resource that yields the highest gains on average (a strategy called averaging). However, when persistence increases, the varying resource switches between long runs of good and bad, and now it makes sense to keep track of the varying resource's state. Recognizing that 'averaging' is the alternative to sampling, one can readily see that tracking will be most useful when the forager's alternatives are about the same on average. If they are quite different on average, then a nonsampling strategy that sticks with the better of the two options will often be the most sensible choice.

A handful of experimental studies have tested the predictions of these optimal tracking models (Tamm, 1987; Shettleworth et al., 1988; Inman, 1990). A recent review by Stephens (2007) found that animals tend to sample less frequently when environmental persistence is high, as these models predict. In addition, they sample less when we experimentally increase the value of the mediocre-stable resource. Again, this is as we would predict, because when the constant resource is good, there is less value in detecting the onset of a good state. On the other hand, our models predict that increasing the value of the varying resource's good state should increase the sampling rate, but the three experimental studies we have on the topic show no consistent effect of this variable. While our economic model agrees qualitatively with observations, Shettleworth et al. (1988) reported that a mechanistic model based on scalar expectancy gave a better quantitative fit to their data.

1.20.3.3   Optimal Memory

The tracking models discussed in the previous section greatly oversimplify how animals respond to experience. For example, they often assume that a single 'sample' is sufficient to instantly change a forager's behavior. An obvious next step asks how animals integrate information from many experiences, and specifically how foragers should combine past and current experience. This leads us to questions about the economics of memory in changing environments. While there is comparatively little work on the behavioral ecology of memory, those studies which have modeled memory have taken one of two approaches. One family of models (e.g., Cowie, 1977) represents memory as a sliding window, e.g., all experience from the last 4 days is weighted equally. These models typically try to understand how the optimal length of the memory window depends on the properties of environment (e.g., rates of change, reliability of experience, and so on). The second approach uses a past versus present weighting system to represent memory (McNamara and Houston, 1987). This approach is reminiscent of Bush and Mosteller's old stochastic learning rules (Bush and Mosteller, 1955). At each trial the animal's judgment (say x) of the current state of the environment is updated via a linear weighting

scheme that puts some weight on the previous judgment and some weight on the animal's most recent experience. In these models, one tries to find the optimal past/present weighting. Of course, both approaches are simplistic mathematical expedients that caricature memory. Both schemes can be extended and elaborated in various ways. For example, one can create a hybrid model by adding a weighting scheme (which weights recent experience more heavily than past experience) to the memory window formulation (see, for example, Hirvonen et al., 1991).

Two economic variables should, in theory, affect how foragers should strike a balance between past and present information. The first key variable is the environmental rate of change. Animals that experience high rates of change should weight recent experience heavily and devalue past experience (i.e., they should have a short memory window). The second key variable is the reliability of experience. Consider a situation with two prey types: good and bad. However, the world is a noisy place, so our hypothetical forager experiences the good state as a distribution of qualities from very good to relatively poor. When the resource quality varies like this, a single experience will not be enough to discriminate between good and bad states. The logic here parallels the statistical concept of standard error: the variance of the measured quantity and the sample size combine to determine the error in our estimate of the mean. When experience is an unreliable guide to the underlying state, then foragers need past information (i.e., a larger sample size) to reasonably characterize the current state. So when experience is unreliable, we expect foragers to weight past experience more heavily (i.e., to have longer memory windows).

Two empirical studies support the idea that change 'shortens' an animal's time horizon. Devenport and Devenport (1994) studied ground squirrels foraging from two baited feeding stations. In one treatment the quality of the stations changed frequently (Left-best, then Right-best, and so on), but in the second treatment the good station was always the same. Next, Devenport and Devenport observed which station the squirrels selected after an experimentally imposed retention interval. Squirrels in the stable environment group always returned to the site that had been best regardless of the retention interval. However, squirrels in the varying environment treatment returned to the old 'best site' after short retention intervals but choose randomly after long intervals. In a similar set of studies Cuthill and colleagues tested the effects of varying travel time on the patch exploitation behavior of starlings. In one study Cuthill et al. (1994) slowly changed the experimentally imposed travel time (from long to short or from short to long). In this slowly changing environment regime, they found that starlings needed experience with several 'long' travel times to appropriately change their patch exploitation behavior. In another study, however, Cuthill et al. (1990) created a rapidly changing environment by alternating long and short travel times. In this situation, they found that starlings adjusted their patch exploitation behavior after a single experience with a 'long' travel time. We readily acknowledge that these studies do not necessarily show differences in memory. It could be for example, that the Devenports' variable-environment squirrels remember the previous state perfectly, but somehow choose not to act on it (a variant of the well-known learning-performance distinction). However, the observation that environmental change influences how the animals integrate information across various time scales seems important and basic regardless of whether this happens via memory or some other mechanism. Although we do not discuss specific mechanisms here, one potential mechanism may not even be through the weighting of specific memories, but in the processes by which these memories are formed, with regards to time course, stages, and the use of multiple sites and substrates (see Menzel, 1999).

1.20.3.4 What Not to Learn and Remember

As students of learning and memory we tend to assume that these fundamental abilities serve animals effectively in many situations, including, but not limited to, foraging behavior. Yet the models reviewed here reveal many situations where it does not pay to attend to experience: there is no benefit in attending to information that cannot change behavior; when the environment changes frequently, simple fixed strategies can often outperform learning; similarly in an environment with rapid change, the contents of long-term memory will often be hopelessly out of date and misleading. Indeed, if we considered the costs of implementing learning and memory (Dukas, 1999), the conditions that favor learning would be even more restrictive. We do not want to overstate the case, however. Animals clearly derive benefits from learning and memory in many situations, but animals do not learn and remember everything. The ideas presented here provide a useful starting point for analyses that consider the ecological relevance of learning and memory. Do animals adaptively forget in changing

environments? Do they filter out experiences that cannot change behavior? A research program that considers the role of learning and memory in foraging and other significant natural contexts may help answer questions like these.

1.20.4 How Learning Constrains Foraging

The previous section discussed how models and data from foraging can inform our thinking about learning and memory. The interactions between foraging and learning, however, run in two directions. This section briefly discusses how results from the study of learning and memory can refine the study of foraging. Consider a migrating bird arriving in a new location. Likely, it will be familiar with the types of prey available at the new site: beetles look very much like beetles everywhere. While many of the new beetle prey will be nutritious and edible, some will probably taste bad or spray noxious chemicals that our hypothetical immigrant has never experienced before. Clearly, the basic models of foraging theory offer us no help in trying to describe or analyze this situation. The prey model, for example, will tell us whether our bird should attack a novel noxious prey from an economic perspective, but clearly this is irrelevant until the forager has an opportunity to adjust to the properties of the prey in its new location. In most situations, these 'adjustments' will occur via learning. It follows that a complete understanding of animal foraging behavior will need to incorporate learning to accommodate situations like our migrating bird's dilemma and probably a great many others.

Unfortunately, the path connecting animal psychology and behavioral ecology has not always been smooth. Early behavioral ecologists advocated a mechanistically agnostic perspective that continues to influence many behavioral ecologists. This perspective recognized that natural selection directly favors behavioral outcomes and acts only indirectly on behavioral mechanisms. According to this view, the prey model (to take a specific example) can be correct and useful regardless of how animals adjust to the properties of prey. Biology is, of course, hierarchical, and one can offer biological explanations at many different levels (e.g., cellular, physiological, population, and so on). Behavioral ecology's mechanistic agnosticism wanders into error, in our opinion, when it seems to diminish the importance of integrating approaches from different levels of biological explanation. The need for studies that combine foraging and psychology illustrates this point eloquently. This section asks how the properties of learning and memory constrain animal foraging behavior. Of course, learning and memory influence virtually every aspect of foraging. To reduce the problem to manageable size we will focus on the problem of prey choice.

1.20.4.1 Acquisition: The Most Basic Constraint

Our migrating bird cannot adjust to new prey types instantaneously. Learning takes time. During acquisition a learning animal's behavior becomes increasingly appropriate for the new situation. It follows that behavior during acquisition is something less than completely appropriate. Thorndike's fundamental observation that learning proceeds incrementally therefore provides the most basic mechanism through which learning constrains foraging. The next few paragraphs review several ways in which acquisition constrains foraging.

1.20.4.1.1 Search image

The insects that form the basic diet for nesting birds vary in abundance throughout the nesting season. In the 1960s Luuk Tinbergen (Tinbergen, 1960) noticed that there was a considerable lag between the first appearance of prey type and its inclusion in the diet. Tinbergen compared prey choice to prey abundance, and he observed that foragers took fewer prey than expected when few prey were present, but they took more than expected when the prey type became abundant. In a now famous paper, Tinbergen argued that this transition reflected a sort of perceptual learning that we now call search image. This is an intuitive idea for many people: when searching for your lost keys, you barely notice the pencils and paper clips on your desk. The search image hypothesis asserts that foraging animals, like the human key-loser, use a perceptual template of the items they are searching for, and as a consequence their perception of objects that do not fit the search image is reduced. Establishing that this appealing idea applies to foraging animals proved to be an arduous process. One reason for this is that many nonperceptual phenomena could account for Tinbergen's observations. For example, if emerging prey items occur in a different habitat (say under rocks), it may be quite reasonable for birds to continue to glean insects from leaves until prey 'under rocks' are abundant enough to justify a change in foraging habitat.

However, careful experimental studies (e.g., Pietrewicz and Kamil, 1979; Bond and Kamil, 1999) have demonstrated that the search image phenomenon is real. Kamil and colleagues have shown that recognition of cryptic prey improves with experience (See Chapter 1.22). However, these effects only appear for cryptic prey; animals do not show the same improvements with experience when tested with noncryptic stimuli of the type commonly used in psychological studies (e.g., red circles vs. green triangles). From the perspective of a cryptic prey species, this 'learning to see' phenomenon means that abundance reduces the protective effect of crypticity. In the course of evolution this can produce polymorphisms (i.e., a prey species with two or more cryptic forms), because an abundant form loses its advantage, while less abundant forms gain an advantage. In an extremely creative set of studies, Bond and Kamil (2002) have demonstrated this effect by training captive blue jays to peck at virtual 'moths' on a computer screen. Bond and Kamil arranged a situation in which the population of virtual moths evolved (in the computer). Using this technique, Bond and Kamil showed that the jay's perceptual learning did, indeed, select for prey polymorphisms.

1.20.4.1.2 Learning to handle prey

Monk's hood (genus *Aconitum*) flowers have an unusual shape. The face of the flower is normal enough, with a patch of stamens in the center; above this is the 'hood' that gives the flowers their common name. The flowers hold their nectar in a pair of receptacles that are 'under the hood' and above the face of the flower. A bee extracting nectar must land on the center of the flower (where its body touches the stamens), crawl up into the hood, and finally extend its tongue upward into the nectar receptacles. Given the complexity of this extractive task, it is not surprising that bumblebees must learn how to exploit monk's hood flowers. Indeed, studies by Laverty (1994) show classical acquisition curves for bumblebees exploiting monk's hood. Experience increases handling accuracy and reduces handling time. While Laverty's work showed that learning plays a critical role in extracting nectar from a complex flower like monk's hood, he also found that experience reduced handling time for simple cup-shaped flowers.

Situations like this must be common. Experience must often improve foragers' abilities to handle prey, but this requires a little rethinking of our standard prey selection model. Handling time is a basic parameter in the standard model, but what happens if handling changes with experience? Which handling time matters: the handling of a naive forager or the handling that an experienced forager can achieve? Students of foraging think that this learning tends to favor diet specialization, because this process tends to make familiar items profitable (low handling times) and unfamiliar items unprofitable (high handling times). Although foragers could improve their handling times by exploiting unfamiliar prey, the comparative advantage of exploiting familiar types provides a sort of dietary inertia that encourages specialization.

This dietary inertia appears to be important in the flower exploitation choices of honeybees and bumblebees. In a phenomenon called flower-constancy or majoring, individual bees often seem to stick with a single species of flower, even when better flowers become available (Heinrich, 1976) (*See* Chapter 1.29). Given the start-up costs associated with learning to exploit a new flower and relatively short life spans of foraging workers, it is probably better (from the hive's perspective) to have older workers continue their foraging specializations while younger bees adapt to changes in the local flora by forming their own specializations. Another level of specialization is at the species level. How does acquisition apply to a species which specializes on only one type of flower? Laverty and Plowright (1988) compared the learning of a specialist species of bumblebee with that of a generalist species. They found that the specialist bumblebees acquired handling skills specific to its specialized flower more quickly than generalist bumblebees did. Many of the generalist bumblebees give up before locating the nectar, as one might expect for a species having to optimize the ability to learn about a large variety of flower morphologies.

1.20.4.1.3 The generality of the 'acquisition constraint'

These two topics – search image learning and learning to handle prey – represent only two ways in which learning can constrain animal foraging. In both cases the time lags involved in learning mean that foragers must be slightly out of sync with the current economic situation. This scenario must play out in many other contexts. To give two examples, studies of aversion learning suggest that animals are well equipped to learn that certain feeding resources should be avoided, and studies of spatial behavior show that animals learn the locations of food resources. In all these 'learning' situations the basic acquisition constraint applies. The behavior of learning foragers will often be on its way to somewhere, rather than in 'optimal' alignment with the current situation.

1.20.5 Emerging Topics

Using the basic models (discussed in the section titled 'Foraging basics') as a starting point, students of foraging have developed several new topics that make connections with learning and memory. This section reviews two of these topics – predator avoidance and social foraging. Although existing approaches to predator avoidance do not make significant connections to learning and memory, we feel there is enormous potential for studies that combine studies of appetitive learning (e.g., learning about food) with fear conditioning and avoidance learning. These two phenomena must frequently be in conflict in natural situations. Social foraging makes important connections with learning and memory because many animals forage in groups (notably many common 'model' organisms such as rats, pigeons, and humans). There is, of course, a well-developed and fascinating literature of social learning. We argue, in this section, that a deeper understanding of learning in social contexts will result when studies of social learning are informed by an understanding of the economic costs and conflicts inherent in group foraging.

1.20.5.1 Foraging and Predator Avoidance

The basic models outlined in the section titled 'Foraging basics' consider the economics of foraging decisions isolated and abstracted from the world in which foragers live. For muddy-boots biologists the most glaring oversight of this approach is that most animals live with the constant threat of predation. To make matters worse, the options that are the best economically are often the most dangerous. The site that provides the most food typically attracts the most foragers, and since these foragers are food for predators, it also attracts the most predators. In other cases the best feeding strategies expose foragers to the risk of predation. For grazing aquatic invertebrates like snails or caddis fly larvae the safest place is typically under rocks or deep in the substrate, but the algae that these organisms feed on grows in the sunlight on the exposed tops of rocks – ideal hunting conditions for a visual predator.

Animals do, of course, respond to the presence of predators. The crude effects are obvious and easily demonstrated. Guppies forage nearly 24 h per day in streams without predators, but they restrict their foraging to the daylight hours when predators are present (Fraser et al., 2004). Juvenile sunfish forage in the weeds along lake shores even though they could obtain food at a faster rate in the open water (Werner et al., 1983; Werner and Gilliam, 1984). Tadpoles restrict their movements when predators are in the vicinity (Anholt et al., 2000). Many birds, from ostriches to chickadees, increase their vigilance (looking up) in risky situations, and clearly time 'looking up' is time that must be subtracted from feeding. Many small mammals organize their activities around a central refuge, such as a burrow or nest. Obviously, these animals quickly deplete the resources near their refuge, and so they face a trade-off between poor feeding close to their safe haven and richer pickings at riskier distances. Finally, many animals can dramatically reduce the risk of predation by foraging in groups. Groups allow foragers to spread the risk of predation and share the costs of vigilance, even though they can increase competition for food and other resources.

A striking finding is that the indirect effects of predation (e.g., the changes in behavior caused by predation) can often be more important ecologically than the direct effects of predation (i.e., the direct reduction in population that occurs when predators kill prey). For example, in 1995 the US National Park Service reintroduced wolves into Yellowstone National Park, where they could prey on the abundant herds of elk. Of course, the wolves have killed many elk, but this does not seem to be nearly as important as how wolves have changed the elk's behavior. Since the reintroduction, park biologists have observed a dramatic change in the riparian (streamside) habitats of the park: willow and aspen have proliferated, and streams meander more and beavers are more abundant. Without wolves, elk grazed everywhere, preventing regeneration of willows and aspens that beavers depend on. Now, elk spend more time in groups, more time being vigilant, and they forage less efficiently. They avoid dangerous thickets where predators might lurk (Laundre et al., 2001). In the words of Brown and Kotler (2007): "Fear can be a powerful ecological force."

1.20.5.1.1 Modeling predator avoidance

We can express the qualitative logic of foraging/predation trade-offs in succinct caveman grammar: food good, death bad. But how do we combine the value of food and threat of death by predation into logically coherent common currency? The breakthrough comes

when we realize that food and death both connect to fitness via the fundamental life history parameters of survival and reproduction. Imagine, for example, that we can divide an animal's life into a sequence of equal time intervals. For an animal outside of the breeding season, we can write the benefits derived from the current interval as the product SV, where S represents the probability of survival to the next interval, and V represents the expected future reproduction of an individual who survives to the next interval. Foraging and predation combine to influence both the probability of survival and the expected value of future reproduction. To survive to the next period, an animal must obtain a minimum amount of food and avoid being killed by a predator. In addition, the animal's nutritional status and overall well-being determine the expected value of future reproduction V. Models of predation–foraging trade-offs typically proceed by specifying the relationship between foraging behavior (feeding site choice, patch use, etc.) and these two basic life history variables (survival and future reproduction). An especially illuminating case occurs with animals, like fish, that have indeterminate growth. These animals grow continuously, so food intake today leads to a larger body tomorrow, which ultimately leads to more reproduction. For these animals, reasonable assumptions about the effects of foraging on survival and future reproduction lead to the so-called μ over g rule (Gilliam, 1982; Stephens and Krebs, 1986). This formulation predicts that animals foraging under predation risk should forage in a way that minimizes the ratio of mortality rate (μ) divided by growth rate (g). To be explicit, imagine a juvenile fish that can choose to feed in any of three habitats. We can, in theory, express how risky each habitat is in terms of the mortality rate experienced there, and we can express the benefits of foraging there in terms of growth rate. The μ-over-g rule tells us that our hypothetical fish should choose the habitat with the smallest mortality rate to growth rate quotient. Although modelers derived this simple result from fairly restrictive assumptions, it seems to be fairly robust, and it provides a useful and elegant way to think about the trade-off between predation and foraging.

1.20.5.1.2 Learning about predators

Obviously enough, animals cannot learn very effectively from the experience of being eaten by a predator. Yet experience clearly plays an important role in anti-predator behavior. Vervet monkeys, for example, learn that some individuals give unreliable alarm calls (Cheney and Seyfarth, 1988). European blackbirds learn to fear 'harmless' objects, if they observe others reacting fearfully to them (Curio et al., 1978). In widely cited studies, Cook and Mineka (1990) showed that monkeys could easily learn to fear snakes by observing the fearful reactions of conspecifics, but did not learn to fear plastic flowers from similar experiences. Although most published examples deal with social learning (see the next section), animals must learn about the risk of predation from many other unconditioned stimuli (e.g., moving shadows, the odor of a freshly killed conspecific, and so on). The study of escape responses, startle responses, and fear has a long history in the literature of learning (*See* Chapter 4.11; Bolles, 1970; Cook and Mineka, 1991; Davis, 2006). The lesson that emerges from studies of foraging is that resource acquisition and predator avoidance represent a fundamental and evolutionarily ancient trade-off. We argue, therefore, that a research program that considers the balance between learning about food and learning to avoid danger may reveal important new connections.

1.20.5.2 Social Foraging

In the autumn and winter nearly everyone in the northern hemisphere can observe large aggregations of starlings wheeling in the sky and foraging across lawns and agricultural fields like a hungry army. This is not unusual, of course; many animals feed in groups, including troops of capuchin monkeys, fishing pelicans, and swarms of army ants. Yet behavioral ecology's basic models of foraging focus on isolated individuals foraging as 'economically independent entities' (Waite and Field, 2007). In recognition of this, the topic of social foraging has been a growth area over the last 15–20 years. How does foraging in groups change the dynamics of foraging behavior? Unfortunately, we can only give a complicated answer to this simple question. As we will explain, the presence of others can influence foraging in many ways. Conspecifics can reduce feeding opportunities via competition, but they may also confer benefits such as enhanced predator avoidance and increased rates of food discovery. Perhaps the most interesting complication, from the perspective of learning and memory, is the problem of information transfer within foraging groups. A key advantage of grouping is that animals can benefit from the predator detection abilities of their group mates, and many studies show that group foragers reduce their personal vigilance (compared to individuals foraging alone). On the other hand, sharing information with group mates

is not always in an animal's best interest. Group mates who are too well informed might interfere with your food discoveries or block the best escape routes when a predator appears.

1.20.5.2.1 Group size

The key to understanding the economic complexities of social foraging is a game theoretical approach. Game theoretical analyses of adaptation differ from the simpler optimization approaches because they recognize that the advantages of a forager's actions will depend on how others act. We already saw this principle when we considered the ideal-free model of habitat choice: the value of a feeding site depends on the number of competitors present. Among the most basic questions one can ask about social foraging is what determines group size? We typically address this question by plotting the relationship between the intake rate each group member obtains and the group size. In the ideal-free distribution, the simple inverse r/n describes this relationship, and the feeding rate always decreases as the group size increases. In situations like this more group mates are always bad, and we call this a 'dispersion economy.' Given that many animals are solitary foragers, this situation must be quite common in nature. Indeed, students of social foraging think that increasing group size must eventually reduce foraging benefits, even for animals adapted to large aggregations. In many situations, we believe that foraging benefits increase with group size (at least initially), and we call this an 'aggregation' economy. **Figure 3** shows the typical situation for an aggregation economy.

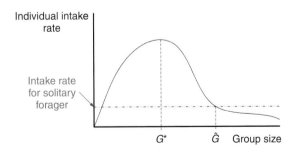

Figure 3 Graphical analysis of foraging group size. The plot shows the relationship between group size and individual intake rate for a so-called aggregation economy (see text). Initially, the per capita intake rate increases with increasing group size to a peak when the group size equals G^*. After that it declines with increasing group size. The dashed horizontal line shows the intake that a solitary forager can achieve. If the group grows beyond $\hat{G}$, then group members can benefit by leaving the group. We generally expect that stable groups should be between G^* and $\hat{G}$ in size.

Initially, individual foraging rates increase with group size, possibly due to the reduced cost of vigilance or the benefits of shared food discovery. During this increasing phase, adding a new member to the group is in the interests of current group members and prospective joiners. Indeed, existing members may even try to recruit new members during this 'increasing benefit' stage. Eventually, however, the foraging benefits will peak, and the mundane negative effects of feeding more mouths will decrease foraging benefits. One might expect groups to converge on the group size that maximizes feeding benefits (G^* in **Figure 3**), but this logic only holds up if existing members can control group entry. If, instead, individuals can join the group freely, then the group size can continue to increase because solitary foragers can still benefit by joining the group. In the language of game theory, one says that the benefit-maximizing group size is unstable. In general we expect to see groups larger than the benefit-maximizing group size (G^*) but smaller than the group size where individuals could do better by foraging on their own ($\hat{G}$ in **Figure 3**). In theory, the degree of control that group members can exert over group entry will determine stable group size: more control will push the predicted value toward the benefit-maximizing group size (G^*), and less will shift things toward larger group sizes near the theoretical maximum $\hat{G}$.

1.20.5.2.2   Producers and scroungers

While animals often benefit from foraging in groups, this does not preclude conflict between group members. The phenomenon of scrounging or kleptoparasitism provides a simple and important example. When one member of a group discovers food, others often parasitize this discovery. One can easily observe this among pigeons feeding in a city park. The mad rush of pigeons toward a successful forager often seems quite comical. From the food discoverer's (or producer's) point of view, scroungers represent a cost of group foraging, but from the scroungers' perspective this 'information sharing' is a distinct advantage. Behavioral ecologists, led primarily by Giraldeau and his colleagues (see Giraldeau and Livoreil, 1998, for review), have investigated this phenomenon in some detail both theoretically and experimentally. To begin, we imagine that group-feeding animals can choose between the producer and scrounger strategies. A producer always finds its own food, and a scrounger feeds by joining producers. So while a producer forages by looking for food, we

imagine that a scrounger forages by looking for successful producers. (The reader may object that it is unreasonable to think of producer and scrounger as hard and fast categories, because individuals can easily switch between producer and scrounger tactics, and of course, that is correct, but it turns out that this premise still leads to a useful and empirically successful model.) Now, obviously, a group with only scroungers is a nonstarter, because no one would find anything to eat. The presence of producers makes scrounging a viable strategy, but what mix of producers and scroungers would we expect? Again, this requires a game theoretical approach. The stable mix depends, it turns out, on how much food a producer can obtain – a quantity that we typically call the producer's advantage. If a producer must share everything it finds equally with its group mates, then we predict a minimal number of producers. At the other extreme, if producers can completely monopolize their discoveries, then we expect all group members to act as producers and no scroungers.

In what is perhaps the most elegant study of this problem, Mottley and Giraldeau (2000) created an experimental situation that allowed only certain group members to act as producers and forced others to act as scroungers. By doing this, they established that the benefits derived from scrounging decreased as the number of scroungers increased. After establishing that the basic features of the model applied, they modified the situation to allow animals to switch between producer and scrounger. This study found, as predicted, a higher frequency of producers when producers got a larger share of discovered food and a lower frequency of producers when the experiment forced producers to share most of the discovered food with scroungers.

1.20.5.2.3   Social information use

Foraging animals, like human shoppers, seldom have complete information about their options. So they must often use experience to respond appropriately to changes in prey quality or the properties of a food patch. Often animals will use direct ('personal') experience with food resources to adjust their behavior, but group-foraging animals have another option. The behavior of group mates often provides information about resources. The producer-scrounger situation, we discussed above, provides a simple example; scroungers exploit information about food patches obtained by producers. There are, however, many other examples. Rats may change their foraging preferences when they smell a new food type on a group mate's breath (Galef and Stein, 1985; Galef and Giraldeau, 2001). Honeybees indicate the distance and direction of food resources by performing their famous waggle dance (*See* Chapter 1.25; von Frisch, 1950). Honeybees may often return to the hive with only partially filled crops, and an interesting explanation for this is that bees foraging in suboptimal patches may be returning early to hive to gain information about better patches from other bees (Varjú and Núñez, 1991, 1993). In parallel with the distinction between personal and social sources of information, behavioral ecologists distinguish between private and public information. Every member of a social group can act on public information, but only the possessor of private information can act on private information, and of course, a key question for the private information possessor is whether to act in way that makes its 'knowledge' public (see, for example, Valone, 1989; Templeton and Giraldeau, 1995).

Social influences on foraging behavior range from the simple (e.g., local enhancement) to the comparatively elaborate (e.g., true imitation, see Galef, 1988). While we leave a complete review of social learning and related phenomena to others (Galef and Giraldeau, 2001) (*See* Chapter 1.16 for a discussion of social learning in primates), we note here that many examples of social learning involve foraging behavior: British titmice opening milk bottles (Sherry and Galef, 1990), quail pecking or stepping on a treadle to obtain food (Zentall, 2004). A full development of the connections between the behavioral ecology of foraging and social learning remains, in our view, an unexploited opportunity. The following paragraphs give two examples, both from work with foraging starlings, that suggest how one might combine social learning and foraging studies.

Templeton and Giraldeau (1996) studied the effects of a partner on patch exploitation. They created experimental patches with discrete holes in which they placed food. Patches varied in that some patches were completely empty (no holes had food), while in others some holes (1 in 10) contained food. This arrangement sets up a classic patch sampling problem that behavioral ecologists have often used to study the behavior of solitary foragers (e.g., Lima, 1983). In this situation the forager must somehow decide how many empty holes to tolerate before leaving to find a new patch. Templeton and Giraldeau's findings suggested that foragers used the explorations of the others to make patch departure decisions. They found that animals foraging in pairs typically probed fewer holes

before leaving than animals foraging alone, and that they probed more holes when their companion probed few. Perhaps the most intriguing finding of this study, however, was that the complexity of the sampling task seems to influence the degree to which starlings use social information. Templeton and Giraldeau found that partners influenced patch sampling as described here when they presented patches that were rectangular arrays of 'food holes.' However, partners had no effect on patch departure when patches were simple linear arrays of holes. This suggests that the importance of social learning may depend on the costs and reliability of individual experience.

Krebs and Inman (1992) studied how the presence of a partner changed the basic problem of tracking a varying resource. As explained in more detail above, subjects in tracking studies must choose between two feeding sites. One site is always the same but mediocre, while the other changes from good (better than the mediocre site) to bad (worse than the mediocre site) unpredictably. Here the question is how frequently should one check (or sample) the varying resource? When two animals do this together, however, only one needs to sample. And Krebs and Inman found that, in pairs of starlings, one typically sampled and the other simply followed the behavior of the sampler. This is an extremely intriguing result in several ways. First, if only some members of a group act as 'information gatherers,' this would seem to diminish the information sharing advantage of group foraging. Second, if some individuals in a group simply play follow the leader, then we would expect that followers obtain lower quality information than leaders. Finally, one has to wonder how the asymmetry between followers and leader develops. How, for example, would a prospective follower choose between two tutors performing conflicting actions?

1.20.5.2.4 Intelligence, foraging, and sociality

We end our discussion of 'emerging topics' with a brief mention of possible connections between foraging and general cognitive abilities (i.e., intelligence). We use the word 'intelligence' here fairly uncritically, acknowledging that a rigorous definition eludes us but that most readers will understand our general meaning. Many students of comparative cognition ascribe to the social intelligence hypothesis, which holds that interactions within social groups have favored increased intelligence. The focus of this hypothesis has typically been on the role of intelligence in disputes about rank and the formation of alliances (Harcourt, 1988; Dunbar, 1998; Reader and Laland, 2002). An alternative hypothesis focuses on the role of foraging and resource extraction (King, 1986). The growing sophistication of social foraging theory suggests that these may be false alternatives. Social behavior does not exist in a vacuum; social interactions are typically about resources. It does not seem far-fetched to speculate that interactions among social foragers have played a role in the evolution of advanced cognitive abilities.

1.20.6 Summary and Conclusions

Behavioral ecologists have developed a large family of foraging models that focus on costs and benefits. These models consider diet selection, patch exploitation, and habitat use. There are many important connections between foraging and learning. Experimental studies of foraging decisions typically depend on animal learning abilities, and many studies of learning focus on situations in which subjects learn about food resources. Students of foraging behavior have considered the adaptive value of learning and memory by constructing models in which hypothetical animals can use or ignore their experience. A surprising result is that it often pays to act without experience. For example, if the environment changes frequently a fixed choice strategy will often serve a forager best. Animals, of course, face many problems other than foraging. They must, for example, avoid being eaten. Unfortunately, the best places to feed are frequently also the most dangerous, so foragers must somehow balance the need to obtain food with the risk of predation. Learning clearly plays a role in predator avoidance. While behavioral ecologists have studied the trade-off between foraging and predator avoidance extensively, we know relatively little about possible interactions between avoidance learning and learning about food. Many animals forage in groups, and this introduces several complications. Group foragers can use the behavior of their group mates to find food or avoid predators, but the availability of the public information can create conflicts of interest within the group.

A complete understanding of learning and memory needs to go beyond an understanding of mechanism and develop an understanding of how these mechanisms serve animals in nature. Foraging is a defining property of animals, and as such it represents an important natural context for learning and memory.

At the same time, students of foraging can benefit from an understanding of the basic principles of learning and how these apply in natural situations.

References

Anholt BR, Werner E, and Skelly DK (2000) Effect of food and predators on the activity of four larval ranid frogs. *Ecology* 81: 3509–3521.

Bateson M and Kacelnik A (1998) Risk-sensitive foraging: Decision making in variable environments. In: Dukas R (ed.) *Cognitive Ecology: The Evolutionary Ecology of Information Processing and Decision Making*, pp. 297–420. Chicago: The University of Chicago Press.

Bolles RC (1970) Species-specific defense reactions and avoidance learning. *Psychol. Rev.* 77: 32–48.

Bond AB and Kamil AC (1999) Searching image in blue jays: Facilitation and interference in sequential priming. *Anim. Learn. Behav.* 27(4): 461–471.

Bond AB and Kamil AC (2002) Visual predators select for crypticity and polymorphism in virtual prey. *Nature* 415(6872): 609–613.

Brown JS and Kotler BP (2007) Foraging and the ecology of fear. In: Stephens DW, Brown JS, and Ydenberg RC (eds.) *Foraging: Behavior and Ecology*, pp. 437–480. Chicago: University of Chicago Press.

Bush RR and Mosteller F (1955) *Stochastic Models for Learning*. New York: John Wiley and Sons.

Cheney DL and Seyfarth RM (1988) Assessment of meaning and detection of unreliable signal by vervet monkeys. *Anim. Behav.* 36: 477–486.

Clayton NS and Dickinson A (1998) Episodic-like memory during cache recovery by scrub jays. *Nature* 395: 272–274.

Cook M and Mineka S (1990) Selective associations in the observational condition of fear in rhesus monkeys. *J. Exp. Psychol. Anim. Behav. Process* 16(4): 372–389.

Cook M and Mineka S (1991) Selective associations in the origins of phobic fears and their implications for behavior therapy. In: Martin PR (ed.) *Handbook of Behavior Therapy and Psychological Science: An Integrative Approach*, pp. 413–434. New York: Pergamon Press, Inc.

Cowie RJ (1977) Optimal foraging in great tits (*Parus major*). *Nature* 268: 137–139.

Curio EB, Ernst U, and Vieth W (1978) Cultural transmission of enemy recognition: One function of mobbing. *Science* 202: 899–901.

Cuthill IC, Haccou P, and Kacelnik A (1994) Starlings (*Sturnus vulgaris*) exploiting patches: Response to long-term changes in travel time. *Behav. Ecol.* 5: 81–90.

Cuthill IC, Haccou P, Kacelnik A, Krebs JR, and Iwasa Y (1990) Starlings exploiting patches: The effect of recent experience on foraging decisions. *Anim. Behav.* 40: 625–640.

Dall SRX, Giraldeau LA, Olsson O, McNamara JM, and Stephens DW (2005) Information and its use in evolutionary ecology. *Trends Ecol. Evol.* 20: 187–193.

Davis M (2006) Neural systems involved in fear and anxiety measured with fear-potentiated startle. *Am. Psychol.* 61(8): 741–756.

Devenport LD and Devenport JA (1994) Time-dependent averaging of foraging information in least chipmunks and golden-mantled ground squirrels. *Anim. Behav.* 47: 787–802.

Dukas R (1999) Costs of memory: Ideas and predictions. *J. Theor. Biol.* 197(1): 41–50.

Dunbar RM (1998) The social-brain hypothesis. *Evol. Anthropol.* 6: 178–190.

Fraser DF, Gilliam JF, Akkara JT, Albanese BW, and Snider SB (2004) Night feeding by guppies under predator release: Effects on growth and daytime courtship. *Ecology* 85(2): 312–319.

Galef BG, Jr. (1988) Imitation in animals: History, definition, and interpretation of data for the psychological laboratory. In: Zentall TR and Galef BG, Jr. (eds.) *Social Learning: Psychological and Biological Perspectives*, pp. 3–28. Hillsdale, NJ: Lawrence Erlbaum Associates.

Galef BG, Jr. and Giraldeau L-A (2001) Social influences on foraging in vertebrates: Causal mechanisms and adaptive functions. *Anim. Behav.* 61: 3–15.

Galef BG, Jr. and Stein M (1985) Demonstrator influence on observer diet preferences: Analyses of critical social interactions and olfactory signals. *Anim. Learn. Behav.* 13: 31–38.

Gilliam JF (1982) *Habitat Use and Competitive Bottlenecks in Size-Structured Fish Populations.* PhD Thesis, Michigan State University.

Giraldeau L-A and Livoreil B (1998) Game theory and social foraging. In: Dugatkin LA and Reeve HK (eds.) *Social Foraging Theory*. Princeton, NJ: Princeton University Press.

Harcourt AH (1988) Alliances in contests and social intelligence. In: Byrne RW and Whiten A (eds.) *Machiavellian Intelligence: Social Intelligence and the Evolution of Intellect in Monkeys, Apes and Humans*, pp. 132–152. Oxford: Oxford University Press.

Heinrich B (1976) The foraging specialization of individual bumblebees. *Ecol. Monogr.* 46: 105–128.

Herrnstein RJ (1974) Formal properties of the matching law. *J. Exp. Anal. Behav.* 21: 159–164.

Hirvonen H, Ranta E, Rita H, and Peuhkuri N (1991) Significance of memory properties in prey choice decisions. *Ecol. Model.* 115: 177–189.

Holling CS (1959) Some characteristics of simple types of predation and parasitism. *Can. Entomol.* 91: 385–398.

Illius AW, Jessop NS, and Gill M (2000) Mathematical models of food intake and metabolism in ruminants. In: Cronje P and Boomker EA (eds.) *Ruminant Physiology: Digestion, Metabolism, Growth and Reproduction*, pp. 21–40. Wallingford: CAB International.

Inman AJ (1990) *Foraging Decisions: The Effects of Conspecifics and Environmental Stochasticity.* PhD Thesis, University of Oxford.

King BJ (1986) Extractive foraging and the evolution of primate intelligence. *Hum. Evol.* 4: 361–372.

Krebs JR and Inman AJ (1992) Learning and foraging: Individuals groups and populations. *Am. Nat.* 140: S63–S84.

Krebs JR, Kacelnik A, and Taylor P (1978) Test of optimal sampling by foraging great tits. *Nature* 275: 27–31.

Krebs JR, Webber MI, Erichsen JT, and Charnov EL (1977) Optimal prey-selection by the great tit (*Parus major*). *Anim. Behav.* 25: 30–38.

Laundre JW, Hernandez L, and Altendrof KB (2001) Wolves, elk and bison: Reestablishing the "landscape of fear" in Yellowstone National Park, USA. *Can. J. Zool.* 79: 1401–1409.

Laverty TM (1994) Bumble bee learning and flower morphology. *Anim. Behav.* 47: 531–545.

Laverty TM and Plowright RC (1988) Flower handling by bumblebees: A comparison of specialists and generalists. *Anim. Behav.* 36: 733–740.

Lima SL (1983) Downy woodpecker foraging behavior: Efficient sampling in simple stochastic environments. *Ecology* 65: 166–174.

Lima SL (1985) Sampling behavior of starlings foraging in simple patch environments. *Behav. Ecol. Sociobiol.* 16: 135–142.

McNamara JM and Houston AI (1987) Memory and the efficient use of information. *J. Theor. Biol.* 125: 385–395.

Menzel R (1999) Memory dynamics in the honeybee. *J. Comp. Physiol. A* 185: 323–340.

Mottley K and Giraldeau L-A (2000) Experimental evidence that group foragers can converge on predicted producer-scrounger equilibria. *Anim. Behav.* 60: 341–350.

Pietrewicz AT and Kamil AC (1979) Search image formation in the blue jay (*Cyanocitta cristata*). *Science* 204(4399): 1332–1333.

Reader SM and Laland KN (2002) Social intelligence, innovation and enhanced brain size in primates. *Proc. Natl. Acad. Sci. USA* 99: 4436–4441.

Sherry DF and Galef BG (1990) Social learning without imitation: More about milk bottle opening by birds. *Anim. Behav.* 40(5): 987–989.

Shettleworth SJ, Krebs JR, Stephens DW, and Gibbon J (1988) Tracking a fluctuating environment: A study of sampling. *Anim. Behav.* 36: 87–105.

Spalinger DE and Hobbs NT (1992) Mechanisms of foraging in mammalian herbivores: New models of functional response. *Am. Nat.* 140: 325–348.

Stephens DW (1987) On economically tracking a variable environment. *Theor. Popul. Biol.* 32: 15–25.

Stephens DW (1989) Variance and the value of information. *Am. Nat.* 134: 128–140.

Stephens DW (1991) Change, regularity and value in the evolution of animal learning. *Behav. Ecol.* 2: 77–89.

Stephens DW (2007) Models of information use. In: Stephens DW, Brown JS, and Ydenberg RC (eds.) *Foraging: Behavior and Ecology*, pp. 31–58. Chicago: University of Chicago Press.

Stephens DW, Brown JS, and Ydenberg RC (eds.) (2007) *Foraging: Behavior and Ecology*. Chicago: University of Chicago Press.

Stephens DW and Krebs JR (1986) *Foraging Theory*. Princeton, NJ: Princeton University Press.

Tamm S (1987) Tracking varying environments: Sampling by hummingbirds. *Anim. Behav.* 35: 1725–1734.

Templeton JJ and Giraldeau LA (1995) Patch assessment in foraging flocks of European starlings: Evidence for public information use. *Behav. Ecol.* 6: 65–72.

Templeton JJ and Giraldeau LA (1996) Vicarious sampling: The use of personal and public information by starlings in a simple patchy environment. *Behav. Ecol. Sociobiol.* 38: 105–113.

Tinbergen L (1960) The natural control of insects in pinewoods: I. Factors influencing the intensity of predation by songbirds. *Arch. Neerlandaises Zool.* 13: 265–343.

Valone TJ (1989) Group foraging, public information and patch estimation. *Oikos* 56: 357–363.

Varjú D and Núñez J (1991) What do foraging honeybees optimize? *J. Comp. Physiol. A* 169: 729–736.

Varjú D and Núñez J (1993) Energy balance versus information exchange in foraging honeybees. *J. Comp. Physiol. A* 172: 257–261.

von Frisch K (1950) *Bees. Their Vision, Chemical Senses, and Language.* Ithaca, NY: Cornell University Press.

Waite TA and Field KL (2007) Foraging with others: Games social foragers play. In: Stephens DW, Brown JS, and Ydenberg RC (eds.) *Foraging: Behavior and Ecology*, pp. 331–362. Chicago: University of Chicago Press.

Werner EE and Gilliam JF (1984) The ontogenetic niche and species interactions in size-structured populations. *Ann. Rev. Ecol. Syst.* 15: 393–425.

Werner EE, Gilliam JF, Hall DL, and Mittelbach GG (1983) An experimental test of the effects of predation risk on habitat use in fish. *Ecology* 64: 1540–1548.

Zentall TR (2004) Action imitation in birds. *Learn. Behav.* 32(1): 15–23.

1.21 Navigation and Episodic-Like Memory in Mammals

N. Fortin, Boston University, Boston, MA, USA

1.21.1 Navigation

The word navigation is derived from the Latin 'navis' (ship) and 'agere' (to drive), and in the classic sense, refers to the science of directing a craft by determining its position, course, and distance traveled (*Encyclopedia Britannica*). In ethological terms, navigation refers to self-controlled movement in space toward an unseen goal (Alyan and Jander, 1994; Alyan and McNaughton, 1999). Although habitats vary substantially between species, the navigational demands are fundamentally similar across mammals (Mackintosh, 2002). All mammals must learn and remember locations of importance and compute trajectories that minimize risk given their size, mode of transportation, the characteristics of their environment, and their specific needs. Although such navigational behavior unfolds seamlessly, it reflects the use of multiple strategies based on different types of representation of the environment (O'Keefe and Nadel, 1978; Mackintosh, 2002; *See* Chapters 1.12, 1.20, 1.22, 1.23, 1.25, 1.26). Under some circumstances, a navigational strategy based on a detailed and flexible representation may be ideal (e.g., to find a different way to get to work when one's habitual route is blocked), whereas simpler strategies and representations may be preferable in others (e.g., to tell a tourist how to get to the zoo).

1.21.1.1 Types of Mental Representations That Can Support Navigation

1.21.1.1.1 Egocentric versus allocentric

Egocentric representations encode relations between landmarks in the environment and the organism (e.g., shelter is 30 m to my left, food source is 40 m straight ahead). In contrast, allocentric representations depict exclusively the relations among landmarks in the environment, without consideration of their relation to the organism (e.g., food source is 50 m northeast of shelter). Allocentric representations are more flexible, since a single representation can be used to calculate trajectories between any landmarks, regardless of changes in the position or orientation of the animal.

1.21.1.1.2 Route versus map

A typical example of a route representation is a set of verbal turn-by-turn directions. More formally, according to O'Keefe and Nadel (1978), a route representation consists of information for a trajectory between a start and goal location that is based on the identification of specific landmarks in the environment (e.g., a particular store on one corner) and the performance of the appropriate behavioral response in relation to each landmark (e.g., turn right; O'Keefe and Nadel, 1978). Because routes simply direct attention to particular objects and specify turns within egocentric space, they can be learned rapidly and require very little skill. However, the information provided in a route representation is very inflexible; the information must be used in the proper sequence and allows no freedom of choice. Their accuracy also depends on the stability of the landmarks (e.g., particular store not going out of business) and on the ability to adequately perceive the landmarks (e.g., darkness can complicate their use). Finally, calculating a return trajectory using a route representation is often challenging and prone to errors, an all-too-familiar experience for some.

In contrast, a mental map has the same properties as a real-world road map; namely, it is an allocentric representation of places in terms of distances and directions among items in the environment (O'Keefe and Nadel, 1978). Mental maps are built out of the integration of multiple trajectories within a specific environment, and consequently, require considerable experience with the environment in order to form. Nonetheless, their flexibility is a distinctive advantage, in that they support the calculation of detours, shortcuts, and novel trajectories. Finally, contrary to routes, maps are not disrupted by alteration or disappearance of individual cues, and provide unambiguous directions on the return trajectory (O'Keefe and Nadel, 1978).

1.21.1.2 Strategies for Navigation

Perhaps the most impressive spatial behavior is the seasonal long-distance migration observed in a number of species of birds (e.g., Berthold, 1996; See Chapter 1.22) and some mammals (e.g., Berger, 2004). Migrating animals use cues, such as the position of the sun and stars at specific times of the day or gradients in the Earth's magnetic field, to orient themselves and maintain that orientation over hundreds or thousands of kilometers to their destination (Sherry, 1998). Although many nonmigrating mammals, including rodents and primates, have been shown to be sensitive to those same celestial and geomagnetic cues (Baker, 1980; Mather and Baker, 1980; Levine and Bluni, 1994), mammals are not believed to rely on those strategies for their usual navigational needs, and the use of such global-reference cues will not be further discussed here (for a review see Sherry, 1998). Instead, mammals have been shown to rely on three main strategies for navigation: piloting, path integration, and the use of guidances and orientations.

1.21.1.2.1 Piloting

Piloting refers to the use of allothetic (external or distal) cues for navigation (Gallistel, 1990; Whishaw and Wallace, 2003; See Chapter 1.12). More specifically, it involves computing relations among cues, usually visual landmarks, to determine one's current position in the environment and plan a trajectory. Although under some circumstances mammals could use a single landmark to calculate their position, experimental manipulations have shown that they instinctively use all available landmarks as a unit (O'Keefe and Nadel, 1978; Suzuki et al., 1980). For instance, spatial performance is not impaired by removing a few of all the available distal landmarks, but it is compromised when one interferes with the relations among landmarks by randomizing their arrangement (Suzuki et al., 1980). Piloting is generally associated with, but is not limited to, navigation based on a mental map of the environment.

1.21.1.2.2 Path integration

Path integration, also known as 'dead reckoning' (from deduced reckoning, or reasoning), is a navigation strategy used by sailors hundreds of years ago to estimate their ship's position using information about speed of movement, travel time, and directional change whenever visible landmarks were unavailable (Whishaw and Wallace, 2003). From an ethological perspective, Darwin (1873) was the first to propose such a mechanism as a navigational strategy in animals. Path integration is currently defined as the capacity to use idiothetic cues, or cues generated by the animal's movements, to calculate the updated position of the animal by monitoring its trajectory in relation to a start location (Gallistel, 1990; Whishaw and Wallace, 2003). Idiothetic cues include information about self-movement from proprioceptive and vestibular systems (Wallace et al., 2002), sensory flow (e.g., optic flow, odor, or sound gradients; Wylie et al., 1999), and perhaps efferent copies of movement commands (Whishaw and Wallace, 2003). Importantly, the use of such egocentric cues does not imply a lack of flexibility in navigation, as animals using path integration can adjust their trajectory according to unexpected obstacles or changed task demands (Whishaw and Wallace, 2003; McNaughton et al., 2006). Finally, path integration is both automatic and constant, and since it does not require the use of visible landmarks, it can support navigation in case piloting fails due to the unavailability of distal cues (Etienne and Jeffery, 2004).

1.21.1.2.3 Guidances and orientations

As first described by O'Keefe and Nadel (1978), guidances refer to landmarks to be approached or followed, while orientations consist of particular movements in egocentric space to be made in the presence of particular guidances. The defining characteristic of this strategy is that, even though it can be used to solve spatial problems, it is not a spatial strategy per se (O'Keefe and Nadel, 1978; Mackintosh, 2002). A specific example of this strategy would be navigation based on approach or avoidance of specific visible landmarks or other cues such as an odor gradient (e.g., a predator following the odor trace of a prey), or navigation based on route representations consisting of a list of stimulus–response (or guidance-orientation) associations inflexibly leading from one point to another.

It is important to note that these strategies are not necessarily used in a mutually exclusive manner; on the contrary, mammals presumably use all of them simultaneously (Etienne et al., 1998; Eichenbaum and Cohen, 2001). For instance, mammals have been shown to predominantly rely on piloting to distal cues to navigate, but if such cues unexpectedly become unreliable or unavailable, animals will readily switch to path integration and demonstrate precise navigation despite the impoverished stimulus conditions (Whishaw and Wallace, 2003). Furthermore, there are distinct advantages to the concurrent use of multiple strategies. The main limitation of piloting is that distal cues are not always available, whereas path integration has been shown to be progressively degraded by the accumulation of error (Etienne and Jeffery, 2004); optimal navigation may therefore be achieved by relying on 'episodic fixes' (Gallistel, 1990), by which the position calculated via path integration is periodically updated by the position calculated from the distal landmarks through piloting.

1.21.1.3 Neural Basis of Navigation

In recent years, navigation research has focused primarily on elucidating its neural substrate, such that there are now few purely behavioral studies. Consequently, further development in our understanding of the navigational capabilities of mammals is intimately associated with the progress of our knowledge of the contribution of different neural systems. Although crucial to all mammalian species, navigational capacities have been most extensively investigated in rodents, presumably because their small size facilitates the manipulation of their spatial environment in a laboratory setting. Naturally, this focus on rodents raises the concern that our extensive understanding of navigational behavior may not extend to other mammals. However, comparative studies have shown that, despite significant differences in niche or specific adaptations, different mammalian species are remarkably similar in terms of neuroanatomy (Sherry and Healy, 1998) and in the way they solve spatial problems (Save et al., 1998), thereby lending support to the validity of cross-species comparisons (*See* Chapters 1.22, 1.25, 1.26).

After millions of years of evolution, it seems unlikely that the brain regions responsible for navigation are a 'tabula rasa'; instead, spatial behaviors and neural systems themselves are more likely to have been preorganized by evolutionary history (Whishaw and Wallace, 2003). The result of such evolution is a set of distinct navigational strategies, which, because each entails unique types of computation, requires the use of distinct neural systems (Sherry and Schacter, 1987). This section will discuss the role of a number of neural systems in supporting navigational behavior.

1.21.1.3.1   The hippocampus as a cognitive map

The hippocampus of food-storing birds and mammals has been shown to be up to twice as large as the hippocampus of species that do not rely on retrieving food they previously cached (Krebs et al., 1989; Sherry et al., 1989; *See* Chapters 1.22, 1.23). Similarly, anatomical scans have shown that humans with advanced navigational capabilities, such as London taxi drivers, may have bigger hippocampi as well (Maguire et al., 2000). Given the biological costs associated with maintaining a larger hippocampus, these findings indicate that this neural structure must play crucial role in navigation ability.

Elucidating the specific role of the hippocampus in spatial memory has been the main focus of navigation research for almost 30 years. The main inspiration for this line of research is a highly influential book by O'Keefe and Nadel (1978) entitled *The Hippocampus as a Cognitive Map*. In this book, O'Keefe and Nadel provided an extensive review of the anatomical, electrophysiological, and neuropsychological literature pertaining to the hippocampus. Based on the evidence they reviewed, they proposed the theory that the hippocampus specifically mediates the construction and use of a cognitive map, an allocentric topographical map of the physical environment that animals use to navigate among salient locations and other important cues in a flexible manner. In the framework of the present chapter, the cognitive map of the hippocampus is best characterized as supporting the navigational strategy of piloting to landmarks (*See* Chapter 1.33).

1.21.1.3.1.(i)   Anatomy of the hippocampal memory system

The hippocampus is a structure located deep in the brain, with its name derived from its curved shape in a coronal section, which resembles a seahorse. It is generally defined as consisting of the CA fields (cornu ammonis; CA1-CA3) and the dentate gyrus. The hippocampus receives highly processed sensory information, and as such should be described in the context of a larger system of cortical areas (Amaral and Witter, 1989; **Figure 1(a)**). This connectivity pattern between the hippocampus and cortical areas (**Figure 1(a)**), as well as the local hippocampal architecture circuitry (**Figure 1(b)**), has been shown to be remarkably conserved across mammalian species (Manns and Eichenbaum, 2006).

Individual perceptual and mnemonic representations from virtually all higher-order cortical processing areas are funneled into the parahippocampal region, which consists of the entorhinal, perirhinal, and parahippocampal (postrhinal in rodents) cortices, and in turn, information is then funneled into the hippocampus. This strong convergence of diverse inputs to the hippocampus, combined with the rapid and stable synaptic plasticity characterizing hippocampal circuits (e.g., Bliss and Collingridge, 1993), allows the hippocampus to rapidly form stable associations among previously unrelated elements from disparate cortical areas. A critical feature of the system is that the connections are reciprocated in a topographic manner, such that a representation at every level could reactivate elements of the higher level representation that originally activated it (Amaral and Witter, 1989;

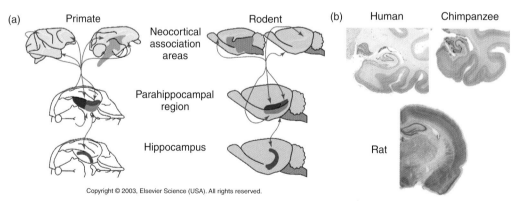

Figure 1   Similarity in the anatomy of the hippocampal system in primates and rodents. (a) Reciprocal connections between the neocortex, the parahippocampal region, and the hippocampus. From Squire LR, Bloom FE, McConnell SK, Roberts JL, Spitzer NC, and Zigmond MJ (2003) *Fundamental Neuroscience,* 2nd edn., p. 1305. New York: Academic Press, copyright Elsevier (2003). (b) Coronal sections of the hippocampus revealing the similarities in the structure of the hippocampus itself, such as the two interlocking c-shaped sectors consisting of the dense cell layers of the CA fields and dentate gyrus. The chimpanzee and human brain slices were cropped to focus on the region of interest; used with permission from www.brainmuseum.org, supported by the National Science Foundation.

Lavenex and Amaral, 2000). This organization may be important for consolidating associations formed in the hippocampus back into cortical areas (Buzsaki, 1996). These distinctive features of the anatomy of the hippocampal system suggest that it would be well suited to act as a cognitive map (O'Keefe and Nadel, 1978).

1.21.1.3.1.(ii) Experimental analysis of navigation

A number of field studies have shown natural behavior indicative of navigation based on a cognitive map (see O'Keefe and Nadel, 1978). For instance, analysis of the spatial behavior of wolf packs in the wild indicates a flexible maplike representation of the environment. Wolves have been reported to return to their pups from any direction, to take necessary shortcuts or detours, and to be able to divide and regroup as a pack over large distances (presumably beyond the range of howling; Peters, 1973). Menzel (1973) has reported similar abilities in chimpanzees. When chimps were carried around an environment and allowed to observe an experimenter hiding food rewards, they subsequently ran directly between food locations and rarely returned to locations where food had already been obtained. Such efficient navigation, not shown in chimps that did not observe the experimenter hiding the food, demonstrates a clear mental representation of the food locations.

Though valuable insight has been obtained from field studies, the vast majority of studies characterizing the navigational capacities of mammals were performed in controlled experimental settings. The laboratory setting confers an advantage because it allows more control over the cues animals may use to navigate and facilitates measurements of navigation capacity. Importantly, the artificial nature of the laboratory experiment does not seem to be a significant concern, as evidenced by studies showing that spatial behavior does not differ between field and laboratory contexts (e.g., Jacobs and Shiflett, 1999). This section will review the behavioral paradigms that provided evidence suggesting that animals use a cognitive map for navigation. Consideration of all paradigms is beyond the scope of this chapter; consequently, only the most widely used will be discussed. Readers are referred to O'Keefe and Nadel (1978) and Eichenbaum and Cohen (2001) for extensive reviews.

1.21.1.3.1.(ii).(a) Evidence from rodent studies

• *Complex maze learning.* Inspired by the famous maze at Hampton Court Palace in England, Small (1901) introduced the use of complex mazes to study

animal intelligence (see **Figure 2**). The method was quite simple. After being placed at the start of the maze, the rat had to learn through trial and error the trajectory that led to the goal, learning being indicated by a gradual decrease in the number of entries in blind (incorrect) alleys across trials.

Though extensively used to study animal learning, the nature of the task emphasized the learning of series of egocentric left and right turns and as such is not optimally designed to measure navigational capacities. However, careful analysis of the behavior of animals suggested that rats 'navigated' through the maze by relying to some extent on visual landmarks in the room to locate the general direction of the reward. In fact, manipulations such as rotating the maze seemed to disrupt performance (Watson, 1907), and rats were more likely to enter blind alleys

(a)

(b)

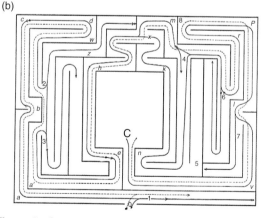

Figure 2 Complex maze learning. (a) Hampton Court Palace maze outside London, which served as inspiration; used with permission from Google Earth mapping service. (b) Diagram of one of the mazes used by Small WS (1901) Experimental study of the mental processes of the rat. II. *Am. J. Psychol.* 12: 206–239.

that pointed toward the goal than those pointing away from the goal (Tolman, 1932). Furthermore, damage to the hippocampus leads to deficits in complex maze learning in a number of studies (see table A20 in O'Keefe and Nadel, 1978), suggesting that the ability of rats to use distal cues to establish their position in relation to the goal location is an important source of information that complements the learning of left- and right-turn associations.

• *Detours and shortcuts: Cognitive maps in rats and humans.* Instead of accepting the commonly held notion from behaviorism that animal learning is based on an assortment of stimulus–response associations which are subsequently triggered by environment stimuli, Tolman demonstrated that rats can learn the spatial layout of a maze as stimulus–stimulus associations and express their knowledge in a flexible manner. In fact, Tolman and Honzik (1930) showed that rats familiar with an environment spontaneously take the shortest detour when their habitual route is blocked (**Figure 3(a)**), and subsequently, Tolman and colleagues (Tolman et al., 1946) used the 'sun-burst' maze to show that rats can select the optimal

shortcut when the longer habitual route is suddenly unavailable (**Figure 3(b)**).

Based on these findings, Tolman (1948) was the first to propose that rats (and humans) use cognitive maps of their environment to get from one place to another. The impact of Tolman's work diminished in the 1950s and 1960s but increased in the late 1970s, as his description of cognitive maps inspired the influential work of O'Keefe and Nadel (1978).

• *Radial-arm maze.* Inspired by the natural behavior of rats, Olton and colleagues (Olton and Samuelson, 1976; Olton et al., 1977) designed the radial-arm maze, a formal testing paradigm to study the ability of rats to collect food efficiently from several locations. The maze is composed of a central platform, out of which runway arms extend radially (typically eight arms). In the original version, a food reward is initially placed at the end of each arm, and optimal foraging performance would consist of running down the end of each arm only once. Since arms are not rebaited, revisiting an arm is considered an error (**Figure 4(a)**).

Experimental manipulations have shown that distal (extra-maze) cues control behavior (Olton

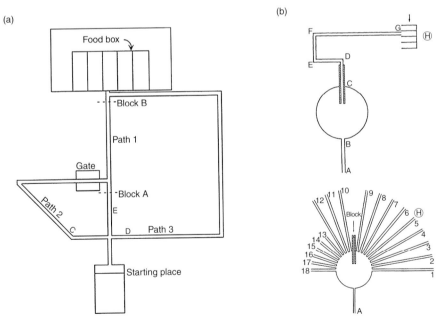

Figure 3 Detours and shortcuts as evidence for a cognitive map. (a) Diagram of the maze used to test the ability of rats to infer a required detour. From Tolman EC (1951/1966) *Collected Papers in Psychology*, p. 74. Berkeley, CA: University of California Press. (b) Diagrams of the maze used to test the ability of rats to infer a shortcut. Top: animals learned this particular trajectory to the goal (H). Bottom: The learned trajectory was blocked and rats could choose from arms 1 to 18. The largest number of rats chose arm 6, which led most directly to the trained goal site. Adapted from Tolman EC, Ritchie BF, and Kalish D (1946) Studies in spatial learning. I. Orientation and the short-cut. *J. Exp. Psychol.* 36: 13–24, with permission from the American Psychological Association. The use of APA information does not imply endorsement by the APA.

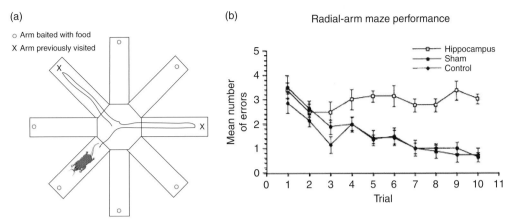

Figure 4   Radial-arm maze task. (a) The maze consists of eight arms radially extending from a central platform. Before each session, all arms were baited with a food reward, and optimal foraging performance would consist of running down the end of each arm only once. (Olton and Samuelson, 1976). (b) Animals with hippocampal damage were severely impaired in learning the task compared to control groups. Adapted from McDonald RJ and White NM (1993) A triple dissociation of memory systems: Hippocampus, amygdala, and dorsal striatum. *Behav. Neurosci.* 107(1): 3–22, with permission from the American Psychological Association. The use of APA information does not imply endorsement by the APA.

and Samuelson, 1976; Suzuki et al., 1980). Indeed, eliminating local odor cues by washing the maze does not affect performance, and animals are not affected by rotations of the maze on its central axis (i.e., they continue to use the distal cues in the room to orient themselves). Disruptions of the hippocampus severely impair performance on this task, suggesting that the hippocampus plays an important role in the processing of information about spatial location supporting navigation (Olton et al., 1978; Olton and Werz, 1978; **Figure 4(b)**). Although it was shown that the deficits of hippocampal animals in the task may not be indicative of a spatial memory deficit per se (Olton and Feustle, 1981, discussed later), this paradigm has been used extensively and represents an important step in our understanding of the neural basis of navigation.

- *Morris water maze.* The water maze task, developed by Morris (1981), is the quintessential navigational paradigm in behavioral research. It measures the ability of rats to remember the location of an escape platform in a large swimming pool (usually >2 m in diameter). Rats are capable swimmers but, as one would expect, prefer not to swim and instead search for solid ground. To ensure that animals rely on extra-maze cues to find the platform location, the water is made opaque by adding powdered milk, and the escape platform is placed arbitrarily in the pool just below the surface. Unlike spatial paradigms that rely on a limited number of choices (left or right turns, or arms in the radial-arm maze), the water maze tests spatial

acuity and requires constant monitoring on the part of the animal (Morris, 1981). Furthermore, rats must use a flexible spatial representation to solve the task, since they are placed in different starting locations at the periphery of the pool on each trial, to avoid the establishment of a rigid swim route, and are also very efficient from novel starting points even if they were trained from a consistent starting point (Morris, 1981; **Figure 5(a)**).

Morris and colleagues (1982) have shown that damage to the hippocampus results in severe impairments in the water maze task (**Figure 5(b)**), providing strong support for the theory that the hippocampus implements a cognitive map of the environment. On the initial trial, control animals could take up to 1 or 2 min to find the platform, but on subsequent trials this latency was reduced considerably to approximately 10–15 s from all starting positions (**Figure 5(c)**). Rats with hippocampal damage also showed some improvement in finding the platform, but their performance reached an asymptote (~35 s), and unlike control animals, they never swam directly to the platform. The trajectories of the rats were also monitored during 'transfer tests,' during which the escape platform was removed (**Figure 5(d)**). Whereas normal rats swam around where the platform should have been (indicating strong memory), hippocampal rats showed no preference for the quadrant where the platform should have been located. Finally, in a control condition in

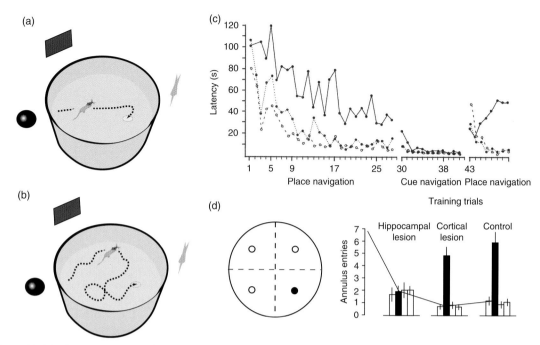

Figure 5   Morris water maze task (Morris, 1981). (a) Example swim path of a control rat. (b) Example swim path of a rat with damage to the hippocampus. (c) Performance of rats with hippocampal lesions (filled circles and lines), cortical lesions (filled circle and dashed lines), and normal controls (open circle) in acquiring the water maze task. Place navigation refers to the condition in which the platform is hidden under the surface; cue navigation refers to a control condition in which the platform is visible to the animals. (d) Performance on transfer test in which the platform was removed. Hippocampal animals were no more likely to pass over the trained location of the platform (filled circle and bar) than the corresponding location in other quadrants (open circles and bars) (c, d) Adapted from Morris RG, Garrud P, Rawlins JN, and O'Keefe J (1982) Place navigation impaired in rats with hippocampal lesions. *Nature* 297(5868): 681–683, with permission from Macmillan Publishers Ltd.

which the escape platform is visible to the rats (cue navigation; **Figure** 5(c)), both groups rapidly learned to swim directly to it, suggesting that hippocampal rats do not suffer from visual or motivational deficits.

The main assets of the water maze task are the speed of training and the robustness of the impairments shown in animals with damage to the hippocampus. For these reasons, the water maze task has become a benchmark test of hippocampal function in rodents (Eichenbaum and Cohen, 2001).

1.21.1.3.1.(ii).(b)   Evidence from primate studies

A number of experimental studies in humans and monkeys have also implicated the hippocampus in learning spatial information essential for navigation. Neuropsychological studies have shown that the integrity of the hippocampus is essential for spatial memory, as demonstrated by the deficits of amnesic patients (Smith and Milner, 1981, 1989; Maguire et al., 1996) or monkeys with dysfunctional hippocampi (Murray et al., 1989; Lavenex et al., 2006) in

different spatial tests. Functional neuroimaging studies have also identified the hippocampus as part of network of structures important for navigation in large-scale environments. For instance, Maguire and colleagues (1997) scanned London taxi drivers with years of experience while they recalled complex routes around the city. Compared with baseline and other nontopographical memory tasks, such route recall resulted in activation of a network of brain regions, including the right hippocampus. Furthermore, in a different study, Maguire and colleagues (1998) developed a test in which normal human subjects explored an imaginary town using virtual reality technology, and reported that activation of the right hippocampus was strongly associated with remembering where specific places were located and navigating accurately between them.

1.21.1.3.1.(iii)   Electrophysiological evidence supporting the cognitive map theory

The concept of a cognitive map has been refined over the years (McNaughton et al., 1996; Muller et al., 1996; O'Keefe and Burgess, 1996) but remains fundamentally similar to O'Keefe and Nadel's (1978) original description. Conceptually, the cognitive map is a two-dimensional Cartesian reconstruction of the environment, in that it provides metric representations of distances and angles between the relevant stimuli (*See* Chapters 1.33, 1.35).

The discovery of place cells in the hippocampus was a crucial piece of evidence supporting the cognitive map theory of the hippocampus. *Place cells* are hippocampal neurons, typically from regions CA1 and CA3, that fire at a high rate whenever the animal is in a specific location in the environment, called the place field (**Figure 6(a)**). Their existence was first described by O'Keefe and Dostrovsky (1971) in rats, but was later confirmed in numerous more systematic studies (e.g., O'Keefe, 1976; Olton et al., 1978; O'Keefe and Conway, 1980; Hill and Best, 1981; Best and Ranck, 1982) and in other mammalian species (humans: Ekstrom et al., 2003; monkeys: Ludvig et al., 2004; mice: Rotenberg et al., 1996). A number of properties of place cells are suggestive of a cognitive map representation of a specific environment. First, their firing pattern is determined by the global spatial relations among landmarks, not simply associated with a particular cue in the environment. For instance, place cell firing is maintained even if individual distal cues are removed, or if all distal cues are rotated as a unit (the place field rotates with the cues; O'Keefe and Conway, 1978; Miller and Best, 1980; Hill and Best, 1981). Second, many place cells reflect the overall topography of the environment, as

they were shown to scale their size to reflect changes in the size of the environment (Muller and Kubie, 1987; O'Keefe and Burgess, 1996). Third, once established, the spatial representation of a specific environment coded by place cell is stable over long periods of time (at least 5 months; Thompson and Best, 1990).

At the conceptual level, a place cell is thought to construct the notion of a place in the environment by encoding the multisensory input pattern that can be perceived when the animal is in a specific part of the environment (O'Keefe, 1979). Each place cell is hypothesized to represent the position of the rat at a particular coordinate position in the map of the environment, and as a population, place cells could underlie a mechanism by which information about the spatial layout of the environment could be used to compute the flexible trajectories required by navigation.

1.21.1.3.2 Processing of spatial information in other brain regions

Despite an intense focus on the role of the hippocampus, it is clear that navigation is a capacity that requires other brain systems as well. In addition to the role of sensory systems to process and represent environmental stimuli, and the involvement of the prefrontal cortex in providing executive control of response selection and planning through interactions with cortico-striatal loops (e.g., De Bruin et al., 1994; Alexander et al., 1986; Dunnett et al., 2005), a number

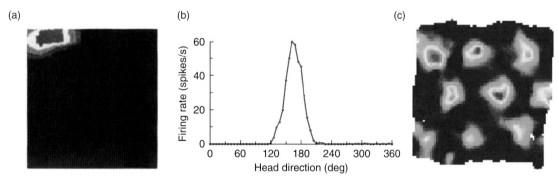

Figure 6 Neurons with spatial firing properties. (a) Place cell: Hippocampal neuron showing an increase in firing rate whenever the animal enters the North-West corner of an open-field environment. Adapted from O'Keefe J and Burgess N (1996) Geometric determinants of the place fields of hippocampal neurons. *Nature* 381(6581): 425–428, with permission from Macmillan Publishers Ltd. (b) Head-direction cell: Postsubicular neuron increasing its firing rate whenever the animal's head is facing a particular direction (60 degrees). Taken from Taube JS (2007) The head direction signal: Origins and sensory-motor integration. *Annu. Rev. Neurosci.* 30: 181–207, with permission from the Annual Review of Neuroscience. (c) Grid cell: Dorsocaudal medial entorhinal cortex neuron exhibiting multiple spatial firing fields arranged in a hexagonal grid in an open field. Taken from Hafting T, Fyhn M, Molden S, Moser MB, and Moser EI (2005) Microstructure of a spatial map in the entorhinal cortex. *Nature* 436(7052): 801–806, with permission from Macmillan Publishers Ltd.

of structures are thought to be critical for navigation, either by having a role associated with that of the hippocampus or by supporting navigational strategies independent of the hippocampus.

1.21.1.3.2.(i) Brain systems associated with the role of the hippocampus

1.21.1.3.2.(i).(a) Parahippocampal region

Although the perirhinal, parahippocampal, and entorhinal regions make significant contributions on their own to information processing (Suzuki et al., 1993; Brown and Aggleton, 2001; Burwell et al., 2004), a major role of these regions is to act as a necessary intermediary link between the complex representations in cortical association areas and the hippocampus itself. According to McClelland and Goddard (1996), the parahippocampal region is important for 'compressing' representations of the complex information contained in numerous cortical associational areas, which allows the hippocampus to access and create associations between those complex representations. This network organization would provide a mechanism by which complex visuospatial representations of the environment in the parietal and retrosplenial cortices shown to be important for spatial information processing (Kolb et al., 1994; Ennaceur et al., 1997; Maguire, 2001; Mesulam et al., 2001; Whishaw et al., 2001; Parron and Save, 2004; Vann and Aggleton, 2004; Goodrich-Hunsaker et al., 2005) could reach the hippocampus. This proposal is supported by evidence demonstrating that the entorhinal (Parron et al., 2004; Parron and Save, 2004) and postrhinal/parahippocampal regions (Maguire et al., 1997; Liu and Bilkey, 2002) are important for performance of spatial tasks.

1.21.1.3.2.(i).(b) Areas with spatial coding complementing that of the hippocampus

Though the representations are typically not as precise and sparse as those of the hippocampus, consistent place-related firing has been observed in the lateral septum (Zhou et al., 1999; Leutgeb and Mizumori, 2002), ventromedial entorhinal cortex (Mizumori et al., 1992; Quirk et al., 1992), subiculum (Sharp and Green, 1994; Martin and Ono, 2000), postsubiculum (Sharp, 1996), and parasubiculum (Taube, 1995a; Hargreaves et al., 2005). Such spatial representations in many distinct regions associated with the hippocampus may imply some degree of redundancy in the nervous system, but more likely it reflects the complementary contribution of each of those areas in representing or operating on aspects of the organism's representation of space.

Directional heading is another type of spatial coding important for navigation. It is coded by *head-direction cells*, which are neurons that discharge when the animal points its head in a particular direction and, similar to place cells, are responsive to allothetic and idiothetic cues (**Figure 6(b)**). Head direction cells were initially discovered in the post-subiculum of rats (Taube et al., 1990), but were since then reported in the parasubiculum (Taube, 1995a), anterior thalamus (Taube, 1995b), laterodorsal thalamus (Zugaro et al., 2004), retrosplenial cortex (Chen et al., 1994), and medial entorhinal cortex (Sargolini et al., 2006), as well as in the primate presubiculum (Robertson et al., 1999; see Knierim, 2006, for a review). Information about directional heading is thought to provide an 'internal compass' or an orientation framework for our representation of space, and thus to be important for navigation through piloting (Goodridge et al., 1998) and path integration (Golob and Taube, 1999; Sargolini et al., 2006).

Finally, the most recently discovered type of spatial coding is an environment-independent coordinate system. The key units of this system are *grid cells*, cells located in the dorsocaudal medial entorhinal cortex that exhibit multiple spatial firing fields arranged in a hexagonal grid (Fyhn et al., 2004; Hafting et al., 2005; **Figure 6(c)**). The grid cell representation may offer a robust metric for calculating position, and since the dorsocaudal medial entorhinal cortex projects to the hippocampus, this information must be important for the development of sparse representations of spatial information in the hippocampus.

1.21.1.3.2.(ii) Brain systems implementing alternative navigational strategies

Although navigation research has predominantly focused on the hippocampus, there is considerable evidence that efficient navigational behavior can be supported by strategies other than piloting or the use of a cognitive map.

1.21.1.3.2.(ii).(a) Guidances and orientations

Consider the example of a spatial discrimination task in which an animal is required to learn to turn left on a T-maze in order to obtain a reward. One obvious strategy would be for the animal to use cues surrounding the maze to orient himself and learn that he must choose the arm on the left side of the room in order to be reinforced, that is, to use a piloting strategy thought to be dependent on the hippocampus. However, the animal could also use at least two other approaches to solve the task, which would fall under the guidances and orientations strategy. First, the animal could develop an attraction, or bias, toward the goal arm, approach it, and obtain a reward.

This navigational strategy of approaching or avoiding particular stimuli depends on the amygdala, a region known to be important for processing the emotional valence of stimuli (McDonald and White, 1993) and other aspects of emotional memory (McGaugh, 2005; Schafe et al., 2005). Alternatively, the animal could also solve the task by learning to perform an egocentric response (i.e., a left turn) at the choice point, a strategy that reflects the use of stimulus–response associations and depends on the integrity of the striatum (McDonald and White, 1993; Packard and McGaugh, 1996). The striatum is best known for its role in planning and modulation of movements, but has been shown to be important for associating specific stimuli or representations to complex behavioral responses, such as forming habits and skills (Graybiel, 1995; White, 1997). The parietal cortex has also been shown to be implicated in the processing of egocentric representations and computation of body turns necessary for navigation (Burgess et al., 1997; Maguire et al., 1998) and displays firing properties that are thought to underlie route representation (Nitz, 2006).

1.21.1.3.2.(ii).(b) Path integration The neural implementation of path integration is not yet well understood. In addition to the neural systems responsible for processing the idiothetic cues (proprioceptive, vestibular, and sensory flow information), behavioral evidence suggests that the parietal (Parron and Save, 2004), entorhinal (Parron and Save, 2004), and retrosplenial cortices (Cooper and Mizumori, 1999) are important for successful path integration (see Etienne and Jeffery, 2004).

The recent discovery of grid cells may help further our understanding of path integration by providing insight into its potential neuronal mechanisms. Grid cells are part of an environment-independent spatial coordinate system that integrates information about location, direction, distance, and speed. In addition to the grid cells previously reported in superficial layers (Fyhn et al., 2004; Hafting et al., 2005), the deep layers of the medial entorhinal cortex contains grid cells that are colocalized with head-direction cells, as well as

conjunctive grid X head-direction cells, with all cell types modulated by running speed (Sargolini et al., 2006). Such colocalized representations of location, distance, speed, and direction information have been proposed to be necessary for the neural computations required by path integration (Fuhs and Touretzky, 2006; McNaughton et al., 2006).

The parallel nature of the contribution of distinct strategies to navigation has been cleverly demonstrated experimentally, by creating conditions that expose either their synergistic or their conflicting interactions (McDonald and White, 1993; Packard and McGaugh, 1996). For instance, McDonald and White (1993) designed a simple stimulus–response task in which rats were required to enter arms identified with a light cue (stimulus–response, or habit, learning). As expected, the performance of control animals incrementally improved with training, and animals with damage to the dorsal striatum were severely impaired in learning the task. Interestingly, animals with hippocampal damage outperformed even control animals, implying that the use of a 'hippocampal' strategy, such as trying to remember the location of specific arms entered, is counterproductive in this particular task. This facilitation effect reflects the conflicting contribution of different strategies to solve the same navigation problem.

These findings help clarify the need for distinct neural systems encoding distinct behavioral strategies. For instance, a piloting strategy supported in part by the hippocampus can be employed quickly, but it requires intensive use of the animal's cognitive demands. In contrast, a stimulus–response strategy develops more slowly, but because of its 'habit' nature can support navigation with little mental effort. The latter strategy is particularly advantageous on highly familiar terrain in that navigation can be accomplished on 'automatic pilot,' and can also explain the common human behavior of following a habitual route in error if our concentration wanders.

1.21.1.3.3 Shortcomings of the cognitive map theory: Evidence for an alternative framework

1.21.1.3.3.(i) Navigation by piloting to landmarks does not always require a cognitive map, and navigation reflecting the use of a cognitive map does not always require the hippocampus First, tasks requiring animals to pilot to landmarks do not necessarily require following a unified cognitive map representation of the environment, as different types of associative learning may often support performance (Mackintosh, 2002). For instance, in the radial-arm maze task, animals could use information from (nonunified) local visual scenes specific to one or a few arms to remember the individual arms already visited on a given trial. Second, elaborate spatial processing indicative of a cognitive map representation can be accomplished in subjects with damage to the hippocampus. For instance, amnesics are impaired at learning new environments but can flexibly recall the spatial layout of a region learned prior to brain damage onset (Teng and Squire, 1999; Rosenbaum et al., 2000), and hippocampectomized animals are able to use the relations between distal landmarks to successfully navigate to an unseen food location (Alyan et al., 2000).

1.21.1.3.3.(ii) Neural representations in the hippocampus are not limited to a faithful Cartesian representation of the layout of the environment The only behavioral protocol in which the firing properties of place cells reflect an allocentric representation, independent of viewpoint and ongoing behavior ('true' place cells; O'Keefe, 1979), is when rats randomly forage for food in an open field environment (e.g., Muller and Kubie, 1987). This experimental protocol is unique in that every task component (e.g., location of reward, direction of trajectory, behavior) is randomized, and consequently most neurons show spatial specificity and no other behavioral correlate. In more elaborate behavioral paradigms, firing patterns of hippocampal neurons can be characterized as encoding task 'regularities' in a variety of paradigms (Eichenbaum et al., 1999). The activity of hippocampal neurons can reflect specific spatial regularities systematically embedded in the task protocol, such as particular speed and direction of movement or angle of turn (McNaughton et al., 1983; Wiener et al., 1989; Markus et al., 1995), but also extends to nonspatial regularities as well. Perhaps the clearest example was provided by Wood and colleagues (1999) in a study in which rats were required to perform the same recognition memory judgment (i.e., is the current odor a match/nonmatch to the previous odor?) in nine distinct locations in a rich spatial environment. They showed that some hippocampal cells fired only in a specific location, others only for one of the nine odors, others to the match/nonmatch status of the presented odor, and others to conjunctions of those task elements. These results indicate that hippocampal neurons encode a broad range of spatial and

nonspatial stimuli, behavioral events, and contingencies that characterize the task at hand.

1.21.1.3.3.(iii) The hippocampus is critical for nonspatial memory Accumulating evidence confirms that the role of the hippocampus is not limited to the processing of spatial information. In fact, though the radial-arm maze was designed to take advantage of rats' spatial abilities and was initially discussed as supporting evidence for the role of the hippocampus in processing spatial information (Olton et al., 1978; Olton and Werz, 1978; see earlier section titled 'Radial-arm maze'), Olton's subsequent work suggests that the hippocampus is not crucial for spatial processing per se, but rather plays a specific role in remembering trial-unique information for both the spatial and nonspatial domains (Olton and Papas, 1979; Olton and Feustle, 1981). In addition, the hippocampus has been shown to be important for creating representations of nonspatial information that can be expressed flexibly, in that they support novel generalizations and inferences from the acquired knowledge (e.g., Bunsey and Eichenbaum, 1996; Dusek and Eichenbaum, 1997; Dusek and Eichenbaum, 1998; Alvarez et al., 2002). These studies will be further discussed in later sections.

1.21.1.4 Conclusions

Navigation is a capacity crucial to mammals' survival that depends on the use of multiple strategies and types of representation, and thus emerges from the contribution of distinct neural systems. Striking parallels in neuroanatomy, neurophysiology, and behavior indicate that these navigational principles are fundamentally the same across mammalian species.

The prominent theory of the neural basis of navigation proposed that the hippocampus represents a cognitive map of the environment (O'Keefe and Nadel, 1978). The hippocampus was later shown to have a more limited role in spatial processing than originally envisaged, and to process nonspatial information as well, suggesting that the hippocampus is important for, but not dedicated to, spatial computations (Mackintosh, 2002). Conversely, recent studies have demonstrated that the full extent of the contribution of extra-hippocampal areas in the service of navigation has been underappreciated. Although elements of the cognitive map theory were incorrect, it should be considered a significant accomplishment in that it acted as a catalyst and generated considerable research evidence on the neural basis of navigation.

Finally, experimental research on navigation has provided a significant contribution to our understanding of general learning and memory principles in mammals. First, it demonstrated that animal learning is not limited to specific stimulus–response associations, but that animals can also internally reorganize information to form cognitive, or stimulus–stimulus, representations (Poucet, 1993). Second, it helped dissociate multiple memory systems by identifying some of their neural substrates and revealing conditions in which they may compete. Finally, because navigation tests such as the watermaze are easy to implement and quick to perform, they are currently being used extensively as a screening tool for learning and memory deficits for a variety of experimental groups (e.g., effects of drug compounds, effects of aging).

1.21.2 Episodic Memory

Unlike the study of navigation, which emphasized research in rodents, episodic memory research has its roots in the study of human cognitive psychology. Unfortunately, the concept of episodic memory is perhaps not as intuitive as the capacity for navigation. Navigation is a behavior that can be accomplished using distinct capacities or strategies, whereas episodic memory should be viewed as a specific memory capacity among many that are essential for adaptive behavior. The precise nature of episodic memory may be better understood by comparisons with other memory systems in a multiple memory system framework, which is the approach taken in this section.

1.21.2.1 Multiple Forms of Memory

1.21.2.1.1 Historical perspective

The existence of multiple forms of memory gained widespread acceptance rather recently, but some prescient thinkers proposed similar ideas a long time ago. Writings from Aristotle (circa 350 BC; translated in Aristotle, 1984), Maine de Biran (1804/1929), Gall (1835), William James (1890), and certainly many others have offered meritorious descriptions of the organization of memory (for reviews, see Schacter and Tulving, 1994; Eichenbaum and Cohen, 2001). Most of these proposals contrast forms of memory that support 'conscious' memory, with other forms

which characteristically do not reach consciousness, that are more of a 'habit' nature. In a manner akin to current accounts, some even distinguished capacities similar to our current concepts of 'knowing' and 'recollecting' (Eichenbaum et al., 2005). Although these early accounts relied on introspection and observation rather than experiments, they successfully capture the essence of the idea of multiple forms of memory as it is known today. At the same time, they also offer a sense of the considerable progress made in recent years in refining these ideas, especially in terms of delineating their respective neural substrates.

1.21.2.1.2 Modern taxonomy of memory systems

In recent years, a new memory taxonomy has emerged from the experimental work of several laboratories (e.g., Cohen and Squire, 1980; Squire and Zola-Morgan, 1991; Schacter and Tulving, 1994). Despite evolving primarily from human studies, this classification has been shown to extend to other mammals as well (Eichenbaum and Cohen, 2001), and considerable research evidence indicates that these phenomenologically distinct forms of memory are supported by distinct memory systems (**Figure 7**; Squire, 2004). The two major types of memory, declarative and nondeclarative, are distinguished according to criteria such as the speed of information acquisition, the nature of their represented information, and the means of expression (Squire, 1992).

Declarative memory, also called explicit memory, refers to the memory for facts and events that can be brought into consciousness and expressed explicitly (Cohen and Squire, 1980; Cohen, 1984; Squire and Cohen, 1984; Cohen and Eichenbaum, 1993; Tulving and Markowitsch, 1998). The stored information is of propositional nature (i.e., can be 'declared'), such that one could describe it symbolically and infer relationships among memories. It is a large, complex, and highly structured system with a presumed unlimited capacity, which allows information from all modalities to be stored, often after a single exposure to an event or a fact. A critical feature of the declarative memory representation is its flexibly of access and expression, which allows memories to be retrieved from various logical associations and expressed through a variety of behaviors. Declarative memory is further divided into episodic and semantic memory (Tulving, 1983; Tulving, 1991; Squire et al., 1993), and their distinction has received considerable interest in recent years. In broad terms, episodic memory

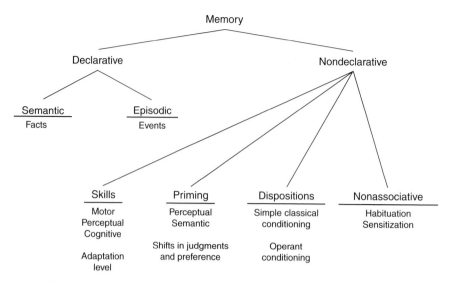

Figure 7 Taxonomy of memory systems. Adapted from Squire LR (1992) Memory and the hippocampus: A synthesis from findings with rats, monkeys, and humans. *Psychol. Rev.* 99: 195–231, with permission from the American Psychological Association. The use of APA information does not imply endorsement by the APA.

refers to the memory for personal experiences (or autobiographical memory for events), while semantic memory is the memory for facts or general knowledge about the world (Squire et al., 1993).

Nondeclarative (implicit) memory, in contrast, consists of a broad set of learning capabilities that involve acquisition of skills and preferences that can be expressed unconsciously by changes in the speed or biasing of performance; they include motor, perceptual, and cognitive skills; habituation and sensitization; sensory adaptations; and priming of perceptual and lexical stimuli (Squire, 1992). Unlike declarative memories, for which the products of retrieval can be consciously 'thought about' and may not lead to overt behavior, retrieval of nondeclarative memories must be expressed through a change in performance (Tulving and Markowitsch, 1998).

1.21.2.1.3 *Episodic and semantic memory*

Although these two forms of declarative memory have many characteristics in common, they are distinguishable on a number of features (Tulving, 1972, 1993a; Tulving and Markowitsch, 1998). In his earlier work, Tulving (1972) suggested that they differed in their relationship to the context in which information was acquired, in that episodic memories were intrinsically tied to the context, whereas semantic memories were essentially context-free. Recent developments in the definition of episodic memory have focused on differences in the 'experiential' nature of episodic and semantic memory as revealed by careful introspective

analysis. According to Tulving and Markowitsch (1998), episodic memory involves 'remembering' specific personal past experiences, whereas semantic memory involves 'knowing' impersonal facts. More precisely, the fundamental difference between episodic and semantic memory lies in the basis of the type of awareness that accompanies recall: episodic memory requires an awareness of personal experience (autonoetic awareness), whereas semantic memory is characterized by the conscious feeling of knowing (noetic awareness; Tulving, 2002). In addition, Tulving (2002) also emphasized that episodic memory is unique in that it is the only form of memory oriented toward the past at the time of retrieval, in the sense that our 'self' must 'mentally time travel' through one's past, in order to 'reexperience' a specific event. In contrast, semantic memory, or knowing, occurs in the present, as one needs not think back to earlier experiences to confirm knowledge of a fact (e.g., knowing that Paris is the capital of France does not require memory for a specific experience).

Annual scientific conferences provide a concrete example of the distinction between the two types of declarative memory. Seeing a particular face may trigger retrieval of an episodic memory, as you think back and distinctly remember having spoken to this person in front of their research poster toward the end of the session on the first day of the meeting. In contrast, seeing another face may simply bring forth a feeling of familiarity as you know you have met this person before but cannot retrieve the specific experience, a situation with the potential to be quite embarrassing. This ability of normal individuals to discriminate between 'remembering' and 'knowing' has been used to operationalize whether particular recalled memories originated from the episodic or semantic domain, providing evidence that the types of memory can be experimentally dissociated at the phenomenological level ('remember/know' distinction; Tulving, 1993b; Knowlton and Squire, 1995).

1.21.2.2 Role of the Hippocampus in Episodic Memory

As in the study of navigation, the main focus of episodic memory research has been to clarify its neural substrate. Therefore, progress in our understanding of the nature of episodic memory will be discussed along with developments in our knowledge of its neural implementation.

As mentioned earlier, the strong convergence of diverse inputs to the hippocampus, combined with the rapid and stable synaptic plasticity characterizing hippocampal circuits (e.g., Bliss and Collingridge, 1993), allow the hippocampus to rapidly form stable associations among previously unrelated elements from disparate cortical areas. Although such associations could be created in the service of creating a cognitive map, as discussed in the previous section, they could also support episodic memory coding by associating environmental stimuli that constitute elements of individual episodic memories.

1.21.2.2.1 Evidence from human studies

The first insight into the neural implementation of episodic memory came from case studies of neurological patients reported to have a memory deficit for daily life events (Tulving et al., 1988; Vargha-Khadem et al., 1997). In one study, patients who suffered neurological damage selective to the hippocampus demonstrated a pronounced amnesia for the episodes of everyday life, but attained relatively normal levels of speech and language competence, literacy, and factual knowledge (Vargha-Khadem et al., 1997). These findings suggested that episodic and semantic memory differ in their neural implementation, with only the episodic component being fully dependent on the hippocampus.

The evidence provided by these case studies is supported by more formal experiments. First, evidence suggests that the hippocampus is important for tests of recall, which are thought to depend exclusively on episodic memory retrieval (Mandler, 1980), but not for recognition tests, which may be solved in nonepisodic ways (for a review, see Aggleton and Shaw, 1996). Second, using the 'remember/know' method to distinguish episodic and semantic memory, Eldridge and colleagues (2000) demonstrated that the hippocampus was selectively activated when sample items were consciously recollected ('remember'), but not when they were simply recognized ('know'). Unfortunately, the use of these paradigms is unlikely to be the key to determine the role of the hippocampus in episodic memory, as similar studies have failed to show a selective role for the hippocampus in episodic processes (e.g., Squire and Zola, 1998; Manns and Squire, 1999; Manns et al., 2003). These inconsistent findings are in part due to the fact that these paradigms provide inadequate measures of episodic memory capacity. Comparisons between tests of recall and recognition are not sensitive enough to clearly distinguish the contribution of episodic and semantic processes, such that slight changes in methodological details can affect the performance of control and amnesic subjects (Squire and Zola, 1998), and although the 'remember/know' approach may capture the phenomenological distinction between episodic and semantic retrieval, its use of introspective judgments cannot be considered an infallible operational definition, as human subjects are notorious for creating false memories (see Eichenbaum and Fortin, 2003).

Recent approaches focusing on objective and measurable observations to assess episodic memory performance have shown promising results. In line with Tulving's (1972) early proposal that the context in which events are experienced is an integral part of episodic memories, functional imaging studies have shown that the hippocampus is involved in remembering the specific relationships among elements of an episodic memory (Davachi and Wagner, 2002) and the episodic context in which specific items were presented (Davachi et al., 2003). Another approach consists of using *receiver operating characteristics* (ROC) analyses to measure the relative contribution of episodic and semantic processes to recognition memory, which are based on the pattern of correct and incorrect responses across confidence levels or biases (Yonelinas, 2001, 2002; procedures described in further detail in the following). Such studies have also shown that the hippocampus is selectively important for episodic memory (Yonelinas et al., 2002; Daselaar et al., 2006).

Unfortunately, even if considerable progress were made in establishing clear experimental measures of episodic memory capacity, the exclusive use of human studies may not be sufficient to determine the precise contribution of the hippocampus to episodic and semantic processes. First, studies of neurological patients present a number of limitations. The brain damage patients suffered is rarely circumscribed to one specific area, which hinders the establishment of clear structure–function relationships. Conversely, brain damage to one specific area is rarely complete such that remaining fragments with residual function may or may not contribute to memory (Squire and Zola, 1998; Maguire et al., 2001). Second, advances in functional neuroimaging may be able to address some of those issues, but like any experimental technique, it has limitations on its own. The primary concern is that resolving the role of specific structures in different types of memory may be beyond the anatomical and temporal resolution of functional imaging techniques.

In light of these difficulties in providing unambiguous evidence from studies of amnesia or functional brain imaging in humans, it is clear that the development of an animal model of episodic memory to use in convergence with human studies is essential. As demonstrated in the navigation section earlier, animal studies directly compensate for the limitations of human studies by allowing much greater control over the anatomical specificity of the brain lesions and the amount of information learned before and after the damage. Also, the activity of individual neurons in multiple brain areas can be directly observed in animals, and the findings may reveal qualitative as well as quantitative distinctions in the nature of memory representations in these areas.

1.21.2.2.2 Evidence from nonhuman mammals

Do animals have episodic memory? One point of view, proposed by Tulving and others (Tulving, 1972, 2002; Tulving and Markowitsch, 1998), is that episodic memory is unique to humans. Tulving and Markowitsch (1998) claimed that the distinction between remembering and knowing simply does not exist in animals, and that declarative memory in animals corresponds to semantic memory in humans. The opposite position emphasizes parsimony in evolutionary design, which suggests that the antecedents of human forms of episodic memory should be found in animals (Morris, 2001; Whishaw and Wallace, 2003). Evolutionary parsimony implies that a similar

algorithm is being used by the hippocampus and its related structures across mammalian species, a proposal supported by the high degree of conservation of the hippocampal system across mammalian species in terms of cell types, connectional architecture, and basic structure (Amaral and Witter, 1989; Lavenex and Amaral, 2000; Manns and Eichenbaum, 2006). Even if the information to be operated upon is different in humans because of language, consciousness, or autonoetic awareness, there are no obvious cellular, connectional, or biochemical differences that would suggest that the computations are of a different nature (Morris, 2001).

According to Tulving (2002), concepts unique to humans such as self, autonoetic awareness, subjectively sensed time, mental time travel, language, and consciousness are all critical to episodic memory. However, though it is clear that these elements of episodic memory cannot be addressed in animals, their absence does not necessarily invalidate attempts to model episodic memory in animals. For instance, language is clearly important for episodic memory in humans, but species that cannot communicate through language are not logically prevented from having private recollective experiences, as experiencing events and recalling them later is certainly independent of their overt communication to conspecifics (see Morris, 2001). In order to develop an animal model of episodic memory, we must operationally define species-independent features of episodic memory that can be tested experimentally by objective behavioral measures reflecting the subject's knowledge of its experiences. Recent theoretical work has identified a number of such features of episodic memory that can be tested in animals (Griffiths et al., 1999; Aggleton and Pierce, 2001; Morris, 2001; Roberts, 2002; Eichenbaum and Fortin, 2003; Whishaw and Wallace, 2003), and four experimental approaches testing the following features will be discussed here: (1) episodic memories are acquired in a single experience, (2) episodic memories contain information about the context in which experiences occurred, (3) episodic memories are structured sequences of events, and (4) episodic memories are characterized by a recollective process with distinct retrieval dynamics.

1.21.2.2.2.(i) Episodic memories are acquired in a single experience
The first approach focuses on the fact that episodic memories are formed after a single experience (e.g., Tulving, 1972, 2002; Tulving and Markowitsch, 1998). The main experimental

paradigm used in this approach is the delayed nonmatch-to-sample task, which tests the capacity of animals to remember a single exposure to a novel stimulus (Gaffan, 1974; Mishkin and Delacour, 1975). This recognition task starts with a sample phase in which the animal is presented with a single stimulus, followed by a delay period in which the stimulus is not present, and ends with a test phase in which the animal is required to select the novel stimulus over the sample stimulus (that is, to 'nonmatch' to the sample) in order to be reinforced. A substantial literature in rats and monkeys shows that damage to the medial temporal lobe region (hippocampus and parahippocampal region), or damage selective to the parahippocampal region, produces a severe delay-dependent impairment. In fact, animals perform normally when the delay period lasts a few seconds, but their accuracy declines rapidly with longer delays (Suzuki et al., 1993; Mumby and Pinel, 1994; Zola-Morgan et al., 1994; Murray, 1996). However, selective damage to the hippocampus results in modest (Mumby et al., 1992; Zola et al., 2000; Clark et al., 2001) or no deficit on delayed performance even when the memory load is very high (Murray and Mishkin, 1998; Dudchenko et al., 2000), suggesting that parahippocampal cortical areas can support this form of simple recognition without critical hippocampal involvement.

In contrast, different results have emerged using the visual paired-comparison task, a recognition test similar in memory demands, but with slightly different behavioral procedures. In this test, animals are simply exposed to a novel visual stimulus and then, following a delay, are tested for time spent visually investigating the same stimulus versus a novel stimulus. In this test, selective damage to the hippocampus produces a severe delay-dependent impairment (Clark et al., 2000; Zola et al., 2000). These mixed findings among recognition tests in animals parallel the inconsistent results reported in recall and recognition tests in human neurological patients mentioned above.

At first, such inconsistent findings in recognition tests seemed difficult to reconcile with emerging theories of the role of the hippocampus in episodic memory. However, it has become clear that recognition paradigms can be solved by ways other than episodic memory (e.g., Griffiths et al., 1999). In fact, analogous to the 'remember/know' distinction reported earlier, performance on simple recognition tasks can be supported by at least two processes, one involving a hippocampal-dependent recollective (episodic) process and another involving

hippocampal-independent familiarity-based (semantic) processing (Eichenbaum et al., 1994; Griffiths et al., 1999; Fortin et al., 2004; Brown and Aggleton, 2001). Methodological differences between recognition studies may change the degree to which subjects rely on episodic recall or on alternative strategies, a likely explanation for the conflicting results in subjects with damage to the hippocampus.

In conclusion, the formation of a memory after a single experience is not a capacity exclusive to episodic memory, as it can be supported by a number of other memory capacities (e.g., familiarity, imprinting, fear conditioning, taste aversion). Tests of memory for single experiences are not sensitive enough to distinguish the individual contribution of these processes and thus are not optimal for investigating episodic memory.

1.21.2.2.2.(ii) Episodic memories contain information about the context in which experiences occurred

In order to be exclusively episodic in nature, experimental paradigms must have behavioral requirements unlikely to be fully subserved by other memory systems. A new approach pioneered by Clayton and Dickinson (1998) is to take advantage of the contextual differences between episodic and semantic memory to contrast them. According to Tulving (1972), episodic memories are tied to the context in which experiences occur, as if labeled for when and where they were acquired, whereas semantic memories are timeless and not bound to the place or other aspects of the context where knowledge was gained. Therefore, tests requiring animals to remember information about the context in which episodes occurred may be successful in measuring episodic memory capacity.

1.21.2.2.2.(ii).(a) What-where-when

Clayton and Dickinson (1998) were the first to show that episodic memory may not be a uniquely human phenomenon, by providing behavioral evidence that animals can recall a unique past experience. They investigated memory for when and where events occurred in a clever experiment that utilized the natural caching behavior of scrub jays. Initially, jays cached both worms and peanuts in an array of locations. Jays prefer worms to peanuts, so if recovery is allowed within a few hours after caching, the jays will recover worms first. However, if a multiday interval is imposed between caching and recovery, the jays know that the worms are degraded and proceed to recover peanuts first. Scrub jays were capable of selecting either type of food depending on the time since caching, leading the authors to conclude the jays remembered *what* had been cached, as well as *where* and *when* each item was cached (what-where-when). Importantly, because the stimuli are equally familiar at the time of test, subjects cannot choose on the basis of differential familiarity, unlike in radial-arm maze and delayed nonmatching tests.

This capacity to retrieve information about the time and place of occurrence of a unique experience has also been shown in rodents (Ergorul and Eichenbaum, 2004), suggesting that it extends to nonhuman mammals as well. However, there are a number of limitations to this model. First, as mentioned by Roberts (2002), the '*when*' component of the study is more a reflection of the jays' sense of how much time has passed since the caching events rather than a measure of a temporally organized memory structure representing when specific experiences occurred in relation to each other, as described by Tulving (1983). Furthermore, the capacity to judge how much time has passed since caching could be guided by signals about the trace strengths of the caching memories instead of episodic recall. Thus, jays may learn to prefer worms 4 hours post-caching when their memory for the caching memory is very strong, but not after a few days when the memory is weaker (Eichenbaum and Fortin, 2003). Second, the requirement for 'what,' 'where,' *and* 'when' is arbitrary and, with regard to the role of the hippocampus, appears inconsistent with the findings of patients and animals with hippocampal damage. In fact, subjects with damage to the hippocampus are impaired when required to remember *where or when* specific events occurred (see below), suggesting that episodic recall is needed to retrieve either type of information associated with the original experience (not necessarily a combination of the two). It therefore appears that the proposal that episodic memories consist of a conjunction of *what*, *where*, and *when* may be too stringent. Overall, however, the demonstration by Clayton and Dickinson (1998) of a possible operational measure of episodic memory has been very influential and generated considerable interest in developing a more complete animal model of episodic memory (*See* Chapter 1.23).

1.21.2.2.2.(ii).(b) *Context in which experiences occur*

There are a number of experimental situations in which animals are required to remember the context in which specific events occurred, and evidence suggests that this capacity depends on the hippocampus. It is important to note that, in this chapter, context is broadly defined as the set of background features, external or internal to the subject, that are present when an event occurs (Ferbinteanu et al., 2006). The context of interest can be a particular visual scene (Gaffan and Parker, 1996) or the environment itself, as in the case of contextual fear conditioning paradigms in which damage to the hippocampus impairs the ability of animals to remember the testing box in which they received a foot shock (Phillips and LeDoux, 1992, 1995). Alternatively, the context may also be more abstract, in the sense that the hippocampus may be critical to remember the relevant component or feature of a particular task. For instance, the hippocampus has been shown to be important for the ability to choose the response that is correct given a specific behavioral context, such as which of two sequences is being completed (Agster et al., 2002), or to remember the task context in which a particular item was presented (e.g., source identification; Davachi et al., 2003). The context can also refer to internal sensations, as demonstrated by a study in which the hippocampus was critical to remember which behavioral response is appropriate, depending on rats' current internal motivational state (i.e., hunger or thirst; Kennedy and Shapiro, 2004).

Another line of evidence came into focus after recent models of episodic memory emphasized the importance of the spatial context of episodic memories (Clayton and Dickinson, 1998). In fact, when reinterpreted within an episodic memory framework, a number of spatial memory deficits in hippocampal animals alluded to previously in the navigation section can be better described as deficits in remembering the spatial location (spatial context) where specific events occurred. For instance, the hippocampus does not seem to be critical for spatial processing per se, but is important for remembering the spatial locations of individual arm entries in the radial-arm maze task (Olton and Papas, 1979), the trial-unique location of the escape platform in the watermaze (Steele and Morris, 1999), and the location where a trial-unique paired-associate was presented (Day et al., 2003). The relationship between navigation and episodic and semantic memory will be further discussed in the final section of this chapter.

In summary, these findings suggest that the experimental approach of testing the memory for the context in which specific events occurred, a function dependent on the hippocampus, is a feature of episodic memory that can be successfully tested in animals.

1.21.2.2.2.(iii) Episodic memories are structured as sequences of events The first two approaches were based on distinctions of episodic memory that have been emphasized explicitly by Tulving and, for the most part, described experimental paradigms already prominent in memory research. This novel approach captures a defining feature of episodic memory, but the formal details of the theory emerged from computational models of hippocampal function (Levy, 1996; Wallenstein et al., 1998; Lisman, 1999). As mentioned earlier, the neural architecture of the hippocampal system is rather unique. Of particular interest is region CA3 of the hippocampus, which has the highest density of recurrent connections in the brain and as such has been proposed to act as a heteroassociative network allowing successive events to be bound together into sequences (Levy, 1996; Wallenstein et al., 1998; Lisman, 1999). In line with Tulving's views (1983) that episodic memories are organized in the temporal dimension and that the central organizing feature of episodic memory is "one event precedes, co-occurs, or follows another," the fundamental principle underlying this approach is that each individual episode is organized as a sequence of events unfolding over time. Thus, this approach tests whether episodic memories contain not only a particular item or items that one is attempting to recall, but also the full sequence of events that precede and follow.

1.21.2.2.2.(iii).(a) Learning new sequences of events To investigate the specific role of the hippocampus in remembering the order of events in unique experiences, recent studies have employed a behavioral protocol that assesses memory for episodes composed of a unique sequence of olfactory stimuli (Fortin et al., 2002; Kesner et al., 2002). In one of these studies, memory for the sequential order of odor events was directly compared with recognition of the odors in the list independent of memory for their order (Fortin et al., 2002; **Figure 8(a)**). On each trial, animals were presented with a series of five odors, selected randomly from a large pool of common household scents. Memory for sequential order was probed using a choice test in which the animal was presented with two odors from the series and was reinforced for selecting the odor that appeared earlier. Similarly, recognition memory for the items in the series was probed using a choice between one of the odors from the series and another odor from the pool that was not in the series, and reinforcement was given for selecting the odor not presented in the

series. Normal rats performed well on sequential order judgments across all lags (temporal distance between probed odors; **Figure 8(b)**), and performance on probes was dependent on the lag, indicating that order judgments were easier for more widely separated items. By contrast, rats with hippocampal lesions performed the sequential order task at near-chance levels and were impaired at all lags. However, both control rats and rats with selective hippocampal damage acquired the recognition task rapidly, and no overall difference in performance was observed between the two groups (**Figure 8(c)**).

As mentioned earlier, a potential confound in any study that employs time as a critical dimension in episodic memory is that, due to the inherent decremental nature of memory traces, memories obtained at different times are likely to differ in terms of their trace strength. However, in the study of Fortin and colleagues (2002), both the control and the hippocampal groups demonstrated a temporal gradient in recognition performance (**Figure 8(c)**), suggesting that memories were in fact stronger for the more recently presented items in each sequence (e.g., performance on E vs. X is better than on A vs. X). Therefore, their finding that only hippocampal animals were impaired in sequential order judgments (**Figure 8(b)**) suggests that this capacity cannot be fully supported by the use of relative strengths of memories traces, but rather depends on episodic recall of the odor sequence.

Contrary to the argument that animals lack episodic memory because they are 'stuck in time' (Roberts, 2002; Tulving, 2002), these observations suggest that animals have the capacity to recollect the flow of events in unique experiences. Finally, reports of a similar pattern of findings in subjects with damage to the hippocampus (Spiers et al., 2001; Downes et al., 2002; but see also Hopkins et al., 1995) support the validity of this approach as an animal model of episodic memory.

1.21.2.2.2.(iii).(b) Disambiguating learned sequences of events A major challenge for a robust model of episodic memory is the requirement for a capacity to develop representations that can distinguish two experiences that share common elements (Shapiro and Olton, 1994). Levy (1989, 1996) proposed that memory for the ordering of events mediated by the hippocampus may be especially important when the event sequences have overlapping elements through which memory of earlier elements must be remembered to complete each

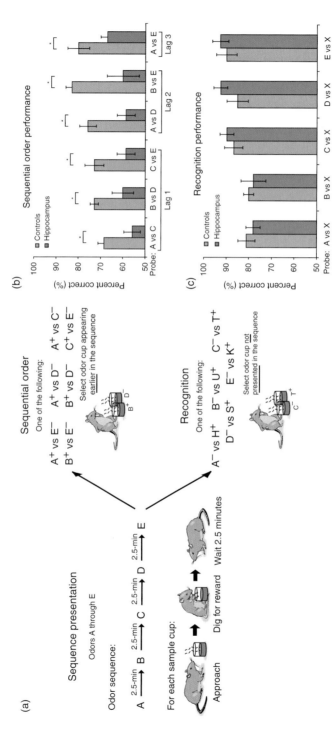

Figure 8 Sequential order and recognition tasks. (a) On each trial the animal was presented with a series of five odors (e.g., odors A through E). The animal was then either probed for its memory of the order of the items in the series (*top*) or its memory of the items presented (*bottom*). +, rewarded odor, −, nonrewarded odor. (b) Hippocampal animals were impaired on all sequential order probes. Performances on different probes are grouped according to the lag (number of intervening elements). (c) Hippocampal animals performed as well as controls on the recognition probes. 'X' designates a randomly selected odor that was not presented in the series and used as the alternative choice. *, $p < .05$. (a–c) Adapted from Fortin NJ, Agster KL, and Eichenbaum H (2002) Critical role of the hippocampus in memory for sequences of events. *Nat. Neurosci.* 5: 458–462, with permission from Macmillan Publishers Ltd.

distinct sequence. In order to test whether such sequence disambiguation is a fundamental feature of memory processing dependent on the hippocampus, Agster et al. (2002) trained rats on a sequence disambiguation task designed after Levy's (1996) formal model that involved two partially overlapping sequences of events (**Figure 9(a)**). The sequences were presented as a series of six pair-wise odor choices where, for each sequence, selection of the appropriate odor at each choice was rewarded (e.g., first choice being A vs. L). Each trial began with two forced choices that initiated production of one of the two sequences (e.g., A then B for Sequence 1). Then the animal was presented with two forced choices that were the same for both sequences (i.e., X then Y). Subsequently, the subject was allowed a free choice and was rewarded for selecting the odor assigned to the ongoing sequence (e.g., if given A→B→X→Y, then select E to complete Sequence 1). Finally the animal completed that sequence with one more forced choice (e.g., F for Sequence 1). The critical feature of this task was the free choice. On that test, animals were required to remember their choices from the first two pairings of the current sequence during the ambiguous components of the trial and then to use the earlier information to guide the correct odor selection.

Rats with damage to the hippocampus were impaired when sequences were presented in rapid succession (**Figure 9(b)**). However, hippocampal rats performed as well as controls in a version of the task in which proactive interference was reduced by increasing the inter-sequence delay (**Figure 9(c)**), but they were subsequently impaired when a 30-min delay was introduced before the free choice (**Figure 9(c)**). These findings suggest that, when memory demands are minimal, as in conditions of low proactive interference or no demand to hold information through ambiguous material, other brain systems, such as corticostriatal pathways, can succeed in coding sequences in which each segment rapidly or unambiguously leads to the next (Nissen and Bullemer, 1987; Reber and Squire, 1998). Conversely, under memory demands characteristic of episodic memory function, such as when proactive interference is high or when a substantial delay is

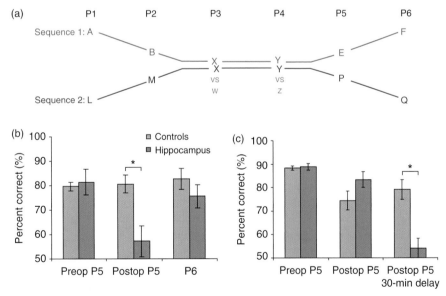

Figure 9 Sequence disambiguation task. (a) The two odor sequences are indicated by letters (Seq1: ABXYEF; Seq2: LMXYPQ). In performing each sequence, the rat selected between vertically aligned odors (e.g., for sequence 1 presentation, the rat should have selected A over L, B over M, X over W, Y over Z, E over P, and F over Q). Note that in both sequences, X was to be selected over W, and Y over Z. (b) When sequences were presented in rapid succession, hippocampal rats were impaired on P5, but not on P6, suggesting that their deficit is limited to a failure to remember the current sequence through the overlapping segment. (c) However, hippocampal rats performed as well as controls in a version of the task in which proactive interference was reduced by increasing the intersequence delay, but were subsequently impaired when a 30-min delay was introduced before the free choice. Modified from Agster KL, Fortin NJ, and Eichenbaum H (2002) The hippocampus and disambiguation of overlapping sequences. *J. Neurosci.* 22: 5760–5768, with permission from the Society for Neuroscience.

imposed between sequential experiences, a representation mediated by the hippocampus is required to disambiguate sequences of events.

In conclusion, the proposal that individual episodic memories are encoded as sequence of events, a hypothesis derived from computational models of hippocampal function, is in agreement with Tulving's view (1983) that the preservation of the temporal structure of events in experience is a central organizing feature of episodic memory. This approach has been successful in showing that the hippocampus of mammals is important for learning new sequences of events (in rodents: Fortin et al., 2002; Kesner et al., 2002; in primates: Spiers et al., 2001; Downes et al., 2002) and for disambiguating overlapping sequences of events (in rodents: Agster et al., 2002; in primates: Kumaran and Maguire, 2006).

1.21.2.2.2.(iv)   Episodic memories are characterized by a recollective process with distinct retrieval dynamics

The most recently developed approach to investigate episodic memory in animals focuses on mathematically deducing from objective behavioral measures the relative contribution of the two processes underlying recognition memory mentioned earlier: *recollection,* which corresponds to the recall of the original experience characteristic of episodic memory, and *familiarity,* which refers to nonepisodic recognition based on a general sense that an item has been previously experienced. In humans, signal detection techniques have been used to distinguish recollection and familiarity based on the shape of their receiver operating characteristic (ROC) curves, standard curves that represent item recognition across different levels of confidence or bias (Yonelinas, 2001; **Figures 10(a)–10(c)**). In such ROC curves, asymmetry (Y-intercept > 0) is viewed as an index of recollection, whereas the degree of curvature reflects the contribution of familiarity to recognition performance.

In order to determine whether animals also employ multiple processes in recognition memory and to explore the anatomical basis of this distinction, Fortin and colleagues (2004) adapted these techniques to examine odor recognition memory in rats (see **Figure 10(g)** for details). The ROC curve obtained in rats had asymmetrical (Y-intercept > 0) and curvilinear components, indicating the existence of both recollection and familiarity in rats (**Figure 10(d)**). Furthermore, following selective damage to the hippocampus, the ROC curve became entirely symmetrical (Y-intercept = 0) and remained curvilinear,

indicating selective loss of recollection capacity but preserved familiarity (**Figure 10(e)**). To further compare the performance of the two groups, the control group was subsequently tested with a longer memory delay (75 min instead of 30 min) to have its overall level of performance (averaged across biases) match that of the hippocampal group. In contrast to the hippocampal group (**Figure 10(e)**), the ROC curve of normal rats at 75 min delay remained asymmetric but showed little curvilinearity (**Figure 10(f)**), indicative of recognition performance mostly based on recollection.

The pattern of findings in this study strongly suggest (1) that the ROC approach, developed in humans, can be used to investigate episodic memory in rodents as well; (2) that rodents also use both episodic recollection and familiarity in recognition memory, providing an explanation for the mixed findings in the recognition tests mentioned; and (3) that, as in humans (Yonelinas et al., 2002), the hippocampus plays a predominant role in episodic recollection compared to familiarity (but see also Wais et al., 2006).

1.21.2.2.3   Hippocampal neuronal mechanisms underlying episodic memory

In addition to the behavioral and neuropsychological findings described, characterizations of the firing patterns of hippocampal neurons in animals performing memory tasks have helped clarify the role of the hippocampus in episodic memory by shedding light on its information processing mechanisms. Observations from rats, monkeys, and humans, and across many different behavioral protocols, show that important attributes of episodic memory are encoded in hippocampal neuronal activity: (1) hippocampal neurons code for the context in which specific events occur, (2) hippocampal neurons encode episodes as sequences of events, and (3) hippocampal neurons disambiguate and link distinct episodic memories (see **Figure 11**).

1.21.2.2.3.(i)   Coding of specific events or experiences in their context

In this chapter, context is defined as the set of background features, external or internal to the subject, that are present when an event occurs (Ferbinteanu et al., 2006). It includes the spatial location where an event took place, but extends to other aspects of context as well, such as the behavioral significance of particular stimuli in the task, or the emotional or motivational states experienced during specific events. As

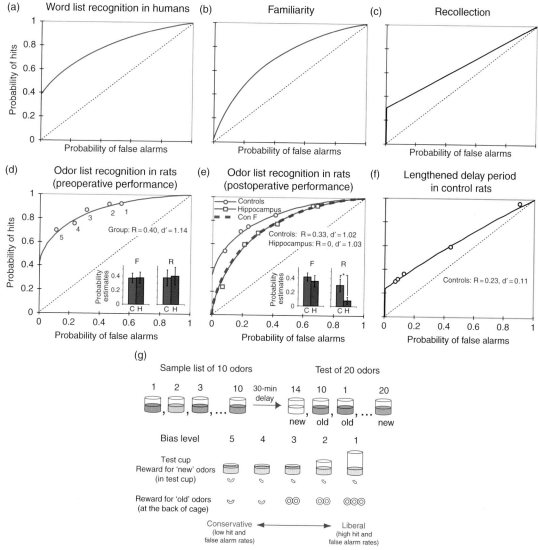

Figure 10 ROCs for recognition performance in humans and rats. (a–c) Performance of humans in verbal recognition. In a typical experiment, human subjects initially study a sample list of words and then are presented with a larger list containing the sample words intermixed with new ones and asked to identify each word as old or new. The resulting ROC analysis plots hits (correct identifications of old items) against false alarms (incorrect identifications of new items as old) across a range of confidence levels or response bias. The data points are then curve fitted by a model with two parameters (Y intercept and d′) using a least-squares method (see Yonelinas et al., 1998, for details). (d–f) Performance of rats in odor recognition (Fortin et al., 2004). (d) Normal rats tested with a 30-min delay. Insets: recollection (R) and familiarity (F) estimates. (e) Postoperative performance with a 30-min delay, including an estimated curve for controls based on familiarity alone (con F). (f) Control rats tested with a 75-min memory delay. Diagonal dotted lines represent chance performance across criterion levels. C, control group; H, hippocampal group. Error bars indicate SEM; *, p < .05. (g) Odor recognition task. The behavioral procedures remained fundamentally similar to those used in human studies but were adapted to take advantage of the natural behavior of rats. On each daily test session, rats initially sampled ten common household scents mixed with playground sand in a plastic cup containing a cereal reward. Following a 30-min memory delay, the same odors plus ten additional odors were presented in random order, and animals were required to identify each odor as old or new. To plot ROC curves, hit and false alarm rates were obtained under a range of response criteria, from conservative to liberal. To achieve this, different response criteria were encouraged for each daily session using a combination of variations in the height of the test cup (making it more or less difficult to respond to that cup), and manipulations of the reward magnitudes associated with correct responses to the test and the unscented cup. Top: Sequence of odor presentation. Bottom: Test cup heights and reward payoffs for each bias level. (a–g) Adapted from Fortin NJ, Wright SP, and Eichenbaum H (2004) Recollection-like memory retrieval in rats is dependent on the hippocampus. *Nature* 431(7005): 188–191, with permission from Macmillan Publishers Ltd.

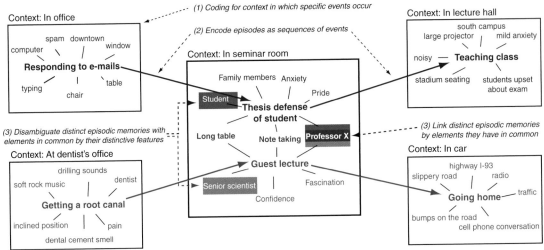

Figure 11   Hippocampal neuronal mechanisms underlying episodic memory. Characteristic features of episodic memories are encoded in hippocampal neuronal activity: (1) hippocampal neurons code for the context in which specific events occur, (2) hippocampal neurons encode episodes as sequences of events, and (3) hippocampal neurons disambiguate and link episodic memories with elements in common.

described in the previous section, a plethora of studies have described the spatial coding properties of hippocampal neurons; however, the focus of the vast majority of these studies was the coding of space itself (e.g., cognitive mapping), not the spatial context of unique experiences, and as such most paradigms had very little memory requirement.

The role of the hippocampus in representing different elements of the context in which specific events take place was first demonstrated by the study of Wood and colleagues (1999) mentioned earlier, in which rats were required to perform the same behavioral judgments (match or nonmatch to the previous odor) at many locations in the same environment. In addition to the cells coding for task regularities, such as specific locations, odors, or match/nonmatch status discussed earlier, they reported other hippocampal cells that fired in association with combinations of events and the context in which they occurred. For instance, some cells fired only if the animal began the approach from a particular location, or fired only for a particular conjunction of the odor, the place where it was sampled, and the match/nonmatch status of the odor. This conjunctive coding representing spatial and nonspatial features of specific events suggests that the hippocampus encodes the context of individual experiences.

A recent study reported very similar results in humans (Ekstrom et al., 2003). The activity of hippocampal neurons was recorded as subjects played a taxi driver game, searching for passengers picked up and dropped off at various locations in a virtual-reality town. Some cells fired when subjects viewed particular scenes, occupied particular locations, or had particular goals in finding passengers or locations for drop off. Many of these cells fired in association with specific conjunctions of a place and the view of a particular scene or a particular goal. Similar coding reflecting context-specific activity in the hippocampus has been reported in a number of other studies as well (e.g., Moita et al., 2003; Wirth et al., 2003). Thus, in rats, monkeys, and humans, a prevalent property of hippocampal firing patterns involves the representation of unique conjunctions of elements reflecting the context in which specific events occur (**Figure 11**).

1.21.2.2.3.(ii)   Coding of episodes as sequences of events   Computational models have hypothesized that the unique neural architecture of the hippocampus would be well suited for coding individual episodes as sequences of events (Levy, 1996; Lisman, 1999), a prediction supported by aforementioned behavioral studies (Agster et al., 2002; Fortin et al., 2002). Although unequivocal evidence for coding of sequences of individual events is not available at this time, this hypothesis has received experimental support. In fact, hippocampal neurons show activity patterns reflecting sequential coding of locations (Mehta et al., 1997, 2000) and have been shown to preserve the sequential order in which locations were visited (Lee and Wilson, 2002; 2004; Foster and Wilson, 2006). Moreover, every behavioral event of significance is encoded by individual hippocampal neurons (e.g., presentation of a specific stimulus, response to a cue), such that different subsets of hippocampal neurons are sequentially activated as the animal performs the task at hand (Wiener et al., 1989; Eichenbaum et al., 1999), providing the hippocampal network as a whole with a representation of the full sequences of events composing individual episodes (**Figure 11**).

1.21.2.2.3.(iii) Disambiguating and linking distinct episodic memories
Since a large number of episodic memories have elements in common, the neural systems responsible for the encoding and retrieval of episodic memories must use neuronal mechanisms that minimize interference between such similar episodic memories but also preserve the integrity of the relations among dissimilar episodes, which support the flexibility of access and expression as well as comparisons within the episodic memory network (Eichenbaum, 2004). According to

the current framework, this can be accomplished by *disambiguating* the representation of similar episodes by emphasizing their differences, and by *linking* common elements between distinct episodic memories to emphasize their similarity (**Figure 11**).

A recent study by Wood and colleagues (2000; see also Frank et al., 2000) lent support to this characterization by recording from hippocampal neurons as rats performed a spatial alternation task in the T-maze. Performance on this task requires that animals distinguish left-turn and right-turn episodes and remember the immediately preceding episode so as to select the other option on the current trial, task demands reflecting the use of episodic memory (Olton, 1984, 1986). The key comparisons focused on the central 'stem' of the maze, which is common to both left- and right-turn trajectories (**Figure 12(a)**). They reported firing patterns that emphasize the distinctiveness between similar episodes, indicative of *disambiguation* coding. In fact, many of the cells that fired when the rat was running down the stem fired differentially on left-turn versus right-turn trials (**Figure 12(b)**), and this differential activity was shown not to be due to differences in head direction, running speed, or location on the two trial types. Thus, even though the behavior and external stimuli were held constant, these cells provided a representation that disambiguated two otherwise identical trajectories on the stem according

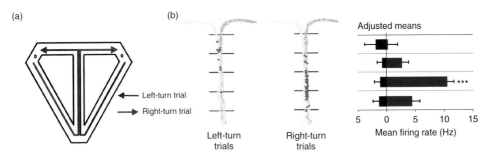

Figure 12 Disambiguation coding in hippocampal neurons. (a) Rats performed a continuous alternation task in which they traversed the central stem of the apparatus on each trial and then alternated between left and right turns at the T junction. Rewards for correct alternations were provided at water ports (small circles) on the end of each choice arm. The rat returned to the base of the stem via connecting arms and then traversed the central stem again on the next trial. For analysis of neural firing patterns, left-turn (blue arrow) and right-turn (red arrow) trials were distinguished. (b) Example of a hippocampal neuron disambiguating between left- and right-turn episodes. This cell fired almost exclusively during right-turn trials. Plots on the left show the location of the rat when individual spikes occurred for left-turn trials (blue dots) and right-turn trials (red dots). In the right panel, the mean firing rate of the cell for each sector, adjusted for variations in firing associated with covariates, is shown separately for left-turn trials (blue) and right-turn trials (red). Adapted from Wood E, Dudchenko P, Robitsek JR, and Eichenbaum H (2000) Hippocampal neurons encode information about different types of memory episodes occurring in the same location. *Neuron* 27: 623–633, with permission from Elsevier.

to the cognitive demands of the task, that is, to remember which turn was performed last. In addition, Wood and colleagues also reported coding patterns reflecting *links* between similar elements of distinct episodes. In fact, they recorded from cells that fired in the same location on the stem for both trial types, potentially providing a link between left-turn and right-turn representations by the common places traversed on both trial types.

In summary, the firing properties of hippocampal ensembles underlie episodic memory by encoding individual episodes as sequences of events as well as the common stimuli, places, and events that are shared across episodes, providing a framework for linking related memories and disambiguating overlapping ones (Eichenbaum et al., 1999; **Figure 11**).

1.21.2.3 Contribution of Other Neural Systems to Episodic Memory

In addition to the hippocampus, a number of other neural systems are important for episodic memory. Evidence from both neuropsychological studies and functional brain imaging indicates that the prefrontal cortex plays a role in the strategic or organizational aspects of episodic retrieval (Milner et al., 1985; Gershberg and Shimamura, 1993; Wheeler et al., 1995; see Buckner and Wheeler, 2001, for a review). The parahippocampal region also plays a crucial role in episodic memory by combining multimodal representations of stimulus details in neocortical areas to form representations of individual items and contextual elements (see Eichenbaum et al., 1994, for a review). These elemental representations in parahippocampal areas would then be combined in the hippocampus to form episodic memories by encoding individual experiences with the context in which they were experienced. Such representations in the parahippocampal region are also thought to underlie nonepisodic recognition memory based on a sense of familiarity, by allowing comparisons between a recently presented item and the current item (Suzuki et al., 1993; Stern et al., 1996; Henson et al., 2003).

1.21.2.4 Conclusions

The idea of multiple memory systems has now gained wide acceptance, and considerable evidence

suggests that these memory systems are fundamentally similar across mammalian species. However, the episodic memory system was initially thought to be unique to humans because of its dependence on human-centric faculties such as self, mental time travel, and consciousness. This section reviewed the fundamental features of episodic memory that can be operationally defined and tested in nonhuman animals as well and presented accumulating evidence from behavioral and electrophysiological studies demonstrating that animals are capable of episodic memory, and that, as in humans, this capacity depends on the integrity of the hippocampus. These findings suggest that we are making considerable progress in developing an animal model of episodic memory function, which will help uncover its underlying neuronal mechanisms.

1.21.3 Reconciling the Role of the Hippocampus in Navigation and Episodic Memory

In the service of clarity, this chapter has described the capacities for navigation and episodic memory separately, which parallels the relative independence of the two respective domains until recently. However, accumulating evidence indicates that the two capacities are related. As mentioned in the previous section, the role of the hippocampus in episodic memory can be responsible for deficits observed in a number of spatial paradigms, such as those requiring the animal to remember the trial-unique locations where specific events occurred (Olton and Papas, 1979; Steele and Morris, 1999; Day et al., 2003), though such an account fails to fully capture the extent of all navigational deficits reported in subjects with damage to the hippocampus. In fact, other navigational deficits appear to result from a failure to create a trial-independent mental representation of the environment that the subject can use to navigate flexibly (e.g., a stable cognitive map of a particular environment), suggesting that the hippocampus is critical for some aspects of semantic memory as well.

A careful review of the literature confirmed that subjects with hippocampal damage are indeed impaired at creating a stable memory structure that supports *flexibility* of access and expression, but, more importantly, also revealed that this deficit extends to memories of both spatial and nonspatial nature

(Eichenbaum and Cohen, 2001). For instance, animals with hippocampal damage can use simple strategies to solve spatial tasks, such as learning to approach a specific set of stimuli, but are severely impaired compared to controls when the start location or the destination is changed and a novel trajectory must be conceived (Eichenbaum et al., 1990; Whishaw et al., 1995; Whishaw and Tomie, 1997). Similarly, hippocampal rats perform as well as controls in nonspatial paradigms that require learning of consistent and nonambiguous reward or response associations to individual cues, such as discrimination learning (e.g., learning to select the always-rewarded item 'A' over the never-rewarded item 'B'; e.g., Dusek and Eichenbaum, 1998; Kesner et al., 2002) and recognition memory tasks (e.g., learning that item 'C' was presented earlier in the session, but that item 'X' was not; Dudchenko et al., 2000; Fortin et al., 2002), but are impaired when required to process relations among individual stimuli and use such information in novel situations (e.g., Bunsey and Eichenbaum, 1996; Dusek and Eichenbaum, 1997). For instance, in the transitive inference task, hippocampal rats could learn a series of discriminations involving overlapping elements as well as control animals (i.e., $A > B$, $B > C$, $C > D$, $D > E$; in which '>' corresponds to 'must be selected over'). However, when confronted with novel pairings (e.g., B vs. D), only control animals could successfully process the relations among all individual items ($A > B > C > D > E$) and correctly identify the indirect relationship between the items (i.e., $B > D$; Dusek and Eichenbaum, 1997).

1.21.3.1 Cognitive Maps as Semantic Knowledge Structures Extracted from Individual Episodic Memories

Although aspects of semantic memory can be learned without the hippocampus (e.g., Vargha-Khadem et al., 1997), the hippocampus appears to be important for the process of developing relations among individual episodic and semantic memories, crucial to support the flexibility of declarative memory representations (Eichenbaum et al., 1999; Eichenbaum, 2004). According to the relational theory of hippocampal function, this process occurs by linking common elements between individual memories (e.g., a location, or a person), which ultimately leads to the creation of the large multidimensional relational network of declarative memories (Cohen,

1984; Eichenbaum et al., 1999; Eichenbaum, 2004). According to this model, spatial representations of the environment, or cognitive maps, are simply one type of semantic knowledge represented in the network.

How are mammals creating cognitive maps of their environment to optimize navigational behavior? In humans, there are two ways to create a mental representation of a specific environment (Shelton and McNamara, 2001). The first is to use a 'survey' strategy, which is characterized by an external perspective, such as a bird's eye view, and allows direct access to the global spatial layout. This strategy is predominantly used when subjects are studying an actual map to learn the layout of the environment. The alternative is a 'route-based' strategy, which is characterized by knowledge of spatial layout from the perspective of a ground-level observer navigating the environment. In this case, initial knowledge is represented as individual trajectories or routes (e.g., airport → hotel, hotel → convention center, convention center → restaurant, restaurant → hotel), but with enough experience with routes within a specific environment, subjects can successfully construct a maplike representation out of those individual routes (or episodic memories).

Since most mammals do not have access to aerial views of their environment, nor have the capacity to read a map, it is clear that the survey strategy is not common to all mammals. The route-based strategy, in contrast, takes advantage of the instinctive behavior of mammals to actively explore their environment (O'Keefe and Nadel, 1978) and uses the same circuitry in humans as it does in animals. In fact, in a recent functional neuroimaging study, the survey representation was shown to activate inferior temporal and posterior parietal regions, suggesting that such information is acquired as complex visual scenes, whereas the route-based strategy recruited regions not activated in survey encoding, including the hippocampus and parahippocampal region (Shelton and Gabrieli, 2002). The strong consistency in data on route encoding from studies on hippocampal neuronal firing patterns in rats and hippocampal activation in human functional imaging support the notion that hippocampal representations of space, like those for nonspatial memory, are created from individual sequences of events and places where they occur (see **Figure 13**).

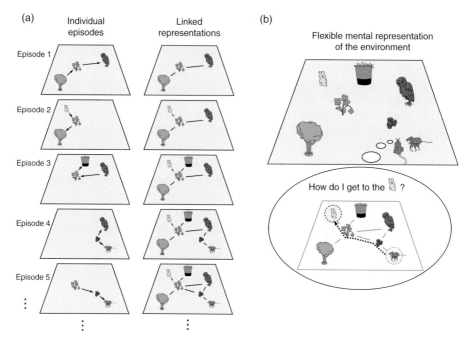

Figure 13 Cognitive map of the environment built out of individual episodes. (a) The column on the left represents individual episodes, each consisting of a particular trajectory in the animal's environment. The column on the right shows the representation that gradually forms as the common features between individual episodic memories (in this case, locations) are linked together. (b) After extensive experience in the environment, the linked representations can support flexible navigation by allowing the animal to determine a novel trajectory between two known points.

References

Aggleton JP and Pierce JM (2001) Neural systems underlying episodic memory, insights from animal research. *Philos. Trans. R. Soc. Lond. B Biol. Sci.* 356: 1467–1482.

Aggleton JP and Shaw C (1996) Amnesia and recognition memory, a reanalysis of psychometric data. *Neuropsychologia* 34: 51–62.

Agster KL, Fortin NJ, and Eichenbaum H (2002) The hippocampus and disambiguation of overlapping sequences. *J. Neurosci.* 22: 5760–5768.

Alexander GE, DeLong MR, and Strick PL (1986) Parallel organization of functionally segregated circuits linking basal ganglia and cortex. *Annu. Rev. Neurosci.* 9: 357–381.

Alvarez P, Wendelken L, and Eichenbaum H (2002) Hippocampal formation lesions impair performance in an odor-odor association task independently of spatial context. *Neurobiol. Learn. Mem.* 78: 470–476.

Alyan S and Jander R (1994) Short-range homing in the house mouse, *Mus musculus*: Stages in the learning of directions. *Anim. Behav.* 48: 285–298.

Alyan SH, Jander R, and Best PJ (2000) Hippocampectomized rats can use a constellation of landmarks to recognize a place. *Brain Res.* 876: 225–237.

Alyan S and McNaughton BL (1999) Hippocampectomized rats are capable of homing by path integration. *Behav. Neurosci.* 113(1): 19–31.

Amaral DG and Witter MP (1989) The three-dimensional organization of the hippocampal formation: A review of anatomical data. *Neuroscience* 31(3): 571–591.

Aristotle (350 BC/1984) *On Memory and Reminiscence*, Beare JI (trans.). Available at: http://classics.mit.edu/Aristotle/memory.html.

Baker RR (1980) Goal orientation by blindfolded humans after long-distance displacement: Possible involvement of a magnetic sense. *Science* 210(4469): 555–557.

Berger J (2004) The last mile: How to sustain long-distance migration in mammals. *Conserv. Biol.* 18: 320–331.

Berthold P (1996) *Control of Bird Migration.* London: Chapman & Hall.

Best PJ and Ranck JB Jr. (1982) Reliability of the relationship between hippocampal unit activity and sensory-behavioral events in the rat. *Exp. Neurol.* 75(3): 652–664.

Bliss TV and Collingridge GL (1993) A synaptic model of memory: Long-term potentiation in the hippocampus. *Nature* 361(6407): 31–39.

Brown MW and Aggleton JP (2001) Recognition memory: What are the roles of the perirhinal cortex and hippocampus? *Nat. Rev. Neurosci.* 2: 51–61.

Buckner RL and Wheeler ME (2001) The cognitive neuroscience of remembering. *Nat. Rev. Neurosci.* 2: 624–634.

Bunsey M and Eichenbaum H (1996) Conservation of hippocampal memory function in rats and humans. *Nature* 379: 255–257.

Burgess N, Donnett JG, Jeffery KJ, and O'Keefe J (1997) Robotic and neuronal simulation of the hippocampus and rat navigation. *Philos. Trans. R. Soc. Lond. B Biol. Sci.* 352(1360): 1535–1543.

Burwell RD, Saddoris MP, Bucci DJ, and Wiig KA (2004) Corticohippocampal contributions to spatial and contextual learning. *J. Neurosci.* 24(15): 3826–3836.

Buzsaki G (1996) The hippocampo-neocortical dialogue. *Cereb. Cortex* 6(2): 81–92.

Chen LL, Lin LH, Green EJ, Barnes CA, and McNaughton BL (1994) Head-direction cells in the rat posterior cortex. I. Anatomical distribution and behavioral modulation. *Exp. Brain Res.* 101(1): 8–23.

Clark RE, West AN, Zola SM, and Squire LR (2001) Rats with lesions of the hippocampus are impaired on the delayed nonmatching-to-sample task. *Hippocampus* 11(2): 176–186.

Clark RE, Zola SM, and Squire LR (2000) Impaired recognition memory in rats after damage to the hippocampus. *J. Neurosci.* 20(23): 8853–8860.

Clayton NS and Dickinson A (1998) Episodic-like memory during cache recovery by scrub jays. *Nature* 395(6699): 272–274.

Cohen NJ (1984) Preserved learning capacity in amnesia: Evidence for multiple memory systems. In: Butters N and Squire LR (eds.) *The Neuropsychology of Memory*, pp. 83–103. New York: Guilford Press.

Cohen NJ and Eichenbaum H (1993) *Memory, Amnesia, and the Hippocampal Memory System.* Cambridge, MA: MIT Press.

Cohen NJ and Squire LR (1980) Preserved learning and retention of a pattern-analyzing skill in amnesia: Dissociation of knowing how and knowing that. *Science* 210: 207–210.

Cooper BG and Mizumori SJ (1999) Retrosplenial cortex inactivation selectively impairs navigation in darkness. *Neuroreport* 10(3): 625–630.

Darwin D (1873) Origin of certain instincts. *Nature (Lond.)* 7: 417–418.

Daselaar SM, Fleck MS, Dobbins IG, Madden DJ, and Cabeza R (2006) Effects of healthy aging on hippocampal and rhinal memory functions: An event-related fMRI study. *Cereb. Cortex* 16(12): 1771–1782.

Davachi L, Mitchell JP, and Wagner AD (2003) Multiple routes to memory: Distinct medial temporal lobe processes build item and source memories. *Proc. Natl. Acad. Sci. USA* 100(4): 2157–2162.

Davachi L and Wagner AG (2002) Hippocampal contributions to episodic encoding, insights from relational and item-based learning. *J. Neurophysiol.* 88: 982–990.

Day M, Langston R, and Morris RG (2003) Glutamate-receptor-mediated encoding and retrieval of paired-associate learning. *Nature* 424(6945): 205–209.

De Bruin JP, Sanchez-Santed F, Heinsbroek RP, Donker A, and Postmes P (1994) A behavioural analysis of rats with damage to the medial prefrontal cortex using the Morris water maze: Evidence for behavioural flexibility, but not for impaired spatial navigation. *Brain Res.* 652(2): 323–333.

Downes JJ, Mayes AR, MacDonald C, and Humkin NM (2002) Temporal order memory in patients with Korsakoff's syndrome and medial temporal amnesia. *Neuropsychologia* 40: 853–861.

Dudchencko P, Wood E, and Eichenbaum H (2000) Neurotoxic hippocampal lesions have no effect on odor span and little effect on odor recognition memory, but produce significant impairments on spatial span, recognition, and alternation. *J. Neurosci.* 20: 2964–2977.

Dunnett SB, Meldrum A, and Muir JL (2005) Frontal-striatal disconnection disrupts cognitive performance of the frontal-type in the rat. *Neuroscience* 135(4): 1055–1065.

Dusek JA and Eichenbaum H (1997) The hippocampus and memory for orderly stimulus relations. *Proc. Natl. Acad. Sci. USA* 94: 7109–7114.

Dusek JA and Eichenbaum H (1998) The hippocampus and transverse patterning guided by olfactory cues. *Behav. Neurosci.* 112: 762–771.

Eichenbaum H (2004) Hippocampus: Cognitive processes and neural representations that underlie declarative memory. *Neuron* 44(1): 109–120.

Eichenbaum H and Cohen NJ (2001) *From Conditioning to Conscious Recollection: Memory Systems of the Brain.* New York: Oxford University Press.

Eichenbaum H, Dudchenko P, Wood E, Shapiro M, and Tanila H (1999) The hippocampus, memory, and place cells: Is it spatial memory or a memory space? *Neuron* 23(2): 209–226.

Eichenbaum H and Fortin NJ (2003) Episodic memory and the hippocampus: It's about time. *Curr. Dir. Psych. Res.* 12(2): 53–57.

Eichenbaum H, Fortin NJ, Ergorul C, Wright SP, and Agster KL (2005) Episodic recollection in animals: "If it walks like a duck and quacks like a duck…" *Learn. Motiv.* 36: 190–207.

Eichenbaum H, Otto T, and Cohen NJ (1994) Two functional components of the hippocampal memory system. *Brain Behav. Sci.* 17: 449–518.

Eichenbaum H, Stewart C, and Morris RG (1990) Hippocampal representation in place learning. *J. Neurosci.* 10(11): 3531–3542.

Ekstrom AD, Kahana MJ, Caplan JB, et al. (2003) Cellular networks underlying human spatial navigation. *Nature* 425(6954): 184–188.

Eldridge LL, Knowlton BJ, Furmanski CS, Brookheimer SY, and Engel SA (2000) Remembering episodes: A selective role for the hippocampus during retrieval. *Nat. Neurosci.* 3: 1149–1152.

Ennaceur A, Neave N, and Aggleton JP (1997) Spontaneous object recognition and object location memory in rats: The effects of lesions in the cingulate cortices, the medial prefrontal cortex, the cingulum bundle and the fornix. *Exp. Brain Res.* 113(3): 509–519.

Ergorul C and Eichenbaum H (2004) The hippocampus and memory for "what," "where," and "when." *Learn. Mem.* 11(4): 397–405.

Etienne AS, Berlie J, Georgakopoulos J, and Maurer R (1998) Role of dead reckoning in navigation. In: Healy S. (ed.) *Spatial Representation in Animals*, pp. 54–68. Oxford: Oxford University Press.

Etienne AS and Jeffery KJ (2004) Path integration in mammals. *Hippocampus* 14(2): 180–192.

Ferbinteanu J, Kennedy PJ, and Shapiro ML (2006) Episodic memory – from brain to mind. *Hippocampus* 16(9): 691–703.

Fortin NJ, Agster KL, and Eichenbaum H (2002) Critical role of the hippocampus in memory for sequences of events. *Nat. Neurosci.* 5: 458–462.

Fortin NJ, Wright SP, and Eichenbaum H (2004) Recollection-like memory retrieval in rats is dependent on the hippocampus. *Nature* 431(7005): 188–191.

Foster DJ and Wilson MA (2006) Reverse replay of behavioural sequences in hippocampal place cells during the awake state. *Nature* 440(7084): 680–683.

Frank LM, Brown EN, and Wilson M (2000) Trajectory encoding in the hippocampus and entorhinal cortex. *Neuron* 27: 169–178.

Fuhs MC and Touretzky DS (2006) A spin glass model of path integration in rat medial entorhinal cortex. *J. Neurosci.* 26(37): 9352–9354.

Fyhn M, Molden S, Witter MP, Moser EI, and Moser MB (2004) Spatial representation in the entorhinal cortex. *Science* 305(5688): 1258–1264.

Gall FG (1835) *The Influence of the Brain on the Form of the Head.* Boston: Marsh, Capen, and Lion.

Gaffan D (1974) Recognition impaired and association intact in the memory of monkeys after transection of the fornix. *J. Comp. Physiol. Psychol.* 86: 1100–1109.

Gaffan D and Parker A (1996) Interaction of perirhinal cortex with the fornix-fimbria: Memory for objects and "object-in-place" memory. *J. Neurosci.* 16(18): 5864–5869.

Gallistel CR (1990) *The Organization of Learning.* Cambridge, MA: MIT Press.

Gershberg FB and Shimamura AP (1995) Impaired use of organizational strategies in free recall following frontal lobe damage. *Neuropsychologia* 33: 1305–1333.

Golob EJ and Taube JS (1999) Head direction cells in rats with hippocampal or overlying neocortical lesions: Evidence for impaired angular path integration. *J. Neurosci.* 19(16): 7198–7211.

Goodrich-Hunsaker NJ, Hunsaker MR, and Kesner RP (2005) Dissociating the role of the parietal cortex and dorsal hippocampus for spatial information processing. *Behav. Neurosci.* 119(5): 1307–1315.

Goodridge JP, Dudchenko PA, Worboys KA, Golob EJ, and Taube JS (1998) Cue control and head direction cells. *Behav. Neurosci.* 112(4): 749–761.

Google Maps – http://maps.google.com

Graybiel AM (1995) Building action repertoires: Memory and learning functions of the basal ganglia. *Curr. Opin. Neurobiol.* 5(6): 733–741.

Griffiths D, Dickinson A, and Clayton N (1999) Episodic memory, What can animals remember about their past? *Trends Cogn. Sci.* 3: 74–80.

Hafting T, Fyhn M, Molden S, Moser MB, and Moser EI (2005) Microstructure of a spatial map in the entorhinal cortex. *Nature* 436(7052): 801–806.

Hargreaves EL, Rao G, Lee I, and Knierim JJ (2005) Major dissociation between medial and lateral entorhinal input to dorsal hippocampus. *Science* 308: 1792–1794.

Henson RN, Cansino S, Herron JE, Robb WG, and Rugg MD (2003) A familiarity signal in human anterior medial temporal cortex? *Hippocampus* 13(2): 301–304.

Hill AJ and Best PJ (1981) Effects of deafness and blindness on the spatial correlates of hippocampal unit activity in the rat. *Exp. Neurol.* 74(1): 204–217.

Hopkins RO and Kesner RP (1995) Item and order recognition memory in subjects with hypoxic brain injury. *Brain Cogn.* 27: 180–201.

Jacobs LF and Shiflett MW (1999) Spatial orientation on a vertical maze in free-ranging fox squirrels (*Sciurus niger*). *J. Comp. Psychol.* 113: 116–127.

James W (1890) *The Principles of Psychology.* New York: Henry Holt.

Kennedy PJ and Shapiro ML (2004) Retrieving memories via internal context requires the hippocampus. *J. Neurosci.* 24(31): 6979–6985.

Kesner RP, Gilbert PE, and Barua LA (2002) The role of the hippocampus in memory for the temporal order of a sequence of odors. *Behav. Neurosci.* 116: 286–290.

Knierim JJ (2006) Neural representations of location outside the hippocampus. *Learn. Mem.* 13(4): 405–415.

Knowlton BJ and Squire LR (1995) Remembering and knowing: Two different expressions of declarative memory. *J. Exp. Psychol. Learn. Mem. Cogn.* 21(3): 699–710.

Kolb B, Buhrmann K, McDonald R, and Sutherland RJ (1994) Dissociation of the medial prefrontal, posterior parietal, and posterior temporal cortex for spatial navigation and recognition memory in the rat. *Cereb. Cortex* 4(6): 664–680.

Krebs JR, Sherry DF, Healy SD, Perry VH, and Vaccarino AL (1989) Hippocampal specialization of food-storing birds. *Proc. Natl. Acad. Sci. USA* 86(4): 1388–1392.

Kumaran D and Maguire EA (2006) The dynamics of hippocampal activation during encoding of overlapping sequences. *Neuron* 49(4): 617–629.

Lavenex P and Amaral DG (2000) Hippocampal-neocortical interaction: A hierarchy of associativity. *Hippocampus* 10: 420–430.

Lavenex PB, Amaral DG, and Lavenex P (2006) Hippocampal lesion prevents spatial relational learning in adult macaque monkeys. *J. Neurosci.* 26(17): 4546–4558.

Lee AK and Wilson MA (2002) Memory of sequential experience in the hippocampus during slow wave sleep. *Neuron* 36: 1183–1194.

Lee AK and Wilson MA (2004) A combinatorial method for analyzing sequential firing patterns involving an arbitrary

number of neurons based on relative time order. *J. Neurophysiol.* 92(4): 2555–2573.

Leutgeb S and Mizumori SJ (2002) Context-specific spatial representations by lateral septal cells. *Neuroscience* 112(3): 655–663.

Levine RL and Bluni TD (1994) Magnetic field effects on spatial discrimination learning in mice. *Physiol. Behav.* 55(3): 465–467.

Levy WB (1989) A computational approach to hippocampal function. In: Hawkins RD and Bower GH (eds.) *Computational Models of Learning in Simple Systems*, pp. 243–305. New York: Academic Press.

Levy WB (1996) A sequence predicting CA3 is a flexible associator that learns and uses context to solve hippocampal-like tasks. *Hippocampus* 6(6): 579–590.

Lisman JE (1999) Relating hippocampal circuitry to function: Recall of memory sequences by reciprocal dentate-CA3 interactions. *Neuron* 22: 233–242.

Liu P and Bilkey DK (2002) The effects of NMDA lesions centered on the postrhinal cortex on spatial memory tasks in the rat. *Behav. Neurosci.* 116(5): 860–873.

Ludvig N, Tang HM, Gohil BC, and Botero JM (2004) Detecting location-specific neuronal firing rate increases in the hippocampus of freely-moving monkeys. *Brain Res.* 1014(1–2): 97–109.

Mackintosh NJ (2002) Do not ask whether they have a cognitive map, but how they find their way about. *Psicológica* 23: 165–185.

Maguire EA (2001) Neuroimaging studies of autobiographical event memory. *Philos. Trans. R. Soc. Lond. B Biol. Sci.* 356(1413): 1441–1451.

Maguire EA, Burgess N, Donnett JG, Frackowiak RS, Frith CD, and O'Keefe J (1998) Knowing where and getting there: A human navigation network. *Science* 280(5365): 921–924.

Maguire EA, Burke T, Phillips J, and Staunton H (1996) Topographical disorientation following unilateral temporal lobe lesions in humans. *Neuropsychologia* 34(10): 993–1001.

Maguire EA, Frackowiak RS, and Frith CD (1997) Recalling routes around London: Activation of the right hippocampus in taxi drivers. *J. Neurosci.* 17(18): 7103–7110.

Maguire EA, Gadian DG, Johnsrude IS, et al. (2000) Navigation-related structural change in the hippocampi of taxi drivers. *Proc. Natl. Acad. Sci. USA* 97(8): 4398–4403.

Main de Biran FPG (1804/1929) *The Influence of Habit on the Faculty of Thinking.* Baltimore: Williams and Wilkins.

Mandler G (1980) Recognizing: The judgment of previous occurrence. *Psychol. Rev.* 87(3): 252–271.

Manns JR and Eichenbaum H (2006) Evolution of declarative memory. *Hippocampus* 16(9): 795–808.

Manns JR, Hopkins RO, Reed JM, Kitchener EG, and Squire LR (2003) Recognition memory and the human hippocampus. *Neuron* 37: 171–180.

Manns JR and Squire LR (1999) Impaired recognition memory on the Doors and People test after damage limited to the hippocampal region. *Hippocampus* 9(5): 495–499.

Markus EJ, Qin Y-L, Leonard B, Skaggs WE, McNaughton BL, and Barnes CA (1995) Interactions between location and task affect the spatial and directional firing of hippocampal neurons. *J. Neurosci.* 15: 7079–7094.

Martin PD and Ono T (2000) Effects of reward anticipation, reward presentation, and spatial parameters on the firing of single neurons recorded in the subiculum and nucleus accumbens of freely moving rats. *Behav. Brain Res.* 116(1): 23–38.

Mather JG and Baker RR (1980) A demonstration of navigation by small rodents using an orientation cage. *Nature* 284(5753): 259–262.

McClelland JL and Goddard NH (1996) Considerations arising from a complementary learning systems perspective on hippocampus and neocortex. *Hippocampus* 6(6): 654–665.

McDonald RJ and White NM (1993) A triple dissociation of memory systems: Hippocampus, amygdala, and dorsal striatum. *Behav. Neurosci.* 107(1): 3–22.

McGaugh JL (2005) Emotional arousal and enhanced amygdala activity: New evidence for the old perseveration-consolidation hypothesis. *Learn. Mem.* 12(2): 77–79.

McNaughton BL, Barnes CA, Gerrard JL, et al. (1996) Deciphering the hippocampal polyglot: The hippocampus as a path integration system. *J. Exp. Biol.* 199(Pt 1): 173–185.

McNaughton BL, Barnes CA, and O'Keefe J (1983) The contributions of position, direction, and velocity to single unit activity in the hippocampus of freely-moving rats. *Exp. Brain Res.* 52: 41–49.

McNaughton BL, Battaglia FP, Jensen O, Moser EI, and Moser MB (2006) Path integration and the neural basis of the 'cognitive map.' *Nat. Rev. Neurosci.* 7(8): 663–678.

Mehta MR, Barnes CA, and McNaughton BL (1997) Experience-dependent, asymmetric expansion of hippocampal place fields. *Proc. Natl. Acad. Sci. USA* 94(16): 8918–8921.

Mehta MR, Quirk MC, and Wilson MA (2000) Experience-dependent asymmetric shape of hippocampal receptive fields. *Neuron* 25(3): 707–715.

Menzel EW (1973) Chimpanzee spatial memory organization. *Science* 182: 943–945.

Mesulam MM, Nobre AC, Kim YH, Parrish TB, and Gitelman DR (2001) Heterogeneity of cingulate contributions to spatial attention. *Neuroimage* 13(6 Pt. 1): 1065–1072.

Miller VM and Best PJ (1980) Spatial correlates of hippocampal unit activity are altered by lesions of the fornix and entorhinal cortex. *Brain Res.* 194(2): 311–323.

Milner B, Petrides M, and Smith ML (1985) Frontal lobes and the temporal organization of memory. *Hum. Neurobiol.* 4: 137–142.

Mishkin M and Delacour J (1975) An analysis of short-term visual memory in the monkey. *J. Exp. Psychol. Anim. Behav. Process.* 1: 326–334.

Mizumori SJ, Ward KE, and Lavoie AM (1992) Medial septal modulation of entorhinal single unit activity in anesthetized and freely moving rats. *Brain Res.* 570(1–2): 188–197.

Moita MAP, Moisis S, Zhou Y, LeDoux JE, and Blair HT (2003) Hippocampal place cells acquire location specific location specific responses to the conditioned stimulus during auditory fear conditioning. *Neuron* 37: 485–497.

Morris RGM (1981) Spatial localization does not require the presence of local cues. *Learn. Motiv.* 12: 239–260.

Morris RGM (2001) Episodic-like memory in animals, psychological criteria, neural mechanisms and the value of episodic-like tasks to investigate animal models of neurodegenerative disease. *Philos. Trans. R. Soc. Lond. B Biol. Sci.* 356: 1453–1465.

Morris RG, Garrud P, Rawlins JN, and O'Keefe J (1982) Place navigation impaired in rats with hippocampal lesions. *Nature* 297(5868): 681–683.

Muller RU and Kubie JL (1987) The effects of changes in the environment on the spatial firing of hippocampal complex-spike cells. *J. Neurosci.* 7(7): 1951–1968.

Muller RU, Stead M, and Pach J (1996) The hippocampus as a cognitive graph. *J. Gen. Physiol.* 107(6): 663–694.

Mumby DG and Pinel PJ (1994) Rhinal cortex lesions and object recognition in rats. *Behav. Neurosci.* 108: 11–18.

Mumby DG, Wood ER, and Pinel JP (1992) Object recognition memory is only mildly impaired in rats with lesions of the hippocampus and amygdala. *Psychobiology* 20: 18–27.

Murray EA (1996) What have ablation studies told us about the neural substrates of stimulus memory? *Semin. Neurosci.* 8: 13–22.

Murray EA, Davidson M, Gaffan D, Olton DS, and Suomi S (1989) Effects of fornix transection and cingulate cortical ablation on spatial memory in rhesus monkeys. *Exp. Brain Res.* 74(1): 173–186.

Murray EA and Mishkin M (1998) Object recognition and location memory in monkeys with excitotoxic lesions of the amygdala and hippocampus. *J. Neurosci.* 18: 6568–6582.

Nissen MJ and Bullemer P (1987) Attentional requirements of learning: Evidence from performance measures. *Cogn. Psychol.* 19: 1–32.

Nitz DA (2006) Tracking route progression in the posterior parietal cortex. *Neuron* 49(5): 747–756.

O'Keefe J (1976) Place units in the hippocampus of the freely moving rat. *Exp. Neurol.* 51(1): 78–109.

O'Keefe J (1979) A review of the hippocampal place cells. *Prog. Neurobiol.* 13(4): 419–439.

O'Keefe J and Burgess N (1996) Geometric determinants of the place fields of hippocampal neurons. *Nature* 381(6581): 425–428.

O'Keefe J and Conway DH (1978) Hippocampal place units in the freely moving rat: Why they fire where they fire. *Exp. Brain Res.* 31(4): 573–590.

O'Keefe J and Conway DH (1980) On the trail of the hippocampal engram. *Physiol. Psychol.* 8: 229–238.

O'Keefe J and Dostrovsky J (1971) The hippocampus as a spatial map. Preliminary evidence from unit activity in the freely-moving rat. *Brain Res.* 34(1): 171–175.

O'Keefe J and Nadel L (1978) *The Hippocampus as a Cognitive Map.* Oxford: Oxford University Press.

Olton DS (1984) Comparative analyses of episodic memory. *Brain Behav. Sci.* 7: 250–251.

Olton DS (1986) Hippocampal function and memory for temporal context. In: Isaacson RL and Pribram KH (eds.) *The Hippocampus*, Vol. 4, pp. 281–298. New York: Plenum Press.

Olton DS, Branch M, and Best PJ (1978) Spatial correlates of hippocampal unit activity. *Exp. Neurol.* 58(3): 387–409.

Olton DS, Collison C, and Werz MA (1977) Spatial memory and radial arm maze performance of rats. *Learn. Motiv.* 8: 289–314.

Olton DS and Feustle WA (1981) Hippocampal function required for nonspatial working memory. *Exp. Brain Res.* 41(3–4): 380–389.

Olton DS and Papas BC (1979) Spatial memory and hippocampal function. *Neuropsychologia* 17(6): 669–682.

Olton DS and Samuelson RJ (1976) Remembrance of places passed: Spatial memory in rats. *J. Exp. Psychol. Anim. Behav. Process.* 2: 97–116.

Olton DS, Walker JA, and Gage FH (1978) Hippocampal connections and spatial discrimination. *Brain Res.* 139(2): 295–308.

Olton DS and Werz MA (1978) Hippocampal function and behavior: Spatial discrimination and response inhibition. *Physiol. Behav.* 20(5): 597–605.

Packard MG and McGaugh JL (1996) Inactivation of hippocampus or caudate nucleus with lidocaine differentially affects expression of place and response learning. *Neurobiol. Learn. Mem.* 65(1): 65–72.

Parron C, Poucet B, and Save E (2004) Entorhinal cortex lesions impair the use of distal but not proximal landmarks during place navigation in the rat. *Behav. Brain Res.* 154(2): 345–352.

Parron C and Save E (2004) Evidence for entorhinal and parietal cortices involvement in path integration in the rat. *Exp. Brain Res.* 159(3): 349–359.

Peters R (1973) Cognitive maps in wolves and men. In: Preiser WFE (ed.) *Environmental Design Research*, vol. 2, pp. 247–253. Stroudburg: Dowden, Hutchinson and Ross.

Phillips RG and LeDoux JE (1992) Differential contribution of amygdala and hippocampus to cued and contextual fear conditioning. *Behav. Neurosci.* 106(2): 274–285.

Phillips RG and LeDoux JE (1995) Lesions of the fornix but not the entorhinal or perirhinal cortex interfere with contextual fear conditioning. *J. Neurosci.* 15(7 Pt 2): 5308–5315.

Poucet B (1993) Spatial cognitive maps in animals: New hypotheses on their structure and neural mechanisms. *Psychol. Rev.* 100(2): 163–182.

Quirk GJ, Muller RU, Kubie JL, and Ranck JB Jr. (1992) The positional firing properties of medial entorhinal neurons: Description and comparison with hippocampal place cells. *J. Neurosci.* 12(5): 1945–1963.

Reber PJ and Squire LR (1998) Encapsulation of implicit and explicit memory in sequence learning. *J. Cogn. Neurosci.* 10: 248–263.

Roberts WA (2002) Are animals stuck in time? *Psychol. Bull.* 128(3): 473–489.

Robertson RG, Rolls ET, Georges-Francois P, and Panzeri S (1999) Head direction cells in the primate pre-subiculum. *Hippocampus* 9(3): 206–219.

Rosenbaum RS, Priselac S, Kohler S, et al. (2000) Remote spatial memory in an amnesic person with extensive bilateral hippocampal lesions. *Nat. Neurosci.* 3: 1044–1048.

Rotenberg A, Mayford M, Hawkins RD, Kandel ER, and Muller RU (1996) Mice expressing activated CaMKII lack low frequency LTP and do not form stable place cells in the CA1 region of the hippocampus. *Cell* 87(7): 1351–1361.

Sargolini F, Fyhn M, Hafting T, et al. (2006) Conjunctive representation of position, direction, and velocity in entorhinal cortex. *Science* 312(5774): 680–681.

Save E, Poucet B, and Thinus-Blanc C (1998) Landmarks use and the cognitive map in the rat. In: Healy S (ed.) *Spatial Representation in Animals*, pp. 119–132. Oxford: Oxford University Press.

Schacter DL and Tulving E (1994) *Memory Systems.* Cambridge, MA: MIT Press.

Schafe GE, Doyere V, and LeDoux JE (2005) Tracking the fear engram: The lateral amygdala is an essential locus of fear memory storage. *J. Neurosci.* 25(43): 10010–10014.

Shapiro ML and Olton DS (1994) Hippocampal function and interference. In: Schacter DL and Tulving E (eds.) *Memory Systems*, p. 87–117. Cambridge, MA: MIT Press.

Sharp PE (1996) Multiple spatial/behavioral correlates for cells in the rat postsubiculum: Multiple regression analysis and comparison to other hippocampal areas. *Cereb. Cortex* 6: 238–259.

Sharp PE and Green C (1994) Spatial correlates of firing patterns of single cells in the subiculum of the freely moving rat. *J. Neurosci.* 14(4): 2339–2356.

Shelton AL and Gabrieli JD (2002) Neural correlates of encoding space from route and survey perspectives. *J. Neurosci.* 22(7): 2711–2717.

Shelton AL and McNamara TP (2001) Systems of spatial reference in human memory. *Cogn. Psychol.* 43(4): 274–310.

Sherry DF (1998) The ecology and neurobiology of spatial memory. In: Dukas R (ed.) *Cognitive Ecology*, pp. 261–296. Chicago: University of Chicago Press.

Sherry D and Healy S (1998) Neural mechanisms of spatial representation. In: Healy S (ed.) *Spatial Representation in Animals*, p. 133–157. Oxford: Oxford University Press.

Sherry DF and Schacter DL (1987) The evolution of multiple memory systems. *Psychol. Rev.* 94(4): 439–454.

Sherry DF, Vaccarino AL, Buckenham K, and Herz RS (1989) The hippocampal complex of food-storing birds. *Brain Behav. Evol.* 34(5): 308–317.

Small WS (1901) Experimental study of the mental processes of the rat. II. *Am. J. Psychol.* 12: 206–239.

Smith ML and Milner B (1981) The role of the right hippocampus in the recall of spatial location. *Neuropsychologia* 19(6): 781–793.

Smith ML and Milner B (1989) Right hippocampal impairment in the recall of spatial location: Encoding deficit or rapid forgetting? *Neuropsychologia* 27(1): 71–81.

Spiers HJ, Burgess N, Hartley T, Vargha-Khadem F, and O'Keefe J (2001) Bilateral hippocampal pathology impairs topographical and episodic memory but not visual pattern matching. *Hippocampus* 11(6): 715–725.

Squire LR (1992) Memory and the hippocampus: A synthesis from findings with rats, monkeys, and humans. *Psychol. Rev.* 99: 195–231.

Squire LR (2004) Memory systems of the brain: A brief history and current perspective. *Neurobiol. Learn. Mem.* 82: 171–177.

Squire LR and Cohen NJ (1984) Human memory and amnesia. In: Lynck G, McGaugh JL, and Weinberger NM (eds.) *Neurobiology of Learning and Memory*, pp. 3–64. New York: Guilford.

Squire LR, Knowlton B, and Musen G (1993) The structure and organization of memory. *Annu. Rev. Psychol.* 44: 453–495.

Squire LR and Zola SM (1998) Episodic memory, semantic memory, and amnesia. *Hippocampus* 8(3): 205–211.

Squire LR and Zola-Morgan S (1991) The medial temporal lobe memory system. *Science* 253(5026): 1380–1386.

Steele RJ and Morris RG (1999) Delay-dependent impairment of a matching-to-place task with chronic and intrahippocampal infusion of the NMDA-antagonist D-AP5. *Hippocampus* 9(2): 118–136.

Stern CE, Corkin S, Gonzalez RG, et al. (1996) The hippocampal formation participates in novel picture encoding: Evidence from functional magnetic resonance imaging. *Proc. Natl. Acad. Sci. USA* 93: 8660–8665.

Suzuki S, Augerinos G, and Black AH (1980) Stimulus control of spatial behavior on the eight-arm maze in rats. *Learn. Motiv.* 11: 1–8.

Suzuki WA, Zola-Morgan S, Squire LR, and Amaral DG (1993) Lesions of the perirhinal and parahippocampal cortices in the monkey produce long-lasting memory impairment in the visual and tactual modalities. *J. Neurosci.* 13: 2430–2451.

Taube JS (1995a) Place cells recorded in the parasubiculum of freely moving rats. *Hippocampus* 5(6): 569–583.

Taube JS (1995b) Head direction cells recorded in the anterior thalamic nuclei of freely moving rats. *J. Neurosci.* 15: 70–86.

Taube JS, Muller RU, and Ranck JB Jr. (1990) Head-direction cells recorded from the postsubiculum in freely moving rats. I. Description and quantitative analysis. *J. Neurosci.* 10(2): 420–435.

Teng E and Squire LR (1999) Memory for places learned long ago is intact after hippocampal damage. *Nature* 400: 675–677.

Thompson LT and Best PJ (1990) Long-term stability of the place-field activity of single units recorded from the dorsal hippocampus of freely behaving rats. *Brain Res.* 509(2): 299–308.

Tolman EC (1932) *Purposive Behaviour in Animals and Men.* New York: Century.

Tolman EC (1948) Cognitive maps in rats and men. *Psychol. Rev.* 55: 189–208.

Tolman EC and Honzik CH (1930) 'Insight' in rats. *Univ. Calif. Publ. Psychol.* 4: 215–232.

Tolman EC, Ritchie BF, and Kalish D (1946) Studies in spatial learning. I. Orientation and the short-cut. *J. Exp. Psychol.* 36: 13–24.

Tulving E (1972) Episodic and semantic memory. In: Tulving E and Donaldson W (eds.) *Organization of Memory*, pp. 381–403. New York: Academic Press.

Tulving E (1983) *Elements of Episodic Memory.* Oxford: Oxford University Press.

Tulving E (1991) Concepts in human memory. In: Squire LR, Weinberger NM, Lynch G, and McGaugh JL (eds.) *Memory: Organization and Locus of Change*, pp. 3–32. New York: Oxford University Press.

Tulving E (1993a) What is episodic memory? *Curr. Perspect. Psychol. Sci.* 2: 67–70.

Tulving E (1993b) Varieties of consciousness and levels of awareness in memory. In: Baddeley A and Weiskrantz L (eds.) *Attention: Selection, Awareness, and Control*, pp. 53–71. New York: Oxford University Press.

Tulving E (2002) Episodic memory: From mind to brain. *Annu. Rev. Psychol.* 53: 1–25.

Tulving E and Markowitsch HJ (1998) Episodic and declarative memory: Role of the hippocampus. *Hippocampus* 8(3): 198–203.

Tulving E, Schacter DL, McLachlan DR, and Moscovitch M (1988) Priming of semantic autobiographical knowledge: A case study of retrograde amnesia. *Brain Cogn.* 8(1): 3–20.

University of Wisconsin, Michigan State University, and National Museum of Health and Medicine, Comparative Mammalian Brain Collections – http://www.brainmuseum.org

Vann SD and Aggleton JP (2004) Testing the importance of the retrosplenial guidance system: Effects of different sized retrosplenial cortex lesions on heading direction and spatial working memory. *Behav. Brain Res.* 155(1): 97–108.

Vargha-Khadem F, Gadin DG, Watkins KE, Connelly A, Van Paesschen W, and Mishkin M (1997) Differential effects of early hippocampal pathology on episodic and semantic memory. *Science* 277: 376–380.

Wais PE, Wixted JT, Hopkins RO, and Squire LR (2006) The hippocampus supports both the recollection and the familiarity components of recognition memory. *Neuron* 49(3): 459–466.

Wallace DG, Hines DJ, Pellis SM, and Whishaw IQ (2002) Vestibular information is required for dead reckoning in the rat. *J. Neurosci.* 22(22): 10009–10017.

Wallenstein GV, Eichenbaum H, and Hasselmo ME (1998) The hippocampus as an associator of discontiguous events. *Trends Neurosci.* 21: 315–365.

Watson JB (1907) Kinaesthetic and organic sensations: Their role in the reactions of the white rat. *Psychol. Rev. Monogr.* 8(2): 1–100.

Wheeler MA, Stuss DT, and Tulving E (1995) Frontal lobe damage produces episodic memory impairment. *J. Int. Neuropsychol. Soc.* 1: 525–536.

Wiener SI, Paul CA, and Eichenbaum H (1989) Spatial and behavioral correlates of hippocampal neuronal activity. *J. Neurosci.* 9: 2737–2763.

Whishaw IQ, Cassel JC, and Jarrad LE (1995) Rats with fimbria-fornix lesions display a place response in a swimming pool: A dissociation between getting there and knowing where. *J. Neurosci.* 15(8): 5779–5788.

Whishaw IQ, Maaswinkel H, Gonzalez CL, and Kolb B (2001) Deficits in allothetic and idiothetic spatial behavior in rats with posterior cingulate cortex lesions. *Behav. Brain Res.* 118(1): 67–76.

Whishaw IQ and Tomie JA (1997) Perseveration on place reversals in spatial swimming pool tasks: Further evidence for place learning in hippocampal rats. *Hippocampus* 7(4): 361–370.

Whishaw IQ and Wallace DG (2003) On the origins of autobiographical memory. *Behav. Brain Res.* 138(2): 113–119.

White NM (1997) Mnemonic functions of the basal ganglia. *Curr. Opin. Neurobiol.* 7(2): 164–169.

Wirth S, Yanike M, Frank LM, Smith AC, Brown EN, and Suzuki WA (2003) Single neurons in the monkey hippocampus and learning of new associations. *Science* 300(5625): 1578–1581.

Wood E, Dudchenko PA, and Eichenbaum H (1999) The global record of memory in hippocampal neuronal activity. *Nature* 397: 613–616.

Wood E, Dudchenko P, Robitsek JR, and Eichenbaum H (2000) Hippocampal neurons encode information about different types of memory episodes occurring in the same location. *Neuron,* 27: 623–633.

Wylie DR, Glover RG, and Aitchison JD (1999) Optic flow input to the hippocampal formation from the accessory optic system. *J. Neurosci.* 19(13): 5514–5527.

Yonelinas AP (2001) Components of episodic memory: The contribution of recollection and familiarity. *Philos. Trans. R. Soc. Lond. B Biol. Sci.* 356: 1363–1374.

Yonelinas AP (2002) The nature of recollection and familiarity: A review of 30 years of research. *J. Mem. Lang.* 46: 441–517.

Yonelinas AP, Kroll NE, Dobbins I, Lazzara M, and Knight RT (1998) Recollection and familiarity deficits in amnesia: Convergence of remember-know, process dissociation, and receiver operating characteristic data. *Neuropsychology* 12(3): 323–339.

Yonelinas AP, Kroll NEA, Quamme JR, et al. (2002) Effects of extensive temporal lobe damage or mild hypoxia on recollection and familiarity. *Nat. Neurosci.* 5: 1236–1241.

Zhou TL, Tamura R, Kuriwaki J, and Ono T (1999) Comparison of medial and lateral septal neuron activity during performance of spatial tasks in rats. *Hippocampus* 9(3): 220–234.

Zola SM, Squire LR, Teng E, Stefanacci L, Buffalo EA, and Clark RE (2000) Impaired recognition memory in monkeys after damage limited to the hippocampal region. *J. Neurosci.* 20: 451–463.

Zola-Morgan S, Squire LR, and Ramus SJ (1994) Severity of memory impairment in monkeys as a function of locus and extent of damage within the medial temporal lobe memory system. *Hippocampus* 4(4): 483–495.

Zugaro MB, Arleo A, Dejean C, Burguiere E, Khamassi M, and Wiener SI (2004) Rat anterodorsal thalamic head direction neurons depend upon dynamic visual signals to select anchoring landmark cues. *Eur. J. Neurosci.* 20(2): 530–536.

1.22 Memory in Food Caching Animals

A. C. Kamil, University of Nebraska-Lincoln, Lincoln, NE, USA

K. L. Gould, Luther College, Decorah, IA, USA

1.22.1 Introduction

One of the more interesting developments in the study of learning and cognition over the past 25 years has been the realization that learning and memory play an important role in the natural world of many animals (e.g., Balda et al., 1998). As this realization led to research into animal cognition in natural settings, it became clear that such research can make important contributions to our understanding of animal and human cognition. In this chapter, we review one of the areas of research that originally stimulated interest in the role of memory in the field, the ability of many food-storing animals to remember where they have cached their food (*See also* Chapter 1.23).

We will begin our review of research in this area with a brief review of the natural history and ecological significance of food-caching. We will then review the evidence demonstrating the use of memory for accurate cache recovery, followed by a discussion of the characteristics of cache site memory and the comparative evidence for differences in memory among caching and noncaching species. We will conclude with reviews of how caching animals encode spatial information and the neural substrates for spatial memory in caching animals.

1.22.2   The Natural History of Food Storage

Animals face many problems obtaining food. Food may vary in abundance on a daily or seasonal basis, or even unpredictably, in boom–bust cycles. Even when food is abundant, there may be fierce competition for access to the food. And animals have evolved a number of strategies to cope with these problems, such as migration, hibernation, and torpor to deal with variability and food-caching and/or territoriality to deal with competition. Food hoarding is a strategy that can help an animal cope effectively with both variability in food availability and competition. By gathering food and hiding it, an animal can simultaneously store food against lean times and gain control over food against competitors.

Food storing takes many forms, from the nest of eusocial bumble bees to the grain silos of the human farmer (see Vander Wall, 1990, for a comprehensive review). The food storage patterns seen in nature vary considerably in the degree of dispersion among caches. At one extreme is larder-hoarding, in which food is gathered during times of plenty and placed into one or a few large larders. The hive and honeycombs of the honey bee (*Apis mellifera*), the granaries of acorn woodpeckers (*Melanerpes formicivorus*), or the middens of red squirrels (*Tiamiasciuris hudsonicus*) are excellent examples of this type of food storage. Once created, of course, these large caches require defense against competitors. Indeed, it would appear that one of the potential disadvantages of larder-hoarding is that loss of a larder incurs high cost to the original hoarder, since each larder site contains a large proportion of the animal's stored food.

The other extreme, in which food is stored in a large number of widely dispersed locations, is referred to as scatter-hoarding. Examples include fox squirrels (*Sciuris niger*), which store many of their walnuts singly; chickadees and tits, which store single seeds in moss and crevices; and nutcrackers, which store one to 14 pine seeds in each cache site. Larder- and scatter-hoarding define a continuum, not a dichotomy, and some mammals such as fox squirrels and yellow pine chipmunks (*Tamias*

amoenus) store both singly and in larders (Vander Wall, 1990). These two storage strategies require quite different defense strategies. The scatter-hoarder creates more caches, each containing less food, over a much larger area than does the larder-hoarder. The caches of a scatter-hoarder cannot be physically defended since they are highly dispersed, but the loss of any single cache site is much less significant for the scatter- than for the larder-hoarder. But scatter-hoarding does raise an interesting question, with intriguing cognitive possibilities. How does the scatter-hoarder relocate the large number of cache sites it has created?

Logically, there are three general classes of answer to this question. We present them in decreasing order of the cognitive demands needed for hoarders to successfully recover their own caches.

1. Memory for cache sites: If the hoarder could remember individual cache sites, it could then use this memory to recover the caches. This would, however, require considerable memory capacity.
2. Site preferences or movement rules: Suppose an animal had certain locations that it preferred to visit or specific paths which it regularly followed, then stored food in those locations or along those paths. If it searched those places, it would be able to find the stored food at a much greater rate than could be achieved by random search. This strategy would require that the animal remember the preferred sites or paths, but it would not be necessary to remember individual cache sites. If, however, the site or path preferences could be learned by an observing competitor, then the potential for loss would be great.
3. Direct cues: The hoarder could relocate its food through detection of cues (such as odor) emanating directly from the cached food itself. While this recovery mechanism would require little cognitive ability except perhaps specialized sensory capacities, it would have a large potential downside. Any animal capable of detecting the cues could recover the cache, with potentially disastrous effects for the animal that originally created the cache.

Interestingly, there appears to be a negative correlation between the cognitive demands of the strategy and the resistance of the strategy to competitors for the caches. This implies that under appropriate conditions – a high risk of loss of scatter-hoarded food – the use of increased cognitive capacities might be favored, even though cognitive abilities involve heavy metabolic costs (Attwell and Laughlin, 2001).

The results of a field study of cache recovery and pilfering in small mammals (Vander Wall, 2000) is quite interesting from this point of view. Vander Wall allowed some yellow pine chipmunks (*Tamias amoenus*) or deer mice (*Peromyscus maniculatus*) to cache pine seeds in a large outdoor cage and then search for their own caches (knowledgeable foragers), while additional animals searched for caches created by others (naive foragers). The experiment was conducted in the Carson mountain range of western Nevada, where the climate is usually quite dry. Under dry conditions, knowledgeable animals were much more successful finding their own caches than naive animals searching for the caches of others. When conditions were wet, such as following rain, however, the chipmunks and mice found all caches, their own, those of conspecifics, or those of the other species, with equal facility (**Figure 1**). The superiority of the knowledgeable over the naive cachers under dry conditions demonstrates the advantage that detailed spatial memory can give. On the other hand, the ability of the naive foragers to locate the caches created by others demonstrates the potential liabilities of relying on direct cues to relocate cache sites.

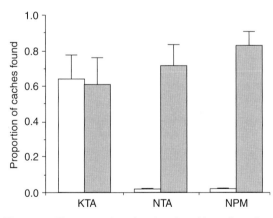

Figure 1 The proportion of caches found by yellow pine chipmunks (TA) and deer mice (PM) who either knew the locations of the caches (K) or were naive about the cache locations (N) under either dry conditions (open bars) or wet conditions (filled-in bars). From Vander Wall SB (2000) The influence of environmental conditions on cache recovery and cache pilferage by yellow pine chipmunks (*Tamias amoenus*) and deer mice (*Peromyscus maniculatus*). *Behav. Ecol.* 11: 544–549; used with permission from Oxford University Press.

1.22.3 Establishing the Role of Memory

Until recently, it was thought unlikely that scatter-hoarders used spatial memory for the recovery of cached food (e.g., Gibb, 1960). Gradually, however, evidence mounted that spatial memory for specific cache sites could be important to accurate cache recovery in a number of species of birds and mammals. Field studies provided suggestive evidence. For example, Tomback (1980) developed a technique for roughly estimating the accuracy of cache recovery by Clark's nutcrackers (*Nucifraga columbiana*) in the field. Tomback's estimated probabilities were quite high, much higher than could be expected by chance. In another field study, Cowie et al. (1981) placed mildly radioactive seeds in a feeder, and they were taken and cached by marsh tits and a scintillation counter used to locate cached seeds in the area around the feeder. A control seed was then placed 100 cm from each cached seed and survivorship of the seeds monitored. The cached seeds disappeared much more rapidly than control seeds, strongly suggesting removal by cachers and consistent with memory for specific cache sites.

MacDonald (1976) conducted similar experiments with a vixen, which almost always found dead mice she had cached but almost never found dead mice cached 1–2 m away by the experimenter.

1.22.3.1 Experimental Evidence for Spatial Memory

Although these types of field studies yielded results consistent with the use of spatial memory for specific cache sites, field studies lack the capacity for experimental control necessary to fully rule out alternative hypotheses. The breakthrough came with a series of laboratory studies that showed that many parids and corvids would cache and recover seeds under laboratory/aviary conditions. In this section, we briefly review the major findings of some of these studies that established the role of spatial memory in the relocation of cached foods.

Balda (1980) tested a single Eurasian nutcracker (*Nucifraga caryocatactes*) in a room with a dirt floor. The bird readily cached and accurately recovered seeds in this room. The search was accurate even when seeds had been removed from caches before recovery, demonstrating that cues emanating directly from caches were not necessary for recovery. Vander

Wall (1982) extended these findings by letting two Clark's nutcrackers individually cache and recover cached seeds in the same aviary. In virtually every case, each bird recovered only its own caches. This also provides strong evidence against direct cues, as well as against site preferences or paths unless these are idiosyncratic.

At the same time as studies were proceeding with nutcrackers, researchers in Canada and England were developing laboratory-based procedures to study cache recovery in chickadees and tits. Sherry et al. (1981) gave marsh tits (*Parus palustris*) sunflower seeds to store in moss-filled trays in an aviary. The birds revisited the areas of the trays used to cache seeds significantly more often than would be expected by chance 3 and 24 h after original storage of the seeds, even though the seeds had been removed. Sherry et al. (1981) also found that the probability of visiting those quadrants in which cache sites were located was higher following caching than it had been during a precaching exploratory session, suggesting that site preferences were not responsible for the performance. Sherry (1984) extended these results in an aviary study with black-capped chickadees (*Parus atricapillus*) by giving the birds specific potential cache sites (as opposed to areas in a tray). The chickadees cached readily in these sites and recovered the caches more accurately than would be expected by chance or by precaching exploratory patterns.

Kamil and Balda (1985) took a more direct approach to the control of site preferences during cache recovery by Clark's nutcrackers. They used a room with 180 holes in the floor, each of which could either be filled with sand for caching/recovery or be capped with a wooden plug. This made it possible to limit the number of sites available for caching sessions, forcing the birds to cache in sites essentially chosen by the experimenters. Even under these conditions, nutcrackers were able to recover caches accurately, demonstrating that site preferences are not necessary to accurate cache recovery by nutcrackers.

Three studies in the early 1990s demonstrated the use of spatial memory to relocate caches in scatter-hoarding rodents. Jacobs and Liman (1991) had gray squirrels cache hazelnuts in an outdoor arena. The squirrels found significantly more of their own caches than the caches of other squirrels that had stored food in the same arena. Vander Wall (1991) allowed yellow pine chipmunks to cache seeds in an arena filled with dry sand. The chipmunks were significantly more likely to find their own caches than caches of other chipmunks. Jacobs (1992) allowed Merriam's

kangaroo rats to cache and retrieve sunflower seeds in an arena with plastic cups filled with sand for caching sites (much like Kamil and Balda, 1985). Before retrieval, she removed half of the caches made by each rat. The rats searched significantly more in locations where they buried seeds, whether the seeds had been removed or not. Jacobs also found that a naive rat searching in the arena found significantly fewer caches than the rat that had made the caches.

It is clear that some form of spatial memory for cache sites is used to find cached seeds by members of several taxa (see Vander Wall, 1990, for a broad survey of food-hoarding in animals). Although other mechanisms such as olfaction or site preferences may play a role, many food-storing corvids and parids and rodents can find their food when these mechanisms are controlled for or eliminated. We now turn our attention to what is known about spatial memory in food-storing species.

1.22.3.2 The Characteristics of Cache Memory and Retrieval

It seems likely that the characteristics of cache site memory in any particular species of scatter-hoarders will be a function of a complex interaction between functional and mechanistic variables. For example, as caches are created, they are necessarily created in some sequence. A large psychological literature indicates that in the case of such serial lists, the order in which the items to be remembered are presented can have important effects on how well they are remembered, the serial position effect well known to students of memory (e.g., Wright et al., 1984; Wright, 2006). On the other hand, different orders of recovery may be most adaptive under different circumstances (Andersson and Krebs, 1978). Duration of memory may be another example. In this section, we briefly survey what is known about the duration, contents, and dynamics of cache memory.

1.22.3.2.1 Memory duration

Balda and Kamil (1992) tested four groups of nutcrackers, each at a different amount of time after caching, from 11 to 285 days. All four groups performed well above chance levels. Bednekoff et al. (1997a) used a repeated-measures design in a comparative study with nutcrackers, pinyon jays (*Gymnorhinus cyanocephalus*), Mexican jays (*Aphelocoma ultramarina*), and Western scrub jays (*A. californica*; note that the classification of *Aphelocoma* species was modified several years ago; we use the current nomenclature throughout this chapter) and found that the birds were still performing above chance after 250 days. In contrast, most studies with parids have suggested much shorter memory durations. For example, Hitchcock and Sherry (1990) found that black-capped chickadees did not find their caches at better than chance levels after postcaching intervals over 28 days, and Brodin and Kunz (1997) obtained similar results in willow tits (*Parus montanus*).

These differences in memory duration correspond with differences in natural history. Many corvids cache in the fall and then depend on their cached food throughout winter into the spring (Vander Wall, 1990). In contrast, within the parids many species cache for shorter periods of time, caching and recovering throughout the winter (e.g., marsh tits, *P. palustris*; Cowie et al., 1981), although there are some parids that cache in fall and use those caches for some months (e.g., crested tits, *P. cristatus*, Haftorn, 1954). Brodin (2005) has suggested that corvids possess a site-specific, accurate long-term memory, whereas parids may use a more general memory along with area-restricted search.

1.22.3.2.2 Memory for cache contents
Several studies indicate that cachers can remember the contents of their caches. Sherry (1984) allowed black-capped chickadees to cache two types of seed and found that they recovered the type they preferred before the nonpreferred type. Clayton and Dickinson (1999) extended this methodology by allowing Western scrub jays to cache two types of food, then prefeeding one of the foods before recovery testing. During recovery, the birds preferentially searched sites in which they had cached (but not retrieved) the food that had not been preferred (*See* Chapter 1.23, research by Clayton and her colleagues on episodic-like memory). This suggests a memory process more dynamic than a simple association of foods and the locations of their caches.

Moller et al. (2001) gave Clark's nutcrackers small and large pine seeds to cache and videotaped recovery sessions. They measured the size of the gape, the distance between the upper and lower bills when beginning to dig out the cache. Gape size was reliably larger for caches containing the larger seeds than for caches containing the smaller seeds.

1.22.3.2.3 Order of recovery
As a number of authors have pointed out (e.g., Vander Wall, 1990), since caches are created

sequentially, the psychological literature on memory suggests that there ought to be some relationship between order of cache creation and order of cache recovery, either primacy (first recovering the caches that were created first) or recency (first recovering the most recently made caches). Psychological studies of memory for serial lists regularly find both of these effects in a wide variety of contexts in humans and animals (see recent review by Wright, 2006).

It has also been argued on functional grounds that there should be recency effects in cache recovery (e.g., Shettleworth and Krebs, 1982). The more time that has passed since a cache was created, the less likely that cache is to still be available to the cacher. As time passes, the probability of the cache having been pilfered increases and the chances of the cache location having been forgotten also may increase. Thus, recovery of the most recent caches first could maximize the total number retrieved. There has, however, been no consistent evidence of such effects. For example, when black-capped chickadees stored and recovered sunflower seeds in Sherry (1984, experiment 2), 24 correlation coefficients between cache and recovery orders were calculated. Two were significant in the positive direction, one was significant in the negative direction, and the remainder were not significant.

In a comparative study with Clark's nutcrackers, pinyon jays, and western scrub jays, Balda and Kamil (1989) calculated 42 correlation coefficients between cache order and recovery order. Twenty-five were above zero, one equaled zero, and the remaining 16 were below zero. Six of the positive correlations were significant, as was one of the negative correlations, indicative of a tendency toward recency effects, which was not statistically significant overall.

1.22.3.2.4 Proactive and retroactive interference
Serial position effects are often interpreted as due to the effects of interference, at least in part (see Shettleworth, 1998, for discussion; *See also* Chapters 1.06, 1.10). Two types of interference are generally recognized. If the target information was experienced before the interfering information, the effects of the interfering information are called retroactive interference. If the target was experienced after the interfering information, it is called proactive interference. As might be expected from the failure to find strong serial-position effects during cache recovery, attempts to document retroactive and proactive interference during caching have also yielded only

424 Memory in Food Caching Animals

weak evidence for such effects. Bednekoff et al. (1997b) explicitly tested for interference in nutcrackers' cache memory by allowing caches to be made at different times. They found no evidence of interference between the two sets of caches.

Experiments using techniques other than cache recovery have found clear evidence for interference effects in parids and corvids. For example, when black-capped chickadees were presented with three-item lists in an operant associative task, they showed clear primacy and recency effects (Crystal and Shettleworth, 1994). And when Lewis and Kamil (2006) gave Clark's nutcrackers separate lists of locations to remember, they showed clear retroactive and proactive interference effects between the lists. These results raise the question of why such effects are weak in cache recovery but prevalent with other measures of memory performance.

1.22.3.2.5 Dynamism of memory

As caches are recovered, an additional problem arises: not only are there caches to remember but there are emptied caches to avoid. Do cachers avoid revisiting sites which have been emptied? Sherry (1982) examined this question by allowing marsh tits to cache in moss-filled trays then recover about half these caches 3 h later. Twenty-four hours after the initial caching, he allowed the tits to recover more caches. The birds clearly made more visits and spent more time at sites which had been cached in but not recovered from than sites that had been cached in and recovered from. Sherry (1984, experiment 2) obtained similar results in black-capped chickadees.

Frequent revisits to emptied cache sites have been observed in Clark's nutcrackers (e.g., Balda, 1980; Kamil and Balda, 1985). These studies, however, were not primarily intended to measure revisit probabilities against appropriate controls, so the implications of the frequent revisits were not clear. Balda et al. (1986) found that revisits to emptied caches by nutcrackers were much more frequent than expected by chance, and that revisit probability was not affected either by leaving signs of previous recoveries on the surface of the sand around cache sites or by reducing the number of seeds in a cache.

From a functional perspective, these observations are a puzzle since revisits increase foraging effort and may also increase predation risk. These considerations led Kamil et al. (1993) to take another look at revisits by Clark's nutcrackers, using a technique which allowed independent estimates of search accuracy and of preference. When they tested sites with cached seeds (good sites) vs. sites with cached seeds that had been removed by the birds (old sites) vs. holes that never had seeds in them (bad sites), the results clearly demonstrated that nutcrackers treated old sites differently than good sites. When they visited a cluster that contained an old site, they probed more of the alternative sites than when they visited good sites that contained seeds. In addition, they visited clusters containing good sites earlier than those containing old sites. They also found that old sites were visited earlier than clusters containing bad sites. Once the good sites have been exploited, the birds are more likely to visit old sites where they cached and then removed seeds than to visit bad sites that never contained seeds.

1.22.3.2.6 Are all caches created equal?

In the Balda and Kamil (1992) study of long-term memory for cache sites, the group of birds tested at the longest cache-retrieval interval showed an interesting pattern of errors. Their error rate per recovery was approximately equal to that of the groups with the shorter retention interval until about 75% of their caches had been recovered. After that, they began to make more errors. This pattern suggested that after 280 days, the nutcrackers had begun to forget some of their cache locations and had recovered those that they remembered most accurately first.

Kamil and Balda (1990) controlled the order of cache recovery by covering the floor in one-quarter of the caching room with canvas. Over four recovery sessions, each quarter of the room was covered once. The accuracy of recovery of this group was compared to that of a control group for whom all cache sites were always available. As predicted, the experimental group showed an initial recovery accuracy that was lower than that of the controls. But this accuracy level was constant over the four sessions, whereas the accuracy of the controls declined, so that during the fourth session the experimental group was more accurate than the controls. This clearly supports the hypothesis that some sites are remembered better than others, and then recovered first.

1.22.3.3 Coding of Cache Site Locations

When a scatter-hoarding animal remembers sites at which it has stored food, just what is it about the cache location that is remembered? Just how is the location encoded in memory? This raises basic questions about orientation and navigation. There is an enormous literature on the cues that animals in a wide variety of taxa use to find locations during, for example, foraging, homing, or migration (*See* Chapters 1.12, 1.20, 1.25). In this section we will focus on studies that relate to how caching animals use landmarks to find locations and divide our review into studies that study cache recovery and studies that use other techniques.

1.22.3.3.1 Landmark use during the recovery of stored food

Many studies have demonstrated that landmarks play a crucial role in accurate cache recovery. For example, animals have been tested for their ability to find their caches when most or all of the landmarks present during caching have been removed from the caching area during recovery testing. If landmarks are important, this should produce substantial decrements in the ability to relocate caches, and it does (e.g., nutcrackers, Balda and Turek, 1984; parids, Herz et al., 1994). Barkley and Jacobs (1998) took a slightly different approach, allowing Merriam's kangaroo rats to cache and recover with either no or with many landmarks present. While the number of landmarks had no effect after a 1-day retention interval, there were large effects after 10 days. The kangaroo rats that had cached and recovered with no landmarks performed at much lower levels than those who had cached and recovered with 16 landmarks present. While such studies establish the role of landmarks in cache recovery, they tell us little about what mechanisms might be used. Few studies, however, have attempted to determine the mechanisms that are used during cache recovery.

The first attempt to do so of which we are aware was by Bossema and Pot (1974). They compared the routes used by individual Eurasian jays (*Garrulus glandarius*) when making and recovering caches. They found that the jays tended to use the same route during recovery as during caching more often than would be expected by chance. Bossema and Pot suggested that the birds used a snapshot of the scene from the cache site when they cached, then matched what they saw to the snapshot during recovery.

Kamil et al. (1999) found the Bossema and Pot interpretation unconvincing. There are many other reasons that could result in use of the same path during caching as during recovery. They conducted an intensive videotape study of movement patterns by nutcrackers during caching and recovery, using a technique that allowed estimates of the accuracy of recovery of each individual cache. Like Bossema and

Pot (1974), Kamil et al. (1999) found that the birds tended to frequently use the same path during caching and recovery, but differing paths and body orientations were also often used. Because their procedure allowed cache-by-cache estimates of accuracy, Kamil et al. (1999) were able to determine the effect of consistency of direction on recovery accuracy. There were none: Birds were equally accurate regardless of the path used. This result argues directly against the snapshot hypothesis.

Bossema (1979) looked at the locations of caches and the accuracy of recovery relative to the positions of landmarks. He found that Eurasian jays cached more near vertical objects and were more accurate at retrieving their caches when vertical objects were available as beacons, as opposed to horizontal objects. Similar results have been found in studies in which caching animals have been trained to find food in specific locations (see following). In a second test, he taught the birds to find hidden food in a specific spatial location relative to two vertical landmarks. He performed tests in which one landmark was removed or the landmarks were moved further apart or closer together. From these tests, he concluded that the jays were using the distance between the spatial location and the line between the landmarks to orient.

Vander Wall (1982) took a different approach. After Clark's nutcrackers had cached food in an arena with an array of landmarks, he displaced the landmarks in one half of the room 20 cm from their original location during cache recovery (**Figure 2**). During the subsequent recovery session, the birds shifted their searching approximately 20 cm in the direction of the displacement in that half of the room. When the birds searched for caches made in the center of the room, where some of the nearby landmarks had been displaced and others had not, their search was displaced approximately 10 cm in the direction of the displacement. This suggests that the birds were integrating information from multiple landmarks (shifted and nonshifted) and searching at some kind of averaged location.

One of the ways to use landmarks to find a location is to use the directional relationship between the cache site and one or more landmarks (e.g., Kamil and Cheng, 2001). The use of directional information requires a compass. In a series of studies, Wiltschko and Balda (1989) and Wiltschko et al. (1999) have used clock-shift procedures in outdoor aviaries to demonstrate the use of a sun compass by scrub jays and nutcrackers. For example, Wiltschko and Balda (1989) had scrub jays cache in a 90° sector of a

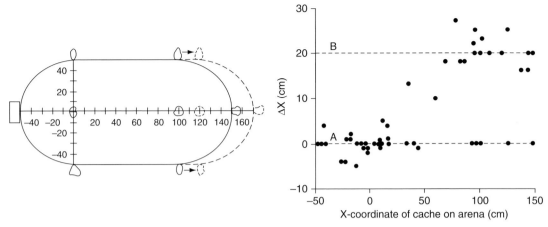

Figure 2 The left panel shows the caching arena during control (solid lines) and during landmark-shift (dashed lines) conditions. The right panel shows the distance between a probe and the nearest cache on the y-axis as a function of the original position of the cache in the x-axis. If the birds followed the shift, a Δx score of 20 cm would be expected. Reprinted from Vander Wall SB (1982) An experimental analysis of cache recovery in Clark's nutcracker. *Anim. Behav.* 30: 84–94, copyright 1982, with permission from Elsevier.

circular outdoor arena and then recover after being clock-shifted 6 h. When clock-shifted, the search was concentrated in an adjacent 90° sector, as would be expected if the sun compass was being used. Although these experiments clearly establish the use of sun compass under some conditions, caches can be recovered in the absence of information from the sun (e.g., indoors). Furthermore, when multiple landmarks are used to encode locations, clock shifts should produce conflicting effects (Kamil and Cheng, 2001).

Another issue that has been investigated both during cache recovery and during other tests of spatial memory in seed-caching animals is the relative importance of local versus global (or distal) cues. Local cues are those located relatively close to the goal location, while global or distal cues are generally larger, but further away. Several studies have found that birds seem to have some preference for caching near objects in the environment, suggesting that local cues may be quite important (e.g., Bossema, 1979). On the other hand, Balda et al. (1986) found that Clark's nutcrackers ignored local cues on the surface when making revisits to cache sites. The results of Herz et al. (1994) suggest the importance of global cues. Black-capped chickadees stored food on artificial trees placed within a symmetrical enclosure that had large global cues on each wall. There were unique color place cues located by each potential cache site. The removal of the place cues did not affect retrieval accuracy, but when the global cues were removed, search accuracy decreased. In a

second study, when birds were only given global cues during caching, displacement of those cues during recovery produced a displacement of the search behavior. Watanabe (2005) has also shown the importance of global cues in remembering cache locations in Western scrub jays.

Results from mammals also suggest distal cues are important. Lavenex et al. (1998) found that fox squirrels use distal environmental cues rather than proximal cues to find food in a field experiment. Even when proximal spatial information was available, the squirrels chose to use the environment surrounding the apparatus to gain spatial information, presumably directional information or bearings. Jacobs and Shiflett (1999) devised an outdoor vertical maze to mimic the vertical structure of the squirrel's environment. They found that fox squirrels used distal cues to orient within this maze as well.

1.22.3.3.2 Landmarks and the coding of spatial locations

Cache recovery procedures are very limited for studies on how cachers encode spatial locations. As several of the studies reviewed suggest, the geometrical relationships among landmarks and between landmarks and the location of a cache are important. But it is very difficult to control location-landmark geometry when the caching animal is free to cache throughout the test arena. Therefore, many investigators have used procedures in which animals are trained to find buried food in a location defined by a set of local/global landmarks or other cues.

Bennett (1993a,b) trained Eurasian jays to find hidden food within an array of landmarks on the floor of an arena. The array consisted of landmarks that were either short or tall and either near or far from the hidden food location. He found that the birds relied more heavily on near, tall landmarks to find the food, a finding similar to that of Bossema (1979), described in the section titled 'Landmark use during the recovery of stored food.' This suggests that local cues are most important, especially if tall.

Other experiments, however, suggest that low horizontal features that define an edge can also be important. Cheng and Sherry (1992) trained black-capped chickadees to find food buried in a location defined relative to the locations of a cylindrical landmark and an edge (**Figure 3**). Then, when the landmark was shifted in a direction either parallel or perpendicular to the edge during probe trials, the birds followed parallel shifts more strongly. This was particularly clear during probe trials in which the landmark was shifted in a diagonal direction, which produced more parallel than perpendicular shifts in search. As Cheng and Sherry pointed out, these results suggest that perpendicular distance from an edge can serve as an important means of encoding spatial locations and are consistent with the results of Bossema (1979).

Similar studies with Clark's nutcrackers (Gould-Beierle and Kamil, 1996, 1998), pinyon jays, and scrub jays (Gould-Beierle and Kamil, 1998) have also found that the distance from an edge is important. In all three of these studies, birds found hidden food whose location was defined relative to the locations of an edge and a cylindrical landmark. As in the parids studied by Cheng and Sherry (1992), these

corvids followed parallel shifts and shifted more readily in the parallel direction when given diagonal shifts. However, when the landmark was shifted in a direction perpendicular to the edge, nutcrackers, pinyon jays, and scrub jays did not shift their searching in that direction, in contrast to the results of Cheng and Sherry (1992).

Gould-Beierle and Kamil (1998) extended the conditions originally tested by Cheng and Sherry (1992) by testing the effects of varying the position and orientation of an edge and landmark across training trials with nutcrackers, pinyon jays, and scrub jays. Following this training, the birds were more sensitive to shifts in the position of the cylindrical landmark, shifting their search with each landmark shift to a much greater extent than birds trained with a nonshifting edge and landmark. The shifting of the relationship between the local cues (edge and cylinder) and the global cues (features of the room) appeared to result in a devaluation of both the global cues and distance from the edge. The extent to which distance from a line or edge is used thus depends upon the salience and location of other, more distal or global landmarks.

The relative importance of local versus more distal or global cues depends on context and on the distance between the local cues and the target location. Gould-Beierle and Kamil (1999) trained three groups of Clark's nutcrackers to find a hidden food site within an open room filled with wood chips. Two local cues were available near the food site, a cylindrical landmark and a horizontal piece of wood (much like the edge of a tray in previous studies). The groups varied in the distance the cylinder and edge were from the target location. They found that the

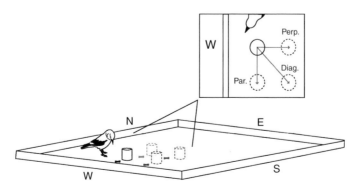

Figure 3 Typical setup (not to scale) for experiments on landmark displacement with an edge and a single landmark present. The birds are initially trained with the cylinder in the location indicated by the solid circle (top left in the inset). They are then tested with occasional nonrewarded trials at each of the three test positions, representing displacements perpendicular (Perp.), parallel (Par.), and diagonal (Diag.) to the long axis of the nearest edge. Drawing by Karina I. Helm.

group with these cues closest to the target used them more heavily to find the location, while the other two groups relied more on information from global cues within the room.

Goodyear and Kamil (2004) extended these results with a study in which different groups of Clark's nutcrackers were trained to find a buried seed at a location defined by an array of four landmarks, each of which was at a different distance from the goal, followed by probe tests with each of the individual landmarks. The groups differed in the mean distance from the landmarks to the goal location. For the group for whom the nearest landmark was quite close to the goal, the presence of the closest landmark had the greatest effect on search accuracy, an effect reminiscent of the overshadowing effect in Pavlovian conditioning (Gallistel, 1990). However, at longer goal–landmark distances, this overshadowing effect disappeared, and each landmark controlled search roughly equally.

Since geometry clearly affects search, there has been some interest in the ability of caching animals to directly learn geometric relationships. Kamil and Jones (1997) tested the ability of Clark's nutcrackers to learn a general geometric rule for spatial locations. They trained nutcrackers to find a seed that was always located halfway between two landmarks whose position in the room and interlandmark distance varied from trial to trial. The birds learned the task readily and searched extremely accurately when tested with new interlandmark distances. Follow-up studies demonstrated that nutcrackers could learn other geometrical rules (Kamil and Jones, 2000), including the use of relative bearings (Jones and Kamil, 2001). Comparative studies found that nutcrackers performed these tasks much more accurately than pigeons (Jones et al., 2002; Spetch et al., 2003).

One of the things that makes the location of cached food so interesting from a coding/navigation and orientation perspective is that successful cache recovery requires a very accurate search. Given the size of a nutcracker's beak and the size of pine seeds, for example, the bird must dig within 1–2 cm of the center of a cache in order to find it. This led Kamil and Cheng (2001) to hypothesize that nutcrackers encode the directional relationship between the goal and multiple landmarks. This was based on a combination of known features of search accuracy and a logical consideration. When nutcrackers are looking for a cache site that is not close to a landmark, the use of directional information results in a more accurate search than the use of distance information.

But all compasses have error, and compensation for such error can be achieved by taking bearings to multiple landmarks. Although there are some data that support the model (Kamil et al., 2001), there are, as yet, insufficient data to fully evaluate the hypothesis.

1.22.4   The Evolution of Spatial Memory in Seed-Caching Animals

The capacity, duration, and dynamics of the memory that seed-caching animals use to relocate stored food seem quite impressive compared to the results of many studies of animal memory using standard psychological procedures such as the radial maze or matching-to-sample (*See* Chapters 1.20, 1.21, 1.23, 1.25, 1.26). This led to the development of the hypothesis that dependence on memory for the location of cached food would be associated with heightened memory abilities. This hypothesis, sometimes referred to as the ecological hypothesis, has led to many studies of memory comparing species that differ in their degree of dependence on cached food. We will divide our review of this literature by methodology, first discussing studies that used cache recovery as their measure of memory, then reviewing studies that used measures of spatial memory that do not depend on the caching and recovery of food.

1.22.4.1   Cache-Site Memory

There are relatively few comparative studies involving cache site memory. This is probably because such studies require the availability of a set of closely related species (or populations) which cache, but vary in some dimension of cache-related natural history, and there are few such instances. We are only aware of four such studies, two with corvids and two with parids.

Balda and Kamil (1989) compared the cache recovery accuracy of three corvid species that differ in their degree of dependence on stored food, Clark's nutcrackers, pinyon jays, and Western scrub jays, after a relatively short retention interval of 7 days. They found that the more cache-dependent species, nutcrackers and pinyon jays, recovered their caches more accurately and more rapidly than Western scrub jays. Bednekoff et al. (1997a) tested the same three species as well as Mexican jays after retention intervals of 10–250 days. They found that cache recovery performance of the two *Aphelocoma* species

(Mexican and Western scrub jays) was lower that that of the nutcrackers or pinyon jays, but that all four species performed with only modest accuracy levels (although still significantly better than chance) after the two longest retention intervals (of 150 and 250 days).

Healy and Suhonen (1996) compared marsh tits and willow tits. Willow tits live in harsher environments than marsh tits and are thought to retrieve their caches after longer retention intervals than marsh tits. In this study, however, no differences in the accuracy of cache recovery were found after either a short (1- to 2-h) or a long (17-day) retention interval. Pravosudov and Clayton (2002) compared two populations of black-capped chickadees, one from Alaska and the other from Colorado. They found that the birds from the harsher environment of Alaska cached more food and recovered it more efficiently than the birds from Colorado, demonstrating that different ecological pressures within this single species are correlated with differences in spatial memory ability. Thus three of these four studies found differences in cache recovery accuracy that were correlated with differences in dependence on stored food.

1.22.4.2   Noncache-Site Memory

Most comparative work on spatial memory involving scatter-hoarding species has been based on procedures that do not depend on caching. Such procedures are necessary to compare spatial memory between caching and noncaching species. In addition, data from such tests could address the question of just how specialized the spatial memory abilities of food-caching animals may be. A variety of techniques were applied, and we have organized our review of these comparative studies by the procedures used to test memory.

1.22.4.2.1   Window shopping

The window shopping task is probably the noncaching task most similar to cache memory. Instead of storing food in a location to be remembered, the bird encounters the seed, either behind a transparent window or a seed wedged into a small hole so tightly that it cannot be removed. Shettleworth et al. (1990) showed that memory for such encountered seeds appeared to be similar to that for stored seeds in black-capped chickadees and coal tits. Krebs et al. (1990) used the technique to test coal tits against nonstoring great tits. They found somewhat better

performance in the storing coal tits. Coal tits were more likely than great tits to return to sites at which they had seen seeds. They were also better at discriminating between sites seen to contain seeds and those seen to be empty.

1.22.4.2.2   One-trial associative tasks

In one-trial associative tasks, two or more stimuli are all associated with a correct location. Following a single experience at that location, the subject is given test trials in which it chooses between the spatial location or the nonspatial stimuli (which are now presented in a new location; see **Figure 4**). A number of one-trial associative studies have used a variation of window shopping in which the bird finds food at a specific location which is also indicated by cues from an object. The bird is allowed to begin to eat, but is interrupted (removed from the experimental situation) before completely consuming the food. The test is to see where the birds will return to look for the seed, to the correct spatial location or the correct location based on object cues. In comparisons of food-storing and nonstoring species in both parid and corvid families (Clayton and Krebs, 1994), the food-storing birds (marsh tits and jays) went first to the correct spatial location, whereas the nonstorers (blue tits, *Parus caeruleus*, and jackdaws, *Corvus monedula*) went equally as often on their first choice to the correct spatial or object-specific location. When comparing food-storing chickadees to nonstoring dark-eyed juncos (*Junco hyemalis*), Brodbeck (1994) found similar results, with the chickadees responding preferentially to spatial cues and the juncos responding equally to spatial and object cues. These studies provide further evidence that food-storing birds focus heavily on spatial memory when returning to food sites.

In another variation on this theme, Brodbeck and Shettleworth (1995) placed spatial and object-related cues in conflict in the choice phase of test trials in a matching-to-sample experiment. With this technique, they found that while space was the first choice of food-storing chickadees, nonstoring juncos chose space and color equally. They also demonstrated that when shown a compound stimulus of both spatial location and color and tested on each element of the compound alone, chickadees performed better on the spatial element, while juncos performed equally well on both elements. This, along with the other one-trial associative memory experiments, demonstrates the importance of spatial information to food-storing birds.

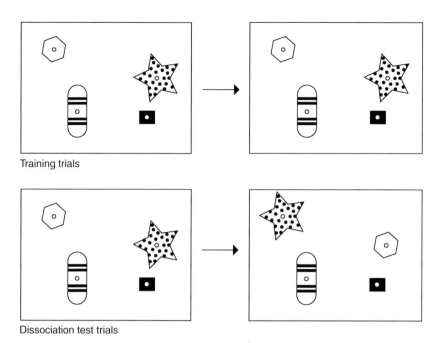

Training trials

Dissociation test trials

Figure 4 Diagrammatic representation of the logic of one-trial associative tasks. The top pair of figures shows training trials. One of the stimuli is randomly designated correct on each trial (with new, trial-unique stimuli used for each trial). The bird is then rewarded when it pecks the correct stimulus. The display then disappears for a retention interval, and the same display is presented for choice, and the bird is rewarded for pecking at the same stimulus. Once this training is complete, the bird receives occasional dissociation test trials, as shown in the bottom pair of figures. These trials differ from training trials in that the spatial locations of two of the stimuli are switched. If the bird pecks at the same visual stimulus (the dot-filled star, in this case), this indicates control by the stimulus. But if the bird pecks at the old location (the hexagon), it suggests spatial control. Spatial location and visual stimulus have been dissociated. Drawings by Karina I. Helm.

Lavenex et al. (1998) used an approach similar to that of one-trial associative tests in a field experiment. Although their training task involved multiple trials, they gave fox squirrels different spatial and nonspatial relational proximal cues that could be used to predict the locations of nuts buried by experimenters. The squirrels used spatial over nonspatial information to solve the task, even when both were available, a result similar to the results of laboratory one-trial associative experiments just reviewed.

1.22.4.2.3 Open-room radial maze

In an open-room radial maze procedure, Hilton and Krebs (1990) tested two storing parid species, two nonstoring parid species, and a nonstoring greenfinch in an open-room analog of the radial maze. They found decreasing performance as the retention interval increased from 30 s to 24 h. The food-storing tits (marsh and coal tits) performed above chance after 24 h, although the extent to which their performance exceeded chance was modest. In contrast, neither the nonstoring tits (blue and great tits) nor the finches performed above chance after 24 h.

Kamil et al. (1994) tested four corvids who vary in dependence on stored food in their version of an open-room analog of the radial maze. They found that the two species most dependent on stored food, Clark's nutcrackers and pinyon jays, acquired the task to higher levels than the less dependent species, Mexican and Western scrub jays. When retention intervals of 30–300 min were tested (in ascending order), the species differences tended to disappear as the retention interval got longer. Only the most dependent species, the nutcrackers, performed above chance after a 24-h retention interval, although, as in the marsh and coal tits, their performance was only modestly better than chance.

Gould-Beierle (2000) also tested four corvid species – nutcrackers, pinyon jays, Western scrub jays, and jackdaws – on a version of the open-room radial maze task. She included both a reference memory and a working memory component by having 12 holes in the floor, four of which were never correct while the other eight were used in the usual way as working memory locations. She found that pinyon jays and scrub jays performed better than nutcrackers and jackdaws in both the working and reference memory aspects of the procedure. When looking at the first four searches in the maze, however, the nutcrackers performed as well as the two jay species in working memory and there were no species differences in reference memory. The performance of the scrub jays was not expected and suggests further exploration into the spatial memory abilities of this species. Perhaps combining both a working and reference memory task simultaneously affects spatial memory differentially in these species.

Barkley and Jacobs (2007) used an open-room task similar to a radial maze analog. They trained two species of kangaroo rat in a task in which the animal was shown four locations (randomly chosen out of 128) and then tested for their ability to remember the four 24 h later. One species was the scatter-hoarding Merriam's kangaroo rat (*Dipodomys merriami*), a species that hoards intensively. The other was the leaf-eating specialist Great Basin kangaroo rat (*D. microps*), which relies less on scatter-hoarding than Merriam's. Merriam's kangaroo rat performed considerably better than the Great Basin kangaroo rat on this task.

1.22.4.2.4   Operant tasks

A number of investigators have used several different operant tasks to measure differences in memory ability among storing species and between storing and nonstoring species. The most commonly used procedure has been spatial delayed nonmatching- or matching-to-sample. In this task, each trial consists of two parts: the presentation of the sample followed by the presentation of a choice test. Thus, for example, Olson (1989, 1991) had two keys on the front wall of an operant chamber. Each trial began with the illumination of one of those keys, chosen at random on each trial. After the bird had pecked at that key and moved to the back of the box to peck at another, single key located there (to break up any patterns of settling in front of the to-be-correct key), the bird was presented with two keys and rewarded only for pecking at the key that had not been pecked at earlier in the trial (nonmatching). Olson (1989) tested Clark's nutcrackers, scrub jays, and pigeons (*Columba livia*). Although all three learned the task with equal facility, the nutcrackers outperformed the other two species when the task was made more difficult by either titrating the delay between sample and choice test or by introducing multiple samples to be remembered.

These results were extended in a subsequent study (Olson et al., 1995) with nutcrackers, pinyon jays, scrub jays, and Mexican jays. In this study, a computer monitor and touch screen were used. When the delay interval was titrated, the nutcrackers performed at much higher levels than the other three species. After completing this spatial nonmatching test, the birds were then tested on an almost exactly equivalent nonspatial task. In this experiment, the samples could be either red or green and the bird had to remember the color rather than the location. Under these conditions, the ordering of the species changed completely, and none of the species differences were statistically significant (**Figure 5**).

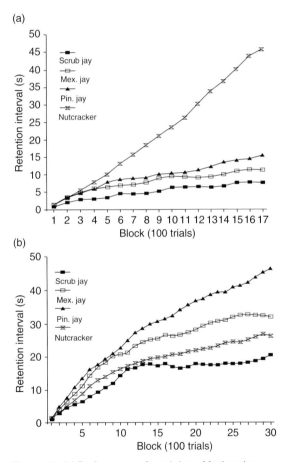

Figure 5   (a) Performance of scrub jays, Mexican jays, pinyon jays, and nutcrackers during spatial nonmatching-to-sample titration. (b) Performance of each species during color nonmatching-to-sample titration. Data are presented as averages of blocks of 100 trials. From Olson DJ, Kamil AC, Balda RP, and Nims PJ (1995) Performance of four seed-caching corvid species in operant tests of nonspatial and spatial memory. *J. Comp. Psychol.* 109: 173–181; used with permission from the American Psychological Association.

Healy and Krebs (1992) studied matching-to-sample in marsh tits and great tits, using a choice apparatus attached to the birds' home cage. The birds took a seed from the correct location, which was signaled both by location and by a visual object, then returned to their home cage to consume the object. They were then given a choice test, and the two species performed very similarly. The only significant different between the species was superior performance by the storing marsh tits early in acquisition of the task. Healy (1995) used a more traditional nonmatching-to-sample (NMTS) test on a computer monitor with four parid species, two storing species (coal and marsh tits) and two nonstoring species (blue and great tits). The birds performed well at retention intervals as long as 100 s, but there were no differences between the storers and nonstorers. This may have been due to the presence of spatial and nonspatial cues. It is also possible that storing and nonstoring tits perform similarly during matching-to-sample type procedures.

1.22.5   Neural Substrates

The central role of spatial memory in the recovery of scatter-hoarded food raises a number of questions about neural substrates. Which areas of the brain are used during cache recovery? What types of species differences in neural structure are associated with the evident differences between species in performance on cache recovery and other tests of spatial memory? In this section we review the literature relevant to these questions.

1.22.5.1   Role of the Hippocampus in Spatial Memory

O'Keefe and Nadel (1978) first proposed a central role for mammalian hippocampus in spatial memory. This hypothesis has been confirmed by experiments in many different laboratory tasks (*See* Chapters 1.33, 2.11). Most of these experiments, however, have been carried out in mammals, while most research on spatial memory in scatter-hoarders has been carried out in birds. What is known about the avian hippocampus (**Figure 6**)?

In this context, it is interesting to note that there is a radically new view of brain evolution and the structure of the avian cerebrum, a view that emphasizes the large number of avian–mammalian homologies (Jarvis et al.,

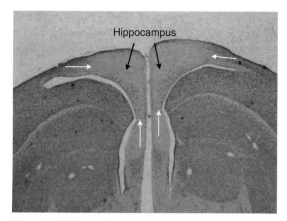

Figure 6   A photomicrograph of a coronal section through the avian hippocampus, with boundaries indicated by the white arrows. (Photograph by Kristy Gould.)

2005). This view has led to a proposal for a radical revision of the nomenclature for avian cerebrum, a nomenclature that "better reflects these functions and the homologies between avian and mammalian brains" (Jarvis et al., 2005: 2). Research with scatter-hoarding birds and mammals is consistent with this revision. The dorsomedial region of the avian telencephalon has been shown to be homologous to the mammalian hippocampal formation in many regards. This includes connectivity (Krayniak and Siegel, 1978; Casini et al., 1986; Szkeley and Krebs, 1996), distribution of neuropeptides and neurotransmitters (Erichsen et al., 1991; Krebs et al., 1991; Gould et al., 2001), generation of long-term potentiation (Shapiro and Wieraszko, 1996) and a theta rhythm (Siegel et al., 2000), electrophysiology (Siegel et al., 2002), and *N*-methyl-D-aspartate (NMDA) receptor activation (Shiflett et al., 2004) and immediate early gene expression (Smulders and DeVoogd, 2000b; Shimizu et al., 2004) during spatial tasks. Behaviorally, lesions to pigeon hippocampus disrupt performance on a variety of spatial memory tasks such as learning spatial representations in homing (reviewed in Bingman et al., 2005), spatial reversal learning (Good, 1987), spatial alternation (Reilly and Good, 1987), and spatial delayed matching-to-sample (Good and Macphail, 1994).

1.22.5.2   The Hippocampus in Food-Storing Birds

In the case of food-storing birds, hippocampal lesions disrupt cache retrieval. Krushinskaya (1966) lesioned the dorsomedial and dorsolateral sections of the hippocampus of Eurasian nutcrackers after they had stored food in a dirt-floored laboratory room. When given the opportunity to recover, lesioned birds retrieved 13% of their caches while nonlesioned controls recovered around 90% of theirs. Although Krushinskaya's lesion methods were crude, and she may have inadvertently damaged areas outside of the hippocampus, later research has confirmed the role of hippocampus in cache recovery and spatial memory using lesion techniques on black-capped chickadees during both food storing (Sherry and Vaccarino, 1989) and delayed spatial matching-to-sample tasks (Hampton and Shettleworth, 1996). Temporary inactivation of the hippocampus in black-capped chickadees also produces memory impairment in a spatial associative task (Shiflett et al., 2003), indicating hippocampal involvement in storing and retrieving spatial information in the short term.

These results strongly suggest that the species differences in spatial memory and cache recovery should be reflected in differences in hippocampal structure. Comparative studies of avian hippocampus have found that species that store food have a larger relative hippocampal size than those that do not (Krebs et al, 1989; Sherry et al., 1989; Garamszegi and Eens, 2004; Lucas et al., 2004; but see Brodin and Lundberg, 2003). Correlations are also found between food storing behavior, spatial memory performance, and relative hippocampal volume for food-storing birds within corvids (Healy and Krebs, 1992; Basil et al., 1996) and parids (Hampton et al., 1995; Healy and Krebs, 1996), as well as in food-storing rodents within the kangaroo rat family (Jacobs and Spencer, 1994).

There are also population differences in hippocampal volume within species. Black-capped chickadees that live further north, in harsher climates (e.g., Alaska), store more food, perform better on spatial tasks, and have a larger hippocampus than birds living further south (e.g., Colorado) (Pravosudov and Clayton, 2002; but see Brodin et al., 1996). Similar population differences may exist in other species. For example, Pravosudov and de Kort (2006) analyzed the brains of a large number of scrub jays, which have been classified as storing fewer seeds (Balda and Kamil, 1989) and performing less accurately during many spatial memory tasks (e.g., Balda and Kamil, 1989; Olson, 1991, see previous); they have been found to have a smaller hippocampus than other food-storing corvids (Basil et al., 1996). Their data indicated a significantly larger relative hippocampal volume than the scrub jays in Basil et al. (1996). This difference in results may be due to methodological differences (paraffin-embedded vs. frozen tissue). On the other hand, the scrub jays used

in the two studies came from different regions (northern Arizona and northern California), and there may be population differences within scrub jays in hippocampal size correlated with natural history.

1.22.5.3 Experience, Seasonality, and Neurogenesis in Birds

There are also important interactions between early environment, seasonality, and hippocampal growth. In at least some food-storing birds, early experience with food storing contributes to the development and ultimate size of adult hippocampus. When juvenile food-storing parids are given the opportunity to store food, they perform better on tests of spatial memory (Clayton, 1995, 2001) and develop larger hippocampi with more neurons and an increased cell proliferation rate compared to food-storing parids that are not allowed to store food (Clayton, 1996; Patel et al., 1997). Juveniles given the opportunity to perform noncaching spatial memory tasks also perform better and have a larger hippocampus than those that were not (Clayton, 1995). The developing hippocampus seems to be sensitive to experience with tasks that require the recall of spatial locations, at least in food-storing parids. However, food-storing experience during adulthood does not change the volume or number of hippocampal neurons (Cristol, 1996). This all suggests that early experience with food storing leads to the development of a larger adult hippocampus with more neurons (Healy and Krebs, 1993, Healy et al., 1994) and a high cell proliferation rate (Patel et al., 1997).

Seasonal changes in the neural tissue associated with birdsong in species that sing seasonally are well known (Nottebohm, 1981). Similar phenomena have been demonstrated in birds that cache/recover seasonally. Barnea and Nottebohm (1994) studied hippocampal neurogenesis in adult black-capped chickadees and found a seasonal difference in neuronal recruitment, with more new neurons in October than any other time of year. This corresponds to a time of seasonal diet change, from insects to seeds, with many of the seeds being stored (see Pravosudov, 2006, for discussion of a bimodal peak in food storing among parids). Barnea and Nottebohm did not, however, find a seasonal difference in total number of hippocampal neurons. They hypothesized that seasonal recruitment is part of a neuronal replacement process important for the acquisition of new spatial memories. As seeds begin to be stored in October, new memories are established, requiring new neurons. Without a change in total neuron number, however, there must be apoptosis occurring as the new neurons are recruited.

Smulders et al. (1995) reported a seasonal change in the relative volume of the hippocampus in black-capped chickadees, with the peak in October. This seemed to complement the results of Barnea and Nottebohm (1994). Smulders et al. (2000), however, concluded that this change in volume was related to an increase in the total number of neurons in the hippocampus. Barnea and Nottebohm did not find seasonal changes in total neuron number, only in the number of new neurons. Smulders and DeVoogd (2000a) hypothesized that the overall increase in neurons they found was the mechanism allowing greater processing of spatial information in the fall. The more neurons, the more spatial information can be processed. This differs from Barnea and Nottebohm's hypothesis of neuron replacement with no net gain in number of neurons.

Hoshooley and Sherry (2004) attempted to distinguish between the hypotheses of Barnea and Nottebohm (1994) and Smulders et al. (2000) by determining if the seasonal changes in chickadee hippocampus were a result of more 'new' neurons or an increase in the actual 'production' of neurons. They found no seasonal change in hippocampal volume, total neuron number, or neuron production, which suggests enhanced survival of new neurons in the fall, not an increase in neuron production. Smulders (2006), however, has pointed out that the birds used by Hoshooley and Sherry (2004) were held in captivity for up to 2 weeks before they were sacrificed and that captivity can cause decreases in neurogenesis (Barnea and Nottebohm, 1994) and hippocampal volume (Smulders and DeVoogd, 2000a) in birds.

There appear to be two mechanisms affecting hippocampal size in food-storing parids. First, food storing experience early in life increases adult hippocampal volume by influencing the total number of neurons and the extent of cell proliferation. Second, in adults, when demand for spatial memory increases because of food-storing, either the number of hippocampal neurons increases or the number of new neurons that survive increases, resulting in a larger population of new hippocampal neurons to process new memories being formed. Further work will be necessary to fully understand the reasons for the increase in neuronal recruitment found by Barnea and Nottebohm (1994).

A possible complication is that cell proliferation is correlated with spatial memory and social status in mountain chickadees (*Parus gambeli*; Pravosudov and Omanska, 2005). Subordinate mountain chickadees performed worse on spatial memory tasks (Pravosudov et al., 2003) and also had lower cell proliferation rates (Pravosudov and Omanska, 2005) than their dominant counterparts. Individual birds that performed better on spatial memory tasks also had higher cell proliferation rates, suggesting a strong correlation between proliferation and spatial memory. However, no differences were found in hippocampal volume or total neuron number.

Other hippocampal differences have been found between food-storing and nonstoring birds. This includes larger calbindin-immunoreactive neurons in the hippocampus of food-storing than nonstoring corvids and parids (Montagnese et al., 1993) and significantly lower levels of NMDA-binding receptor sites in the hippocampus of food-storing parids (Stewart et al., 1999). How these differences might be related to food-storing is unclear. However, blocking NMDA receptors when black-capped chickadees are learning a one-trial spatial association task prevents the retrieval of the food after either 3 or 24 h. It also blocks learning about a new spatial location within the context of an already learned array of locations (Shiflett et al., 2004). This suggests that the avian hippocampus plays a role in linking new spatial locations into preexisting spatial memories (Smulders, 2006) and that NMDA receptor activation is important only in processing spatial information over the long term. Food-storing birds have fewer hippocampal NMDA receptor sites, which seems contradictory to these results. But this highlights the complexity of the relationship between the NMDA system and food-storing and the need for future work in this area.

1.22.5.4 Role of the Hippocampus in Mammals

In food-storing mammals, three studies have addressed species and seasonal differences in hippocampal neuroanatomy. Lavenex et al. (2000a,b) found no seasonal variations in hippocampal volume, total neuron number, or cell proliferation rates in the adult scatter-hoarding eastern gray squirrel (*Sciurus carolinensis*), an interesting contrast with the results from birds (Smulders et al. 1995, 2000) in terms of seasonal changes in volume and neuron number. Barker et al. (2005) compared the yellow pine chipmunk, both a larder- and scatter-hoarder, to the scatter-hoarding eastern gray squirrel during the fall when both species were actively collecting and storing food for winter. Gray squirrels had three times the number of proliferating cells in the dentate gyrus of the hippocampus, but no significant difference in the number of new neurons compared to the yellow pine chipmunk. There was a nonsignificant trend suggesting gray squirrels had more new neurons, and Barker et al. (2005) hypothesized that the greater number of proliferating cells provided a larger population from which to recruit new neurons into the hippocampus.

The Barker et al. (2005) results were quite different from those of Lavenex et al. (2000a) in terms of cell proliferation rates, but there were two major methodological differences. While Barker et al. used free-living animals sacrificed within 2 h of capture, Lavenex et al. used animals that had been in captivity for days before sacrificing. In addition, Barker et al. analyzed endogenous proteins that are indicators of neurogenesis, proteins that would be conserved at time of capture regardless of stress due to capture. Lavenex et al. assessed neurogenesis with a mitotic marker, which can be affected by stress of captivity (Barker et al., 2005). The results of Barker et al. (2005) were also different from those of Hoshooley and Sherry (2004), in that cell proliferation was related to spatial memory, but not the number of new neurons. These differences may also be the result of differences in stress due to captivity. It is also possible that there are different mechanisms producing hippocampal seasonal changes in mammals and birds.

1.22.5.5 Other Brain Areas

Brain areas other than the hippocampus play important roles in processing spatial information. However, the contribution of these areas to the recovery of scatter-hoarded food has not been investigated very thoroughly. These areas include the parahippocampal region (or Wulst in birds), the prefrontal cortex (or caudolateral nidopallium in birds), the septum, and visual areas. All of these brain regions have connections with the hippocampus in both mammals and birds and their contribution to spatial memory in mammals has been extensively studied. But we have little understanding of their contribution to spatial memory in birds or to scatter-hoarding in general for either rodents or birds. A handful of studies show

general differences in the volume of two of these structures in food-storing birds. Gould et al. (2001) show that the medial substance P receptor field within the parahippocampal area of the food-storing black-capped chickadee is larger than that found in the nonstoring blue tit and great tit. Shiflett et al. (2002) showed that the septum is larger in chickadees than in blue and great tits. What these results mean in relation to food-storing is not clear, but research investigating brain regions connected with the hippocampus and their contributing role to spatial memory should be continued.

1.22.5.6 Cognitive Pleiotropy

Like genes, cognitive abilities can affect more than one trait. Spatial memory, for example, can facilitate territoriality or migration as well as cache recovery. This complicates the analysis of the relationship between natural history and cognition/neuroanatomy. If evolution has favored larger hippocampal volumes in some species, there must be strong advantages to such investment for those species, given the high cost of maintaining neural tissue (Attwell and Laughlin, 2001). But the hippocampus undoubtedly plays a significant role in behaviors other than relocating stored food. For example, Volman et al. (1997) looked at hippocampal volume in two species in each of two genera of woodpeckers. In *Melanerpes*, they found a larger hippocampus in a scatter-hoarding species than a larder-hoarder. But in *Picoides*, they found generally large hippocampal volumes even though neither *Picoides* species scatter-hoards. They suggest that factors other than scatter-hoarding may influence hippocampal size.

One such factor is migration. Healy et al. (1996) demonstrated that experience with migration has an impact on the size of the hippocampus in Garden warblers (*Sylvia borin*), who normally migrate from Europe to tropical Africa. They found that warblers at least 1 year old that have experience migrating have a larger hippocampus after at least one migration trip than 3-month-old, naive birds. In contrast, no age effect was found in nonmigratory Sardinian warblers (*S. melanocephala momus*), who had relatively small hippocampi, suggesting that it is the migratory experience and not some other maturational factor that affects hippocampus size.

Mettke-Hofmann and Gwinner (2003) extended these results with behavioral measures. They found better long-term spatial memory in migratory garden warblers than nonmigratory Sardinian warblers. Taken together, these studies suggest a picture for these migratory and nonmigratory congeners similar to that found for storing and nonstoring parids by Clayton and her colleagues (reviewed in the section titled 'Memory for cache contents'). The connection between migration, spatial memory, and hippocampal structure is further indicated by the research of Cristol et al. (2003).

1.22.6   Conclusions

The study of spatial memory in scatter-hoarding animals has enriched the scientific understanding of animal cognition. The duration, capacity, and dynamism of this memory have driven impressive, stimulating research into both ultimate-evolutionary and proximate-neurophysiological explanations. The most important impact of this research has probably been its contribution toward integrating biological and psychological approaches to animal cognition, combining concepts and designs from psychology with those from biology in a broadly evolutionary framework, leading to a better understanding of the complex relationships between natural history, cognition, and brain structure and function.

At another level, the cache recovery context has proved an extremely valuable setting for experiments on animal cognition. As our review has hopefully demonstrated, experiments on caching and recovery have extended ideas about the memorial capacities of animals. Many interesting questions about cache memory remain, questions such as the role of interference in forgetting, how information about the emptying of cache sites affects cache site memory, and exactly how cache site locations are encoded. In addition, caching and recovery are also providing an extremely useful context in which to study other important aspects of animal cognition such as episodic-like memory and social cognition (*See* Chapter 1.23).

Acknowledgments

Preparation of this manuscript was supported by NIMH grant MH61810.

References

Andersson M and Krebs J (1978) On the evolution of hoarding behaviour. *Anim. Behav.* 26: 707–711.

Attwell D and Laughlin SB (2001) An energy budget for signaling in the grey matter of the brain. *J. Cereb. Blood Flow Metab.* 21: 1133–1145.

Balda RP (1980) Recovery of cached seeds by a captive *Nucifraga caryocatactes*. *Z. Tierpsychol.* 52: 331–346.

Balda RP and Kamil AC (1989) A comparative study of cache recovery by three corvid species. *Anim. Behav.* 38: 486–495.

Balda RP and Kamil AC (1992) Long-term spatial memory in Clark's nutcracker. *Anim. Behav.* 44: 761–769.

Balda RP and Turek RJ (1984) The cache-recovery system as an example of memory capabilities in Clark's nutcrackers. In: Roitblat HL, Bever TG, and Terrace HS (eds.) *Animal Cognition*, pp. 513–532. Hillsdale, NJ: Lawrence Erlbaum Associates.

Balda RP, Kamil AC, and Grim K (1986) Revisits to emptied cache sites by Clark's nutcrackers (*Nucifraga columbiana*). *Anim. Behav.* 34: 1289–1298.

Balda RP, Pepperberg I, and Kamil AC (1998) *Animal Cognition in Nature.* New York: Academic Press.

Barker JM, Wojtowicz JM, and Boonstra R (2005) Where's my dinner? Adult neurogenesis in free-living food-storing rodents. *Genes Brain Behav.* 4: 89–98.

Barkley CL and Jacobs LF (1998) Visual environment and delay affect cache retrieval accuracy in a food-storing rodent. *Anim. Learn. Behav.* 26: 439–447.

Barkley CL and Jacobs LF (2007) Sex and species differences in spatial memory in food-storing kangaroo rats. *Anim. Behav.* 73: 321–329.

Barnea A and Nottebohm F (1994) Seasonal recruitment of hippocampal neurons in adult free-ranging black-capped chickadees. *Proc. Natl. Acad. Sci. USA* 91: 11217–11221.

Basil JA, Kamil AC, Balda RP, and Fite KV (1996) Differences in hippocampal volume among food storing corvids. *Brain Behav. Evol.* 47: 156–164.

Bednekoff PA, Balda RP, Kamil AC, and Hile AG (1997a) Long-term spatial memory in four seed-caching corvid species. *Anim. Behav.* 53: 335–341.

Bednekoff PA, Kamil AC, and Balda RP (1997b) Clark's nutcracker (*Aves: Corvidae*) spatial memory: Interference effects on cache recovery performance? *Ethology* 103: 554–565.

Bennett ATD (1993a) Remembering landmarks. *Nature* 364: 293–294.

Bennett ATD (1993b) Spatial memory in a food storing corvid. I. Near tall landmarks are primarily used. *J. Comp. Physiol. A Sens. Neural Behav. Physiol.* 173: 193–207.

Bingman VP, Gagliardo A, Hough GE, Paolo I, Kahn MC, and Siegel JJ (2005) The avian hippocampus, homing in pigeons and the memory representation of large-scale space. *Integr. Comp. Biol.* 45: 555–564.

Bossema I (1979) Jays and oaks: An eco-ethological study of a symbiosis. *Behaviour* 70: 1–117.

Bossema I and Pot W (1974) Het terugvinden van verstopt voedsel door de Vlaamse gaai (*Garrulus g. glandarius* L). *De Levende Natuur* 77: 265–279.

Brodbeck DR (1994) Memory for spatial and local cues: A comparison of a storing and a nonstoring species. *Anim. Learn. Behav.* 22: 119–133.

Brodbeck DR and Shettleworth SJ (1995) Matching location and color of a compound stimulus: Comparison of a food-storing and a nonstoring bird species. *J. Exp. Psychol. Anim. Behav. Process.* 21: 64–77.

Brodin A (2005) Mechanisms of cache retrieval in long-term hoarding birds. *J. Ethol.* 23: 77–83.

Brodin A and Kunz C (1997) An experimental study of cache recovery by hoarding willow tits after different retention intervals. *Behaviour* 134: 881–890.

Brodin A and Lundborg K (2003) Is hippocampal volume affected by specialization for food hoarding in birds? *Proc. R. Soc. Lond. B Biol. Sci.* 270: 1555–1563.

Brodin A, Lahti K, Lens L, and Suhonen J (1996) A northern population of willow tits *Parus montanus* did not store more food than southern ones. *Ornis Fennica* 73: 114–118.

Casini G, Bingman VP, and Bagnoli P (1986) Connections of the pigeon dorsomedial forebrain studies with WGA-HRP and 3H-proline. *J. Comp. Neurol.* 245: 454–470.

Cheng K and Sherry DF (1992) Landmark-based spatial memory in birds (*Parus atricapillus* and *Columba livia*): The use of edges and distances to represent spatial positions. *J. Comp. Psychol.* 106: 331–341.

Clayton NS (1995) Development of memory and the hippocampus: Comparison of food-storing birds on a one-trial associative memory task. *J. Neurosci.* 15: 2796–2807.

Clayton NS (1996) Development of food-storing and the hippocampus in juvenile marsh tits. *Behav. Brain Res.* 74: 153–159.

Clayton NS (2001) Hippocampal growth and maintenance depend on food-caching experience in juvenile mountain chickadees (*Poecile gambeli*). *Behav. Neurosci.* 115: 614–625.

Clayton NS and Dickinson A (1999) Memory for the content of caches by scrub jays (*Aphelocoma coerulescens*). *J. Exp. Psychol. Anim. Behav. Process.* 25: 82–91.

Clayton NS and Krebs JR (1994) One-trial associative memory: Comparison of food-storing and nonstoring species of birds. *Anim. Learn. Behav.* 22: 366–372.

Cowie RJ, Krebs JR, and Sherry DF (1981) Food storing by marsh tits. *Anim. Behav.* 29: 1252–1259.

Cristol D (1996) Food storing does not affect hippocampal volume in experienced adult willow tits. *Behav. Brain Res.* 81: 233–236.

Cristol DA, Reynolds EB, LeClerc JE, Donner AH, Farabaugh CS, and Ziegenfus CWS (2003) Migratory dark-eyed juncos, (*Junco hyemails*), have better spatial memory and denser hippocampal neurons than nonmigratory conspecifics. *Anim. Behav.* 66: 317–328.

Crystal JD and Shettleworth SJ (1994) Spatial list learning in black-capped chickadees. *Anim. Learn. Behav.* 22: 77–83.

Erichsen JT, Bingman VP, and Krebs JR (1991) The distribution of neuropeptides in the dorsomedial telencephalon of the pigeon (*Columba livia*): A basis for regional subdivisions. *J. Comp. Neurol.* 314: 478–492.

Gallistel CR (1990) *The Organization of Learning*. Cambridge, MA: MIT Press.

Garamszegi LZ and Eens M (2004) The evolution of hippocampus volume and brain size in relation to food hoarding in birds. *Ecol. Lett.* 7: 1216–1224.

Gibb J (1960) Populations of tits and goldcrests and their food supply in pine plantations. *Ibis* 102: 163–208.

Good M (1987) The effects of hippocampal-area parahippocampalis lesions on discrimination learning in the pigeon. *Behav. Brain Res.* 26: 171–184.

Good M and Macphail EM (1994) The avian hippocampus and short-term memory for spatial and non-spatial information. *Q. J. Exp. Psychol.* 47B: 293–317.

Goodyear AJ and Kamil AC (2004) Clark's nutcrackers (*Nucifraga columbiana*) and the effects of goal-landmark distance on overshadowing. *J. Comp. Psychol.* 118: 258–264.

Gould KL, Newman SW, Tricomi EM, and DeVoogd TJ (2001) The distribution of substance P and neuropeptide Y in four songbird species: A comparison of food-storing and non-storing birds. *Brain Res.* 918: 80–95.

Gould-Beierle KL (2000) A comparison of four corvid species in a working and reference memory task using a radial maze. *J. Comp. Psychol.* 114: 347–356.

Gould-Beierle KL and Kamil AC (1996) The use of local and global cues by Clark's nutcrackers *Nucifraga columbiana*. *Anim. Behav.* 52: 519–528.

Gould-Beierle KL and Kamil AC (1998) Use of landmarks in three species of food-storing corvids. *Ethology* 104: 361–378.

Gould-Beierle KL and Kamil AC (1999) The effect of proximity on landmark use in Clark's nutcrackers. *Anim. Behav.* 58: 477–488.

Haftorn S (1954) Contribution to the food biology of tits especially about storing of surplus food. Part 1. The crested tit (*Parus c. cristatus* L). *Det Kgl Norske Videnskabers Selskabs Skrifter 1953 Nr* 4: 1–123.

Hampton RR and Shettleworth SJ (1996) Hippocampal lesions impair memory for location but not color in passerine birds. *Behav. Neurosci.* 110: 831–835.

Hampton RR, Sherry DF, Shettleworth SJ, Khurgel M, and Ivy G (1995) Hippocampal volume and food-storing behavior are related in parids. *Brain Behav. Evol.* 45: 54–61.

Healy SD (1995) Memory for objects and positions: Delayed-non-matching-to-sample in storing and non-storing tits. *Q. J. Exp. Psychol.* 48B: 179–191.

Healy SD and Krebs JR (1992) Food storing and the hippocampus in corvids: Amount and volume are correlated. *Proc. R. Soc. Lond. B Biol. Sci.* 248: 241–245.

Healy SD and Krebs JR (1993) Development of hippocampal specialisation in a food-storing bird. *Behav. Brain Res.* 53: 127–131.

Healy SD and Krebs JR (1996) Food storing and the hippocampus in Paridae. *Brain Behav. Evol.* 47: 195–199.

Healy SD and Suhonen J (1996) Memory for locations of stored food in willow tits and marsh tits. *Behaviour* 133: 71–80.

Healy SD, Clayton NS, and Krebs JR (1994) Development of hippocampal specialisation in two species of tit (*Parus* spp.). *Behav. Brain Res.* 61: 23–28.

Healy SD, Gwinner E, and Krebs JR (1996) Hippocampal volume in migratory and non-migratory warblers: Effects of age and experience. *Behav. Brain Res.* 81: 61–68.

Herz RS, Zanette L, and Sherry DF (1994) Spatial cues for cache retrieval by black-capped chickadees. *Anim. Behav.* 48: 343–351.

Hilton SC and Krebs JK (1990) Spatial memory of four species of *Parus*: Performance in an open-field analogue of a radial maze. *Q. J. Exp. Psychol.* 42B: 345–368.

Hitchcock CL and Sherry DF (1990) Long-term memory for cache sites in the black-capped chickadee. *Anim. Behav.* 40: 701–712.

Hoshooley JS and Sherry DF (2004) Neuron production, neuron number, and structure size are seasonally stable in the hippocampus of the food-storing black-capped chickadee (*Poecile atricapillus*). *Behav. Neurosci.* 118: 345–355.

Jacobs LF (1992) Memory for cache locations in Merriam's kangaroo rats. *Anim. Behav.* 43: 585–593.

Jacobs LF and Liman ER (1991) Grey squirrels remember the locations of buried nuts. *Anim. Behav.* 41: 103–110.

Jacobs LF and Shiflett MW (1999) Spatial orientation on a vertical maze in free-ranging fox squirrels (*Sciurus niger*). *J. Comp. Psychol.* 113: 116–127.

Jacobs LF and Spencer WD (1994) Natural space-use patterns and hippocampal size in kangaroo rats. *Brain Behav. Evol.* 44: 125–132.

Jarvis E, Gunturkun O, Bruce L, et al. (2005) Avian brains and a new understanding of vertebrate brain evolution. *Nature Rev. Neurosci.* 6: 151–159.

Jones JE and Kamil AC (2001) The use of relative and absolute bearings by Clark's nutcrackers *Nucifraga columbiana*. *Anim. Learn. Behav.* 29: 120–132.

Jones JE, Antoniadis E, Shettleworth SJ, and Kamil AC (2002) A comparative study of geometric rule learning by nutcrackers (*Nucifraga columbiana*), pigeons (*Columba livia*), and jackdaws (*Corvus monedula*). *J. Comp. Psychol.* 116: 350–356.

Kamil AC and Balda RP (1985) Cache recovery and spatial memory in Clark's nutcrackers *Nucifraga columbiana*. *J. Exp. Psychol. Anim. Behav. Process.* 11: 95–111.

Kamil AC and Balda RP (1990) Differential memory for cache sites in Clark's nutcrackers *Nucifraga columbiana*. *J. Exp. Psychol. Anim. Behav. Process.* 16: 162–168.

Kamil AC and Cheng K (2001) Way-finding and landmarks: The multiple-bearings hypothesis. *J. Exp. Biol.* 204: 103–113.

Kamil AC and Jones JE (1997) The seed-caching corvid Clark's nutcracker learns geometric relationships among landmarks. *Nature* 390: 276–279.

Kamil AC and Jones JE (2000) Geometric rule learning by Clark's nutcrackers *(Nucifraga columbiana)*. *J. Exp. Psychol. Anim. Behav. Process.* 26: 439–453.

Kamil AC, Balda RP, Olson DJ, and Good S (1993) Revisits to emptied cache sites by Clark's nutcrackers (*Nucifraga columbiana*): A puzzle revisited. *Anim. Behav.* 45: 241–252.

Kamil AC, Balda RP, and Olson DJ (1994) Performance of four seed-caching corvid species in the radial-arm maze analog. *J. Comp. Psychol.* 108: 385–393.

Kamil AC, Balda RP, and Good S (1999) Patterns of movement and orientation during caching and recovery by Clark's nutcrackers *Nucifraga columbiana*. *Anim. Behav.* 57: 1327–1335.

Kamil AC, Goodyear AJ, and Cheng K (2001) The use of landmarks by Clark's nutcrackers: First tests of a new model. *J. Navigation* 54: 429–435.

Krayniak PF and Siegel A (1978) Efferent connections of the hippocampus and adjacent regions in the pigeon. *Brain Behav. Evol.* 15: 372–388.

Krebs JR, Healy SD, and Shettleworth SJ (1990) Spatial memory of Paridae: Comparison of a storing and a non-storing species, the coal tit *Parus ater*, and the great tit *P. major*. *Anim. Behav.* 39: 1127–1137.

Krebs JR, Sherry DF, Healy SD, Perry VH, and Vaccarino AL (1989) Hippocampal specialization of food-storing birds. *Proc. Natl. Acad. Sci. USA* 86: 1388–1392.

Krebs JR, Erichsen JT, and Bingman VP (1991) The distribution of neurotransmitters and neurotransmitter-related enzymes in the dorsomedial telencephalon of the pigeon *(Columba livia)*. *J. Comp. Neurol.* 314: 467–477.

Krushinskaya NL (1966) Some complex forms of feeding behavior of nutcrackers *Nucifraga caryocatactes*, after removal of their old cortex. *J. Evol. Biochem. Physiol.* 11: 564–568.

Lavenex P, Shiflett MW, Lee RK, and Jacobs LF (1998) Spatial versus nonspatial relational learning in free-ranging fox squirrels *(Sciurus niger)*. *J. Comp. Psychol.* 112: 127–136.

Lavenex P, Steele MA, and Jacobs LF (2000a) The seasonal pattern of cell proliferation and neuron number in the dentate gyrus of wild adult eastern grey squirrels. *Eur. J. Neurosci.* 12: 643–648.

Lavenex P, Steele MA, and Jacobs LF (2000b) Sex differences, but no seasonal variations in the hippocampus of food-caching squirrels: A stereological study. *J. Comp. Neurol.* 425: 152–166.

Lewis JL and Kamil AC (2006) Interference effects in the memory for serially presented locations in Clark's nutcrackers. *J. Exp. Psychol. Anim. Behav. Process.* 32: 407–418.

Lucas JR, Brodin A, DeKort SR, and Clayton NS (2004) Does hippocampal size correlate with the degree of caching specialization? *Proc. R. Soc. Lond. B Biol. Sci.* 271: 2433–2429.

MacDonald DW (1976) Food-caching by red foxes and some other carnivores. *Z. Tierpsychol.* 42: 170–185.

Macdonald IMV (1997) Field experiments on duration and precision of grey and red squirrel spatial memory. *Anim. Behav.* 54: 879–891.

Mettke-Hofmann C and Gwinner E (2003) Long-term memory for a life on the move. *Proc. Natl. Acad. Sci. USA* 100(10): 5863–5866.

Moller A, Pavlick B, Hile AG, and Balda RP (2001) Clark's nutcrackers *Nucifraga columbiana* remember the size of their cached seeds. *Ethology* 107: 451–461.

Montagnese CM, Krebs JR, Szekely AD, and Csillag A (1993) A subpopulation of large calbindin-like immunopositive neurones is present in the hippocampal formation in food-storing but not in non-storing species of bird. *Brain Res.* 614: 291–300.

Nottebohm F (1981) A brain for all seasons: Cyclical anatomical changes in song control nuclei of the canary brain. *Science* 214: 1368–1370.

O'Keefe J and Nadel L (1978) *The Hippocampus as a Cognitive Map*. Oxford: Clarendon Press.

Olson D (1989) *Comparative Spatial Memory in Birds*. PhD Thesis, University of Massachusetts Amherst.

Olson DJ (1991) Species differences in spatial memory among Clark's nutcrackers, scrub jays, and pigeons. *J. Exp. Psychol. Anim. Behav. Process.* 17: 363–376.

Olson DJ, Kamil AC, Balda RP, and Nims PJ (1995) Performance of four seed-caching corvid species in operant tests of nonspatial and spatial memory. *J. Comp. Psychol.* 109: 173–181.

Patel SN, Clayton NS, and Krebs JR (1997) Spatial learning induces neurogenesis in the avian brain. *Behav. Brain Res.* 89: 115–128.

Pravosudov VV (2006) On seasonality in food-storing behaviour in parids: Do we know the whole story? *Anim. Behav.* 71: 1455–1460.

Pravosudov VV and Clayton NS (2002) A test of the adaptive specialization hypothesis: Population differences in caching, memory, and the hippocampus in black-capped chickadees *(Poecile atricapilla)*. *Behav. Neurosci.* 116: 515–522.

Pravosudov VV and de Kort SR (2006) Is the western scrub-jay (*Aphelocoma californica*) really an underdog among food-caching corvids when it comes to hippocampal volume and food caching propensity? *Brain Behav. Evol.* 67: 1–9.

Pravosudov VV and Omanska A (2005) Dominance-related changes in spatial memory are associated with changes in hippocampal cell proliferation rats in mountain chickadees. *J. Neurobiol.* 62: 31–41.

Pravosudov VV, Mendoza SP, and Clayton NS (2003) The relationship between dominance, corticosterone, memory, and food caching in mountain chickadees. *Horm. Behav.* 44: 93–102.

Reilly S and Good M (1987) Enhanced DRL and impaired forced-choice alternation performance following hippocampal lesions in the pigeon. *Behav. Brain Res.* 26: 185–197.

Shapiro E and Wieraszko A (1996) Comparative, in vitro, studies of hippocampal tissue from homing and non-homing pigeon. *Brain Res.* 725: 199–206.

Sherry DF (1982) Food storage, memory and marsh tits. *Anim. Behav.* 30: 631–633.

Sherry DF (1984) Food storage by black-capped chickadees: Memory for the location and contents of caches. *Anim. Behav.* 32: 451–464.

Sherry DF and Vaccarino AL (1989) Hippocampus and memory for food caches in black-capped chickadees. *Behav. Neurosci.* 103: 308–318.

Sherry DF, Krebs JR, and Cowie RJ (1981) Memory for the location of stored food in marsh tits. *Anim. Behav.* 29: 1260–1266.

Sherry DF, Vaccarino AL, Buckenham K, and Herz RS (1989) The hippocampal complex of food-storing birds. *Brain Behav. Evol.* 34: 308–317.

Shettleworth SJ (1998) *Cognition Evolution and Behavior*. Oxford: Oxford University Press.

Shettleworth SJ and Krebs JR (1982) How marsh tits find their hoards: The roles of site preference and spatial memory. *J. Exp. Psychol. Anim. Behav. Process.* 8: 354–375.

Shettleworth SJ, Krebs JR, Healy SD, and Thomas CM (1990) Spatial memory of food-storing tits (*Parus ater* and *Patricapillus*): Comparison of storing and nonstoring tasks. *J. Comp. Psychol.* 104: 71–81.

Shiflett MW, Gould KL, Smulders TV, and DeVoogd TJ (2002) Septum volume and food-storing behavior are related in Parids. *J. Neurobiol.* 51: 215–222.

Shiflett MW, Smulders TV, Benedict L, and DeVoogd TJ (2003) Reversible inactivation of the hippocampal formation in food-storing black-capped chickadees (*Poecile atricapillus*). *Hippocampus* 13: 437–444.

Shiflett MWT, Tomaszycki ML, Rankin AZ, and DeVoogd TJ (2004) Long-term memory for spatial locations in a food-storing bird (*Poecile atricapilla*) requires activation of NMDA receptors in the hippocampal formation during learning. *Behav. Neurosci.* 118: 121–130.

Shimizu R, Bowers AN, Budzynski CA, Kahn MC, and Bingman VP (2004) What does a pigeon (*Columba livia*) brain look like during homing? Selective examination of ZENK expression. *Behav. Neurosci.* 118: 845–851.

Siegel JJ, Nitz D, and Bingman VP (2000) Hippocampal theta rhythm in awake, freely moving homing pigeons. *Hippocampus* 10: 627–231.

Siegel JJ, Nitz D, and Bingman VP (2002) Electrophysiological profile of avian hippocampal unit activity: A basis for regional subdivisions. *J. Comp. Neurol.* 445: 256–268.

Smulders TV (2006) A multi-disciplinary approach to understanding hippocampal function in food-hoarding birds. *Rev. Neurosci.* 17: 53–69.

Smulders TV and DeVoogd TJ (2000a) The avian hippocampal formation and memory for hoarded food: Spatial learning out in the real world. In: Bolhuis J (ed.) *Brain Perception Memory. Advances in Cognitive Neuroscience*, pp. 127–148. Oxford: Oxford University Press.

Smulders TV and DeVoogd TJ (2000b) Expression of immediate early genes in the hippocampal formation of the

black-capped chickadee (*Poecile atricapillus*) during a food-hoarding task. *Behav. Brain Res.* 114: 39–49.

Smulders TV, Sasson AD, and Devoogd TJ (1995) Seasonal variation in hippocampal volume in a food-storing bird, the black-capped chickadee. *J. Neurobiol.* 27: 15–25.

Smulders TV, Shiflett MW, Sperling AJ, and DeVoogd TJ (2000) Seasonal changes in neuron numbers in the hippocampal formation of a food-hoarding bird: The black-capped chickadee. *J. Neurobiol.* 44: 414–422.

Spetch ML, Rust TB, Kamil AC, and Jones JE (2003) Searching by rules: Pigeons' (*Columba livia*) landmark-based search according to constant bearing or constant distance. *J. Comp. Psychol.* 117: 123–132.

Stewart MG, Cristol D, Philips R, et al. (1999) A quantitative autoradiographic comparison of binding to glutamate receptor sub-types in hippocampus and forebrain regions of a food-storing and a non-food-storing bird. *Behav. Brain Res.* 98: 89–94.

Szekely AD and Krebs JR (1996) Efferent connectivity of the hippocampal formation of the zebra finch (*Taenopygia guttata*): An anterograde pathway tracing study using *Phaseolus vulgaris leucoagglutinin*. *J. Comp. Neurol.* 368: 198–214.

Tomback DF (1980) How nutcrackers find their seed stores. *Condor* 82: 10–19.

Vander Wall SB (1982) An experimental analysis of cache recovery in Clark's nutcracker. *Anim. Behav.* 30: 84–94.

Vander Wall SB (1990) *Food Hoarding in Animals*. Chicago: University of Chicago Press.

Vander Wall SB (1991) Mechanisms of cache recovery by yellow pine chipmunks. *Anim. Behav.* 41: 851–863.

Vander Wall SB (2000) The influence of environmental conditions on cache recovery and cache pilferage by yellow pine chipmunks (*Tamias amoenus*) and deer mice (*Peromyscus maniculatus*). *Behav. Ecol.* 11: 544–549.

Volman SF, Grubb TC, and Schuett KC (1997) Relative hippocampal volume in relation to food-storing behavior in four species of woodpeckers. *Brain Behav. Evol.* 49: 110–120.

Watanabe S (2005) Strategies of spatial learning for food storing in scrub jays. *J. Ethol.* 23: 181–187.

Wiltschko W and Balda RP (1989) Sun compass orientation in seed-caching scrub jays. *J. Comp. Physiol. A* 164: 717–721.

Wiltschko W, Balda RP, Jahnel M, and Wiltschko R (1999) Sun compass orientation in seed-caching corvids: Its role in spatial memory. *Anim. Cogn.* 2: 215–221.

Wright AA (2006) Memory processing. In: Wasserman EA and Zentall TR (eds.) *Comparative Cognition: Experimental Explorations of Animal Intelligence*, pp. 164–185. New York: Oxford University Press.

Wright AA, Santiago HC, Sands SF, and Urcuioli PJ (1984) Pigeon and monkey serial probe recognition: Acquisition, strategies, and serial position effects. In: Roitblat HL, Bever TG, and Terrace HS (eds.) *Animal Cognition*, pp. 353–374. Hillsdale, NJ: Erlbaum Associates.

1.23   What Do Animals Remember about Their Past?

L. H. Salwiczek, A. Dickinson, and N. S. Clayton, Cambridge University, Cambridge, UK

1.23.1   Introduction

Episodic memory refers to the ability to remember specific personal happenings from the past. Ever since Tulving first made the distinction between episodic memory and other forms of declarative memory in 1972, most cognitive psychologists and neuroscientists have assumed that episodic recall is unique to humans, in part because our reminiscences are accompanied by the subjective awareness of remembering (e.g., Tulving, 1983; Suddendorf and Corballis, 1997; Wheeler, 2000; *See also* Chapters 1.02, 1.04, and 1.21). Tulving argues that, like many animals, his pet cat can acquire and retrieve all kinds of information about events that have happened in the past, but only in a way that is devoid of any awareness of remembering such events. So while his cat may know that she caught a mouse, what she does not recall is the personal experience of having caught that mouse. To be fair, humans also have many instances of knowledge acquisition in which we do not remember the episode in which we acquired that information. For example, although most of us know when and where we were born, we do not remember the birth itself or the episode in which we were told when our birthday is.

According to Tulving, the retrieval of semantic factual knowledge and episodic memories can be differentiated in terms of the remember-know distinction. To *know* that the Psychological Laboratory was opened in Cambridge in 1912 is semantic knowledge, whereas *remembering* having attended a comparative cognition lecture at Cambridge University is an episodic memory. Remembering and knowing are thought to be two separate subjective states of awareness, the former being an awareness of reliving past events in the mind's eye (what he later called mental time travel; Tulving, 2000), whereas the latter only involves an awareness of knowledge without any requirement to travel mentally back in time to reexperience the past (Gardiner and Richardson-Klavehn, 2000).

In humans, these episodic memories are often recalled vividly and contain a rich representation of the past event. Furthermore, the memories may appear quite suddenly, and out of the blue. In his autobiographical novel *Remembrance of Things Past*, Marcel Proust (1922) described such a moment of episodic recall:

> And suddenly the memory returns. . . . The taste was that of the little crumb of madeleine which . . . my aunt Léonie used to give me, dipping it first in her own cup of real or of lime-flower tea. And once I had recognized the taste of the crumb of madeleine soaked in her decoction of lime-flowers which my aunt used to give me . . . immediately the old grey house upon the street, where her room was, rose up like the scenery of a theatre to attach itself to the little pavilion, opening on to the garden, which had been built out behind it for my parents (the isolated segment which until that moment had been all that I could see); and with the house the town, from morning to night and in all weathers, the Square where I

used to be sent before lunch, the streets along which I used to run errands, the country roads we took when it was fine.

One of the cardinal features of episodic memory is that it operates in what Tulving (2002) calls "subjective time," namely that remembering the event is always accompanied by an awareness of traveling back to the past time in which the experiences were recorded (see also Hampton and Schwartz, 2004). Episodic memory differs from all other kinds of memory in being oriented to the past, and specifically in the past of the owner of that memory. So while some factual memories do involve a datable occurrence, they are fundamentally different from episodic memories. Indeed, as William James so aptly wrote:

> Memory requires more than the mere dating of a fact in the past. It must be dated in *my* past. (James, 1890: 650)

Tulving (2002) argues that episodic remembering requires a specific form of self-consciousness, *chronesthesia*, that enables an individual to address her own, personally experienced past, which "does not reside in memory traces as such; it emerges as the phenomenally apprehended product of episodic memory system" (Tulving, 2000: 17), much like the piece of madeleine dipped in linden tea enabled Proust to consciously relive the past as a simultaneous part of his present. Many cognitive neuropsychologists have argued that this ability to travel back in time in the mind's eye to reexperience the past is unique to humans; animals, by contrast, are stuck in the seemingly eternal present (e.g., Tulving, 1983; Suddendorf and Corballis, 1997; Roberts, 2002). So according to Tulving (1983), his pet cat does not recall the personal experience of having caught the mouse, nor is she aware that the event is explicitly located in her past.

Language-based reports of episodic recall suggest not only that the retrieved experiences are explicitly located in the past but that they are also accompanied by the conscious experience of one's recollections (e.g., Wheeler, 2000), of feeling that one is the author of the memory, what Tulving (1985) called *autonoetic consciousness*. It is this feature of episodic recollection that William James referred to when describing what he called the "warmth and intimacy" of one's episodic memories (James, 1890).

This phenomenological definition makes it impossible to assess the claim that episodic memory is unique to humans, because there are no agreed nonlinguistic behavioral markers of these kinds of conscious

experiences in nonhuman animals (Griffiths et al., 1999), and therefore we have no way of assessing whether Tulving's cat, or any other animal, does or does not experience an awareness of the passing of time and of reexperiencing one's own memories while retrieving information about a specific past event. This dilemma can be resolved to some degree, however, by using Tulving's original definition of episodic memory (Tulving, 1972), according to which he identified episodic recall as the retrieval of information about where a unique event occurred, what happened during the episode, and when it took place. The advantage of using this definition is that the simultaneous retrieval and integration of information about these three features of a single, unique experience may be demonstrated behaviorally in animals. We refer to this ability as *episodic-like memory* (Clayton and Dickinson, 1998) rather than episodic memory, because we have no way of knowing whether or not this form of remembering is accompanied by the various phenomenological aspects that accompany conscious recollection in humans.

1.23.2 Animal Studies

Some of the earliest evidence that animals may be capable of episodic-like recall came from studies of rats foraging in a radial arm maze (*See* Chapter 1.22). In a paper entitled "Remembrance of places passed: Spatial memory in rats," Olton and Samuelson (1976) argued their laboratory rats could remember which arms had already been chosen and/or which had not in order to forage efficiently by avoiding those arms they had visited previously. Another potential example of episodic-like memory came from studies of visual short-term memory in which rhesus monkeys (*Macaca mulatto*) had to choose, for example, either the previously presented stimulus or the novel stimulus in a delayed matching or nonmatching to sample task (Mishkin and Delacour, 1975). In both of these studies, the animals may have solved the task by remembering the specific past event – about which arms had been visited in the case of the rats, and which stimuli had been seen in the case of the monkeys. There is a simpler alternative, however, namely that the animals could have based their decision of where to search in the maze or which stimulus to choose in the matching tasks on familiarity rather than recall; for example, they could simply have learned to avoid stimuli that look familiar, arms in the case of a rat in the radial maze and objects in the case of the monkey performing the matching task (see Griffiths et al., 1999).

There is growing evidence that familiarity and episodic recall are separate cognitive processes, both psychologically (Mandler 1980; Jacoby and Dallas, 1981; Kelley and Jacoby, 2000) and neurobiologically (Aggleton and Brown, 1999, 2006; Wheeler, 2000), and that they have different retrieval dynamics (e.g., Yonelinas, 2001; Yonelinas et al., 2002, 2005, for humans; Fortin et al., 2004, for rats). For example, Yonelinas (2001) has argued that the receiver operating characteristic (ROC) of human recognition memory consists of two components. The first is a *familiarity* component, which is mediated by a standard signal-detection process, whereas the second is an *episodic recollection* component that reflects a high-threshold process in which recollection only occurs once the strength of the episodic memory trace exceeds a threshold. Given this analysis, there is no need to appeal to anything more than the discriminative control exerted by the familiarity of an arm in the radial maze task or of the sample stimulus in a delayed matching task.

Fortin and colleagues used Yonelinas' analysis to determine whether rats were capable of episodic recollection using an odor recognition paradigm (Fortin et al., 2004). Importantly, the rats produced an asymmetrical ROC curve that is characteristic of the conjoint control of recognition by familiarity and episodic recollection. Moreover, their assessment of the two processes through the ROC analysis allowed the authors to dissociate the two processes, by both brain lesions and retention interval (*See* Chapter 1.21).

Clayton and Dickinson (1998) adopted a different approach to the question of whether or not animals other than humans are capable of episodic recall. Rather than applying a theoretically derived analysis, they considered cases in nature in which an animal might need to rely on episodic recall as opposed to other forms of memory. They suggested that the food-caching behavior of Western scrub-jays (*Aphelocoma californica*) might be one such example, because this species of bird hides both perishable food items (e.g., insect larvae) and nonperishable food items (e.g., nuts) for later consumption (for other potential candidates, see discussion by Clayton et al., 2001a). A suite of studies have shown that Western scrub-jays, like many other food-caching animals, have highly accurate and long-lasting spatial memories for the locations of their caches (Bednekoff et al. (1997) for Western scrub-jays; see review by Shettleworth (1995) for food-caching

animals in general; *See also* Chapter 1.22). As these jays rely on their caches for survival in the wild, the selection pressure for remembering which caches were hidden where and how long ago might have been particularly strong (Griffiths et al., 1999), particularly since they cache year round (Curry et al., 2002). Furthermore, the birds also cache reliably in the laboratory, providing both ethological validity and experimental control (Clayton, 1999).

Rather than identifying episodic-like memory by its retrieval characteristic, Clayton and colleagues focused on the behavioral criteria for episodic-like memory, namely that the animal must be capable of remembering what happened where and when on the basis of a single past experience and in a way that cannot be explained in terms of relative familiarity. Clayton et al. (2003a) argued, however, that this criterion was insufficient; rather, an animal's *episodic-like* memory must fulfill three criteria: content, structure, and flexibility. In terms of the content of an episodic-like memory, we have argued that it is the 'when' component that is critical, since episodic memory is the only kind of memory to be explicitly located in the past. Furthermore, the what-where-and-when components form an integrated structure, and this feature of episodic memory is important because it permits discrimination between similar episodes that occurred at different times and possibly different places. Finally, the third criterion is one of flexibility, namely that the information can be represented in memory in a form that allows it to be used in a number of different ways, depending on the context. This flexibility arises from the fact that episodic memories are embedded within a larger declarative system that also encodes factual knowledge (e.g., Tulving and Markowitsch, 1998), and consequently the information can be updated and generalized across situations (*See* Chapters 1.04 and 1.21).

1.23.3 The Critical Components of Episodic-Like Memory

In the following section we discuss each of these three key features of episodic-like memory in turn in order to assess the evidence that some nonhuman animals do have episodic-like memory and, if so, which ones. We shall start our analysis by reviewing what is known about the memories of food-caching jays and then discuss subsequent studies that have been conducted on other animals, primarily rodents and primates.

1.23.3.1 The Content Criterion: The Importance of Pastness

Episodic memory is the only memory to be oriented in time (Tulving, 2000), and more precisely, in subjective time. Semantic and other memories do contain information that was acquired in the past, but without any notion of when they had been acquired, and thus these memories are timeless. As we argued in the introduction, having an awareness of the passage of time ('pastness') is a critical feature of episodic memory, one that distinguishes it from all other forms of memory, so it is therefore essential that any demonstration of episodic-like memory must show that the animal remembers when a particular event occurred in the past as well as what happened where (Clayton, 2004).

1.23.3.1.1 The what-where-and-when memories of food-caching Western scrub-jays

When investigating food-caching by Western scrub-jays as a natural candidate for episodic-like memory in animals, Clayton and Dickinson reasoned that, as these birds do not eat rotten insects, the recovery of perishable items is only valuable as long as they are still fresh. Consequently, a jay should remember not only the location of a cached food item but also the content (perishable or nonperishable food item), in addition to keeping track of the time since caching. Clayton and Dickinson (1998) gave the jays a series of trials in which they cached both their preferred food wax worms (wax moth larvae), and the less-preferred peanuts in two sand-filled ice cube trays, both of which were made visuospatially distinct and trial-unique by structures of children's building blocks (Lego Duplo) attached to the sides of the trays. Consequently, the jays cached in different pairs of trays on different trials so that each caching episode was unique (**Figure 1**). Although the birds had no cue predicting whether or not the wax worms were perished other than the passage of time, the birds quickly learnt that wax worms were available and fresh when recovered 4 h after caching, but rotten after 124 h, while peanuts were always fresh (Clayton and Dickinson, 1998).

Having received four pairs of training trials, the birds were given a pair of test trials, in which the caches were removed prior to recovery and the trays were filled with fresh sand to ensure that the birds could not use any cues emanating directly from the hidden food. The birds' search patterns at recovery demonstrated that they did remember which caches they had hidden in which particular trays and when, because they

Figure 1 Sweetie Pie, one of the Western scrub-jays in Clayton's colony, is about to cache one of the wax worms in one of the visuospatially unique caching trays. Photo courtesy of Ian Cannell and Dean Alexis, University of Cambridge, UK, with permission.

looked primarily in the places in which they had hidden the wax worms when the food had been cached 4 h ago, but redirected their search to peanut sites when the food had been cached 124 h ago. Note that the recoveries after both short and long retention intervals (RIs) always occur at the same time of day (4 h after caching on the same day as caching or 5 days after caching), and therefore neither circadian rhythms nor the state of hunger at the time of recovery could provide cues to guide the jays' searching behavior (see de Kort et al. (2005) for further discussion).

At issue, however, is whether the birds really remembered the specific past caching episodes or whether they simply knew what had been cached where and when. In order to search in the correct cache sites that were unique to that specific caching event, the jays had to retain information about which caches they had placed where. However, it is possible that rather than remembering how long ago they had cached, the birds relied on familiarity judgments with the caching trays in order to decide whether to search for worms or peanuts. When caching had occurred just 4 h previously, the trays are presumably much more familiar than when caching occurred 124 h ago, and so the jays might have used a conditional rule, "if the trays look familiar search for worms, but if the trays look relatively unfamiliar search for peanuts."

To investigate this issue, Clayton and Dickinson (1999a) then gave the jays a second test trial (i.e., with no food actually present at recovery to test for memory), using an interleaved trial procedure shown in **Figure 2**. The jays were allowed to cache one food type on one side of a tray, while the other side of the tray was made inaccessible for caching by attaching a transparent strip of Plexiglas to cover all the caches sites on that side of the tray. The birds then got their trays back in the morning of the fifth day, prepared so that the birds

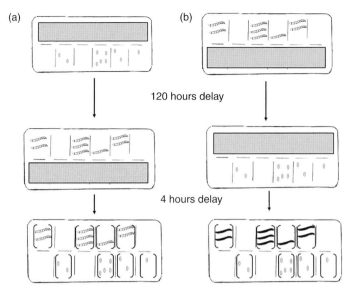

Figure 2 The food caching what-where-when memory paradigm used to test the content criterion of episodic-like memory by Western scrub-jays. Having received a series of training trials in which the birds could cache and recover peanuts and wax worms, the birds received an interleaved trials procedure in which they cached peanuts in one side of a caching tray and then wax worms in the other side of the tray 120 h later (a) or vice versa (b). On test, 4 h later, they then were given the opportunity to search in both sides of the tray. The brackets indicate the fact that the food caches were not present at recovery in order to test for memory. The open symbols represent fresh wax worms, the black symbols illustrate rotten wax worms, and the grey filled circles denote peanuts. The grey bar indicates the side of the tray that was blocked by a Plexiglas strip (the unavailable cache site) during each of the two caching events.

could cache the second food type in the previously inaccessible side of the very same tray, and they were prevented from recovering the previous caches by our attaching the Plexiglas strip to the other side of the caching tray. In the afternoon of this day 5, the jays were allowed to search in both sides of the tray. What is important here is that the interleaved procedure removes the differential relative familiarity of the tray because the temporal pattern of exposures to the tray was the same irrespective of whether or not the worms had been cached first, 124 h ago, or second, just 4 h ago. And since the caches were not present at recovery, the birds would have to rely on their memory of the previous caching episodes in order to search appropriately.

This they did: the jays spontaneously searched for the worms they had cached 4 h earlier, whereas on the trial in which they had cached the worms 5 days ago they ignored searching in the worm sites and instead searched for peanuts. This pattern of recovery searches suggests that the birds were not using tray familiarity as a cue but, rather, that they were remembering specific past caching episodes in terms of where they had hidden the peanuts and worms, and how long ago. Subsequent work established that the jays could also keep track of two perishable foods that decayed at different rates (Clayton et al., 2001b).

Several authors have argued that, as the jays had received a number of training trials in which they could cache and recover the various food items, they may have learned to solve the task by learning semantic factual rules about when to recover the particular foods rather than episodically recalling which foods had been cached where and how long ago (e.g., Zentall et al., 2001; Dere et al., 2005; Hampton et al., 2005). However, such claims misunderstand the theoretical interpretations of the role of semantic and episodic-like memory in the control of caching. Clayton and colleagues have argued that, to search in a particular tray for the perishable caches only when fresh and not when degraded, the birds must integrate a semantic-like rule about how long each food type remains fresh with a specific episodic-like memory of which caches they hid where in a given tray on a specific day (Clayton et al., 2003b).

1.23.3.1.2 Evidence of what-where-and-when memories in other animals

There have been a number of attempts to assess the content criterion of episodic-like memory in other animals (*See* Chapter 1.22). For example, Hampton and colleagues (Hampton et al., 2005) adopted our scrub-jay paradigm to test what rhesus monkeys remember about specific foraging events. The test room contained three foraging sites, two baited and one unbaited, and what the monkeys had to learn was that all food was fresh after 1 h, but their preferred food was rotten after 25 h, while the less-preferred food remained fresh. The monkeys rapidly learned to search first for their preferred food, and to avoid the empty foraging location. However, although rhesus monkeys rejected the rotten food much like the jays did, they did not reverse their search patterns after the long delay, but instead they revisited those locations that contained their preferred food irrespective of the length of the delay. Like the jays, the monkeys remembered the what-and-where of trial-unique events; however, unlike the jays, there was no evidence that they encoded temporal information.

Perhaps the foraging paradigm might be less suitable for testing episodic-like memory in rhesus monkeys, given that they do not naturally cache perishable and nonperishable foods, although they do have specialized cheek-pouches that allow them to hoard food and eat it later in safe surroundings. But certainly their survival does not depend on them caching food for later, and their feeding ecology does not require them to keep track of decay rates, as they are primarily herbivorous (Hampton et al., 2005). Given the complexity of their social lives (e.g., Humphrey, 1976; Tomasello and Call,

1997; Whiten and Byrne, 1997), however, tests of episodic-like memory in primates that involve a social component, such as who was present in a particular social setting, may be more salient.

Roberts and colleagues found no evidence that rats could remember when they had cached various food types (Bird et al., 2003; McKenzie et al., 2005). However, most species of rat do not store much food in the wild (Vander Wall, 1990), and like primates, but unlike the jays, they do not rely on their caches for survival (Vander Wall, 1990). When viewed in this light, perhaps it is not so surprising that the rats behaved like the monkeys rather than like the jays, preferentially searching at recovery in those locations in which they had hidden food more often than other locations that had not been associated with food. Yet there was no evidence that they encoded the 'when,' because they did so even when items repeatedly degraded or were pilfered before recovery (Bird et al., 2003; McKenzie et al., 2005).

By contrast, recent work by Babb and Crystal (2005) did provide some evidence that rats could remember the what-where-and-when of specific past events. Instead of hoarding the food items themselves, the rats were trained to remember where they had previously encountered food that they could subsequently recover after either 1 h (the short RI) or after 25 h (the long RI). As shown in **Figure 3**, using a

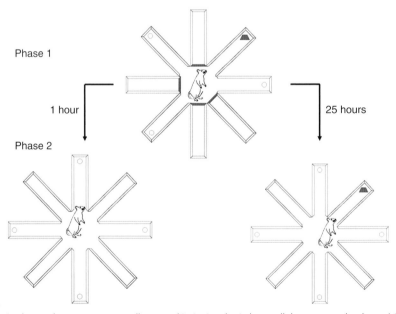

Figure 3   The what-where-when memory paradigm used to test rodents in a radial arm maze. In phase 1 the rats were given the opportunity to explore four of eight arms, three of which contain rat pellets, and one of which contains chocolate. During phase 2, the rats were allowed to explore all eight arms. The delay between phase 1 and phase 2 was either 1 h or 25 h, and rats received training with both the short and the long delay. The black bars show entrances that were inaccessible during phase 1; open circles represent rat pellets, and solid symbols denote chocolate pieces.

standard eight-arm radial maze, the rats were allowed to search during phase 1 for food located at the ends of four arms of the maze (the other four arms were blocked): three of them with regular pellets and one with highly preferred chocolate pellets. During phase 2, the rats were returned to the maze with all eight arms accessible, and the four previously inaccessible arms were baited with regular pellets. In addition the chocolate pellets were replenished if the rats were returned to the maze after a long delay, but not after a short RI. If the rats remembered which arms they had visited and eaten food from in phase 1, then they should selectively search in the previously inaccessible arms, because these are the ones that still contain food. If they also remembered which foods were available where and how long ago they had visited the maze in phase 1 then they should prefer to visit the arm containing the chocolate pellets after the long RI, but avoid that arm after the short RI.

Babb and Crystal found that the rats did learn to avoid the previously baited arms and to revisit the chocolate arm after a long RI only, demonstrating that rats could use the length of the retention interval as a cue to guide their choice of where to search, a finding that has also been replicated by Roberts' group (Naqshbandi et al., 2007). In both studies, however, the issue is whether the rats also remembered the specific contents of the encountered food. Although the rats may have remembered that a particular arm they had visited during phase 1 specifically contained chocolate, it is also possible that they simply encoded that the arm contained something more preferred than rat chow as opposed to encoding the precise type of food. Actually Clayton and Dickinson (1999b) already made a similar argument in the case of the jays' memories for what they had cached where. To establish that the jays did remember the content of their caches, the jays were given the opportunity to cache two equally preferred foods, and then just prior to recovery they were fed one of the two foods until sated. The jays searched preferentially for the non-prefed food at recovery, even on test trials in which no food items were present during recovery, thereby demonstrating that the jays did remember which particular foods they had cached where.

Babb and Crystal (2006b) addressed this question in an elegant satiation study. In phase 1, rats found three arms baited with regular food, and two of the other arms were each baited with a particular flavored food (grape, raspberry), both of which were equally preferred over regular pellets and both replenished after the long, but not short, RI. The rats were more likely to revisit the flavored arms and avoid the other previously baited arms after the long delay, just as they had done in the previous study. However, when the rats were sated on one flavor shortly before phase 2, the rats avoided that arm but revisited the arm containing the other flavored food, suggesting that they remembered not only which arms contained preferred food but that they also recalled the specific food contents of these arms. A transfer experiment using banana chips and chocolate, the latter devalued by pairing it with a lithium chloride injection after phase 1, produced the same results.

Crystal (2006) argued that these experiments provide evidence of episodic-like memory in rats. Only by remembering what happened where and when could the rats return reliably to the replenishing chocolate arm after the long interval, but avoid this arm when the chocolate was devalued. However, this experiment does not control for relative familiarity. It is not clear whether the rats really remembered when to visit the chocolate arm or whether the rats could have solved the task by learning a rule that it is only when the arm appears to be relatively unfamiliar that the rats should search for the chocolate, or grape, or raspberry. As the lithium chloride treatment may have caused a general aversion to chocolate, the rats had to return only to the previously blocked arm, and since that arm had not been visited during phase 1, it may have been less familiar to the rat than the arms that had been visited in phase 1.

The results of the satiation study, although more convincing, can still be explained in terms of familiarity. Although rats do not use time of day or state of hunger as cues guiding their behavior (Babb and Crystal, 2006a), the relative familiarity of the maze itself could function as a cue to avoid or to revisit arms with preferred food in just the same way as we argued for the jays and their trays in the first experiment, namely that when the maze cues are highly familiar, then avoid all familiar arms, and when the maze cues are much less familiar, then revisit the arm containing the preferred food. Clearly what is needed to discriminate between these two possibilities is an interleaved trial procedure of the kind described for the jays in **Figure 2**.

Eichenbaum and colleagues used a different approach when developing their rodent model of episodic-like memory, with a focus on resolving the recollection versus familiarity dispute (*See* Chapter 1.21 for detailed discussion). Their sequence learning paradigm is based on the assumption that humans may infer the sequence of events by their relative times of occurrence (Roberts, 2002), because "one event precedes, co-occurs, or succeeds another in time" (Tulving, 1983: 38). For example, Ergorul and Eichenbaum (2004) trained their rats to learn unique sequences of four odors in terms of which odors the rats encountered where and in what order ('when'). On test, two of the four odors were presented, and the rats were reinforced for choosing the location of the cup containing the odor that had occurred earlier in the sequence. This they did. However, when the rats were given a probe test, in which the cups that had previously contained the odors were placed in the correct locations but the odors had been removed so that they did not provide scent cues, then the rats failed to make the correct choice. Consequently, the rats may have solved this task by remembering which odors they had encountered earliest in the sequence without any recourse to remembering where.

A similar rational was adopted by Schwartz and Evans (2001), who tested the 31-year-old gorilla, King, for his ability to remember a temporal sequence of specific past feeding events. Specifically, they argued that "the animal's response should provide information about its past rather than about the current state of knowledge" (Schwartz et al., 2005: 231). King received three types of food in succession, each 5 min after finishing eating the former one. On test, a few minutes later, the experimenter asked King what he had eaten and in what order. Although King was able to answer correctly, he itemized the food in reversed order only, from the most familiar to the least familiar item. Consequently, his performance could be explained in terms of relative familiarity rather than episodic-like recall.

To summarize this section, attempts to establish models of episodic-like memory in nonhuman animals other than Western scrub-jays suggest that the 'when' component is by far the most challenging feature. In some studies, the animals failed to show any sensitivity to the temporal relationships between events (Bird et al., 2003; Hampton et al., 2005). Of course, the absence of evidence is not evidence of absence, and the fact that rats do appear to remember what happened where and how long ago when tested for the memory of food they have seen previously (Babb and Crystal, 2005, 2006b; Naqushbandi et al., 2007), but have not cached previously (Bird et al., 2003), suggests that the ecological salience of the task may be critical. One advantage of the caching paradigm when employed with Western scrub-jays is that it taps into this particular species' natural propensity – if not

obsession – to cache and efficiently recover perishable as well as nonperishable food. That said, an outstanding issue in the rodent memory models is whether the animals may have solved these tasks using relative familiarity or rule learning after intensive training instead of episodic recall (Schwartz and Evans, 2001; Babb and Crystal, 2005, 2006a), and the extent to which an animal's ability to remember and discriminate between sequences (e.g., Schwartz and Evans, 2001; Agster et al., 2002; Ergorul and Eichenbaum, 2004; *see also* Chapter 1.21) depends on episodic-like recall.

1.23.3.1.3   *Challenging the "when" component*

Other researchers have questioned whether the encoding of the 'when' component is central to the concept of episodic-like memory, or whether in fact it is the context in which the event occurred that is critical. Although human memories are usually rich and detailed in some aspects, the quality of the temporal information may be rather poor (e.g., Friedman, 1993, 2001; Simpson et al., 1998; Eacott and Norman, 2004). This does not remove our own sense of the pastness of a memory, however, just as Proust was fully aware of the concurrence of his present and the mentally relived past. Furthermore, most humans have seemingly little difficulty in discriminating between memories that have the same 'what' and 'where' contents but different 'when' components. For example, most of us find it easy to differentiate between memories of two different meals with the same friend. In this case the 'when' component may simply be a temporal form of the occasion setting 'which,' and we distinguish between our memories of the two events by binding each episode to the different contexts provided by the two restaurants. Eacott and Norman (2004) therefore suggested that the behavioral criteria for episodic-like memory should not be restricted to what-where-and-when but should also include what-where-and-which, with the 'which' component functioning as the occasion-specific context (see also Kart-Teke et al., 2006).

The what-where-and-which concept of episodic memory has been exploited by capitalizing on the rodent's propensity to seek out novelty (e.g., Eacott and Norman, 2004; Dere et al., 2005; Norman and Eacott, 2005; Kart-Teke et al., 2006). The most convincing example is that conducted by Eacott and her colleagues (2005), because they were able to control for relative familiarity. To do so, they built a maze in the shape of an E so that they could place two different novel objects at the two outside ends of the E-maze, out of sight of the rats at their starting point, as shown in **Figure 4**. The rats were given the opportunity to explore the two different objects in one specific context before being allowed to investigate them again in a different configuration in a second context that was texturally different from the first (plain grey and smooth to the touch versus wire mesh). Following this episode, the rats were exposed to one of the objects outside the two contexts until they had become habituated to it, an experience that enhanced their propensity to explore the other object when returned to one of the two E-maze contexts. A rat could only do so, however, if it had remembered where the objects were located in the E-maze in a particular context during the initial episode. Their rats' success at this task led Eacott and colleagues to argue that the rats recollected the object (what) and its location (where) in a particular context (which) on the basis of unique what-where-and-which memories. Note that, because the objects were out of sight at the starting point, the rat's choice to turn right or left could not have been based on relative familiarity of the object.

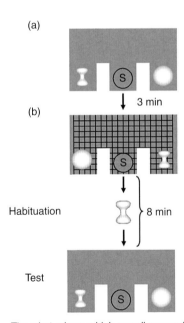

Figure 4 The what-where-which paradigm used to test rodents in the E-maze. The rats explored two different objects placed in a certain spatial configuration in a particular context (a), before investigating them again in a different configuration in a second context (b). Following this episode, the rats were exposed to one of the objects in a different place until they were habituated. On test they were placed back in either context (a) or (b), but the objects were not visible from the starting point (S) in order to test for memory.

1.23.3.1.4   Differential forgetting or remembrance of times past?

Although we have argued strongly for the importance of the 'when' component of an episodic-like memory, several researchers have suggested that demonstrations of an animal's ability to remember the what-where-and-when of a specific past event may not be sufficient to claim that the animal is capable of episodic recall. In the case of our jays, it is argued that, instead of traveling back in time, the birds might have used the strengths or ages of memory traces in order to know when to search for the food items at particular locations.

There are two ways in which a jay could use the strength or vividness of the memory trace to date its memory of a particular caching event: spontaneous forgetting and directed forgetting (for detailed discussion see de Kort et al., 2005). Consider the case of the jays that learned that if there was a short delay between caching and recovery then their worms would still be fresh at the time of recovery, whereas if a long interval had elapsed between caching and recovery then the worms would have degraded. In terms of spontaneous forgetting, the bird might simply forget the location of degraded worms because the event happened a relatively long time ago. Alternatively, rather than having an all-or-none response (remember–forget), the bird might use forgetting, just like familiarity, as a conditional cue to control its pattern of searches at recovery. The birds learn to search for the worms when they recall a vivid memory of the caching episode, whereas they learn to avoid attempting to recover the worms when they recall a less vivid or partially forgotten memory. Staddon and Higa (1999) have recently proposed an account of interval timing based upon conditional control by the strength of the memory for a time marker.

If the jays use vividness to date the caching episode, we should expect the birds to show some evidence of forgetting for other aspects of the content of the memory, specifically the location and types of caches, at longer delays. Even if the worms did not degrade with time since caching, the time-dependent forgetting of the memory representation should be accompanied by a loss in accuracy for locating the different caches of food. To assess this possibility, Clayton and colleagues (Clayton and Dickinson, 1998, 1999a; Clayton et al., 2001b) tested the cache recovery behavior of a second group of jays, whose potentially perishable caches did not in fact degrade. These birds showed no loss in accuracy of locating the food caches at the retention intervals for which the putative forgetting should have been controlling the recovery choice of the birds whose caches did degrade. Furthermore, the jays were just as accurate at locating caches after 5 days as they were after 4 h (Clayton and Dickinson, 1999b), even though we should have to assume that the strength of the cache memory after 5 days was significantly weaker than after 4 h if this strength difference is to control a complete reversal in recovery patterns. Consequently we think that it is unlikely that the jays' temporal control of caching was mediated by memory decay.

Although spontaneous forgetting is unlikely to account for the behavior of the jays, perhaps directed forgetting (Roper and Zentall, 1993) may be more plausible. Consider, once again, the case in which jays cache and recover worms and peanuts after a short and a long delay. As the peanuts never perish, the jays always recover fresh peanuts. However, this is not the case for their worm caches, which are found to be degraded at recovery on half of the trials (i.e., those in which recovery occurs after a long delay). According to the directed forgetting account, experience with unpalatable worms on half of the recovery trials causes the jays to forget the location of these caches more rapidly. For example, perhaps having experienced degraded, unpalatable worms at recovery, the jays subsequently devote less processing of the location of these caches on subsequent caching episodes, which in turn leads to more rapid forgetting of those caches.

A test of this hypothesis would be to establish whether the jays could learn the opposite profile for when worms are edible, namely one in which worms ripen rather than degrade over time (de Kort et al., 2005). To do so the jays received a series of trials in which they could cache peanuts and worms as before, but this time the worms were degraded after the short delay but were fresh after the long delay. de Kort and colleagues found that the jays rapidly learned to avoid searching for worms after the short retention interval, while preferentially searching for them after the long one. The fact that jays' performance could not be explained by either spontaneous or directed forgetting strongly suggests that jays encode time specifically within their episodic-like memory of events (de Kort et al., 2005).

As explained in the first section, we can never ascertain whether or not an animal is aware of the past while retrieving a memory. All we know is that animals can discriminate among events which occurred at different times in the past. One way to tackle this issue would be to devise an experiment in which the animal is given the opportunity to report that it knows whether or not it has remembered using an uncertainty monitoring paradigm (Smith, 2005), just as Hampton (2001) did when testing whether his rhesus monkeys knew what they had and had not remembered.

1.23.3.2 The Structural Criterion of Episodic-Like Memories: An Integrated Representation

In humans, the content of an episodic memory is usually a rich representation of what happened, where, and when. Imagine the moment when handing over a carefully chosen present to a special person. We not only remember where and when we bought this present, and of course what we have chosen, but we may spontaneously remember a number of other details about the event, such as whether it was a rainy or a sunny day, and whether the shop was overcrowded or completely empty, and some of us might remember other seemingly trivial details such as what shoes we were wearing.

One of the cardinal features of human episodic memory is that, when we come to recall the event to mind, we retrieve all these components together as a gestalt image. This reflects the structure of episodic memory, namely that the 'what,' 'where,' and 'when' components are not encoded separately but are bound together in an integrated representation, and consequently the retrieval of one component elicits the retrieval of the others. Contrast this integrated representation with a linear one in which the components are not directly linked. If we were to remember the episode as a series of separate components, then we would not be able to distinguish between episodes that have similar contents and locations but different temporal contexts, such as family Christmas dinners that occurred in different years. It is this feature that led Clayton et al. (2003a) to argue that the criterion of remembering what-where-and-when is not, by itself, sufficient to characterize a memory as episodic-like if, by this term, we mean that the memory has the behavioral properties of human episodic memory.

To illustrate this point, let us consider another food-caching scrub-jay scenario in which the birds cache the same foods in two trays at different times. The design is illustrated in **Figure 5**. Briefly, the trained jays were allowed to cache peanuts and worms in one tray on one day, and then at a later time they cache the same food types in a second tray, after which the jays are allowed to recover from both

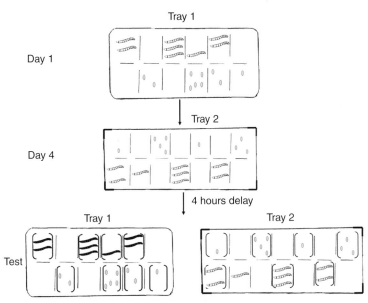

Figure 5 The food caching what-where-when memory paradigm used to test the structure criterion of episodic-like memory by Western scrub-jays. The jays cached peanuts and wax worms in one caching tray on day 1, and then again in a second tray on day 4. On test, 4 h later, the jays were given the opportunity to search in both trays. The brackets indicate the fact that the food caches were not present at recovery in order to test for memory. The open worms represent fresh wax worm caches, the black worm symbols denote rotten wax worm caches, and the grey filled circles illustrate peanut caches.

trays. The retention intervals are such that the worms will be decayed in the first tray while still being fresh in the second tray, and the critical question is whether the jays show the appropriate search pattern for each of the two trays.

If the birds retrieved the 'when' component separately, they could not have distinguished between the caching episodes because, by that account, the jays would simply associate caching the worms with a temporal tag, and the memory of caching worms at recovery would retrieve temporal tags for both the long and short RIs. In short, a linear mnemonic structure does not support the appropriate recovery pattern, namely searching for peanuts in the first tray and worms in the second tray. However, the jays do in fact search appropriately (Clayton et al., 2001b), a result that suggests that they do form integrated memories, because they can distinguish in memory between the two caching episodes in terms of their time and location, even though they involved the same food items.

Clayton and colleagues interpreted this finding as evidence that the jays' behavior met what they called the *structural* criterion for episodic-like memory (Clayton et al., 2003a,b). Not only must a memory have the what-where-when representational *content* to be episodic-like, but that content must be bound in a

form that yields a unique memory for each caching episode. It is this representational binding that allows the jays, like humans, to discriminate between similar episodes that occurred at different times and possibly different places.

What of other animals? So far, the only other study to test the structural criterion of episodic-like memory is that by Shettleworth and colleagues (Skov-Rackett et al., 2006). In a series of delayed matching to sample tasks on a touch screen, they tested their pigeons' memory of all three features independently: on some trials they had to select the correct 'what' in terms of an object's identity, on other trials they had to select the correct 'where' in terms of an item's location on the screen, and on yet other trials they were tested for their memory of 'when' in terms of the time intervals passed since presentation of items. The pigeons performed well above chance on all three types of trials, which suggests that the pigeons could encode all three features during a single presentation. However, further tests established that the pigeons' memories were stored independently in a linear rather than in an integrated structure. It remains to be seen whether the rodent what-where-when and even what-where-which memories possess an integrated structure like those of jays and humans, or whether they are linear, like those of pigeons.

Further evidence for the integrated structure of scrub-jay episodic-like memories comes from studies of the social context of caching (reviewed by Clayton et al., 2007). These birds readily steal one another's caches (e.g., Clayton and Emery, 2004) and go to great lengths to protect their own caches from being stolen by another bird, hiding them behind barriers (e.g., Dally et al., 2005) and moving those caches another individual has seen them make once that other individual has left the scene (Emery and Clayton, 2001). Of particular relevance to the issue of integrated memories is the finding that these jays recognize particular individuals and remember which particular individual was watching them cache during specific past caching episodes and take protective action accordingly (Dally et al., 2006). It is this integrated structure of their episodic-like memories that allows them to discriminate between caching episodes that differed only in terms of who was watching when.

The only other published study that tested an animal's episodic-like memory with a 'who' component was conducted on the gorilla King (Schwartz et al., 2002), who was trained to associate five food types and their respective English words with five wooden cards carrying a picture of each food in question. In addition, he was trained to associate each of two human trainers who were present during the trials with a card carrying the name of that person. To test King's episodic-like social memory, the "to-be-remembered trainer" handed the gorilla one piece of food through the bars of the cage, while the second trainer was present but did not do anything. On test, either about 10 min later or on the next day, King received five cards for the various food types plus the two cards for the two trainers. In response to the questions "What did you eat?" and "Who gave you the food?" King was expected to hand over the card that corresponded to the food he had eaten and the card with the name of the trainer who had given him the food, which he did for the most part accurately (see also Schwartz et al., 2004). However, the issue remains as to whether King episodically recalled the specific past event or whether King's performance could have been based on relative familiarity, given that he simply needed to select the cards that matched the stimuli he had encountered most recently (for detailed discussion see Schwartz, 2005; Schwartz et al., 2005).

To summarize this section, we have argued in order to demonstrate episodic-like memory in an animal requires not only evidence that the animal

remember the what-where-and-when of a specific past event, and in a way that cannot be explained by relative familiarity, but that the structure of this memory requires an integrated representation. To our knowledge, so far only the jay studies provide evidence for all features. Even less well studied than the structural criterion is the third key feature of episodic-like memory – its flexibility.

1.23.3.3 The Flexibility Criterion

As we argued at the end of the section titled 'Animal studies,' there is a third defining feature of episodic-like memory, namely that it should be capable of flexible deployment (Clayton et al., 2003a). This term refers to the fact that the use of the information encoded in a memory can vary depending on the context. Because episodic memories are embedded within a larger declarative memory system that also encodes factual knowledge (e.g., Tulving and Markowitsch, 1998), the information can not only be generalized across situations but also updated when new information is acquired after the encoding of the original memory.

Evidence for the updating of episodic-like memories comes from a study by Clayton and Dickinson (1999b) in which the jays cached two types of food, peanuts and dog kibble, in both of two trays. They then allowed the jays to recover the peanuts from tray A and the dog kibble from tray B. If the birds could update their original cache memories in light of these recoveries, they should have represented tray A as containing only kibble and tray B only peanuts following the recovery episodes. To test whether this was so, one of the foods was then devalued by allowing the jays to consume it to satiety before they once again searched for their caches. Evidence for mnemonic updating came from the observation that the jays searched the kibble sites when prefed peanuts and peanut sites when prefed kibble, thereby demonstrating that they integrated the memories of the caching and recovery episodes in a way that enabled them to know the identity of the food items remaining in the trays.

This study also illustrated a second form of flexibility. The fact that the jays searched preferentially for the nondevalued food types shows that the deployment of cache memories is sensitive to changes in the incentive values of the caches. There is now good evidence that rats are also capable of this form of mnemonic flexibility. Eacott and colleagues have argued that their rats do show flexibility because the demonstration of the what-where-and-which depended upon devaluing one of the objects as a target of exploration by habituation. A similar claim was made by Babb and Crystal (2006a) on the basis of the fact that, when their rats acquired taste aversion to chocolate after the memorization phase, they subsequently avoided the chocolate arm.

A final form of flexibility illustrates the fact that episodic memory is embedded with a general declarative system and that episodic information interacts with semantic knowledge in the control of behavior. Again this point can be illustrated with the scrub-jay food-caching paradigm. Across a series of training trials, the jays learned that different types of perishable food decayed at different rates – mealworms were rotten just 1 day later, whereas crickets, like wax worms, took longer to degrade (Clayton et al., 2001b). Clayton and colleagues argued that, in order to adopt the appropriate recovery strategy of recovering perishable caches while they are still fresh but avoiding them once they have perished, the jays would need to acquire a semantic-like knowledge about the rates at which various cached foods decay and to combine this with an episodic-like memory for each particular caching event (Clayton et al., 2001b, 2003b). The basic idea is that degrade rates of the different foods are extracted across a number of caching-and-recovery bouts and stored in a semantic-like representation, but that this information needs to be coupled with a particular episodic-like memory of the caching event if the jay is to know what to search for and where. The flexibility of this declarative memory system arises from the fact that the same episodic-like memory can support different recovery strategies depending upon the jay's semantic-like knowledge of when the caches degrade.

A strong test of this declarative flexibility asks whether the deployment of a cache memory is sensitive to new information about perishability, even though this information is not available until after the caching has occurred. Clayton et al. (2003b) assessed this form of flexibility. To do so, the jays first received a series of training trials in which they learned that crickets remain fresh for 1 day but have degraded after 4 days. On the basis of a temporal generalization test, it was then established that the birds behaved as though they expected the crickets to remain fresh for up to 3 days after caching, even though they had not been trained with these retention intervals and had no direct information upon which to base these expectations, merely an interpolation from the differential training at the

1- and 4-day intervals. At issue was whether the birds would change their strategy of where to search at recovery if they obtained subsequent information after they had already cached the food that their expectation about the durability of the cricket caches was, in fact, false.

In order to provide this information, the jays were given the opportunity to cache crickets in three different trays on three successive days. The critical design of this test is illustrated in **Figure 6**. On the fourth and fifth days the jays recovered the crickets from each of the first two trays, one per day, so that the jays had experienced a 3-day retention interval between each caching and recovery episode. During these two recovery episodes, the jays discovered to their surprise that the crickets were degraded. Note that this information was acquired a long time after the birds had formed the episodic-like memory of caching crickets in a particular tray on a given day.

At issue was whether the birds in this group would integrate this new, semantic-like information with the episodic-like memory of caching in the third tray on day 3. On the sixth day the birds received the final tray back, but no caches were present in order to test for memory. All the birds avoided searching in the cricket sites on test, a result which demonstrates that such integration occurred and attests to the declarative nature of the jay's memory for caching in particular trays. By contrast, a control group whose caches perished at the expected rate showed the same recovery pattern as before, preferentially searching for crickets.

1.23.3.4 Incidental and Automatic Encoding

So far we have argued that there are three key features of the behavioral components of episodic memory. The first – in terms of content – is that the subject recalls a specific event that happened in the past and in a way that cannot be explained in terms of discrimination by relative familiarity. Second, the representation of that past event should contain multiple features (e.g., where, what, who) in addition to 'when,' which are bound in an integrated structure. The third pertains to the flexible deployment of information acquired after encoding of the original memory, which allows memories to be embedded within a broader declarative memory structure and allows the subject to keep track and update information accordingly. However, several

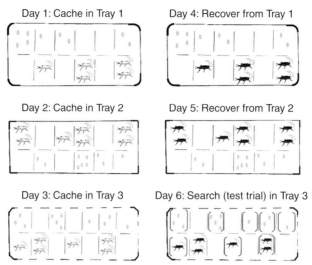

Figure 6   The food caching what-where-when memory paradigm used to test the flexibility criterion of episodic-like memory by Western scrub-jays. The jays cached peanuts and crickets in one caching tray on day 1, and then again in a second tray on day 2, and in a third tray on day 3. The birds were given the opportunity to recover the caches they had hidden in tray 1 on day 4, and in tray 2 on day 5. On test, on day 6, the jays were allowed to search in tray 3. The brackets indicate the fact that the food caches were not present at recovery on day 6 in order to test for memory. The open symbols represent fresh cricket caches, the black symbols represent rotten cricket caches, and the grey filled circles represent peanut caches.

other facts of human episodic memory remain to be explored.

When addressing the issue of an integrated representation, for example, we noted the richness of many episodic representations, of how we typically encode many seemingly incidental features of an event, without any deliberate intent to do so. So what is the origin that causes the flood of memories during episodic recall? In their "automatic recording of attended experience" hypothesis, which they invoked to explain the function of synaptic plasticity in the hippocampus, Morris and Frey (1997) emphasized this feature of episodic memory.

Zentall and colleagues (Zentall et al., 2001) have made a similar point by noting that, when animals receive a number of training trials, they may come to expect a test of their memory even though the event may be novel. For example, in the case of the jays, the birds may come to expect that their caches will be available for recovery, and that the expectation of this recovery test may lead to a semantic memory rather episodically encoding the unique features of that particular caching event. He argues that it is only when asked an unexpected question that one has to travel mentally back in time to reexperience the event in question and find the correct answer. We remain to be convinced, however, that incidental encoding is a defining feature of episodic memory. While many

features of an event may indeed be encoded automatically, it does not follow that a prior request to remember specific aspects of an event preclude it from being encoded as an episodic memory. Consider a special event, a wedding, for example. Knowing that one may be asked to describe the event to others later does not prevent one from reexperiencing that episode each time one is asked to do so.

Perhaps some of the most convincing work on spontaneous episodic recall comes from C. Menzel's (1999, 2005) studies of Panzee, an 11-year-old female chimpanzee, who was trained to use a lexigram as well as gestures in her daily encounters with her human caretakers (**Figure 7**). Panzee could regularly watch from indoors how a human caretaker in the outdoor area kept a particular object in his hand and then hid it under a natural cover before leaving the outdoor area. Later, Panzee would spontaneously initiate contact with the caretaker, showing that person the lexigram of the hidden food type, and subsequently guiding the trainer outdoors, giving the gesture for 'hide,' and eventually pointing in the direction where she had observed the object being hidden. Of course Panzee's own initiative in catching the caretaker's attention and communicating is not without nonepisodic explanations (for discussion, see Menzel, 2005), but it may provide a promising avenue for future studies on this issue.

Figure 7 Panzee, the chimpanzee, using the lexigram to communicate with her human caretakers. Photo courtesy of Charles Menzel and Carolyn Richardson, Georgia State University, USA.

1.23.4 The Distribution and Evolution of Episodic Memory

Many people share Nietzsche's view that animals are stuck in the present and thus cannot episodically recall specific events that happened in their past because they have no sense of possessing a personalized past:

> they do not know what is meant by yesterday or today, they leap about, eat, rest, digest, leap about again, and so from morn till night and from day to day, fettered to the moment and its pleasure or displeasure, and thus neither melancholy nor bored. (Nietzsche, 1983: 60)

Such an ability to acquire and retrieve information about the world in a seemingly depersonalized timeless zone may have its advantages, for as Nietzsche pointed out:

> This is a hard sight for man to see; for, though he thinks himself better than the animals because he is human, he cannot help envying them in their happiness – what they have, a life neither bored nor painful, is precisely what he wants. (Nietzsche, 1983: 60)

The problem with such an account is that it is essentially untestable. As we pointed out at the start of the introduction, we can probably never know whether any nonhuman animal is capable of episodic recall, at least in the form that we humans experience, with the associated conscious experiences of chronesthesia and autonoesis.

By turning our focus to the behavioral criteria for episodic memory, we can at least assess which animals possess these elements of episodic memory that, in the absence of any assessment of phenomenological criteria, we call episodic-like memory. This perspective may in turn provide clues as to how and why episodic memory evolved. After all, it seems unlikely that episodic memory evolved in humans *de novo*, without any precursors in the rest of the animal kingdom.

What does an understanding of the distribution of episodic-like memory among animals tell us about the evolution of episodic memory? If we accept that episodic-like memory is present in at least one species of corvid (i.e., the Western scrub-jay) and at least one species of ape (i.e., humans), then it follows that this ability might have arisen through convergent evolution (similarities that arise as a result of adaptation to similar selection pressures in distantly related species) rather than through a shared common ancestor (homology). However, if we were to show that all birds and mammals possess episodic-like memory, then the parsimonious explanation would be that they share a common ancestor who also possessed the same traits. The answer to this question will only be known when studies have been conducted on a wider sample of species.

So far the attempts to establish models of episodic-like memory in nonhuman animals are still in their relative infancy, and perhaps this is not too surprising given that the initial paper on episodic-like memory in jays was published about 10 years ago (Clayton and Dickinson, 1998). Our review of the available evidence to date suggests that a strong case can be made for the scrub-jays, and a promising case for the chimpanzees, yet there is no evidence that rhesus monkeys remember when as well as what and where, and for rats the results are mixed. Rats do appear to remember what happened where and how long ago when tested for the memory of food they have seen previously (Babb and Crystal, 2005, 2006b;

Naqshbandi et al., 2006), but not that they have cached previously (Bird et al., 2003), suggesting that ecological salience may be critical in designing and developing the appropriate tasks.

As we noted earlier in this chapter, an outstanding issue in the rodent memory models is whether the animals may have solved these tasks using relative familiarity or rule learning after intensive training instead of episodic recall (Schwartz and Evans, 2001; Babb and Crystal, 2005, 2006a), and the extent to which an animals' ability to remember and discriminate between sequences (e.g., Schwartz and Evans, 2001; Agster et al., 2002; Ergorul and Eichenbaum, 2004; *See also* Chapter 1.21) depends on episodic-like recall. Furthermore, with the exception of the scrub-jay studies, most of the experiments have focused on the content criterion for episodic-like memory, rather than on its structure or flexibility of deployment. So clearly there is much more work to be done. A key question for future research will be to make sense of these apparently conflicting results, perhaps by using similar paradigms with different species. But this pattern of mixed results provides a cautionary note that even species that can remember the what, where, and when of a specific past experience may not necessarily express this ability under all conditions (Clayton, 2007).

The other point worthy of mention, and one we alluded to earlier, is that of ecological salience. Perhaps it is no coincidence that the evidence for episodic-like memory in the jays comes from studies of their natural propensity to cache and form rich representations of previous caching events in order to recover their food efficiently in the future. There are a number of features of the food-caching behavior of scrub-jays that might be rather special. The first is that there is no need to train the animals to perform a caching and recovery task, as these are behaviors that the animals do for a living. Moreover, Western scrub-jays are highly motivated to do so and will go to great lengths to protect their caches from being stolen by conspecifics (see review by Clayton et al., 2007), and so presumably there was intense selection pressure on mnemonic processing by jays. McKenzie et al. came to a similar conclusion when arguing that the observed differences in chronesthesia between rats and scrub-jays

> favor greater fitness for birds through sooner and greater acquisition of food. . . . Food hoarding and retrieval behaviors inherited by rats from rodent ancestors may not have been fine-tuned by the same demands placed on food-storing birds. (McKenzie et al., 2005: 24)

Perhaps it is not surprising that the scrub-jays show such rapid learning about the fate of their caches over just two or three trials.

Indeed, the jays cache perishable foods in an environment where the rate at which foods decay changes across the year, and from day to day, depending on the weather conditions between caching and recovery, so fast that flexible learning may be essential to their survival. For jays that live in the Central Valley (California, USA), the ambient temperatures rarely fall below 10 °C but may rise to over 40 °C between July and September. At such temperatures, caches that consist of various invertebrates, for example, will degrade rapidly in the heat and more slowly in cold. So the problem for a scrub-jay is not only to learn how quickly a particular food type degrades but also to be capable of updating information in a flexible manner, based on the ecological conditions that occur in the interim between caching the item and recovering it (de Kort et al., 2005).

Not all animals cache food, but there are a number of others that forage for food that degrades, ripens, or replenishes, providing another potential candidate for studying episodic memory that could be investigated experimentally (for suggestions of other candidates, see Clayton et al., 2001a; Griffiths and Clayton, 2001; Clayton and Griffiths, 2002). Nectar-feeding hummingbirds and bats, for example, could increase their food intake by taking into account a given flower's secretion rate to guide an individual's revisiting schedule. Henderson et al. (2006) tested whether free-living, territorial Rufous hummingbirds (*Selasphorus rufus*) could keep track of when the flowers refilled with nectar. The animals quickly learned the different refilling rates of the two types of flowers and roughly adjusted their revisiting schedules accordingly. Furthermore, the birds appeared to remember which particular flower they had emptied recently (Jones and Healy, 2006). Similarly, Gonzalez-Gomez and Vasquez (2006) found that green-backed firecrown hummingbirds (*Sephanoides sephaniodes*) remembered not only the location of a particular flower but also the locations of the most rewarding nectar sources among less-rewarding flowers. The flower bats (Phyllostomidae, Glossophaginae), for example, *Glossophaga soricina*, may also be a promising candidate for testing episodic-like memory, especially given that these bats can hold more than 40 feeder visits in working memory without indication of memory decay (Winter and Stich, 2005), and would allow a second test of convergence of episodic-like memory in birds and mammals.

If convergent evolution is the most likely process, then what are the common selective pressures shared between the ape and corvid species (see Emery and Clayton, 2004), or between the hummingbirds and bats? One direction for future research will be to characterize what advantages the possession of episodic memory might have, and this is where comparisons of different behavioral systems may be particularly informative. It is important to note at this point that similarity arising as a result of convergence need not lead to identical solutions (e.g., Salwiczek and Wickler, 2004), and therefore episodic-like memory in different groups may have similar functional properties without necessarily having similar neurobiological structures (de Kort and Clayton, 2006). A second direction for future research will be to ask questions about the brain systems necessary to support the various kinds of memory and the extent to which convergently evolved brain systems are similar in their details. For example, although there is good evidence that the hippocampus plays an important role in spatial memory processing in both birds and mammals, the two types of hippocampi differ in structure, with the avian one being nuclear and the mammalian one being laminar (see Emery and Clayton, 2005).

References

Aggleton JP and Brown MW (1999) Episodic memory, amnesia and the hippocampal-anterior thalamic axis. *Behav. Brain Sci.* 22: 425–489.

Aggleton JP and Brown MW (2006) Interleaving brain systems for episodic and recognition memory. *Trends Cogn. Sci.* 10: 455–463.

Agster KL, Fortin NJ, and Eichenbaum H (2002) The hippocampus and disambiguation of overlapping sequences. *J. Neurosci.* 22: 5760–5768.

Babb SJ and Crystal JD (2005) Discrimination of what, when, and where: Implications for episodic-like memory in rats. *Learn. Motiv.* 36: 177–189.

Babb SJ and Crystal JD (2006a) Discrimination of what, when, and where is not based on time of day. *Learn. Behav.* 34: 124–130.

Babb SJ and Crystal JD (2006b) Episodic-like memory in the rat. *Curr. Biol.* 16: 1317–1321.

Bednekoff PA, Balda RP, Kamil AC, and Hile AG (1997) Long term spatial memory in four seed caching corvid species. *Anim. Behav.* 53: 335–341.

Bird LR, Roberts WA, Abroms B, Kit KA, and Crupi C (2003) Spatial memory for food hidden by rats (*Rattus norvegicus*) on the radial maze: Studies of memory for where, what, and when. *J. Comp. Psychol.* 117: 176–187.

Clayton NS (1999) What animals can remember about past events: An ethological approach. In: Crusio WE and Gerlai R (eds.) *Handbook of Molecular-Genetic Techniques for Brain and Behavior Research*, chap. 4.2, pp. 614–626. Amsterdam: Elsevier.

Clayton NS (2004) Elements of mental time travel by food-caching Western scrub-jays. In: *Comparative Analysis of Mind*, pp. 15–29. Tokyo: Keio University Press.

Clayton NS (2007) Phylogeny and evolution: How an understanding of both contributes to the science of memory. In: Roediger R, Dudai Y, and Fitzpatrick S (eds.) *Science of Memory: Concepts*, pp. 367–370. Oxford: Oxford University Press.

Clayton NS, Bussey TJ, and Dickinson A (2003a) Can animals recall the past and plan for the future? *Nat. Rev. Neurosci.* 4: 685–691.

Clayton NS, Dally JM, and Emery NJ (2007) Social cognition by food-caching corvids: The Western scrub-jay as a natural psychologist. *Philos. Trans. R. Soc. Lond. B Biol Sci.* 362: 507–522.

Clayton NS and Dickinson A (1998) Episodic-like memory during cache recovery by scrub jays. *Nature* 395: 272–274.

Clayton NS and Dickinson A (1999a) Scrub jays (*Aphelocoma coerulescens*) remember the relative time of caching as well as the location and content of their caches. *J. Comp. Psychol.* 113: 403–416.

Clayton NS and Dickinson A (1999b) Memory for the content of caches by scrub jays (*Aphelocoma coerulescems*). *J. Exp. Psychol. Anim. Behav.* 25: 82–91.

Clayton NS and Emery NJ (2004) Cache robbing. In: Bekoff M and Goodall J (eds.) *Encyclopedia of Animal Behaviour*, pp. 251–252. Westport, CT: Greenwood Publishing Group.

Clayton NS and Griffiths DP (2002) Testing episodic-like memory in animals. In: Squire L and Schacter D (eds.) *The Neuropsychology of Memory*, 3rd edn., chap. 38, pp. 492–507. New York: Guilford Publications Inc.

Clayton NS, Griffiths DP, Emery NJ, and Dickinson A (2001a) Elements of episodic-like memory in animals. *Philos. Trans. R. Soc. Lond. B Biol Sci.* 356: 1483–1491.

Clayton NS, Yu KS, and Dickinson A (2001b) Scrub jays (*Aphelocoma coerulescens*) form integrated memories of the multiple features of caching episodes. *J. Exp. Psychol. Anim. Behav.* 27: 17–29.

Clayton NS, Yu KS, and Dickinson A (2003b) Interacting cache memories: Evidence for flexible memory use by Western scrub-jays (*Aphelocoma californica*). *J. Exp. Psychol. Anim. Behav.* 29: 14–22.

Crystal JD (2006) Time, place, and content. *Comp. Cogn. Behav. Rev.* 1: 53–76.

Curry RK, Peterson AT, and Langen TA (2002) Western Scrub-Jay. In: Poole A and Gill F (eds.) *The Birds of North America*, 712, pp. 1–35. Philadelphia: The Birds of North America, Inc.

Dally JM, Emery NJ, and Clayton NS (2005) Cache protection strategies by Western scrub-jays: Implications for social cognition. *Anim. Behav.* 70: 1251–1263.

Dally JM, Emery NJ, and Clayton NS (2006) Food-caching Western scrub-jays keep track of who was watching when. *Science* 312: 1662–1665.

de Kort SR and Clayton NS (2006) An evolutionary perspective on caching by corvids. *Proc. Biol. Soc.* 273: 417–423.

de Kort SR, Dickinson A, and Clayton NS (2005) Retrospective cognition by food-caching Western scrub-jays. *Learn. Motiv.* 36: 159–176.

Dere E, Huston JP, and De Souza Silva MA (2005) Episodic-like memory in mice: Simultaneous assessment of object, place and temporal order memory. *Brain Res. Brain Res. Prot.* 16: 10–19.

Eacott MJ, Easton A, and Zinkivskay A (2005) Recollection in an episodic-like memory task in the rat. *Learn. Mem.* 12: 221–223.

Eacott MJ and Norman G (2004) Integrated memory for object, place, and context in rats: A possible model of episodic-like memory? *J. Neurosci.* 24: 1948–1953.

Emery NJ and Clayton NS (2001) Effects of experience and social context on prospective caching strategies by scrub jays. *Nature* 414: 443–446.

Emery NJ and Clayton NS (2004) The mentality of crows. Convergent evolution of intelligence in corvids and apes. *Science* 306: 1903–1907.

Emery NJ and Clayton NS (2005) Evolution of the avian brain and intelligence. *Curr. Biol.* 15: 946–950.

Ergorul C and Eichenbaum H (2004) The hippocampus and memory for "what," "where," and "when." *Learn. Mem.* 11: 397–405.

Fortin NJ, Wright SP, and Eichenbaum H (2004) Recollection-like memory retrieval in rats is dependent on the hippocampus. *Nature* 431: 188–191.

Friedman WJ (1993) Memory for the time of past events. *Psychol. Bull.* 113: 44–66.

Friedman WJ (2001) Memory processes underlying humans' chronological sense of the past. In: Hoerl C and McCormack T (eds.) *Time and Memory: Issues in Philosophy and Psychology*, pp. 139–168. Oxford: Clarendon Press.

Gardiner JM and Richardson-Klavehn A (2000) Remembering and knowing. In: Tulving E and Craik FIM (eds.) *The Oxford Handbook of Memory*, pp. 229–244. Oxford: Oxford University Press.

Gonzalez-Gomez PL and Vasquez RA (2006) A field study of spatial memory in green-backed firecrown hummingbirds (*Sephanoides Sephaniodes*). *Ethology* 112: 790–795.

Griffiths DP and Clayton NS (2001) Testing episodic memory in animals: A new approach. *Physiol. Behav.* 73: 755–762.

Griffiths D, Dickinson A, and Clayton NS (1999) Episodic memory: What can animals remember about their past? *Trends Cogn. Sci.* 3: 74–80.

Hampton RR (2001) Rhesus monkeys know when they remember. *Proc Nat Acad Sci U.S.A.* 98: 5359–5362.

Hampton RR, Hampstead BM, and Murray EA (2005) Rhesus monkeys (*Macaca mulatta*) demonstrate robust memory for what and where, but not when, in an open-field test of memory. *Learn. Motiv.* 36: 245–259.

Hampton RR and Schwartz BL (2004) Episodic memory in nonhumans: What, and where, is when? *Curr Opin Neurobiol* 14: 192–197.

Henderson J, Hurly TA, Bateson M, and Healy SD (2006) Timing in free-living rufous hummingbirds, *Selasphorus rufus. Curr. Biol.* 16: 512–515.

Humphrey N (1976) The social function of intellect. In: Bateson PPG and Hinde RA (eds.) *Growing Points in Ethology*, pp. 303–317. Cambridge: Cambridge University Press.

Jacoby LL and Dallas M (1981) On the relationship between autobiographical memory and perceptual learning. *J. Exp. Psychol. Gen.* 3: 306–340.

James W (1890) *The Principles of Psychology.* New York: Dover Publications Inc.

Jones CM and Healy SD (2006) Differences in cue use and spatial memory in men and women. *Proc. Biol. Soc.* 273: 2241–2247.

Kart-Teke E, De Souza Silva MA, Huston JP, and Dere E (2006) Wistar rats show episodic-like memory for unique experiences. *Neurobiol. Learn. Mem.* 85: 173–182.

Kelley CM and Jacoby LL (2000) Recollection and familarity. In: Tulving E and Craik FIM (eds.) *The Oxford Handbook of Memory*, pp. 215–228. Oxford: Oxford University Press.

Mandler G (1980) Recognising: The judgement of previous experience. *Psychol. Rev.* 87: 252–271.

McKenzie TLB, Bird LR, and Roberts WA (2005) The effects of cache modification on food caching and retrieval behavior by rats. *Learn. Motiv.* 36: 260–278.

Menzel CR (1999) Unprompted recall and reporting of hidden objects by a chimpanzee (*Pan troglodytes*) after extended delays. *J. Comp. Psychol.* 113: 426–434.

Menzel C (2005) Progress in the study of chimpanzee recall and episodic memory. In: Terrace HS and Metcalfe J (eds.) *The Missing Link in Cognition. Origins of Self-Reflective Consciousness*, pp. 188–224. Oxford: Oxford University Press.

Mishkin M and Delacour J (1975) An analysis of short-term visual memory in the monkey. *J. Exp. Psychol. Anim. Behav.* 1: 326–334.

Morris RGM and Frey U (1997) Hippocampal synaptic plasticity: Role in spatial learning or the automatic recording of attended experience? *Philos. Trans. R. Soc. Lond. B Biol Sci.* 352: 1489–1503.

Naqshbandi M, Feeney MC, McKenzie TLB, and Roberts WA (2007) Testing for episodic-like memory in rats in the absence of time of day cues: Replication of Babb and Crystal. *Behav. Processes* 74: 217–225.

Nietzsche F (1983) *Untimely Meditations*, Hollingdale RJ (trans). Cambridge: Cambridge University Press.

Norman G and Eacott MJ (2005) Dissociable effects of lesions to the perirhinal cortex and the postrhinal cortex on memory for context and objects in rats. *Behav. Neurosci.* 119: 557–566.

Olton DS and Samuelson RJ (1976) Remembrance of places passed: Spatial memory in rats. *J. Exp. Psychol. Anim. Behav.* 2: 97–116.

Proust M (1922) *Remembrance of Things Past.* Hertfordshire, UK: Wordsworth Editions Ltd.

Roberts WA (2002) Are animals stuck in time? *Psychol. Bull.* 128: 473–489.

Roper KL and Zentall TR (1993) Directed forgetting in animals. *Psychol. Bull.* 113: 513–532.

Salwiczek LH and Wickler W (2004) Birdsong: An evolutionary parallel to human language. *Semiotica* 151: 163–182.

Schwartz BL (2005) Do nonhuman primates have episodic memory? In: Terrace HS and Metcalfe J (eds.) *The Missing Link in Cognition. Origins of Self-Reflective Consciousness*, pp. 225–241. Oxford: Oxford University Press.

Schwartz BL, Colon MR, Sanchez IC, Rodriguez I, and Evans S (2002) Single-trial learning of "what" and "who" information in a gorilla (*Gorilla gorilla gorilla*): Implications for episodic memory. *Anim. Cogn.* 5: 85–90.

Schwartz BL and Evans S (2001) Episodic memory in primates. *Am. J. Primatol.* 55: 71–85.

Schwartz BL, Hoffman ML, and Evans S (2005) Episodic-like memory in a gorilla: A review and new findings. *Learn. Motiv.* 36: 226–244.

Schwartz BL, Meissner CA, Hoffman M, Evans S, and Frazier LD (2004) Event memory and misinformation effects in a gorilla (*Gorilla gorilla gorilla*). *Anim. Cogn.* 7: 93–100.

Shettleworth SJ (1995) Comparative studies of memory in food storing birds – From the field to the Skinner box. In: Alleva EEA (ed.) *Behavioural Brain Research in Naturalistic and Semi-Naturalistic Settings*, pp. 159–219. Dordrecht, The Netherlands: Kluwer Academic Publishers.

Simpson EL, Gaffan EA, and Eacott MJ (1998) Rats' object-in-place encoding and the effect of fornix transection. *Psychobiol.* 26: 190–204.

Skov-Rackette SI, Miller NY, and Shettleworth SJ (2006) What-where-when memory in pigeons. *J. Exp. Psychol. Anim. Behav.* 32: 345–358.

Smith DJ (2005) Studies of uncertainty monitoring and metacognition in animals and humans. In: Terrace HS and Metcalfe J (eds.) *The Missing Link in Cognition. Origins of Self-Reflective Consciousness*, pp. 242–271. Oxford: Oxford University Press.

Staddon JER and Higa JJ (1999) Time and memory: Towards a pacemaker-free theory of interval timing. *J. Exp. Anal. Behav.* 71: 215–251.

Suddendorf T and Corballis MC (1997) Mental time travel and the evolution of the human mind. *Genet. Soc. Gen. Psych.* 123: 133–67.

Tomasello M and Call J (1997) *Primate Cognition.* Oxford: Oxford University Press.

Tulving E (1972) Episodic and semantic memory. In: Tulving E and Donaldson W (eds.) *Organisation of Memory*, pp. 381–403. New York: Academic Press.

Tulving E (1983) *Elements of Episodic Memory.* New York: Clarendon Press.

Tulving E (1985) Memory and consciousness. *Can Psychol* 26: 1–12.

Tulving E (2000) Concepts of Memory. In: Tulving E and Craik FIM. (eds.) *The Oxford Handbook of Memory*, pp. 33–43. Oxford: Oxford University Press.

Tulving E (2002) Episodic memory: From mind to brain. *Annu. Rev. Psychol.* 53: 1–25.

Tulving E and Markowitsch HJ (1998) Episodic and declarative memory: Role of the hippocampus. *Hippocampus* 8: 198–204.

Vander Wall SB (1990) *Food Hoarding in Animals.* Chicago: University of Chicago Press.

Wheeler MA (2000) Episodic memory and autonoetic awareness. In: Tulving E and Craik FIM (eds.) *The Oxford Handbook of Memory*, pp. 597–608. New York: Oxford University Press.

Whiten A and Byrne RW (1997) *Machiavellian Intelligence II.* Cambridge: Cambridge University Press.

Winter Y and Stich KP (2005) Foraging in a complex naturalistic environment: Capacity of spatial working memory in flower bats. *J. Exp. Biol.* 208: 539–548.

Yonelinas AP (2001) Components of episodic memory: The contribution of recollection and familiarity. *Philos. Trans. R. Soc. Lond. B Biol. Sci.* 356: 1363–1374.

Yonelinas AP, Kroll NEA, Quamme JR, et al. (2002) Effects of extensive temporal lobe damage or mild hypoxia on recollection and familiarity. *Nat. Neurosci.* 5: 1236–1241.

Yonelinas AP, Otten LJ, Shaw KN, and Rugg MD (2005) Separating the brain regions involved in recollection and familiarity in recognition memory. *J. Neurosci.* 25: 3002–3008.

Zentall TR, Clement TS, Bhat RS, and Allen J (2001) Episodic-like memory in pigeons. *Psychon. Bull. Rev.* 8: 685–690.

1.24 Reconsolidation: Historical Perspective and Theoretical Aspects

S. J. Sara, Collège de France, Paris, France

Everything flows and nothing abides; everything gives way and nothing stays fixed. (Heraclitus 535–475 BC)

1.24.1 Historical Background: Thinking About Memory

Memory is dynamic, in that it is constantly being updated as it is retrieved. Heraclitus was the first writer to insist on this dynamic nature of memory with his metaphor cited above or with the more familiar,

> You can never step twice into the same river as other waters are ever flowing on you. (Heraclitus 535–475 BC).

William James (1892) updated this view, arguing that memory was a dynamic property of the nervous system, in constant flux as a result of being retrieved within current cognitive environments. These speculations were largely supported by the seminal experiments of Bartlett (1932), showing that information was gradually biased toward the subjects' cultural expectations as it was repeatedly recalled. Extensive evidence for this comes from laboratory studies of human memory processes over the past three decades, where old memories have been shown to be profoundly influenced by information in the retrieval environment, particularly if this information is in contradiction of the old memory (see Loftus, 2005a,b for reviews; *See also* Chapters 1.02, 1.04).

1.24.1.1 Reconsolidation: A Hypothetical Construct

Postretrieval retrograde amnesia was demonstrated experimentally in rats several decades ago, but the term 'reconsolidation' was introduced more recently, as a hypothetical construct to account for amnesia after cued recall (Pryzbyslawsky and Sara, 1997). Reconsolidation has attracted wide interest among contemporary neurobiologists for a number of reasons, including broad therapeutic applications (Pryzbyslawsky and Sara, 1997; Debiec and Ledoux, 2006). There has been a proliferation of papers appearing in the literature in the past decade, mostly addressed at understanding the molecular and cellular mechanisms underlying this still-hypothetical process. As with any area of scientific inquiry, as the number of investigators addressing the question increases, so do discrepancies in results, alternative explanations of the data, and definitions of constraints. Several reviews of this recent literature are available (Nader, 2003; Dudai, 2004, 2006; Alberini, 2005; Alberini et al., 2006; *See* Chapters 1.27, 4.14). The purpose of this chapter is to provide a deeper historical perspective from which to understand and evaluate current issues.

1.24.2 The Consolidation Hypothesis

1.24.2.1 Origins and Fate of the Consolidation Hypothesis

To understand the significance of the growing literature and issues being raised around the reconsolidation construct requires a brief reminder concerning the origins and fate of the consolidation hypothesis (for recent, more extensive, reviews see Dudai, 2004; Sara and Hars, 2006). Scientific investigation of memory processes was initiated at the end of the nineteenth century by German psychologists, first Ebbinghaus (1885) and then Mueller and Pilzecker (1900). Their studies of verbal learning and retention in human subjects led them to suggest that a memory trace was formed gradually over time after acquisition, and they introduced the term 'consolidation.' Contemporary with this were the very influential clinical observations and theoretical elaborations of the French psychiatrist, Ribot (1882). From his studies of amnesic patients, he formulated 'La loi de regression' that simply notes that as memories age, they become more resistant to trauma-induced amnesia. The origins of the

neurobiological studies of memory processes can be found in early animal models of experimental amnesia (Duncan, 1945, 1948, 1949). Based on a clear temporal gradient of efficacy of the amnestic treatment, these early investigators concluded that retrograde amnesia experiments provided direct evidence for Mueller and Pilzecker's hypothesis stating that postlearning neural perseveration was necessary for consolidating memory. Electroconvulsive shock treatments (ECS) disrupted this activity, thereby preventing postacquisition memory consolidation. In the same year, and quite independently of Duncan's results, Hebb (1949) formalized the idea that propagating or recurrent impulses of a specific spatiotemporal pattern underlie initial memory. This provided the rationale for the use of ECS as an amnesic agent to study the temporal dynamics of consolidation, since such a specific spatiotemporal pattern of neural activity could hardly survive the electrical storm induced by ECS.

Thus the study of memory became, for the most part, a study of function through dysfunction. Investigators overwhelmingly relied on amnesia – either clinical studies of amnesic patients or animal models of experimental amnesia. The protocol of retrograde amnesia, indeed, opened a door on a neurobiological approach to the study of memory, evaluating the efficacy and temporal dynamics of diverse physiological treatments to disrupt memory without interfering with acquisition. The common feature of these experiments is that amnesic agents lose their ability to respectively impair memory as the interval between memory acquisition and treatment is increased, defining a temporal gradient. This large body of data supported the consolidation hypothesis, which stipulates that (1) memories are fixated or consolidated over time; (2) once consolidated, memories are then stable; and (3) acquisition of a new memory and its consolidation together form a unique event. Consolidation happens only once (McGaugh, 1966, 2000).

1.24.2.2 Challenges to the Consolidation Hypothesis

Embedded in the extensive literature on memory consolidation generated during the 1970s, however, were a myriad of studies challenging the interpretation of these retrograde amnesia experiments (*See also* Chapters 1.04, 1.05, 1.14). These include scores of demonstrations of recovery from retrograde amnesia over time or after a reminder. Spontaneous recovery at various times after ECS-induced amnesia was reported by Cooper and Koppenaal (1964), Kohlenberg and Trabasso (1968), Young and Galluscio, (1971), and D'andrea and Kesner (1973). There were similar reports of spontaneous recovery after protein-synthesis-induced amnesia as well (Quartermain et al., 1970; Serota, 1971; Squire and Barondes, 1972). Moreover, reminders before the retention test in the form of exposure to the conditioned stimulus (CS) or the unconditioned stimulus (US) (Koppenaal et al., 1967; Galluscio, 1971; Miller and Springer, 1972; Quartermain et al., 1972) or to the training context (Quartermain et al., 1970; Sara, 1973; Sara and David-Remacle, 1974) could effectively promote expression of memory in rats that had been submitted to an amnestic treatment after learning. Later, pharmacological studies added particularly strong arguments for the contention that the amnesic agent did not prevent formation of a memory trace. Drug treatment given before the retention test could attenuate or reverse amnesia (Gordon and Spear, 1973; Sara and Remacle, 1977; Rigter and VanRiezen, 1979; Quartermain et al., 1988). If the animal could express memory after a drug treatment, with no further exposures to the elements of the learning situation, then the recovery could not be attributed to new learning.

This large and growing body of literature benefited from a thorough and thoughtful review by Donald Lewis as early as 1976, in a paper titled "A cognitive approach to experimental amnesia." His conclusion at that time was that memory 'fixation' was very rapid – a matter of seconds, and that the extended retrograde amnesia gradient was due to the effect of the treatments on retrieval (Lewis, 1976). Indeed, if memory disruption after ECS, hypothermia, or protein synthesis inhibition is alleviated by reminders or drugs given before the test, then the sparing of the original memory trace would be a logical imperative, requiring an alternative explanation for the behavioral deficit. Reconsolidation has awakened new interest in this literature, generated more than 30 years ago, and several reviews by those very investigators who contributed the initial studies 30 years ago have been published recently (Gold, 2006; Riccio, 2006; Sara and Hars, 2006).

Many clinical investigators dealing with human amnesic patients also argued convincingly that amnestic syndromes were, for the most part, due to retrieval dysfunction (*See* Chapters 1.14, 1.15). This was based on experiments showing that profoundly

amnesic patients were able to benefit as much as healthy volunteers from partial cuing in a memory test of previously acquired word lists. This retrieval facilitation by cuing occurred even though the patients did not remember ever having learned the list. Such a phenomenon led to the conclusion that the memory deficit was due to a retrieval dysfunction rather than a failure to consolidate the new memory (Warrington and Weiskrantz, 1970). This naturally led to a call for consideration of retrieval, itself, as an intricate part of the memory process. Warrington and Weiskrantz went on to warn against any interpretation of behavioral deficits after amnestic treatments in animals as failure to consolidate, because it was impossible to demonstrate experimentally the absence of a memory trace. On the other hand, their studies clearly demonstrated that memory traces could be revealed by appropriate retrieval cues.

1.24.2.3 Amnesia and Forgetting As Retrieval Failure

Norman Spear took the position, with Weiskrantz, that all memory deficits, including forgetting, should be considered as retrieval failure, since it was impossible to prove the absence of a memory trace (Spear, 1971). He argued in several monographs published in the 1970s that memory studies should focus on retrieval. Remote memory is always apprehended through its retrieval and, especially in animal studies, through its expression as adaptive behavior. Thus the context in which the retention test is administered can play a determinant role in the behavioral expression of memory (or amnesia). The retrieval context includes the learning-associated environmental cues, and also the internal state of the animal, including motivational and attentional factors (Spear, 1971, 1973, 1976, 1981; Spear and Mueller, 1984). Indeed, many studies were later to confirm this hypothesis: Spontaneous forgetting of a complex maze task could be reversed by exposure to contextual cues just before the retention test (Deweer et al., 1980; Deweer and Sara, 1984; Gisquet-Verrier and Alexinsky, 1986). Furthermore, electrical stimulation of the mesencephalic reticular formation (MRF) (Sara et al., 1980; Dekeyne et al., 1987) or the noradrenergic nucleus locus coeruleus (Sara and Devauges, 1988; Devauges and Sara, 1991) also facilitated the retrieval of the a 'forgotten' maze task when administered before the retention test. All of these experiments used the same appetitively reinforced maze task adapted from that described by Donald Lewis in his earlier 'cue-dependent amnesia' studies (see below).

While emphasizing the 'lability' of the retrieval process and its dependence on the information in the retrieval environment, Spear's main thesis was that "consolidation occurs when memory is retrieved, as well as when it was stored originally" (Spear and Mueller, 1984, p. 116; see also Spear, 1981). Nevertheless, it is nowhere specified in Spear's writings that retrieval processes trigger time-dependent neurobiological processes identical to that occurring after learning, nor does he suggest experimental protocols that would test this thesis. The experiments cited above, demonstrating a facilitation of retrieval by pretest manipulations, do not directly address the issue of consolidation occurring at retrieval, because the retention test occurs within a time frame when one would expect residual effects of the memory-modulating treatment on behavior. The adequate protocol to test treatment effects on a putative post-retrieval consolidation would be to reactivate the memory by means of a retrieval cue, administer the treatment, and then test for retention at some later time, when the effects of the treatment would have dissipated. A change in memory expression, compared with a nontreated control group, could then be attributed to reinforcement or disruption of a postretrieval consolidation process.

1.24.3 Cue-Dependent Amnesia

1.24.3.1 Seminal Studies by Donald Lewis

Such experiments, carried out independently by Donald Lewis and his colleagues, demonstrated 'cue-dependent amnesia' in the rat. These studies showed that a temporally graded retrograde amnesia could be obtained when the memory trace was activated by a reminder of the original learning event, just before the amnestic treatment. While the 'recovery' studies, discussed above, challenged the consolidation hypothesis' claim that experimental amnesia procedures block the time-dependent formation of the memory trace, the 'cue-dependent amnesia' studies challenged the corollary that consolidation occurs only once, that is, that consolidated trace is fixed and impervious to further disruption (McGaugh, 1966, 2000; Dudai, 2004).

These studies of Lewis are really at the origin of today's 'reconsolidation' hypothesis, so it is appropriate to examine these experiments in detail to determine to what extent they already addressed some of the current issues being raised. In the first series of experiments from the Lewis laboratory, rats were trained in conditioned lick-suppression protocol. Thirsty rats learned to lick a drinking spout; when this behavior was well established, a tone (conditioned stimulus, CS), followed by a footshock (unconditioned stimulus, US), was presented during the ongoing licking behavior. Subsequent presentations of the tone alone elicited suppression of licking. A day after training, when memory expression was robust and reliable in control rats, the CS was presented alone, followed by electroconvulsive shock, a treatment that produces amnesia when administered after learning. Those rats that were 'reminded' by the CS, before ECS, showed a significant behavioral deficit when tested the following day. ECS in absence of the cue had no effect on subsequent behavior. These investigators referred to the phenomenon as 'cue-dependent amnesia.' Their interpretation was that the cue reinstated the memory, putting it in an active state and making it labile, as it was immediately after acquisition (Lewis and Maher, 1965, 1966; Misanin et al., 1968; Lewis, 1969, for Review). Cue-dependent amnesia was replicated by Mactutus et al. (1979), see Lewis 1969 for review using hypothermia as the amnesic agent.

Cue-dependent amnesia could likewise be induced by protein synthesis inhibition in much the same way that newly acquired memories are. Judge and Quartermain (1982) trained mice on the conditioned lick suppression task used by Lewis. The protein synthesis inhibitor anisomycin was injected systemically at different time intervals after a single memory reactivation, consisting of a brief exposure to the training context. There was a clear renewed efficacy of the treatment after reactivation, although the temporal gradient was steeper than for that generated after initial learning. (It can be noted that the conditioned lick suppression is a Pavlovian conditioning protocol based on the tone-shock association and, as such, is perfectly analogous to the 'conditioned fear' protocol that is now almost universally used in reconsolidation studies. In both cases the response to presentation of the CS alone is behavioral inhibition; i.e., lick suppression or freezing.)

Later experiments from the Lewis laboratory showed that the phenomenon of cue-dependent amnesia was not limited to aversive Pavlovian conditioning protocols. In a series of experiments, rats were trained in a complex maze consisting of four consecutive left–right choices, using food reward as the incentive (see **Figure 1**). The training procedure

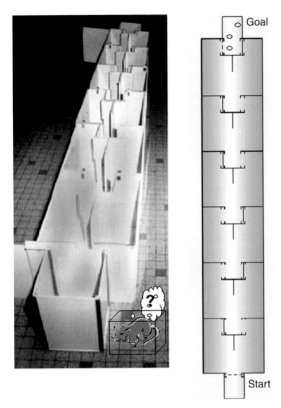

Figure 1 Krechevsky maze consisting of a series of left–right choices to reach a goal box containing palatable food. In the six-unit version, shown here, exposure to contextual cues in the experimental room, combined with stimulation of the reticular formation or the locus coeruleus just before the retention test, alleviated forgetting. A four-unit version of the task was used by Lewis to show cue-dependent amnesia. Adapted from Sara SJ (2000b) Strengthening the shaky trace through retrieval. *Nat. Rev. Neurosci.* 1: 212–213.

Goal

Start

involved 10 days of elaborate pretraining, and then rats were trained for ten trials/day over several days until they reached the stringent behavioral criterion of 11/12 correct choices on three successive trials. During a 7-day rest period, rats were handled several times daily in order to extinguish handling-associated arousal. The following day, rats were exposed to the start box of the maze and the click of the door opening to provide reinstatement cues for the memory of the maze. This procedure was followed by electroconvulsive shock treatment. Retention was assessed 24 h later by counting the number of errors made before attaining the initial training criterion. Rats subjected to the reactivation procedure followed by ECS expressed profound amnesia compared with those subjected to ECS alone in the absence of the reactivation. A series of careful control experiments eliminated motivational and arousal confounds and explored the nature

of the relevant cues in the start box. It was determined in this case that the click of the door opening in the start box was the salient feature in reinstating the memory (Lewis et al., 1972; Lewis and Bregman, 1973).

1.24.3.2 Behavioral Studies

Purely behavioral studies, in animals and humans, further confirmed that retrieval induces memory lability. Gordon and Spear (1973), in a series of experiments in rats, showed that reactivation of memory by various reminders makes it vulnerable to interference by another task, or to distortion by nonrelevant cues present at the moment of reactivation. This approach has been used recently with human subjects, showing that the memory for a list of junk objects can be distorted by intrusions from a second list presented right after the memory of the first list was reactivated by a reminder cue. An important observation in the latter series was that the disruption of memory was only expressed after a delay of 1 day; subjects tested right after learning the second list showed good retention (Hupbach et al., 2007). This experiment not only illustrates that memory can be distorted by intrusions but, on a more positive note, also shows how new information is integrated into an existing functional memory system when it is in an active state. This is the kind of analysis and approach advocated by Lewis several decades ago in his monograph entitled "A cognitive approach to experimental amnesia" (Lewis, 1976).

These studies are compatible with a long line of human studies suggesting that memory is substantially modified by the incorporation of new information during retrieval (Loftus, 1979, 1981). In the view of all these authors, the modulation of long-term memory is not an ongoing continuous process but occurs at transient windows of opportunity when the trace is in an active state. Reactivation can be spontaneous or triggered by external or internal events and, as discussed below, may even occur during sleep (see Sara and Hars, 2006, for review).

1.24.4 Cue-Dependent Amnesia: Neurobiological Hypotheses

Thus it was clearly established, by broad experimental evidence, as early as the late 1960–1970s, that well-consolidated memories are vulnerable to interference in a time-dependent manner when they were in an active state. Unfortunately, little attempt was made at the time to integrate this phenomenon of 'cue-dependent amnesia' into the rapidly developing neurobiological hypotheses of memory formation.

1.24.4.1 NMDA Receptors in Cue-Dependent Amnesia

In 1997, our interest in cue-dependent amnesia was rekindled by some unexpected results that would provide the opportunity for such integration. The initial purpose of our experiments had been to study the effect of N-methyl-D-aspartate (NMDA) receptor blockade on various stages of acquisition of a spatial reference memory task to fix a critical time point during the multisession acquisition when these receptors might play a specific role. The surprising result of the initial experiment was that not only did the NMDA receptor antagonist, MK-801, disrupt performance of a well-trained spatial task but the rats continued to show a decrement on the subsequent trial, 24 h later. Follow-up experiments showed that posttrial injections of the antagonist up to 2 h after the training trial likewise induced the performance decrement the following day. Given our long-standing interest in the dynamics of memory retrieval and recovery from amnesia, we interpreted these unexpected results within Lewis' conceptual framework of 'cue-dependent amnesia.' Since there were no previous reports of long-lasting effects of MK-801, we performed a series of experiments to confirm that a well-consolidated spatial memory, acquired over many days, reactivated by a single errorless trial, was somehow dependent upon intact NMDA receptors to maintain stability. The memory deficit was robust, in that there was no spontaneous recovery 48 h later (Przybyskawski and Sara, 1997, Exp4). Amnesia was, however, only partial, in that drug-treated rats could relearn the task and attain asymptotic levels of performance in only a few massed trials (Przybyskawski and Sara, 1997, Exp3). Extrapolating from these data, we suggested that

> memory is reconsolidated, so to speak, each time it is retrieved and these reconsolidation processes are dependent on the NMDA receptor for at least 2 h after the reactivation. (Przybyskawski and Sara, 1997, p. 245)

To our knowledge, this is the first use of the term 'reconsolidation' in the literature in relation to the well-established phenomenon of cue-dependent amnesia.

1.24.4.2 Role of the Noradrenergic System

We went on to investigate the role of beta-adrenergic receptors in this putative reconsolidation process and showed that postreactivation, a systemically injected beta antagonist, propranolol, induced amnesia in the spatial memory task protocol. Memory had to be reactivated by a single reminder trial for the drug to induce amnesia, expressed 24 h later.

As the spatial discrimination task is acquired over many trials, it does not lend itself to comparison of the temporal dynamics of postretrieval reconsolidation with that of postacquisition consolidation. This is an essential step in establishing that reconsolidation involves cellular processes similar to those occurring during the initial consolidation. Injection of propranolol after reactivation of a single-trial passive avoidance task also induced amnesia. In this case the effect of the beta receptor antagonist was even more robust after reactivation than after original training (Przybyskawski et al., 1999, Figs. 4 and 5).

Both the spatial memory task and passive avoidance memory formation depend upon hippocampal activity. To investigate the temporal dynamics of NMDA and beta receptors in reconsolidation in a task that does not involve the hippocampus, we used a simple, rapidly learned odor-reward association task (Tronel and Sara, 2002). Rats were extensively handled, mildly food deprived, and familiarized with the palatable reinforcement. Three sponges, each impregnated with a different odor, are arranged symmetrically within a wooden box; the spatial configuration of the sponges within the box are changed from trial to trial. Chocokrispies are hidden in the hole of the sponge with the target odor. The response is measured as a nose poke into the correct hole. Rats are very proficient at this task, learning the three-way discrimination in only three trials (for further details see Tronel and Sara, 2002). Intracerebroventricular (ICV) injections of an NMDA receptor antagonist induce amnesia not only when the injections are made immediately after learning (Tronel and Sara, 2003) but also when drug treatment is administered after a reminder cue consisting of the target odor presented in the experimental context (Torras-Garcia et al., 2005). In this task, ICV injection of beta receptor antagonists induces amnesia when the injection is made within a narrow time window around 2 h after learning, and the rat is tested 48 h later (**Figure 2**, top). Quite strikingly, the same temporal dynamic of involvement of beta receptors is seen after memory reactivation (**Figure 2**, bottom);

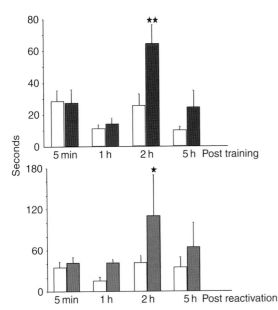

Figure 2 Retention performance in terms of latency to find the reward in an odor-reward association task 24 h after learning (top) or 24 h after memory reactivation by a brief exposure to the CS in the experimental context (bottom). Rats were injected with saline (white bars) or a beta receptor antagonist (red bars) at times indicated after training. There was a narrow time window at 2 h after training when the initial memory required beta receptors and a strikingly similar time window after reactivation when the drug treatment was effective in producing amnesia. Adapted from Tronel S, Feenstra MG, and Sara SJ (2004) Noradrenergic action in prefrontal cortex in the late stage of memory consolidation. *Learn. Mem.* 11: 453–458.

thus, the noradrenergic system appears to be involved in a late phase of memory consolidation, and again in reconsolidation (Tronel et al., 2004).

Based on the data from these studies, we proposed that treatment with propranolol in conjunction with psychotherapeutic memory reactivation could serve to attenuate the compulsive traumatic memories associated with posttraumatic stress disorder (Przybyskawski et al., 1999).

1.24.5 Rebirth of Reconsolidation

These pharmacological data, showing cue-dependent amnesia effects of NMDA and beta antagonists, merely confirmed and extended results obtained by many others nearly three decades earlier. Donald Lewis had proposed, in light of the large amount of data already available at this early date, to replace the consolidation paradigm by a conceptual framework of active and inactive memory in labile and stable states

and to open the way for a more cognitive interpretation of amnestic syndromes (Lewis, 1979). It is truly ironic that the Lewis cue-dependent amnesia studies are at the origin of the current 'reconsolidation' hypothesis, as it is clear that the phenomenon of postreactivation lability cannot be understood by a simple extension of the consolidation concept. The problem is that cue-dependent amnesia is not predicted by the consolidation hypothesis and is, in fact, in direct contradiction of it. Neither Lewis nor his contemporaries used the term reconsolidation, and they were generally not interested in such questions as "does reconsolidation recapitulate consolidation?" Their aim had been merely to show that the amnesia gradient did not reflect the duration of a consolidation process and that consolidation was not a unique event. Memory was labile when in an active state, and lability was not time bound to acquisition. Indeed, the initial series of experiments was explicitly designed by Lewis and colleagues to challenge the interpretation of retrograde amnesia as consolidation failure and to inspire a more cognitive interpretation of memory function and dysfunction.

Nevertheless, there has been a surge of interest in 'reconsolidation' initiated by elegant experiments from the Ledoux laboratory. These investigators found that amnesia could be obtained after reactivation of conditioned fear by injecting, directly into the amygdala, the protein synthesis inhibitor anisomycin (Nader et al., 2000). The results obtained were similar to those of Judge and Quartermain (1982), except that now the protein synthesis inhibition was limited to a structure that is part of the neural circuit underlying the fear conditioning.

1.24.6 Neurobiological Substrates and Boundaries of Reconsolidation

The decade since this report has seen a proliferation of studies of cue-dependent amnesia that fall into two categories. One approach has been to study the cellular and molecular processes implicated in putative reconsolidation and to investigate to what extent they recapitulate consolidation processes occurring after initial learning. The second, and by far the more controversial, approach lies in an attempt to firmly establish (or repudiate) reconsolidation as a real phenomenon in memory processing by delineating the 'boundaries' within which cue-dependent amnesia can be obtained and sustained.

1.24.6.1 Neurobiological Substrates

The search for cellular and molecular substrates of reconsolidation has produced a myriad of results delineating neuromodulatory systems, neurotransmitters, intracellular signaling pathways, transcription factors, and brain regions that are necessary for both posttraining and postretrieval memory stabilization. Others seem to be specific to one or the other stage of memory processing. For example, NMDA receptors are necessary for both consolidation and reconsolidation across tasks and species (Pryzbyslawski and Sara, 1997; Perdreia et al., 2002; Torras-Garcia, 2005; Akirav and Maroun, 2006; Lee et al., 2006). The role of beta noradrenergic receptors, on the other hand, seems to be restricted to postretrieval memory processing (Debiec and LeDoux, 2006; Pryzbyslawski et al., 1999; Roullet and Sara, 1998; Diergaarde et al., 2006). Early implication of the transcription factor cAMP response element binding protein (CREB) in the stabilization of both new and reactivated fear memory was established by experiments using transgenic mice with inducible and reversible CREB repressor (Kida et al., 2002). This burgeoning literature concerning neurobiological substrates of postretrieval memory processes, focusing, for the most part, on intracellular cascades and immediate early gene expression, has been subject to several recent comprehensive reviews (Alberini, 2005; Alberini et al., 2006; Dudai and Eisenberg, 2004) and has been updated in the present volume (*See* Chapter 4.14).

1.24.6.2 Boundaries of Reconsolidation

It is becoming increasingly evident, as the literature grows, that the same old questions raised during the consolidation era, concerning the nature of the memory deficit after an amnestic treatment, persist, although the discussion lacks the strong polemics of the past generation. Does the amnestic agent block consolidation, or now reconsolidation, or does it impair retrieval (*See* Chapters 1.04, 1.05, 1.14)? The single-trial inhibitory avoidance protocol that was used almost exclusively in earlier consolidation studies has been replaced by a simplified version of conditioned fear, in which a CS is associated with footshock to produce a conditioned emotional response measured as freezing behavior. The protein synthesis inhibitor, anisomycin, has largely replaced ECS as the generic amnestic agent in these reconsolidation boundary studies.

1.24.6.2.1 A note on the action of anisomycin

The increasing use of anisomycin as a generic amnestic agent to study boundaries and temporal dynamics of postretrieval memory processing is based on the widely held assumption that *de novo* protein synthesis is the final step of the intracellular cascade triggered by a learning or retrieval event and necessary for the consolidation or reconsolidation of long-term memory. This recent literature largely ignores the fact that caution was urged by the early users of protein synthesis inhibitors as amnestic agents in behavioral experiments, because of toxicity and ability to induce behavioral aversion. Thus, special care must be taken, especially in avoidance experiments, to dissociate aversive and amnestic effects of the drugs on behavior (Squire et al., 1975; Davis et al., 1980). Furthermore, several early investigators provided evidence that memory impairment attributed to protein synthesis inhibitors could be accounted for, at least in part, by specific effects on brain catecholamine systems (Flexner and Goodman, 1975; Quartermain et al., 1977; Flood et al., 1980; Altman and Quartermain, 1983; Davis and Squire, 1984, for review). These data take on particular importance in the light of several recent studies reporting the amnestic effects of the beta adrenergic antagonist propranolol after memory retrieval (see preceding paragraph).

More recent literature has underlined the fact that anisomycin activates the MAPkinase intracellular signaling pathway and causes apoptosis at doses lower that those that inhibit protein synthesis (Routtenberg and Rekart, 2005; Rudy et al., 2006). So, while the behavioral deficits associated with administration of anisomycin after memory reactivation are quite reliable, they may be caused by effects other than the inhibition of protein synthesis. This underlines the caveats inherent in elaborating a theory of memory function relying exclusively on a single paradigm that includes fear conditioning and anisomycin-induced amnesia.

1.24.6.2.2 Permanence of cue-dependent amnesia?

Is the memory deficit permanent, or is there spontaneous recovery or the possibility of recovering the memory by further treatments or reminders? Quartermain showed early on that postretrieval anisomycin-induced memory deficits in mice were less persistent than the deficits obtained by the same dose administered after training (Judge and Quartermain, 1982). They found spontaneous recovery of memory in mice 4 days after the reactivation-drug treatment, while behavioral expression of amnesia was still present in those mice receiving the anisomycin after training. In more recent studies, in mice submitted to context fear conditioning and systemic injection of anisomycin, amnesia is durable after acquisition, but after reactivation it is necessary to use repeated injections, and the amnesia is transitory (seen at 1 day but not at 21 days; Lattal and Abel, 2004; Prado-Alcala et al., 2006). Spontaneous recovery from cue-dependent amnesia has been confirmed by others using either systemic or locally injected anisomycin in rats, mice, chicks, or fish (Anokhin et al., 2002; Eisenberg and Dudai, 2004; Power et al., 2006). On the other hand, at least one group reports persistent amnesia even several weeks after retrieval and treatment by anisomycin (Duvarci and Nader, 2004). These discrepancies are similar to those reported decades ago concerning the nature and permanence of the memory dysfunction in experimental amnesia studies, as discussed above. Moreover, the same logical objection voiced by Warrington and Weiskrantz (1970) years ago can be raised here. Experimental amnesia studies are fatally flawed from the outset, since it is not possible to prove the null hypothesis (i.e., the absence of a memory trace).

1.24.6.2.3 Age and strength of the memory

The ease with which cue-dependent amnesia can be obtained may depend upon the age and the strength of the memory. Newer memories appear to be more susceptible to disruption after their retrieval than are older memories (Milekic and Alberini, 2002; Eisenberg and Dudai, 2004; Suzuki et al., 2004). Moreover, the strength of the memory, as revealed by the probability of its behavioral expression, also determines its vulnerability at retrieval. This has been shown by manipulating the number of unreinforced reminder trials to yield either reactivation or extinction (Eisenberg et al., 2003; Stollhoff et al., 2005; *See* Chapter 1.27). With a weak memory, resulting from a single training trial, in a conditioned taste aversion task, unreinforced presentation of the CS results in extinction. If this is followed by an amnestic treatment, extinction is blocked, and retention for initial learning is expressed at retention test. If the initial memory is strong, presentation of the CS reactivates the memory, rendering it labile, and amnesia is expressed at retention test (Eisenberg et al., 2003).

Another way to shift from retrieval to extinction in behavioral control is to modify the duration or the repetition of the cuing episode: a brief retrieval will reactivate the memory, making it labile. A long or repeated retrieval will lead to extinction (i.e., new learning, with its requirement for consolidation). Using a fear conditioning to context protocol, Suzuki et al. (2004) show that there is no amnesia with brief exposure to the CS (1 min), amnesia with a moderate exposure (3 min), or retention with a long CS exposure (30 min). This retention is interpreted as an amnesia for the extinction induced by the 30-min unreinforced CS exposure. Interestingly, they observe that the effective duration of cuing to induce lability increases with either the strength or the age of the memory.

1.24.6.2.4 Task- and species-related boundaries

Although most of the studies of cue-dependent amnesia use fear conditioning, the phenomenon can readily be obtained after different forms of appetitive and aversive learning in many species: rodents (Lewis et al., 1972; Lewis and Bregman, 1973; Pryzbyslawski and Sara, 1997; Pryzbyslawski et al., 1999; Torras-Garcia et al., 2005; Wang et al., 2005; *See* Chapter 1.09), and even in the honeybee (Stollhof et al., 2005), crab (Frenkel et al., 2005), slug (Sangha et al., 2003), and snail (Gainutdinova et al., 2005; Kemenes et al., 2006) (*See* Chapter 1.27). Behavioral tasks used in these studies have included conditioned taste aversion (Eisenberg et al., 2003; Gruest et al., 2004a,b), object recognition (Kelly et al., 2003), inhibitory avoidance (Milekic and Alberini, 2002), instrumental incentive learning (Wang et al., 2005), odor reward association (Torras-Garcia et al., 2005), and eyelid conditioning (Inda et al., 2005). Moreover, at least in the case of rodents, this aspect of memorization is already present at the beginning of life, showing that it is a fundamental aspect of memory (Gruest et al., 2004a,b).

Despite generality of the cue-dependent amnesia phenomenon across species and tasks, some important constraints have recently been reported. Biedenkapp and Rudy (2004) attempted to induce amnesia by injecting anisomycin after reactivating a memory for a context. Rats received six massed exposures to a specific context in which they would be later receive tone–shock fear conditioning. In this particular protocol, the context preexposure is necessary for the rat to subsequently learn the tone–shock association. The authors clearly showed that intra-hippocampal anisomycin induces amnesia for the context when injections are made immediately after the preexposure. However, they failed to obtain cue-dependent amnesia if the injections were made after a 5-s or a 1-min reactivation of the context memory. One explanation that they offer to account for their negative findings is the 'significant event hypothesis.' A significant event is one that has been associated with a reinforcement, giving it predictive value. This hypothesis is quite appealing in light of the strong evidence for a major role for the locus-coeruleus noradrenergic system in memory retrieval and putative reconsolidation processes, as discussed above. It would take a 'significant event' to elicit the attention or arousal response associated with the activation of neuromodulatory systems (Sara, 1985, 1991; Bouret and Sara, 2004, 2006).

A related determinant of the lability of a reactivated memory is the extent to which a new encoding mode is solicited at the time of retrieval (Morris et al., 2006). These authors show that a reactivated spatial reference memory, learned in the water maze over several days, is not susceptible to amnesia induced by injection of a protein synthesis inhibitor into the hippocampus. It is only when new information must be integrated into the existing memory that amnesia follows such injections. These data fit nicely with the 'significant event' hypothesis. New information requiring behavioral adaptation should elicit attention and activate neuromodulatory systems necessary for stabilization of the reorganized memory.

1.24.6.2.5 A note on the problem with negative results

Cue-dependent amnesia studies lead to the conclusion that memory in an active state is labile and can be disrupted by a wide range of treatments, many of which are effective in producing amnesia when applied after new learning, as well. If an animal expresses amnesia after training and amnestic treatment, one concludes that memory consolidation was blocked by the treatment. If the memory is subsequently expressed after a reminder or a pharmacological treatment, one must conclude that the trace was there, but for some reason the animal could not express it behaviorally. What about possible outcomes of experiments evaluating the putative reconsolidation processes? There the amnestic agent is applied after a reminder that is supposed to reactivate the memory. If the rat expresses amnesia on a retention test, can it be taken as proof that the treatment erased or weakened the reactivated, labile trace

by preventing reconsolidation? Suppose the memory is expressed at some later test? Or after a reminder? So, as Weiskrantz warned, we are faced with the impossible challenge of proving that the memory trace does not exist. When no cue-dependent amnesia is expressed on the retention test, there are several possible conclusions: (1) the amnestic agent was not effective in blocking reconsolidation because of, for example, inappropriate dose), (2) the reactivation treatment was not sufficient to elicit the memory to put it into an active labile state, or (3) postreactivation reconsolidation processes are not necessary.

1.24.7 Beyond Cue-Dependent Amnesia: Retrieval Strengthens Memory

This large body of literature concerned with cue-dependent amnesia confirms the *lability* of a memory trace after its reactivation, but it should not lead to the counterintuitive conclusion that retrieval weakens memory. Memory lability has always been easier to document behaviorally through amnesic rather than through promnesic treatments, which is why most investigators have chosen this research strategy. We know, however, that retrieval of memory does not usually result in wiping it out or even weakening it. On the contrary, a high level of attention or arousal during retrieval, a more likely real-life scenario, should *reinforce* the labile active memory. Remembering, especially when it involves effortful retrieval, usually occurs in an attentive, motivated behavioral state. During such states, neuromodulatory systems are activated (Bouret and Sara, 2004), releasing noradrenaline, dopamine, and other neuromodulators in the forebrain structures involved in the ongoing sensory processing and retrieval. These neuromodulators act to promote synaptic plasticity and trigger intracellular processes leading to new protein synthesis, upon which stable long-term memory is dependent (Sara, 2000a,b) (*See* Chapter 1.27 for a discussion of the internal reinforcement theory).

1.24.7.1 Cue-Dependent Enhancement

1.24.7.1.1 Enhancement by MRF stimulation

Although the strengthening of a memory trace by repeated remembering seems intuitively valid, experimental documentation of retrieval-associated memory improvement is rather sparse. There are a few reports of marked improvement of memory in the rat when retrieval is accompanied by arousal. Experiments by DeVietti et al. (1977) demonstrated that electrical stimulation of the mesencephalic reticular formation (MRF), which improves memory consolidation when administered within a short time after acquisition, improved memory for a well-consolidated conditioned fear response when it was applied after memory reactivation. The reactivation treatment consisted of a 15-s exposure to the tone in the training chamber; the rat was tested 24 h later. The shorter the interval between the reactivation and the MRF stimulation, the better the memory enhancement, the temporal gradient of efficacy being strikingly similar to the postacquisition gradient (**Figure 3**).

1.24.7.1.2   Enhancement by activation of the noradrenergic system

It has been shown repeatedly that stimulation of the noradrenergic system will enhance memory retrieval when given before the retention test (reviewed above), but it is only recently that the effects of pharmacologically increasing noradrenergic tonus on putative reconsolidation processes have been investigated. The alpha 2 receptor antagonist, idazoxan, increases firing of noradrenergic neurons of the locus coeruleus twofold at a dose that has no detectable effect on overt behavior such as locomotor activity (Sara, 1991). Rats were trained in the odor-reward association task used in the timolol studies described above. Forty-eight hours later, they were exposed to the odor in a neutral cage, located in the experimental room. This was followed by an injection of idazoxan; control rats were handled in the colony room before injection. Idazoxan enhanced performance when the rat was tested 48 h later, but only when the injection was given after memory reactivation (**Figure 4**). These data complement studies showing cue-dependent amnesia induced by beta adrenergic antagonists, discussed earlier. Together they lend support to the notion that the locus-coeruleus-noradrenergic system is activated by cues associated with target memories and contributes to the postreactivation stabilization or reinforcement of the memory (Sara, 2000b; see also Sara, 1985).

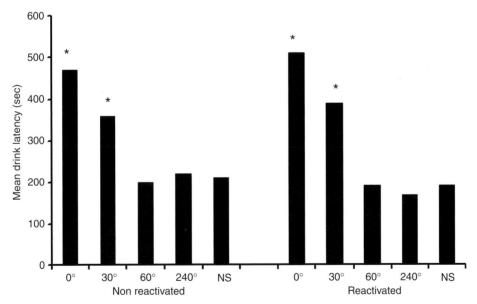

Figure 3 Retention performance in a lick suppression task after training and electrical stimulation of the mesencephalic reticular formation (MRF) (left) or after memory reactivation by the tone conditioned stimulus and (MRF) stimulation (right). In each condition one group of rats received no stimulation, to provide a baseline performance (NS). Histograms from left to right represent data from rats stimulated immediately after training or exposure to the tone or progressively longer delays. The treatment was effective in improving retention when applied up to 30 min after training; behavioral performance of rats stimulated after that was indistinguishable from that of NS rats. Note the striking similarity between the temporal gradient of efficacy after training and after reactivation. Figure adapted from Devietti TL, Conger GL, and Kirkpatrick BR (1977). Comparison of the enhancement gradients of retention obtained with stimulation of the mesencephalic reticular formation after training or memory reactivation. *Physiol. Behav.* 19: 549–554, with permission from Elsevier.

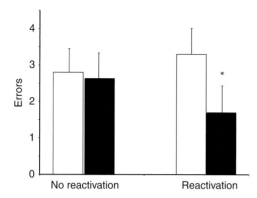

Figure 4 Retention performance in terms of errors before finding the reward in a retention test, 3 weeks after learning the odor-reward association test. Left: data from rats receiving no reactivation on the day before the test. Right: data from rats exposed for a few minutes to the target odor in the experimental room, 24 h before the retention test. White bars: saline injections after reactivation or no reactivation. Black bars: rats injected with idazoxan (an alpha 2 receptor antagonist that increases release of NE), 2 mg kg^{-1} ip, after no reactivation or reactivation.

1.24.7.1.3 Enhancement by activation of PKA

The beta adrenergic receptor is one of a family of receptors positively linked to G proteins that serve to activate the cyclic AMP intracellular signaling cascade, leading to gene induction by the transcription factor CREB. The resulting *de novo* protein synthesis is thought to be essential for the stabilization of long-term memory. Activation of protein kinase A (PKA) is an important step in this cyclic AMP intracellular signaling cascade. A recent study by Tronson et al. (2006) has shown that pharmacologically activating PKA within the rat amygdala can facilitate fear memory if and only if the memory has been reactivated by a reminder. These results, taken together with the studies showing enhancement of reactivated memory by beta adrenergic agonists, lend support to the notion that the noradrenergic system, activated at retrieval, serves to reinforce memories rendered labile by reactivation.

1.24.7.2 Clinical Significance of Cue-Dependent Enhancement

Clinical syndromes such as posttraumatic stress disorder (PTSD), phobias, obsessive compulsion, and craving in addiction share the common feature of underlying compelling, persistent memories. The possibility that memory may be rendered labile under controlled conditions has broad therapeutic applications for these disorders, accounting for the increasing number of investigators interested in this aspect of memory.

In particular, the susceptibility of reactivated memories to noradrenergic manipulation sheds some light on the underlying mechanisms of pathological persistence of memory. In the case of PTSD, it has already been established that there is greater noradrenergic (NE) activity under baseline conditions in patients with chronic PTSD than in healthy subjects, with a direct relationship of NE activity to the severity of the clinical syndrome (Geracioti et al., 2001). Further activation of this system during stress could recreate the internal state induced by the original trauma and thereby reinstate the memory (Grillon et al., 1996). The demonstrated role of the intracellular pathway activated by this system in reinforcing reactivated memories (Tronson et al., 2006) suggests that the memory recalled in the presence of a high level of NE will be reinforced each time (see also **Figure 3**).

The potential usefulness of noradrenergic receptor–blocking agents in PTSD has already been pointed out by Cahill (1997), who suggested that treatment with beta blockers as soon as possible after the traumatic event might prevent the development of PTSD. The recent 'rediscovery' of the phenomenon of lability of memory in its active state adds a new dimension to this potential use. Treatment with beta receptor antagonists, at the time of spontaneous or clinically elicited reinstatement of the traumatic memory, should serve to attenuate the active memory by blocking reconsolidation processes (Przybyskawski et al., 1999).

1.24.8 New Look at Retrieval and 'Reconsolidation'

Memory only lends itself to study through its retrieval; as William James underlined more than a century ago, "the only proof of there being retention is that recall actually takes place" (James, 1892). Although some memory retrieval is likely to occur spontaneously as a result of random fluctuations of network activity in the brain, retrieval is usually brought about with effort, as a result of integration of incoming environmental information with the 'memory network' driven by that information (Tulving and Thomson, 1973). It follows from this that the formation of new memories will always be made on the background of retrieved information. Recent functional imaging studies in humans are, indeed, confirming these earlier theoretical speculations (e.g., Cabeza et al., 2002; Nyberg et al., 1996a,b). They are providing clear evidence that it is memory of the past that organizes and provides meaning to the present perceptual experience. Borrowing Tulving's terminology, new episodic memory, to be remembered in a meaningful way, must be consolidated within a preexisting semantic memory (Tulving, 2002).

This analysis does not allow a clear demarcation between consolidation and retrieval processes, and in this view, it can be assumed that every retrieval operation should trigger a reconsolidation process. This is a view similar to that of Spear, although he never used the term 'reconsolidation' (Spear and Mueller, 1984). It follows from this that retrieval will change the information content of the 'trace' such that memory can be viewed as an emergent, dynamic, adaptive property of the nervous system. It is in that sense that

> Everything flows and nothing abides; everything gives way and nothing stays fixed.

References

Akirav I and Maroun M (2006) Ventromedial prefrontal cortex is obligatory for consolidation and reconsolidation of object recognition memory. *Cereb. Cortex* 16: 1759–1765.

Alberini CM (2005) Mechanisms of memory stabilization: Are consolidation and reconsolidation similar or distinct processes? *Trends Neurosci.* 28: 51–56.

Alberini CM, Milekic MH, and Tronel S (2006) Memory: Mechanisms of memory stabilization and de-stabilization. *Cell. Mol. Life Sci.* 63: 999–1008.

Altman HJ and Quartermain D (1983) Facilitation of memory retrieval by centrally administered catecholamine stimulating agents. *Behav. Brain Res.* 7: 51–63.

Anokhin KV, Tiunova AA, and Rose SP (2002) Reminder effects – Reconsolidation or retrieval deficit? Pharmacological dissection with protein synthesis inhibitors following reminder for a passive-avoidance task in young chicks. *Eur. J. Neurosci.* 15: 1759–65.

Bartlett FC (1932) *Remembering: A Study in Experimental and Social Psychology*. Cambridge: Cambridge University Press.

Biedenkapp JC and Rudy JW (2004) Context memories and reactivation, constraints on the reconsolidation hypothesis. *Behav. Neurosci.* 118: 956–964.

Bouret S and Sara SJ (2004) Reward expectation, orientation of attention and locus coeruleus-medial frontal cortex interplay during learning. *Eur. J. Neurosci.* 20: 791–802.

Bouret S and Sara SJ (2006) Network reset, a simplified overarching theory of locus coeruleus noradrenaline function. *Trends Neurosci.* 28: 574–582.

Cabeza R, Dolcos F, Graham R, and Nyberg L (2002) Similarities and differences in the neural correlates of episodic memory retrieval and working memory. *Neuroimage* 16: 317–30.

Cahill L (1997) The neurobiology of emotionally influenced memory. Implications for understanding traumatic memory. *Ann. N.Y. Acad. Sci.* 821: 238–246.

Cooper RM and Koppenaal RJ (1964) Suppression and recovery of a one-trial avoidance response after a single ECS. *Psychon. Sci.* 303–304.

D'Andrea J and Kesner R (1973) The effects of ECS and hypoxia on information retrieval. *Physiol. Behav.* 11: 747–752.

Davis HP, Rosenzweig MR, Bennett EL, and Squire LR (1980) Inhibition of cerebral protein synthesis, dissociation of nonspecific effects and amnesic effects. *Behav. Neural Biol.* 28: 99–104.

Davis HP and Squire LR (1984) Protein synthesis and memory, a review. *Psychol. Bull.* 96: 518–559.

Debiec J and LeDoux JE (2006) Noradrenergic signaling in the amygdala contributes to the reconsolidation of fear memory: Treatment implications for PTSD. *Ann. N.Y. Acad. Sci.* 1071: 521–524.

Dekeyne A, Deweer B, and Sara SJ (1987) Background stimuli as a reminder after spontaneous forgetting: Potentiation by stimulation of the mesencephalic reticular formation. *Psychobiology* 15: 161–166.

Devauges V and Sara SJ (1991) Memory retrieval enhancement by locus coeruleus stimulation, evidence for mediation by beta receptors. *Behav. Brain Res.* 43: 93–97.

DeVietti TL, Conger GL, and Kirkpatrick BR (1977) Comparison of the enhancement gradients of retention obtained with stimulation of the mesencephalic reticular formation after training or memory reactivation. *Physiol. Behav.* 19: 549–554.

Deweer B and Sara SJ (1984) Background stimuli as a reminder after spontaneous forgetting, Role of duration of cuing and cuing-test interval. *Anim. Learn. Behav.* 12: 238–247.

Deweer B, Sara SJ, and Hars B (1980) Contextual cues and memory retrieval in rats. Alleviation of forgetting by a pretest exposure to background stimuli. *Anim. Learn. Behav.* 8: 265–272.

Diergaarde L, Schoffelmeer AN, and De Vries TJ (2006) Beta-adrenoceptor mediated inhibition of long-term reward-related memory reconsolidation. *Behav. Brain Res.* 170: 333–336.

Dudai Y (2004) The neurobiology of consolidations, or, how stable is the engram? *Annu. Rev. Psychol.* 55: 51–86.

Dudai Y (2006) Reconsolidation, the advantage of being refocused. *Curr. Opin. Neurobiol.* 16: 174–178.

Dudai Y and Eisenberg M (2004) Rites of passage of the engram, reconsolidation and the lingering consolidation hypothesis. *Neuron* 44: 93–100.

Duncan CP (1945) The effect of electroshock convulsions on the maze habit in the white rat. *J. Exp. Psychol.* 35: 267–278.

Duncan C (1948) Habit reversal deficit induced by electroshock in the rat. *J. Comp. Physiol. Psychol.* 41: 11–16.

Duncan CP (1949) The retroactive effect of electroshock on learning. *J. Comp. Physiol. Psychol.* 42: 32–44.

Duvarci S and Nader K (2004) Characterization of fear memory reconsolidation. *J. Neurosci.* 24: 9269–9275.

Ebbinghaus H (1885) *Uber des Gedachtnis, untcuchungen zur experimentellen Psychologie*. Berlin: Dunker & Humbolt.

Eisenberg M and Dudai Y (2004) Reconsolidation of fresh, remote, and extinguished fear memory in Medaka: Old fears don't die. *Eur. J. Neurosci.* 20: 3397–3403.

Eisenberg M, Kobilo T, Berman DE, and Dudai Y (2003) Stability of retrieved memory, inverse correlation with trace dominance. *Science* 301: 1102–1104.

Flexner LB and Goodman RH (1975) Studies on memory, inhibitors of protein synthesis also inhibit catecholamine synthesis. *Proc. Natl. Acad. Sci. USA* 72: 4660–4663.

Flood JF, Smith GE, and Jarvik ME (1980) A comparison of the effects of localized brain administration of catecholamine and protein synthesis inhibitors on memory processing. *Brain Res.* 197: 153–165.

Frenkel L, Maldonado H, and Delorenzi A (2005) Memory strengthening by a real-life episode during reconsolidation, an outcome of water deprivation via brain angiotensin II. *Eur. J. Neurosci.* 22: 1757–1766.

Gainutdinova TH, Tagirova RR, Ismailova AI, et al. (2005) Reconsolidation of a context long-term memory in the terrestrial snail requires protein synthesis. *Learn. Mem.* 12: 620–625.

Galluscio E (1971) Retrograde amnesia induced by electroconvulsive shock and carbon dioxyde anesthesia in rats, an attempt to stimulate recovery. *J. Comp. Physiol. Psychol.* 75: 136–140.

Geracioti TD Jr., Baker DG, Ekhator NN, et al. (2001) CSF norepinephrine concentrations in posttraumatic stress disorder. *Am. J. Psychiatry* 158: 1227–1230.

Gisquet-Verrier P and Alexinsky T (1986) Does contextual change determine long-term forgetting? *Anim. Learn. Behav.* 14: 349–358.

Gold PE (2006) The many faces of amnesia. *Learn. Mem.* 13: 506–514.

Gordon WC and Spear NE (1973) The effects of strychnine on recently acquired and reactivated passive avoidance memories. *Physiol. Behav.* 10: 1071–1075.

Grillon C, Southwick SM, and Charney DS (1996) The psychobiological basis of posttraumatic stress disorder. *Mol. Psychiatry* 1: 278–297.

Gruest N, Richer P, and Hars B (2004a) Emergence of long-term memory for conditioned aversion in the rat fetus. *Dev. Psychobiol.* 44: 189–198.

Gruest N, Richer P, and Hars B (2004b) Memory consolidation and reconsolidation in the rat pup require protein synthesis. *J. Neurosci.* 24: 10488–10492.

Hebb DO (1949) *The Organisation of Behavior.* New York: John Wiley.

Hupbach A, Gomez R, Hardt O, and Nadel L (2007) Reconsolidation of episodic memories: A subtle reminder triggers integration of new information. *Learn. Mem.* 14: 47–53.

Inda MC, Delgado-Garcia JM, and Carrion AM (2005) Acquisition, consolidation, reconsolidation, and extinction of eyelid conditioning responses require *de novo* protein synthesis. *J. Neurosci.* 25: 2070–2080.

James W (1892) *The Principles of Psychology.* New York: Henry Holt.

Judge ME and Quartermain D (1982) Characteristics of retrograde amnesia following reactivation of memory in mice. *Physiol. Behav.* 28: 585–590.

Kelly A, Laroche S, and Davis S (2003) Activation of mitogen-activated protein kinase/extracellular signal-regulated kinase in hippocampal circuitry is required for consolidation and reconsolidation of recognition memory. *J. Neurosci.* 23: 5354–5360.

Kemenes G, Kemenes I, Michel M, Papp A, and Muller U (2006) Phase-dependent molecular requirements for memory reconsolidation: Differential roles for protein synthesis and protein kinase A activity. *J. Neurosci.* 26: 6298–6302.

Kida S, Josselyn SA, de Ortiz SP, et al. (2002) CREB required for the stability of new and reactivated fear memories. *Nat. Neurosci.* 5: 348–355.

Kohlenberg R and Trabasso T (1968) Recovery of a conditioned emotional response after one or two electro-convulsive shocks. *J. Comp. Physiol. Psychol.* 65: 270–273.

Koppenaal R, Jogoda E, and Cruce JA (1967) Recovery from ECS produced amnesia following a reminder. *Psychon. Sci.* 9: 293–294.

Lattal KM and Abel T (2004) Behavioral impairments caused by injections of the protein synthesis inhibitor anisomycin after contextual retrieval reverse with time. *Proc. Natl. Acad. Sci. USA* 101: 4667–4672.

Lee JL, Milton AL, and Everitt BJ (2006) Reconsolidation and extinction of conditioned fear: Inhibition and potentiation. *J. Neurosci.* 26: 10051–6.

Lewis DJ (1969) Sources of experimental amnesia. *Psychol. Rev.* 76: 461–472.

Lewis DJ (1976) A cognitive approach to experimental amnesia. *Am. J. Psychol.* 89: 51–80.

Lewis DJ (1979) Psychobiology of active and inactive memory. *Psychol. Bull.* 86: 1054–1083.

Lewis DJ and Bregman NJ (1973) Source of cues for cue-dependent amnesia in rats. *J. Comp. Physiol. Psychol.* 85: 421–6.

Lewis DJ, Bregman NJ, and Mahan JJ, Jr. (1972) Cue-dependent amnesia in rats. *J. Comp. Physiol. Psychol.* 81: 243–247.

Lewis DJ and Maher BA (1965) Neural consolidation and electroconvulsive shock. *Psychol. Rev.* 72: 225–239.

Lewis DJ and Maher BA (1966) Electroconvulsive shock and inhibition, some problems considered. *Psychol. Rev.* 73: 388–392.

Loftus EF (1979) The malleability of human memory. *Am. Sci.* 67: 312–320.

Loftus EF (1981) Natural and unnatural cognition. *Cognition* 10: 193–196.

Loftus EF (2005a) Planting misinformation in the human mind: A 30-year investigation of the malleability of memory. *Learn. Mem.* 12: 361–366.

Loftus EF (2005b) Searching for the neurobiology of the misinformation effect. *Learn. Mem.* 12: 1–2.

Mactutus CF, Riccio DC, and Ferek JM (1979) Retrograde amnesia for old reactivated memory, some anomalous characteristics. *Science* 204: 1319–1320.

McGaugh JL (1966) Time dependent processes in memory storage. *Science* 153: 1351–1358.

McGaugh JL (2000) Memory – A century of consolidation. *Science* 287: 248–51.

Milekic MH and Alberini CM (2002) Temporally graded requirement for protein synthesis following memory reactivation. *Neuron* 36: 521–525.

Miller RR and Springer AD (1972) Induced recovery of memory in rats following electroconvulsive shock. *Physiol. Behav.* 8: 645–651.

Misanin JR, Miller RR, and Lewis DJ (1968) Retrograde amnesia produced by electroconvulsive shock after reactivation of a consolidated memory trace. *Science* 160: 554–555.

Morris RG, Inglis J, Ainge JA, et al. (2006) Memory reconsolidation, sensitivity of spatial memory to inhibition of protein synthesis in dorsal hippocampus during encoding and retrieval. *Neuron* 50: 479–489.

Mueller GE and Pilzecker A (1900) Experimentelle Beitrage zur Lehre vom Gedachtniss. *Z. Psychol.* 10: 388–394.

Nader K (2003) Memory traces unbound. *Trends Neurosci.* 26: 65–72.

Nader K, Schafe GE, and Le Doux JE (2000) Fear memories require protein synthesis in the amygdala for reconsolidation after retrieval. *Nature* 406: 722–726.

Nyberg L, McIntosh AR, Cabeza R, et al. (1996a) Network analysis of positron emission tomography regional cerebral blood flow data, ensemble inhibition during episodic memory retrieval. *J. Neurosci.* 16: 3753–3759.

Nyberg L, McIntosh AR, Houle S, Nilsson LG, and Tulving E (1996b) Activation of medial temporal structures during episodic memory retrieval. *Nature* 380: 715–717.

Pedreira M, Perez-Cuesta LM, and Maldonado H (2002) Reactivation and reconsolidation of long-term memory in the crab *Chasmagnathus*: Protein synthesis requirement and mediation by NMDA-type glutamate receptors. *J. Neurosci.* 22: 8305–8311.

Power AE, Berlau DJ, McGaugh JL, and Steward O (2006) Anisomycin infused into the hippocampus fails to block "reconsolidation" but impairs extinction: The role of re-exposure duration. *Learn. Mem.* 13: 27–34.

Prado-Alcala RA, Diaz Del Guante MA, Garin-Aguilar ME, Diaz-Trujillo A, Quirarte GL, and McGaugh JL (2006) Amygdala or hippocampus inactivation after retrieval induces temporary memory deficit. *Neurobiol. Learn. Mem.* 86: 144–149.

Przybyslawski J, Roullet P, and Sara SJ (1999) Attenuation of emotional and nonemotional memories after their reactivation, role of beta adrenergic receptors. *J. Neurosci.* 19: 6623–6628.

Przybyslawski J and Sara SJ (1997) Reconsolidation of memory after its reactivation. *Behav. Brain Res.* 84: 241–246.

Quartermain D, Freedman LS, Botwinick CY, and Gutwein BM (1977) Reversal of cycloheximide-induced amnesia by adrenergic receptor stimulation. *Pharmacol. Biochem. Behav.* 7: 259–267.

Quartermain D, Judge ME, and Jung H (1988) Amphetamine enhances retrieval following diverse sources of forgetting. *Physiol. Behav.* 43: 239–241.

Quartermain D, McEwen B, and Azmita E (1970) Amnesia produced by electroconvulsive shock or cycloheximide, conditions for recovery. *Science* 169: 683–686.

Quartermain D, McEwen B, and Azmita E (1972) Recovery of memory following amnesia in the rat and mouse. *J. Comp. Physiol. Psychol.* 79: 360–379.

Ribot T (1882) *Diseases of Memory.* New York: Appleton-Century Crofts.

Riccio DC, Millin PM, and Bogart AR (2006) Reconsolidation: A brief history, a retrieval view, and some recent issues. *Learn. Mem.* 13: 536–544.

Rigter H and Van Riezen H (1979) Pituitary hormones and amnesia. *Curr. Dev. Psychopharmacol.* 5: 67–124.

Roullet P and Sara S (1998) Consolidation of memory after its reactivation, involvement of beta noradrenergic receptors in the late phase. *Neural Plast.* 6: 63–68.

Routtenberg A and Rekart JL (2005) Post-translational protein modification as the substrate for long-lasting memory. *Trends Neurosci.* 28: 12–19.

Rudy JW, Biedenkapp JC, Moineau J, and Bolding K (2006) Anisomycin and the reconsolidation hypothesis. *Learn. Mem.* 13: 1–3.

Sangha S, Scheibenstock A, and Lukowiak K (2003) Reconsolidation of a long-term memory in *Lymnaea* requires new protein and RNA synthesis and the soma of right pedal dorsal 1. *J. Neurosci.* 23: 8034–8040.

Sara SJ (1973) Recovery from hypoxia and ECS-induced amnesia after a single exposure to training environment. *Physiol. Behav.* 10: 85–89.

Sara SJ (1985) Noradrenergic modulation of selective attention, its role in memory retrieval. *Ann. N.Y. Acad. Sci.* 444: 178–193.

Sara SJ (1991) Noradrenaline and memory: Neuromodulatory effects on retrieval. In: Weinman J and Hunter J (eds.) *Memory: Neurochemical and Clinical Aspects*, pp. 105–128. London: Harwood Academic.

Sara SJ (2000a) Retrieval and reconsolidation: Toward a neurobiology of remembering. *Learn. Mem.* 7: 73–84.

Sara SJ (2000b) Strengthening the shaky trace through retrieval. *Nat. Rev. Neurosci.* 1: 212–213.

Sara SJ and David-Remacle M (1974) Recovery from electroconvulsive shock-induced amnesia by exposure to the training environment, pharmacological enhancement by piracetam. *Psychopharmacologia* 36: 59–66.

Sara SJ and Devauges V (1988) Priming stimulation of locus coeruleus facilitates memory retrieval in the rat. *Brain Res.* 438: 299–303.

Sara SJ and Devauges V (1989) Idazoxan, an alpha-2 antagonist, facilitates memory retrieval in the rat. *Behav. Neural Biol.* 51: 401–411.

Sara SJ, Deweer B, and Hars B (1980) Reticular stimulation facilitates retrieval of a "forgotten" maze habit. *Neurosci. Lett.* 18: 211–217.

Sara SJ and Hars B (2006) In memory of consolidation. *Learn. Mem.* 13: 515–521.

Sara SJ and Remacle JF (1977) Strychnine-induced passive avoidance facilitation after electroconvulsive shock or undertraining, a retrieval effect. *Behav. Biol.* 19: 465–475.

Serota RG (1971) Acetoxycycloheximide and transient amnesia in the rat. *Proc. Natl. Acad. Sci. USA* 68: 1249–1250.

Spear NE (1971) *Animal Memory.* New York: Academic Press.

Spear NE (1973) Retrieval of memory in animals. *Psychol. Rev.* 80: 163–194.

Spear NE (1976) Ontogenetic factors in the retrieval of memories. *Act. Nerv. Super. Praha.* 18: 302–311.

Spear NE (1981) Extending the domain of memory retrieval. In: Spear NE and Miller RR (eds.) *Information Processing in Animals, Memory Mechanisms*, pp. 341–378. Hillsdale NJ: Lawrence Erlbaum Associates.

Spear NE and Mueller CW (1984) Consolidation as a function of retrieval. In: Weingartner H and Parker ES (eds.) *Memory Consolidation, Psychobiology of Cognition*, pp. 111–147. Hillsdale, NJ: Lawrence Erlbaum Associates.

Squire LR and Barondes SH (1972) Variable decay of memory and its recovery in cycloheximide-treated rats. *Proc. Natl. Acad. Sci. USA* 69: 1416–1420.

Squire LR, Emanuel CA, Davis HP, and Deutsch JA (1975) Inhibitors of cerebral protein synthesis, dissociation of aversive and amnesic effects. *Behav. Biol.* 14: 335–341.

Stollhoff N, Menzel R, and Eisenhardt D (2005) Spontaneous recovery from extinction depends on the reconsolidation of the acquisition memory in an appetitive learning paradigm in the honeybee *Apis Mellifera*. *J. Neurosci.* 25: 4485–4492.

Suzuki A, Josselyn SA, Frankland PW, Masushige S, Silva AJ, and Kida S (2004) Memory reconsolidation and extinction have distinct temporal and biochemical signatures. *J. Neurosci.* 24: 4787–4795.

Torras-Garcia M, Lelong J, Tronel S, and Sara SJ (2005) Reconsolidation after remembering an odor-reward association requires NMDA receptors. *Learn. Mem.* 12: 18–22.

Tronel S, Feenstra MG, and Sara SJ (2004) Noradrenergic action in prefrontal cortex in the late stage of memory consolidation. *Learn. Mem.* 11: 453–458.

Tronel S and Sara SJ (2002) Mapping of olfactory memory circuits, region-specific c-fos activation after odor-reward associative learning or after its retrieval. *Learn. Mem.* 9: 105–111.

Tronel S and Sara SJ (2003) Blockade of NMDA receptors in prelimbic cortex induces an enduring amnesia for odor-reward associative learning. *J. Neurosci.* 23: 5472–5476.

Tronson NC, Wiseman SL, Olausson P, and Taylor JR (2006) Bidirectional behavioral plasticity of memory reconsolidation depends on amygdalar protein kinase A. *Nat. Neurosci.* 9: 167–169.

Tulving E (2002) Episodic memory: From mind to brain. *Annu. Rev. Psychol.* 53: 1–25.

Tulving E and Thomson D (1973) Encoding specificity and retrieval processes in episodic memory. *Psychol. Rev.* 80: 352–372.

Wang SH, Ostlund SB, Nader K, and Balleine BW (2005) Consolidation and reconsolidation of incentive learning in the amygdala. *J. Neurosci.* 25: 830–835.

Warrington EK and Weiskrantz L (1970) Amnesic syndrome, consolidation or retrieval? *Nature* 228: 628–630.

Young AG and Galluscio EH (1971) Recovery from ECS produced amnesia. *Psychon. Sci.* 22: 149–151.

1.25   Learning and Memory in Communication and Navigation in Insects

R. J. De Marco and R. Menzel, Freie Universität Berlin, Berlin, Germany

1.25.1   Introduction

The distinction between instinctive and learned behavior is a fundamental issue in behavioral research. A major difficulty in addressing it relies on the fact that labeling behaviors as either instinctive or learned is in most cases a merely analytical approach to the problem. Behavior develops on the basis of the interplay between an animal's phylogenetic boundaries and the sources of external signals that belong to its specific sensory world (Tinbergen, 1963; Lorenz, 1981; Shettleworth, 1998; Macphail and Bolhuis, 2001). It follows that when an animal computes the differences between stimuli activating the same or different sensory modalities, its subsequent behavior will be the outcome of an unbroken succession of possible responses, whose particular boundaries have been modified by selection in the course of evolution. Learning is embedded into this continuousness, and its effects on the animal's instantaneous performance will be superimposed onto those of its specific phylogenetic boundaries. This is why it is so fundamental to focus on salient responses invariably linked to the animal's previous experience when distinguishing between instinctive and learned behaviors. From a behavioral point of view, this leads to the search for the mechanisms underlying the animal's decision, a notion that denotes the process of parsing complexes of stimuli into equivalent options and the control of the subsequent responses that arise from the corresponding choices.

A central argument advanced in this chapter is that some invertebrate taxa constitute powerful model systems for the study of the teamwork between these two modes of behaviors, instinctive and learned, and for the analysis of basic principles of learning and memory, particularly within the context of communication and spatial cognition, where the possibility of revealing decisions might be within reach. Our focus is on social insects, animals that form societies and appear to have been exposed to higher cognitive demands during the course of evolution, perhaps due to their long lifetime, the diversity and complexity of the signals involved in their social interactions, and the development of counterresponses. In fact, "if Earth's social organisms are scored by complexity of communication, division of labor and intensity of group integration, three pinnacles of evolution stand out: humanity, the jelly-fish-like siphonophores, and a select assemblage of social insect species" (Wilson, 2006). Within this insect group, emphasis is on the honeybee, *Apis mellifera*, simply because its communication and navigation skills are impressive (e.g., von Frisch, 1967; Seeley, 1995; Menzel et al., 2005). Furthermore, because their brains are small, bees appear to be suitable subjects for studying system-level neural correlates of learning and memory through robust behavioral approaches, both at the level of single neurons and neural networks.

1.25.2   Communication

Since its early days, ethology has nurtured the study of learning and memory phenomena, and a great deal of its classical ideas "emerged or crystallized from the study of animal communication" (Konishi, 1999). It follows, therefore, that communication in nonlinguistic animals has been at the center of many of the current behavioral approaches to learning and memory. The study of animal communication is concerned with the production of and the responses to signals, including adaptive advantages and mechanisms of central processing, motor coordination, and peripheral detection and filtering. In invertebrates, it is in the context of communication and navigation that learning transcends elementary forms of association in particularly clear ways (Menzel et al., 2006). The evaluating signal for storing experience must come from internal nervous system conditions at the time of learning, depends considerably on the motivational level, requires attention to a subset of stimuli, and is adjusted to the animal's own behavior in an intricate way. The signals learned are usually composed of multimodal inputs, which cannot be isolated from each other, and the motor performances involve sophisticated sequences of programs. Insects make use of all sensory channels for communication and evolved sophisticated sender–receiver systems serving mate recognition and sexual selection, predator–prey relationships, and complex social interactions. Although the sensory, ecological, and evolutionary aspects of these communication systems have long been studied in detail (see the following discussion), little is known about the cognitive dimensions of these communication systems (e.g., how innate mechanisms interact with experience-dependent developmental

processes, how these mechanisms depend on internal and external conditions, and how learning actually shapes a communication process). In the present context the neural mechanisms of insect communication will henceforth be eschewed altogether. We shall describe a few examples from several taxa illustrating the dominance of innate behaviors with regard to communication with conspecifics; these examples will be listed according to the sensory modalities involved in the processing of communicating signals. We will then focus on a few examples illustrating simple forms of learning in a selected group of insects, and finally, we will focus on the study case of the honeybee dance communication system, with special emphasis on the structure and content of the spatial memory underlying such complex phenomenon.

1.25.2.1   The Dominance of Innately Programmed Responses in Communication

1.25.2.1.1   Chemical
In highly eusocial species, the interplay between innate and learned behaviors becomes evident through group recognition, which greatly depends on smell and genetically programmed responses to information gathered in specific, innately recognized behavioral contexts (Lindauer, 1961; Wilson, 1971; Michener, 1974; Barrows et al., 1975; Oster and Wilson, 1978; Fletcher and Ross, 1985; Hölldobler and Wilson, 1990). Within an insect society, conspecific individuals respond differently to age, sex, and physiological groups, and the task of recognizing queens, males, workers (both egg-layers and infertile individuals), as well as intruders, strongly relies on volatile pheromones, variations in hydrocarbon cuticular profiles, and environmental odors (e.g., Eberhard, 1969; Bell, 1974; Franks and Scovell, 1983; Wagner et al., 1998; Liebig et al., 2000).

Individually distinctive or colony odors are frequent across highly eusocial insects and constitute the basis of colony integration and social organization (Hölldobler and Michener, 1980). Foragers from many ant species, for example, resume their field excursions by following trails chemically marked with colony-specific components (Hölldobler and Wilson, 1990; Billen and Morgan, 1998). Research on the harvesting ant *Pogonomyrmex*, for example, shows how context-dependent innate responses to olfactory stimuli lead to adaptive behavioral flexibility during foraging (Greene and Gordon, 2003). A colony of these ants consists of a single queen and several thousand workers, including foragers and patrollers. Patrollers scout the foraging area before foragers leave the nest; if they do not return from their early excursions, the foragers will not begin to work. Recently, Greene and Gordon (2003) first blocked a *Pogonomyrmex* colony's foraging activity by removing its patrollers and then presented the foragers with glass beads at the nest's entrance. These beads had previously been coated with cuticular lipids from patrollers, hydrocarbon profiles from either patrollers or within-the-nest ants, and plain solvent; they also used live patrollers as a positive control. The authors thus found that task-specific cuticular hydrocarbons from patrollers were sufficient to rescue the colony's foraging activity, and that the foragers' responses depended not only on the patrollers' hydrocarbon profiles, but also on whether or not they were presented at the nest's entrance and at the right time of day (Greene and Gordon, 2003). The question remains of to what degree simple forms of learning, such as habituation (Barrows et al., 1975), underlie these responses to colony and individually distinctive odors.

1.25.2.1.2 Visual

Visual stimuli also control innate responses in communicating insects. Fireflies use luminescent signals for attracting mates (Lloyd, 1983). Butterflies use bright colors, iridescence, and polarized light in the context of long-range mate recognition and sexual selection (e.g., Vane-Wright and Boppre, 1993; Sweeney et al., 2003). Males of the hoverfly *Syritta pipiens* closely track the movements of conspecifics (Collett and Land, 1975), a skill that seemingly serves copulatory functions. Male flies of the genus *Lispe* perform a dancelike motion pattern during courtship that is seemingly perceived through vision (Frantsevich and Gorb, 2006). Visual cues enhance recruitment orientation to food sources in stingless bees (Nieh, 2004), that is, several species of these highly social insects exhibit local enhancement and orient toward the visual presence of foraging conspecifics (Slaa et al., 2003), a phenomenon also found in honeybees (Tautz and Sandeman, 2002) and wasps (D'Adamo and Lozada, 2005). Furthermore, stingless bees also appear to visually track the piloting flights of experienced conspecifics, and these movements can guide them for at least part of the distance to a food source (Esch et al., 1965; Esch, 1967; Kerr, 1969), although the role of learning in this intriguing form of recruitment has yet to be analyzed.

1.25.2.1.3 Mechanosensory

The use of air pressure waves, substrate-born vibrations, and touching is widespread in sexual selection, alarm and defensive behavior, and complex social interactions in insects (e.g., Webster et al., 1992; Fullard and Yack, 1993; Michelsen, 1999; Hölldobler and Roces, 2001; Virant-Doberlet and Cokl, 2004). Complex behaviors involving these types of signals vary considerably across species. Female crickets, for example, orient toward males by recognizing and localizing the sound signals they produce. Their auditory orientation emerges from mechanisms detecting species-specific temporal structures of the males' sound signals, as well as reactive motor responses to individual sound pulses (Webster et al., 1992; Stumpner and von Helversen, 2001; Hedwig and Poulet, 2004). Leaf-cutting ants are highly sensitive to substrate-borne vibrations (Markl, 1965) and possess stridulatory organs that produce such vibrations when the animals are engaged in leaf-cutting (Tautz et al., 1995; Hölldobler and Roces, 2001). It has been shown that these substrate-born stridulatory vibrations operate as short-range recruitment signals that enhance the effect of recruitment pheromones (Hölldobler and Roces, 2001).

Moreover, the exchange of liquid food by mouth is widespread among highly eusocial species of insects (Wilson, 1971), and these social interactions depend strongly on intense antennal contacts that occur between donor and food-receivers (Free, 1956; Montagner and Galliot, 1982). In the honeybee, antennal interactions are also important in the transmission of waggle dance information (Rohrseitz and Tautz, 1999). Ants recruit nest-mates to newly discovered food sources as well as possible nest sites by means of tandem running (Hingston, 1928), a behavioral mechanism that strongly relies on mechanosensory cues (e.g., Wilson, 1959; Hölldobler et al., 1974; Möglich et al., 1974; Traniello and Hölldobler, 1984). Camponotus ants returning from successful field excursions stimulate nest-mates through fast directed movements of their front legs or even their entire bodies, as well as food samples; they then present the nest-mates with their gasters, and tandem running begins between pairs of leaders and followers (Hingston, 1928; Hölldobler et al., 1974; Hölldobler and Wilson, 1990). Hölldobler (1974) and colleagues demonstrated that tactile signals from the follower's antennae are sufficient to trigger an ant's leadership behavior, and that the subsequent following behavior relies on mechanical stimulation based on contact with a leader's gaster. Tandem running is especially interesting in the context of genetically programmed mechanosensory communication because it clearly exposes the bidirectionality of the communication process. It has recently been shown through the behaviors of both the leader and the follower in a pair of tandemly running *Temnothorax* ants how they depend on each other (Franks and Richardson, 2006), that is, there is an evident feedback between both ants that relies on mechanical stimuli and helps in maximizing the speed at which the two of them can travel their path. It remains open whether and how the follower gathers path-related information during tandem running that might subsequently be used in solitary excursions.

1.25.2.2   Learning in Communication

1.25.2.2.1   Chemical

Some animals imprint on salient aspects of their sensory world pre- and postnatally. Slave-making ants provide an interesting example of imprinting. These ants invade colonies of other ant species and transport the pupae back to their own nest. Adults emerging from these pupae behave and work for the slave-making species as if it were its own species (Isingrini et al., 1985; Carlin and Schwartz, 1989). Evidence indicates that this phenomenon depends on a process of imprinting, by which the slave ants learn to recognize the slave-makers as members of their own species. This process involves learning about the slave-makers' hydrocarbon cuticular profiles, a distinctive olfactory mark of the species. Apparently, imprinting is successfully accomplished when the hydrocarbon cuticular profiles of both ant species, the slave-makers and the slaves, do not differ markedly (Lenoir et al., 2001; D'Ettorre et al., 2002).

Communicating insects also benefit from anticipatory behavior based on simple associative principles. In the honeybee, for example, and probably also in many other social species, the exchange of liquid food by mouth, called trophallaxis, allows individuals to assign nectar odors with predictive values. Animals associate the odor (as the conditioned stimulus or CS) and the sucrose (as the unconditioned stimulus or US) present in the nectar they receive through these social interactions. This form of learning leads to long-term olfactory memories after a single learning trial – even when trophallaxis is brief – and the strength of association depends on CS and US intensity, as well as on the animals' past foraging experience (Gil and De Marco, 2005). Olfactory memories established in this manner

may have important implications in the organization of foraging (Gil and De Marco, 2006): First, foragers and food-receivers may benefit from learned odors in searching for a transfer partner, eliciting trophallaxis, or even avoiding it; second, currently unemployed foragers as well as nonexperienced foragers may benefit from a highly prevalent CS available within the colony to resume their subsequent foraging flights (e.g., the higher the rate of encounter with a rewarding olfactory CS the higher the probability of flying out to search for the prospective nectar source).

1.25.2.2.2   Visual

Polistes wasps provide an example of selective learning, which develops around innate responsiveness to simple sign stimuli: the yellow-black patterns of the wasps' faces and abdomens (Tibbetts, 2002). These patterns vary across individuals and correlate well with a wasp's ranking in a colony's hierarchy based on body size and dominance. Manipulating them induces aggressive responses in staged contests between pairs of unfamiliar individuals, and subordinate wasps with experimentally altered facial color patterns are targets of considerably more aggression from the dominant individuals than sham controls (Tibbetts and Dale, 2004). The question of whether these observations reveal individual recognition in insects remains open, but the wasps' behavior in the staged contests indicates that these animals learn about visual signals of quality that convey information on conspecifics on the basis of a colony's inherent hierarchy. Another interesting example of visual learning involved in communication may arise from the dance behavior of the Asian honeybee, *Apis florea*. In contrast to *Apis mellifera* bees, these animals do not dance on a vertical plane, but on the flattened tops of their open combs, which are directly exposed to a view of the sky (Lindauer, 1956; Koeniger et al., 1982; Dyer, 1985). These bees orient their dances on the horizontal plane according to both celestial cues and landmarks (Dyer, 1985), and the bees that closely follow these communicating dances might use their vision to collect information from them.

1.25.2.2.3   Mechanosensory and combined modalities

The seemingly ritualized movements or dances that honeybees use to recruit nest-mates from the colony – or the swarm – to the location of a desirable resource involve multiple signals, including mechanosensory stimuli (von Frisch, 1967). The role of learning in the context of dance communication was initially dismissed (Lindauer, 1952), but we shall see that this system's functioning may depend strongly on the structure and content of the honeybees' spatial memory.

Karl von Frisch (1946) revealed that a highly stereotyped, still variable motion pattern that honeybees perform on the comb surface conveys to the human observer the position of a well-defined target at the endpoint of an average vector in a two-dimensional egocentric system of coordinates. Since its early days, von Frisch's (1946) discovery was recognized as one of the most impressive achievements of twentieth-century behavioral biology. This motion pattern involves finely controlled repetitive movements and can therefore be described on the basis of its inherent, well-defined features: orientation in space and tempo. The term waggle dance denotes a form of this pattern that conveys information about targets located fairly far from the hive, whereas the term round dance refers to a slightly different form that the animals perform after returning from nearby locations (von Frisch, 1967). Honeybees also use other stereotyped motion patterns when engaged in cooperative work that have also been called dances (von Frisch, 1967; Seeley, 1998). For example, a honeybee may shake its body back and forth, also rotating its body axis every second or so, and walk slowly in all directions across the comb (Seeley 1992). This type of motion pattern has been called tremble dance (von Frisch, 1923), and it helps the colony members to coordinate their activities while handling the collected nectar, both outside and inside the nest (Seeley, 1992). When a forager returns from a highly desirable nectar source and has problems searching for a food receiver (a younger bee that receives its load and eventually stores it in the honeycombs) (Doolittle, 1907; Lindauer, 1952), it usually performs a tremble dance, which may last several tens of minutes. These dances are followed by a rise in the number of available food-receivers and a drop in recruitment of additional foragers to nectar sources, thereby helping the colony to maintain its rate of nectar processing matched with its rate of nectar gathering (Seeley, 1992). In another intriguing example of these dances, a honeybee remains stationary and briefly vibrates its body laterally at a frequency of 4–9 Hz, sometimes alternating brief periods of self-grooming. This pattern has been called the grooming invitation dance (Haydak, 1945) and increases the workers' chances of being rapidly groomed by a nest-mate (Bozic and Valentincic, 1995; Land and Seeley, 2004). These two later forms of dances,

however, do not convey spatial information. Our focus is therefore on the waggle dance, which does convey spatial information and is perhaps the most intriguing form of these complex, iterative movements.

The homeostasis of a honeybee colony greatly depends on cooperative work and efficient communication (e.g., Lindauer, 1961). Compelling evidence indicates that the waggle dance is embedded in a series of communication systems that enables the colony to coordinate the activity of its members during foraging and nest-site selection (e.g., Seeley, 1995). Hence dancing honeybees have their own spectators. The colony members that keep close contact with a dancing bee, usually called dance followers or recruits, appear to detect a variety of signals emitted by the dancer and process them in such a way that their ensuing behaviors may greatly vary due to the content of these signals (von Frisch, 1967). Nevertheless, the way in which the followers detect the dance signals is not yet well understood, but the diversity of these signals indicates that multiple sensory modalities are involved in dance communication (Michelsen, 1999). Mechanical stimuli derived from the body contacts between dancers and followers are certainly involved, as well as environmental chemical cues brought into the colony by the dancers, and most likely also semiochemicals coupled to the dancer's wagging movements. Three-dimensional fields of air currents surrounding the body of the dancing bees and substrate-borne vibrations caused by the wagging movements of the abdomen also seem to play a role in dance communication (Esch, 1961; Wenner, 1962; von Frisch, 1967; Michelsen et al., 1987, 1992; Bozic and Valentincic, 1991; Kirchner and Towne, 1994; Tautz, 1996; Rohrseitz and Tautz, 1999). In addition to these external stimuli, propioceptive signals enable both dancers and followers to process mechanosensory information derived from the position of their body relative to the direction of gravity (von Frisch, 1967). Because the dance in *Apis mellifera* takes place on the vertical surface of the comb, the dancers have to transfer visual information gathered during their foraging flights to a reference system primarily defined by mechanosensory stimulation, a process called transposition also found in other insects (von Frisch, 1967). We shall focus on a few selected features of the waggle dance because they illustrate how learning may be involved in this form of social communication and also pose the question of how space is represented in the honeybee brain. Obviously, both sides of the communication process, those from dancers and followers, must be taken into account if one is to understand what a successful follower actually learns from a dancing bee and how it combines the information available via the dance signals with that of its own spatial memory.

In the waggle dance (von Frisch, 1946, 1948, 1967), the dancer moves forward on the comb surface while moving its abdomen from side to side at about 15 times per second. This straight portion of the dance is called waggle-run. Without interruption, it then moves in a semicircular trajectory and returns to the starting point of its recent waggle-run; this portion is called return-phase. Once at this position, it repeats the forward, wagging portion of the dance. The dancer also tends to alternate clockwise and counterclockwise throughout successive return-phases. The followers tend to approach the dancer's body during the return-phase, which indirectly restricts the area on the comb in which the dance takes place, and if they begin following the dance maneuvers, their movements during a given return-phase will determine their subsequent position with respect to the dancer's body during the following waggle-run. Moreover, during the return-phase, dancers and followers interact repeatedly with their antennae and mouthparts, allowing mutual stimulation through chemical and mechanical signals. Finally, consecutive waggle-runs are performed with some directional scatter, which decreases when the distance to the indicated goal increases.

A major feature of the dance is that it can be triggered by different constellations of external stimuli, thereby conveying information about different types of goals. Honeybees dance for desirable sources of nectar and pollen (von Frisch, 1967), thus improving the colony's food collection (Sherman and Visscher, 2002), and also for water, essential to downregulate the nest's temperature when the hive gets overheated (Lindauer, 1954). This undoubtedly speaks about how versatile the dance communication system is. But perhaps the most striking example of this versatility relies on its role during swarming (Lindauer, 1951, 1953, 1955). Upon leaving their old nest during a colony's seasonal division, honeybees rely on a complex group decision-making process for selecting a new nest site. Their ultimate success depends on an accurate, fast, and unified collective decision (Seeley and Visscher, 2004). During this process, numerous colony members locate and dance on the surface of the swarm for potential nest sites. The decision process thus relies on several

groups of dancers indicating different sites and recruiting uncommitted bees to follow their own dancing; most of the swarm's members remain in place until all dancers achieve unanimity by indicating the same goal, then the swarm lifts off (Seeley and Visscher, 2004).

The number of dancing events varies across dances, thereby revealing the regulatory responses and amplification phenomena that operate on the signal production side of the communication process. The strength of the dance depends on the flow rate (Núñez, 1970) and sugar content (von Frisch, 1967) of the nectar that the dancers bring into the colony; the flown distance (Seeley, 1986) and the nature of the indicated goal, that is, either a nest site or a food source (Seeley and Buhrman, 2001); the colony's nectar influx (Lindauer, 1948; Núñez, 1970; Seeley, 1995; De Marco, 2006); the dancer's past foraging experience (Raveret-Richter and Waddington, 1993; De Marco and Farina, 2001; De Marco et al., 2005); and even weather conditions (Lindauer, 1948; Boch, 1956). Honeybees also adjust the rate of waggle-run production by modifying the duration of the return-phase based on specific properties of the indicated goal (Seeley et al., 2000; Seeley and Buhrman, 2001) and by means of signals derived from their interactions with their fellow mates (Lindauer, 1948, 1954; Núñez, 1970; Seeley, 1986; De Marco, 2006) and time-based cues coupled to the current foraging status of the colony as a whole (Lindauer, 1948, 1954; Seeley, 1995). These relations enable the dance communication system to be tuned according to both colony demands and availability of resource opportunities.

1.25.2.2.4   What is the information content of the honeybee waggle dance?

So far, we have briefly described the waggle dance as an intriguing example of multisensory convergence, central processing, and motor coordination. We shall now focus on how it relates to navigation. Flying bees are able to use the sun as a reference to maintain a course, a mechanism referred to as the sun-compass (von Frisch, 1967), and also recognize the sun's azimuth by the pattern of polarized light in the blue sky (von Frisch, 1949, 1967; Rossel and Wehner, 1984). They also compensate for the sun's time-dependent movement, even when neither the sun nor the pattern of polarized light is visible (Lindauer 1957, 1959). For this task to be accomplished, they must learn the sun's azimuth as a function of the time of the day during their initial orientation flights (Dyer and Dickinson, 1996).

A waggle dance encodes the direction and distance of a goal. First, the average orientation of the successive waggle-runs relative to the direction of gravity approximates the angle between the direction toward the goal and toward the sun (von Frisch, 1949, 1967; Lindauer, 1963). Second, the average length of the waggle-runs increases together with the distance from the hive to the goal (von Frisch and Jander, 1957). Early studies suggested that a honeybee's estimate of the flight length depends on gauging the amount of energy expended while flying (Heran, 1956; Scholze et al., 1964). Cumulating evidence now suggests that honeybees gauge and control the distance that they travel by integrating self-induced optic flow during flight (i.e., the net amount of image motion over the retina accumulated during movement) (Esch et al., 1994; Esch and Burns, 1996; Srinivasan et al., 1996, 2000; Tautz et al., 2004; De Marco and Menzel, 2005). The functioning of this mechanism is not yet fully understood, but it seems to depend on flight height and initial calibration based on landscape features (Esch and Burns, 1996; Esch et al., 2001). These two correlations convey to a human observer the circular coordinates of specific locations in a two-dimensional space and also provide a direct access into the dancer's perceptual world.

Evidence indicates that some of the followers that keep close contact with a dancing bee subsequently fly the approximate direction and distance that the dance conveys to the researcher (Lindauer, 1967; Esch and Bastian, 1970; Gould, 1975; Judd, 1995; Riley et al., 2005). They also use additional cues (i.e., semiochemicals and visual cues provided by other colony members, as well as environmental odors) to pinpoint the location of the targeted goal (e.g., von Frisch, 1967; Tautz and Sandeman, 2002). Six decades after von Frisch's (1946) original discovery, however, the process of decoding information in the dance still remains obscure (Michelsen, 1999). Some reasons are probably to be found in the striking variability of the multiple dance signals (e.g., von Frisch and Lindauer, 1961; Esch, 1978), the rather suboptimal methods that have been used so far to record the movements of both dancers and followers, and the lack of suitable tools to track the behavior of the followers after they depart from the hive. Improvements arise along with new methods (see the following discussion).

However, it is also worthwhile to consider a general aspect of the dance communication system that has received little attention, namely, the interaction between two different sources of spatial information that the followers might be able to access simultaneously: (1) the actual dance signals and (2) their own spatial memory store, as derived from their previous flights and reward experience; we shall refer to this putative store as the animal's spatial knowledge. The interaction between these two sources of information refers to a fundamental question in any process of communication. Communication depends on reproducing at one point an abstract entity selected at and sent from another point, but the entity that is finally reproduced on the receiver's side also depends on stored variants of this entity, which the receiver computes together with the signals it receives from the sender. In other words, one needs to ask whether a follower recollects stored information while decoding information in the dance.

The extent to which individual honeybees are exposed to the waggle dance throughout their foraging life has been addressed only recently (Biesmeijer and Seeley, 2005). In their study, Biesmeijer and Seeley (2005) reported that no more than a quarter of an average bee's lifetime field excursions was preceded by dance following, and in most of the instances in which the bees did follow dances before resuming their field excursions, they did so by following those that appeared to be indicating the goals that they were already familiar with. These findings are in close agreement with previous results by von Frisch (1968), who reported that the followers' response to the dance depends on their background of experience with the indicated goal, and that dances for familiar goals lead to more effective recruitment. Biesmeijer and Seeley (2005) also reported that the honeybees with field experience followed an average of only two to four dance circuits before resuming their new flights to the target. This small number of dance circuits provides spatial information only roughly to a human observer (**Figure 1**) and poses the question how informative this sample can be to the followers (Haldane and Spurway, 1954). Taken together, the results of this study suggest that the most advantageous functioning of the dance communication system will depend not only on the dancer's ability to keep record and derive spatial features of its recent field excursion, but also on the follower's ability to acquire, store, and recall specific navigational memories in the dance context (Menzel et al., 2006).

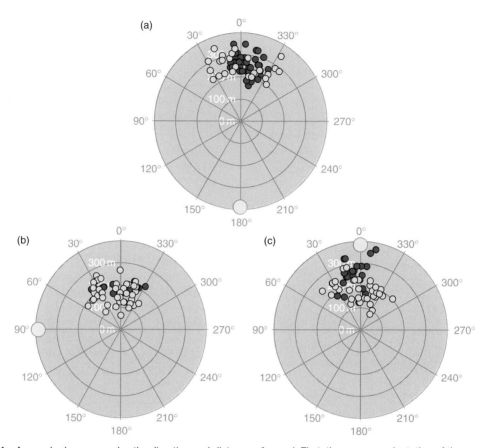

Figure 1 A waggle dance encodes the direction and distance of a goal: First, the average orientation of the successive waggle-runs relative to the direction of gravity approximates the angle between the directions toward the goal and toward the sun. Second, the average length of the waggle-runs increases together with the distance from the hive to the goal. These two correlations convey to a human observer the circular coordinates of specific locations in a two-dimensional space. The figure depicts radial maps indicating vectors' endpoints (in yellow and red) from waggle-runs performed by two dancing bees during single dances. These bees foraged regularly on a feeder placed 225 m west of an observation hive (52° 27′ 25″ N, 13° 17′ 46″ E) whose entrance pointed toward the north. In the radial maps, the direction of the feeder corresponds to 0°. Dances were video-recorded (at 88 frames s^{-1}) on the same day, in the morning (a), and the early (b) and late (c) afternoon, meaning that the sun (indicated by a yellow circle) was behind (a), to the side (b), or in front of the bees (c) during their flights toward the feeder, respectively. The coordinates indicated by the single waggle-runs are widely scattered around the actual position of the goal.

But is there any indication of some form of persisting spatial memory available to transitorily uncommitted honeybees (either dancers or followers)? Sometimes the waggle dance occurs in the absence of foraging. Under these conditions, it is performed in accordance with the current position of the sun and without any view of the sky, even during the night. These dances encode spatial information about goals that the dancers would have visited if they were guided by their sense of time (Lindauer, 1957, 1960; von Frisch, 1967). Furthermore, dancers seem to recall information related to goals visited several weeks earlier and

estimate, at night, the closest goal in time after being trained to two different feeding places at two different times during the day (von Frisch, 1967). It follows, therefore, that honeybees use persisting memories to control their dances, which can be retrieved by specific stimuli (e.g., odors associated with the prospective goal) and whose content is appropriately combined with the time of day and complexes of signals that determine the animal's overall motivational state. The retrieval of long-term spatial memories has been observed in navigating bees (e.g., Menzel et al., 1998, 2000), but its appropriate incorporation into the dance context poses additional questions. One of these questions is whether the waggle dance conveys to a follower only the approximate direction of and distance to the goal, or whether it also encodes a constellation of signals embedded in the follower's spatial knowledge, built throughout its previous flights and organized by reference to topographical features of the hive's surroundings. The structure of the spatial memory in honeybees will be addressed in the section titled 'Memory Structure'; we shall see that there is convincing evidence indicating that navigating bees may benefit from a topological representation of the environment, or a maplike spatial memory. It is thus conceivable that if honeybees are able to store spatial memories linked to specific locations in the field, and perhaps memories on specific features of their targets (e.g., food availability at a certain time of the day), the dance followers might also be able to combine information available through the dance with information from their own spatial memory, either already associated with the goals being indicated or in spatial relation to landmarks embedded in the seemingly topological structure of their spatial memory. What kind of spatial memory may be necessary for the waggle dance to encode information on past goals? How do these memories develop throughout the dancer's foraging life? These questions refer to the cognitive complexity underlying dance communication in honeybees. Future research on dance communication will certainly profit from the analysis of the interplay between the process of encoding and decoding spatial information in the dance and the structure and content of the honeybees' spatial memory.

1.25.3 Navigation

The term navigation denotes an animal's ability to efficiently travel between at least two specific distributions of concurrent signals (locations), even without having sensory access to the signals that define its targeted location. This notion removes any reference to the sensory modalities involved in gauging compass directions and distances and the control of the motor programs underlying the subject's locomotion. For the location to be reached, therefore, a navigating subject must be able to detect whether or not the immediate distribution of signals available within its current sensory horizon corresponds to the location it has been traveling to, a process that, in principle, only depends on innately

stored information and programmed responses. In most animal species, however, survival involves moving regularly from and to several locations. It follows that to cope with such a complex navigational task, the single distributions of signals defining these locations (available from either idiothetic or allothetic sources or from both) must be stored in specific forms of persistent memories. Differences in the content and the organization of these complexes of memories may arise as long as task complexity varies across taxa.

1.25.3.1 Typology

Different classification schemes are used in the analysis of spatial behavior. Kühn's (1919) attempt to conceptualize orientation mechanisms on the basis of the relationship between sensory stimuli and an animal's response to them is an early example of these schemes. In recent decades, research on spatial behavior has also nurtured the development of biologically inspired artificial navigation systems. This gave researchers an opportunity to classify several theoretical accounts of spatial behavior within a single unifying framework centered on the structure and content of the information used by the navigating agents. The ensuing classification schemes are based on task complexity and experimentally tested features of an agent's spatial behavior (Trullier et al., 1997; Franz and Mallot, 2000); they tend to be purposely broad, ignore endogenously coordinated performances, and dissect complex behaviors found in nature into motor programs that can be reliably implemented in artificial systems. Although somewhat crude, these typologies provide a suitable basis for analyzing basic strategies of spatial behavior, feature detectors, and navigation learning. Their most salient characteristic is that they account for complex navigational tasks by means of hierarchically organized, interacting strategies. For example, Trullier et al. (1997) conceive taxes (Kühn, 1919; Fraenkel and Gunn, 1961) as the basic machinery of all navigating agents and then distinguish between local navigation and way-finding. Local navigation accounts for orientation in the immediate environment, where the agent acts based on information available within its perceptual range, whereas way-finding involves moving in a large-scale environment, where relevant cues lie beyond the perception range, and the goal is not in the immediate environment. Technically speaking, each of these categories can still be divided into several levels: search, direction-following, aiming and guidance for local navigation, and recognition-triggered responses, topological, and survey navigation for way-finding (Franz and Mallot, 2000). Due to their hierarchical organization, way-finding relies on local navigation, but it is not yet clear how these strategies may interact in the brain, or how animals recognize specific locations, let alone how they may assign specific identities to these locations, a prerequisite of some high-level navigational tasks. Evidence indicates, however, that a hierarchical array of seemingly different, interacting strategies underlies the spatial behavior of some species of navigating insects (Wehner et al., 1996; Menzel et al., 2005). In the present context, we will use this basic typology to survey the structure and content of the spatial memory used by desert ants and honeybees, because data from these two navigating insects are frequently discussed using different terminologies and approached from different conceptual frameworks.

1.25.3.2   Navigation in Desert Ants

Desert ants of the genus *Cataglyphis* live in subterranean nests surrounded by relatively flat and featureless areas. They forage individually and travel over distances of hundreds of meters along circuitous paths during their foraging excursions. After grasping a food item, they quickly return in a straight line to the proximity of the starting point of their journey, where they finally break off their homeward runs and start a systematic search aimed at pinpointing the entrance of the nest; avoiding overheating is crucial in their environment. These ants primarily benefit from path integration (Mittelstaedt and Mittelstaedt, 1980), also referred as to dead-reckoning (*See* Chapter 1.12), to accomplish their remarkable homing performances (Wehner, 1992; Collett and Collett, 2000). This means that a navigating ant iteratively computes all its rotational and translational motion components, integrating them into a sort of global vector (Wehner, 2003) that connects, at any time, its current location and that of the starting point of the excursion. This navigation strategy can easily be revealed by displacing the animal over some distance; after being released, it chooses a compass direction and walks an approximate distance that brings it to a predictable, virtual reference point (Pièron, 1904; Santschi, 1911).

Desert ants appear to inexorably compute this type of vectorial information and are incapable of using more than one vector simultaneously. They benefit from inverse forms of these home vectors and efficiently move from the nest to previously visited field locations. Global vectors also appear to be stored and recalled in accordance with specific contexts, meaning, for instance, that when a returned ant is moved back to a recently visited location, it does not apply its recent home vector to once again navigate its way to the nest. Instead, it uses a systematic, time-consuming search strategy to find the nest's entrance (unless it navigates in familiar terrain offering conspicuous landmarks, as we will see). Under these circumstances, however, the information about its recent home vector does not disappear, and the ant is able to subsequently use an inverse form of it to quickly find its way to the previously visited location. This indicates, in turn, that path integration information is transferred from some form of working memory into a different, more persisting memory stage, from which it can be later recalled on the basis of context-dependent signals (Wehner, 2003).

In order to use path integration, a desert ant must be able to align its trajectory with a locally available compass direction and to reliably acquire distance information. *Cataglyphis* ants do not acquire directional information by means of idiothetic sources, such as an inertial compass or proprioceptive signals; they do it using a celestial compass based on a specialized set of polarization-sensitive ultraviolet receptors located within a particular portion of the retina (Wehner, 1994, 1997), which detect the pattern of polarized light in the blue sky (Wehner and Müller, 2006). The functioning of this celestial compass involves an internal ephemeris function (Wehner and Müller, 1993) and demands recalibrations due to the inexorable changes in the pattern of polarized skylight that take place during the day. Desert ants do use idiothetic sources to compute translational motion: Distance information appears to be gauged by means of a step integrator (Wittlinger et al., 2006), and the control of distance by self-induced optic flow seems to be only slightly modified under specific test procedures (Ronacher and Wehner, 1995). These two path-related components – distances and directions – are combined via some sort of accumulator, the state of which encodes the ant's current coordinates relative to the reference point. The task of surveying the possible computational boundaries of this hardwired accumulator lies beyond the scope of this chapter (for comprehensive accounts of this issue, see Wehner 1997, 1999, 2003). In the present context, let us simply say that its functioning directly depends on locomotion (Seidl et al., 2006), that it must process distance and compass information simultaneously (Sommer and Wehner, 2004), and that it allows an ant to gauge the ground distance while traveling undulating paths (Wohlgemuth et al., 2001; Grah et al., 2005). Its output can also be combined with external, sensory cues, thereby reducing search costs and improving the ants' general foraging strategy (Wolf and Wehner, 2000, 2005). This accumulator or path integrator also appears to continuously process information, that is, when homing ants are captured at the nest's entrance and displaced several times in a row to the initial position of their homeward runs, they move away from their reference location (the proximity of a virtual nest) when transferred to a featureless test channel (Andel and Wehner, 2004).

The findings described earlier illustrate how path integration, a basic local navigation strategy, enables *Cataglyphis* ants to reliably find the proximity of a virtual nest in unfamiliar terrain. Things are different in familiar terrain, however. The use of landmark-based information improves the efficiency of an ant's path integrator because the number of inaccurate alignments increases together with the length of the animal's excursion (Wehner and Wehner, 1986). Due to these unavoidable computational errors, a cross talk between path integration and guidance decreases the chance of missing the goal (Collett and Collett, 2000). Provided with an irregular environment, homing ants use landmarks while on their way to the nest's immediate surroundings (Bregy and Wehner, 2003; Knaden and Wehner, 2005), thus following well-defined paths or routes (Collett et al., 1992; Wehner et al., 1996; Kohler and Wehner, 2005). Moreover, it has recently been shown that they can also use memories of minute ground features to pinpoint the entrance of the nest (Seidl and Wehner, 2006). Guidance, therefore, leads navigating ants to locations where they have acquired a certain egocentric relationship with respect to a specific configuration of external signals (Wehner et al., 1996; Collett and Collett, 2000). They thus take advantage of a store of reliable landmark-based memories, which can be associated with specific motor routines and recalled in the appropriate context, and exhibit goal-directed movements at different locations (Collett et al., 1998; Collett and Collett, 2000, 2002; Åkesson and Wehner, 2002). Research on other ant species (e.g., Jander, 1957; Graham and Collett, 2002; Wehner et al., 2006) also provides evidence of local navigation and even more complex navigation strategies based on (1) the recognition of a

catchment area from which a configuration of landmarks is perceived to be identical, (2) successful orientation within this area, and (3) the subsequent selection of a goal-directed movement. These strategies, therefore, rely on the combination of several recognizable areas associated with specific goals and directed actions (Barto and Sutton, 1981; Trullier et al., 1997; Collett and Collett, 2000).

The study of navigation in desert ants has led to a remarkable understanding of the basic mechanisms that these animals use for setting a directional bearing in the field (Wehner, 2003). Experience-dependent behavioral flexibility is conceived as a calibration process of path integration computations. Next, a context-dependent recollection of path integration coordinates may eventually lead to the ants' seemingly idiosyncratic routes. Landmarks provide information about turns to make and distances to travel next (Collett, 1996, 1998; Collett and Collett, 2000; Kohler and Wehner, 2005), such that seemingly complex performances might be based on simple rules that depend on learning sensory-motor routines. This is frequently referred to as procedural learning. Traditional thinking on ant navigation therefore conceives a toolbox of sensorimotor routines, whose stepwise application enables the animals to solve seemingly complex navigational tasks. Moreover, the recollection of single vectors does not require an overall representation of multiple locations, and the selection of goal-directed actions may exclusively depend on innately stored, calibrating information. This corresponds to the fact that ants do not appear to make decisions involving equivalent options. The question remains how ants use external signals to map several recognizable places. None of the current approaches to navigation in several ant species has yet reached the level of analysis achieved in the study of homing by desert ants, let alone the principles of navigation learning in walking insects.

Honeybees also exhibit procedural learning. They learn to negotiate complex mazes of adjacent boxes by associating colored disks with right or left turns, for example (Zhang et al., 2000; Srinivasan and Zhang, 2004), and also refer to compass directions in their dances on overcast days (von Frisch, 1967; Dyer and Gould, 1981). The latter result reveals that landmarks serve as a backup system, which conveys direction information to navigating bees and poses the question of how external signals are actually incorporated into the bees' representation of space (Gallistel, 1990). Interpretations from the study of ant navigation have often been transferred to bees. In contrast to ants, however, bees fly over distances of a few kilometers, cruising well aboveground; they also use depth information extracted from motion parallax (Lehrer, 1996) and learn about the absolute size of landmarks (Horridge et al., 1992). Furthermore, honeybee foraging behavior involves a remarkable diversity of responses, including those underlying cooperative work during food gathering (see earlier discussion). When an experienced worker forages on a given flower species, for example, it leaves the colony and flies toward its targeted location for a certain amount of time, without interrupting its flight even when alternative flowers of the same species might be within reach. Once this motor program is extinguished, it begins searching for the flowers it recognizes according to their odors, colors, and shapes and inspects them by means of specific motor commands that allow it to efficiently find and collect the offered nectar (von Frisch, 1967). Meanwhile, it adjusts its estimate of how much nectar ought to be collected (Núñez, 1966). Finally, it initiates its return flight to the hive. Although exaggeratedly simplistic, this scheme illustrates an intriguing feature of the honeybee foraging strategy: each animal leaves the colony with a large – and diverse – amount of information, which is used in context-specific ways and involves expected outcomes of particular behaviors. The contexts are defined by both time and space, a fact that becomes strikingly evident when bees forage on multiple locations throughout the same day. Furthermore, there is a cross talk between navigation and collective foraging (see earlier discussion), which involves specific responses to numerous features and dynamic components of the animal's sensory world. As we shall see next, the repertoire of navigational performances in honeybees is far from simple. Together with complex modulatory processes, learning is at the heart of the animals' navigation skills.

1.25.3.3 Navigation in Honeybees

Foraging honeybees usually follow straight flight trajectories between specific locations and the hive (Beutler, 1954; von Frisch, 1967). If they are caught at the moment they depart from the hive and then released at a different spot in the field, they fly in the direction they would have taken if they had not been moved to the release site, meaning that they fly in the correct compass direction but along a false route relative to the goal they were originally traveling to. They perform in a similar manner when

caught at the beginning of their homeward flight. Once again, they fly in the predisplacement compass direction which might have connected their foraging location and the hive, but along a false route with respect to the actual location of the colony (Wolf, 1927; Menzel et al., 2005). The bees' flown distances and compass bearings in this type of experiment resemble the global vectors observed in desert ants (see the section titled 'Navigation in desert ants'), supporting the view that honeybees also use vector memories that develop through their regular flights. Furthermore, when bees arriving at a foraging spot are held captive for several hours, they subsequently fly farther outward from the hive along the same hive-target direction (Dyer et al., 2002). After being trained along a fixed route, therefore, vector memories will reliably guide honeybees back to the hive and toward specific field locations; unless they have been artificially displaced.

In fact, navigation research in flying hymenoptera has long been based on displacement experiments and the analysis of the animals' homing abilities (Tinbergen and Kruyt, 1938; Thorpe, 1950; von Frisch, 1967; Tinbergen, 1972; Menzel et al., 2000, 2005). If navigating bees only rely on global vectors and random searches, displaced foragers might have trouble rapidly finding their way back to the colony. They do return home when released at a new, unexpected location, however, and they do it reliably and relatively fast when released within the range of approximately 1 km from the hive (Capaldi and Dyer, 1999; Menzel et al., 2000). Consider the following experiment: One group of bees was trained to forage on a stationary feeder placed 300 m away from the hive, and another group was trained to forage on a close feeder that rotated around the hive at a constant radius of only 10 m. Hence, the foragers from the latter group had not experienced a flight vector connecting the hive and a fixed, distant foraging location. However, despite lacking this experience, they returned home equally well from various possible directions and as quickly as the animals from the former group, which had experienced a predisplacement route training (Menzel et al., 2000). Furthermore, the results of this experiment could not be explained by reference to local navigation strategies, due to the lack of landmarks in the vicinity of the hive and the actual distance to the different released sites (Menzel et al., 2000). This indicates that successful homing in honeybees does not necessarily depend on a random, time-consuming search strategy. Recently, radar traces of the full flight trajectories of displaced honeybees revealed that the last phase of homing is eventually accomplished by straight, goal-directed flights toward the hive (Menzel et al., 2005), supporting the view that honeybees are able to store and retrieve allocentric cues that help in defining compass directions in the field (Menzel et al., 1998).

The results described, in addition, pose the question of how the forager's working memory is organized and what role its content actually plays during navigation. Path integration is the subject of computational errors (Benhamou et al., 1990) and controls navigation as long as the animal combines it with multiple environmental cues. It is therefore reasonable to ask how landmarks provide honeybees with a basis for accurate homing. The complexity underlying such a strategy still remains open. How does it rely on guidance? How many configurations of landmarks can be processed and stored? How much does the animal perceive about these configurations, and how does it relate them? Are sequentially learned configurations generalized in such a way that they can be categorized, or counted, or even embedded into a more general, combined representation of space (Menzel et al., 2006; *see also* Chapter 1.12)? These questions are also at the heart of a long-lasting controversy (Wehner and Menzel, 1990), namely, whether navigating insects have at their disposal only minimal cognitive modules enabling them to store and retrieve ordered sequences of context-dependent actions (Wehner, 1999), or whether they also store and retrieve relations among points, lines, and surfaces somehow embedded in an internal representation of space (Menzel et al., 2006; *see also* Chapter 1.12 for a detailed account of this issue). Answering these questions, however, would only be possible after revealing the mechanisms underlying what we now merely label as specific responses to specific configurations of external signals, such as the response of a navigating bee to a familiar visual scene. Consider the term snapshot (Cartwright and Collett, 1983), for example; it denotes an insect's memory of visual landmarks, and it helps in formulating hypotheses based on matching algorithms and behavioral data, but its neurobiological basis is yet to be established. Similarly, we simply do not know how multiple and complex procedures might be combined in a common spatial memory store.

One of the reasons that led to differences in conceptualizing navigation in flying insects lies in the fact that most experiments were performed with animals trained along fixed, predisplacement routes and subsequently observed only during their initial postdisplacement flight paths. Most likely, only the motor routines based on the actual content of the animals' working memory can be revealed in this manner. The bees' exploration of the environment, however, does not begin with flights along fixed routes, which develop relatively late in the animals' foraging careers, and it is the spatial memory that develops during the bees' exploratory flights that might supply the animals with information for successful homing when vector memories fail. Therefore, an important aspect related to the questions listed earlier might be at stake – how spatial behavior develops.

Honeybees begin foraging only after executing a series of exploratory flights of increasing lengths (Becker, 1958; Vollbehr, 1975; Winston, 1987; Capaldi and Dyer, 1999), normally on several consecutive days (von Frisch, 1967). Using harmonic radar, Capaldi et al. (2000) showed that when honeybees are engaged in these exploratory flights, they keep the trip duration constant, but fly faster with increased experience of the terrain, so that the later flights cover a larger area than the earlier flights. Each flight, in addition, is typically restricted to a well-defined, narrow sector around the hive, and changes in this respect appear to be related to the number of previous flights. Taken together, these results indicate that early flights provide honeybees with repeated opportunities to become exposed to different landscape features (including the hive's position) from different viewpoints, supporting the view that they may store landscape information in a progressive fashion (Capaldi et al., 2000). At the individual level, however, the ontogeny of these flights remains a mystery, and the question of how the animals use information available throughout successive flights is still unanswered.

Tracing the full flight trajectories of free-flying bees allows evaluation of the complexity of the animals' spatial memory, and this is now possible using harmonic radar techniques (Riley et al., 1996). Menzel (2005) and colleagues recorded more than 200 flight trajectories in this manner (Menzel et al., 2005) and analyzed the flight paths of three different groups of animals: (1) honeybees that had been trained to forage on a stationary feeder located 200 m east of the hive, thereby repeatedly following a well-defined predisplacement route; we shall call them SF-bees; (2) honeybees trained to forage on a feeder that circled around the hive within a distance of 10 m, thereby experiencing no route prior to displacement; here we call them VF-bees; and (3) honeybees that lacked training and had closely followed a waggle dance for the feeder placed 200 m east of the hive; we shall call these bees R-bees. Three phases of navigation can be distinguished among these groups of honeybees (Menzel et al., 2005): (1) vector flights, (2) circuitous flights, and (3) straight homeward flights. Vector flights were apparent in the SF- and R-bees, but not in VF-bees. Those from SF-bees showed compass directions and distances that matched the predisplacement route, and those from R-bees matched the spatial information that the waggle dances conveyed to a human observer (Riley et al., 2005). Hence, it follows that, when accessible, route memories are invariably applied first, and vector flights are based on directions and distances from these memories. The circuitous flights showed multiple returns to the release site and to the end of the vector flights in the case of SF- and R-bees. During this phase, the flight speed was significantly lower than during phases of straight flights. These flights were also considerably longer for the SF- and VF-bees (carrying full crops) and shorter for R-bees (captured before getting in contact with any sugar reward), suggesting that this type of motion might not only underlie a process of reorientation (necessary after displacement), but also some sort of exploratory behavior (Menzel et al., 2005).

The honeybees from all these three groups returned to the hive by means of fast, straight homeward flights, and a detailed analysis of the straightness of these flights led to a clear distinction between the second and third navigation phases, thereby revealing the field locations where the straight homeward flights began (Menzel et al., 2005). They originated along different directions relative to the hive's position and usually began far outside a radius of 60 m, where the animals might have used visual cues to find their way back to the colony by means of aiming or guidance or both. Furthermore, they also began at locations with conspicuous, artificial landmarks, and when these landmarks were either displaced or removed, the animals were equally successful during homing. The most consistent hypothesis that accounts for these homing performances is that the ground structure itself provided the displaced honeybees with reliable information to find their way back to the hive (Menzel et al., 2000, 2005). Most significant is this: A third of the SF-bees made straight and fast flights directed not only to the hive but also first to the feeder and then to the hive (**Figure 2**). This latter result fits well with a

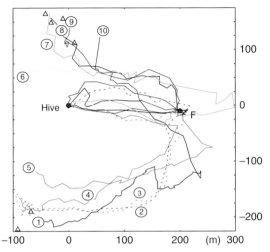

Figure 2   The homing flights via the feeder. Ten SF-bees (of the 29 bees tested under similar conditions) performed their homing flights via the feeder. Bees released south of the hive are shown by flight paths 1–5, and those released north of the hive are indicated by flight paths 6–10. The bee from flight path 4 landed at the feeder and flew to the hive after filling its crop. All bees were tested with the normal arrangement of tents under sunny weather conditions (for details see Menzel R, Greggers U, Smith A, et al. (2005) Honeybees navigate according to a map-like spatial memory. *Proc. Natl. Acad. Sci. USA* 102: 3040–3045).

topological representation of the environment (Trullier et al., 1997) and can also be explained by two mutually related hypotheses. First, homing bees might be able to integrate at least two vector memories. Assume the following premises: (I) they are able to associate vector memories defining homeward flights with specific configurations of external signals, and (II) when exposed to these signals, the corresponding vector memories can be recollected from a memory store. Next, if two of these memories are simultaneously recollected and transferred to the animal's active working memory, they might be combined to steer a seemingly new flight trajectory. The second hypothesis can be thought of as a more complex form of the first one. It assumes that the bees' orientation flights, together with their initial foraging excursions, lead to a memory of a network of several homeward vectors connecting specific distributions of external signals, including the hive's location. Such a process is believed to be possible in mammals and birds (Gallistel, 1989; O'Keefe and Nadel, 1978).

These concepts are closely interconnected to several issues about the honeybee dance communication system, somehow embedded in the following question: Do dancers and followers have analogous memories? When von Frisch (1967) compelled honeybees to fly a two-legged detour path to reach an artificial feeder, the trained animals indicated in their dances the direction of a straight line toward the goal. They might have computed this compass direction from the two legs of the detour, but they also indicated the actual flown distance, and not the distance of the segment connecting the feeder and the hive. Thus the bees encoded in their dances the direction of a virtual flight vector, but not its length (von Frisch, 1967). This poses the question whether it is the outbound or the inbound flight or both that provides the dancer with the spatial information that is finally conveyed to the human observer. If spatial information available during the homeward flight (a directional bearing, for example) can successfully be incorporated into the dancer's maneuvers, the waggle dance might also be capable of conveying information that the dancer (and probably also a follower) has already linked to a specific spot in the field. It follows, therefore, that the efficiency of the dance communication system would greatly depend on the way in which both dancers and followers acquire, store, and retrieve navigational memories.

Behavioral studies of self-induced optic flow in honeybees (e.g., Srinivasan et al., 1997) take advantage of the following fact: Flying a short distance close to a surface gives the same integrated optic flow as flying a longer distance further from the surface. As a result, when honeybees fly through narrow tunnels with visually textured walls, they experience a subjectively flown distance that is greater than that actually flown (Srinivasan et al., 1996), also indicating a longer distance in their dances (Srinivasan et al., 2000). This allows manipulation of a bee's navigational experience of a subjective flight path (De Marco and Menzel, 2005). Honeybees perform longer waggle phases when they fly through a visually patterned tunnel on their outbound flight (Figure 3(a)–(c)). Thus, when the tunnel is set perpendicular to the straight line connecting its entrance and that of the hive, a mismatch arises between the animals' estimate of the goal's location (derived from path integration information from the outbound flight) and its actual location in the field. Under such conditions, the bees' waggle dances indicate a direction close to that of the straight line connecting the hive and the actual goal's location (Figure 3(d)–(i)), and the virtual detour has no significant effect on

the duration of the bees' homeward flights, indicating that they fly directly back to the hive after leaving the tunnel through its far end. Moreover, path integration coordinates appear to be more strongly weighted in the dance maneuvers only with increasing experience of the terrain (Figure 3(j)–(l)), thus supporting previous interpretations (Otto, 1959; Edrich and Scheske, 1988) of the relationship between information available on-site and the encoding of direction in the dance. These results indicate that (1) a discrepancy between subjective measures of distances and directions and path integration coordinates already linked to visual scenes has no significant effect on the triggering of the waggle dance, and (2) the process of encoding spatial information in the dance involves detecting and processing such a discrepancy (De Marco and Menzel, 2005). It is not yet clear to what degree honeybees might refer in their dances to the inbound component of their journeys, or whether they embed the encoding spatial information in the dance into their maplike spatial memory.

1.25.3.3.1 Memory structure

It appears that honeybees develop spatial memories in three different contexts: (1) during their initial orientation flights, (2) while flying repeatedly from and to a specific field location, and (3) while following dances. We refer to these memories as (1) the general landscape memory, (2) the route memory, and (3) the dance memory, respectively. Note that the term general landscape memory makes no assumptions about the structure of the spatial information accessible through it, and that route memories may involve vector memories as well as procedures based on sequences of context-dependent actions. This typology, therefore, denotes processes not yet understood, but accounts for predictable actions. These memories might have different properties. Route memories provide information about directions and distances, and the same may be true for a dance memory, although the extent to which the latter may be combined with spatial information accessible from the bees' memory store remains an open question. Honeybees seem to transfer these two memory forms into their active working memory and apply them first. Once applied, however, they lose their influence on behavior. The directional component of these memories, in addition, is susceptible to updates according to changes in the animal's motivation. When at least two route memories are accessible, it becomes feasible to recognize that they have been linked to landmark-based information.

This led to the concept that honeybees use their route memories to estimate the sun's azimuth (von Frisch, 1967; Dyer and Gould, 1981), and that they may integrate at least two of them under specific circumstances (Menzel et al., 1998, 2005). The general landscape memory might be thought of as a structure of several recognizable locations within the range of the animals' orientation flights. It might arise through the integration of information provided by two or more route memories (Menzel et al., 2005)

or by a process by which the bees innately store specific distributions of external signals and assign them specific identities based on idiothetic and allothetic cues. According to these hypotheses, honeybees may use their general landscape memory only when their active working memory has no access to route or dance memories.

The concept of multiple memories hierarchically organized is a generally accepted mind-set in neurosciences. Implicit and explicit knowledge, or

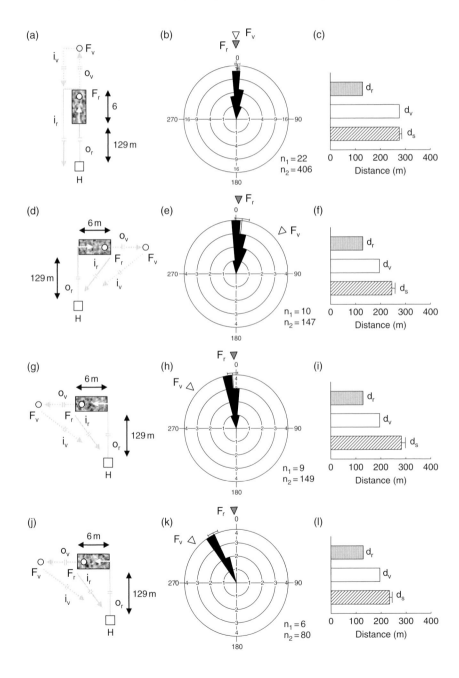

declarative and nondeclarative knowledge, develop from the various learning strategies, which involve various brain structures in mammals, including humans (Cohen and Squire, 1980; Packard and McGaugh, 1996; Schroeder et al., 2002; Chang and Gold, 2003). Navigation in mice and rats, intensively studied with respect to the role of the hippocampus and striatum, is actually embedded in a convincing theoretical framework, whereas hippocampal place cells are responsible for orientation based on specific distribution of signals and sequences of experiences that help in defining geometric relations among landmarks, and the striatum is responsible for those forms of learning based on signals sent by the goal (O'Keefe and Nadel, 1978; Moser and Paulsen, 2001; McNaughton et al., 2006; Witter and Moser, 2006). It might be interesting to evaluate whether and how the seemingly different navigational memories described earlier rely on the various neuronal structures in the bee brain. What can be behaviorally tested in the near future is whether dance memories are coupled to the general landscape memory.

1.25.3.4 Insect Migrations

Several insect orders exhibit far-distance movements referred to as migrations (Drake and Gatehouse,

1995). Populations of butterflies, moths, dragonflies, and locusts are seasonally engaged in far-distance migrations (e.g., Williams, 1958; Johnson, 1969; Holland et al., 2006). Costs and adaptations have long been addressed in migrating insects (e.g., Rankin and Burchsted, 1992), but the selective forces behind these movements are not yet fully understood. The distribution of offspring across a range of areas and conditions favorable for future reproduction might have played an important role in the evolutionary development of these movements (Wilson, 1995; Holland et al., 2006). At least two distinctive features of these far-distance movements distinguish them from the regular excursions of the central place (Orians and Pearson, 1979) foraging hymenopterans (i.e., bees, wasps, and ants). First, return migration has yet to be documented in insects (Holland et al., 2006), meaning that with a few exceptions (e.g., Urquhart and Urquhart, 1979), migrating individuals do not perform round-trip journeys that bring them into the areas from which they previously departed (Holland et al., 2006). In monarch butterflies, for example, several generations are produced during their northward migrations (Brower, 1995, 1996). Second, although migrating insects compensate for wind drift and maintain a heading using the sun compass (Srygley and Oliveira, 2001; Mouritsen

---

Figure 3 Experimental layout and results of an investigation of the encoding of spatial information in the waggle dance. A visually patterned tunnel was used to create a virtual detour. By compelling the bees to fly through such a tunnel, set up outdoors in various configurations, it is possible to add a virtual distance to the journey from the hive to the feeder – either straight ahead or to the right or left. Bees were trained to forage on a feeder placed at the far end of a 6-m-long, 30-cm-wide, and 30-cm-high tunnel. The tunnel's entrance was located 129 m away from the hive, and its walls and floor were decorated with a random visual pattern. (a) Experimental arrangements first had the tunnel oriented at 0° with respect to the direct line connecting its near entrance and the hive (h). The bees flew through the tunnel during their outbound flights (o_r) but not during their inbound flights (i_r). F_r and F_v correspond to the real and the virtual location of the feeder (white circle), respectively; whereas o_v and i_v correspond to the virtual outbound and inbound flights, respectively, as derived from the overestimated distance flown inside the tunnel. (b) Distribution of the individual mean directions signaled in the waggle dances recorded in the tunnel experiment described in (a), mean vector direction $\mu = 1.33°$, $r = 0.99$, $P < 0.001$, n_1 (number of animals analyzed) $= 22$, n_2 (number of waggle-runs analyzed) $= 406$. The frequencies within 10° class ranges are shown as the areas of the dark wedges. The dark spoke and segment indicate the mean vector μ and 95% confidence interval, respectively. The gray and white arrows indicate the directions toward the real (F_r) and the virtual (F_v) feeders shown in (a), respectively. (c) Shown are the flown distance (mean $\pm$ SE) signaled in the waggle dances recorded in the tunnel experiment described in (a) (d_s, striped bar), the distance to the virtual feeder (d_v, white bar, in this case equivalent to the signaled distance), and the real distance from the hive to the food site (d_r, gray bar). (d–f) Experimental arrangements and results as in (a–c) with the tunnel rotated 90° to the right. The distance flown inside the tunnel oriented at 0° (c) was used to compute the location to be signaled (F_v: direction and d_v: distance) if the global vector computed by the path integration of the outbound flight provides the dancers with the spatial information encoded in the waggle dance. In (e), mean vector direction $\mu = 6.77°$, $r = 0.98$, $P < 0.001$, $n_1 = 10$, $n_2 = 147$. (g–i) Experimental arrangements and results as in (d–f) with the tunnel rotated 90° to the left. In (h), mean vector direction $\mu = 356.1°$, $r = 0.99$, $P < 0.001$, $n_1 = 9$, $n_2 = 149$. (j–l) Experimental arrangements and results as in (g–i), obtained with the experienced bees. In (k), mean vector direction $\mu = 333.99°$, $r = 0.99$, $P < 0.001$, $n_1 = 6$, $n_2 = 80$. The reader will find a detailed description of this experiment in De Marco RJ and Menzel R (2005) Encoding spatial information in the waggle dance. *J. Exp. Biol.* 208: 3885–3894.

and Frost, 2002) and possibly also a magnetic compass (Etheredge et al., 1999), their flight routes depend strongly on atmospheric conditions and seasonal wind patterns (e.g., Rainey, 1951, 1976; Kanz, 1977; Drake and Farrow, 1988; Gatehouse, 1997; Chapman et al., 2002). It thus appears that insect migration is basically controlled by innate mechanisms and does not rely on learning, although the genetic control of flight direction in migrating insects has yet to be confirmed (Holland et al., 2006).

1.25.4 Conclusions and Future Prospects

We have argued that a distinction between instinctive and learned behaviors, a fundamental issue in behavioral research, is not possible without thoughtfully considering the interplay between an animal's possible phylogenetic boundaries and the sources of the external signals that belong to its specific sensory world, simply because the effects of learning on a subject's performance will always be superimposed onto those of its phylogenetic boundaries. We also claimed that it is in the context of communication and navigation that learning transcends elementary forms of association in particularly clear ways. Communication and navigation in insects have been extensively studied on the sensory processing level, but the structure and content of the spatial knowledge underlying such phenomena have yet to be addressed. This might be particularly feasible in honeybees, due to their extensive behavioral repertoire, which also seems to involve decisions, and their small, experimentally accessible brains, which allow the study of system-level neural correlates of learning and memory. In honeybees, in addition, these two behavioral domains appear strictly related to each other via the famous waggle dance, although their relation is not fully understood. We have explored new findings (Menzel et al., 2005) indicating that the spatial knowledge used by honeybees to navigate within the range of their orientation flights is much more complex than hitherto thought. Several interacting – and probably competing – memory systems seem to be at work. These findings also raise questions about the process of encoding and decoding information in the waggle dance (De Marco and Menzel, 2005). We reviewed published data (von Frisch, 1968) and recent evidence (Biesmeijer and Seeley, 2005) suggesting that the spatial knowledge available to followers is also involved in dance

communication and that learning might be at the heart of this impressive communicating system. The flight paths of navigating bees can now be traced with radar techniques. Mechanical models of dancing bees and virtual environments allowing navigation experiments under controlled experimental situations can also be developed. Thus tools are available to tackle these questions.

References

Åkesson S and Wehner R (2002) Visual navigation in desert ants *Cataglyphis fortis*: Are snapshots coupled to a celestial system of reference? *J. Exp. Biol.* 205: 1971–1978.

Andel D and Wehner R (2004) Path integration in desert ants, *Cataglyphis*: How to make a homing ant run away from home. *Proc. R. Soc. Lond. (B)* 1547: 1485–1489.

Barrows EM, Bell WJ, and Michener CD (1975) Individual odor differences and their social functions in insects. *Proc. Natl. Acad. Sci. USA* 72: 2824–2828.

Barto AG and Sutton RS (1981) Landmark learning: An illustration of associative search. *Biol. Cybern.* 42: 1–8.

Becker L (1958) Untersuchungen über das Heimwendevermögen der Bienen. *Z. Vergl. Physiol.* 41: 1–25.

Bell WJ (1974) Recognition of resident and non-resident individuals in intraspecific nest defence of a primitively eusocial Halictine bee. *J. Comp. Physiol.* 93: 173–181.

Benhamou S, Sauvé J-P, and Bovet P (1990) Spatial memory in large scale movements, efficiency and limitation of the egocentric coding process. *J. Theor. Biol.* 145: 1–12.

Beutler R (1954) Über die Flugweite der Bienen. *Z. Vergl. Physiol.* 36: 266–298.

Biesmeijer JC and Seeley TD (2005) The use of waggle dance information by honey bees throughout their foraging careers. *Behav. Ecol. Sociobiol.* 59: 133–142.

Billen J and Morgan ED (1998) Pheromone communication in social insects: Sources and secretions. In: Vander Meer RK, Breed MD, Espelie KE, and Winston ML (eds.) *Pheromone Communication in Social Insects*, pp. 3–33. Boulder, CO: Westview Press.

Boch R (1956) Die Tänze der Bienen bei nahen und fernen Trachtquellen. *Z. Vergl. Physiol.* 38: 136–167.

Bozic J and Valentincic T (1991) Attendants and followers of honeybee waggle dances. *J. Apicult. Res.* 30: 125–131.

Bozic J and Valentincic T (1995) Quantitative analysis of social grooming behavior of the honey bee *Apis mellifera carnica*. *Apidologie* 26: 141–147.

Bregy P and Wehner R (2003) Beacon versus vector navigation in homing ants *Cataglyphis fortis*. *Neurobiol. Conf.* 29: 574.

Brower LP (1995) Understanding and misunderstanding the migration of the monarch butterfly (*Nymphalidae*) in North America: 1857–1995 *J. Lepid. Soc.* 49: 304–385.

Brower LP (1996) Monarch butterfly orientation: Missing pieces of a magnificent puzzle. *J. Exp. Biol.* 199: 93–103.

Capaldi EA and Dyer FC (1999) The role of orientation flights on homing performance in honeybees. *J. Exp. Biol.* 202: 1655–1666.

Capaldi EA, Smith AD, Osborne JL, et al. (2000) Ontogeny of orientation flight in the honeybee revealed by harmonic radar. *Nature* 403: 537–540.

Carlin NF and Schwartz PH (1989) Pre-imaginal experience and nestmate brood recognition in the carpenter ant *Camponotus floridanus*. *Anim. Behav.* 38: 89–95.

Cartwright BA and Collett TS (1983) Landmark learning in bees: Experiments and models. *J. Comp. Physiol.* 151: 521–543.

Chang Q and Gold PE (2003) Intra-hippocampal lidocaine injections impair acquisition of a place task and facilitate acquisition of a response task in rats. *Behav. Brain. Res.* 144: 19–24.

Chapman JW, Reynolds DR, Smith AD, Riley JR, Pedgley DE, and Woiwod IP (2002) High-altitude migration of the diamondback moth *Plutella xylostella* to the U.K.: A study using radar, aerial netting, and ground trapping. *Ecol. Entomol.* 27: 641.

Cohen NJ and Squire LR (1980) Preserved learning and retention of pattern-analyzing skill in amnesia: Dissociation of knowing how and knowing that. *Science* 210: 207–210.

Collett M, Collett TS, Bisch S, and Wehner R (1998) Local and global vectors in desert ant navigation. *Nature* 394: 269–272.

Collett TS (1996) Insect navigation en route to the goal: Multiple strategies for the use of landmarks. *J. Exp. Biol.* 199: 227–235.

Collett TS (1998) Rapid navigational learning in insects with a short lifespan. *Connect. Sci.* 10: 255–270.

Collett TS and Collett M (2000) Path integration in insects. *Curr. Opin. Neurobiol.* 10: 757–762.

Collett TS and Collett M (2002) Memory use in insect visual navigation. *Nat. Rev. Neurosci.* 3: 542–552.

Collett TS, Dillmann E, Giger A, and Wehner R (1992) Visual landmarks and route following in desert ants. *J. Comp. Physiol. (A)* 170: 435–442.

Collett TS and Land MF (1975) Visual spatial memory in hoverfly. *J. Comp. Physiol. (A)* 100: 59–84.

D'Adamo P and Lozada M (2005) Conspecific and food attraction in the wasp *Vespula germanica* (Hymenoptera: Vespidae), and their possible contributions to control. *Ann. Entomol. Soc. Am.* 98: 236–240.

D'Ettorre P, Mondy N, Lenoir A, and Errard C (2002) Blending in with the crowd: Social parasites integrate into their host colonies using a flexible chemical signature. *Proc. Biol. Sci.* 269: 1911–1918.

De Marco RJ (2006) How bees tune their dancing according to their colony's nectar influx: Re-examining the role of the food-receivers' 'eagerness.' *J. Exp. Biol.* 209: 421–432.

De Marco RJ and Farina WM (2001) Changes in food source profitability affect the trophallactic and dance behavior of forager honeybees (*Apis mellifera* L.). *Behav. Ecol. Sociobiol.* 50: 441–449.

De Marco RJ, Gil M, and Farina WM (2005) Does an increase in reward affect the precision of the encoding of directional information in the honeybee waggle dance? *J. Comp. Physiol. (A)* 191: 413–419.

De Marco RJ and Menzel R (2005) Encoding spatial information in the waggle dance. *J. Exp. Biol.* 208: 3885–3894.

Doolittle GM (1907) Where do the field-bees deposit their loads? *Am. Bee J.* 42: 653–654.

Drake VA and Farrow RA (1988) The influence of atmospheric structure and motions on insect migration. *Annu. Rev. Entomol.* 33: 183–210.

Drake VA and Gatehouse AG (eds.) (1995) *Insect Migration: Tracking Resources through Space and Time.* Cambridge, UK: Cambridge University Press.

Dyer FC (1985) Mechanisms of dance orientation in the Asian honey bee *Apis florea* L. *J. Comp. Physiol. A* 157: 183–198.

Dyer FC and Dickinson JA (1996) Sun-compass learning in insects: Representation in a simple mind. *Curr. Dir. Psychol. Sci.* 5: 67–72.

Dyer FC, Gill M, and Sharbowski J (2002) Motivation and vector navigation in honey bees. *Naturwiss.* 89: 262–264.

Dyer FC and Gould JL (1981) Honey bee orientation: A backup system for cloudy days. *Science* 214: 1041–1042.

Eberhard MJW (1969) The social biology of polistine wasps. *Misc. Publ. Mus. Zool. Univ. Mich.* 140: 1–101.

Edrich W and Scheske C (1988) Umwegversuche mit Bienen auf Dreieckförmiger Sammeltour. *BIONA Rep.* 6: 17–27.

Esch H (1961) Über die Schallerzeugung beim Werbetanz der Honigbiene. *Z. Vergl. Physiol.* 45: 1–11.

Esch H (1967) The sounds produced by swarming honey bees. *Z. Vergl. Physiol.* 56: 408–411.

Esch H (1978) On the accuracy of the distance message in the dance of honey bees. *J. Comp. Physiol. (A)* 123: 339–347.

Esch H and Bastian JA (1970) How do newly recruited honey bees approach a food site? *Z. Vergl. Physiol.* 68: 175–181.

Esch HE and Burns JE (1996) Distance estimation by foraging honeybees. *J. Exp. Biol.* 199: 155–162.

Esch H, Esch I, and Kerr WE (1965) Sound: An element common to communication of stingless bees and to dances of the honey bee. *Science* 149: 320–321.

Esch H, Goller F, and Burns JE (1994) Honeybee waggle dances: The 'energy hypothesis' and thermoregulatory behavior of foragers. *J. Comp. Physiol. (B)* 163: 621–625.

Esch HE, Zhang S, Srinivasan MV, and Tautz J (2001) Honeybee dances communicate distances measured by optic flow. *Nature* 411: 581–583.

Etheredge JA, Perez SM, Taylor OR, and Jander R (1999) Monarch butterflies (*Danaus plexippus* L.) use a magnetic compass for navigation. *Proc. Natl. Acad. Sci. USA* 96: 13845–13846.

Fletcher DJC and Ross KG (1985) Regulation of reproduction in eusocial Hymenoptera. *Ann. Rev. Entomol.* 30: 319–343.

Fraenkel GS and Gunn DL (1961) *The Orientation of Animals.* New York: Dover Publications.

Franks NR and Richardson T (2006) Teaching in tandem-running ant. *Nature* 439: 153.

Franks NR and Scovell E (1983) Dominance and reproductive success among slave-making worker ants. *Nature* 304: 724–725.

Frantsevich L and Gorb S (2006) Courtship dances in the flies of the genus Lispe (Diptera: Muscidae): From the fly's viewpoint. *Arch. Insect Biochem. Physiol.* 62: 26–42.

Franz MO and Mallot HA (2000) Biomimetic robot navigation. *Robotics Auton. Syst.* 30: 133–153.

Free JB (1956) A study of the stimuli which release the food begging and offering responses of worker honey-bees. *Br. J. Anim. Behav.* 4: 94–101.

Fullard JH and Yack JE (1993) The evolutionary biology of insect hearing. *Trends Ecol. Evol.* 8: 248–252.

Gallistel CR (1989) Animal cognition: The representation of space, time, and number. *Annu. Rev. Psychol.* 40: 155–189.

Gallistel CR (1990) *The Organization of Learning.* Cambridge, MA: MIT Press.

Gatehouse AG (1997) Behavior and ecological genetics of wind-borne migration by insects. *Annu. Rev. Entomol.* 42: 475–502.

Gil M and De Marco RJ (2005) Olfactory learning by means of trophallaxis in *Apis mellifera*. *J. Exp. Biol.* 208: 671–680.

Gil M and De Marco RJ (2006) *Apis mellifera* bees acquire long-term olfactory memories within the colony. *Biol. Lett.* 2: 98–100.

Gould JL (1975) Honey bee recruitment: The dance-language controversy. *Science* 189: 685–693.

Grah G, Wehner R, and Ronacher B (2005) Path integration in a three-dimensional maze: Ground distance estimation keeps desert ants *Cataglyphis fortis* on course. *J. Exp. Biol.* 208: 4005–4011.

Graham P and Collett TS (2002) View-based navigation in insects: How wood ants (*Formica rufa L.*) look at and are guided by extended landmarks. *J. Exp. Biol.* 205: 2499–2509.

Greene MJ and Gordon DM (2003) Cuticular hydrocarbons inform task decisions. *Nature* 423: 32.

Haldane JBS and Spurway H (1954) A statistical analysis of communication in 'Apis mellifera' and comparison with communication in other animals. Ins. Soc. 1: 247–283.

Haydak MH (1945) The language of the honeybees. Am. Bee J. 85: 316–317.

Hedwig B and Poulet JF (2004) Complex auditory behaviour emerges from simple reactive steering. Nature 430: 781–785.

Heran H (1956) Ein Beitrag zur Frage nach der Wahrnehmungsgrundlage der Entfernungsweisung der Bienen. Z. Vergl. Physiol. 38: 168–218.

Hingston RWG (1928) Problems of Instinct and Intelligence among Tropical Insects. London: Edward Arnold.

Holland RA, Wikelski M, and Wilcove DS (2006) How and why do insects migrate? Science 313: 794–796.

Hölldobler B (1974) Communication by tandem running in the ant Camponotus sericeus. J. Comp. Physiol. 90: 105–127.

Hölldobler B and Michener CD (1980) Mechanisms of identification and discrimination in social Hymenoptera. In: Markl H (ed.) Evolution of Social Behavior: Hypotheses and Empirical Tests, pp. 35–38. Weinheim: Verlag Chemie.

Hölldobler B, Möglich M, and Maschwitz U (1974) Communication by tandem running in the ant Camponotus sericeus. J. Comp. Physiol. 90: 105–127.

Hölldobler B and Roces F (2001) The behavioral ecology of stridulatory communication in leafcutting ants. In: Dugatkin LA (ed.) Model Systems in Behavioral Ecology, pp. 92–109. Princeton, NJ: Princeton University Press.

Hölldobler B and Wilson EO (1990) The Ants. Cambridge, MA: Harvard University Press.

Horridge GA, Zhang S-W, and Lehrer M (1992) Bees can combine range and visual angle to estimate absolute size. Phil. Trans. R. Soc. Lond. B 337: 49–57.

Isingrini M, Lenoir A, and Jaisson P (1985) Pre-imaginal learning for colony brood recognition in the ant Cataglyphis cursor. Proc. Natl. Acad. Sci. USA 82: 8545–8547.

Jander R (1957) Die optische Richtungsorientierung der Roten Waldameise. Z. Vergl. Physiol. 40: 162–238.

Johnson CG (1969) Migration and Dispersal of Insect by Flight London: Methuen.

Judd TM (1995) The waggle dance of the honey bee: Which bees following a dancer successfully acquire the information? J. Insect. Behav. 8: 342–355.

Kanz JE (1977) The orientation of migrant and non-migrant monarch butterflies. Psyche 84: 120–141.

Kerr WE (1969) Some aspects of the evolution of social bees (Apidae). Evol. Biol. 3: 119–175.

Kirchner WH and Towne WF (1994) The sensory basis of the honeybee's dance language. Sci. Am. 52–59.

Knaden M and Wehner R (2005) Nest mark orientation in desert ants Cataglyphis: What does it do to the path integrator? Anim. Behav. 70: 1349–1354.

Koeniger N, Koeniger G, Punchuhewa RKW, Fabritius MO, and Fabritius MI (1982) Observations and experiments on dance communication of Apis florea in Sri Lanka. J. Apic. Res. 21: 45–52.

Kohler M and Wehner R (2005) Idiosyncratic route-based memories in desert ants, Melophorus bagoti: How do they interact with path-integration vectors? Neurobiol. Learn. Mem. 83: 1–12.

Konishi M (1999) Preface. In: Hauser MD and Konishi M (eds.) The Design of Animal Communication. Cambridge, MA: MIT Press.

Kühn A (1919) Die Orientierung der Tiere im Raum. Jena, Germany: G. Fisher.

Land BB and Seeley TD (2004) The grooming invitation dance of the Honey Bee. Ethology 110: 1–10.

Lehrer M (1996) Small-scale navigation in the honeybee: Active acquisition of visual information about the goal. J. Exp. Biol. 199: 253–261.

Lenoir A, D'Ettorre P, Errard C, and Hefetz A (2001) Chemical ecology and social parasitism in ants. Annu. Rev. Entomol. 46: 573–599.

Liebig J, Peeters C, Oldham NJ, Markstädter C, and Hölldobler B (2000) Are variations in cuticular hydrocarbons of queens and workers a reliable signal of fertility in the ant Harpegnathos saltator? Proc. Natl. Acad. Sci. USA 97: 4124–4131.

Lindauer M (1948) Über die Einwirkung von Duft- und Geschmackstoffen sowie anderer Faktoren auf die Tänze der Bienen. Z. Vergl. Physiol. 31: 348–412.

Lindauer M (1951) Bienentänze in der Schwarmtraube. Naturwiss. 38: 509–513.

Lindauer M (1952) Ein Beitrag zur Frage der Arbeitsteilung im Bienenstaat. Z. vergl. Physiol. 34: 299–345.

Lindauer M (1953) Bienentänze in der Schwarmtraube. II. Naturwiss. 40: 379–385.

Lindauer M (1954) Dauertänze im Bienenstock und ihre Beziehung zur Sonnenbahn. Naturwiss. 41: 506–507.

Lindauer M (1955) Schwarmbienen auf Wohnungssuche. Z. Vergl. Physiol. 37: 263–324.

Lindauer M (1956) Über die Verständigung bei indischen Bienen. Z. Vergl. Physiol. 38: 521–557.

Lindauer M (1957) Sonnenorientierung der Bienen unter der Äguatorsonne und zur Nachtzeit. Naturwiss. 44: 1–6.

Lindauer M (1959) Angeborene und erlernte Komponenten in der Sonnenorientierung der Bienen. Z. Vergl. Physiol. 42: 43–62.

Lindauer M (1960) Time-compensated sun orientation in bees. Cold Spring Harb. Symp. Quant. Biol. 25: 371–377.

Lindauer M (1961) Foraging and homing flight of the honeybee (Apis mellifera): Some general problems of orientation. R. Entomol. Soc. Lond. 7: 199–216.

Lindauer M (1963) Allgemeine Sinnesphysiologie. Orientierung im Raum. Fortschr. Zool. 16: 58–140.

Lindauer M (1967) Recent advances in bee communication and orientation. Annu. Rev. Entomol. 12: 439–470.

Lloyd JE (1983) Bioluminescence and communication in insects. Ann. Rev. Entomol. 28: 131–160.

Lorenz K (1981) The Foundations of Ethology. New York: Springer.

Macphail EM and Bolhuis JJ (2001) The evolution of intelligence: Adaptive specializations versus general process. Biol. Rev. 76: 341–364.

Markl H (1965) Stridulation in leaf-cutting ants. Science 149: 1392–1393.

McNaughton BL, Battaglia FP, Jensen O, Moser EI, and Moser M-B (2006) Path integration and the neural basis of the 'cognitive map'. Nat. Rev. Neurosc. 7: 663–678.

Menzel R, Brandt R, Gumbert A, Komischke B, and Kunze J (2000) Two spatial memories for honeybee navigation. Proc. R. Soc. Lond. (B) 267: 961–968.

Menzel R, Brembs B, and Giurfa M (2006) Cognition in invertebrates. In: Kaas JH (ed.) Evolution of Nervous Systems, Vol. II: Evolution of Nervous Systems in Invertebrates, pp. 403–422. Oxford, UK: Academic Press.

Menzel R, De Marco RJ, and Greggers U (2006) Spatial memory, navigation and dance behaviour in Apis mellifera. J. Comp. Physiol. (A) 192: 889–903.

Menzel R, Geiger K, Müller U, Joerges J, and Chittka L (1998) Bees travel novel homeward routes by integrating separately acquired vector memories. Anim. Behav. 55: 139–152.

Menzel R, Greggers U, Smith A, et al. (2005) Honeybees navigate according to a map-like spatial memory. Proc. Natl. Acad. Sci. USA 102: 3040–3045.

Michelsen A (1999) The dance language of honeybees: recent findings and problems. In: Hauser MD and Konishi M (eds.) The Design of Animal Communication, pp. 111–131. Cambridge, MA: MIT Press.

Michelsen A, Andersen BB, Storm J, Kirchner WH, and Lindauer M (1992) How honeybees perceive communication dances, studied by means of a mechanical model. *Behav. Ecol. Sociobiol.* 30: 143–150.

Michelsen A, Towne WF, Kirchner WH, and Kryger P (1987) The acoustic near field of a dancing honeybee. *J. Comp. Physiol. (A)* 161: 633–643.

Michener CD (1974) *The Social Behavior of the Bees*. Cambridge, MA: Harvard University Press.

Mittelstaedt H and Mittelstaedt ML (1980) Homing by path integration in mammal. *Naturwiss.* 67: 566.

Möglich M, Maschwitz U, and Hölldobler B (1974) Tandem calling: A new kind of signal in ant communication. *Science* 186: 1046–1047.

Montagner H and Galliot G (1982) Antennal communication and food exchange in the domestic bee *Apis mellifera L.* In: Breed MD, Michener CD, and Evans ME (eds.) *The Biology of Social Insects*, pp. 302–306. Boulder, CO: Westview Press.

Moser EI and Paulsen O (2001) New excitement in cognitive space: Between place cells and spatial memory. *Curr. Opin. Neurobiol.* 11: 745–751.

Mouritsen H and Frost BJ (2002) Virtual migration in tethered flying monarch butterflies reveals their orientation mechanisms. *Proc. Natl. Acad. Sci. USA* 99: 10162–10166.

Nieh JC (2004) Recruitment communication in stingless bees (*Hymenoptera, Apidae, Meliponinae*). *Apidologie* 35: 159–182.

Núñez JA (1966) Quantitative Beziehungen zwischen den Eigenschaften von Futterquellen und dem Verhalten von Sammelbienen. *Z. Vergl. Physiol.* 53: 142–164.

Núñez JA (1970) The relationship between sugar flow and foraging and recruiting behaviour of honey bees (*Apis mellifera* L.). *Anim. Behav.* 18: 527–538.

O'Keefe J and Nadel J (1978) *The Hippocampus as a Cognitive Map*. Oxford, UK: Oxford University Press.

Orians GH and Pearson NE (1979) On the theory of central place foraging. In: Horn DJ, Stairs GR, and Mitchell RD (eds.) *Analysis of Ecological Systems*, pp. 155–177. Columbus: Ohio State University Press.

Oster GF and Wilson EO (1978) *Caste and Ecology in the Social Insects*. Princeton, NJ: Princeton University Press.

Otto F (1959) Die Bedeutung des Rückfluges für die Richtungs und Entfernungsangabe der Bienen. *Z. Vergl. Physiol.* 42: 303–333.

Packard MG and McGaugh JL (1996) Inactivation of hippocampus or caudate nucleus with lidocaine differentially affects expression of place and response learning. *Neurobiol. Learn. Mem.* 65: 65–72.

Pièron H (1904) Contribution à la biologie de la Patelle et la Calyptreé. I. L'éthologie, les phénomènes sensoriels. *Bull. Sci. Fr. Belg.* 43: 183–202. II. Le sens du retour et la mémoire topographique. *Arch. Zool. Exp. Gén.* (5) Notes et Revues 18–29.

Rainey RC (1951) Weather and the movement of locust swarms: A new hypothesis. *Nature* 168: 1057–1060.

Rainey RC (1976) Flight behaviour and features of the atmospheric environment. In: Rainey RC (ed.) *Symposia of the Royal Entomological Society of London, Vol. 7: Insect Flight*, pp. 74–112. London: Blackwell Scientific.

Rankin MA and Burchsted JCA (1992) The cost of migration in insects. *Ann. Rev. Entomol.* 37: 533–559.

Raveret-Richter M and Waddington KD (1993) Past foraging experience influences honeybee dance behavior. *Anim. Behav.* 46: 123–128.

Riley JR, Greggers U, Smith AD, Reynolds DR, and Menzel R (2005) The flight paths of honeybees recruited by the waggle dance. *Nature* 435: 205–207.

Riley JR, Smith AD, Reynolds DR, et al. (1996) Tracking bees with harmonic radar. *Nature* 379: 29–30.

Rohrseitz K and Tautz J (1999) Honey bee dance communication: Waggle run direction coded in antennal contacts? *J. Comp. Physiol.* 184: 463–470.

Ronacher B and Wehner R (1995) Desert ants, *Cataglyphis fortis*, use self-induced optic flow to measure distances travelled. *J. Comp. Physiol. (A)* 177: 21–27.

Rossel S and Wehner R (1984) Celestial orientation in bees: The use of spectral cues. *J. Comp. Physiol. (A)* 155: 605–613.

Santschi F (1911) Observations et remarques critiques sur le mécanisme de l'orientation chez les fourmis. *Rév. Suisse Zool.* 19: 305–338.

Scholze E, Pichler H, and Heran H (1964) Zür Entfernungsschätzung der Bienen nach dem Kraftaufwand. *Naturwiss.* 51: 69–70.

Schroeder PJ, Wingard JC, and Packard MG (2002) Post-training reversible inactivation of hippocampus reveals interference between memory systems. *Hippocampus* 12: 280–284.

Seeley TD (1986) Social foraging by honeybees: How colonies allocate foragers among patches of flowers. *Behav. Ecol. Sociobiol.* 19: 343–354.

Seeley TD (1992) The tremble dance of the honey bee: Message and meanings. *Behav. Ecol. Sociobiol.* 31: 375–383.

Seeley TD (1995) *The Wisdom of the Hive: The Social Physiology of Honey Bee Colonies*. Cambridge, MA: Harvard University Press.

Seeley TD (1998) Thoughts on information and integration in honey bee colonies. *Apidologie* 29: 67–80.

Seeley TD and Buhrman SC (2001) Group decision making in swarms of honey bees. *Behav. Ecol. Sociobiol.* 45: 19–31.

Seeley TD, Mikheyev AS, and Pagano GJ (2000) Dancing bees tune both duration and rate of waggle-run production in relation to nectar-source profitability. *J. Comp. Physiol. (A)* 186: 813–819.

Seeley TD and Visscher PK (2004) Group decision making in nest-site selection by honey bees. *Apidologie* 35: 101–116.

Seidl T, Knaden M, and Wehner R (2006) Desert ants: Is active locomotion a prerequisite for path integration? *J. Comp. Physiol. (A)* 192: 1125–1131.

Seidl T and Wehner R (2006) Visual and tactile learning of ground structures in desert ants. *J. Exp. Biol.* 209: 3336–3344.

Sherman G and Visscher PK (2002) Honeybee colonies achieve fitness through dancing. *Nature* 419: 920–922.

Shettleworth SJ (1998) *Cognition, Evolution and Behaviour*. Oxford, UK: Oxford University Press.

Slaa EJ, Wassenberg J, and Biesmeijer JC (2003) The use of field-based social information in eusocial foragers: Local enhancement among nestmates and heterospecifics in stingless bees. *Ecol. Entomol.* 28: 369–379.

Sommer S and Wehner R (2004) The ant's estimation of distance travelled: Experiments with desert ants, *Cataglyphis fortis*. *J. Comp. Physiol. (A)* 190: 1–6.

Srinivasan MV and Zhang S (2004) Visual motor computations in insects. *Annu. Rev. Neurosci.* 27: 679–696.

Srinivasan MV, Zhang SW, Lehrer M, and Collett TS (1996) Honeybee navigation en route to the goal: Visual flight control and odometry. *J. Exp. Biol.* 199: 237–244.

Srinivasan MV, Zhang SW, and Bidwell NJ (1997) Visually mediated odometry in honeybees. *J. Exp. Biol.* 200: 2513–2522.

Srinivasan MV, Zhang S, Altwein M, and Tautz J (2000) Honeybee navigation: Nature and calibration of the 'odometer.' *Science* 287: 851–853.

Srygley RB and Oliveira EG (2001) Sun compass and wind drift compensation in migrating butterflies. *J. Navig.* 54: 405–417.

Stumpner A and von Helversen D (2001) Evolution and function of auditory systems in insects. *Naturwiss.* 88: 159–170.

Sweeney A, Jiggins C, and Johnsen S (2003) Polarized light as a butterfly mating signal. *Nature* 423: 31–32.

Tautz J (1996) Honey bee waggle dance: Recruitment success depends on the dance floor. *J. Exp. Biol.* 199: 1375–1381.

Tautz J, Roces F, and Hölldobler B (1995) Use of a sound-based vibratome by leaf-cutting ants. *Science* 267: 84–87.

Tautz J and Sandeman DC (2002) Recruitment of honeybees to non-scented food sources. *J. Comp. Physiol. (A)* 189: 293–300.

Tautz J, Zhang S, Spaethe J, Brockmann A, Si A, and Srinivasan MV (2004) Honeybee odometry: Performance in varying natural terrain. *PLoS Biol.* 2(7), e211.

Thorpe W (1950) A note on detour behaviour with *Ammophila pubescens*. *Behav.* 2: 257–264.

Tibbetts EA (2002) Visual signals of individual identity in the wasp *Polistes fuscatus*. *Proc. Biol. Sci.* 269: 1423–1428.

Tibbetts EA and Dale J (2004) A socially enforced signal of quality in a paper wasp. *Nature* 432: 218–222.

Tinbergen N (1963) On aims and methods in ethology. *Z. Tierpsychol.* 20: 410–433.

Tinbergen N (1972) *The Animal in Its World, Vol. 1: Field Studies.* Oxford, UK: Alden Press.

Tinbergen N and Kruyt W (1938) Über die Orientierung des Bienenwolfes. III. Die Bevorzugung bestimmter Wegmarken. *Z. Vergl. Physiol.* 25: 292–334.

Traniello JFA and Hölldobler B (1984) Chemical communication during tandem running in *Pachycondyla obscuricornis* (Hymenoptera: Formicidae). *J. Chem. Ecol.* 10: 783–794.

Trullier O, Wiener SI, Berthoz A, and Meyer J-A (1997) Biologically based artificial navigation systems: Review and prospects. *Prog. Neurobiol.* 51: 483–544.

Urquhart FA and Urquhart NR (1979) Breeding areas and overnight roosting locations in the northern range of the monarch butterfly (*Danaus plexippus plexippus*) with a summary of associated migratory routes. *Can. Field-Nat.* 93: 41–47.

Vane-Wright RI and Boppre M (1993) Visual and chemical signalling in butterflies: Functional and phylogenetic perspectives. *Philos. Trans. Biol. Sci.* 340: 197–205.

Virant-Doberlet M and Cokl A (2004) Vibrational communication in insects. *Neotrop. Entomol.* 33: 121–134.

Vollbehr J (1975) Zür Orientierung junger Honigbienen bei ihrem ersten Orientierungsflug. *Zool. Jahrb. Abt. Allg. Zool. Physiol. Tiere* 79: 33–69.

von Frisch K (1923) Über die 'Sprache' der Bienen, eine tierpsychologische Untersuchung. *Zool. Jb. Physiol.* 40: 1–186.

von Frisch K (1946) Die Tänze der Bienen. *Osterr. Zool. Z.* 1: 1–48.

von Frisch K (1948) Gelöste und ungelöste Rätsel der Bienensprache. *Naturwiss.* 35: 12–23.

von Frisch K (1949) Die Polarisation des Himmelslichtes als orientierender Faktor bei den Tänzen der Bienen. *Experientia* 5: 142–148.

von Frisch K (1967) *The Dance Language and Orientation of Bees.* Cambridge, MA: Harvard University Press.

von Frisch K (1968) The role of dances in recruiting bees to familiar sites. *Anim. Behav.* 16: 531–533.

von Frisch K and Jander R (1957) Über den Schwanzeltanz der Bienen. *Z. Vergl. Physiol.* 4: 1–21.

von Frisch K and Lindauer M (1961) Über die 'Mißweisung' bei den richtungsweisenden Tänzen der Bienen. *Naturwiss.* 4: 585–594.

Wagner D, Brown MJF, Broun P, et al. (1998) Task-related differences in the cuticular hydrocarbon composition of harvester ants, *Pogonomyrmex barbatus*. *J. Chem. Ecol.* 24: 2021–2037.

Webster DB, Fay RR, and Popper AN (1992) *The Evolutionary Biology of Hearing.* New York: Springer.

Wehner R (1992) Arthropods. In: Papi F (ed.) *Animal Homing*, pp. 45–144. New York: Chapman and Hall.

Wehner R (1994) Himmelsbild und kompaßauge-neurobiologie eines navigationssystems. *Verh. Dtsch. Zool. Ges.* 87: 9–37.

Wehner R (1997) The ant's celestial compass system: Spectral and polarization channels. In: Lehrer M (ed.) *Orientation and Communication in Arthropods*, pp. 145–185. Basel, Switzerland: Birkhäuser Verlag.

Wehner R (1999) Large-scale navigation: The insect case. In: Freksa C and Mark DM (eds.) *Spatial Information Theory. Cognitive and Computational Foundations of Geographic Information Science. International Conference COSIT'99, Germany: Proceedings.* Heidelberg, Germany: Springer Berlin.

Wehner R (2003) Desert ant navigation: How miniature brains solve complex tasks. *J. Comp. Physiol. (A)* 189: 579–588.

Wehner R, Boyer M, Loertscher F, Sommer S, and Menzi U (2006) Ant navigation: One-way routes rather than maps. *Curr. Biol.* 16: 75–79.

Wehner R and Menzel R (1990) Do insects have cognitive maps? *Annu. Rev. Neurosci.* 13: 403–414.

Wehner R, Michel B, and Antonsen P (1996) Visual navigation in insects: Coupling of egocentric and geocentric information. *J. Exp. Biol.* 199: 129–140.

Wehner R and Müller M (1993) How do ants acquire their celestial ephemeris function? *Naturwiss.* 80: 331–333.

Wehner R and Müller M (2006) The significance of direct sunlight and polarized skylight in the ant's celestial system of navigation. *Proc. Natl. Acad. Sci. USA* 103: 12575–12579.

Wehner R and Wehner S (1986) Path integration in desert ants. Approaching a long-standing puzzle in insect navigation. *Monitore Zool. Ital. (NS)* 20: 309–331.

Wenner A (1962) Sound production during the waggle dance of the honeybee. *Anim. Behav.* 10: 79–95.

Williams CB (1958) *Insect Migration.* London: Collins.

Wilson EO (1959) Communication by tandem running in the ant genus *Cardiocondyla*. *Psyche (Cambridge)* 66: 29–34.

Wilson EO (1971) *The Insect Societies.* Cambridge, MA: Harvard University Press.

Wilson EO (2006) How to make a social insect. *Nature* 443: 919–920.

Wilson K (1995) Insect migration in heterogeneous environments. In: Drake VA and Gatehouse AG (eds.) *Insect Migration: Tracking Resources through Space and Time*, pp. 243–264. Cambridge, UK: Cambridge University Press.

Winston ML (1987) *The Biology of the Honey Bee.* Cambridge, MA: Harvard University Press.

Witter MP and Moser EI (2006) Spatial representation and the architecture of the entorhinal cortex. *Trends Neurosci.* 29(12): 671–678.

Wittlinger M, Wehner R, and Wolf H (2006) The ant odometer: Stepping on stilts and stumps. *Science* 312: 1965–1967.

Wohlgemuth S, Ronacher B, and Wehner R (2001) Ant odometry in the third dimension. *Nature* 411: 795–798.

Wolf E (1927) Heimkehrvermögen der Bienen. II. *Z. Vergl. Physiol.* 6: 221–254.

Wolf H and Wehner R (2000) Pinpointing food sources: Olfactory and anemotactic orientation in desert ants, *Cataglyphis fortis*. *J. Exp. Biol.* 203: 857–868.

Wolf H and Wehner R (2005) Desert ants compensate for navigation uncertainty. *J. Exp. Biol.* 208: 4223–4230.

Zhang S, Mizutani A, and Srinivasan MV (2000) Maze navigation by honeybees: Learning path regularity. *Learn. Mem.* 7: 363–374.

1.26 Spatial Learning in Fish

C. Salas, C. Broglio, E. Durán, A. Gómez, and F. Rodríguez, Universidad de Sevilla, Sevilla, Spain

1.26.1 Introduction

Fish represent the largest and most diverse vertebrate radiation. Members of this taxonomic group have inhabited the earth for more than 500 million years, occupying an immense range of aquatic habitats and ecological niches and achieving an enormous diversity of morphological and functional adaptations. The prevailing views on vertebrate brain and behavior evolution have largely considered fish as the most primitive and least evolved vertebrate group. According to these rooted evolutionary notions that dominated neuroscience virtually to the present, vertebrate brain and behavior evolution occurred in successive stages of increasing complexity and advancement (fishes, amphibians, reptiles and birds, and finally mammals, to reach the superior cerebral and cognitive level of humans). In this context, fishes were thought to have developed relatively simple neural circuits allowing only elemental forms of behavior and extremely limited cognitive capabilities. Consequently, their behavior was considered as essentially reflex or instinctive. However, during the last few years a wealth of new comparative developmental, neuroanatomical, functional, and behavioral evidence has strongly contradicted this anthropocentric and misleading view, showing that vertebrate brain and behavior evolution has been far more conservative than previously thought. The new evidence shows that fishes exhibit a wide assortment of highly sophisticated behavioral and cognitive capabilities (Rodríguez et al., 2006), indicating that these

vertebrate groups share with land vertebrates (including birds and mammals) a number of brain and behavioral organization features (for reviews, see Nieuwenhuys et al., 1998; Broglio et al., 2005; Butler and Hodos, 2005; Striedter, 2005; Salas et al., 2006). We review here the evidence available on spatial learning and memory capabilities in fish and on their neural basis. For this review, we concentrate mainly on ray-finned fishes and especially the teleost fish, because considerably more research has been conducted on this taxonomic group, which makes up nearly half of all vertebrate species.

1.26.2 Spatial Cognition in Fish: Observations in the Natural Environment

Naturalistic studies show that fishes, similar to mammals and birds, possess impressive spatial abilities for orienting, piloting, and navigating (*See also* Chapters 1.21, 1.25). Although traditionally research in this field has been focused mainly on the description of the innate fixed patterns of behavior and on the study of sensory and ecological factors involved in navigation, a number of naturalistic studies suggest the possibility that fish spatial behavior is a flexible and adaptive process that involves a variety of cognitive phenomena and diverse learning and memory mechanisms (for reviews, see Dodson, 1988; Kiefer and Colgan, 1992; Quinn, 1992; Dittman and Quinn, 1996; Odling-Smee and Braithwaite,

2003). For example, many fish species are territorial and remain within a restricted home range, guarding sites and resources from competitors (Hallacher, 1984; Matthews, 1990a; Kroon et al., 2000), whereas others perform intercontinental migrations (Quinn and Dittman 1990; Dittman and Quinn, 1996). Foraging, reproduction, and predator avoidance require accurate knowledge of the spatial distribution of resources, mates, and refuge areas obtained through spatial learning and memory and based on well-developed orientation and navigation capabilities (Dodson, 1988; Brown and Laland, 2006; Kelly and Magurran, 2006; Odling-Smee et al., 2006; Warburton, 2006; Witte, 2006).

Some fish species accomplish large-scale navigation, including transoceanic migrations, and spatial learning and memory could play an important role in this ability (for a review, see Quinn, 1982; Dodson, 1988). One of the best-studied long-distance migratory fish is the salmon. Salmon return to their natal stream for reproduction after long foraging migrations in the sea, and during these migrations, they travel through diverse habitats such as oceans, lakes, and rivers. The precision of the salmon homing ability is remarkable, with approximately 95% of the ocean survivors returning to their natal streams (Quinn and Dittman, 1990; Dittman and Quinn, 1996). A variety of navigational mechanisms underlie salmon migration and homing. Salmon navigation in the open ocean seems to be based on the use of celestial and magnetic compasses as well as on olfactory cues and pheromone tracking (Quinn and Dittman, 1990; Dittman and Quinn, 1996). Navigation based on odor memories associated with their natal-stream sites seems to be essential during the final freshwater phase of the migration (Scholtz et al., 1976; Hasler and Scholtz, 1983; Hansen et al., 1993; Unwin and Quinn, 1993; Pascual and Quinn, 1994; Heard, 1996; Hard and Heard, 1999). Home-stream odor imprinting appears to occur at the time of peak thyroid hormone levels during the smolt transformation process that prepares salmon for ocean navigation (Morin and Doving, 1992; Hasler and Scholtz, 1983). However, odor learning also seems to take place many times during migration, and thus salmon can use a sequence of learned odors to guide the homeward journey (Quinn, 1985; Hansen et al., 1987; Dittman and Quinn, 1996; Heard, 1996).

Other interesting examples suggesting well-developed spatial cognition capabilities in fish are provided by experimental studies conducted in natural environments. For example, studies on homing behavior showed that relocated intertidal rockpool fishes are able to accurately return to familiar hiding places even after 6 months of absence (Aronson, 1971; Green, 1971; Griffiths, 2003). The benthic fish *Ulvaria subbifurcata*, which lives in small home ranges, can home even after displacements of several hundred meters (Green and Fisher, 1977). Furthermore, this work showed that fish were significantly well oriented in the homeward direction at the release time, suggesting that they were able to determine their actual location with respect to home. Some sedentary and territorial rockfishes of different species, displaced from their home sites, navigate back home from long distances, in some cases even more than 20 km away (Carlson and Haight, 1972; Hallacher, 1984; Quinn and Ogden, 1984; Markevich, 1988; Matthews, 1990a,b).

Fish discover and remember the location of profitable food patches and prey location by exploration and individual sampling as well as by observing other foragers (Hart, 1986; Pitcher and Magurran, 1983; Pitcher and House, 1987; Hart, 1993; Warburton, 2006). Learning and remembering the location of particular food patches and mapping their status and renewal rates, as well as identifying and remembering the predation risk associated with different locations, improve fish foraging efficiency and survival probabilities. For example, butterflyfishes (*Chaetodontidae*) follow predictable paths as they swim from one food patch to another within their territories. When a coral outcrop is removed, the fish look for it in its former location before resuming their route along the reef (Reese, 1989). For these displacements, Reese (1989) suggested that butterflyfishes use a system of spatially learned route-specific landmarks, possibly in conjunction with sun compass orientation, and a cognitive map of their territories. Brown surgeon fish (*Acanthurus nigrofuscus*) undergo daily migrations of up to 1.5 km to feeding and spawning sites apparently following a sequence of landmarks (Mazeroll and Montgomery, 1998). Interestingly, the migrating brown surgeon fish changed direction in accordance with the position of experimentally displaced landmarks. The reliance of the migrating brown surgeon fish on particular landmarks could be reduced by moving the landmarks more than 6 m from their original location; nonetheless, the animals still accurately navigate to the feeding or spawning sites after key landmarks had been manipulated, suggesting that there were redundancies in the cues used.

Social transmission of foraging routes provides other interesting examples of the role of learning and cognition in fish spatial behavior (Hobson, 1972; Ogden and Ehrlich, 1977; Gladfelter, 1979;

MacFarland, 1980; Mainardi, 1980; Helfman, 1981; Helfman et al., 1982; Helfman and Schultz, 1984). For example, French grunts (*Haemulon flavolineatum*) introduced to new schooling sites and initially allowed to follow residents in their displacements, rapidly learn to use the novel foraging routes even in absence of the residents (Helfman et al., 1982; Helfman and Schultz, 1984). Laland and Williams (1997, 1998) reported that naïve guppies could learn a route to a foraging patch by observing and following experienced fish. When the experienced fish were removed, the observers continued using the same routes even when alternative itineraries were available. Warner (1988, 1990) reported culturally transmitted migratory traditions in bluehead wreasse (*Thalassoma bifasciatum*). These coral reef fish establish mating-site locations that remain constant over several generations. The experimental replacement of entire local populations led to the use of new sites, which remained constant over subsequent generations.

Field studies and experiments in natural environments provide a broad range of suggestive observations and raise interesting insights into the biological and ecological significance of fish spatial cognition capabilities. Frequently, however, given the enormous difficulty of defining, isolating, and controlling important variables in the field, these studies do not provide clear-cut conclusions on the nature of the cues and spatial strategies being used by the fish. Thus, controlled laboratory experiments are called for, as they can overcome some of these difficulties and provide optimal conditions to reveal the mechanisms that fish use for orientation and navigation.

1.26.3 Exploration and Environment Investigation

Fish apply systematic exploration in unfamiliar environments in order to acquire spatial knowledge. When introduced into a novel environment, most fish display an intensive exploratory activity, which progressively decreases. This decrease could correspond to a state in which the processing of the initial spatial information has been completed (Wilz and Bolton, 1971; Poucet et al., 1986; Thinus-Blanc et al., 1987). For example, when introduced into a novel environment, goldfish engage in an organized and systematic pattern of exploration, avoiding previously visited locations (Kleerekoper et al., 1974; Rodríguez, 1996). After performing a few ample initial turns near the edges of the tank, the fish thoroughly explore a particular area before moving to the next one, in a rather systematic way, thus exploring the entire tank (**Figure 1**). This pattern of exploration, area by area, which is never replaced by random exploration, requires some degree of spatial memory. According to this view, through its exploration behavior, the goldfish becomes familiar with a new environment faster when salient visual cues reduce the spatial (geometric) ambiguity of the environment (Warburton, 1990). A similar pattern of exploratory activity has also been observed in fish foraging in their natural environment. The planktivorous reef fish, the stout-body chromis (*Chromis chrysurus*), use a local search strategy consisting in swimming in a circuitous and stereotypic pattern over a specific foraging region, completing the search before moving to the next foraging area (Noda et al., 1994). The use of such an organized search pattern prevents revisiting depleted foraging areas and provides the basis for exploring and mapping unfamiliar areas.

In addition, the rate of activity of different species of fish correlates inversely with the degree of environmental novelty. Moreover, the fish show increases in exploratory activity in response to changes in familiar environments, indicating that these animals detect environmental modifications, be it in the location of the objects or in the identity of the objects themselves (Breder and Halpern, 1946; Breder, 1950; Welker and Welker, 1958; Russell, 1967; Kleerekoper et al., 1974). Blind cave fish (*Anoptichthys jordani*) orient and navigate accurately in the environment and can find a well-known place in the tank, even when that place is not directly accessible (Campenhausen et al., 1981). Interestingly, the swimming behavior of the blind cave fish differs in familiar and unfamiliar environments. When introduced into an unfamiliar environment, and also after alterations of a well-known one, these fish swim through it for several hours, exploring the surfaces of the walls and objects, using their lateral line to sense self-induced perturbations in the surrounding flow field. For this activity, fish increase their swimming speed, supposedly to optimize the stimulation of the organ of the lateral line. Campenhausen and coworkers suggested that during this high-speed swimming phase blind cave fish build a memory representation of the environment (i.e., an internal map). Once the representation has been elaborated, the fish can rely on this internal map to navigate and therefore can reduce the swimming speed below the optimal required by the lateral line organ,

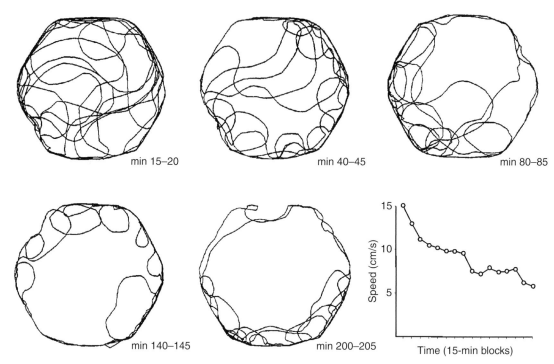

Figure 1 Exploratory behavior in goldfish. Examples of the exploratory pattern of a goldfish during a 4-h session of free exploration in a large open field. Each figure shows the fish trajectories during 5-min intervals throughout the session. Note the organized and systematic pattern of exploration area by area. The plot in the bottom right shows the mean swimming speed during the entire session of exploration in consecutive 15-min blocks.

without observable deficits in avoiding obstacles (Campenhausen et al., 1981; Teyke, 1989). Note that accurate navigation at speeds that are suboptimal for lateral-line organ stimulation implies that fish are using the internal map via feedback from senses other than those primarily used for map development (Demski and Beaver, 2001). Some additional evidence supports this hypothesis. For example, blind cave fish react by increasing swimming speed when changes are introduced in a familiar environment, such as the removal or the displacement of a familiar cue or the introduction of new objects in a well-known tank (Campenhausen et al., 1981; Teyke, 1985; Burt de Perera, 2004b). Teyke (1985) showed that the duration of the exploratory activity of the blind cave fish, *Anoptichthys jordani*, depends on the shape of the experimental tank, with bilaterally symmetrical tanks explored during longer periods of time than asymmetrical tanks or tanks in which objects have been introduced near the walls in asymmetrical positions (Teyke, 1985). Burt de Perera (2004a) showed that blind cave fish, *Astyanax fasciatus*, are able to remember the order of a landmark sequence. The ability to represent the order in which a series of places are

spatially linked could be a mechanism that allows these animals to orient beyond the limits of their perceptual range. In addition, Teyke (1989) obtained evidence suggesting that the elaboration of these hypothetical internal maps by blind cave fish is a memory phenomenon that occurs in two phases, an initial volatile phase (short-term memory) and a resistant phase after consolidation (long-term memory). In fact, Teyke (1989) showed that if the fish is anesthetized by cooling only 4 h after the exploration of a new environment, when the animal recovers from the anesthesia it explores that environment again as if it were a completely unfamiliar one. However, a reactivation of the exploration is not observed when the anesthesia is produced 6–30 h after the habituation to the environment.

1.26.4 Spatial Learning in Fish: Cues and Strategies

Fish use diverse sources of spatial information, such as self-generated movement cues from different sensory modalities, directional cues that polarize the environment, or positional landmarks that enable inferring the place locations relative to distances, angles, and the geometry of objects within an array (Thinus-Blanc, 1996; Burgess et al., 1999; Jacobs, 2003).

Teleost fish learn spatial tasks using visual cues and landmarks (Huntingford and Wright, 1989; Rodríguez et al., 1994; Girvan and Braithwaite, 1998; López et al., 1999; Hughes and Blight, 2000), as well as using nonvisual senses, such as olfaction (Quinn, 1985; Hansen et al., 1987; Dittman and Quinn, 1996; Heard, 1996), audition (Tolimieri et al., 2000; Simpson et al., 2004, 2005), the lateral line system (Campenhausen et al., 1981; Teyke, 1985, 1989), or electrolocation (Cain et al., 1994; Cain, 1995). Fish also use a variety of sources of directional information to orient and navigate, for example, sun position (Schwassmann and Braemer, 1961; Goodyear and Ferguson, 1969; Goodyear, 1970; Hasler, 1971; Loyacano et al., 1971; Goodyear and Bennet, 1979), polarized light (Dill, 1971; Davitz and McKaye, 1978; Hawryshyn et al., 1990), the earth's magnetic field (Kalmijn, 1978; Quinn, 1980; Quinn and Brannon, 1982), or water flow direction (Jonsson et al., 1994; Kaya and Jeanes, 1995; Smith and Smith, 1998; Girvan and Braithwaite, 2000; Braithwaite and Girvan, 2003; Hunter et al., 2004).

Fish learn and remember the location of profitable food patches. Pitcher and Magurran (1983) showed that goldfish (*Carassius auratus*) remember the spatial position of food patches in a tank and are able to shift to a different foraging strategy when the location of the feeders has been changed. The spined sticklebacks (*Gasterosteus aculeatus*) remember which of two patches were baited with food during training for at least 8 days (Milinski, 1994). Atlantic salmon (*Salmo salar*) trained in an artificial stream remembered the location of two feeding sites in the stream and were able to shift between these two alternative sites to continue feeding (Gotceitas and Godin, 1992).

A number of pioneering studies provide notable evidence on fish spatial learning and memory capabilities. For example, Aronson (1951, 1971) reported that gobiid fishes learn and remember the geographic features of their environment. The tide-pool-dwelling gobiid fish *Bathygobius soporator* leap with surprising accuracy from one pool to another, jumping over ledges and other obstacles. Although neighboring pools are not visible at the onset of the leap, the fish rarely, if ever, jump onto dry land, suggesting that these animals build a precise memory representation of the local topography during high

tide. More recently, it has been reported that black-eye gobies (*Coryphopterus nicholsi*) increase their accuracy in escaping to their burrows if they previously had the opportunity to become familiar with the environment (Markel, 1994). Animals that were allowed to spend additional exploration time in the test tank were quicker to find the burrow. In addition, when the burrow position was shifted to a new location, the more experienced animals took longer than the less experienced fish to find the shifted burrow, suggesting that they have learned the spatial location of the burrow.

Goldfish use landmarks as direct cues or beacons but also are able to learn more complex spatial relationships and to use visual cues as indirect spatial reference points (Warburton, 1990), and they can also learn to swim in a constant direction relative to visual cues, even when their approach to the goal is from the opposite direction (Ingle and Sahagian, 1973). These abilities could reflect the capability of fish to discriminate spatial relationships in the environment independently of a body-centered reference system. Goldfish are able to use the visual angle of a familiar landmark to locate a food source (Douglas, 1996). Goldfish trained to search for food buried 20 cm from a landmark still searched in the correct location when the food was absent. Halving either the width or height of the landmark resulted in searches significantly closer to the landmark, suggesting that these animals determined their position relative to the landmark using their horizontal and vertical visual angles. In addition, fish use route-based orientation strategies, that is, a learned sequence of cues or an algorithm based on a sequence of turns (Braithwaite, 1998).

Roitblat et al. (1982) showed that Siamese fighting fish need fewer trials to learn a T-maze task when it is compatible with a win-shift strategy (i.e., to avoid revisiting the previously depleted maze arms) than in another task compatible with a win-stay strategy (to visit previously visited maze arms repeatedly). Mammals and birds typically use a win-shift strategy when solving T-maze tasks (Dember and Fowler, 1958; Uster et al., 1976; Olton et al., 1977; Withem, 1977; Kamil, 1978; Olton et al., 1981). More recently, it has been reported that spined sticklebacks (*Spinachia spinachia*) and corkwing wrase (*Crenilabrus melops*) can readily use visual cues to locate food sources in a radial maze and adequately track renewal frequencies and site productivity. These animals distinguished between renewable food sources differing in productivity, preferentially visiting those containing more food. Fish showed preferentially win-shift strategies, avoiding recently visited locations, but switched from win-shift to win-stay strategies when appropriate (Hughes and Blight, 2000).

Roitblat et al. (1982) analyzed features of the Siamese fighting fish's (*Betta splendens*) spatial memory strategies using an aquatic version of a procedure widely used to test spatial memory in mammals, the Olton eight-arm radial maze (Olton, 1979). In this procedure, the optimal performance is achieved when the animals visit each arm only once, as the previously visited arms have already been depleted of the reinforcer. This study showed that although the performance of Siamese fighting fish in this task is characterized by a strong algorithmic component, it also involves some measure of spatial memory. The fish showed a strong tendency to choose the adjacent maze arms, turning in a consistent direction, either clockwise or counter-clockwise. This algorithmic behavior plays an important role in the sequential choice of the arms. However, the algorithmic component alone does not completely explain the performance of the *Betta splendens* in this radial arm maze task, and memory of the recently visited places is necessary to explain the fish's accurate behavior. Roitblat et al. (1982) suggested that the algorithmic component of the fish behavior in these training conditions could represent a choice strategy more than memory limitations. The fish could be using a list of the previously visited and already depleted arms or a list of the baited arms (probably including three or four items). That is, although the fish may be able to remember more information, in the Olton task they use the apparently rigid, but highly efficient, algorithmic search pattern, shadowing the use of spatial memory. In a follow-up experiment, the same researchers confirmed the participation of short-term memory in the Siamese fighting fish's performance in the radial arm maze procedure. They used a standard procedure consisting of confining the animals in the maze's central platform between choices 4 and 5 during periods of 0 s (no confinement), 30 s, and 5 min. This procedure assesses the memory component relative to the algorithm component in the eight-arm maze performance: Because the accuracy of the algorithm-based performance depends on a continuous chain of choices, any interference would restart the algorithm, increasing the number of errors after the interruption. Thus, it can be expected that the interruption by itself, independently of the confinement time, will produce greater deleterious effects if the performance

only depends on a strategy based on algorithms. On the contrary, if the performance has a memory component, the effects of the interruption *per se* will be smaller, and they will depend on the duration of the confinement period. The results of this test showed that the performance accuracy depended on the duration of the confinement period as it deteriorated progressively with increasing durations. This indicates that the fish retain information on their previous choices for some time during the confinement period (spatial working memory). More recently, Hughes and Blight (1999) provided converging evidence as they observed that 15-spined sticklebaks and corkwing wrasse adopted an algorithmic strategy to solve an eight-arm maze task consisting of visiting every third arm in absence of spatial cues, but in the presence of visual cues they used spatial memory. The imposition of a delay within trials reset the algorithm, decreasing foraging behavior efficiency, but the delay in itself had no effects on performance if spatial cues could be used.

1.26.5 Separating Egocentric and Allocentric Navigation

A growing amount of evidence indicates that fish, like land vertebrates, are able to orient and navigate using a variety of cognitive mechanisms based on distinct spatial learning and memory systems (*See also* Chapters 1.20, 1.21). Fish use multiple, parallel spatial learning and memory systems to orient and navigate that show distinctive properties and depend on separate neural substrata. These multiple spatial orientation mechanisms range from simple reflex egocentric orientation mechanisms and stimulus–response simple associations to allocentric, map-like representations of the environment.

Several experiments provide direct evidence on the use of multiple spatial learning strategies in fish. For example, Rodríguez et al. (1994) aimed to ascertain whether goldfish are able to use egocentric (turn) or extramaze visual cue–based navigation strategies. The fish were trained to locate a baited feeder in a four-arm maze surrounded by an array of widely distributed distal visual cues, in one of the three following tasks (see **Figure 2(a)**):

1. an egocentric task, in which two opposite start arms were randomly used (50% each), but for all trials, the goal arm was determined by a fixed-turn

relative to the start arm (e.g., always right). As the extramaze cues were irrelevant for solving the task, this procedure made it possible to determine whether or not the fish could choose the correct arm on the basis of a particular turn response.

2. an extramaze visual cue task, in which two opposite start points were also randomly used (50% each), but the fish were always rewarded in the arm with the end located in a determined, stable place in the room. This procedure was used to determine whether or not the fish could learn to go to a rewarded place solely on the basis of the information provided by widely distributed (extramaze) cues. No fixed-turn direction was relevant to task solution, because, depending on the location of the start-box, the subjects were required to make a left- or a right-hand turn.

3. a mixed egocentric–extramaze visual cue task, in which the fish, in contrast to the procedures described previously, always left from the same start box and were rewarded exclusively in a goal arm ending in another constant place. This task thus allowed selecting the correct arm on the basis of a specific turn direction and/or extramaze cues.

The animals in all the groups quickly learned to reach the goal (**Figure 2(b)**). Interestingly, although the fish in the different groups achieved similar levels of performance, the transfer and probe tests revealed that these animals were using very different spatial strategies.

The test trials revealed that the goldfish trained in the extramaze visual cue procedure navigate directly to the rewarded place regardless of start position and swimming direction, even during the trials when the maze was displaced and they were required to start from previously unvisited locations (**Figure 2(d)**). In addition, these animals were able to accurately reach the goal when the extramaze cues were individually removed but not when all of them were occluded by a curtain that surrounded the maze (**Figure 2(c)**). The fish trained in the egocentric task also performed with accuracy, although they used a very different strategy. These animals mainly chose the arm corresponding with the fixed 90° turn learned during training, independently of the starting point and maze location (**Figure 2(d)**). Moreover, the performance of these animals was not affected by removing any one of the extramaze cues or all of them simultaneously. Thus, the choices of these animals were purely egocentric, and the environmental information was not taken into account for selecting the arm. Moreover, the results of the ego-allocentric group indicate that fish are also able to use both types of

strategies (body-centered orientation and extramaze visual cue–based navigation) simultaneously, to solve spatial tasks, and use one or the other according to task requirements (**Figure 2(d)**). The use of both types of strategy simultaneously could explain the tendency of this group to perform more accurately and steadily than the other groups.

López et al. (2000a) also obtained evidence on the simultaneous and cooperative use of multiple spatial learning strategies in fish. In this study, goldfish were trained in a mixed place-cue procedure to find food at the end of a maze arm that occupied a constant room location, and that was, in addition, signaled by a distinct intramaze visual cue (**Figure 3**). That is, the fish were trained in a test environment where they could simultaneously rely on the spatial information provided by the extramaze distal landmarks and on a single intramaze cue that directly indicated the location of food. Subsequent probe trials were conducted in which the two sources of spatial information were set in conflict (the local cues were switched between sides; **Figure 3(a)**) or one of the two sources, the extramaze distal cues or the intramaze proximal cue, were removed (**Figure 3(b,c)**). When the intramaze visual cue was eliminated, the goldfish were still able to locate the goal using a place strategy based on the information provided by the extramaze visual cues (**Figure 3(c)**). Conversely, when the use of the extramaze distal visual cues was precluded by means of a curtain that surrounded the maze, the animals relied exclusively on the intramaze visual cue signaling the goal during training to accurately reach the goal (**Figure 3(b)**). These results indicate that goldfish implement place and guidance strategies simultaneously to solve spatial problems, and that they switch from one strategy to the other depending on the available information. Convergent results were obtained using a different apparatus and experimental procedure (Salas et al., 1996b; López et al., 1999; see **Figure 4**). Goldfish trained in a spatial constancy task or in a cue task to locate a goal in a small, stimulus-controlled enclosure, where only proximal visual cues were available, implemented guidance (orientation) or spatial relational strategies according to task demands. Whereas the performance of the fish in the cue task was dramatically impaired when the cue associated directly with the goal was removed (López et al., 1999), goldfish in the spatial constancy task navigated accurately to the goal from different start locations regardless of route direction and response requirements (Salas et al., 1996b) and despite the partial deletion of any subset of visual cues (López et al.,

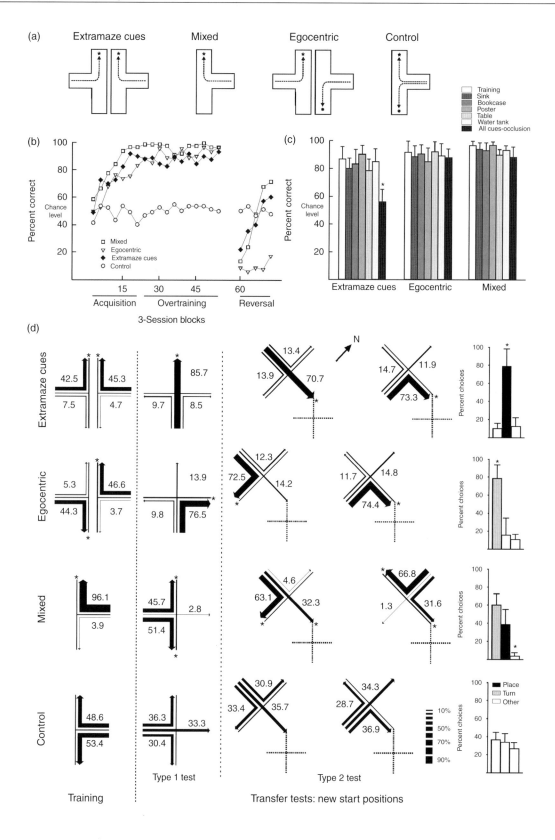

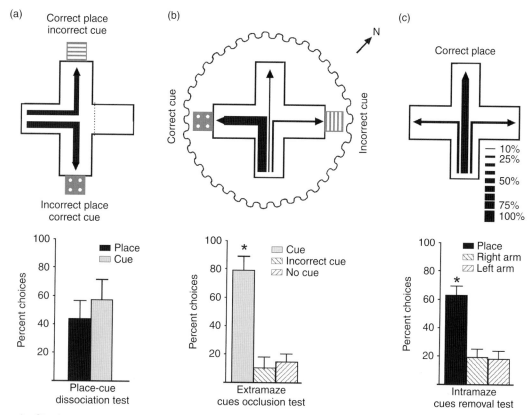

Figure 3 Simultaneous use of multiple spatial learning strategies in goldfish trained in a mixed place-cue procedure in a plus maze. In this experiment, the goal was in the arm end situated in a constant location in the room, and was, in addition, signaled by an intramaze visual cue. The figure shows the results of three different probe tests conducted following learning: (a) place-cue dissociation test; (b) extramaze cues occlusion test; (c) intramaze cues removal test. In the upper diagrams, the arrows show the trajectories chosen during each test from the start position, and their relative thickness denotes the percentage of times that each choice was made. The histograms show the mean percentage of choices to the various arms. Asterisks denote significant differences. Modified from López JC, Bingman VP, Rodríguez F, Gómez Y, and Salas C (2000a) Dissociation of place and cue learning by telencephalic ablation in goldfish. *Behav. Neurosci.* 114: 687–699.

Figure 2 Spatial learning strategies used by goldfish to find a goal in a plus arm maze. (a) Schematic diagrams of the four training procedures. The arrows mark the most appropriate trajectory from the start to the goal (asterisks) for each group. Note that for the extramaze cues and egocentric tasks two opposite start positions (50% each) were employed (see text for more details). The fish in the control group left from a start box always situated in a fixed place of the room. However, their training involved two possible correct goals, which were randomly assigned across trials. This group was used to ascertain whether or not the goal was reached by attending to odor or other uncontrolled variables. (b) Mean percentage of correct choices of goldfish trained in the four different experimental conditions, during acquisition, overtraining, and reversal of the task. (c) Percentage of correct choices when one salient cue was hidden or removed from the room and when all distal cues were removed by curtains surrounding the maze. The percentage of correct choices during training is also shown for comparison. (d) Trajectories chosen by the animals in the different groups during training and transfer trials. Once the animals learned their task, transfer tests were run to elucidate whether the animals of the different groups solved their respective tasks on the basis of turn or place strategies. In the type 1 transfer tests, the maze remained in its usual position but the animals were released from a novel start position. In the type 2 tests, the maze was displaced in the room in such a way that the end of one arm was located in the same place where the fish was rewarded during training trials, but the start positions were different from those used during training. The numbers and the relative thickness of the arrows denote the percentage of times that a particular choice was made. The dashed lines indicate the position of the maze before it was displaced for type 2 tests, and the asterisks mark the goal location. The histograms on the right show the accumulated mean percentage of choices for both types of transfer tests. Note that the animals in the allocentric group consistently chose the arm with the end at the place rewarded during training trials. In contrast, the arm most frequently chosen by the fish in the egocentric group was the one coinciding with the learned turn, independently of the location of the start arm. Asterisks on the histograms denote significant differences. Modified from Rodríguez F, Durán E, Vargas J, Torres B, and Salas C (1994) Performance of goldfish trained in allocentric and egocentric maze procedures suggests the presence of a cognitive mapping system in fishes. *Anim. Learn. Behav.* 22: 409–420.

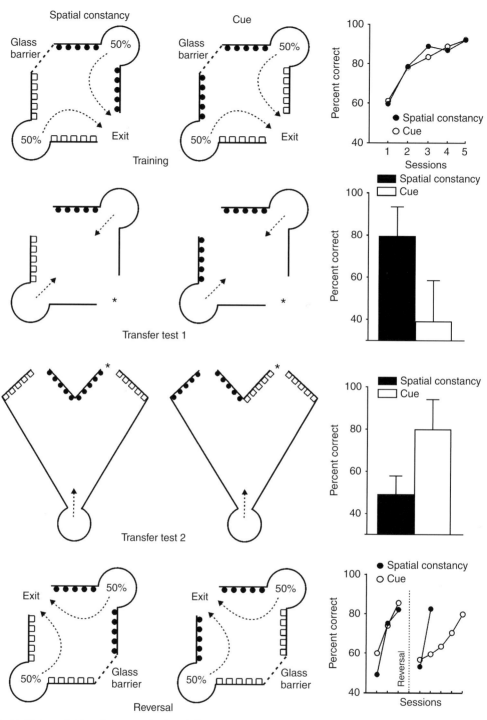

Figure 4 Multiple spatial learning strategies in goldfish trained in a spatial constancy or a cue task to locate a goal in a small, stimulus-controlled enclosure. The access from the start compartments, the distribution of the experimental visual cues (black circles and hollow squares), the position of the glass barrier, and the location of the goal (asterisk) are shown for the two experimental training conditions, transfer tests, and task reversal. The numbers indicate the percentage of trials initiated from each starting compartment. The arrows show the most efficient routes to the goal. The figures on the right show the percentage of correct responses during each experimental situation. Asterisks denote significant differences. Modified from López JC, Broglio C, Rodríguez F, Thinus-Blanc C, and Salas C (1999) Multiple spatial learning strategies in goldfish (*Carassius auratus*). *Anim. Cogn.* 2: 109–120.

1999). In fact, one might expect that the use of multiple orientation systems would increase navigational efficiency in an environment with redundant cues. The cooperative use of different spatial strategies has been described previously in other vertebrate groups (Schenk and Morris, 1985; Whishaw and Mittleman, 1986; Able, 1991).

1.26.6 Map-like Memory Representations of the Environmental Space

In the preceding sections, we mentioned the possibility that, in addition to using egocentrically referenced mechanisms for orienting, fish may also use allocentric spatial representations. In the present section, we discuss this point in more detail. Although this has been one of the most controversial topics in animal spatial cognition research, thorough studies carried out during the last few decades indicate that mammals, birds, and reptiles can use allocentric representations of space for navigation (O'Keefe and Nadel, 1978; Eichenbaum et al., 1990; Sherry and Duff, 1996; Bingman et al., 1998; Burgess et al., 1999; López et al., 2000b, 2001; Salas et al., 2003; Chapters 1.20, 1.22, 1.25). These allocentric representations, defined as map-like, world-centered cognitive representations (i.e., cognitive maps; Tolman, 1948; O'Keefe and Nadel, 1978), are the result of processing and encoding the properties and features of the environment in terms of the spatial relationships between multiple cues. These memory representations allow the subject to represent itself within a stable spatial framework and navigate accurately and flexibly within it, regardless of its own actual position and local view. These map-like spatial memory representations, which can be considered true relational memories, show some of the properties that distinguish the human declarative or episodic memory (Clayton and Dickinson, 1998; Eichenbaum, 2000; Chapters 1.22, 1.23). In comparative psychology and neuroscience, relational and allocentric spatial memories have long been considered attributes that distinctly characterize humans and other mammals, as these high-order cognitive capabilities are assumed to require complex associational brain structures, in particular the hippocampus and the six-layered neocortex. However, the results of some experiments indicate that teleost fish can implement allocentric, map-like spatial representations to navigate, based on processing multiple, reciprocal associations among different environmental features (for reviews, see Broglio et al., 2003; Salas et al., 2003).

For example, the results from the above-cited study by Rodríguez and coworkers (1994) showed that goldfish trained in an allocentric procedure were able to navigate directly to the rewarded place independently of start position and swimming direction, since they were able to reach the goal even when released from novel start arms (**Figure 2(d)**; transfer test, type 1) and from previously unvisited room locations (**Figure 2(d)**; transfer test, type 2). In fact, these animals chose spontaneously the most direct trajectory to the goal place from different, never experienced start locations, establishing new routes without a history of previous training (see trajectories in **Figure 2(d)**) The results of the probe and transfer trials are especially significant because they can rule out the possibility that these fish could be using guidance or other egocentric referenced orientation mechanisms, by relying on a particular landmark or in a direction sense, for example, approaching or avoiding a sensory cue, be it visual, auditory, odor, polarized light, or geomagnetic gradients. These results show that goldfish spontaneously use the most appropriate of the available routes from previously unvisited places, using shortcuts or detours, as convenient, although the new trajectories imply new, never experienced, egocentric relations to landmarks. These data provide solid evidence of the fish's capacity to represent spatial relationships in the environment independently of a body-centered reference system, that is, to perform place responses by using allocentric frames of reference.

Another important property proposed for map-like, relational spatial memory representations is the storage of redundant information on the encoded cues and environmental features. This property implies that the disappearance of any subset of environmental cues will not impair accurate navigation, because the animals can rely on the remaining cues (Suzuki et al., 1980; Morris, 1981; Mazmanian and Roberts, 1983). The study by Rodríguez et al. (1994) provided interesting evidence in this regard (**Figure 2(c)**): On the one hand, the performance of the fish trained in the allocentric task did not deteriorate when the most salient visual cues were individually removed or hidden, and on the other hand, when all the cues were simultaneously removed, performance became as poor as that of the control fish, indicating that the performance of the allocentric group was based on the knowledge of the relationships among the goal location and many environmental cues. These data agree with the above-mentioned requirement for cognitive mapping, concerning the encoding of redundant information, as it was not impaired by the removal or occlusion of any one of the component elements of the landmark array, that is, none of those cues, taken individually, was essential to locate the goal.

Recently, Schluessel and Bleckmann (2005), using behavioral procedures that closely match those used in the above-cited study by Rodríguez et al. (1994), have obtained results that indicate that elasmobranchs, a sister group of actinopterygian and sarcopterygian vertebrates, can also use allocentric strategies for navigation. Rays (*Potamotrygon motoro*), in addition to using egocentric strategies, use the information provided by the extramaze visual cues to reach the goal using novel routes starting from unfamiliar locations, suggesting that the spatial mapping could be a widely extended cognitive capability in vertebrates.

Further studies have provided direct evidence of additional characteristics of the allocentric strategies in fish. For example, a number of recent studies indicate that besides using landmarks to build map-like spatial representations, fish can use the geometry or the shape of the environmental boundaries (Broglio et al., 2000; Sovrano et al., 2003; Vargas et al., 2004; Sovrano et al., 2007). In fact, these studies showed that fish match birds, rodents, monkeys, and humans in the capability to encode geometric spatial information for orientation and navigation (Tinklepaugh, 1932; Cheng, 1986; Vallortigara et al., 1990; Hermer and Spelke, 1994; Kelly et al., 1998; Gouteaux et al., 2001; Gouteaux and Spelke, 2001). These results are specially relevant, because the capability to encode and use the geometrical features of the environment for allocentric navigation reflects the knowledge of the spatial features as a whole, that is, the metric and geometrical relationships among the constituent elements (Cheng and Gallistel, 1984; Cheng, 1986; Hughey and Koppenaal, 1987; Gallistel, 1990; Cheng and Sherry, 1992; Cheng, 1994; Hermer and Spelke, 1994; Kamil and Jones, 1997).

Lopez et al. (1999) showed that goldfish trained in a spatial constancy task were impaired when a spatial modification was introduced in the experimental apparatus that altered the global shape (geometry) and the topography of the apparatus, although it left unchanged the local visual and geometric features of the areas corresponding to each of the doors. In contrast, the performance of the fishes trained in a cue task using the same apparatus was unimpaired by the global topographical alteration if the local cues were maintained

(López et al., 1999, see **Figure 4**). In addition, recent experimental studies, directly addressing this issue in fish, demonstrated that fish use the geometry of the surroundings for spatial orientation. For example, Sovrano et al. (2003) showed that, when disoriented in a closed rectangular tank, redtail splitfin (*Xenotoca eiseni*) are able to reorient according to the shape of the environment and to combine geometric and nongeometric information of the environment such as the color of the walls or the features provided by the visual cues. Fish encode geometric information even when distinct feature information is sufficient to solve the task. In addition, Vargas et al. (2004) showed that goldfish locate a place in an environment by encoding the goal location with respect to the geometrical features of the experimental space, even in the absence of feature information. Goldfish trained in a symmetrical, rectangular apparatus, and in the absence of additional visual cues, made systematic rotational errors by confusing geometrically equivalent places (**Figure 5(a)**). In the test trials in which the geometric features were modified by means of replacing the rectangular apparatus used during training by a square one, the performance was significantly impaired, indicating that the fish used no other source of spatial information but the geometry of the rectangular arena (**Figure 5(a)**). In addition, the results of this study indicate that goldfish encode geometric and nongeometric information simultaneously when the environment provides both types of information and use one or the other according to task requirements. The dissociation tests showed that goldfish encoded the geometric information even when information provided by distinct visual cues was sufficient to solve the task, and that the fish's representation of the spatial environment was flexible and resistant to losses of redundant but relevant spatial information (**Figure 5(b)**, geometry test and feature test). However, the performance was disrupted when the metric and topological relationships among the composing elements were altered (**Figure 5(b)**, dissociation test). In fact, whereas the fish were able to solve the task successfully by using either the geometrical (**Figure 5(b)** geometry test) or the featural cues (**Figure 5(b)**, feature test), they chose at random between the possible exits when the information provided by both types of cues was dissociated and made contradictory (**Figure 5(b)**, dissociation test). Furthermore, this pattern of results suggests that goldfish elaborate a complex representation of the environment, in which the different elements and properties of the environmental space (geometry and featural information) are not only simultaneously

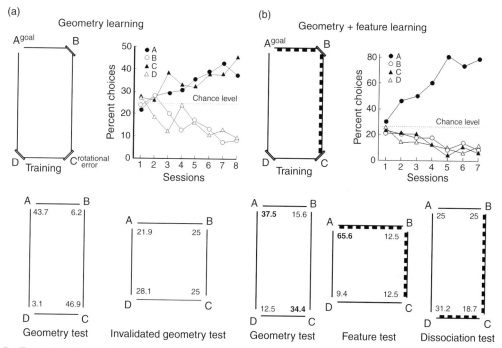

Figure 5 Encoding of geometric and featural spatial information by goldfish. (a) Geometry task. Fish were trained to find the exit door (goal) placed in a corner (A) of a rectangular arena that had three identical blocked openings in the other three corners (B, C, and D). Because of the geometric properties of the apparatus, the correct corner was indistinguishable from the diagonally opposite corner (rotational error). The curves show the percentage of choices for the four corners during training. The diagrams in the bottom show the percentage of choices (numbers) for each corner during the two different probe tests conducted for this group. (b) Geometry + feature task. Fish were trained in the same rectangular box but in which additional feature information was provided by alternate dark grey and white vertical stripes on two walls. The curves show the percentage of choices for the four corners during training. The diagrams on the bottom show the percentage of choices (numbers) for each corner during the three different probe tests conducted for this group. Modified from Vargas JP, Lopez JC, Salas C, and Thinus-Blanc C (2004) Encoding of geometric and featural spatial information by Goldfish (*Carassius auratus*). *J. Comp. Psychol.* 118: 206–216.

encoded but also are probably integrated in a single configuration, a relational, map-like representation (O'Keefe and Nadel, 1978; Eichenbaum et al., 1990; Poucet, 1993; Eichenbaum et al., 1994; Thinus-Blanc, 1996).

These data show that some significant features of the spatial capabilities of fish resemble those of reptiles, birds, and mammals, including primates (O'Keefe and Nadel, 1978; Schenk and Morris, 1985; Whishaw and Mittleman, 1986; Sherry and Vaccarino, 1989; Whishaw, 1989; Sherry and Duff, 1996; Bingman et al., 1998; López et al., 2000c, 2001) and suggest that spatial cognition is organized in a similar way in every vertebrate radiation. Such striking cognition similarities in vertebrate groups that diverged millions of years ago from a common evolutionary ancestor suggest the possibility that these multiple spatial memory systems may be a primitive feature in vertebrates, that is, that all of them could have inherited some common features in the behavioral and neural organization, maintained

with little modification through phylogenetic branching. However, if the cognitive capabilities observed in fish and amniotes really have a common evolutionary origin, then they must stem from a conserved neural basis. This possibility is discussed in the next section.

1.26.7 Neural Basis of Spatial Cognition in Teleost Fish

In the preceding sections, we reviewed evidence suggesting that spatial orientation and navigation in teleost fish, as in land vertebrates, involves a variety of cognitive, perceptive, and motor mechanisms. We now summarize experimental evidence showing that these spatial cognition processes and memory systems are based on separate brain substrata and outline the central question of whether they are supported by neural centers and circuits equivalent to those that underline spatial cognition in land vertebrates.

Comparative evidence shows that separate brain systems contribute in different ways to spatial orientation and navigation in vertebrates, such that sensorimotor information is processed and integrated by a number of brain mechanisms, and the information about environmental space and the position of the body and body parts in space is coded and translated into a series of coordinate systems, from the receptive surfaces to head-centered and body-centered coordinates and to allocentric, world-centered coordinate systems. For example, in mammals, perception and action based on egocentric frames of spatial reference depend on brain circuits that involve the superior colliculus, cerebellum, basal ganglia, and parietal and frontal motor cortical areas (Stein and Meredith, 1993; Burgess et al., 1999). However, the use of allocentric frames of reference for navigation, based on the encoding of the reciprocal spatial relationships between the goal and multiple sensory and spatial features, depends on other neural systems, mainly the hippocampal formation and associated brain circuits (O'Keefe and Nadel, 1978; Burgess et al., 1999; Chapters 1.21, 1.33).

Unfortunately, the psychological and neurobiological research concerning the neural basis of learning and memory in fish has been largely limited by the misleading, but very common and deeply rooted, idea that vertebrate evolution occurred in successive stages of increasing complexity and advancement in brain organization and cognitive capabilities, following a lineal progression from inferior to superior forms (i.e., fishes, amphibians, reptiles, birds, and mammals; *Scala naturae*, Hodos and Campbell, 1969; Deacon, 1990; Hodos and Campbell, 1990; Preuss, 1995; Butler and Hodos, 2005). Thus, the classical theories on vertebrate brain and behavior evolution propose that fishes, the most primitive and least evolved vertebrate group, have developed relatively simple neural circuits. According to these theories, the forebrain of fishes was thought to consist mainly of a subpallium (paleostriatum) and a very reduced and primitive pallium (paleocortex), both entirely dominated by olfactory inputs and consequently allowing only elemental forms of behavior and learning capabilities. In fact, these theories considered that neural structures equivalent to the hippocampus and the neocortex were completely absent in the fish telencephalon. All these telencephalic structures (the neoencephalon) were thought to have evolved later, in supposedly more recent and complex vertebrate groups. However, by the end of the twentieth century, a fast-growing amount of comparative developmental, neuroanatomical, and

functional evidence had led to an entirely different understanding of vertebrate brain and behavior evolution, as the traditional, anthropocentric view of linear brain evolution was consistently contradicted by the data: Vertebrates have not evolved linearly, but the lineage initiated in a remote common ancestor branched in different radiations, which evolved independently, and increases in brain size and complexity occur in every one of these branches. Furthermore, this new evidence reveals that the evolution of the vertebrate brain has likely been more conservative than previously thought and that the extant vertebrates share some inherited features of brain and behavior organization. Thus, although showing conspicuous morphological and cytoarchitectural differences, their brains can be considered as variations of a common vertebrate plan (Wiley, 1981; Northcutt, 1995; Nieuwenhuys et al., 1998; Butler and Hodos, 2005). The comparative evidence reveals not only that the central nervous system of vertebrates is organized in homologous main subdivisions (i.e., telencephalon, diencephalon, mesencephalon, rhombencephalon, and spinal cord) but also that the telencephalon of every vertebrate group, including fish, consists of equivalent pallial and subpallial zones. Moreover, we now know that the olfactory areas represent only a limited portion of the fish telencephalic pallium and that the main pallial subdivisions in the actinopterygian fish telencephalon are likely to be homologous to the main pallial subdivisions of tetrapods (Braford, 1995; Northcutt, 1995; Wulliman and Rink, 2002; Butler and Hodos, 2005).

1.26.8 Teleost Fish Telencephalon and Spatial Cognition

The results of the initial studies on the neural basis of behavior in teleost fish seemed consistent with the theories on vertebrate brain evolution prevailing at the time. For example, early studies reported that ablation of the entire telencephalon in teleost fish produced few (if any) deleterious effects on fish behavior, that gross sensory or motor deficits were not apparent, and that the motivation of the ablated animals appeared to remain at normal levels (see, e.g., Polimanti, 1913; Nolte, 1932; Janzen, 1933; Hosch, 1936; Hale, 1956; Savage, 1969b). However, more careful analyses revealed that telencephalon ablation causes profound learning and memory deficits in fishes as well as significant alterations in emotional and social behavior (Aronson, 1970; Hollis and

Overmier, 1978; de Bruin, 1980; Davis and Kassel, 1983; for revisions, see Savage 1980; Overmier and Hollis 1983, 1990). These studies showed that whereas telencephalon ablation in fish does not impair simple instrumental learning and classical conditioning (Overmier and Curnow, 1969; Flood and Overmier, 1971; Frank et al., 1972; Overmier and Savage, 1974; Farr and Savage, 1978; Hollis and Overmier, 1982), it does produce severe impairments in other learning instances, such as avoidance learning (Hainsworth et al., 1967; Savage, 1968; Overmier and Flood, 1969; Savage, 1969a), as well as instrumental learning when there is a delay between the response and the reward (Savage and Swingland, 1969; Overmier and Patten, 1982).

Interestingly, the involvement of the teleost fish telencephalon in spatial cognition was also already suggested by early ablation studies, although the initial reports were often contradictory. Thus, no deficits, impairments, or even improvement in spatial learning have been observed following telencephalon ablation in fish trained in alleys and mazes (Hosch, 1936; Zunini, 1954; Hale, 1956; Warren, 1961; Ingle, 1965; Frank et al., 1972; Flood et al., 1976; Farr and Savage, 1978). The inconsistency of the reports could be attributed to the fact that these experiments were not specifically aimed to analyze spatial cognition and therefore did not include a precise definition of the spatial requirements of the tasks nor adequate control tests, which are essential for identifying the effects of ablation on spatial performance. Moreover, spatial learning and memory and spatial cognition frequently involve somewhat confusing concepts that include a mixture of still poorly characterized perceptive and cognitive processes actually based in separate neural substrata.

More recent studies, designed specifically to analyze the nature of the spatial cognition deficits produced by telencephalic lesions, have provided strong evidence for the central role of the telencephalon in spatial cognition in teleosts. The data from the more recent ablation studies show that the teleost telencephalon is necessary for some specific spatial learning and memory functions, as it contains essential components of the neural network that underlies map-like spatial memories in fish (Rodríguez et al., 1994; Salas et al., 1996a, 1996b). For example, Salas et al. (1996b) trained goldfish in place (allocentric), turn (egocentric), or mixed place–turn procedures in a four-arm maze. After the animals had mastered their task, they were subjected to complete telencephalic ablation or sham operations. The results showed that

the ablation dramatically and irreversibly impaired the ability of the fish trained in the place procedure to recognize goal location during postsurgery training (**Figure 6**). In contrast, telencephalon ablation did not alter the performance of the animals using egocentric orientation strategies. Interestingly, the lesion appeared to produce no deficit in the fish trained in the mixed place–turn procedure, as during postsurgery training their performance remained at the previous levels. However, the transfer trials revealed that the telencephalon ablation did produce a remarkable spatial cognition impairment: Whereas before ablation these animals used place (allocentric) or turn (egocentric) strategies in a flexible and cooperative way according to the experimental conditions, after surgery, their performance was based exclusively on turn responses (**Figure 6**).

Consistent results were obtained in an experiment in which intact and telencephalon-ablated goldfish were trained in a mixed place–cue procedure (López et al., 2000a). Sham-operated and telencephalon-ablated goldfish were trained in a test environment where they could simultaneously rely on the spatial information provided by a number of extramaze distal landmarks on the periphery of the experimental room and on an intramaze single cue that directly indicated the location of food. Paradoxically, telencephalon-ablated goldfish showed better performance during training relative to sham-operated animals (see **Figure 7(a)**). However, the results of the probe tests designed to examine the relative importance of the two sources of information (extra- vs. intramaze cues) revealed that these animals suffered a profound spatial learning deficit: their performance was based exclusively on egocentric strategies (**Figure 7(b)**). In the place–cue dissociation tests, in which the two sources of information were set in conflict (the place and the cue responses were incompatible), the control fish did not have a significant preference for either the cue or the place responses. In contrast, the performance of the telencephalon-ablated fish was notably biased in these test trials; they showed a significant preference for the arm containing the cue that signaled the goal during training. In the extramaze occlusion tests, when the maze was completely surrounded by curtains precluding the use of the extramaze visual cues, both telencephalic and control fish showed a strong preference for the arm containing the cue associated with the goal during training. However, in the intramaze cue-removal test, whereas the control goldfish consistently chose the arm placed at the location of the room where they were rewarded during training, the

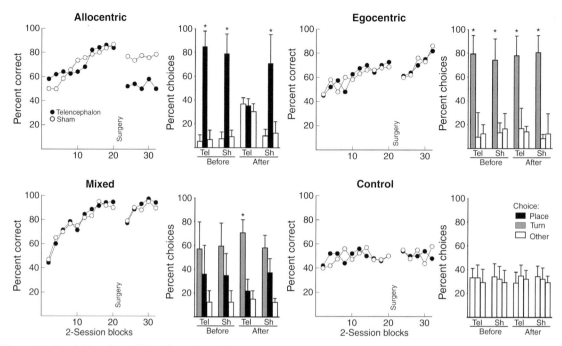

Figure 6 Spatial learning deficits after telencephalic ablation in goldfish trained in egocentric and allocentric maze procedures. The curves show the mean percentage of correct choices of telencephalon-ablated and sham-operated goldfish trained in different spatial procedures as described in **Figure 2**. The bars show the percentage of choices during the transfer tests conducted before and after surgery for each experimental group. Asterisks denote significant differences. Modified from Salas C, Rodríguez F, Vargas JP, Durán E, and Torres B (1996b) Spatial learning and memory deficits after telencephalic ablation in goldfish trained in place and turn maze procedures. *Behav. Neurosci.* 110: 965–980.

telencephalon-ablated fish chose at random between the maze arms, indicating that these animals were not able to use the array extramaze cues as a source of useful spatial information. These results indicate that although both groups learned the task, the sham-operated and the telencephalon-ablated goldfish differed in their capacity to use complementary navigational strategies; the control animals used both place and cue strategies, but the telencephalon-ablated animals solved the task exclusively on the basis of a cue strategy. Additional experiments using different behavioral procedures provided converging evidence on the role of the teleost fish telencephalon in spatial cognition. Thus, telencephalon ablation disrupted the postsurgery performance (Salas et al., 1996b) and reversal learning (López et al., 2000b) of goldfish trained in a spatial constancy task but did not produce any observable deficit in a cue procedure (Salas et al., 1996b). In summary, the place memory impairments observed in these experiments strongly suggest that forebrain ablation in fish produces a selective but severe disruption in a telencephalon-dependent spatial memory system, which sustains the use of allocentric, relational map-like representations of space.

In mammals, birds, and reptiles, map-like or relational spatial memories depend on the hippocampus and associated structures (O'Keefe and Nadel, 1978; Sherry and Duff, 1996; Bingman et al., 1998; Burgess et al., 1999; Rodríguez et al., 2002a, b; López et al., 2003a, b; Chapters 1.21, 1.22, 1.33). Similarly, compelling evidence suggests that specific areas and circuits of the teleost forebrain, in particular the lateral pallium, proposed as homologous with the hippocampus of land vertebrates, provide an essential neural substratum for cognitive mapping abilities in fish (Salas et al., 1996a, b; López et al., 2000a, b; Rodríguez et al., 2002b; Salas et al., 2003, Broglio et al., 2005; Salas et al., 2006).

1.26.9 Telencephalic Hippocampal Pallium and Map-like Memories in Teleost Fish

The telencephalon of ray-finned fishes presents morphological features that are unique among vertebrates; for instance, it consists of solid telencephalic hemispheres separated by a single ventricular cavity, instead of hemispheres with internal ventricles.

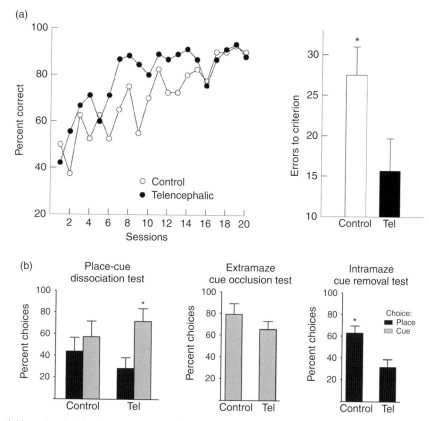

Figure 7 Spatial learning deficits by telencephalic ablation in goldfish trained in a mixed place–cue arm-maze procedure. (a) Percentage of correct choices and errors to criterion of sham-operated and telencephalon-ablated goldfish trained in a mixed place–cue procedure as described in **Figure 3**. (b) Mean percentage of choices in the three different probe tests conducted following learning of the task by both groups. Asterisks denote significant differences. Modified from López JC, Bingman VP, Rodríguez F, Gómez Y, and Salas C (2000a) Dissociation of place and cue learning by telencephalic ablation in goldfish. *Behav. Neurosci.* 114: 687–699.

Ray-finned fishes represent a particular case because their telencephalon develops by a process of eversion or bending outward of the embryonic prosencephalic alar plate, contrasting with the evagination that characterizes the telencephalic development of every other vertebrate group (Nieuwenhuys, 1963; Northcutt and Braford, 1980; Braford, 1995; Northcutt, 1995, 2006; Striedter and Northcutt, 2006). This developmental peculiarity implies that the medial-to-lateral topography of the pallial areas observed in the vertebrates with evaginated telencephalon is reversed in ray-finned fishes. In fact, the ray-finned fish's lateral telencephalic pallium (i.e., the embryonary distal pallium) is considered homologous to the medial pallium or hippocampus of the tetrapods (Northcutt and Braford, 1980; Nieuwenhuys and Meek, 1990; Braford, 1995; Northcutt, 1995; Butler, 2000; Northcutt, 2006; see **Figure 8**). This hypothesis of homology of

hippocampus is supported by the neuroanatomical and developmental data (Northcutt, 1995; Wulliman and Mueller, 2004; Northcutt, 2006). Like the hippocampus, the lateral pallium is characterized by widespread reciprocal connections with other pallial areas, as well as with the contralateral lateral pallium, by means of commissural projections. In addition, the lateral pallium is reciprocally connected with the ventral nucleus of the area ventralis (Vv) considered homologous to the septal nucleus (Butler and Hodos, 2005), from which it receives a cholinergic input. The extratelencephalic pattern of connectivity of the lateral pallium is also similar to that of the hippocampus, as it projects to the preoptic area and other diencephalic regions and receives inputs from the preoptic area, the locus coeruleus, and the superior raphe. Particularly, the ventral subdivision of the lateral pallium (Dlv) is the most likely candidate as the specific homolog of the

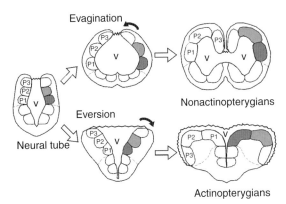

Figure 8 Schematic representation of the process of evagination and inversion that occurs in the telencephalon of nonactinopterygian vertebrates during embryonic development compared with the process of eversion or bending outward that occurs in actinopterygians. P1, P2, and P3 correspond to the three main subdivisions of the pallium. V, ventricle.

tetrapod medial pallium; it occupies the most distal topological position in the pallium and has extensive interconnections with the likely homologs of the septal nuclei and preoptic area. The hypothesis of homology concerning the teleost fish Dlv region and the hippocampus is also supported by the distribution pattern of several histochemical and molecular markers. For example, the dopamine receptor subtype D1B, which is characteristic of the mammalian hippocampus, is selectively expressed in the Dlv subdivision of the teleost pallium (Kapsimali et al., 2000), and this area, like the mammalian dentate gyrus, shows neurogenesis and migration of interneurons (Grandel et al., 2006).

Functional evidence also supports the hypothesis of homology between the lateral pallium of teleost fish and the hippocampus, as the ventral lateral pallium of teleost fish, like the amniote hippocampus, is selectively involved in spatial cognition (Rodríguez et al., 2002b; Broglio et al., 2005). Extensive lesions to the lateral pallium produce a dramatic impairment in place memory in goldfish trained in a plus maze surrounded by widely distributed distal visual cues (Rodriguez et al., 2002b; see **Figure 9(a)**). Following surgery, lateral pallium–lesioned fish showed a severe and permanent impairment to reaching well-trained goal locations. In addition, these animals were not able to locate the goal from new starting places during transfer tests in which reaching the goal involved the use of novel routes. The spatial learning and memory deficits following lesions restricted to the lateral pallium in goldfish are as severe as those

produced by the ablation of the entire telencephalon (Salas et al., 1996b; López et al., 2000a; Rodríguez et al., 2002a,b). In addition, the involvement of the lateral pallium in spatial cognition is highly selective, as the damage to this area does not disrupt cue learning or other egocentrically referenced spatial behaviors (Salas et al., 1996a,b; López et al., 2000a; Rodríguez et al., 2002b; see **Figure 9(b)**). These results indicate that, like the hippocampal pallium of land vertebrates, the lateral pallium of teleost fish is selectively involved in the use of map-like or relational spatial memory representations for allocentric navigation, but it is not critical for simple stimulus–response associations or cue learning. In contrast, the medial and dorsal pallium lesions do not produce any observable impairment in spatial memory in goldfish (Rodríguez et al., 2002b; see **Figure 9**). In contrast, the teleost fish medial pallium, likely homologous to the pallial amygdala of amniotes (Northcutt and Braford, 1980; Northcutt, 1995; Wulliman and Mueller 2004; Yamamoto et al., 2007), seems to be involved in emotional behavior (Portavella et al., 2004a,b; Broglio et al., 2005; Salas et al., 2006), and the dorsal pallium, which contains several multisensory and motor representations, appears to be the homolog of the amniote dorsal cortex or isocortex (Northcutt, 1995; Prechtl et al., 1998; Saidel et al., 2001; Northcutt, 2006; Yamamoto et al., 2007).

The involvement of the lateral telencephalic pallium of teleost fish in spatial cognition is suggested also by studies using complementary techniques to reveal neural activity. Vargas et al. (2000) showed that training goldfish in a spatial task induces a significant and selective spatial learning-related increase in the transcription activity (protein synthesis) of the neurons in the lateral pallium, evaluated by means of a silver stain with high affinity for the argyrophilic proteins of the nucleolar organizing region (AgNORs). The size of the AgNORs in the cell nucleus indicates the level of transcriptive activity of rDNA, and heightened rDNA activity indicates increases in protein synthesis (Davis and Squire, 1984; Crocker and Nar, 1987; Dámaso et al., 1988; Lafarga et al., 1991; Underwood, 1992; González-Pardo et al., 1994). Vargas et al. (2000) showed that the size of the AgNORs in the neurons of the ventral part of the goldfish telencephalic lateral pallium (Dlv region) increased significantly and selectively after learning a spatial constancy task, compared with the same area of the brain in the animals of the control group (trained in a noncontingent procedure) or with the neurons of the medial pallium of both groups (see **Figure 10**). An interesting result is also provided by Carneiro et al. (2001), who showed spatial cognition-related sex differences in the lateral pallium of Azorean rock-pool blennies (*Parablennius parvicornis*). In this species, males establish nest sites and remain in their nest area during the entire breeding season. In contrast, females need to move relatively long distances in order to visit different nests and spawn with males. Interestingly, Carneiro et al. (2001) found that female blennies have a larger lateral pallium compared to males. These authors related the greater size of the female blennies' lateral pallium with the increased spatial cognition demand on females, which need to displace greater distances than males and need to remember the nest location of different males.

Recently, Saito and Watanabe (2004, 2006) reported results apparently contradictory to this view, as they found that not lateral but, rather, medial pallium lesions produced spatial memory deficits in goldfish tested in a hole-board analog task. However, these experiments lack an adequate set of test trials to identify the spatial strategies used by the animals; therefore, the possible deficits observed in these experiments cannot have been clearly defined. In fact, the performance deficits observed in the medial pallium-lesioned animals in these studies could be better explained by nonspatial impairments, such as motivation, attention, and general activity alterations (Davis and Kassel, 1983; Riedel, 1998). Furthermore, the lateral pallium lesions in the experiment by Saito and Watanabe do not include the ventral portion of the lateral pallium but affect mostly the pallial region extending between the lateral and the medial pallium, which is most likely homologous with the dorsal cortex of land vertebrates (Northcutt, 1995; Pretchtl et al., 1998; Butler, 2000; Saidel et al., 2001; Northcutt, 2006; Yamamoto et al., 2007). In fact, it has not been possible to replicate the results of Saito and Watanabe in experiments when care was taken to lesion the medial pallium and the ventral part of lateral pallium selectively (Durán, 2004; Rodríguez et al., 2005). Durán (2004) trained lateral and medial pallium-lesioned goldfish to locate one baited feeder (goal) within a 25-feeder matrix surrounded by an array of intramaze visual cues, in a procedure analogous to the hole-board task used with rats and similar to the procedure and apparatus used by Saito and Watanabe. In this experiment, transfer and probe tests were performed to analyze carefully and identify the spatial strategies used by the animals. The results of this work are consistent with previous lesion

studies and do not support Saito and Watanabe's conclusions. The lateral pallium-lesioned goldfish, as well as the medial pallium-lesioned and the control animals learned to solve the task with accuracy. However, the test trials when the different visual cues were independently removed showed that the lateral pallium-but not the medial pallium-lesioned fish suffered a spatial learning impairment. Thus, the lateral pallium-lesioned animals, but not the medial pallium-lesioned and the control fish, failed to reach the goal when the particular subset of visual cues situated in the proximity of the goal was excluded. These results reveal that the lateral pallium animals relied on a guidance strategy to solve the task (i.e., they learned to approach a particular visual cue that they associated with the goal), suggesting that these animals lack the capacity to encode the goal location relative to multiple environmental features in a map-like representation (place learning). The probe tests also showed that, in contrast, the medial pallium-lesioned goldfish are able to navigate readily to the goal independently of the removal of any particular subset of visual cues. These data clearly indicate that the lateral pallium of teleost fish, but not the medial pallium, provides the neural substratum for the ability of fish to use allocentric, relational representations of the environment.

1.26.10 Neural Mechanisms for Egocentrically Referenced Spatial Orientation

Fish spatial cognition also involves a variety of egocentrically referenced perceptive and motor mechanisms based on the function of different neural centers and circuits, for example, the reticulospinal and vestibular circuits, the cerebellum, and the optic tectum.

The optic tectum is a crucial center for the generation of egocentrically referenced actions in space. The anatomical and functional organization of the optic tectum (superior colliculus in mammals) appears to be quite well conserved in vertebrates (Vanegas, 1984; Stein and Meredith, 1993). The teleost optic tectum is a crucial center for sensorimotor integration and for the generation of egocentrically referenced actions in space. As in other vertebrates, the optic tectum of teleost fish presents a spatially ordered motor map in the deep tectal layers in correspondence with the retinotopic visual map in the superficial layers (Salas et al., 1997; Sparks, 2002). For example,

(a)

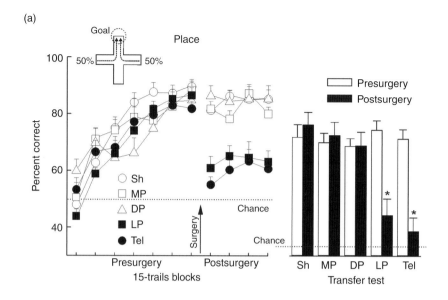

(b)

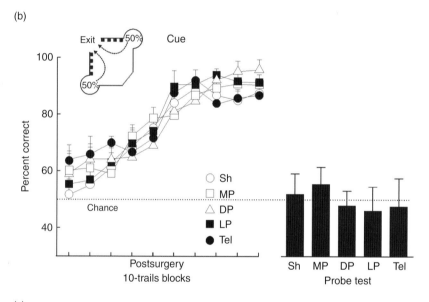

(c)

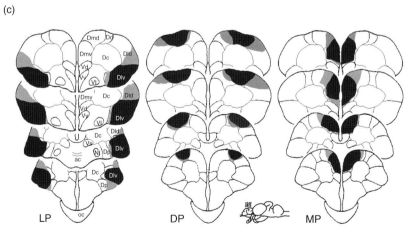

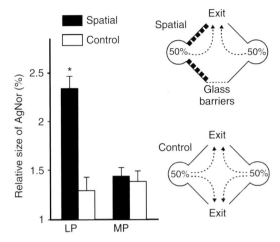

Figure 10 Spatial learning induced a significant increase in protein synthesis in the neurons of the lateral pallium of goldfish trained in a spatial task. The figure shows the size of the nucleolar organizing regions (NORs) relative to the size of the nucleus in lateral (LP) and medial (MP) pallium neurons of goldfish trained in a spatial or a control task as described in the diagrams. Asterisks denote significant differences. Modified from Vargas JP, Rodríguez F, López JC, Arias JL, and Salas C (2000) Spatial learning-induced increase in the argyrophilic nucleolar organizer region of dorsolateral telencephalic neurons in goldfish. *Brain Res.* 865: 77–84.

electrical microstimulation in the optic tectum elicited egocentrically referenced coordinated eye and body movements and postural adjustments in teleost fish (Meyer et al., 1970; Demski, 1983; Al-Akel et al., 1986; Salas et al., 1995, 1997; Herrero et al., 1998; see **Figure 11**). The optic tectum provides common body-centered frames of reference for multisensory integration and for sensorimotor transformation, based in their specialized intrinsic circuits and in their profuse connectivity with other motor and sensorial centers (Vanegas, 1984; Stein and Meredith, 1993; Salas et al., 1997), and probably participates in a neural interface for transforming the tectal information, coded in spatial coordinates, into a temporal signal in separate brainstem generators in the reticular premotor centers (Torres et al., 2002, 2005).

However, the distinction between only two main types of reference frames (egocentric vs. allocentric) is probably too restrictive. For example, both the egocentric and allocentric reference frames require a geocentric frame based on the invariant direction of the gravity forces (Trevarthen, 1968; Paillard, 1991; Berthoz, 1999). The vestibular information is essential in orientation and perceptual and motor stabilization, by providing an egocentric reference frame for orientation (Paillard, 1991), and is also likely to have a role in navigation based on inertial information (Mittelstaedt and Glasauer, 1991). In addition, different egocentrically referenced orientation mechanisms can interact to provide integrated behavioral outputs. For example, in the dorsal light response (DLR), the incident angle of the light, in addition to gravity, determines the postural position of fish (Holst, 1950). When the light angle of incidence is not completely vertical, fish assume a tilted posture, with the dorsal body area oriented somewhat toward the light source. The exact angle of deviation from the vertical position depends on light incidence angle and light intensity. Thus, this relatively simple reflex response involves an interaction between the visual and vestibular sensory inputs. Lesion studies in goldfish indicated that this response is abolished after lateral valvula cerebelli or pretectal nuclei lesions, but not after optic tectum lesions (Watanabe et al., 1989; Yanagihara et al., 1993b,c). The visual information is relayed to the cerebellum by the pretectal nuclei, which project to the valvula cerebelli directly, not via the optic tectum. In addition, the lateral valvula cerebelli receives vestibular and lateral line inputs indirectly, via the eminentia granularis and the medial nucleus of the octavolateralis column (Yanagihara et al., 1993a). As in land vertebrates, even these relatively simple and apparently mechanical fish reflexes are submitted to learning and memory modulation and undergo plastic modifications, adjustments, and recalibrations, with the cerebellum playing a central role in such plasticity (Löwenstein, 1932; Holst, 1935; Paul and Roberts,

Figure 9 Spatial memory deficits after lateral pallium lesion in goldfish. (a) Left, mean percentage of correct choices during pre- and postsurgery training in an arm-maze place task by goldfish with different pallial lesions or sham-operated goldfish. Right, mean percentage of correct choices during pre- and postsurgery transfer trials in which new start positions were used (see **Figure 2**). (b) Left, mean percentage of correct responses during postsurgery training in a cue task as described in **Figure 4**. Right, percentage of correct responses in the cue removal probe test. (c) Schematic representation of the largest (grey shading) and smallest (black shading) extent of the lateral (LP), dorsal (DP), and medial (MP) pallium lesions in goldfish, reconstructed in coronal sections. Asterisks denote significant differences. Modified from Rodríguez F, López JC, Vargas JP, Gómez Y, Broglio C, and Salas C (2002b) Conservation of spatial memory function in the pallial forebrain of amniotes and ray-finned fishes. *J. Neurosci.* 22: 2894–2903.

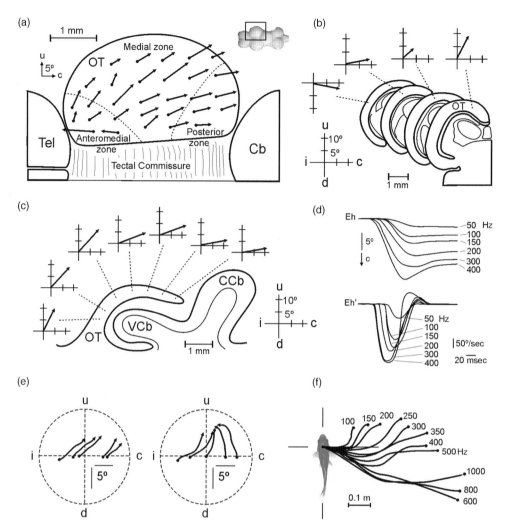

Figure 11 Focal electrical stimulation in the optic tectum of goldfish elicits coordinated eye and body movements, revealing that the optic tectum of teleost fish is a crucial center for the generation of egocentrically referenced actions in space. The amplitude and direction of eye movement vectors depend on the stimulation site within the tectum (a). Varying the stimulation site in the medial-lateral axis produces an increase in the vertical component (b), whereas varying the stimulation site in the rostrocaudal axis produces a systematic change in the amplitude of the horizontal component of the saccade (c). Varying the stimulation parameters (v.g. frequency) produces systematic changes in the metric and kinetic of the evoked orientation responses (d). Stimulating anatomically separated tectal areas evokes different types of eye movements (e). The electrical microstimulation of the optic tectum in free-swimming fish elicits body movements (f). Evoked movements consist of complete orientation responses including coordinated movements of the axial musculature, fins, and eyes, which closely resemble the natural responses. The direction and amplitude of the orienting responses depend on both the tectal stimulation site and the stimulus parameters. Abbreviations: Cb, cerebellum; CCb, corpus cerebellum; Eh, horizontal component of eye position; Eh', eye velocity trace; OT, optic tectum; St, electrode for microstimulation; Tel, telencephalon; VCb, valvula cerebellum; d, u, i, c, downward, upward, ipsiversive, and contraversive direction of evoked eye saccade, respectively. Modified from Herrero L, Rodríguez F, Salas C, and Torres B (1998) Tail and eye movements evoked by electrical microstimulation of the optic tectum in goldfish. *Exp. Brain Res.* 120: 291–305; Salas C, Herrero L, Rodríguez F, and Torres B (1997) Tectal codification of eye movements in goldfish studied by electrical microstimulation. *Neuroscience* 78: 271–288.

1979; Burt and Flohr, 1988; Ott and Platt, 1988; Burt and Flohr, 1991; Pastor et al., 1994; Li et al., 1995; McElligott et al., 1998; Straka et al., 2006). However, like the mammalian cerebellum, the teleost fish cerebellum is likely not only an essential center for motor coordination and adjustment but is also involved in learning and memory and in spatial cognition. For example, the goldfish cerebellum is involved in eye blink–like classical conditioning (Rodríguez et al., 2005; Salas et al., 2006). In addition, cerebellum lesions produce profound spatial cognition deficits in goldfish (Durán, 2004; Rodríguez et al., 2005, 2006). In this study, when goldfish were required to learn the location of a baited feeder within a 25-feeder matrix surrounded by a stable array of visual cues, the cerebellum-lesioned animals never reached the level of accuracy of the control and sham-operated animals. This could be due to the fact that their search pattern is stereotyped and inefficient. The results of test trials showed that the performance of the cerebellum-lesioned fish depends on approaching a particular subset of cues, suggesting that they are unable to use the entire array. These data indicate that these animals are impaired in their ability to generate or use map-like representations of the environment. Interestingly, the cerebellum lesions also impair orientation based on egocentric frames of reference. Durán (2004) showed that whereas telencephalic lesions disrupt goldfish performance in a spatial constancy task but spare cue orientation learning (see also Salas et al., 1996b), cerebellum lesions are equally disruptive in both tasks. These results indicate that the teleost cerebellum is also involved in the association of motor responses with single landmarks and in other egocentric orientation mechanisms. Remarkably, whereas the effects of cerebellum lesions in goldfish are profound and widespread in spatial learning, they do not produce observable sensorimotor impairments or deficits in posture, swimming ability, or obstacle avoidance, indicating that also in teleost fish the role of the cerebellum goes far beyond just motor-control modulation.

1.26.11 Concluding Remarks

The data presented here show that the complexity and plasticity of spatial behavior in fish parallels that of mammals and birds. Moreover, as in land vertebrates, spatial behavior in fish depends on a variety of learning and memory mechanisms and cognitive processes, supported by particular brain circuits. The fish's lateral pallium, likely homologous to the hippocampus of amniotes, is essential for simultaneously processing and encoding spatial information from multiple sources and forming map-like or relational representations of the environment. Also as in land vertebrates, other brain circuits, involving, for example, the optic tectum or the cerebellum, underlie egocentrically referenced spatial orientation. The notable similarity observed in the spatial cognition capabilities and their neural substrates in groups that diverged millions of years ago suggest that some features of these spatial learning and memory systems and their neural basis might be a primitive feature in vertebrates, conserved through evolution.

References

Able KP (1991) Common themes and variations in animal orientation systems. *Am. Zool.* 31: 157–167.
Al-Akel AS, Guthrie DM, and Banks JR (1986) Motor responses to localized electrical stimulation of the tectum in the freshwater perch (*Perca fluviatilis*). *Neuroscience* 19: 1381–1391.
Aronson LR (1951) Orientation and jumping behavior in the gobiid fish *Bathygobius soporator*. *Am. Mus. Nov.* 1586: 1–22.
Aronson LR (1970) Functional evolution of the forebrain in lower vertebrates. In: Aronson E, Toback E, Lehrman DS, and Rosenblatt J (eds.) *Development and Evolution of Behavior*, p. 75. San Francisco: WH Freeman.
Aronson LR (1971) Further studies on orientation and jumping behaviour in the Gobiid fish *Bathygobius soporator*. *Ann. N. Y. Acad. Sci.* 188: 378–392.
Berthoz A (1999) Hippocampal and parietal contribution to topokinetic and topographic memory. In: Burgess N, Jeffery KJ, and O'Keefe J (eds.) *The Hippocampal and Parietal Foundations of Spatial Cognition*, pp. 381–403. Oxford: Oxford University Press.
Bingman VP, Riters LV, Strasser R, and Gagliardo A (1998) Neuroethology of avian navigation. In: Balda R, Pepperberg I, and Kamil A (eds.) *Animal Cognition in Nature*, pp. 201–226. New York: Academic Press.
Braford MR (1995) Comparative aspects of forebrain organization in the ray-finned fishes: Touchstones or not? *Brain Behav. Evol.* 46: 259–274.
Braithwaite VA (1998) Spatial memory, landmark use and orientation in fish. In: Healy S (ed.) *Spatial Representation in Animals*, pp. 86–102. Oxford: Oxford University Press.
Braithwaite VA and Girvan JR (2003) Use of waterflow to provide spatial information in a small-scale orientation task. *J. Fish Biol.* 63: 74–83.
Breder CM (1950) Factors influencing the establishment of residence in shells by tropical shore fishes. *Zoologica* 35: 153–158.
Breder CM and Halpern E (1946) Innate and acquired behavior affecting the aggregation of fishes. *Physiol. Zool.* 19: 154–190.
Broglio C, Gómez Y, López JC, Rodríguez F, Salas C, and Vargas JP (2000) Encoding of geometric and featural properties of a spatial environment in teleostean fish (*Carassius auratus*). *Int. J. Psychol.* 35: 195–195.
Broglio C, Rodríguez F, and Salas C (2003) Spatial cognition and its neural basis in teleost fishes. *Fish Fisher* 4: 247–255.
Broglio C, Gómez A, Durán E, et al. (2005) Hallmarks of a common forebrain vertebrate plan: Specialized pallial areas for spatial, temporal and emotional memory in actinopterygian fish. *Brain Res. Bull.* 66: 277–281.
Brown C and Laland K (2006) Social learning in fishes. In: Brown C, Laland K, and Krause J (eds.) *Fish Cognition and Behaviour*, pp. 186–202. Oxford: Blackwell.
Burgess N, Jeffery KJ, and O'Keefe J (1999) *The Hippocampal and Parietal Foundations of Spatial Cognition*. London: Oxford University Press.
Burt A and Flohr H (1988) "Acute" vestibular compensation in the goldfish: A visual substitution process? In: Flohr H (ed.) *Postlesion Neural Plasticity*, pp. 393–410. Berlin: Springer.

Burt A and Flohr H (1991) Role of the visual input in recovery of function following unilateral vestibular lesion in the goldfish. I. Short-term behavioural changes. *Behav. Brain Res.* 42: 201–211.

Burt de Perera T (2004a) Fish can encode order in their spatial map. *Proc. Roy. Soc. Lond. B Biol. Sci.* 271: 2131–2134.

Burt de Perera T (2004b) Spatial parameters encoded in the spatial map of blind Mexican cave fish *Astynax fasciatus*. *Anim. Behav.* 68: 291–295.

Butler AB (2000) Topography and topology of the teleost telencephalon: A paradox resolved. *Neurosci. Lett.* 293: 95–98.

Butler AB and Hodos H (2005) *Comparative Vertebrate Neuroanatomy: Evolution and Adaptation*, 2nd edn. New York: Wiley-Liss.

Cain P (1995) Navigation in familiar environments by the weakly electric fish *Gnathonemus petersii* L (Mormyriformes Teleostei). *Ethology* 99: 332–349.

Cain P, Gerin W, and Moller P (1994) Short-range navigation of the weakly electric fish *Gnathonemus petersii* L (Mormyridae Teleostei) in novel and familiar environments. *Ethology* 96: 33–45.

Campenhausen CV, Riess I, and Weissert R (1981) Detection of stationary objects by the blind cave fish *Anoptichtys jordani* (Characidae). *J. Comp. Physiol.* 143: 369–374.

Carlson HR and Haight RE (1972) Evidence for a home site and homing of adult yellowtail rockfish *Sebastes flavidus*. *J. Fish Res. Board Canada* 29: 1011–1014.

Carneiro LA, Andrade RP, Oliveira RF, and Kotrschal K (2001) Sex differences in home range and dorso-lateral telencephalon in the azorean rock-pool blenny. *Soc. Neurosci. Abstr.* 27: Program No. 535.4.

Cheng K (1986) A purely geometric module in the rat's spatial representation. *Cognition* 23: 149–178.

Cheng K (1994) The determination of direction and landmark based spatial search in pigeons: A further test of the vector sum model. *Anim. Learn. Behav.* 22: 291–301.

Cheng K and Gallistel CR (1984) Testing the geometric power of an animal's spatial representation. In: Roitblat HL, Bever TG, and Terrace HS (eds.) *Animal Cognition*, pp. 409–423. Hillsdale, NJ: Erlbaum.

Cheng K and Sherry DF (1992) Landmark-based spatial memory in birds (*Parus atricapillus*) and distances to represent spatial position. *J. Comp. Psychol.* 106: 331–341.

Clayton NS and Dickinson A (1998) Episodic-like memory during cache recovery by scrub jays. *Nature* 395: 272–274.

Crocker J and Nar P (1987) Nucleolar organizer regions in lymphomas. *J. Pathol.* 151: 111–118.

Dámaso C, Viadero CF, Villegas J, and Lafarga M (1988) Nucleoli numbers and neuronal growth in supraoptic nucleus neurons during postnatal development in the rat. *Dev. Brain Res.* 44: 151–155.

Davis HP and Squire LR (1984) Protein synthesis and memory: A review. *Psychol. Bull.* 96: 518–559.

Davis RE and Kassel J (1983) Behavioral functions of the teleost telencephalon. In: Northcutt RG and Davis RE (eds.) *Fish Neurobiology*, pp. 237–264. Ann Arbor: The University of Michigan Press.

Davitz MA and McKaye KR (1978) Discrimination between vertically and horizontally polarized light by the cichlid fish *Pseudotropheus macrophthalmus*. *Copeia* 190: 333–334.

De Bruin JPC (1980) Telencephalon and behavior in teleost fish. A neuroethological approach. In: Ebbesson SOE (ed.) *Comparative Neurology of the Telencephalon*, New York: Plenum Press.

Deacon TW (1990) Rethinking mammalian brain evolution. *Am. Zool.* 30: 629–705.

Dember WN and Fowler H (1958) Spontaneous alternation behavior. *Psychol. Bull.* 55: 412–428.

Demski LS (1983) Behavioral effects of electrical stimulation of the brain. In: Davis RE and Northcutt RG (eds.) *Fish Neurobiology, vol 2. Higher Brain Areas and Functions*, pp. 317–359. Ann Arbor: Michigan University Press.

Demski LS and Beaver JA (2001) Brain and cognitive function in teleost fishes. In: Roth G and Wulliman MF (eds.) *Brain Evolution and Cognition*, pp. 297–332. New York: Wiley.

Dill PA (1971) Perception of polarized light by yearling sockeye salmon (*Oncorhynchus nerka*). *J. Fish Res. Board Canada* 28: 1319–1322.

Dittman AH and Quinn TP (1996) Homing in pacific salmon: Mechanisms and ecological basis. *J. Exp. Biol.* 199: 83–91.

Dodson JJ (1988) The nature and role of learning in the orientation and migratory behavior of fishes. *Environ. Biol. Fish* 23: 161–182.

Douglas RH (1996) Goldfish use the visual angle of a familiar landmark to locate a food source. *J. Fish Biol.* 49: 532–536.

Durán E (2004) Neural bases of spatial learning in goldfish. PhD Thesis, University of Sevilla.

Eichenbaum H (2000) A cortical-hippocampal system for declarative memory. *Nat. Rev. Neurosci.* 1: 41–50.

Eichenbaum H, Stewart C, and Morris RGM (1990) Hippocampal representation in spatial memory. *J. Neurosci.* 10: 3531–3542.

Eichenbaum H, Otto T, and Cohen NJ (1994) Two functional components of the hippocampal memory system. *Behav. Brain Sci.* 17: 449–518.

Farr EJ and Savage GE (1978) First- and second-order conditioning in the goldfish and their relation to the telencephalon. *Behav. Biol.* 22: 50–59.

Flood NB and Overmier JB (1971) Effects of telecephalic and olfactory lesions on appetitive learning in goldfish. *Physiol. Behav.* 6: 35–40.

Flood NB, Overmier JB, and Savage GE (1976) The teleost telencephalon and learning: An interpretative review of data and hypotheses. *Physiol. Behav.* 16: 783–798.

Frank AH, Flood NC, and Overmier JB (1972) Reversal learning in forebrain ablated and olfactory tract sectioned teleost *Carassius auratus*. *Psychon. Sci.* 26: 149–151.

Gallistel CR (1990) *The Organization of Learning*. Cambridge, MA: MIT Press.

Girvan JR and Braithwaite VA (1998) Population differences in spatial learning in three-spined sticklebacks. *Proc. R. Soc. Lond. B Biol. Sci.* 265: 913–919.

Girvan JR and Braithwaite VA (2000) Orientation behavior in sticklebacks: Modified by population or specific? *Behaviour* 137: 833–843.

Gladfelter WB (1979) Twilight migrations and foraging activities of the Copper Sweeper *Pempheris schombergki* (Teleostei, Pempheridae). *Mar. Biol.* 50: 109–119.

González-Pardo H, Gutiérrez-Sánchez JM, Menéndez-Patterson A, and Arias JL (1994) Postnatal development of argyrophilic nucleolar organizer regions in the mammillary body of undernourished rats. *Brain Res.* 654: 75–80.

Goodyear CP (1970) Terrestrial and aquatic orientation in the starthead topminnow *Fundulus notti*. *Science* 168: 2220–2224.

Goodyear CP and Bennett DH (1979) Sun-compass orientation of inmature bluegill. *Trans. Am. Fish Soc.* 108: 555–559.

Goodyear CP and Ferguson DE (1969) Sun-compass orientation in mosquitofish *Gambusia affinis*. *Anim. Behav.* 17: 636–640.

Gotceitas V and Godin JG (1992) Effects of location of food delivery and social status on foraging-site selection by juvenile Atlantic salmon. *Environ. Biol. Fish* 35: 291–300.

Gouteux S and Spelke ES (2001) Children's use of geometry and landmarks to reorient in an open space. *Cognition* 81: 119–148.

Gouteux S, Thinus-Blanc C, and Vauclair J (2001) Rhesus monkeys use geometric and nongeometric information during a reorientation task. *J. Exp. Psychol Gen.* 130: 505–519.

Grandel H, Kaslin J, Ganz J, Wenzel I, and Brand M (2006) Neural stem cells and neurogenesis in the adult zebrafish brain: Origin, proliferation dynamics, migration and cell fate. *Dev. Biol.* 295: 263–77.

Green JM (1971) High tide movements and homing behaviour of the tidepool sculping *Oligocottus maculosus*. *J. Fish Res. Board Canada* 28: 383–389.

Green JM and Fisher R (1977) A field study of homing and orientation to the home site in *Ulvaria subbifurcata* (Pisces: Stichaeidae). *Can. J. Zool.* 55: 1551–1556.

Griffiths SP (2003) Homing behaviour of intertidal rockpool fishes in south-eastern New South Wales Australia. *Aust. J. Zool.* 51: 387–398.

Hainsworth FR, Overmier JB, and Snowdon CT (1967) Specific and permanent deficits in instrumental avoidance responding following forebrain ablation in the goldfish. *J. Comp. Physiol. Psychol.* 63: 111–116.

Hale EB (1956) Social facilitation and forebrain function in maze performance of green sunfish *Lepomis cyanellus*. *Physiol. Zool.* 29: 93–106.

Hallacher LE (1984) Relocation of original territories by displaced black-and-yellow rockfish *Sebastes chrysomelas*, from Carmel Bay California. *Calif. Fish Game* 7: 158–162.

Hansen LP, Doving KB, and Jonsson B (1987) Migration of farmed adult Atlantic salmon with and without olfactory sense, released on the Norwegian coast. *J. Fish Biol.* 30: 713–720.

Hansen LP, Doving KB, and Jonsson B (1993) Oceanic migration in homing Atlantic salmon. *Anim. Behav.* 45: 927–941.

Hard JJ and Heard WR (1999) Analysis of straying variation in Alaskan hatchery Chinook salmon (*Oncorhynchus tshawytscha*) following transplantation. *Can. J. Fish Aquat. Sci.* 56: 578–589.

Hart PJB (1986) Foraging in teleost fishes. In: Pitcher TJ (ed.) *The Behaviour of Teleost Fishes*, pp. 211–252. London: Croom-Helm.

Hart PJB (1993) Teleost foraging: facts and theories. In: Pitcher TJ (ed.) *The Behaviour of Teleost Fishes,* 2nd ed., pp. 253–284. London: Chapman and Hall.

Hasler AD (1971) Orientation and fish migration. In: Hoar WS and Randall WJ (eds.) *Fish Physiology*, pp. 429–510. London: Academic Press.

Hasler AD and Scholz AT (1983) *Olfactory imprinting and homing in Salmon*. Berlin: Springer-Verlag.

Hawryshyn CW, Arnold MG, Bowering E, and Cole RL (1990) Spatial orientation of rainbow trout to plane-polarised light: the ontogeny of E-vector discrimination and spectral sensitivity characteristics. *J. Comp. Physiol A* 166: 565–574.

Heard WR (1996) Sequential imprinting in Chinook salmon: Is it essential for homing fidelity? *Bull. Nat. Res. Inst. Aquac. Suppl.* 2: 59–64.

Helfman GS (1981) Twilight activities and temporal structure in a freshwater fish communitiy. *Can. J. Fish Aquat. Sci.* 38: 1405–1420.

Helfman GS and Schultz ET (1984) Social transmission of behavioral traditions in a coral reef fish. *Anim. Behav.* 32: 379–384.

Helfman GS, Meyer JL, and McFarland WN (1982) The ontogeny of twilight migration patterns in grunts (pisces: Haemulidae). *Anim. Behav.* 30: 317–326.

Hermer L and Spelke S (1994) A geometric process for spatial reorientation in young children. *Nature* 370: 57–59.

Herrero L, Rodríguez F, Salas C, and Torres B (1998) Tail and eye movements evoked by electrical microstimulation of the optic tectum in goldfish. *Exp. Brain Res.* 120: 291–305.

Hobson ES (1972) Activity of Hawaiian reef fishes during the evening and morning transitions between daylight and darkness. *US Nat. Mar. Fish Ser. Bull.* 70: 715–740.

Hodos W and Campbell CBG (1969) The scala naturae: Why there is no theory in comparative psychology. *Psychol. Rev.* 76: 337–350.

Hodos W and Campbell CBG (1990) Evolutionary scales and comparative studies of animal cognition. In: Kesner RP and Olton DS (eds.) *Neurobiology of Comparative Cognition*, pp. 1–20. Hillsdale: Lawrence Erlbaum.

Hollis KL and Overmier JB (1978) The function of the teleost telencephalon in behavior: A reinforcement mediator. In: Distofsky DI (ed.) *The Behavior of Fishes and Other Aquatic Animals*, pp. 137–195. New York: Academic Press.

Hollis KL and Overmier JB (1982) Effect of telencephalon ablation on the reinforcing and eliciting properties of species specific events in *Betta splendens*. *J. Comp. Physiol. Psychol.* 96: 574–590.

Holst E (1935) Über den lichtrückenreflex bei fischen. *Publ. Staz. Zool. Nopoli* 15: 143–158.

Holst EV (1950) Die Tätigkeit des Statolithenapparates im Wirbeltierlabyrinth. *Naturwissenschaften* 37: 265–272.

Hosch L (1936) Untersuchungen über Grosshirnfunktion der Elritze (*Phoxinus laevis*) und des grundlings (*Gobio fluviatilis*). Zoolgische Jarhb Abten Zoologie und Physiologie. *Zool. Jarhb.* 57: 57–70.

Hughes RN and Blight CM (1999) Algorithmic behaviour and spatial memory are used by two intertidal fish species to solve the radial maze. *Anim. Behav.* 58: 601–613.

Hughes RN and Blight CM (2000) Two intertidal fish species use visual association learning to track the status of food patches in a radial maze. *Anim. Behav.* 59: 613–621.

Hughey DJ and Koppenaal RJ (1987) Hippocampal lesions in rats alter learning about intramaze cues. *Behav. Neurosci.* 101: 634–643.

Hunter E, Metcalfe JD, Arnold GP, and Reynolds JD (2004) Impacts of migratory behaviour on population structure in North Sea plaice. *J. Anim. Ecol.* 73: 377–385.

Huntingford FA and Wright PJ (1989) How sticklebacks learn to avoid feeding patches. *Behav. Process* 19: 181–189.

Ingle DJ (1965) Behavioral effects of forebrain lesions in goldfish. In: *Proceedings of the 73rd Annual Convention of the American Psychological Association*, pp. 143–144.

Ingle DJ and Sahagian D (1973) Solution of a spatial constancy problem by goldfish. *Physiol. Psychol.* 1: 83–84.

Jacobs LF (2003) The evolution of the cognitive map. *Brain Behav. Evol.* 62: 128–139.

Janzen W (1933) Untersuchungen über Grosshirnfunktionen des Goldfisches (*Carassius auratus*). *Zool. Jahrb.* 52: 591–628.

Jonsson N, Jonsson B, Skurdal J, and Hansen LP (1994) Differential response to water current in offspring of inlet- and outlet-spawning brown trout *Salmo trutta*. *J. Fish Biol.* 45: 356–359.

Kalmijn A (1978) Experimental evidence of geomagnetic orientation in elasmobranch fishes. In: Schmidt-Koenig K and Keeton WT (eds.) *Animal Migration, Navigation and Homing*, pp. 347–355. Berlin: Springer.

Kamil AC (1978) Systematic foraging by a nectar-feeding bird *Loxops virens*. *J. Comp. Physiol. Psychol.* 92: 388–396.

Kamil AC and Jones JE (1997) The seed-storing corvid Clarks's nutcracker learns geometric relationships among landmarks. *Nature* 390: 276–279.

Kapsimali M, Vidal B, Gonzalez A, Dufour S, and Vernier P (2000) Distribution of the mRNA encoding the four dopamine D(1) receptor subtypes in the brain of the European eel (*Anguilla anguilla*): Comparative approach to the function of D(1) receptors in vertebrates. *J. Comp. Neurol.* 419: 20–43.

Kaya CM and Jeanes ED (1995) Retention of adaptive rheotactic behaviour by F$_1$ fluvial Arctic grayling. *Trans. Am. Fish Soc.* 124: 453–457.

Kelley JL and Magurran AE (2006) Learned defences in predator-prey interactions. In: Brown C, Laland K, and Krause J (eds.) *Fish Cognition and Behaviour*, pp. 28–48. Oxford: Blackwell.

Kelly DM, Spetch ML, and Heth CD (1998) Pigeons' (*Columba livia*) encoding of geometric and featural properties of a spatial environment. *J. Comp. Psychol.* 112: 259–269.

Kieffer JD and Colgan PW (1992) The role of learning in fish behaviour. *Rev. Fish Biol. Fisher* 2: 125–143.

Kleerekoper H, Matis J, Gensler P, and Maynard P (1974) Exploratory behaviour of goldfish *Carassius auratus*. *Anim. Behav.* 22: 124–132.

Kroon FJ, de Graaf M, and Liley NR (2000) Social organisation and competition for refuges and nest sites in *Coryphopterus nicholsii* (Gobiidae), a temperature protogynous reef fish. *Environ. Biol. Fish* 57: 401–411.

Lafarga M, Andrés MA, Berciano MT, and Maquieri E (1991) Organization of nucleoli and nuclear bodies in osmotically stimulated supraoptic neurons in the rat. *J. Comp. Neurol.* 308: 329–333.

Laland KN and Williams K (1997) Shoaling generates social learning of foraging information in guppies. *Anim. Behav.* 53: 1161–1169.

Laland KN and Williams K (1998) Social transmission of maladaptive information in the guppy. *Behav. Ecol.* 9: 493–499.

Li J, Smith SS, and McElligott JG (1995) Cerebellar nitric oxide is necessary for vestibulo-ocular reflex adaptation, a sensorimotor model of learning. *J. Neurophysiol.* 74: 489–494.

López JC, Broglio C, Rodríguez F, Thinus-Blanc C, and Salas C (1999) Multiple spatial learning strategies in goldfish (*Carassius auratus*). *Anim. Cogn.* 2: 109–120.

López JC, Bingman VP, Rodríguez F, Gómez Y, and Salas C (2000a) Dissociation of place and cue learning by telencephalic ablation in goldfish. *Behav. Neurosci.* 114: 687–699.

López JC, Broglio C, Rodríguez F, Thinus-Blanc C, and Salas C (2000b) Reversal learning deficit in a spatial task but not in a cued one after telencephalic ablation in goldfish. *Behav. Brain Res.* 109: 91–98.

López JC, Rodríguez F, Gómez Y, Vargas JP, Broglio C, and Salas C (2000c) Place and cue learning in turtles. *Anim. Learn. Behav.* 28: 360–372.

López JC, Gómez Y, Rodríguez F, Broglio C, Vargas JP, and Salas C (2001) Spatial learning in turtles. *Anim. Cogn.* 4: 49–59.

López JC, Gómez Y, Vargas JP, and Salas C (2003a) Spatial reversal learning deficit after medial cortex lesion in turtles. *Neurosci. Lett.* 341: 197–200.

López JC, Vargas JP, Gómez Y, and Salas C (2003b) Spatial and non-spatial learning in turtles: The role of medial cortex. *Behav. Brain Res.* 143: 109–120.

Löwenstein O (1932) Experimentelle untersuchungen über den gleichgewitchssinn der elritze (*Phoxinus laevis*). *Zh. Verg. Physiol.* 17: 806–854.

Loyacano HA, Chappell JA, and Gauthreaux SA (1971) Sun-compass orientation of juvenile largemouth bass *Micropterus salmoides*. *Trans. Am. Fish Soc.* 106: 77–79.

MacFarland WN (1980) Observations on recruitment in haemulid fishes. *Proc. Gulf Carib. Fisher. Inst.* 32: 132–138.

Mainardi D (1980) Tradition and social transmission of behavior in animals. In: Barlow GW and Siverberg J (eds.) *Sociobiology: Beyond Nature/Nurture?* pp. 227–255. Boulder CO: Westview Press.

Markel RW (1994) An adaptive value of spatial learning and memory in the blackeye goby *Coryphoterus nicholsi*. *Anim. Behav.* 47: 1462–1464.

Markevich AI (1988) Nature of territories and homing in the eastern sea-perch *Sebastes taczanowski*. *J. Ichthyol.* 28: 161–163.

Matthews KR (1990a) An experimental study of the habitat preferences and movement patterns of copper, quillback, and brown rockfishes (*Sebastes* spp.). *Environ. Biol. Fish* 29: 161–178.

Matthews KR (1990b) A telemetric study of the home ranges and homing of cooper and quillback, and brown rockfishes on shallows rocky reefs. *Can. J. Fish Aquat. Sci.* 68: 2243–2250.

Mazeroll AI and Montgomery WL (1998) Daily migrations of a coral reef fish in the Red Sea (Gulf of Aqaba Israel): Initiation and orientation. *Copeia* 4: 893–905.

Mazmanian DS and Roberts WA (1983) Spatial memory in rats under restricted viewing conditions. *Learn. Motiv.* 14: 123–139.

McElligott JG, Beeton P, and Polk J (1998) Effect of cerebellar inactivation by lidocaine microdialysis on the vestibuloocular reflex in goldfish. *J. Neurophysiol.* 79: 1286–1294.

Meyer DL, Schott D, and Schaefer KP (1970) Brain stimulation in the tectum opticum of freely swimming cods (*Gadus morrhua* L.). *Pflüg. Archiv.* 314: 240–252.

Milinski M (1994) Long-term memory for foods patches and implications for ideal free distributions in sticklebacks. *Ecology* 75: 1150–1156.

Mittelstaedt ML and Glasauer S (1991) Idiothetic navigation in gerbils and humans. *Zool. J. Physiol.* 95: 427–435.

Morin PP and Doving KB (1992) Changes in the olfactory function of Atlantic salmon *Salmo salar*, in the course of smoltification. *Can. J. Fish Aquat. Sci.* 49: 1704–1713.

Morris RGM (1981) Spatial localization does no require the presence of local cues. *Learn. Motiv.* 12: 239–260.

Nieuwenhuys R (1963) The comparative anatomy of the actynopterigian forebrain. *J. Hirnf.* 6: 171–192.

Nieuwenhuys R and Meek J (1990) The telencephalon of actinopterygian fishes. In: Jones EG and Peters A (eds.) *Comparative Structure and Evolution of the Cerebral Cortex*, p. 31. New York: Plenum.

Nieuwenhuys R, ten Donkelaar HJ, and Nicholson C (1998) *The Central Nervous System of Vertebrates*. Berlin: Springer.

Noda M, Gushima K, and Kakuda S (1994) Local prey search based on spatial memory and expectation in the planktivorous fish *Chromis chrysurus* (Pomacentridae). *Anim. Behav.* 47: 1413–1422.

Nolte W (1932) Experimentelle Untersuchungen zum Problem der Lokalisation des Assoziationsvermogens im Fischgehirn. *Zeits. Verg. Physiol.* 18: 255–279.

Northcutt RG (1995) The forebrain of gnathostomes: In search of a morphotype. *Brain Behav. Evol.* 46: 275–318.

Northcutt RG (2006) Connections of the lateral and medial divisions of the goldfish telencephalic pallium. *J. Comp. Neurol.* 494: 903–943.

Northcutt RG and Braford MR (1980) New observations on the organization and evolution of the telencephalon in actinopterygian fishes. In: Ebbesson SOE (ed.) *Comparative Neurology of the Telencephalon*, pp. 41–98. New York: Plenum Press.

Ogden JC and Ehrlich PR (1977) The behavior of heterotypic resting schools of juvenile grunts (Pomadasyidae). *Mar. Biol.* 42: 273–280.

Odling-Smee L and Braithwaite VA (2003) The role of learning in fish orientation. *Fish Fisher* 4: 235–246.

Odling-Smee L, Simpson SD, and Braithwaite VA (2006) The role of learning in fish orientation. In: Brown C, Laland K, and Krause J (eds.) *Fish Cognition and Behavior*, pp. 119–138. Blackwell.

O'Keefe J and Nadel L (1978) *The Hippocampus as a Cognitive Map*. Oxford: Clarendon Press.

Olton DS (1979) Mazes, maps and memory. *Am. Psychol.* 34: 583–596.

Olton DS, Walker JA, Gage FH, and Johnson CT (1977) Choice behavior of rats searching for food. *Learn. Motiv.* 8: 315–331.

Olton DS, Handelmann GE, and Walker JA (1981) Spatial memory and food searching strategies. In: Kamil AC and Sargent TD (eds.) *Foraging Behavior: Ecological Ethological and Psychological Approaches*, pp. 333–354. New York: Garland Press.

Ott JF and Platt C (1988) Early abrupt recovery from ataxia during vestibular compensation in goldfish. *J. Exp. Biol.* 138: 345–357.

Overmier JB and Curnow PF (1969) Classical conditioning, pseudoconditioning, and sensitization in "normal" and forebrainless goldfish. *J. Comp. Physiol. Psychol.* 68: 193–198.

Overmier JB and Flood NB (1969) Passive avoidance in forebrain ablated teleost fish (*Carassius auratus*). *Physiol. Behav.* 4: 791–794.

Overmier JB and Hollis KL (1983) The teleostean telencephalon in learning. In: Northcutt RG and Davis RE (eds.) *Fish Neurobiology*, pp. 265–284. Ann Arbor: University of Michigan Press.

Overmier JB and Hollis KL (1990) Fish in the think tank: Learning, memory and integrated behavior. In: Kesner DS and Olton DS (eds.) *Neurobiology of Comparative Cognition*, pp. 204–236. Hillsdale, NJ: Lawrence Erlbaum.

Overmier JB and Patten RL (1982) Teleost telencephalon and memory for delayed reinforcers. *Physiol. Psychol.* 10: 74–78.

Overmier JB and Savage GE (1974) Effects of telencephalic ablation on trace classical conditioning of heart rate in goldfish. *Exp. Neurol.* 42: 339–346.

Paillard J (1991) Motor and representational framing of space. In: Paillard J (ed.) *Brain and Space*, pp. 163–182. Oxford: Oxford University Press.

Pascual MA and Quinn TP (1994) Geographical patterns of straying of fall Chinook salmon *Oncorhynchus tshawytscha* (Walbaum), from Columbia River (USA) hatcheries. *Aquac. Fish Manag.* 25: 17–30.

Pastor AM, De La Cruz RR, and Baker R (1994) Cerebellar role in adaptation of the goldfish vestibuloocular reflex. *J. Neurophysiol.* 72: 1383–1394.

Paul DH and Roberts BL (1979) The significance of cerebellar function for a reflex movement of the dogfish. *J. Comp. Physiol.* 134: 69–74.

Pitcher TJ and House AC (1987) Foraging rules for group feeders: Area copying depends upon food density in shoaling goldfish. *Ethology* 76: 161–167.

Pitcher TJ and Magurran AE (1983) Shoal size, patch profitability and information exchange in foraging goldfish. *Anim. Behav.* 31: 546–555.

Polimanti O (1913) Contributions a la physiologie du système nerveux central et du mouvement des poissons. *Arch. Ital. Biol.* 59: 383–401.

Portavella M, Torres B, and Salas C (2004a) Avoidance response in goldfish: Emotional and temporal involvement of medial and lateral telencephalic pallium. *J. Neurosci.* 24: 2335–2342.

Portavella M, Torres B, Salas C, and Papini MR (2004b) Lesions of the medial pallium, but not of the lateral pallium, disrupt spaced-trial avoidance learning in goldfish (*Carassius auratus*). *Neurosci. Lett.* 362: 75–78.

Poucet B (1993) Spatial cognitive maps in animals: New hypotheses on their structure and neural mechanisms. *Psychol. Rev.* 100: 163–182.

Poucet B, Chapuis N, Durup M, and Thinus-Blanc C (1986) A study of exploratory behavior as an index of spatial knowledge in hamsters. *Anim. Learn. Behav.* 14: 93–100.

Prechtl JC, von der Emde G, Wolfart J, et al. (1998) Sensory processing in the pallium of a mormyrid fish. *J. Neurosci.* 18: 7381–7393.

Preuss TM (1995) The argument from animals to humans in cognitive neuroscience. In: Gazzaniga MS (ed.) *The Cognitive Neurosciences*, pp. 1227–1241. Cambridge, MA: MIT Press.

Quinn TP (1980) Evidence for celestial and magnetic compass orientation in lake migrating sockeye salmon fry. *J. Comp. Physiol.* 137: 243–248.

Quinn TP (1982) An experimental approach to fish compass and map orientation. In: McLeave JD and Arnold JJ (eds.) *Mechanisms of Migration in Fishes*, pp. 113–123. New York: Plenum Press.

Quinn TP (1985) Salmon homing: Is the puzzle complete? *Environ. Biol. Fish* 12: 315–317.

Quinn TP (1992) Fishes. In: Papi F (ed.) *Animal Homing* (Ed. F. Papi), pp. 145–211. London: Chapman and Hall.

Quinn TP and Brannon EL (1982) The use of celestial and magnetic cues by orienting sockeye salmon smolts. *J. Comp. Physiol A* 147: 547–552.

Quinn TP and Dittman AH (1990) Pacific salmon migrations and homing: Mechanisms and adaptive significance. *Trends Ecol. Evol.* 5: 174–177.

Quinn TP and Ogden JC (1984) Field evidence of compass orientation in migrating juvenile grunts (Haemulidae). *J. Exp. Mar. Biol. Ecol.* 81: 181–192.

Reese ES (1989) Orientation behavior of butterflyfishes (family Chaetodontidae) on coral reefs: Spatial learning of route specific landmarks and cognitive maps. *Environ. Biol. Fishes* 25: 79–86.

Riedel G (1998) Long-term habituation to spatial novelty in blind cave fish (*Astyanax hubbsi*): Role of the telencephalon and its subregions. *Learn. Mem.* 4: 451–461.

Rodríguez F (1996) Mecanismos Tectales implicados en la orientación espacial en el carpín dorado (*Carassius auratus*): un estudio mediante técnicas de lesión y de microestimulación eléctrica localizada. PhD Thesis. Universidad de Sevilla.

Rodríguez F, Durán E, Vargas J, Torres B, and Salas C (1994) Performance of goldfish trained in allocentric and egocentric maze procedures suggests the presence of a cognitive mapping system in fishes. *Anim. Learn. Behav.* 22: 409–420.

Rodríguez F, López JC, Vargas JP, Broglio C, Gómez Y, and Salas C (2002a) Spatial memory and hippocampal pallium through vertebrate evolution: Insights from reptiles and teleost fish. *Brain Res. Bull.* 57: 499–503.

Rodríguez F, López JC, Vargas JP, Gómez Y, Broglio C, and Salas C (2002b) Conservation of spatial memory function in the pallial forebrain of amniotes and ray-finned fishes. *J. Neurosci.* 22: 2894–2903.

Rodríguez F, Durán E, Gómez A, et al. (2005) Cognitive and emotional functions of the teleost fish cerebellum. *Brain Res. Bull.* 66: 365–370.

Rodríguez F, Broglio C, Durán E, Gómez A, and Salas C (2006) Neural mechanisms of learning in teleost fishes. In: Brown C, Laland K, and Krause J (eds.) *Fish Cognition and Behaviour*, pp. 243–277. Oxford: Blackwell.

Roitblat HL, Tham W, and Golub L (1982) Performance of *Betta splendens* in a radial arm maze. *Anim. Learn. Behav.* 10: 108–114.

Russell EM (1967) The effect of experience of surroundings on the response of *Lebistes reticulatus* to a strange object. *Anim. Behav.* 15: 586–594.

Saidel WM, Marquez-Houston K, and Butler AB (2001) Identification of visual pallial telencephalon in the goldfish *Carassius auratus*: A combined cytochrome oxidase and electrophysiological study. *Brain Res.* 919: 82–93.

Saito K and Watanabe S (2004) Spatial learning deficits after the development of dorsomedial telencephalon lesions in goldfish. *Neuroreport* 15: 2695–2699.

Saito K and Watanabe S (2006) Deficits in acquisition of spatial learning after dorsomedial telencephalon lesions in goldfish. *Behav. Brain Res.* 172: 187–194.

Salas C, Herrero L, Rodríguez F, and Torres B (1995) On the role of goldfish optic tectum in the generation of eye movements. In: Delgado-Garcia JM and Godaux E (eds.) *Information Processing Underlying Gaze Control*, pp. 87–95. Oxford: Pergamon.

Salas C, Broglio C, Rodríguez F, López JC, Portavella M, and Torres B (1996a) Telencephalic ablation in goldfish impairs performance in a spatial constancy problem but not in a cued one. *Behav. Brain Res.* 79: 193–200.

Salas C, Rodríguez F, Vargas JP, Durán E, and Torres B (1996b) Spatial learning and memory deficits after telencephalic ablation in goldfish trained in place and turn maze procedures. *Behav. Neurosci.* 110: 965–980.

Salas C, Herrero L, Rodríguez F, and Torres B (1997) Tectal codification of eye movements in goldfish studied by electrical microstimulation. *Neuroscience* 78: 271–288.

Salas C, Broglio C, and Rodríguez F (2003) Evolution of forebrain and spatial cognition in vertebrates: Conservation across diversity. *Brain Behav. Evol.* 62: 72–82.

Salas C, Broglio C, Durán E, et al. (2006) Neuropsychology of learning and memory in teleost fish. *Zebrafish* 3: 157–171.

Savage GE (1968) Temporal factors in avoidance learning in normal and forebrainless goldfish (*Carassius auratus*). *Nature* 218: 1168–1169.

Savage GE (1969a) Telencephalic lesions and avoidance behaviour in the goldfish (*Carassius auratus*). *Anim. Behav.* 17: 362–373.

Savage GE (1969b) Some preliminary observations on the role of the telencephalon in food-reinforced behaviour in the goldfish *Carassius auratus*. *Anim. Behav.* 17: 760–772.

Savage GE (1980) The fish telencephalon and its relation to learning. In: Ebbesson SOE (ed.) *Comparative Neurology of the Telencephalon*, pp. 129–174. New York: Plenum.

Savage GE and Swingland IR (1969) Positively reinforced behaviour and the forebrain in goldfish. *Nature* 221: 878–879.

Schenk F and Morris RGM (1985) Dissociation between components of spatial memory in rats after recovery from the effects of the retrohippocampal lesions. *Exp. Brain Res.* 58: 11–28.

Schluessel V and Bleckmann H (2005) Spatial memory and orientation strategies in the elasmobranch *Potamotrygon motoro*. *J. Comp. Physiol A* 191: 695–706.

Schwassmann HO and Braemer W (1961) The effect of experimentally changed photoperiod on the sun orientation rhythm of fish. *Physiol. Zool.* 34: 273–326.

Scholz AT, Horrall RM, Cooper JC, and Hasler AD (1976) Imprinting to chemical cues: The basis for home stream selection in salmon. *Science* 192: 1247–1249.

Sherry DF and Duff SJ (1996) Behavioral and neural bases of orientation in food storing birds. *J. Exp. Biol.* 199: 165–172.

Sherry DF and Vaccarino AL (1989) Hippocampus and memory for food caches in black-capped chickadees. *Behav. Neurosci.* 103: 308–318.

Simpson SD, Meekan MG, McCauley RD, and Jeffs AG (2004) Attraction of settlement-stage coral reef fishes to reef noise. *Mar. Ecol. Prog. B* 276: 263–268.

Simpson SD, Meekan MG, Montgomery JC, McCauley RD, and Jeffs AG (2005) Home ward sound. *Science* 308: 221.

Smith RJF and Smith MJ (1998) Rapid acquisition of directional preferences by migratory juveniles two amphidromous Hawaiian gobies *Awaous guamensis* and S*icyopterus stimpsoni*. *Environ. Biol. Fish* 53: 275–282.

Sovrano VA, Bisazza A, and Vallortigara G (2003) Modularity as a fish (*Xenotoca eiseni*) views it: Conjoining geometric and nongeometric information for spatial reorientation. *J. Exp. Psychol. Anim. Behav. Process* 29: 199–210.

Sovrano VA, Bisazza A, and Vallortigara G (2007) How fish do geometry in large and in small spaces. *Anim. Cogn.* 10: 47–54.

Sparks DL (2002) The brainstem control of saccadic eye movements. *Nat. Rev. Neurosci.* 3: 952–964.

Stein BE and Meredith MA (1993) *The Merging of the Senses*. Cambridge, MA: MIT Press.

Straka H, Beck JC, Pastor AM, and Baker R (2006) Morphology and physiology of the cerebellar vestibulolateral lobe pathways linked to oculomotor function in the goldfish. *J. Neurophysiol.* 96: 1963–1980.

Striedter GF (2005) *Principles of Brain Evolution*. Sunderland: Sinauer Associates.

Striedter GF and Northcutt RG (2006) Head size constrains forebrain development and evolution in ray-finned fishes. *Evol. Dev.* 8: 215–22.

Suzuki S, Augerinos G, and Black AH (1980) Stimulus control of spatial behavior on the eight-arm maze in rats. *Learn. Motiv.* 11: 1–18.

Teyke T (1985) Collison and avoidance of obstacles in blind cave fish *Anoptichthys jordani* (Characidae). *J. Comp. Physiol. A* 157: 837–843.

Teyke T (1989) Learning and remembering the environment in the blind cave fish *Anoptichthys jordani*. *J. Comp. Physiol. A* 164: 655–662.

Thinus-Blanc C (1996) *Animal Spatial Cognition. Behavioral and neural approaches*. Singapore: World Scientific.

Thinus-Blanc C, Bouzouba L, Chaix K, Chapuis N, Durup M, and Poucet B (1987) A study of spatial parameters encoded during exploration in hamsters. *J. Exp. Psychol. Anim. B* 13: 418–427.

Tinklepaugh O (1932) Multiple delayed reaction with chimpanzees and monkeys. *J. Comp. Psychol.* 13: 207–243.

Tolimieri N, Jeffs A, and Montgomery JC (2000) Ambient sound as a cue for navigation by the pelagic larvae of reef fishes. *Mar. Ecol. Prog.* 207: 219–224.

Tolman EC (1948) Cognitive maps in rats and men. *Psychol. Rev.* 55: 189–208.

Torres B, Pérez-Pérez MP, Herrero L, Ligero M, and Núñez-Abades PA (2002) Neural substrate underlying tectal eye movement codification in goldfish. *Brain Res. Bull.* 57: 345–348.

Torres B, Luque MA, Perez-Perez MP, and Herrero L (2005) Visual orienting response in goldfish: A multidisciplinary study. *Brain Res. Bull.* 66: 376–380.

Trevarthen C (1968) Vision in fish: the origins of the visual frame for action in vertebrates. In: Ingle D (ed.) *The Central Nervous System and Fish Behavior*, pp. 61–94. Chicago: University of Chicago Press.

Underwood JCE (1992) Nucleolar organizer regions. In: Hall AP, Levison DA, and Wright NA (eds.) *Assessment of Cell Proliferation in Clinical Practice*, pp. 161–175. London: Springer-Verlag.

Unwin MJ and Quinn TP (1993) Homing and straying patterns of Chinook salmon (*Oncorhynchus tshawytscha*) from a New Zealand hatchery: Spatial distribution of strays and effects of release date. *Can. J. Fish Aquat. Sci.* 50: 1168–1175.

Uster HJ, Battig K, and Nageli HH (1976) Effects of maze geometry and experience on exploratory behavior in the rat. *Anim. Learn. Behav.* 4: 84–88.

Vallortigara G, Zanforlin M, and Pasti G (1990) Geometric modules in animals' spatial representations: A test with chicks (*Gallus gallus domesticus*). *J. Comp. Psychol.* 104: 248–254.

Vanegas H (1984) *Comparative Neurology of the Optic Tectum*. New York: Plenum Press.

Vargas JP, Rodríguez F, López JC, Arias JL, and Salas C (2000) Spatial learning-induced increase in the argyrophilic nucleolar organizer region of dorsolateral telencephalic neurons in goldfish. *Brain Res.* 865: 77–84.

Vargas JP, Lopez JC, Salas C, and Thinus-Blanc C (2004) Encoding of geometric and featural spatial information by

Goldfish (*Carassius auratus*). *J. Comp. Psychol.* 118: 206–216.

Warburton K (1990) The use of local landmarks by foraging goldfish. *Anim. Behav.* 40: 500–505.

Warburton K (2006) Learning of foraging skills by fishes. In: Brown K, Laland K, and Krause J (eds.) *Fish Cognition and Behaviour*, pp. 9–27. Oxford: Blackwell.

Warner RR (1988) Traditionality of mating-site preferences in a coral reef fish. *Nature* 335: 719–721.

Warner RR (1990) Male versus female influences on mating-site determination in a coral-reef fish. *Anim. Behav.* 39: 540–548.

Warren JM (1961) The effects of telencephalic injuries on learning by Paradise fish *Macropodus opercularis*. *J. Comp. Physiol. Psychol.* 54: 130–132.

Watanabe S, Takabayashi A, Takagi S, von Baumgarten R, and Wetzig J (1989) Dorsal light response and changes of its responses under varying acceleration conditions. *Adv. Space Res.* 9: 231–240.

Welker WI and Welker J (1958) Reaction of fish (*Eucinostomus gula*) to environmental changes. *Ecology* 39: 283–288.

Whishaw IQ (1989) Dissociating performance and learning deficits on spatial navigation tasks in rats subjected to cholinergic muscarinic blockade. *Brain Res. Bull.* 23: 347–358.

Whishaw IQ and Mittleman G (1986) Visits to starts, routes and places by rats (*Rattus norvegicus*) in swimming pool navigation tasks. *J. Comp. Psychol.* 100: 422–431.

Wiley EO (1981) *Phylogenetics. The Theory and Practice of Phylogenetic Systematics.* New York: Wiley.

Wilz KJ and Bolton RL (1971) Exploratory behavior in response the spatial rearrangement of familiar stimuli. *Psychon. Sci.* 24: 177–181.

Withem TG (1977) Coevolution of foraging in Bombus and nectar dispensing in Chilopsis. A last dreg theory. *Science* 197: 593–595.

Witte K (2006) Leaning and mate choice. In: Brown K, Laland K, and Krause J (eds.) *Fish Cognition and Behaviour*, pp. 70–95. Oxford: Blackwell.

Wulliman MF and Mueller T (2004) Teleostean and mammalian forebrains contrasted: Evidence from genes to behavior. *J. Comp. Neurol.* 75: 143–162.

Wullimann MF and Rink E (2002) The teleostean forebrain: A comparative and developmental view based on early proliferation Pax6 activity and catecholaminergic organization. *Brain Res. Bull.* 57: 363–370.

Yamamoto N, Ishikawa Y, Yoshimoto M, et al. (2007) A new interpretation on the homology of the teleostean telencephalon based on hodology and a new eversion model. *Brain Behav. Evol.* 69: 96–104.

Yanagihara D, Watanabe S, and Mitarai G (1993a) Neuroanatomical substrate for the dorsal light response. I. Differential afferent connections of the lateral lobe of the valvula cerebelli in goldfish (*Carassius auratus*). *Neurosci. Res.* 16: 25–32.

Yanagihara D, Watanabe S, Takagi S, and Mitarai G (1993b) Neuroanatomical substrate for the dorsal light response. II. Effects of kainic acid-induced lesions of the valvular cerebelli on the goldfish dorsal light response. *Neurosci. Res.* 16: 33–37.

Yanagihara D, Watanabe S, and Takagi S (1993c) Functional participation of the valvular cerebelli on the goldfish dorsal light response. *Physiologist* 36: 83–84.

Zunini G (1954) Researches on fish's learning. *Arch. Néerl. Zool.* 10: 127–140.

1.27 Reconsolidation in Invertebrates

D. Eisenhardt and N. Stollhoff, Freie Universität Berlin, Berlin, Germany

1.27.1 Introduction

1.27.1.1 Memory Consolidation after Training and Retrieval

Formation of long-term memories (LTMs) can be disturbed during a discrete time window after learning with amnestic agents. It has been therefore concluded that LTMs undergo a labile phase of memory fixation, which is termed consolidation, and that an LTM, once consolidated, is stable (Dudai, 2004). Nevertheless, it has been known since the late 1960s that retrieving a memory in combination with the application of a consolidation inhibitor disturbs memory retention in a later memory test (Misanin et al., 1968; *See* Chapter 1.24) (**Figure 1(a)**). This observation of a retrieval-dependent amnesia first resulted in the theory that memories do not undergo a consolidation process but, rather, exist in an active or an inactive state (Lewis, 1979). In the active state, memories are vulnerable to inhibitors; in the inactive state, inhibitors have no effect. Memory retrieval transfers an inactive memory into an active memory, which makes the memories vulnerable again. Some years ago Nader and colleagues (2000) took on the issue of retrieval-dependent amnesia. They interpreted their findings in combining the consolidation theory with the hypothesis of active and

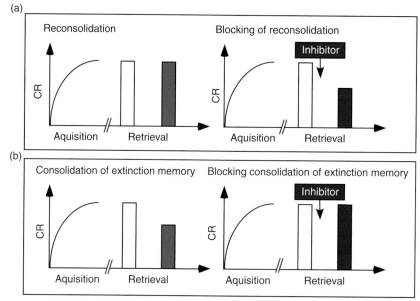

Figure 1 Consolidation processes following memory retrieval. Schematic diagram of the behavioral outcome of consolidation processes following memory retrieval. (a) Reconsolidation. The combination of memory retrieval and the application of an inhibitor of consolidation leads to a decrease of the conditioned response (CR) (right) in comparison to animals that are retrieved but not treated with the inhibitor (left). (b) Consolidation of an extinction memory. The CR is decreased after memory retrieval (left). This reduction of the CR is blocked by application of an inhibitor of consolidation after the first memory retrieval. Blocking is visible at the second retrieval trial (which is a retention test for the memory following memory retrieval) (right).

inactive memories (Nader, 2003). They proposed that retrieval makes the consolidated memory labile and that a second consolidation round is required to stabilize the retrieved memory. This second round of consolidation is targeted by the inhibitor, resulting in a decrease of the conditioned response (CR) at a later memory test. Accordingly, the process in question is called reconsolidation (Spear, 1973; Przybyslawski and Sara, 1997; Sara, 2000; Nader, 2003; Dudai and Eisenberg, 2004; *See also* Chapter 1.24). Meanwhile, an extensive study began of the neuronal and molecular basis of reconsolidation in vertebrates and invertebrates, and it is under dispute whether this hypothesis holds true. Several other hypotheses have been put forward to explain this phenomenon either based on the consolidation theory (Dudai and Eisenberg, 2004; Alberini, 2005; Eisenhardt and Menzel, 2007) or based on the assumption that the retrieval rather then the memory itself is affected (Riccio et al., 2002).

Sometimes memory retrieval leads to a decrease of the CR. This phenomenon is termed extinction (Pavlov, 1927). When a consolidation inhibitor like a protein synthesis inhibitor is applied around the time point of memory extinction, the CR increases in a later memory test (**Figure 1(b)**). It has therefore been

concluded that the extinction memory undergoes a consolidation process that is blocked by the application of the inhibitor (Berman and Dudai, 2001; Vianna et al., 2001, 2003; Pedreira and Maldonado, 2003; Power et al., 2006). Accordingly, retrieving a memory induces two processes that result in contrasting behavioral phenomena – reconsolidation and consolidation of an extinction memory.

Meanwhile, reconsolidation has been described in several invertebrate model organisms, namely, four gastropod species, *Hermissenda* (Child et al., 2003), *Lymnaea stagnalis* (Sangha et al., 2003a; Kemenes et al., 2006), *Helix lucorum* (Gainutdinova et al., 2005), and *Limax flavus* (Sekiguchi et al., 1997); the crab, *Chasmagnathus granulatus* (Pedreira et al., 2002); and the honeybee, *Apis mellifera* (Stollhoff et al., 2005). Findings in each of these organisms contributed to the study of the reconsolidation phenomenon. Many of the results known from vertebrates have also been found in invertebrates, demonstrating generalities and differences in the reconsolidation phenomenon and its underlying mechanisms. To illustrate the generalities and differences, we present experiments on reconsolidation in gastropods, the crab *Chasmagnathus*, and the honeybee, *Apis mellifera*.

1.27.2 Studies on Reconsolidation in Invertebrates

1.27.2.1 The Terrestrial Slug *Limax flavus*

1.27.2.1.1 Memory for aversive odor-taste conditioning is cooling sensitive

The slug *Limax flavus* (**Figure 2(a)**) is native to Europe but has been imported throughout the world. To study memory formation in *Limax flavus*, an odor-avoiding paradigm is used (Yamada et al., 1992). A starved animal is placed in a box lined with carrot juice–moistened filter paper. Carrot juice is

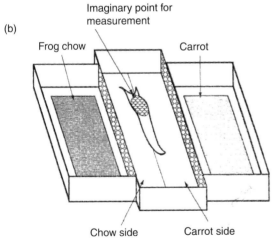

Figure 2 The slug *Limax flavus*: The odor-avoidance paradigm. (a) The yellow garden slug *Limax flavus*. Photo provided by Rolf Kirch. (b) The three-part test chamber: Carrot and frog chow are placed in opposite side chambers. The walls of the center chamber are perforated. A center line divides the room into a chow side and a carrot side. Individual slugs, marked with a dot on the head, which is used for measurement, are placed into the center chamber; the time the slug's head spent on the carrot side is recorded during three testing trials. Adapted from Figure 1 in Yamada A, Sekiguchi T, Suzuki H, and Mizukami A (1992) Behavioral analysis of internal memory states using cooling-induced retrograde amnesia in *Limax flavus. J. Neurosci.* 12: 729–735.

used as the CS. After a 2-min exposure, the animal is immediately transferred to another box with bitter-tasting quinidine sulfate, which presents the unconditioned stimulus (US). For memory testing a slug is placed into the center of a three-chambered apparatus (**Figure 2(b)**). The walls of the center chamber are perforated to allow odor sensing. The two side chambers contain moistened filter-paper with the trained carrot juice or frog chow, which is normally fed to the snails.

After a single CS–US pairing, slugs show an avoidance behavior for the trained carrot odor. Cooling the animal within 1 min after training induces retrograde amnesia, but later cooling has no effect (Yamada et al., 1992).

1.27.2.1.2 Reconsolidation in Limax flavus

The first study that found the reconsolidation phenomenon in an invertebrate was done in *Limax flavus*. In this study the authors focused on the temporal evolution of a memory (Sekiguchi et al., 1997). Although the authors did not term their findings reconsolidation, they revealed retrieval-dependent amnesia when trained snails were exposed to the CS and were cooled immediately afterward.

The combination of memory retrieval and cooling was applied at different time points after training, and the resulting memory was tested 1 day later. It turned out that by memory retrieval, a cooling-sensitive process can be induced until 3 days after training (**Figure 3**). After 3 days the memory becomes insensitive to retrieval-dependent amnesia. Nevertheless, when an additional CS–US pairing was presented before combining memory retrieval and cooling, a retrieval-dependent amnesia occurred even though the initial training had been applied more than 3 days before (**Figure 4**).

Interestingly, this induced susceptibility for retrieval-dependent amnesia followed the same temporal gradient as occurred after initial training, and it was supposed that the additional CS–US pairing results in a new memory with the same temporal gradient as the initial memory. To test this, a second-order conditioning trial, where a CS (CS 2) is paired with the formerly reinforced CS (CS 1), was presented instead of the additional CS–US pairing. The presentation of the CS1 in combination with cooling after the second-order conditioning resulted in a retrieval-dependent amnesia for the initial memory. But the presentation of the CS 2 in combination with cooling leads to retrieval-dependent amnesia for the initial memory and the

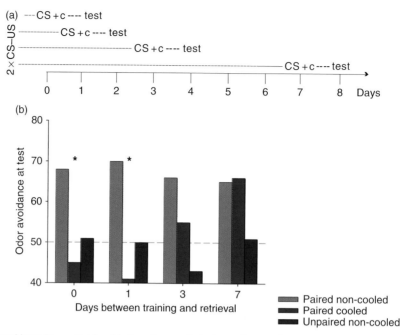

Figure 3 The slug *Limax flavus*: Retrieval-induced amnesia is dependent on the age of the memory (a) experimental schedule: Animals were trained to avoid an odor on day 0 by pairing the odor (conditioned stimulus, CS) with quinidine sulfate (unconditioned stimulus, US). Animals were divided into four experimental groups. For each group the memory was retrieved once by CS presentation at different time points (on day 0, 1, 3, or 7) followed immediately by a cooling procedure (CS + c). The slugs were tested 24 hours later in the three-chambered apparatus. Their odor avoidance behavior in the test was measured; the means are presented in (b) (paired cooled, violet bars). An additional group of slugs was trained, but not retrieved and cooled (paired noncooled, green bars). A second control group received unpaired presentation of the CS–US on day 0, but was not retrieved and cooled (unpaired noncooled, blue bars). The odor avoidance behavior of the experimental group (violet bars) is significantly decreased (indicated by an asterisk) in comparison to the trained noncooled group if the memory was retrieved > 3 days after training. Afterward, the reconsolidation phenomenon is not visible. The gray dashed line at 50% indicates no odor preference. Adapted from Figure 1 of Sekiguchi T, Yamada A, and Suzuki H (1997) Reactivation-dependent changes in memory states in the terrestrial slug *Limax flavus*. *Learn. Mem.* 4: 356–364.

second-order conditioned memory. Sekiguchi et al. (1997) concluded that the CS 1 in the second-order conditioning trial activates the initial memory. Accordingly, an additional CS–US pairing should also activate the initial memory rather than resulting in the formation of a new memory. According to this conclusion, Sekiguchi et al. (1997) stated that a memory becomes inactive after it matures and can no longer be inhibited by cooling. When the memory is retrieved, it becomes active again but might still be insensitive to cooling, depending on its age. Only additional CS–US pairings or second-order conditioning trials activate the initial memory that was insensitive to cooling, pushing it from a cooling-insensitive state back to a cooling-sensitive state. This model is based on Lewis's theory of activated and inactivated memories (1979) (see section titled "Memory Consolidation after Training and Retrieval") but extends beyond it. In contrast to Lewis (1979), Sekiguchi et al. (1997) posed an active and an inactive memory state, but in addition,

showed a cooling-sensitive and a cooling-insensitive state. Accordingly, although memories are retrieved and are thus activated, they are not necessarily cooling sensitive. Only additional CS–US pairing or second-order conditioning leads to a memory that gets cooling sensitive by retrieval 24 h later. Interestingly, the findings by Sekiguchi et al. (1997) cannot be easily explained by the reconsolidation theory (Nader, 2003). The reconsolidation theory proposes a direct reactivation of a consolidated memory by a retrieval trial. Here, instead, the additional CS–US pairing enables a memory to be reactivated 24 h later.

1.27.2.2 The Pond Snail *Lymnaea stagnalis*

To study the reconsolidation phenomenon in the snail *Lymnaea stagnalis*, two learning paradigms have been used: the operant aerial respiration paradigm and the classical chemosensory conditioning paradigm.

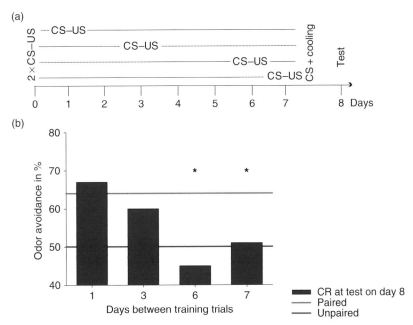

Figure 4 The slug *Limax flavus*: Additional training reactivates the memory. (a) Experimental schedule. Slugs received two conditioned stimulus (CS)–unconditioned stimulus (US) pairings on day 0. Afterward the animals were divided into four subgroups. Additional CS–US pairings were applied at varied time points (1, 3, 6, 7 days) after training. Memory was retrieved by CS presentation on day 7, and slugs were immediately cooled afterward. (b) Memory avoidance behavior was tested on day 8. Retrieval-induced amnesia is only detectable if an additional training was applied on day 6 and day 7. Significant difference in response between experimental group (bars) and paired control group are indicated by asterisks. The means of paired and unpaired control groups are presented as a blue or a green line, respectively. Adapted from Figure 2 in Sekiguchi T, Yamada A, and Suzuki H (1997) Reactivation-dependent changes in memory states in the terrestrial slug *Limax flavus*. *Learn. Mem.* 4: 356–364.

1.27.2.2.1 Lymnaea stagnalis: *The operant aerial respiration paradigm*

Lymnaea stagnalis is an aquatic pulmonate snail (**Figure 5**). It is a bimodal breather and can breathe via its skin (cutaneous respiration) or through a simple lung (aerial respiration). When the animal stays in stagnant water where the oxygen content is low, it becomes hypoxic. Then the snail comes to the water

Figure 5 The snail *Lymnaea stagnalis* The snail *Lymnaea stagnalis* sinks from the water surface to the ground of the pond. Photo by Kathrin Spöcker.

surface for aerial respiration. It opens and closes its respiratory orifice, the pneumostome, and breathes through the lung (**Figure 6(a)**). This behavior by the snail is used in the operant aerial respiration paradigm (Lukowiak et al., 1996). Here the snails are put in beakers of water, which is made hypoxic by bubbling N_2 through it. When the animal attempts to open its pneumostome as a reaction to the hypoxic water, it receives a gentle tactile stimulus to the pneumostome area, reducing its aerial respiration, without affecting cutaneous respiration. The number of openings is recorded during training periods and retention tests. Learning takes place if the number of attempted pneumostome openings is significantly decreased between the first and the last training trial. It is important to note that in this paradigm memory retrieval and retention tests consist of the same procedure as the training sessions. They are only designated differently for the reader's convenience.

1.27.2.2.2 A long-term memory for the tactile stimulus is already formed after 4 h

Memory for the tactile stimulation of the pneumostome is defined by two criteria: (1) the number of

(a)

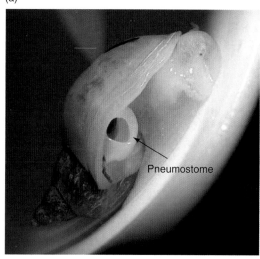

Pneumostome

(b)

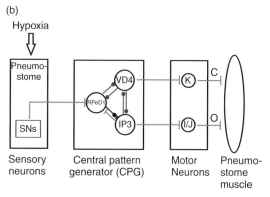

Figure 6 The snail *Lymnaea stagnalis*: Neuronal network underlying respiratory behavior. (a) *Lymnaea stagnalis* with opened pneumostome (arrow). From Lukowiak K, Sangha S, Scheibenstock A, et al. (2003) A molluscan model system in the search for the engram. *J. Physiol.* 69–76. (b) Schematic drawing of the central pattern generator (CPG). A chemosensory stimulus (here hypoxia) activates sensory neurons (SNs) in the pneumostome area, which in turn provide excitatory input (green line) to the right pedal dorsal 1 interneuron (RPeD1). Once stimulated, RPeD1 activates the input3 interneuron (IP3) via a biphasic effect (inhibition followed by excitation) (blue line) and inhibits visceral dorsal 4 interneuron (VD4) (red line). IP3 in turn excites both RPeD1 and the I/J motor neurons involved in pneumostome openings (O). IP3 also produces an inhibitory effect on VD4, and after release from this inhibition, VD4 fires, resulting in pneumostome closure (C). Tactile stimulation of the pneumostome area evokes closure of the pneumostome, and the aerial respiratory behavior stops. Adapted from Figure 1 in Sangha S, Varshney N, Fras M, et al. (2004) Memory, reconsolidation and extinction in *Lymnaea* require the soma of RPeD1. *Adv. Exp. Med. Biol.* 551: 311–318. Syed NI Winlow W (1991) Coordination of locomotor and cardiorespiratory networks of *Lymnaea stagnalis* by a pair of identified interneurones. J. Exp. Biol. 158: 37–62.

pneumostome openings is significantly reduced between the memory test and the first training session, and (2) the number of pneumostome openings at the memory test is not significantly different from the last training session (Lukowiak et al., 1996). Memory persists for at least 4 weeks if a spaced training protocol is used (Lukowiak et al., 1998). Within 1 h after the last training session, the consolidation process is susceptible for amnesic treatment. Memory that lasts beyond 4 h is considered long-term memory (LTM) because its consolidation depends on protein synthesis and RNA synthesis (Sangha et al., 2003b).

1.27.2.2.3 The neuronal network underlying the aerial respiration paradigm

One advantage of the aerial respiration paradigm is that the circuit of neurons controlling this behavior is known. Rhythmic behaviors like respiration and feeding are often controlled by neurons known as central pattern generators (CPGs). The respiratory CPG in *Lymnaea* consists of three neurons, named right pedal dorsal 1 (RPeD1), input 3 (IP3), and visceraldorsal 4 (VD4) interneurons. The latter two provide synaptic inputs to identified motor neurons, which mediate the opening movement (expiration) and the closing movement (inspiration) of the pneumostome (Syed et al., 1991; Syed and Winlow, 1991). The third neuron, RPeD1, receives excitatory chemosensory and mechanosensory input from the pneumostome area, which in turn initiates the CPG activity, and hence the respiratory behavior (**Figure 6(b)**).

Procedural memories are thought to be stored within the same network that mediates behavior (Milner et al., 1998), and therefore learning-induced changes were believed to be stored in the CPG. Indeed, neural correlates of learning and memory have been found in RPeD1 (Spencer et al., 1999). Removing the soma of RPeD1 by poking it gently with a glass microelectrode does not alter aerial respiratory behavior in a hypoxic environment, and the remaining neurite is electrophysiologically functional for at least 10 days after ablation (Scheibenstock et al., 2002). This preparation allows analyzing the function of RPeD1 in LTM formation in the aerial respiration paradigm. Snails with a soma-less RPeD1 are able to learn, but an LTM is not formed. Nevertheless, when RPeD1's soma is ablated after LTM consolidation has occurred, LTM can still be accessed. Accordingly, the soma of RPeD1 is a site of LTM consolidation but is not needed for memory retrieval (Scheibenstock et al., 2002).

1.27.2.2.4 Reconsolidation in the aerial respiration paradigm

To test for a possible reconsolidation process, snails are cooled in 4°C cold water immediately after memory retrieval. The memory of the control group is not retrieved, but the animal is also cooled. Memory retention is tested 4 hours after memory retrieval. The retrieved and cooled animals do not demonstrate memory. In contrast, the control group, which was cooled but was not retrieved, shows a memory for the tactile stimulus. Therefore, the reconsolidation process induced by memory retrieval is disturbed by the cooling procedure (Sangha et al., 2003a).

Similar results are obtained with the systemic application of the RNA synthesis-inhibitor, actinomycin D, after memory retrieval (**Figure 7(a)**). Only

animals receiving the retrieval in conjunction with the actinomycin D treatment do not show memory in a test 4 hours later. Comparable to the results with this RNA inhibitor, RPeD1 soma ablation after retrieval blocks memory retention at the later test (**Figure 7(b)**). The memory remains intact in RPeD1 soma-ablated snails that were not retrieved before the ablation. Accordingly, the soma of RPeD1 is required for reconsolidation.

These experiments demonstrate that a single neuron is necessary for consolidation and reconsolidation. Accordingly, in *Lymnaea* both processes take place not only in the same structure but also in the same neuron (Sangha et al., 2003a, 2004). Interestingly, vertebrate studies on this issue reach contradicting results. Some demonstrate that consolidation and

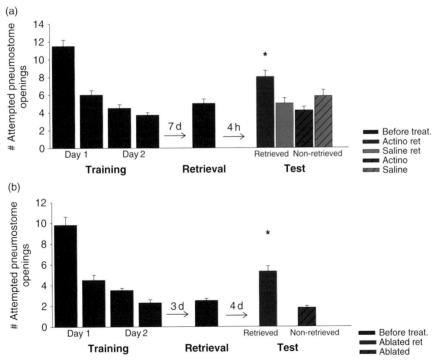

Figure 7 *Lymnaea stagnalis*: Reconsolidation is RNA syntheses dependent and takes place in a single neuron. (a) Training consisted of 4 45-min sessions in N_2-enriched hypoxic water. Sessions were dispersed over 2 days. On a single day the intertraining interval was 1 h. The memory was retrieved 7 days after training, and snails were injected with actinomycin D (Actino ret, violet bar) or saline (Saline ret, green bar) immediately after retrieval. The control groups (striped bars) received the injection (Actino ret, striped violet bar; Saline, striped green bar), but not the retrieval session. Memory retention was tested 4 h later. The retrieved and actinomycin D–injected animals (Actino ret) did not demonstrate memory. In contrast, the control group, which received the actinomycin D but was not retrieved, showed a memory for the conditioned response. (b) Operant training was administered as described above. Three days later half of the animals received the retrieval session immediately followed by the ablation of the soma of RPeD1 (Ablated ret, violet bar), whereas the other half was not reminded but underwent the ablation procedure (Ablated, striped violet bar). Animals were tested 4 days later. Memory was not observed in retrieved and ablated snails, whereas ablated snails that did not receive the retrieval procedure showed memory. Adapted from Figures 3 and 4 in Sangha S, Scheibenstock A, and Lukowiak K (2003a) Reconsolidation of a long-term memory in *Lymnaea* requires new protein and RNA synthesis and the soma of right pedal dorsal 1. *J. Neurosci.* 23: 8034–8040.

reconsolidation take place in different brain structures (Tronel and Sara, 2002; Salinska et al., 2004), whereas others find that reconsolidation can be disrupted with protein synthesis inhibitors targeting the same brain structure as in consolidation experiments (Rose and Benjamin, 1979; Nader et al., 2000; Debiec et al., 2002; Koh and Bernstein, 2003).

1.27.2.2.5 Lymnaea stagnalis: *The classical chemosensory conditioning paradigm*

The second paradigm used in *Lymnaea* is an appetitive classical conditioning based on its feeding behavior. Feeding behavior consists of a series of rasps that can be divided into three phases: (1) protraction phase, in which the animal opens the mouth and the radula, a toothed chitinous tissue, is extended to contact the food; (2) retraction phase, when the food substrate is grazed and lifted into the mouth; and (3) the swallow phase, during which the mouth is closed and the food is swallowed (Rose and Benjamin, 1979; Benjamin et al., 2000; Elliott and Susswein, 2002). Similar to the respiratory behavior described earlier, a known network driven by a CPG controls this behavior (Benjamin et al., 2000: *See also* Chapter 1.30).

Using sucrose as a stimulus increases the feeding behavior in terms of the number of rasps (Kemenes et al., 1986; *See also* Chapter 4.09). Therefore, sucrose is used as a US in an appetitive classical conditioning paradigm. Here food-deprived snails are put into a Petri dish with water and are allowed to acclimatize. Amyl acetate, used as the CS, and the sucrose solution are added to the Petri dish, one after another and the animals are exposed to the CS–US mixture for 10 s. Afterward, the trained snails are transferred to their home tanks. To test the taste memory, the animals are put back into the Petri dish, the CS (amyl acetate) is added after a resting period, and the number of rasps is counted. Following a single paired CS–US presentation, animals show significant higher feeding response to amyl acetate compared with their own naïve response and with that of control groups (unpaired, CS alone, US alone) (Fulton et al., 2005).

1.27.2.2.6 A consolidated long-term memory in the appetitive chemosensory conditioning paradigm is formed after 5 hours

An LTM is formed about the amyl acetate-sucrose association that lasts at least 19 days (Alexander et al., 1984). Applying the widely used protein synthesis-

inhibitor anisomycin at different time points after single-trial training demonstrates a protein-dependent consolidation phase 10 min after training, whereas later tested time points (1–6 hours) no longer reveal any sensitivity to the inhibitor. An impairment of memory retention can be seen already 5 h after training and injection. Therefore, memory retention 5 h after learning is protein synthesis dependent (Fulton et al., 2005).

1.27.2.2.7 Reconsolidation in the appetitive chemosensory conditioning paradigm

A study by Kemenes et al. (2006) asked if the age of a memory has an influence on the molecular mechanisms that underlie a reconsolidation process. This study distinguishes between fresh and old memories. Protein synthesis shortly after conditioning (between 10 min and 1 h) is required for the formation for a memory expressed more than 5 h after training (Fulton et al., 2005). Therefore, a 6-h memory was considered to be a freshly consolidated memory, whereas a 24-h memory was regarded as an old consolidated memory. To demonstrate the reconsolidation phenomenon, the animals receive a CS presentation to retrieve the memory 6 or 24 h after conditioning, followed by an injection of the protein synthesis inhibitor anisomycin. At a retention test 18 h after the injection, the CR (number of rasps) of the anisomycin-injected and retrieved animals was reduced in comparison to the control groups. This demonstrates that protein synthesis is required for reconsolidation when a 6-h or a 24-h memory is retrieved (Kemenes et al., 2006).

A follow-up experiment directly measured the retrieval-induced activation of cAMP-dependent protein kinase A (PKA) in the cerebral ganglia. The cerebral ganglia were chosen because they are known to be a site for neuronal plasticity (Straub et al., 2004). Again the study differentiated between fresh and old memories (Kemenes et al., 2006). Interestingly, the PKA activity was increased in the group with trained animals subjected to a CS presentation 6 h after training in comparison to nonretrieved or unpaired trained control groups. This retrieval-induced increase of PKA activity was not found if the memory was retrieved 24 h after CS–US pairing. A PKA inhibitor was used to verify that retrieval-induced PKA activity is dependent on the age of the memory. Animals showed a reduced CR at the retention test if a freshly consolidated memory was retrieved followed by an injection of the PKA inhibitor. If the memory was retrieved 24 h after training, the application of the PKA inhibitor did not lead to a reduced CR (**Figure 8**).

This confirmed the biochemical data. Accordingly, retrieval of a consolidated memory induces a protein synthesis–dependent reconsolidation process, but only reconsolidation of freshly consolidated memories requires the activation of PKA. It can be concluded that the molecular requirements for reconsolidation depend on the age or the maturation of the retrieved memory (Kemenes et al., 2006).

Reconsolidation's dependency on the age of the retrieved memory has been reported before, although on a different timescale. Rats trained in an inhibitory avoidance task, show the reconsolidation phenomenon only when a recent memory has been retrieved in combination with the application of a protein synthesis-inhibitor. When the memory for the inhibitory

avoidance task is 14 days old or older, a decrease of the CR can no longer be observed after combining memory retrieval with a systemic application of a protein synthesis inhibitor (Milekic and Alberini, 2002). Similar results have been demonstrated by other authors in several paradigms in vertebrates (e.g., Eisenberg and Dudai, 2004; Suzuki et al., 2004; Frankland et al., 2006; Power et al., 2006). Nevertheless, contrasting findings have also been reported (Nader et al., 2000; Debiec et al., 2002). Debiec et al. (2002) demonstrated in rats that retrieval of a 45-day-old memory for contextual fear conditioning, in combination with protein synthesis inhibition in the hippocampus, still results in the reconsolidation phenomenon (Debiec et al., 2002). Taken together the reason for different temporal requirements for reconsolidation remains unknown.

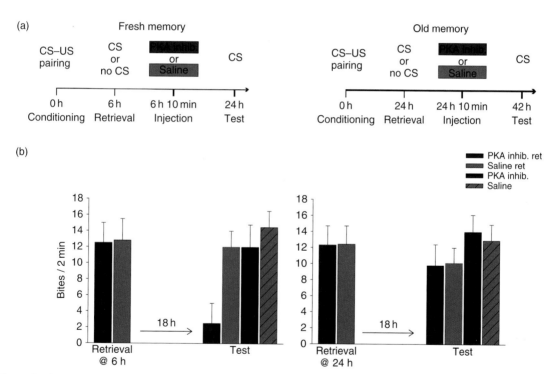

Figure 8 *Lymnaea stagnalis*: Reconsolidation in an appetitive conditioning paradigm. (a) The experimental scheme. Food-deprived snails were put in a Petri dish with water. Amyl acetate, as conditioned stimulus (CS), was added to a final concentration of 0.004%. After 15 s, a the sucrose solution was added and the animals remained in this CS + unconditioned stimulus (US) mixture for an additional 105 s. After this single CS–US pairing, the animals were rinsed. Animals were divided into two groups, and half of the animals received a CS presentation to retrieve the memory 6 h (fresh memory, left panel) or 24 (old memory, right panel) hours after conditioning. The other half received no CS stimulation. Ten minutes later, all animals were injected with PKA inhibitor (violet) or saline (green). All animals were tested 18 h after injection for their response to the CS in a 2-min test. (b) Animals that were retrieved at 6 h after training followed by an injection of the PKA inhibitor (PKA Inhib. ret, violet bars) show reduced conditioned response (number of rasps) during testing in comparison to retrieved and saline-injected (Saline ret, green bars) animals or to the nonretrieved groups (striped bars) (left panel). This significant reduction of CR of the retrieved and inhibited group is not observable if the memory is retrieved 24 h after training (right panel). Adapted from Figures 1 and 3 in Kemenes G, Kemenes I, Michel M, Papp A, and Muller U (2006) Phase-dependent molecular requirements for memory reconsolidation: Differential roles for protein synthesis and protein kinase A activity. *J. Neurosci.* 26: 6298–6302.

But the study in *Lymnaea stagnalis* illustrates that differences in the molecular events induced by memory retrieval might play a role.

1.27.2.3 The Terrestrial Snail *Helix lucorum*

1.27.2.3.1 *Context memory in* Helix lucorum *is protein synthesis dependent*

Helix lucorum is an edible snail, sometimes called escargot turc (**Figure 9(a)**). It is found in central Italy, from Yugoslavia through the Crimea to Turkey, and around the Black Sea. *Helix lucorum* is trained in an aversive conditioning paradigm, where it learns to associate the context, a rotating ball, with an electric shock (Gainutdinova et al., 2005). To do so, the animals receive an electric shock to the dorsal surface of their foot after they are fixed at their shell and placed on a ball, which rotates in water (**Figure 9(b)**). To test for the acquired context memory, the animals are placed onto the ball (the reinforced context) again or on a flat glass plate (the nonreinforced context), and a tactile stimulus is applied to the skin in both contexts. The defensive tentacle withdrawal amplitude is measured. A significantly different withdrawal amplitude between the reinforced and the nonreinforced context indicates an associative memory for the context.

To study memory consolidation, animals are trained over 5 days and receive an injection of anisomycin or saline every day after the first shock. Memory is tested 2 days after the last training day

(**Figure 10**). Saline-injected snails show a significantly higher response to tactile stimulation in the trained context compared to the nonreinforced context. Therefore, the animals are able to differentiate between the context in which they get a sensitizing shock and the control context. Anisomycin-injected snails show no significant difference in the withdrawal amplitude between the two contexts. This indicates that the formation of a context memory depends on protein synthesis (Gainutdinova et al., 2005).

1.27.2.3.2 *Reconsolidation in* Helix lucorum

The training protocol used in the reconsolidation experiments is the same as in the consolidation experiment (see previous section). To remind the animals of the training situation, they are placed in the reinforced context, and neither a shock nor a tactile stimulus for testing is delivered. Anisomycin or saline are applied immediately after the reminding procedure. Testing the animals the next day does not reveal context memory in reminded and anisomycin-injected snails (**Figure 11**). In contrast, animals treated with saline show context memory. If the reminding process is omitted, the injection of anisomycin does not affect the context memory. Therefore, the reminder procedure induces a protein synthesis–dependent process, and hence reconsolidation. If in the reminding situation (the reexposure to the context) the reinforcing stimulus (the shock) is applied in combination with a protein synthesis inhibitor, the reconsolidation

(a)

(b)

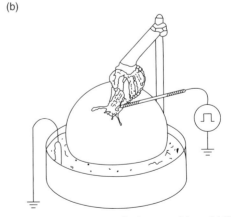

Figure 9 *Helix lucorum*: Aversive context learning. (a) *Helix lucorum* is sometimes called escargot turc. (b) The training apparatus. A snail is fixed at its shell and placed on a ball in a manner that allows crawling. The ball rotates freely in water and is laced with stainless steel wire to complete an electrical circuit between the animal's foot and a carbon electrode placed in the water. Electric shock is delivered through a macroelectrode applied manually to the dorsal surface of the foot. Adapted from Figure 1 in Gainutdinova TH, Tagirova RR, Ismailova AI, et al. (2005) Reconsolidation of a context long-term memory in the terrestrial snail requires protein synthesis. *Learn. Mem.* 12: 620–625.

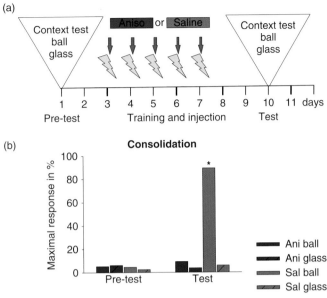

Figure 10 *Helix lucorum*: Memory consolidation. (a) Protocol of context conditioning. Snails received a pretest. Two days later all animals received five electrical shocks (flash) per day with a 20-min interval for 5 days. Every day, 3–5 min after the first shock, they were injected (arrow) with anisomycin (aniso, violet) or saline (green). A test was applied 3 days later. (b) Average of withdrawal response in the two contexts, reinforced context ball (plain) and nonreinforced context flat glass (striped). No difference in response to test stimulus was found in anisomycin-injected groups (Ani, violet bar), whereas the control group (Sal, green bar) showed context memory. Adapted from Figure 3 in Gainutdinova TH, Tagirova RR, Ismailova AI, et al. (2005) Reconsolidation of a context long-term memory in the terrestrial snail requires protein synthesis. *Learn. Mem.* 12: 620–625.

phenomenon is not visible (e.g., the animal can discriminate the two contexts) (Gainutdinova et al., 2005). This finding resembles a result in the crab *Chasmagnathus granulatus* (described in the next section), showing that reconsolidation can only be induced when the reminder is not accompanied by the reinforcer.

1.27.2.4 The Crab *Chasmagnathus granulatus*

1.27.2.4.1 Learning about a visual danger stimulus (VDA) leads to an associative and a nonassociative memory component

Chasmagnathus granulatus is a semiterrestrial crab that lives at the coast of South Brazil, Uruguay, and Argentina. Memory formation is studied on adult, male crabs (**Figure 12(a)**). They are caught in their natural habitat and transferred to the laboratory, where they are tested in an aversive learning paradigm. In this paradigm a danger stimulus (an opaque screen termed the visual danger stimulus = VDS) is passed over an animal that sits in a plastic container (**Figure 12(b)**).

The movement of this danger stimulus leads to an escape response that declines with further movements of the stimulus (Brunner and Maldonado, 1988). This decrease in the escape response has been initially assigned to habituation (Brunner and Maldonado, 1988). Depending on the training protocol, the decline of the escape response to the presentation of the VDS persists for several days (Lozada et al., 1990; Pedreira et al., 1995, 1998). Accordingly, a long-term memory about the VDS has been formed, which is termed long-term habituation (LTH). It consists of an associative component and a nonassociative component (Hermitte et al., 1999). The associative component is based on an association between the context and the signal (the VDS), and the resulting memory is termed context-signal memory (CSM) (Hermitte et al., 1999; Tomsic et al., 1998).

It is only induced by spaced training, depends on protein synthesis (**Figure 13(a)**), and lasts at least 5 days (Pedreira et al., 1995). The nonassociative component depends on the invariance of the VDS and is independent of the context of training. It is termed signal memory (SM). Massed training is sufficient to induce this nonassociative component of

(a)

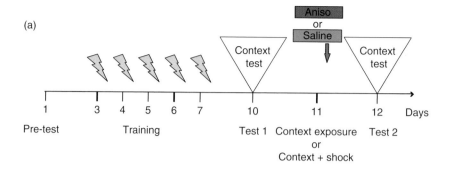

(b)

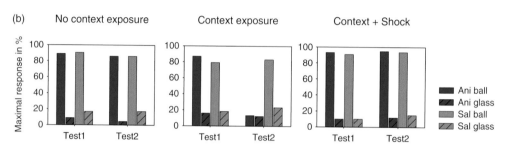

Figure 11 *Helix lucorum:* Reconsolidation. (a) Protocol of reminded context conditioning. Snails received a pretest on day 1 and were trained with five electrical shocks (flash) per day over 5 days. Three days later they received the test stimulus (test 1) to control if the animals had learned. Next day snails were reminded of training by placing them in the same context (context exposure, b middle panel) for 20 min or administering an electrical shock during the exposure (context + shock, b right panel), or as a control group received no context exposure (b left panel). All groups were injected (arrow) immediately afterward with anisomycin (aniso, violet) or saline (green). Next day all groups were tested again (Test 2) in both contexts. (b) Average response of withdrawal response in the two contexts, reinforced context ball (plain bars) and nonreinforced context glass (striped bars) before treatment (Test 1) and afterward (Test 2). In all experiments the context memory was intact in test 1. When the context exposure is omitted, injection of anisomycin (Ani, violet bars) or saline (Sal, green bars) has no influence on the context memory in test 2 (left panel: no context exposure). But reminded and anisomycin-treated snails show no context memory on test 2 to the trained context (ball), in contrast to the reminded saline-injected snails (middle panel: context exposure). If the reinforcer (shock) is presented during context exposure, injecting anisomycin does not lead to a loss of context memory (right panel: context + shock). Adapted from Figures 1, 2, and 4 in Gainutdinova TH, Tagirova RR, Ismailova AI, et al. (2005) Reconsolidation of a context long-term memory in the terrestrial snail requires protein synthesis. *Learn. Mem.* 12: 620–625.

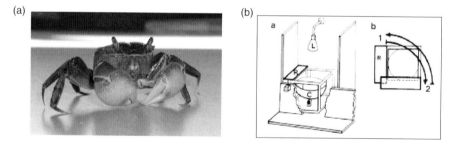

Figure 12 The crab *Chasmagnathus granulatus*: Learning about a visual danger stimulus (VDA). (a) The crab *Chasmagnathus granulatus*. (b) Left: The actometer, one of 40 units of the apparatus in which the crabs are trained. C, plastic container; R, rectangular screen used for the visual danger stimulus; M, motor; L, lamp; P, pizoelectric transducer; Right: Movement of the screen during a trial cycle (from 1 to 2 and vice versa). From Beron de Astarda M and Maldonado H (1999) Two related forms of long-term habituation in the crab *Chasmagnathus* are differentially affected by scopolamine. *Pharmacol. Biochem. Behav.* 63: 109–118.

the LTH (Pedreira et al., 1998; Hermitte et al., 1999) (**Figure 13(b)**).

It is important to note that memory for habituation can only be tested if the VDS is presented to the trained animals. Only then do the crabs show the learned freezing response. This means that retrieval of the initial memory and retraining occur in the same test session. Accordingly, when the usual series

(a)

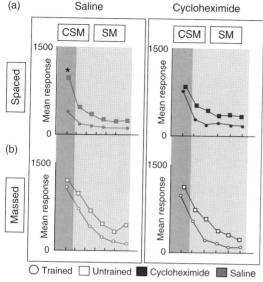

○ Trained □ Untrained ■ Cycloheximide ■ Saline

Figure 13 The crab *Chasmagnathus granulatus*: The induction of the context-signal memory (CSM) depends on the training protocol and is inhibited by a protein synthesis inhibitor. Crabs were systemically injected with 15 μg Cycloheximide (Cycloheximide; violet) or saline (Saline; green) immediately after spaced training (spaced, filled symbols) or massed training (massed, open symbols). Memory retention was tested 24 h later with six trials with the same intertrial interval that was used during training. Conditioned responses (mean response) at each test trial are shown here. The first test uncovers memory retention of the context-signal memory (CSM; dark gray); five following tests show memory retention of the signal memory (SM, light gray) and include a retraining phase. In each of the experiments, a trained group (trained, circles) is compared with an untrained control group (untrained, squares). (a) Memory retention after spaced training (15 trials; intertrial interval 171 s). The CSM is induced in the trained group in comparison to the untrained group (saline) and CSM but not SM depend on protein-synthesis (Cycloheximide). (b) Memory retention after massed training (300 training trials without intertrial interval). The CSM is not induced in the trained group in comparison to the untrained group (saline) and CSM and SM do not depend on protein synthesis (Cycloheximide). Adapted from Figure 3 in Hermitte G, Pedreira ME, Tomsic D, and Maldonado H (1999) Context shift and protein synthesis inhibition disrupt long-term habituation after spaced, but not massed, training in the crab *Chasmagnathus*. *Neurobiol. Learn. Mem.* 71: 34–49.

of six memory tests is applied, only memory retention at the first memory test resembles the memory for the initial training, and only this memory is based on the associative component of the LTM, the context-signal memory (CSM). Further memory tests in the same test session resemble a retraining phase (Pedreira et al., 1998).

1.27.2.4.2 Reconsolidation of the CSM

CSM retention can be observed 24 h after spaced training when the crabs are exposed to the VDS in the training context. When the crabs are exposed to the training context without the presentation of the VDS, a conditioned response is not elicited (Pedreira et al., 2002). Nevertheless, this exposure to the training context has an impact on subsequent memory retention. Namely, the combination of a 5-min context exposure 24 h after training with an injection of protein synthesis inhibitor leads to the inhibition of CSM memory retention 1 day later (Pedreira et al., 2002) (**Figure 14(a)**). The reconsolidation phenomenon has been induced accordingly.

1.27.2.4.3 The duration of the reexposure defined by its offset is critical for reconsolidation to occur

The reconsolidation phenomenon is only induced when reexposure to the training context endures for less then 40 min. A longer reexposure to the training context leads to a new, context–no signal association, and hence extinction learning. This extinction learning results in an extinction memory that depends on protein synthesis (Pedreira and Maldonado, 2003) (**Figure 14(b)**). Also in studies on vertebrates, the reconsolidation phenomenon becomes apparent when extinction is weak (Eisenberg et al., 2003; Suzuki et al., 2004; Power et al., 2006). On the basis of these findings, Nader (2003) and Dudai (2004) proposed the hypothesis of trace dominance. They interpreted these results as indicating a competition between two consolidation processes, the consolidation of extinction memory and the consolidation process underlying the reconsolidation phenomenon (Eisenberg et al., 2003; Nader, 2003). However, in the meantime, two studies, one in the honeybee and one in rats, reveal that the hypothesis of trace dominance is only half of the truth (see "The Honeybee *Apis mellifera*").

In crabs, the duration of the reexposure of the training context is critical for the consolidation process induced by the reminder. Accordingly, it has been found that the offset of the reminder stimulus without the appearance of the VDS is critical for either reconsolidation or consolidation of the extinction memory to occur (Pedreira et al., 2004). These data suggest that reconsolidation or the consolidation of an extinction memory occurred only when the nonoccurrence of the reinforcement (here the VDS) is irreversible due to the termination of the reminder (Pedreira et al., 2004). Accordingly, Pedreira et al. (2004) concluded

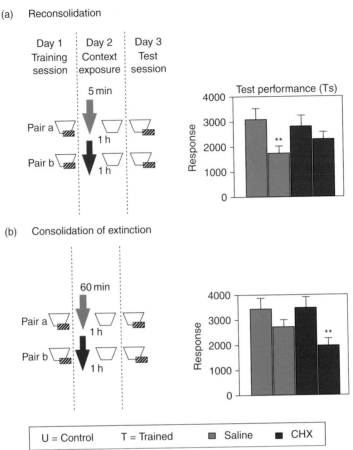

Figure 14 The crab *Chasmagnathus granulatus*: Reconsolidation and consolidation of extinction memory depend on the duration of the reexposure to the training context. Day 1: Training with 15 9-s presentations of the visual danger stimulus (striped bar), separated by 3 min; Day 2: Systemic injection (arrow) of Cycloheximid (CYX; violet arrow and bars) or saline (green arrow and bars) 1 h prior to reexposure to the training context trapeze for either 5 min (reconsolidation) or 60 min (consolidation of extinction); Day 3: Memory retention test: a single 9-s VDS presentation (striped bar). A significant difference between the untrained group (U) and the trained group (T) (U > T) at the memory retention test indicates memory retention. The trapeze stands for the container where a crab is placed during each of the experimental phases. Adapted from Figure 2 in Pedreira ME and Maldonado H (2003) Protein synthesis subserves reconsolidation or extinction depending on reminder duration. *Neuron* 38: 863–869.

that the mismatch between what is expected and what actually occurs triggers memory reconsolidation or extinction. Interestingly, a similar finding has been recently reported in an aversive paradigm in the gastropod *Helix lucorum*, namely, that the reconsolidation phenomenon is not visible when in the reminding situation (the reexposure to a context) the reinforcing stimulus (a shock) is applied in combination with a protein synthesis inhibitor (Gainutdinova et al., 2005) (see "The Terrestrial Snail *Helix lucorum*"). This is in contrast to findings in *Limax flavus* (see "The Terrestrial Slug *Limax flavus*") and in rats. In *Limax flavus* amnesia can be induced by retrieval with the CS alone or with an additional CS–US pairing followed by a cooling procedure (Sekiguchi et al., 1997). A similar result has been reported in an aversive conditioning paradigm in rats (Duvarci and Nader, 2004), namely, that the injection of anisomycin in selected brain regions after retrieval with and without reinforcement inhibits reconsolidation (Nader et al., 2000; Duvarci and Nader, 2004). The reason for this contradiction is not known. One could assume that the type of paradigm used in the different experiments is critical. In context conditioning (used in *Chasmagnathus granulatus* and *Helix lucorum*) memory retrieval that is accompanied by the reinforcement does not lead to reconsolidation. In contrast, the reconsolidation phenomenon is detectable after retrieval with or without reinforcing stimulus in cue-dependent conditioning (used in *Limax flavus* and rats).

1.27.2.4.4 CSM consolidation and reconsolidation share molecular mechanisms

Several molecules have been identified that are involved in the consolidation of the associative CSM (Romano et al., 2006). Presently it is not known if this holds true for reconsolidation and if the same molecular mechanisms underlie both the consolidation of the CSM and the reconsolidation. Growing evidence in vertebrates demonstrates that reconsolidation is not a faithful recapitulation of consolidation, but each process is mediated by distinct intracellular signaling cascades, which might overlap (Kelly et al., 2003; Lee et al., 2004). Findings in *Chasmagnathus* are in accordance with this in demonstrating that molecular mechanisms are shared by both consolidation processes, but differences between both processes have not yet been demonstrated.

Consolidation of the CSM and reconsolidation are sensitive to inhibitors of translation. In accordance with these results, a transcription factor, the nuclear factor κB (NF-κB), (*See* Chapter 4.28), has been found to be involved in the consolidation of the CSM and in reconsolidation (Freudenthal et al., 1998; Freudenthal and Romano, 2000; Merlo et al., 2002). After training, NF-κB is activated in two phases, directly and 6 h after spaced training (Freudenthal and Romano, 2000). This parallels activity of the cAMP-dependent protein-kinase A (PKA) after spaced training (Locatelli et al., 2002; Locatelli and Romano, 2005), suggesting a causal relationship between these processes, which nevertheless remains to be demonstrated. Also, reconsolidation depends on NF-κB activity during a 5-min reexposure to the trained context (Merlo et al., 2005), but it is unknown whether NF-κB is activated 6 h after memory retrieval as it is after training, and whether PKA plays a role in reconsolidation.

Are the same transmitters and receptors involved in consolidation and reconsolidation? Application of the *N*-methyl-D-aspartate (NMDA)-receptor antagonists during training up to 4 h after training inhibits the formation of CSM (Troncoso and Maldonado, 2002). This holds true for reconsolidation (Pedreira et al., 2002). Interestingly, the involvement of NMDA receptors in reconsolidation processes (and consolidation processes) has also been demonstrated in appetitive and aversive paradigms in several studies on vertebrates (Przybyslawski and Sara, 1997; Przybyslawski et al., 1999; Torras-Garcia et al., 2005; Akirav and Maroun, 2006; Lee et al., 2006). Accordingly, the involvement of the NMDA receptor might be an evolutionarily conserved feature of the reconsolidation processes.

The endogenous peptide angiotensin II, which plays a role in regulating fluid homeostasis and is present in higher amounts after water shortage in the crab brain, facilitates the consolidation of CSM (Delorenzi and Maldonado, 1999; Delorenzi et al., 2000; Frenkel et al., 2002). This memory enhancement is mediated by NF-κB that is activated by angiotensin II following water shortage (Frenkel et al., 2002). Angiotensin II is also involved in reconsolidation because its inhibition leads to retrieval-induced amnesia (Frenkel et al., 2005).

1.27.2.5 The Honeybee *Apis mellifera*

1.27.2.5.1 The appetitive, olfactory conditioning of the proboscis extension response

The honeybee is one of the oldest – if not the oldest – invertebrate models in learning and memory research. Its pronounced learning ability is used in a classical, Pavlovian conditioning paradigm in the laboratory, the olfactory conditioning of the proboscis extension response, where honeybee learning and memory formation are studied in single, restrained bees (**Figure 15(a)**) (*See also* Chapters 1.29 and 4.06).

Honeybees reflexively extend their proboscis when their antennae are touched with a drop of sucrose solution. This response to sucrose solution is called the proboscis extension response (PER) (**Figure 15(b)**). When the presentation of an odor precedes the sucrose reward (**Figure 15(c)**), honeybees learn to associate the odorant (CS) with the sucrose reward (US) (Menzel et al., 1974; Bitterman et al., 1983). After an association has formed, the odor alone elicits the proboscis extension. This reaction toward the odor is the CR. The CR can be elicited by the learned odor immediately after the acquisition and up to several days later, indicating the formation of short as well as long-lasting memories for this odor-sucrose association (Menzel, 1999; Eisenhardt, 2006).

1.27.2.5.2 A consolidated LTM is formed after three CS–US pairings

Three CS–US pairings are sufficient to induce a consolidated LTM. Two LTMs have been characterized so far by means of their sensitivity to systemically injected inhibitors. One and 2 days after three CS–US pairings, an LTM has been formed depending on translation during acquisition (Friedrich et al., 2004;

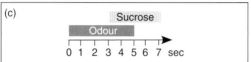

Figure 15 The honeybee *Apis mellifera*: Olfactory conditioning of the proboscis extension response. (a) Single honeybees are restrained in small tubes to condition the proboscis extension response (PER). Adapted from Bitterman ME, Menzel, R, Fietz, A, and Schäfer S (1983) Classical conditioning of proboscis extension in honeybees (*Apis mellifera*). *J. Comp. Psychol.* 97: 107–119. (b) Honeybees reflexively elicit their proboscis when the antennae and the proboscis are touched with sugar water. Here a toothpick that is moistened with sucrose solution is used to touch the honeybee's proboscis. After the PER is elicited, the honeybee licks sucrose solution from the toothpick. (c) Schematic diagram of the olfactory conditioning of the PER. An odor (conditioned stimulus) is presented for 5 s; after 3 s the PER is elicited with sucrose solution (unconditioned stimulus), and the honeybee is allowed to lick the sucrose solution for 4 s.

Stollhoff et al., 2005) (**Figure 16(a)**). A second long-lasting memory, formed 3–4 days after three CS–US pairings, depends on translation, but also on transcription. Inhibition of transcription and translation during acquisition, 1 h and 6 h after acquisition, results in an inhibition of this LTM (translation, 6 h: Eisenhardt & Stollhoff, unpublished data; Grünbaum and Müller, 1998; Wüstenberg et al., 1998; Friedrich et al., 2004). Thus, the activation of both processes for at least 6 h after acquisition is necessary for the formation of this later LTM. Interestingly, both LTMs are formed in parallel. They are induced by two different mechanisms that both depend on the cAMP-dependent protein kinase A (PKA) (Fiala et al., 1999; Müller, 2000; Friedrich et al., 2004).

1.27.2.5.3 Retrieval of a consolidated olfactory LTM

When a consolidated LTM is retrieved 1 day after training, two different consolidation processes can be induced, and the consolidation of an extinction memory and reconsolidation (Stollhoff et al., 2005). A series of experiments with one, two, and five retrieval trials that were applied 1 day after the initial training revealed that the resulting memory is dependent on the number of retrieval trials. Memory retention was

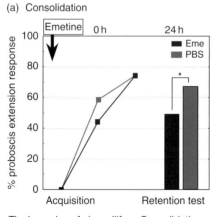

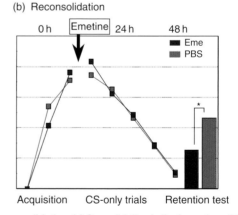

Figure 16 The honeybee *Apis mellifera*: Consolidation and reconsolidation. (a) Consolidation in the honeybee. 0 h: Emetine or PBS were systemically injected 30 min before honeybees were conditioned with three trials with an intertrial interval of 10 min (acquisition); 24 h: Memory retention was tested 1 day after acquisition by one 5-s presentation of the conditioned odor (CS). Eme: Animals that were injected with emetine; PBS: Control group; Animals that were injected with PBS. (b) Reconsolidation in the honeybee occurs after extinction. 0 h: Honeybees were conditioned with three trials with an intertrial interval of 10 min (acquisition); Emetine or PBS were systemically injected 30 min before the initial memory was retrieved with five conditioned stimulus (CS)-only trials with an intertrial interval of 10 min (CS-only trials); 48 h: memory retention was tested with one CS-only trial Eme: Emetine; PBS: Control group injected with saline. Adapted from Stollhoff N, Menzel R, and Eisenhardt D (2005) Spontaneous recovery from extinction depends on the reconsolidation of the acquisition memory in an appetitive learning paradigm in the honeybee (*Apis mellifera*). *J. Neurosci.* 25: 4485–4492.

tested 24 h after the initial memory retrieval. It turned out that one retrieval trial induced neither an extinction memory nor a reconsolidation phenomenon. Two retrieval trials led to significant extinction, and application of protein synthesis inhibitor before this memory retrieval resulted in an inhibition of the extinction memory. Five retrieval trials also induced significant extinction and spontaneous recovery of the CR (**Figure 16(b)**). After the application of the protein synthesis inhibitor, the amount of spontaneous recovery from extinction was reduced, but inhibition of the extinction memory was not observed. Hence, reconsolidation was induced after five retrieval trials (**Figure 16(b)**). Accordingly, although extinction was induced, the reconsolidation phenomenon was observed (Stollhoff et al., 2005).

These data contrast to those gathered in studies of the crab *Chasmagnathus* and in vertebrates (Eisenberg et al., 2003; Pedreira and Maldonado, 2003; Suzuki et al., 2004). Reconsolidation was induced in these studies only when extinction did not take place, and it was concluded that extinction is a boundary condition for reconsolidation (Nader, 2003).

The reason for this contradiction remains unclear, but only recently a study in vertebrates revealed a similar phenomenon, namely, the occurrence of reconsolidation after extinction (Duvarci et al., 2006). Hence extinction is not always a boundary condition for reconsolidation.

Spontaneous recovery from extinction after five retrieval trials in the honeybee is not complete (**Figure 16(b)**). From that it was concluded that after five retrieval trials, an extinction memory has been found, although spontaneous recovery occurred. Because this spontaneous recovery is based on reconsolidation, it seems likely that consolidation of the extinction memory and reconsolidation are two parallel processes (Stollhoff et al., 2005). What might be the mechanisms generating two parallel memory traces? A new hypothesis was put forward to explain the existence of these two memory traces (Eisenhardt and Menzel, 2007). This internal reinforcement hypothesis is substantially different from the original reconsolidation hypothesis (Nader, 2003) because it proposes that memory retrieval initiates new learning rather then activating and destabilizing the original CS–US memory trace. The hypothesis is based on the assumption that mechanisms underlying the reconsolidation phenomenon can be ascribed to basic neuronal mechanisms that are found in both vertebrates and invertebrates. The central tenet refers to the properties of reinforcement-predicting neurons, such as the dopamine neurons of the ventral tegmentum (Schultz, 2006) and the VUMmx1 neuron in the honeybee (Hammer, 1993). Neurons with comparable properties are assumed to exist also in the fruit fly *Drosophila melanogaster* (Riemensperger et al., 2005) and the molluscs (e.g., Aplysia et al., 1984). The internal reinforcement hypothesis proposes that two learning processes take place when memory is retrieved: one based on the lack of reinforcement (extinction learning) and one based on the internal existence of the reinforcement, which is activated by the CS (reminder learning) (Eisenhardt and Menzel, 2007). This internal existence of the reinforcement is proposed to be due to neuronal activity that is induced by memory retrieval, like the activity that can be observed in the honeybee's Vum$_{mx1}$ neuron (Hammer, 1993). When retrieving a memory, the presentation of the CS and the activation of these neurons at the same time should then result in excitatory learning comparable to physical CS–US pairing. This form of learning should lead to a consolidation process underlying the reconsolidation phenomenon. Accordingly, reminder learning and extinction learning induce the formation of two memories that are consolidated in parallel and together constitute controlling behavior.

1.27.3 Conclusion

Several invertebrate species are currently used to study the reconsolidation phenomenon: the gastropods *Helix lucorum*, *Limax flavus*, *Lymnaea stagnalis*, the crab *Chasmagnathus granulatus*, and the honeybee, *Apis mellifera*. Findings from each of these organisms contribute to elucidate the reconsolidation phenomenon and its underlying mechanisms.

The slug *Helix lucorum* was the first invertebrate for which the reconsolidation phenomenon was demonstrated (Sekiguchi et al., 1997). In addition, the study of an odor-avoidance paradigm revealed that the age of the retrieved memory is important for the reconsolidation process to occur. It is only when fresh memories are retrieved that reconsolidation occurs. When retrieving an old memory, reconsolidation occurs only when either an additional training trial or a second-order conditioning was applied shortly before (Sekiguchi et al., 1997).

Furthermore, a study of an appetitive classical conditioning paradigm in the snail *Lymnaea stagnalis* revealed that the age of the retrieved memory is important for the reconsolidation process. Retrieval of fresh and old memories induces a reconsolidation process that depends on protein synthesis. But only retrieval of a fresh memory induces a reconsolidation process that depends on the cAMP-dependent PKA (Kemenes et al., 2006). Accordingly, the molecular mechanisms underlying the reconsolidation processes depend on the age of the retrieved memory (*See* Chapter 4.09).

The neuronal network underlying reconsolidation in an aversive, operant conditioning paradigm has been studied in *Lymnaea stagnalis*. It has been demonstrated that only a single neuron is necessary for reconsolidation. In this paradigm, the reconsolidation phenomenon has been uncovered by cooling and using a transcription inhibitor. In accordance with this, reconsolidation is not induced when the nucleus of the relevant neuron has been ablated. Nevertheless, the nucleus is not needed to retrieve the inhibited reconsolidated memory (Sangha et al., 2003a).

In an aversive context conditioning paradigm in the snail *Helix lucorum*, the exposure to a context as a reminder elicits the reconsolidation phenomenon (Gainutdinova et al., 2005). But if the reinforcer is presented during the exposure to the reminder, reconsolidation cannot be observed.

A similar result has been found in the crab *Chasmagnathus granulatus*. Work on an aversive classical conditioning paradigm revealed that the duration of the CS presentation when retrieving a consolidated memory is critical for the induction of the reconsolidation phenomenon: Only a short exposure to the CS results in reconsolidation, whereas a long exposure leads to extinction and the consolidation of an extinction memory (Pedreira and Maldonado, 2003). Accordingly, it is only when the CS exposure is terminated without the occurrence of the US that reconsolidation and the consolidation of an extinction memory occur (Pedreira et al., 2004). In contrast to the findings in *Chasmagnathus*, a study on an appetitive classical conditioning paradigm in the honeybee demonstrates that – although extinction was induced – reconsolidation occurs after many CS presentations (Stollhoff et al., 2005). These results do not support the hypothesis of trace dominance that derives from studies in *Chasmagnathus* and vertebrates stating that extinction is a boundary condition for reconsolidation. It rather suggests that reconsolidation and the consolidation of an extinction memory are two parallel processes.

References

Akirav I and Maroun M (2006) Ventromedial prefrontal cortex is obligatory for consolidation and reconsolidation of object recognition memory. *Cereb. Cortex* 16(12): 1759–1765.

Alberini C (2005) Mechanisms of memory stabilization: Are consolidation and reconsolidation similar or distinct processes? *Trends Neurosci.* 28: 51–56.

Alexander J Jr, Audesirk TE, and Audesirk GJ (1984) One-trial reward learning in the snail *Lymnea stagnalis*. *J. Neurobiol.* 15: 67–72.

Benjamin PR, Staras K, and Kemenes G (2000) A systems approach to the cellular analysis of associative learning in the pond snail *Lymnaea*. *Learn. Mem.* 7: 124–131.

Berman DE and Dudai Y (2001) Memory extinction, learning anew, and learning the new: Dissociations in the molecular machinery of learning in cortex. *Science* 291: 2417–2419.

Beron de Astarda M and Maldonado H (1999) Two related forms of long-term habituation in the crab *Chasmagnathus* are differentially affected by scopolamine. *Pharmacol. Biochem. Behav.* 63: 109–118.

Bitterman ME, Menzel R, Fietz A, and Schäfer S (1983) Classical conditioning of proboscis extension in honeybees (*Apis mellifera*). *J. Comp. Psychol.* 97: 107–119.

Brunner D and Maldonado H (1988) Habituation in the crab *Chasmagnathus-Granulatus* – Effect of morphine and naloxone. *J. Comp. Physiol. A. Neuroethol. Sens. Neural. Behav. Physiol.* 162: 687–694.

Child FM, Epstein HT, Kuzirian AM, and Alkon DL (2003) Memory reconsolidation in *Hermissenda*. *Biol. Bull.* 205: 218–219.

Debiec J, Ledoux JE, and Nader K (2002) Cellular and systems reconsolidation in the hippocampus. *Neuron* 36: 527–538.

Delorenzi A, Dimant B, Frenkel L, Nahmod VE, Nassel DR, and Maldonado H (2000) High environmental salinity induces memory enhancement and increases levels of brain angiotensin-like peptides in the crab *Chasmagnathus granulatus*. *J. Exp. Biol.* 203: 3369–3379.

Delorenzi A and Maldonado H (1999) Memory enhancement by the angiotensinergic system in the crab *Chasmagnathus* is mediated by endogenous angiotensin II. *Neurosci. Lett.* 266: 1–4.

Dudai Y (2004) The neurobiology of consolidations, or, how stable is the engram? *Annu. Rev. Psych.* 55: 51–86.

Dudai Y and Eisenberg M (2004) Rites of passage of the engram: Reconsolidation and the lingering consolidation hypothesis. *Neuron* 44: 93–100.

Duvarci S, Mamou CB, and Nader K (2006) Extinction is not a sufficient condition to prevent fear memories from undergoing reconsolidation in the basolateral amygdala. *Eur. J. Neurosci.* 24: 249–260.

Duvarci S and Nader K (2004) Characterization of fear memory reconsolidation. *J. Neurosci.* 24: 9269–9275.

Eisenberg M and Dudai Y (2004) Reconsolidation of fresh, remote, and extinguished fear memory in medaka: Old fears don't die. *Eur. J. Neurosci.* 20: 3397–3403.

Eisenberg M, Kobilo T, Berman DE, and Dudai Y (2003) Stability of retrieved memory: Inverse correlation with trace dominance. *Science* 301: 1102–1104.

Eisenhardt D (2006) Learning and memory formation in the honeybee (*Apis mellifera*) and its dependency on the cAMP-protein kinase A pathway. *Animal Biology* 56: 259–278.

Eisenhardt D and Menzel R (2007) Extinction learning, reconsolidation and the internal reinforcement hypothesis. *Neurobiol. Learn. Mem.* 87: 167–173.

Elliott CJH and Susswein AJ (2002) Comparative neuroethology of feeding control in molluscs. *J. Exp. Biol.* 205: 877–896.

Fiala A, Muller U, and Menzel R (1999) Reversible downregulation of protein kinase A during olfactory learning using antisense technique impairs long-term memory formation in the honeybee, *Apis mellifera*. *J. Neurosci.* 19: 10125–10134.

Frankland PW, Ding HK, Takahashi E, Suzuki A, Kida S, and Silva AJ (2006) Stability of recent and remote contextual fear memory. *Learn. Mem.* 13: 451–457.

Frenkel L, Freudenthal R, Romano A, Nahmod VE, Maldonado H, and Delorenzi A (2002) Angiotensin II and the transcription factor Rel/NF-kappa B link environmental water shortage with memory improvement. *Neuroscience* 115: 1079–1087.

Frenkel L, Maldonado H, and Delorenzi A (2005) Memory strengthening by a real-life episode during reconsolidation: An outcome of water deprivation via brain angiotensin II. *Eur. J. Neurosci.* 22: 1757–1766.

Freudenthal R, Locatelli F, Hermitte G, et al. (1998) Kappa-B like DNA-binding activity is enhanced after spaced training that induces long-term memory in the crab *Chasmagnathus*. *Neurosci. Lett.* 242: 143–146.

Freudenthal R and Romano A (2000) Participation of Rel/NF-kappa B transcription factors in long-term memory in the crab *Chasmagnathus*. *Brain Res.* 855: 274–281.

Friedrich A, Thomas U, and Muller U (2004) Learning at different satiation levels reveals parallel functions for the cAMP-protein kinase A cascade in formation of long-term memory. *J. Neurosci.* 24: 4460–4468.

Fulton D, Kemenes I, Andrew RJ, and Benjamin PR (2005) A single time-window for protein synthesis-dependent long-term memory formation after one-trial appetitive conditioning. *Eur. J. Neurosci.* 21: 1347–1358.

Gainutdinova TH, Tagirova RR, Ismailova AI, et al. (2005) Reconsolidation of a context long-term memory in the terrestrial snail requires protein synthesis. *Learn. Mem.* 12: 620–625.

Grünbaum L and Müller U (1998) Induction of a specific olfactory memory leads to a long-lasting activation of protein kinase C in the antennal lobe of the honeybee. *J. Neurosci.* 18: 4384–4392.

Hammer M (1993) An identified neuron mediates the unconditioned stimulus in associative olfactory learning in honeybees. *Nature* 366: 59–63.

Hawkins RD and Kandel ER (1984) Is there a cell-biological alphabet for simple forms of learning? *Psychol. Rev.* 91(3): 375–91.

Hermitte G, Pedreira ME, Tomsic D, and Maldonado H (1999) Context shift and protein synthesis inhibition disrupt long-term habituation after spaced, but not massed, training in the crab *Chasmagnathus*. *Neurobiol. Learn. Mem.* 71: 34–49.

Kelly A, Laroche S, and Davis S (2003) Activation of mitogen-activated protein kinase/extracellular signal-regulated kinase in hippocampal circuitry is required for consolidation and reconsolidation of recognition memory. *J. Neurosci.* 23: 5354–5360.

Kemenes G, Elliott CJH, and Benjamin PR (1986) Chemical and tactile inputs to the *Lymnaea* feeding system – Effects on behavior and neural circuitry. *J. Exp. Biol.* 122: 113–137.

Kemenes G, Kemenes I, Michel M, Papp A, and Muller U (2006) Phase-dependent molecular requirements for memory reconsolidation: Differential roles for protein synthesis and protein kinase A activity. *J. Neurosci.* 26: 6298–6302.

Koh MT and Bernstein IL (2003) Inhibition of protein kinase A activity during conditioned taste aversion retrieval: Interference with extinction or reconsolidation of a memory? *Neuroreport* 14: 405–407.

Lee JL, Everitt BJ, and Thomas KL (2004) Independent cellular processes for hippocampal memory consolidation and reconsolidation. *Science* 304: 839–843.

Lee JL, Milton AL, and Everitt BJ (2006) Reconsolidation and extinction of conditioned fear: Inhibition and potentiation. *J. Neurosci.* 26: 10051–10056.

Lewis DJ (1979) Psychobiology of active and inactive memory. *Psychol. Bull.* 86: 1054–1083.

Locatelli F, Maldonado H, and Romano A (2002) Two critical periods for cAMP-dependent protein kinase activity during long-term memory consolidation in the crab *Chasmagnathus*. *Neurobiol. Learn. Mem.* 77: 234–249.

Locatelli F and Romano A (2005) Differential activity profile of cAMP-dependent protein kinase isoforms during long-term memory consolidation in the crab *Chasmagnathus*. *Neurobiol. Learn. Mem.* 83: 232–242.

Lozada M, Romano A, and Maldonado H (1990) Long-term habituation to a danger stimulus in the crab *Chasmagnathus-Granulatus*. *Physiol. Behav.* 47: 35–41.

Lukowiak K, Cotter R, Westly J, Ringseis E, Spencer G, and Syed N (1998) Long-term memory of an operantly conditioned respiratory behaviour pattern in *Lymnaea stagnalis*. *J. Exp. Biol.* 201: 877–882.

Lukowiak K, Ringseis E, Spencer G, Wildering W, and Syed N (1996) Operant conditioning of aerial respiratory behaviour in *Lymnaea stagnalis*. *J. Exp. Biol.* 199: 683–691.

Lukowiak K, Sangha S, Scheibenstock A, et al. (2003) A molluscan model system in the search for the engram. *J. Physiol.* 69–76.

Menzel R, Erber J, and Masuhr T (1974) Learning and memory in the honeybee. In: Barton-Browne L (ed.) *Experimental Analysis of Insect Behaviour*, pp. 195–217. Berlin: Springer.

Menzel R (1999) Memory dynamics in the honeybee. *J. Comp. Physiol. [A]* 185: 323–340.

Merlo E, Freudenthal R, Maldonado C, and Romano A (2005) Activation of the transcription factor NF-kappa B by retrieval is required for long-term memory reconsolidation. *Learn. Mem.* 12: 23–29.

Merlo E, Freudenthal R, and Romano A (2002) The I kappa B kinase inhibitor sulfasalazine impairs long-term memory in the crab *Chasmagnathus*. *Neuroscience* 112: 161–172.

Milekic MH and Alberini CM (2002) Temporally graded requirement for protein synthesis following memory reactivation. *Neuron* 36: 521–525.

Milner B, Squire LR, and Kandel ER (1998) Cognitive neuroscience and the study of memory. *Neuron* 20: 445–468.

Misanin JR, Miller RR, and Lewis DJ (1968) Retrograde amnesia produced by electroconvulsive shock after reactivation of a consolidated memory trace. *Science* 160: 554–555.

Müller U (2000) Prolonged activation of cAMP-dependent protein kinase during conditioning induces long-term memory in honeybees. *Neuron* 27: 159–168.

Nader K (2003) Memory traces unbound. *Trends Neurosci.* 26: 65–72.

Nader K, Schafe GE, and Le Doux JE (2000) Fear memories require protein synthesis in the amygdala for reconsolidation after retrieval. *Nature* 406: 722–726.

Pavlov IP (1927) *Conditioned Reflexes: An Investigation of the Physiological Activity of the Cerebral Cortex*. London: Oxford University Press.

Pedreira ME, Dimant B, Tomsic D, Quesada-Allue LA, and Maldonado H (1995) Cycloheximide inhibits context memory and long-term habituation in the crab *Chasmagnathus*. *Pharmacol. Biochem. Behav.* 52: 385–395.

Pedreira ME and Maldonado H (2003) Protein synthesis subserves reconsolidation or extinction depending on reminder duration. *Neuron* 38: 863–869.

Pedreira ME, Perez-Cuesta LM, and Maldonado H (2002) Reactivation and reconsolidation of long-term memory in the crab *Chasmagnathus*: Protein synthesis requirement and mediation by NMDA-type glutamatergic receptors. *J. Neurosci.* 22: 8305–8311.

Pedreira ME, Perez-Cuesta LM, and Maldonado H (2004) Mismatch between what is expected and what actually occurs triggers memory reconsolidation or extinction. *Learn. Mem.* 11: 579–585.

Pedreira ME, Romano A, Tomsic D, Lozada M, and Maldonado H (1998) Massed and spaced training build up different components of long-term habituation in the crab *Chasmagnathus*. *Anim. Learn. Behav.* 26: 34–45.

Power AE, Berlau DJ, McGaugh JL, and Steward O (2006) Anisomycin infused into the hippocampus fails to block "reconsolidation" but impairs extinction: The role of re-exposure duration. *Learn. Mem.* 13: 27–34.

Przybyslawski J, Roullet P, and Sara SJ (1999) Attenuation of emotional and nonemotional memories after their reactivation: role of beta adrenergic receptors. *J. Neurosci.* 19: 6623–6628.

Przybyslawski J and Sara SJ (1997) Reconsolidation of memory after its reactivation. *Behav. Brain Res.* 84: 241–246.

Riccio DC, Moody EW, and Millin PM (2002) Reconsolidation reconsidered. *Integr. Physiol. Behav. Sci.* 37: 245–253.

Riemensperger T, Voller T, Stock P, Buchner E, and Fiala A (2005) Punishment prediction by dopaminergic neurons in *Drosophila*. *Curr. Biol.* 15: 1953–60.

Romano A, Locatelli F, Freudenthal R, et al. (2006) Lessons from a crab: Molecular mechanisms in different memory phases of *Chasmagnathus*. *Biol. Bull.* 210: 280–288.

Rose RM and Benjamin PR (1979) Relationship of the central motor pattern to the feeding cycle of *Lymnaea stagnalis*. *J. Exp. Biol.* 80: 137–163.

Salinska E, Bourne RC, and Rose SP (2004) Reminder effects: The molecular cascade following a reminder in young chicks does not recapitulate that following training on a passive avoidance task. *Eur. J. Neurosci.* 19: 3042–3047.

Sangha S, Scheibenstock A, and Lukowiak K (2003a) Reconsolidation of a long-term memory in *Lymnaea* requires new protein and RNA synthesis and the soma of right pedal dorsal 1. *J. Neurosci.* 23: 8034–8040.

Sangha S, Scheibenstock A, McComb C, and Lukowiak K (2003b) Intermediate and long-term memories of associative learning are differentially affected by transcription versus translation blockers in *Lymnaea*. *J. Exp. Biol.* 206: 1605–1613.

Sangha S, Varshney N, Fras M, et al. (2004) Memory, reconsolidation and extinction in *Lymnaea* require the soma of RPeD1. *Adv. Exp. Med. Biol.* 551: 311–318.

Sara SJ (2000) Retrieval and reconsolidation: Toward a neurobiology of remembering. *Learn. Mem.* 7: 73–84.

Scheibenstock A, Krygier D, Haque Z, Syed N, and Lukowiak K (2002) The soma of RPeD1 must be present for long-term memory formation of associative learning in *Lymnaea*. *J. Neurophysiol.* 88: 1584–1591.

Schultz W (2006) Behavioral Theories and the Neurophysiology of Reward. *Annu. Rev. Psychol.* 57: 87–115.

Sekiguchi T, Yamada A, and Suzuki H (1997) Reactivation-dependent changes in memory states in the terrestrial slug *Limax flavus*. *Learn. Mem.* 4: 356–364.

Spear NE (1973) Retrieval of memory in animals. *Psychol. Rev.* 80: 163–194.

Spencer GE, Syed NI, and Lukowiak K (1999) Neural changes after operant conditioning of the aerial respiratory behavior in *Lymnaea stagnalis*. *J. Neurosci.* 19: 1836–1843.

Stollhoff N, Menzel R, and Eisenhardt D (2005) Spontaneous recovery from extinction depends on the reconsolidation of the acquisition memory in an appetitive learning paradigm in the honeybee *(Apis mellifera)*. *J. Neurosci.* 25: 4485–4492.

Straub VA, Styles BJ, Ireland JS, O'Shea M, and Benjamin PR (2004) Central localization of plasticity involved in appetitive conditioning in Lymnaea. *Learn. Mem.* 11: 787–793.

Suzuki A, Josselyn SA, Frankland PW, Masushige S, Silva AJ, and Kida S (2004) Memory reconsolidation and extinction have distinct temporal and biochemical signatures. *J. Neurosci.* 24: 4787–4795.

Syed NI, Harrison D, and Winlow W (1991) Respiratory behavior in the pond snail *Lymnaea-Stagnalis*.1. Behavioral-analysis and the identification of motor neurons. *J. Comp. Physiol. A Neuroetheol. Sens. Neural. Behav. Physiol.* 169: 541–555.

Syed NI and Winlow W (1991) Coordination of locomotor and cardiorespiratory networks of *Lymnaea stagnalis* by a pair of identified interneurones. *J. Exp. Biol.* 158: 37–62.

Tomsic D, Pedreira ME, Romano A, Hermitte G, and Maldonado H (1998) Context – US association as a determinant of long-term habituation in the crab *Chasmagnathus*. *Anim. Learn. Behav.* 26: 196–209.

Torras-Garcia M, Lelong J, Tronel S, and Sara SJ (2005) Reconsolidation after remembering an odor-reward association requires NMDA receptors. *Learn. Mem.* 12: 18–22.

Troncoso J and Maldonado H (2002) Two related forms of memory in the crab *Chasmagnathus* are differentially affected by NMDA receptor antagonists. *Pharmacol. Biochem. Behav.* 72: 251–265.

Tronel S and Sara SJ (2002) Mapping of olfactory memory circuits: Region-specific c-fos activation after odor-reward associative learning or after its retrieval. *Learn. Mem.* 9: 105–111.

Vianna MR, Igaz LM, Coitinho AS, Medina JH, and Izquierdo I (2003) Memory extinction requires gene expression in rat hippocampus. *Neurobiol. Learn. Mem.* 79: 199–203.

Vianna MRM, Szapiro G, McGaugh JL, Medina JH, and Izquierdo I (2001) Retrieval of memory for fear-motivated training initiates extinction requiring protein synthesis in the rat hippocampus. *Proc. Natl. Acad. Sci. USA* 98: 12251–12254.

Wüstenberg D, Gerber B, and Menzel R (1998) Short communication: Long- but not medium-term retention of olfactory memories in honeybees is impaired by actinomycin D and anisomycin. *Eur. J. Neurosci.* 10: 2742–2745.

Yamada A, Sekiguchi T, Suzuki H, and Mizukami A (1992) Behavioral analysis of internal memory states using cooling-induced retrograde amnesia in Limax flavus. *J. Neurosci.* 12: 729–735.

1.28 Behavioral Analysis of Learning and Memory in *Drosophila*

M. Heisenberg and B. Gerber, Universität Würzburg, Würzburg, Germany

Associative learning is supposed to come about through changes in neurons, and it is believed that memory-guided behavior relies on these changes (Lechner and Byrne, 1998; Martin et al., 2000; Cooke and Bliss, 2006). Thus, in terms of physiology, past experiences would leave traces in terms of altered properties of neuronal circuits (*See* Chapters 1.02, 1.04, 1.33, 1.34). Here, we discuss whether it is possible to assign such changes to specific cells in the brain and, in this sense, to localize those memory traces underlying conditioned behavioral modifications. What could be the criteria for an accomplished localization of such a memory trace? As argued elsewhere (Gerber et al., 2004), if a certain set of cells were said to be the site of a memory trace, one should be able to show that:

1. Neuronal plasticity occurs in these cells and is sufficient for memory.
2. The neuronal plasticity in these cells is necessary for memory.
3. Memory cannot be expressed if these cells cannot provide output during test.
4. Memory cannot be established if these cells do not receive input during training.

If these criteria are met, it must be concluded that the group of cells in question is the one and only site of the memory trace under investigation. Clearly, neither of these criteria alone is sufficient to draw this conclusion; in particular, despite claims to the contrary (e.g., Yu et al., 2004, 2005; Liu and Davis, 2007), the mere observation of altered neuronal activity after some training regime in imaging experiments, albeit indispensable for the argument, is in itself not sufficient to localize a memory trace. This is because such data allow concluding that some memory trace must be residing between the stimulation site (i.e., the sensory level in Yu et al., 2004, 2005; Liu and Davis, 2007) and the site of the measurement, but more specific conclusions cannot be drawn.

In *Drosophila*, three different learning paradigms have been used in efforts to localize memory traces according to these criteria (Zars et al., 2000a,b; Liu et al., 2006). We will go through the available evidence, restricting ourselves to short-term (3–30 min) memory throughout, unless explicitly stated otherwise. *See* Chapter 4.07 for additional information on mechanisms of olfactory memory in *Drosophila*.

1.28.1 Neural Plasticity?

Criteria (1) and (2) rely on the ability to measure the plasticity of candidate neurons during the learning process, as well as on the manipulation of these neurons *in vivo*. In *Drosophila*, no method is available to directly measure neural plasticity *in vivo* in adult central brain neurons, despite impressive advances in physiological techniques (Fiala et al., 2002; Ng et al., 2002; Hallem et al., 2004; Wang et al., 2004; Wilson et al., 2004). In a strict sense, this makes it difficult to test for criteria (1) and (2). Actually, the only way to directly observe neural plasticity in flies to date is to study the larval neuromuscular junction (Koh et al., 2000; Schuster, 2006). Being left with inferences from larval motor neuron-to-muscle synapses to central brain neurons in adults, however, is unsatisfying. Therefore, as a second best approach, genetic intervention was used to locally manipulate molecular components underlying neural plasticity. The process of choice was the cAMP/PKA signaling cascade. It had been shown to be required for learning as well as for neuronal plasticity in various paradigms

throughout the animal kingdom (Byrne et al., 1991; Davis et al., 1995; Renger et al., 2000; Davis, 2005; Hawkins et al., 2006). More specifically, *in vitro* studies in *Aplysia* suggest that the type I adenylyl cyclase (in flies encoded by the *rutabaga* gene, *rut*) might act as a timing-specific molecular coincidence detector for the stimuli to be associated (Abrams et al., 1998). Hence, by an admittedly indirect argument, one is inclined to attribute an impaired or restored capacity to learn, caused by a genetic manipulation of the cAMP cascade in specific brain regions, to impaired or restored neural plasticity in that region (Zars et al., 2000a,b; McGuire et al., 2003; Mao et al., 2004; Liu et al., 2006).

As will be discussed later, such local *rut* rescues were successful for all three learning paradigms covered here (**Figure 1**). We therefore tentatively assume that indeed a lack of *rut* impairs neuronal plasticity and that a local rescue of *rut* does rescue

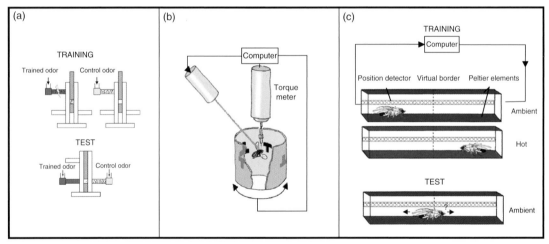

Figure 1 Behavioral procedures for measuring associative learning and memory. In all three cases flies are tested for memory by choosing between two conditions, of which they previously experienced one together with the reinforcer. In all cases, the *rutabaga* adenylyl cyclase is necessary for learning/memory, presumably via its role in synaptic plasticity. (a) Odor discrimination learning. Two experimental groups are run that undergo reciprocal training: One group of flies is exposed to odor A (green) and the reinforcer (in this case electric shock, but sucrose as appetitive reinforcer works as well). Next, the flies are exposed to odor B (yellow) without reinforcer. For testing, flies are shaken into the elevator (grey) and placed between two tubes simultaneously presenting the odors A and B; then flies on either side are counted and the difference in the number of flies on the control versus the trained side is calculated. For the other group of flies, the shock is presented with the respective other odor. Performance indices then present the mean of the odor choice scores in these reciprocally trained groups. (b) Visual pattern memory in the flight simulator. Tethered flies are suspended at a torque meter such that their yaw torque drives the angular velocity of a rotating panorama surrounding the fly. The wall of the panorama is decorated by two alternating patterns spaced by 90°. Flies can choose their direction of flight with respect to the patterns. Flies that are heated by a laser beam while heading toward one of the patterns subsequently avoid that pattern. The paradigm also uses a reciprocal training design; performance indices are calculated as in (a). (c) Heat box learning. Flies walk in a dark alley, and their position is monitored. During training they are heated if they enter one half of the chamber, some flies on the left side, some on the right side. During the memory test, flies still avoid the side where they had previously been heated. Again, the performance index is calculated as in (a).

this plasticity in the respective neurons. Clearly, the scope of conclusions thus is limited to those kinds of neuronal plasticity that involve *rut* and that are impaired in the available *rut* mutants. Still, as criteria (3) and (4) do not rely on any knowledge of the biochemistry underlying memory, they can serve to independently validate claims of localization of a memory trace.

1.28.2 Olfactory Learning

In odor discrimination learning (**Figure 1**), flies receive one odor together with an electric shock, and later another odor without shock. In a subsequent binary choice test, flies avoid the previously punished odor (Tully and Quinn, 1985). A similar paradigm can be used with sugar instead of electric shock, making flies approach the trained odor (Tempel et al., 1983; Schwaerzel et al., 2003). Within this section, however, we refer to odor-shock learning throughout unless explicitly stated otherwise.

Odors are detected (reviews by Stocker, 1994, 2001; Hallem et al., 2006) by receptor neurons, each expressing a single functional receptor gene of the *Or* gene family; receptor neurons expressing the same *Or* gene converge to one so-called glomerulus in the antennal lobe. Hence, the glomeruli represent the fly's primary odor qualities. The glomerular patterns of activity are shaped in addition by local interneurons. Projection neurons then relay the primary odor qualities to two sites, the lateral horn, a presumed premotor center, and the mushroom body calyx. Output from the mushroom bodies projects to a variety of target regions, including premotor areas. Thus, the mushroom bodies constitute a side branch of the olfactory pathway.

A memory trace underlying conditioned odor avoidance was proposed to be localized within the mushroom body neurons, also called Kenyon cells (reviews by Heisenberg, 2003; Gerber et al., 2004): Whenever the activation of a pattern of Kenyon cells elicited by a given odor coincides with a modulatory reinforcement signal impinging onto the Kenyon cells, future output from these activated Kenyon cells onto mushroom body output neurons is suggested to be strengthened. This facilitated output is thought to subsequently mediate conditioned behavior in response to the odor alone. The following data are the basis for this working model.

1.28.2.1 Sufficiency of Neuronal Plasticity in the Mushroom Bodies

In *rut* mutants, local transgenic expression of an intact *rut* cDNA can fully rescue the learning impairment (Zars et al., 2000a); notably, such rescue requires *rut* expression in the γ- and α/β-lobes of the mushroom bodies (GAL4 driver lines mb247, c772, 30y, 238y, and H24; for the GAL4/UAS technique, see Brand and Perrimon, 1993). A partial rescue is observed with the driver line 201y. In contrast, three drivers not expressing in the mushroom body γ-lobes (c232, 189y, and 17d) do not rescue (Zars et al., 2000a) (concerning H24, see also supplementary material provided with McGuire et al., 2003). The driver line mb247 also rescues sugar reward learning (Schwaerzel et al., 2003). Furthermore, Davis and colleagues (McGuire et al., 2003; Mao et al., 2004) showed that providing the *rut* cDNA during adulthood is sufficient for rescuing short-term memory. These results argue that the mushroom bodies are a site at which restoring neuronal plasticity is sufficient to restore olfactory learning, and that criterion (1) for the localization of a memory trace to the mushroom bodies is met. It needs to be emphasized that neuronal plasticity related to the *rut* adenylyl cyclase (rut-AC) can account for only about 50% of memory in conditioned odor discrimination; under the assumption that the used *rut* mutants completely lack the type I adenylate cyclase function required in this task, this would imply a distinct *rut* independent memory trace.

1.28.2.2 Necessity of Neuronal Plasticity in the Mushroom Bodies

Transgenic mushroom body expression of a dominant negative $G\alpha_s$ protein subunit ($G\alpha_s^*$), which constitutively activates the type I adenylyl cyclase, completely abolishes learning (Connolly et al., 1996) (driver lines 238y, c309, and c747). The driver line 201y that provides a partial rescue also inhibits partially (about 50%) when driving $G\alpha_s^*$ expression. Two lines with expression outside of the mushroom bodies (c232 and ok348) were normal. Under the plausible assumption that a constitutively activated cyclase prevents regulation of cAMP levels, and hence regulation of neuronal efficacy, this argues that plasticity within the mushroom body Kenyon cells is necessary for memory trace formation and that criterion (2) for the localization of a memory trace to these cells is met. Strikingly, expression of the $G\alpha_s{}^*$ transgene in the mushroom bodies completely blocks 3-min memory in odor-shock learning, but *rut* mutants show only a 50% reduction, suggesting that any potentially *rut*-independent memory trace is also blocked by $G\alpha_s{}^*$ and is also located in the Kenyon cells.

In contrast, odor-sugar learning is only partially suppressed by $G\alpha_s{}^*$ expression in the mushroom bodies (A. Thum and H. Tanimoto, personal communication), suggesting that the memory trace in the Kenyon cells is not the only one underlying the odor-reward association. Indeed, a second memory trace may be located in projection neurons connecting the antennal lobe to the calyx and lateral protocerebrum (Thum, 2006). Whether these two traces are functionally redundant remains to be investigated; that is, do they differ in terms of the kinds of behavior supported, in their role during different memory phases, or the specificity of their 'content' (see Menzel, 2001 for such analyses in the honeybee; *See also* Chapter 1.29)?

1.28.2.3 Blocking Mushroom Body Output during Test

In flies it is possible to within minutes reversibly turn off the output of chemical synapses using a dominant negative, temperature-sensitive dynamin transgene, Shi^{ts} (Kitamoto, 2002). If Shi^{ts} is expressed in the mushroom bodies, flies can be trained with mushroom body output enabled, but tested with mushroom body output blocked. Three different laboratories have independently found that flies do not express odor memory if the temperature is raised to the off-condition 15 min prior to the test (driver lines c739, c747, c309, mb247, and c772) (Dubnau et al., 2001; McGuire et al., 2001; Schwaerzel et al., 2002; see Krashes et al., 2007, for a specific role of output from the $\alpha'\beta'$ lobes for stabilizing short- into longer-term memory). Apparently, criterion (3) for the localization of memory traces of odor-shock and odor-sugar learning to the Kenyon cells is met. Because the Shi^{ts} method is unspecific with regard to the biochemical mechanism(s) of memory trace formation, this supports the conclusions discussed earlier and, moreover, indicates that any *rut*-independent memory trace is unlikely to be located downstream of the Kenyon cell output synapses.

1.28.2.4 Blocking Input to the Mushroom Body during Training

Olfactory input to the mushroom bodies is carried by the uniglomerular projection neurons from the antennal lobes. If, by means of Shi^{ts} expression, synaptic output during training is blocked in approximately 60% of these projection neurons (driver line GH 146; Stocker et al., 1997), flies do not show any sign of memory during subsequent test (Schwaerzel, 2003), suggesting that criterion (4) for the localization of a memory trace to the mushroom bodies is met as well. However, the projection neurons provide input not only to the mushroom bodies but also to the lateral protocerebrum (Yasuyama et al., 2003) (and presumably even the antennal lobe; Ng et al., 2002). Therefore, this conclusion needs to be taken with caution, as we are still lacking appropriate tools to specifically block mushroom body input.

Concerning reinforcer-related input to the mushroom bodies, Riemensperger et al. (2005) showed that dopaminergic neurons, which impinge onto the mushroom body lobes, are activated by electric shock. Concerning behavior, Schwaerzel et al. (2003) found that for aversive learning dopamine (driver line TH-Gal4) but not octopamine signaling is necessary, and that in turn for appetitive learning, octopamine but not dopamine signaling is necessary. Furthermore, as shown in the *Drosophila* larva by using the 'remote control' of neuronal activation with a transgenically expressed light-gated ion channel (channelrhodopsin; Schroll et al., 2006), the respective catecholaminergic neurons also are sufficient to substitute for reinforcement in appetitive and aversive training, respectively. In the adult fly, both dopamine and octopamine signaling were shown to be specifically required during training, but not during test (Schwaerzel et al., 2003). The Kenyon cells clearly express octopamine and dopamine receptors and are targets of dopamine- and octopamine-immunoreactive neurons (Han et al., 1996, 1998; Friggi-Grelin et al., 2003; Kim et al., 2003; Strausfeld et al., 2003); notably, the antennal lobe receives strikingly little if any dopaminergic innervation (Riemensperger et al., 2005). However, whether specifically those octopaminergic and/or dopaminergic neurons that carry the reinforcing information do indeed directly impinge onto the mushroom bodies is at present unknown. Interestingly, using Ca^{++} imaging, Riemensperger et al. (2005) have reported that dopaminergic neurons innervating the mushroom body lobes acquire increased responsiveness specifically to the learned odor, suggesting that training confers the reinforcing function of the shock to the odor. Thus, in keeping with the seminal work on reinforcement processing in bees (Hammer, 1997; Menzel, 2001; see also Schultz, 2006, for analogous results concerning dopaminergic neurons in monkeys), it seems likely that (i) also in flies (and fly larvae), signaling via aminergic neurons carries a prediction error–like internal reinforcement signal, (ii) these neurons impinge onto the mushroom bodies, and (iii) these neurons act during acquisition to induce, but not during retention to express, olfactory memory traces.

1.28.2.5 A Memory Trace Downstream of the Mushroom Bodies?

Three different laboratories found that blocking Kenyon cell output during odor-shock training (in the driver lines c739, c747, c309, mb247, and c772) leaves performance during test intact (Dubnau et al., 2001; McGuire et al., 2002; Schwaerzel et al., 2003; but see Krashes et al., 2007). Thus, for learning to occur, olfactory information needs to enter but does not need to leave the Kenyon cells. In fact, any kind of plasticity underlying learning, be it *rut* dependent or *rut* independent, thus seems to occur upstream of mushroom body output and, as argued in the previous paragraph, likely downstream of projection neuron output.

1.28.2.6 A Memory Trace in the Projection Neurons and/or Antennal Lobes?

Concerning an additional memory trace established in the projection neurons (for review of the work in honeybees, see Menzel, 2001), Yu et al. (2004) reported that two identified glomeruli (D and VA1) in the *Drosophila* antennal lobe are more strongly activated by the odor after training than before. This effect is stimulus specific, in that training with either of two different odors (3-octanol or 4-methylcyclohexanol) leads to the recruitment of either of the two glomeruli; it is also associative, as it is seen after odor-shock training, but not after a reversed order of stimulus presentation (i.e., shock-odor training); it is cell specific in that neither olfactory receptor neurons nor local antennal lobe interneurons show such recruitment; and it is specific for very short term memory, as after 7 min the effect has waned. Thus, there must be a memory trace

somewhere between olfactory input and the projection neurons. As neither the olfactory sensory neurons nor the local interneurons, which are canonically acknowledged as inputs to the projection neurons, show any training-induced change, Yu et al. (2004) are inclined to conclude that a memory trace for very short term memory is located within the projection neurons themselves.

However, some caveats may warrant an alternative explanation. First, in naïve flies, neither of the odors induces excitation in either of these glomeruli (Wang et al., 2003; Yu et al., 2006); rather, olfactory sensory neurons innervating VA1 likely respond by inhibition (Hallem and Carlson, 2006), so that a specific explanation is required as to how an inhibited projection neuron could be the site of coincidence detection of odor and shock. Second, the antennal lobe is receiving little if any dopaminergic input (Riemensperger et al., 2005), so that one may need to invoke a dopamine-independent internal reinforcement signal to induce a memory trace in the antennal lobe. Third, $G\alpha_s^*$ expression in the mushroom bodies completely blocks learning (Connolly et al., 1996), and fourth, attempts to rescue aversive learning using *rut*-AC expression in the projection neurons have failed (H. Tanimoto, personal communication; A. Keene and S. Waddell, personal communication). The latter two arguments suggest that in electric shock learning any projection-neuron memory trace in itself would be insufficient for behavior control. Fifth, blocking projection neuron output during training completely abolishes learning (Schwaerzel, 2003), arguing against a cell-autonomous memory trace within the projection neurons. Finally, blocking mushroom body output during test completely blocks expression of memory (Dubnau et al., 2001; McGuire et al., 2001; Schwaerzel et al., 2002), which is difficult to reconcile with a memory trace located in the projection neurons because such a trace could be read-out directly via the lateral protocerebrum, independently of the mushroom bodies.

These caveats may prompt the question of whether the recruitment of antennal lobe glomeruli may be explained without reference to an antennal-lobe memory trace. Could it be that the two glomeruli are activated by a memory trace located elsewhere? It was shown in honeybees that mushroom body output neurons feed back onto the antennal lobe (Rybak and Menzel, 1993; loc. cit. Figure 4b, 16; Kirschner et al., 2006); thus, at the moment of test the learned odor may activate its memory trace in the mushroom body, which by virtue of this feedback loop could disinhibit antennal lobe glomeruli to indicate the odors' behavioral relevance. Such a scenario predicts that glomerular recruitment would not be inducible if projection neuron output was blocked during training and would not be observed if it were blocked during test.

1.28.2.7 A Memory Trace in the DPM Neurons?

In a seminal discovery, Waddell et al. (2000) found that a single pair of identified, dorsal paired medial neurons (DPM neurons) are expressing the *amnesiac* gene product, the lack of which leads to an unusually fast decay of memory. That is, retention is more or less normal right after training but has completely waned already after 60 min. Restoring *amnesiac* function in these cells is sufficient to overcome this defect. However, given that output from the DPM neurons is dispensable at the moment of test (Keene et al., 2004, 2006; Yu et al., 2004). by our criteria they cannot be the site of a memory trace underlying retention (criterion [3]).

In summary, concerning short-term memory after odor-shock training, the *rut*^{2080}-dependent memory trace can be assigned to the Kenyon cells with reasonable confidence because this hypothesis accommodates all available experimental data.

1.28.3 Learned Visual Pattern Preference

Visual pattern learning at the flight simulator (**Figure 1**) involves an association between the heat of a laser beam and a specific visual feature of a landmark in the panorama (Ernst and Heisenberg, 1999; Tang et al., 2004). Landmark features so far have been found to fall into five classes (parameters): the height of the pattern in the panorama, its size, its color, the vertical distance between its components, and the orientation of its contour. Flies can be conditioned to discriminate landmarks according to any of these parameters if the landmarks have different values for them (how high? how big? etc.). This kind of learning, at the very least concerning pattern height, clearly is independent of the mushroom bodies, as their ablation leaves this task unaffected (Wolf et al., 1998). Until recently it had remained elusive which parts of the brain might house the corresponding memory traces.

Genetically, visual pattern recognition requires *rut* (Liu et al., 2006), allowing the application of a similar mapping strategy as in the case of olfactory memory. A total of 27 driver lines with different expression profiles were used to locally supply *rut*-AC to the brain of the *rut*^{2080} mutant. Seven of them restored the learning defect. What distinguishes the expression patterns in these seven lines from those of the 20 nonrescuing lines seems to be a group of about 15 neurons on either side of the protocerebrum (the so-called F5 neurons), forming a sharp horizontal layer of fibers in the upper fan-shaped body. All flies with *rut*-AC in F5 neurons were able to learn to avoid flying toward a pattern previously combined with heat. No fly without *rut*-AC in F5 neurons was able to perform this learning task (Liu et al., 2006).

In these experiments the authors used pairs of patterns that the flies could possibly distinguish only by their height in the panorama. However, *rut*-AC expression in the F5 neurons failed to restore pattern learning when the patterns were distinguishable only by their size or only by the orientation of their contours. Hence, the rescuing effect of *rut*-AC in the F5 neurons was specific for the pattern parameter 'height.' Subsequently, two driver lines were investigated that showed transgene expression in a horizontal fiber layer of the fan-shaped body that was different from that of the F5 neurons. This layer is formed by two clusters of about 10 neurons each (F1 neurons). Strikingly, expression of *rut*-AC in these cells did not rescue the memory defect for height or size but did restore the memory for contour orientation. Both rescue effects, that for height and that for contour orientation, are adult specific, as was shown by temporal and regional expression of *rut*-AC using tub-GAL80^{ts} (Liu et al., 2006), a temperature-sensitive silencer of GAL4 (McGuire et al., 2003).

These results argue that by criterion (1), two further memory traces can tentatively be localized, the memory trace for the pattern parameter height in F5 neurons and that for the parameter contour orientation in F1 neurons of the fan-shaped body. Moreover, *rut*-AC also seems to be necessary in these neurons (criterion [2]), as expression of Gα_s* in the F5 and F1 neurons specifically interferes with the corresponding pattern memories but leaves the memories for the other pattern parameters unaffected. Thus, these memory traces appear to be the only ones for the respective tasks. Regarding criteria (3, 4), we cannot make any conclusion, as using heat as the punishing stimulus in pattern learning may interfere with *Shi^ts* function, at present precluding this kind of experimental strategy.

1.28.4 Heat Box

Historically, the first attempt at mapping a memory trace was conducted for place memory in the so-called heat box (Zars et al., 2000b). In this paradigm, single flies walk in a small dark box that can be quickly heated and cooled between 24 °C and 37 °C (**Figure 1**). The position of the fly in the box is monitored, and the fly is heated when it is located on one side of the box but not when located on the other. Flies quickly learn to avoid being heated and retain their side preference for some minutes even after place-dependent heating has ceased. Clearly, this kind of learning is independent of the mushroom bodies (Wolf et al., 1998).

By mutant analysis, it turned out that *rut* mutant flies show reduced acquisition and memory scores, allowing for local rescue experiments. Seventeen driver lines with transgene expression in various parts of the central nervous system were used to restore the *rut*-AC in the mutant. In four lines the learning/memory defect was rescued. All four lines had substantial, potentially overlapping expression in the median bundle and more subtle overlapping expression in the antennal lobes and ventral ganglion. Of five mushroom body expressing lines that rescue olfactory learning, four do not rescue heat-box learning (30y, 238y, 201y, and H24); one line (c772) rescues in both paradigms. A refined anatomical assessment of the expression patterns in rescuing and nonrescuing lines is still pending, but neither the mushroom bodies nor the central complex seem to contribute to heat-box learning. The most likely sites thus include the median bundle and/or the antennal lobes and the ventral ganglion. So far, experiments neither using $G\alpha_s{}^*$ nor tub-GAL80^ts have been performed. Moreover, as in the case of visual pattern learning, the use of *Shi^ts* is not readily possible. In all, exactly where the memory trace for place learning is localized remains poorly resolved.

1.28.5 Selectivity of Rescue Effects

In the studies reviewed here (**Figure 2**), 33 selected lines were tested in *rut* rescue experiments, 16 of them successfully. A total of 60 rescue experiments were performed. Of these, 18 were positive.

Seventeen lines were tested in more than one memory task. Only two (c772 and c271) rescued in two tasks, and none of the 11 lines that were used in all three tasks rescued in all three of them. These numbers document the high local specificity of the rescue effects by GAL4 expression.

Taking into account that the used GAL4 lines typically express the transgene in much less than 1% of the brain neurons, one might wonder why that many positive results were obtained. It is likely that, in the studies on olfactory and visual memory, the choice of driver lines was biased toward the mushroom bodies and central complex, respectively, because previous studies on HU-ablation as well as structural brain mutants in which the mushroom bodies or the central complex were affected had pointed to these structures. In any event, the amazing selectivity of the rescue effects, even for different parts of the fan-shaped body housing traces for different visual parameter memories, is independent of such bias in the choice of lines.

1.28.6 Assessing Gene Expression Patterns

The most important caveat for memory mapping – and actually for any circuit analysis in the fly brain using the GAL4/UAS approach – is that the spatial expression patterns of driver lines are difficult to reliably assess (Ito et al., 2003; Saper and Swachenko, 2003). Neither for *Shi^ts* nor $G\alpha_s{}^*$ are any means available to directly detect the transgenically expressed effector proteins. Regarding the *rut*-AC, the *rut* mutant used for rescue experiments (*rut^{2080}*) most likely is no protein-null mutant (H. Tanimoto and T. Zars, personal communication). This leaves us with inferences from the expression patterns of reporter genes like GFP. However, this again is no reliable approach. First, the expression of the reporter may alter connectivity, as was shown for *tau* (Wittmann et al., 2001); second, with the same GAL4 driver line, the expression pattern of different effectors and – even the expression pattern for the same effector construct at different insertion sites (e.g., UAS-GFP on different chromosomes; A. Jenett and M. H., unpublished) – can be different. The construction of tagged transgenes and appropriate immunocytochemistry will be a major advance in this field, in particular when it comes to arguing about levels of transgene expression. At present, using multiple GAL4 lines for answering the same question seems the best way to deal with these concerns.

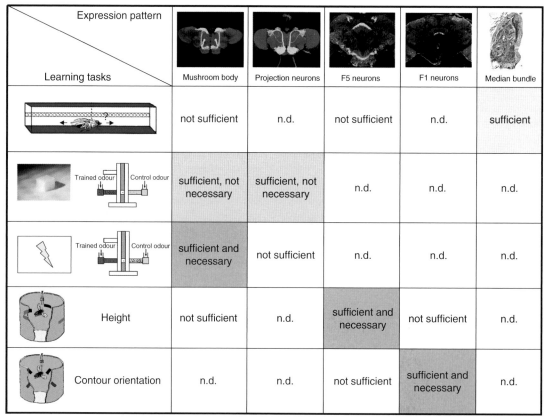

Expression pattern / Learning tasks	Mushroom body	Projection neurons	F5 neurons	F1 neurons	Median bundle
	not sufficient	n.d.	not sufficient	n.d.	sufficient
Trained odour / Control odour	sufficient, not necessary	sufficient, not necessary	n.d.	n.d.	n.d.
Trained odour / Control odour	sufficient and necessary	not sufficient	n.d.	n.d.	n.d.
Height	not sufficient	n.d.	sufficient and necessary	not sufficient	n.d.
Contour orientation	n.d.	n.d.	not sufficient	sufficient and necessary	n.d.

Figure 2 Locally restoring the *rutabaga* adenylyl cyclase (*rut*-AC) rescues specific memory tasks. Top row: Five different groups of neurons (yellow in columns 2–5 and black in column 6). Leftmost column: Five learning paradigms requiring *rut*-AC (see **Figure 1** for further details). The matrix shows in which of the above neuronal groups *rut*-AC is sufficient and necessary to allow for the respective task. Odor–reward learning/memory can be rescued at either of two places.

1.28.7 Memory Mapping Reveals Functional Architecture

Contemplating the sites for olfactory and visual memory traces (**Figures 2, 3**), one notices interesting parallels and deviations. In both cases the memory trace is known from the behavioral analysis to be specific for a particular learned stimulus, whereas the neurons highlighted in the rescuing lines likely contribute to processing of many stimuli from the same sensory modality. In other words, the precise set of neurons housing a particular memory trace most likely is smaller than the group of neurons genetically highlighted in a certain driver line. Searching through more driver lines one might gradually approach the minimal set. Yet, at least in the mushroom bodies, the GAL4/UAS approach may fall short of reaching the resolution of individual memory traces: GAL4 expression patterns highlight groups of Kenyon cells that are genetically defined,

whereas the sets representing given odors are functionally specified.

Odor quality appears to be coded in a combinatorial way such that the primary odor qualities constitute the coordinates of one multidimensional feature space. To accommodate a memory trace for a given odor quality within this feature space, the output of a subset from one common pool of Kenyon cells is strengthened.

In contrast, visual processing is parametrical in the sense that it is subdivided into several parameters (e.g., height and contour orientation). For visual memory, the values for each of these parameters need to be stored; consequently, each of these parameters has its own feature space employing distinct sets of neurons (e.g., F1 and F5 neurons for contour orientation and height, respectively); each of these feature spaces typically has a low dimensionality tailored toward storing parameter values. In short, olfaction employs one multidimensional feature space, whereas vision

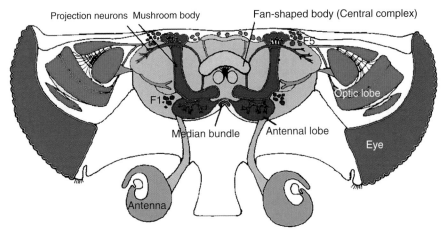

Projection neurons Mushroom body

Fan-shaped body (Central complex)

F5

Optic lobe

F1

Median bundle   Antennal lobe

Eye

Antenna

Figure 3 Schematic horizontal section of the *Drosophila* head showing some of the brain structures indicated in **Figure 2**. The Median bundle runs perpendicular to the plane of section. In the fan-shaped body, the horizontal strata of the F5 and F1 neurons lie about parallel to, but above and below, the plane of section.

appears to work in multiple, low-dimensional feature spaces. This example shows that beyond localizing the engram, memory mapping can elucidate the functional organization of the brain at the circuit level.

1.28.8 Conclusions

We have suggested a set of criteria for localizing a site of neuronal plasticity as the one and only trace (engram) underlying an associative memory. These criteria are that plasticity in a given group of cells be (i) sufficient and (ii) necessary for memory, and that memory be abolished if (iii) these cells could not output during test, and/or (iv) would not receive input during training. Regarding short-term memory for odor quality in aversive conditioning, the working hypothesis of the underlying memory trace being localized to Kenyon cells of the mushroom body is holding up well. Regarding visual pattern recognition, restoring the *rut*-AC is sufficient and presumably necessary in the F1 and F5 neurons of the fan-shaped body to restore memory for contour orientation and height, respectively. However, the containment of the engram in these neurons using temporally specific blockade of synaptic output has not yet been verified. For place learning in the heat box, the situation is less clear. Most likely, neither mushroom body nor central complex play a role; candidate structures are neurons in the median bundle, the antennal lobe, and the ventral ganglion.

These data altogether show that memory traces for different simple learning tasks reside in distinct parts of the brain, and that for any given learning task, the site of the underlying memory trace can be amazingly local. It should be interesting to see whether this kind of conclusion may hold up generally (i.e., also for memory traces in bees, snails, rabbits, mice, and humans). Keeping the neuronal changes of elemental memory traces locally confined may be a general operating principle of brains.

References

Abrams TW, Yovell Y, Onyike CU, Cohen JE, and Jarrard HE (1998) Analysis of sequence-dependent interactions between transient calcium and transmitter stimuli in activating adenylyl cyclase in *Aplysia*: Possible contribution to CS–US sequence requirement during conditioning. *Learn. Mem.* 4: 496–509.

Brand AH and Perrimon N (1993) Targeted gene expression as a means of altering cell fates and generating dominant phenotypes. *Development* 118: 401–415.

Byrne JH, Baxter DA, Buonomano DV, et al. (1991) Neural and molecular bases of nonassociative and associative learning in *Aplysia*. *Ann. N. Y. Acad. Sci.* 627: 124–149.

Connolly JB, Roberts IJ, Armstrong JD, et al. (1996) Associative learning disrupted by impaired Gs signaling in *Drosophila* mushroom bodies. *Science* 274: 2104–2107.

Cooke SF and Bliss TV (2006) Plasticity in the human central nervous system. *Brain* 129: 1659–1673.

Davis RL (2005) Olfactory memory formation in *Drosophila*: From molecular to systems neuroscience. *Annu. Rev. Neurosci.* 28: 275–302.

Davis RL, Cherry J, Dauwalder B, Han PL, and Skoulakis E (1995) The cyclic AMP system and *Drosophila* learning. *Mol. Cell. Biochem.* 149–150: 271–278.

Dubnau J, Grady L, Kitamoto T, and Tully T (2001) Disruption of neurotransmission in *Drosophila* mushroom body blocks retrieval but not acquisition of memory. *Nature* 411: 476–480.

Ernst R and Heisenberg M (1999) The memory template in *Drosophila* pattern vision at the flight simulator. *Vis. Res.* 39: 3920–3933.

Fiala A, Spall T, Diegelmann S, et al. (2002) Genetically expressed cameleon in *Drosophila* melanogaster is used to visualize olfactory information in projection neurons. *Curr. Biol.* 12: 1877–1884.

Friggi-Grelin F, Coulom H, Meller M, Gomez D, Hirsh J, and Birman S (2003) Targeted gene expression in *Drosophila* dopaminergic cells using regulatory sequences from tyrosine hydroxylase. *J. Neurobiol.* 54: 618–627.

Gerber B, Tanimoto H, and Heisenberg M (2004) An engram found? Evaluating the evidence from fruit flies. *Curr. Opin. Neurobiol.* 14: 737–744.

Hallem EA and Carlson JR (2006) Coding of odors by a receptor repertoire. *Cell* 125: 143–160.

Hallem EA, Dahanukar A, and Carlson JR (2006) Insect odor and taste receptors. *Annu. Rev. Entomol.* 51: 113–135.

Hallem EA, Ho MG, and Carlson JR (2004) The molecular basis of odor coding in the *Drosophila* antenna. *Cell* 117: 965–979.

Hammer M (1997) The neural basis of associative reward learning in honeybees. *Trends Neurosci.* 20: 245–252.

Han KA, Millar NS, and Davis RL (1998) A novel octopamine receptor with preferential expression in *Drosophila* mushroom bodies. *J. Neurosci.* 18: 3650–3658.

Han KA, Millar NS, Grotewiel MS, and Davis RL (1996) DAMB, a novel dopamine receptor expressed specifically in *Drosophila* mushroom bodies. *Neuron* 16: 1127–1135.

Hawkins RD, Kandel ER, and Bailey CH (2006) Molecular mechanisms of memory storage in *Aplysia*. *Biol. Bull.* 210: 174–191.

Heisenberg M (2003) Mushroom body memoir: From maps to models. *Nat. Rev. Neurosci.* 4: 266–275.

Ito K, Okada R, Tanaka NK, and Awasaki T (2003) Cautionary observations on preparing and interpreting brain images using molecular biology-based staining techniques. *Microsc. Res. Tech.* 62: 170–186.

Keene AC, Krashes MJ, Leung B, Bernard JA, and Waddell S (2006) *Drosophila* dorsal paired medial neurons provide a general mechanism for memory consolidation. *Curr. Biol.* 16: 1524–1530.

Keene AC, Stratmann M, Keller A, Perrat PN, Vosshall LB, and Waddell S (2004) Diverse odor-conditioned memories require uniquely timed dorsal paired medial neuron output. *Neuron* 44: 521–533.

Kirschner S, Kleineidam CJ, Zube C, Rybak J, Grunewald B, and Rossler W (2006) Dual olfactory pathway in the honeybee Apis mellifera. *J. Comp. Neurol.* 499: 933–952.

Kitamoto T (2002) Targeted expression of temperature-sensitive dynamin to study neural mechanisms of complex behavior in *Drosophila*. *J. Neurogenet.* 16: 205–228.

Kim YC, Lee HG, Seong CS, and Han KA (2003) Expression of a D1 dopamine receptor dDA1/DmDOP1 in the central nervous system of *Drosophila* melanogaster. *Gene Expr. Patterns* 3: 237–245.

Koh YH, Gramates LS, and Budnik V (2000) *Drosophila* larval neuromuscular junction: Molecular components and mechanisms underlying synaptic plasticity. *Microsc. Res. Tech.* 49: 14–25.

Krashes MJ, Keene AC, Leung B, Armstrong JD, and Waddell S (2007) Sequential use of mushroom body neuron subsets during *Drosophila* odor memory processing. *Neuron* 53: 103–115.

Lechner HA and Byrne JH (1998) New perspectives on classical conditioning: A synthesis of Hebbian and non-Hebbian mechanisms. *Neuron* 20: 355–358.

Liu G, Seiler H, Wen A, et al. (2006) Distinct memory traces for two visual features in the *Drosophila* brain. *Nature* 439: 551–556.

Liu X and Davis RL (2007) Insect olfactory memory in time and space. *Curr. Opin. Neurobiol.* 16: 679–685.

Mao Z, Roman G, Zong L, and Davis RL (2004) Pharmacogenetic rescue in time and space of the rutabaga memory impairment by using Gene-Switch. *Proc. Natl. Acad. Sci. USA* 101: 198–203.

Martin SJ, Grimwood PD, and Morris RG (2000) Synaptic plasticity and memory: An evaluation of the hypothesis. *Annu. Rev. Neurosci.* 23: 649–711.

McGuire SE, Le PT, and Davis RL (2001) The role of *Drosophila* mushroom body signaling in olfactory memory. *Science* 293: 1330–1333.

McGuire SE, Le PT, Osborn AJ, Matsumoto K, and Davis RL (2003) Spatiotemporal rescue of memory dysfunction in *Drosophila*. *Science* 302: 1765–1768.

Menzel R (2001) Searching for the memory trace in a mini-brain, the honeybee. *Learn. Mem.* 8: 53–62.

Ng M, Roorda RD, Lima SQ, Zemelman BV, Morcillo P, and Miesenbock G (2002) Transmission of olfactory information between three populations of neurons in the antennal lobe of the fly. *Neuron* 36: 463–474.

Renger JJ, Ueda A, Atwood HL, Govind CK, and Wu CF (2000) Role of cAMP cascade in synaptic stability and plasticity: Ultrastructural and physiological analyses of individual synaptic boutons in *Drosophila* memory mutants. *J. Neurosci.* 20: 3980–3992.

Riemensperger T, Voller T, Stock P, Buchner E, and Fiala A (2005) Punishment prediction by dopaminergic neurons in *Drosophila*. *Curr. Biol.* 15: 1953–1960.

Rybak J and Menzel R (1993) Anatomy of the mushroom bodies in the honey bee brain: The neuronal connections of the alpha-lobe. *J. Comp. Neurol.* 334: 444–465.

Saper CB and Sawchenko PE (2003) Magic peptides, magic antibodies: Guidelines for appropriate controls for immunohistochemistry. *J. Comp. Neurol.* 465: 161–163.

Schroll C, Riemensperger T, Bucher D, et al. (2006) Light-induced activation of distinct modulatory neurons triggers appetitive or aversive learning in *Drosophila* larvae. *Curr. Biol.* 16: 1741–1747.

Schuster CM (2006) Glutamatergic synapses of *Drosophila* neuromuscular junctions: A high-resolution model for the analysis of experience-dependent potentiation. *Cell Tissue Res.* 326: 287–299.

Schultz W (2006) Behavioral theories and the neurophysiology of reward. *Annu. Rev. Psychol.* 57: 87–115.

Schwaerzel M (2003) Localizing engrams of olfactory memories in *Drosophila*. PhD Thesis, Universität Würzburg.

Schwaerzel M, Heisenberg M, and Zars T (2002) Extinction antagonizes olfactory memory at the subcellular level. *Neuron* 35: 951–960.

Schwaerzel M, Monastirioti M, Scholz H, Friggi-Grelin F, Birman S, and Heisenberg M (2003) Dopamine and octopamine differentiate between aversive and appetitive olfactory memories in *Drosophila*. *J. Neurosci.* 23: 10495–10502.

Stocker RF (1994) The organization of the chemosensory system in *Drosophila* melanogaster: A review. *Cell Tissue Res.* 275: 3–26.

Stocker RF (2001) *Drosophila* as a focus in olfactory research: Mapping of olfactory sensilla by fine structure, odor specificity, odorant receptor expression, and central connectivity. *Microsc. Res. Tech.* 55: 284–296.

Stocker RF, Heimbeck G, Gendre N, and de Belle JS (1997) Neuroblast ablation in *Drosophila* P(GAL4) lines reveals origins of olfactory interneurons. *J. Neurobiol.* 32: 443–456.

Strausfeld NJ, Sinakevitch I, and Vilinsky I (2003) The mushroom bodies of *Drosophila* melanogaster: An immunocytological and Golgi study of Kenyon cell organization in the calyces and lobes. *Microsc. Res. Tech.* 62: 151–169.

Tang S, Wolf R, Xu S, and Heisenburg M (2004) Visual pattern recognition in _Drosophila_ is invariant for retinal position. _Science_ 305: 1020–1022.

Tempel BL, Bonini N, Dawson DR, and Quinn WG (1983) Reward learning in normal and mutant _Drosophila_. _Proc. Natl. Acad. Sci. USA_ 80: 1482–1486.

Thum A (2006) _Sugar Reward Learning in_ Drosophila. PhD Thesis, Universität Würzburg.

Tully T and Quinn WG (1985) Classical conditioning and retention in normal and mutant _Drosophila_ melanogaster. _J. Comp. Physiol. (A)_ 157: 263–277.

Waddell S, Armstrong JD, Kitamoto T, Kaiser K, and Quinn WG (2000) The amnesiac gene product is expressed in two neurons in the _Drosophila_ brain that are critical for memory. _Cell_ 103: 805–813.

Wang Y, Guo HF, Pologruto TA, et al. (2004) Stereotyped odor-evoked activity in the mushroom body of _Drosophila_ revealed by green fluorescent protein-based Ca2+ imaging. _J. Neurosci._ 24: 6507–6514.

Wang JW, Wong AM, Flores J, Vosshall LB, and Axel R (2003) Two-photon calcium imaging reveals an odor-evoked map of activity in the fly brain. _Cell_ 112: 271–282.

Wilson RI, Turner GC, and Laurent G (2004) Transformation of olfactory representations in the _Drosophila_ antennal lobe. _Science_ 303: 366–370.

Wittmann CW, Wszolek MF, Shulman JM, et al. (2001) Tauopathy in _Drosophila_: Neurodegeneration without neurofibrillary tangles. _Science_ 293: 711–714.

Wolf R, Wittig T, Liu L, Wustmann G, Eyding G, and Heisenberg M (1998) _Drosophila_ mushroom bodies are dispensable for visual, tactile, and motor learning. _Learn. Mem._ 5: 166–178.

Yasuyama K, Meinertzhagen IA, and Schurmann FW (2003) Synaptic connections of cholinergic antennal lobe relay neurons innervating the lateral horn neuropile in the brain of _Drosophila_ melanogaster. _J. Comp. Neurol._ 466: 299–315.

Yu D, Keene AC, Srivatsan A, Waddell S, and Davis RL (2005) _Drosophila_ DPM neurons form a delayed and branch-specific memory trace after olfactory classical conditioning. _Cell_ 123: 945–957.

Yu D, Ponomarev A, and Davis RL (2004) Altered representation of the spatial code for odors after olfactory classical conditioning; memory trace formation by synaptic recruitment. _Neuron_ 42: 437–449.

Zars T, Fischer M, Schulz R, and Heisenberg M (2000a) Localization of a short-term memory in _Drosophila_. _Science_ 288: 672–675.

Zars T, Wolf R, Davis R, and Heisenberg M (2000b) Tissue-specific expression of a type I adenylyl cyclase rescues the rutabaga mutant memory defect: In search of the engram. _Learn. Mem._ 7: 18–731.

1.29 Behavioral and Neural Analysis of Associate Learning in the Honeybee

M. Giurfa, CNRS, Université Paul Sabatier, Toulouse, France

1.29.1 Introduction

French naturalist Georges-Louis Leclerc Buffon (1707–1788) became famous for the 36 volumes of his *Natural History*, an entire life's work, in which he covered subjects as diverse as the origin of the solar system, the fossilization processes, the classification of flora and fauna, and the origin of humans. Following a peculiar vision of animal intelligence, he expressed admiration for some creatures but fervently rejected others. Among the despised animals, an insect gathered his anger and devastating criticisms. It was neither an irritating mosquito nor a creeping cockroach. It was the honeybee. Buffon was impressed by the reproductive capabilities of a honeybee queen, which "produces thirty or forty thousand flies" (bees were indistinctly called bees and flies in his works), thus constituting "the largest known multiplication in the animal kingdom." This led him to conclude that "the most abject, vilest and smallest species are the most abundant ones" (Buffon, 1749a: 13–14). He went further and argued that "it is forceful to conclude that

bees, taken individually, have less genius than a dog, a monkey and the vast majority of living animals; we shall also agree that they have less docility, less attachment and fewer feelings, in a word, fewer qualities relative to our own" (Buffon, 1749b: 93–94).

This animadversion contrasts with the admiration expressed by another famous scientist, who devoted his life to the study of honeybees. Karl von Frisch (1886–1982) became famous for the discovery of the honeybee dance, a ritualized behavior that allows a successful bee forager to inform other bees within the hive about the distance and direction of a profitable food source (von Frisch, 1967). This was not the only contribution made by von Frisch. He left us an amazingly rich and accurate body of evidence on honeybee behavior that spans studies on honeybee navigation, vision, olfaction, taste, and magnetic sensing, among other things (Frisch, 1967). Von Frisch liked to describe honeybees as a 'magic well' for discoveries in biology because the more that is drawn from it, the more there is to draw. Surprisingly, this fascination ended at a particular point, in which, ironically, von Frisch could be said to approach some of Buffon's ideas. He expressed his view on the plasticity underlying honeybee behavior in the following way: "The brain of a bee is the size of a grass seed and is not made for thinking. The actions of bees are mainly governed by instinct" (Frisch, 1962, p. 78). Admittedly, von Frisch expressed this view in relation to communication behavior, but it is nevertheless striking that a tendency to dismiss the cognitive capacities of bees – and insects in general – has been perpetuated for centuries.

Despite this prolonged skepticism, in the last three decades honeybees have become a useful model for the study of learning and memory (Menzel and Erber, 1978; Menzel, 1985; Menzel et al., 1993). More recently, they have also acquired a new reputation in studies addressing higher-order cognitive capacities that have long seemed to exclusively belong to vertebrates such as monkeys, pigeons, or dolphins, which are known for their learning abilities. In this chapter, I analyze the contributions made by research on honeybee learning and memory that have facilitated this progress. I present findings and open questions that show the extent to which honeybees have increased our current understanding of cognitive processing at both the behavioral and the cellular levels, in hopes of underlining the power and potential of the honeybee in cognitive neurosciences. Chapter 4.06 provides a detailed description of the molecular mechanisms of bee learning.

1.29.2 Elemental and Nonelemental Forms of Associative Learning

Because this chapter intends to present the different levels of complexity that honeybees can reach in mastering different learning tasks, it is worth starting with operational definitions that allow discerning the simple from the complex. I focus on associative learning and introduce the distinction between elemental and nonelemental learning, which may be useful as a boundary between simple and complex forms of learning.

Associative learning is a capacity that is widespread among living animals and that allows extracting the logical structure of the world. It consists in establishing predictive relationships between contingent events in the environment so that uncertainty is reduced and adaptive behavior results from individual experience with such events. Two major forms of associative learning are usually recognized: In classical

conditioning (Pavlov, 1927), animals learn to associate an originally neutral stimulus (conditioned stimulus, CS) with a biologically relevant stimulus (unconditioned stimulus, US); in operant conditioning (Skinner, 1938), they learn to associate their own behavior with a reinforcer. Both forms of learning, therefore, reliably predict reinforcement, either appetitive or aversive, and admit different levels of complexity. In their most simple version, both rely on the establishment of elemental links connecting two specific and unambiguous events in the animal's world. What has been learned for a given tone in terms of its outcome is valid for that tone but not necessarily for another stimulus, such as a light. The outcome of a given behavior, such as pressing a lever, is valid for that behavior but not for a different one such as pulling a chain (*See* Chapters 1.03, 1.07, 1.08). These forms of learning, which have been intensively studied by experimental psychologists, are also particularly interesting for neuroscientists interested in the neural bases of learning because they allow tracing to the level of neural circuits and single neurons the basis of associations underlying learning. Because these forms of learning rely on specific stimuli (e.g., a given CS and a given US), it is possible to study where and how in the central nervous system such stimuli are represented, where and how their neural pathways interact in order to facilitate association, and how experience modifies their respective neural representations. Both at the behavioral and neural level, these forms of learning have in common the univocal and unambiguous relationships established between events in the world. Because they can be characterized through specific links between unique events, simple forms of associative learning are termed elemental learning forms. Typical examples of elemental learning are absolute conditioning (A+), in which a single stimulus A is reinforced (+), and differential conditioning (A+ vs. B−), in which one stimulus, A, is reinforced (+), while another stimulus, B, is nonreinforced (−) (see **Table 1**). In the former, an animal has to learn to respond to A, which is unambiguously associated with reinforcement; in the latter, it has to learn to respond to A and not to B because both are unambiguously associated with reinforcement and with the absence of it, respectively.

However, other forms of associative learning are possible, in which unique links connecting specific events are useless because ambiguity characterizes the events under consideration (see **Table 1**). For instance, in the so-called patterning problems, animals have to learn to discriminate a stimulus

Table 1 Examples of elemental and nonelemental conditioning protocols[a]

Conditioning task	Training	Processing
Absolute conditioning	A+	Elemental
Differential conditioning	A+ vs. B−	Elemental
Feature positive discrimination	AB+ vs. B−	Elemental
Negative patterning	A+, B+ vs. AB−	Nonelemental
Biconditional discrimination	AB+, CD+ vs. AC−, BD−	Nonelemental

[a]In absolute conditioning, the subject has to learn to respond to stimulus A, which is unambiguously associated with reinforcement (+); in differential conditioning, the subject has to learn to respond to stimulus A and not to B; A is unambiguously associated with reinforcement (+), whereas B is unambiguously associated with the absence of reinforcement (−); in feature-positive discrimination, the subject has to learn to respond to the compound AB, which is reinforced (+), and not to B (−), which is nonreinforced; although B is ambiguous because it appears as often reinforced as nonreinforced, the fact that A is unambiguously associated with the reinforcement allows solving the problem. Simple links between a stimulus and reinforcement allow solving these three elemental problems. Elemental solutions cannot account for negative patterning solving, in which the subject has to learn to respond to the single stimuli A+ and B+ but not to their compound AB−, because elements are as often reinforced as nonreinforced. The same remark applies to biconditional discrimination, in which the subject has to learn to respond to the compounds AB+ and CD+ but not to AC− and BD−.

compound from its components, a task that is not necessarily trivial. Consider, for example, negative patterning, a problem in which an animal has to learn to discriminate two single components reinforced from their nonreinforced binary compound (A+, B+ vs. AB−). This situation is challenging because each element A and B appears as often reinforced as nonreinforced. Relying on elemental links between A (or B) and reinforcement (or absence of reinforcement) cannot solve this problem. Different strategies, such as treating the binary compound in a nonlinear form (i.e., as being different from the simple sum of A and B) have to be implemented to solve this kind of problem. A profuse literature has shown that some vertebrates can solve this kind of nonlinear processes and has put the accent on the nervous circuits and brain structures required for this kind of cognitive processing (Rudy and Sutherland, 1995; O'Reilly and Rudy, 2001; Bucci et al., 2002; Alvarado and Bachevalier, 2005; Moses et al., 2005; Borlikova et al., 2006; Jacobs, 2006; *See* Chapter 1.10).

Having introduced these two forms of learning, which define different levels of complexity in cognitive processing in a formalized and operational way, I present findings showing that it is possible to dissect and understand the basic mechanisms underlying these two levels of processing, using honeybees as a model system. I demonstrate that this insect exhibits elemental and nonelemental forms of learning that are relevant in its natural life and that are amenable to the laboratory, thus allowing controlled study and access to the underlying nervous system.

1.29.3 The Honeybee as a Natural Model for Studies on Learning and Memory

Several reasons warrant the use of the honeybee as a model for the study of learning abilities. In a natural context and despite their small size, honeybees exhibit an extremely rich behavioral repertoire (von Frisch, 1967). A social lifestyle is obligatory, and a single bee cannot survive very long separated from its mates. Outside of the hive, a bee travels over distances of several kilometers and visits hundreds of flowers in quick and efficient succession for gathering food (nectar and/or pollen). It also collects resin or water or roams for information-gathering purposes. Sensory capacities and motor performance are highly developed. Bees see the world in color (Menzel and Backhaus, 1991), perceive shapes and patterns (Srinivasan, 1994; Giurfa and Lehrer, 2001), and resolve movements with a high temporal resolution (Srinivasan et al., 1999). Their olfactory sense is able to distinguish a wide range of odors (Guerrieri et al., 2005b), and their mechanosensory perception is also extremely rich because of thousands of hair cells all around the body and proprioceptors inside the body.

In a natural context, bees learn and memorize the local cues characterizing the places of interest, which are essentially the hive and the food sources (Menzel, 1985; Menzel et al., 1993). In the case of food sources, learning and memory are the very basis of floral constancy, a behavior exhibited by foragers that consists of foraging on a unique floral species as long as it offers profitable nectar and/or pollen reward (Grant,

1951). Only when such an offer becomes unprofitable will bees switch to a different species. Learning and memorizing the sensory cues of the exploited flower through their association with nectar and/or pollen reward is what allows a bee forager to track a particular species in the field. Similarly, learning abilities for landmark constellations and for celestial cues used in navigation (azimuthal position of the sun, polarized light pattern of the blue sky) ensure a safe return to the nest and enhance foraging efficiency (Collett et al., 2003).

Honeybees communicate information about important locations around the hive through ritualized body movements, called the waggle dance, a communication system that transmits information on the vector flown toward an attractive food source or nest site (von Frisch, 1967). Hive bees attending such a dance decode from the speed of dance movement the distance to the food source, and from the angle of the waggling phase relative to gravity, the flight direction relative to the sun. In this context, specific associations are built as dance followers learn to associate the odor of nectar brought by a dancer with the nectar that it regurgitates and passes them through trophallactic contacts (Farina et al., 2005, 2007; Gil and de Marco, 2005, 2006; *See* Chapter 1.25). Usually, many such dances occur in parallel within a colony. Individual and collective decision-making result from multiple and independent decisions without reference to full knowledge of all potential options available (Seeley, 1995).

The complexity and richness of the honeybee's natural life is therefore appealing in terms of the opportunities it offers for the study of natural learning and memory. Such an appeal would be, however, useless if these phenomena were not amenable to controlled laboratory conditions. However, several protocols have been developed to allow experimental access in terms of controlled training and testing conditions, thus underscoring the remarkable plasticity of this insect, which can learn even under restrictive (in terms of movement, for instance) or stressful (in terms of the aversive reinforcement experienced) conditions.

1.29.4 Experimental Access to Learning and Memory in Honeybees

Honeybees can be easily trained individually to solve different kinds of discrimination problems (von Frisch, 1967). Different from the en-masse training

commonly used in other insects (e.g., *Drosophila*; Tully and Quinn, 1985), which does not always allow controlling the exact experience of the experimental subjects, different experimental protocols have been implemented to study learning and memory in honeybees at the individual level. This individual approach is important because learning and memory result from individual experience and because a neurobiological approach can then be undertaken and correlated with individual learning and memory scores only if such scores have been recorded in a precise way. Three main protocols developed to study honeybee learning and memory can be mentioned here: (1) conditioning of the approach flight toward a visual target in free-flying bees, (2) olfactory conditioning of the proboscis extension reflex in harnessed bees, and (3) olfactory conditioning of the sting extension reflex in harnessed bees. The first two protocols exploit the appetitive context of food search, as in both cases bees are rewarded with sucrose solution as an equivalent of nectar. The third protocol represents a case of aversive learning, as bees learn to associate odorants paired with the noxious reinforcement of an electric shock. In all three cases, and with different possible modifications derived from particular experimental needs, the basic experimental design comprises an acquisition or training phase in which the bees experience a particular stimulus or perform a given task that is reinforced, and a test or retrieval phase without reinforcement in which the bees are presented with the trained situation in order to assess the memory created by training. Eventually, novel stimuli can be presented in the test phase together with the trained stimulus in order to study generalization and discrimination capabilities. Transfer to novel stimuli (i.e., in absence of the trained stimulus) can also be tested to characterize the flexibility of the bee's choice (see below).

1.29.4.1 Conditioning of the Approach Flight Toward a Visual Target in Free-Flying Bees

Free-flying honeybees can be conditioned to visual stimuli such as colors, shapes and patterns, and depth and motion contrast, among others (von Frisch, 1914; Wehner, 1981; Giurfa and Menzel, 1997; Lehrer, 1997; Giurfa and Lehrer, 2001). In such a protocol, each bee is individually marked by means of a color spot on the thorax or the abdomen so that individual performance can be recorded. The marked bee is generally displaced by the experimenter toward the training/test place, where it is rewarded with sucrose solution to promote its regular return (**Figure 1(a)**). Such pretraining is provided without presenting the training stimuli in order to avoid uncontrolled learning. When the bee starts visiting the experimental place actively (i.e., nondisplaced to it by the experimenter), the training stimuli are presented and the choice of the appropriate visual target reinforced with sucrose solution. As pointed out above, bees have to be trained and tested individually to achieve a precise control of the experience of each subject when it enters into a particular test. It is also important to control the distance at which a choice is made

because orientation and choice are mediated by different visual cues at different distances or angles subtended by the target (Giurfa and Menzel, 1997; Giurfa and Lehrer, 2001). The time between visits to the experimental place is also an important variable to be recorded, because it reflects the appetitive motivation of the bee (Núñez, 1982), and thus its motivation to learn. For a food source approximately 100 m from the hive, motivated bees take between 3 and 10 min between foraging bouts. Longer intervals reflect a lower appetitive motivation and thus unreliable data.

Several behaviors can be used to quantify the bees' choice in these experiments. Touches (i.e., the flights

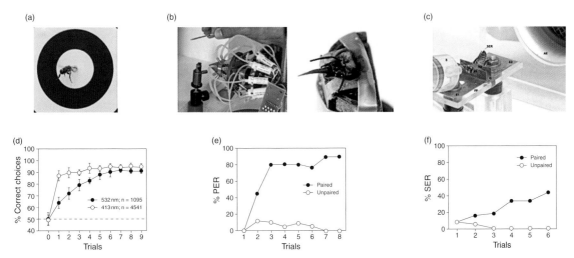

Figure 1 Experimental protocols for the study of learning and memory in honeybees. (a) Visual appetitive conditioning of free-flying bees. A bee marked with a green spot on the abdomen is trained to collect sugar solution in the middle of a ring pattern. (b) Olfactory appetitive conditioning of harnessed bees. The left panel shows a bee immobilized in a metal tube facing an olfactory stimulation device controlled by a computer. The toothpick soaked in sucrose solution held by the experimenter allows delivering reward to the antennae and mouthparts. The right panel shows the proboscis extension reflex (PER) of a trained bee to an odorant previously paired with sucrose solution. (c) Olfactory aversive conditioning of harnessed bees. A bee is immobilized by an elastic girdle (G) between two metal plates (E1, E2) on a plexiglas plate (pp) through which a mild electric shock is delivered. Odorant presentation is achieved by a syringe (S), and olfactory contamination is avoided by an air extractor (AE) placed behind the bee. Bees learn to extend the sting (sting extension reflex, SER) to the odorant aversively reinforced. (d) Acquisition curves for bees trained with colors in dual-choice experiments. Adapted from Figure 4 in Menzel R (1967) Untersuchungen zum Erlernen von Spektralfarben durch die Honigbiene (*Apis mellifica*) *Z. Vergl. Physiol.* 56: 22–62. The curves depict the percentage of correct choices along conditioning for two wavelengths, 413 nm (human violet) and 532 nm (human green). Trial 0 constitutes a spontaneous-choice test in which bees freely choose between the color that will be trained and an alternative. Although bees reached comparable levels of correct choices at the end of training, they learned 413 nm faster than 532 nm. n, number of choices recorded. (e) Acquisition curves for bees trained to associate an odorant with sucrose solution. Adapted from Figure 2 in Bitterman ME, Menzel R, Fietz A, and Schäfer S (1983) Classical conditioning of proboscis extension in honeybees (*Apis mellifera*) *J. Comp. Psychol.* 97: 107–119. The curves depict the percentage of PER along conditioning trials for two groups of bees, one trained with explicitly paired presentations of odorant and reward (paired, black dots), and another trained with explicitly unpaired presentations of odorant and reward (unpaired, white dots). Only the paired group learned the odorant–reward association, thus showing that learning has an associative basis and is not merely a result of experience with the stimuli independently of their temporal relation. (f) Acquisition curves for bees trained to associate an odorant with an electric shock. Adapted from Figure 2 in Vergoz V, Roussel E, Sandoz JC, and Giurfa M (2007a) Aversive learning in honeybees revealed by the olfactory conditioning of the sting extension reflex. *PLoS ONE* Mar 14 2: e288. The curves depict the percentage of SER along conditioning trials for two groups of bees, one paired (black dots) and another unpaired (white dots). Only the paired group learned the odorant–reward association, thus showing that learning has an associative basis.

toward a target that end with a contact of the bee's antennae or legs with the stimulus surface) and landings on a given stimulus are usually recorded to this end. The associations built in these contexts can be either operant, classical, or both; that is, they may link visual stimuli (CS) and reward (US), the response of the animal (e.g., landing) and the US, or both. The experimental framework is nevertheless mainly operant, as the bee's behavior is determinant for obtaining or not the sucrose reinforcement.

1.29.5 Olfactory Conditioning of the Proboscis Extension Reflex in Harnessed Bees

Apart from visual stimuli, honeybees can be conditioned to olfactory stimuli (Takeda, 1961; Bittermann et al., 1983). In this type of protocol, each bee is restrained in an individual harness such that it can only freely move its antennae and mouth parts (mandibles and proboscis) (**Figure 1(b)**). The antennae are the bees' main chemosensory organs. When the antennae of a hungry bee are touched with sucrose solution, the animal reflexively extends its proboscis to reach out to and suck the sucrose (proboscis extension reflex, PER). Neutral odorants blown to the antennae do not release such a reflex in naive animals. If, however, an odorant is presented immediately before sucrose solution (forward pairing), an association is formed that enables the odorant to release the PER in a following test (**Figure 1(b)**) This effect is clearly associative and constitutes a case of classical conditioning (Bittermann et al., 1983); that is, the odorant can be viewed as the conditioned stimulus (CS) and the sucrose solution as the rewarding, unconditioned stimulus (US). Within this framework, bees learn to associate the odorant with the sucrose reward.

As in any learning protocol, it is important to ensure the appropriate appetitive motivation of the experimental subjects. Immobilized bees in the laboratory therefore have to be starved prior to conditioning. A period of 2–3 h or a whole night is usually used as a starvation period in which bees have to be kept in a calm, darkened, humid environment. In olfactory PER conditioning, the response recorded is the extension of the proboscis, which is a dichotomous response (1 or 0). The duration of PER can also be recorded in order to provide a continuous, instead of a discrete, measure of acquisition (Hosler and Smith, 2000). To quantify learning,

responses to the CS (the odorant) have to be measured before US delivery in each acquisition trial. In quantifying responses to the US, it is also important to control for the presence of the unconditioned reaction, and thus for the maintenance of the appetitive motivation of the bee throughout the experiment. A useful practice is to check the integrity of PER before and after the experiment by touching the antennae with sucrose solution. Animals not exhibiting PER in these control assays should not be included in the experimental analyses, as negative responses during acquisition and/or retrieval can be caused by sensory-motor deficits instead of learning and/or memory deficits.

1.29.5.1 Olfactory Conditioning of the Sting Extension Reflex in Harnessed Bees

Contrary to the previous protocols, this new form of conditioning (Vergoz et al., 2007a) offers the opportunity to study aversive instead of appetitive learning in honeybees. In this case, each bee is restrained in an individual harness such that it builds a bridge between two metallic plates through which an electric shock can be delivered (**Figure 1(c)**). Bees stimulated in this way exhibit an unconditioned, defensive reaction, which is the extension of the sting (sting extension reflex, SER) (Núñez et al., 1997). Using odorants paired with electric shocks, it is possible to condition the SER so that bees learn to extend their sting in response to the odorants previously punished (Vergoz et al., 2007a). Because no appetitive responses are involved in this protocol, true aversive learning can be characterized in this way.

As in appetitive olfactory conditioning of PER, the experimenter controls the stimulus contingency and can therefore vary the interstimulus interval and/or the intertrial interval in order to study the impact of these variations on aversive olfactory memory. Responses recorded are also dichotomous (1 or 0), but continuous measures can be obtained by recording SER duration. To quantify learning, responses to the CS (the odorant) have to be measured before shock delivery in each acquisition trial. Quantifying responses to the shock is also important to control for the presence of the unconditioned reaction, and thus for the aversive motivation of the bee throughout the experiment. As for PER conditioning, the integrity of SER has to be checked before and after the experiment to ensure the use of reliable data for the experimental analyses.

1.29.6 Accessibility of the Central Nervous System

The brain of a honeybee has a volume of approximately $1 \, mm^3$ and contains around 960 000 neurons (**Figure 2**). Despite this apparent simplicity, the bee brain is capable of supporting learning and memory under simplified and restrictive conditions such as those described above. Accessing it in order to understand how neural architecture relates to cognitive processing is therefore possible, and several approaches can be employed to this end.

Although the free-flying visual conditioning protocol offers the obvious advantage of keeping the bee free, and thus allows visualizing the richness of its natural learning abilities, it is not helpful to uncover the neural bases of such abilities. Appetitive and aversive olfactory PER and SER conditioning, respectively, have the advantage of being controlled learning protocols precluding the bees' movement so that they can be easily combined with physiological approaches allowing *in vivo* the study of cellular and

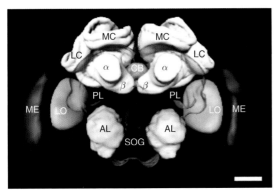

Figure 2 Three-dimensional reconstruction of a honeybee brain in frontal view based on confocal microscopy. Different neuropiles are indicated: ME, medulla, together with the lamina (not shown); LO, lobula; together with the lamina (not shown), both constitute the visual lobes in which visual processing occurs; AL, antennal lobe, the primary olfactory neuropile; PL, protocerebral lobe (lateral horn), a neuropile whose function is unclear; SOG, subesophageal ganglion, a region of the brain related to gustatory input; CB, a region of the brain related to motor responses; the two prominent, lighter symmetric structures in the middle of the brain are the mushroom bodies. Each mushroom body consists of two subunits, the calyces, lateral (LC) and median (MC) that constitute the input region of the mushroom bodies. Two lobes α and β constitute their output. Bar $= 200 \, \mu m$. From Malun D, Giurfa M, Galizia CG, et al. (2002) Hydroxyurea-induced partial mushroom body ablation does not affect acquisition and retention of olfactory differential conditioning in honeybees. *J. Neurobiol.* 53: 343–360.

molecular substrates of learning and memory. This is a considerable advantage offered by bees and other invertebrate models with respect to some vertebrates, namely the possibility of an on-line access to the nervous system of a nonanesthetized animal while it learns and memorizes. It is possible to expose the bee brain through a small window cut in the cuticle of the head and to employ several invasive methods to study the bases of learning and memory. Physiological correlates of these different forms of olfactory conditioning can be found at different levels, ranging from the molecular and pharmacological levels to single identified neurons and neuronal ensembles whose activity can be visualized using electrophysiological or optophysiological techniques (Menzel, 1999, 2001). Neuropharmacological approaches based on the injection of agonists or antagonists of neurotransmitters or receptors into the brain can also be employed. Furthermore, RNAi can also be injected into the bee brain to characterize the role of certain receptor molecules functionally (Farooqui et al., 2003).

Experimental access to the bee brain has characterized its basic architectural principles (Menzel and Giurfa, 2001). It comprises (1) dedicated neuropiles (i.e., brain regions devoted to the processing of specific sensory information [vision, olfaction, etc.]), (2) dedicated neurons (i.e., neurons that can be recurrently identified from bee to bee and within the same bee because of their unique morphology and because they accomplish specific functions in sensory-motor routines), and (3) higher-order integration centers (i.e., centers in which different sensory pathways converge such that multimodal integration takes place in them). Examples of these elements are provided when discussing the neural substrates of elemental and nonelemental learning in bees.

1.29.7 Elemental Appetitive Learning in Bees

Having described the main protocols used for the study of learning in honeybees, in this section I outline the main findings that have characterized elemental forms of learning at the behavioral and the cellular levels.

1.29.7.1 Elemental Color Learning and Memory in Free-Flying Honeybees

The first pioneering study on honeybee learning and memory that used controlled protocols for characterizing individual acquisition and retention employed colors as rewarding stimuli (Menzel, 1967). Free-flying bees were trained to choose a rewarded monochromatic light and were then presented in dual-choice situations with the rewarded light vs. an alternative color. This study reported acquisition curves for different wavelengths and showed that bees learned all wavelengths after few (generally three) learning trials (**Figure 1(d)**). Performance was independent of the alternative, nonrewarded wavelength presented in the test. Moreover, some wavelengths, particularly 413 nm, were learned faster than others, especially after a first acquisition trial (Menzel, 1967). This result argued in favor of innate biases in color learning, probably reflecting the intrinsic biological relevance of the color signals that are learned faster (Menzel, 1985). Indeed, color-naïve honeybees in their first foraging flight prefer these colors, which experienced bees learn faster (Giurfa et al., 1995), and preliminary findings indicate that these colors could correspond to floral colors that are highly associated with a profitable nectar reward (Giurfa et al., 1995).

Menzel's (1968) experiments determined that one learning trial leads to a memory trace that fades a few days after learning if the animal is not allowed to learn anything else during this time, but three learning trials lead to a lifelong color memory. This was the very basis for discovering the existence of different memory phases in honeybees, some of which are short-term memories susceptible to interferences from additional color trials, and others are long-term memories that are resistant to such interferences. Short-term memories that allow keeping memory active during shorter periods of time are dominated by nonassociative processes such as sensitization. It was shown that at intervals of 24 h, memory formation is not protein-synthesis dependent, thus leading to the conclusion that long-term visual memories were not dependent on protein synthesis (Wittstock and Menzel, 1994). However, this conclusion is only valid for early components of long-term memory, as bees in these experiments were only tested 24 h after conditioning. Results from olfactory conditioning (see below) have shown that olfactory memories older than 4 days are indeed dependent on protein synthesis (Wüstenberg et al., 1998). A similar dependence on color memory is expected, given the parallels in dynamics between olfactory and visual memories. However, the demonstration that later components of long-term color memory do indeed depend on protein synthesis is still pending.

Color conditioning of free-flying bees was used to characterize other elemental learning phenomena such as overshadowing, the fact that after learning a color compound a bee responds significantly more to one color at the expense of the other (Couvillon and Bittermann, 1980; Couvillon et al., 1983), and blocking, the fact that after learning a single color and being then trained with a color compound made of the previously rewarded color and a new color, a bee may not learn the new color despite its close association with reward in the second training phase (Couvillon et al., 1997). Often, studies addressing these phenomena did not consider important stimulus characteristics that could bias performance, such as chromatic salience and detectability. They nevertheless had the merit of underlining that general principles of learning studied in vertebrates could be also found in honeybees.

In the 1980s and 1990s, visual learning was mainly used as a tool to answer questions on orientation close to the goal and visual perception and discrimination. The questions raised by these studies (see Lehrer, 1997; Srinivasan and Zhang, 1997, for reviews) focused on visual capabilities such as visual spatial resolution, shape discrimination, orientation detection, and movement perception and parallax, among others, and were not concerned by learning itself. Not surprisingly, none of these investigations quantified individual acquisition performance in order to present acquisition curves. This is a critical point because the visual strategies used by bees to solve a visual discrimination may be affected by the amount of accumulated experience at the moment of a test (Giurfa et al., 2003; Stach and Giurfa, 2005).

Because of obvious limitations, color learning in honeybees was never amenable at the cellular level because of the free-flying activity of the bees under study. Stages of central color processing such as color opponent neurons (Kien and Menzel, 1977; Yang et al., 2004) are known in the bee brain (Menzel and Backhaus, 1991), but there is no evidence on the possible interactions between the known neural elements of the color processing circuit and a reward-processing pathway. Recently, a protocol for color conditioning of the proboscis extension reflex has been proposed (Hori et al., 2006), based on pioneer findings by Kuwabara (1957). This protocol consists of training harnessed bees to extend the proboscis to color signals paired with sucrose solution.

1.29.7.2 Elemental Olfactory Learning and Memory in Harnessed Bees

The first study on olfactory PER conditioning was conducted by Takeda (1961) and was inspired by Kuwabara (1957), who reported PER conditioning using colors as CS. Olfactory PER conditioning was first used to assess olfactory discrimination capabilities in bees. These were typically trained with one rewarded odor and then tested for their choice of different odors, which differed from the rewarded one in structure (Vareschi, 1971). Even now, the protocol continues to serve this purpose and has provided a description of a putative olfactory space for the honeybee (Guerrieri et al., 2005b). This space was established by quantifying similarity and difference relationships between several odorants through olfactory PER conditioning. However, the protocol turned out to be the most powerful tool to characterize elemental olfactory learning after Bitterman et al. (1983) characterized it as a case of classical conditioning in which bees learn a CS (odorant)–US (sucrose solution) association. Forward (CS precedes US) but not backward (US precedes CS) pairing results in acquisition and learning of the trained odorant (**Figure 1(e)**). The memory trace initiated by a single CS–US pairing follows a biphasic memory function similar to that found for color learning of free-flying bees. The initial high response level is dominated by a nonassociative sensitization component, because a single US alone also arouses the animal for a short period of time, leading to a transient increase in response to many stimuli, including the CS.

A single learning trial results in a medium-term memory that fades away after a few days, whereas three learning trials lead to a stable long-term memory that is resistant to different forms of interference. Olfactory memory and its different phases (short-term, early and long; medium-term, early and long; and long-term, early and long; see Menzel, 1999) have been accurately described in terms of their dynamics (Menzel, 1999). The molecular bases of these phases are currently either known or being explored (Menzel, 2001), but this subject will not be reviewed here. The fact that similar dynamics underlie color and olfactory memory can be related to the natural lifestyle of the honeybee. Indeed, olfactory memory phases correspond to the temporal dynamics of foraging activities in the field (Menzel, 1999), such that early components of memory can be related to the fast succession of experiences that a bee gathers while foraging within a patch or when moving between close patches, whereas medium-term memory corresponds, because of its intrinsic

dynamic, to the intervals occurring between foraging bouts. Long-term memory relates to foraging bouts that are spaced in time and that may occur in different days or after long-interrupted bouts (Menzel, 1999).

As in other classical (Pavlovian) protocols, olfactory memory acquired through PER conditioning is dependent on variables such as the kind of CS, US intensity (i.e., the amount and/or quality of sucrose solution received during conditioning), the number of conditioning trials, and the intertrial interval; Menzel et al., 2001). Trial spacing is the dominant factor for both acquisition and retention. Generally, massed trials (i.e., trials succeeding each other in a fast sequence) lead to impaired memory performance compared with spaced trials (i.e., trials separated in time). Longer-intertrial intervals lead to better acquisition and higher retention. Several studies on olfactory memory dynamics (reviewed in Menzel, 1999) showed that memories in bees pass through an early consolidation phase and that memories are fragile before consolidation is completed. Transfer from short-term memory to long-term memory via medium-term memory is not a purely sequential process but also includes parallel processes (Menzel, 1999). As in color learning, olfactory short-term memories are dominated by a nonassociative sensitization component, and long-term memory at its latest phase is protein synthesis dependent (Wüstenberg et al., 1998). The main conclusion arising from studies on honeybee olfactory memory (Menzel, 1999, 2001) is that behavioral performance reflecting memory storage and retrieval is guided by multiple and discrete memory traces rather than by a single, continuously decaying memory trace.

Olfactory conditioning of PER allowed studying associative phenomena such as overshadowing (Smith, 1998), blocking (Smith and Cobey, 1994; Gerber and Ullrich, 1999; Hosler and Smith, 2000; Guerrieri et al., 2005a), and other forms of compound conditioning (e.g., sensory preconditioning; Müller et al., 2000; backward blocking, Blaser et al., 2004) in a more controlled way. In some cases, clear effects were found (e.g., overshadowing, sensory preconditioning), whereas in others (e.g., blocking), the responses were rather inconsistent (Guerrieri et al., 2005a).

1.29.7.3 Cellular Bases of Appetitive Olfactory Proboscis Extension Reflex Conditioning

Apart from behavioral studies, the significant advance yielded by olfactory PER conditioning was

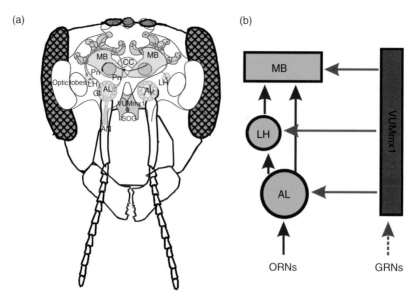

Figure 3 CS–US associations in the honeybee brain. (a) Scheme of a frontal view of the bee brain showing the olfactory (CS, in blue on the left) and gustatory (US, in red on the right) central pathways. The CS pathway: olfactory sensory neurons send information to the brain via the antennal nerve (AN). In the antennal lobe (AL), these neurons synapse at the level of glomeruli (Gl) onto local interneurons (not shown) and projection neurons (Pn) conveying the olfactory information to higher-order centers, the lateral horn (LH) and the mushroom bodies (MB). MBs are interconnected through commissural tracts (in violet).The US pathway: this circuit is partially represented by the VUMmx1 neuron, which converges with the CS pathway at three main sites: the AL, the LH, and the MB. CC, central complex, SOG, subesophageal ganglion. (b) Localization and distribution of CS–US associations in the bee brain. ORNs, olfactory receptor neurons; GRNs, gustatory receptor neurons. The dashed line between GRNs and VUMmx1 indicates that this part of the circuit is actually unknown. Adapted from a scheme provided courtesy of B. Gruenewald.

the possibility of tracing CS and US pathways in the honeybee brain and integratively studying the neural circuits underlying elemental associative learning. Odorants are processed in a neural pathway (the CS processing pathway) characterized by different processing stages (**Figure 3(a)**). Olfactory perception starts at the level of the antennae, where olfactory receptor neurons are located within specialized hairs called sensilla. Sensory neurons endowed with molecular olfactory receptors convey information on odorants to the antennal lobe. This structure is a good example of dedicated neuropile (see above), as it is the primary olfactory center of the bee brain. Antennal lobes are made up of globular structures called glomeruli, which are synaptic interaction sites between olfactory receptors, with local inhibitory interneurons connecting glomeruli laterally and projection neurons conveying processed olfactory information to higher-order centers such as the lateral horn or the mushroom bodies. The latter are higher-order integration centers, as they receive input from visual and mechanosensory pathways apart from the olfactory pathway.

Optophysiological studies based on recording calcium activity at the level of the antennal lobe following olfactory stimulation have shown that in naïve (i.e., nontrained) honeybees, odors are represented in terms of glomerular activity patterns (Joerges et al., 1997; Galizia and Menzel, 2000). Activity patterns for a given odor are symmetric between brain hemispheres and are conserved between individuals (Galizia et al., 1998, 1999). The pattern of active glomeruli tells the brain the identity of the odorant processed. When two odorants are presented in a mixture, the glomerular representation resembles the sum of the responses to the components or the response of the strongest component (Deisig et al., 2006). As more components are added, the picture changes and inhibitory interactions become apparent (Joerges et al., 1997). This across-fiber pattern coding is maintained upstream (Faber and Menzel, 2001), but there are differences in odor coding between the antennal lobes and the mushroom bodies. Indeed, odors evoke combinatorial activity patterns also at the level of the calyces, the input region of the mushroom bodies, but these are substantially sparser (Szyszka et al., 2005). Moreover, the Kenyon cells, the neurons that constitute the mushroom bodies, exhibit a temporal sharpening of responses in response to odorants.

Although some parts of the CS pathway are still superficially characterized (e.g., the lateral horn), and although we are only starting to understand the dynamic aspects of odorant processing in several of the stages of this pathway (Szyszka et al., 2005), an integrative view of the CS circuit is already available. How does learning modify neural activity in this circuit? Faber et al. (1999) found that olfactory differential conditioning induces an increase in the intensity of the glomerular activation pattern for a rewarded odorant but not a qualitative change in its global nature. The nonrewarded odorant induced no change in glomerular activity. This conclusion has been recently challenged by experiments that showed no change in activity in a subpopulation of uniglomerular output neurons (projection neurons) after different elemental olfactory conditioning protocols (Peele et al., 2006). How olfactory representations are modified by associative learning therefore remains to be determined. In doing this, changes at the different stages of the olfactory pathway have to be studied at different intervals after conditioning. Moreover, the effect of different conditioning protocols of varying complexity should also be considered as a possible determinant of the olfactory representation achieved.

In the case of the US processing pathway, our knowledge is only partial, at least in neuroanatomical terms, as it has thus far been restricted to a unique neuron that is necessary and sufficient to substitute for the sucrose reward in the honeybee brain. This neuron, which constitutes a good example of dedicated neuron (see above), is called VUMmx1 (ventral unpaired median neuron of the maxillary neuromere 1) and responds with long-lasting spike activity to sucrose solution delivered both at the antennae and the proboscis (Hammer, 1993). The dendrites of VUMmx1 arborize symmetrically in the brain and converge with the olfactory pathway at three sites: the antennal lobes; the calyces, which are the olfactory input areas of the mushroom bodies; and the lateral horns (**Figure 3(a)**). This convergence is particularly remarkable in the case of a neuron coding for sucrose solution because it provides the structural basis for CS–US associations. That VUMmx1 indeed constitutes the neural representation of the US in olfactory PER conditioning was shown through an elegant substitution experiment conducted by Hammer (1993). He showed that behavioral learning

of an olfactory stimulus can be induced by substituting the sucrose reward in PER conditioning with an artificial depolarization of VUMmx1 immediately after olfactory stimulation (forward pairing). If depolarization, and thus spike activity, precedes olfactory stimulation (backward pairing), no learning was observed. The same forward–backward effect was seen when sucrose was used as the reward under similar experimental conditions. These results showed that VUMmx1 constitutes the neural correlate of the US in associative olfactory learning.

This conclusion was reaffirmed by neuropharmacological experiments aimed at discovering the neurotransmitter acting as appetitive reinforcement in olfactory PER conditioning. As VUMmx1 belongs to a group of octopamine-immunoreactive neurons (Kreissl et al., 1994), it was hypothesized that octopamine, a biogenic amine usually associated with increased levels of arousal and behavioral facilitation in invertebrates (Libersat and Pflüger, 2004; Huber, 2005), acts as the neurotransmitter necessary and sufficient to substitute for the sucrose reward (Hammer and Menzel, 1998). Indeed, pairing an odorant with injections of octopamine as a substitute for sucrose into the mushroom bodies or the antennal lobes (but not the lateral horn lobe) produced a lasting, learning-dependent enhancement of proboscis extension (Hammer and Menzel, 1998). Thus, octopamine signaling via VUMmx1 is sufficient to substitute for sugar reinforcement in honeybees. This conclusion was confirmed by silencing octopaminergic receptor expression in the honeybee antennal lobe using double-stranded RNA (Farooqui et al., 2003). This treatment inhibited olfactory acquisition and recall but did not disrupt odorant discrimination. This result underscores that appetitive reinforcer function in the invertebrate brain is subserved by specific neurons and associated biogenic amines (here octopamine), which act as value systems in associative learning phenomena (i.e., as systems allowing ordering, prioritizing and assigning good or bad labels to odorants; Giurfa, 2006).

We still lack a more integrative view of the US pathway. Although gustatory receptor neurons tuned to sucrose have been located on specialized sensilla on the antennae, mouth parts, and tarsi (Whitehead and Larsen, 1976; Whitehead, 1978; Haupt, 2004; de Brito Sanchez et al., 2005), less is known about the circuit allowing these receptors to convey US information to the central level, and more specifically to VUMmx1. This circuit is probably localized in the subesophageal ganglion, which is the first synaptic relay in the gustatory pathway (Altman and Kien, 1987). Despite this incomplete view of the US pathway, an important principle of classical conditioning was verified by studying VUMmx1 activity, namely, stimulus substitution. Classical conditioning relies on a CS acquiring the capacity of replacing the US as it becomes a reliable predictor of reinforcement. This was evident in recordings of VUMmx1 activity after olfactory conditioning (Hammer, 1993). After training a bee to discriminate a rewarding (CS1) from a nonrewarded odorant (CS2), it was found that VUMmx1 fired to CS1 and not to CS2 (Hammer, 1993). Thus, CS1, the odorant that reliably predicted the US, acquired the capacity of activating VUMmx1. At the same time, VUMmx1 continues to respond to the US when it is presented unexpectedly (i.e., not preceded by a predictive odorant; Menzel and Giurfa, 2001). Thus, the VUMmx1 neuron has the characteristic properties of a system that provides reinforcement prediction error information that is critical to associative learning (e.g., Schultz and Dickinson, 2000). In other words, it provides information on the discrepancy between the expected and delivered values of a reinforcing event (the prediction error), which determines the effective reinforcement value of that event (Rescorla and Wagner, 1972).

The picture emerging from these and other studies is one in which elemental, associative, olfactory learning can be accurately characterized at both the behavioral and cellular levels in order to understand the mechanisms of this simple form of learning. The honeybee offers the unique chance of dissecting elemental olfactory learning and identifying its building blocks. From this dissection, it appears that learning relies on distributed, but localized, interactions between CS and US pathways throughout the brain (**Figure 3(b)**). Distribution is reflected by the fact that interactions between these pathways occur in at least three different regions of the brain, the antennal lobes, the mushroom bodies, and the lateral horns (see **Figure 3(b)**). Localization is reflected by the fact that these interactions are spatially delimited. Redundancy could also be designated as a principle because of the repetition of synaptic interactions between CS and US pathways, but so far it remains unknown whether the interactions occurring at one of these three sites are equivalent to those occurring in another site (i.e., whether different memory contents are formed and stored in the antennal lobes, mushroom bodies, and lateral horns). Instead, it appears that these different brain structures intervene in different forms of learning (see below) so that the concept of redundancy would not be appropriated.

1.29.8 Elemental Aversive Learning in Bees

The previous sections underline that for almost a century research on honeybees has made significant contributions to our general understanding of learning and memory but that such an understanding is restricted to appetitive learning. As mentioned above, olfactory conditioning of PER has been used for 45 years (beginning in 1961; Takeda, 1961) as the only tool to access the neural and molecular bases of learning in honeybees.

Recently, aversive learning could be studied in honeybees in such a way that both behavioral and neural levels were made accessible to experimentation (Vergoz et al., 2007a). Pairing an odorant with an electric shock resulted in associative learning, in which bees learned to extend their sting (SER) in response to the odorant previously punished (**Figure 1(f)**). They were also able to learn to master appetitive and aversive associations simultaneously and exhibited the appropriate response, PER or SER, to the appropriate odorant. Moreover, neuropharmacological experiments addressed the question of modularity of appetitive and aversive learning and the possible dependency of this modularity on two different biogenic amines subserving appetitive and aversive reinforcement. Indeed, although octopamine has been shown to substitute for appetitive reinforcement (Hammer and Menzel, 1998; see above), it was found that blocking of dopaminergic, but not octopaminergic, receptors suppresses aversive olfactory learning. Thus, octopamine and dopamine subserve appetitive and aversive reinforcement in the honeybee, respectively. Again, this finding emphasizes the conclusion that dedicated biogenic amines act as value systems in the invertebrate brain and that they fulfill different reinforcing roles in different forms of learning.

This finding brought the honeybee closer to other insect models such as the fruit fly *Drosophila melanogaster* and the cricket *Gryllus bimaculatus*. In crickets, pharmacological experiments showed that octopamine and dopamine subserve the appetitive and aversive reinforcing functions, respectively (Unoki et al., 2005). In fruit flies, the same result was previously found using mutants with inactivated dopaminergic or octopaminergic neurons (Schwaerzel et al., 2003). Recently,

Schroll et al. (2006) showed that octopamine and dopamine are necessary and sufficient to substitute for appetitive and aversive reinforcement in *Drosophila* larvae. Furthermore, neurons capable of mediating and predicting aversive reinforcement have been found in the *Drosophila* brain (Riemensperger et al., 2005; *See* Chapter 1.28). These neurons may be a general feature of the insect brain, and dopamine may underlie other forms of aversive learning involving stimuli of different sensory modalities (e.g., visual stimuli associated with aversive gustatory reinforcements; Unoki et al., 2006). Interestingly, dopaminergic neurons in the fly brain exhibit the same functional principle as the VUMmx1 neuron in the bee brain, namely, stimulus substitution. Here too, dopaminergic neurons did not respond to the odorant used for aversive conditioning before conditioning and acquired this property after conditioning (Riemensperger et al., 2005). Similarly to the VUMmx1 neuron, dopaminergic neurons in the fly brain provide, therefore, reinforcement prediction error information that is critical to associative learning.

The study of aversive learning in honeybees is just starting. As this form of conditioning uses odorants as CS, it is possible to ask how odorant representations are modified by aversive experiences compared with appetitive experiences. An important goal is to identify dopaminergic neurons in the bee brain whose morphology and functional properties make them candidates for integrating the aversive US pathway. Furthermore, characterizing aversive olfactory memory at both the cellular and molecular levels is crucial for a comparative analysis of appetitive and aversive learning and memory in bees, which can now be performed. The usefulness of the aversive learning protocol has been demonstrated by the finding that green mandibular pheromone, the pheromone that is responsible for social dominance and control exerted by the queen within the hive, inhibits selectively olfactory aversive learning in young bees (Yugoz et al., 2007b). In this way, young bees, which have to stay closer to the queen are prevented from forming any aversive experience that could result from such an important bond. This fascinating result could only be accessed thanks to the aversive learning protocol, as no significant effect of the pheromone was found in the case of the appetitive olfactory learning.

1.29.9 Nonelemental Learning in Bees

Elemental appetitive and aversive learning, as discussed above, rely on the establishment of elemental associative links connecting two specific and unambiguous events in the bee's world. What has been learned for a given color in terms of its outcome is valid for that color but not for a different one. The sucrose reward that follows a given behavior, such as contacting a given surface with the left antenna, is valid for that behavior but not for a different one such as contacting the same surface with the right antenna. However, in the forms of associative learning that we discuss here, unique links connecting specific events are not useful because the events under consideration are ambiguous in terms of their outcome. A typical case introduced above is negative patterning, in which the subject needs to learn to discriminate a nonreinforced compound from its components (A+, B+, AB−). This problem does not admit elemental solutions because the animal has to learn that AB is necessarily different from the linear sum of A and B. In biconditional discrimination, the subject has to learn to respond to the compounds AB and CD and not to the compounds AC and BD (AB+, CD+, AC−, BD−). As in negative patterning, each element, A, B, C, and D, appears as often reinforced as nonreinforced, so that it is impossible to rely on the associative strength of a given stimulus to solve the task. These examples show that more elaborated computational strategies are necessary in the case of nonelemental discrimination problems.

Treating compound stimuli as entities different from the simple sum of their components (e.g., $AB = X \neq A + B$) constitutes the basis of the configural learning theory proposed to account for the solving of these nonlinear discrimination problems (Pearce, 1994). For this account, animals trained with AB can respond to A or B only to a low extent. Another theory, the unique-cue theory, proposes that a mixture is processed as the lineal sum of its components plus a stimulus (u) that is unique to the joint presentation of the elements in the mixture (e.g., $AB = A + B + u$) (Whitlow and Wagner, 1972). The unique cue is what gives a unique signature to a compound, which differentiates it from the linear sum of its components. For this account, animals trained with AB can respond to A or B to a relatively high extent.

Probably because of their inherent complexity, these problems have been rarely studied in invertebrates. However, several recent studies have addressed the issue of elemental vs. nonelemental learning in honeybees, using visual conditioning of free-flying animals and olfactory PER conditioning (Giurfa, 2003). In both experimental protocols, bees were shown to solve a biconditional discrimination (AB+, CD+, AC−, BD−). In the visual modality, free-flying bees had to discriminate complex patterns that were arranged to fulfill the principles of this discrimination problem (Schubert et al., 2005). In the olfactory modality, olfactory compounds were used (Hellstern et al., 1995; Chandra and Smith, 1998), and bees learned to respond appropriately to each compound, independent of the ambiguity inherent to the components. This capacity demonstrates that under certain circumstances both visual and olfactory compounds are learned as entities different from the simple sum of their components.

This conclusion is underlined by studies showing that bees can solve a negative patterning discrimination (A+, B+, AB−) both in the visual (Schubert et al., 2005) and the olfactory (Deisig et al., 2001, 2002, 2003) modality. Solving this problem is possible if the compound AB is treated as being different from the simple sum of its elements. In the case of olfactory compound learning, experiments were conceived to discern between the two nonelemental theories mentioned above, the configural and the unique-cue theory. It was shown (Deisig et al., 2003) that the bees' performance was consistent with the unique-cue theory (i.e., when bees perceive an olfactory compound they detect the presence of the components in it, but they also assign a unique identity to the compound, resulting from the interaction of its components).

Another study used an original protocol, side-specific olfactory PER conditioning, which posed a nonlinear discrimination problem (Sandoz and Menzel, 2001). In this case, a thin plastic wall separated the honeybee's antennae during olfactory stimulation (**Figure 4(a)**). Bees were differentially conditioned using two odors (A and B). When odorants were delivered to one antenna, the contingency was A+ vs. B−, but it was reversed (A− vs. B+) when they were delivered to other antenna. This discrimination resembles a form of contextual learning, as the context of each antennal side (left vs. right) determines the contingency of the stimuli. Bees learned to respond appropriately to the rewarded odor and to inhibit their reaction to the nonrewarded odor on each side (Sandoz and Menzel, 2001). They thus solved this side-specific, nonelemental discrimination and remembered the contingencies learned 24 h later (**Figure 4(b)**). In this case, insight into the neural bases of this type of nonelemental problem solving was obtained by combining this protocol with *in vivo* calcium imaging recordings of glomerular activity at the level of both antennal lobes (**Figure 4(c)**). It was found that in naïve bees, odor

response patterns were highly symmetrical (i.e., before conditioning, the same odorant elicited the same activation pattern in both antennal lobes). In conditioned bees, topical differences between sides were found. After side-specific conditioning, the left and right representations of the same odorant became slightly different, thus allowing differentiation between sides (Sandoz et al., 2003). Thus, this form of nonelemental learning resulted in a decorrelation of the representations of the conditioning odors between sides (**Figure 4(d)**). This result emphasizes that bees may form odor/side associations of the type AS1+/AS2− and BS1−/BS2+ (S1: side 1, S2: side 2). It is thus conceivable that structures situated upstream of the antennal lobes (e.g., the mushroom bodies or the lateral horn) are crucial for decoding differences in neural representations, such as those generated in side-specific conditioning.

Komischke et al. (2003) showed that bilateral olfactory input is required for solving a negative patterning discrimination. Given that the olfactory circuit remains practically unconnected between hemispheres to the mushroom bodies, this result suggests that the reading of a unique cue, arising from odorant interaction within the mixture, occurs upstream of the antennal lobes (i.e., at the level of the mushroom bodies). Komischke et al. (2005) used mushroom body–ablated honeybees to determine whether intact mushroom bodies are necessary to solve nonelemental olfactory discriminations. Bees were treated with hydroxyurea, which partially or totally removes the calyces (the input region to the mushroom bodies) (Malun, 1998). In previous studies, Scheiner et al. (2001) and Malun et al. (2002) showed that such ablations do not affect elemental forms of learning. Scheiner et al. (2001) showed that tactile learning, a form of elemental learning in which bees learn to associate an object within the range of one antenna with sucrose solution and discriminate it from an object presented to the opposite side, was unaffected in ablated bees. Malun et al. (2002) studied olfactory learning and showed that the presence of ablations did not impair acquisition of an elemental olfactory discrimination in which one odor was rewarded and another odor was nonrewarded (A+ vs. B−).

In the experiments of Komischke et al. (2005), bees with unilateral lesions of the mushroom bodies (a median calyx was usually absent) were trained in different olfactory discrimination problems. When odorants were delivered in a side-specific manner, bees with mushroom body lesions could not solve an

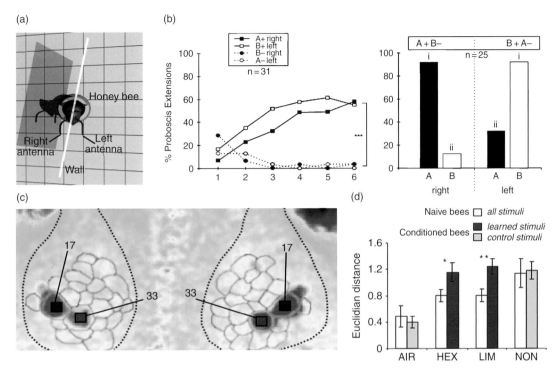

Figure 4 Side-specific olfactory conditioning of harnessed bees. (a) In this protocol, a harnessed bee is conditioned to discriminate two odorants A and B, which, depending on the presentation side (the antenna to which they are delivered), have different contingencies. To this end, the left and right antennae are separated by a thin wall glued along the bee body. Bees have to learn that when odorants are delivered to the right antenna, the contingency is A+ vs. B−, but it is A− vs. B+ if they are delivered to the left antenna. (b) Bees learn to solve this nonelemental double discrimination. The acquisition curves display the responses (% PER) to the rewarded odorants (A+ right and B+ left) and to the nonrewarded odorants (B− right and A− left). At the end of training, bees discriminate the rewarding from the nonrewarding stimuli. Twenty-four hours later, they still remember the appropriate contingencies on the appropriate side (histogram); n, number of bees trained or tested. (c) Simultaneous calcium imaging recording of both antennal lobes (delimited by the dashed lines). In this case, the response of naïve (nontrained) bees to Nonanol is shown. Glomeruli 17 and 33 are activated by this odor, and this activation is symmetric between sides. (d) The effect of side-specific conditioning on odor representation. The perceptual distance between the left and right representations of the same odorant was measured in a putative olfactory space, calculated for the honeybee. Odor representations differing perceptually are separated by a larger Euclidian distance in that space. For Hexanol and Limonene, the two odors used in the side-specific conditioning, the distance between left and right representations increased significantly as a consequence of training (red bars), thus showing that left and right representations of the same odorant became more different. For a control odorant, Nonanol, and for a clean-air control, the responses on the right and left antennal lobes were the same. Adapted from Sandoz JC and Menzel R (2001) Side-specificity of olfactory learning in the honeybee: Generalization between odors and sides. *Learn. Mem.* 8: 286–294 and Sandoz JC, Galizia CG, and Menzel R (2003) Side-specific olfactory conditioning leads to more specific odor representations between sides but not within sides in the honeybee antennal lobes. *Neuroscience* 120: 1137–1148; courtesy of J.C. Sandoz.

unambiguous double discrimination (Problem 1: A+ vs. B− on one antenna, C+ vs. D− on the other; A + B−/C + D−), even though each of the four odorants had an unambiguous outcome. When confronted with the ambiguous side-specific discrimination (Problem 2: A + vs. B− on one antenna, A− vs. B+ on the other; see above and **Figure 4**), bees were also impaired because they could only learn the discrimination proposed to their intact brain side. Nonablated bees could master both side-specific discriminations. When odorants were delivered

simultaneously to both antennae (Problem 3: A + B−C + D−), ablated bees learned slower than normal bees.

Thus, in all three cases, the unilateral loss of a median calyx affected olfactory learning (Komischke et al., 2005). It was proposed that mushroom bodies are required for solving nonelemental discriminations but also elemental tasks whose complexity is enhanced by virtue of the number of stimuli involved (Problems 1 and 3: 4 stimuli). To solve an A + B−/A−B+ discrimination, information exchange between brain hemispheres has to be inhibited such that A on the right side is not generalized to A on the left side, and vice versa. Mushroom body ablations could have an effect on this inhibition; in normal bees conditioning would result in inhibition of interhemispheric transfer. Ablations would restore the transfer from the intact side, thus creating confusion on the ablated side.

Cumulative experience seems to play a critical role for adopting elemental or nonelemental learning strategies (Giurfa et al., 2003). When free-flying bees are trained to fly into a Y-maze to collect sucrose solution on a rewarded visual target presented in one of the arms of the maze, the strategy underlying the choice of visual compounds changes along training. Bees were trained with color stimuli that were color disks violet (V), green (G), or yellow (Y), which were of equal salience for honeybees. Training followed an A+, BC+ design, followed by an AC vs. BC test. Training consisted of six (three A+ and three BC+), 20 (10 A+ and 10 BC+), or 40 (20 A+ and 20 BC+) acquisition trials, thus increasing the amount of experience on the same problem. Elemental models of compound processing predict that in the test (AC vs. BC), a preference for the nontrained stimulus AC should occur, whereas configural models predict a preference for the trained stimulus BC (Giurfa et al., 2003). After six training trials, bees favored an elemental strategy and preferred AC to BC during the tests. Increasing the number of training trials resulted in an increase of the choice of BC. Thus, short training favored processing the compound as the sum of its elements (elemental theory), whereas long training favored its processing as being different from the sum of its elements (configural theory). It was also observed that the change in stimulus processing was influenced by stimulus similarity. Color similarity favored configural processing with increasing experience (Giurfa et al., 2003), a result that was consistent with the results of honeybee olfactory compound conditioning (Deisig et al., 2002). Further factors favoring nonelemental compound processing and learning could be the spatial and temporal proximity of elements and the animals' previous experience.

There is, however, a limitation in these studies that has to be overcome in future research, namely that all compound stimuli used were of the same modality, either visual or olfactory. It would be important to verify that similar rules apply for intermodal compounds. This goal is particularly important in the context of searching for the neural substrates of nonelemental learning forms. If mushroom bodies, which are multimodal sensory integration structures, are indeed an important center for achieving nonlinear processing, affecting their normal function could have more dramatic consequences in the case of bimodal than unimodal compounds. In studying nonelemental learning with stimuli from different modalities, one should guarantee comparable salience between stimuli, because differences at this level may lead to overshadowing or blocking.

1.29.10   Positive Transfer of Learning in Honeybees

In this section, I focus on problem solving in which animals respond in an adaptive manner to novel stimuli that they have never encountered before and that do not predict a specific outcome *per se* based on the animals' past experience. Such a positive transfer of learning (Robertson, 2001) is therefore different from elemental forms of learning, which link known stimuli or actions to specific reinforcers. In the cases considered in this section, the response can attain levels in which it becomes independent of the physical nature of the stimuli presented so that it acts as a rule guiding the animal's behavior (like relational rules such as 'on top of' or 'larger than,' which can be applied irrespective of the similarity of the stimuli considered).

1.29.10.1   Categorization of Visual Stimuli

Positive transfer of learning is a distinctive characteristic of categorization performance. Categorization refers to the classification of perceptual input into defined functional groups (Harnard, 1987). It can be defined as the ability to group distinguishable objects or events on the basis of a common feature or set of features, and therefore to respond similarly to them (Troje et al., 1999; Delius et al., 2000; Zentall et al., 2002; *See* Chapter 1.08). Categorization deals, therefore, with the extraction of these defining features from objects of the subject's environment. A typical categorization experiment trains an animal to extract the basic attributes of a category and then tests it with novel stimuli that were never encountered before and that may or may not present the attributes of the category learned. If the animal chooses the novel stimuli based on these attributes, it classifies them as belonging to the category and therefore exhibits positive transfer of learning.

Using this basic design in which procedural modifications can be introduced, several studies have recently shown the ability of visual categorization in free-flying honeybees trained to discriminate different patterns and shapes. For instance, van Hateren et al. (1990) trained bees to discriminate two given gratings presented vertically and differently oriented (e.g., 45° vs. 135°) by rewarding one of these gratings with sucrose solution and not rewarding the other. Each bee was trained with a changing succession of pairs of different gratings, one of which was always rewarded, while the other was not. Despite the difference in pattern quality, all the rewarded patterns had the same edge orientation, and all the nonrewarded patterns also had a common orientation, perpendicular to the rewarded one. Under these circumstances, the bees had to extract and learn the orientation that was common to all rewarded patterns to solve the task. This was the only cue predicting reward delivery. In the tests, bees were presented with novel patterns, to which they had never been exposed, and that were all nonrewarded, but that exhibited the same stripe orientations as the rewarding and nonrewarding patterns employed during the training. In such transfer tests, bees chose the appropriate orientation despite the novelty of the structural details of the stimuli. Thus, bees could categorize visual stimuli on the basis of their global orientation.

They can also categorize visual patterns based on their bilateral symmetry. When trained with a succession of changing patterns to discriminate bilateral symmetry from asymmetry, bees learn to extract this information from very different figures and transfer it to novel symmetrical and asymmetrical patterns (Giurfa et al., 1996). Similar conclusions apply to other visual features such as radial symmetry, concentric pattern organization and pattern disruption (see Benard et al., 2006 for review), and even photographs belonging to a given class (e.g., radial flower, landscape, plant stem) (Zhang et al., 2004).

How could bees appropriately classify different photographs of radial flowers if these vary in color, size, dissection, and so on? An explanation is provided by Stach et al. (2004), who expanded the demonstration that bees can categorize visual stimuli based on their global orientation to show that different coexisting orientations can be considered at a time and integrated into a global stimulus representation that is the basis for the category (Stach et al., 2004). Thus, a radial flower would be, in fact, the conjunction of five or more radiating edges. Besides

focusing on a single orientation, honeybees were shown to assemble different features to build a generic pattern representation, which could be used to respond appropriately to novel stimuli sharing this basic layout. Honeybees trained with a series of complex patterns sharing a common layout comprising four edge orientations remembered these orientations simultaneously in their appropriate positions and transferred their response to novel stimuli that preserved the trained layout (**Figure 5**). Honeybees also transferred their response to patterns with fewer correct orientations, depending on their match with the trained layout. These results show that honeybees extract regularities in their visual environment and establish correspondences among correlated features such that they generate a large set of object descriptions from a finite set of elements.

Thus, honeybees show positive transfer of learning from a trained to a novel set of stimuli, and their performance is consistent with the definition of categorization. Visual stimulus categorization is not, therefore, a prerogative of certain vertebrates. However, this result might not be surprising because it admits an elemental learning interpretation. To explain this interpretation, the possible neural mechanisms underlying categorization should be considered. If we admit that visual stimuli are categorized on the basis of specific features such as orientation, the neural implementation of category recognition could be relatively simple. The feature(s) allowing stimulus classification would activate specific neuronal detectors in the optic lobes, the visual areas of the bee brain. Examples of such feature detectors are the orientation detectors whose orientation and tuning have been already characterized by means of electrophysiological recordings in the honeybee optic lobes (Yang and Maddess, 1997). Thus, responding to different gratings with a common orientation of, say, 60° is simple because all these gratings will elicit the same neural activation in the same set of orientation detectors despite their different structural quality. In the case of category learning, the activation of an additional neural element is needed. This type of element would be a reinforcement neuron equivalent to VUMmx1 (Hammer, 1993; see above) but contacting the visual circuits at its relevant processing stages. Other VUM neurons whose function is still unknown are present in the bee brain (Schroter et al., 2006). It could be conceived that one of them (or more than one) acts as the neural basis of reinforcement in associative visual learning. Category learning could thus be reduced to the progressive reinforcement of an associative neural

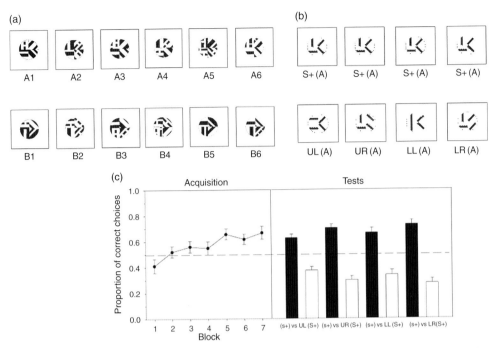

Figure 5 Categorization of visual patterns based on sets of multiple features. (a) Training stimuli used in Stach et al.'s experiments (2004). Bees were trained to discriminate A from B patterns during a random succession of A vs. B patterns. A patterns (A1–A6) differed from each other but shared a common layout defined by the spatial arrangement of orientations in the four quadrants. B patterns (B1–B6) shared a common layout perpendicular to that of A patterns. (b) Test stimuli used to determine whether or not bees extract the simplified layout of four bars from the rewarded A patterns. The four test pairs shown correspond to the honeybees trained with A patterns. Equivalent tests were performed with the honeybees trained with B patterns (not shown). S+, simplified layout of the rewarded A patterns; UL, upper-left bar rotated; UR, upper-right bar rotated; LL, lower-left bar rotated; LR, lower-right bar rotated. (c) Left panel: acquisition curve showing the pooled performance of bees rewarded on A and B patterns. The proportion of correct choices along seven blocks of six consecutive visits is shown. Bees learned to discriminate the rewarding patterns (A or B) used for the training and significantly improved their correct choices along training. Right panel: proportion of correct choices in the tests with the novel patterns. Bees always preferred the simplified layout of the training patterns previously rewarded (S+) to any variant in which one bar was rotated, thus showing that they were using the four bars in their appropriate spatial locations and orientations. Adapted from Stach S, Benard J, and Giurfa M (2004) Local-feature assembling in visual pattern recognition and generalization in honeybees. *Nature* 429: 758–761.

circuit relating visual-coding and reinforcement-coding neurons, similar to that underlying simple associative (e.g., Pavlovian) conditioning. From this perspective, even if categorization is viewed as a nonelemental learning form because it involves positive transfer of learning, it may simply rely on elemental links between CS and US.

1.29.10.2   Rule Learning

This argument is not applicable to rule learning in which positive transfer occurs independently of the physical nature of the stimuli considered. In this case, the animal learns relations between objects and not the objects themselves. Typical examples are the so-called rules of sameness and difference. These rules are

demonstrated through the protocols of delayed matching to sample (DMTS) and delayed nonmatching to sample (DNMTS), respectively. In DMTS, animals are presented with a sample and then with a set of stimuli, one of which is identical to the sample and is reinforced. Since the sample is regularly changed, animals must learn the sameness rule, that is, always choose what is shown to you (the sample), independent of what else is shown to you. In DNMTS, the animal has to learn the opposite, that is, always choose the opposite of what is shown to you (the sample). Honeybees foraging in a Y-maze learn both rules (Giurfa et al., 2001). Bees were trained in a DMTS problem in which they were presented with a changing nonrewarded sample (i.e., one of two different color disks or one of two different black-and-white gratings,

(a)

(b)

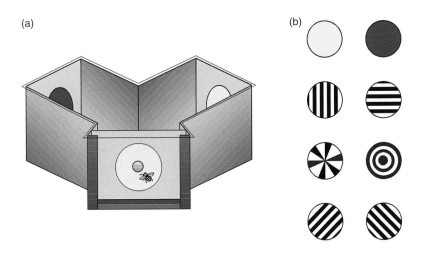

(c) Transfer tests with patterns (d) Transfer tests with colours
(Training with colours)   (Training with patterns)

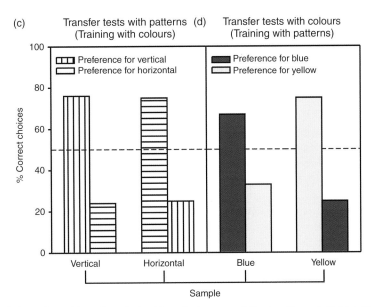

Figure 6 Rule learning in honeybees. Honeybees trained to collect sugar solution in a Y-maze (a) on a series of different patterns (b) learn a rule of sameness. Learning and transfer performance of bees in a delayed matching-to-sample task in which they were trained to colors (Experiment 1) or to black-and-white, vertical and horizontal gratings (Experiment 2). (c, d) Transfer tests with novel stimuli. (c) In Experiment 1, bees trained on the colors were tested on the gratings. (d) In Experiment 2, bees trained on the gratings were tested on the colors. In both cases, bees chose the novel stimuli corresponding to the sample, although they had no experience with such test stimuli. n denotes number of choices evaluated. Adapted from Giurfa M, Zhang S, Jenett A, Menzel R, and Srinivasan MV (2001) The concepts of 'sameness' and 'difference' in an insect. *Nature* 410: 930–933.

vertical or horizontal) at the entrance of a maze (**Figure 6**). The bees were rewarded only if they chose the stimulus identical to the sample once within the maze. Bees trained with colors and presented in transfer tests with black-and-white gratings that they had not experienced before solved the problem and chose the grating identical to the sample at the entrance of the maze. Similarly, bees trained with the gratings and tested with colors in transfer tests also solved the problem and chose the novel color corresponding to that of the sample grating at the maze entrance. Transfer was not limited to different kinds of modalities (pattern vs. color) within the visual domain, but it could also operate between drastically different domains such as olfaction and vision (Giurfa et al., 2001). Furthermore, bees also mastered a DNMTS task, thus showing that they learn a rule of difference between stimuli (Giurfa et al., 2001). These results document that bees learn rules relating stimuli in their environment. The capacity of honeybees to solve a DMTS task has recently been verified and studied with respect to the working memory underlying it (Zhang et al., 2004, 2005). It was found that the working memory for the sample underlying the solving of DMTS lasts approximately 5 s (Zhang et al., 2005) and coincides with the duration of other visual and olfactory short-term memories characterized in simpler forms of associative learning in honeybees (Menzel, 1999; see above). Moreover, bees trained in a DMTS task can learn to pay attention to one of two different samples presented successively in a flight tunnel (either to the first or to the second) and can transfer the learning of this sequence weight to novel samples (Zhang et al., 2005).

Despite the honeybees' evident capacity to solve relational problems such as the DMTS or the DNMTS tasks, such capacities are not unlimited. In some cases, biological constraints may impede the solving of a particular problem for which rule extraction is necessary. It is therefore interesting to focus on a different example of rule learning that bees could not master, the transitive inference problem (Benard and Giurfa, 2004). In this problem, animals have to learn a transitive rule (i.e., A > B, B > C, then A > C). Preference for A over C in this context can be explained by two strategies: (1) deductive reasoning (Fersen et al., 1990), in which the experimental subjects construct and manipulate a unitary and linear representation of the implicit hierarchy A > B > C, or (2) responding as a function of reinforced and not reinforced experiences (Terrace and McGonigle, 1994), in which case animals choose among stimuli based on their associative strength (i.e., on the effective number of reinforced and nonreinforced experiences with the stimuli; A is always reinforced, and B is always nonreinforced).

To determine whether bees learn a transitive rule, they were trained using five different visual stimuli A, B, C, D, and E in a multiple discrimination task: A+ vs. B−, B+ vs. C−, C+ vs. D−, D+ vs. E− (Benard and Giurfa, 2004). Training involved overlapping of adjacent premise pairs (A > B, B > C, C > D, D > E), which underlie a linear hierarchy A > B > C > D > E. After training, bees were tested with B vs. D, a nonadjacent

pair of stimuli that were never explicitly trained together. In theory, B and D have equivalent associative strengths because they are, in principle, equally associated with reinforcement or absence of it during training. Thus, if bees were guided by the stimulus's associative strength, they should choose randomly between B and D. If, however, bees used a transitive rule, they should prefer B to D. Honeybees learned the premise pairs as long as these were trained as uninterrupted, consecutive blocks of trials (Benard and Giurfa, 2004). But if shorter and interspersed blocks of trials were used, such that bees had to master all pairs practically simultaneously, performance collapsed, and bees did not learn the premise pairs. The bees' choice was significantly influenced by their experience with the last pair of stimuli (D+ vs. E−), such that they preferred D and avoided E. In the tests, no preference for B over D was found. Although this result agrees with an evaluation of stimuli in terms of their associative strength (see above), during training bees visited B more when it was rewarding than D, such that a preference for B should have been expected only if the associative strength were guiding the bees' choices. It was then concluded that bees do not establish transitive inferences between stimuli but, rather, guide their choices by the joint action of a recency effect (preference for the last rewarded stimulus, D) and by an evaluation of the associative strength of the stimuli (in which case preference for B should be evident). As the former supports choosing D while the latter supports choosing B, choosing B and D equally in the tests could be explained (Benard and Giurfa, 2004). At any rate, memory constraints (in this case, that simultaneous mastering of the different premise pairs was not possible and that the last excitatory memory seems to predominate over previous memories) impeded learning the transitive rule. Recently, Chen (2006) demonstrated that failure to master several consecutive visual discriminations is a result of the response competition occurring when animals are tested. This may explain why bees in the transitive inference protocol were unable to master the successive short blocks of training with different premise pairs.

1.29.11 Distributed Cognition in Honeybees

So far, we have concentrated on individual cognitive capabilities, but bees live in societies and therefore face problems that require coordination, task sharing, and collective decision making. From this perspective, it is legitimate to ask whether collective behaviors reflect or even surpass individual plasticity, because of, for instance, the possible additive effect of individual cognitive capacities.

This question has been the subject of debate in the case of social insects in which colonies were considered superorganisms (Southwick, 1983; Seeley, 1989). It has been argued that the superorganism protects and constitutes itself from colony recognition systems based on cuticular hydrocarbons that are transferred between individuals within the colony, thus obscuring, in theory, individual identity. The metaphor of the superorganism may be in a sense misleading because an individually behaving organism is made from cells and structures that are tightly interconnected by complex neuronal, circulatory, and regulatory networks and has a central brain that commands and produces behavior. The superorganism, on the other hand, is made up of individuals that may be interconnected by complex chemical interactions but that are rather autonomous and can hardly be compared to constituent cells. The essential difference, however, is that although an insect colony produces collective behavior, it does not have a central brain to command and control such behavior. On the contrary, studies on collective decision making in social insects show that collective behavioral patterns can arise from simple interactions between individuals, without any central control and without memory (Theraulaz et al., 2003).

From this point of view, the sophisticated cognitive capacities that honeybees exhibit in individual tests are not required for the close coordination of the social group. Differences in individual thresholds for reacting to environmental sensory stimuli seem to be a critical factor for the emergence of collective behaviors based on task partitioning. This may account, for instance, for the collective behavior of nest choice by a honeybee swarm. Group decision making in honeybee swarms has been studied (see Seeley and Vischer, 2004) to determine the rules underlying collective choice. It was found that the essence of a swarm's decision making relies on sensing a quorum (a sufficient number of scouts) at one of the nest sites rather than sensing a consensus (agreement of dancing scouts) at the swarm cluster. By this quorum-sensing hypothesis, a scout bee votes for a site by spending time at it. Somehow the scouts act and interact so that their numbers rise faster at superior sites, and somehow the bees at each site monitor their numbers there so that they know whether they have reached the threshold number (quorum) and can proceed to initiating the swarm's move to this site. Exactly

how scout bees sense a quorum remains an enigma (Seeley and Visscher, 2004). They may use visual, olfactory, or even tactile information to assess the number of fellow scouts at a site. But the complex migration pattern involving the coordinate displacement of thousands of bees does not require sophisticated mechanisms such as dance comparisons or verifying the reliability of information conveyed by a hive mate. In short, the bees appear to begin preparations for liftoff as soon as enough of the scout bees, but not all of them, have approved of one of the potential nest sites.

The interesting conclusion emerging from studies on social insect collective behavior is that individuals, who may be viewed as extremely sophisticated at the cognitive level when performing some individual tasks, appear to be automatons with limited cognitive capacities when performing collective tasks. This difference may seem puzzling and could be the result of cognitive richness being lost or at least temporally inhibited in a social context. However, a possible explanation is that in an individual and in a social context, the animal will adopt the behavioral strategies leading to adaptive solutions, either boosting or sacrificing what researchers would view as cognitive sophistication. Whenever simple behaviors can lead to adaptive solutions, they are adopted. When, on the contrary, cognitive abilities are required, they are used. The critical question in this context is therefore what determines the adoption of one or the other level of cognitive complexity? Which factors are responsible for the fact that an ant or a bee that can learn and memorize several cues while foraging, solve complex discriminations, and generate novel behaviors leading to adaptive solutions behaves like an automaton following a reduced set of repetitive patterns and simple rules in a social context? Which physiological changes, if any, determine the passage from one state to the other? Do social regulation pheromones intervene in the expression or inhibition of behavioral autonomy in a social context by acting on neurotransmitter levels in the insect nervous system? Do social pheromones determine changes in immediate early gene (IEG) expression in the brain affecting cognitive processing? So far, we have no answers to these questions, but they can be approached experimentally. Studying whether or not individual learning and memory are modified by exposure to social pheromones or by chemosensory cues within a group and whether or not biogenic amine and neurotransmitter levels and IEG expression are changed in the presence of a group of cospecifics are just some of the questions that need to be considered.

1.29.12   Conclusion

This chapter underlines the enormous richness of experience-dependent behavior in honeybees, its high flexibility, and the fact that it is possible to formalize and characterize in controlled laboratory protocols some forms of cognitive processing. Adopting rigorous definitions from elemental and nonelemental learning is useful to determine the extent to which honeybees can go beyond simple forms of associative learning. This type of experimental approach is possible, as illustrated by the numerous examples reviewed here, which have made it possible to appreciate the sophistication of cognitive processing in a honeybee, which, as most insects, was traditionally considered as being limited in terms of its cognitive capabilities.

Contrary to simple forms of associative learning for which specific neural circuits have been identified, more work is needed to relate complex problem solving to neural structures of the honeybee brain. The existing evidence points toward the mushroom bodies, a central structure in the insect brain that has been repeatedly associated with learning and memory capabilities (Menzel, 1999). It has been shown that some elemental discriminations can be achieved without the mushroom bodies (Malun et al., 2002), but this does not seem to be so obvious in the case of nonelemental discriminations. Although specific substrates or circuits for complex problem solving in the bee brain are still unknown, it is possible to be optimistic with respect to their future identification. In this case, what is delaying our understanding of cognitive brain processing is not the technical level but, rather, that up to now researchers have not dared to raise questions on complex cognitive processing in an insect.

What are the specific limitations of the bee brain when compared with larger brains, and what might the structural/functional basis be? To address this question, one would need to know more about its deficiencies, an area that has so far been investigated very little (but see Benard and Giurfa, 2004). Because of obvious limitation in space, we have not discussed the role of different forms of learning in natural contexts such as navigation and communication. These contexts also offer promising frameworks for the study of cognitive processing. Questions such as the nature of space representation and the flexibility of communication strategies are important to characterize the potential of the bee brain. They need to be related, when possible, to underlying neural circuits and structures, a task that has been impossible until now.

Studies on honeybee behavior allow researchers to be optimistic in view of these questions. Moreover, as learning in honeybees can be compared to that of vertebrates in many senses, the honeybee may serve as a model system for understanding intermediate levels of complexity of cognitive functions and their neural substrates.

References

Abel R, Rybak J, and Menzel R (2001) Structure and response patterns of olfactory interneurons in the honeybee, *Apis mellifera*. *J. Comp. Neurol.* 437: 363–383.

Alvarado MC and Bachevalier J (2005) Selective neurotoxic damage to the hippocampal formation impairs performance of the transverse patterning and location memory tasks in rhesus macaques. *Hippocampus* 15: 118–131.

Altman JS and Kien J (1987) Functional organization of the subesophageal ganglion in arthropods. In: Gupta AP (ed.) *Arthropod Brain: Its Evolution, Development, Structure and Function*, pp. 265–301. New York: Wiley.

Benard J and Giurfa M (2004) A test of transitive inferences in free-flying honeybees: Unsuccessful performance due to memory constraints. *Learn. Mem.* 11: 328–336.

Benard J, Stach S, and Giurfa M (2006) Categorization of visual stimuli in the honeybee *Apis mellifera*. *Anim. Cogn.* 9: 257–270.

Bitterman ME, Menzel R, Fietz A, and Schäfer S (1983) Classical conditioning of proboscis extension in honeybees (*Apis mellifera*). *J. Comp. Psychol.* 97: 107–119.

Blaser RE, Couvillon PA, and Bitterman ME (2004) Backward blocking in honeybees. *Q. J. Exp. Psychol. B* 57: 349–360.

Borlikova GG, Elbers NA, and Stephens DN (2006) Repeated withdrawal from ethanol spares contextual fear conditioning and spatial learning but impairs negative patterning and induces over-responding: Evidence for effect on frontal cortical but not hippocampal function? *Eur. J. Neurosci.* 24: 205–216.

Bucci DJ, Saddoris MP, and Burwell RD (2002) Contextual fear discrimination is impaired by damage to the postrhinal or perirhinal cortex. *Behav. Neurosci.* 116: 479–488.

Buffon (Leclerc GL) (1749a) *Histoire Naturelle Générale et Particulière: Avec la Description du Cabinet du Roy*, vol. II. Paris: Imprimerie Royale.

Buffon (Leclerc GL) (1749b) *Histoire Naturelle Générale et Particulière: Avec la Description du Cabinet du Roy*, vol. IV. Paris: Imprimerie Royale.

Chandra S and Smith BH (1998) An Analysis of synthetic processing of odor mixtures in the honeybee. *J. Exp. Biol.* 201: 3113–3121.

Cheng K and Wignall AE (2006) Honeybees (*Apis mellifera*) holding on to memories: Response competition causes retroactive interference effects. *Anim. Cogn.* 9: 141–150.

Collett TS, Graham P, and Durier V (2003) Route learning by insects. *Curr. Opin. Neurobiol.* 13: 718–725.

Couvillon PA, Arakaki L, and Bitterman ME (1997) Intramodal blocking in honeybees. *Anim. Learn. Behav.* 25: 277–282.

Couvillon PA and Bitterman ME (1980) Some phenomena of associative learning in honey bees. *J. Comp. Physiol. Psychol.* 94: 878–885.

Couvillon PA, Klosterhalfen S, and Bitterman ME (1983) Analysis of overshadowing in honeybees. *J. Comp. Psychol.* 97: 154–166.

De Brito Sanchez MG, Giurfa M, de Paula Mota TR, and Gauthier M (2005) Electrophysiological and behavioural characterization of gustatory responses to antennal 'bitter' taste in honeybees. *Eur. J. Neurosci.* 22: 3161–3170.

Deisig N, Lachnit H, Hellstern F, and Giurfa M (2001) Configural olfactory learning in honeybees: Negative and positive patterning discrimination. *Learn. Mem.* 8: 70–78.

Deisig N, Lachnit H, and Giurfa M (2002) The effect of similarity between elemental stimuli and compounds in olfactory patterning discriminations. *Learn. Mem.* 9: 112–121.

Deisig N, Lachnit H, Sandoz JC, Lober K, and Giurfa M (2003) A modified version of the unique cue theory accounts for olfactory compound processing in honeybees. *Learn. Mem.* 10: 199–208.

Deisig N, Giurfa M, Lachnit H, and Sandoz JC (2006) Neural representation of olfactory mixtures in the honeybee antennal lobe. *Eur. J. Neurosci.* 24: 1161–1174.

Delius JD, Jitsumori M, and Siemann M (2000) Stimulus equivalences through discrimination reversals. In: Heyes C and Huber L (eds.) *The Evolution of Cognition*, pp. 103–122. Cambridge, MA: MIT Press.

Faber T and Menzel R (2001) Visualizing mushroom body response to a conditioned odor in honeybees. *Naturwissenschaften* 88: 472–476.

Faber T, Joerges J, and Menzel R (1999) Associative learning modifies neural representations of odors in the insect brain. *Nat. Neurosci.* 2: 74–78.

Farina W, Gruter C, and Diaz PC (2005) Social learning of floral odours inside the honeybee hive. *Proc. Biol. Sci.* 272: 1923–1928.

Farina W, Gruter C, Acosta L, and Mc Cabe S (2007) Honeybees learn floral odors while receiving nectar from foragers within the hive. *Naturwissenschaften* 94: 55–60.

Farooqui T, Robinson K, Vaessin H, and Smith BH (2003) Modulation of early olfactory processing by an octopaminergic reinforcement pathway in the honeybee. *J. Neurosci.* 23: 5370–5380.

Fersen L von, Wynne CDL, and Delius JD (1990) Deductive reasoning in pigeons. *Naturwissenschaften* 77: 548–549.

Galizia CG and Menzel R (2000) Odour perception in honeybees: coding information in glomerular patterns. *Curr. Opin. Neurobiol.* 10: 504–510.

Galizia CG, Nägler K, Hölldobler B, and Menzel R. (1998) Odour coding is bilaterally symmetrical in the antennal lobes of honeybees (*Apis mellifera*). *Eur. J. Neurosci.* 10: 2964–2974.

Galizia CG, Sachse S, Rappert A, and Menzel R (1999) The glomerular code for odor representation is species specific in the honeybee *Apis mellifera*. *Nat. Neurosci.* 2: 473–478.

Gerber B and Ullrich J (1999) No evidence for olfactory blocking in honeybee classical conditioning. *J. Exp. Biol.* 202: 1839–1854.

Gil M and de Marco RJ (2005) Olfactory learning by means of trophallaxis in *Apis mellifera*. *J. Exp. Biol.* 208: 671–680.

Gil M and de Marco RJ (2006) *Apis mellifera* bees acquire long-term olfactory memories within the colony. *biol. Lett* 2: 98–100.

Giurfa M (2003) Cognitive neuroethology: Dissecting non-elemental learning in a honeybee brain. *Curr. Opin. Neurobiol.* 13: 726–735.

Giurfa M (2006) Associative learning: The instructive function of biogenic amines. *Curr. Biol.* 16: R892–R895.

Giurfa M and Lehrer M (2001) Honeybee vision and floral displays: From detection to close-up recognition. In: Chittka L and Thomson J (eds.) *Cognitive Ecology of Pollination*, pp. 61–82. Cambridge: Cambridge University Press.

Giurfa M and Menzel R (1997) Insect visual perception: Complex abilities of simple nervous systems. *Curr. Opin. Neurobiol.* 7: 505–513.

Giurfa M, Núñez JA, Chittka L, and Menzel R (1995) Colour preferences of flower-naive honeybees. *J. Comp. Physiol. A* 177: 247–259.

Giurfa M, Eichmann B, and Menzel R (1996) Symmetry perception in an insect. *Nature* 382: 458–461.

Giurfa M, Hammer M, Stach S, Stollhoff N, Muller-deisig N, and Mizyrycki C (1999) Pattern learning by honeybees: Conditioning procedure and recognition strategy. *Anim. Behav.* 57: 315–324.

Giurfa M, Zhang S, Jenett A, Menzel R, and Srinivasan MV (2001) The concepts of 'sameness' and 'difference' in an insect. *Nature* 410: 930–933.

Giurfa M, Schubert M, Reisenman C, Gerber B, and Lachnit H (2003) The effect of cumulative experience on the use of elemental and configural visual discrimination strategies in honeybees. *Behav. Brain Res.* 145: 161–169.

Grant V (1951) The fertilization of flowers. *Sci. Am.* 12: 1–6.

Guerrieri F, Lachnit H, Gerber B, and Giurfa M (2005a) Olfactory blocking and odorant similarity in the honeybee. *Learn. Mem.* 12: 86–95.

Guerrieri F, Schubert M, Sandoz JC, and Giurfa M (2005b) Perceptual and neural olfactory similarity in honeybees. *PLoS Biol.* 3: e60.

Hammer M (1993) An identified neuron mediates the unconditioned stimulus in associative olfactory learning in honeybees. *Nature* 366: 59–63.

Hammer M and Menzel R (1998) Multiple sites of associative odor learning as revealed by local brain microinjections of octopamine in honeybees. *Learn. Mem.* 5: 146–156.

Harnard S (1987) *Categorical Perception. The Groundwork of Cognition.* Cambridge: Cambridge University Press.

Hateren JH, Srinivasan MV, and Wait PB (1990) Pattern recognition in bees: Orientation discrimination. *J. Comp. Physiol. A* 197: 649–654.

Haupt SS (2004) Antennal sucrose perception in the honey bee (*Apis mellifera* L): Behaviour and electrophysiology. *J. Comp. Physiol. A* 190: 735–745.

Hellstern F, Wüstenberg D, and Hammer M (1995) Contextual learning in honeybees under laboratory conditions. In: Elsner N and Menzel R (eds.) *Learning and Memory. Proceedings of the 23rd Göttingen Neurobiology Conference*, p. 30. Stuttgart: Georg Thieme.

Hori S, Takeuchi H, Arikawa K, et al. (2006) Associative visual learning, color discrimination, and chromatic adaptation in the harnessed honeybee *Apis mellifera* L. *J. Comp. Physiol. A* 192: 691–700.

Hosler JS and Smith BH (2000) Blocking and the detection of odor components in blends. *J. Exp. Biol.* 203: 2797–2806.

Huber R (2005) Amines and motivated behaviors: A simpler systems approach to complex behavioral phenomena. *J. Comp. Physiol. A* 191: 231–239.

Jacobs LF (2006) From movement to transitivity: The role of hippocampal parallel maps in configural learning. *Rev. Neurosci.* 17: 99–109.

Joerges J, Küttner A, Galizia CG, and Menzel R (1997) Representation of odours and odour mixtures visualized in the honeybee brain. *Nature* 387: 285–288.

Kien J and Menzel R (1977) Chromatic properties of interneurons in the optic lobes of the bee. II. Narrow band and colour opponent neurons. *J. Comp. Physiol. A* 113: 35–53.

Komischke B, Sandoz JC, Lachnit H, and Giurfa M (2003) Non-elemental processing in olfactory discrimination tasks needs bilateral input in honeybees. *Behav. Brain Res.* 145: 135–143.

Komischke B, Sandoz JC, Malun D, and Giurfa M (2005) Partial unilateral lesions of the mushroom bodies affect olfactory learning in honeybees *Apis mellifera* L. *Eur. J. Neurosci.* 21: 477–485.

Kreissl S, Eichmüller S, Bicker G, Rapus J, and Eckert M (1994) Octopamine-like immunoreactivity in the brain and suboesophageal ganglion of the honeybee. *J. Comp. Neurol.* 348: 583–595.

Kuwabara M (1957) Bildung des bedingten Reflexes von Pavlovs Typus bei der Honigbiene, *Apis mellifica*. *J. Fac. Sci. Hokkaido Univ. Ser. VI. Zool.* 13: 458–464.

Lehrer M (1997) Honeybee's visual orientation at the feeding site. In: Lehrer M (ed.) *Orientation and Communication in Arthropods*, pp. 115–144. Basel: Birkhäuser.

Libersat F and Pflüger H-J (2004) Monoamines and the orchestration of behavior. *Bioscience* 54: 17–25.

Malun D (1998) Early development of mushroom bodies in the brain of the honeybee *Apis mellifera* as revealed by BrdU incorporation and ablation experiments. *Learn. Mem.* 5: 90–101.

Malun D, Giurfa M, Galizia CG, et al. (2002) Hydroxyurea-induced partial mushroom body ablation does not affect acquisition and retention of olfactory differential conditioning in honeybees. *J. Neurobiol.* 53: 343–360.

Menzel R (1967) Untersuchungen zum Erlernen von Spektralfarben durch die Honigbiene (*Apis mellifica*). *Z. Vergl. Physiol.* 56: 22–62.

Menzel R (1968) Das Gedächtnis der Honigbiene für Spektralfarben. IKurzzeitiges und langzeitiges Behalten. *Z. Vergl. Physiol.* 60: 82–102, 1968.

Menzel R (1985) Learning in honey bees in an ecological and behavioral context. In: Hölldobler B and Lindauer M (eds.) *Experimental Behavioral Ecology and Sociobiology*, pp. 55–74. Stuttgart: Fischer Verlag.

Menzel R (1999) Memory dynamics in the honeybee. *J. Comp. Physiol. A* 185: 323–340.

Menzel R (2001) Searching for the memory trace in a mini-brain, the honeybee. *Learn. Mem.* 8: 53–62.

Menzel R and Backhaus W (1991) Colour vision in insects. In: Gouras P (ed.) *Vision and Visual Dysfunction. The Perception of Colour*, pp. 262–288. London: MacMillan Press.

Menzel R and Erber J (1978) Learning and memory in bees. *Sci. Am.* 239: 80–87.

Menzel R and Giurfa M (2001) Cognitive architecture of a mini-brain: The honeybee. *Trends Cogn. Sci.* 5: 62–71.

Menzel R, Greggers U, and Hammer M (1993) Functional organization of appetitive learning and memory in a generalist pollinator, the honey bee. In: Papaj D and Lewis AC (eds.) *Insect Learning: Ecological and Evolutionary Perspectives*, pp. 79–125. New York: Chapman & Hall.

Menzel R, Manz G, Menzel R, and Greggers U (2001) Massed and spaced learning in honeybees: The role of CS, US, the intertrial interval, and the test interval. *Learn. Mem.* 8: 198–208.

Moses SN, Cole C, Driscoll I, and Ryan J (2005) Differential contributions of hippocampus, amygdala and perirhinal cortex to recognition of novel objects, contextual stimuli and stimulus relationships. *Brain Res. Bull.* 67: 62–76.

Müller D, Gerber B, Hammer M, and Menzel R (2000) Sensory preconditioning in honeybees. *J. Exp. Biol.* 203: 1351–1356.

Müller D, Abel R, Brandt R, Zöckler M, and Menzel R (2002) Differential parallel processing of olfactory information in the honeybee, *Apis mellifera* L. *J. Comp. Physiol. A* 188: 359–370.

Núñez JA (1982) Honeybee foraging strategies at a food source in relation to its distance from the hive and the rate of sugar flow. *J. Apicult. Res.* 21: 139–150.

Núñez JA, Almeida L, Balderrama N, and Giurfa M (1997) Alarm pheromone induces stress analgesia via an opioid system in the honeybee. *Physiol. Behav.* 63: 75–80.

O'Reilly RC and Rudy JW (2001) Conjunctive representations in learning and memory: Principles of cortical and hippocampal function. *Psychol. Rev.* 108: 311–345.

Pavlov IP (1927) *Lectures on Conditioned Reflexes.* New York: International Publishers.

Pearce JM (1994) Similarity and discrimination: A selective review and a connectionist model. *Psychol. Rev.* 101: 587–607.

Peele P, Ditzen M, Menzel R, and Galizia G (2006) Appetitive odor learning does not change olfactory coding in a subpopulation of honeybee antennal lobe neurons. *J. Comp. Physiol. A* 192: 1083–1103.

Rescorla RA and Wagner AR (1972) A theory of Pavlovian conditioning: variations in the effectiveness of reinforcement and nonreinforcement. In: Black AH and Prokasy WF (eds.) *Classical Conditioning II*, pp. 64–99. New York: Appleton-Century-Crofts.

Riemensperger T, Völler T, Stock P, Buchner E, and Fiala A (2005) Punishment prediction by dopaminergic neurons in *Drosophila*. *Curr. Biol.* 15: 1953–1960.

Robertson I (2001) *Problem Solving.* Hove, UK: Psychology Press.

Rudy JW and Sutherland RJ (1992) Configural and elemental associations and the memory coherence problem. *J. Cogn. Neurosci.* 4: 208–216.

Rudy JW and Sutherland RJ (1995) Configural association theory and the hippocampal formation: An appraisal and reconfiguration. *Hippocampus* 5: 375–389.

Sandoz JC, Galizia CG, and Menal R (2003) Side-specific olfactory conditioning leads to more specific odor representations between sides but not within sides in the honeybee antennal lobes. *Neuroscience* 120: 1137–1148.

Sandoz JC and Menzel R (2001) Side-specificity of olfactory learning in the honeybee: Generalization between odors and sides. *Learn. Mem.* 8: 286–294.

Scheiner R, Weiß A, Malun D, and Erber J (2001) Learning in honey bees with brain lesions: How partial mushroom-body ablations affect sucrose responsiveness and tactile antennal learning. *Anim. Cogn.* 4: 227–235.

Schroll C, Riemensperger T, Bucher D, et al. (2006) Light-induced activation of distinct modulatory neurons substitutes for appetitive or aversive reinforcement during associative learning in larval *Drosophila*. *Curr. Biol.* 16: 1741–1747.

Schroter U, Malun D, and Menzel R (2006) Innervation pattern of suboesophageal ventral unpaired median neurones in the honeybee brain. *Cell Tissue Res.* 327: 647–667.

Schubert M, Francucci S, Lachnit H, and Giurfa M (2005) Nonelemental visual learning in honeybees. *Anim. Behav.* 64: 175–184.

Schultz W and Dickinson A (2000) Neuronal coding of prediction errors. *Ann. Rev. Neurosci.* 23: 473–500.

Schwaerzel M, Monastirioti M, Scholz H, Friggi-Grelin F, Birman S, and Heisenberg M (2003) Dopamine and octopamine differentiate between aversive and appetitive olfactory memories in *Drosophila*. *J. Neurosci.* 23: 10495–10502.

Seeley TD (1989) The honey bee colony as a superorganism. *Am. Sci.* 77: 546–553.

Seeley TD (1995) *The Wisdom of the Hive – The Social Physiology of Honey Bee Colonies.* London: Harvard University Press.

Seeley TD and Visscher K (2004) Quorum sensing during nest site selection by honeybee swarms. *Behav. Ecol. Sociobiol.* 56: 594–601.

Skinner BF (1938) *The Behavior of Organisms.* New York: Appleton.

Smith BH (1998) Analysis of interaction in binary odorant mixtures. *Physiol. Behav.* 65: 397–407.

Smith BH and Cobey S (1994) The olfactory memory of the honeybee *Apis mellifera*. II. Blocking between odorants in binary mixtures. *J. Exp. Biol.* 195: 91–108.

Southwick EE (1983) The honey bee cluster as a homeothermic superorganism. *Comp. Biochem. Physiol.* 75: 641–645.

Srinivasan MV (1994) Pattern recognition in the honeybee: Recent progress. *J. Insect Physiol.* 40: 183–194.

Srinivasan MV and Zhang SW (1997) Visual control of honeybee flight. In: Lehrer M (ed.) *Orientation and Communication in Arthropods*, pp. 95–114. Basel: Birkhäuser.

Srinivasan MV, Poteser M, and Kral K (1999) Motion detection in insect orientation and navigation. *Vision Res.* 39: 2749–2766.

Stach S and Giurfa M (2005) The influence of training length on generalization of visual feature assemblies in honeybees. *Behav. Brain Res.* 161: 8–17.

Stach S, Benard J, and Giurfa M (2004) Local-feature assembling in visual pattern recognition and generalization in honeybees. *Nature* 429: 758–761.

Szyszka P, Ditzen M, Galkin A, Galizia G, and Menzel R (2005) Sparsening and temporal sharpening of olfactory representations in the honeybee mushroom bodies. *J. Neurophysiol.* 94: 3303–3313.

Takeda K (1961) Classical conditioned response in the honey bee. *J. Insect Physiol.* 6: 168–179.

Terrace HS and McGonigle B (1994) Memory and representation of serial order by children, monkeys and pigeons. *Curr. Dir. Psychol. Sci.* 3: 180–185.

Theraulaz G, Gautrais J, Camazine S, and Deneubourg JL (2003) The formation of spatial patterns in social insects: From simple behaviours to complex structures. *Phil. Trans. R. Soc. Lond. A* 361: 1263–1282.

Troje F, Huber L, Loidolt M, Aust U, and Fieder M (1999) Categorical learning in pigeons: The role of texture and shape in complex static stimuli. *Vis. Res.* 39: 353–366.

Tully T and Quinn WG (1985) Classical conditioning and retention in normal and mutant *Drosophila melanogaster*. *J. Comp. Physiol. Psychol.* 156: 263–277.

Unoki S, Matsumoto Y, and Mizunami M (2005) Participation of octopaminergic reward system and dopaminergic punishment system in insect olfactory learning revealed by pharmacological study. *Eur. J. Neurosci.* 22: 1409–1416.

Unoki S, Matsumoto Y, and Mizunami M (2006) Roles of octopaminergic and dopaminergic neurons in mediating reward and punishment signals in insect visual learning. *Eur. J. Neurosci.* 24: 2031–2038.

Vareschi E (1971) Duftunterscheidung bei der Honigbiene – Einzelzell-Ableitungen und Verhaltensreaktionen. *Z. Vergl. Physiol.* 75: 143–173.

Vergoz V, Roussel E, Sandoz JC, and Giurfa M (2007a) Aversive learning in honeybees revealed by the olfactory conditioning of the sting extension reflex. *PLoS ONE* Mar 14 2: e288.

Vergoz V, Schreurs HA, and Merur A (2007b) Queen pheromone blocks aversive learning in young worker bees. *Science* 317: 384–386.

Von Frisch K (1914) Der Farbensinn und Formensinn der Biene. *Zool. Jb. Physiol.* 37: 1–238.

Von Frisch K (1962) Dialects in the language of the bees. *Sci. Am.* 207: 78–87.

Von Frisch K (1967) *The Dance Language and Orientation of Bees.* Cambridge, MA: Belknap Press.

Wehner R (1981) Spatial vision in arthropods. In: Autrum HJ (ed.) *Handbook of Sensory Physiology VIc*, pp. 287–616. Berlin: Springer.

Whitehead AT (1978) Electrophysiological response of honey bee labial palp contact chemoreceptors to sugars and electrolytes. *Physiol. Entomol.* 3: 241–248.

Whitehead AT and Larsen JR (1976) Electrophysiological responses of galeal contact chemoreceptors of *Apis mellifera* to selected sugars and electrolytes. *J. Insect Physiol.* 22: 1609–1616.

Whitlow JW and Wagner AR (1972) Negative patterning in classical conditioning: Summation of response tendencies to isolable and configural components. *Psychon. Sci.* 27: 299–301.

Wittstock S and Menzel R (1994) Color learning and memory in honey bees are not affected by protein synthesis inhibition. *Behav. Neural Biol.* 62: 224–229.

Wüstenberg D, Gerber B, and Menzel R (1998) Long- but not medium-term retention of olfactory memories in honeybees is impaired by actinomycin D and anisomycin. *Eur. J. Neurosci.* 10: 2742–2745.

Yang EC and Maddess T (1997) Orientation-sensitive neurons in the brain of the honey bee (*Apis mellifera*) *J. Insect. Physiol.* 43: 329–336.

Yang EC, Lin HC, and Hung YS (2004) Patterns of chromatic information processing in the lobula of the honeybee, *Apis mellifera* L. *J. Insect Physiol.* 50: 913–925.

Zentall TR, Galizio M, and Critchfield TS (2002) Categorization, concept learning and behavior analysis: An introduction. *J. Exp. Anal. Behav.* 78: 237–248.

Zhang SW, Srinivasan MV, Zhu H, and Wong J (2004) Grouping of visual objects by honeybees. *J. Exp. Biol.* 207: 3289–3298.

Zhang S, Bock F, Si A, Tautz J, and Srinivasan M (2005) Visual working memory in decision making by honey bees. *Proc. Natl. Acad. Sci. USA* 102: 5250–5255.

1.30 Behavioral and Circuit Analysis of Learning and Memory in Mollusks

P. R. Benjamin and G. Kemenes, University of Sussex, East Sussex, UK

1.30.1 Introduction

The major advantage of using gastropod mollusks for investigating neural mechanisms underlying learning and memory is that behavioral studies can be linked to circuit analysis by taking advantage of the ability to identify individual neurons with known electrical properties and synaptic connectivity (Benjamin et al., 2005). Simple forms of associative learning such as classical and operant conditioning and nonassociative forms such as habituation and sensitization have been extensively investigated. The use of a wide variety of learning paradigms in a number of different gastropod species allows comparisons to be made of underlying neural mechanisms involved in memory formation in different types of learning (e.g., associative versus nonassociative, classical versus operant

conditioning). Important progress has been made in understanding the mechanisms of synaptic plasticity in gastropod memory formation, but nonsynaptic (cellular) mechanisms such as changes in excitability also have been increasingly recognized as contributing to memory formation. These data on gastropod molluscs are of general importance in understanding the mechanisms of memory formation in the brain.

1.30.2 Model Circuits

A brief review of the four molluscan circuits most useful for learning and memory studies will be given next because the synaptic and cellular changes that underlie memory formation are located within these circuits. Two general types of circuit will be described: defensive reflexes in *Aplysia* and *Hermissenda* and the more complex central pattern generator (CPG)-mediated feeding and respiratory circuits of *Lymnaea*.

1.30.2.1 *Aplysia* Gill-Siphon Defensive Withdrawal Reflex

A brief tactile stimulus applied to the siphon of *Aplysia* elicits gill and siphon withdrawal into the protective mantle cavity (**Figure 1(ai)**). The withdrawal responses in these two organs are mediated by identified sensory and motor neurons located in the abdominal ganglia (**Figure 1(aii)**), and because the strength of these responses is modified by experience, they have been extensively used to study the mechanisms underlying both associative and nonassociative forms of learning (Hawkins et al., 2006). Early studies of habituation focused on gill withdrawal plasticity, but the ease of identifying siphon responses in the live animal and the identification of a distinct set of siphon motor neurons (the LFS cells, **Figure 1(aii)**) has meant that the siphon circuit has been used mainly for more recent studies of sensitization and classical conditioning (Antonov et al., 2003). A variety of centrally located siphon sensory neurons and excitatory and inhibitory interneurons provide synaptic input to the LFS motor neurons but the direct LE mechanosensory to LFS monosynaptic pathway (**Figure 1(aii)**) has been the main focus of attention for learning studies, although sensorimotor synapses in the pleural and pedal ganglia also have been used. Monosynaptic excitatory connections from the LE to LFS motor neurons have been estimated to mediate about one-third of the siphon reflex response that corresponds to siphon flaring in the intact animal. The remainder of the response is mediated by peripheral motor neurons (Hawkins et al., 2006).

For habituation studies, sequences of weak touch stimuli are applied to the siphon, and the strength of the gill/siphon withdrawal reflex is measured either mechanically or by using a photocell to record displacement. Electrical shocks are applied to the tail or neck for sensitization of the siphon reflex, and repeated shocks (unconditioned stimulus, US) are paired with siphon touch (conditioned stimulus, CS) for behavioral studies of aversive classical conditioning. The detailed pathway by which the electrical stimuli influence the gill-siphon circuitry is not known for certain, although it may recruit the serotonergic cerebral CB1 neurons that have projections to the abdominal ganglion (Mackey et al., 1989).

1.30.2.2 *Hermissenda* Statocyst-Mediated Behaviors

High-speed rotation or orbital shaking elicits two types of behavioral response in *Hermissenda*: foot shortening (**Figure 1(bi)**) and inhibition of the normally positive phototactic response, indicated by a reduced forward locomotion toward light (Crow, 2004). The type of stimuli used to elicit this response in the laboratory mimics the natural response to mechanical turbulence caused by wave action that results in the animal clinging to the substrate for protection. The sensory response is mediated by a pair of gravity detector organs called the statocysts that have hair cell receptors analogous in function to the vestibular hair cells of vertebrates. In *Hermissenda*, depolarization of the hair cells by rotation generates responses in interneurons in the central ganglia that excite foot motor neurons responsible for foot shortening and inhibit ciliary motor neurons to inhibit forward locomotion (**Figure 1(bii)**). The interneurons involved in the two behavioral responses are different, giving independent pathways for the control of the two unconditioned responses.

Rotation of the body is used as the aversive US in behavioral associative conditioning studies, and a light flash is used as the CS. Repeated pairing of these two stimuli over several days leads to a reduction of the phototactic response to the CS and foot shortening similar to the previously described response to the US. Photoreceptors in the eye respond to the light CS, and these cells have a variety of excitatory and inhibitory synaptic connections with sensory receptors and interneurons of the US statocyst pathway. However, these synaptic connections are ineffective in eliciting unconditioned responses in naive animals (Crow, 2004).

1.30.2.3 *Lymnaea* Feeding

Feeding in *Lymnaea* consists of a sequence of repetitive movements called rasps. During each rasp, the mouth opens (**Figure 1(ci)**), and a toothed radula is scraped forward over the food substrate (protraction phase). Food is then lifted into the mouth (retraction phase), which closes while the food is being swallowed (swallow phase), and the sequence is repeated. Rhythmic movements of the feeding muscles are driven by a network of motor neurons (B1 to B10) that, in turn, are driven by synaptic inputs from a feeding CPG network of interneurons (**Figure 1(cii)**). Each phase of the feeding rhythm is generated by one of three main types of CPG interneurons, N1 (protraction), N2 (retraction), N3 (swallow), providing sequences of excitatory and inhibitory synaptic inputs to motor neurons active in different phases of the feeding rhythm (Benjamin and Elliott, 1989). CPG-driven rhythmic electrical activity can be recorded in the feeding network even in the absence of feeding muscles, and this is called fictive feeding. Activity in the motor neurons and CPG neurons is modulated by identified higher-order interneurons (**Figure 1(cii)**), such as the cerebral giant cells (CGCs) and cerebral ventral 1 cells (CV1s). These higher-order neurons have been the major focus of learning and memory studies (Benjamin et al., 2000). The CGCs act as gating neurons in the feeding circuit. Increased CGC spiking activity during feeding facilitates feeding responses to food. The CV1 cells are members of a larger population of neurons called the cerebrobuccal interneurons (CBIs) (**Figure 1(cii)**) that are commandlike neurons involved in the activation of feeding.

Sucrose is an effective chemical stimulus for feeding and is therefore used as the US for reward conditioning. At the cellular level, sucrose applied to the lips in semi-intact preparations induces fictive feeding in motor neurons and interneurons of the feeding network. The CPG neurons are activated in the sucrose-driven fictive feeding rhythm, along with the modulatory CGC and CV1 cells.

The CS used for reward conditioning in *Lymnaea* is either a chemical (amyl acetate) or a tactile stimulus (a gentle brushstroke applied to the lips). The chemical CS was previously thought to have no effect on feeding ('neutral stimulus'), either at the behavioral or electrophysiological levels, but has recently been shown to have stimulatory or inhibitory effects in naive animals, depending on concentration (Straub et al., 2006). Touch to the lips, monitored either at the behavioral or the electrophysiological level, cannot initiate or maintain feeding, but nevertheless touch produced a complex sequence of inhibitory and excitatory synaptic inputs on all neurons of the feeding network (Staras et al., 1999b).

1.30.2.4 *Lymnaea* Respiration

The aquatic pulmonate snail *Lymnaea* can breathe either through the skin or through a simple lung. As

their name implies, *Lymnaea stagnalis* populations often live in stagnant water, and when the environment becomes hypoxic, the snails float to the surface and perform rhythmic opening and closing movements of their pulmonary opening, the pneumostome (**Figure 1(di)**). This aerial respiration behavior is controlled by a respiratory CPG, the three main components of which are the right pedal dorsal 1 (RPeD1), input 3 (IP3), and visceral dorsal 4 (VD4) interneurons (**Figure 1(dii)**). These components provide synaptic inputs to identified motor neurons (I and J, opener, and K, closer) innervating pneumostome opener and closer muscles (**Figure 1(dii)**). The chemosensory stimulus (hypoxia) that triggers pneumostome opening first activates sensory cells in the pneumostome–osphradial area, which in turn provides excitatory afferent inputs to RPeD1. Through its synaptic connections with the other members of the CPG network, activation of RPeD1 initiates CPG activity, which underlies the respiratory rhythm. Tactile stimulation of the pneumostome area evokes pneumostome closure and stops aerial respiratory behavior. This type of tactile stimulation is used as the positive punishment in behavioral operant conditioning studies (Lukowiak et al., 2003).

1.30.3 Nonassociative Learning: Habituation and Sensitization in the Gill-Siphon Withdrawal Reflex

The gill-siphon withdrawal reflex of *Aplysia* shows both habituation and sensitization (Kandel, 1976). When a weak touch (usually by a calibrated water jet) is applied repeatedly to the siphon or adjacent mantle skin at intervals of between 30 s and 3 min, the gill withdrawal response habituates (decrements) to about 30% of control values after 10–15 trials. This short-term habituation lasts for several hours, but if these trials (10 per day) are repeated over 4 days then a long-term habituation of the gill withdrawal response is induced that lasts for up to 3 weeks. If, prior to touch, a single strong noxious stimulus, such as an electric shock, is applied to the tail or neck, the subsequent touch-evoked response is enhanced or sensitized for a few hours. Long-term sensitization can be induced by the application of multiple shocks. Applying four shocks a day to the head for 4 days significantly increased the duration of withdrawal so that it was greater than in controls up to 1 week after training. Both of these nonassociative phenomena are central processes that involve changes in synaptic strength at the sensory level to motor synapses that mediate the normal gill-siphon withdrawal reflex.

1.30.3.1   Habituation

Behavioral habituation was found to be paralleled by suppression of neurotransmitter release from the presynaptic terminals of the touch-sensitive

(ai) *Aplysia* defensive reflexes

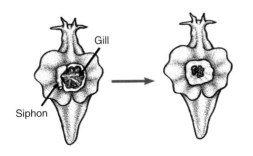

(aii) *Aplysia* siphon and gill withdrawal networks

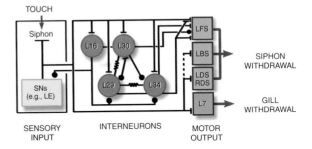

(bi) *Hermissenda* defensive reflexes

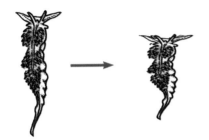

(bii) *Hermissenda* foot contraction and ciliary inhibition networks

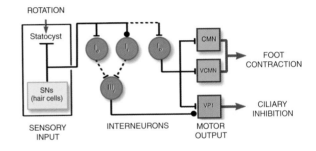

(ci) *Lymnaea* feeding behavior

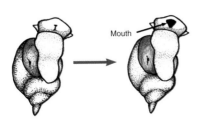

(cii) *Lymnaea* feeding network

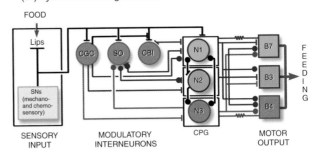

(di) *Lymnaea* aerial respiration

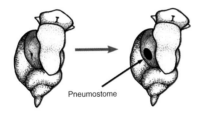

(dii) *Lymnaea* respiratory network

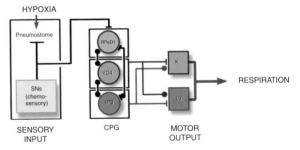

mechanosensory neurons resulting in homosynaptic depression (HSD). A consequent reduction in the size of the motor neuron excitatory postsynaptic potential (EPSP) is followed by a reduction in the activation of the motor neurons, which consequently fires less. Both calcium-dependent and -independent mechanisms have been suggested to underlie HSD, the cellular mechanism of habituation.

There appears to be a consensus that short-term habituation (STH) involved purely presynaptic mechanisms (Armitage and Siegelbaum, 1998; Ezzeddine and Glanzman, 2003), but recent work by Ezzeddine and Glanzman (2003) suggests that long-term habituation (LTH) may involve postsynaptic mechanisms as well. In a behavioral preparation, these authors showed that induction of LTH depended on the activation of specific types of glutamate receptors presumed to be located on the postsynaptic motor neurons. LTH was blocked either in the presence of the *N*-methyl-D-aspartate (NMDA) antagonist 2-amino-5-phosphonopentanoic acid (APV) or the alpha-amino-3-hydroxy-5-methyl-4-isoxazole propionic acid (AMPA) antagonist 6,7-dinitroquinoxaline-2,3-dione (DNQX) (Ezzeddine and Glanzman, 2003). DNQX had no effects on STH, as shown in earlier experiments (Armitage and Siegelbaum, 1998).

1.30.3.2 Sensitization

Sensitizing stimuli have the opposite effect of habituation, causing an increase in transmitter release (reviewed in Carew and Sahley, 1986). Sensitizing stimuli cause the release of the transmitter serotonin (5-hydroxytryptamine, 5-HT) from facilitatory interneurons onto the sensory neuron terminals of the mechanosensory neurons, and this transmitter acts presynaptically to facilitate synaptic transmission at the sensorimotor junction. This causes the motor neurons to fire more after sensitization, thereby increasing the strength of the withdrawal reflex. This type of heterosynaptic facilitation can be mimicked in reduced preparations and in a simplified cell culture system if tail shock is replaced by brief applications of 5-HT to the sensory neurons. The mechanisms underlying presynaptic facilitation involve two types of synaptic mechanisms that result in an increase in transmitter release (reviewed in Hawkins et al., 2006). The first synaptic mechanism involves an increase in the duration of the spike in the sensory neuron. A second synaptic mechanism is independent of spike broadening and is thought to involve vesicle mobilization. A nonsynaptic mechanism increases the excitability of the sensory neurons, making it more likely that the

Figure 1 Molluscan behaviors and underlying neural circuitries most widely used in studies of the cellular mechanisms of learning and memory. (ai) Touch-evoked withdrawal reflex of the gill and siphon in *Aplysia californica* (drawing by Dr. I. Kemenes). (aii) Sensory neurons (SNs, yellow square) activated by touch to the siphon provide direct excitatory synaptic inputs to motor neurons innervating the gill and siphon (green and blue squares, respectively). In addition, there are indirect excitatory and inhibitory connections from the sensory to the motor neurons, which are mediated by a set of interneurons (orange circles) interconnected by both chemical and electrical synapses. Touch can normally only evoke a weak contraction of the siphon and gill, but the reflex becomes stronger after sensitization and classical conditioning (see **Figure 2**). (bi) Foot contraction and ciliary inhibition evoked by rotation in *Hermissenda crassicornis* (drawing by Dr. I. Kemenes). (bii) Sensory cells activated by rotation provide polysynaptic excitatory and inhibitory inputs to motor neurons responsible for foot contraction (green squares) and ciliary inhibition (blue square). Dashed lines represent polysynaptic connections with potential interneurons not yet identified. When a visual input is repeatedly paired with rotation, it will become effective in evoking both foot contraction and ciliary inhibition (see **Figure 3**). (ci) Feeding behavior in *Lymnaea stagnalis* (drawing by Dr. I. Kemenes). (cii) Chemosensory neurons located in the lip structures detect the presence of food or chemostimulants, such as sucrose. Excitatory inputs from the sensory pathways are distributed in parallel to modulatory interneurons (orange circles) and also to central pattern generators (CPG) neurons (green, blue, and pink circles). The cerebral giant cells (CGCs) may presynaptically modulate certain types of chemosensory inputs to the cerebrobuccal interneurons (CBIs) (see **Figure 4**). The complex synaptic connectivity between the modulatory and N1 interneurons leads to activation of the whole CPG, with the protraction (N1), rasp (N2), and swallow (N3) phases of the feeding cycle following in sequence due to the synaptic connectivity within the CPG and their intrinsic properties. Several subtypes of each of the N cells have been characterized, but because of the complexity of their synaptic connections with modulatory interneurons and motor neurons, only a generalized representative of each N-type is shown. The rhythmic pattern generated by the CPG drives protraction, rasp, and swallow phase motor neurons, such as B7 (green squares), B3 (blue squares), and B4 (pink squares), leading to sequences of muscular activity and feeding movements executed by the mouth (shown in drawing), the radula, and the buccal mass. Reward classical conditioning leads to an enhanced activation of the feeding network by tactile or chemically (see **Figure 4**) conditioned stimuli. (di) Hypoxia-evoked opening of the pneumostome in *Lymnaea stagnalis* (drawing by Dr. I. Kemenes). (dii) The motor neurons are excited or inhibited by a three-neuron CPG network activated by chemosensory inputs. Operant conditioning leads to the suppression of pneumostome opening and aerial respiration (see text). Dots indicate inhibitory chemical synapses, bars excitatory chemical synaptic connections, and resistor symbols electrotonic (electrical) synapses.

sensory neurons will respond to siphon touch after sensitization. These types of presynaptic mechanisms are produced by single brief applications of 5-HT (1 min) or single shocks to the tail, and they are believed to underlie behavioral short-term sensitization or short-term facilitation (STF) of synaptic transmission seen in reduced preparations and in cell culture.

Long term-facilitation (LTF) of synaptic responses in culture is induced by repeated and spaced application of 5-HT and lasts for as long as the cells survive in culture. Its behavioral equivalent, long-term sensitization, lasting for days or weeks, requires repetitive sensitizing stimuli lasting for 1 to 1.5 h. Recently, an intermediate-term memory (ITM) for sensitization and correlated intermediate-term synaptic facilitation (ITF) have been identified, lasting for up to 85 minutes (Ghirardi et al., 1995; Sutton and Carew, 2000).

There is a consensus that short-term sensitization and STF are due to purely presynaptic mechanisms (Glanzman, 2006; Hawkins et al., 2006) and until recently this was also thought to be the case for other forms of sensitization, such as ITM. However, important work by the Glanzman laboratory in culture and in reduced preparations (e.g., Lin and Glanzman, 1994; Li et al., 2005) and now confirmed by simultaneous behavioral and electrophysiological investigations by Antonov et al. in a more intact preparation (reviewed in Hawkins et al., 2006) have clearly shown that postsynaptic mechanisms are also involved in ITF.

A 10-minute application of serotonin in culture induced synaptic ITF, after a delay of about 5 minutes, and facilitated synaptic transmission for at least 50 minutes without decrement (reviewed in Glanzman, 2006). This ITF induced by serotonin application was found to depend on the activation of AMPA-like glutamate receptors in the motor neurons because it was blocked by DNQX. Prior injection of exocytotic inhibitors into the motor neurons blocked this facilitation, suggesting that 5-HT might stimulate the insertion of AMPA receptors into the motor neuron membrane. This trafficking of AMPA receptors is known to involve calcium/cal-modulin-dependent protein kinase II (CaMKII) in vertebrate systems, so it is interesting that injecting inhibitors of this kinase into *Aplysia* motor neurons reduced synaptic ITF (see Hawkins et al., 2006). ITF also depends on the elevation of calcium levels in the motor neurons. Injection of BAPTA (1,2-bis(o-aminophenoxy)ethane-N,N,N′,N′-tetra-acetic acid), a rapid chelator of intracellular calcium,

blocked the delayed facilitation of the sensorimotor synapse *in vitro* (Li et al., 2005), induced by a 10-min application of 5-HT. 5-HT causes a release of intracellular calcium, mediated by both IP3 and ryanodine receptors (Li et al., 2005). ITF produced by 10-min applications of 5-HT also involves presynaptic mechanisms because injection of protein kinase C (PKC) inhibitors into the sensory neurons in culture also reduces the facilitatory effects of 5-HT on synaptic transmission (Hawkins et al., 2006).

In summary, ITF of sensorimotor synapses, a mechanism thought to underlie behavioral sensitization, involves both presynaptic (PKC-dependent) and postsynaptic (calcium- and CaMKII-dependent) mechanisms with CaMKII suggested to be linked to insertion of AMPA receptors in the postsynaptic membrane. Short-term sensitization involves only presynaptic mechanisms, mainly involving a cyclic adenosine monophosphate (cAMP)-dependent protein kinase A (PKA) pathway.

Long-term sensitization has also been investigated for changes in postsynaptic mechanisms. In a pioneering study, Cleary et al. (1998) showed that the biophysical properties of tail motor neurons were changed after behavioral long-term sensitization, resulting in hyperpolarization of the resting membrane potential and a decrease in spike threshold. This suggests that these postsynaptic neurons are a locus for memory and provides evidence for the importance of postsynaptic mechanisms in both long-term and intermediate-term sensitization (*See* Chapters 4.03 and 4.38 for additional details on the molecular mechanisms of short-, intermediate-, and long-term sensitization).

1.30.4 Associative Learning

1.30.4.1 Aversive Classical Conditioning of the *Aplysia* Gill-Siphon Withdrawal Reflex

Carew and colleagues (see Carew and Sahley, 1986) showed that the gill and siphon withdrawal reflex is subject to aversive classical conditioning as well as habituation and sensitization. In their associative conditioning paradigm, they paired a weak tactile stimulus (the CS) to the siphon with a strong electric shock to the tail (the US). After 15 trials, the CS came to elicit a stronger gill withdrawal than controls; the effect lasted for several days. Later they showed that differential classical conditioning also worked. A weak tactile stimulus applied to the siphon or mantle shelf was either paired with shock (CS+) or not paired (CS−) in the same animal. Differences between the effects on gill withdrawal at the two sites were enhanced, even after a single trial. Cellular analysis of differential conditioning, using a reduced preparation, showed that the mechanism underlying classical conditioning of the gill withdrawal response was the elaboration of presynaptic facilitation that was previously shown to underlie sensitization, except that the effect of the pairing of CS and US produced an even greater facilitation of the withdrawal response. This effect was called activity-dependent presynaptic facilitation (ADPF) (Hawkins et al., 1983). Evidence for this mechanism was obtained in a reduced preparation where the effects of touch were mimicked by stimulation of two different sensory neurons that made excitatory synaptic connections with siphonal motor neurons. Differential conditioning produced a significantly greater enhancement of the sensorimotor synapse if weak sensory neuron spike activation (by current injection) was followed by the tail shock (CS+) than if the sensory neuron stimulation was unpaired (CS−) or if shock occurred alone (sensitization). This result supported the notion of ADPF because of its dependence on temporal pairing. Like sensitization, this mechanism was shown to be presynaptic and could also be mimicked by the application of serotonin. With a larger number of pairings, a longer-term form of synaptic plasticity is induced

underpinned by changes in gene regulation and synaptic remodeling (*See* Chapter 4.10).

As was the case with sensitization, the early model for aversive classical conditioning was entirely presynaptic, but the discovery that sensorimotor synapses in culture or in reduced preparations exhibit NMDA-dependent long-term potentiation (LTP) (Glanzman, 1995; Roberts and Glanzman, 2003) led to the now generally accepted hypothesis that associative learning involves postsynaptic processes utilizing Hebbian-type LTP as well as presynaptic ADPF (**Figure 2(a)**). Use of the more intact preparation by Antonov et al. (2003) allowed classical conditioning of the behavioral siphonal withdrawal reflex to be correlated with synaptic plasticity. Pairing siphonal touch with tail shock induced a parallel associative enhancement of siphonal withdrawal and synaptic strength. Application of the NMDA receptor blocker APV to the ganglion or injection of the calcium chelator BAPTA into the siphonal motor neurons blocked conditioning, providing direct evidence that Hebbian LTP is part of the mechanism for behavioral classical conditioning. To compare the role of pre- and postsynaptic mechanisms in synaptic plasticity, Antonov et al. (2003) injected the peptide inhibitor of PKA (PKAi) into LE sensory neurons and BAPTA into LFS siphonal motor neurons. Both procedures reduced the pairing specific facilitation of

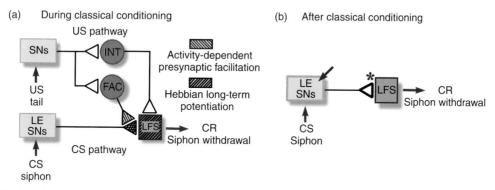

Figure 2 Aversive classical conditioning of the siphon withdrawal reflex in *Aplysia*. (a) During aversive classical conditioning, the conditioned stimulus (CS, touch to the siphon) weakly activates LE sensory neurons (SNs), which make monosynaptic connections onto LFS motor neurons. The unconditioned stimulus (US, electric shock to the tail) strongly activates tail sensory neurons. These sensory neurons excite both facilitatory interneurons (FAC) that produce presynaptic facilitation at the LE-to-LFS synapse and other types of interneurons (INT) that postsynaptically excite the LFS motor neurons. Thus, both the sensory neurons and the motor neurons are sites of CS and US pathway convergence and can act as coincidence detectors. The shading indicates neuronal elements that must be activated conjointly for the induction of either activity-dependent presynaptic facilitation (red) or Hebbian LTP (black) at the LE-LFS synapses (from Antonov I, Antonova I, Kandel ER, and Hawkins RD (2003) Activity-dependent presynaptic facilitation and hebbian LTP are both required and interact during classical conditioning in *Aplysia*. *Neuron* 37: 135–147; used with permission from Elsevier). (b) After aversive classical conditioning the synaptic connections of the LE sensory neurons with the LFS motor neurons are strengthened (synaptic plasticity, green asterisk and bold outline) and the excitability of the LE sensory neurons is increased (cellular plasticity, green arrow and bold outline). These changes lead to an increased siphon withdrawal response to the touch CS.

postsynaptic potentials (PSPs) in the motor neurons during conditioning. Thus pre- and postsynaptic mechanisms appear to be contributing (**Figure 2(a)**) to the plastic changes in synaptic strength between the sensory neurons and the motor neurons (**Figure 2(b)**). There also appears to be a retrograde signal involved, as well as orthograde, because injecting BAPTA into the motor neurons blocks the changes in the cellular membrane properties of the sensory neurons (increase in membrane resistance), so some of the changes occurring in the two sides of synapse following conditioning are coordinated. The nature of the retrograde signal is unknown, but it could be the diffusible gas nitric oxide (NO), as injecting the NO scavenger myoglobin into the sensory neuron blocks the facilitation of the PSP during conditioning (Hawkins et al., 2006). Whether both presynaptic and postsynaptic mechanisms are active together at all phases of synaptic facilitation is still an open question. On the basis of experiments where 5-HT is used to mimic classical conditioning, Roberts and Glanzman (2003) have speculated that the rapid-onset ADPF mechanism is responsible for short-term synaptic facilitation. Hebbian LTP has a longer onset and leads to more persistent synaptic plasticity for medium-term and perhaps long-term synaptic facilitation.

1.30.4.2 Aversive Classical Conditioning of *Hermissenda* Phototactic Behavior

Behavioral training in *Hermissenda* involves the pairing of the CS, a light flash, with the US, a mechanical perturbance such as rotation. This induces a short-term memory that can last for a few minutes (e.g., single trial) or long-term memory lasting for days and weeks, depending on the number of trials (e.g., 150 trials per day over 3 days gives a week-long memory). Neural correlates can be studied in semi-isolated central nervous system (CNS) preparations made from behaviorally trained animals, or single-trial *in vitro* conditioning can be induced by pairing a light flash with CNS application of 5-HT, a key transmitter in the US pathway. Conditioning in the *Hermissenda* system involves the development of two different behavioral responses to the CS, foot contraction and inhibition of ciliary locomotion (Crow, 2004). Both these conditioned responses are thought to develop independently due to the involvement of different components of the central circuit involved in the two behaviors (see earlier discussion). Functionally, there is a learning-induced 'transfer' of the ability to activate these circuits from the US to the CS. We

will focus on the part of the circuit that underlies the conditioned inhibition of ciliary motor neurons, responsible for the cessation of forward locomotion in the intact animal, because most is known about how conditioning changes this circuit. After conditioning, the CS is able to activate the same interneuronal pathway that normally mediates the inhibition of ciliary motor neurons by the mechanical US in naive animals. Earlier, it was proposed that changes in the cellular properties of photoreceptor cells and the strength of synaptic connections between the two classes of photoreceptors' synaptic connections solely could account for the changes underlying behavioral conditioning (Goh and Alkon, 1984), but more recent identification of elements of the interneuronal circuit that forms an intermediate level of processing between sensory and ciliary motor neurons (Crow and Tian, 2002) has identified further sites of synaptic and nonsynaptic plasticity that are also involved in the conditioned response so that a more complex multisite model for associative conditioning in *Hermissenda* has emerged (Crow, 2004; Crow and Tian, 2006).

The electrical changes following conditioning are thought to be due to interactions between convergent CS (photic) and US (mechanical) synaptically mediated pathways that exist at various levels in the ciliary control network (**Figure 3(a)**). There are two types of synaptic connections between the CS and US pathways at the level of the sensory receptors. Reciprocal inhibitory monosynaptic connections occur between the statocyst hair cells and the B-type photoreceptors in the eye, and another unidirectional excitatory polysynaptic pathway, mediated by 5-HT, exists between the hair cells and the photoreceptors (**Figure 3(a)**). The presence of this US excitatory pathway mediated by 5-HT is of particular significance because this chemical is thought to underlie the ability of the US to induce changes in the CS photoreceptor pathway following conditioning. Conditioning induces cellular changes in both the type A and type B photoreceptors, which increase the firing of the cells in response to the CS. The CS evokes a larger receptor potential and an enhanced excitability in the B cells as tested by the response to a standard applied depolarizing pulse. An increase in membrane resistance contributes to this increase in spike activity, and a decrease in spike accommodation is also important in producing a sustained response to receptor depolarization in response to the CS. Conditioning reduces the peak amplitude of several types of potassium conductances in the B-type photoreceptors, including calcium-dependent and voltage-dependent types.

(a) During classical conditioning

(b) After classical conditioning

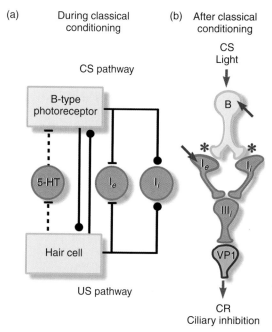

Figure 3 Aversive classical conditioning of the phototactic response in *Hermissenda*. (a) Sites of convergence between identified components of the CS and US pathways. Statocyst hair cells project have indirect excitatory synaptic connections with B-type photoreceptors through a proposed 5-HT-mediated interneuronal pathway. Hair cells and photoreceptors also have reciprocal inhibitory monosynaptic connections. Both hair cells and B-type photoreceptors form monosynaptic connections with both type I_e and type I_i interneurons (see also **Figure 1(b)**), which are therefore further sites of synaptic interactions between the CS and the US pathway (from Crow, 2004). Dots indicate inhibitory chemical synaptic connections and bar excitatory synaptic connections. (b) Components of the CS pathway involved in ciliary inhibition after classical conditioning. Changes in both cellular excitability (bold outlines, green arrow) and synaptic efficacy (bold outline, green asterisk) contribute to CS-elicited inhibition of ciliary locomotion. The net effect of cellular and synaptic plasticity is to increase the spike activity of type III_i inhibitory interneurons (see **Figure 1(b)**), during which light produces an inhibition of VP1 ciliary activating motor neurons (see **Figure 1(b)**) in conditioned animals. From Crow T (2004) Pavlovian conditioning of *Hermissenda*: Current cellular, molecular, and circuit perspectives. *Learn. Mem.* 11: 229–238; used with permission from Cold Spring Harbor Laboratory Press.

Importantly, these conductance changes can be mimicked by the application of 5-HT, providing evidence that the increased release of this transmitter via the hair cell polysynaptic pathway might be responsible for the changes in the intrinsic properties of the photoreceptors following conditioning. The molecular mechanisms underlying the effects of 5-HT on long-term memory are reviewed elsewhere (*See* Chapter 4.08).

The role of these convergent inputs in conditioning is best understood at the level of the primary sensory neurons, but convergent interactions may also be important at the level of the cerebropleural interneurons known as the I_e and I_i cells. Both cell types receive conjoint synaptic input from the photoreceptors and statocyst hair cells (**Figure 3(a)**). Photoreceptors and statocysts form monosynaptic excitatory connections with the I_e interneurons and monosynaptic inhibitory connections with the I_i interneurons.

Both I-cell types receive larger compound synaptic inputs in response to the CS in conditioned animals compared with controls (Crow and Tian, 2002). Larger EPSPs in the I_e cells increase spike activity, and larger inhibitory postsynaptic potentials (IPSPs) in the I_i cells reduce ongoing spike activity. This increase in the amplitude of the PSPs in the I-cells is due not only to increased CS-induced spike activity in the photoreceptors following conditioning but also to an increase in the strength of the B photoreceptor monosynaptic connections to both I-cell types (**Figure 3(b)**). In addition, the intrinsic excitability of the I_e interneurons also appears to be increased after conditioning, a third mechanism leading to the increased spike response of the I_e cells to the CS (**Figure 3(b)**). The mechanism increasing the excitability of the I_e cells has yet to be investigated.

Recording the VP1 ciliary motor neurons shows that light inhibits the tonic spike activity in conditioned animals compared with controls. Reduction of VP1 spiking reduces foot ciliary activity and inhibits forward locomotion. Facilitation of the synaptic connection between the B-type photoreceptors and type I_e interneurons in conjunction with intrinsic enhanced excitability in type B photoreceptors and type I_e interneurons would result in an increase in spike activity in the type III_i inhibitory interneurons and inhibition of the VP1 ciliary interneurons via the III_i-to-VP1 monosynaptic connection (**Figure 3(b)**). Thus, this combined set of synaptic and cellular changes located within the ciliary control circuit can elegantly account for the light-elicited inhibition of locomotion following associative conditioning. In the *Hermissenda* system, conditioning increases both the strength of already existing synapses by presynaptic mechanisms and postsynaptically by increasing the excitability of neurons in the circuit (Crow, 2004).

1.30.4.3 Aversive and Appetitive Conditioning of Chemosensory Responses in Terrestrial Slugs and Snails

Terrestrial slugs and snails show striking changes in the preference for food odors as a result of experience. Simply allowing the land snail *Achatina* to feed on a specific food, such as carrot, for 48 h leads to a preferential orientation of the snails toward odors of these foods, compared with the odors of a novel food, for up to 21 days after exposure to the food (Croll and Chase, 1980). Formation of food preferences depended on the consumption of food and does not occur by exposure to food odors alone, so an associative memory trace appears to have been formed between the odors and the consumption of the food, perhaps its nutritional value. Odor preferences have also been extensively investigated in the slug, *Limax*, but the emphasis in this mollusk has been on aversive classical conditioning. Slugs are attracted by odor to locomote toward a food source, such as carrot or potato, and when the food is located, they will evert their lips to taste the food and then consume the food with rhythmic feeding movements. If the food odors are paired with the bitter taste of quinidine, then the slug learns to avoid the food odor when compared with naive and unpaired groups of slugs that show no change in their food preference (Sahley et al., 1981a). A single pairing of a CS odor (carrot or potato) and the aversive US can reduce the time spent near the CS form by 80% in control groups to 20% for conditioned animals. The association of the food odor (CS) with the bitter taste (US) is an example of first-order classical conditioning, but the paradigm can also be extended to demonstrate second-order conditioning in the slug (Sahley et al., 1981b). Slugs are first presented with carrot/quinidine (phase 1) and then given the same number of pairings of two odors, potato and carrot (phase 2). To ensure that changes in the slug's preference for potato depended on it receiving both the phase 1 and phase 2 pairings, control groups were included. One control group received paired presentations of odor and quinidine in phase 1, but during phase 2, potato and carrot were unpaired. The other control group received unpaired carrot odor and quinidine in phase 1 but paired carrot and potato odor in phase 2. Slugs that received pairings during both phases of training displayed a reduced preference for potato odor when presented alone compared with slugs from the two control groups, indicating that second-order conditioning had occurred.

Another type of higher-order conditioning behavior shown by slugs is known as 'blocking' (*See* Chapter 1.18). Sahley et al. (1981b) showed that prior conditioning to one stimulus, carrot odor, reduced or blocked learning to a second stimulus, potato odor, when a compound odor consisting of both carrot and potato odors was subsequently paired with quinidine. In contrast, control groups of slugs without prior training to carrot learned to avoid both carrot odor and potato odor when the compound presentation of both odors was paired with quinidine.

As might be expected from such complex chemosensory behavior, *Limax* has an elaborate olfactory system for processing odor signals and the elaboration of memory traces. *Limax* and other terrestrial slugs and snails have two pairs of chemosensory tentacles located on the head, the 'superior' being responsible for sensing airborne odorous signals (Chase, 2002). At the tip of the tentacles is a large tentacle ganglion organized in glomeruli, and these structures contain primary olfactory neurons that are thought to code the airborne odor stimuli. These primary olfactory neurons project to a large CNS processing center, the procerebrum (PC), which is involved in odor discrimination as well as odor learning. Gelperin and Tank (1990) demonstrated the existence of synchronized neuronal oscillations in the PC of *Limax* that could be recorded as a local oscillatory field potential (LFP) with a frequency of about 0.7 Hz. This LFP is modulated by odor stimuli applied to the tentacle. As well as local potentials, waves of hyperpolarization and depolarization can be recorded that propagate continuously at 1 mm/s across the whole PC structure from the apical end of the PC to the basal end. The oscillatory activity is thought to be due to the bursting properties and inhibitory synaptic connections of the two types of neurons that form the PC (reviewed in Gelperin, 1999).

Evidence that the PC is involved on odor memories came from experiments where the fluorescent dye Lucifer yellow (LY) was used as a measure of neuronal activity (Kimura et al., 1998a). When LY was injected into the body cavity of intact *Limax* just after conditioning, many cells of the PC were stained. This was not observed in unpaired controls, so the incorporation of the dye was specific to the odor conditioning. The dye-stained clusters of neurons formed a characteristic beltlike structure transverse to the axis of wave propagation. If two different odors were used as the CS for aversive conditioning, then different clusters of cells showed dye labeling, suggesting that memory traces for different odors were stored in distinct populations of PC cells. In related experiments (Kimura et al., 1998b), electrical activity in the PC was recorded following aversive odor conditioning using voltage-sensitive dyes. Presentation of an aversively conditioned odor to the tentacle modulated the spontaneous oscillatory activity. Initially a depolarization of the basal level of oscillation occurred in specific belt-shaped regions of the PC (cf. LY staining), and then a later phase of hyperpolarization occurred that covered a wider area. Different odors produced different patterns of spatial modulation of oscillatory activity. Spatial and temporal modulation was not observed when unpaired control odors were tested, suggesting that the electrical changes were specific to conditioning. It appears from this work that olfactory memories are stored as spatial and temporal activity patterns of oscillators that form a coherent network.

In more recent work an *in vitro* version of odor conditioning has been developed where it is possible to stimulate the olfactory organs with odors and record motor output (Inoue et al., 2006). In this preparation it was also possible to record a behavioral correlate of PC oscillation. After odor-aversion conditioning, shortening of mantle muscles was recorded *in vitro* that form part of the conditioned response in the whole animal. This was accompanied by increased activity in the parietal motor nerves that innervate the mantle. In a differential conditioning paradigm two attractive odors (carrot and cucumber) were used as CSs; one was paired with the US (CS+), and the other was applied alone (CS–). The US was an electrical stimulus applied to pedal and lip sensory nerves. Before conditioning, neither CS caused activity in the motor nerves innervating the mantle. After one pairing, the CS+ increased larger-amplitude discharges in the motor nerve but the CS– did not. In addition, LFPs were recorded from the PC during conditioning. Before conditioning, attractive odors caused little change in the PC oscillations, but after conditioning, the PC oscillation frequency doubled with increases in activity in the motor nerves. Only the aversively conditioned CS+ increased the frequency of PC oscillation with no effect from application of the CS–. Whether the changes in PC oscillation are due purely to learning-related events is still an open question, because natively aversive odors (say onion or garlic) also cause increases in PC oscillation in naive animals (Inoue et al., 2006) similar to those produced by the CS+ odors (say, cucumber) that are made aversive by conditioning.

1.30.4.4 Reward Classical Conditioning of *Lymnaea* and *Aplysia* Feeding Behavior

In the original successful formulation of chemical reward conditioning in *Lymnaea*, snails were subjected to a multi-trial chemical conditioning protocol (15 trials, 5 trials per day for 3 days) using amyl acetate as a neutral CS and sucrose as the US (Audesirk et al., 1982). Following training, the explicitly paired (CS-US) experimental group showed significantly greater feeding responses to amyl acetate over their own naive responses and all the standard control groups (random, explicitly unpaired, CS alone, US alone). As might be predicted for appetitive conditioning, both age and motivational state (hunger versus satiety) influenced learning. Both hungry and sated young snails could acquire the conditioned response, but in the latter group, its expression was only apparent when the animals were starved before testing. On the other hand, old snails could only acquire the conditioned response if they were maintained in a hungry state during training (Audesirk et al., 1982). The significance of motivational state became even more apparent when it was realized that if snails were starved long enough (for 5 days) before and throughout the experiment, even a single pairing of amyl acetate and sucrose resulted in long-term memory (LTM), which lasted for at least 19 days (Alexander et al., 1984). This is a remarkable example of single-trial learning, which is used now for analyses of the time course of the mechanisms underlying LTM formation.

An electrophysiological correlate of the conditioned response to amyl acetate was recorded as changes in the fictive feeding responses in motor neurons (Kemenes et al., 2002), but electrical activity following conditioning has also been recorded in other parts of the feeding system in attempts to localize sites of plasticity. The cell bodies of chemosensory neurons are located in lip epithelial tissue and project to the cerebral ganglia via the lip nerves, where they synapse with cerebral ganglion neurons like the CBIs (Straub et al., 2004). Extracellularly recorded spike responses to both the CS and US can be recorded in the lip nerves from naive animals, and these responses do not change after conditioning. In contrast, neuronal output from the cerebral ganglia is significantly enhanced in response to the CS after conditioning (Straub et al., 2004). This indicates that chemical conditioning affects central but not peripheral processing of chemosensory information, with the cerebral ganglia being an important site of plasticity. The fibers that were recorded extracellularly to indicate cerebral plasticity were originating from the CBI interneurons, so their activation is particularly significant. Confirmation that the CBIs do increase their activity after conditioning was obtained by showing increases in feeding patterns to the CS in CV1 neurons, a specific CBI cell type. From this work, it is suggested that the synapses between the primary chemosensory neurons and the CBIs are increased in strength. Two other CS pathways are present in naive animals, but these are not affected by conditioning (Straub et al., 2006).

The current network model for chemical conditioning (**Figure 4(a)**, **(b)**) includes nonsynaptic plasticity. The CGCs are persistently depolarized by about 10 mV after behavioral conditioning. This indirectly increases the strength of postsynaptic responses to CGC stimulation by a process that involves an increase in intracellular calcium concentration (Kemenes et al., 2006). The local target for CGC depolarization is the CBI cells, and artificial depolarization of the CGCs in naive snails increases the response of the CBI cells to the CS, mimicking the effects of behavioral conditioning. It appears that the CGCs are increasing the strength of the CS-to-CBI synapse by presynaptic facilitation (**Figure 4(b)**). The onset of the CGC depolarization is between 16–24 h after training, and it persists for at least 14 days, as long as the behavioral memory trace is present. There is an early behavioral memory trace from 2 h after conditioning, so the CGCs cannot be involved in memory expression immediately after training. It is more likely that the CGCs are involved in the maintenance of the LTM after the trace has already been consolidated and encode information that is important for memory recall. Interestingly, the CV1 cells that show a persistent change in membrane potential after tactile conditioning (see later discussion) show no change after chemical conditioning. A variety of molecular pathways are involved in chemical conditioning in *Lymnaea*, and these are reviewed elsewhere (*See* Chapter 4.09).

Lymnaea can also be classically conditioned to a lip touch CS by repeatedly pairing a touch to the lip with food (5–15 trials over 3 days). This type of reward learning shares important characteristics with associative conditioning in vertebrates, such as

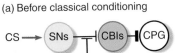
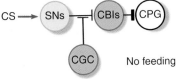
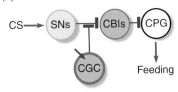

Figure 4 A cellular model for long-term memory after chemical classical conditioning in *Lymnaea*. (a) In naive animals, the excitatory connections between the sensory neurons (SNs) and the command-like cerebrobuccal interneurons (CBIs) are weak, and the chemical CS (amyl acetate) cannot activate feeding. The cerebral giant cells (CGCs) are at normal membrane potential (~65 mV), and the presynaptic modulatory input from the CGCs to the SNs is inactive or weak. (b) In conditioned animals, the CGC soma is depolarized by ~10 mV compared to naive animals, and this leads to an enhancement of the CGC presynaptic modulatory inputs to SNs and a strengthening of the SN-to-CBI excitatory synapse, which results in a feeding response to the CS. Black lines, inactive connections; green lines, active connections. Thin bars, weak chemical excitatory synapses; thicker bars, stronger/enhanced excitatory synapses. The thicker outline of the CGC and the green arrow in (b) indicate learning-induced nonsynaptic plasticity (membrane depolarization), which increases the strength of CGC-to-SN synaptic connections. CPG, central pattern generator.

stimulus generalization and discriminative learning, classical-operant interactions, and strong dependence on both external and internal background variables (Kemenes and Benjamin, 1989a,b, 1994).

Two approaches have been used to investigate the neural basis of tactile reward classical conditioning in *Lymnaea*. One approach was based on the development of an *in vitro* preparation where electrophysiological manipulation of neuronal pathways aims to mimic the behavioral conditioning paradigm (Kemenes et al., 1997). In this study a lip touch stimulus was paired with intracellular activation of the modulatory slow oscillator neuron, which can drive fictive feeding. After 6–10 pairings, presentation of the touch stimulus could activate a robust fictive feeding rhythm in feeding motor neurons.

A second approach used behavioral conditioning followed by electrophysiological analysis to record changes in electrical activity that follows LTM formation. Using the lip touch behavioral training protocol, snails were subjected to 15 training trials over 3 days, and then these and control animals were dissected for electrophysiological analysis, starting on the day after the last training trial. Touching the lips of the intact snails from the experimental group after training induced a pattern of feeding movements significantly greater than controls. Similar significant differences were seen between experimental and control animals at the level of the electrophysiologically recorded fictive feeding pattern in motor neurons made from the same snails (Staras et al., 1998, 1999a).

The CPG-driven activity in the motor neurons depends ultimately on activity of neurons at all levels of the feeding network, so the conditioned fictive feeding recorded in the motor neurons is a systems level 'readout' of the memory trace in the whole feeding system. However, more detailed changes can also be recorded in different parts of the network (Staras et al., 1999a). One of these is the early EPSP that occurs in the B3 motor neuron before the onset of the fictive feeding pattern. The amplitude, but not the latency and duration of the EPSP, was significantly enhanced after conditioning. In sated snails the conditioned fictive feeding response to touch was lost, but the increase in the EPSP amplitude persisted. This suggests that there is unlikely to be a causal link between increases in amplitude in B3 and generation of the fictive feeding pattern.

Electrical correlates of tactile conditioning were also recorded at other levels within the feeding circuit, and these could all be potential sites of plasticity. That sites quite early in the CS pathway could be involved in conditioning was revealed by extracellularly recording mechanosensory fibers located in the connective between the cerebral and buccal ganglia. Tactile responses could be recorded in these fibers, and following conditioning, the number of spikes occurring early in this response increased, compared with controls (Staras et al., 1999a).

Interestingly, a correlate of tactile conditioning could also be recorded in the CPG network. A long-lasting sequence of inhibitory synaptic inputs that occurs in the N1 CPG interneurons in response to lip touch in naive animals changes to a strong sustained depolarizing synaptic input after *in vitro* conditioning, and this drives a sustained plateauing pattern in the N1 cell (Kemenes et al., 1997). This is an example of synaptic plasticity affecting an important CPG component of the feeding network.

One candidate for initiating CPG activity following conditioning is the CBI cell type known as CV1. This neuron is capable of driving a fictive feeding pattern via its connections with the N1M cells of the CPG network, and activity in these cells normally accompanies unconditioned feeding patterns stimulated by sucrose (Kemenes et al., 2001). After conditioning, the CV1 cells are significantly more active following touch in conditioned snails compared with controls, and they show the typical patterned activity seen with sucrose (US) application (Jones et al., 2003). More detailed experiments on the role of CV1 cells in tactile conditioning have revealed that nonsynaptic electrical changes play a role in memory (Jones et al., 2003). A long-lasting membrane depolarization of 11 mV on average was recorded in CV1s from conditioned compared with control snails that persisted for as long as the electrophysiological and behavioral memory trace. The depolarization makes the cells more responsive to the CS and can account for the activation of the feeding response after conditioning via the CV1 cell's strong excitatory synaptic connection with the CPG. The importance of this result is emphasized by experiments in which the membrane potential of the CV1 cells is manipulated to either reverse the effect of behavioral conditioning or to mimic the effects of conditioning in naive snails. These experiments showed that the persistent depolarization of the CV1 cells was both sufficient and necessary for the conditioned tactile response in the feeding network.

Like *Lymnaea*, the *Aplysia* feeding system has also been subjected to behavioral and electrophysiological analysis of reward conditioning using lip touch as the CS and food reinforcement (seaweed) as the US. An *in vitro* electrophysiological analogue of classical conditioning employed electrical stimulation of nerves to activate the CS and US pathways. Lesions of the En (esophageal nerve) blocked classical conditioning and suggested that this nerve mediates the effects of the US (Lechner et al., 2000). This nerve also contains dopamine (DA) immunofluorescent fibers, so it was interesting that the DA antagonist, methylergonovine, blocked the acquisition of the *in vitro* analogue of reward conditioning. Thus the behavioral, immunostaining, and pharmacological data are consistent with the hypothesis that DA located within nerve fibers in the En nerve mediates the actions of the US during conditioning.

Individual neurons of the *Aplysia* feeding circuit have been analyzed for changes occurring during conditioning. Buccal neurons B31/32 play a key role in initiating buccal motor programs, and these neurons were significantly more depolarized by the CS after conditioning, although their intrinsic properties were unaffected. This suggests that there is greater excitation of the B31/B32 neurons after conditioning due to an enhancement of the CS pathway. Another neuron that plays a key role in expression of the buccal feeding program is B51. In preparations made from behaviorally trained animals, this cell type showed a greater number of plateau potentials compared with controls, and it was depolarized more by the CS. Neither the input resistance nor resting potential of the B51 was affected by conditioning, but another intrinsic property, the threshold for plateau initiation, was increased. This would make the cell less responsive to excitatory synaptic input, but nevertheless, the cell still showed more plateau potentials after conditioning, so some other unknown factor must overcome this diminished excitability (Baxter and Byrne, 2006). Similar results were obtained in both *in vivo* and *in vitro* conditioning. Recently, the CBI-2 cell type has been examined after *in vitro* conditioning and shown to increase its activity after conditioning. CBI-2 has the ability to initiate ingestive feeding motor programs, and this may contribute to the increased activation of the buccal B31/32 interneurons after conditioning (Mozzachiodi et al., 2003). No changes in the nonsynaptic cellular properties of the CBIs was reported, which contrasts with the results from *Lymnaea*, where the homologs of the CBIs, the CV1a cells, were shown to be persistently depolarized after tactile reward conditioning (Jones et al., 2003, see earlier discussion).

1.30.4.5   Reward Operant Conditioning of *Aplysia* Feeding Behavior

Brembs et al. (2002) developed a behavioral paradigm for operant conditioning using the consummatory (ingestive) phase of the feeding cycle as the operant. Contingent electrical stimulation of the En nerve that carries the US pathway from the esophagus, using implanted electrodes, was used to positively reinforce spontaneous extracellular recorded feeding bursts of activity monitored on the same nerve in freely moving animals. These extracellularly recorded bursts occurred at the same time as feeding ingestion movements and so acted as a direct monitor of the behavior. The number of spontaneous feeding bursts was increased compared with nonstimulated or yoked

controls after 10 min of training immediately after the training period and when measured 24 h later. This indicates that operant conditioning was successful in producing both short-term and long-term memory. A cellular correlate of operant conditioning was monitored by intracellularly recording the B51 feeding interneuron in isolated buccal ganglia made from behaviorally trained animals. Cells from the contingent group showed a significant decrease in threshold for plateau formation and a significant increase in input resistance compared with cells from yoked controls. To test whether this was due to an intrinsic change in the B51 cell rather than changes in input originating from outside the cell, an analogue of conditioning was developed where B51 was grown in culture and electrically triggered burst of spikes paired with 6-s puffs of DA applied close to the isolated cell over a 10-min training period. Contingent application of these two stimuli produced a significant reduction in plateau threshold and a significant increase in input resistance compared with unpaired controls similar to that occurring in the previous intact buccal ganglion preparation (Brembs et al., 2002). These results indicate that intrinsic changes are induced in B51 by operant conditioning. How these changes in B51 contribute to the network and behavioral expression of the conditioned response are yet to be determined. Some of the molecular changes involving the effects of DA have been elucidated (reviewed in Baxter and Byrne, 2006).

1.30.4.6   Aversive Operant Conditioning of *Lymnaea* Breathing Behavior

The aerial respiratory behavior of *Lymnaea stagnalis* has been used to investigate the behavioral and neuronal mechanisms of operant conditioning (Lukowiak et al., 2003). Hypoxia triggers pneumostome opening, and this was used as the operant for behavioral conditioning. Tactile stimulation of the pneumostome area evokes pneumostome closure and stops aerial respiratory behavior. Animals were tested and trained in an artificially created hypoxic N_2-rich environment to increase the level of respiratory behavior. In the operantly trained group a tactile stimulus was applied to the pneumostome area each time aerial respiration was attempted by the animal. Suitable yoked and hypoxic control groups were also used. The number of openings, latency to first opening, and total breath durations were recorded in pre- and posttraining periods. Only the operantly conditioned group showed significant changes between the pre- and posttraining behaviors, with significant reductions in openings and total breathing time and significant increases in the latency to first breath. It has since been demonstrated that a memory for this conditioned response could persist for at least 4 weeks when a spaced training procedure was used. Both intermediate memory (ITM) and LTM have been described based not only partly on the length of time the memory persists but also on the sensitivity to protein and mRNA synthesis blockers. Anisomycin prevents the formation of both ITM and LTM, whereas actinomycin-D only prevents LTM. Both reconsolidation and extinction have been studied following operant conditioning, and both have been shown to be dependent on new RNA and protein synthesis (Sangha et al., 2003a,b; See Chapters 1.24, 1.27). Extinction is viewed as a new type of associative memory that 'covers up' but does not replace the original memory. Thus, following extinction trials, a loss of memory at 2 h is followed by full 'spontaneous recovery' at 24 h (Sanga et al., 2003b).

Neural changes associated with this learned behavior have been identified in the isolated CNS derived from operantly conditioned animals. Specifically, spontaneous patterned activity in the IP3 interneuron, which is involved in pneumostome opening (see **Figure 1(dii)**), showed a significant reduction compared to activity in the IP3 neurons of brains derived from yoked controls. Furthermore, a higher percentage of RPeD1 CPG interneurons, which are important in the onset of the respiratory cycle, were silent in conditioned versus control preparations (Spencer et al., 1999). A reduction in the ability of the RPeD1 cells to induce IP3 activity was also observed. More direct evidence for the role of RPeD1 in memory formation came from somal ablation experiments. Removal of the soma 2 h prior to conditioning prevented LTM but had no effect on ITM, without affecting the ability of the snail to carry out respiratory behavior, suggesting that the RPeD1 soma was necessary for LTM formation (Scheibenstock et al., 2002). Removal of the RPeD1 soma 1 h after conditioning had no effect on LTM, indicating that the effects of soma ablation were not related to memory access or retrieval. Interestingly, both extinction and reconsolidation also require the presence of the soma of RPeD1, indicating that RPeD1 is involved in the formation of more than one type of memory trace (Sangha et al., 2003a,b).

1.30.5 Discussion

1.30.5.1 The Complexity of Molluscan Learning

Molluscan studies are focused on implicit forms of memory such as classical/operant conditioning and sensitization. Initially, simple forms of associative and nonassociative learning behavior were investigated. However, gastropod mollusks are capable of showing more complex types of associative learning behavior with features that are similar to those found in vertebrates (See Chapters 1.18, 1.36). For instance, differential conditioning has been described in a number of mollusks (Hawkins et al., 1983; Kemenes et al., 1989a; Jones et al., 2001; Inoue et al., 2006). In addition, second-order conditioning and blocking of aversive-odor conditioning has been demonstrated in *Limax* (Sahley et al., 1981b), and stimulus generalization, goal tracking, and context dependence (increased learning in a novel environment) were found in *Lymnaea* tactile conditioning (Kemenes and Benjamin, 1989a,b, 1994). The circuits underlying these behaviors are more complicated than those originally used for the study of reflexive defensive withdrawal responses and require the understanding of CPG and other interneuronal circuits mediating multimodality sensory responses. A key finding in these studies is that conditioning-induced synaptic and nonsynaptic changes occur at several sites within the same network (Benjamin et al., 2000; Crow, 2004; Baxter and Byrne, 2006; Kemenes et al., 2006; Straub et al., 2006). These include sensory neurons, modulatory and pattern-generating interneurons, and motor neurons. A future task will require us to understand how these various changes may be integrated to generate the final behavioral output.

1.30.5.2 Comparison of Nonsynaptic Electrical Mechanisms in Different Types of Molluscan Learning

It has long been recognized that changes in synaptic plasticity play a major role in molluscan learning and memory, but an increasing number of examples of nonsynaptic plasticity have been discovered that are known to be involved in circuits underlying behavioral learning. These include changes in input resistance, membrane potential, and threshold for plateau initiation. Examples of input resistance increases induced by conditioning occur in the B-type photoreceptor cells of *Hermissenda* (Crow, 2004). This leads to an increase in excitability of the photoreceptors so that they fire more in response to the light CS. Similar input resistance increases have been described in the LE mechanoreceptors of the gill-siphon reflex of *Aplysia* following sensitization and classical conditioning (Hawkins et al., 2006). In both examples, a reduction in the size of intrinsic potassium channel conductances appears to be involved.

Persistent changes in membrane potential occur in whole body withdrawal interneurons in *Helix* (Gainutdinov et al., 1998) and in feeding command-like CV1 interneurons in *Lymnaea* (Jones et al., 2003). In both snails, the cells are depolarized following conditioning, and this lowers the threshold for firing in response to the CS, thus allowing the command cells to directly activate the motor circuits. The CGCs in *Lymnaea* also show persistent changes in membrane potential (Kemenes et al., 2006) after conditioning, but this does not lead to an increase in spiking responses to the CS. Instead, the 10-mV depolarization facilitates CS responses in the chemosensory pathway by increasing presynaptic release of transmitter at the sensory-to-command-neuron synapse. The CGCs are extrinsic to the feeding circuit, and so the change of membrane potential activates feeding responses indirectly by affecting command interneurons intrinsic to the circuit. Interestingly, the CGC's changes occur in chemically conditioned snails but not those subjected to tactile conditioning. For tactile conditioning the CV1 cells are depolarized but not the CGCs. The reason for this difference in the two types of classical reward conditioning is unclear but is probably linked to differences in the neural pathways activated by sucrose versus lip touch.

Changes in the threshold for plateau formation in the pattern generation occurs in the same *Aplysia* interneuron (B51) in both classical and operant conditioning of feeding, allowing comparisons to be made of the intrinsic changes occurring in B51 in the two different types of learning (Lorenzetti et al., 2006). The two types of conditioning have the opposite types of effect – increasing the plateau membrane potential threshold in classical conditioning and decreasing it in operant conditioning. This is despite the increase in overall plateauing frequency in both types of conditioning in the intact network. B51 is thought to have some type of 'decision-making role' in the feeding circuit but how the differential effects of conditioning on plateauing translate to differences in the type of conditioning used is unclear.

1.30.5.3 Comparison of Synaptic Mechanisms

Changes in synaptic strength have been described in several molluscan systems following training. In *Aplysia*, the gill-siphon withdrawal response is present in naive animals and is enhanced by learning (Hawkins et al., 2006). In contrast, *Hermissenda* phototactic conditioning causes a different response to the CS in naive animals compared with after conditioning, and so a new response has to be learned (Crow, 2004). There are weak synaptic responses to the photic CS-conditioned response in *Hermissenda*, but they are too ineffective in naive animals to generate a network inhibitory response in the ciliary motor neurons. It might have been expected that there might be formation of novel synapses or activation of 'silent synapses' in the circumstances where there is no behavioral response prior to conditioning, but this does not appear to be the case. In *Lymnaea* there are two alternative CS pathways, one excitatory and one inhibitory, that can be activated by the chemical CS in naive animals (Straub et al., 2006). At high concentrations the inhibitory effect is predominant on feeding behavior. Following reward conditioning, the CS becomes overall excitatory on feeding responses to high CS concentrations, but this is not due to any change in the preexisting pathways, but a previously ineffective excitatory pathway becomes predominant over the inhibitory pathway. These results from *Hermissenda* and *Lymnaea* make it clear that there are no simple rules so far elucidated that can predict whether new synapses will be formed or already-existing synapses strengthened following associative conditioning.

References

Alexander J, Audesirk TE, and Audesirk GJ (1984) One-trial reward learning in the snail *Lymnea stagnalis*. *J. Neurobiol.* 15: 67–72.

Antonov I, Antonova I, Kandel ER, and Hawkins RD (2003) Activity-dependent presynaptic facilitation and hebbian LTP are both required and interact during classical conditioning in *Aplysia*. *Neuron* 37: 135–147.

Armitage BA and Siegelbaum SA (1998) Presynaptic induction and expression of homosynaptic depression at *Aplysia* sensorimotor neuron synapses. *J. Neurosci.* 18: 8770–8779.

Audesirk TE, Alexander JE, Audesirk GJ, and Moyer CM (1982) Rapid, nonaversive conditioning in a freshwater gastropod. I. Effects of age and motivation. *Behav. Neur. Biol.* 36: 379–390.

Baxter DA and Byrne JH (2006) Feeding behavior of *Aplysia*: A model system for comparing mechanisms of classical and operant conditioning. *Learn. Mem.* 13: 669–680.

Benjamin PR and Elliott CJ (1989) Snail feeding oscillator: The central pattern generator and its control by modulatory interneurons. In: Jacklet J (ed.) *Neuronal and Cellular Oscillators*, p. 173. New York: Dekker.

Benjamin PR, Kemenes G, and Staras K (2005) *Molluscan nervous systems*. In: *Encyclopedia of Life Sciences.* Chichester: John Wiley. Available at: http://www.mrw.interscience.wiley.com/emrw/047001590x/home.

Benjamin PR, Staras K, and Kemenes G (2000) A systems approach to the cellular analysis of associative learning in the pond snail *Lymnaea*. *Learn. Mem.* 7: 124–231.

Brembs B, Lorenzetti FD, Reyes FD, Baxter D, and Byrne JH (2002) Operant reward learning in *Aplysia*: Neuronal correlates and mechanisms. *Science* 296: 1706–1709.

Carew TJ and Sahley CL (1986) Invertebrate learning and memory: From behavior to molecules. *Annu. Rev. Neurosci.* 9: 435–487.

Chase R (2002) *Behavior and Its Neural Control in Gastropod Molluscs.* New York: Oxford University Press.

Cleary LJ, Lee WL, and Byrne JH (1998) Cellular correlates of long-term sensitization in *Aplysia*. *J. Neurosci.* 18: 5988–5998.

Croll RP and Chase R (1980) Plasticity of olfactory orientation to foods in the snail *Achatina fulica*. *J. Comp. Physiol.* 136: 267–277.

Crow T (2004) Pavlovian conditioning of *Hermissenda*: Current cellular, molecular, and circuit perspectives. *Learn. Mem.* 11: 229–238.

Crow T and Tian L-M (2002) Facilitation of monosynaptic and complex PSPs in Type I interneurons of conditioned *Hermissenda*. *J. Neurosci.* 22: 7818–7824.

Crow T and Tian L-M (2006) Pavlovian conditioning in *Hermissenda*: A circuit analysis. *Biol. Bull.* 210: 289–297.

Ezzeddine Y and Glanzman DL (2003) Prolonged habituation of the gill-withdrawal reflex in *Aplysia* depends on protein synthesis, protein phosphatase activity and postsynaptic glutamate receptors. *J. Neurosci.* 23: 9585–9594.

Gainutdinov KL, Chekmarev LJ, and Gainutdinova TH (1988) Excitability increase in withdrawal interneuron after conditioning in the snail. *Neuroreport* 16: 517–520.

Gelperin A (1999) Oscillatory dynamics and information processing in olfactory systems. *J. Exp. Biol.* 202: 1855–1864.

Gelperin A and Tank DW (1990) Odor-modulated collective network oscillations by olfactory interneurons in a terrestrial mollusc. *Nature* 345: 437–440.

Ghirardi M, Montorola PG, and Kandel ER (1995) A novel intermediate stage in the transition between short- and long-term facilitation in the sensory to motor neuron synapse in *Aplysia* sensory neurons. *Neuron* 14: 413–420.

Glanzman DL (1995) The cellular basis of classical conditioning in *Aplysia californica* – It's less simple than you think. *Trends Neurosci.* 18: 30–36.

Glanzman DL (2006) The cellular mechanisms of learning in *Aplysia*: Of blind men and elephants. *Biol. Bull.* 271–279.

Hawkins RD, Abrahams TW, Carew TJ, and Kandel ER (1983) A cellular mechanism of classical conditioning of Aplysia. *Science* 219: 400–405.

Hawkins RD, Kandel ER, and Bailey CH (2006) Molecular mechanisms of memory storage in *Aplysia*. *Biol. Bull.* 210: 174–191.

Inoue T, Murakami M, Watanabe S, Inokuma Y, and Kirino Y (2006) *In vitro* odor-aversion conditioning in a terrestrial mollusc. *J. Neurophysiol.* 95: 3898–3903.

Kandel ER (1976) *Cellular Basis of Behavior. An Introduction to Behavioral Biology.* San Francisco: W. H. Freeman.

Kemenes G and Benjamin PR (1989a) Appetitive learning in snails shows characteristics of conditioning in vertebrates. *Brain Res.* 489: 163–166.

Kemenes G and Benjamin PR (1989b) Goal-tracking behavior in the pond snail, *Lymnaea stagnalis. Behav. Neur. Biol.* 52: 260–270.

Kemenes G and Benjamin PR (1994) Training in a novel environment improves the appetitive learning performance of the snail, *Lymnaea stagnalis. Behav. Neur. Biol.* 61: 139–149.

Kemenes G, Staras K, and Benjamin PR (1997) *In vitro* appetitive classical conditioning of the feeding response in the pond snail *Lymnaea stagnalis. J. Neurophysiol.* 78: 2351–2362.

Kemenes G, Staras K, and Benjamin PR (2001) Multiple types of control by identified interneurons in a sensory-activated rhythmic motor pattern. *J. Neurosci.* 21: 2903–2911.

Kemenes I, Kemenes G, Andrew RJ, Benjamin PR, and O'Shea M (2002) Critical time-window for NO-cGMP-dependent long-term memory formation after one-trial appetitive conditioning. *J. Neurosci.* 22: 1414–1425.

Kemenes I, Straub VA, Nikitin ES, et al. (2006) Role of delayed nonsynaptic neuronal plasticity in long-term associative memory. *Curr. Biol.* 16: 1269–1279.

Kimura T, Suzuki H, Kono E, and Sekiguchi T (1998a) Mapping of interneurons that contribute to food aversive conditioning in the slug brain. *Learn. Mem.* 4: 376–388.

Kimura T, Toda S, Sekiguchi T, Kawahara S, and Kirino Y (1998b) Optical recording analysis of olfactory response of the procerebral lobe in the slug brain. *Learn. Mem.* 4: 389–400.

Jones NG, Kemenes G, and Benjamin PR (2001) Selective expression of electrical correlates of differential appetitive classical conditioning in a feeding network. *J. Neurophysiol.* 85: 89–97.

Jones NG, Kemenes I, Kemenes G, and Benjamin PR (2003) A persistent cellular change in a single modulatory interneuron contributes to associative long-term memory. *Curr. Biol.* 13: 1064–1069.

Lechner H, Baxter DA, and Byrne JH (2000) Classical conditioning of feeding in *Aplysia*: I. behavioral analysis. *J. Neurosci.* 20: 3369–3376.

Li Q, Roberts AC, and Glanzman DL (2005) Synaptic facilitation and behavioral dishabituation in *Aplysia*: Dependence on release form postsynaptic intracellular stores, postsynaptic exocytosis, and modulation of postsynaptic AMPA receptor efficacy. *J. Neurosci.* 25: 5623–5637.

Lin XL and Glanzman DL (1994) Hebbian induction of long-term potentiation of *Aplysia* sensorimotor synapses: Partial requirement for activation of an NMDA-related receptor. *Proc. Roy. Soc. B.* 255: 215–221.

Lorenzetti FD, Mozzachiodi R, Baxter D, and Byrne JH (2006) Classical and operant conditioning differentially modify the intrinsic properties of an identified neuron. *Nat. Neurosci.* 9: 17–19.

Lukowiak K, Sangla S, Scheibenstock A, et al. (2003) A molluscan model system in the search for the engram. *J. Physiol.* (Paris) 97: 69–76.

Mackey SL, Kandel ER, and Hawkins RD (1989) Identified serotonergic neurons LCB1 and RCB1 in the cerebral ganglia of *Aplysia* produce presynaptic facilitation of siphon sensory neurons. *J. Neurosci.* 9: 4227–4235.

Mozzachiodi R, Lechner H, Baxter DA, and Byrne JH (2003) *In vitro* analogue of classical conditioning of feeding behavior in *Aplysia. Learn. Mem.* 10: 478–494.

Roberts AC and Glanzman DL (2003) Learning in *Aplysia*: Looking at synaptic plasticity from both sides. *Trends Neurosci.* 26: 662–670.

Sahley CL, Gelperin A, and Rudy J (1981a) One-trial associative learning modifies food odor preference of a terrestrial mollusc. *Proc. Nat. Acad. Sci. USA* 78: 640–642.

Sahley CL, Rudy JW, and Gelperin A (1981b) An analysis of associative learning in a terrestrial mollusc: Higher order conditioning, blocking and a transient US exposure effect. *J. Comp. Physiol.* 144: 1–8.

Sangha S, Scheibenstock A, and Lukowiak K (2003a) Reconsolidation of a long-term memory in *Lymnaea* requires new protein and RNA synthesis and the soma of Right Pedal Dorsal 1. *J. Neurosci.* 23: 8034–8040.

Sangha S, Scheibenstock A, Morrow R, and Lukowiak K (2003b) Extinction requires new RNA and protein synthesis and the soma of the cell Right Pedal Dorsal 1 in *Lymnaea stagnalis*. *J. Neurosci.* 23: 9842–9851.

Scheibenstock A, Krygier D, Haque Z, Syed N, and Lukowiak K (2002) The soma of RPeD1 must be present for long-term memory formation of associative learning in *Lymnaea*. *J Neurophysiol.* 88: 1584–1591.

Spencer GE, Syed NI, and Lukowiak K (1999) Neural changes after operant conditioning of the aerial respiratory behaviour in *Lymnaea stagnalis*. *J. Neurosci.* 19: 1836–1843.

Spencer GE, Kazmi MH, Syed NI, and Lukowiak K (2002) Changes in the activity of a CPG neuron after the reinforcement of an operantly conditioned behavior *Lymnaea*. *J. Neurophysiol.* 88: 1915–1923.

Staras K, Kemenes G, and Benjamin PR (1998) Neurophysiological correlates of unconditioned and conditioned feeding behavior in the pond snail *Lymnaea stagnalis*. *J. Neurophysiol.* 79: 3030–3040.

Staras K, Kemenes G, and Benjamin PR (1999a) Cellular traces of behavioral classical conditioning can be recorded at several specific sites in a simple nervous system. *J. Neurosci.* 19: 347–357.

Staras K, Kemenes G, and Benjamin PR (1999b) Electrophysiological and behavioral analysis of lip touch as a component of the food stimulus in the snail *Lymnaea*. *J. Neurophysiol.* 81: 1261–1273.

Straub VA, Kemenes I, O'Shea M, and Benjamin PR (2006) Associative memory stored by functional novel pathway rather than modifications of preexisting neuronal pathways. *J. Neurosci.* 26: 4139–4146.

Straub VA, Styles BJ, Ireland JS, O'Shea M, and Benjamin PR (2004) Central localization of plasticity involved in appetitive conditioning in *Lymnaea*. *Learn. Mem.* 11: 787–793.

Sutton MA and Carew TJ (2000) Parallel molecular pathways mediate expression of distinct forms of intermediate-term facilitation at a tail sensory-motor synapse in *Aplysia*. *Neuron* 26: 219–231.

1.31 Behavioral Analysis of Learning and Memory in Cephalopods

L. Borrelli and G. Fiorito, Stazione Zoologica A. Dohrn, Naples, Italy

1.31.1 An Historical Overview

The ancient civilizations of the Mediterranean, whose lives were closely linked to the sea, were clearly aware of the existence and beauty of cephalopods. Exquisite motifs and sketches of marine creatures were recurrent in the well-known Middle and Late Minoan pottery (approximately 2000–1000 BC) and also in the probably less famous Chiriquian art, typical of northwest Panama (approximately 300 BC). Both made extensive use of lozenge-shaped figures from which eight waving arms emerged. Independent of their realistic or stylized rendering, common characters such as dots, spots, and circles of various shades and colors convinced archeologists, anthropologists, and art historians that the figures were artistic representations of the same peculiar marine creature: the octopus.

This brings our attention to the fact that, among living organisms, cephalopods have been familiar to man since antiquity. In his *Historia Animalium*, Aristotle (fourth century BC) described the difference in occurrence between the inking response of cuttlefishes (concealment and fear) and that of squids and octopuses (fear only), together with the changing of the patterns of their skin to match the background and disguise themselves from predators and prey. He also mentioned the octopus's strong curiosity (or stupidity, to put it in his words), which made it an easy catch since a hand shaking under the water surface was sufficient to elicit its exploratory drive (Aristotle, 1910). Cephalopods' behavior even intrigued Darwin, who gave a detailed account of his observations of octopuses and cuttlefishes in the waters of the islands of Cape Verde (Darwin, 1870).

Many other anecdotal and popular reports are known from the classic literature (review in Cousteau and Diolé, 1973; see also Borrelli et al., 2006).

1.31.1.1   The Role of the Zoological Stations in Cephalopod Research

It is without doubt, however, that the scientific and systematic analysis of cephalopods' anatomy, physiology, and behavior started near the beginning of the twentieth century, mainly from initiatives of the Zoological Station of Naples (Stazione Zoologica di Napoli) and its outstanding guests.

The Stazione, with its strategic position on the seafront, fleet of fishing boats, and professional personnel, gave foreign scientists the unique opportunity to combine leisure and work as temporary guests of the institute. Since its foundation, octopuses were among its favorite research models; moreover, they figured as a symbol of the Stazione, as is clear from the decorations on the wrought-iron gates of the main entrance to the institute (**Figure 1**) and from the numerous old postcards of the Naples Aquarium, which often depicted them. This stemmed mainly from the the long-standing tradition of Neapolitan fishermen to catch live cephalopods, always considered a prime delicacy (for review, see Lo Bianco, 1909; Lane, 1960).

Figure 1   The gate of the main entrance to the Stazione Zoologica A. Dohrn, built during the final phase of the construction of the institute (1905–1910). It is embellished with motifs of traditional fishing tools, such as the fishing net (bottom) and the row of spears and tridents (top), the latter being a symbol of the Greek sea god Poseidon. Marine creatures, such as crabs and octopuses (detail on right), are carefully depicted by Neapolitan craftsmen.

During this period, the outstanding studies of Giuseppe Jatta (1896) and Adolf Naef (1923, 1928) on the anatomy, systematics, and ontogeny of cephalopods, conducted and published at the Stazione, formed the groundwork for further studies. In addition, the first observations of cephalopods living in captive conditions (in tanks at the Naples Aquarium) gave an idea of the complexity of their behavior and learning capabilities (e.g., Piéron, 1911; for review see Boycott, 1954). Dr. Ariane Droescher referred to a description by Anton Dohrn, who tried to avoid octopuses feeding on lobsters kept in adjacent tanks. Solid cement walls, raised several centimeters above the water surface, separated the aquarium's tanks. However, his attempts proved to be unsuccessful. In fact, as observed by Dohrn, the "same day, one of [the octopuses] climbed over the wall, attacked the unsuspecting crayfish and, after a short battle, tore him into two pieces! ... The octopus [could] have seen that the crab [was] set by the keeper into the neighbouring tank, or he [could have] smelled the prey in the circulating water of the tanks. Anyhow, the event shows that the octopus [was] able to deduce from a sensual impression that there [was] a prey that he did not see, to conclude and, finally, to perform an air-jump in the right direction" (Salvini-Plawen, 1979, pp. 218–219).

Research on the biology and behavior of cephalopods was not confined to the Stazione but attracted the attention of and flourished in many other marine laboratories, both in Europe and the United States. As an example, a thorough description of the chromatic changes and behavioral repertoire of *Octopus vulgaris* was carried out by Cowdry (1911) at the Bermuda Biological Station for Research. Similar studies were conducted on *Loligo pealeii* by Williams (1909) at the Marine Biological Laboratory (Woods Hole, MA, USA) and by Stevenson (1934) at the Biological Station of St. Andrews (Scotland). Finally, the behavior and complexity of body patterning of *Sepia officinalis* was described by Bert (1867) at Arcachon (France), by Tinbergen (1939) at the Aquarium of the Zoological Station of Der Helder (The Netherlands), and finally by Holmes (1940) and Sanders and Young (1940), who carried out their studies at the Marine Biological Laboratory in Plymouth (UK).

1.31.1.2   A Research Effort Lasting Over a Century

In order to evaluate the research on cephalopods from the pioneering studies to the present day, we counted the number of publications cited in the Zoological

Record on a yearly basis for over a century, from 1900 to 2006 (**Figure 2**). Only publications concerning the anatomy and physiology of the central nervous system, the behavioral responses to learning paradigms, or living habits of cephalopods were considered pertinent and were accounted for. The number and distribution of papers over years clearly shows the prominent role achieved by the octopus in the study of learning and memory in cephalopods in the 15 years spanning from 1955 to 1970 (**Figure 2**).

1.31.1.2.1 The contribution of J. Z. Young

After the Second World War, the insight into the octopus rose mainly by the initiative of the British anatomist and zoologist John Zachary Young. On a yearly basis, JZ (as he was commonly called), together with a plethora of students and co-workers, was hosted by the Stazione Zoologica, where he systematically studied the anatomy and physiology of cephalopods' nervous system, increasing the knowledge on the behavior and learning capabilities

of these animals. Many people were involved in these and related physiological studies: Brian B. Boycott, Francesco Ghiretti, Pasquale Graziadei, Nicolas J. Mackintosh, Hector Maldonado, John B. Messenger, William R.A. Muntz, Andrew Packard, Geoffrey D. Sanders, Norman S. Sutherland, and Martin J. Wells are but a few names.

The impressive bulk of knowledge gained over these years at the Stazione and in other laboratories around the world has confirmed the old view of cephalopod preparations as marine guinea pigs (A. Droescher, personal communication) or as primates of the sea (Kerstitch, 1988). In fact, Young became more and more conscious of the fact that the "brain of the octopus has already abundantly proved its value for the study of behaviour. It is perhaps the type most divergent from that of mammals that is really suitable for study of the learning process" (Young, 1971: p. vii).

Apart from a few other contributions (for review, see Boycott, 1954), when J. Z. Young and Brian

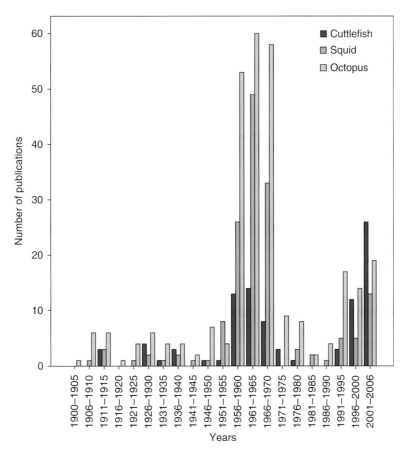

Figure 2 Number of publications per quinquennium on behavior, learning, and memory in cephalopods (cuttlefish, squid, and octopus) indexed in the Zoological Record from 1900 to 2006.

Boycott started their adventure with *Octopus vulgaris* at the Stazione Zoologica, two major works were available to them: a comprehensive overview of the brains of different cephalopod species (*Sepia officinalis, Sepiola robusta, Loligo vulgaris, Illex coindetii, Argonauta argo, O. vulgaris, Eledone moschata, Ocythoe tuberculata*; Thore, 1939) and an experimental study on the effects of the removal of certain lobes of the brain of *S. officinalis* on the behavior and learning of the cuttlefish (Sanders and Young, 1940).

Their aim was to study the learning capabilities of these animals by combining behavioral observations and lesions of the neural centers in order to disclose the functional organization of the cephalopod brain involved in the control of different behaviors; essentially, the predatory response.

O. vulgaris appeared to them as the ideal candidate for a series of reasons. First, because it was easy to maintain in aquaria. A tank of relatively reduced space ($30 \times 100 \times 40$ cm) with running seawater and a pair of bricks as shelter was (and still is) sufficient to make an octopus happy and at home. In this type of experimental setting, an initially scared, hiding, and pale octopus, as it commonly appears on the day it is captured becomes a tame, pet-like animal with time (Buytendijk, 1933; Hochner et al., 2006). Second, because of its natural curiosity. A few days in captivity are normally enough for the octopus to show its intrinsic attitude to attend to any object placed in its aquaria, which is largely a result of its voracity and exploratory drive toward natural (or artificial) objects. Third, because of its resilience to recover from massive brain surgery, contrary to what Young and coworkers experienced with *S. officinalis* (Sanders and Young, 1940).

The advantage of the octopus preparation became clear when Boycott introduced an efficient training technique. *O. vulgaris*'s hunting behavior was utilized as biological drive to teach animals to discriminate between stimuli that were positively and negatively reinforced. In the first experiments, octopuses were presented with crabs alone or associated with a white square; every attack on the latter was negatively reinforced (6–12 V AC). Several dozen trials were enough for the animals to learn the task and to respond correctly in quite a stable and predictive way.

In a series of subsequent experiments, it was demonstrated that octopuses were able to distinguish between different shapes by successive presentation of the two objects. The octopus was allowed to eat the crab when it attacked the positive figure, but an electric shock was delivered to the animal by a probe when it attacked the negative stimulus (Boycott and Young, 1956; for review, see Sanders, 1975; Hanlon and Messenger, 1996). Following this initial set of experiments, the protocol was improved by giving the animal a piece of anchovy as positive reinforcement instead of crabs, which could reduce the octopuses' predatory response because of satiety (Young, 1961).

1.31.1.3   The Breadth of the Studies on Octopus and Other Cephalopods

The versatility of this training protocol allowed a rapid growth of the field up to the 1960s (see also **Figure 2**). In fact, different research directions emerged from the original study by Boycott and Young (for review, see also Wells, 1965b).

For example, the first were centered on the study of the different sensorial capabilities (orientation in space, vision, chemotaxis, touch, and proprioception) and of the structures devoted to their control using different approaches (e.g., behavioral, ablation, and stimulation). Subsequent attention was focused on disclosing the role of the lobes of the brain (essentially the vertical and the peduncle lobes) in the learning and behavioral responses and in the motor coordination.

All these studies allowed Young and coworkers to produce a model of the brain of a learning (and behaving) octopus (Young, 1964; Clymer, 1973). In addition, these studies demonstrated that the animals were capable of sensitization, habituation, associative learning (passive avoidance, visual and tactile discrimination), and spatial learning (for a review, see Young, 1961; Sanders, 1975; Wells, 1978; Boyle, 1986; Boal, 1996; Hanlon and Messenger, 1996; Hochner et al., 2006). As clearly stated by Wells, "Octopuses can be taught to make a wide variety of tactile and visual discriminations. They learn rapidly under conditions that would lead to learning by mammals, and they achieve similar standards of accuracy of performance. This places them in a different category from many invertebrates, where research has tended to concentrate on demonstrating that the animals can learn at all. In the case of *Octopus* there is now no doubt that the species can learn, whatever definition of learning one cares to employ. One is free to pass on to considerations of *what* these animals can detect and learn about the world around them and what *we* can learn about the organisation of the cephalopod brain from their successes and failures" (Wells, 1965a, p. 115).

The analysis of the literature clearly shows what cephalopod workers (and modern neuroscientists) know well: The octopus, as a model, was almost (and suddenly) abandoned by the end of the 1960s (**Figure 2**).

This was mainly a result of:

- The relatively poor control by experimenters of the behavioral training procedures (Bitterman, 1966, 1975);
- The lack of appropriate tools to explore the neurophysiological properties of cells within certain lobes of the brain (e.g., amacrine cells in the vertical lobe; Young, 1985); and
- The inability of octopuses to pick up kinesthetic cues and the lack of proprioceptive feedback of the higher centers of the octopus brain (review in Wells, 1978).

Controlled handling, maintenance, and training procedures (Walker et al., 1970) and the thorough knowledge of the behavior and learning capabilities of cephalopods (Maldonado, 1963a; Packard, 1963; Messenger, 1968, 1977; Packard and Sanders, 1969, 1971; Packard and Hochberg, 1977; Hanlon, 1978; Hanlon and Messenger, 1988) have allowed subsequent workers to cope with the difficulties implicit in the training protocols and to produce renovated experimental approaches to the study of the behavioral biology of learning in these animals. This has led to a growing number of publications over the last 20 years (**Figure 2**) that are not necessarily focused on the octopus model but on different cephalopod species.

1.31.2 The Cephalopod Brain and Its Learning Capabilities

Dramatic evolutionary changes in the body plan and in the gross morphology of the nervous system (and of its relative organization) led to the origin and diversification of the phylum Mollusca (Kandel, 1979; Lee et al., 2003).

The nervous system, in particular, varies greatly in complexity and in the number of neurons among taxa (Bullock, 1965a,b,c,d). However, it is in cephalopods that this complexity reaches its highest degree within the phylum – a complexity that can be recognized at three levels. First, the brain size (relative to body weight) is comparable to that of vertebrate brains and positions cephalopods just below higher vertebrates (i.e., birds and mammals; Packard, 1972). Second, an

average-sized octopus presents roughly 500 million neurons. More than one-third (roughly 200 million cells) are recruited to form its central nervous system (Young, 1963), a number that appears to be from 200 to 10 000 times higher when compared with the brains of other invertebrates (*Apis* and *Aplysia*, respectively). Finally, the degree of complexity of the nervous system is not only limited to the relative size and number of neurons within the brain but also stems from its neuroanatomical organization (for review, see Young, 1971; Budelmann, 1995; Williamson and Chrachri, 2004).

1.31.2.1 General Organization of the Brain

In cephalopods, the ganglia recruited to form the central nervous system may be considered homologous to the labial, buccal, cerebral, pedal, pleural, and visceral ganglia of gastropod mollusks. Contrary to what occurs in the typical molluscan design, in a cephalopod the ganglia are fused together and clustered around the most anterior part of the esophagus (for a review, see Bullock, 1965b; Budelmann, 1995). The agglomeration of the ganglia, which happened by the shortening of the connectives and commissures, form three almost distinct parts: the supra- and the subesophageal masses, and a pair of optic lobes that emerge laterally from the supraesophageal mass (one for each side positioned just behind the eyes).

The supraesophageal mass originated from the ancestral labial, buccal, and cerebral ganglia. The main lobes constituting it are the inferior, superior, and posterior buccal; the inferior frontal, subfrontal, and superior frontal; the vertical; and the basal lobes (**Figure 3**). Moreover, certain lobes of the supraesophageal mass (e.g., the optic and olfactory lobes) are of more recent neural formation. The subesophageal mass, instead, essentially derived from the paired pedal, pleural, and visceral ganglia that fused together to a different extent within and between cephalopod species (Nixon and Young, 2003). Again, neural masses of more recent origin were added to the ganglia listed above to form the brachial ganglion, mainly devoted to the control of the actions of arms and suckers.

Altogether, this provides cephalopods with the highest degree of centralization compared with any other mollusk and with the vast majority of other invertebrate phyla. Nevertheless, the nervous system keeps the basic invertebrate organization with layers of cell bodies distributed externally and with an inner neuropil.

(a)

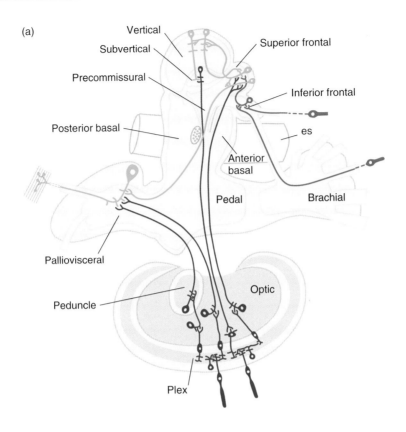

(b)

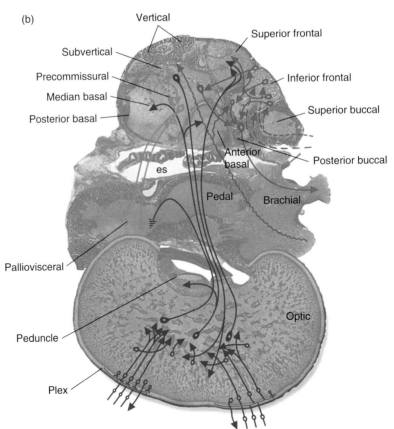

A thorough description of the gross morphology, neuroanatomy, and organization of the cephalopod brain is known for *O. vulgaris* (Young, 1971) and for decapods (Young, 1974, 1976, 1977, 1979; Messenger, 1979). (Reviews on this topic are available in Bullock, 1965b; Budelmann, 1995; Nixon and Young, 2003; but see also Budelmann et al., 1997). In addition, quantitative data on the relative size of the different brain lobes of various species of cephalopods is also available following the contributions of Wirz (1959) and Maddock and Young (1987). Information on the relative size of the lobes in hatchlings has been determined for several Mediterranean species by Frösch (1971; for review see also Nixon and Young, 2003).

Taken as a whole, these studies have shown that the Cephalopoda present a marked diversification of cerebrotypes that should correspond to differences in the habitats occupied within the marine environment (Nixon and Young, 2003; Borrelli, 2007). For example, the brachial and inferior frontal lobes are highly diverse between octopods and decapods, with those in the former being considerably larger than in the latter as a consequence of their benthic lifestyle (and tactile sensorial modality). On the other hand, the vertical lobe (as integrative center, see Sections 1.31.2.2, 1.31.2.3) shows greater variability among species both in relative size and gross morphology (Young, 1979; Maddock and Young, 1987; for a review, see Nixon and Young, 2003).

Finally, as mentioned above, the arms of an octopus contain about two-thirds of the some 500 million neurons in total. The arms can thus work rather autonomously (following a hierarchical functional control of the higher motor centers), as they can generate highly stereotyped movements (Altman, 1971; Sumbre et al., 2001, 2005, 2006).

Moreover, we now know the possible function of roughly 40 lobes within the cephalopod brain by stimulation experiments carried out in *S. officinalis* (Boycott, 1961) and *O. vulgaris* (Boycott and Young, unpublished data: cited in Young, 1963, 1971).

These studies have shown that the supraesophageal mass is responsible for sensory processing and analysis and control of behavior, and it also provides motor commands and coordination to the higher motor centers (i.e., basal lobes). The subesophageal mass, instead, provides the control of particular sets of effectors via intermediate and lower motor centers.

1.31.2.2 Neural Substrates of Behavior

The analysis of hundreds of lesion experiments conducted on octopuses (mostly), squids, and cuttlefishes (review in Sanders, 1975; Boyle, 1986) and of several dozen serial histological sections of cephalopod brains allowed Young and coworkers not only to describe the anatomy of the nervous system of these animals (for a review, see Nixon and Young, 2003) but also to unravel the circuit leading to their visual and tactile learning capabilities (**Figure 3**). In Young's view, learning and memory are achieved in cephalopods by "a series of matrices of intersecting axes, which find associations between the signals of input events and their consequences" (Young, 1991: p. 200).

1.31.2.2.1 Tactile information
During tactile processing (and learning), the decision to grasp or reject an object by an octopus is made on the basis of the interaction of a network made up by the following eight matrices:

- Lateral inferior frontal lobes
- Median inferior frontal lobe
- Subfrontal lobe
- Posterior buccal lobes
- Lateral superior frontal lobes
- Median superior frontal lobe
- Vertical lobe
- Subvertical lobe

The system, which corresponds to roughly six lobes of the supraesophageal mass, is tuned to take any object touched (i.e., tactile exploratory drive) unless pain signals are conveyed.

Figure 3 A schematic representation of the neural pathways for the visual (blue) and tactile (red) sensorimotor systems in the brains of *Sepia officinalis* (a) and *Octopus vulgaris* (b). Possible integrations (or shared pathways) between the two systems are indicated in green. In the supraesophageal mass, several matrices of the two systems overlap, particularly in *Octopus* (see text for details). The optic lobes (bottom) are depicted from horizontal sections. The reciprocal positions and sizes are not in scale. The supra- and subesophageal masses of the two species are drawn or photographed from a sagittal section: (*Sepia* (a) after Sanders FK and Young JZ (1940). Learning and other functions of the higher nervous centres of *Sepia*. *J. Neurophysiol.* 3: 501–526. *Octopus* (b); after Young JZ (1991) Computation in the learning system of cephalopods. *Biol. Bull.* 180: 200–208). Esophagus (es); plexiform zone (plex).

The interaction between the inferior frontal (positive signals) and the subfrontal (negative signals) plays the major role in decision making (i.e., take/reject) by the animal.

Finally, the inferior frontal system (in decapods, the posterior buccal and the lateral inferior frontal lobes; in octopods, the posterior buccal, the lateral and median inferior frontal, and the subfrontal lobes) is qualified as the main site of the long-term memory storage for tactile information, as roughly 60% of the total tactile learning capacity is thought to reside in this brain region (Young, 1983). The remaining quota is distributed between the superior frontal and vertical lobes (approximately 25%) and, to a limited extent, in areas of the subesophageal mass (the remaining 15%; Young, 1983; see also Budelmann and Young, 1985; for a review, see Wells, 1978; Young, 1991, 1995; Williamson, 1995; Williamson and Chrachri, 2004).

In decapods, the so-called inferior frontal lobe is more comparable to the posterior buccal lobe of *Octopus* than to the inferior frontal lobe *sensu stricto* (Young, 1971, 1979), which is lacking in cuttlefishes and squids. However, the distribution and interchange of fibers originating from the arms make the inferior frontal lobe of decapods appear close to the median inferior frontal lobe of *O. vulgaris* (see p. 350 and p. 314 of Young, 1971, 1979, respectively).

From a functional point of view, the fact that cuttlefishes and squids detect their prey visually and capture it with the arms or by ejection of the tentacles (depending on the prey species; see a review in Hanlon and Messenger, 1996) makes us assume that they have only a limited need and capacity for learning tactile information. Manipulatory activities related to feeding are considered largely programmed and based on reflexes (but see Halm et al., 2000, 2002, 2003), with some inhibitory pathways (i.e., reciprocal inhibition) from the small amacrine cells that are distributed among the large motor neurons of the buccal and subesophageal centers (Young, 1976, 1991), in close resemblance to the spinal cord of mammals (Young, 1995).

1.31.2.2.2 Visual information

Like the tactile learning system, visual stimuli are classified and processed behaviorally by a network composed of the following four matrices:

- Lateral superior frontal lobes
- Median superior frontal lobe
- Vertical lobe
- Subvertical lobe

The optic lobe also plays a major role in the visual learning system but was excluded by Young from the assemblage of matrices because of its location outside of the supraesophageal mass.

Again, like before, the system of matrices is tuned to promote the animal to attack the stimulus unless unpleasant feelings are perceived. At the level of the optic lobes, the cells from the retina reach the outer plexiform zone, where they make contact with a large number of cells (second-order visual cells; see **Figure 3**) that act as feature detectors. They constitute dendritic fields of various shapes and extensions that allow the recognition of "the relevant features of objects and scenes" (Young, 1995, p. 434) encountered by the animals during their everyday life (see also Deutsch, 1960; Sutherland, 1960; for a review, see Sanders, 1975; Hanlon and Messenger, 1996). The axons of the second-order cells "form columns proceeding to the center of the [optic] lobe, where they interact in an interweaving matrix of cells and fibers" (Young, 1991, p. 205).

Outputs of the neurons of the optic lobe proceed toward various areas of the brain (**Figure 3**). Some go directly to the magnocellular lobe, which is considered to act in situations where rapid escape reactions are needed (Young, 1971, 1973, 1991, 1995). Other fibers proceed to the peduncle and basal lobes, thus serving to regulate movements, and finally the third pathway goes toward the core of the visual matrices. It is at this level that the interaction between the lateral superior frontal (promoting the attack) and the median superior frontal and vertical lobes (inhibiting the attack) regulates the animal's behavior. Finally, according to Young, memory formation for visual experiences and their outcome take place within the optic lobes, with active participation of the supraesophageal centers (Young, 1991, 1995).

As is shown in **Figure 3**, the neural organization of the visual system of decapods has close affinities to that of octopods (Cajal, 1917; Sanders and Young, 1940; Young, 1973; for a review, see Nixon and Young, 2003; Williamson and Chrachri, 2004). Perhaps the system works in a similar way in cuttlefishes and squids, although it has not yet been extensively studied in the learning context, as has been done for octopuses (see a review in Young, 1991; Agin et al., 2006a).

1.31.2.3 How Computation in the Learning System Is Achieved

The idea promoted by Young and colleagues on the existence of multiple matrices in the central nervous system, working in the control of behavioral responses, found its roots in the pioneering studies of Cajal (1917) and Sanders and Young (1940). The model proposed by Young was deduced essentially on the basis of morphological and experimental evidence (see the review in Young, 1961).

Following Young, the two systems work on similar principles. The information is processed through a series of matrices that allow signals of different types (and meanings) to interact to some extent with each other and to regulate subsequent behavior for attack/take and retreat/reject responses (**Figure 3**). In addition, the modulation between promotion and inhibition is tuned in order to facilitate exploratory behavior. According to Young, the systems are designed with a close similarity with complex nervous systems such as the mammalian hippocampus and neocortical centers (Young, 1995). This system seems to be limited in that a complete integration (transfer) between visual and tactile information is relegated only at the level of the effectors (Allen et al., 1986), although limited cross-modality has been shown in *O. digueti* at higher neural levels (Michels et al., 1987). Similar findings are reported for *O. vulgaris* by Robertson and Young (in preparation, cited by Michels et al., 1987) but unfortunately are unpublished as far as we know.

Wells (1978) published an alternative hypothesis worthy of mention based on the response of animals to an associative learning context. In his opinion, the sensorial inputs (visual system) reach the vertical lobe, where they are modulated on the basis of the effects of positive or negative signals (tactile system). Here the system is tuned to sensitize by raising or lowering the level of response on the basis of previous experiences. In this way, new information is added to the long-term cumulative experience, allowing short-term fluctuations and flexible and adaptive behavior (Wells, 1978).

The hierarchical control of motor patterns (described earlier) with lower (i.e., arms), intermediate (i.e., subesophageal), and higher (i.e., supraesophageal) motor centers (Boycott, 1961; Young, 1971, 1991) has been updated by experimental evidence (Plän, 1987). According to this view, different motor areas work in consensus, contributing to a more democratic concept of neuronal assembly. In other words, parallel central sensorimotor pathways cooperate synaptically to produce a given motor pattern (i.e., behavior; Plän, 1987), which appears to be similar to what has been shown in other invertebrates (for a review, see Getting, 1989; Leonard and Edstrom, 2004; Calabrese, 2007).

These models should be validated (hierarchical vs. democratic) in view of modern experimental approaches.

The compartmentalization (or certain modularity of the system) achieved by the multiple matrices may correspond well to the lifestyle adaptations of cephalopod species in different environments and niches (Nixon and Young 2003; **Figure 4**), as recently tested by combining ecological and neuroanatomical data (Borrelli, 2007).

As solicited in several occasions by Young himself (1985, 1995), a physiological investigation of the responses of the cells within the various regions of the brain is necessary to disclose the functional characteristics of the system. It is only relatively recently that attention has been focused on studies of this kind, starting from the pioneering studies on *S. officinalis* (Bullock and Budelmann, 1991) and *O. vulgaris* (Williamson and Budelmann, 1991) up to the latest findings of Hochner and coworkers (2003, 2006).

Figure 4 Old drawing by Comingio Merculiano (188?, unpublished) of octopuses (*Octopus vulgaris*), squids (probably *Loligo vulgaris*), and cuttlefishes (*Sepia officinalis*) expressing their different behavioral adaptations. Stazione Zoologica Archives, ASZN: Ua.I.506.

The most recent electrophysiological studies in the octopus confirm the view that convergent evolution has led to the selection of similar networks and synaptic plasticity in remote taxa (i.e., cephalopods and higher vertebrates), contributing to the production of complex behavior and learning capabilities (for review, see Hochner et al., 2006). A similar architecture and physiological connectivity of the vertical lobe system (i.e., median superior frontal and vertical lobes) of the octopus with the mammalian hippocampus, together with the large number of small neurons acting as interneurons, suggest a typical structure with high redundancy of connections working with en passant innervations. This makes it possible to create large-capacity memory associations (Hochner et al., 2003, 2006). However, the analogy between the octopus and mammalian systems is not complete, the major differences being in the morphological organization and biophysical characteristics (see a review in Bullock, 1965b; Williamson and Chrachri, 2004; Hochner et al., 2006).

Finally, it is important to underline that a system similar to *Octopus* has been found in *S. officinalis*, but with differences emerging at various levels (morphological, physiological, and behavioral; Agin et al., 2006a; Graindorge et al. 2006; B. Hochner, personal communication). The present results, although promising, must be taken with caution since they are preliminary at this stage.

Last, it is worth mentioning that a computer simulation model of the predatory response of *O. vulgaris* (attack behavior *sensu*: Maldonado, 1963a; Packard, 1963; for a review, see also Borrelli et al., 2006) has been developed (Clymer, 1973).

In the model, a mnemon (i.e., a visual feature with associated memory value resulting from experience; Young, 1965) is activated by a given visual input to a specific set of classifying cells and switched on/off on the basis of other inputs that depend on the taste–pain circuits. The output of these units (i.e., attack command) is summed up to produce an overall attack strength, in contrast to the opposite units (retreat command) that in a similar way build an overall retreat strength. These values (or strengths) are combined in the model and determine the final attack/retreat response (Clymer, 1973).

The model proposed by Clymer was based on the knowledge of *O. vulgaris*'s predatory behavior (also as a result of the discrimination experiments) as deduced by Young (1964, 1965) and Maldonado (1963b). Interestingly, the results produced from the model are comparable to those obtained from proper experiments with live animals, including the

responses resulting from short- and long-term changes in behavior and interference on learning performance when spacing between trials is reduced in time (Clymer, 1973). In addition, the model has been recently reviewed and modified on the basis of the most advanced findings on neural networks and learning in simulated environments (Myers, 1992).

1.31.3 Learning in Cephalopods

Many reviews centered on the biology and learning capabilities of cephalopods have been published during the course of the last 50 years. An analysis of the literature indexed in both the Zoological Record and the Web of Science (from 1950 to 2007) selected roughly 100 reviews regarding the topic. Several other reference works (e.g., *The Mollusca* by Wilbur, 1983–1988) with chapters relevant to the subject must also be taken into consideration.

Over the last few decades, different workers have attempted to synthesize the knowledge on the behavioral biology of cephalopods and its flexibility (Packard and Hochberg, 1977; Hanlon, 1988; Mather, 1995, 2007; Boal, 1996; Messenger, 1996, 2001; Williamson and Chrachri, 2004; Borrelli et al., 2006; Hochner et al., 2006, to cite just a few). The most significant and comprehensive reviews published on cephalopod biology, learning, and memory are those by Young (1961), Sanders (1975), Wells (1978), Boyle (1986), and Hanlon and Messenger (1996).

In this chapter, we are deliberately not summarizing the information provided by the papers listed above, as this would necessarily result in redundancy. Our aim is simply to offer the reader with a general overview of what is known on the subject, which phenomena/mechanisms have been described and analyzed in detail, and which cephalopod species have been chosen as models for studies on the learning and memory capabilities of this taxon (**Table 1**). In the following pages, we focus our attention on the results and directions of the most recent advancements on the behavioral biology of learning and memory in cephalopods.

As thoroughly reviewed by Hanlon and Messenger (1996), various forms of learning (**Table 1**) have been demonstrated in cephalopods, from simple sensitization, to associative learning and problem solving, to more complex forms such as spatial and social learning and tool use. In essence, a large number of the entities proposed by Moore (2004) in his cladogram of learning processes have been shown in some of the 780 cephalopod species known to date. It is a pity that

Table 1 Breadth of the learning paradigms shown in cephalopods, by species[a]

	Habituation	Sensitization	Classical conditioning	Instrumental conditioning	Avoidance learning	Spatial learning	Mazes and problem solving	Social learning	Perceptual processes in visual learning
Sepia officinalis	X		√	√	X	X		X	√
Loligo vulgaris	√								
Lolliguncula brevis			√						
Todarodes pacificus			√						
Octopus vulgaris	√	√	√	√	√	√	√	√	√
Octopus bimaculatus			√						
Octopus bimaculoides			√			X			√
Octopus cyanea			√	√					
Octopus joubini					√				
Octopus maorum					√				
Octopus maya			√				√		√
Enteroctopus dofleini			√						
Eledone moschata			√		√				

[a]Data are arranged following Hanlon RT and Messenger JB (1996) *Cephalopod Behaviour*. Cambridge: Cambridge University Press. The learning capabilities (√) by species are deduced from reviews (Sanders GD [1975] The cephalopods. In: Corning WC, Dyal JA, and Willows AOD [eds.] *Invertebrate Learning. Cephalopods and Echinoderms*, pp. 1–101. New York: Plenum Press, and Hanlon RT and Messenger JB [1996] *Cephalopod Behaviour*. Cambridge: Cambridge University Press), with the exception of more recent findings (X) that are also described in the text. It is important to underline that certain paradigms, such as discrimination learning, are here classified as classical conditioning, although they could also be considered as cases of operant (or Thorndikian) conditioning (see Moore, 2004).

learning (and behavior) studies are still restricted to a limited number of representatives (**Table 1**). In fact, a detailed description of the behavioral repertoire is available for only roughly 30 species (review in Hanlon and Messenger, 1996; Borrelli et al., 2006). Another problem inherent to the cephalopod literature is that some phenomena have been relegated to anecdotal accounts (e.g., tool use: Power, 1857; Pliny the Elder, 1961) and that experimentally controlled observations on such capabilities remain to be done.

1.31.3.1 Sensitization

Following our everyday practice with octopuses, the daily presentation of food increases the chance of the animal attacking, so that its predatory performance (measured as the time to attack the prey from its appearance in the tank) improves with time. This is a clear case of sensitization, similar to what was tested empirically in the past by Wells and coworkers, who showed that food could enhance the probability to attack the stimuli (as much as shock depressed it; Wells, 1967a, cited in Hanlon and Messenger, 1996), or as was demonstrated in conditions where chemotactic behavior was studied (Chase and Wells, 1986).

This phenomenon has recently been confirmed in our laboratory for *O. vulgaris* following the classic acclimatization phase to the experimental setting. The continuous administration of a reward (food) over days improves the predatory performance that reaches a steady-state level during consecutive attacks. However, it is difficult to rule out whether different speeds in the attack curves (when interindividual variability is evaluated) may be related to food preferences, novelty, or familiarity toward food items, or to individual differences in the capability to cope with contextual learning processes, and so on (see also Section 1.31.4.1).

Finally, it could be extremely interesting to explore whether the relative length of time in the laboratory has an effect on octopuses' performance in a learning paradigm, say, for example, on the individual preferences in a simultaneous visual discrimination task. This concept should not be underestimated, also considering that as the positive learning process (see Section 1.31.4.1) proceeds with time, differences between individuals may be reduced to a few clear-cut responses and other characteristics of the subjects may emerge. Such processes may be easily extended to other cephalopods, although significant differences between species are expected as a result of different lifestyles and adaptive capabilities (for a review, see Packard, 1972; Nixon and Young, 2003).

1.31.3.2 Various Forms of Associative Learning

A new set of learning protocols (or variations on the theme) has recently been developed successfully in cephalopods. We provide a few examples below.

Painting quinine on the carapax of prey items (crabs, shrimps) was sufficient to show simple and rapid taste aversion learning in *S. officinalis* (Darmaillacq et al., 2004). This produced significant shifts in prey choice that were retained over the long term (for at least 3 days; Darmaillacq et al., 2004).

Calvé (2005) showed that the cutout of a bird (predator) gliding over individual cuttlefishes elicited startling reactions of different intensities. The startling stimulus significantly affected the cuttlefishes' hunting behavior, although evidence suggests that the animals habituated to it (Calvé, 2005).

Plastic spheres were utilized in successive visual discrimination tasks in order to test whether classical conditioning could change the species-specific predatory (or hunting) behavior; the results suggest that autoshaping occurs in *S. officinalis* (Cole and Adamo, 2005).

All the cases mentioned above represent innovations in the practice of learning studies with *Sepia* and clear additions to the classic prawn-in-the-tube training procedure pioneered by Sanders and Young (1940) and modified by successive authors (Wells, 1962; Messenger, 1973; see also Chichery and Chichery, 1992a,b; **Figure 5**). Notwithstanding, this procedure promoted a large number of studies on associative learning in the cuttlefish and on the biological machinery involved (e.g., Agin et al., 2000, 2001, 2003; Bellanger et al., 1997, 1998, 2003, 2005; Halm et al., 2003). Recent findings in *S. officinalis* strongly support the view that learning not to attack prey trapped in a transparent tube (inhibitory learning) corresponds to associative learning (Agin et al., 2006b; Purdy et al., 2006).

The number of training protocols available for *Octopus* is traditionally greater than for other species, mainly as a result of the animal's behavioral flexibility and feasibility of experimental studies with this species (see also **Table 1**). Moreover, recent protocols such as passive avoidance, additional problem-solving tasks (e.g., jars with multiple openings, black boxes; Borrelli, 2007), and even habituation tests have extended the repertoire of training paradigms that may be utilized to find answers to the fundamental question of how and to what extent *O. vulgaris* is capable of learning to modify its behavioral response.

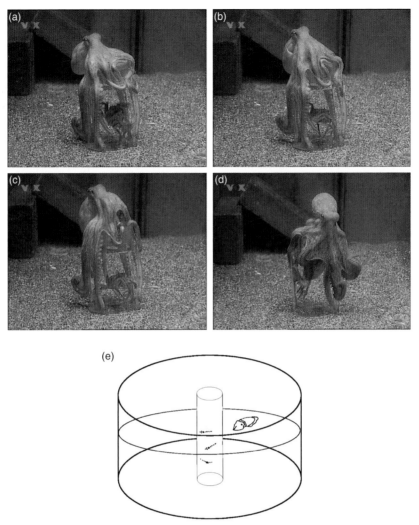

Figure 5 Two examples of classic tasks utilized to study learning and memory recall in *Octopus* and *Sepia*. (a)–(d) A sequence of frames taken from video recordings of the problem-solving experiment in *O. vulgaris* (classic jar). Courtesy of Mr. M. Schumacher, RS-Film. (e) A sketch of the prawn-in-the-tube protocol utilized with *S. officinalis* (after Wells MJ (1962) Early learning in *Sepia*. *Symp. Zool. Soc. Lond.* 8: 149–169).

1.31.3.3   Development of the Learning Capabilities

The prawn-in-the-tube protocol, which was and is still utilized to study associative learning in *S. officinalis*, disclosed important details on how cuttlefishes' behavioral plasticity changes during ontogeny. The analysis of this phenomenon made it possible to find significant correlations with the development (and maturation) of the neural circuitry, considered to play a role in the processing of behavioral responses and learned changes (Wells, 1962; Messenger, 1973; Chichery and Chichery, 1992a,b; Dickel et al., 1997, 1998, 2001; Agin et al., 2006a,c; for review see also Dickel et al., 2006).

In a similar way, the predatory efficiency of *Loligo* spp. on copepod swarms is reported to improve with age. It was found that the mastery of copepod capture develops progressively from the initial basic attack type up to more specialized strategies that effectively extend the range of capture to both longer and shorter distances, culminating in the adult-like prey capture behavior (Chen et al., 1996).

Similar changes of behavior with experience have also been described for octopuses; the optimization of the site and number of holes drilled in bivalve preys, for example, distinguishes juvenile from adult performance (see a review in Mather, 1995, 2007).

1.31.3.4 Spatial Learning

Spatial learning was originally tested in cephalopods using mazes, which led to a heated debate as to whether octopuses were capable or not of learning a detour (Bierens de Haan, 1926; Buytendijk, 1933; Schiller, 1949; Boycott, 1954; Wells, 1965a; but see Walker et al., 1970; Moriyama and Gunji, 1997).

During the last few decades, studies on the problem-solving abilities of these animals have been frequently confused and erroneously attributed to spatial learning processes (Piéron, 1911; Fiorito et al., 1990, 1998b; but for critiques, see Mather, 1995; Hanlon and Messenger, 1996).

Nevertheless, spatial learning *sensu stricto* has been shown in several species over the last few years. Apart from the pioneering studies of Mather (1991) on *O. vulgaris*, learning to orient and navigate in space is reported for *O. bimaculoides* (Boal et al., 2000a) and *S. officinalis* (Karson, 2003; Karson et al., 2003; Graindorge et al., 2006; Alves et al., 2007). However, our knowledge is probably underestimated relative to the large number of cephalopods that are known to cover short and/or long distances in space (e.g., Shevtsov, 1996; Sims et al., 2001; Arkhipkin and Middleton, 2002; Oosthuizen and Smale, 2003; Arkhipkin et al., 2004, 2006; Olyott et al., 2006; Smith et al., 2006; Watanabe et al., 2006; for a review, see also Hanlon and Messenger, 1996).

Such studies should be encouraged to increase our knowledge on the differences in the spatial capabilities among cephalopod species. In addition, this new avenue of research could facilitate comparative analysis to answer questions relative to the neural structures (i.e., the hippocampus and possibly the vertical lobe system; Graindorge et al., 2006) involved in the processing of such a sophisticated ability, as recently found in other animals (Jacobs, 2003; Frost and Mouritsen, 2006).

1.31.3.5 Other Learning Capabilities

Problem solving and social learning have mostly been studied in *O. vulgaris*. These learning paradigms have often been debated and criticized for not providing clear evidence of learning in these animals (Mather, 1995, 2007; Hanlon and Messenger, 1996; but see also Biederman and Davey, 1993; Suboski et al., 1993).

1.31.3.5.1 Problem solving

The task traditionally utilized to test the problem-solving capabilities of *O. vulgaris* (Fiorito et al., 1990), derived from the pioneering experiments by Piéron

(1911), uses the well-known skills of octopuses with jars (Cousteau and Diolé, 1973). In the classic experiment, the animal is faced with a transparent glass jar, closed with a plug, containing a live prey. The octopus generally attacks the object at first glance, with the attack elicited by visual cues (the sight of the prey). The physical contact with the jar makes the animal switch to the tactile-driven exploration of the stimulus (**Figure 5**). While manipulating the jar, the octopus must solve two problems: the operandum (i.e., removing the plug by pulling), and the detour (i.e., the blind exploration of the inside of the jar with the arms to reach for the prey).

It was shown that octopuses spent significantly less time on the two motor components of the task with trials, thus suggesting that learning is involved in solving the problem (Fiorito et al., 1990, 1998b).

The switch between the two modalities (from visual to tactile) that controls and determines the octopus' performance in the task is not automatic and occurs at different instances in different animals. This further supports the view that learning of the task is required in order to sort out the motor programs (probably species specific) that are necessary to solve the paradigm. In fact, the pulling action, which is required by an animal dealing with the operandum, is already present in the species' behavioral repertoire, as the same technique is adopted by octopuses preying upon bivalves (McQuaid, 1994; Fiorito and Gherardi, 1999; Steer and Semmens, 2003). Moreover, the detour may be compared to the so-called speculative pounce (e.g., Yarnall, 1969), a common foraging strategy in which animals mostly use a tactile-driven manipulation and blind exploration of the sea bottom in search of edible items hidden under rocks or in crevices (for a review, see Hanlon and Messenger, 1996; Borrelli et al., 2006).

Different tasks (e.g., jars with multiple openings and boxes with drawers) have recently been designed to further explore *O. vulgaris'* problem-solving capabilities.

Similar objects could be used with other octopod species, facilitating comparative analysis of the taxon's behavioral flexibility. In addition, such tasks may provide more general information on the biological correlates involved in the two modalities (visual and tactile) that govern such behavioral responses.

1.31.3.5.2 Social learning

Fiorito and Scotto (1992) provided experimental evidence of social learning in *O. vulgaris*. They showed that naïve animals were able to discriminate and choose between two stimuli following observation of trained conspecifics. The observer octopuses appeared to follow the model witnessed, and their choice seemed to be stable over time. The original work was replicated to test the role of the neural circuit considered to be involved in social learning (Fiorito and Chichery, 1995) and to study the attention and memory retrieval capabilities of this kind of learning after a pharmacological interference (Fiorito et al., 1998a).

The results of social learning in *O. vulgaris* were debated and criticized in a number of publications (e.g., Biederman and Davey, 1993; Hanlon and Messenger, 1996).

Future studies are required to reply to the many questions that remain open on this peculiar learning capability, since it is possible that certain other factors may act in favor of or against the outcome of the observation of the conspecific's behavior by naïve observers (e.g., reproductive drive, social dominance, territoriality; for review, see also Boal, 2006). This, at least, appears to be the case in *S. officinalis*, where social experience promotes (Warnke, 1994) or inhibits (Boal et al., 2000b) social facilitation in the feeding behavior of cuttlefishes, probably depending on the relative age of the animals.

1.31.4 Neglected Issues in the Study of Cephalopod Learning

As amply discussed above, most of our knowledge on the learning capabilities and memory recall in cephalopods derives from experiments conducted in the laboratory, the sole exception being the field studies on *O. vulgaris* carried out in the waters of Bermuda (Mather, 1991; Mather and O'Dor, 1991). Mather and colleagues demonstrated that octopuses acquire information and keep memories of their surroundings to navigate during foraging trips (i.e., spatial learning; Mather, 1991; see also Hanlon and Messenger, 1996; Forsythe and Hanlon, 1997). Moreover, *O. vulgaris* is capable of behavioral plasticity in lifestyle resulting from changes in foraging needs and predation pressure (Mather and O'Dor, 1991).

Despite the growing number of publications on the habits and adaptive responses of cephalopods in the wild (e.g., Smale and Buchan, 1981; Moynihan and Rodaniche, 1982; Roper and Hochberg, 1988; Mather and Mather, 1994; Hanlon et al., 1999), our inference on learning in cephalopods is still largely biased by laboratory evidence. Whether this is the result of the behavioral flexibility (neural and

behavioral) of the cephalopod system to the new context (captive situation), or whether it corresponds to the animals' real needs in the wild, still remains an open question.

1.31.4.1 Effect of Acclimatization: Contextual Learning

Following capture, the animals are generally immediately brought by the fishermen to the laboratory, where they are exposed to the experimental setting (i.e., a novel environment). In the case of an octopus, the animal is thus constrained to a tank that represents a foraging area about 300 times smaller than that required by the animal in natural conditions. In addition, the scenery to which the animal is exposed is somewhat dull and uniform, independent of whether it is designed to provide an enriched or an impoverished environment (e.g., Dickel et al., 2000; Anderson and Wood, 2001; Poirier et al., 2004). We may therefore hypothesize that the new context has only a poor resemblance to the seascape the cephalopod had experienced until then.

This is true not only for octopuses but also for other cephalopod species. A rough analysis of the literature on cephalopods published over the last 10 years has provided exhaustive examples and confirms this view.

The animal must adapt to this novel environment, which is achieved in a variable amount of time and is generally referred as acclimatization. During the acclimatization phase, a common practice is to expose cephalopods to live prey (for exceptions, see, e.g., Boletzky and Hanlon, 1983; Boal, 1993; Koueta et al., 2006), not only to maintain the animals in captivity but also to test their recovery in motivation to attack (i.e., well-being; for a review, see Boyle, 1991). In addition, the animals are exposed to experiments that study their predatory behavior (attack/not attack or take/reject responses). Thus, they must be able to face the task and plastically adapt their species-specific predatory behavior to the new context. As already mentioned above, this phase takes a variable length of time and depends (from species to species) on the animals' previous experience, the individual variability resulting from biological and possibly ecological factors (differences in age, sex, maturity, etc.), and the common practice of experimenters, to cite a few examples.

It has been recently demonstrated that during the acclimatization phase, the animal is exposed to a positive learning process, which is a form of contextual learning. As described by Maldonado (1963a,b, 1964), at the beginning of acclimatization (or training), the time spent by an octopus to attack the stimulus is relatively long, and the behavior (in terms of types of attack) is highly variable. However, as the animal becomes more and more accustomed to the experimental setting (or paradigm), its attacks on the stimulus become faster and faster, a process known as the positive learning process. Moreover, this reduces the types of attack curves to nearly a stereotype, that is, the full attack in the octopus (Maldonado, 1963a; Packard, 1963) and the tentacle attack in decapods (e.g., *S. officinalis*: Messenger, 1968; *Loligo vulgaris*: Neill and Cullen, 1974; *L. pealeii* and *L. plei*: Kier, 1982; *Illex illecebrosus*: Foyle and O'Dor, 1988).

In sum, during the positive learning process (*sensu* Maldonado, 1963a), behavioral syndromes are generally reduced to a few broad types representing populational differences (within a species). These differences are recognized to play important ecological and evolutionary roles, mainly during the adaptation to environmental changes (Sih et al., 2004a,b).

In addition, there is evidence in *O. vulgaris* that this phenomenon is directly linked to a more general form of contextual learning, as recently shown in other invertebrates (e.g., Tomsic et al., 1998; Liu et al., 1999; Haney and Lukowiak, 2001; Menzel, 2001; Law et al., 2004; Skow and Jakob, 2006; Zhang et al., 2006).

A series of factors may interfere in this process, such as:

- The time of day at which the experiment is conducted (which does not necessarily correspond to the animal's peak of activity in natural conditions);
- The feeding regime;
- The experimental setting to which the animal is exposed; and
- The prey types utilized in captivity that do not necessarily correspond to those fed upon in the wild.

Concerning this last point, for example, the animals' performance in the new context may be affected by individual dietary preferences derived from previous feeding habits (e.g., for *S. officinalis* Darmaillacq et al., 2006), which have also been shown to influence the performance in visual and tactile discrimination tasks during associative learning (e.g., for *O. vulgaris*: Messenger and Sanders, 1972; Bradley and Messenger, 1977).

1.31.4.2 Neophobia/Neophilia and the Shy–Bold Continuum

Another neglected issue in the study of learning in cephalopods is whether novelty may interfere with

the animals' decision-making processes (Greenberg and Mettke-Hofmann, 2001). In other words, familiar objects or prey types should be preferred to novel ones, and the natural exploratory drive, connected to cephalopods' voracious appetite, should be reduced by the presence of novel stimuli.

In *O. vulgaris*, for example, the behavioral flexibility (in terms of learning capabilities) of this species corresponds to ecological plasticity, where opportunistic behaviors and reduced neophobia are exhibited (see also Section 1.31.2.3). *O. vulgaris* seems to show less feeding specialization and a higher versatility in foraging than other cephalopods. This appears to be related to the changes in the lifestyle during ontogeny (Hanlon and Messenger, 1996; Nixon and Mangold, 1998) and to the frequent horizontal and vertical migrations by the different age classes moving in the water column (e.g., Oosthuizen and Smale, 2003). Therefore, octopuses have to deal with different environments both at a small and a large time scale (seasons and life history, respectively) that expose them to potentially different degrees of complexity. Under such circumstances, a low neophobia is expected for *O. vulgaris*, as results from current experimental work.

On the other hand, ecological stereotypy may favor individuals (or species) that contrast novel situations by exhibiting less flexible behaviors. This should be investigated.

A consequence of the neophobia/neophilia behavioral types discussed above, at any level (from the individual to the species), leads to the shy–bold continuum (or in the cephalopod sense, to the approach–withdrawal axis *sensu*; Packard, 1963). This has been shown in several cephalopods: *S. officinalis* (Hanlon and Messenger, 1988; Calvé, 2005), *Euprymna tasmanica* (Sinn and Moltschaniwskyj, 2005), *O. vulgaris* (Packard, 1963; Borrelli, 2007), and *O. rubescens* (Mather and Anderson, 1993).

As described by Calvé (2005), cuttlefishes are classified as shy when they mostly remain inactive and when, following stimulation, respond by inking and jetting away. At the opposite end of the spectrum, bold animals appear active in the tank and interact more with humans (i.e., are tame; Buytendijk, 1993; Hochner et al., 2006). Of course, individuals will respond differently to the same tests on the basis of whether their behavioral traits tend more toward one or the other of the opposite shy–bold extremes of the axis.

Similar findings have been shown for *O. rubescens*, where individuals were classified into three major behavioral components (activity, reactivity, avoidance; Mather and Anderson, 1993).

As already mentioned, the individual differences of behavioral traits in cephalopods confirm the phenomenon to be widespread among different taxa, ranging from invertebrates to vertebrates (e.g., Armitage, 1986; Kagan et al., 1988; Coleman and Wilson, 1998; López et al., 2005; Mettke-Hofmann et al., 2005a; for a review, see also Gosling, 2001; Sih et al., 2004b; Mettke-Hofmann et al., 2005b).

In planning future studies testing neophobia/neophilia in cephalopods, the importance of population differences (i.e., genetic polymorphism) and individual experience on environmental factors should be considered, as has been done in other animals. For example, it could be interesting to test how the response of individuals captured with different fishing methods in the wild would appear along the shy–bold continuum in laboratory conditions, taking advantage of what is known in the pumpkinseed sunfish (Coleman and Wilson, 1998). Moreover, Coleman and Wilson (1998) discovered that animals that behaved boldly in threatening contexts did not act necessarily the same when exposed to novel foods (i.e., foraging contexts). Would it not be intriguing to find similar – or even contrasting – results in cephalopods?

1.31.5 Memory in Cephalopods

Despite the considerable number of studies published on the extent of memory recall and on the effects of its impairment induced by experimental interference (for a review, see Sanders, 1975; Wells, 1978), very little is known on the ability of cephalopods to encode and retrieve information.

From the classic works of Sanders and Young (1940) and Schiller (1949), it was shown that cuttlefishes and octopuses are capable of short- and long-term memory, although differences emerged between the two species and among paradigms (**Table 2**).

It is astonishing that in many cases the memory trace was reported to last for a very long time (e.g., in octopus for weeks, according to Boal, 1991; Fiorito and Scotto, 1992; for months, according to Sanders,

Table 2 Summary of studies on the time course of memory recall in *Sepia officinalis* (*So*) and *Octopus vulgaris* (*Ov*)

Paradigm	Species	Training	STM	MTM	ARM	LTM	PSD	Refs
Prawn-in-the tube	*So*	1-t	20 m			48 h		6
Prawn-in-the tube	*So*	1-t	5 m					7
Prawn-in-the tube	*So*	1-t				24 h	+	8
Prawn-in-the tube	*So*	Spaced				24 h		6
Instrumental conditioning	*So*	Spaced				14 d		10
Avoidance	*So*	Spaced				3 d		9
Classical conditioning	*Ov*	Massed				2 d		2
Classical conditioning	*Ov*	Massed				2 d		4
Classical conditioning	*Ov*	Massed				24 h	–	11
Classical conditioning	*Ov*	Spaced				4 w		1
Classical conditioning	*Ov*	Spaced				16 w		3
Avoidance	*Ov*	Massed	1 h	8 h		1 d		5
Avoidance	*Ov*	Massed			+	24 h	–	11

Different learning paradigms and training procedures with different intervals (massed vs. spaced) or length (single trial, 1-t vs. training to criterion) produce memories of variable time span. Moreover, the extent of the recall at each stage (STM, short term; MTM, medium term; LTM, long term) has not been systematically measured by each of the cited papers (see following, so a blank cell stands for missing data). Finally, only a handful of studies have addressed questions on whether long-term memory is anesthesia resistant (ARM; +, resistance) or protein synthesis dependent (PSD; + dependence; – no effect). Time units are as follows: minutes (m), hours (h), days (d), weeks (w). The references (Refs) included are: 1. Sutherland, 1957a, cited in Sanders GD (1975) The Cephalopods. In: Corning WC, Dyal JA, and Willows AOD (eds.) *Invertebrate Learning. Cephalopods and Echinoderms*, pp. 1–101. New York: Plenum Press; 2. Maldonado H (1968) Effect of electroconvulsive shock on memory in *Octopus vulgaris* Lamarck. *Z. Vgl. Physiol.* 59: 25–37; 3. Sanders, 1970b, cited in Sanders GD (1975) The Cephalopods. In: Corning WC, Dyal JA, and Willows AOD (eds.) *Invertebrate Learning. Cephalopods and Echinoderms*, pp. 1–101. New York: Plenum Press; 4. Wells MJ and Young JZ (1970) Single-session learning by octopuses. *J. Exp. Biol.* 53: 779–788; 5. Sanders GD and Barlow JJ (1971) Variations in retention performance during long-term memory formation. *Nature* 232: 203–204; 6. Messenger JB (1973) Learning in the cuttlefish *Sepia*. *Anim. Behav.* 21: 801–826; 7. Agin V, Dickel L, Chichery R, and Chichery MP (1998) Evidence for a specific short-term memory in the cuttlefish *Sepia*. *Behav. Process.* 43: 329–334; 8. Agin V, Chichery R, Maubert E, and Chichery MP (2003) Time-dependent effects of cycloheximide on long-term memory in the cuttlefish. *Pharmacol. Biochem. Behav.* 75: 141–146; 9. Darmaillacq A-S, Dickel L, Chichery MP, Agin V, and Chichery R (2004) Rapid taste aversion learning in adult cuttlefish *Sepia officinalis*. *Anim. Behav.* 68: 1291–1298; 10. Cole PD and Adamo SA (2005) Cuttlefish (*Sepia officinalis*: Cephalopoda) hunting behavior and associative learning. *Anim. Cogn.* 8: 27–30; 11. Zarrella, unpublished.

1970). Many unpublished observations carried out in our laboratory confirm this view. However, it was found that this remarkably long memory trace is not common to all individuals that learn a given task (Sanders, 1970). The reasons behind this surprising result of only certain individuals having a particularly long memory should be further investigated.

Unfortunately, the systematic analysis of the memory phases (**Table 2**), together with the time course of retention and memory consolidation (and perhaps reconsolidation), in cephalopods remains insufficient, especially when compared with the knowledge currently available for other taxa (for a review, see, e.g., McGaugh, 2000; Dudai, 2004).

Whether the memory recall observed in cephalopods corresponds to a more phylogenetically conserved consolidation mechanism is an issue that has been tested in *O. vulgaris* using several approaches (Maldonado, 1968, 1969; Zarrella, unpublished data). The data suggest that the establishment of long memory traces, to learn conditioned or associative responses, is maintained in *Octopus* following anesthetic treatments and protein synthesis inhibition (Zarrella, unpublished data) applied before or after training (massed intervals). In contrast, electroconvulsive shocks cause significant deficits in retention of previously learned paradigms (spaced intervals: Maldonado, 1968, 1969).

Moreover, protein synthesis inhibition was found to impair memory recall for the prawn-in-the-tube protocol in *S. officinalis* (Agin et al., 2003).

The above studies, although limited in number and species studied, show how promising it could be to test the role of the biological machinery in the establishment of long-term memories in cephalopods, especially when considering the contrasting evidence between species that has emerged so far.

1.31.6 Concluding Remarks

Whoever has had the chance to interact with a cephalopod, in the tank or at sea, remains struck by the richness of its behavioral repertoire, its distinct personality traits, and its penetrating gaze, which make it an extraordinary and fascinating creature. There is no doubt that cephalopods are learning animals, although it is difficult to give an objective view of the variety and extent of their learning capabilities.

What is still lacking in the field is more communication and exchange of ideas among cephalopod researchers and the focus on common aims or objectives that could strengthen the work in these animal

models. The contribution to the knowledge of the behavioral biology in cephalopods should not be restricted to a handful of workers but be of interest to a greater number of scientists.

Through our behavioral analysis of learning and memory in cephalopods, we hope to have contributed to increasing the understanding and scientific interest and awareness of these animals.

As a last note, the study of cephalopods, despite the long historical tradition, suffers from the lack (or incomplete) availability of tools that are now available for other invertebrate models (such as *Apis*, *Aplysia*, *Caenorhabditis*, and *Drosophila*). The approach and direction of studies such as those pioneered and masterly conducted by Maldonado and coworkers on *Chasmagnathus* should be the example (see the review in Romano et al., 2006). The recent work on *Octopus'* genomics (Ogura et al., 2004; Choy et al., 2006) has contributed outstanding results that give us hope for the future.

Acknowledgments

Research in our laboratory was partly supported by Istituto Banco di Napoli, Fondazione.

References

Agin V, Dickel L, Chichery R, and Chichery MP (1998) Evidence for a specific short-term memory in the cuttlefish *Sepia*. *Behav. Process.* 43: 329–334.

Agin V, Chichery R, and Chichery MP (2000) Effects of learning and memory on regional brain variations of cytochrome oxidase activity in *Sepia officinalis*. *Eur. J. Neurosci.* 12: 91.

Agin V, Chichery R, and Chichery MP (2001) Effects of learning on cytochrome oxidase activity in cuttlefish brain. *Neuroreport* 12: 113–116.

Agin V, Chichery R, Maubert E, and Chichery MP (2003) Time-dependent effects of cycloheximide on long-term memory in the cuttlefish. *Pharmacol. Biochem. Behav.* 75: 141–146.

Agin V, Chichery R, Chichery MP, Dickel L, Darmaillacq AS, and Bellanger C (2006a) Behavioural plasticity and neural correlates in adult cuttlefish. *Vie Milieu* 56: 81–87.

Agin V, Chichery R, Dickel L, and Chichery MP (2006b) The "prawn-in-the-tube" procedure in the cuttlefish: Habituation or passive avoidance learning? *Learn. Mem.,* 13: 97–101.

Agin V, Poirier R, Chichery R, Dickel L, and Chichery MP (2006c) Developmental study of multiple memory stages in the cuttlefish *Sepia officinalis. Neurobiol. Learn. Mem.* 86: 264–269.

Allen A, Michels J, and Young JZ (1986) Possible interactions between visual and tactile memories in *Octopus. Mar. Behav. Physiol.* 12: 81–97.

Altman JS (1971) Control of accept and reject reflexes in the octopus. *Nature* 229: 204–206.

Alves C, Chichery R, Boal JG, and Dickel L (2007) Orientation in the cuttlefish *Sepia officinalis*: Response versus place learning. *Anim. Cogn.* 10: 29–36.

Anderson RC and Wood JB (2001) Enrichment for giant pacific octopuses: Happy as a clam? *J. Appl. Anim. Welf. Sci.* 4: 157–168.

Aristotle (1910) Historia Animalium English Translation by D'Arcy Wenthworth Thompson, Vol. IV. Oxford: Clarendon Press.

Arkhipkin AI and Middleton DAJ (2002) Sexual segregation in ontogenetic migrations by the squid *Loligo gahi* around the Falkland Islands. *Bull. Mar. Sci.* 71: 109–127.

Arkhipkin AI, Middleton DAJ, Sirota AM, and Grzebielec R (2004) The effect of Falkland Current inflows on offshore ontogenetic migrations of the squid *Loligo gahi* on the southern shelf of the Falkland Islands. *Estuar. Coast. Shelf S* 60: 11–22.

Arkhipkin AI, Laptikhovsky VV, Sirota AM, and Grzebielec R (2006) The role of the Falkland Current in the dispersal of the squid *Loligo gahi* along the Patagonian Shelf. *Estuar. Coast. Shelf S.* 67: 198–204.

Armitage KB (1986) Individuality, social behavior, and reproductive success in yellow-bellied marmots. *Ecology* 67: 1186–1193.

Bellanger C, Dauphin F, Belzunces LP, Cancian C, and Chichery R (1997) Central acetylcholine synthesis and catabolism activities in the cuttlefish during aging. *Brain Res.* 762: 219–222.

Bellanger C, Dauphin F, Belzunces LP, and Chichery R (1998) Parallel regional quantification of choline acetyltransferase and cholinesterase activity in the central nervous system of an invertebrate (*Sepia officinalis*). *Brain Res. Protoc.* 3: 68–75.

Bellanger C, Dauphin F, Chichery MP, and Chichery R (2003) Changes in cholinergic enzyme activities in the cuttlefish brain during memory formation. *Physiol. Behav.* 79: 749–756.

Bellanger C, Halm MP, Dauphin F, and Chichery R (2005) *In vitro* evidence and age-related changes for nicotinic but not muscarinic acetylcholine receptors in the central nervous system of *Sepia officinalis*. *Neurosci. Lett.* 387: 162–167.

Bert P (1867) Mémoire sur la physiologie de la seiche (*Sepia officinalis* Linn.). *Memoires Soc. Sci. Physi. Nat. Bordeaux* 5: 115–138.

Biederman GB and Davey VA (1993) Social learning in invertebrates. *Science* 259: 1627–1628.

Bierens de Haan JA (1926) Versuche über den Farbensinn und das psychische Leben von *Octopus vulgaris*. *Z. Vgl. Physiol.* 4: 766–796.

Bitterman ME (1966) Learning in the lower animals. *Am. Psychol.* 21: 1073.

Bitterman ME (1975) Critical commentary. In: Corning WC and Dyal JA (eds.) *Invertebrate Learning*, pp. 139–145. New York: Plenum.

Boal JG (1991) Complex learning in *Octopus bimaculoides*. *Am. Malacol. Bull.* 9: 75–80.

Boal JG (1993) An assessment of complex learning in octopuses. PhD Thesis, The University of North Carolina Chapel Hill, Chapel Hill, NC.

Boal JG (1996) A review of simultaneous visual discrimination as a method of training octopuses. *Biol. Rev.* 71: 157–190.

Boal JG (2006) Social recognition: A top down view of cephalopod behaviour. *Vie Milieu* 56: 69–79.

Boal JG, Dunham AW, Williams KT, and Hanlon RT (2000a) Experimental evidence for spatial learning in octopuses (*Octopus bimaculoides*). *J. Comp. Psychol.* 114: 246–252.

Boal JG, Wittenberg KM, and Hanlon RT (2000b) Observational learning does not explain improvement in predation tactics by cuttlefish (Mollusca: Cephalopoda). *Behav. Process.* 52: 141–153.

Boletzky SV and Hanlon RT (1983) A review of the laboratory maintenance, rearing and culture of cephalopod molluscs. *Mem. Mus. Vic.* 44: 147–187.

Borrelli L (2007) Testing the contribution of relative brain size and learning capabilities on the evolution of *Octopus vulgaris* and other cephalopods. PhD Thesis, The Open University London UK and Stazione Zoologica A Dohrn Napoli Italy.

Borrelli L, Gherardi F, and Fiorito G (2006) *A Catalogue of Body Patterning in Cephalopoda*. Napoli, Italy: Stazione Zoologica A Dohrn, Firenze University Press.

Boycott BB (1954) Learning in *Octopus vulgaris* and other cephalopods. *Pubbl. Staz. Zool. Napoli* 25: 67–93.

Boycott BB (1961) The functional organization of the brain of the cuttlefish *Sepia officinalis*. *Proc. R. Soc. Lond. B* 153: 503–534.

Boycott BB and Young JZ (1956) Reactions to shape in *Octopus vulgaris* Lamarck. *Proc. Zool. Soc. Lond.* 126: 491–547.

Boyle PR (1986) Neural control of cephalopod behavior. In: Williams AOD (ed.) *The Mollusca. Neurobiology and Behaviour, Part 2*, pp. 1–99. Orlando: Academic Press.

Boyle PR (1991) *The UFAW Handbook on the Care and Management of Cephalopods in the Laboratory*. Potters Bar: Universities Federation for Animal Welfare.

Bradley EA and Messenger JB (1977) Brightness preference in *Octopus* as a function of the background brightness. *Mar. Behav. Physiol.* 4: 243–251.

Budelmann BU (1995) The cephalopod nervous system: What evolution has made of the molluscan design. In: Briedback O and Kutsch W (eds.) *The Nervous Systems of Invertebrates: An Evolutionary and Comparative Approach*, pp. 115–138. Basel: Birkhäuser Verlag.

Budelmann BU and Young JZ (1985) Central pathways of the nerves of the arms and mantle of *Octopus*. *Philos. Trans. R. Soc. Lond. B* 310: 109–122.

Budelmann BU, Schipp R, and Boletzky SV (1997) Cephalopoda. In: Harrison FW and Kohn AJ (eds.) *Microscopic Anatomy of Invertebrates*, pp. 119–414. New York: Wiley-Liss Inc.

Bullock TH (1965a) Mollusca: Amphineura and Monoplacophora. In: Bullock TH and Horridge GA (eds.) *Structure and Function in the Nervous Systems of Invertebrates*, pp. 1273–1281. San Francisco: WH Freeman.

Bullock TH (1965b) Mollusca: Cephalopoda. In: Bullock TH and Horridge GA (eds.) *Structure and Function in the Nervous Systems of Invertebrates? (eds.* TH Bullock and GA Horridge), pp. 1433–1515. San Francisco: WH Freeman.

Bullock TH (1965c) Mollusca: Gastropoda. In: Bullock TH and Horridge GA (eds.) *Structure and Function in the Nervous Systems of Invertebrates*, pp. 1283–1386. San Francisco: WH Freeman.

Bullock TH (1965d) Mollusca: Pelecypoda and Scaphopoda. In: Bullock TH and Horridge GA (eds.) *Structure and Function in the Nervous Systems of Invertebrates*, pp. 1387–1431. San Francisco: WH Freeman.

Bullock TH and Budelmann BU (1991) Sensory evoked potentials in unanesthetized unrestrained cuttlefish: A new preparation for brain physiology in cephalopods. *J. Comp. Physiol. A* 168: 141–150.

Buytendijk FJJ (1933) Das Verhalten von Octopus nach teilweiser Zerstörung des "Gehirns." *Arch. Néerl. Physiol.* 18: 24–70.

Cajal SR (1917) Contribución al conocimento de la retina y centros opticos de los Cephalopodos. *Trab. Lab. Invest. Biol. Univ. Madrid* 15: 1–83.

Calabrese RL (2007) Motor networks: Shifting coalitions. *Curr. Biol.* 17: R139–R141.

Calvé MR (2005) Individual differences in the common cuttlefish *Sepia officinalis*. MS Thesis, Dalhousie University, Halifax, Nova Scotia.

Chase R and Wells MJ (1986) Chemotactic behavior in octopus. *J. Comp. Physiol. A* 158: 375–381.

Chen DS, VanDykhuizen G, Hodge J, and Gilly WF (1996) Ontogeny of copepod predation in juvenile squid (*Loligo opalescens*). *Biol. Bull.* 190: 69–81.

Chichery MP and Chichery R (1992a) Behavioural and neurohistological changes in aging *Sepia*. *Brain Res.* 574: 77–84.

Chichery R and Chichery MP (1992b) Learning performances and aging in cuttlefish (*Sepia officinalis*). *Exp. Gerontol.* 27: 233–239.

Choy KW, Wang CC, Ogura A, et al. (2006) Molecular characterization of the developmental gene in eyes: Through data-mining on integrated transcriptome databases. *Clin. Biochem.* 39: 224–230.

Clymer JC (1973) A computer simulation model of attack-learning behavior in the octopus. PhD Thesis, University of Michigan, Ann Arbor.

Cole PD and Adamo SA (2005) Cuttlefish (*Sepia officinalis*: Cephalopoda) hunting behavior and associative learning. *Anim. Cogn.* 8: 27–30.

Coleman K and Wilson DS (1998) Shyness and boldness in pumpkinseed sunfish: Individual differences are context-specific. *Anim. Behav.* 56: 927–936.

Cousteau J-Y and Diolé P (1973) *Octopus and Squid. The Soft Intelligence*. Bernard JF (trans).Garden City, NY: Doubleday.

Cowdry EV (1911) The colour changes in *Octopus vulgaris* Lmk. *Contrib. Bermuda Biol. Station Res.* 2: 1–52.

Darmaillacq A-S, Dickel L, Chichery MP, Agin V, and Chichery R (2004) Rapid taste aversion learning in adult cuttlefish *Sepia officinalis*. *Anim. Behav.* 68: 1291–1298.

Darmaillacq A-S, Chichery R, Shashar N, and Dickel L (2006) Early familiarization overrides innate prey preference in newly hatched *Sepia officinalis* cuttlefish. *Anim. Behav.* 71: 511–514.

Darwin C (1870) *Journal of the Researches into the Natural History and Geology of the Countries Visited During the Voyage of HMS Beagle Round the World Under the Command of Capt. Fitz Roy RN*. London: John Murray Albemarle Street.

Deutsch JA (1960) The plexiform zone and shape recognition in the octopus. *Nature* 185: 443–446.

Dickel L, Chichery MP, and Chichery R (1997) Postembryonic maturation of the vertical lobe complex and early development of predatory behavior in the cuttlefish (*Sepia officinalis*). *Neurobiol. Learn. Mem.* 67: 150–160.

Dickel L, Chichery MP, and Chichery R (1998) Time differences in the emergence of short- and long-term memory during post-embryonic development in the cuttlefish *Sepia*. *Behav. Process.* 44: 81–86.

Dickel L, Boal JG, and Budelmann BU (2000) The effect of early experience on learning and memory in cuttlefish. *Dev. Psychobiol.* 36: 101–110.

Dickel L, Chichery MP, and Chichery R (2001) Increase of learning abilities and maturation of the vertical lobe complex during postembryonic development in the cuttlefish *Sepia*. *Dev. Psychobiol.* 39: 92–98.

Dickel L, Darmaillacq AS, Poirier R, Agin V, Bellanger C, and Chichery R (2006) Behavioural and neural maturation in the cuttlefish *Sepia officinalis*. *Vie Milieu* 56: 89–95.

Dudai Y (2004) The neurobiology of consolidation, or, how stable is the engram? *Ann. Rev. Psychol.* 55: 51–86.

Fiorito G and Chichery R (1995) Lesions of the vertical lobe impair visual discrimination learning by observation in *Octopus vulgaris*. *Neurosci. Lett.* 192: 117–120.

Fiorito G and Gherardi F (1999) Prey-handling behaviour of *Octopus vulgaris* (Mollusca Cephalopoda) on Bivalve preys. *Behav. Process.* 46: 75–88.

Fiorito G and Scotto P (1992) Observational learning in *Octopus vulgaris*. *Science* 256: 545–547.

Fiorito G, von Planta C, and Scotto P (1990) Problem solving ability of *Octopus vulgaris* Lamarck (Mollusca Cephalopoda). *Behav. Neural Biol.* 53: 217–230.

Fiorito G, Agnisola C, d'Addio M, Valanzano A, and Calamandrei G (1998a) Scopolamine impairs memory recall in *Octopus vulgaris*. *Neurosci. Lett.* 253: 87–90.

Fiorito G, Biederman GB, Davey VA, and Gherardi F (1998b) The role of stimulus preexposure in problem solving by *Octopus vulgaris*. *Anim. Cogn.* 1: 107–112.

Forsythe JW and Hanlon RT (1997) Foraging and associated behavior by *Octopus cyanea* Gray (1849) on a coral atoll French Polynesia. *J. Exp. Mar. Biol. Ecol.* 209: 15–31.

Foyle TP and O'Dor RK (1988) Predatory strategies of squid (*Illex illecebrosus*) attacking small and large fish. *Mar. Behav. Physiol.* 13: 155–168.

Frösch D (1971) Quantitative Untersuchungen am Zentralnervensystem der Schlüpfstadien von zehn mediterranen Cephalopodenarten. *Rev. Suisse Zool.* 78: 1069–1122.

Frost BJ and Mouritsen H (2006) The neural mechanisms of long distance animal navigation. *Curr. Opin. Neurobiol.* 16: 481–488.

Getting PA (1989) Emerging principles governing the operation of neural networks. *Ann. Rev. Neurosci.* 12: 185–204.

Gosling S (2001) From mice to men: What we can learn about personality from animal research. *Psychol. Bull.* 127: 45–86.

Graindorge N, Alves C, Darmaillacq AS, Chichery R, Dickel L, and Bellanger C (2006) Effects of dorsal and ventral vertical lobe electrolytic lesions on spatial learning and locomotor activity in *Sepia officinalis*. *Behav. Neurosci.* 120: 1151–1158.

Greenberg R and Mettke-Hofmann C (2001) Ecological aspects of neophobia and neophilia in birds. In: Nolan V Jr. and Thompson CH (eds.) *Current Ornithology*, pp. 119–178. New York: Kluwer Academic/Plenum.

Halm MP, Agin V, Chichery MP, and Chichery R (2000) Effect of aging on manipulative behavior in the cuttlefish *Sepia*. *Physiol. Behav.* 68: 543–547.

Halm MP, Chichery MP, and Chichery R (2002) The role of cholinergic networks of the anterior basal and inferior frontal lobes in the predatory behaviour of *Sepia officinalis*. *Comp. Biochem. Physiol. A* 132: 267–274.

Halm MP, Chichery MP, and Chichery R (2003) Effect of nitric oxide synthase inhibition on the manipulative behaviour of *Sepia officinalis*. *Comp. Biochem. Physiol. C* 134: 139–146.

Haney J and Lukowiak K (2001) Context learning and the effect of context on memory retrieval in *Lymnaea*. *Learn. Mem.* 8: 35–43.

Hanlon RT (1978) Aspects of the biology of the squid *Loligo (Doryteuthis) plei* in captivity. PhD Thesis, University of Miami, Coral Gables, FL.

Hanlon RT (1988) Behavioral and body patterning characters useful in taxonomy and field identification of cephalopods. *Malacologia* 29: 247–264.

Hanlon RT and Messenger JB (1988) Adaptive coloration in young cuttlefish (*Sepia officinalis* L): The morphology and development of body patterns and their relation to behaviour. *Philos. Trans. R. Soc. Lond. B* 320: 437–487.

Hanlon RT and Messenger JB (1996) *Cephalopod Behaviour*. Cambridge: Cambridge University Press.

Hanlon RT, Forsythe JW, and Joneschild DE (1999) Crypsis, conspicuousness, mimicry and polyphenism as antipredator defences of foraging octopuses on Indo-Pacific coral reefs, with a method of quantifying crypsis from video tapes. *Biol. J. Linn. Soc.* 66: 1–22.

Hochner B, Brown ER, Langella M, Shomrat T, and Fiorito G (2003) A learning and memory area in the octopus brain manifests a vertebrate-like long-term potentiation. *J. Neurophysiol.* 90: 3547–3554.

Hochner B, Shomrat T, and Fiorito G (2006) The octopus: A model for a comparative analysis of the evolution of learning and memory mechanisms. *Biol. Bull.* 210: 308–317.

Holmes W (1940) The colour changes and colour patterns of *Sepia officinalis* L. *Proc. Zool. Soc. Lond.* 110: 17–35.

Jacobs LF (2003) The evolution of the cognitive map. *Brain Behav. Evol.* 62: 128–139.

Jatta G (1896) *I Cefalopodi viventi nel Golfo di Napoli. Sistematica.* Fauna und Flora des Golfes von Neapel. Monographie 23, Stazione Zoologica di Napoli. Berlin: Friedländer & Sohn.

Kagan J, Reznick JS, and Snidman N (1988) Biological bases of childhood shyness. *Science* 240: 167–171.

Kandel ER (1979) *Behavioral Biology of Aplysia. A Contribution to the Comparative Study of Opisthobranch Molluscs.* San Francisco: WH Freeman.

Karson MA (2003) Simultaneous discrimination learning and its neural correlates in the cuttlefish *Sepia officinalis* (Mollusca: Cephalopoda). PhD Thesis, Michigan State University, East Lansing, MI.

Karson MA, Boal JG, and Hanlon RT (2003) Experimental evidence for spatial learning in cuttlefish (*Sepia officinalis*). *J. Comp. Psychol.* 117: 149–155.

Kerstitch A (1988) Primates of the sea. *Freshwater Mar. Aquar.* 11: 8–10.

Kier WM (1982) The functional morphology of the musculature of squid (Loliginidae) arms and tentacles. *J. Morphol.* 172: 179–192.

Koueta N, Alorend E, Noel B, and Boucaud-Camou E (2006) Earlier acceptance of frozen prey by juvenile cuttlefish *Sepia officinalis* in experimental rearing: Effect of previous enriched natural diet. *Vie Milieu* 56: 147–152.

Lane FW (1960) *Kingdom of the Octopus: the Life History of the Cephalopoda.* New York: Sheridan House.

Law E, Nuttley WM, and van der Kooy D (2004) Contextual taste cues modulate olfactory learning in *C. elegans* by an occasion-setting mechanism. *Curr. Biol.* 14: 1303–1308.

Lee PN, Callaerts P, de Couet HG, and Martindale MQ (2003) Cephalopod *Hox* genes and the origin of morphological novelties. *Nature* 424: 1061–1065.

Leonard JL and Edstrom JP (2004) Parallel processing in an identified neural circuit: The *Aplysia californica* gill-withdrawal response model system. *Biol. Rev.* 79: 1–59.

Liu L, Wolf R, Ernst R, and Heisenberg M (1999) Context generalization in *Drosophila* visual learning requires the mushroom bodies. *Nature* 400: 753–756.

Lo Bianco S (1909) Notizie biologiche riguardanti specialmente il periodo di maturità sessuale degli animali del Golfo di Napoli. *Mitt. Zool. Stat. Neapel* 19: 513–763.

López P, Hawlena D, Polo V, Amo L, and Martín J (2005) Sources of individual shy-bold variations in antipredator behaviour of male Iberian rock lizards. *Anim. Behav.* 69: 1–9.

Maddock L and Young JZ (1987) Quantitative differences among the brains of cephalopods. *J. Zool.* 212: 739–767.

Maldonado H (1963a) The positive learning process in *Octopus vulgaris*. *Z. Vgl. Physiol.* 47: 191–214.

Maldonado H (1963b) The visual attack learning system in *Octopus vulgaris*. *J. Theor. Biol.* 5: 470–488.

Maldonado H (1964) The control of attack by *Octopus*. *Z. Vgl. Physiol.* 47: 656–674.

Maldonado H (1968) Effect of electroconvulsive shock on memory in *Octopus vulgaris* Lamarck. *Z. Vgl. Physiol.* 59: 25–37.

Maldonado H (1969) Further investigations on the effect of electroconvulsive shock (ECS) on memory in *Octopus vulgaris*. *Z. Vgl. Physiol.* 63: 113–118.

Mather JA (1991) Navigation by spatial memory and use of visual landmarks in octopuses. *J. Comp. Physiol. A* 168: 491–497.

Mather JA (1995) Cognition in cephalopods. *Adv. Stud. Behav.* 24: 317–353.

Mather JA (2007) Cephalopod consciousness: Behavioural evidence. *Conscious. Cogn.* doi:10.1016/j.concog.2006.11.006: 1–12.

Mather JA and Anderson RC (1993) Personalities of octopuses (*Octopus rubescens*). *J. Comp. Psychol.* 107: 336–340.

Mather JA and Mather DL (1994) Skin colours and patterns of juvenile *Octopus vulgaris* (Mollusca Cephalopoda) in Bermuda. *Vie Milieu* 44: 267–272.

Mather JA and O'Dor RK (1991) Foraging strategies and predation risk shape the natural history of juvenile *Octopus vulgaris*. *Bull. Mar. Sci.* 49: 256–269.

McGaugh JL (2000) Memory – A century of consolidation. *Science* 287: 248–251.

McQuaid CD (1994) Feeding behaviour and selection of bivalve prey by *Octopus vulgaris* Cuvier. *J. Exp. Mar. Biol. Ecol.* 177: 187–202.

Menzel R (2001) Searching for the memory trace in a mini-brain, the honeybee. *Learn. Mem.* 8: 53–62.

Messenger JB (1968) The visual attack of the cuttlefish *Sepia officinalis*. *Anim. Behav.* 16: 342–357.

Messenger JB (1973) Learning in the cuttlefish *Sepia*. *Anim. Behav.* 21: 801–826.

Messenger JB (1977) Prey-capture and learning in the cuttlefish *Sepia*. *Symp. Zool. Soc. Lond.* 38: 347–376.

Messenger JB (1979) The nervous system of *Loligo* IV. The peduncle and olfactory lobes. *Philos. Trans. R. Soc. Lond. B* 285: 275–309.

Messenger JB (1996) Neurotransmitters of cephalopods. *Invertebr. Neurosci.* 2: 95–114.

Messenger JB (2001) Cephalopod chromatophores: Neurobiology and natural history. *Biol. Rev.* 76: 473–528.

Messenger JB and Sanders GD (1972) Visual preference and two-cue discrimination learning in *Octopus*. *Anim. Behav.* 20: 580–585.

Mettke-Hofmann C, Ebert C, Schmidt T, Steiger S, and Stieb S (2005a) Personality traits in resident and migratory warbler species. *Behaviour* 142: 1357–1375.

Mettke-Hofmann C, Wink M, Winkler H, and Leisler B (2005b) Exploration of environmental changes relates to lifestyle. *Behav. Ecol.* 16: 247–254.

Michels J, Robertson JD, and Young JZ (1987) Can conditioned aversive tactile stimuli affect extinction of visual responses in octopus? *Mar. Behav. Physiol.* 13: 1–11.

Moore BR (2004) The evolution of learning. *Biol. Rev.* 79: 301–335.

Moriyama T and Gunji YP (1997) Autonomous learning in maze solution by *Octopus*. *Ethology* 103: 499–513.

Moynihan M and Rodaniche AF (1982) The behavior and natural history of the Caribbean reef squid *Sepioteuthis sepioidea*. With a consideration of social, signal and defensive patterns for difficult and dangerous environments. *Adv. Ethol.* 25: 1–150.

Myers CE (1992) *Delay Learning in Artificial Neural Networks*. London: Chapman & Hall.

Naef A (1923) *Die Cephalopoden. Systematik*. Fauna und Flora des Golfes von Neapel. Monographie 35, Stazione Zoologica di Napoli. Berlin: Friedländer & Sohn.

Naef A (1928) *Die Cephalopoden. Embryologie*. Fauna und Flora des Golfes von Neapel. Monographie 35, Stazione Zoologica di Napoli. Berlin: Friedländer & Sohn.

Neill SR and Cullen JM (1974) Experiments on whether schooling by their prey affects the hunting behaviour of cephalopods and fish predators. *J. Zool.* 172: 549–569.

Nixon M and Mangold K (1998) The early life of *Sepia officinalis*, and the contrast with that of *Octopus vulgaris* (Cephalopoda). *J. Zool.* 245: 407–421.

Nixon M and Young JZ (2003) *The Brains and Lives of Cephalopods*. New York: Oxford University Press.

Ogura A, Ikeo K, and Gojobori T (2004) Comparative analysis of gene expression for convergent evolution of camera eye between octopus and human. *Genome Res.* 14: 1555–1561.

Olyott LJH, Sauer WHH, and Booth AJ (2006) Spatio-temporal patterns in maturation of the chokka squid (*Loligo vulgaris reynaudii*) off the coast of South Africa. *ICES J. Mar. Sci.* 63: 1649–1664.

Oosthuizen A and Smale MJ (2003) Population biology of *Octopus vulgaris* on the temperate south-eastern coast of South Africa. *J. Mar. Biol. Assoc. UK* 83: 535–541.

Packard A (1963) The behaviour of *Octopus vulgaris*. *Bull. Inst. Oceanogr. (Monaco)* 1D: 35–49.

Packard A (1972) Cephalopods and fish: The limits of convergence. *Biol. Rev.* 47: 241–307.

Packard A and Hochberg FG (1977) Skin patterning in *Octopus* and other genera. *Symp. Zool. Soc. Lond.* 38: 191–231.

Packard A and Sanders G (1969) What the octopus shows to the world. *Endeavour* 28: 92–99.

Packard A and Sanders GD (1971) Body patterns of *Octopus vulgaris* and maturation of the response to disturbance. *Anim. Behav.* 19: 780–790.

Piéron H (1911) Contribution a la psychologie du poulpe. L'acquisition d'habitudes. *Bull. Inst. Psych. Internat. Paris* 11: 111–119.

Plän T (1987) Funktionelle Neuroanatomie sensorisch/motorischer Loben im Gehirn von *Octopus vulgaris*. PhD Thesis, Universität Regensburg Regensburg, Germany.

Pliny the Elder (1961) *Naturalis Historia*. H Rackham (trans.)Cambridge, MA: Harvard University Press.

Poirier R, Chichery R, and Dickel L (2004) Effects of rearing conditions on sand digging efficiency in juvenile cuttlefish. *Behav. Process.* 67: 273–279.

Power J (1857) Observations on the habits of various marine animals. Observations upon *Octopus vulgaris* and *Pinna nobilis*. *Ann. Mag. N. Hist.* 20: 336.

Purdy JE, Dixon D, Estrada A, Peters A, Riedlinger E, and Suarez R (2006) Prawn-in-a-tube procedure: Habituation or associative learning in cuttlefish? *J. Gen. Psychol.* 133: 131–152.

Romano A, Locatelli F, Freudenthal R, et al. (2006) Lessons from a crab: Molecular mechanisms in different memory phases of *Chasmagnathus*. *Biol. Bull.* 210: 280–288.

Roper CFE and Hochberg FG (1988) Behavior and systematics of cephalopods from Lizard Island Australia, based on color and body patterns. *Malacologia* 29: 153–193.

Salvini-Plawen Von L (1979) Die Kopftüsser. In: Grzimek B (ed.) *Grzimeks Tierleben. Enzyklopädie des Tierreichs*. Vol. 3 (Weichtiere und Stachelhäuter). Munich: Deutscher Taschentavch.

Sanders FK and Young JZ (1940) Learning and other functions of the higher nervous centres of *Sepia*. *J. Neurophysiol.* 3: 501–526.

Sanders GD (1970) The retention of visual and tactile discrimination by *Octopus vulgaris*. PhD Thesis. The University of London, London, UK.

Sanders GD (1975) The Cephalopods. In: Corning WC, Dyal JA, and Willows AOD (eds.) *Invertebrate Learning. Cephalopods and Echinoderms*, pp. 1–101. New York: Plenum Press.

Sanders GD and Barlow JJ (1971) Variations in retention performance during long-term memory formation. *Nature* 232: 203–204.

Schiller PH (1949) Delayed detour response in the octopus. *J. Comp. Physiol. Psychol.* 42: 220–225.

Shevtsov GA (1996) On possible migration of cuttlefish from the family Sepiidae (Cephalopoda) into southern regions of Primorye (Russian zone of the Japan Sea). *Zool. Zh.* 75: 939–941.

Sih A, Bell A, and Johnson JC (2004a) Behavioral syndromes: An ecological and evolutionary overview. *Trends Ecol. Evol.* 19: 372–378.

Sih A, Bell AM, Johnson JC, and Ziemba RE (2004b) Behavioral syndromes: An integrative overview. *Q. Rev. Biol.* 79: 241–277.

Sims DW, Genner MJ, Southward AJ, and Hawkins SJ (2001) Timing of squid migration reflects North Atlantic climate variability. *Proc. R. Soc. Lond. B* 268: 2607–2611.

Sinn DL and Moltschaniwskyj NA (2005) Personality traits in Dumpling squid (*Euprymna tasmanica*): Context-specific traits and their correlation with biological characteristics. *J. Comp. Psychol.* 119: 99–110.

Skow CD and Jakob EM (2006) Jumping spiders attend to context during learned avoidance of aposematic prey. *Behav. Ecol.* 17: 34–40.

Smale MJ and Buchan PR (1981) Biology of *Octopus vulgaris* off the east coast of South Africa. *Mar. Biol.* 65: 1–12.

Smith CD, Groeneveld JC, and Maharaj G (2006) The life history of the giant octopus *Octopus magnificus* in South African waters. *Afr. J. Mar. Sci.* 28: 561–568.

Steer MA and Semmens JM (2003) Pulling or drilling, does size or species matter? An experimental study of prey handling in *Octopus dierythraeus* (Norman, 1992). *J. Exp. Mar. Biol. Ecol.* 290: 165–178.

Stevenson JA (1934) On the behaviour of the long-finned squid (*Loligo pealii* (Lesueur)). *Can. Field Nat.* 48: 4–7.

Suboski MD, Muir D, and Hall D (1993) Social learning in invertebrates. *Science* 259: 1628–1629.

Sumbre G, Gutfreund Y, Fiorito G, Flash T, and Hochner B (2001) Control of octopus arm extension by a peripheral motor program. *Science* 293: 1845–1848.

Sumbre G, Fiorito G, Flash T, and Hochner B (2005) Motor control of flexible octopus arms. *Nature* 433: 595–596.

Sumbre G, Fiorito G, Flash T, and Hochner B (2006) Octopuses use a human-like strategy to control precise point-to-point arm movements. *Curr. Biol.* 16: 767–772.

Sutherland NS (1960) Theories of shape discrimination in *Octopus*. *Nature* 186: 840–844.

Thore S (1939) Beiträge zur Kenntnis der vergleichenden Anatomie des zentralen Nervensystems der dibranchiaten Cephalopoden. *Pubbl. Staz. Zool. Napoli* 17: 313–506.

Tinbergen L (1939) Zur Fortpflanzungsethologie von *Sepia officinalis* L. *Arch. Néerl. Zool.* 3: 323–364.

Tomsic D, Pedreira ME, Romano A, Hermitte G, and Maldonado H (1998) Context-US association as a determinant of long-term habituation in the crab *Chasmagnathus*. *Anim. Learn. Behav.* 26: 196–209.

Walker JJ, Longo N, and Bitterman ME (1970) The octopus in the laboratory. Handling, maintenance, training. *Behav. Res. Methods Instrum.* 2: 15–18.

Warnke K (1994) Some aspects of social interaction during feeding in *Sepia officinalis* (Mollusca: Cephalopoda) hatched and reared in the laboratory. *Vie Milieu* 44: 125–131.

Watanabe H, Kubodera T, Moku M, and Kawaguchi K (2006) Diel vertical migration of squid in the warm core ring and cold water masses in the transition region of the western North Pacific. *Mar. Ecol. Prog. Ser.* 315: 187–197.

Wells MJ (1962) Early learning in *Sepia*. *Symp. Zool. Soc. Lond.* 8: 149–169.

Wells MJ (1965a) Learning and movement in octopuses. *Anim. Behav. Suppl.* 1: 115–128.

Wells MJ (1965b) Learning in the octopus. *Symp. Soc. Exp. Biol.* 20: 477–507.

Wells MJ (1978) *Octopus: Physiology and Behaviour of an Advanced Invertebrate*. London: Chapman and Hall.

Wells MJ and Young JZ (1970) Single-session learning by octopuses. *J. Exp. Biol.* 53: 779–788.

Wilbur KM (1983–1988) *The Mollusca*. New York: Academic Press.

Williams LW (1909) *The Anatomy of the Common Squid Loligo pealii Lesueur*. Leiden, The Netherlands: EJ Brill.

Williamson R (1995) A sensory basis for orientation in cephalopods. *J. Mar. Biol. Assoc. UK* 75: 83–92.

Williamson R and Budelmann BU (1991) Convergent inputs to *Octopus* oculomotor neurons demonstrated in a brain slice preparation. *Neurosci. Lett.* 121: 215–218.

Williamson R and Chrachri A (2004) Cephalopod neural networks. *NeuroSignals* 13: 87–98.

Wirz K (1959) Étude biométrique du système nerveux des Céphalopodes. *Bull. Biol. Fr. Belg.* 93: 78–117.

Yarnall JL (1969) Aspects of behaviour of *Octopus cyanea* Gray. *Anim. Behav.* 17: 747–754.

Young JZ (1961) Learning and discrimination in the octopus. *Biol. Rev.* 36: 32–96.

Young JZ (1963) The number and sizes of nerve cells in *Octopus*. *Proc. Zool. Soc. Lond.* 140: 229–254.

Young JZ (1964) *A Model of the Brain*. Oxford: Clarendon Press.

Young JZ (1965) The organization of a memory system. *Proc. R. Soc. Lond. B* 163: 285–320.

Young JZ (1971) *The Anatomy of the Nervous System of Octopus vulgaris*. London: Oxford University Press.

Young JZ (1973) Receptive fields of the visual system of the squid. *Nature* 241: 469–471.

Young JZ (1974) The central nervous system of *Loligo*. I. The optic lobe. *Philos. Trans. R. Soc. Lond. B* 267: 263–302.

Young JZ (1976) The nervous system of *Loligo*. II. Suboesophageal centres. *Philos. Trans. R. Soc. Lond. B* 274: 101–167.

Young JZ (1977) The nervous system of *Loligo*. III. Higher motor centres: The basal supraoesophageal lobes. *Philos. Trans. R. Soc. Lond. B* 276: 351–398.

Young JZ (1979) The nervous system of *Loligo*. V. The vertical lobe complex. *Philos. Trans. R. Soc. Lond. B* 285: 311–354.

Young JZ (1983) The distributed tactile memory system of *Octopus*. *Proc. R. Soc. Lond. B* 218: 135–176.

Young JZ (1985) Cephalopods and neuroscience. *Biol. Bull.* 168: 153–158.

Young JZ (1991) Computation in the learning system of cephalopods. *Biol. Bull.* 180: 200–208.

Young JZ (1995) Multiple matrices in the memory system of *Octopus.*. In: Abbott JN, Williamson R, and Maddock L (eds.) *Cephalopod Neurobiology*, pp. 431–443. Oxford: Oxford University Press.

Zhang SW, Schwarz S, Pahl M, Zhu H, and Tautz J (2006) Honeybee memory: A honeybee knows what to do and when. *J. Exp. Biol.* 209: 4420–4428.

1.32 Behavioral Analysis of Learning and Memory in *C. elegans*

A. C. Giles and C. H. Rankin, University of British Columbia, Vancouver, BC, Canada

1.32.1 Introduction

Caenorhabditis elegans was first developed as a model system by Sydney Brenner in the 1960s, with the goal of having a simple multicellular system in which to study the cellular and molecular mechanisms of development using modern genetic and molecular biological techniques. *C. elegans* is a 1-mm soil-dwelling nematode. In the laboratory it lives on a bacterial lawn of *Escherichia coli* in an agar-filled Petri dish. Brenner, along with John Sulston, who mapped the complete cell lineage of the organism, and Robert Horvitz, who elucidated the first programmed cell death mechanisms, won the Nobel Prize in Physiology or Medicine in 2002 for this work. For our purposes *C. elegans* is an excellent model for studying the behavioral, cellular, and molecular mechanisms involved in learning and memory.

Rankin et al. (1990) were the first to recognize *C. elegans* as a model for learning and memory when they showed that *C. elegans* is capable of both short- and long-term memory for the nonassociative form of learning known as habituation. Since 1990, many labs have investigated a variety of types (i.e., mechanosensory, chemosensory, and thermosensory) of both nonassociative (habituation) and associative learning (classical conditioning) in *C. elegans*. As a model of the cellular and molecular mechanisms of learning and

memory *C. elegans* has many advantageous qualities. Composed of only 302 neurons, with only 5000 synaptic connections, all of which are identified, the *C. elegans* nervous system offers an opportunity to study a system in which all the neurons that mediate a learned behavior or memory can be identified (keep in mind that even the simplest mammals have nervous systems containing millions of neurons, between which are billions of synaptic connections). *C. elegans* can serve as a model of the mammalian nervous system because many of the elements that constitute the *C. elegans* nervous system are homologous to those of mammals, and these elements are incorporated into conserved pathways for many cellular functions, such as neurotransmission and intracellular signaling. *C. elegans* is an excellent subject for techniques that probe into cellular mechanisms because they have a short life cycle, they live in clonal populations, and their bodies are transparent. Because of this transparency, manipulations of the neural circuitry can easily be performed using techniques such as laser ablation. In addition, the worm's genome has been sequenced; there are thousands of identified mutants available for analysis, and there is a knockout consortium that accepts gene knockout requests at no cost. Finally, and most importantly for this chapter, *C. elegans* exhibits well-described and measurable behaviors, and these behaviors can change with experience.

It is absolutely crucial to understand the behavioral characteristics of learning and memory in *C. elegans* to properly elucidate the molecular mechanisms involved. The focus of this chapter is the behavioral analysis of the different types of learning and memory that have been discovered in *C. elegans*; however, we also briefly touch on how these behavioral studies have already begun to help elucidate cellular and molecular mechanisms of learning and memory. In the first section, we discuss how *C. elegans* changes with the experience of individual stimuli that it encounters in its environment, such as a mechanical tap or exposure to a certain chemical stimulus. The second section is an overview of how *C. elegans* learns to predict the presence of food using cues like chemical concentration and temperature. The third and final section reviews how *C. elegans* learns to avoid harmful stimuli such as pathogenic bacteria.

1.32.2 Learning about the Environment

During an organism's life, it is constantly bombarded with stimuli. To be successful, it needs to allocate energy, resources, and attention appropriately. One way to achieve this is by learning to ignore stimuli that are irrelevant, thereby avoiding the waste of energy caused by unnecessary responses; this is known as habituation. More objectively, it is a decrease in response to an irrelevant stimulus over repeated stimulation (Groves and Thompson, 1970). Habituation is considered a nonassociative form of learning. This phenomenon can be distinguished from decreases in response resulting from sensory adaptation or motor fatigue (or both) by the process of dishabituation. Dishabituation is achieved by following habituation training with a novel or noxious stimulus, such as electric shock used for dishabituation of the gill withdrawal response in *Aplysia* (Carew et al., 1971). If a habituated animal is given a dishabituating stimulus, its response to the initial stimulus will immediately increase above the habituated level. In contrast, sensory adaptation or motor fatigue will only recover after a period of rest.

1.32.2.1 Mechanical Stimuli

In its natural environment, *C. elegans* can sense mechanical forces that might include bumping into subterranean obstacles in their path of travel,

bumping into other similarly sized organisms, or even vibration of the surrounding environment from a close encounter with a larger organism. In the laboratory, these stimuli can be mimicked by touching the anterior or posterior body with a hair or by a discreet tap to the side of the Petri dish in which they live. To study habituation, the latter of these stimuli was used because the frequency and intensity of the stimulus could be easily controlled and manipulated. *C. elegans* responds to this stimulus with a reversal, which is called the tap withdrawal response (Rankin et al., 1990). When this stimulus was repeated at a constant interstimulus interval (ISI) of 10 s, the magnitude of the response significantly decreased over a period of 40 stimuli (Rankin et al., 1990). An analysis across 60 trials showed that habituation consisted of an initial steep downward slope of decreasing response magnitude during the first 10–20 stimuli, followed by a relatively flat asymptotic stage for the remainder of the stimuli (Rankin and Broster, 1992). The response to tap was also measured at various time intervals (30 s, 10 min, 20 min, and 30 min) after the 60th stimulus, and it was observed that the response magnitude spontaneously recovered over time (Rankin and Broster, 1992). Dishabituation was observed by applying an electrical shock to the agar near the worm immediately after the taps; response magnitude to subsequent taps significantly increased (Rankin et al., 1990). Dishabituation indicates that the response decrement observed after repeated stimuli was in fact habituation and not a form of sensory adaptation or motor fatigue.

The most important procedural factor that affects habituation of the tap withdrawal response in *C. elegans* is the length of the ISI. Short ISIs (i.e., 10 s) produced steep slopes in the initial stage of habituation and very low asymptotic levels of response during the second stage, whereas long ISIs (i.e., 60 s) produced shallow slopes and high asymptotic levels (Rankin and Broster, 1992). Variations in ISI also affected the spontaneous recovery after habituation; spontaneous recovery was faster and more complete after short ISIs than after long ISIs (Rankin and Broster, 1992). This was an important finding because it provided an alternate and more elegant way to distinguish habituation from sensory adaptation and motor fatigue than dishabituation, which can be quite variable. The rate of recovery following sensory adaptation or motor fatigue is determined by the degree of decrement, and so greater decrement, which is observed at short ISIs, would take longer to recover than long ISIs, and this is opposite to what is observed after habituation.

Rankin and Broster (1992) investigated the effects of habituation level, achievement of the asymptotic level, and number of missed stimuli before the recovery test on the rate of spontaneous recovery. To test the effects of habituation level, they set a criterion for the level of decrement *C. elegans* had to reach before recovery began, regardless of ISI. *C. elegans* stimulated at a 10 s ISI achieved the criterion level after fewer stimuli than those tapped at a 60 s ISI; however, the 10-s ISI group still showed faster and more complete spontaneous recovery than the 60-s ISI group, even though they were habituated to the same response level.

Although the level of habituation did not affect spontaneous recovery, whether *C. elegans* had reached the asymptotic stage of habituation was found to be an important factor. *C. elegans* that reached asymptote after only 8 stimuli recovered at the same ISI dependent rate as worms that had received 60 stimuli (Rankin and Broster, 1992). This result supports the idea that reaching the asymptotic level of habituation is an important factor in determining rate of spontaneous recovery, but the number of stimuli an animal experiences after reaching the asymptotic stage has very little effect on the spontaneous recovery of the behavior.

Finally, Rankin and Broster (1992) tested how the number of missed stimuli affected recovery. For example, at the 10-min recovery test worms habituated at a 10-s ISI would have missed 60 stimuli, whereas worms habituated at a 60-s ISI would only have missed 10 stimuli. Spontaneous recovery of *C. elegans* trained at a 10-s ISI still showed significantly greater recovery at 5 min (30 missed stimuli) compared to worms trained at a 60-s ISI after 30 min of recovery (also 30 missed stimuli; Rankin and Broster, 1992). Therefore, ISI length is a crucial factor for both habituation and spontaneous recovery from habituation in *C. elegans*, regardless of the habituated level, the number of stimuli (as long as asymptote is achieved), or the number of missed stimuli during recovery.

The purpose of studying *C. elegans* as a simple model of learning is to be able to more easily research questions involving the cellular and molecular mechanisms that mediate learning. These behavioral analyses have created a foundation that can now be used to conduct this investigation. In fact, one of the most important mechanistic hypotheses regarding habituation has been identified by these behavioral analyses: That is, that habituation is not a single process but, instead, habituation at different ISIs must be mediated at least in part by different mechanisms (Rankin and Broster, 1992). This hypothesis has been supported by the identification of mutations that selectively disrupt habituation at either short or long ISIs, but not both (*See* Chapter 4.04).

The neural circuit that mediates the tap withdrawal response has been described in detail (Wicks and Rankin, 1995). It consists of five sensory neurons and four pairs of command interneurons; the most likely site for plasticity has been identified as the chemical synapses between the mechanosensory neurons and the command interneurons within the circuit (Wicks and Rankin, 1997). The chemical synapses between these sensory neurons and interneurons, as well as some of the synapses between interneurons, are glutamatergic (Brockie and Maricq, 2006), suggesting a possible role for glutamate in habituation. This was confirmed by a study that found that mutants that lack a glutamate vesicular transporter (*eat-4*), which is important for loading vesicles ready for neurotransmission, showed abnormal habituation (Rankin and Wicks, 2000). Recently, dopamine has been shown to play a role in habituation because mutants with disrupted dopamine neurotransmission (*dop-1* and *cat-2*) show abnormal habituation (Sanyal et al., 2004). Together these results are of general interest because glutamate–dopamine interactions have been noted in other animal learning and are associated with human disorders that are usually associated with learning and memory deficits (Palomo et al., 2004; David et al., 2005). More research is necessary to fully understand the mechanisms of habituation; however, it is clear that glutamate, dopamine, and the synapses between the mechanosensory neurons and the command interneurons are important for habituation of the tap withdrawal response in *C. elegans*.

So far this section has focused on the short-term effects of habituation to a mechanosensory stimulus. Under the right conditions *C. elegans* can also show long-term memory for this mechanosensory habituation. This was first observed by Rankin et al. (1990) and then studied in more detail by Beck and Rankin (1995, 1997) using a protocol adapted from a study of long-term memory for habituation, in *Aplysia*. Beck and Rankin (1997) investigated the parameters necessary for long-term memory for habituation in *C. elegans*. They tested distributed training, which features a number of blocks of stimuli separated by hour-long rest periods, and massed training, in which the same number of stimuli is administered without any rest periods (a longer single block). Distributed versus massed training appears to be a fundamental feature of memory because it has been shown to enhance long-term memory in many other training paradigms in a number of other organisms, such as habituation in *Aplysia* (Carew et al., 1972), classical conditioning in *Drosophila* (Tully et al., 1994), and memorization of lists of nonsense syllables in humans (Ebbinghaus 1885). The ISI within blocks was either 10 s or 60 s, and the number of taps varied between 40 (10 per block) and 60 (20 per block). Only distributed training at a 60-s ISI with either 40 (4 blocks of 10 taps) or 60 (3 blocks of 20 taps) stimuli was capable of reliable expression of memory 24 h after training. In general, more stimulation (60 stimuli) was better at producing long-term memory than less stimulation (40 stimuli). Beck and Rankin (1997) concluded that training protocols with a high total number of stimuli, long ISIs, and distributed training produced significant long-term memory of habituation in *C. elegans*.

One very important aspect that defines long-term memory and helps distinguish it from shorter forms is the fact that the mechanisms that store long-term memory are protein synthesis dependent. Long-term memory for habituation in *C. elegans* was found to be protein synthesis dependent by a set of heat shock experiments (Beck and Rankin, 1995). Heat shock is a technique that can block protein synthesis in the worm because at high temperatures (32 °C), all non-essential protein synthesis is stopped to give way to the synthesis of a set of heat shock proteins important for protection against cellular stress (Lindquist, 1986). Heat shock for the first 45 min during each of the 1-h rest periods of the long-term protocol blocked the formation of the long-term memory without disrupting the short-term effects of habituation (Beck and Rankin, 1995). Heat shock immediately prior to training or testing had no effect on long-term memory formation. This suggests that the protein synthesis that is taking place during the rest periods after each training block leads to consolidation of long-term memory for habituation of the tap withdrawal response in *C. elegans*. Interestingly, 15 min of heat shock exposure during either the first 15 min of the period or the second 15 min of the period is enough to disrupt the formation of long-term memory, whereas heat shock during the last 15 min of the rest period had no effect (Beck and Rankin, 1995). This suggests that the protein synthesis portion of the molecular mechanism responsible for the formation of long-term memory takes place during the first 30 min after each training block.

The consolidation of this long-term memory is not always permanent. If the memory is recalled by 10 reminder taps 24 h after the training, the memory becomes labile and must undergo consolidation again (Rose and Rankin, 2006); this is known as reconsolidation (Nader et al., 2000). By blocking protein synthesis immediately after the reminder, the memory is lost; nontrained worms showed similar responses to the trained worms 48 h after training (24 h after reminder). Protein synthesis blockade 24 h after training in the absence of a set of reminder taps has no effect on the long-term memory; trained animals had significantly lower magnitudes of response than nontrained animals.

Similar to short-term habituation, glutamate appears to be an important molecule for the consolidation of long-term memory. Mutants with defective glutamate neurotransmission (*eat-4* and *glr-1*) cannot form long-term memory for habituation, and pharmacological agents that disrupt glutamate neurotransmission block the formation of long-term memory (Rose et al., 2002, 2003). Also, pharmacological blockade of glutamate neurotransmission during 10 reminder taps 24 h after training blocks the reconsolidation of the long-term memory (Rose and Rankin, 2006). A subunit of an AMPA-like glutamate receptor (*glr-1*) appears to play an especially important role in the mechanism of long-term memory consolidation, as its expression, assessed by quantitative measurements of a GLR-1::GFP fusion construct using confocal imaging, was significantly decreased 24 h after the administration of the long-term memory protocol, which strongly correlates with the observed behavior (Rose et al., 2003). Similarly, GLR-1::GFP levels return to nontrained levels if reconsolidation is disrupted following a reminder 24 h after training (Rose and Rankin, 2006), again directly correlating with the behavior. This evidence supports the idea that the level of expression of these glutamate receptors mediates the level of response to tap, and a portion of the mechanism that mediates the long-term memory is a downregulation of expression of these receptors.

In summary, both short- and long-term habituation of the tap withdrawal response in *C. elegans* have been well characterized at the behavioral level. This behavioral analysis has been an important foundation on which to build a strong investigation for the mechanisms that mediate it, and a number of clues into this mechanism have been uncovered.

1.32.2.2 Chemical Stimuli

The first evidence that behavioral responses to chemical cues are also plastic in *C. elegans* was olfactory adaptation (Colbert and Bargmann, 1995). Usually, *C. elegans* exposed to a concentration gradient of a chemical (such as benzaldehyde and diacetyl) will move up the concentration gradient toward the chemical stimulus. This is known as chemotaxis and is usually measured by placing a group in a gradient and observing the fraction that migrates toward the stimulus. If *C. elegans* is exposed to a strong uniform concentration of the chemical prior to the chemotaxis assay, the fraction that migrates toward the stimulus significantly decreases, indicating that *C. elegans* decreases its response to the chemical stimulus after the preexposure treatment (Colbert and Bargmann, 1995).

This decrease was assumed to always be adaptation until Wen et al. (1997) first suggested it was possible to see habituation to a chemical stimulus by using a longer preexposure with a relatively weaker concentration than that used in the sensory adaptation paradigm. They used solubilized Na^+ as the chemical stimulus and found that a smaller number of *C. elegans* migrated toward the Na^+ spot during the chemotaxis assay compared to naïve controls. Importantly, this decrease in approach behavior could be immediately reversed or dishabituated by a short exposure to a high concentration of Na^+ solution, indicating that the change in approach behavior was habituation and not fatigue.

Bernhard and van der Kooy (2000) investigated the difference between chemosensory habituation and adaptation by using various preexposure concentrations. High preexposure concentrations of diacetyl (like those used in the sensory adaptation paradigm) led to a chemotaxis decrement that is irreversible, whereas low concentrations caused a decreased chemotaxis response that was immediately reversible by a dishabituating stimulus. These results suggest that habituation to chemical stimuli can occur in *C. elegans*; however, unless tests for dishabituation are done, the results observed in the sensory adaptation paradigms cannot be considered habituation. Similar to mechanosensory habituation, chemical habituation to diacetyl requires normal glutamate neurotransmission because *C. elegans* mutants lacking the AMPA-type glutamate receptor subunit *glr-1* are not capable of diacetyl habituation (Morrison and van der Kooy, 2001). This is an interesting similarity, but more research needs to be conducted to understand whether the mechanism for habituation is conserved across sensory modalities.

1.32.2.3 Context Conditioning for Habituation

Although habituation and other forms of nonassociative learning are initially dependent only on a single stimulus, later learning concerning the same stimulus can be dependent on environmental conditions during the initial training session (Wagner, 1976, 1978, 1979). One example of this is context conditioning in which there is greater retention of the initial learning during a later training session if some contextual cue was present in the environment during both the initial and later training sessions. This has been observed in a number of organisms, including rats (Evans and Hammond, 1983), crabs (Tomsic et al., 1998), and *Aplysia* (Colwill et al., 1988). *C. elegans* is also capable of such context conditioning using habituation of the response (Rankin, 2000). Worms habituated in the presence of sodium acetate showed greater retention of habituation during a later habituation session only if they were also exposed to sodium acetate during the second session (**Figure 1(a)** and (**b**)). It was very important that the worms experience this contextual environment only during the habituation sessions to form the association, as Rankin (2000) showed that if this was not the case, latent inhibition and extinction blocked the enhanced learning (**Figure 1(c)**). Latent inhibition occurs when the animal is preexposed to the contextual cue for a period of time before it is used in training. When *C. elegans* was exposed to the sodium acetate for 1 h prior to habituation training, there was no difference between the initial training session and the later test session. Extinction occurs when the contextual cue remains present in the absence of habituation after the initial training. This was done by leaving the worms on sodium acetate between the training session and the test; no difference was observed between sessions in this case either. Finally, reverse context conditioning was observed when worms were reared on sodium acetate plates and then trained and tested on normal growth medium (**Figure 1(c)**). Therefore, *C. elegans* is capable of associating a chemical concentration with habituation of the tap withdrawal response, and this context conditioning is sensitive to latent inhibition and extinction.

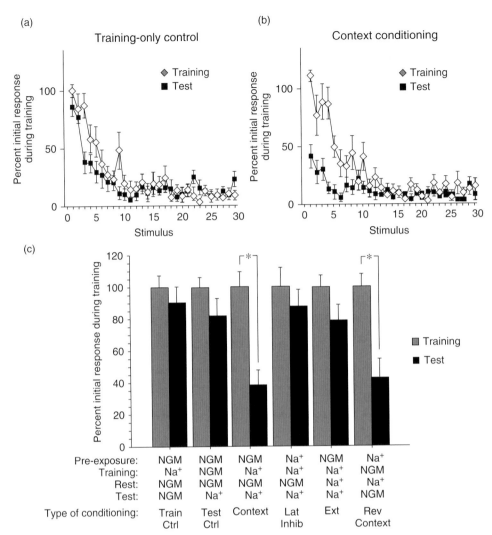

Figure 1   Context conditioning of habituation of the tap withdrawal response. (a and b) Habituation curves during the initial training (light diamonds) and later testing (dark squares) sessions for *C. elegans* that experienced sodium acetate context only during the training session (training-only control; (a)) and *C. elegans* that experienced the sodium acetate context during training and testing (context conditioning; (b)). (c) Initial responses during the initial training (light bars) and later testing (dark bars) habituation sessions for all conditioned groups: training-only control (Train Ctrl; sodium acetate only during training), testing-only control (Test Ctrl; sodium acetate only during testing), context (sodium acetate during training and during testing), latent inhibition (Lat Inhib; sodium acetate for 1 h prior to training, during training and during testing), extinction (Ext; sodium acetate during training, during the 1 h between training and testing, and during testing), reverse context (Rev Context; sodium acetate for the 1 h prior to training and for the 1 h between training and testing). *C. elegans* were exposed to either the sodium acetate (Na^+) context cue or to standard nematode growth medium (NGM) during preexposure, training, testing, and the period in between the training and test sessions (rest). * indicates significant difference between the initial response during training and test sessions. Rankin CH (2000) Context conditioning in habituation in the nematode *C. elegans. Behav. Neurosci.* 114: 496–505. Adapted from APA.

1.32.2.4   State-Dependent Learning

A similar form of learning is known as state-dependent learning because it uses a physiological state within the organism to act as a cue for a nonassociative learning behavior. One method of artificially manipulating internal state in an organism is with the use of neuroactive drugs. Ethanol exposure during the chemotaxis assay did not affect the naïve attraction toward benzaldehyde, nor did it affect benzaldehyde adaptation; however, if *C. elegans* was preexposed to benzaldehyde in the presence of etha-nol, then it would only show adaptation if it was also exposed to ethanol during the chemotaxis assay (Bettinger and McIntire, 2004). This suggests that *C. elegans* can learn to associate a physiological state with a nonassociative training paradigm and that this training will only be expressed when experiencing that same physiological state.

1.32.3 Predicting Food

Associative learning involves the formation of an association between two previously unrelated stimuli. The common stimulus used in most of the associative learning paradigms for *C. elegans* is food. Food is an extremely important resource for any animal; therefore, it is not surprising that most animals studied have the ability to learn to associate specific sensory cues with food. In 1997, Wen et al. were the first to show that even an organism as simple as *C. elegans* can learn to predict the location of food based on previous experience.

1.32.3.1 Appetitive Classical Conditioning using Chemical Cues

Classical conditioning is a form of associative learning that involves presentation of a conditioned stimulus (CS) with an unconditioned stimulus (US) so that an association between the CS and the presence of the US is learned. Wen et al. (1997) used a discriminative classical conditioning paradigm, which involves two CSs, one paired with the US and the other unpaired. They incorporated this paradigm into a chemotaxis assay to investigate associative learning in *C. elegans*. Sodium acetate and lithium chloride concentrations were chosen as the CSs such that *C. elegans* shows the same preference to them; if sodium acetate and lithium chloride are spotted on opposite ends of a chemotaxis plate, 50% of a naïve group will migrate toward sodium, and 50% will migrate toward chloride. When worms were preexposed to sodium paired with food, followed by chloride paired without food, 70–80% of the group migrated toward sodium during the chemotaxis assay; similar results were observed when chloride was paired with food and sodium was unpaired, except the majority of the group moved toward the chloride (Wen et al., 1997).

Using slight variations on this original paradigm, many researchers are now investigating the cellular and molecular mechanisms involved in the association of chemical cues with prediction of food source. For example, genetic screens have been conducted to identify mutants with defects in this behavior (Wen et al., 1997; Saeki et al., 2001); however, the function of the genes identified in these screens (such as *lrn-1* and *lrn-2*) has not yet been identified. Another study found a secretory protein with a low-density lipoprotein receptor (LDLR) motif (*hen-1*) that is important for sensory integration and that played a role in food-related associative learning (Ishihara et al., 2002). It is difficult to understand how these molecules and genes might fit together into a possible mechanism, but as more molecules are identified, the pathway(s) will be more apparent.

1.32.3.2 Thermotaxis

In 1975, Hedgecock and Russell discovered that worms could track changes in temperature and move toward or away from temperatures; they called this behavior thermotaxis. They found that thermotaxis could be altered by experience: *C. elegans* would migrate toward a preferred temperature on a concentration gradient, and the preferred temperature was the temperature at which it is cultivated from hatching until the test assay. Interestingly, animals starved during cultivation would avoid the temperature at which they were cultivated, whereas well-fed worms could change their temperature preference after cultivation in a well-fed environment at a new temperature for several hours. This behavior was investigated using genetic and neural circuit analysis to understand the cellular and molecular mechanisms that mediate it (Hedgecock and Russell, 1975; Mori and Ohshima, 1995), but it was not recognized as a form of learning until several reviews were published in the late 1990s (Bargmann and Mori, 1997; Mori, 1999). In the more recent review, Mori (1999) suggested that for thermotaxis to occur, two processes must take place: first, *C. elegans* must be able to memorize its current cultivation temperature, and then it must be able to associate that temperature with the state of food in its current environment. If there is an abundance of food, then the worms will migrate toward this cultivation temperature in the future. If there is no food, and the worms are starving, this cultivation temperature will be avoided.

After the identification of an intriguing mutant (*aho-2*) that was capable of memorizing a cultivation temperature but was defective at associating that temperature with the food state, thereby always migrating to its cultivation temperature regardless of whether it was well fed or starved during its previous exposure, Mori and colleagues conducted an elegant behavior dissection of the two processes involved in thermotaxis (Mohri et al., 2005). This was accomplished by cultivating *C. elegans* at a particular temperature (17 °C vs. 25 °C) with a particular food condition (well fed vs. starved). Groups of worms were then switched in one of the conditions, and worms were tested using the thermotaxis assay at various time intervals after the switch (**Figure 2**). This allowed Mohri et al. (2005) to watch as either the new temperature was learned or the new food state was associated as time passed. The results

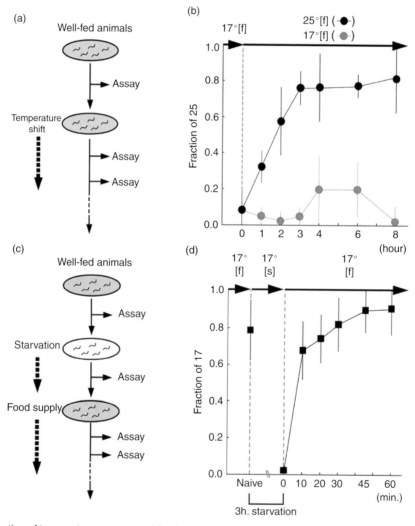

Figure 2   Dissection of temperature memory and food-temperature association of thermotaxis. (a) Procedural diagram for observing the kinetics for learning a new cultivation temperature; *C. elegans* was cultivated at 17 °C on plates with food, assayed, and then switched to a new cultivation temperature of 25 °C and then assayed every hour. (b) The fraction of worms that migrate toward 25 °C during each of the thermotaxis assays for the temperature switch paradigm (upper dark circles). *C. elegans* worms kept at 17 °C were assayed as a control (lower light circles). (c) Procedural diagram for observing the kinetics for association of a new feeding state; *C. elegans* cultivated at 17 °C on a well-fed plate was assayed, transferred to plates with no food for 3 h, assayed again, then transferred back to food and assayed every 10–15 min. (d) The fraction of *C. elegans* that migrates toward 17 °C during each of the thermotaxis assays for the feeding-state switch paradigm. Note that the time scale for (b) is in hours, and (d) is in minutes. Adapted from Mohri A, Kodama E, Kimura KD, Koike M, Mizuno T, and Mori I (2005) Genetic control of temperature preference in the nematode *Caenorhabditis elegans*. *Genetics* 169: 1437–1450.

suggested that it takes *C. elegans* roughly 3 h to learn and memorize a cultivation temperature, whereas it can change the food-state association with that memorized temperature in a matter of minutes (10–25 min, depending on the direction of the switch). This study was instrumental in raising our level of understanding of this behavior, which will be crucial as we attempt to understand the molecular mechanisms that mediate the thermosensory learning and memory of which *C. elegans* is capable.

The neural circuit underlying thermotaxis has been determined (Mori and Oshima, 1995). A number of genes expressed in these neurons have been found to play a role in thermotaxis learning. These include a calcium sensor, *nsc-1* (Gomez et al., 2001); a secretory protein with a LDLR motif, *hen-1* (Ishihara et al., 2002); a LIM homeobox gene, *ceh-1* (Cassata et al., 2000); genes that affect the amount of oxidative stress; and genes that disrupt the insulin/IGF-1/TGF-β endocrine pathway (Murakami and Murakami, 2005; Murakami et al., 2005). A number of mutations have been discovered to disrupt normal thermotaxis as well (such as *aho-2*); however, their respective genes have not yet been identified (Mohri et al., 2005). Unfortunately, to date no relationship between these molecules has been identified, so the mechanisms involved in thermotaxis learning are still unclear.

1.32.3.3   Aerotaxis

C. elegans can also sense oxygen concentrations in their environment (Gray et al., 2004). Cheung et al. (2005) invested the effects of oxygen on the behavior of *C. elegans*, as well as the preference for different concentrations of oxygen. Given a concentration gradient, *C. elegans* will migrate toward a preferred oxygen level of 7–12%. This preference is exaggerated by a natural genetic variant found in a strain of *C. elegans* from Hawaii, such that a much larger fraction of the Hawaiian strain accumulates in the 7–12% oxygen content region of the assay plate. These *C. elegans* worms were all cultivated in the laboratory at a standard oxygen concentration of 21%; however, when the worms were cultivated at 1% oxygen concentration, a shift in the oxygen preference was observed during the aerotaxis assay. These hypoxia-reared *C. elegans* migrated to the 0–5% region of the assay plate (**Figure 3**), suggesting that the *C. elegans* learned that a low concentration of oxygen predicts the occurrence of food. Oddly, this learned behavior was only observed in the worms

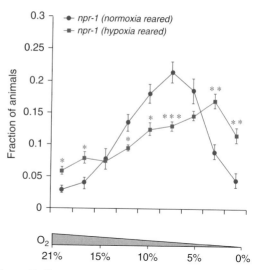

Figure 3   Experience-dependent behavioral plasticity of aerotaxis for *npr-1* mutant *C. elegans*. Fraction of *npr-1* mutant *C. elegans* (similar variant to Hawaiian strain) that migrate to different oxygen concentrations (0–21%) after being cultivated in normoxia (21%; circles) versus hypoxia (1%; squares) conditions. Asterisks indicate significant differences between fractions at each oxygen concentration. Reprinted from Cheung BH, Cohen M, Rogers C, Albayram O, and de Bono M (2005) Experience-dependent modulation of *C. elegans* behavior by ambient oxygen. *Curr. Biol.* 15: 905–917. Copyright (2005), with permission from Elsevier.

with the recessive Hawaiian genotype, which carry a mutation in a gene called *npr-1* that is homologous to a mammalian neuropeptide Y receptor, and not in the worms with the standard laboratory wild-type (from Bristol, England). This is not surprising, considering that the Bristol strain lacks other oxygen-related behaviors, such as social aggregation during feeding at high levels of oxygen (Cheung et al., 2005). Cheung et al. (2005) identify a set of neurons responsible for the behavior and a set of soluble guanylyl cyclases that are expressed in these neurons that play a role in this learned behavior, suggesting the beginnings of a putative mechanism.

1.32.4   Predicting Harm

Being able to predict the presence of food is not the only thing that is advantageous for survival. The foresight and avoidance of harm or death would also increase the chances of a long and successful reproductive life.

1.32.4.1 Aversive Learning toward Pathogenic Food

One important source of potential harm is food. When *C. elegans* is in its natural environment in the soil, it encounters various types of bacteria, some of which it approaches and some of which it avoids; the types that it is attracted to, it will consume. Unfortunately, a number of these bacteria are pathogenic to *C. elegans*, causing harm and even death. Zhang et al. (2005) investigated whether *C. elegans* could learn to avoid these pathogenic bacteria after a period of preexposure long enough to lead to harmful infection.

Zhang et al. (2005) choose pathogenic bacterial strains, *Pseudomonas aeruginosa* and *Serratia marcescens*, to which *C. elegans* is naively attracted. These bacteria proliferate within the digestive tract of the nematode, causing a harmful infection that can lead to death after long exposures. Zhang et al. (2005) modified the standard chemotaxis assay by using small bacterial lawns grown on opposite sides of the testing plate instead of chemical solutions; one lawn was the test bacteria, and there other was *E. coli* OP50 (a standard food source for *C. elegans* in the laboratory) as a control. Naive *C. elegans* worms (cultivated on *E. coli* OP50) tested in this assay were equally attracted to *P. aeruginosa* and *E. coli* and showed a slight preference for *S. marcescens* compared to *E. coli*. When *C. elegans* was cultivated in an environment that included *E. coli* and *P. aeruginosa* (cultivation in *P. aeruginosa* alone caused severe infections that lead to death), significantly fewer animals migrated toward *P. aeruginosa* during the taxis assay compared to naive worms, suggesting after preexposure to the pathogenic bacteria, the worms now strongly preferred the *E. coli*; the same was true when they were preexposed and tested with *S. marcescens*. This strongly supports the hypothesis that *C. elegans* learns to avoid bacteria that cause infectious harm.

In the preceding experiments *C. elegans* worms were preexposed to the test bacteria for their entire development, which is approximately 4 days. To test the kinetics of this olfactory avoidance learning, Zhang et al. (2005) cultivated *C. elegans* worms on *E. coli* until they were adults and then preexposed animals to the test conditioning environment (test bacteria plus *E. coli*) or a control conditioning environment (*E. coli* alone) for various amounts of time and then tested the groups using the taxis assay. They found that the shortest preexposure time that achieved a similar difference in preference to that observed after preexposure during all of development was 4 h of conditioning. Therefore, adult *C. elegans* worms needed to be exposed to pathogenic bacteria for at least 4 h to learn to avoid it.

This paradigm does not address the question of whether the learning that is occurring is strengthening the aversion toward the pathogenic bacteria, the attraction toward the control bacteria, or both. Zhang et al. (2005) tested this by developing a multiarm maze that contained four types of bacteria, the pathogenic test bacteria, the nonpathogenic control bacteria, novel pathogenic bacteria, and novel nonpathogenic bacteria (**Figure 4(a)**). A group of *C. elegans* was placed in a central decision area and then had to choose an arm to move down to get to a bacterial lawn; the percentage of worms that ended up at each bacterial lawn was measured. A greater percentage chose the control bacterial lawn, and a lesser percentage chose the test bacterial lawn in the preexposed group compared to the naive group (**Figure 4(b)**). The percentage of worms found in both of the novel bacterial lawns was found to be the same between groups. This suggests that this pathogenesis-induced olfactory aversive learning is caused by both an increase in aversion to the previously experienced pathogenic bacteria and an increase in attraction to the previously experienced nonpathogenic bacteria. Interestingly, Zhang et al. (2005) found that the kinetics of these different aspects were not the same because *C. elegans* worms that were exposed to the pathogenic bacteria for only 4 h showed aversion to the pathogenic test bacterial lawn but not an increased attraction to the nonpathogenic control lawn. This suggests that *C. elegans* can learn the aversive aspect more quickly than it can learn the attractive aspect of this behavior.

Serotonin is an important neurotransmitter for food-related behaviors in *C. elegans* (Croll, 1975; Horvitz et al., 1982; Avery and Horvitz, 1990), so it is not surprising that mutations that affect serotonin neurotransmission disrupt learning of pathogenic bacteria avoidance (Zhang et al., 2005). Using neuron-specific expression of wild-type constructs that rescue these serotonin deficits, the site of plasticity was identified. The researchers believe the ADF serotonergic chemosensory neuron is activated during bacterial infection and releases serotonin onto the interneurons involved in integrating chemosensory information, AIY and AIZ. The serotonin induces some sort of neural plasticity, not yet understood, that leads to the behavioral plasticity observed during the behavior.

(a)

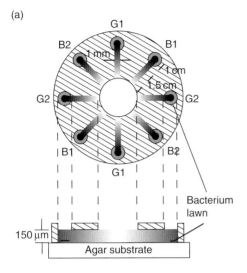

(b)

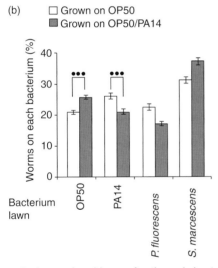

Figure 4 Learned avoidance of pathogenic bacteria. (a) Multiarm maze for testing attractive versus aversive nature of pathogenic bacteria avoidance. *E. coli* OP50, previously experienced nonpathogenic bacteria, was placed at G1; *P. aeruginosa* PA14, previously experienced pathogenic bacteria, was placed at B1; *P. fluorescens*, novel nonpathogenic bacteria, was placed at G2; *S. marcescens*, novel pathogenic bacteria, was placed at B2. *C. elegans* worms were placed in the center of the apparatus and allowed to choose which bacterial lawn to migrate toward. (b) Fraction of *C. elegans* worms, which were preexposed only to *E. coli* OP50 (light bars) versus preexposed to *E. coli* OP50 and *P. aeruginosa* PA14 (dark bars), that migrated to the different bacterial lawn. *** indicates significant differences ($p < 0.05$) between different preexposure conditions. Zhang Y, Lu H, and Bargmann CI (2005) Pathogenic bacteria induce aversive olfactory learning in *Caenorhabditis elegans*. *Nature* 438: 179–184. Adapted by permission from Macmillan Publishers Ltd: Nature, Copyright (2005).

1.32.5   Summary

C. elegans possesses a plethora of behaviors that can change with experience, which covers every aspect of its sensory abilities that has been investigated. Understanding the details of this learning and memory is much easier than understanding the complex behavioral repertoire of higher-order organisms. This detailed understanding is essential for helping to understand the mechanisms that mediate these organisms because a mechanism must be able to explain all aspects of the learning to be complete. *C. elegans* also offers the advantage of accessible manipulation at the molecular level, which allows for investigation of cellular and molecular mechanisms of learning and memory. These results can then be carefully extended from this model system to higher-order organisms in the hopes of better understanding the biological foundations of learning and memory.

References

Avery L and Horvitz HR (1990) Effects of starvation and neuroactive drugs on feeding in *Caenorhabditis elegans*. *J. Exp. Zool.* 253: 263–270.

Bargmann CI and Mori I (1997) Chemotaxis and thermotaxis. In: Riddle DL, Blumenthal T, Meyer BJ, and Preiss JR (eds.) *C. elegans II*, pp. 717–737. Plainview, NY: Cold Spring Harbor Laboratory Press.

Beck CDO and Rankin CH (1995) Heat shock disrupts long-term memory consolidation in *Caenorhabditis elegans*. *Learn. Mem.* 2: 161–177.

Beck CDO and Rankin CH (1997) Long-term habituation is produced by distributed training at long ISIs and not by massed training at short ISIs in *Caenorhabditis elegans*. *Anim. Learn. Behav.* 25: 446–457.

Bernhard N and van der Kooy D (2000) A behavioural and genetic dissection of two forms of olfactory plasticity in *Caenorhabditis elegans*: Adaptation and habituation. *Learn. Mem.* 7: 199–212.

Bettinger JC and McIntire SL (2004) State-dependency in *C. elegans*. *Genes Brain Behav.* 3: 266–272.

Brockie PJ and Maricq AV (2006) Ionotropic glutamate receptors: Genetics, behavior and electrophysiology. In: The *C. elegans* Research Community (eds.) *WormBook*, http://www.wormbook.org.

Carew TJ, Castellucci VF, and Kandel ER (1971) An analysis of dishabituation and sensitization of the gill-withdrawal reflex in *Aplysia*. *Int. J. Neurosci.* 2: 79–98.

Carew TJ, Pinsker HM, and Kandel ER (1972) Long-term habituation of a defensive withdrawal reflex in *Aplysia*. *Science* 175: 451–454.

Cassata G, Kagoshima H, Andachi Y, et al. (2000) The LIM homeobox gene ceh-14 confers thermosensory function to the AFD neurons in *Caenorhabditis elegans*. *Neuron* 25: 587–597.

Cheung BH, Cohen M, Rogers C, Albayram O, and de Bono M (2005) Experience-dependent modulation of *C. elegans* behavior by ambient oxygen. *Curr. Biol.* 15: 905–917.

Colbert HA and Bargmann CI (1995) Odorant-specific adaptation pathways generate olfactory plasticity in *C. elegans*. *Neuron* 14: 803–812.

Colwill RM, Absher RA, and Roberts ML (1988) Context-US learning in *Aplysia californica*. *J. Neurosci.* 8: 4434–4439.

Croll NA (1975) Indolealkylamines in the coordination of nematode behavioral activities. *Can. J. Zool.* 53: 894–903.

David HN, Ansseau M, and Abraini JH (2005) Dopamine-glutamate reciprocal modulation of release and motor responses in the rat caudate-putamen and nucleus accumbens of "intact" animals. *Brain Res. Brain Res. Rev.* 50: 336–360.

Ebbinghaus H (1885) Retention as a function of repeated learning. In: *Memory* (reprint edition, 1964), pp. 81–89. New York: Dover.

Evans JGM. and Hammond GR (1983) Differential generalization of habituation across contexts as a function of stimulus significance. *Anim. Learn. Mem.* 11: 431–434.

Gomez M, De Castro E, Guarin E, et al. (2001) Ca^{2+} signaling via the neuronal calcium sensor-1 regulates associative learning and memory in *C. elegans*. *Neuron* 30: 241–248.

Gray JM, Karow DS, Lu H, et al. (2004) Oxygen sensation and social feeding mediated by a *C. elegans* guanylate cyclase homologue. *Nature* 430: 317–322.

Groves PM and Thompson RF (1970) Habituation: A dual-process theory. *Psychol. Rev.* 77: 419–450.

Hedgecock EM and Russell RL (1975) Normal and mutant thermotaxis in the nematode *Caenorhabditis elegans*. *PNAS* 72: 4061–4065.

Horvitz HR, Chalfie M, Trent C, Sulston JE, and Evans PD (1982) Serotonin and octopamine in the nematode *Caenorhabditis elegans*. *Science* 216: 1012–1014.

Ishihara T, Iino Y, Mohri A, et al. (2002) HEN-1: A secretory protein with an LDL receptor motif, regulates sensory integration and learning in *Caenorhabditis elegans*. *Cell* 109: 639–649.

Lindquist S (1986) The heat shock response. *Annu. Rec. Biochem.* 55: 1151–1191.

Mohri A, Kodama E, Kimura KD, Koike M, Mizuno T, and Mori I (2005) Genetic control of temperature preference in the nematode *Caenorhabditis elegans*. *Genetics* 169: 1437–1450.

Mori I (1999) Genetics of chemotaxis and thermotaxis in the nematode *Caenorhabditis elegans*. *Annu. Rev. Genet.* 33: 399–422.

Mori I and Oshima Y (1995) Neural regulation of thermotaxis in *Caenorhabditis elegans*. *Nature* 376: 344–348.

Morrison GE and van der Kooy D (2001) A mutation in the AMPA-type glutamate receptor, *glr-1*, blocks olfactory associative and nonassociative learning in *Caenorhabditis elegans*. *Behav. Neurosci.* 115: 640–649.

Murakami H, Bessinger K, Hellmann J, and Murakami S (2005) Aging-dependent and -independent modulation of associative learning behavior by insulin/insulin-like growth factor-1 signal in *Caenorhabditis elegans*. *J. Neurosci.* 25: 10894–10904.

Murakami S and Murakami H (2005) The effects of aging and oxidative stress on learning behavior in *C. elegans*. *Neurobiol. Aging* 26: 899–905.

Nader K, Schafe GE, and LeDoux JE (2000) The labile nature of consolidation theory. *Nat. Rev. Neurosci.* 1: 216–219.

Palomo T, Archer T, Kostrzewa RM, and Beninger RJ (2004) Gene-environment interplay in schizopsychotic disorders. *Neurotox. Res.* 6: 1–9.

Rankin CH (2000) Context conditioning in habituation in the nematode *C. elegans*. *Behav. Neurosci.* 114: 496–505.

Rankin CH, Beck CDO, and Chiba CM (1990) *Caenorhabditis elegans*: A new model system for the study of learning and memory. *Behav. Brain Res.* 37: 89–92.

Rankin CH and Broster BS (1992) Factors affecting habituation and recovery from habituation in the nematode *Caenorhabditis elegans*. *Behav. Neurosci.* 106: 239–242.

Rankin CH and Wicks SR (2000) Mutations of the *C. elegans* brain-specific inorganic phosphate transporter, *eat-4*, affect habituation of the tap-withdrawal response without affecting the response itself. *J. Neurosci.* 20: 4337–4344.

Rose JK, Kaun KR, Chen SH, and Rankin CH (2003) GLR-1, a non-NMDA glutamate receptor homolog, is critical for long-term memory in *Caenorhabditis elegans*. *J. Neurosci.* 23: 9595–9599.

Rose JK, Kaun KR, and Rankin CH (2002) A new group training procedure for habituation demonstrates that presynaptic glutamate release contributes to long-term memory in *C. elegans*. *Learn. Mem.* 9: 130–137.

Rose JK and Rankin CH (2006) Blocking memory reconsolidation reverses memory-associated changes in glutamate receptor expression. *J. Neurosci.* 26: 11582–11587.

Saeki S, Yamamoto M, and Iino Y (2001) Plasticity of chemotaxis revealed by paired presentation of a chemoattractant and starvation in the nematode *Caenorhabditis elegans*. *J. Exp. Biol.* 204: 1757–1764.

Sanyal S, Wintle RF, Kindt KS, et al. (2004) Dopamine modulates the plasticity of mechanosensory responses in *Caenorhabditis elegans*. *EMBO* 23: 473–482.

Tomsic D, Pedreira ME, Romano A, Hermitte G, and Maldonado H (1998) Context–US association as a determinant of long-term habituation in the crab *Charmagnathus*. *Anim. Learn. Behav.* 26: 196–204.

Tully T, Preat T, Boynton SC, and Del Vecchio M (1994) Genetic dissection of consolidated memory in *Drosophila*. *Cell* 79: 35–47.

Wagner AR (1976) Priming in STM: An information-processing mechanism for self-generated or retrieval-generated depression in performance. In: Tighe TJ and Leaton RN (eds.) *Habituation: Perspective from Child Development, Animal Behavior and Neurophysiology*, pp. 95–128. Hillsdale, NJ: Erlbaum.

Wagner AR (1978) Expectancies and priming of STM. In: Hulse SH, Fowler H, and Honig WR (eds.) *Cognitive Processes in Animal Behavior*, pp. 177–209. Hillsdale, NJ: Erlbaum.

Wagner AR (1979) Habituation and memory. In: Dickinson A and Boakes RA (eds.) *Mechanisms of Learning and Motivation*, pp. 53–82. Hillsdale, NJ: Erlbaum.

Wen JYM, Kumar N, Morrison G, et al. (1997) Mutations that prevent associative learning in *C. elegans*. *Behav. Neurosci.* 111: 354–368.

Wicks SR and Rankin CH (1995) Integration of mechanosensory stimuli in *Caenorhabditis elegans*. *J. Neurosci.* 15: 2434–2444.

Wicks SR and Rankin CH (1997) The effects of tap withdrawal response habituation on other withdrawal behaviors: The localization of habituation in *C. elegans*. *Behav. Neurosci.* 111: 1–12.

Wood WB (1988) *The nematode Caenorhabditis elegans*. Plainview, NY: Cold Spring Harbor Laboratory Press.

Zhang Y, Lu H, and Bargmann CI (2005) Pathogenic bacteria induce aversive olfactory learning in *Caenorhabditis elegans*. *Nature* 438: 179–184.

1.33 Computational Models of Hippocampal Functions

E. T. Rolls, University of Oxford, Oxford, UK

1.33.1 Introduction

In this chapter, a computational approach to the function of the hippocampus in memory is described and compared to other approaches. The theory is quantitative and takes into account the internal and systems-level connections of the hippocampus, the effects on memory of damage to different parts of the hippocampus, and the responses of hippocampal neurons recorded during memory tasks. The theory was developed by Rolls (1987, 1989a,b,c, 1996b, 2007), Treves and Rolls (1992, 1994), and with other colleagues (Rolls et al., 2002; Rolls and Stringer, 2005; Rolls and Kesner, 2006). The theory was preceded by the work of Marr (1971), who developed a mathematical model, which, although not applied to particular networks within the hippocampus and dealing with binary neurons and binary synapses that utilized heavily the properties of the binomial distribution, was important in utilizing computational concepts and in considering how recall could occur in a network with recurrent collateral connections. Analyses of these autoassociation or attractor networks developed rapidly (Gardner-Medwin, 1976; Kohonen, 1977; Hopfield, 1982; Amit, 1989; Treves and Rolls, 1991; Rolls and Treves, 1998). Rolls (1987, 1989b) produced a theory of the hippocampus in which the CA3 neurons operated as

an autoassociation memory to store episodic memories including object and place memories, and the dentate granule cells operated as a preprocessing stage for this by performing pattern separation so that the mossy fibers could act to set up different representations for each memory to be stored in the CA3 cells. He suggested that the CA1 cells operate as a recoder for the information recalled from the CA3 cells to a partial memory cue, so that the recalled information would be represented more efficiently to enable recall, via the backprojection synapses, of activity in the neocortical areas similar to that which had been present during the original episode. At about the same time, McNaughton and Morris (1987) suggested that the CA3 network might be an autoassociation network, and that the mossy fiber-to-CA3 connections might implement detonator synapses. The concepts that the diluted mossy fiber connectivity might implement selection of a new random set of CA3 cells for each new memory and that a direct perforant path input to CA3 was needed to initiate retrieval were introduced by Treves and Rolls (1992). Since then, many investigators have contributed to our understanding of hippocampal computation, with some of these approaches described in the section titled 'Comparison with other theories of hippocampal function' and throughout the chapter.

1.33.2   A Theory of Hippocampal Function

1.33.2.1   Systems-Level Functions of the Hippocampus

Any theory of the hippocampus must state at the systems level what is computed by the hippocampus. Some of the relevant evidence comes from the effects of damage to the hippocampus, the responses of neurons in the hippocampus during behavior, and the systems-level connections of the hippocampus, described in more detail elsewhere (Rolls and Kesner, 2006; Rolls, 2007).

1.33.2.1.1   Evidence from the effects of damage to the hippocampus

Damage to the hippocampus or to some of its connections such as the fornix in monkeys produces deficits in learning about the places of objects and about the places where responses should be made (Buckley and Gaffan, 2000). For example, macaques and humans with damage to the hippocampal system or fornix are impaired in object–place memory tasks in which not only the objects seen but where they were seen must be remembered (Gaffan, 1994; Burgess et al., 2002; Crane and Milner, 2005). Posterior parahippocampal lesions in macaques impair even a simple type of object-place learning in which the memory load is just one pair of trial-unique stimuli (Malkova and Mishkin, 2003). Further, neurotoxic lesions that selectively damage the primate hippocampus impair spatial scene memory, tested by the ability to remember where in a scene to touch to obtain reward (Murray et al., 1998). Rats with hippocampal lesions are impaired in using environmental spatial cues to remember particular places (O'Keefe and Nadel, 1978; Jarrard, 1993; Cassaday and Rawlins, 1997; Martin et al., 2000; Kesner et al., 2004). These memory functions are important in event or episodic memory, in which the ability to remember what happened where on typically a single occasion is important.

It will be suggested below that an autoassociation memory implemented by the CA3 neurons enables event or episodic memories to be formed by enabling associations to be formed between spatial and other including object representations.

1.33.2.1.2   The necessity to recall information from the hippocampus

Information stored in the hippocampus will need to be retrieved and affect other parts of the brain in order to be used. The information about episodic events recalled from the hippocampus could be used to help form semantic memories (Rolls, 1989b,d, 1990a; Treves and Rolls, 1994). For example, remembering many particular journeys could help to build a geographic cognitive map in the neocortex. The hippocampus and neocortex would thus be complementary memory systems, with the hippocampus being used for rapid, on-the-fly, unstructured storage of information involving activity potentially arriving from many areas of the neocortex, while the neocortex would gradually build and adjust the semantic representation on the basis of much accumulating information (Rolls, 1989b; Treves and Rolls, 1994; McClelland et al., 1995; Moscovitch et al., 2005). The present theory shows how information could be retrieved within the hippocampus and how this retrieved information could enable the activity in neocortical areas that was present during the original storage of the episodic event to be reinstated, thus implementing recall, by using hippocampo-neocortical backprojections (see **Figure 1**).

1.33.2.1.3   Systems-level neurophysiology of the primate hippocampus

The systems-level neurophysiology of the hippocampus shows what information could be stored or processed by the hippocampus. To understand how the hippocampus works, it is not sufficient to state just that it can store information – one needs to know what information. The systems-level neurophysiology of the primate hippocampus has been reviewed recently by Rolls and Xiang (2006), and a brief summary is provided here because it provides a perspective relevant to understanding the function of the human hippocampus that is somewhat different from that provided by the properties of place cells in rodents, which have been reviewed elsewhere (see McNaughton et al., 1983; O'Keefe, 1984; Muller et al., 1991; Jeffery et al., 2004; Jeffery and Hayman, 2004).

The primate hippocampus contains spatial cells that respond when the monkey looks at a certain part of space, for example, at one quadrant of a video monitor, while the monkey is performing an object–place memory task in which he must remember where on the monitor he has seen particular images (Rolls et al., 1989). Approximately 9% of the hippocampal neurons have such spatial view fields, and about 2.4% combine information about the position in space with information about the object that is in that position in space (Rolls et al., 1989). The representation of space is for the majority of hippocampal

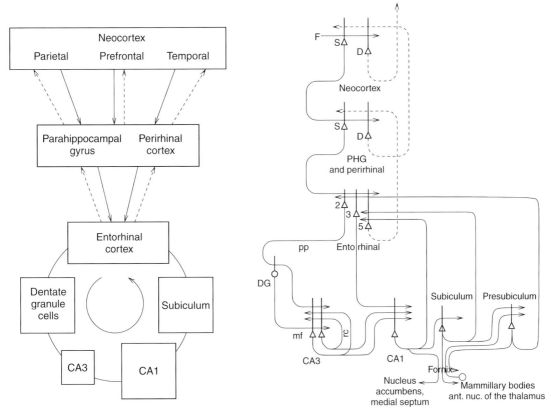

Figure 1 Forward connections (solid lines) from areas of cerebral association neocortex via the parahippocampal gyrus and perirhinal cortex, and entorhinal cortex, to the hippocampus; and backprojections (dashed lines) via the hippocampal CA1 pyramidal cells, subiculum, and parahippocampal gyrus to the neocortex. There is great convergence in the forward connections down to the single network implemented in the CA3 pyramidal cells and great divergence again in the backprojections. Left: block diagram. Right: more detailed representation of some of the principal excitatory neurons in the pathways. Abbreviations: D, deep pyramidal cells; DG, dentate granule cells; F, forward inputs to areas of the association cortex from preceding cortical areas in the hierarchy; mf, mossy fibers. PHG, parahippocampal gyrus and perirhinal cortex; pp, perforant path; rc, recurrent collateral of the CA3 hippocampal pyramidal cells; S, superficial pyramidal cells; 2, pyramidal cells in layer 2 of the entorhinal cortex; 3, pyramidal cells in layer 3 of the entorhinal cortex. The thick lines above the cell bodies represent the dendrites.

neurons in allocentric – not egocentric – coordinates (Feigenbaum and Rolls, 1991). These spatial view cells can be recorded while monkeys move themselves round the test environment by walking (or running) on all fours (Rolls et al., 1997a, 1998; Robertson et al., 1998; Georges-François et al., 1999). These hippocampal spatial view neurons respond significantly differently for different allocentric spatial views, and have information about spatial view in their firing rate, but do not respond differently just on the basis of eye position, head direction, or place. If the view details are obscured by curtains and darkness, then some spatial view neurons (especially those in CA1 and less those in CA3) continue to respond when the monkey looks toward the spatial view field, showing that these

neurons can be updated for at least short periods by idiothetic (self-motion) cues including eye position and head direction signals (Rolls et al., 1997b; Robertson et al., 1998).

A fundamental question about the function of the primate including human hippocampus is whether object as well as allocentric spatial information is represented. To investigate this, Rolls et al. (2005) made recordings from single hippocampal formation neurons while macaques performed an object–place memory task that required the monkeys to learn associations between objects, and where they were shown in a room. Some neurons (10%) responded differently to different objects independently of location; other neurons (13%) responded to the spatial view independently of which object was present at the location; and some neurons (12%) responded to a combination of a particular object and the place where it was shown in the room. These results show that there are separate as well as combined representations of objects and their locations in space in the primate hippocampus. This is a property required in an episodic memory system, for which associations between objects and the places where they are seen are prototypical. The results thus show that a requirement for a human episodic memory system, separate and combined neuronal representations of objects and where they are seen out there in the environment, are present in the primate hippocampus (Rolls et al., 2005). What may be a corresponding finding in rats is that some rat hippocampal neurons respond on the basis of the conjunction of location and odor (Wood et al., 1999).

Primate hippocampal neuronal activity has also been shown to be related to the recall of memories. In a one–trial object place recall task, images of an object in one position on a screen and of a second object in a different position on the screen were shown successively. Then one of the objects was shown at the top of the screen, and the monkey had to recall the position in which it had been shown earlier in the trial and to touch that location (Rolls and Xiang, 2006). In addition to neurons that responded to the objects or places, a new type of neuronal response was found in which 5% of hippocampal neurons had place-related responses when a place was being recalled by an object cue.

The primate anterior hippocampus (which corresponds to the rodent ventral hippocampus) receives inputs from brain regions involved in reward processing such as the amygdala and orbitofrontal cortex (Pitkanen et al., 2002). To investigate how this affective input may be incorporated into primate hippocampal function, Rolls and Xiang (2005) recorded neuronal activity while macaques performed a reward-place association task in which each spatial scene shown on a video monitor had one location, which if touched yielded a preferred fruit juice reward, and a second location that yielded a less preferred juice reward. Each scene had different locations for the different rewards. Of 312 hippocampal neurons analyzed, 18% responded more to the location of the preferred reward in different scenes, and 5% to the location of the less preferred reward (Rolls and Xiang, 2005). When the locations of the preferred rewards in the scenes were reversed, 60% of 44 neurons tested reversed the location to which they responded, showing that the reward–place associations could be altered by new learning in a few trials. The majority (82%) of these 44 hippocampal reward–place

neurons tested did not respond to object–reward associations in a visual discrimination object–reward association task. Thus the primate hippocampus contains a representation of the reward associations of places out there being viewed, and this is a way in which affective information can be stored as part of an episodic memory, and how the current mood state may influence the retrieval of episodic memories. There is consistent evidence that rewards available in a spatial environment can influence the responsiveness of rodent place neurons (Hölscher et al., 2003; Tabuchi et al., 2003).

1.33.2.1.4 *Systems-level anatomy*

The primate hippocampus receives inputs via the entorhinal cortex (area 28) and the highly developed parahippocampal gyrus (areas TF and TH) as well as the perirhinal cortex from the ends of many processing streams of the cerebral association cortex, including the visual and auditory temporal lobe association cortical areas, the prefrontal cortex, and the parietal cortex (Van Hoesen, 1982; Amaral, 1987; Amaral et al., 1992; Suzuki and Amaral, 1994b; Witter et al., 2000b; Lavenex et al., 2004) (see **Figure 1**). The hippocampus is thus by its connections potentially able to associate together object and spatial representations. In addition, the entorhinal cortex receives inputs from the amygdala and the orbitofrontal cortex, which could provide reward-related information to the hippocampus (Suzuki and Amaral, 1994a; Carmichael and Price, 1995; Stefanacci et al., 1996; Pitkanen et al., 2002).

The primary output from the hippocampus to neocortex originates in CA1 and projects to subiculum, entorhinal cortex, and parahippocampal structures (areas TF-TH), as well as prefrontal cortex (Van Hoesen, 1982; Witter, 1993; Delatour and Witter, 2002; van Haeften et al., 2003) (see **Figure 1**), though there are other outputs (Rolls and Kesner, 2006).

1.33.2.2 The Operation of Hippocampal Circuitry as a Memory System

1.33.2.2.1 *Hippocampal circuitry*
(see Figure 1; Amaral and Witter, 1989; Storm-Mathiesen et al., 1990; Amaral, 1993; Witter et al., 2000b; Naber et al., 2001; Lavenex et al., 2004)

Projections from the entorhinal cortex layer 2 reach the granule cells (of which there are 10^6 in the rat) in the dentate gyrus (DG), via the perforant path (pp) (Witter, 1993). The granule cells project to CA3 cells via the mossy fibers (mf), which provide a sparse but possibly powerful connection to the $3 \cdot 10^5$

CA3 pyramidal cells in the rat. Each CA3 cell receives approximately 50 mf inputs, so that the sparseness of this connectivity is thus 0.005%. By contrast, there are many more – possibly weaker – direct perforant path inputs also from layer 2 of the entorhinal cortex onto each CA3 cell, in the rat on the order of $4 \cdot 10^3$. The largest number of synapses (approximately $1.2 \cdot 10^4$ in the rat) on the dendrites of CA3 pyramidal cells is, however, provided by the (recurrent) axon collaterals of CA3 cells themselves (rc) (see **Figure 2**). It is remarkable that the recurrent collaterals are distributed to other CA3 cells throughout the hippocampus (Amaral and Witter, 1989; Amaral et al., 1990; Ishizuka et al., 1990; Amaral and Witter, 1995), so that effectively the CA3 system provides a single network, with a connectivity of approximately 2% between the different CA3 neurons given that the connections are bilateral. The neurons that comprise CA3, in turn, project to CA1 neurons via the Schaffer collaterals. In addition, projections that terminate in the CA1 region originate in layer 3 of the entorhinal cortex (see **Figure 1**).

1.33.2.2.2   *Dentate granule cells*

The theory is that the dentate granule cell stage of hippocampal processing that precedes the CA3 stage acts in a number of ways to produce during learning

the sparse yet efficient (i.e., nonredundant) representation in CA3 neurons that is required for the autoassociation implemented by CA3 to perform well (Rolls, 1989b; Treves and Rolls, 1992; Rolls and Kesner, 2006; Rolls et al., 2006).

The first way is that the perforant path – the dentate granule cell system with its Hebb-like modifiability is suggested to act as a competitive learning network to remove redundancy from the inputs producing a more orthogonal, sparse, and categorized set of outputs (Rolls, 1987, 1989a,b,d, 1990a,b, Rolls and Treves, 1998; Rolls, 2007). (Competitive networks are described elsewhere: Hertz et al., 1991; Rolls and Treves, 1998; Rolls and Deco, 2002; Rolls, 2008). The nonlinearity in the N-methyl-D-aspartate (NMDA) receptors may help the operation of such a competitive net, for it ensures that only the most active neurons left after the competitive feedback inhibition have synapses that become modified and thus learn to respond to that input (Rolls, 1989a). Because of the feedback inhibition, the competitive process may result in a relatively constant number of strongly active dentate neurons relatively independently of the number of active perforant path inputs to the dentate cells. The operation of the dentate granule cell system as a competitive network may also be facilitated by a Hebb rule of the form:

$$\delta w_{ij} = k \cdot r_i \left(r'_j - w_{ij} \right), \qquad [1]$$

where k is a constant, r_i is the activation of the dendrite (the postsynaptic term), r'_j is the presynaptic firing rate, w_{ij} is the synaptic weight, and r'_j and w_{ij} are in appropriate units (Rolls, 1989a). Incorporation of a rule such as this which implies heterosynaptic long-term depression (LTD) as well as long-term potentiation (LTP) (see Levy and Desmond, 1985; Levy et al., 1990) makes the sum of the synaptic weights on each neuron remain roughly constant during learning (cf. Oja, 1982; see Rolls, 1989a; Rolls and Treves, 1998; Rolls, 2008; Rolls and Deco, 2002).

This functionality could be used to help build hippocampal place cells in rats from the grid cells present in the medial entorhinal cortex (Hafting et al., 2005). Each grid cell responds to a set of places in a spatial environment, with the places to which a cell responds set out in a regular grid. Different grid cells have different phases (positional offsets) and grid spacings (or frequencies) (Hafting et al., 2005). We (Rolls et al., 2006) have simulated the dentate granule cells as a system that receives as inputs the activity of a population of entorhinal cortex grid cells as the animal traverses a spatial environment and

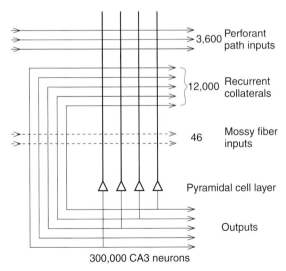

Figure 2 The numbers of connections from three different sources onto each CA3 cell from three different sources in the rat. After Treves A and Rolls ET (1992) Computational constraints suggest the need for two distinct input systems to the hippocampal CA3 network. *Hippocampus* 2: 189–199; Rolls ET and Treves A (1998) *Neural Networks and Brain Function*. Oxford: Oxford University Press.

have shown that the competitive net builds dentate-like place cells from such entorhinal grid cell inputs (see **Figure 3**). This occurs because the firing states of entorhinal cortex cells that are active at the same time when the animal is in one place become associated together by the learning in the competitive net, yet each dentate cell represents primarily one place because the dentate representation is kept sparse, thus helping to implement symmetry breaking (Rolls et al., 2006).

The second way is also a result of the competitive learning hypothesized to be implemented by the dentate granule cells (Rolls, 1987, 1989a,b,d, 1990a,b, 1994). It is proposed that this allows overlapping (or very similar) inputs to the hippocampus to be separated in the following way (see also Rolls, 1996b). Consider three patterns B, W, and BW, where BW is a linear combination of B and W. (To make the example very concrete, we could consider binary patterns where B = 10, W = 01, and BW = 11.) Then the memory system is required to associate B with reward and W with reward, but BW with punishment. Without the hippocampus, rats might have more difficulty in solving such problems, particularly when they are spatial, for

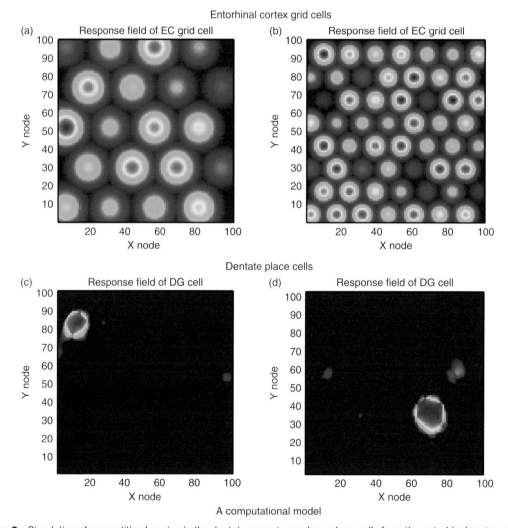

Figure 3   Simulation of competitive learning in the dentate gyrus to produce place cells from the entorhinal cortex grid cell inputs. (a), (b). Firing rate profiles of two entorhinal cortex grid cells with frequencies of four and seven cycles. In the simulation, cells with frequencies of four to seven cycles were used, and with 25 phases or spatial offsets. (A phase is defined as an offset in the X and Y directions, and five offset values were used in each direction.) The standard deviation of the peak heights was set to 0.6. (c), (d): Firing rate profiles of two dentate gyrus cells after competitive network training with the Hebb rule. After Rolls ET, Stringer SM, and Elliot T (2006) Entorhinal cortex grid cells can map to hippocampal place cells by competitive learning. *Netw. Comput. Neural Sys.* 17: 447–465.

the dentate/CA3 system in rodents is characterized by being implicated in spatial memory. However, it is a property of competitive neuronal networks that they can separate such overlapping patterns, as has been shown elsewhere (Rolls, 1989a; Rolls and Treves, 1998; Rolls, 2008); normalization of synaptic weight vectors is required for this property. It is thus an important part of hippocampal neuronal network architecture that there is a competitive network that precedes the CA3 autoassociation system. Without the dentate gyrus, if a conventional autoassociation network were presented with the mixture BW having learned B and W separately, then the autoassociation network would produce a mixed output state and would therefore be incapable of storing separate memories for B, W, and BW. It is suggested, therefore, that competition in the DG is one of the powerful computational features of the hippocampus and could enable it to help solve spatial pattern separation tasks (Rolls and Kesner, 2006).

This computational hypothesis and its predictions have been tested. Rats with DG lesions are impaired at a metric spatial pattern separation task (Gilbert et al., 2001; Goodrich-Hunsaker et al., 2005) (see **Figure 4**). The recoding of grid cells in the entorhinal cortex (Hafting et al., 2005) into small place field cells in the dentate granule cells that has been modeled (Rolls et al., 2006) can also be considered to be a case where overlapping inputs must be recoded so that different spatial components can be treated

differently. I note that Sutherland and Rudy's configural learning hypothesis was similar but was not tested with spatial pattern separation. Instead, when tested with, for example, tone and light combinations, it was not consistently found that the hippocampus was important (Sutherland and Rudy, 1991; O'Reilly and Rudy, 2001). I suggest that application of the configural concept, but applied to spatial pattern separation, may capture part of what the DG – acting as a competitive network – could perform, particularly when a large number of such overlapping spatial memories must be stored and retrieved.

The third way in which the DG is hypothesized to contribute to the sparse and relatively orthogonal representations in CA3 arises because of the very low contact probability in the mf–CA3 connections and is described in the section titled 'Mossy fiber inputs to the CA3 cells' and by Treves and Rolls (1992).

A fourth way is that, as suggested and explained in the section titled 'Mossy fiber inputs to the CA3 cells,' the dentate granule cell–mf input to the CA3 cells may be powerful, and its use, particularly during learning, would be efficient in forcing a new pattern of firing onto the CA3 cells during learning.

In the ways just described, the dentate granule cells could be particularly important in helping to build and prepare spatial representations for the CA3 network. The actual representation of space in the primate hippocampus includes a representation of spatial view, whereas in the rat hippocampus it is of the place where the rat is. The representation in the rat may be related to the fact that with a much less developed visual system than the primate, the rat's representation of space may be defined more by the olfactory and tactile as well as distant visual cues present and may thus tend to reflect the place where the rat is. However, the spatial representations in the rat and primate could arise from essentially the same computational process as follows (Rolls, 1999; de Araujo et al., 2001). The starting assumption is that in both the rat and the primate, the dentate granule cells (and the CA3 and CA1 pyramidal cells) respond to combinations of the inputs received. In the case of the primate, a combination of visual features in the environment will, because of the fovea providing high spatial resolution over a typical viewing angle of perhaps $10°–20°$, result in the formation of a spatial view cell, the effective trigger for which will thus be a combination of visual features within a relatively small part of space. In contrast, in the rat, given the very extensive visual field

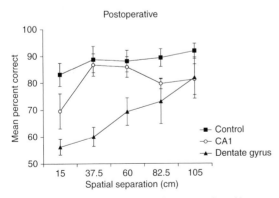

Figure 4 Pattern separation impairment produced by dentate gyrus lesions. Mean percent correct performance as a function of spatial separation of control group, CA1 lesion group, and dentate gyrus lesion group on postoperative trials. A graded impairment was found as a function of the distance between the places only following dentate gyrus lesions. After Gilbert PE, Kesner RP, and Lee I (2001) Dissociating hippocampal subregions: Double dissociation between dentate gyrus and CA1. *Hippocampus* 11: 626–636.

subtended by the rodent retina, which may extend over 180°–270°, a combination of visual features formed over such a wide visual angle would effectively define a position in space that is a place (de Araujo et al., 2001).

Although spatial view cells are present in the parahippocampal areas (Rolls et al., 1997a, 1998; Robertson et al., 1998; Georges-François et al., 1999), and neurons with place-like fields (though in some cases as a grid [Hafting et al., 2005]) are found in the medial entorhinal cortex (Moser and Moser, 1998; Brun et al., 2002; Fyhn et al., 2004; Moser, 2004), there are backprojections from the hippocampus to the entorhinal cortex and thus to parahippocampal areas, and these backprojections could enable the hippocampus to influence the spatial representations found in the entorhinal cortex and parahippocampal gyrus. On the other hand, as described above, the grid-like place cells in the medial entorhinal cortex could, if transformed by the competitive net functionality of the dentate cells, result in the place cell activity (without a repeating grid) that is found in dentate and rat hippocampal neurons.

1.33.2.2.3 CA3 as an autoassociation memory

1.33.2.2.3.(i) Arbitrary associations and pattern completion in recall Many of the synapses in the hippocampus show associative modification as shown by long-term potentiation, and this synaptic modification appears to be involved in learning (see Morris, 1989, 2003; Morris et al., 2003; Lynch, 2004). On the basis of the evidence summarized above, Rolls (1987, 1989a,b,d, 1990a,b, 1991) and others (McNaughton and Morris, 1987; Levy, 1989; McNaughton, 1991) have suggested that the CA3 stage acts as an autoassociation memory that enables episodic memories to be formed and stored in the CA3 network, and that subsequently the extensive recurrent collateral connectivity allows for the retrieval of a whole representation to be initiated by the activation of some small part of the same representation (the cue). The crucial synaptic modification for this is in the recurrent collateral synapses. A description of the operation of autoassociative networks is provided by Hertz et al. (1991), Rolls and Treves (1998), Rolls and Deco (2002), and Rolls (2007). The architecture of an autoassociation network is shown in **Figure 2**, and the learning rule is as shown in eqn [1], except that the subtractive term could be the presynaptic firing rate (Rolls and Treves, 1998; Rolls and Deco, 2002).

The hypothesis is that because the CA3 operates effectively as a single network, it can allow arbitrary associations between inputs originating from very different parts of the cerebral cortex to be formed. These might involve associations between information originating in the temporal visual cortex about the presence of an object, as well as information originating in the parietal cortex about where it is. I note that although there is some spatial gradient in the CA3 recurrent connections, so that the connectivity is not fully uniform (Ishizuka et al., 1990), nevertheless the network will still have the properties of a single interconnected autoassociation network allowing associations between arbitrary neurons to be formed, given the presence of many long-range connections that overlap from different CA3 cells.

Crucial issues include how many memories could be stored in this system (to determine whether the autoassociation hypothesis leads to a realistic estimate of the number of memories that the hippocampus could store); whether the whole of a memory could be completed from any part; whether the autoassociation memory can act as a short-term memory, for which the architecture is inherently suited, and whether the system could operate with spatial representations, which are essentially continuous because of the continuous nature of space. These and related issues are considered in the remainder of this section and in more detail elsewhere (Rolls and Kesner, 2006; Rolls, 2008).

1.33.2.2.3.(i).(a) Storage capacity We have performed quantitative analyses of the storage and retrieval processes in the CA3 network (Treves and Rolls, 1991, 1992). We have extended previous formal models of autoassociative memory (see Amit, 1989) by analyzing a network with graded response units, so as to represent more realistically the continuously variable rates at which neurons fire, and with incomplete connectivity (Treves, 1990; Treves and Rolls, 1991). We have found that in general, the maximum number p_{max} of firing patterns that can be (individually) retrieved is proportional to the number C^{RC} of (associatively) modifiable recurrent collateral synapses per cell, by a factor that increases roughly with the inverse of the sparseness a of the neuronal representation (Each memory is precisely defined in the theory: It is a set of firing rates of the population of neurons – which represent a memory – that can be stored and later retrieved, with retrieval being possible from a fraction of the originally stored set of neuronal firing rates.) The sparseness of response (or selectivity) of a single cell to a set of stimuli (which in the brain has approximately the same value as the sparseness of the response of the population of neurons to any one stimulus, which can in turn be thought of as the proportion of neurons that is active to any one stimulus if the neurons had binary responses; see Franco et al., 2007) is defined as

$$a = \left(\sum_{i=1,n} r_i/n \right)^2 \Big/ \sum_{i=1,n} \left(r_i^2/n \right), \qquad [2]$$

where r_i is the firing rate to the ith stimulus in the set of n stimuli. The sparseness ranges from $1/n$, when the cell responds to only one stimulus, to a maximal value of 1.0, attained when the cell responds with the same rate to all stimuli. Approximately,

$$p_{max} \cong \frac{C^{RC}}{a \ln(1/a)} k, \qquad [3]$$

where k is a factor that depends weakly on the detailed structure of the rate distribution, on the connectivity pattern, and so on, but is roughly on the order of 0.2–0.3 (Treves and Rolls, 1991). The sparseness a in this equation is strictly the population sparseness (Treves and Rolls, 1991; Franco et al., 2007). The population sparseness a^p would be measured by measuring the distribution of firing rates of all neurons to a single stimulus at a single time. The single-cell sparseness or selectivity a^s would be measured by the distribution of firing rates to a set of stimuli, which would take a long time. These concepts are elucidated by Franco et al. (2007). The sparseness estimates obtained by measuring early gene changes, which are effectively population sparsenesses, would thus be expected to depend greatly on the range of environments or stimuli in which these were measured. If the environment was restricted to one stimulus, this would reflect the population sparseness. If the environment was changing, the measure from early gene changes would be rather undefined, as all the populations of neurons activated in an undefined number of testing situations would be likely to be activated. For example, for $C^{RC} = 12{,}000$ and $a = 0.02$, p_{max} is calculated to be approximately 36,000. This analysis emphasizes the utility of having a sparse representation in the hippocampus, for this enables many different memories to be stored. Third, in order for most associative networks to store information efficiently, heterosynaptic LTD (as well as LTP) is required (Fazeli and Collingridge, 1996;

Rolls and Deco, 2002; Rolls and Treves, 1990, 1998; Treves and Rolls, 1991). Simulations that are fully consistent with the analytic theory are provided by Simmen et al. (1996) and Rolls et al. (1997b).

We have also indicated how to estimate I, the total amount of information (in bits per synapse) that can be retrieved from the network. I is defined with respect to the information i_p (in bits per cell) contained in each stored firing pattern, by subtracting the amount i_l lost in retrieval and multiplying by p/C^{RC}:

$$I = \frac{p}{C^{RC}} (i_p - i_l) \qquad [4]$$

The maximal value I_{max} of this quantity was found (Treves and Rolls, 1991) to be in several interesting cases around 0.2–0.3 bits per synapse, with only a mild dependency on parameters such as the sparseness of coding a.

We may then estimate (Treves and Rolls, 1992) how much information has to be stored in each pattern for the network to efficiently exploit its information retrieval capacity I_{max}. The estimate is expressed as a requirement on i_p:

$$i_p > a \ln(1/a) \qquad [5]$$

As the information content of each stored pattern i_p depends on the storage process, we see how the retrieval capacity analysis, coupled with the notion that the system is organized so as to be an efficient memory device in a quantitative sense, leads to a constraint on the storage process.

A number of points that arise are treated elsewhere (Rolls and Kesner, 2006; Rolls, 2007). Here I note that given that the memory capacity of the hippocampal CA3 system is limited, it is necessary to have some form of forgetting in this store, or another mechanism to ensure that its capacity is not exceeded. (Exceeding the capacity can lead to a loss of much of the information retrievable from the network.) Heterosynaptic LTD could help this forgetting, by enabling new memories to overwrite old memories (Rolls, 1996a, 2007). The limited capacity of the CA3 system does also provide one of the arguments that some transfer of information from the hippocampus to neocortical memory stores may be useful (see Treves and Rolls, 1994). Given its limited capacity, the hippocampus might be a useful store for only a limited period, which might be on the order of days, weeks, or months. This period may well depend on the acquisition rate of new episodic memories. If the animal were in a constant and limited environment, then as new information is not being added to the hippocampus, the representations in the hippocampus would remain stable and persistent. These hypotheses have clear experimental implications, both for recordings from single neurons and for the gradient of retrograde amnesia, both of which might be expected to depend on whether the environment is stable or frequently changing. They show that the conditions under which a gradient of retrograde amnesia might be demonstrable would be when large numbers of new memories are being acquired, not when only a few memories (few in the case of the hippocampus being less than a few hundred) are being learned.

1.33.2.2.3.(i).(b) Recall A fundamental property of the autoassociation model of the CA3 recurrent collateral network is that the recall can be symmetric, that is, the whole of the memory can be retrieved from any part. For example, in an object–place autoassociation memory, an object could be recalled from a place retrieval cue, and vice versa. This is not the case with a pattern association network. If, for example, the CA3 activity represented a place–spatial view, and perforant path inputs with associative synapses to CA3 neurons carried object information (consistent with evidence that the lateral perforant path [LPP] may reflect inputs from the perirhinal cortex connecting via the lateral entorhinal cortex [Hargreaves et al., 2005]), then an object could recall a place, but a place could not recall an object.

A prediction of the theory is thus that the CA3 recurrent collateral associative connections enable arbitrary associations to be formed between whatever is represented in the hippocampus, in that, for example, any place could be associated with any object, and in that the object could be recalled with a spatial recall cue, or the place with an object recall cue.

In one test of this, Day et al. (2003) trained rats in a study phase to learn in one trial an association between two flavors of food and two spatial locations. During a recall test phase they were presented with a flavor that served as a cue for the selection of the correct location. They found that injections of an NMDA blocker (AP5) or alpha-amino-3-hydroxy-5-methyl-isoxazole-4-propionic acid (AMPA) blocker (CNQX) to the dorsal hippocampus prior to the study phase impaired encoding, but injections of AP5 prior to the test phase did not impair the place recall, whereas injections of CNQX did impair the place recall. The interpretation is that somewhere in the hippocampus NMDA

receptors are necessary for forming one-trial odor–place associations, and that recall can be performed without further involvement of NMDA receptors.

In a hippocampus subregion test of this, rats in a study phase are shown one object in one location, and then a second object in another location. (There are 50 possible objects and 48 locations.) In the test phase, the rat is shown one object in the start box and then after a 10-s delay must go to the correct location (choosing between two marked locations). CA3 lesions made after training in the task produced chance performance on this one-trial object–place recall task. A control, fixed visual conditional-to-place task (Rolls and Kesner, 2006) with the same delay was not impaired, showing that it is recall after one-trial (or rapid) learning that is impaired. In the context of arbitrary associations between whatever is represented in CA3, the theory also predicts that cued place–object recall tasks and cued place–odor recall tasks should be impaired by CA3 lesions.

Evidence that the CA3 system is not necessarily required during recall in a reference memory spatial task, such as the water maze spatial navigation for a single spatial location task, is that CA3-lesioned rats are not impaired during recall of a previously learned water maze task (Brun et al., 2002; Florian and Roullet, 2004). However, if completion from an incomplete cue is needed, then CA3 NMDA receptors are necessary (presumably to ensure satisfactory CA3–CA3 learning), even in a reference memory task (Nakazawa et al., 2002). Thus, the CA3 system appears to be especially needed in rapid, one-trial object–place recall and when completion from an incomplete cue is required.

In a neurophysiological investigation of one-trial object–place learning followed by recall of the spatial position in which to respond when shown the object, Rolls and Xiang (2005) showed that some primate hippocampal (including CA3) neurons respond to an object cue with the spatial position in which the object had been shown earlier in the trial. Thus, some hippocampal neurons appear to reflect spatial recall given an object recall cue.

1.33.2.2.3.(i).(c) Completion Another fundamental property is that the recall can be complete even from a small fragment. Thus, it is a prediction that when an incomplete retrieval cue is given, CA3 may be especially important in the retrieval process. Tests of this prediction of a role for CA3 in pattern completion have been performed, as follows.

Rats were tested on a cheese board with a black curtain with four extramaze cues surrounding the apparatus. (The cheese board is like a dry-land water maze with 177 holes on a 119-cm-diameter board.) Rats were trained to move a sample phase object covering a food well that could appear in one of five possible spatial locations. During the test phase of the task, following a 30-s delay, the animal needs to find the same food well in order to receive reinforcement with the object now removed. After reaching stable performance in terms of accuracy to find the correct location, rats received lesions in CA3. During postsurgery testing, four extramaze cues were always available during the sample phase. However, during the test phase zero, one, two, or three cues were removed in different combinations. The results indicate that controls performed well on the task regardless of the availability of one, two, three, or all cues, suggesting intact spatial pattern completion. Following the CA3 lesion, however, there was an impairment in accuracy compared to the controls especially when only one or two cues were available, suggesting impairment in spatial pattern completion in CA3-lesioned rats (Gold and Kesner, 2005) (see **Figure 5**). A useful aspect of this task is that the test

for the ability to remember a spatial location learned in one presentation can be tested with a varying number of available cues, and many times in which the locations vary, to allow for accurate measurement of pattern completion ability when the information stored on the single presentation must be recalled.

In another study, Nakazawa et al. (2002) trained CA3 NMDA receptor-knockout mice in an analogous task, using the water maze. When the animals were required to perform the task in an environment where some of the familiar cues were removed, they were impaired in performing the task. The result suggests that the NMDA receptor–dependent synaptic plasticity mechanisms in CA3 are critical to perform the pattern completion process in the hippocampus.

1.33.2.2.3.(ii) Continuous spatial patterns and CA3 representations

The fact that spatial patterns, which imply continuous representations of space, are represented in the hippocampus has led to the application of continuous attractor models to help understand hippocampal function. This has been necessary because space is inherently continuous, because the firing of place and spatial view cells is approximately Gaussian as a function of the distance away from the preferred spatial location, because these cells have spatially overlapping fields, and because the theory is that these cells in CA3 are connected by Hebb-modifiable synapses. This specification would inherently lead the system to operate as a continuous attractor network. Continuous attractor network models have been studied by Amari (1977), Zhang (1996), Taylor (1999), Samsonovich and McNaughton (1997), Battaglia and Treves (1998), Stringer et al. (2002a,b, 2004), Stringer and Rolls (2002), and Rolls and Stringer (2005) (see Rolls, 2007; Rolls and Deco, 2002) and are described next.

A continuous attractor neural network (CANN) can maintain the firing of its neurons to represent any location along a continuous physical dimension such as spatial position and head direction. It uses excitatory recurrent collateral connections between the neurons (as are present in CA3) to reflect the distance between the neurons in the state space of the animal (e.g., place or head direction). These networks can maintain the bubble of neural activity constant for long periods wherever it is started, to represent the current state (head direction, position, etc.) of the animal, and are likely to be involved in many aspects of spatial processing and memory, including spatial vision. Global inhibition is used to keep the number

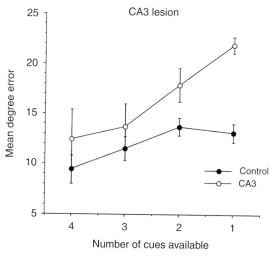

Figure 5 Pattern completion impairment produced by CA3 lesions. The mean (and SEM) degree of error in finding the correct place in the cheeseboard task when rats were tested with 1, 2, 3, or 4 of the cues available. A graded impairment in the CA3 lesion group as a function of the number of cues available was found. The task was learned in the study phase with the four cues present. The performance of the control group is also shown. After Gold AE and Kesner RP (2005) The role of the CA3 subregion of the dorsal hippocampus in spatial pattern completion in the rat. *Hippocampus* 15: 808–814.

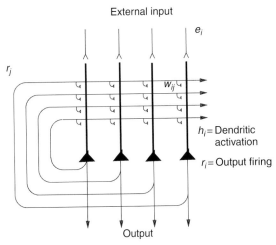

Figure 6   The architecture of a continuous attractor neural network. The architecture is the same as that of a discrete attractor neural network.

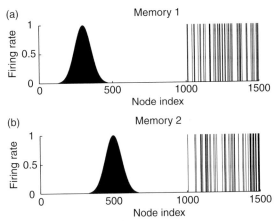

Figure 7   The types of firing patterns stored in continuous attractor networks are illustrated for the patterns present on neurons 1–1000 for Memory 1 (when the firing is that produced when the spatial state represented is that for location 300), and for Memory 2 (when the firing is that produced when the spatial state represented is that for location 500). The continuous nature of the spatial representation results from the fact that each neuron has a Gaussian firing rate that peaks at its optimal location. This particular mixed network also contains discrete representations that consist of discrete subsets of active binary firing rate neurons in the range 1001–1500. The firing of these latter neurons can be thought of as representing the discrete events that occur at the location. Continuous attractor networks by definition contain only continuous representations, but this particular network can store mixed continuous and discrete representations, and is illustrated to show the difference of the firing patterns normally stored in separate continuous attractor and discrete attractor networks. For this particular mixed network, during learning, Memory 1 is stored in the synaptic weights, then Memory 2, etc., and each memory contains a part that is continuously distributed to represent physical space and a part that represents a discrete event or object.

of neurons in a bubble or packet of actively firing neurons relatively constant and to help to ensure that there is only one activity packet. Continuous attractor networks can be thought of as very similar to autoassociation or discrete attractor networks (see Rolls and Deco 2002) and have the same architecture, as illustrated in **Figure 6**. The main difference is that the patterns stored in a CANN are continuous patterns, with each neuron having broadly tuned firing that decreases with, for example, a Gaussian function as the distance from the optimal firing location of the cell is varied, and with different neurons having tuning that overlaps throughout the space. Such tuning is illustrated in **Figure 7**. For comparison, autoassociation networks normally have discrete (separate) patterns (each pattern implemented by the firing of a particular subset of the neurons), with no continuous distribution of the patterns throughout the space (see **Figure 7**). A consequent difference is that the CANN can maintain its firing at any location in the trained continuous space, whereas a discrete attractor or autoassociation network moves its population of active neurons toward one of the previously learned attractor states, and thus implements the recall of a particular previously learned pattern from an incomplete or noisy (distorted) version of one of the previously learned patterns.

The energy landscape of a discrete attractor network (see Rolls and Deco 2002) has separate energy minima, each one of which corresponds to a learned pattern, whereas the energy landscape of a continuous attractor network is flat, so that the activity

packet remains stable with continuous firing wherever it is started in the state space. (The state space refers to the set of possible spatial states of the animal in its environment, e.g., the set of possible places in a room.)

So far we have said that the neurons in the continuous attractor network are connected to each other by synaptic weights w_{ij} that are a simple function, for example, Gaussian, of the distance between the states of the agent in the physical world (e.g., head directions, spatial views, etc.) represented by the neurons. In many simulations, the weights are set by formula to have weights with these appropriate Gaussian values. However, Stringer et al. (2002b) showed how the appropriate weights could be set up by learning. They started with the fact that since the neurons have broad tuning that may be Gaussian in shape, nearby neurons in the state space will have overlapping spatial fields, and will thus be coactive to a degree that depends on the distance between them. The authors postulated that therefore the synaptic weights could be set up by associative learning based on the coactivity of the neurons produced by external stimuli as the animal moved in the state space. For example, head direction cells are forced to fire during learning by visual cues in the environment that produces Gaussian firing as a function of head direction from an optimal head direction for each cell. The learning rule is simply that the weights w_{ij} from head direction cell j with firing rate r_j^{HD} to head direction cell i with firing rate r_i^{HD} are updated according to an associative (Hebb) rule:

$$\delta w_{ij} = k r_i^{HD} r_j^{HD},\qquad [6]$$

where δw_{ij} is the change of synaptic weight and k is the learning rate constant. During the learning phase, the firing rate r_i^{HD} of each head direction cell i might be the following the Gaussian function of the displacement of the head from the optimal firing direction of the cell:

$$r_i^{HD} = e^{-s_{HD}^2/2\sigma_{HD}^2},\qquad [7]$$

where s_{HD} is the difference between the actual head direction x (in degrees) of the agent and the optimal head direction x_i for head direction cell i, and σ_{HD} is the standard deviation. Stringer et al. (2002b) showed that after training at all head directions, the synaptic connections develop strengths that are an almost Gaussian function of the distance between the cells in head direction space.

1.33.2.2.3.(iii) Combined continuous and discrete memory representations in the same (e.g., CA3) network, and episodic memory

Space is continuous, and object representations are discrete. If these representations are to be combined in, for example, an object–place memory, then we need to understand the operation of networks that combine these representations. It has now been shown that attractor networks can store both continuous patterns and discrete patterns (as illustrated in **Figure** 7) and can thus be used to store, for example, the location in (continuous, physical) space (e.g., the place out there in a room represented by spatial view cells) where an object (a discrete item) is present (Rolls et al., 2002).

1.33.2.2.3.(iv) The capacity of a continuous attractor network, and multiple charts

If spatial representations are stored in the hippocampus, the important issue arises in terms of understanding memories that include a spatial component or context of how many such spatial representations could be stored in a continuous attractor network. The very interesting result is that because there are in general low correlations between the representations of places in different maps or charts (where each map or chart might be of one room or locale), very many different maps can be simultaneously stored in a continuous attractor network (Battaglia and Treves, 1998a).

1.33.2.2.3.(v) Idiothetic update by path integration

We have considered how spatial representations could be stored in continuous attractor networks and how the activity can be maintained at any location in the state space in a form of short-term memory when the external (e.g., visual) input is removed. However, many networks with spatial representations in the brain can be updated by internal, self-motion (i.e., idiothetic) cues even when there is no external (e.g., visual) input. The way in which path integration could be implemented in recurrent networks such as the CA3 system in the hippocampus or in related systems is described next.

Single-cell recording studies have shown that some neurons represent the current position along a continuous physical dimension or space even when no inputs are available, for example, in darkness. Examples include neurons that represent the positions of the eyes (i.e., eye direction with respect to the head), the place where the animal is looking in space, head direction, and the place where the animal is located. In particular, examples of such classes of cells include head direction cells in rats (Ranck, 1985; Taube et al., 1990; Muller et al., 1996; Taube et al., 1996) and primates (Robertson et al., 1999), which respond maximally when the animal's head is facing in a particular preferred direction; place cells in rats (O'Keefe and Dostrovsky, 1971; McNaughton et al., 1983; O'Keefe, 1984; Muller et al., 1991; Markus et al., 1995) that fire maximally when the animal is in a particular location; and spatial view cells in primates that respond when the monkey is looking toward a particular location in space (Rolls et al., 1997a; Robertson et al., 1998; Georges-François et al., 1999).

One approach to simulating the movement of an activity packet produced by idiothetic cues (which is a form of path integration whereby the current location is calculated from recent movements) is to employ a look-up table that stores (taking head direction cells as an example), for every possible head direction and head rotational velocity input generated by the vestibular system, the corresponding new head direction (Samsonovich and McNaughton, 1997). An analogous approach has been described for entorhinal cortex grid cells (McNaughton et al., 2006). Another approach involves modulating the strengths of the recurrent synaptic weights in the continuous attractor on one but not the other side of a currently represented position, so that the stable position of the packet of activity, which requires symmetric connections in different directions from each node, is lost, and the packet moves in the direction of the temporarily increased weights, although no possible biological implementation was proposed of how the appropriate dynamic synaptic weight changes might be achieved (Zhang, 1996). Another mechanism (for head direction cells) (Skaggs et al., 1995) relies on a set of cells, termed (head) rotation cells, which are coactivated by head direction cells and vestibular cells and drive the activity of the attractor network by anatomically distinct connections for clockwise and counterclockwise rotation cells, in what is effectively a look-up table. However, these proposals did not show how the synaptic weights for this path integration could be achieved by a biologically plausible learning process.

Stringer et al. (2002b) introduced a proposal with more biological plausibility about how the synaptic connections from idiothetic inputs to a continuous attractor network can be learned by a self-organizing learning process. The mechanism associates a short-term memory trace of the firing of the neurons in the attractor network reflecting recent movements in the state space (e.g., of places) with an idiothetic velocity of movement input (see **Figure 8**). This has been applied to head direction cells (Stringer et al., 2002b), rat place cells (Stringer et al., 2002a,b), and primate spatial view cells (Stringer et al., 2004, 2005; Rolls and Stringer, 2005). These attractor networks provide a basis for understanding cognitive maps and how they are updated by learning and by self-motion. The implication is that to the extent that path integration of place or spatial view representations is performed within the hippocampus itself, then the CA3 system is the most likely part of the hippocampus to be involved in this, because it has

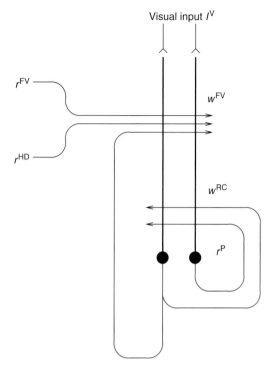

Figure 8 Neural network architecture for two-dimensional continuous attractor models of place cells. There is a recurrent network of place cells with firing rates r^P, which receives external inputs from three sources: (i) the visual system I^V, (ii) a population of head direction cells with firing rates r^{HD}, and (iii) a population of forward velocity cells with firing rates r^{FV}. The recurrent weights between the place cells are denoted by w^{RC}, and the idiothetic weights to the place cells from the forward velocity cells and head direction cells are denoted by w^{FV}.

the appropriate recurrent collateral connections. Consistent with this, Whishaw and colleagues (Maaswinkel et al., 1999; Whishaw et al., 2001; Wallace and Whishaw, 2003) have shown that path integration is impaired by hippocampal lesions. Path integration of head direction is reflected in the firing of neurons in the presubiculum, and mechanisms outside the hippocampus probably implement path integration for head direction.

1.33.2.2.3.(vi)   The dynamics of the recurrent network   The analysis described earlier of the capacity of a recurrent network such as the CA3 considered steady-state conditions of the firing rates of the neurons. The question arises of how quickly the recurrent network would settle into its final state. With reference to the CA3 network, how long does it take before a pattern of activity, originally evoked in

CA3 by afferent inputs, becomes influenced by the activation of recurrent collaterals? In a more general context, recurrent collaterals between the pyramidal cells are an important feature of the connectivity of the cerebral neocortex. How long would it take these collaterals to contribute fully to the activity of cortical cells? If these settling processes took on the order of hundreds of milliseconds, they would be much too slow to contribute usefully to cortical activity, whether in the hippocampus or the neocortex (Rolls, 1992; Panzeri et al., 2001; Rolls and Deco, 2002; Rolls, 2003).

It has been shown that if the neurons are not treated as McCulloch-Pitts neurons, which are simply updated at each iteration, or cycle of time steps (and assume the active state if the threshold is exceeded), but instead are analyzed and modeled as integrate-and-fire neurons in real continuous time, then the network can effectively relax into its recall state very rapidly in one or two time constants of the synapses (Treves, 1993; Battaglia and Treves, 1998b; Rolls and Treves, 1998; Rolls and Deco, 2002). This corresponds to perhaps 20 ms in the brain. One factor in this rapid dynamics of autoassociative networks with brain-like integrate-and-fire membrane and synaptic properties is that with some spontaneous activity, some of the neurons in the network are close to threshold already before the recall cue is applied, and hence some of the neurons are very quickly pushed by the recall cue into firing, so that information starts to be exchanged very rapidly (within 1–2 ms of brain time) through the modified synapses by the neurons in the network. The progressive exchange of information starting early on within what would otherwise be thought of as an iteration period (of perhaps 20 ms, corresponding to a neuronal firing rate of 50 spikes/s) is the mechanism accounting for rapid recall in an autoassociative neuronal network made biologically realistic in this way. Further analysis of the fast dynamics of these networks if they are implemented in a biologically plausible way with integrate-and-fire neurons, is provided in Section 7.7 of Rolls and Deco (2002), in Appendix A5 of Rolls and Treves (1998), by Treves (1993), and by Panzeri et al. (2001).

1.33.2.2.3.(vii) Mossy fiber inputs to the CA3 cells

We hypothesize that the mf inputs force efficient information storage by virtue of their strong and sparse influence on the CA3 cell firing rates (Rolls, 1987, 1989b,d; Treves and Rolls, 1992). (The strong effects likely to be mediated by the mfs were also emphasized by McNaughton and Morris [1987] and McNaughton and Nadel [1990].) We hypothesize that the mf input appears to be particularly appropriate in several ways.

First of all, the fact that mf synapses are large and located very close to the soma makes them relatively powerful in activating the postsynaptic cell. (This should not be taken to imply that a CA3 cell can be fired by a single mf excitatory postsynaptic potential [EPSP].)

Second, the firing activity of dentate granule cells appears to be very sparse (Jung and McNaughton, 1993), and this, together with the small number of connections on each CA3 cell, produces a sparse signal, which can then be transformed into an even sparser firing activity in CA3 by a threshold effect. For example, if only one granule cell in 100 were active in the dentate gyrus, and each CA3 cell received a connection from 50 randomly placed granule cells, then the number of active mf inputs received by CA3 cells would follow a Poisson distribution of average $50/100 = 1/2$, that is, 60% of the cells would not receive any active input, 30% would receive only one, 7.5% two, little more than 1% would receive three, and so on. (It is easy to show from the properties of the Poisson distribution and our definition of sparseness that the sparseness of the mf signal as seen by a CA3 cell would be $x/(1 + x)$, with $x = C^{MF} a_{DG}$, assuming equal strengths for all mf synapses.) If three mf inputs were required to fire a CA3 cell and these were the only inputs available, we see that the activity in CA3 would be roughly as sparse, in the example, as in the dentate gyrus. C^{MF} is the number of mf connections to a CA3 neuron, and a_{DG} is the sparseness of the representation in the dentate granule cells.

Third, nonassociative plasticity of mfs (see Brown et al., 1989, 1990) might have a useful effect in enhancing the signal-to-noise ratio, in that a consistently firing mf would produce nonlinearly amplified currents in the postsynaptic cell, which would not happen with an occasionally firing fiber (Treves and Rolls, 1992). This plasticity, and also learning in the dentate, would also have the effect that similar fragments of each episode (e.g., the same environmental location) recurring on subsequent occasions would be more likely to activate the same population of CA3 cells, which would have potential advantages in terms of economy of use of the CA3 cells in different memories, and in making some link between different episodic memories with a common feature, such as the same location in space.

Fourth, with only a few, and powerful, active mf inputs to each CA3 cell, setting a given sparseness of the representation provided by CA3 cells would be simplified, for the EPSPs produced by the mfs would be Poisson distributed with large membrane potential differences for each active mf. Setting the average firing rate of the dentate granule cells would effectively set the sparseness of the CA3 representation, without great precision being required in the threshold setting of the CA3 cells (Rolls et al., 1997b). Part of what is achieved by the mf input may be setting the sparseness of the CA3 cells correctly, which, as shown above, is very important in an autoassociative memory store.

Fifth, the nonassociative and sparse connectivity properties of the mf connections to CA3 cells may be appropriate for an episodic memory system that can learn very fast, in one trial. The hypothesis is that the sparse connectivity would help arbitrary relatively uncorrelated sets of CA3 neurons to be activated for even somewhat similar input patterns without the need for any learning of how best to separate the patterns, which in a self-organizing competitive network would take several repetitions (at least) of the set of patterns.

The mf solution may thus be adaptive in a system that must learn in one trial, and for which the CA3 recurrent collateral learning requires uncorrelated sets of CA3 cells to be allocated for each (one-trial) episodic memory. The hypothesis is that the mf sparse connectivity solution performs the appropriate function without the mf system having to learn by repeated presentations of how best to separate a set of training patterns. The perforant path input would, the quantitative analysis shows, not produce a pattern of firing in CA3 that contains sufficient information for learning (Treves and Rolls, 1992).

On the basis of these points, we predict that the mfs may be necessary for new learning in the hippocampus but may not be necessary for recall of existing memories from the hippocampus. Experimental evidence consistent with this prediction about the role of the mfs in learning has been found in rats with disruption of the dentate granule cells (Lassalle et al., 2000).

As acetylcholine turns down the efficacy of the recurrent collateral synapses between CA3 neurons (Hasselmo et al., 1995), then cholinergic activation also might help to allow external inputs rather than the internal recurrent collateral inputs to dominate the firing of the CA3 neurons during learning, as the current theory proposes. If cholinergic activation at the same time facilitated LTP in the recurrent collaterals (as it appears to in the neocortex), then cholinergic activation could have a useful double role in facilitating new learning at times of behavioral activation, when presumably it may be particularly relevant to allocate some of the limited memory capacity to new memories.

1.33.2.2.3.(viii)   Perforant path inputs to CA3 cells   By calculating the amount of information that would end up being carried by a CA3 firing pattern produced solely by the perforant path input and by the effect of the recurrent connections, we have been able to show (Treves and Rolls, 1992) that an input of the perforant path type, alone, is unable to direct efficient information storage. Such an input is too weak, it turns out, to drive the firing of the cells, as the dynamics of the network are dominated by the randomizing effect of the recurrent collaterals. This is the manifestation, in the CA3 network, of a general problem affecting storage (i.e., learning) in all autoassociative memories. The problem arises when the system is considered to be activated by a set of input axons making synaptic connections that have to compete with the recurrent connections, rather than having the firing rates of the neurons artificially clamped into a prescribed pattern.

An autoassociative memory network needs afferent inputs also in the other mode of operation, that is, when it retrieves a previously stored pattern of activity. We have shown (Treves and Rolls, 1992) that the requirements on the organization of the afferents are in this case very different, implying the necessity of a second, separate input system, which we have identified with the perforant path to CA3. In brief, the argument is based on the notion that the cue available to initiate retrieval might be rather small, that is, the distribution of activity on the afferent axons might carry a small correlation, $q \ll 1$, with the activity distribution present during learning. In order not to lose this small correlation altogether, but rather transform it into an input current in the CA3 cells that carries a sizable signal – which can then initiate the retrieval of the full pattern by the recurrent collaterals – one needs a large number of associatively modifiable synapses. This is expressed by the formulas that give the specific signal S produced by sets of associatively modifiable synapses, or by nonassociatively modifiable synapses: If C^{AFF} is the number of afferents per cell,

$$S_{\mathrm{ASS}} \sim \frac{\sqrt{C^{\mathrm{AFF}}}}{\sqrt{p}} q \quad S_{\mathrm{NONASS}} \sim \frac{1}{\sqrt{C^{\mathrm{AFF}}}} q. \qquad [8]$$

Associatively modifiable synapses are therefore needed and are needed in a number C^{AFF} of the same order as the number of concurrently stored patterns p, so that small cues can be effective, whereas nonassociatively modifiable synapses – or even more so, nonmodifiable ones – produce very small signals, which decrease in size the larger the number of synapses. In contrast with the storage process, the average strength of these synapses does not play now a crucial role. This suggests that the perforant path system is the one involved in relaying the cues that initiate retrieval.

1.33.2.2.4   CA1 cells

1.33.2.2.4.(i)   Associative retrieval at the CA3 to CA1 (Schaffer collateral) synapses   The CA3 cells connect to the CA1 cells by the Schaeffer collateral synapses. The following arguments outline the advantage of this connection being associatively modifiable and apply independently of the relative extent to which the CA3 or the direct entorhinal cortex inputs to CA1 drive the CA1 cells during the learning phase.

The amount of information about each episode retrievable from CA3 has to be balanced against the number of episodes that can be held concurrently in storage. The balance is regulated by the sparseness of the coding. Whatever the amount of information per episode in CA3, one may hypothesize that the organization of the structures that follow CA3 (i.e., CA1, the various subicular fields, and the return projections to neocortex) should be optimized so as to preserve and use this information content in its entirety. This would prevent further loss of information, after the massive but necessary reduction in information content that has taken place along the sensory pathways and before the autoassociation stage in CA3. We have proposed (Treves and Rolls, 1994; Treves, 1995) that the need to preserve the full information content present in the output of an autoassociative memory requires an intermediate recoding stage (CA1) with special characteristics. In fact, a calculation of the information present in the CA1 firing pattern, elicited by a pattern of activity retrieved from CA3, shows that a considerable fraction of the information is lost if the synapses are nonmodifiable, and that this loss can be prevented only if the CA3 to CA1 synapses are associatively modifiable. Their modifiability should match the plasticity of the CA3 recurrent collaterals. The additional information that can be retrieved beyond that retrieved by CA3 because the CA3 to CA1 synapses

are associatively modifiable is strongly demonstrated by the hippocampal simulation described by Rolls (1995) and is quantitatively analyzed by Schultz and Rolls (1999).

1.33.2.2.4.(ii)   Recoding in CA1 to facilitate retrieval to the neocortex   If the total amount of information carried by CA3 cells is redistributed over a larger number of CA1 cells, less information needs to be loaded onto each CA1 cell, rendering the code more robust to information loss in the next stages. For example, if each CA3 cell had to code for two bits of information, for example, by firing at one of four equiprobable activity levels, then each CA1 cell (if there were twice as many as there are CA3 cells) could code for just 1 bit, for example, by firing at one of only two equiprobable levels. Thus, the same information content could be maintained in the overall representation while reducing the sensitivity to noise in the firing level of each cell. In fact, there are more CA1 cells than CA3 cells in rats (2.5×10^5). There are even more CA1 cells (4.6×10^6) in humans (and the ratio of CA1 to CA3 cells is greater). The CA1 cells may thus provide the first part of the expansion for the return projections to the enormous numbers of neocortical cells in primates, after the bottleneck of the single network in CA3, the number of neurons in which may be limited because it has to operate as a single network.

Another argument on the operation of the CA1 cells is also considered to be related to the CA3 autoassociation effect. In this, several arbitrary patterns of firing occur together on the CA3 neurons and become associated together to form an episodic or whole scene memory. It is essential for this CA3 operation that several different sparse representations are present conjunctively in order to form the association. Moreover, when completion operates in the CA3 autoassociation system, all the neurons firing in the original conjunction can be brought into activity by only a part of the original set of conjunctive events. For these reasons, a memory in the CA3 cells consists of several different simultaneously active ensembles of activity. To be explicit, the parts A, B, C, D, and E of a particular episode would each be represented, roughly speaking, by its own population of CA3 cells, and these five populations would be linked together by autoassociation. It is suggested that the CA1 cells, which receive these groups of simultaneously active ensembles, can detect the conjunctions of firing of the different ensembles that represent the episodic memory and allocate by competitive learning neurons to represent at least larger parts of each episodic memory (Rolls, 1987, 1989a,b,d, 1990a,b). In relation to the simple example above, some CA1 neurons might code for ABC, and others for BDE, rather than having to maintain independent representations in CA1 of A, B, C, D, and E. This implies a more efficient representation, in the sense that when eventually, after many further stages, neocortical neuronal activity is recalled (as discussed later), each neocortical cell need not be accessed by all the axons carrying each component A, B, C, D, and E but, instead, by fewer axons carrying larger fragments, such as ABC and BDE. This process is performed by competitive networks, which self-organize to find categories in the input space, where each category is represented by a set of simultaneously active inputs (Rolls and Treves, 1998; Rolls, 2000; Rolls and Deco, 2002).

1.33.2.2.4.(iii)   CA1 inputs from CA3 vs direct entorhinal inputs
Another feature of the CA1 network is its double set of afferents, with each of its cells receiving most synapses from the Schaeffer collaterals coming from CA3, but also a proportion (about 1/6; Amaral et al., 1990) from direct perforant path projections from entorhinal cortex. Such projections appear to originate mainly in layer 3 of entorhinal cortex (Witter et al., 1989) from a population of cells only partially overlapping with that (mainly in layer 2) giving rise to the perforant path projections to DG and CA3. This suggests that it is useful to include in CA1 not only what it is possible to recall from CA3 but also the detailed information present in the retrieval cue itself (see Treves and Rolls, 1994).

Another possibility is that the perforant path input provides the strong forcing input to the CA1 neurons during learning and that the output of the CA3 system is associated with this forced CA1 firing during learning (McClelland et al., 1995). During recall, an incomplete cue could then be completed in CA3, and the CA3 output would then produce firing in CA1 that would correspond to that present during the learning. This suggestion is essentially identical to that of Treves and Rolls (1994) about the backprojection system and recall, except that McClelland et al. (1995) suggest that the output of CA3 is associated at the CA3 to CA1 (Schaeffer collateral) synapses with the signal present during training in CA1, whereas in the theory of Treves and Rolls (1994), the output of the hippocampus consists of CA1 firing, which is associated in the entorhinal cortex and earlier cortical stages with the firing present during learning, providing a theory of how the correct recall is implemented at every backprojection stage though the neocortex (see the next section).

1.33.2.2.5 Backprojections to the neocortex – a hypothesis
The need for information to be retrieved from the hippocampus to affect other brain areas was noted in the introduction. The way in which this could be implemented via backprojections to the neocortex is now considered.

It is suggested that the modifiable connections from the CA3 neurons to the CA1 neurons allow the whole episode in CA3 to be produced in CA1. This may be assisted as described above by the direct perforant path input to CA1. This might allow details of the input key for the recall process, as well as the possibly less information-rich memory of the whole episode recalled from the CA3 network, to contribute to the firing of CA1 neurons. The CA1 neurons would then activate, via their termination in the deep layers of the entorhinal cortex, at least the pyramidal cells in the deep layers of the entorhinal cortex (see **Figure 1**). These entorhinal cortex layer 5 neurons would then, by virtue of their backprojections (Lavenex and Amaral, 2000; Witter et al., 2000a) to the parts of cerebral cortex that originally provided the inputs to the hippocampus, terminate in the superficial layers (including layer 1) of those neocortical areas, where synapses would be made onto the distal parts of the dendrites of the (superficial and deep) cortical pyramidal cells (Rolls, 1989a, 1989b, 1989d). The areas of cerebral neocortex in which this recall would be produced could include multimodal cortical areas (e.g., the cortex in the superior temporal sulcus, which receives inputs from temporal, parietal, and occipital cortical areas, and from which it is thought that cortical areas such as 39 and 40, related to language, developed), and also areas of unimodal association cortex (e.g., inferior temporal visual cortex). The backprojections, by recalling previous episodic events, could provide information useful to the neocortex in the building of new representations in the multimodal and unimodal association cortical areas, which by building new long-term representations can be considered as a form of memory consolidation (Rolls, 1989a,b,d, 1990a,b), or in organizing actions.

The hypothesis of the architecture with which this would be achieved is shown in **Figure 1**. The feed-forward connections from association areas of the cerebral neocortex (solid lines in **Figure 1**) show major convergence as information is passed to CA3, with the CA3 autoassociation network having the smallest number of neurons at any stage of the processing. The backprojections allow for divergence back to neocortical areas. The way in which I suggest that the backprojection synapses are set up to have the appropriate strengths for recall is as follows (Rolls, 1989a,b,d). During the setting up of a new episodic memory, there would be strong feedforward activity progressing toward the hippocampus. During the episode, the CA3 synapses would be modified, and via the CA1 neurons and the subiculum, a pattern of activity would be produced on the backprojecting synapses to the entorhinal cortex. Here the backprojecting synapses from active backprojection axons onto pyramidal cells being activated by the forward inputs to entorhinal cortex would be associatively modified. A similar process would be implemented at preceding stages of neocortex, that is, in the parahippocampal gyrus/perirhinal cortex stage, and in association cortical areas, as shown in **Figure 1**.

The concept is that during the learning of an episodic memory, cortical pyramidal cells in at least one of the stages would be driven by forward inputs but would simultaneously be receiving backprojected activity (indirectly) from the hippocampus, which would, by pattern association from the backprojecting synapses to the cortical pyramidal cells, become associated with whichever cortical cells were being made to fire by the forward inputs. Then, later on, during recall, a recall cue from perhaps another part of cortex might reach CA3, where the firing during the original episode would be completed. The resulting backprojecting activity would then, as a result of the pattern association learned previously, bring back the firing in any cortical area that was present during the original episode. Thus, retrieval involves reinstating the activity that was present in different cortical areas during the learning of an episode. (The pattern association is also called heteroassociation, to contrast it with autoassociation. The pattern association operates at multiple stages in the backprojection pathway, as made evident in **Figure 1**.) If the recall cue was an object, this might result in recall of the neocortical firing that represented the place in which that object had been seen previously. As noted elsewhere in this chapter and by McClelland et al. (1995), that recall might be useful to the neocortex to help it build new semantic memories, which might

inherently be a slow process and is not part of the theory of recall.

1.33.2.2.6 Backprojections to the neocortex – quantitative aspects

A plausible requirement for a successful hippocampus-directed recall operation is that the signal generated from the hippocampally retrieved pattern of activity, and carried backward toward neocortex, remains undegraded when compared to the noise due, at each stage, to the interference effects caused by the concurrent storage of other patterns of activity on the same backprojecting synaptic systems. That requirement is equivalent to that used in deriving the storage capacity of such a series of heteroassociative memories, and it was shown in Treves and Rolls (1991) that the maximum number of independently generated activity patterns that can be retrieved is given, essentially, by the same formula as eqn (3) above where, however, a is now the sparseness of the representation at any given stage and C is the average number of (back)projections each cell of that stage receives from cells of the previous one. (k' is a similar, slowly varying factor to that introduced above.) If p is equal to the number of memories held in the hippocampal memory, it is limited by the retrieval capacity of the CA3 network, p_{max}. Putting together the formula for the latter with that shown here, one concludes that, roughly, the requirement implies that the number of afferents of (indirect) hippocampal origin to a given neocortical stage (C^{HBP}), must be $C^{HBP} = C^{RC} a_{nc}/a_{CA3}$, where C^{RC} is the number of recurrent collaterals to any given cell in CA3, the average sparseness of a representation is a_{nc}, and a_{CA3} is the sparseness of memory representations there in CA3.

This requirement is very strong: Even if representations were to remain as sparse as they are in CA3, which is unlikely, to avoid degrading the signal, C^{HBP} should be as large as C^{RC}, that is, 12,000 in the rat. If then C^{HBP} has to be of the same order as C^{RC}, one is led to a very definite conclusion: A mechanism of the type envisaged here could not possibly rely on a set of monosynaptic CA3-to-neocortex backprojections. This would imply that, to make a sufficient number of synapses on each of the vast number of neocortical cells, each cell in CA3 has to generate a disproportionate number of synapses (i.e., C^{HBP} times the ratio between the number of neocortical and the number of CA3 cells). The required divergence can be kept within reasonable limits only by assuming that the backprojecting system is polysynaptic, provided that the number of cells involved grows gradually at each stage, from CA3 back to neocortical association areas (Treves and Rolls, 1994) (cf. **Figure 1**).

The theory of recall by the backprojections thus provides a quantitative account of why the cerebral cortex has as many backprojection as forward projection connections. Further aspects of the operation of the backprojecting systems are described elsewhere (Rolls, 2008).

1.33.3   Comparison with Other Theories of Hippocampal Function

The overall theory described here is close in different respects to those of a number of other investigators (Marr, 1971; Brown and Zador, 1990; McNaughton and Nadel, 1990; Eichenbaum et al., 1992; Gaffan, 1992; Squire, 1992; Moscovitch et al., 2005), and of course priority is not claimed on all the propositions put forward here.

Some theories postulate that the hippocampus performs spatial computation. The theory of O'Keefe and Nadel (1978), that the hippocampus implements a cognitive map, placed great emphasis on spatial function. It supposed that the hippocampus at least holds information about allocentric space in a form that enables rats to find their way in an environment even when novel trajectories are necessary, that is, it permits an animal to "go from one place to another independent of particular inputs (cues) or outputs (responses), and to link together conceptually parts of the environment which have never been experienced at the same time" (O'Keefe and Nadel, 1978). O'Keefe (1990) extended this analysis and produced a computational theory of the hippocampus as a cognitive map, in which the hippocampus performs geometric spatial computations. Key aspects of the theory are that the hippocampus stores the centroid and slope of the distribution of landmarks in an environment and stores the relationships between the centroid and the individual landmarks. The hippocampus then receives as inputs information about where the rat currently is and where the rat's target location is and computes geometrically the body turns and movements necessary to reach the target location. In this sense, the hippocampus is taken to be a spatial computer, which produces an output that is very different from its inputs. This is in contrast to the present theory, in which the hippocampus is a memory device that is able to recall what was stored in it, using as input a partial cue. A prototypical example in Rolls' theory is the learning of object–place

association memory and the recall of the whole memory from a part, which can be used as a model of event or episodic memory. O'Keefe's theory postulates that the hippocampus actually performs a spatial computation. A later theory (Burgess et al., 1994, 2000) also makes the same postulate, but now the firing of place cells is determined by the distance and approximate bearing to landmarks, and the navigation is performed by increasing the strength of connections from place cells to goal cells and then performing a gradient-ascent style search for the goal using the network.

McNaughton et al. (1991) have also proposed that the hippocampus is involved in spatial computation. They propose a compass solution to the problem of spatial navigation along novel trajectories in known environments, postulating that distances and bearings (i.e., vector quantities) from landmarks are stored, and that computation of a new trajectory involves vector subtraction by the hippocampus. They postulate that a linear associative mapping is performed, using as inputs a cross-feature (combination) representation of (head) angular velocity and (its time integral) head direction, to produce as output the future value of the integral (head direction) after some specified time interval. The system can be reset by learned associations between local views of the environment and head direction, so that when later a local view is seen, it can lead to an output from the network that is a (corrected) head direction. They suggest that some of the key signals in the computational system can be identified with the firing of hippocampal cells (e.g., local view cells) and subicular cells (head direction cells). It should be noted that this theory requires a (linear) associative mapping with an output (head direction) different in form from the inputs (head angular velocity over a time period, or local view). This is pattern association (with the conditioned stimulus local view and the unconditioned stimulus head direction), not autoassociation, and it has been postulated that this pattern association can be performed by the hippocampus (cf. McNaughton and Morris, 1987). This theory is again in contrast to the present theory, in which the hippocampus operates as a memory to store events that occur at the same time and can recall the whole memory from any part of what was stored. (A pattern associator uses a conditioned stimulus to map an input to a pattern of firing in an output set of neurons, which is like that produced in the output neurons by the unconditioned stimulus. A description of pattern associations and autoassociators in a neurobiological context is provided by Rolls (1996a, 2007) and Rolls and Treves (1998). The present theory is fully consistent with the presence of spatial view cells and whole-body motion cells in the primate hippocampus (Rolls, 1999; Rolls and O'Mara, 1993; Rolls and Xiang, 2006) (or place or local view cells in the rat hippocampus, and head direction cells in the presubiculum), for it is often important to store and later recall where one has been (views of the environment, body turns made, etc.), and indeed such (episodic) memories are required for navigation by dead reckoning in small environments.

The present theory thus holds that the hippocampus is used for the formation of episodic memories using autoassociation. This function is often necessary for successful spatial computation but is not itself spatial computation. Instead, I believe that spatial computation is more likely to be performed in the neocortex (utilizing information if necessary recalled from the hippocampus). Consistent with this view, hippocampal damage impairs the ability to learn new environments but not to perform spatial computations such as finding one's way to a place in a familiar environment, whereas damage to the parietal cortex and parahippocampal cortex can lead to problems such as topographical and other spatial agnosias in humans (see Gruesser and Landis, 1991; Kolb and Whishaw, 2003). This is consistent with spatial computations normally being performed in the neocortex. In monkeys, there is evidence for a role of the parietal cortex in allocentric spatial computation. For example, monkeys with parietal cortex lesions are impaired at performing a landmark task in which the object to be chosen is signified by the proximity to it of a landmark (another object; Ungerleider and Mishkin, 1982).

A theory closely related to the present theory of how the hippocampus operates has been developed by McClelland et al. (1995). It is very similar to the theory we have developed (Rolls, 1987, 1989a,b,d; Treves and Rolls, 1992, 1994; Rolls, 2007) at the systems level, except that it takes a stronger position on the gradient of retrograde amnesia, emphasizes that recall from the hippocampus of episodic information is used to help build semantic representations in the neocortex, and holds that the last set of synapses that are modified rapidly during the learning of each episode are those between the CA3 and the CA1 pyramidal cells, as described above (see **Figure 1**). It also emphasizes the important point that the hippocampal and neocortical memory systems may be quite different, with the hippocampus specialized for the rapid learning of single events or

episodes and the neocortex for the slower learning of semantic representations, which may necessarily benefit from the many exemplars needed to shape the semantic representation.

Lisman and colleagues (2005) have considered how the memory of sequences could be implemented in the hippocampus. This theory of sequential recall within the hippocampus is inextricably linked to the internal timing within the hippocampus imposed, he believes, by the theta and gamma oscillations, and this makes it difficult to recall each item in the sequence as it is needed. It is not specified how one would read out the sequence information, given that the items are only 12 ms apart. The Jensen and Lisman (1996) model requires short, time constant NMDA channels and is therefore unlikely to be implemented in the hippocampus. Hasselmo and Eichenbaum (2005) have taken up some of these sequence ideas and incorporated them into their model, which has its origins in the Rolls and Treves model (Rolls, 1989b; Treves and Rolls, 1992, 1994), but proposes, for example, that sequences are stored in entorhinal cortex layer III. The proposal that acetylcholine could be important during encoding by facilitating CA3–CA3 LTP, and should be lower during retrieval (Hasselmo et al., 1995), is an important concept.

Another type of sequence memory uses synaptic adaptation to effectively encode the order of the items in a sequence (Deco and Rolls, 2005). This could be implemented in recurrent networks such as the CA3 or the prefrontal cortex.

In this chapter, we have seen that quantitative approaches to the functions of the hippocampus in memory are being developed by a number of investigators and that these theories are consistent with the quantitative circuitry of the hippocampus as well as with neuronal recordings and the effects of lesions. Moreover, we have seen that the predictions of these theories are now being tested.

Acknowledgments

Different parts of the research described here were supported by Programme Grants from the Medical Research Council, a Human Frontier Science program grant, an EEC BRAIN grant, the MRC Oxford Interdisciplinary Research Centre in Cognitive Neuroscience, and the Oxford McDonnell-Pew Centre in Cognitive Neuroscience.

References

Amaral DG (1987) Memory: Anatomical organization of candidate brain regions. In: Mountcastle VB (ed.) *Handbook of Physiology. Section 1, The Nervous System*, pp. 211–294. Washington DC: American Physiological Society.

Amaral DG (1993) Emerging principles of intrinsic hippocampal organisation. *Curr. Opin. Neurobiol.* 3: 225–229.

Amaral DG and Witter MP (1989) The three-dimensional organization of the hippocampal formation: A review of anatomical data. *Neuroscience* 31: 571–591.

Amaral DG and Witter MP (1995) The hippocampal formation. In: Paxinos G (ed.) *The Rat Nervous System*, pp. 443–493. San Diego: Academic Press.

Amaral DG, Ishizuka N, and Claiborne B (1990) Neurons, numbers, and the hippocampal network. *Prog. Brain Res.* 83: 1–11.

Amaral DG, Price JL, Pitkanen A, and Carmichael ST (1992) Anatomical organization of the primate amygdaloid complex. In: Aggleton JP (ed.) *The Amygdala*, pp. 1–66. New York: Wiley-Liss.

Amari S (1977) Dynamics of pattern formation in lateral-inhibition type neural fields. *Biol. Cybern.* 27: 77–87.

Amit DJ (1989) *Modeling Brain Function*. Cambridge University Press: Cambridge.

Battaglia FP and Treves A (1998a) Attractor neural networks storing multiple space representations: A model for hippocampal place fields. *Phys. Rev.* 58: 7738–7753.

Battaglia FP and Treves A (1998b) Stable and rapid recurrent processing in realistic auto-associative memories. *Neural Comput.* 10: 431–450.

Brown TH and Zador A (1990) The hippocampus. In: Shepherd G (ed.) *The Synaptic Organisation of the Brain*, pp. 346–388. New York: Oxford University Press.

Brown TH, Ganong AH, Kairiss EW, Keenan CL, and Kelso SR (eds.) (1989) *Long-Term Potentiation in Two Synaptic Systems of the Hippocampal Brain Slice*. San Diego: Academic Press.

Brown TH, Kairiss EW, and Keenan CL (1990) Hebbian synapses: Biophysical mechanisms and algorithms. *Annu. Rev. Neurosci.* 13: 475–511.

Brun VH, Otnass MK, Molden S, et al. (2002) Place cells and place recognition maintained by direct entorhinal-hippocampal circuitry. *Science* 296: 2243–2246.

Buckley MJ and Gaffan D (2000) The hippocampus, perirhinal cortex, and memory in the monkey. In: Bolhuis JJ (ed.) *Brain Perception, and Memory: Advances in Cognitive Neuroscience*, pp. 279–298. Oxford: Oxford University Press.

Burgess N, Recce M, and O'Keefe J (1994) A model of hippocampal function. *Neural Netw.* 7: 1065–1081.

Burgess N, Jackson A, Hartley T, and O'Keefe J (2000) Predictions derived from modelling the hippocampal role in navigation. *Biol. Cybern.* 83: 301–312.

Burgess N, Maguire EA, and O'Keefe J (2002) The human hippocampus and spatial and episodic memory. *Neuron* 35: 625–641.

Carmichael ST and Price JL (1995) Limbic connections of the orbital and medial prefrontal cortex in macaque monkeys. *J. Comp. Neurol.* 346: 403–434.

Cassaday HJ and Rawlins JN (1997) The hippocampus, objects, and their contexts. *Behav. Neurosci.* 111: 1228–1244.

Crane J and Milner B (2005) What went where? Impaired object-location learning in patients with right hippocampal lesions. *Hippocampus* 15: 216–231.

Day M, Langston R, and Morris RG (2003) Glutamate-receptor-mediated encoding and retrieval of paired-associate learning. *Nature* 424: 205–209.

de Araujo IET, Rolls ET, and Stringer SM (2001) A view model which accounts for the spatial fields of hippocampal primate spatial view cells and rat place cells. *Hippocampus* 11: 699–706.

Deco G and Rolls ET (2005) Sequential memory: A putative neural and synaptic dynamical mechanism. *J. Cogn. Neurosci.* 17: 294–307.

Delatour B and Witter MP (2002) Projections from the parahippocampal region in the rat: Evidence of multiple pathways. *Eur. J. Neurosci.* 15: 1400–1407.

Eichenbaum H, Otto T, and Cohen NJ (1992) The hippocampus – What does it do? *Behav. Neural Biol.* 57: 2–36.

Fazeli MS and Collingridge GL (eds.) (1996) *Cortical Plasticity: LTP and LTD*. Oxford: Bios Scientific.

Feigenbaum JD and Rolls ET (1991) Allocentric and egocentric spatial information processing in the hippocampal formation of the behaving primate. *Psychobiology* 19: 21–40.

Florian C and Roullet P (2004) Hippocampal CA3-region is crucial for acquisition and memory consolidation in Morris water maze task in mice. *Behav. Brain Res.* 154: 365–374.

Franco L, Rolls ET, Aggelopoulos NC, and Jerez JM (2007) *Neuronal Selectivity, Population Sparseness, and Ergodicity in the Inferior Temporal Visual Cortex*. New York: Springer-Verlag.

Fyhn M, Molden S, Witter MP, Moser EI, and Moser MB (2004) Spatial representation in the entorhinal cortex. *Science* 305: 1258–1264.

Gaffan D (1992) The role of hippocampo-fornix-mammillary system in episodic memory. In: Squire LR and Butters N (eds.) *Neuropsychology of Memory*, pp. 336–346. New York: Guilford.

Gaffan D (1994) Scene-specific memory for objects: A model of episodic memory impairment in monkeys with fornix transection. *J. Cogn. Neurosci.* 6: 305–320.

Gardner-Medwin AR (1976) The recall of events through the learning of associations between their parts. *Proc. R. Soc. Lond. B* 194: 375–402.

Georges-François P, Rolls ET, and Robertson RG (1999) Spatial view cells in the primate hippocampus: Allocentric view not head direction or eye position or place. *Cereb. Cortex* 9: 197–212.

Gilbert PE, Kesner RP, and Lee I (2001) Dissociating hippocampal subregions: Double dissociation between dentate gyrus and CA1. *Hippocampus* 11: 626–636.

Gold AE and Kesner RP (2005) The role of the CA3 subregion of the dorsal hippocampus in spatial pattern completion in the rat. *Hippocampus* 15: 808–814.

Goodrich-Hunsaker NJ, Hunsaker MR, and Kesner RP (2005) Effects of hippocampus sub-regional lesions for metric and topological spatial information processing. *Soc. Neurosci. Abst.* 647.1.

Gruesser O-J and Landis T (1991) *Visual Agnosias*. London: Macmillan.

Hafting T, Fyhn M, Molden S, Moser MB, and Moser EI (2005) Microstructure of a spatial map in the entorhinal cortex. *Nature* 436: 801–806.

Hargreaves EL, Rao G, Lee I, and Knierim JJ (2005) Major dissociation between medial and lateral entorhinal input to dorsal hippocampus. *Science* 308: 1792–1794.

Hasselmo ME and Eichenbaum HB (2005) Hippocampal mechanisms for the context-dependent retrieval of episodes. *Neural Netw.* 18: 1172–1190.

Hasselmo ME, Schnell E, and Barkai E (1995) Dynamics of learning and recall at excitatory recurrent synapses and cholinergic modulation in rat hippocampal region CA3. *J. Neurosci.* 15: 5249–5262.

Hertz J, Krogh A, and Palmer RG (1991) *An Introduction to the Theory of Neural Computation*. Wokingham: Addison-Wesley.

Hölscher C, Jacob W, and Mallot HA (2003) Reward modulates neuronal activity in the hippocampus of the rat. *Behav. Brain Res.* 142: 181–191.

Hopfield JJ (1982) Neural networks and physical systems with emergent collective computational abilities. *Proc. Natl. Acad. Sci. USA* 79: 2554–2558.

Ishizuka N, Weber J, and Amaral DG (1990) Organization of intrahippocampal projections originating from CA3 pyramidal cells in the rat. *J. Comp. Neurol.* 295: 580–623.

Jarrard EL (1993) On the role of the hippocampus in learning and memory in the rat. *Behav. Neural Biol.* 60: 9–26.

Jeffery KJ and Hayman R (2004) Plasticity of the hippocampal place cell representation. *Rev. Neurosci.* 15: 309–331.

Jeffery KJ, Anderson MI, Hayman R, and Chakraborty S (2004) A proposed architecture for the neural representation of spatial context. *Neurosci. Biobehav. Rev.* 28: 201–218.

Jensen O and Lisman JE (1996) Theta/gamma networks with slow NMDA channels learn sequences and encode episodic memory: Role of NMDA channels in recall. *Learn. Mem.* 3: 264–278.

Jung MW and McNaughton BL (1993) Spatial selectivity of unit activity in the hippocampal granular layer. *Hippocampus* 3: 165–182.

Kesner RP, Lee I, and Gilbert P (2004) A behavioral assessment of hippocampal function based on a subregional analysis. *Rev. Neurosci.* 15: 333–351.

Kohonen T (1977) *Associative Memory: A System Theoretical Approach*. New York: Springer.

Kolb B and Whishaw IQ (2003) *Fundamentals of Human Neuropsychology*. New York: Worth.

Lassalle JM, Bataille T, and Halley H (2000) Reversible inactivation of the hippocampal mossy fiber synapses in mice impairs spatial learning, but neither consolidation nor memory retrieval in the Morris navigation task. *Neurobiol. Learn. Mem.* 73: 243–257.

Lavenex P and Amaral DG (2000) Hippocampal-neocortical interaction: A hierarchy of associativity. *Hippocampus* 10: 420–430.

Lavenex P, Suzuki WA, and Amaral DG (2004) Perirhinal and parahippocampal cortices of the macaque monkey: Intrinsic projections and interconnections. *J. Comp. Neurol.* 472: 371–394.

Levy WB (1989) A computational approach to hippocampal function. In: Hawkins RD and Bower GH (eds.) *Computational Models of Learning in Simple Neural Systems*, pp. 243–305. San Diego: Academic Press.

Levy WB and Desmond NL (1985) The rules of elemental synaptic plasticity. In: Levy WB, Anderson JA, and Lehmkuhle S (eds.) *Synaptic Modification Neuron Selectivity, and Nervous System Organization*, pp. 105–121. Hillsdale, NJ: Erlbaum.

Levy WB, Colbert CM, and Desmond NL (1990) Elemental adaptive processes of neurons and synapses: A statistical/computational perspective. In: Gluck MA and Rumelhart DE (eds.) *Neuroscience and Connectionist Theory*, pp. 187–235. Hillsdale, NJ: Erlbaum.

Lisman JE, Talamini LM, and Raffone A (2005) Recall of memory sequences by interaction of the dentate and CA3: A revised model of the phase precession. *Neural Netw.* 18: 1191–1201.

Lynch MA (2004) Long-term potentiation and memory. *Physiol. Rev.* 84: 87–136.

Maaswinkel H, Jarrard LE, and Whishaw IQ (1999) Hippocampectomized rats are impaired in homing by path integration. *Hippocampus* 9: 553–561.

Malkova L and Mishkin M (2003) One-trial memory for object-place associations after separate lesions of hippocampus and posterior parahippocampal region in the monkey. *J. Neurosci.* 23: 1956–1965.

Markus EJ, Qin YL, Leonard B, Skaggs W, McNaughton BL, and Barnes CA (1995) Interactions between location and task affect the spatial and directional firing of hippocampal neurons. *J. Neurosci.* 15: 7079–7094.

Marr D (1971) Simple memory: A theory for archicortex. *Phil. Trans. Roy. Soc. Lond. B* 262: 23–81.

Martin SJ, Grimwood PD, and Morris RG (2000) Synaptic plasticity and memory: An evaluation of the hypothesis. *Annu. Rev. Neurosci.* 23: 649–711.

McClelland JL, McNaughton BL, and O'Reilly RC (1995) Why there are complementary learning systems in the hippocampus and neocortex: Insights from the successes and failures of connectionist models of learning and memory. *Psychol. Rev.* 102: 419–457.

McNaughton BL (1991) Associative pattern completion in hippocampal circuits: New evidence and new questions. *Brain Res. Rev.* 16: 193–220.

McNaughton BL and Morris RG M (1987) Hippocampal synaptic enhancement and information storage within a distributed memory system. *Trends Neurosci.* 10: 408–415.

McNaughton BL, Barnes CA, and O'Keefe J (1983) The contributions of position, direction, and velocity to single unit activity in the hippocampus of freely-moving rats. *Exp. Brain Res.* 52: 41–49.

McNaughton BL and Nadel L (1990) Hebb-Marr networks and the neurobiological representation of action in space. In: Gluck MA and Rumelhart DE (eds.) *Neuroscience and Connectionist Theory*, pp. 1–63. Hillsdale, NJ: Erlbaum.

McNaughton BL, Chen LL, and Markus EJ (1991) "Dead reckoning", landmark learning, and the sense of direction: A neurophysiological and computational hypothesis. *J. Cogn. Neurosci.* 3: 190–202.

McNaughton BL, Battaglia FP, Jensen O, Moser EI, and Moser M-B (2006) Path integration and the neural basis of the "cognitive map." *Nat. Rev. Neurosci.* 7: 663–678.

Morris RG (2003) Long-term potentiation and memory. *Philos. Trans. R. Soc. Lond. B Biol. Sci.* 358: 643–647.

Morris RGM (1989) Does synaptic plasticity play a role in information storage in the vertebrate brain? In: Morris RGM (ed.) *Parallel Distributed Processing: Implications for Psychology and Neurobiology*, pp. 248–285. Oxford: Oxford University Press.

Morris RG, Moser EI, Riedel G, et al. (2003) Elements of a neurobiological theory of the hippocampus: The role of activity-dependent synaptic plasticity in memory. *Philos. Trans. R. Soc. Lond. B Biol. Sci.* 358: 773–786.

Moscovitch M, Rosenbaum RS, Gilboa A, et al. (2005) Functional neuroanatomy of remote episodic, semantic and spatial memory: A unified account based on multiple trace theory. *J. Anat.* 207: 35–66.

Moser EI (2004) Hippocampal place cells demand attention. *Neuron* 42: 183–185.

Moser MB and Moser EI (1998) Functional differentiation in the hippocampus. *Hippocampus* 8: 608–619.

Muller RU, Kubie JL, Bostock EM, Taube JS, and Quirk GJ (1991) Spatial firing correlates of neurons in the hippocampal formation of freely moving rats. In: Paillard J (ed.) *Brain and Space*, pp. 296–333. Oxford: Oxford University Press.

Muller RU, Ranck JB Jr, and Taube JS (1996) Head direction cells: Properties and functional significance. *Curr. Opin. Neurobiol.* 6: 196–206.

Murray EA, Baxter MG, and Gaffan D (1998) Monkeys with rhinal cortex damage or neurotoxic hippocampal lesions are impaired on spatial scene learning and object reversals. *Behav. Neurosci.* 112: 1291–1303.

Naber PA, Lopes da Silva FH, and Witter MP (2001) Reciprocal connections between the entorhinal cortex and hippocampal fields CA1 and the subiculum are in register with the projections from CA1 to the subiculum. *Hippocampus* 11: 99–104.

Nakazawa K, Quirk MC, Chitwood RA, et al. (2002) Requirement for hippocampal CA3 NMDA receptors in associative memory recall. *Science* 297: 211–218.

Oja E (1982) A simplified neuron model as a principal component analyser. *J. Math. Biol.* 15: 267–273.

O'Keefe J (1984) Spatial memory within and without the hippocampal system. In: Seifert W (ed.) *Neurobiology of the Hippocampus*, pp. 375–403. London: Academic Press.

O'Keefe J (1990) A computational theory of the hippocampal cognitive map. *Prog. Brain Res.* 83: 301–312.

O'Keefe J and Dostrovsky J (1971) The hippocampus as a spatial map: Preliminary evidence from unit activity in the freely moving rat. *Brain Res.* 34: 171–175.

O'Keefe J and Nadel L (1978) *The Hippocampus as a Cognitive Map*. Oxford: Clarendon Press.

O'Reilly RC and Rudy JW (2001) Conjunctive representations in learning and memory: Principles of cortical and hippocampal function. *Psychol. Rev.* 108: 311–345.

Panzeri S, Rolls ET, Battaglia F, and Lavis R (2001) Speed of information retrieval in multilayer networks of integrate-and-fire neurons. *Netw. Comput. Neural Sys.* 12: 423–440.

Pitkanen A, Kelly JL, and Amaral DG (2002) Projections from the lateral, basal, and accessory basal nuclei of the amygdala to the entorhinal cortex in the macaque monkey. *Hippocampus* 12: 186–205.

Ranck JBJ (1985) Head direction cells in the deep cell layer of dorsolateral presubiculum in freely moving rats. In: Buzaki G and Vanderwolf CH (eds.) *Electrical Activity of the Archicortex*. Budapest: Akademiai Kiado.

Robertson RG, Rolls ET, and Georges-François P (1998) Spatial view cells in the primate hippocampus: Effects of removal of view details. *J. Neurophysiol.* 79: 1145–1156.

Robertson RG, Rolls ET, Georges-François P, and Panzeri S (1999) Head direction cells in the primate pre-subiculum. *Hippocampus* 9: 206–219.

Rolls ET (1987) Information representation, processing and storage in the brain: Analysis at the single neuron level. In: Changeux J-P and Konishi M (eds.) *The Neural and Molecular Bases of Learning*, pp. 503–540. Chischester: Wiley.

Rolls ET (1989a) Functions of neuronal networks in the hippocampus and cerebral cortex in memory. In: Cotterill RMJ (ed.) *Models of Brain Function*, pp. 15–33. Cambridge: Cambridge University Press.

Rolls ET (1989b) Functions of neuronal networks in the hippocampus and neocortex in memory. In: Byrne JH and Berry WO (eds.) *Neural Models of Plasticity: Experimental and Theoretical Approaches*, pp. 240–265. San Diego: Academic Press.

Rolls ET (1989c) Parallel distributed processing in the brain: Implications of the functional architecture of neuronal networks in the hippocampus. In: Morris RGM (ed.) *Parallel Distributed Processing: Implications for Psychology and Neurobiology*, pp. 286–308. Oxford: Oxford University Press.

Rolls ET (1989d) The representation and storage of information in neuronal networks in the primate cerebral cortex and hippocampus. In: Durbin R, Miall C, and Mitchison G (eds.) *The Computing Neuron*, pp. 125–159. Wokingham, UK: Addison-Wesley.

Rolls ET (1990a) Functions of the primate hippocampus in spatial processing and memory. In: Olton DS and Kesner RP (eds.) *Neurobiology of Comparative Cognition*, pp. 339–362. Hillsdale, NJ: Erlbaum.

Rolls ET (1990b) Theoretical and neurophysiological analysis of the functions of the primate hippocampus in memory. *Cold Spring Harb. Symp. Quant. Biol.* 55: 995–1006.

Rolls ET (1991) Functions of the primate hippocampus in spatial and non-spatial memory. *Hippocampus* 1: 258–261.

Rolls ET (1992) Neurophysiological mechanisms underlying face processing within and beyond the temporal cortical visual areas. *Philos. Trans. R. Soc. Lond. B* 335: 11–21.

Rolls ET (1994) Neurophysiological and neuronal network analysis of how the primate hippocampus functions in memory. In: Delacour J (ed.) *The Memory System of the Brain*, pp. 713–744. London: World Scientific.

Rolls ET (1995) A model of the operation of the hippocampus and entorhinal cortex in memory. *Int. J. Neural Sys.* 6: 51–70.

Rolls ET (1996a) Roles of long term potentiation and long term depression in neuronal network operations in the brain. In: Fazeli GL and Collingridge GL (eds.) *Cortical Plasticity*, pp. 223–250. Oxford: Bios Scientific.

Rolls ET (1996b) A theory of hippocampal function in memory. *Hippocampus* 6: 601–620.

Rolls ET (1999) Spatial view cells and the representation of place in the primate hippocampus. *Hippocampus* 9: 467–480.

Rolls ET (2000) Memory systems in the brain. *Annu. Rev. Psychol.* 51: 599–630.

Rolls ET (2003) Consciousness absent and present: A neurophysiological exploration. *Prog. Brain Res.* 144: 95–106.

Rolls ET (2008) *Memory Attention, and Decision-Making: A Unifying Computational Neuroscience Approach*. Oxford: Oxford University Press.

Rolls ET and Deco G (2002) *Computational Neuroscience of Vision*. Oxford: Oxford University Press.

Rolls ET and Kesner RP (2006) A computational theory of hippocampal function, and empirical tests of the theory. *Prog. Neurobiol.* 79: 1–48.

Rolls ET and O'Mara S (1993) Neurophysiological and theoretical analysis of how the primate hippocampus functions in memory. In: Ono T, Squire LR, Raichle ME, Perret DI, and Fukuda M (eds.) *Brain Mechanisms of Perception and Memory: From Neuron to Behavior*, pp. 276–300. New York: Oxford University Press.

Rolls ET and Stringer SM (2005) Spatial view cells in the hippocampus, and their idiothetic update based on place and head direction. *Neural Netw.* 18: 1229–1241.

Rolls ET and Treves A (1990) The relative advantages of sparse versus distributed encoding for associative neuronal networks in the brain. *Network* 1: 407–421.

Rolls ET and Treves A (1998) *Neural Networks and Brain Function*. Oxford: Oxford University Press.

Rolls ET and Xiang J-Z (2005) Reward-spatial view representations and learning in the hippocampus. *J. Neurosci.* 25: 6167–6174.

Rolls ET and Xiang J-Z (2006) Spatial view cells in the primate hippocampus, and memory recall. *Rev. Neurosci.* 17: 175–200.

Rolls ET, Miyashita Y, Cahusac PMB, et al. (1989) Hippocampal neurons in the monkey with activity related to the place in which a stimulus is shown. *J. Neurosci.* 9: 1835–1845.

Rolls ET, Robertson RG, and Georges-François P (1997a) Spatial view cells in the primate hippocampus. *Eur. J. Neurosci.* 9: 1789–1794.

Rolls ET, Treves A, Foster D, and Perez-Vicente C (1997b) Simulation studies of the CA3 hippocampal subfield modelled as an attractor neural network. *Neural Netw.* 10: 1559–1569.

Rolls ET, Treves A, Robertson RG, Georges-François P, and Panzeri S (1998) Information about spatial view in an ensemble of primate hippocampal cells. *J. Neurophysiol.* 79: 1797–1813.

Rolls ET, Stringer SM, and Trappenberg TP (2002) A unified model of spatial and episodic memory. *Proc. R. Soc. Lond. B* 269: 1087–1093.

Rolls ET, Xiang J-Z, and Franco L (2005) Object, space and object-space representations in the primate hippocampus. *J. Neurophysiol.* 94: 833–844.

Rolls ET, Stringer SM, and Elliot T (2006) Entorhinal cortex grid cells can map to hippocampal place cells by competitive learning. *Netw. Comput. Neural Sys.* 17: 447–465.

Samsonovich A and McNaughton BL (1997) Path integration and cognitive mapping in a continuous attractor neural network model. *J. Neurosci.* 17: 5900–5920.

Schultz S and Rolls ET (1999) Analysis of information transmission in the Schaffer collaterals. *Hippocampus* 9: 582–598.

Simmen MW, Treves A, and Rolls ET (1996) Pattern retrieval in threshold-linear associative nets. *Network* 7: 109–122.

Skaggs WE, Knierim JJ, Kudrimoti HS, and McNaughton BL (1995) A model of the neural basis of the rat's sense of direction. In: Tesauro G, Touretzky DS, and Leen TK (eds.) *Advances in Neural Information Processing Systems*, pp. 173–180. Cambridge, MA: MIT Press.

Squire LR (1992) Memory and the hippocampus: A synthesis from findings with rats, monkeys and humans. *Psychol. Rev.* 99: 195–231.

Stefanacci L, Suzuki WA, and Amaral DG (1996) Organization of connections between the amygdaloid complex and the perirhinal and parahippocampal cortices in macaque monkeys. *J. Comp. Neurol.* 375: 552–582.

Storm-Mathiesen J, Zimmer J, and Ottersen OP Eds. (1990) *Understanding the Brain Through the Hippocampus*. Oxford: Elsevier.

Stringer SM and Rolls ET (2002) Invariant object recognition in the visual system with novel views of 3D objects. *Neural Comput.* 14: 2585–2596.

Stringer SM, Rolls ET, Trappenberg TP, and Araujo IE T (2002a) Self-organizing continuous attractor networks and path integration. Two-dimensional models of place cells. *Netw. Comput. Neural Sys.* 13: 429–446.

Stringer SM, Trappenberg TP, Rolls ET, and Araujo IE T (2002b) Self-organizing continuous attractor networks and path integration: One-dimensional models of head direction cells. *Netw. Comput. Neural Sys.* 13: 217–242.

Stringer SM, Rolls ET, and Trappenberg TP (2004) Self-organising continuous attractor networks with multiple activity packets, and the representation of space. *Neural Netw.* 17: 5–27.

Stringer SM, Rolls ET, and Trappenberg TP (2005) Self-organizing continuous attractor network models of hippocampal spatial view cells. *Neurobiol. Learn. Mem.* 83: 79–92.

Sutherland RJ and Rudy JW (1991) Exceptions to the rule of space. *Hippocampus* 1: 250–252.

Suzuki WA and Amaral DG (1994a) Perirhinal and parahippocampal cortices of the macaque monkey – cortical afferents. *J. Comp. Neurol.* 350: 497–533.

Suzuki WA and Amaral DG (1994b) Topographic organization of the reciprocal connections between the monkey entorhinal cortex and the perirhinal and parahippocampal cortices. *J. Neurosci.* 14: 1856–1877.

Tabuchi E, Mulder AB, and Wiener SI (2003) Reward value invariant place responses and reward site associated activity in hippocampal neurons of behaving rats. *Hippocampus* 13: 117–132.

Taube JS, Muller RU, and Ranck JB J (1990) Head-direction cells recorded from the postsubiculum in freely moving rats 1: Description and quantitative analysis. *J. Neurosci.* 10: 420–435.

Taube JS, Goodridge JP, Golob EJ, Dudchenko PA, and Stackman RW (1996) Processing the head direction signal: A review and commentary. *Brain Res. Bull.* 40: 477–486.

Taylor JG (1999) Neural "bubble" dynamics in two dimensions: Foundations. *Biol. Cybern.* 80: 393–409.

Treves A (1990) Graded-response neurons and information encodings in autoassociative memories. *Phys. Rev. A* 42: 2418–2430.

Treves A (1993) Mean-field analysis of neuronal spike dynamics. *Network* 4: 259–284.

Treves A (1995) Quantitative estimate of the information relayed by Schaffer collaterals. *J. Comp. Neurosci.* 2: 259–272.

Treves A and Rolls ET (1991) What determines the capacity of autoassociative memories in the brain? *Network* 2: 371–397.

Treves A and Rolls ET (1992) Computational constraints suggest the need for two distinct input systems to the hippocampal CA3 network. *Hippocampus* 2: 189–199.

Treves A and Rolls ET (1994) A computational analysis of the role of the hippocampus in memory. *Hippocampus* 4: 374–391.

Ungerleider LG and Mishkin M (1982) Two cortical visual systems. In: Ingle DJ, goodale MA, and Mansfield RJW (eds.) *Analysis of Visual Behavior*, pp. 549–586. Cambridge, MA: MIT Press.

van Haeften T, Baks-te-Bulte L, Goede PH, Wouterlood FG, and Witter MP (2003) Morphological and numerical analysis of synaptic interactions between neurons in deep and superficial layers of the entorhinal cortex of the rat. *Hippocampus* 13: 943–952.

Van Hoesen GW (1982) The parahippocampal gyrus. New observations regarding its cortical connections in the monkey. *Trends Neurosci.* 5: 345–350.

Wallace DG and Whishaw IQ (2003) NMDA lesions of Ammon's horn and the dentate gyrus disrupt the direct and temporally paced homing displayed by rats exploring a novel environment: Evidence for a role of the hippocampus in dead reckoning. *Eur. J. Neurosci.* 18: 513–523.

Whishaw IQ, Hines DJ, and Wallace DG (2001) Dead reckoning (path integration) requires the hippocampal formation: Evidence from spontaneous exploration and spatial learning tasks in light (allothetic) and dark (idiothetic) tests. *Behav. Brain Res.* 127: 49–69.

Witter MP (1993) Organization of the entorhinal-hippocampal system: A review of current anatomical data. *Hippocampus* 3: 33–44.

Witter MP, Van Hoesen GW, and Amaral DG (1989) Topographical organisation of the entorhinal projection to the dentate gyrus of the monkey. *J. Neurosci.* 9: 216–228.

Witter MP, Naber PA, van Haeften T, et al. (2000a) Cortico-hippocampal communication by way of parallel parahippocampal-subicular pathways. *Hippocampus* 10: 398–410.

Witter MP, Wouterlood FG, Naber PA, and Van Haeften T (2000b) Anatomical organization of the parahippocampal-hippocampal network. *Ann. NY Acad. Sci.* 911: 1–24.

Wood ER, Dudchenko PA, and Eichenbaum H (1999) The global record of memory in hippocampal neuronal activity. *Nature* 397: 613–616.

Zhang K (1996) Representation of spatial orientation by the intrinsic dynamics of the head-direction cell ensemble: A theory. *J. Neurosci.* 16: 2112–2126.

1.34   Neural Computation Theories of Learning

S. B. Moldakarimov, Salk Institute for Biological Studies, La Jolla, CA, USA

T. J. Sejnowski, Salk Institute for Biological Studies and University of California at San Diego, La Jolla, CA, USA

1.34.1   Introduction

The anatomical discoveries in the nineteenth century and the physiological studies in the twentieth century showed that brains were networks of neurons connected through synapses. This led to the theory that learning could be the consequence of changes in the strengths of the synapses.

The best-known theory of learning based on synaptic plasticity is that proposed by Donald Hebb, who postulated that connection strengths between neurons are modified based on neural activities in the presynaptic and postsynaptic cells:

> When an axon of cell A is near enough to excite cell B and repeatedly or persistently takes part in firing it, some growth process or metabolic change takes place in one or both cells such that A's efficiency, as one of the cells firing B, is increased. (Hebb, 1949)

This postulate was experimentally confirmed in the hippocampus with high-frequency stimulation of a presynaptic neuron that caused long-term potentiation (LTP) in the synapses connecting it to the postsynaptic neuron (Bliss and Lomo, 1973). LTP takes place only if the postsynaptic cell is also active and sufficiently depolarized (Kelso et al., 1986). This is due to the *N*-methyl-D-aspartate (NMDA) type of glutamate receptor, which opens when glutamate is bound to the receptor, and the postsynaptic cell is sufficiently depolarized at the same time (*See* Chapters 1.33, 1.35).

Hebb's postulate has served as the starting point for studying the learning capabilities of artificial neural networks (ANN) and for the theoretical analysis and computational modeling of biological neural systems. The architecture of an ANN determines its behavior and learning capabilities. The architecture of a network is defined by the connections among the artificial neural units and the function that each unit performs on its inputs (*See* Chapter 1.35). Two general classes are feedforward and recurrent architecture.

The simplest feedforward network has one layer of input units and one layer of output units (**Figure 1**, left). All connections are unidirectional and project from the input units to the output units. The perceptron is an example of a simple feedforward network (Rosenblatt, 1958). It can learn to classify patterns from examples. It turned out that the perceptron can only classify patterns that are linearly separable – that is, if the positive patterns can be separated from all negative patterns by a plane in the space of input patterns. More powerful multilayer feedforward networks can discriminate patterns that are not linearly separable. In a multilayer feedforward network, the 'hidden' layers of units between the input and output layers allow more flexibility in learning features. Multilayer feedforward networks have also been applied to solve some other difficult problems (Rumelhart and McClelland, 1986).

In contrast to strictly feedforward network models, recurrent networks also have feedback connections

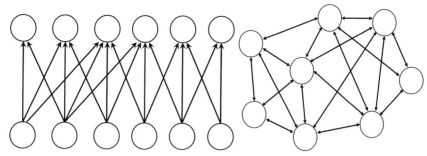

Figure 1 Network architectures. Left: Feedforward network. Right: Recurrent network. Open circles represent neuronal units, and arrowhead lines represent synaptic connections.

among units in the network (**Figure 1**, right). A simple recurrent network can have a uniform architecture such as all-to-all connectivity combined with symmetric weights between units, as in a Hopfield network (Hopfield, 1982), or it can be a network with specific connections designed to model a particular biological system.

Modeling learning processes in networks implies that the strengths of connections and other parameters are adjusted according to a learning rule (*See* Chapter 1.33). Other parameters that may change include the threshold of the unit, time constants, and other dynamical variables. A learning rule is a dynamical equation that governs changes in the parameters of the network. There are three main categories of learning rules: unsupervised, supervised, and reinforcement. Unsupervised learning rules are those that require no feedback from a teaching signal. Supervised learning rules require a teacher, who provides detailed information on the desired values of the output units of the network, and connections are adjusted based on discrepancies between the actual output and the desired one. Reinforcement learning is also error correcting but involves a single scalar signal about the overall performance of the network. Thus, reinforcement learning requires less-detailed information than supervised learning.

A learning algorithm specifies how and under what conditions a learning rule or a combination of learning rules should be applied to adjust the network parameters. For a simple task, it is possible to invent an algorithm that includes only one type of learning rule, but for more complex problems, an algorithm may involve a combination of several different learning rules.

In the following sections, we give an overview of basic learning rules and examples of learning algorithms used in neural network models, and describe specific problems solved by neural networks with adjustable parameters.

1.34.2 Hebbian Learning

Implementations of Hebb's rule can take different forms (Sejnowski and Tesauro, 1988). Simple associative Hebbian learning is based on the coincidence of activities in presynaptic and postsynaptic neurons. The dynamics of Hebbian learning are governed by a differential equation:

$$\frac{\mathrm{d}w_{ij}}{\mathrm{d}t} = \alpha \cdot v_i \cdot u_j$$

where w_{ij} is the weight of a connection from an input unit j with activity u_j to an output unit i with activity v_i, and α is a learning rate.

The Hebbian learning rule has been used to model a wide variety of problems, including feature selectivity and cortical map development.

Cortical neurons respond selectively to particular feature stimuli, such as selectivity for ocular dominance and orientation in the visual cortex. To understand challenges of modeling the development of feature selectivity, consider a network with many input units and one output unit. We would like to explore under what conditions the output unit will respond well to few input units and less to the others. If we apply a stimulus to the input units and allow the connections to develop according to the Hebbian learning rule, then all connections will grow and eventually saturate, and no selectivity will emerge. To develop selectivity, some dependencies among weights are needed, so that changes at one connection will influence the others. There are many different ways to introduce dependencies. One approach is to introduce weight normalization (Miller and Mackay, 1994). A different approach, based on competition among input patterns, called the BCM (Bienenstock, Cooper, and Munro) rule (Bienenstock et al., 1982), has been used to model the development of orientation selectivity and ocular dominance in neural networks.

Neuronal response selectivity varies across the cortex in regular patterns called cortical maps. Although some aspects of cortical map formation during development are activity independent, neuronal activity can modify the maps. Hebbian learning rules have also been applied to model the effects of cortical activity on map formations. For comprehensive overviews of neural network models that develop orientation selectivity maps and ocular dominance columns, see Swindale (1996) and Ferster and Miller (2000).

Models of cortical map formation can become extremely complex when multiple features, such as retinotopic location, ocular dominance, orientation preference, and others, are considered simultaneously. To deal with such problems, a more abstract class of models was developed by Kohonen (1982). The Kohonen algorithm is usually applied to two-layer networks with feedforward connections from an input layer to an output layer. The input layer is an N-dimensional vector layer. The output layer is normally a one- or two-dimensional array. There are no lateral connections in the output layer, but the algorithm can accomplish what models with lateral connections can achieve at less computational cost. The algorithm does this by a weight updating procedure that involves neighboring units. At every step, it chooses a 'winner' among output units whose weights are closest to the input pattern. Then it updates the weights of the winner and the nearby neighbors of the winner. The number of neighbors that participate in weight updating is controlled through a neighborhood function, which is dynamically changed during learning to ensure convergence. The neighborhood function starts out long range and is reduced as learning proceeds. This allows the network to organize a map rapidly and then refine it more slowly with subsequent learning.

Models based on the Kohonen algorithm perform dimensionality reduction, which facilitates data analysis, taking input vectors from a high-dimensional feature space and projecting them onto a low-dimensional representation.

1.34.3 Unsupervised Hebbian Learning

If the goal of learning is to discover the statistical structure in unlabeled input data, then the learning is said to be unsupervised. A common method for unsupervised learning is principal component analysis (PCA). Suppose the data are a set of N-dimensional input vectors. The task is to find an $M < N$ dimensional representation of N-dimensional input vectors that contains as much information as possible of the input data. This is an example of dimensionality reduction, which can significantly simplify subsequent data analysis.

A simple network that can extract the first principal component (the one with the maximal variance) is a network with N input units and one output unit. At each time step an N-dimensional input vector is applied to the input layer. If we allow the connections to be modified according to the Hebbian learning rule, then in the case of zero mean value of the input vector, the weights will form an N-dimensional vector, along which the variance will be the largest. This is the principal eigenvector or component. A network with N input and M output units, augmented with a generalized Hebbian learning rule, can learn first M components. The projections of the input data onto the components give us M-dimensional representation of the N-dimensional input data.

PCA is appropriate when the data obey Gaussian statistics, but images, audio recordings, and many types of scientific data often do not have Gaussian distributions. As an example of such a problem, consider a room where a number of people are talking simultaneously (cocktail party), and the task is to focus on one of the speakers. The human brain can, to some extent, solve this auditory source separation problem by using knowledge of the speaker, but this becomes a more difficult problem when the signals are arbitrary. The goal of blind source separation (BSS) is to recover source signals given only sensor signals that are linear mixtures of the independent source signals. Independent component analysis (ICA) is a method that solves the BSS problem for non-Gaussian signals. In contrast to correlation-based algorithms such as PCA and factor analysis, ICA finds a nonorthogonal linear coordinate system such that the resulting signals are as statistically independent from each other as possible.

One approach to BSS derives unsupervised learning rules based on information theory. The input is assumed to be N mixtures of N independent sources, and the goal is to maximize the mutual information between the inputs and the outputs of a two-layer neural network. The resulting stochastic gradient learning rules are highly effective in the blind separation and deconvolution of hundreds of non-Gaussian sources (Bell and Sejnowski, 1995).

ICA is particularly effective at analyzing electro-encephalograms (EEG) and functional magnetic resonance imaging (fMRI) data (Jung et al., 2001). Consider, for example, electrical recordings of brain activity at many different locations on the scalp. These EEG potentials are generated by underlying components of brain activity and various muscle and eye movements. This is similar to the cocktail-party problem: We would like to recover the original components of the brain activity, but we can only observe mixtures of the components. ICA can reveal interesting information of the brain activity by giving access to its independent components. ICA also gives useful insights into task-related human brain activity from fMRI recordings when the underlying temporal structure of the sources is unknown.

Another application of ICA is feature extraction (Lee, 1998). A fundamental problem in signal processing is to find suitable representations for images, audio recordings, and other kinds of data. Standard linear transformations used in image and auditory processing, such the Fourier transforms and cosine transforms, may not be optimal, and but it would be useful to find the most efficient linear transformation, based on the statistics of the data, to optimally compress the data.

1.34.4 Supervised Learning

Consider the problem of learning to retrieve an output pattern given an input pattern. To remember the patterns, the Hebbian rule can be applied to adjust weights between input and output units. As mentioned earlier, however, the associative Hebbian learning rule will lead to saturation with multiple repetitions, which reduces the capacity of the network. To resolve this problem, one can augment the Hebbian rule with a weight normalization algorithm as in the case of unsupervised learning algorithms.

Another disadvantage of using the associative Hebbian learning rule is that weight adjustments do not depend on the actual performance of the network. An effective way to adjust weights would be by using information of the actual performance of the network. Supervised learning can do this. Supervised learning requires a teacher, who provides detailed information of the desired outputs of the network and adjusts the connections based on discrepancies between the actual outputs and the desired ones.

The perceptron uses a supervised learning rule to learn to classify input patterns (Rosenblatt, 1958). The perceptron is a two-layer network with one output unit that can classify input patterns into two categories. The Hebbian learning rule can be used to solve the task, but the perceptron with the Hebbian learning rule works well only if the number of input patterns is significantly less than the number of input units. An error-correcting supervised learning algorithm for weight adjustments is more effective for a large number of input patterns:

$$\frac{\mathrm{d}w_{ij}}{\mathrm{d}t} \propto u_j \cdot (R_i - v_i)$$

where w_{ij} is a weight of a connection from the input unit j with activity u_j to an output unit i with activity v_i, R_i is a target value of the output unit, and

$$v_i = \sum_j w_{ij} \cdot u_j$$

The perceptron learning rule uses the performance of the network to decide how much adjustment is needed and in which direction the weights should be changed to decrease the discrepancy between the actual network outputs and the desired ones. If input patterns are linearly separable, then the perceptron learning rule guarantees to find a set of weights that allow pattern classification.

A simple unsupervised Hebbian learning rule adjusts synaptic weights based on correlations between presynaptic and postsynaptic neurons. However, this approach is inefficient when the goal of the network is to perform a specific function, rather than simply represent data. To perform a specific task, the network should receive some information about the task.

An example of how Hebbian plasticity can be incorporated into a supervised learning framework is a two-layer network that was trained to perform a function approximation task (Swinehart and Abbott, 2005). The feedforward connections from input units to output units were modified according to an unsupervised Hebbian rule, and a supervised learning mechanism was used to adjust connections from a supervisor to the network. The supervisor is a network that assesses the performance of the training network and, based on that information, modifies the gains of the input units using an error-correcting learning rule. The purpose of the supervised modulation was to enhance connections between the input and the output units to facilitate the synaptic plasticity needed to learn the task. Thus, Hebbian plasticity did not have direct access to the supervision, and the supervised modulations did not produce any permanent changes. Nonetheless, this network could learn to approximate different functions. In the initial phase the improvement in the network performance was mostly due to the gain modulation, and the synaptic adjustments were minimal. But later, the synaptic adjustments and the gain modulation were equally involved in shaping the performance. Once the network learned the task with the supervisor, it was possible to turn off the supervision, relying only on further Hebbian plasticity to refine the approximation.

The role of the supervisor in the model was to compute an error by comparing the actual and the desired output of the network and to use this error to direct the modification of network parameters such that the network performance improves. Conventionally, the major targets of this process were the synaptic weights. The novel feature of this supervised learning scheme was that supervision took place at the level of neuronal responsiveness rather than synaptic plasticity.

A simple two-layer perceptron cannot solve higher-order problems, but adding additional layers to the feedforward network provides more representational power. Then new learning algorithms are needed to train multilayer networks. The simple error-correcting learning rule was effective for training two-layer networks. With the rule, the connections from the input layer to the output one are adjusted based on discrepancies between the desired output and the actual output produced by the network. In a multilayer network, however, there are intermediate 'hidden' layers that also need to be trained. The backpropagation learning algorithm was developed to train multilayer networks (Rumelhart and McClelland, 1986). The learning rule relies on passing an error from the output layer back to the input layer. Multilayer networks trained with the back-propagation learning rule have been effective in solving many difficult problems.

An example of a multilayer network that was trained using a back-propagation algorithm is a model of song learning in songbirds (Fiete et al., 2004). Juvenile male songbirds learn their songs from adult male tutors of the same species. Birdsong is a learned complex motor behavior driven by a discrete set of premotor brain nuclei with well-studied anatomy (*See* Chapter 1.17). Syringeal and respiratory motor neurons responsible for song production are driven by precisely executed sequences of neural activity in the premotor nucleus robustus archistriatalis (RA) of songbirds (**Figure 2**). Activity in RA is driven by excitatory feedforward inputs from the forebrain nucleus high vocal center (HVC), whose RA-projecting neural population displays temporally sparse, precise, and stereotyped sequential activity. Individual RA-projecting HVC neurons burst just once in an entire song motif and fire almost no spikes elsewhere in the motif. The temporal sparseness of HVC activity implies that these HVC–RA synapses are used in a special way during song; that is, each synapse is used only once during the motif. The goal of the work was to study the effect of HVC sparseness on the learning speed of the network. They studied multilayer feedforward network with an HVC layer that provides input to a

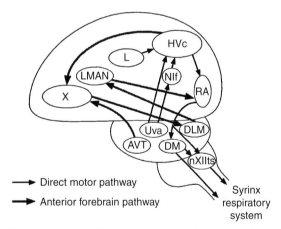

Figure 2 Schematic diagram of the major songbird brain nuclei involved in song control (*See also* Chapter 1.17). The thinner arrows show the direct motor pathway, and the thicker arrows show the anterior forebrain pathway. Abbreviations: Uva, nucleus uvaeformis of the thalamus; NIf, nucleus interface of neostriatum; L, field L (primary auditory area of the forebrain); HVc, higher vocal center; RA, robust nucleus of the archistriatum; DM, dorsomedial part of the nucleus intercollicularis; nXIIts, tracheosyringeal part of the hypoglossal nucleus; AVT, ventral area of Tsai of the midbrain; X, area X of lobus parolfactorius; DLM, medial part of the dorsolateral nucleus of the thalamus; LMAN, lateral magnocellular nucleus of the anterior neostriatum. From Doya K and Sejnowski TJ (2000) A computational model of avian song learning. In: Gazzaniga MS (ed.) *The New Cognitive Neurosciences*, 2nd edn., p. 469. Cambridge, MA: MIT Press; used with permission.

'hidden' RA layer and RA projecting to an output layer of motor units. Song learning is thought to involve plasticity of synapses from HVC to RA because these synapses display extensive synaptic growth and redistribution during the critical period. So in the model, the weights from HVC layer to RA layer were modified. Because there is no evidence of plasticity in the synapses from RA to motor neurons, those connections in the model were kept fixed. For learning, the connections from HVC to RA were adjusted to minimize discrepancy between the desired outputs and the actual outputs produced by the network. They used the back-propagation gradient descent rule and varied the number of bursts in HVC neurons per motif. The network learned the motif for any number of bursts in HVC neurons, but the learning time for two bursts per motif nearly doubled compared to the one burst case and increased rapidly with the number of bursts. Based on these simulations, they concluded that the observed sparse coding in HVC minimized interference and the time needed for learning. It is important to note here that the back-propagation learning algorithm was not used to model the biological learning process itself, but rather to determine if the network architecture can solve the problem and what constraints the representation may have on the speed of learning.

1.34.5   Reinforcement Learning

Learning about stimuli or actions based solely on rewards and punishments is called reinforcement learning. Reinforcement learning is minimally supervised because animals are not told explicitly what actions to take in a particular situation. The reinforcement learning paradigm has attracted considerable interest because of the notion that the learner is able to learn from its own experience at attempting to perform a task without the aid of an intelligent 'teacher.' In contrast, in the more commonly employed paradigm of supervised learning, a detailed 'teacher signal' is required that explicitly tells the learner what the correct output pattern is for every input pattern.

A computational model of birdsong learning based on reinforcement learning has been proposed (Doya and Sejnowski, 2000). A young male songbird learns to sing by imitating the song of a tutor, which is usually the father or other adult males in the colony. If a young bird does not hear a tutor song during a

critical period, it will sing short, poorly structured songs. If a bird is deafened during the period when it practices vocalization, it develops highly abnormal songs. Thus, there are two phases in song learning – the sensory learning phase, when a young bird memorizes song templates, and the sensorimotor learning phase, in which the bird establishes the motor programs using auditory feedback. These two phases can be separated by several months in some species, implying that birds have remarkable capability for memorizing complex temporal sequences. Once a song is crystallized, its pattern is very stable. Even deafening the bird has little immediate effect.

The anterior forebrain pathway, which is not involved in song production, is necessary for song learning. In the previously discussed model (Fiete et al., 2004), it was assumed that HVC is a locus of pattern memorization during the first phase of learning, song acquisition, and RA is a motor command area (*See* Chapter 1.17). Therefore, the patterns stored in HVC serve as inputs to RA to produce motor commands. It was also assumed that evaluation of the similarity of the produced song to the memorized tutor song takes place in area X in the anterior forebrain. This assumption is supported by a finding that area X receives dopaminergic input. Depending on how closely the produced song is to the tutor's song, the connections from HVC to RA are modulated via the lateral magnocellular nucleus (LMAN).

The learning algorithm consisted of making small random changes in the HVC to RA synapses and keeping the new weights only if overall performance was improved. The network learned artificial song motifs and was even able to replicate realistic birdsongs within the number of trials that birds take to learn their songs.

Reinforcement learning has thus far had few practical successes in solving large-scale complex real-world problems. In the case of reinforcement learning with delay, the temporal credit assignment aspect of the problem has made learning very slow. However, a method called temporal difference (TD) learning has overcome some of these limitations (Sutton and Barto, 1998). The basic idea of TD learning is to compute the difference between temporally successive predictions. In other words, the goal of learning is to make the learner's current prediction for the current input pattern more closely match the prediction at the next time step. One of the most effective of these TD methods is an algorithm called TD(λ), in which there is an exponentially decaying feedback of the error in time, so that previous estimates for previous states are also corrected. The time scale of the exponential decay is governed by the λ parameter.

Perhaps the most successful application of TD(λ) is TD-Gammon, which was designed for networks to learn to play backgammon (Tesauro, 1995). Backgammon is an ancient two-player game that is played on an effectively one-dimensional track. The players take turns rolling dice and moving their checkers in opposite directions along the track as allowed by the dice roll. The first player to move all his checkers all the way forward and off his end of the board is the winner.

At the heart of TD-Gammon is a neural network with a standard multilayer architecture. Its output is computed by a feedforward flow of activation from the input nodes, representing the game position, to the output node, which evaluates the strength of the position. Each of the connections in the network is parameterized by a real valued weight. Each of the nodes in the network outputs a real number equal to a weighted linear sum of inputs feeding into it, followed by a nonlinear sigmoid operation. At each time step, the TD(λ) algorithm is applied to the output, which is then back-propagated to change the network's weights.

During training, the neural network selects moves for both sides. At each time step during the course of a game, the neural network scores every possible legal move. The move that is then selected is the move with maximum expected outcome for the side making the move. In other words, the neural network learns by playing against itself. At the start of self-play, the network's weights are random, and hence its initial strategy is random. But after a few hundred thousand games, TD-Gammon played significantly better than any previous backgammon program, equivalent to an advanced level of play. In particular, it is not dependent on a human teacher, which would limit the level of play it can achieve (Tesauro and Sejnowski, 1989). After one million games, TD-Gammon was playing at a championship level.

One of the essential features of reinforcement learning is a trade-off between exploration and exploitation. The learning system should exploit a successful strategy to reach the goal of the task it learns, but it should also explore other strategies to find out if there is a better one. In models, exploration has been implemented by stochasticity. The source of such stochasticity in the brain remains unclear. A model implementing this trade-off between exploration and exploitation has been proposed (Seung,

2003). The model is based on the probabilistic nature of synaptic release by a presynaptic terminal when an action potential arrives at the terminal. The model combines this local synaptic release-failure event and a global reward signal received outside based on the output of the model. The main assumption is that synapses are hedonistic: they increase their probabilities of release or failure depending on which action immediately preceded reward. This concept of the hedonistic synapse is potentially relevant to any brain area in which a global reinforcement signal is received (Klopf, 1982).

This version of reinforcement learning was used to address the matching law phenomenon (Seung, 2003). When animals are presented with repeated choices between competing alternatives, they distribute their choices so that returns from two alternatives are approximately the same. A return is the total reward obtained from an alternative divided by the number of times it was chosen. Before trials, the alternatives are baited with unequal probabilities. The network had to learn a probabilistic strategy in which one alternative is favored over the other one. The network started from equal choices for both alternatives, but over time, it learned a preference that satisfied the matching law.

In the present model, stochastic vesicle release was assumed to be a source of stochasticity in the brain. However, there might be many other possible sources of noise, such as fluctuations in quantal size, irregular action potential firing, and on a slower time scale, the stochastic creation and destruction of synapses. Thus, identifying specific sources of randomness is essential for connecting mathematical models and neurobiology.

1.34.6 Spike-Timing Dependent Plasticity

The traditional coincidence version of the Hebbian learning rule implies simply that the correlation of activities of presynaptic and postsynaptic neurons drives learning. This approach has been implemented in many types of neural network models using average firing rate or average membrane potentials of neurons (*See* Chapter 1.35). Although Hebb's formulation implicitly recognized the idea of causality and relative spike timing (Hebb, 1949; Sejnowski, 1999), this was not appreciated by a generation of modelers because rate coding was generally accepted as the primary form of information processing, and high-frequency stimulation protocols were used to induce plasticity at synapses. More recently, the relative timing of spikes has been shown to be critical for the direction and magnitude of synaptic plasticity in the cortex as well as the hippocampus (Markram et al., 1997; Bi and Poo, 1998). Potentiation of a synapse takes place if the presynaptic spike precedes the postsynaptic spike, and depression occurs when presynaptic spike follows the postsynaptic spike. This spike-timing dependent plasticity (STDP) is an asymmetric function of relative spike times in the presynaptic and postsynaptic neurons. The time window for the plasticity can be as short as 10 ms and as long as 100 ms, depending on the synapse.

A natural application for STDP is temporal sequence learning (*See* Chapters 1.34, 1.35). If neurons are activated in a sequential manner then, due to the asymmetry of the learning rule, synapses from previously activated neurons to following active neurons will be strengthened. For example, such a spike-timing dependent learning algorithm has been used to train a network to link sequential hippocampal place cells while a rat navigates a maze (Blum and Abbott, 1996). The goal was to predict the direction of a future motion on the basis of a previous experience. Asymmetric synaptic weights develop in the model because of the temporal asymmetry of LTP induction and because place fields are activated sequentially during locomotion. This learning algorithm closely resembles the STDP learning rule. The only essential difference is time scale, which in the model was 200 ms, longer than the STDP windows found in cortical or hippocampal neurons.

This model of a navigational map was based on three observations. First, NMDA-dependent LTP in hippocampal slices occurs only if presynaptic activity precedes postsynaptic activity by less than approximately 200 ms. Presynaptic activity following postsynaptic firing produces either no LTP or long-term depression (LTD). Second, place cells are broadly tuned and make synaptic connections with each other both within the CA3 region and between CA3 and CA1. Third, a spatial location can be determined by appropriately averaging the activity of an ensemble of hippocampal place cells. These three observations imply that when an animal travels through its environment, causing different sets of place cells to fire, information about both temporal and spatial aspects of its motion will be reflected in changes of the strengths of synapses between place cells. Because this LTP affects a subsequent place cell firing, it can shift the spatial location coded by the

place cell activity. These shifts suggest that an animal could navigate by heading from its present location toward the position coded by the place cell activity. To illustrate both how a spatial map arises and how it can be used to guide movement, these ideas were applied to navigation in the Morris maze. The network was trained using this spike-timing dependent learning algorithm to form a direction map, which improved with training.

Timing is important in auditory processing, and a number of perceptual tasks, such as sound localization, explicitly use temporal information. Sound localization is important to the survival of many species, in particular to those that hunt in the dark. Interaural time differences (ITD) are often used as a spatial cue. However, the question of how temporal information from both ears can be transmitted to a site of comparison, where neurons are tuned to ITDs, and how those ITD-tuned neurons can be organized in a map remains unclear. A network model based on STDP can successfully account for a fine precision of barn owl sound localization (Kempter et al., 2001). The model converts ITDs into a place code by combining axonal delay lines from both ears and STDP in synapses with distributed delays. The neurons are organized as a single-layer network for each frequency and receive inputs from both ears through axonal arbors. The axons have different time delays. After training, each neuron adjusts its connections to axons with the appropriate time delays in agreement with the neuron's spatial position. In this way, a map with neurons tuned to particular ITDs can be formed.

There is an interesting connection between STDP and TD learning at the computational level (Rao and Sejnowski, 2003). If, consistent with TD learning, synaptic weights between Hodgkin–Huxley type spiking neurons are updated based on the difference in the postsynaptic voltage at time $t + \Delta t$ and at time t, where t is the time when the presynaptic neuron fired a spike, and Δt is a fixed time interval, then the learning rule resembles the conventional STDP learning rule. Networks with this spike-dependent TD learning rule are able to learn and predict temporal sequences, as demonstrated by the development of direction selectivity in a recurrent cortical network. The network consisted of a single chain of recurrently connected excitatory neurons. Each neuron initially received symmetric excitatory and inhibitory inputs of the same magnitude. For training, the neurons in the network were exposed to 100 trials of retinotopic sensory inputs consisting of moving pulses of excitation in the rightward direction.

The effect of learning on the network was in developing a profound asymmetry in the pattern of excitatory connections from preceding and successor neurons. The synaptic conductances of excitatory connections from the left side were strengthened, whereas the ones from the right side were weakened. Because neurons on the left side fired (on average) a few milliseconds before a considered neuron, whereas neurons on the right side fired (on average) a few milliseconds after, as a result, the synaptic strengths of connections from the left side were increased, whereas the synaptic strengths for connections from the right side were decreased. As expected from the learned pattern of connections, the neuron responded vigorously to rightward motion but not to leftward motion.

To investigate the question of how selectivity for different directions of motion may emerge simultaneously, they also simulated a network comprising two parallel chains of neurons, with mutual inhibition between corresponding pairs of neurons along the two chains. As in the previous simulation, a given excitatory neuron received both excitation and inhibition from its predecessors and successors. To break the symmetry between the two chains, they provided a slight bias in the recurrent excitatory connections, so that neurons in one chain fired slightly earlier than neurons in the other chain for a given motion direction. To evaluate the consequences of spike-based TD learning in the two-chain network, the model neurons were exposed alternately to leftward- and rightward-moving stimuli for a total of 100 trials. As in the previous simulation, the excitatory and inhibitory connections to a neuron in one chain showed asymmetry after training, with stronger excitatory connections from the left neurons and stronger inhibitory connections from the right neurons. A corresponding neuron in the other chain exhibited the opposite pattern, and as expected from the learned patterns of connectivity, neurons in one chain were selective to rightward motion, and neurons in the other chain were selective to the leftward motion. This explanation was consistent with the development of directionally selective neurons in the visual cortex of kittens.

1.34.7 Plasticity of Intrinsic Excitability

Several lines of evidence argue for the presence of activity-dependent modification of intrinsic neuronal excitability during development and learning (Daoudal and Debanne, 2003; *See* Chapter 4.40). In the dentate gyrus of the hippocampus, for example, in addition to homosynaptic LTP of excitatory synaptic transmission, the probability of discharge of the postsynaptic neurons to a fixed excitatory synaptic input is enhanced by high-frequency stimulation (HFS, 100 Hz) of the afferent fibers (Bliss et al., 1973). This second component has been called excitatory postsynaptic potential (EPSP)-to-spike potentiation (E-S potentiation) (Frick et al., 2004). Synaptic plasticity (LTP) and nonsynaptic E-S potentiation are complementary. As in LTP, E-S potentiation requires the activation of NMDA receptor (NMDAR) for its induction. These two forms of plasticity may share common induction pathways. In a recent study of deep cerebellar nuclei neurons, tetanization of inputs to these neurons produces a rapid and long-lasting increase in intrinsic excitability that depends on NMDAR activation (Aizenman and Linden, 2000). These studies suggest that plasticity of intrinsic excitability may be important in developmental plasticity and information storage.

Another form of plasticity in intrinsic excitability has been demonstrated in spontaneously firing vestibular nucleus neurons, which may be responsible for learning of the vestibuloocular reflex. Purkinje cells, which are inhibitory, contact a subset of the neuron in the vestibular nucleus, which receive direct vestibular input and project to the oculomotor nuclei. Brief periods of synaptic inhibition or membrane hyperpolarization produced a dramatic increase in both spontaneous firing rate and responses to intracellularly injected current (Gittis and du Lac, 2006). A similar change occurred after silencing the vestibular nerve. Neurons in the vestibular system fire at remarkably high rates in the intact animal, with resting rates on the order of 50–100 spikes/s and responses to head movements ranging up to 300 spikes/s. Loss of peripheral vestibular function silences the vestibular nerve, resulting in a significant loss of spontaneous firing in the neurons of the vestibular nucleus, which then returns to control values within about a week, even in the absence of vestibular nerve recovery. This plasticity of intrinsic excitability could potentially contribute either to adaptive changes in vestibular function during recovery from peripheral damage or to oculomotor learning in intact animals.

A similar phenomenon has been demonstrated in cultured neocortical pyramidal neurons (Desai et al., 1999). Prolonged activity blockade lowers the threshold for spike generation, and neurons fire at a higher frequency for any given level of current injection. These changes occurred through selective modifications in the magnitude of voltage-dependent currents: sodium currents increase and persistent potassium currents decrease, whereas calcium currents and transient potassium currents are unaltered. Increase of neuronal excitability in response to reduced activity may contribute to the activity-dependent stabilization of firing rates. The stability in neuronal firing rates is maintained through many mechanisms, and regulation of neuronal excitability may be one of them.

Information about the outside world is transformed into spike trains in the nervous system. How do the neurons learn to represent the information, and do they change their behavior based on changing external stimuli? In the discussion of unsupervised learning and the ICA algorithm, it was shown that information theoretical approaches can be effective in solving real-world problems. A similar information theoretical approach can be implemented to search for an optimal representation. A Hodgkin–Huxley type model of a neuron that can adjust its membrane conductances to maximize information transfer has been proposed (Stemmler and Koch, 1999). The slope of the neuronal gain function should line up with the peak of the input to maximize information transfer. The learning rules they implemented in the model performed this matchup by adjusting the membrane conductances. The conductance modulations did not require calculation of mutual information but were based solely on local characteristics of the neuron. They showed that for different input distributions the model could successfully line up the gain function and the input distributions leading to maximization of information transfer. Thus, the ability of activity-dependent selective modification of the gain functions based on the active balance of inward and outward ion channels could serve a number of important functions, including fine-tuning of the output properties of neurons to match the properties of their inputs.

Plasticity of intrinsic excitability can also participate in regulating the conventional synaptic plasticity. For details, see the previously discussed model, which combines Hebbian and supervised learning (Swinehart and Abbott, 2005), in the section titled 'Supervised learning.'

synaptic connections. However, correlation-based learning in neural networks can be unstable. According to the Hebb rule, if a presynaptic neuron participates in firing of a postsynaptic neuron, it leads to strengthening the synapses between the neurons. This makes it more likely that next time the presynaptic neuron fires, it will cause firing in the postsynaptic neuron, which leads to further strengthening of the synapse. Simple associative Hebbian algorithm causes instability in the network by increasing the total activity of the network and losing selectivity among synapses. To keep the network stable and maintain the selectivity of the network, an additional mechanism must stabilize the properties of neuronal networks.

Homeostatic plasticity is a mechanism by which the neurons regulate the network's activity (Turrigiano and Nelson, 2000). There are many different ways neural activities could be regulated to keep them within a functional dynamical range. One mechanism that could maintain relatively constant activity levels is to increase the strength of all excitatory connections into a neuron in response to a prolonged drop in firing rates, and vice versa. This form of homeostatic plasticity is called synaptic scaling.

Regulating synaptic strength is not the only mechanism by which homeostatic activity can be maintained. Previously discussed plasticity of intrinsic excitability also contributes to the homeostatic regulation by controlling the firing rates of the neurons.

All theoretical models implementing associative Hebbian learning rule have to deal with the instability problem. For example, the BCM learning rule deals with unconstrained growth of synaptic weights by dynamically adjusting the threshold between potentiation and depression (Bienenstock et al., 1982). This algorithm is biologically plausible and reflects experimental findings indicating that calcium level is crucial for the direction of plasticity. The dynamical threshold modulation implemented in the BCM rule not only prevents the synapses from unconstrained growth but also maintains the activity level of the units at the appropriate value (*See* Chapters 1.33, 1.35).

In the next section we present some other examples of learning algorithms involving homeostatic plasticity as a critical element of learning.

1.34.8 Homeostatic Plasticity

Correlation-based Hebbian plasticity is thought to be crucial for information storage because it produces associative changes in the strength of individual

1.34.9 Complexity of Learning

The learning paradigms discussed earlier were based on a single mechanism for plasticity (e.g., STDP versus homeostatic and synaptic versus intrinsic neuronal). However, many difficult tasks cannot be solved using a single learning rule, but require combinations of several learning rules working together. Another essential element of modeling learning processes is the time scale of learning. There are multiple time scales for plasticity, from milliseconds to years, and depending on the demands of the task, different mechanisms for plasticity with different time scales may be involved.

Long-term memory is vulnerable to degradation from passive decay of the memory trace and ongoing formation of new memories. Memory based on synapses with two states shows exponential decay, but experimental data shows that forgetting (memory degradation) follows a power law. A cascade model was developed to address this problem (Fusi et al., 2005). In the model, synapses had two states, weak and strong, but in addition to transition between these two states, there were metaplastic transitions within each state. Based on the stage of metaplasticity, the synapses showed the range of behavior from being highly plastic to being resistant to any plasticity at all. The metaplastic transitions effectively introduced multiple time scales into the model.

The cascade model outperformed alternative models and exhibited a power law for the decay of memory as a function of time. The dependence of memory lifetime on the number of synapses in the model is also a power law function. Memory lifetimes diminish when the balance between excitation and inhibition is disturbed, but the effect is much less severe in the cascade model than in noncascade models.

The function of homeostatic plasticity is to maintain the activity of the cortex at a functional level. But are there any other computational or functional advantages of such plasticity? One study has shown that a combination of Hebbian and homeostatic plasticity can lead to temporal sharpening in response to multiple applications of transient sensory stimuli (Moldakarimov et al., 2006). The model included two types of homeostatic mechanisms, fast and slow. Relatively fast plasticity was responsible for maintaining the average activity of the units. To maintain activity in the excitatory neurons at a target homeostatic level, they implemented a learning rule, according to which inhibitory connections have been adjusted. The slow plasticity was used to determine the value of the target average activities. Thus, the model had three time scales for synaptic adjustments: Hebbian, fast homeostatic, and slow homeostatic mechanisms. Repeated presentations of

a transient signal taught the network to respond to the signal with a high amplitude and short duration, in agreement with experimental findings. This sharpening enhances the processing of transients and may also be relevant for speech perception.

A standard approach in models of self-organized map (SOM) formation is the application of Hebbian plasticity augmented with a mechanism of weight normalization. A conventional way to normalize weights is based on a sum of weights coming into each neuron: The soma collects information on every weight, sums them, and then decides on the amount of normalization. An alternative approach to weight normalization has been proposed (Sullivan and de Sa, 2006). The normalization algorithm did not need information from every synapse but rather was based on the average activities of the units and homeostatic plasticity. When Hebbian and homeostatic mechanisms were combined, the average activities of the units were better maintained compared to the standard Hebbian models.

Dimensionality reduction facilitates the classification, the visualization, and the storage of high-dimensional data. A simple and widely used method is PCA, which finds the directions of greatest variance in the data set and represents each data point by its coordinates along each of these directions. A new deep network model has been proposed to transform the high-dimensional data into a low-dimensional code (Hinton and Salakhutdinov, 2006). The adaptive multilayer network consisted of two subnetworks, an encoder and decoder. The encoder transformed high-dimensional data into a low-dimensional code. The code layer was then used as the input layer to the decoder network to reconstruct the original input pattern.

The two networks were trained together to minimize the discrepancy between the original data and its reconstruction. The required gradients were obtained using the chain rule to back-propagate error derivatives, first through the decoder network and then through the encoder network. In general, it is difficult to optimize the weights in a multilayer network with many hidden layers. Large initial weights typically lead to poor local minima; with small initial weights, the gradients in the early layers are tiny, making it impossible to train. But if the initial weights are close to a good solution, gradient descent back-propagation works well. A good initial network was obtained with unsupervised learning based on Restricted Boltzmann Machine (RBM) learning algorithm. First, the input layer of the multilayer network was used as a visible layer of RBM, and the next layer served as a feature layer. After learning one layer of feature detectors, the weights were fixed and used for learning a second layer of feature detectors. This layer-by-layer learning was repeated many times. After pretraining multiple layers of feature detectors, the model was unfolded to produce the encoder and decoder networks that initially used the same weights. The global fine-tuning stage used back-propagation through the whole network to adjust the weights for optimal reconstruction.

They applied the algorithm to multiple tasks including handwritten digits visualization, grayscale images, and documents generalization. In all these tasks, the new algorithm outperformed different approaches based on PCA and other supervised algorithms.

1.34.10 Conclusions

We have discussed learning rules and learning algorithms designed for neural network models and described some problems that can be solved by neural networks with modifiable connections. Neural computation is a broad field that continues to grow; only a few selected studies have been used to illustrate general principles.

Although early modeling efforts focused mainly on traditional synaptic plasticity, such as LTP and LTD, relatively new homeostatic plasticity mechanisms are also being explored. Although synaptic plasticity was once presumed to be the primary neural mechanism of learning, recent models have incorporated changes of intrinsic properties of the neurons as well.

Most experimental studies of learning have studied the mechanisms of synaptic plasticity in reduced preparations. Recently the focus has shifted to relating the changes in the synapses with behavioral learning. For example, inhibitory avoidance learning in rats produced the same changes in hippocampal glutamate receptors as induction of LTP with HFS (Whitlock et al., 2006). Because the learning-induced synaptic potentiation occluded HFS-induced LTP, they concluded that inhibitory avoidance training induced LTP in hippocampus.

Theoretical approaches can integrate local mechanisms with whole system behavior. Even after locating particular sites where changes occur, it is still not clear to what degree those changes are directly related to the learning. Building a computational model that integrates learning mechanisms allows one to evaluate the importance of different sites of plasticity. The observed plasticity for some sites may be secondary, or compensatory to the primary sites of learning (Lisberger and Sejnowski, 1992).

References

Aizenman CD and Linden DJ (2000) Rapid, synaptically driven increases in the intrinsic excitability of cerebellar deep nuclear neurons. *Nature Neurosci.* 3: 109–111.

Bell AJ and Sejnowski TJ (1995) An information maximization approach to blind separation and blind deconvolution. *Neural Comput.* 7: 1129–1159.

Bi G-Q and Poo M-M (1998) Synaptic modifications in cultured hippocampal neurons: Dependence on spike timing, synaptic strength, and postsynaptic cell type. *J. Neurosci.* 18: 10464–10472.

Bienenstock E, Cooper LN, and Munro PW (1982) Theory for the development of neuron selectivity: Orientation specificity and binocular interaction in visual cortex. *J. Neurosci.* 2: 32–48.

Bliss TV and Lomo T (1973) Long-lasting potentiation of synaptic transmission in the dentate area of the anaesthetized rabbit following stimulation of the perforant path. *J. Physiol.* 232: 331–356.

Bliss TV, Lomo T, and Gardner-Medwin AR (1973) Synaptic plasticity in the hippocampal formation. In: Ansell G and Bradley PB (eds.) *Macromolecules and Behavior*, pp. 192–303. London: Macmillan.

Blum KI and Abbott LF (1996) A model of spatial map formation in the hippocampus of the rat. *Neural Comput.* 8: 85–93.

Daoudal G and Debanne D (2003) Long-term plasticity of intrinsic excitability: Learning rules and mechanisms. *Learn. Mem.* 10: 456–465.

Desai NS, Rutherford LC, and Turrigiano GG (1999) Plasticity in the intrinsic excitability of cortical pyramidal neurons. *Nature Neurosci.* 2: 515–520.

Doya K and Sejnowski TJ (2000) A computational model of avian song learning. In: Gazzaninga MS (ed.) *The New Cognitive Neurosciences*, 2nd edn., p. 469. Cambridge, MA: MIT Press.

Ferster D and Miller KD (2000) Neural mechanisms of orientation selectivity in the visual cortex. *Annu. Rev. Neurosci.* 23: 441–471.

Fiete IR, Hahnloser RHR, Fee MS, and Seung HS (2004) Temporal sparseness of the premotor drive is important for rapid learning in a neural network model of birdsong. *J. Neurophysiol.* 92: 2274–2282.

Frick A, Magee J, and Johnston D (2004) LTP is accompanied by an enhanced local excitability of pyramidal neuron dendrites. *Nature Neurosci.* 7: 126–135.

Fusi S, Drew PJ, and Abbott LF (2005) Cascade models of synaptically stored memories. *Neuron* 45: 599–611.

Gittis AH and du Lac S (2006) Intrinsic and synaptic plasticity in the vestibular system. *Curr. Opin. Neurobiol.* 16: 385–390.

Hebb DO (1949) *Organization of Behavior: A Neuropsychological Theory.* New York: Wiley.

Hinton GE and Salakhutdinov RR (2006) Reducing the dimensionality of data with neural networks. *Science* 313: 504–507.

Hopfield JJ (1982) Neural networks and physical systems with emergent collective computational abilities. *Proc. Natl. Acad. Sci. USA* 79: 2554–2558.

Jung T-P, Makeig S, McKeown MJ, Bell AJ, Lee T-W, and Sejnowski TJ (2001) Imaging brain dynamics using independent component analysis. *Proc. IEEE* 89: 1107–1122.

Kelso SR, Ganong AH, and Brown TH (1986) Hebbian synapses in hippocampus. *Proc. Natl. Acad. Sci. USA* 83: 5326–5330.

Kempter R, Leibold C, Wagner H, and van Hemmen JL (2001) Formation of temporal-feature maps by axonal propagation of synaptic learning. *Proc. Natl. Acad. Sci. USA* 98: 4166–4171.

Klopf AH (1982) *The Hedonistic Neuron: A Theory of Memory, Learning and Intelligence.* Washington, DC: Hemisphere.

Kohonen T (1982) Self-organized formation of topologically correct feature maps. *Biol. Cybern.* 43: 59–69.

Lee T-W (1998) *Independent Component Analysis. Theory and Applications.* Boston: Kluwer Academic Publishers.

Lisberger SG and Sejnowski TJ (1992) Motor learning in a recurrent network model based on the vestibule-ocular reflex. *Nature* 360: 159–161.

Markram H, Lubke J, Frotscher M, and Sakmann B (1997) Regulation of synaptic efficacy by coincidence of postsynaptic APs and EPSPs. *Science* 275: 213–215.

Miller KD and Mackay DJC (1994) The role of constraints on Hebbian learning. *Neural Comput.* 6: 100–109.

Moldakarimov SB, McClelland JL, and Ermentrout GB (2006) A homeostatic rule for inhibitory synapses promotes temporal sharpening and cortical reorganization. *Proc. Natl. Acad. Sci. USA* 103: 16526–16531.

Rao RP and Sejnowski TJ (2003) Self-organizing neural systems based on predictive learning. *Philos. Trans. R. Soc. Lond.* 361: 1149–1175.

Rosenblatt F (1958) The perceptron: A probabilistic model for information storage and organization in the brain. *Psychol. Rev.* 65: 386–408.

Rumelhart DE and McClelland JL (1986) *Parallel Distributed Processing, Vol. 1: Foundations.* Cambridge, MA: MIT Press.

Sejnowski TJ (1999) The book of Hebb. *Neuron* 24: 773–776.

Sejnowski TJ and Tesauro G (1988) The Hebb rule for synaptic plasticity: Algorithms and implementations. In: Byrne J and Berry WO (eds.) *Neural Models of Plasticity*, pp. 94–103. New York: Academic Press.

Seung HS (2003) Learning in spiking neural networks by reinforcement of stochastic synaptic transmission. *Neuron* 40: 1063–1073.

Stemmler M and Koch C (1999) How voltage-dependent conductances can adapt to maximize the information encoded by neuronal firing rate. *Nature Neurosci.* 2: 521–527.

Sullivan TJ and de Sa VR (2006) Homeostatic synaptic scaling in self-organizing maps. *Neural Networks* 19: 734–743.

Sutton RS and Barto AG (1998) *Reinforcement Learning. An Introduction.* Cambridge, MA: MIT Press.

Swindale NV (1996) The development of topography in the visual cortex: A review of models. *Network* 7: 161–247.

Swinehart CD and Abbott LF (2005) Supervised learning through neuronal responses modulation. *Neural Comput.* 17: 609–631.

Tesauro G (1995) Temporal difference learning and TD-Gammon. *Comm. ACM* 38: 58–68.

Tesauro G and Sejnowski TJ (1989) A parallel network that learns to play backgammon *J. Artif. Intell.* 39: 357–390.

Turrigiano GG and Nelson SB (2000) Hebb and homeostasis in neural plasticity. *Curr. Opin. Neurobiol.* 10: 358–364.

Whitlock JR, Heynen AJ, Shuler MG, and Bear MF (2006) Learning induces long-term potentiation in the hippocampus. *Science* 313: 1093–1097.

1.35   Connectionist Memory Models of Hippocampal Function

R. A. Koene and M. E. Hasselmo, Boston University, Boston, MA, USA

1.35.1   Introduction

Connectionist models of memory function distinguish themselves from other models of memory through their explicit analogy to memory function that may be supported by the anatomy of the neural substrate. Unlike semantic memory models, for example, connectionist models do not generally store explicit semantic pieces of information in individual memory locations. Instead, the expression of concepts in connectionist models relies on the simultaneous activity of a number of units that form a unique pattern. The structure that is needed to elicit such patterns of activity is provided by a corresponding unique arrangement of connection strengths between units. The network of units is therefore analogous to anatomical networks of neurons, and the connections in such models are analogous to the pathways, fibers, and synapses that form connections between neurons and groups of neurons.

The degree of functional similarity between connectionist units and connections and their biological counterparts varies greatly between different models. Connectionist models with abstract functions, such as the error back-propagating functions of Rumelhart units, tend to focus on general concepts of learning in networks with distributed storage resembling neural networks. At the other end of the spectrum, computational models that involve a greater degree of biophysical accuracy generally study neural activity that is comparable with electrophysiological data. It is the latter type of connectionist model that is our principal focus here, as those models are directly applicable to the study of neural activity in the hippocampal system.

We will consider connectionist models of the complex and comparatively well-studied memory binding functions of the medial temporal lobes. The anatomical regions included in the medial temporal lobes are the hippocampus (dentate gyrus, Cornu Ammonis fields CA1–CA3, and CA4, which is also called the hilus, and the subiculum) and the surrounding perirhinal, parahippocampal, and entorhinal cortices (*See* Chapter 1.33 for anatomical details).

Three significant forms of memory function are believed to depend on the function of hippocampal and entorhinal networks in particular: (1) context-dependent memory, which is retrieved by association with specific contextual cues; (2) episodic memory, in which specific associations between temporally ordered events are maintained; and (3) spatial memory, which aids spatial navigation through the retrieval of associated spatial features (*See* Chapters 1.14, 1.15, 1.21, 1.23, 1.33, 1.34). In the following text, we will review a number of theories and models that specifically attempt to model functions that have been proposed to rely on neuronal network activity in the hippocampal and entorhinal regions of the medial temporal lobes.

Connectionist models developed to study different types of learning and memory are evaluated in the context of the computational neurophysiology that underlies function in networks of the entorhinal cortex and hippocampus. Hippocampal function supports specific memory-dependent behaviors in humans and animals. Data are therefore available with which models of the integral system can be tested. The hippocampal system is consequently a rich substrate for studies both at the scale of an individual network and at the scale of dynamic interactions between networks.

Neuropsychological data in human subjects show that lesions of the hippocampus selectively impair specific components of memory function. Hippocampal lesions impair the delayed free recall of information (Scoville and Milner, 1957; Penfield and Milner, 1958; Corkin, 1984). Such lesions have little effect on digit span (Corkin, 1984) or on the recency component of the serial position curve (Baddeley and Warrington, 1970). Neither semantic memory nor consolidated episodic memory appears affected by hippocampal lesions (Zola-Morgan et al., 1983, 1986). As a result of lesion data from nonhuman primates, the impairments seen in patients such as HM have been attributed in part to the removal of perirhinal cortex and parahippocampal gyrus (Suzuki et al., 1993). Lesions that are restricted to the subregions of the hippocampus may, however, cause severe memory impairments, as exhibited by patient RB (Zola-Morgan et al., 1986; Rempel-Clower et al., 1995). For example, in tests of the free recall of ten words from the middle of a 15-word list, patient RB recalls only 10% of the words, whereas controls recall about 40% (Graf et al., 1984). Similar striking differences between controls and patients with hippocampal lesions appear in tests of the free recall of information from a story, which is a common subtest of the Wechsler Memory Scale (Zola-Morgan et al., 1986). The human data support the specific significance of hippocampal subregions for the storage and retrieval of verbal information with context-dependent and episodic associations, as mentioned (*See* Chapters 1.02, 1.14, 1.15).

Memory function in a range of tasks can also be impaired by drug effects and by damage to the cholinergic innervation of regions in the medial temporal lobes. In humans, damage to cortical cholinergic innervation caused by anterior communicating artery aneurysms impairs performance in tests of the free recall of lists of words or information from paragraphs (Heilman and Sypert, 1977; Hodges and Carpenter, 1991), causes enhanced interference in an AB, AC paradigm (van der Linden et al., 1993), and also results in considerable confabulation in memory tasks (DeLuca, 1993). In nonhuman primates, lesions of the fornix, which cuts off most of the cholinergic innervation of the hippocampus, have been shown to impair formation of snapshot memories (Gaffan and Harrison, 1989). In addition to the extensive behavioral data suggesting some role for the hippocampus in human memory function, there is a wealth of data on the anatomy and physiology of this structure, and extensive theoretical work on the function of individual subregions. Here we review simulations of encoding and retrieval of item representations within networks that represent components of the full hippocampal circuit. The connectionist models discussed deal with sequential encoding, delayed free recall, and pattern recognition. In the context of hippocampal learning and memory, we review the published modeling results of many investigators, and in particular the integrative qualities of several system models that include our own work.

1.35.2 Connectionist Modeling of Hippocampal Episodic Memory

The study of memory in neural network models is typically approached in one of two ways: Either a fixed pattern of network connectivity is applied, so that simulations can focus on aspects of the retrieval of information (Hopfield, 1982; Treves and Rolls, 1994), or connectionist models use a protocol of repeated presentations of stimuli, so that they can simulate the training of connection weights by explicitly computing an error during a behavioral task (Schmajuk and DiCarlo, 1992; Gluck and Myers, 1993; Myers and Gluck, 1994). By contrast, recent simulations of hippocampal network activity use Hebbian learning (Jensen and Lisman, 1996; Hasselmo and Wyble, 1997; Koene et al., 2003) and often do not impose learning and recall stages externally (Hasselmo and Wyble, 1997; Koene et al., 2003). Instead, these models explicitly simulate the effect of cholinergic modulation of specific pathways and oscillatory activity at theta rhythm. Electrophysiological evidence suggests that such modulation elicits specific periods of selective suppression of synaptic transmission and of modulated susceptibility to long-term potentiation (LTP) (Hyman et al., 2003). Conditions favor the retrieval of patterns of activity in associative memory when synaptic transmission is cholinergically suppressed (Huerta and Lisman, 1993; Hasselmo, 1995). Conversely, encoding and self-organization are favored in the absence of synaptic suppression and when LTP is facilitated.

In models of hippocampal memory function that simulate neural activity in terms of values for the firing rate, Hebbian learning rules are justified by experimental evidence of firing rate protocols that elicit LTP (McNaughton et al., 1978; Levy and Steward, 1979; Kelso et al., 1986; Wigstrom et al., 1986; *See* Chapter 1.33). Similarly, experimental evidence by Bi and Poo (1998) supports the hypothesis that spike-timing-dependent potentiation (STDP) of synapses is an effect that implements the Hebbian learning rule. Computational equivalents of STDP are applied in integrate-and-fire neural network models of hippocampal function (Jensen et al., 1996; Koene et al., 2003), also known as spiking neuron models (Gerstner, 1998a,b; Gerstner and Kistler, 2002).

In many cases, a theory of hippocampal function focuses exclusively on the function of a specific subregion of the hippocampus. Such theories commonly do not take into account how interactions between the subregions of the hippocampal system affect behavior in specific tasks. This is not a trivial matter, since hippocampal function is characterized by a dynamic interaction between the activity in its various subregions. It is likely that hippocampus-mediated behavior is not simply a consequence of the gathering of communicated results from isolated regional functions, but is instead elicited and modified through interaction and feedback. A number of reviews have previously summarized subregion-specific theories (Levy, 1989; Eichenbaum and Buckingham, 1990; O'Reilly and McClelland, 1994; Treves and Rolls, 1994).

Our models of learning and memory in the hippocampal system explicitly integrate the simulated functions of multiple regions (Hasselmo and Wyble, 1997; Hasselmo et al., 2002b; Koene et al., 2003; Hasselmo and Eichenbaum, 2005). A similar approach has been taken by other investigators, such as Jensen and Lisman (1996). The structure of these integrated system models of hippocampal function was motivated by experimental data about the anatomy and physiology of the hippocampal

formation, and by previous theoretical work on the function of different hippocampal subregions (Marr, 1971; Valentino and Dingledine, 1981; McNaughton and Morris, 1987; Dutar and Nicoll, 1988; Levy, 1989; Eichenbaum and Buckingham, 1990; Levy et al., 1990, 1995; Ratcliff et al., 1990; McNaughton, 1991; Treves and Rolls, 1992, 1994; O'Reilly and McClelland, 1994; Rolls, 1995; Hasselmo et al., 1996, 1998). These models contrast with most earlier simulations in that they do not simulate individual effects and ideas in isolation. Instead, they combine the functions of different regions into a detailed, self-regulated model, generally including network representations of three or more subregions of the hippocampus along with the adjacent entorhinal cortex. Some of these new models address specific human memory tasks, such as free recall and recognition, and the effect of drugs on memory function during such tasks, which was not done in earlier simulations of the full hippocampal network (Rolls et al., 1997). Others address the combination of spatial memory and episodic memory or context-dependent memory tasks involved in rodent spatial navigation behavior. The anatomy of the hippocampal formation and structure of the model are summarized in **Figure 1**.

The hippocampus extends along the ventromedial border of the temporal lobe and receives convergent multimodal input from a wide range of neocortical association areas, most of which project to the hippocampus via neurons of the entorhinal cortex. The hippocampus consists of two interdigitated structures: the dentate gyrus (DG) and cornu ammonis (CA), of which regions CA1 and CA3 feature prominently in many models. Researchers often refer to the classical trisynaptic circuitry of the hippocampus, which consists of a feed-forward flow of information between the different structures (Amaral and Witter, 1989). As shown in **Figure 1**, entorhinal cortex layer II projects via the perforant path to the dentate gyrus. The DG projects via the mossy fibers to region CA3; region CA3 contains extensive excitatory recurrent collaterals (the longitudinal association fibers) and also projects on to region CA1 via the Schaffer collaterals. Region CA1 projects back directly and via the subiculum to entorhinal cortex layer IV. In addition to the trisynaptic circuit, there are also direct projections from entorhinal cortex layers II and III to regions CA3 and CA1 of the hippocampus.

In the recent integrated system models (Hasselmo and Wyble, 1997; Hasselmo and Eichenbaum, 2005),

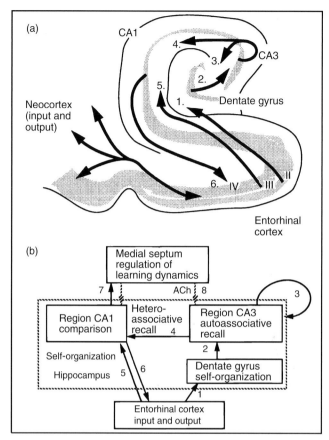

Figure 1 (a) Anatomical connectivity of the hippocampal formation. Connections between the hippocampus and multimodal association cortices pass through the entorhinal cortex. (1) Fibers of the perforant path connect layers II and III of the entorhinal cortex with the dentate gyrus. (2) The dentate gyrus projects to subregion CA3 via the mossy fibers. (3) Longitudinal association fibers connect pyramidal cells within subregion CA3. (4) The Schaffer collaterals connect subregion CA3 with subregion CA1. (5) Perforant path connections also enter subregion CA1 from the entorhinal cortex. (6) Projections back from subregion CA1 enter layer IV of the entorhinal cortex, either directly or via the subiculum. Subregion CA1 can influence activity in the medial septum either directly or via connections with the lateral septum. The medial septum (and the vertical limb of the diagonal band of Broca) provides cholinergic modulation to all hippocampal subregions. (b) Proposed function of individual anatomical subregions in the model by Hasselmo and Wyble (1997). The entorhinal cortex provides input from neocortical structures and transmits output back to neocortical structures. (1) Perforant path synapses undergo rapid self-organization to form new representations of patterns presented sequentially to the entorhinal cortex. (2) Mossy fibers pass the sparse new representation on to subregion CA1 for autoassociative storage. (3) Excitatory feedback in subregion CA3 mediates autoassociative storage and recall of these representations. (4) Schaffer collaterals mediate heteroassociative storage and recall of associations between activity in subregion CA3 and the self-organized representations formed by entorhinal input to subregion CA1. (5) Perforant path inputs to subregion CA1 undergo self-organization, forming new representations of entorhinal cortex input for comparison with recall from subregion CA3. (6) Feedback from subregion CA1 stores associations between activity in CA1 and in entorhinal cortex, allowing representations in subregion CA1 to activate the associated activity patterns in entorhinal cortex layer IV. (7) Output from subregion CA1 regulates cholinergic modulation, allowing a mismatch between recall and input to increase acetylcholine (ACh) and a match between recall and input to decrease ACh. (8) ACh from the medial septum sets appropriate dynamics for learning of new information in the model.

the network representations of individual subregions have the following functions:

1. Entorhinal cortex layer II (ECII). Network activity elicited by input to this model region represents the activity induced in entorhinal cortex in response to experimental stimuli. For example, the presentation of specific words in a behavioral experiment, as well as the shared experimental context, elicits representative patterns of activity in ECII.

2. Dentate gyrus (DG). The network model of this structure forms self-organized representations of each input pattern in ECII. The overlap between stored item and temporal context-specific representations in DG is reduced compared with the corresponding sequence of patterns of activity in ECII. The resulting patterns of output activity in DG target neurons in region CA3.

3. Region CA3. This modeled region encodes and retrieves associations between the shared experimental context (e.g., episode) and the individual items (e.g., words). The CA3 network activity provides the driving force for memory function in the model.

4. Region CA1. This modeled network structure compares the direct input from entorhinal cortex with the output of region CA3. In Hasselmo and Wyble (1997), the output of region CA1 regulates levels of acetylcholine on the basis of how well CA3 retrieval matches direct input. In Hasselmo and Eichenbaum (2005), the convergence of spreading activity in the entorhinal cortex and of episodic retrieval activity in region CA3 generates spiking activity in CA1 that identifies prior temporal context-specific events needed to make a decision at a choice-point in a delayed spatial alternation task.

5. Medial septum. The model network of this region in Hasselmo and Wyble (1997) sets the level of acetylcholine in all the other regions. In our integrated system model of hippocampal function, modulation by acetylcholine influences synaptic modification, synaptic transmission, depolarization, and adaptation.

6. Entorhinal cortex layer IV (ECIV). This modeled region stores associations between the full input patterns and the compressed representations from region CA1, allowing full retrieval of patterns. In prior work by one of the authors (Koene, 2001), this decoding stage emphasized learned connectivity from region CA1 to subiculum and ECIV.

Other connectionist approaches modeling these individual functions are described in the following text.

A number of subregion-specific models have focused on the significance of the perforant path synapses that link the output of entorhinal cortex to the DG (Marr, 1971; McNaughton and Morris, 1987; Eichenbaum and Buckingham, 1990; Treves and Rolls, 1994). It is a common hypothesis that the perforant path synapses encode representations of the patterns of afferent input activity that are manifested by sparse or nonoverlapping, distributed patterns of activity in the DG. Such sparse representations are especially useful to a hippocampal function for the encoding of episodic memory after a single occurrence of a sequence of individual patterns of input activity, in which the individual patterns of simultaneous activity are familiar. This is also called one-shot episodic learning. Recent theory and modeling have begun to address the questions of when and how such sparse representations may be generated and modified in tasks that involve multiple stimulus episodes in which specific patterns of activity may interfere (Koene, 2001; Koene and Hasselmo, 2006). In the section titled 'Dentate gyrus: Generating representations that minimize interference,' we address the issue of 'catastrophic interference' (McCloskey and Cohen, 1989) and the ways in which models of hippocampal memory function deal with that concern.

The Schaffer collateral fibers are another important hippocampal synaptic pathway. Those fibers transfer the output activity of subregion CA3 to subregion CA1. A common hypothesis is that the Schaffer collateral fibers mediate heteroassociative memory function (McNaughton, 1991; Treves, 1995). If this is so, then activity in CA1 may be predicted to a significant degree by the activity in CA3 (Levy, 1989). The involvement of the Schaffer collateral fibers in heteroassociative memory function has been explored in modeling studies with differing hypotheses about their precise role in the process. Possible self-regulation of learning and recall was studied in models specifically of the Schaffer collaterals (Hasselmo and Schnell, 1994), as well as in more inclusive models of the hippocampal network (Hasselmo and Stern, 1996; Hasselmo et al., 1996, 1998). In another set of hippocampal network models, the bulk of heteroassociative memory function was assumed to occur within the CA3 network, and the involvement of the Schaffer collateral fibers was constrained to delivering the activity of heteroassociative memory function to neurons in region CA1 (Jensen and Lisman, 1996; Koene et al., 2003).

The desire to pinpoint the hippocampal structure in which heteroassociative memory function is enabled has frequently focused on the possible function of the third set of significant fibers in the hippocampus, the longitudinal association fibers (or recurrent fibers) within region CA3. One common hypothesis is that the longitudinal association fibers within region CA3 mediate autoassociative memory function (Marr, 1971; McNaughton and Morris, 1987; Eichenbaum and Buckingham, 1990; Treves and Rolls, 1992; Lisman, 1999). The other common hypothesis is that these association fibers mediate episodic memory by encoding temporal sequences of spiking patterns at the synapses of fibers that connect pyramidal neurons within region CA3 (Levy, 1989; Minai and Levy, 1994; Levy et al., 1995; Jensen and Lisman, 1996; Hasselmo and Eichenbaum, 2005). Models that focused exclusively on the recurrent CA3 network have studied autoassociative learning and retrieval (Hasselmo et al., 1995; Levy et al., 1995). More recently, models of autoassociative function mediated by such a recurrent network have been incorporated into more general (hierarchical) models of the integral hippocampal system (Hasselmo and Stern, 1996; Hasselmo et al., 1996, 2002b; Jensen and Lisman, 1996; Koene et al., 2003; Hasselmo and Eichenbaum, 2005; Koene and Hasselmo, 2007b).

The integral system models of hippocampal and entorhinal memory function tend to include a (sub)-set of modeled subregions, most commonly including networks of entorhinal cortex and hippocampal subregions CA3 and CA1. Each subregion is generally represented by local network circuitry. Those networks receive input and deliver output through connections that represent a subset of the known anatomical pathways in the medial temporal lobes. For example, the Hasselmo and Wyble (1997) model of cholinergically modulated learning and recall includes networks representing ECII, ECIII, DG, hippocampal subregions CA3 and CA1, and ECIV.

This system model is depicted in **Figure 2**. A similarly complex model of episodic recall by Lisman et al. (2005) includes networks that represent hippocampal subregion CA3 and that separately represent the mossy and granule cell layers of the DG. In recent models of temporal context-dependent episodic memory in the hippocampus that were used to simulate behavioral experiments with rodents in spatial tasks, modeling involved the specification of networks representing layer II and III of the entorhinal cortex, the DG, and hippocampal subregions CA3 and CA1, as well as the interactions mediated by fiber pathways between the modeled subregions (Hasselmo and Eichenbaum, 2005; Koene and Hasselmo, 2007b).

1.35.3 Encoding and Retrieval of Items within a Context Cue Presented in Layer II of Entorhinal Cortex

Our understanding of the physiology and of the biophysics of neurons in ECII has improved greatly in recent years (Klink and Alonso, 1997; Fransén et al., 2002), as have the available data about the task-specific responses of neurons from electrophysiology performed in ECII (Hafting et al., 2005). It is now known that both the pyramidal and stellate cell types in ECII can exhibit rhythmic activity during specific tasks and can sustain persistent repeated firing following specific stimulation protocols. Klink and Alonso (1997) showed that an after-depolarizing response exhibited by pyramidal cells in ECII can sustain rhythmic spiking once action potentials are elicited by a short period of depolarization or by synaptic input. These characteristic neural responses in ECII resemble earlier findings about neurons in the prefrontal cortex (Andrade, 1991). The apparent possibility that synaptic input can elicit intrinsic spiking without relying on excitatory fiber loops or synfire chains (Abeles et al., 1993) gave rise to a novel mechanistic hypothesis for short-term spike buffering introduced by Lisman and Idiart (1995). Since then, models of working memory that are based on intrinsic neuron dynamics have been investigated and used as networks specially suited to the rapid acquisition and ordered maintenance of sequences or temporal cues of patterns of spikes (Jensen et al., 1996; Koene and Hasselmo, 2007a). A buffered sequence of spike patterns can be repeatedly delivered to the hippocampus for episodic encoding (Jensen and Lisman, 1996; Koene et al., 2003).

In vivo electrophysiology during spatial tasks has shown that neurons in medial ECII respond in a spatial-location-specific manner that has some resemblance with the place cell activity commonly attributed to hippocampal pyramidal cells (Fyhn et al., 2004), although the place fields associated with location-specific activity in ECII can be large and overlapping with multiple peak response locations. Responses of stellate cells in rat layer II of dorsocaudal medial entorhinal cortex also appear to be rhythmic and directly related to location in a spatial task, but in contrast to the activity of the pyramidal cells, Hafting et al. (2005) found that the place-specific responses of the stellate cells in ECII change in spike frequency with distance from spatial grid points of maximum spike frequency. Active grid

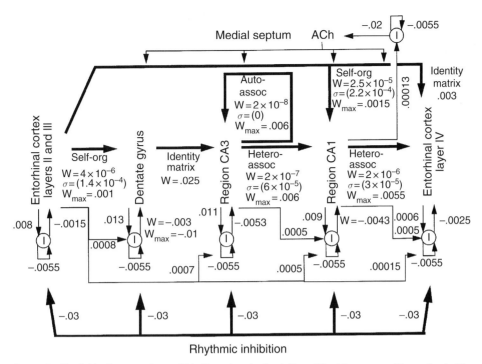

Figure 2 Strength of individual connections within the network simulation of the hippocampal formation in Hasselmo and Wyble (1997). When a single number is specified, this is the homogeneous strength of a set of nonmodifiable connections. When three numbers are specified, these are the mean initial strength, the standard deviation of the initial strength, and the maximum possible strength of a set of modifiable connections. Each modeled layer of entorhinal cortex contained 40 excitatory units, while the other hippocampal subregions each contained ten excitatory context units and 50 excitatory item units. Excitatory connections between regions represent the perforant path projecting from layer III of entorhinal cortex to dentate gyrus, layer III of entorhinal cortex to subregion CA1, the mossy fibers from dentate gyrus to CA3, the recurrent longitudinal association fibers in subregion CA3, the Schaffer collaterals from CA3 to CA1, and projection back from subregion CA1 to layer IV of entorhinal cortex. In each region the pyramidal cells are fully connected with an inhibitory interneuron (marked I) by excitatory connections of the strength shown. The inhibitory interneuron sends back inhibitory connections of the strength shown. In the dentate gyrus and subregion CA1, these inhibitory connections had random initial strength and were modifiable.

points of a particular stellate cell appear throughout an extended spatial field, and the grid points form equilateral triangles. The spatial frequency that is defined by the distance between grid points of an active ECII stellate cell increases when recording from cells in the dorsal medial ECII toward cells in the ventral medial ECII. The possibility that combinations of the rate-coded activity of multiple grid cells can act as a coordinate system that determines a precise spatial location has led to the development of models of path integration that incorporate this stellate activity in ECII as part of the information into the hippocampal system (O'Keefe and Burgess, 2005).

Other connectionist modeling of the memory function of ECII emphasizes encoding of representative patterns for use in hippocampal memory function. In Hasselmo and Wyble (1997), context-

dependent encoding of specific word stimuli is assumed to occur in ECII. The corresponding connectionist network model that does this encoding was tested with regard to its performance in subsequent recognition or free recall of the words. In the simulations, both individual words and experimental contexts were represented by binary patterns of activity that were presented to the ECII and ECIII networks of the model. The binary patterns of activity used were strongly overlapping and were chosen randomly. The assumption that underlies the use of separate item and context representation is that a persevering context, provided by input due to (1) environmental features present during trials, (2) features of the presentation medium, and (3) the presence of the experimenter, results in cortical activity that is largely nonoverlapping with item input activity. Each individual word belonged to a specific list, and the representative patterns of words from the same list were always given in association with the same consistent representation of context. During the presentation of a pattern of activity, which was maintained for 400 time steps of the simulation, the network activity caused by the input propagated to all other subregions of the modeled hippocampal system. In this manner and by manipulation of the model functions, the effects of scopolamine (Ghoneim and Mewaldt, 1975) could be described. A similar representation of stimuli has been used in previous connectionist models of free recall (Metcalfe and Murdock, 1981; Metcalfe Eich, 1982; Gillund and Shiffrin, 1984).

Free recall and recognition test different aspects of memory retrieval. A common means to elicit recognition retrieval in connectionist models is to present partial input patterns. By contrast, free recall tests require that subjects recall items from a list without being given item-specific cues. In the integral hippocampal system model of Hasselmo and Wyble (1997), either type of retrieval could be elicited by providing the corresponding appropriate input to the modeled entorhinal networks. To simulate free recall, only the activity pattern representing a context cue was presented to layers II and III of model entorhinal cortex. The resulting entorhinal activity evoked context-specific activity in the model networks of DG and of hippocampal subregion CA3. In the associative CA3 network, the context cue elicited activity that represents individual items. If one of the item patterns of activity produced in CA3 matched a pattern of activity that was elicited in ECIV in response to the context cue, then successful recall was achieved.

To test the recognition of events in an episode or items from a list in a connectionist model, it is necessary to explicitly avoid presenting a cue that is a partial representation of one learned item. In tests of recognition with human subjects, the subjects are given lists that contain words from a learned list, as well as distractor words. They are instructed to identify words that were encountered during the encoding phase of the experiment. A similar protocol can be simulated in connectionist models. For example, in the model of Hasselmo and Wyble (1997), this was simulated by presenting to layers II and III of the model entorhinal cortex a sequence containing some known and some unknown item patterns. In simulations, the propagation of activity allowed the known item patterns to elicit the retrieval of a corresponding context pattern in the CA3 network. A

recognition process of this sort was first proposed by Hollingworth (1913), which led Tulving and Norman (Norman, 1968; Tulving, 1975) to hypothesize that recognition was the inverse function of recall.

Another issue that concerns the presentation of input at entorhinal cortex layers of a hippocampal system model is the relationship between presentation frequency and recognition, the effect of familiarity. This issue was addressed by several connectionist models (Metcalfe and Murdock, 1981; Gillund and Shiffrin, 1984; Hintzman, 1988; Chappell and Humphreys, 1994) and was restated in the integral system model of Hasselmo and Wyble (1997). There and in similar system models, the effect that cue familiarity has on simulated recognition performance may be observed in terms of the temporal delay before a context or item pattern is reactivated by retrieval. This method has been suggested for studies of temporal delays in ECIV.

The potential roles of the entorhinal cortex in models of learning and memory, as the perforant path input to the integrative processing in the hippocampus, are likely to inspire a major part of the modeling and experimental efforts in coming years. In addition to the sustained and specialized rhythmic responses supported by pyramidal and stellate cells in ECII, novel types of intrinsic spiking responses are now known to occur in ECIII and ECV. In layer III, induced sustained spiking may be maintained until deactivated by an equivalent stimulus, regardless of intervening hyperpolarization (Fransén et al., 2006b). In layer V, successive instances of induced depolarization produce a graded increase in the frequency of a sustained spiking response, while following instances of hyperpolarization cause a graded decrease of the sustained spike frequency (Fransén et al., 2006a). Each of these characteristic responses implies a nonsynaptic neural memory function that can play a specialized role in learning and memory.

1.35.4 Dentate Gyrus: Generating Representations That Minimize Interference

Recent models of learning and memory in the hippocampal system propose that the neurons of the DG may self-organize to form novel and sparse (nonoverlapping) ensembles that are associated with a unique temporal context (Hasselmo and Eichenbaum, 2005). In this case, such a temporal context is identified as a sequence of input activity that originates in the entorhinal cortex, as well as through associations that were established with episodic sequences of patterns of activity in region CA3 of the hippocampus. The unique representations of successive temporal contexts that may be generated in DG could establish associations between those representations within the DG that reflect a specific temporal order. Such associations within the DG may be established through synaptic modification in the fibers that connect the mossy and granule cell layers of DG (Lisman, 1999; Lisman et al., 2005).

Unique coding for temporal context in DG may provide a route of direct access through which input to the DG can cue the retrieval of episodic memory stored by the hippocampus. A process by which unique representations may be generated by coincidental activity has been postulated in earlier studies (Koene, 2001). In connectionist models, a temporal context may be represented as a continually changing sequence of input activity. Presentation of such a sequence to the hippocampus may be aided by a first-in, first-out buffer in ECII, thereby providing a sliding window in which activity is repeatedly presented in order (Koene and Hasselmo, 2007a). The representation of temporal context has been described formally in terms of context drift and its potential significance with respect to the recency and contiguity effects in human recall performance (Howard and Kahana, 2002; Howard et al., in press). Recent unpublished data by J. Manns, obtained by recording in subregion CA1, provides supporting electrophysiological evidence of a mechanism that supports contiguity of context representations.

Connectionist networks, unlike human brains, are prone to a type of forgetting called 'catastrophic interference,' which is not gradual as during normal forgetting observed in experiments with humans (Barnes and Underwood, 1959). When new data interfere catastrophically with existing stored memory in connectionist networks, the earlier memory can be erased rapidly and completely by the interference effects. Attractor neural network models can avoid catastrophic interference by using a protocol of interleaved learning. During interleaved learning, items of a list are presented multiple times in randomized order (McClelland et al., 1995; Hasselmo, 1999).

In humans, interleaved learning may indeed occur during a gradual process of transfer from the hippocampus and memory consolidation in neocortical regions of the brain. For such consolidation to be possible, new information that is generally believed to be processed as part of hippocampal function must first be acquired and encoded in the hippocampal system. During this initial encoding, interleaved learning is not generally feasible, since animals and humans cannot exert absolute control over the environment from which stimuli appear. It will often be impossible or undesirable (as in the case of dangerous events) to repeat stimuli or to randomize their order during repeated presentations (as in the case of causal events). One-shot encoding of episodes is possible without risking catastrophic interference if nonoverlapping representations are involved, as in the case of the unique coding that was hypothesized in DG, as described in preceding paragraphs. A number of spiking neuron models (integrate-and-fire models) of hippocampal function use encoding with sparse patterns in portions of modeled hippocampal network hierarchy to avoid catastrophic interference. In those models, the separated patterns of activity can be maintained in a short-term buffer to repeat ordered presentations that elicit activity in the hippocampus and encode episodic associations (Jensen et al., 1996; Jensen and Lisman, 1996; Koene, 2001; Koene et al., 2003; Hasselmo and Eichenbaum, 2005).

This supposed function of the DG has been described in some connectionist models as a competitive network. There, it is proposed that the divergent connections from entorhinal cortex to DG distribute overlapping input patterns into sparse nonoverlapping representations that reduce interference (McNaughton, 1991; Treves and Rolls, 1994). A detailed analysis of the modification of perforant path synapses by O'Reilly and McClelland (1994) showed that modification can enhance pattern separation, but that study did not explicitly focus on the sequential presentation of different input patterns. A modification of perforant path synapses was explicitly considered when sequences of input were presented in the Hasselmo and Wyble (1997) model. The excitatory perforant path connections from layer II of model entorhinal cortex to the DG network consequently achieved self-organization: random initial connection strengths from ECII to DG resulted in the initial activation of a subset of DG neurons; the connections from active ECII neurons to activated DG neurons were strengthened; the connections from inactive ECII neurons were weakened by synaptic decay in response to the postsynaptic activity; connections from active ECII neurons to inactive DG neurons were weakened due to presynaptically regulated synaptic decay. The effect of these model mechanisms corresponded to experimental evidence, which has shown that strengthening of perforant path synapses depends on pre- and postsynaptic activity (McNaughton et al., 1978; Levy and Steward, 1979), while weakening of connections has been similarly demonstrated (Levy and Steward, 1979). In Hasselmo and Wyble (1997), the model mechanism was able to establish selective patterns of connectivity between active neurons in the ECII network and neurons in the DG network. The process produced sparsified, less overlapping representations for each of the item patterns that were presented in trial sequences.

The model in Hasselmo and Wyble (1997) did require a novel mechanism to prevent previously established representations from dominating the learning elicited by new pattern input. The novel mechanism involved strengthening the connections from active inhibitory interneurons in DG to active neurons in DG (Hasselmo et al., 1996, 1998). Such inhibitory synaptic enhancement has been demonstrated in other regions of the hippocampus (Haas and Rose, 1984; Morishita and Sastry, 1991; Grunze et al., 1996). The resulting suppression of neurons that participated in previously encountered representations insured that different patterns of activity were elicited in DG by subsequent patterns of entorhinal cortex activity.

The connectionist proposal that DG rapidly establishes new memory patterns to represent changing input leads to neural network models that rely of different rates of learning in DG networks and in networks that represent a hippocampal subregion such as CA3. In Hasselmo and Wyble (1997), this need was met by assuming different thresholds for synaptic modification in the two regions. In more recent models, the comparative ease with which spiking has been shown to occur in cells of the dentate granule layer is explicitly taken into consideration, so that the resulting simulations further suggest that comparatively rapid encoding takes place at synapses in the DG (Lisman et al., 2005; Koene and Hasselmo, 2007b).

1.35.5   CA3: Forming Attractors and Associations between Attractors during Rhythmic Oscillation at Theta Frequency

The hippocampus is essential to the ability of humans to easily acquire new episodic memory. One-shot learning is known to occur, in which known stimuli are presented only once in a specific order. One-shot episodic learning may depend critically on a combination of subregion-specific learning functions. In DG, nonoverlapping and therefore noninterfering representations can be made of activity that originates in and may be buffered in the entorhinal cortex. In subregion CA3, associative memory may be encoded by the LTP of the synapses of excitatory recurrent fibers (the longitudinal fibers of subregion CA3). Jensen and Lisman (1996) have demonstrated successful simulations with a model that combines these elements and achieves one-shot learning of novel episodes that are composed of known item patterns. In that integrate-and-fire network model, item representations are patterns of simultaneous spikes, and individual patterns are separated by competitive recurrent inhibition due to the activation of a network of interneurons after each pattern of item spikes. Lisman and Idiart (1995) theorized that the separation of spike patterns by such inhibition may explain the appearance of gamma frequency in the power spectrum during working memory tasks.

A model of episodic acquisition similar to that of Jensen and Lisman (1996) incorporates novel insights about the modulatory effect of theta rhythm in the hippocampus (Hasselmo et al., 2002a; *See* Chapter 1.37). During each cycle of the simulated theta rhythm in this model, the phase of maximum neuronal membrane depolarization in region CA3 coincides with a suppression of the strength of afferent input transmission. Conditions during that phase favor associative retrieval via the recurrent fibers in subregion CA3. Conversely, conditions at the opposite phase of the theta rhythm encourage the receipt and encoding of novel associations in accordance with afferent input. During that opposite phase of rhythmic modulation, recurrent synaptic transmission is suppressed, and LTP of those synapses is more readily elicited (Hyman et al., 2003).

The theory of differential functional modulation during different phase intervals of the theta rhythm that is observed during hippocampal memory tasks inspired the development of a new category of models of hippocampal episodic memory (Hasselmo et al., 2002b,c; Cannon et al., 2003). In these models, memory encoding and memory retrieval alternate within each cycle of the theta rhythm. Complex integral system models include both the proposed neural network mechanism of buffered (Lisman and Idiart, 1995; Koene and Hasselmo, 2007a) one-shot episodic learning (Jensen et al., 1996; Jensen and Lisman, 1996) and the proposed biophysical model mechanism of alternating encoding and retrieval conditions. These system models with integrate-and-fire neurons react dynamically to feedback from the environment in response to actions taken and, therefore, perform successfully in tasks during which the need for memory encoding or memory retrieval may not be easily predicted or may be required in a concurrent or ongoing manner (Hasselmo et al., 2002b; Koene et al., 2003). During phase-locked conditions favorable to memory encoding, buffered sequences of spike patterns cause synaptic modification at recurrent excitatory fibers in model subregion CA3 and in model ECIII. During phase-locked conditions favorable to memory retrieval, activity spreads along strengthened connections within the recurrent networks, thereby retrieving representative spike patterns that provide information about known feature associations and heteroassociative information about encountered episodes.

The allocation of network roles in terms of stored association type is a continuing source of debate. For example, in models by Hasselmo et al. (2002b) and by Koene et al. (2003), feature (or place) associations were stored in a network representing subregion CA3, and heteroassociative storage occurred in a network representing ECIII. In later models by Hasselmo and Eichenbaum (2005) and by Koene and Hasselmo (2007b), the roles of the two recurrent networks were reversed. In either case, it was assumed that a convergence of streams of spreading activity in the two recurrent networks elicited spike activity at pyramidal neurons in hippocampal subregion CA1. The spiking of neurons in subregion CA1 can inform actions to be taken to successfully perform a specific task. The models of rhythmically alternating encoding and retrieval, and of activity that is gated by converging streams of spreading activity during retrieval, were applied together by Koene et al. (2003) to successfully simulate the performance of rat spatial navigation and by McGaughy et al. (2005) to simulate conditioned responses in a delayed nonmatch to sample task.

A number of connectionist models have proposed that hippocampal subregion CA3 provides autoassociative memory function, based on the extensive and strong excitatory recurrent connectivity in that neural network (McNaughton and Morris, 1987; Levy, 1989; Eichenbaum and Buckingham, 1990; Treves and Rolls, 1992; Hasselmo et al., 1995; Hasselmo and Stern, 1996). In contrast to the biophysical and structural complexity of the models described in preceding paragraphs, neural network models with excitatory recurrent connections that focus on the principles of attractor networks have been used extensively to model memory function (Little and Shaw, 1975; Anderson et al., 1977; Hopfield, 1982; Anderson, 1983; Ruppin and Yeshurun, 1991; Chappell and Humphreys, 1994; Hasselmo et al., 1995; *See* Chapters 1.33, 1.34). Those networks have the characteristics of fixed-point attractor models, due to recurrent connections with specific patterns of connection strengths. When network activity settles into final stable states, those stable states represent stored memories. Each final stable state may be reached by a different state of initial activity.

From a computational perspective, fixed-point attractors present an appealing model of human memory function, since the final memory states can exhibit robustness to variation in the input cues. Therefore, attractor dynamics are particularly useful for models that are used to simulate free recall. In tests of free recall, the input cues are relatively weak, and associations with an experimental context are shared by a number of items in the same list. Given initial activity that reflects these item and context input characteristics, free recall performance is simulated when attractor dynamics lead from the initial state to a final stable state that is a known representation in the trial context. It is worth noting that attractor dynamics in a more biophysically detailed model of hippocampal subregion CA3 may mediate the retrieval of autoassociative memory, even if network activity does not settle into persisting fixed-point attractors. The dynamics of activity in subregion CA3 may nonetheless be dominated by the approach to an attractor, during the interval defined by a single oscillation at gamma frequency, or during complex spike activity.

As perpetuated in recent system models (Hasselmo and Eichenbaum, 2005; Koene and Hasselmo, 2007b), the hypothesized role in Hasselmo and Wyble (1997) for the memory function of subregion CA3 was that of an attractor network that specialized in the formation of robust episodic representations of items and context. These associations were learned by modifying excitatory recurrent connection strengths, so that attractor states were encoded. The encoding of weaker associative links between context and item attractors was also assumed. Free recall and recognition were primarily achieved through the attractor dynamics. During encoding, the activity of a sufficiently active unit in model DG propagates through an identity matrix of connections that represent mossy fibers to activate individual CA3 units. In the presence of cholinergic suppression, the pattern of activity in the model is determined primarily by this afferent input, instead of being subject to strong recurrent excitation. Consequently, the connections between neurons that were activated by input from the DG are selectively strengthened, which results in increased activity in model subregion CA3 and a greater output of activity to subregion CA1.

Earlier studies have explored the stability of the CA3 network when modeled with a number of different patterns of connectivity (Minai and Levy, 1994). In comparatively abstract neural network models, the possibility of an exponential explosion of excitatory activity is prevented by assuming that total activity is normalized (Treves and Rolls, 1992). In continuous-firing-rate models, a similar limitation of network activity is achieved through the use of feedback inhibition (Hasselmo et al., 1995; Hasselmo and Wyble, 1997). The same method may be applied in spiking neuron models.

In the Hasselmo and Wyble (1997) integral system model, increased activity in subregion CA1 causes a decrease in simulated cholinergic modulation throughout the model network, which in turn causes greater recurrent excitation in subregion CA3. Therefore, it is possible to enter a stable fixed-point attractor pattern that represents a stored context or item, if a pattern of cue activity is presented. An emerging item or context attractor state can (a) drive ensuing activity into an associated item or context attractor state, and (b) drive output activity in region CA1 and ECIV. Attractor states are terminated in the model by neural adaptation and by the rhythmic inhibition through interneuron activity, which is a model mechanism of hippocampal theta rhythm (Bland and Colom, 1993).

With the model mechanisms in Hasselmo and Wyble (1997), free recall is simulated when a cue elicits a context attractor state in model subregion CA3. The activity spreads into a number of weakly associated item attractor states in CA3. As the activity of item attractor states grows, they compete by inhibiting each other. At most one winning attractor state persists, which represents the free recall of an item. That attractor state is eventually terminated by cyclic inhibition, so that the context attractor can evoke the attractor state of another associated item. Inhibitory oscillations have been shown to provide a potent means of competitive neural network learning (Norman, 2006).

Recognition is simulated when input of an individual learned item pattern of activity in model ECII elicits the corresponding item attractor state in subregion CA3. When a familiar item attractor state is reached, that attractor elicits associated context attractor activity. Such context attractor activity does not appear for novel items.

1.35.6 CA1: Comparing and Gating of Input from Region CA3 and Entorhinal Cortex

There are two common functional hypotheses concerning the arrangement of synapses in the important Schaffer collateral fiber path from hippocampal subregion CA3 to subregion CA1. The first supposes that the Schaffer collaterals undergo a process of self-organization (Treves and Rolls, 1994). The second supposes that the Schaffer collaterals provide a heteroassociative memory function (McNaughton, 1991). The two are not mutually exclusive, and the relative amount of these two functions depends upon how strongly the Schaffer collaterals influence activity in subregion CA1.

If the Schaffer collaterals dominate postsynaptic activity in region CA1 during learning, then they will predominantly undergo self-organization. This must be assumed if no mechanism for the modulation of synaptic transmission is incorporated in models. However, in models that include the cholinergic suppression of synaptic transmission at the Schaffer collaterals, the perforant path input can more strongly influence CA1 activity during learning, thereby allowing heteroassociative memory function. The heteroassociative memory function may be necessary if it is assumed that one of the functions of subregion CA1 is to provide a comparison between the recall activity generated by subregion CA3 and episodes of direct input transferred from entorhinal cortex, as has been proposed by some researchers (Levy, 1989; Eichenbaum and Buckingham, 1990; Lisman, 1999).

Experimental results have shown that the strength of input from entorhinal cortex to subregion CA1 is insufficient to achieve significant activation in subregion CA1, unless supported by converging input from hippocampal subregion CA3. The Schaffer collateral input from CA3 therefore gates the activation of neurons in subregion CA1. In this regard, recent integral system models of the hippocampal system, such as the model of Hasselmo and Eichenbaum (2005) and the model of Koene and Hasselmo (2007b), implement an explicit mechanism of convergence and gating of activity in CA1 by Schaffer collateral input.

The model of Hasselmo and Wyble (1997) proposes that, during sequential self-organization in DG, similar self-organization also takes place in subregion CA1, resulting in a similar modification of excitatory and inhibitory connections. The possibility of long-term changes of inhibitory potentials is supported by considerable data obtained by recording in subregion CA1 (Grunze et al., 1996). During encoding of a novel pattern, random initial connection strengths of the activated Schaffer collateral fibers elicits a distributed pattern of activity in subregion CA1. This postsynaptic activity can interact with the presynaptic activity of input from perforant path fibers to form a new self-organized representation. Hasselmo and Wyble supposed that during recall, even though the perforant path input initially has a greater influence on the activity of subregion CA1, those patterns of Schaffer collateral activity that represent familiar stimuli are a sufficient match to perforant path input, so that the output of CA1 elicits a reduction of the cholinergic modulation. One consequence of this is the removal of cholinergic suppression of synaptic transmission through the Schaffer collateral fibers. Then, the input to CA1 through Schaffer collaterals comes to dominate activity there. The mode suggests that it is through such a mechanism that the output activity of hippocampal subregion CA3 can drive the neural activity in subregion CA1 to produce a pattern of activity that is associated with memory retrieved in CA3.

1.35.7 Medial Septum: Feedback Regulation of Cholinergic Modulation and Selective Emphasis of Encoding or Retrieval

In the regulatory system of cholinergic modulation that was supposed in the models discussed in preceding paragraphs, the propagation of hippocampal activity through the medial septum has been explicitly associated with the feedback regulation and consequent selective emphasis of memory encoding or memory retrieval processes. In recent simulation studies, the proposed selection mechanism has been further refined to include ongoing alternation of preferential encoding and retrieval in separate phase intervals of each cycle of theta rhythm. Rhythmic modulation of hippocampal networks at theta frequency establishes opposing periods of relative

depolarization and relative hyperpolarization of the neural membrane.

In Hasselmo et al. (2002a), this network-wide modulation of membrane potentials is combined with the aforementioned phase-locked selective suppression of recurrent or afferent fiber transmission during distinct intervals of the theta rhythm. Also included was an explicit mechanism of the theta-phase specific effectiveness of LTP in the hippocampus (Hyman et al., 2003). The sum of the theta-modulated transmission and plasticity effects may enable alternation between conditions that favor encoding and conditions that favor retrieval during each theta cycle. This model of ongoing encoding and retrieval has been applied successfully to simulated spatial navigation tasks (Hasselmo et al., 2002b; Koene et al., 2003) and to delayed nonmatch to sample tasks (McGaughy et al., 2005), as well as to a biophysical implementation of reinforcement learning in prefrontal cortex (Koene and Hasselmo, 2005).

According to Hasselmo and Wyble (1997), the level of output activity elicited in subregion CA1 is a direct determinant of activity in the medial septum. That in turn determines the degree of cholinergic modulation that is applied to all modeled subregions through connections from the medial septum. The cholinergic modulation was deemed responsible for all cellular effects of acetylcholine, namely: (1) selective suppression of synaptic transmission at connections from neurons in CA3 through recurrent connections to other neurons in CA3, and at connections from neurons in CA3 to neurons in CA1, as well as at connections from neurons in CA1 to neurons in the entorhinal cortex; (2) network-wide depolarization of all neurons; (3) suppression of adaptation in the response of excitatory neurons; and (4) enhancement of synaptic plasticity (Hyman et al., 2003). In the model implementation, default levels of cholinergic modulation were high, and changes were effected by the active inhibition of cholinergic input. This inhibition was hypothesized to occur due to the activation of interneurons in the medial septum by output activity from subregion CA1.

In summary therefore, when both the output activity from model subregion CA3 to CA1 and the activity delivered to CA1 via the perforant path generate a match and elicit consequent activity in the CA1 network, then the output activity from CA1 feeds back into the hippocampal system in the form of a decrease of cholinergic modulation via the medial septum, which was proposed to effectively switch the modeled hippocampal networks from encoding to retrieval dynamics. This proposed switching system has a slower time course than the rhythmic alternation of modulation that was proposed in Hasselmo et al. (2002a) and subsequent published models.

1.35.8 The Translation of Representations in Layer IV of Entorhinal Cortex and Feedback to the Neocortex

ECIV receives direct input from ECII. For this reason, layer IV may be considered an ideal network in which activity represents the output of the hippocampal system during simulations of tests of free recall and of recognition (Hasselmo and Wyble, 1997). Simulated activity elicited in ECII is transmitted directly to ECIV, propagation that is done through an identity matrix of connections in the model. During the initial learning of a novel pattern, it is that input which dominates activity in layer IV of model entorhinal cortex. After all, feedback from subregion CA1 is suppressed by cholinergic modulation during this time. Associations between the patterns of activity in ECIV and the activity of episodic representations in subregion CA1 are encoded.

During simulated retrieval, partial input cues given to the ECII network result in inactive or incomplete item pattern activity in ECIV. Those patterns of activity can be completed only once output activity spreads from subregion CA1 to ECIV, which can reconstitute previously encoded item or context information. Transmission through the feedback connections from subregion CA1 to ECIV is not suppressed during retrieval. Consequently, recognition tests could be simulated and evaluated with the model by measuring whether activity in the ECIV network generated a known context pattern when individual familiar or novel item patterns were presented (Norman and O'Reilly, 2003).

1.35.9 The Hippocampal Model of Temporal Context-Dependent Episodic Memory

Insights gained in work with earlier integral system models, such as in the models of Hasselmo and Wyble (1997), Jensen and Lisman (1996), and Koene et al. (2003), and through the application of those models to

simulated tasks that depend on the specific functions of each layer of the entorhinal cortex and subregions in the hippocampus, led those researchers to formulate novel hierarchical models. Recent models in Hasselmo and Eichenbaum (2005) and in Lisman et al. (2005) incorporate proposed functions of context-dependent episodic memory that enable complex behavioral performance in tasks such as delayed spatial alternation. Each of these models takes into consideration associative encoding on the recurrent fibers of two networks. In the case of the Hasselmo and Eichenbaum (2005) model, these networks are subregion CA3 and ECIII. In the case of the Lisman et al. (2005) model, they are subregion CA3 and the recurrent network that is formed by the reciprocal synaptic fibers between the mossy and granule cell layers of the DG. Associative encoding on the recurrent fibers in DG was also taken into account for the unique sparse encoding in DG of the models of Hasselmo and Eichenbaum (2005) and Koene and Hasselmo (2007b), although the implementation of the network was more abstract in those models.

The Hasselmo and Eichenbaum (2005) model has been applied to simulated tasks in which performance depends on the ability to concurrently encode and retrieve temporal context-dependent episodic memory. In these simulations, input activity that is elicited by stimuli in a simulated environment causes activity in a layer II network of model entorhinal cortex. In an integrate-and-fire implementation of the model hypotheses (Koene and Hasselmo, 2007b), the ECII network acts as a working memory of short sequences of sequences of spike patterns that are sustained by persistent firing characteristics of the pyramidal neurons in ECII (Koene and Hasselmo, 2007a). Several studies have addressed the possible mechanisms by which executive mechanisms and attention may gate input to working memory (Grossberg and Stone, 1986; O'Reilly and Frank, 2005). The output of the ECII network provides repeated episodes of spiking activity to the model ECIII, as well as to model subregion CA3 and model DG.

Hasselmo and Eichenbaum have proposed that the synapses of recurrent fibers in ECIII encode associations between items distinguished by specific features, such as associations between the place cells of adjacent place fields in spatial navigation tasks. In this model, the associative network properties of the DG are used to generate unique temporal context representations that are associated with a buffered episodic cue of activity in the ECII network. The third associative network, model subregion CA3, was assigned a heteroassociative role, storing episodic memories of the sequences of activity propagated from the output of ECII. During encoding, the modification of synapses at fibers from DG to CA3 creates associations between the unique temporal context-specific representations in DG and the episodic memory traces stored in subregion CA3. In this manner, activating a representation stored in the DG provides a direct way to elicit the retrieval of a specific instance of episodic memory that was stored in the hippocampus.

A significant characteristic of episodic encoding in the CA3 network of the models of Hasselmo and Eichenbaum (2005) and Koene and Hasselmo (2007b) is that episodic order is reversed in the encoded associations at recurrent fibers. Thus, during episodic retrieval in the model CA3 network, the sequence of retrieved activity can trace events in reverse, resembling reversal of activity shown during *in vivo* electrophysiology in linear track experiments (Foster and Wilson, 2006) and during spatial alternation behavior in multiple T-mazes (Johnson and Redish, 2006).

Activity in the model subregion CA1 was elicited by the convergence of spreading activity elicited during retrieval in the ECIII and CA3 recurrent networks. Simulation results with the model showed that it could successfully simulate performance in delayed spatial alternation tasks. The activity of neurons in the model subregion CA1 could be decoded to represent specific spatial locations and, in the stem of a T-maze, exhibited the selective activity and spiking behavior of experimentally observed 'splitter cells' (Hasselmo and Eichenbaum, 2005; Koene and Hasselmo, 2007b). In a spatial alternation task, splitter cells that respond to motion in the same head direction and in the same location of the stem of a T-maze fire selectively, depending on whether an animal must turn left or right at the top of the stem in order to perform a specific run of the alternation task successfully.

With the development of several hierarchical models that include the interacting functions of multiple subregions of the hippocampal system, it has become possible to simulate full-network activity and thereby to study the interactions between the subregions. Early full-network simulations focused either on behavioral phenomena (Schmajuk and DiCarlo, 1992; Gluck and Myers, 1993) or on hippocampal physiology (Rolls, 1995; Hasselmo and Stern,

1996), but the recent models explicitly simulate a combination of system behavior and biophysical detail. That combination of modeling levels has already led to new insights about mechanisms necessitated by the interaction and improved physiological realism of individual subregion networks. Full-network simulations in Hasselmo and Wyble (1997) indicated the need for inclusion of additional hippocampal subregions, so that nonoverlapping representations could be generated (DG), and so that encoding and retrieval conditions could be regulated within the simulations (a comparison function in CA1, plus medial septum). Entorhinal regions were included to decode self-organized representations in the hippocampus and allow the study of the interaction of input and output with neocortical regions. A set of simulations by Jensen et al. (1996) and by Jensen and Lisman (1996) showed how a succession of hippocampal network stages could generate incrementally more complex associative information, from short buffered sequences to auto-associative item representations and sequence representations of episodic memory, and emphasized how the characteristic physiology of N-methyl-D-aspartate (NMDA) receptors in the subregions involved could selectively mediate the different associative functions. Simulations by Koene et al. (2003) clearly demonstrate the involvement of synchronization by theta rhythm throughout the hippocampal system during active task behavior, while simulations by Hasselmo and Eichenbaum (2005) demonstrate the functional significance of spreading retrieval activity in regions CA3 and ECIII that converge in region CA1.

In Hasselmo and Wyble (1997), simulations with the neural network model were able to replicate list length and list strength effects seen in the human data.

The list strength effect appears during free recall, where list strength is the ratio of recall performance between strong items (items presented several times) and weak items (items presented once). There was no effect of list strength on performance during recognition. In the model, items interfere only when simultaneously active, such as when competing during free recall. As more items compete, simulated recall becomes more difficult, with a greater threshold for retrieval in subregion CA3.

This difference in the experimental human data, between free recall and recognition performance, was not replicated by earlier composite models, in which each item contributes to the variance of the entire system. In such models, the variance deteriorates recognition accuracy just as it deteriorates recall accuracy (Ratcliff et al., 1990). The list strength effect has been achieved differently by a model of Chappell and Humphreys (1994), in which the activity of units is controlled by intrinsic dynamics. The list length effect, which is seen during recognition, and the list strength effect are achieved by the same process in composite models. In contrast, the list length effect appears in the Hasselmo and Wyble (1997) model when the chance that a distractor item matches one of the list of items learned by DG is great enough to cause an erroneous recognition. This effect is due to increasing intrusions with longer lists, rather than due to increasing variance assumed in the composite models.

Simulations in full-network, hierarchical models of hippocampal function may also be compared to data on the effect of hippocampal lesions. Removal of a model's ability to rapidly encode episodic memory after a single presentation can simulate anterograde amnesia and partial retrograde amnesia, as experienced by patients such as HM (Scoville and Milner, 1957). Temporally graded, partial retrograde amnesia (McClelland et al., 1995) may result if episodic memories encoded with the hippocampal system are involved in a gradual formation of representations in the neocortex (Buzsáki, 1989; Treves and Rolls, 1994; Hasselmo et al., 1998). A transfer of data back from the hippocampus to deep entorhinal cortex during periods of decreased cholinergic modulation is supported by physiological data (Chrobak and Buzsáki, 1994). Compared to the more abstract and fundamental models of human memory (Gluck and Myers, 1993; Myers and Gluck, 1994), full-network simulations clarify the link between the model and specific anatomical or physiological features of the hippocampal system.

The internal representation of item activity in recent models of hippocampal function, though established through a biologically plausible rationale, has similarities with earlier and nonconnectionist models of human memory. Entorhinal activity resembles coding in composite trace models, where the individual features that compose items elicit subsets of an item representation (Metcalfe and Murdock, 1981; Murdock, 1982). By contrast, after sparse nonoverlapping encoding in DG, representations have more in common with those used in separate trace models (Gillund and Shiffrin, 1984; Hintzman, 1988). For example, the storage of representations in CA3 in (Hasselmo and Wyble, 1997)

resembles that used in the search of associative memory model (Gillund and Shiffrin, 1984), where a matrix of weights between 0 and 1 stores the relative values of associations between different items, but using attractor dynamics for retrieval. To cue retrieval, a number of hippocampal models use context (Hasselmo and Wyble, 1997; Hasselmo and Eichenbaum, 2005; Koene and Hasselmo, 2007b). Such cuing resembles the retrieval mechanism used in convolution-correlation models Metcalfe and Murdock (1981).

During retrieval, a procedure of cleanup, error correction, or pattern completion is used by many models of human memory, from the more abstract approaches (Hintzman, 1988) to those in which dynamic interactions allow activity to spread through different regions (Hasselmo and Wyble, 1997; Hasselmo and Eichenbaum, 2005). In the Lisman (1999) model, the combination of perforant path and Schaffer collateral input to CA1 allows error or novelty detection, while dynamic pattern completion during the retrieval of spiking patterns in episodic recall is enabled by recurrent activation through the reciprocal loop from CA3 to the granule and mossy cell layers of DG and back to CA3. In the Hasselmo and Wyble (1997) model, competition between different patterns in model subregion CA3 must result in a clear winner before the output of CA3 is propagated to subregion CA1 and to the model ECIV, since the model specifies that activity in CA1 can be elicited only by complete retrieved patterns.

In the model of temporal context-dependent episodic memory of Hasselmo and Eichenbaum (2005) and its variant based on integrate-and-fire neurons (Koene and Hasselmo, 2007b), spiking in CA1 can be elicited only when there is a convergence between spreading activity representing the retrieval of feature associations in entorhinal cortex and spreading activity in CA3 that represents retrieved episodic memory in the temporal context. In their implementation of cleanup, those latest models incorporate competition between items retrieved by auto- and heteroassociative attractor processes, as well as the gating of perforant path input by Schaffer collateral input, which had been demonstrated in prior full-network models (Lisman, 1999; Koene et al., 2003). In addition to this, the integrate-and-fire neuron implementation of the model (Koene and Hasselmo, 2007b) of temporal context-dependent episodic memory does not depend on a specific complete pattern size, but instead depends on activity that occurs at specific phases of the cycles of theta rhythm.

Some models of free recall (Metcalfe and Murdock, 1981; Gillund and Shiffrin, 1984) prevent the reactivation of previous responses through a sort of repetitive cued recall, in which previously recalled items provide cues that move recall more efficiently from item to item. In contrast, the cues presented for free recall in the Hasselmo and Wyble (1997) model remain constant during recall. Instead, that model uses adaptation based on previous activation to effectively remove a pattern, once activated, from the pool of possible responses. The adaptation properties of the model have been used to simulate functional magnetic resonance imaging data that showed a decrease in hippocampal activation during the viewing of a single repeated stimulus when compared to the activation during the viewing of different novel stimuli (Stern et al., 1996; Stern and Hasselmo, 1997).

Simulations with neural network models that include mechanisms of interactions between networks with specific characteristics, such as those described in the preceding text, can be used to make specific and testable predictions. For example, in the case of the Hasselmo and Wyble (1997) neural network model, by blocking simulated cholinergic effects, it was possible to make clear and specific predictions of the effects of scopolamine on human memory function. The selectivity of the effects predicted corresponded to effects demonstrated in psychopharmacological experiments (Ghoneim and Mewaldt, 1975, 1977; Peterson, 1977; Mewaldt and Ghoneim, 1979). Specifically, encoding of new words was impaired, but retrieval of words in a free recall test was not, and the recognition of words was not impaired. The connectionist model therefore pointed out a direct link between physiological effects at the level of neurons and synapses and the behavioral effects of drug administration in a human experiment. This example demonstrates how the use of connectionist simulations to link cellular physiology with behavior may be used to constrain models of memory function in accordance with experimental data in neurophysiology and molecular biology.

Acknowledgments

Supported by NIH R01 grants DA16454 (CRCNS), MH60013 and MH61492 to Michael Hasselmo and by NSF Science of Learning Center SBE 0354378 and Conte Center Grant MH60450.

References

Abeles M, Bergman H, Margalit E, and Vaadia E (1993) Spatiotemporal firing patterns in the frontal cortex of behaving monkeys. *J. Neurophysiol.* 70(4): 1629–1638.

Amaral D and Witter M (1989) The three-dimensional organization of the hippocampal formation: A review of anatomical data. *Neuroscience* 31: 571–591.

Anderson J (1983) Cognitive and psychological computation with neural models. *IEEE Trans. Syst. Man Cybern.* 13: 799–815.

Anderson J, Silverstein J, Ritz R, and Jones R (1977) Distinctive features, categorical perception and probability learning: Some applications of a neural model. *Psychol. Rev.* 84: 413–451.

Andrade R (1991) The effect of carbachol which affects muscarinic receptors was investigated in prefrontal layer v neurons. *Brain Res.* 541: 81–93.

Baddeley A and Warrington E (1970) Amnesia and the distinction between long- and short-term memory. *J. Verb. Learning Verb. Behav.* 9: 176–189.

Barnes J and Underwood B (1959) Fate of first-list associations in transfer theory. *J. Exp. Psychol.* 58: 97–105.

Bi G and Poo M (1998) Synaptic modifications in cultured hippocampal neurons: Dependence on spike timing, synaptic strength, and postsynaptic cell type. *J. Neurosci.* 18(24): 10464–10472.

Bland B and Colom L (1993) Extrinsic and intrinsic properties underlying oscillation and synchrony in limbic cortex. *Prog. Neurobiol.* 41: 157–208.

Buzsáki G (1989) Two-stage model of memory trace formation: A role for "noisy" brain states. *Neuroscience* 31: 551–570.

Cannon R, Hasselmo M, and Koene R (2003) From biophysics to behaviour: Catacomb2 and the design of biologically plausible models for spatial navigation. *Neuroinformatics* 1(1): 3–42.

Chappell M and Humphreys M (1994) An auto-associative neural network for sparse representations: Analysis and application to models of recognition and cued recall. *Psych. Rev.* 101: 103–128.

Chrobak J and Buzsáki G (1994) Selective activation of deep layer (V-VI) retrohippocampal cortical neurons during hippocampal sharp waves in the behaving rat. *J. Neurosci.* 14: 1660–1670.

Corkin S (1984) Lasting consequences of bilateral medial temporal lobectomy: Clinical course and experimental findings in H.M. *Semin. Neurol.* 4: 249–259.

DeLuca J (1993) Predicting neurobehavioral patterns following anterior communicating artery aneurysm. *Cortex* 29: 639–647.

Dutar P and Nicoll R (1988) Classification of muscarinic responses in hippocampus in terms of receptor sybtypes and 2nd messenger systems electrophysiological studies in vitro. *J. Neurosci.* 8(11): 4214–4224.

Eichenbaum H and Buckingham J (1990) Studies on hippocampal processing: Experiment, theory and model. In: Gabriel M and Moore J (eds.) *Learning and Computational Neuroscience: Foundations of Adaptive Networks,* pp. 171–231. Cambridge, MA: MIT Press.

Foster D and Wilson M (2006) Reverse replay of behavioural sequences in hippocampal place cells during the awake state. *Nature* 440: 680–683.

Fransén E, Alonso A, and Hasselmo M (2002) Simulations of the role of the muscarinic activated calcium-sensitive nonspecific cation current i_{NCM} in entorhinal neuronal activity during delayed matching tasks. *J. Neurosci.* 22(3): 1081–1097.

Fransén E, Tahvildari B, Egorov A, Hasselmo M, and Alonso A (2006a) Mechanism of graded persistent cellular activity of entorhinal cortex layer V neurons. *Neuron* 49: 735–746.

Fransén E, Tahvildari B, Hasselmo M, and Alonso A (2006b) Mechanisms of persistent plateaus in entorhinal cortex layer III pyramidal neurons. In: Program No. 636.1, 2006 Neuroscience Meeting Planner. Atlanta, GA: Society for Neuroscience. Online.

Fyhn M, Molden S, Witter M, Moser E, and Moser M (2004) Spatial representation in the entorhinal cortex. *Science* 305(5688): 1246–1246.

Gaffan D and Harrison S (1989) Place memory and scene memory effects of fornix transection in the monkey. *Exp. Brain Res.* 74: 202–212.

Gerstner W (1998a) Populations of spiking neurons. In: Maass W and Bishop C (eds.) *Pulsed Neural Networks*, pp. 261–293. Cambridge, MA: MIT Press.

Gerstner W (1998b) Spiking neurons. In: Maass W and Bishop C (eds.) *Pulsed Neural Networks*, pp. 3–54. Cambridge, MA: MIT Press.

Gerstner W and Kistler W (2002) *Spiking Neuron Models: Single Neurons, Populations, Plasticity*. Cambridge, UK: Cambridge University Press.

Ghoneim M and Mewaldt S (1975) Effects of diazepam and scopolamine on storage, retrieval and organization processes in memory. *Psychopharmacologia* 44: 257–262.

Ghoneim M and Mewaldt S (1977) Studies on human memory: The interactions of diazepam, scopolamine and physostigmine. *Psychopharmacology* 52: 1–6.

Gillund G and Shiffrin R (1984) A retrieval model of both recognition and recall. *Psych. Rev.* 91: 1–67.

Gluck M and Myers C (1993) Hippocampal mediation of stimulus representation: A computational theory. *Hippocampus* 3: 491–516.

Graf P, Squire L, and Mandler G (1984) The information that amnesic patients do not forget. *J. Exp. Psychol. Hum. Learn. Mem.* 10: 164–178.

Grossberg S and Stone G (1986) Neural dynamics of attention switching and temporal-order information in short-term memory. *Mem. Cognit.* 14(6): 451–468.

Grunze H, Rainnie D, Hasselmo M, et al. (1996) NMDA-dependent modulation of CA1 local circuit inhibition. *J. Neurosci.* 16: 2034–2043.

Haas H and Rose G (1984) The role of inhibitory mechanisms in hippocampal long-term potentiation. *Neurosci. Lett.* 47: 301–306.

Hafting T, Fyhn M, Molden S, Moser MB, and Moser E (2005) Microstructure of a spatial map in the entorhinal cortex. *Nature* 436: 801–806.

Hasselmo M (1995) Neuromodulation and cortical function: Modeling the physiological basis of behavior. *Behav. Brain Res.* 65: 1–27.

Hasselmo M (1999) Neuromodulation: Acetylcholine and memory consolidation. *Trends Cogn. Sci.* 3: 351–359.

Hasselmo M, Bodelon C, and Wyble B (2002a) A proposed function for hippocampal theta rhythm: Separate phases of encoding and retrieval enhance reversal of prior learning. *Neural Comput.* 14(4): 793–817.

Hasselmo M, Cannon R, and Koene R (2002b) A simulation of parahippocampal and hippocampal structures guiding spatial navigation of a virtual rat in a virtual environment: A functional framework for theta theory. In: Witter M and Wouterlood F (eds.) *The Parahippocampal Region: Organization and Role of Cognitive Functions*, pp. 139–161. Oxford: Oxford University Press.

Hasselmo M and Eichenbaum H (2005) Hippocampal mechanisms for the context-dependent retrieval of episodes. *Neural Netw.* 18(9): 1172–1190.

Hasselmo M, Hay J, Ilyn M, and Gorechetnikov A (2002c) Neuromodulation, theta rhythm and rat spatial navigation. *Neural Netw.* 15: 689–707.

Hasselmo M and Schnell E (1994) Laminar selectivity of the cholinergic suppression of synaptic transmission in rat hippocampal region CA1: Computational modeling and brain slice physiology. *J. Neurosci.* 14: 3898–3914.

Hasselmo M, Schnell E, and Barkai E (1995) Learning and recall at excitatory recurrent synapses and cholinergic modulation in hippocampal region CA3. *J. Neurosci.* 15: 5249–5262.

Hasselmo M and Stern C (1996) Linking LTP to network function: A simulation of episodic memory in the hippocampal formation. In: Baudry M and Davis J (eds.) *Long-Term Potentiation,* vol. 3, pp. 293–325. Cambridge, MA: MIT Press.

Hasselmo M and Wyble B (1997) Free recall and recognition in a network model of the hippocampus: Simulating effects of scopolamine on human memory function. *Behav. Brain Res.* 89: 1–34.

Hasselmo ME, Wyble BP, and Stern CE (1998) A model of human memory based on the cellular physiology of the hippocampal formation. In: Parks R, Levine DS, and Long DL (eds.) *Fundamentals of Neural Network Modeling: Neuropsychology and Cognitive Neuroscience*, pp. 299–329. Cambridge, MA: MIT Press.

Hasselmo M, Wyble P, and Wallenstein G (1996) Encoding and retrieval of episodic memories: Role of cholinergic and GABAergic modulation in the hippocampus. *Hippocampus* 6: 693–708.

Heilman K and Sypert G (1977) Korsakoff's syndrome resulting from bilateral fornix lesions. *Neurology* 27: 490–493.

Hintzman D (1988) Judgements of frequency and recognition memory in a multipletrace memory model. *Psych. Rev.* 95: 528–551.

Hodges J and Carpenter K (1991) Anterograde amnesia with fornix damage following removal of IIIrd ventricle colloid cyst. *J. Neurol. Neurosurg. Psychiatr.* 54: 633–638.

Hollingworth H (1913) Characteristic differences between recall and recognition. *Am. J. Psychol.* 24: 532–544.

Hopfield J (1982) Neural networks and physical systems with emergent collective computational abilities. *Proc. Natl. Acad. Sci. USA* 79: 2554–2558.

Howard M and Kahana M (2002) A distributed representation of temporal context. *J Math. Psychol.* 46(3): 269–299.

Howard MW, Youker TE, and Venkatadass VS (in press) The persistence of memory: Contiguity effects across hundreds of seconds. *Psychon. Bull. Rev.*

Huerta P and Lisman J (1993) Heightened synaptic plasticity of hippocampal ca1 neurons during a cholinergically induced rhythmic state. *Nature* 364: 723–725.

Hyman J, Wyble B, Goyal P, Rossi C, and Hasselmo M (2003) Stimulation in hippocampal region CA1 in behaving rats yields LTP when delivered to the peak of theta and LTD when delivered to the trough. *J. Neurosci.* 23(37): 11725–11731.

Jensen O, Idiart M, and Lisman J (1996) Physiologically realistic formation of autoassociative memory in networks with theta/gamma oscillations: Role of fast NMDA channels. *Learn. Mem.* 3: 243–256.

Jensen O and Lisman J (1996) Theta/gamma networks with slow N-Methyl-D-aspartate channels learn sequences and encode episodic memory: Role of NMDA channels in recall. *Learn. Mem.* 3: 264–278.

Johnson A and Redish A (2006) Neural ensembles in CA3 transiently encode paths forward of the animal at a decision point: A possible mechanism for the consideration of alternatives. In: Program No. 574.2, 2006 Neuroscience Meeting Planner. Atlanta, GA: Society for Neuroscience. Online.

Kelso S, Ganong A, and Brown T (1986) Hebbian synapses in the hippocampus. *Proc. Natl. Acad. Sci. USA* 83: 5326–5330.

Klink R and Alonso A (1997) Muscarinic modulation of the oscillatory and repetitive firing properties of entorhinal cortex layer II neurons. *J. Neurophysiol.* 77(4): 1813–1828.

Koene R (2001) *Functional Requirements Determine Relevant Ingredients to Model for On-Line Acquisition of Context Dependent Memory.* PhD Thesis, McGill University.

Koene R, Gorchetchnikov A, Cannon R, and Hasselmo M (2003) Modeling goal-directed spatial navigation in the rat based on physiological data from the hippocampal formation. *Neural Netw.* 16(56): 577–584.

Koene R and Hasselmo M (2005) An integrate-and-fire model of prefrontal cortex neuronal activity during performance of goal-directed decision making. *Cereb. Cortex* 15(12): 1964–1981.

Koene R and Hasselmo M (2006) Encoding episodes in a specific temporal context depends on the reduction of interference by extending representations in dentate gyrus. Presented at the Tenth International Conference on Cognitive and Neural Systems (ICCNS2006) Boston, MA, USA, 17–20 May.

Koene R and Hasselmo M (2007a) First-in-first-out item replacement in a model of short-term memory based on persistent spiking. *Cereb. Cortex* 17: 1766–1781.

Koene R and Hasselmo M (2007b) A reversing buffer mechanism that enables instances of retrospective activity in hippocampal regions CA3 and CA1. In: *Proceedings of the International Joint Conference on Neural Networks* (IJCNN2007), Orlando, FL. New York: IEEE.

Levy W (1989) A computational approach to hippocampal function. In: Hawkins R and Bower G (eds.) *The Psychology of Learning and Motivation, Vol. 23: Computational Models of Learning in Simple Neural Systems*, pp. 243–305. New York: Academic Press.

Levy W, Colbert C, and Desmond N (1990) Elemental adaptive processes of neurons and synapses: A statistical/computational perspective. In: Gluck M and Rumelhart D (eds.) *Neuroscience and Connectionist Theory*, pp. 187–236. Hillsdale, NJ: Lawrence Erblaum.

Levy W and Steward O (1979) Synapses as associative memory elements in the hippocampal formation. *Brain Res.* 175: 233–245.

Levy W, Wu X, and Baxter R (1995) Unification of hippocampal function via computational/encoding considerations. *Int. J. Neural Syst.* 6: 71–80.

Lisman J (1999) Relating hippocampal circuitry to function: Recall of memory sequences by reciprocal dentate CA3 interactions. *Neuron* 22: 233–242.

Lisman J and Idiart M (1995) Storage of 7 ± 2 short-term memories in oscillatory subcylces. *Science* 267: 1512–1515.

Lisman J, Talamini L, and Raffone A (2005) Recall of memory sequences by interaction of the dentate and CA3: A revised model of the phase precession. *Neural Netw.* 18(9): 1191–1201.

Little W and Shaw G (1975) A statistical theory of short and long-term memory. *Behav. Biol.* 14: 115–133.

Marr D (1971) Simple memory: A theory for archicortex. *Philos. Trans. R. Soc. B Biol. Sci.* 262: 23–81.

McClelland J, McNaughton B, and O'Reilly R (1995) Why there are complementary learning systems in the hippocampus and neocortex: Insights from the successes and failures of connectionist models of learning and memory. *Psychol. Rev.* 102: 419–457.

McCloskey M and Cohen N (1989) Catastrophic interference in connectionist networks: The sequential learning problem. In: Bower G (ed.) *The Psychology of Learning and Motivation*, New York: Academic Press.

McGaughy J, Koene R, Eichenbaum H, and Hasselmo M (2005) Cholinergic deafferentation of the entorhinal cortex in rats impairs encoding of novel but not familiar stimuli in a delayed nonmatch-to-sample task. *J. Neurosci.* 25(44): 10273–10281.

McNaughton B (1991) Associative pattern completion in hippocampal circuits: New evidence and new questions. *Brain Res. Rev.* 16: 193–220.

McNaughton B, Douglas R, and Goddard G (1978) Synaptic enhancement in fascia dentata: Cooperativity among coactive afferents. *Brain Res.* 15: 277–293.

McNaughton B and Morris R (1987) Hippocampal synaptic enhancement and information storage within a distributed memory system. *Trends Neurosci.* 10: 408–415.

Metcalfe J and Murdock B (1981) An encoding and retrieval model of single-trial free recall. *J. Verb. Learn. Verb. Behav.* 20: 161–189.

Metcalfe Eich J (1982) A composite holographic associative recall model. *Psych. Rev.* 89: 627–661.

Mewaldt S and Ghoneim M (1979) The effect and interactions of scopolamine, physostigmine and methamphetamine on human memory. *Pharmacol. Biochem. Behav.* 10: 1205–1210.

Minai A and Levy W (1994) Setting the activity level in sparse random networks. *Neural Comput.* 6: 83–97.

Morishita W and Sastry B (1991) Chelation of postsynaptic Ca2+ facilitates long term potentiation of hippocampal IPSPs. *Neuroreport* 2: 533–536.

Murdock B (1982) A theory for the storage and retrieval of item and associative information. *Psych. Rev.* 89: 609–626.

Myers C and Gluck M (1994) Context, conditioning and hippocampal representation in animal learning. *Behav. Neurosci.* 108: 835–847.

Norman D (1968) Toward a theory of memory and attention. *Psychol. Rev.* 75: 522–536.

Norman K (2006) How inhibitory oscillations can train neural networks and punish competitors. *Neural Comput.* 18: 1577–1610.

Norman K and O'Reilly R (2003) Modeling hippocampal and neocortical contributions to recognition memory: A complementary-learning-systems approach. *Psychol. Rev.* 110(4): 611–646.

O'Keefe J and Burgess N (2005) Dual-phase and rate coding in hippocampal place cells: Theoretical significance and relationship to entorhinal grid cells. *Hippocampus* 15: 853–866.

O'Reilly R and Frank M (2005) Making working memory work: A computational model of learning in the prefrontal cortex and basal ganglia. *Neural Comput.* 18: 283–328.

O'Reilly R and McClelland J (1994) Hippocampal conjunctive encoding, storage, and recall: Avoiding a tradeoff. *Hippocampus* 4: 661–682.

Penfield W and Milner B (1958) Memory deficit produced by bilateral lesions in the hippocampal zone. *Arch. Neurol. Psychiatr.* 79: 475–497.

Peterson R (1977) Scopolamine induced learning failures in man. *Psychopharmacology* 52: 283–289.

Ratcliff R, Clark S, and Shiffrin R (1990) List-strength effect: I. data and discussion. *J. Exp. Psychol. Learn. Mem. Cognit.* 16: 163–178.

Rempel-Clower N, Zola S, Squire L, and Amaral D (1995) Importance of the hippocampal region and entorhinal cortex in human memory: Neuropsychological and neuropathological findings from a new patient. *Soc. Neurosci. Abstr.* 21: 1493. (586.4).

Rolls E (1995) A model of the operation of the hippocampus and entorhinal cortex in memory. *Int. J. Neural Syst.* 6(supplemental): 51–70.

Rolls E, Treves A, Foster D, and Perez-Vincente C (1997) Simulation studies of the CA3 hippocampal subfield modelled as an attractor neural network. *Neural Netw.* 10(9): 1559–1569.

Ruppin E and Yeshurun Y (1991) Recall and recognition in an attractor neural network model of memory retrieval. *Connect. Sci.* 3: 381–399.

Schmajuk N and DiCarlo J (1992) Stimulus configuration, classical conditioning, and hippocampal function. *Psychol. Rev.* 99(2): 268–305.

Scoville W and Milner B (1957) Loss of recent memory after bilateral hippocampal lesions. *J. Neurol. Neurosurg. Psychiatry* 20: 11.

Stern C, Corkin S, Gonzalez R, et al. (1996) The hippocampal formation participates in novel picture encoding: Evidence from functional magnetic resonance imaging. *Proc. Natl. Acad. Sci. USA* 93: 8660–8665.

Stern C and Hasselmo M (1997) Functional magnetic resonance imaging and computational modeling: An integrated study of hippocampal function. In: Bower J (ed.) *Advances in Computational Neuroscience*, pp. 859–865. New York: Plenum Press.

Suzuki W, Zola-Morgan S, and Squire L (1993) Lesions of the perirhinal and parahippocampal cortices in the monkey produce long-lasting memory impairment in the visual and tactual modalities. *J. Neurosci.* 13: 2430–2451.

Treves A (1995) Quantitative estimate of the information relayed by the Schaffer collaterals. *J. Comput. Neurosci.* 2: 259–272.

Treves A and Rolls E (1992) Computational constraints suggest the need for two distinct input systems to the hippocampal CA3 network. *Hippocampus* 2: 189–200.

Treves A and Rolls E (1994) Computational analysis of the role of the hippocampus in memory. *Hippocampus* 4: 374–391.

Tulving E (1975) Ecphoric processes in recall and recognition. In: Brown J (ed.) *Recall and Recognition*, pp. 37–73. London: Wiley.

Valentino R and Dingledine R (1981) Presynaptic inhibitory effect of acetylcholine in the hippocampus. *J. Neurosci.* 1: 784–792.

van der Linden M, Bruyer R, Roland J, and Schils J (1993) Proactive interference in patients with amnesia resulting from anterior communicating artery aneurysm. *J. Clin. Exp. Neuropsychol.* 15: 525–536.

Wigstrom H, Gustafsson B, Huang Y, and Abraham W (1986) Hippocampal long-term potentiation is induced by pairing single afferent volleys with intracellularly injected depolarizing current pulses. *Acta Physiol. Scand.* 126: 317–319.

Zola-Morgan S, Cohen N, and Squire L (1983) Recall of remote episodic memory in amnesia. *Neuropsychologia* 21: 487–500.

Zola-Morgan S, Squire L, and Amaral D (1986) Human amnesia and the medial temporal region: Enduring memory impairment following a bilateral lesion limited to field CA1 of the hippocampus. *J. Neurosci.* 6: 2950–2967.

1.36 Theory of Reward Systems

S. B. Ostlund, N. E. Winterbauer, and B. W. Balleine, University of California, Los Angeles, CA, USA

1.36.1 Introduction

Except, perhaps, for the unabashed moralist, knowledge alone does not determine choice of action, i.e., knowing that "action A leads to X and action B leads to Y" does not 'entail' choosing A or B. What enables choice, given this information, is some nonarbitrary means of establishing the relative merits of achieving X or Y. We argue that it is the reward system that provides this means. From this perspective, although the reward system is an extension of the general motivational processes of animals, its function is limited to actions over which animals can exert control and that are instrumental to achieving some goal or other, i.e., to goal-directed instrumental actions. Of course, although most aspects of an animal's behavioral repertoire can be described in goal-directed terms, many of these activities are not goal-directed at all and are reflexive responses elicited by stimuli or relations between stimuli. Establishing criteria for discerning goal-directed and non-goal-directed actions is a necessary step, therefore, in limiting our discussion of the reward system. In this chapter, we consider first the criteria for defining an action as goal-directed and then use that definition to describe the nature and function of the reward system in establishing primary rewarding events, like foods and fluids, both with

respect to encoding reward value and to retrieving that value in order to choose between competing courses of action.

This research has established that the value of reward is determined by the quality of the emotional response associated with an event, the latter dependent on current motivational state, i.e., value essentially maps onto the relationship between the specific sensory features of an event and the particular, pleasant or unpleasant, emotional feedback generated when that event is contacted. This issue is taken up in more detail in the section titled 'Reward processes,' where we examine one of the main predictions of this account, that, in the context of secondary rewards, any event associated with a pleasant emotional reaction will support the performance of goal-directed actions. These are sensory events that acquire reward value through association with primary rewards (commonly mislabeled conditioned reinforcers). The procedures used to establish secondary rewards are identical to those commonly used to establish Pavlovian conditioned responses to a stimulus, raising the possibility that the functioning of the reward system can be reduced to the motivational processes that support Pavlovian conditioning. In the section titled 'Secondary reward' we examine this possibility and conclude, based on the extensive evidence standing against this claim, that Pavlovian conditioned responses (CRs) and goal-directed actions are controlled by fundamentally distinct incentive processes.

1.36.2 Reward Processes

1.36.2.1 Goal-Directed Actions and Behavioral Control

The critical distinction between reflexive and goal-directed actions is that the latter are controlled by a causal relationship to their consequences, whereas the former are not. There are many illustrations of this distinction but perhaps the most apposite is Sheffield's (1965) analysis based on the salivary response of dogs. Salivation was the conditioned and unconditioned reflex studied by Pavlov (1927). Nevertheless, from a goal-directed perspective, it is possible that dogs control this response in order to facilitate digestion or to improve the taste of food. Sheffield arranged a standard pairing between conditioned and unconditioned stimuli, in this case presentation of a tone followed by food delivery, but with a twist: If the dog salivated during the tone the food was not delivered on that trial. This arrangement maintains a Pavlovian relationship between the tone and food but abolishes any instrumental contingency between salivation and food. He reasoned that, if the salivation was goal-directed then this omission contingency should ensure that they stop salivating; indeed having never had the opportunity to learn that salivating improved the rewarding impact of the food by enhancing its flavor or improving its ingestion, they should never acquire salivation to the tone in the first place. Sheffield found that it was clearly the Pavlovian relationship controlling performance; during the course of over 800 tone-food pairings the dogs acquired and maintained salivation to the tone even though this resulted in them losing most of the food they could otherwise have obtained.

Salivation may be the exception of course, but in numerous studies over the last 40 years it has been established in a range of species that Pavlovian conditioned responses do not adjust to this kind of contingency, i.e., one in which performance of the conditioned response leads to the omission of the unconditioned stimulus. Rats acquire conditioned approach responses during a conditioned stimulus (CS) when doing so omits the food (Holland, 1979), pigeons peck at keys (Williams and Williams, 1969), chicks chase food away (Hershberger, 1986), and so on. In all of these studies, the evidence confirms that

the performance of the Pavlovian CR does not depend on the relationship between the CR and the US. (*See* Chapter 1.03).

In contrast, experiments assessing the performance of actions acquired during instrumental conditioning have found evidence that these responses do indeed depend on the contingency between action and outcome. Take, for example, instrumental lever pressing. Rats will acquire lever pressing for food quickly and without explicit shaping. Putting this response on an omission contingency, in which responding leads to the omission of an otherwise freely delivered food, rapidly reduces the performance of that response, more rapidly than simply delivering the outcome in an unpaired manner (Davis and Bitterman, 1971; Dickinson et al., 1998; *See* Chapter 1.06). Furthermore, numerous studies have demonstrated the exquisite sensitivity of the performance of instrumental lever pressing to changes in the net probability of outcome delivery given the action (i.e., the difference between probability of an outcome given a response and the probability of the outcome given no response). These changes can be highly selective; degrading one action–outcome contingency by delivering the outcome associated with that action noncontingently often has no effect on the performance of other actions (Colwill and Rescorla, 1986; Dickinson and Mulatero, 1989; Balleine and Dickinson, 1998a).

1.36.2.2 The Effect of Changes in Reward Value

Generally, therefore, goal-directed actions are those that, unlike Pavlovian CRs, are sensitive to the causal relation between the performance of the action and its specific outcome. It is important to note, however, that lever press responses can be controlled by two kinds of association. The first is the relationship between action and outcome described earlier. After extensive instrumental training, however, performance of an action can become habitual, elicited by various situational cues connected with the action through a process of sensorimotor association (Adams, 1981; Dickinson, 1985, 1994). Although the formation of these associations diminishes sensitivity to omission (Dickinson et al., 1998), it does not necessarily abolish it and, although this test distinguishes actions from Pavlovian conditioned reflexes, it does not provide an adequate assessment in itself to distinguish goal-directed actions from habits. Fortunately, there is a clear distinction between the functions of the instrumental outcome in the two forms of learning. Whereas the outcome serves as the second term of the action–outcome association that supports the acquisition and performance of goal-directed actions, it serves merely to strengthen or to reinforce the stimulus–response (S–R) associations that form habits. As such, the outcome forms no part of the associative structure that supports habitual performance. Based on this analysis, therefore, and combined with an assessment of sensitivity to changes in the instrumental contingency, the standard test of whether an action is goal-directed or not involves an assessment of the sensitivity of performance to a posttraining change in the reward value of the outcome. From an S–R perspective, when conducted posttraining, i.e., after a substantial S–R association has been established, a change in outcome value should be expected to have little if any effect on the subsequent tendency to perform the action. If an action is goal-directed, however, the change in value should potently alter performance.

Consider the case in which a hungry rat is trained to press a lever for a particular type of food pellet. According to a goal-directed account, it is the reward value of the food pellets that motivates performance. Consequently, if having trained the rat to perform this action, the reward value of the food pellets is reduced in some way, we should expect this devaluation to affect performance, i.e., the rat should be less inclined to press the lever after the devaluation. Given this scenario, the question at issue is whether the devaluation affects performance via the animal's knowledge of the contingency between lever pressing and the food pellets. In the first appropriately controlled study along these lines, Adams and Dickinson (1981) assessed this by training rats with two types of food pellets, sugar and grain, with only one type being delivered by lever pressing. The other type of pellet was presented independently of any instrumental action. Thus, any particular rat might have to work for sugar pellets by lever pressing, while receiving free deliveries of grain pellets every so often. The issue was whether the animals would reduce lever pressing more after the devaluation of the response-contingent pellets, the sugar pellets in our example, than after devaluation of the free pellets, the grain ones. Such an outcome could only occur if the effect of the devaluation was mediated by the instrumental contingency between lever pressing and the sugar pellets.

In this study, the pellets were devalued using conditioned taste aversion procedures; it is well established that a food aversion can be conditioned

by inducing gastric illness, for example by the injection of lithium chloride (LiCl), shortly after the animal has consumed the food (Bernstein, 1999). In the Adams and Dickinson study, having trained the rats to lever press, half had a taste aversion conditioned to the sugar and half to the grain pellets. During aversion conditioning, the levers were withdrawn and the animals were given a series of sessions in each of which they were allowed to eat one type of pellet. The animals in the devaluation group received a LiCl injection after sessions in which they received the pellets that had been contingent on lever pressing during training but not following sessions with the free pellets. The control group, by contrast, had the aversion conditioned to the free pellets rather than the response-contingent ones. Although such food aversions can be established with a single pairing of consumption with illness when the food is novel, the treatment had to be repeated a number of times to suppress consumption in the present study. This is because the pellets were already familiar to the rats, having been presented during instrumental training.

After inducing these aversions, Adams and Dickinson were now in a position to ask whether devaluing the pellets that acted as the reward for lever pressing during training had a greater impact on performance than devaluing the freely delivered pellets. This result would be expected if the motivational properties of rewards are mediated by their instrumental relation to the action. In fact, this is just what Adams and Dickinson found: when subsequently given access to the lever again, the devaluation group pressed significantly less than the control group. Note that this test was conducted in extinction, during which neither type of pellet was presented, for if the pellets had been presented during testing, the reluctance of the devaluation group to press the lever could be explained simply in terms of the direct suppressive effect of presenting this aversive consequence. By testing in extinction, however, different performance in the two groups must have reflected integration of knowledge of the consequences of lever pressing acquired during training with the current reward value of the pellets. This suggestion was further confirmed by Colwill and Rescorla (1986) using a choice test. They trained hungry rats to perform two instrumental actions, lever pressing and chain pulling, with one action earning access to food pellets and the other earning access to a sucrose solution. The rats were then given several trials in which they were allowed to consume one of the outcomes with the levers and chains withdrawn and were then made ill by an injection of LiCl. All animals were then given a choice extinction test on the levers and chains again conducted in extinction, i.e., in the absence of either of the outcomes. Although S–R accounts should predict no effect of this treatment, Colwill and Rescorla found that animals performed less of the action whose training outcome was subsequently paired with LiCl than the other action, indicating that the rats had indeed encoded the consequences of their actions.

The importance of these demonstrations of the outcome devaluation effect lies in the fact that, together, they provide strong evidence that animals encode the specific features of the consequences or outcome of their instrumental actions. Furthermore, these studies show that instrumental performance is not only determined by the encoding of the action–outcome relation but also by the current reward value of the outcome. In recent years, considerable attention has been paid to the processes that contribute to the encoding of reward value, and the advances that have been made have come largely from asking how outcome devaluation works to change instrumental performance: How does taste aversion work to modify the rats' evaluation of the outcome and so change the course of its instrumental performance?

1.36.2.3   Incentive Learning and the Encoding of Reward Value

Perhaps the simplest account of the way taste aversion learning works to devalue the instrumental outcome can be derived from accounts of aversive conditioning generally according to which pairing the instrumental outcome with illness changes the evaluation of the outcome through the formation of a predictive association between the food or fluid and the aversive state induced by illness. The result of an effective pairing of the outcome with illness is, therefore, that the animal learns that the outcome now signals that aversive consequence. From this perspective, the outcome devaluation effect is the product of a practical inference process through which a previously encoded action–outcome relation is combined with learning that the outcome signals an aversive consequence to reduce subsequent performance of the action.

In contrast, Garcia (1989) introduced a more complex account according to which the change in the evaluation of the outcome induced by taste aversion learning is not due to changing what the outcome predicts but due to changes in how it tastes. Garcia related the change in taste to negative feedback from a system sensitive to illness that he identified as inducing a disgust or distaste reaction. It is important to see that this view implies that taste aversion learning involves not one learning process but two: (1) an effective pairing of the outcome with illness initially enables a connection between the sensory properties of the outcome and processes sensitive to illness; (2) this association is activated when the outcome is subsequently contacted to generate a distaste reaction and allow the animal to associate the outcome representation with disgust or distaste. This account predicts that, to induce outcome devaluation, it is not sufficient merely to pair the outcome with an injection of LiCl. Rather, a change in value is not induced until the second process is engaged when the outcome is again contacted.

The procedures employed to induce instrumental outcome devaluation, such as that described by Adams and Dickinson (1981), do not differentiate between these two accounts of taste aversion learning because the conditioning of an aversion to the outcome is usually conducted using multiple pairings of the outcome with illness. Clearly the pairings themselves would be sufficient to establish a signaling relation between the outcome and an aversive consequence. But the fact that the animals were allowed to contact the outcome on subsequent pairings could have provided the opportunity for the animals to associate the outcome representation with distaste. If a substantial aversion to the outcome could be conditioned with a single pairing of the outcome with illness, however, then these accounts of outcome devaluation make divergent predictions: On the signaling account, a devaluation effect should emerge, providing that an effective pairing between the taste and illness was produced; on Garcia's (1989) account it should not emerge until the rats have been reexposed to the devalued outcome. In a test of these divergent predictions, Balleine and Dickinson (1991) trained thirsty rats to lever press for water. After acquisition, the outcome was switched to sugar solution for a single session, after which the rats were given an injection of LiCl either immediately or after a delay (the latter treatment, as an unpaired control, should have induced relatively little aversion to the sucrose on either account). The critical question was whether, in the absence of further contact with the sucrose, the rats in the immediately poisoned group would display reduced performance on the lever relative to the delayed group.

To assess the influence of reexposure to the sucrose, half of each of the immediate and delayed groups were allowed merely to taste the sucrose, whereas the remainder were given water before two tests were conducted on the levers. The first test was conducted in extinction to assess the effects of devaluation and reexposure on the tendency to press. A second, punishment test was then conducted in which responding on the lever again delivered the sucrose, which allowed us to assess the strength of the aversion to sucrose. If a substantial aversion to the sucrose was conditioned in the immediately poisoned groups, then not only should a reliable punishment effect have emerged in the second test, but, on the signaling account, responding should also have been reduced in the extinction test in all of the immediately poisoned rats. In contrast, in Garcia's account, responding in the extinction test should be reduced in those immediately poisoned rats given reexposure to the sucrose. In fact, in this and in several other experiments along similar lines, Balleine and Dickinson (1991) and Balleine (1992) found consistent evidence for Garcia's account; although a single pairing between sucrose and illness invariably produced a reliable punishment effect in immediately poisoned rats, a devaluation effect only emerged in the critical extinction test if reexposure to the sucrose was given prior to the test.

These results suggest that outcome devaluation depends upon the interaction of two learning processes. The first process involves the conditioning of an association between the outcome and processes that are activated by the induction of illness by LiCl. The failure of this learning process to directly affect instrumental performance suggests that it is not, alone, sufficient to induce outcome devaluation. Rather, it appears to be necessary for feedback from this first learning process to become explicitly associated with the specific sensory features of the outcome itself for a change in the reward value of the instrumental outcome to occur and for performance to change. Indeed, considerable evidence now suggests that this second learning process critically determines the encoding of the rewarding properties of the instrumental outcome, a process referred to as incentive learning (Dickinson and Balleine, 1994, 1995).

The reason for emphasizing the role of incentive learning in instrumental outcome-devaluation effects is that it also appears to be the process by which other

primary motivational states, such as hunger and thirst, encode the reward value of other goals such as foods and fluids. It is well established that the motivational state of rats is a major determinant of their instrumental performance; not surprisingly, hungry animals work more vigorously for a food reward than sated ones. But what current evidence suggests is that this is because a food-deprived state induces an animal to assign a higher incentive value to nutritive outcomes when they are contacted in that state and that this high rating of the incentive value of the outcome is then reflected in a more vigorous rate of performance. Although this suggestion stands contrary to general drive theories of motivation that suppose that increments in motivation elicit their effects on performance by increases in general activation (Hull, 1943), there are good empirical grounds for arguing that motivational states do not directly control performance (Dickinson and Balleine, 1994, 2002; Balleine, 2001). Balleine (1992) trained groups of undeprived rats to lever press for a food reward. After training, half of the rats were shifted to a food deprivation schedule, whereas the remainder were maintained undeprived before both groups were given an extinction test on the levers. Balleine found that performance of the groups on test did not differ even though the shift in motivational state was clearly effective. In a subsequent test where the animals could again earn the food pellets, the food-deprived rats pressed at a substantially higher rate than the undeprived rats. Although motivational state clearly did not exert any direct control over performance, as was found in taste aversion conditioning, the motivational state could control performance if the rats were given the opportunity for incentive learning by allowing them consummatory contact with the instrumental outcome in the test motivational state prior to the test. To demonstrate this, Balleine (1992) trained two further groups of rats to lever press when undeprived. Both groups were given prior exposure to the instrumental outcome when food-deprived before the test in which one group was tested undeprived and the other food-deprived. Now a clear difference in performance was found in that the rats tested when food-deprived and allowed to consume the instrumental outcome when food-deprived prior to test pressed at a higher rate than the other three groups that in turn did not differ. Balleine (1992) was able to confirm that this incentive learning effect depended upon the instrumental contingency. He trained undeprived rats to perform two actions, lever pressing and chain pulling, with one action earning access to food pellets and the other to a maltodextrin solution. All rats were then given a choice extinction test on the levers and chains. Prior to the test, however, the animals were given six sessions in which they were allowed to consume one instrumental outcome when food deprived and, on alternate days, the other outcome in the training, i.e., undeprived, state. On test, Balleine found that animals performed more of the action that, in training, had delivered the outcome reexposed in the food-deprived state prior to the test than the other action.

It should be noted that this role for incentive learning in instrumental performance following a shift in motivational state is not confined to posttraining increases in food deprivation. The same pattern of results was also found for the opposite shift, i.e., where rats were trained to lever press for food pellets when food-deprived and then tested when undeprived. In this case, rats only reduced their performance when food deprivation was reduced if they were allowed to consume the instrumental outcome when undeprived prior to the test (Balleine, 1992; Balleine and Dickinson, 1994). Finally, the generality of this role of incentive learning in instrumental performance has been confirmed for a number of different motivational systems and in a number of devaluation paradigms. For example, in addition to taste aversion learning, incentive learning has been found to mediate (1) specific satiety-induced outcome devaluation effects (Balleine and Dickinson, 1998b); (2) shifts from water deprivation to satiety (Lopez et al., 1992); (3) changes in outcome value mediated by drug states (Balleine et al., 1994, 1995a); and changes in the value of (4) thermoregulatory rewards (Hendersen and Graham, 1979) and (5) sexual rewards (Everitt and Stacey, 1987; Woodson and Balleine, 2002) (see Dickinson and Balleine, 1994, 2002; Balleine, 2001, for reviews). In all of these cases, it is clear that animals have to learn about changes in the incentive value of an instrumental outcome through consummatory contact with that outcome before this change will affect performance.

1.36.2.4 Incentive Learning as an Emotional Process

Traditional neobehaviorist learning theories argued that CRs, what were called fractional anticipatory goal responses, could exert a motivating effect on instrumental performance (Hull, 1943, 1952; Spence, 1956). Largely due to the subsequent work of Konorski

(1967) and Mowrer (1960), however, it is now widely accepted that these effects reflect the conditioning of an affective state that can exert a direct modulatory influence over consummatory responses and, through a change in the emotional responses elicited during ingestion, on instrumental performance (Rescorla and Solomon, 1967; Dickinson, 1989). Recent research investigating the microstructure of orofacial taste reactivity responses in rats to various tastes has provided evidence, not only of specific ingestion and rejection responses to sweet and bitter tastes, but also that the ingestive taste reactivity responses are increased in hungry rats to tastes previously paired with nutrients (Myers and Sclafani, 2001). Likewise, rejection-related taste reactivity responses are increased to tastes previously paired with illness (Berridge et al., 1981). With respect to incentive learning, this approach suggests that, during this form of consummatory exposure, activation of the outcome representation activates its associated motivational system, which, through activation of attendant affective processes, generates feedback in the form of an emotional response. This process is illustrated in **Figure 1**. On this account, incentive learning depends on two processes: a feedback process: (**Figure 1 (a), (b)**) and a feedforward process (**Figure 1 (c)**). Presenting the instrumental outcome in some motivational state or other provides the opportunity for the formation of an association between the outcome representation and the motivation system (**Figure 1(a)**) that acts to open a feedback loop (**Figure 1(b)**). When the outcome is subsequently contacted, activation of the outcome representation acts to produce specific motivational activity that results directly in activity in affective structures productive of an emotional response. Incentive learning

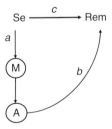

Figure 1 The structure of incentive learning. (a) Sensory features of the instrumental outcome (Se) are associated with a motivational process (M). (b) Through connections with affective structures (A) this connection provides feedback in the form of an emotional response (Rem). (c) Incentive learning reflects the association between Se and Rem based on their contiguous activity.

(**Figure 1**(c)), then, is the formation of a feedforward association between the outcome representation and an emotional response.

Taste aversion-induced outcome devaluation effects provide a good example of this process. In this case, this perspective argues that a taste is first associated with activation of a disgust system induced by LiCl. After this pairing, reexposure to the taste can drive the disgust system to activate the aversive affective system to generate an aversive emotional response. It is the contiguous pairing of the taste and the emotional response that, from this perspective, drives the reduction in reward value induced by reexposure. Notice that, if pairing a taste with illness conditions an association between the taste and disgust, then blocking the activity of the disgust system at the time of conditioning using an antiemetic, i.e., a drug that prevents or relieves illness or nausea, should be predicted to attenuate the formation of that association with the effect that, in the test sessions, rats should prefer a taste poisoned under the antiemetic to some other poisoned taste. But furthermore, if the expression of a previously conditioned aversion, and the consequent change in reward value, depends upon the ability of the taste representation to access the disgust system via an established connection, blocking the activity of the disgust system with an antiemetic during reexposure should be predicted to block the incentive learning effect; see **Figure 2**.

In accord with this suggestion, Limebeer and Parker (2000) reported that the antiemetic ondansetron blocked the expression of the aversive taste reactivity responses induced by a taste previously paired with illness. Furthermore, we have assessed this prediction by assessing the influence of ondansetron on reexposure to a poisoned taste on instrumental choice performance (Balleine et al., 1995b). In this experiment, thirsty rats were trained in a single session to perform two actions, lever pressing and chain pulling, with one action delivering a sucrose solution and the other a saline solution on a concurrent schedule. Immediately after this training session, all of the rats were given an injection of LiCl. Over the next 2 days the rats were given brief periods of reexposure to both the sucrose and the saline solutions. Prior to one reexposure session, rats were injected with ondansetron in an attempt to block the emotional effects of reexposure, whereas prior to the other session they were injected with vehicle. The next day, the rats were given a choice extinction test on the lever and chain. If reexposure devalues the instrumental outcome via the

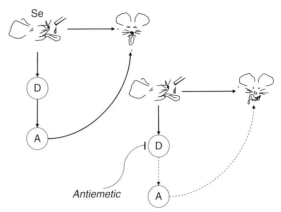

Figure 2 Incentive learning and taste aversion-induced outcome devaluation. The left panel shows the effect of reexposure to a poisoned outcome; the association between the taste (Se) and disgust (D) induced by pairing the taste with illness provokes feedback in the form of a disgust response, allowing the rat to learn about the change in value of the outcome. The right panel shows the predicted effect of an antiemetic on incentive learning. By blocking activity in the disgust system, the antiemetic should reduce the unpleasant emotional feedback and hence the change in value produced during reexposure to the taste. A, affective structures.

ability of the outcome representation to access the disgust system, blocking the activity of that system with ondansetron should attenuate the effects of reexposure such that, on test, the action that, in training, delivered the outcome subsequently reexposed under ondansetron should be performed more than the other action. This is, in fact, exactly what was found (Balleine et al, 1995a). The attenuation of incentive learning by ondansetron provides, therefore, strong confirmation of the suggestion that incentive learning depends critically upon negative feedback generated by an association between the outcome representation and a disgust system.

1.36.2.5 Retrieving Reward Value

Given the role of incentive learning in the encoding of reward, it is interesting to consider how the value conferred by this process is retrieved to determine choice performance. Because the choice tests are often conducted many days after incentive learning, in extinction the rat is forced to rely on their memory of specific action–outcome associations and the current relative value of the instrumental outcomes. So how is value encoded for retrieval during this test?

A currently influential theory, the somatic marker hypothesis (Damasio, 1994), proposes that value is retrieved through the operation of the same processes through which it was encoded. According to this view, decisions based on the value of specific goals are determined by reexperiencing the emotional effects associated with contact with that goal. With regard to outcome devaluation effects, for example, the theory could not be more explicit:

> When a bad outcome connected with a given response option comes to mind, however fleetingly, you experience an unpleasant gut feeling... that forces attention on the negative outcome to which the given action may lead, and functions as an automated alarm signal which says: Beware of danger ahead if you choose the option that leads to this outcome. The signal may lead you to reject, *immediately*, the negative course of action and thus make you choose between other alternatives (Damasio, 1994: 173).

An alternative theory proposes that reward values, once determined through incentive learning, are encoded abstractly (e.g., X is good or Y is bad and so on) and, as such, from this perspective they are not dependent on the original emotional effects induced by contact with the goal during the encoding of incentive value for their retrieval (see Balleine and Dickinson, 1998a; Balleine, 2005, for further discussion).

We have conducted several distinct series of experiments to test these two hypotheses and, in all of these, the data suggest that after incentive learning, incentive values are encoded abstractly and do not involve the original emotional processes that established those values during their retrieval (Balleine and Dickinson, 1994; Balleine et al., 1994, 1995a,b). One test of these two accounts was derived from consideration of the role of associations between the outcome representation and the disgust system in outcome devaluation described in the previous section. If the impact of outcome devaluation on performance is carried by emotional feedback induced by activation of the disgust system by the outcome representation, then, according to the somatic marker hypothesis, reducing the ability of the outcome representation to activate the disgust system during retrieval of incentive value on test by administering ondansetron prior to the test should be predicted to attenuate the effects of outcome devaluation on performance. This experiment replicated the procedures used in the experiment described earlier

(Balleine et al., 1995b) except that, prior to the choice extinction test, half of the animals were injected with ondansetron, whereas the remainder were injected with vehicle. Based on the previous study, it was anticipated that the group given the injection of vehicle prior to the test would perform more of the action that, in training, had delivered the outcome reexposed under ondansetron. More importantly, if activation of the disgust system critically mediates the retrieval of incentive value during the test, as the somatic marker hypothesis suggests, then any difference found in the vehicle group should be attenuated in the group injected with ondansetron on test.

The results of this experiment were very clear; contrary to predictions of the somatic marker hypothesis, the injection of ondansetron on test had no impact whatsoever on performance in the choice extinction test. Whether injected with vehicle or ondansetron prior to the test, the action that, in training, delivered the outcome reexposed under ondansetron was performed more than the other action and to a similar degree. This finding suggests that, although activity in the disgust system determines the effects of incentive learning, the disgust system does not play a role once incentive learning has occurred, i.e., the retrieval of incentive value is not based on the same process through which it was encoded. In line with the proposal that reward value is encoded abstractly or symbolically and in contradiction to predictions from the somatic marker hypothesis position, in this and other similar studies we have found that the processes that determine the encoding of reward value are not required during the retrieval of that value during free choice tests in order for animals to select a course of action.

1.36.3 Secondary Reward

The suggestion that the reward process supporting instrumental conditioning is derived from an association between the sensory features of an event and an emotional response, together with the evidence for the abstract encoding of reward value, provides an immediate explanation as to how events not directly associated with primary motivational systems can serve as the goals of instrumental actions; from this perspective, any stimulus associated with an emotional response should be able to serve as a goal and so support the performance of goal-directed actions. In the past, the seemingly arbitrary nature of goals has been explained in terms of a process called conditioned reinforcement (Skinner, 1938). Within that literature, this process was proposed as the means by which arbitrary things, like colored pieces of paper, could serve as reinforcers supporting the development of new response tendencies through the acquisition of various stimulus-response associations. It is our view that the term conditioned reinforcement is a misnomer; it implies that the actions that they support are no more than habits. Of course, most human actions are acquired and maintained by goals that are associated with primary rewards and so have only an indirect connection to primary motivational systems and as such are more likely to be goal-directed actions than habits. We propose that the process that determines the acquisition of these goals be referred to, therefore, as secondary reward (SdR). Nevertheless, it is clear that the goal-directed status of these actions is something that stands in need of direct assessment.

There is, in addition, a further implication of this account. Although one should anticipate that secondary rewards will be the more potent, what this account of incentive learning portends is that, if the emotional response associated with an event determines whether it can serve as a goal, essentially any event can serve as the goal of an action providing it induces a positive change in emotional tone. In this section we describe research indicating that both stimuli associated with already established rewards and salient sensory events can serve as goals, allowing animals to acquire new responses based on the relationship of actions to these, sometimes weakly but nevertheless apparently rewarding, consequences.

1.36.3.1 Sensory Versus Secondary Reward

As mentioned, the older literature dealing with the phenomenon of conditioned reinforcement proposed that when neutral stimuli were associated with reinforcing ones, they could become conditioned reinforcers. A problem widely neglected within this literature, however, is the fact that apparently neutral stimuli turn out to be very difficult to come by. Indeed, the vast majority of experimentally utilized stimuli are demonstrably not neutral with respect to their ability to support instrumental responding even prior to any pairing with primary reward (Kish, 1966). The capacity of environmental stimuli, or more correctly, of change in the state of environmental stimuli to support instrumental behavior can, however, be well enough handled by the current

claim that reward value is controlled by the emotional response associated with that event providing it is accepted that change in environmental stimuli provides a sufficiently positive change in that response. From this perspective, therefore, events that are sufficiently mild to induce a positive change provide a source of sensory reward (SeR), whether it is derived from generalization or perhaps by another source of motivation, such as a form of preparatory state produced by general affective arousal (Konorski, 1967) or perhaps, as has occasionally been proposed in the past, by a primary motivational process such as curiosity (Berlyne, 1960).

In order to use secondary reward as a tool to establish the way apparently arbitrary events can become the goals of instrumental action, it is important first to compare the influence of secondary and sensory rewards on the performance of actions. The question is, which secondary reward procedure should one employ to do so? The central position of this notion in Hull's conception of learning (Hull, 1943) and Skinner's utilization of it to explain the origin of human actions without apparent reinforcement (Skinner, 1938) drove considerable research during the middle part of the last century intended to establish or to disprove its applicability to the conditioning process. The most commonly used procedure to analyze SdR has been in chain schedules of instrumental reinforcement, where both instrumental training with the SdR and the pairing of the event with reward presumed to support that conditioned reinforcer occurred within a common sequence of behavior. Zimmerman (1969), for instance, gave rats the opportunity to press one lever in order to obtain the presentation of a stimulus light on a fixed interval. Once that stimulus was presented, a response on a second lever would result in the delivery of food. The stimulus light, via its forward pairings with the food, should have accrued associative strength over the course of performance. Because, however, responding on the first component of the chain also activated the second manipulandum in the chain, it is difficult to assert that the animal was responding for the stimulus rather than the opportunity to respond on that second manipulandum. Chain schedules, therefore, typically require some further intervention in order to partition the sources of support for instrumental responding. In this case, Zimmerman took advantage of the fact that the pattern of responding on fixed interval and variable interval schedules differs to assess whether the light was controlling performance on the first lever as a secondary reward.

To do this, he put the rewarding impacts of the light and food into competition with each other on the first lever. In a test phase, the light was presented as a result of responding on the first lever on a variable interval schedule, whereas the food was presented on the fixed interval schedule that had previously delivered the light and the second lever was shifted to an extinction schedule. Zimmerman found that the pattern of responding on the first lever shifted from that typical of a fixed interval schedule to that typical of a variable interval schedule, a finding consistent with the development of conditioned reinforcing properties by the stimulus light.

Although commonly employed, the difficulty of ruling out alternative interpretations of the source of instrumental performance on chain schedules leaves something to be desired. Since the second response, as in Zimmerman's study (1969), often becomes superfluous in the critical phase testing for the presence of SdR, it follows that it may not be necessary at all. Extinction studies of SdR reify this possibility, by utilizing a training phase where an instrumental action is paired with a stimulus that is immediately followed by the delivery of a reward. Because of the presence of the reward during training, the second, third, and higher components of the instrumental chain used to provide further conditioned stimuli and eventual primary reinforcement in chain studies of SdR are eliminated from the outset. A test phase is again required to detect the role of the SdR in the maintenance of that instrumental behavior. If the SdR plays no role in the maintenance of instrumental responding, then with or without its presence at an extinction test phase, animals should extinguish at the same rate. Instead, researchers usually find that animals extinguish much more slowly when the instrumental response leads to the delivery of the putative conditioned reinforcer than when it leads to no stimulus consequences (Bugelski, 1938).

Although these studies appear to confirm the basic effect, the most direct way to demonstrate and compare the secondary or sensory reward value of some event or other is to assess its ability to serve as the goal during the acquisition of a new action. If stimuli acquire the ability to reward instrumental actions in the course of pairing them with a primary reward, then it follows that one should be able to demonstrate the acquisition of instrumental actions that have as their sole outcome the delivery of a stimulus with a history of this pairing. This logic has been frequently employed in the detection of SdR, and procedures employing it have generally been referred to as

acquisition of a new response, or simply, acquisition tests of SdR. Especially attractive is the absence of confounding effects of primary reward during training that could interfere with SdR interpretations of instrumental behaviors (Wike, 1966). Numerous experiments along these lines have been conducted by giving prior stimulus–outcome associations followed by training on a lever that delivers that stimulus. Work by Trevor Robbins and colleagues has demonstrated particularly clear acquisition of lever-press performance when that lever delivered a stimulus that was previously associated with food relative to an inactive lever that the rats could press but that had no scheduled consequences (Taylor and Robbins, 1984; Robbins et al., 1989).

We have conducted a similar experiment to those of Robbins using two different versions of their procedure, firstly to replicate their basic result but also to examine the effects of using a different control condition in which one lever delivered a stimulus that had previously been paired with food and the other lever delivered a familiar stimulus but that had not been paired with any rewarding consequence; a sensory reinforcement control (SeR). The results of this study are presented in **Figure 3**. As is clear from this figure, a good conditioned reinforcement effect was observed in both conditions: responding on the lever delivering the SdR was greater than on the inactive lever (left panel) and greater on the lever delivering the SdR than on the lever delivering the SeR. It is also clear, however, that the net size of the SdR effect is really much smaller than one might be led to believe from the difference between the active and inactive levers.

1.36.3.2   Do Secondary Rewards Reward, Reinstate, or Reinforce?

Describing events associated with primary reward as SdRs suggests that the responses that animals learn to gain access to SdRs are goal-directed. This is, however, a matter of dispute. It has often been argued in the past that, rather than developing reward value, the stimulus acquires the ability to drive instrumental responding in an S–R fashion, i.e., rather than acting as a goal in and of itself, it acts to reinforce the connection between situational cues and the response. That the conditioned reinforcing stimulus itself might not be the object of an instrumental action, but rather an elicitor of that action, is an explanation that has seen some theoretical and experimental exploration. Bugelski (1956), for instance, reinterpreted his

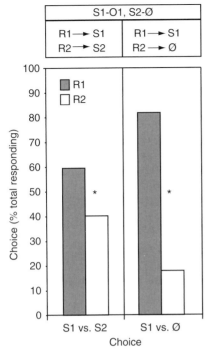

Figure 3 An assessment of secondary reward conducted in a choice test on two levers. Rats were first given pairings between one stimulus (S1) and a rewarding outcome (O1), whereas another stimulus was presented unpaired (S2). Some rats were then allowed to press two levers. In one group, one lever delivered S1 and the other S2 (left panel) in the other group, one lever delivered S1 and the other nothing (Ø). It is clear that both tasks revealed a secondary rewarding effect of S1 on performance. However, the effect is somewhat exaggerated by the choice between S1 and Ø. When sensory reward is taken into consideration, as it is in the choice between S1 and S2, the net secondary reward effect is significantly smaller.

earlier extinction test-conditioned reinforcement data (Bugelski, 1938) using this framework and found that it provided a satisfactory account of the results. During acquisition training, the SdR not only follows the instrumental response as a consequence, but on all trials except the first bears a forward predictive relationship with later occurrences of that response. It is at least possible that during acquisition the instrumental action is reinforced solely by the primary reinforcer, whereas the SdR becomes associated with the response itself. In extinction, it is argued, the conditioned reinforcer then acts, following the first response, to delay extinction through this conditioned ability to evoke or reinstate subsequent instrumental responses.

Wyckoff (1959) attempted to produce a quantitative model of SdR effects emphasizing the eliciting function, or cue properties, of the conditioned reinforcer. This model was based on the results of an experiment reported by Wyckoff et al. (1958) in which rats were given conditioning trials where a buzzer was followed by the delivery of water. Following this training, experimental rats were given the opportunity to press a lever in order to secure the delivery of the buzzer without water, and control rats were placed on an omission schedule, where the buzzer was delivered if they refrained from pressing the lever. Performance between the two groups was not reliably different, which led Wyckoff et al. to conclude that the buzzer functioned primarily not to reward lever pressing, in which case the experimental group should have pressed significantly more than the control animals, but to elicit lever pressing. This result, however, has not been replicated, suggesting that some feature of the experimental design, or a simple lack of power, prevented Wyckoff et al. from observing cue-independent conditioned reinforcing effects. Indeed, Ward (1960) conducted a formally very similar experiment, substituting food reward for water and the random delivery of the cue in the control group for the omission schedule, and demonstrated a reliably greater level of responding in experimental animals than in control animals.

An important source of evidence against the response elicitation account of SdR effects comes from an experimental series performed by Crowder and his colleagues. They employed a yoked control procedure in several different paradigms to demonstrate the existence of secondary reward above and beyond the effects of stimulus-based response elicitation. In all experiments, the experimental animals performed an instrumental action that was followed by the delivery of SdR. At the same time as that delivery, the yoked controls received noncontingent presentation of that same stimulus. If the stimulus elicited or reinstated further responding, it should have done so equally in both groups. Instead, in the extinction test paradigm (Crowder et al., 1959a), the acquisition of a new response paradigm (Crowder et al., 1959b), and in reacquisition (Crowder et al., 1959c) and retention SdR paradigms (Crowder et al., 1959d), they found superior performance in the experimental subjects whose actions were correlated with the delivery of the SdR. Although these results are not completely immune to criticism derived from the analysis of systematic sources of error in the yoked group (Church, 1964), they indicate the relatively small degree of support that elicitation or reinstatement accounts provide for instrumental responding in SdR paradigms.

One published study has attempted to assess whether lever pressing for the SdR is goal-directed by devaluing the primary reward previously associated with the SdR (Parkinson et al., 2005). In this study rats were given pairings of a light stimulus paired with sugar after which the sugar was paired with illness. Although this reduced responding to the sucrose, it did not affect the ability of the light to serve as a secondary reward for lever pressing; lever pressing was acquired and maintained to a comparable degree whether the sucrose had been devalued or not. The authors concluded that, as the lever pressing appeared to be independent of the value of the primary reward, performance acquired through SdR should be considered habitual. But what was not confirmed in this study, however, was whether the devaluation of the sucrose was successful in modifying the reward value of the light. Indeed, as the SdR value depends on the association of the light with the emotional response elicited by the sucrose, rather than by the sucrose itself (see **Figure 4**), it seems unlikely that SdR could be undermined in this way. Rather, what this account predicts is that devaluation of the SdR could only be induced by counterconditioning, i.e., pairing the light previously paired with sucrose with a noxious consequence, such as foot shock. Would lever pressing still have been maintained after this treatment? To date no studies along these lines have been conducted, although there is plenty of evidence from studies of conditioned punishment to conclude that at least the sensory

rewarding component of stimuli is abolished by this means of devaluation (Killcross et al., 1997).

Other studies from our laboratory have, however, confirmed that actions acquired for a secondary reward are essentially goal-directed. As discussed with respect to primary reward, one of the criteria for defining an action as goal-directed is that it is sensitive to the causal relationship between the action and reward. In this experiment, rats were first given pairings between two distinct visual cues with one cue paired with sucrose and the other with food pellets. After this training, the rats were trained to press two levers, each associated with a different visual cue. In these sessions, one of the visual cues was also presented noncontingently; as such the noncontingent cue was the same as that presented contingent on pressing one lever but different from that presented for pressing the other lever. As such the specific R-SdR contingency was maintained on one lever but was degraded on the other. The results of this study are presented in **Figure 5**. As is clear from this figure, the rats were sensitive to the specific lever press–SdR contingency, reducing performance on the action delivering the same SdR as that delivered noncontingently relative to the other action. This result is not consistent with either the reinforcing or reinstating functions of SdRs (Winterbauer, 2006).

An important aspect of the establishment of a secondary reward is its pairing with primary reward. The procedures that establish SdRs are, in fact, identical to those used to establish Pavlovian CRs to a stimulus. The possibility that stimuli require something more than Pavlovian conditioning to become conditioned reinforcers has been entertained; Skinner (1938) proposed, for example, in a thesis later considered in detail in the work of Keller and Schoenfeld (1950), that only stimuli that act to set the occasion for responding to other Pavlovian stimuli could serve as SdRs. Again, as Wike (1966) suggested, although occasion setters may make better SdRs, there seems to be no requirement that all conditioned reinforcers be occasion setters. Work in our laboratory has largely confirmed this view, in that we show perfectly reasonable SdR effects without special modifications to the Pavlovian conditioning phase (Winterbauer, 2006). But this raises an important issue: if SdR can be established using Pavlovian procedures, are the processes underlying reward and those underlying Pavlovian incentive motivation all one and the same? Or is this no more than a superficial, procedural similarity?

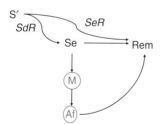

Figure 4   Sensory reward (SeR) is derived from the emotional effects (Rem) of stimulus change that can be produced by the presentation of even quite neutral stimuli (such as S′). Secondary reward (SdR) is derived from the pairing of S′ with an excitatory sensory event (Se in this diagram) previously established as a primary reward and through its association with an emotional response generated by its connection with both motivational (M) and affective (Af) processes (see **Figure 1**).

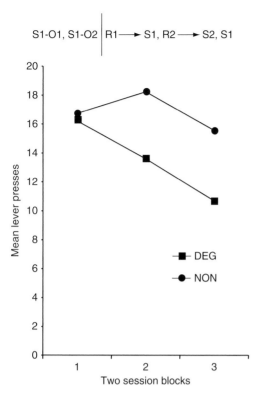

S1-O1, S1-O2 | R1 ⟶ S1, R2 ⟶ S2, S1

Figure 5 Contingency degradation in instrumental conditioning using secondary rewards. After establishing two stimuli (S1 and S2) as secondary rewards by pairing them with primary rewards, rats were trained to perform two lever-press responses (R1 and R2) with one earning S1 and the other S2. Noncontiguous presentations of one secondary reward (e.g., S1) degraded the response–outcome contingency (DEG) and caused a significant reduction in responding on the lever delivering S1 (DEG) relative to that delivering S2 (NON).

1.36.4 Reward and the Anticipation of Reward

The preceding sections have reviewed the considerable evidence suggesting that the influence of changes in reward value on goal-directed instrumental actions is an important determinant of action selection and of instrumental performance generally. Other factors can clearly influence performance, however. One of the most obvious, and perhaps best-documented, influences on action selection is that produced by stimuli 'associated' with reward. Advertising has a clear influence on action selection; if it did not the advertising industry would be a vacuous waste of time and of advertisers' money. Of course, advertisers are hoping that the stimuli that they associate with a particular product will provide

the basis for quite specific changes in choice performance and, of course, by and large they do. It is important to recognize, however, that, despite a superficial similarity in some of the procedures used to establish the reward value of particular events, notably SdRs, there is substantial evidence suggesting that the influence of cues associated with reward on goal-directed instrumental actions is not mediated by the reward system. In this section, we describe this evidence as it has emerged from analyses of the relationship between Pavlovian and instrumental conditioning, particularly those proposing that the motivational processes engaged by reward and by the anticipation of reward are the same or, at the very least, interact with one another.

1.36.4.1 Pavlovian-Instrumental Interactions

In fact, some of the earliest evidence that the representation of the instrumental outcome takes part in action selection was found by studying how Pavlovian and instrumental learning processes interact. For instance, Trapold (1970) trained rats on a biconditional discrimination in which, on any given trial, subjects were allowed to choose between two actions (left and right lever press). Trials were initiated by the presentation of one of two discriminative stimuli (tone and clicker), signaling which of the actions would be rewarded (e.g., S1 → R1 and S2 → R2). The novel feature of this experiment, however, was that these cues also signaled the identity of the outcome that could be earned on that trial. Whereas the control groups earned either food pellets (food control) or sucrose solution (sucrose control) on both actions (e.g., S1 → R1 → O1 and S2 → R1 → O1), the experimental group was rewarded with one outcome (O1; e.g., pellets) for performing one action and a different outcome (O2; e.g., sucrose) for performing the other action (e.g., S1 → R1 → O1 and S2 → R2 → O2). Consequently, the experimental group differed from the control groups in that, for the former, each discriminative stimulus signaled not only a different response but also a different outcome. Interestingly, Trapold (1970) found that the experimental group acquired more rapidly than either control group despite the fact that the S–R arrangements needed to solve the discrimination were the same across conditions.

This phenomenon, known as the differential outcomes effect, provides clear evidence that reward expectations can be used to guide action selection.

Moreover, the representation mediating this effect appears to consist of richly detailed information about the sensory properties of the reward. In Trapold's (1970) study, the sucrose solution and grain-based pellets used to differentially reward the two actions were both nutritive outcomes and so should have held a similar incentive value for hungry rats. Since this motivational variable does not appear to have been used to discriminate between actions, rats probably relied instead on the sensory features (e.g., texture, odor, taste) of the anticipated outcome. There is even evidence that this effect can be obtained using outcomes that differ in one motivationally irrelevant sensory feature. Fedorchak and Bolles (1986) trained thirsty rats on a biconditional lever press discrimination task in which each correct response was rewarded with water. For two groups, the delivery of water was occasionally paired with a flashing light; whereas the light exclusively followed just one of the two S–R arrangements in the differential outcomes group, it followed both responses with an equal probability in the nondifferential control group. For a third group, the light was never paired with water. Once again, the group that received differential outcomes acquired more rapidly than the other two groups, demonstrating that the expectancy of a sensory event extraneous to outcome itself could be used to guide action selection.

How does differential outcomes training provide an advantage in discriminating between two actions? Clearly, it must have something to do with the Pavlovian contingencies embedded in the task (see **Figure 6**, top panel). It has long been argued that Pavlovian learning plays an important role in the control of instrumental performance (Rescorla and Solomon, 1967). Although we will discuss alternative accounts shortly, let us first consider the model Trapold and Overmier (1972) devised to explain the differential outcomes effect and similar findings (see **Figure 6**, middle panel). Their model was built within the general framework of traditional S–R theory (Hull, 1943), and so instrumental learning was assumed to involve the gradual recruitment of S–R associations through a conventional reinforcement process. However, Trapold and Overmier (1972) proposed that reward deliveries engage a second, Pavlovian learning process capable of supporting the acquisition of stimulus–reward associations. It was argued that through such learning, stimuli acquired the capacity to elicit a reward expectancy comprising the sensory features of that event. The final step in their argument was in allowing this reward

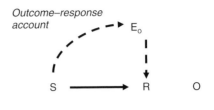

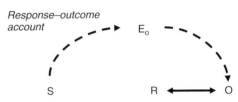

Figure 6 Schematic diagrams illustrating the associative structure proposed to underlie instrumental conditioning on various accounts. As shown in the top panel, the introduction of an instrumental (R–O) contingency is typically accompanied by an imbedded Pavlovian (S–O) contingency, arising from incidental pairings between contextual cues and reward. Two-process accounts of action selection have proposed that Pavlovian learning results in the generation of an outcome expectancy (E_o), which may guide performance by entering into association with the instrumental response (middle panel), or by retrieving any response that had earned the expected outcome (bottom panel).

expectancy to enter into S–R associations like any other sensorial event in the training environment, i.e., the expectation of reward was assumed to acquire discriminative control over performance. According to this analysis, the experimental group in Trapold's (1970) study was provided with an additional source of stimulus support for action selection; the correct choice was signaled by both an auditory cue and an expectation of the reward that could be earned on that trial.

The differential outcomes effect provides strong evidence that the Pavlovian learning can influence instrumental performance through a highly specific representation of the mediating outcome. Further evidence for this claim comes from studies of the so-called Pavlovian-instrumental transfer effect. For instance, Kruse et al. (1983) first trained rats using a biconditional procedure quite similar to that used in differential outcomes studies (e.g., Trapold, 1970;

Fedorchak and Bolles, 1986), such that each stimulus (clicker and tone) signaled both the response (left or right lever) that would be rewarded and the identity of its outcome (pellets or sucrose solution). During a separate Pavlovian training phase, the group of interest to our current discussion received pairings between a stimulus (pause in the background white noise) and one of the two outcomes (either pellets or sucrose). In a subsequent test phase, Kruse et al. (1983) found that presentations of this stimulus facilitated instrumental performance in an outcome-dependent manner; rats preferentially increased their performance of the action that had shared a common outcome with that cue, relative to the other action. Importantly, this test was conducted in extinction, indicating that this effect relied entirely on information acquired during earlier training phases.

Following Kruse et al. (1983), there have been numerous demonstrations of outcome-specific transfer (Colwill and Rescorla, 1988), even using actions that had been acquired through free operant training (Colwill and Motzkin, 1994; Delamater, 1995; Holland, 2004). The latter finding is important because it reveals that Pavlovian learning can influence action selection even under conditions in which anticipating reward provides no obvious advantage in obtaining reward. According to Trapold and Overmier (1972), the transfer effect emerges because the Pavlovian outcome expectancy selectively retrieves the response it signaled during training through the activation of an outcome–response association (see **Figure 6**, top panel). This account applies equally well to the free operant situation. Note that in any instrumental conditioning study there exists an embedded Pavlovian relationship between contextual cues and the reward delivery. In this case, cues that best predict reward should come to elicit an expectancy of reward capable of entering into association with the response.

Of course, the two-process account of Trapold and Overmier (1972) does not provide the only explanation for the influence of Pavlovian reward expectancies over instrumental performance. For instance, several two-process theories have been proposed that assume instrumental learning involves encoding some approximation of the action–outcome contingency arranged by the experimenter (Bolles, 1972; Asratyan, 1974). According to this view, Pavlovian outcome expectancies guide action selection by retrieving the action that had actually earned that outcome during training (see **Figure 6**, bottom panel).

1.36.4.2 The Two-Process Account of Reward Value

How is Pavlovian-instrumental transfer relevant to our interpretation of instrumental performance as an instance of goal-directed action? Recall that in order to be considered goal-directed, a behavior must be performed because of its expected consequences; performance should depend on the subject's capacity to (1) anticipate the outcome of the action (i.e., action–outcome learning) and (2) evaluate the incentive properties of that outcome (i.e., incentive learning). Two-process theories, however, tend to attribute incentive effects, such as the sensitivity of instrumental performance to outcome devaluation, to the Pavlovian process (Rescorla and Solomon, 1967). These accounts typically assume that Pavlovian learning provides the motivational support for instrumental performance. Even Trapold and Overmier (1972), who took an expressly associative approach, entertained the possibility that incentive manipulations have their effect by disrupting the capacity of the Pavlovian outcome expectancy to mediate response selection (e.g., through generalization decrement). Others have taken a more explicitly motivational position. Bolles (1972), for instance, proposed that Pavlovian and instrumental processes interact based on their shared outcome expectancies, but that this interaction is gated by the incentive value of mediating outcome. The two-process approach, therefore, provides a compelling explanation for the influence of reward value over performance. According to this account, instrumental responding is depressed following outcome devaluation, not because of a reduction in the reward value of the outcome and knowledge of the underlying response–outcome contingency, but because this treatment diminishes the Pavlovian support for performance.

The claim that Pavlovian learning plays a part in action selection is beyond doubt. The critical question, however, is whether these processes are responsible for the influence of reward value over performance. If so, it would be necessary to abandon the goal-directed interpretation of instrumental performance altogether. Note that since the two-process account uses the Pavlovian–instrumental interaction responsible for transfer to explain the sensitivity of performance to outcome devaluation, it predicts that these two apparently distinct forms of action selection should share a common associative structure. One way to evaluate this prediction, therefore, is to assess whether the associations guiding transfer and outcome devaluation are acquired at roughly the same rate. For instance, it has been repeatedly shown that, while sensitivity to outcome devaluation emerges with rather limited training (Holland, 2004; Yin et al., 2005), depending on training parameters used (e.g., number of action–outcome contingencies), this effect is either maintained (Colwill and Rescorla, 1985a) or attenuated (Adams, 1981; Holland, 2004) with training that is more extensive. Alternatively, recent evidence suggests that Pavlovian-instrumental transfer increases in magnitude with more extensive instrumental training (Holland, 2004).

It should also be possible to evaluate the two-process account by analyzing the content of the associations that mediate transfer and outcome devaluation. However, it is important to remember that individual two-process theories do not agree on what that content should be. Trapold and Overmier (1972), for instance, argued that the response becomes associated with an expectancy of reward generated by prevailing stimuli, resulting in an outcome–response association. As we have mentioned, others (e.g., Asratyan, 1974; Bolles, 1972) have proposed that the response becomes associated with the outcome it actually produces during training, in the form of a response–outcome association. Two-process theories, therefore, can be distinguished by determining whether the association responsible for action selection reflects the actual response–outcome contingency, or whether it is, instead, the product of the incidental stimulus–outcome contingency present during training. However, investigating the relative contribution of these two contingencies to instrumental learning is no trivial task. In any typical instrumental conditioning study, the outcome earned by the response is also predicted by the prevailing situational cues (i.e., the anticipated and earned outcomes are the same). Thus, one approach to the problem is to create a training situation in which this in not the case.

Several studies have used this basic strategy to assess the associative structure underlying transfer and outcome devaluation. For instance, Colwill (1994) reported evidence of outcome selective transfer with responses that had been concurrently trained on distinct action–outcome contingencies. Similarly, Colwill and Rescorla (1985b) reported that rats display an outcome-specific devaluation effect after concurrent training of this kind. Since rats given concurrent training are allowed to alternate freely between responses, the context should be associated

equally with both outcomes, thereby preventing the development of specific outcome–response associations. The specificity of transfer and outcome devaluation despite this treatment, therefore, seems to suggest that both effects can be supported by response–outcome learning.

Rescorla and Colwill (1989) and Rescorla (1992) have attempted more directly to compare the relative contribution of outcome–response and response–outcome associations to these effects. For instance, Rescorla and Colwill (1989) investigated this issue by first pretraining rats on a common nose-poke response with four distinct stimuli; two stimuli (S1 and S3) signaled a pellet reward and two others (S2 and S4) signaled a sucrose solution. Next, they were given discrimination training on two responses (R1 and R2), such that one response, say R1, earned pellets and the other response, R2, earned sucrose. However, each response was also signaled by a stimulus that had previously been paired with the alternative outcome (i.e., $S2 \rightarrow R1 \rightarrow O1$ and $S1 \rightarrow R2 \rightarrow O2$). According to Trapold and Overmier's (1972) two-process account, this should have resulted in the formation of, for example, a sucrose–R1 association, even though R1 had actually been followed by pellets. During the transfer test, rats were allowed to perform each response in extinction while S3 and S4 were occasionally presented. In contrast to the predictions of the outcome–response view, it was found that stimulus presentations selectively facilitated performance based on the identity of the outcome that 'followed' a response during training (e.g., S3 increased R1 relative to R2). Furthermore, in a separate experiment, Rescorla and Colwill (1989) used the same strategy to investigate the structure underlying outcome devaluation performance. They found that, as with transfer, the sensitivity of instrumental performance to reward value was dominated by response–outcome learning; performance was suppressed by devaluing the outcome that the action had actually earned during training, not the outcome that was signaled by the discriminative stimulus (e.g., devaluing O1 decreased R1 relative to R2).

There is, however, reason to question whether these experiments provide a fair test of the outcome–response account. This basic approach, of course, depends entirely on the experimenter's capacity to create a situation in which the expectation of reward differs from the reward that is obtained by responding. In Rescorla and Colwill's (1989) study, for instance, each discriminative stimulus was pretrained so that it would signal a different outcome from the one that would be earned on that trial. Since this phase of the experiment was conducted over 4 days, however, it is possible that rats were able to learn the new stimulus–outcome relationships (e.g., S1 → O2), nullifying the effects of pretraining. Rescorla (1992) addressed this issue in an experiment otherwise quite similar to the first (Rescorla and Colwill, 1989), except that, during the discrimination phase, each stimulus continued to be paired with the outcome that it predicted during initial pretraining, while at the same time signaling that responding could earn the opposite outcome. These additional Pavlovian trials were added to encourage the persistence of the initial stimulus–outcome learning, thereby providing greater opportunity for any potential outcome–response associations to form during the instrumental discrimination training. Using this new procedure, Rescorla (1992) once again found no evidence that outcome–response associations play a part in outcome devaluation performance. However, the results of transfer testing were less straightforward. He observed that stimulus presentations tended to increase the performance of both responses, although this effect was larger for the response that had 'earned' the outcome signaled by the transfer stimulus than it was for the response that had been trained in 'anticipation' of that outcome. Thus, while these findings suggest that both outcome devaluation and transfer are dominated by response–outcome learning, they also indicate that outcome–response associations may play some, albeit limited, role in the latter.

This conclusion does not help the two-process account of reward value. According to this account, the processes underlying transfer and outcome devaluation should be identical. Perhaps more importantly, however, these studies illustrate the difficulty in attempting to dissociate the contributions of Pavlovian and instrumental learning to performance. Indeed, even in these studies it is possible that the subjects were able to confound the experimenter's intentions and acquire appropriate stimulus–outcome associations during instrumental training based on the relationship between the features of the individual response manipulanda and the outcome earned by those responses. For instance, rats trained to press a lever for pellets and pull a chain for sucrose solution may come to associate the lever itself with pellets and the chain with sucrose. Such learning would ensure that the rat anticipated the reward that they would actually obtain for performing the response, even in the presence of a context

that signaled both rewards (e.g., Colwill and Rescorla, 1985b; Colwill, 1994) or a Pavlovian cue that signaled a different reward (e.g., Rescorla and Colwill, 1989; Rescorla, 1992).

This problem can be avoided, however, by training distinct action–outcome contingencies on a common response manipulandum. For instance, Dickinson et al. (1996) trained rats to push a vertically positioned pole to the left and right for different outcomes; for half the rats, left pushes earned food pellets and right pushes earned a maltodextrin solution, whereas the other half was trained with the opposite arrangement. Rats were then sated on one of the two outcomes in order to selectively reduce its reward value. Immediately after this treatment, they were given an extinction test in which the pole was available and could be pushed freely in either direction without consequence. Dickinson et al. (1996) found that, despite having both actions trained on a common manipulandum, the rats were able to use response–outcome training relationships to guide their action selection according to outcome value; rats were less likely to push the pole in the direction that had earned the now devalued outcome, relative to the other direction. This finding is incompatible with the two-process account, which predicts that outcome-selective devaluation should never emerge in the absence of differential stimulus–outcome contingencies. Instead, it provides strong support for the view that instrumental performance is goal-directed and that its sensitivity to reward value depends on response–outcome learning.

One final method for evaluation of the two-process account of reward value involves assessing the interaction between transfer and outcome devaluation. If these phenomena rely on the same underlying structure, then the capacity of a Pavlovian cue to facilitate performance should depend on the value of the mediating outcome representation. Colwill and Rescorla (1990) directly investigated the role of incentive value in outcome selective transfer. Rats were initially given biconditional discrimination training using differential outcomes, such that one stimulus (S1) signaled that pellets could be earned on one response (R1) and the other stimulus (S2) signaled that sucrose could be earned on a different response (R2). Subsequently, they were given free operant training on two new responses (R3 and R4), such that each earned a unique outcome (either pellets or sucrose). One outcome was then devalued through conditioned taste aversion and then a transfer test was conducted in extinction, with both R3 and R4 available. Although rats were, in general, less likely to perform the response that had earned the devalued outcome than the other response, both responses were selectively facilitated by presentations of the stimulus with which they shared a common outcome. Moreover, the magnitude of this transfer effect, measured in the difference from baseline performance, was comparable across responses. This basic finding, that devaluing an outcome fails to diminish its capacity to mediate Pavlovian-instrumental transfer, has since been replicated in a number of studies (Rescorla, 1994; Holland, 2004).

Altogether, there appears to be scant support for the two-process account of reward value. The associative processes supporting outcome devaluation and transfer appear to be acquired at different rates and encode somewhat different content. Furthermore, instrumental responses remain sensitive to outcome devaluation under conditions that cannot support differential stimulus–outcome learning. Finally, the Pavlovian-instrumental interaction responsible for transfer does not appear to depend on the reward value of the retrieved outcome. Instead, these findings strengthen the goal-directed view of instrumental action and, while demonstrating that reward anticipation influences action selection, it is also clear that this effect is not mediated by the reward system.

1.36.5 Summary and Conclusions

We have argued that the reward system is a specialization that developed in the service of goal-directed action allowing animals to encode the relative values of specific environmental events. These values provide the basis for choice, allowing animals to decide on a course of action based not only on knowledge or information as to the consequences of an action but on the basis of the value of those consequences.

Encoding the reward value of a particular event involves the formation of an association between the specific sensory representation of that event and an emotional response. In the case of primary rewards, the emotional response is directly determined by the activity of specific motivational and affective processes engaged during consummatory contact with the outcome. Thus, by virtue of their biologically active properties (e.g., nutrient, fluidic, pheromonal),

rewarding events (food, fluid, sex objects, and so on) are readily able to activate these underlying systems that modify emotional responses as one of the consequences of that activation. Basing the evaluation of primary rewards on emotional responses is adaptive if those responses are determined by the operation of these basic motivational and affective systems, which is essential if the animal's choice between alternative courses of action is to remain, by and large, adaptive too. In the case of secondary rewards, the emotional response is, of course, determined by the primary reward with which it is paired. By basing the transfer of value from primary to secondary rewards on an emotional response, the selection of actions, even when they are directed toward achieving apparently quite arbitrary goals, can be understood as being constrained by primary motivational processes through their influence on emotional responses.

Finally, we addressed the distinction between the role the reward system plays in assigning reward value and the processes controlling the anticipation of reward. These are quite distinct aspects of behavioral control; although cues that signal forthcoming rewards can provide information that can be used by the goal-directed system, they do not depend, ultimately, on the reward system to play that role. As such, the influence of reward-related cues on action selection does not replace or explain away the functions of the reward system in this regard. Rather, the distinct processes mediating the effects of reward and of the anticipation of reward provides the basis for understanding the role that cognitive processes generally play in goal-directed action. Because it constrains the event relations to which an animal is exposed, there has been a long tradition of using Pavlovian conditioning to model the cognitive control of behavior. The fact that, ultimately, this system is concerned with the production of reflexive responses would, however, appear to render this approach perhaps a little too abstract. It makes more sense to study the role of cognition in a behavioral system within which information can act to influence performance. Based on the evidence reviewed here that animals are able to exert control over their instrumental actions, choose between actions based on the relative value of their consequences, and use predictive information to influence action selection, we suggest that instrumental conditioning provides the more precise model of this capacity.

Acknowledgments

The preparation of this chapter was supported by the National Institute of Mental Health, grant #56446.

References

Adams CD (1981) Variations in the sensitivity of instrumental responding to reinforcer devalaution. *Q. J. Exp. Psychol. B* 34: 77–98.

Adams CD and Dickinson A (1981) Instrumental responding following reinforcer devaluation. *Q. J. Exp. Psychol. B* 33: 109–121.

Asratyan EA (1974) Conditioned reflex theory and motivational behavior. *Acta Neurobiol. Exp.* 34: 15–31.

Balleine B (1992) Instrumental performance following a shift in primary motivation depends on incentive learning. *J Exp Psychol Anim Behav Process* 18: 236–250.

Balleine BW (2001) Incentive processes in instrumental conditioning. In: Klein RMS (ed.) *Handbook of Contemporary Learning Theories*, pp. 307–366. Hillsdale, NJ: Lawrence Erlbaum Associates.

Balleine B and Dickinson A (1991) Instrumental performance following reinforcer devaluation depends upon incentive learning. *Q. J. Exp. Psychol. B* 43: 279–296.

Balleine BW and Dickinson A (1994) The role of cholecystokinin in the motivational control of instrumental action. *Behav. Neurosci.* 108: 590–605.

Balleine BW and Dickinson A (1998a) Goal-directed instrumental action: Contingency and incentive learning and their cortical substrates. *Neuropharmacology* 37: 407–419.

Balleine BW and Dickinson A (1998b) The role of incentive learning in instrumental outcome revaluation by specific satiety. *Anim. Learn. Behav.* 26: 46–59.

Balleine B, Ball J, and Dickinson A (1994) Benzodiazepine-induced outcome revaluation and the motivational control of instrumental action in rats. *Behav. Neurosci.* 108: 573–589.

Balleine B, Davies A, and Dickinson A (1995a) Cholecystokinin attenuates incentive learning in rats. *Behav. Neurosci.* 109: 312–319.

Balleine B, Garner C, and Dickinson A (1995b) Instrumental outcome devaluation is attenuated by the anti-emetic ondansetron. *Q. J. Exp. Psychol.* B 48: 235–251.

Berlyne DEC (1960) *Contact, Arousal and Curiosity*. New York: McGraw-Hill.

Bernstein IL (1999) Taste aversion learning: A contemporary perspective. *Nutrition* 15: 229–234.

Berridge K, Grill HJ, and Norgren R (1981) Relation of consummatory responses and preabsorptive insulin release to palatability and learned taste aversions. *J. Comp. Physiol. Psychol.* 95: 363–382.

Bolles RC (1972) Reinforcement, expectancy, and learning. *Psychol. Rev.* 79: 394–409.

Bugelski BR (1956) *The Psychology of Learning*. New York: Holt.

Bugelski R (1938) Extinction with and without sub-goal reinforcement. *J. Comp. Psychol.* 26: 121–134.

Church RM (1964) Systematic effect of random error in the yoked control design. *Psychol. Bull.* 62.

Colwill RM (1994) Associative representations of instrumental contingencies. In: Medin DL (ed.) *The Psychology of Learning and Motivation*, pp. 1–72. New York: Academic Press.

Colwill RM and Motzkin DK (1994) Encoding of the unconditioned stimulus in Pavlovian conditioning. *Anim. Learn. Behav.* 22: 384–394.

Colwill RM and Rescorla RA (1985a) Instrumental responding remains sensitive to reinforcer devaluation after extensive training. *J. Exp. Psychol. Anim. Behav. Process.* 11: 520–536.

Colwill RM and Rescorla RA (1985b) Postconditioning devaluation of a reinforcer affects instrumental responding. *J. Exp. Psychol. Anim. Behav. Process.* 11: 120–132.

Colwill RM and Rescorla RA (1986) Associative structures in instrumental learning. In: *The Psychology of Learning and Motivation*, pp. 55–104 Orlando: Academic Press.

Colwill RM and Rescorla RA (1988) Associations between the discriminative stimulus and the reinforcer in instrumental learning. *J. Exp. Psychol. Anim. Behav. Process.* 14: 155–164.

Colwill RM and Rescorla RA (1990) Effect of reinforcer devaluation on discriminative control of instrumental behavior. *J. Exp. Psychol. Anim. Behav. Process.* 16: 40–47.

Crowder WF, Morris JB, and McDaniel MH (1959a) Secondary reinforcement or response facilitation? I. Resistance to extinction. *J. Psychol.* 48: 299–302.

Crowder WF, Gill K Jr, Hodge CC, and Nash FA Jr (1959b) Secondary reinforcement or response facilitation? II. Response acquisition. *J. Psychol.* 48: 303–306.

Crowder WF, Gay BR, Bright MG, and Lee MF (1959c) Secondary reinforcement or response facilitation? III. Reconditioning. *J. Psychol.* 48: 307–310.

Crowder WF, Gay BR, Fleming WC, and Hurst RW (1959d) Secondary reinforcement or response facilitation? IV. The retention method. *J. Psychol.* 48: 311–314.

Damasio A (1994) *Descartes' Error*. New York: G.P. Putnam's Sons.

Davis J and Bitterman ME (1971) Differential reinforcement of other behavior (DRO): A yoked-control comparison. *J. Exp. Anal. Behav.* 15: 237–241.

Delamater AR (1995) Outcome-selective effects of intertrial reinforcement in Pavlovian appetitive conditioning with rats. *Anim. Learn. Behav.* 23: 31–39.

Dickinson A (1985) Actions and habits: The development of behavioural autonomy. *Philos. Trans. R. Soc. Lond. B* 308: 67–78.

Dickinson A (1989) Expectancy theory in animal conditioning. In: Klein SB and Mowrer RR (eds.) *Contemporary Learning Theories: Pavlovian Conditioning and the Status of Traditional Learning Theories*, pp. 279–308. Hillsdale, NJ: Lawrence Erlbaum Associates.

Dickinson A (1994) Instrumental conditioning. In: Mackintosh NJ (ed.) *Animal Cognition and Learning*, pp. 4–79. London: Academic Press.

Dickinson A and Balleine BW (1994) Motivational control of goal-directed action. *Anim. Learn. Behav.* 22: 1–18.

Dickinson AB and Balleine B (1995) Motivational control of instrumental action. *Curr. Dir. Psychol. Sci.* 4: 162–167.

Dickinson A and Balleine BW (2002) The role of learning in the operation of motivational systems. In: Gallistel CR (ed.) *Learning, Motivation and Emotion, Vol. 3: Stevens' Handbook of Experimental Psychology*, 3rd edn., pp. 497–533. New York: John Wiley.

Dickinson A, Campos J, Varga Z, and Balleine BW (1996) Bidirectional control of instrumental conditioning. *Q. J. Exp. Psychol.* 49B: 289–306.

Dickinson A and Mulatero CW (1989) Reinforcer specificity of the suppression of instrumental performance on a non-contingent schedule. *Behav. Process.* 19: 167–180.

Dickinson A, Squire S, Varga Z, and Smith JW (1998) Omission learning after instrumental pretraining. *Q. J. Exp. Psychol.* 51B: 271–286.

Everitt BJ and Stacey P (1987) Studies of instrumental behavior with sexual reinforcement in male rats (*Rattus norvegicus*): II. Effects of preoptic area lesions, castration and testosterone. *J. Comp. Psychol.* 101: 407–419.

Fedorchak PM and Bolles RC (1986) Differential outcome effect using a biologically neutral outcome difference. *J. Exp. Psychol. Anim. Behav. Process.* 12: 125–130.

Garcia J (1989) Food for Tolman: Cognition and cathexis in concert. In: Archer T and Nilsson L-G (eds.) *Aversion, Avoidance and Anxiety*, pp. 45–85. Hillsdale, NJ: Lawrence Erlbaum Associates.

Hendersen RW and Graham J (1979) Avoidance of heat by rats: Effects of thermal context on the rapidity of extinction. *Learn. Motiv.* 10: 351–363.

Hershberger WA (1986) An approach through the looking-glass. *Anim. Learn. Behav.* 14: 443–451.

Holland PC (1979) Differential effects of omission contingencies on various components of Pavlovian appetitive conditioned responding in rats. *J. Exp. Psychol. Anim. Behav. Process.* 5: 178–193.

Holland PC (2004) Relations between Pavlovian-instrumental transfer and reinforcer devaluation. *J. Exp. Psychol. Anim. Behav. Process.* 30: 104–117.

Hull CL (1943) *Principles of Behavior*. New York: Appleton.

Hull CL (1952) *A Behavior System*. New York: Wiley.

Keller FS and Schoenfeld WN (1950) *Principles of Psychology: A Systematic Text in the Science of Behavior*. East Norwalk, CT: Appleton-Century-Crofts.

Killcross AS, Everitt BJ, and Robins TW (1997) Symmetrical effects of amphetamine and alpha-flupenthixol on conditioned punishment and conditioned reinforcement: Contrasts with midazolam. *Psychopharmacology (Berl)* 129: 141–152.

Kish GB (1966) Studies of sensory reinforcement. In: Honig WK (ed.) *Operant Behavior: Areas of Research and Application*, pp. 109–159. New York: Appleton-Century-Crofts.

Konorski J (1967) *Integrative Activity of the Brain*. Chicago: University of Chicago Press.

Kruse JM, Overmier JB, Konz WA, and Rokke E (1983) Pavlovian conditioned stimulus effects upon instrumental choice behavior are reinforcer specific. *Learn. Motiv.* 14: 165–181.

Limebeer CL and Parker LA (2000) The antiemetic drug ondansetron interferes with lithium-induced conditioned rejection reactions, but not lithium-induced taste avoidance in rats. *J. Exp. Psychol. Anim. Behav. Process.* 26: 371–384.

Lopez M, Balleine BW, and Dickinson A (1992) Incentive learning and the motivational control of instrumental performance by thirst. *Anim. Learn. Behav.* 20: 322–328.

Mowrer OH (1960) *Learning Theory and the Symbolic Processes*. New York: Wiley.

Myers KP and Sclafani A (2001) Conditioned enhancement of flavor evaluation reinforced by intragastric glucose. II. Taste reactivity analysis. *Physiol. Behav.* 74: 495–505.

Parkinson JA, Roberts AC, Everitt BJ, and Di Ciano P (2005) Acquisition of instrumental conditioned reinforcement is resistant to the devaluation of the unconditioned stimulus. *Q. J. Exp. Psychol. B* 58: 19–30.

Pavlov IP (1927) *Conditioned Reflexes: An Investigation of the Physiological Activity of the Cerebral Cortex*, Anrep GV (trans.). London: Oxford University Press.

Rescorla RA (1992) Response-outcome versus outcome-response associations in instrumental learning. *Anim. Learn. Behav.* 20: 223–232.

Rescorla RA (1994) Transfer of instrumental control mediated by a devalued outcome. *Anim. Learn. Behav.* 22: 27–33.

Rescorla RA and Colwill RM (1989) Associations with anticipated and obtained outcomes in instrumental learning. *Anim. Learn. Behav.* 17: 291–303.

Rescorla RA and Solomon RL (1967) Two-process learning theory: Relationships between Pavlovian conditioning and instrumental learning. *Psychol. Rev.* 74: 151–182.

Robbins TW, Cador M, Taylor JR, and Everitt BJ (1989) Limbic-striatal interactions in reward-related processes. *Neurosci. Biobehav. Rev.* 13: 155–162.

Sheffield FD (1965) Relation between classical and instrumental conditioning. In: Prokasy WF (ed.) *Classical Conditioning*, pp. 302–322. New York: Appleton-Century-Crofts.

Skinner BF (1938) *The Behavior of Organisms: An Experimental Analysis*. New York, London: D. Appleton-Century.

Spence KW (1956) *Behavior Theory and Conditioning*. New Haven: Yale University Press.

Taylor JR and Robbins TW (1984) Enhanced behavioural control by conditioned reinforcers following microinjections of d-amphetamine into the nucleus accumbens. *Psychopharmacology (Berl.)* 84: 405–412.

Trapold MA (1970) Are expectancies based upon different positive reinforcing events discriminably different? *Learn. Motiv.* 1: 129–140.

Trapold MA and Overmier JB (1972) The second learning process in instrumental conditioning. In: Black AA and Prokasy WF (eds.) *Classical Conditioning: II. Current Research and Theory*, pp. 427–452. New York: Appleton-Century-Crofts.

Ward GI (1960) Secondary reinforcement with cue stimulus effects reduced. *Proc. WV Acad. Sci.* 32: 205–208.

Wike EL (1966) *Secondary Reinforcement: Selected Experiments*. New York: Harper and Row.

Williams DR and Williams H (1969) Auto-maintenance in the pigeon: Sustained pecking despite contingent non-reinforcement. *J. Exp. Anal. Behav.* 12: 511–520.

Winterbauer NE (2006) *Conditioned Reinforcement*. PhD Thesis, University of California at Los Angeles.

Woodson JC and Balleine BW (2002) An assessment of factors contributing to instrumental performance for sexual reward in the rat. *Q. J. Exp. Psychol. B* 55: 75–88.

Wyckoff LB (1959) Toward a quantitative theory of secondary reinforcement. *Psychol. Rev.* 66: 68–78.

Wyckoff LB, Sidowski J, and Chambliss DJ (1958) An experimental study of the relationship between secondary reinforcing and cue effects of a stimulus. *J. Comp. Physiol. Psychol.* 51: 103–109.

Yin HH, Knowlton BJ, and Balleine BW (2005) Blockade of NMDA receptors in the dorsomedial striatum prevents action-outcome learning in instrumental conditioning. *Eur. J. Neurosci.* 22: 505–512.

Zimmerman DW (1969) Patterns of responding in a chained schedule altered by conditioned reinforcement. *Psychonom. Sci.* 16: 120–126.

1.37 Synchronous Oscillations and Memory Formation

W. Singer, Max Planck Institute for Brain Research, Frankfurt am Main, Germany

1.37.1 Introduction

It is commonly held that the neuronal mechanisms supporting the formation of memories consist of use-dependent long-term modifications of synaptic transmission. In order to explain the formation of new associations, Donald Hebb had postulated that connections among neurons should strengthen if the coupled neurons are repeatedly active in temporal contiguity (Hebb, 1949). This prediction has been confirmed by the seminal discovery of long-term potentiation (LTP) in the hippocampus by Bliss and Lomo (1973). They had found that tetanic stimulation of excitatory pathways led to a long-lasting enhancement of the efficacy of the synapses between the activated fibers and the respective postsynaptic target cells. Later it had been shown that this increase in synaptic efficacy occurred only if the postsynaptic cells were actually responding with action potentials to the tetanic stimuli, thus fulfilling the criterion of contingent pre- and postsynaptic activation. If postsynaptic cells were prevented from responding, modifications either did not occur or had opposite polarity, i.e., they consisted of a reduction of synaptic efficacy. This phenomenon has become known as long-term depression (LTD). It is now well established that both modifications depend on a surge of calcium in the subsynaptic space of the postsynaptic dendrites and that the polarity of the modifications depends on the rate of rise and the amplitude of this calcium increase (Bröcher et al., 1992b; Hansel et al., 1996, 1997). Fast and strong increases lead to LTP, while slow and smaller increases trigger LTD. Moreover, the source of the calcium increase is of importance. Calcium entering through N-methyl-D-aspartate (NMDA) receptor-associated channels favors the induction of LTP, whereas calcium entering through voltage-dependent calcium channels is more likely to trigger LTD. However, both modifications can be obtained merely by raising intracellular calcium concentrations through the liberation of caged calcium in a concentration-dependent manner (Neveu and Zucker, 1996). A vast number of studies have subsequently been performed in order to elucidate the molecular cascades mediating these use-dependent changes in synaptic transmission which involve both changes in transmitter release and postsynaptic susceptibility. This has led to a deep understanding of the extremely complex regulatory processes that translate neuronal activity into lasting changes of synaptic transmission (*See* Chapters 1.33, 1.34, 1.35).

It had long been held that the polarity of use-dependent synaptic gain changes depended merely on the extent to which pre- and postsynaptic activity was correlated in time as initially proposed by Hebb. The evidence that activation of NMDA receptors was one of the decisive variables in determining the polarity of synaptic gain changes agreed with this notion because these channels open and become permeable for calcium ions only if the excitatory transmitter glutamate is bound to the receptor and if the postsynaptic cell is sufficiently depolarized to remove the magnesium block that makes the channel impermeable at hyperpolarized membrane potential levels (Artola and Singer, 1987; Kleinschmidt et al., 1987; Bear et al., 1990). Thus, LTP would occur in all cases where presynaptic afferents are sufficiently active while the postsynaptic cells are sufficiently depolarized (Artola et al., 1990). Since the level of depolarization of the postsynaptic neuron not only depends on the level of activity of the pathways under consideration, but also on all the other excitatory and inhibitory inputs, this mechanism can also elegantly account for the cooperativity of synaptic modifications. Even weak inputs can increase their gain if at the same time strong inputs are active to assure sufficient depolarization of the postsynaptic membrane to remove the magnesium block. Likewise, concomitant activation of inhibitory inputs can prevent NMDA receptor activation at levels of presynaptic activity that would normally induce LTP. In this case, the outcome is usually LTD (Artola et al., 1990).

In conclusion, this mechanism is ideally suited to strengthening excitatory interactions among pairs of cells that are frequently activated in temporal contiguity, and because of cooperativity, it strengthens excitatory inputs converging on a common target cell if these inputs are frequently active in temporal contiguity. Conversely, modifications of opposite polarity occur if the respective activation patterns are anti-correlated. In this conceptual framework, the crucial variable that determines the occurrence and the polarity of synaptic gain changes is the discharge rate of the pre- and postsynaptic elements and the temporal coherence of fluctuations in discharge rate. The precise timing of individual spikes appeared irrelevant in this context.

1.37.2 Spike Timing Synaptic Plasticity

This notion has changed considerably over the last few years because of three initially independent lines of research that converged in the conclusion that the precise timing of spikes matters both in signal processing and synaptic plasticity (Gray and Singer, 1989; Gray et al., 1989; Markram et al., 1997). In experiments based on paired recordings from coupled neurons in slices, it was deduced that the polarity of synaptic gain changes depended crucially on the temporal relation between excitatory postsynaptic potentials (EPSPs) and postsynaptic action potentials. It was discovered that somatic action potentials can propagate backward into the dendrites because of activation of voltage-dependent dendritic sodium channels and electrotonic propagation and that contingency of this back-propagating action potential with a simultaneously generated EPSP could be sufficient to remove the magnesium block of the NMDA channels and in certain cases even allow for the generation of a dendritic calcium spike, thus allowing for a sufficient increase in postsynaptic calcium to induce LTP (Stuart and Häusser, 2001). By varying the timing between the EPSP and the back-propagating spike, in this case elicited by somatic current injection, it was revealed that the timing between individual EPSPs and back-propagating spikes was critical both for the induction of long-term

modifications and the determination of their polarity. No changes occurred when the interval between the EPSP and the back-propagating spike was longer than about 50 ms. When the EPSP preceded the back-propagating action potential, the probability of obtaining LTP increased with decreasing delays and then there was a sharp transition toward LTD as soon as the EPSP occurred after the back-propagating spike. This discovery of spike timing-dependent plasticity (STDP) had two important implications: First, it showed that the precise timing of spikes matters in determining the occurrence and polarity of synaptic gain changes. Second, the mechanism subserving synaptic modifications not only evaluates simple covariations between pre- and postsynaptic firing rates, but also evaluates causal relations. It increases the gain of excitatory connections whose activity can be causally related to the activation of the postsynaptic neuron and it weakens connections whose activity could not have contributed to the postsynaptic response (Markram et al., 1997; but see Stiefel et al., 2005).

At about the same time, evidence was obtained suggesting that the precise timing of individual spikes is relevant in signal processing. In vivo recordings from higher visual areas, the auditory and the somatic sensory cortex, revealed that the discharge latencies of individual neurons could signal the temporal structure of stimuli with an extreme precision in the millisecond range, suggesting that precise timing of discharges can be preserved despite numerous intervening synaptic transmission steps (Buracas et al., 1998; Reinagel and Reid, 2002). Simulation studies, partly based on the concept of synfire chains proposed by Moshe Abeles (1991), confirmed that conventional integrate-and-fire neurons are capable of transmitting temporal information with the required precision (Mainen and Sejnowski, 1995; Diesmann et al., 1999).

Parallel to these discoveries, evidence has been obtained in the visual system for the existence of mechanisms capable of adjusting the timing of individual spikes, again with millisecond precision independently of external stimuli (Gray and Singer, 1989; Gray et al., 1989; Engel et al., 2001; Fries et al., 2001a). Using multielectrode recording techniques, it was shown that neurons in the visual cortex engage in oscillatory firing patterns in the range of the gamma frequency band and that these periodic discharges are synchronized with a precision in the millisecond range. This synchronization was observed not only between neurons located within the same cortical area, but also between cells in different cortical areas and even among cells in corresponding areas of the two hemispheres (Roelfsema et al., 1997; Singer, 1999). While synchronization probability reflected to some extent the layout of corticocortical association connections (Löwel and Singer, 1992), it soon turned out that this was the result of a highly dynamic self-organizing process that enables rapid reorganization of synchronized cell assemblies as a function of stimulus configuration, central state, and attentional mechanisms (for review, see Singer, 1999; Engel et al., 2001). Initially, this precise synchronization of discharges of spatially distributed neurons was seen mainly in the context of low-level visual processes such as feature binding and figure ground segregation. Later it became clear that it is a ubiquitous phenomenon in most structures of the nervous system (Castelo-Branco et al., 1998; Brecht et al., 1999) and with all likelihood serves a large number of different functions that all have to do with the coordination and selective routing of activity in the context of distributed processing (Womelsdorf et al., 2006). Synchronized discharges have a stronger impact on target neurons than temporally dispersed inputs and this effect means that synchrony can be used as a complementary mechanism to rate increases in order to raise the saliency of neuronal signals (Biederlack et al., 2006). The difference is that synchrony can enhance the saliency of discharge patterns on a spike-by-spike basis with very high temporal resolution.

Extensive experimental and theoretical studies have since demonstrated that the oscillatory patterning of neuronal activity is crucial for the adjustment of precise spike timing (König et al., 1995; Volgushev et al., 1998). Because of reciprocal coupling via chemical and electrical synapses, networks of inhibitory interneurons engage in oscillatory activity, the frequency of which is often characteristic for particular networks and conveys periodic inhibition to excitatory neurons, in the case of the neocortex and the hippocampus pyramidal cells (Whittington et al., 2001). The effect is that the timing of spikes generated by pyramidal cells does not solely depend on the timing of the arriving EPSPs. During the hyperpolarizing phase of the oscillation cycle, arriving EPSPs have only a small chance to drive action potentials in the postsynaptic neuron because of the initial shunting and then hyperpolarizing effect of the barrages of IPSPs. This limits spiking essentially to the depolarizing phase in the peak of the oscillation cycle, causing synchronization of discharges in cells oscillating in phase. Moreover, the precise timing of spikes generated during the depolarizing cycle does

depend on the strength of the excitatory input (Fries et al., 2007). Strong excitatory input will elicit spikes earlier during the depolarizing cycle than a weak input. Thus, the phase relation between the time of occurrence of a spike and the peak of the oscillation cycle does reflect the amplitude of the excitatory drive that generated the spike. Through this mechanism, known as phase precession in the hippocampus for example, rate-coded amplitude values can be converted into a temporal code that is expressed in the timing of spikes relative to the oscillation cycle. As has been shown in numerous theoretical studies, such temporal codes are advantageous for fast processing because information on spike times can be transmitted and read out much more rapidly than information encoded in discharge rates because it does not require temporal integration, neither for transmission nor for readout (for review, see Fries et al., 2007).

There is thus a mechanism that can evaluate the precise temporal relations among individual spikes for the gating of synaptic plasticity, and there is a mechanism to adjust the precise timing of spikes during signal processing and to convert rate-coded information into timing relations. Both the classical Hebbian mechanism as well as STDP, which most certainly do coexist, evaluate temporal relations among activity patterns in order to convert correlations into synaptic gain changes. For these modifications to be meaningful, the signatures of relatedness used for engram formation must be exactly the same as those used for signal processing. Otherwise, correlations occurring spuriously during signal processing would lead to changes in synaptic coupling that are functionally meaningless. Because STDP does depend so critically on the precise timing of spikes and is susceptible to changes in timing relations on the order of the millisecond, relations between the distributed firing of neurons need to be defined and evaluated with similar precision during signal processing. However, this requires that neurons can act as coincidence detectors and distinguish between precisely synchronized and temporally dispersed input activity.

A third line of independent evidence also favors the notion that precise spike timing may play an important role in neuronal processing and memory formation. Data are accumulating which indicate that cortical circuits, synaptic properties, and the characteristics of neurons are optimized for the transmission and detection of coincident activity. A prominent feature of cortical connectivity is sparseness and as proposed by Abeles and confirmed later in extensive simulation studies (Mainen and Sejnowski, 1995; König et al., 1996; Diesmann et al., 1999), such networks strongly favor transmission of synchronized activity over transmission of temporally dispersed activity. Likewise, the frequency adaptation of transmitter release and the adaptation of postsynaptic receptors attenuate transmission of frequency-coded information. These adaptive mechanisms favor transmission of singular synchronized events and tend to filter out discharge sequences occurring at high frequencies. Sensitivity to single but coincident EPSPs is further enhanced by cooperative mechanisms in the postsynaptic dendrites. The existence of voltage-dependent sodium and calcium channels in the dendrites and their ability to convert high-amplitude EPSPs such as result from coincident input into regenerative spikes greatly enhances the coincidence sensitivity of cortical neurons (Stuart and Häusser, 2001; Ariav et al., 2003). Finally, there is evidence that spike thresholds lower as the depolarizing slope preceding the spike becomes steeper. This also favors responses to coincident inputs as compared to temporally dispersed inputs. Last but not least, the membrane time constants of cortical neurons are shorter than previously assumed, especially when the neurons are in the up state: this is due to the reduced membrane resistance caused by the simultaneous bombardment by EPSPs and IPSPs in the up state.

Thus, several lines of evidence indicate that cortical networks that are thought to support memory formation by mechanisms of use-dependent synaptic plasticity are capable of exploiting precise temporal relations among the discharges of interconnected neurons for signal processing, the encoding of information, and the induction of corresponding gain changes.

However, if precise timing of discharges is achieved through an oscillatory modulation of neuronal excitability, especially when it comes to the coordination of timing relations over larger distances, and if synaptic gain changes depend essentially on STDP, a problem arises. If coupled neuron groups engage in oscillatory activity in the same frequency range but oscillate 180 degrees out of phase, one can anticipate situations in which EPSPs always arrive in the trough of the oscillation cycle and hence at equal distance to the preceding and the following peak of enhanced excitability where spikes tend to occur. Thus, EPSPs are preceded and followed by spikes at the same interval. In this case, different outcomes are predicted by the classical Hebbian correlation rule and STDP. If the pre- and postsynaptic neurons discharge at high frequencies, as would be the case, for example, if they are engaged in

gamma oscillations, the classical Hebbian rule would predict LTP because of the contingency of high-frequency pre- and postsynaptic activation. The STDP rule cannot make a clear prediction because EPSPs are preceding and following spikes at about the same interval, which should lead to a cancellation of the antagonistic effects. This problem has recently been addressed in an in vitro study on slices of the visual cortex (Wespatat et al., 2004). The results indicated that inputs oscillating at the same frequency as the target cell (20 or 40 Hz) underwent LTP when they were in phase with the depolarizing peak of the oscillation cycle, whereby it was irrelevant whether the EPSPs arrived shortly before or after the action potentials, whereas the same input underwent LTD when it oscillated 180 degrees out of phase so that the EPSPs arrived during the hyperpolarizing troughs of the oscillation cycle of the postsynaptic neuron.

1.37.3 Evidence for Relations between Oscillatory Activity, Synaptic Plasticity, and Learning

Given that learning mechanisms evaluate temporal correlations among the activity patterns of coupled neurons and that the temporal patterning of neuronal activity is often structured by an oscillatory modulation, one expects to find close relations between memory processes and oscillatory activity. Although research on this issue is still at its very beginning, such evidence is indeed available.

Indirect evidence for a relation between synaptic plasticity and oscillatory patterning comes from studies relating oscillatory activity to central states and attentional mechanisms. While synaptic modifications can be induced with artificial stimulation conditions irrespective of the state of neuronal networks and even in fully deafferented slice preparations, there is consensus that under natural conditions learning-related modifications of synaptic gain occur only when the brain is in an activated state and when attentional mechanisms are functional. The reason is that synaptic modifications require the presence of an appropriate mix of neuromodulators such as acetylcholine, dopamine, and noradrenaline and that these modulators are available in the required concentrations only when the brain is in an awake and activated state. Another likely reason is that the induction of synaptic modifications requires a minimum of cooperativity, for example a sufficient amount of synchronized input activity, and that such cooperativity is only achieved in the activated brain. These activated brain states favor the emergence of oscillatory activity in various frequency bands and the synchronization of the oscillations across structures that need to cooperate for memory processes. In this context, the most important frequency bands appear to be the theta, the beta, and the gamma. Gamma oscillations in the neocortex and the associated precise synchronization of neuronal discharges are greatly facilitated by the presence of acetylcholine and its action on muscarinic receptors (Munk et al., 1996; Herculano-Houzel et al., 1999). Acetylcholine also facilitates use-dependent synaptic modifications and it is likely that there is a relation between the two phenomena (Bröcher et al., 1992a; Wespatat et al., 2004). Likewise, attention facilitates gamma oscillations (Fries et al., 2001b) and favors learning (Bröcher et al., 1992; Wespatat et al., 2004). Preliminary evidence suggests that there may be a causal relation between the occurrence of synchronized oscillatory activity in the gamma-frequency band and the induction of synaptic plasticity. It is possible to modify the receptive fields of neurons in the visual cortex by appropriate visual stimulation even in anesthetized preparations if the brain is concomitantly activated by electrical stimulation of the mesencephalic reticular formation (unpublished observation). This stimulation increases the release of plasticity-enhancing neuromodulators and at the same time favors the occurrence of gamma oscillations in response to the applied stimuli. Post hoc analysis of the neuronal responses to the change-inducing light stimuli revealed that only those trials caused lasting changes in receptive field properties that were associated with a strong oscillatory modulation and synchronization of neuronal responses in the gamma band. A similar relation, albeit in the theta-frequency range, has been found in the hippocampus (Huerta and Lisman, 1995). Here, the so-called beta-burst stimulation that entrains the hippocampus in the characteristic theta rhythm of the structure turned out to be particularly effective for the induction of long-lasting synaptic modifications. Moreover, when the hippocampal circuits were engaged in spontaneous theta oscillations, the effectiveness of the stimuli applied for the induction of synaptic gain changes and the polarity of the resulting synaptic modifications depended critically on the phase relation between the ongoing theta activity and the change-inducing stimuli (Huerta and Lisman, 1995). A similar finding has been obtained in the somatosensory barrel cortex, where synchronous oscillatory activity occurs in conjunction with the whisking movements. Again, the efficacy of the change-inducing electrical stimuli depended

critically on the timing of the stimuli relative to the whisking cycle. Finally, it was shown in experiments in which hippocampus theta was recorded while animals were exposed to classical conditioning paradigms that memory traces could be established only if the conditioning stimuli were given during a particular phase of the theta cycle. While these experiments only showed a relation between the timing of inducing stimuli relative to oscillatory activity, more direct evidence for an instrumental role of long-range synchronization of oscillations in memory processes has been obtained with multielectrode recordings from structures relevant for memory formation (Fell et al., 2001; Tallon-Baudry et al., 2001, 2004). In human subjects implanted with depth electrodes for the localization of epileptic foci, it was found that successful formation of episodic memories was accompanied by transient increases in gamma- and theta-oscillatory synchrony between the hippocampus and neighboring entorhinal cortex, structures known to be involved in memory formation. In trials in which memory formation was not successful, these changes in synchronization were not observed (Fell et al., 2001, 2003). Likewise, simultaneous recordings from limbic structures (amygdala and hippocampus) have shown that fear conditioning is associated with transient synchronization of oscillatory activity between the two structures (Seidenbecher et al., 2003; Narayanan et al., 2007). Electroencephalographic and magneto-encephalographic studies in healthy human subjects revealed that classical Pavlovian conditioning leads to a lasting enhancement of the synchronization of gamma oscillations between cortical areas encoding the conditioned and nonconditioned stimuli, respectively (Miltner et al., 1999).

The recall of memories also appears to be associated with enhanced oscillatory patterning of neuronal responses in the theta, beta, and gamma bands (Raghavachari et al., 2001; Tallon-Baudry et al., 2001; Rizzuto et al., 2003; Sederberg et al., 2003; Herrmann et al., 2004; Guderian and Duzel, 2005). Auditory stimuli that matched a previously stored template led to significantly more gamma band synchrony than those that did not match (Debener et al., 2003). Visual stimuli for which subjects have a long-term memory representation caused significantly greater gamma oscillations in the occipital cortex than similar stimuli that were not stored in long-term memory (Herrmann et al., 2004). A close relation between encoding and retrieval of memory contents and enhanced gamma oscillations has also been found in experiments on working memory (Tallon-Baudry et al., 1997; Strüber et al., 2000;

Tallon-Baudry et al., 2001, 2004). Here, the increase in oscillatory activity was particularly pronounced over parietal, central, and frontal regions of the brain. Finally, there appears to be a relation between the access to declarative memory and long-range synchronization of gamma oscillations (Melloni et al., 2007). In humans performing a delayed matching-to-sample task on stimuli that were only perceived in a subset of trials and gained access to consciousness and declarative recall, it was possible to demonstrate that only those stimuli that were consciously perceived and encoded in declarative memory evoked large-scale phase synchronization of gamma oscillations across distributed cortical networks. In addition, only those trials were associated with sustained, enhanced theta activity throughout the hold period. The latter finding agrees well with the growing evidence that large-scale synchronization in the theta frequency band is closely related to the encoding and recall of stimulus material in declarative memory. Successful recognition of known faces is associated with increased activity in a distributed network that includes prefrontal mediotemporal and visual areas in occipital cortex (Guderian and Duzel, 2005). Finally, invasive recordings in patients suggest that theta band oscillations are implicated in spatial navigation, working memory, and episodic memory (Raghavachari et al., 2001; Caplan et al., 2001, 2003; Rizzuto et al., 2003; Sederberg et al., 2007).

Last but not least, there is recent evidence from studies in human subjects that consolidation of memories during sleep is closely related to an oscillatory patterning of neuronal activity (Marshall et al., 2006).

1.37.4 Conclusion

So far, most of the evidence suggesting a relation between synchronized oscillatory activity in various frequency bands and memory formation is correlative in nature and does not allow one to conclude that synchronized oscillatory activity is a necessary prerequisite for the induction of memory-related synaptic gain changes. However, the evidence reviewed concerning the importance of precise temporal relations in memory processes and the pivotal role of oscillations for the establishment of precise temporal relations between neuronal activities provides strong support for the hypothesis that oscillations and the associated synchronization of spike discharges play a crucial role in the coordination of distributed neuronal processing on the one hand and engram formation on the other. This conclusion is further supported by the growing

evidence that cognitive deficits, including impairments in short- and long-term memory such as occur in schizophrenia, Alzheimer's disease, and epilepsy, are associated with abnormal patterns of neuronal oscillations and reduced synchronization (for review, see Uhlhaas and Singer, 2006).

References

Abeles M (1991) *Corticonics*. Cambridge: Cambridge University Press.

Ariav G, Polsky A, and Schiller J (2003) Submillisecond precision of the input-output transformation function mediated by fast sodium dendritic spikes in basal dendrites of CA1 pyramidal neurons. *J. Neurosci.* 23(21): 7750–7758.

Artola A and Singer W (1987) Long-term potentiation and NMDA receptors in rat visual cortex. *Nature* 330: 649–652.

Artola A, Bröcher S, and Singer W (1990) Different voltage-dependent thresholds for the induction of long-term depression and long-term potentiation in slices of the rat visual cortex. *Nature* 347: 69–72.

Bear MF, Kleinschmidt A, Gu Q, and Singer W (1990) Disruption of experience-dependent synaptic modifications in striate cortex by infusion of an NMDA receptor antagonist. *J. Neurosci.* 10: 909–925.

Biederlack J, Castelo-Branco M, Neuenschwander S, Wheeler DW, Singer W, and Nikolic D (2006) Brightness induction: Rate enhancement and neuronal synchronization as complementary codes. *Neuron* 52: 1073–1083.

Bliss TVP and Lomo T (1973) Long-lasting potentiation of synaptic transmission in the dentate area of the anaesthetized rabbit following stimulation of the perforant path. *J. Physiol.* 232: 331–356.

Brecht M, Singer W, and Engel AK (1999) Patterns of synchronization in the superior colliculus of anesthetized cats. *J. Neurosci.* 19(9): 3567–3579.

Bröcher S, Artola A, and Singer W (1992a) Agonists of cholinergic and noradrenergic receptors facilitate synergistically the induction of long-term potentiation in slices of rat visual cortex. *Brain Res.* 573: 27–36.

Bröcher S, Artola A, and Singer W (1992b) Intracellular injection of Ca^{++} chelators blocks induction of long-term depression in rat visual cortex. *Proc. Natl. Acad. Sci. USA* 89: 123–127.

Buracas G, Zador A, Deweese M, and Albright T (1998) Efficient discrimination of temporal patterns by motion-sensitive neurons in primate visual cortex. *Neuron* 20: 959–969.

Caplan JB, Madsen JR, Raghavachari S, and Kahana MJ (2001) Distinct patterns of brain oscillations underlie two basic parameters of human maze learning. *J. Neurophysiol.* 86: 368–380.

Caplan JB, Madsen JR, Schulze-Bonhage A, Aschenbrenner-Scheibe R, Newman EL, and Kahana MJ (2003) Human theta oscillations related to sensorimotor integration and spatial learning. *J. Neurosci.* 23: 4726–4736.

Castelo-Branco M, Neuenschwander S, and Singer W (1998) Synchronization of visual responses between the cortex, lateral geniculate nucleus, and retina in the anesthetized cat. *J. Neurosci.* 18: 6395–6410.

Debener S, Herrmann CS, Kranczioch C, Gembris D, and Engel AK (2003) Top-down attentional processing enhances auditory evoked gamma band activity. *Neuroreport* 14: 683–686.

Diesmann M, Gewaltig M-O, and Aertsen A (1999) Stable propagation of synchronous spiking in cortical neural networks. *Nature* 402: 529–533.

Engel AK, Fries P, and Singer W (2001) Dynamic predictions: Oscillations and synchrony in top-down processing. *Nat. Rev. Neurosci.* 2: 704–716.

Fell J, Klaver P, Lehnertz K, et al. (2001) Human memory formation is accompanied by rhinal-hippocampal coupling and decoupling. *Nat. Neurosci.* 4(12): 1259–1264.

Fell J, Klaver P, Elfadil H, Schaller C, Elger CE, and Fernández G (2003) Rhinal-hippocampal theta coherence during declarative memory formation: Interaction with gamma synchronization? *Eur. J. Neurosci.* 17: 1082–1088.

Fries P, Neuenschwander S, Engel AK, Goebel R, and Singer W (2001a) Rapid feature selective neuronal synchronization through correlated latency shifting. *Nat. Neurosci.* 4(2): 194–200.

Fries P, Reynolds JH, Rorie AE, and Desimone R (2001b) Modulation of oscillatory neuronal synchronization by selective visual attention. *Science* 291: 1560–1563.

Fries P, Nikolic D, and Singer W (2007) The gamma cycle. *Trends Neurosci.* 30(7): 309–316.

Gray CM and Singer W (1989) Stimulus-specific neuronal oscillations in orientation columns of cat visual cortex. *Proc. Natl. Acad. Sci. USA* 86: 1698–1702.

Gray CM, König P, Engel AK, and Singer W (1989) Oscillatory responses in cat visual cortex exhibit inter-columnar synchronization which reflects global stimulus properties. *Nature* 338: 334–337.

Guderian S and Duzel E (2005) Induced theta oscillations mediate large-scale synchrony with mediotemporal areas during recollection in humans. *Hippocampus* 15: 901–912.

Hansel C, Artola A, and Singer W (1996) Different threshold levels of postsynaptic $[Ca^{2+}]i$ have to be reached to induce LTP and LTD in neocortical pyramidal cells. *J. Physiol. (Paris)* 90: 317–319.

Hansel C, Artola A, and Singer W (1997) Relation between dendritic Ca^{2+} levels and the polarity of synaptic long-term modifications in rat visual cortex neurons. *Eur. J. Neurosci.* 9: 2309–2322.

Hebb DO (1949) *The Organization of Behavior*. New York: John Wiley and Sons.

Herculano-Houzel S, Munk MHJ, Neuenschwander S, and Singer W (1999) Precisely synchronized oscillatory firing patterns require electroencephalographic activation. *J. Neurosci.* 19(10): 3992–4010.

Herrmann CS, Lenz D, Junge S, Busch NA, and Maess B (2004) Memory-matches evoke human gamma-responses. *BMC Neuroscience* 5: 13.

Huerta PT and Lisman JE (1995) Bidirectional synaptic plasticity induced by a single burst during cholinergic theta oscillation in CA1 in vitro. *Neuron* 15: 1053–1063.

Kleinschmidt A, Bear MF, and Singer W (1987) Blockade of "NMDA" receptors disrupts experience-dependent plasticity of kitten striate cortex. *Science* 238: 355–358.

König P, Engel AK, and Singer W (1995) Relation between oscillatory activity and long-range synchronization in cat visual cortex. *Proc. Natl. Acad. Sci. USA* 92: 290–294.

König P, Engel AK, and Singer W (1996) Integrator or coincidence detector? The role of the cortical neuron revisited. *Trends Neurosci.* 19(4): 130–137.

Löwel S and Singer W (1992) Selection of intrinsic horizontal connections in the visual cortex by correlated neuronal activity. *Science* 255: 209–212.

Mainen ZF and Sejnowski TJ (1995) Reliability of spike timing in neocortical neurons. *Science* 268: 1503–1506.

Markram H, Lübke J, Frotscher M, and Sakmann B (1997) Regulation of synaptic efficacy by coincidence of postsynaptic APs and EPSPs. *Science* 275: 213–215.

Marshall L, Helgadóttir H, Mölle M, and Born J (2006) Boosting slow oscillations during sleep potentiates memory. *Nature* 44: 610–613.

Melloni L, Molina C, Pena M, Torres D, Singer W, and Rodriguez E (2007) Synchronization of neural activity across cortical areas correlates with conscious perception. *J. Neurosci.* 27(11): 2858–2865.

Miltner WHR, Braun C, Arnold M, Witte H, and Taub E (1999) Coherence of gamma-band EEG activity as a basis for associative learning. *Nature* 397: 434–436.

Munk MHJ, Roelfsema PR, König P, Engel AK, and Singer W (1996) Role of reticular activation in the modulation of intracortical synchronization. *Science* 272: 271–274.

Narayanan RT, Seidenbecher T, Kluge C, Bergado J, Stork O, and Pape H-C (2007) Dissociated theta synchronization in amygdalo-hippocampal circuits during various stages of fear memory. *Eur. J. Neurosci.* 25(6): 1823–1831.

Neveu D and Zucker RS (1996) Postsynaptic levels of $[Ca^{2+}]_i$ needed to trigger LTD and LTP. *Neuron* 16: 619–629.

Raghavachari S, Kahana MJ, Rizzuto DS, et al. (2001) Gating of human theta oscillations by a working memory task. *J. Neurosci.* 21: 3175–3183.

Reinagel P and Reid RC (2002) Precise firing events are conserved across neurons. *J. Neurosci.* 22(16): 6837–6841.

Rizzuto DS, Madsen JR, Bromfield EB, et al. (2003) Reset of human neocortical oscillations during a working memory task. *Proc. Natl. Acad. Sci. USA* 100: 7931–7936.

Roelfsema PR, Engel AK, König P, and Singer W (1997) Visuomotor integration is associated with zero time-lag synchronization among cortical areas. *Nature* 385: 157–161.

Sederberg PB, Kahana MJ, Howard MW, Donner EJ, and Madsen JR (2003) Theta and gamma oscillations during encoding predict subsequent recall. *J. Neurosci.* 23: 10809–10814.

Sederberg PB, Schulze-Bonhage A, Madsen JR, et al. (2007) Hippocampal and neocortical gamma oscillations predict memory formation in humans. *Cereb. Cortex* 17(5): 1190–1196.

Seidenbecher T, Laxmi TR, Stork O, and Pape H-C (2003) Amygdala and hippocampal theta rhythm synchronization during fear memory retrieval. *Science* 301: 846–850.

Singer W (1999) Neuronal synchrony: A versatile code for the definition of relations? *Neuron* 24: 49–65.

Stiefel KM, Tennigkeit F, and Singer W (2005) Synaptic plasticity in the absence of backpropagating spikes of layer II inputs to layer V pyramidal cells in rat visual cortex. *Eur. J. Neurosci.* 21: 2605–2610.

Strüber D, Basar-Eroglu C, Hoff E, and Stadler M (2000) Reversal-rate dependent differences in the EEG gamma-band during multistable visual perception. *Int. J. Psychophysiol.* 38: 243–252.

Stuart GJ and Häusser M (2001) Dendritic coincidence detection of EPSPs and action potentials. *Nat. Neurosci.* 4(1): 63–71.

Tallon-Baudry C, Bertrand O, Delpuech C, and Permier J (1997) Oscillatory gamma-band (30–70 Hz) activity induced by a visual search task in humans. *J. Neurosci.* 17: 722–734.

Tallon-Baudry C, Bertrand O, and Fischer C (2001) Oscillatory synchrony between human extrastriate areas during visual short-term memory maintenance. *J. Neurosci.* 21: RC177.

Tallon-Baudry C, Mandon S, Freiwald WA, and Kreiter AK (2004) Oscillatory synchrony in the monkey temporal lobe correlates with performance in a visual short-term memory task. *Cereb. Cortex* 14(7): 713–720.

Uhlhaas PJ and Singer W (2006) Neural synchrony in brain disorders: Relevance for cognitive dysfunctions and pathophysiology. *Neuron* 52: 155–168.

Volgushev M, Chistiakova M, and Singer W (1998) Modification of discharge patterns of neocortical neurons by induced oscillations of the membrane potential. *Neuroscience* 83(1): 15–25.

Wespatat V, Tennigkeit F, and Singer W (2004) Phase sensitivity of synaptic modifications in oscillating cells of rat visual cortex. *J. Neurosci.* 24(41): 9067–9075.

Whittington MA, Doheny HC, Traub RD, LeBeau FEN, and Buhl EH (2001) Differential expression of synaptic and nonsynaptic mechanisms underlying stimulus-induced gamma oscillations in vitro. *J. Neurosci.* 21(5): 1727–1738.

Womelsdorf T, Fries P, Mitra PP, and Desimone R (2006) Gamma-band synchronization in visual cortex predicts speed of change detection. *Nature* 439: 733–736.

1.38 The Neuronal Workspace Model: Conscious Processing and Learning

J.-P. Changeux, URACNRS 2182, Collège de France and Institut Pasteur, Paris, France

S. Dehaene, Collège de France, Paris, France; and INSERM-CEA Cognitive Neuroimaging Unit, Neurospin Center, Gif-sur-Yvette, France

1.38.1 Introduction

Researchers in the field of computational biology have mostly focused their attention in the recent years on the sequences of eukaryotic genomes, on their annotation, and on the understanding of how these linear sources of information give rise to the three-dimensional organization of the body and, in particular, of the brain. Ultimately, from the DNA sequences already stored *in silico* of the human genome, one should be able to compute the main features of the species-specific functional organization of our brain. Yet, the brain strikingly differs from the other organs of the body in several respects. First, the complexity of its cellular and supracellular organization is orders of magnitudes higher, and second, it is able to learn and store information from the outside world. Finally, its structure is under constant reorganization as a function of its internal physiological states of activity, either endogenously generated or evoked by signals from the outside world. These are a few of the many reasons why computational neuroscience has recently developed as a rather autonomous and fast-moving discipline. Its principal project is to understand the multiple modes of signal processing by the brain ultimately resulting in behavior and/or tacit mental events. It is also to build up formal models, expressed in terms of neuronal networks, that link the molecular, neuronal, physiological, and behavioral/mental data in a coherent, noncontradictory though minimal form (Changeux and Dehaene, 1989). Ultimately implemented as 'formal organisms' (Changeux et al., 1973), these neurocomputational models should altogether account for the available data and produce experimentally testable predictions at all those levels. Being minimal, they are not anticipated to give an exhaustive description of reality, but nevertheless to validate or invalidate theories and, if necessary, give rise to new ones, thus contributing to our understanding of how the human brain works.

If multiple attempts have been successfully done to model the relationships between the states of activity of neuronal networks and overt behaviors in simple systems (Grillner and Graybiel, 2006), a most fascinating intellectual challenge of today's neuroscience remains to understand the explicit processing of the mental events which invest our brain, in other words to establish a comprehensive theory of consciousness on the basis of the presently available scientific knowledge. As stated by Delacour (1997),

> Multiple explanations have already been suggested like such-and-such a sophisticated algorithm, the oscillation of the extracellular electrical field in the cortex, the probabilistic character of synaptic transmission, or some still mysterious property of 'quantum gravity.' These theories represent little advance over the pineal gland theory of René Descartes. (Delacour, 1997: 127)

The case of consciousness is indeed exceptional. First of all, a fundamental ambiguity exists in the use of the term which, depending on context and author, can equally refer to waking state, personal experience, mental processing, or the multifaceted concept of self. Second, its comprehensive description crosses multiple disciplines ranging from basic neuroscience to molecular biology, psychology, and philosophy which, in the present situation of the academic community, show considerable difficulties to interact and cooperate. Last, any plausible theory on consciousness has to refer to a phenomenal subjective experience reported through introspection that a long tradition, from positivism to behaviorism and, most of all, the current practices of bench work research in neuroscience or pharmacology, has banned from any serious form of scientific enquiry.

Nevertheless, in the past decades, the situation has significantly changed because of a 'renaissance' (Zeman, 2005) of empirical research on consciousness and the proposal of constructive and plausible mechanistic theories, which aim at accounting for the subjective experience of a unified or global 'space or scene,' where some kind of *synthesis* between past, present, and future takes place, where multimodal perceptions, emotions, and feelings (present), and evoked memories of prior experiences (past), together with anticipations of actions (future), become subjectively integrated in a continuously changing and dynamic flow of consciousness, "altogether one and multiple at any of its moments" (Fessard, 1954; Bogen, 1995; Edelman and Tononi, 2000; Crick and Koch, 2003; Dehaene and Changeux, 2004). Among these theories, Zeman (2005) distinguishes the following.

1.38.1.1 Information Processing Theories

Following the lead of William James in associating consciousness with selective attention and memory, Baars (1989) has proposed a psychological model which postulates that the content of consciousness is broadcasted to the whole brain through a 'global workspace' which recruits the operation of multiple unconscious and automatic processors. Yet, Baars proposed as the essential neural basis of his global workspace the ascending reticular formation, the nonspecific nuclei of the thalamus, and only casually mentioned that "it is possible that corticocortical connections should also be included."

Shallice (1988) has also suggested an integrative role of consciousness through a 'supervisory attentive system' which would control the activities of lower level psychological systems mediated by some kind of 'contention scheduling' system and has placed emphasis on parieto-prefrontal networks in relation with the supervisory system (see also Frith et al., 1999).

1.38.1.2 Neurobiological Theories

In their pioneering efforts to specify the neural correlates of consciousness, Crick and Koch (Crick, 1994; Crick and Koch, 1995, 2004) have successively emphasized the importance of gamma-band oscillations around 40 Hz as a correlate of conscious processing; then, successively, the role of connections to and from prefrontal cortex in conscious perception (though more recently they have defended the opposite view that prefrontal cortex works as an 'unconscious homunculus'); and last, the possible role of the claustrum in the integration of conscious percepts (Crick and Koch, 2005).

Edelman and Tononi (2000) and Tononi and Edelman (1998) have emphasized the role of information integration and of reentrant connections in establishing a shifting assembly or 'dynamic core' linking distributed cortical and thalamic neurons. Its representation content, at the same time diversified and unitary, could not be localized to single parts of the brain and would vary significantly among individuals, but yet would correspond to the content of phenomenal consciousness. Lumer et al. (1997a,b) have developed a formalism in their simulations focused on early visual processing, with reentrant connections but without establishing a link with the notion of consciousness and specifically with the dynamic core hypothesis.

The hypothesis of a conscious 'neuronal workspace' (Dehaene et al., 1998; Dehaene and Changeux, 2000; Dehaene and Naccache, 2001; Dehaene et al., 2003b) emphasizes the role of distributed neurons with long-distance connections, particularly dense in prefrontal, cingulate, and parietal regions, interconnecting multiple specialized processors and broadcasting signals at the brain scale in a spontaneous and sudden manner, forming a conscious 'global neuronal workspace.' This model is extensively presented and discussed in this chapter.

1.38.1.3 Social Theories

The philosopher Strawson (1974) has argued that the concept of one's own mind presupposes the concept of other minds. This, together with the notion that language is critical for human consciousness, has led to the notion that conscious experience would be more a social construction than a physiological or psychological phenomenon (Rose, 1999). Without contesting the importance of social relationships and in particular of language (see Edelman, 1989) in human consciousness, one may wonder, however, whether this is the adequate level of explanation for a comprehensive theory of consciousness, which should ultimately capture such basic phenomena as sleep and anesthesia, masking, or attentional blink (see following).

In this chapter we successively analyze: (1) the theoretical premises of the neuronal workspace hypothesis; (2) the formal representation of the neuronal workspace model; (3) simulations with the workspace model of states of consciousness and access to consciousness in cognitive tasks; and (4) the neuronal workspace model and the evolution of consciousness.

1.38.2 The Neuronal Workspace Hypothesis: Premises and Theoretical Statements

The views presented in this chapter developed from three sets of complementary data: anatomical, computational, and psychophysical.

1.38.2.1 Anatomical Data

Early observations by Cajal (1892) (see DeFelipe and Jones, 1988) underlined the 'special morphology' of the pyramidal cells from the cerebral cortex and suggested that they might be "the substratum of the highest nervous activities," calling them '*the psychic cells.*' Cajal mentioned their very numerous and complex dendritic cells and also noted that "the pyramidal cells from cortical layers II and III possess long axons with multiple collaterals." Cajal further distinguished in the white matter: projection fibers which enter the cerebral peduncle, callosal fibers which associate the two hemispheres, and fibers of association that "bring into relation ... different territories and different lobes of the same hemisphere" (Cajal, 1892). He also noted that these fibers of association increase in number in humans and large mammals, where they form "the main mass of the white matter." Recent investigations have confirmed the view that the corticocortical and callosal fibers primarily (though not exclusively) arise from layer II-III pyramids (Jones, 1984) (**Figure 1(d)**).

Furthermore, von Economo (1929), a follower of Brodman, distinguished in his "Cytoarchitectonics of the human cerebral cortex" five "fundamental types of cortical structure" (**Figures 1(a)** and **1(b)**) and among them: the "frontal type 2 (which)... possesses large, well-formed, and well-arranged pyramidal cells in layers III and V" while in the "parietal type 3 (these cells) are smaller, more slender, and numerous...." Von Economo also noted that the type 2 is "spread over the anterior two-thirds of the frontal lobe, over the superior parietal lobule..." as well as over the cingulate cortex, among other cortical areas and concludes that "type 2 and 3 isocortex... are the chief station for the commemorative and higher psychic functions."

Interestingly, recent quantitative analysis of the dendritic field morphology of layer III pyramidal neurons in the occipitofrontal cortical 'stream' revealed a continuous increase of complexity up to the prefrontal cortex within a given species (Elston and Rosa, 1997, 1998; DeFelipe and Farinas, 1992) (**Figure 1(c)**) and from lower species (owl monkey, marmoset) to humans (Elston, 2003). A correlative increase of the relative surface of the prefrontal cortex accompanies this increased complexity (see Changeux, 2004). Moreover, mapping of long-range connections in the monkey cerebral cortex revealed long-range connections linking, among others, the prefrontal cortex (area 46), the superior temporal sulcus, parietal area 7a, and the hippocampus together with the contralateral anterior and posterior cingulum, area 19, and the parahippocampal gyrus (Goldman-Rakic, 1988). These circuits were suggested to contribute to working memory (Goldman-Rakic, 1994) and

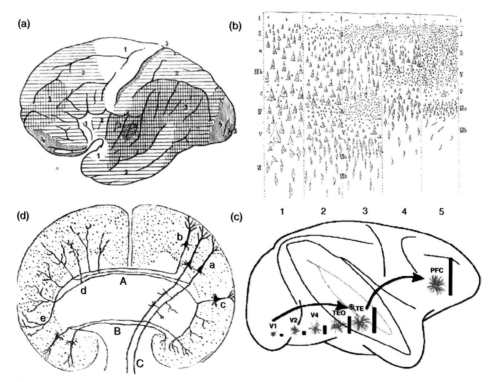

Figure 1 The anatomical basis of the neuronal workspace hypothesis. The pyramidal neurons with long corticocortical axons from layers 2–3 of the cerebral cortex (d) display increased complexity of the basal dendrites (and thus increased connectivity) from primary visual areas (V1) to prefrontal cortex (PFC) (here in the monkey (c)) and from primitive vertebrates to humans. These neurons are particularly abundant in what von Economo referred to as type 2 cortex (b), which primarily occupies the frontal, parietotemporal, and cingulate areas (a). Parts (a) and (b) from von Economo C (1929) *The Cytoarchitectonics of the Human Cerebral Cortex.* London: Oxford University Press; used with permission. (c) from Elston GN (2003) Cortex, cognition and the cell: New insights into the pyramidal neuron and prefrontal function. *Cereb. Cortex* 13: 1124–1138; used with permission from Oxford University Press. (d) from Cajal S (1892) El nuevo concepto de la histologia de los centros nerviosos. *Rev. Ciencias Med.* 18: 457–476; used with permission.

proposed to contribute to the anatomical basis of the neuronal workspace model (Dehaene et al., 1998).

1.38.2.2 Computational Data

The present neurocomputational approach to conscious versus nonconscious processing originates from the design of neural network models that aimed at specifying the contribution of prefrontal cortex to increasingly higher cognitive tasks (Dehaene and Changeux, 1989, 1991, 1997; Dehaene et al., 1998). Successively, these models considered the issues of how a network could retain an active memory across the long delay of a delayed-response task (Dehaene and Changeux, 1989), how it could encode abstract rules that might be selected from external or internal rewards (Dehaene and Changeux, 1991), and finally how networks based on those principles could pass complex planning tasks such as the Tower of London test or the Stroop test (Dehaene and Changeux, 1997; Dehaene et al., 1998). The 'conscious *neuronal* workspace' model (Dehaene et al., 1998; Dehaene and Naccache, 2001; Dehaene et al., 2003b; Dehaene and Changeux, 2005) is the last development of these models which emphasize the role of distributed neurons with long-distance connections, particularly dense in prefrontal, cingulate, and parietal regions, which are capable of interconnecting multiple specialized processors and can broadcast signals at the brain scale in a spontaneous and sudden manner.

1.38.2.3 Cognitive Psychology, Neuropsychology, and Human Neuroimaging

A long psychophysical and neuropsychological tradition, dating back to Hughlings Jackson and perpetuated among others by Baddeley, Shallice, Mesulam, or Posner, has emphasized the hierarchical organization of the brain and separates lower automatized systems from increasingly higher and more autonomous supervisory executive systems. It has also been influenced by Fodor's distinction between the vertical 'modular faculties' and a distinct 'isotropic central and horizontal system' capable of sharing information across modules. Empirically, finally, it has taken advantage of a variety of experimental techniques, starting with behavioral analysis, neuropsychological observation in brain-lesioned patients, and most recently, human neuroimaging with functional magnetic resonance imaging (fMRI) and causal

interference with transcranial magnetic stimulation (TMS).

It is beyond the scope of this chapter to discuss the variety of experimental contributions that are relevant to the ongoing science of consciousness (see, e.g., Laureys, 2005), but they can be briefly sketched as belonging to two main lines of research. The first line, starting with the pioneering research of Weiskrantz on blindsight and Marcel on subliminal priming, has investigated the extent of nonconscious processing in humans. In combination with fMRI, this research has uncovered that not only subcortical, but in fact a variety of specialized cortical systems were capable of activating in the absence of any conscious report of stimulus presence (for review, see Naccache and Dehaene, 2001; Naccache et al., 2005; Dehaene et al., 2006). The second line, exemplified by Posner's or Shallice's work, has studied the properties of a central executive or executive attention system, whose activity seems to index conscious top-down attention and control (Norman and Shallice, 1986; Amati and Shallice, 2007). Through the use of Baars's contrastive method, which consists of opposing two minimally different conditions, one of which is conscious and the other is not, it has been observed that executive control is deployed only following consciously perceived trials (e.g., Kunde, 2004) and is consistently associated with a sharp increase in dorsal and midline prefrontal as well as anterior cingulate and, in many cases, inferior or posterior parietal activation (see Gusnard and Raichle, 2001; Dosenbach et al., 2006).

1.38.2.4 The Model

Inspired by these observations, our theoretical work attempted to capture them within a minimal theoretical model. In the following, the headlines of the theoretical premises will be presented following the initial presentation of Dehaene et al. (1998), yet updated in a few of its formulations in the subsequent papers of Dehaene et al. (2003a) and Dehaene and Changeux (2005).

1.38.2.4.1 Two computational spaces
The neuronal workspace hypothesis distinguishes, in a first approach, two main computational spaces within the brain (**Figure 2**), each characterized by a distinct pattern of connectivity:

a. A processing network, composed of a set of parallel, distributed, and functionally specialized

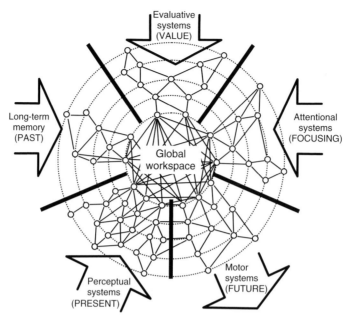

Figure 2 Schematic representation of the neuronal workspace hypothesis as initially proposed by Dehaene et al. (1998). The model distinguishes two computational spaces: (1) specialized processors, which are modular, encapsulated, and automatic, labeled here as perceptual systems, long-term memory (including autobiographic memory and self), and attentional and evaluative systems and (2) the global workspace, with long-range axon neurons broadcasting signals to multiple areas yielding subjective experience and reportability. From Dehaene S, Kerszberg M, and Changeux JP (1998) A neuronal model of a global workspace in effortful cognitive tasks. *Proc. Natl. Acad. Sci. USA* 95: 14529–14534; used with permission from the National Academy of Sciences.

processors (Baars, 1989) or modular subsystems (Shallice, 1988) subsumed by topologically distinct cortical domains with highly specific local or medium-range connections that encapsulate information relevant to its function. This specialized network processes information in a bottom-up manner (see Miyashita and Hayashi, 2000).

b. A global workspace, consisting of a distributed set of cortical neurons characterized by their ability to receive from and send back to homologous neurons in other cortical areas, horizontal projections through long-range excitatory axons (which may as well impinge on excitatory or inhibitory neurons). Such long-range corticocortical tangential connections include callosal connections and mostly originate from the pyramidal cells of layers 2 and 3. We therefore propose that the extent to which a given brain area contributes to the global workspace would be simply related to the fraction of its pyramidal neurons contributing to layers 2 and 3, which is particularly elevated in von Economo's type 2 (dorsolateral prefrontal) and type 3 (inferior parietal) cortical structures (von Economo, 1929). The pyramidal neurons from layers 2 and 3 establish, in addition, vertical and reciprocal connections with layer 5 neurons and thus

corresponding thalamic nuclei. These connections contribute to both the stability and the dynamics of workspace activity, via, for instance, self-sustained circuits, but also mediate the direct access to and from the processing networks (Brecht et al., 2003). The global network neurons typically process information in a top-down manner.

1.38.2.4.2 Content of the global workspace

In the original formulation of the neuronal workspace hypothesis (Dehaene et al., 1998), five major categories of processors were distinguished which could be dynamically mobilized and multiply reconfigured (**Figure 2**).

a. *Perceptual circuits* give the workspace access to the present state of the external world. Empirically, perceptual circuits may include the primary and secondary sensory areas together with the object-oriented ventral and lateral areas of the temporal lobes in both visual (Mishkin and Ungerleider, 1982; Goodale et al., 1991; Fang and He, 2005) and auditory (Rauschecker and Tian, 2000) modalities as well as the temporal and inferior parietal areas involved in language comprehension (including Wernicke's area) (Mesulam, 1998). Accordingly, the content of any external stimulus, attended object, or linguistic input can access the global workspace. Such access may take place stepwise through hierarchical stages of processing through primary and secondary sensory areas such as V1 and FEF (Lamme and Roelfsema, 2000) and then higher association areas of temporal, frontal, and cingulate cortex. In Dehaene et al. (2003a) and Dehaene and Changeux (2005) formulations, each area was further assumed to establish with the neighboring area bottom-up feedforward connections and top-down feedback projections, the top-down connections being slower, more numerous, and more diffuse (Felleman and van Essen, 1991; Salin and Bullier, 1995). Moreover, bottom-up connections were thought to impinge on glutamate α-amino-3-hydroxy-5-methyl-4-isoxazole propionic acid (AMPA) receptors, whereas the top-down ones would primarily mobilize glutamate N-methyl-D-aspartate (NMDA) receptors (see Lumer et al., 1997).

b. *Motor programming circuits* allow the content of the workspace to be used to guide future motor behaviors and actions. A hierarchy of nested circuits implements motor intentions, from the highest level of abstract plans to individual actions, themselves composed of moves and gestures (Jeannerod and Jacob, 2005).

Empirically in humans, these circuits include premotor cortex, posterior parietal cortex, supplementary motor area, basal ganglia (notably the caudate nucleus), and cerebellum, as well as the high-level speech production circuits of the left inferior frontal lobe, including Broca's area. Connections of the workspace to motor and language circuits at the higher levels of this hierarchy endow any active representation in the workspace with the property of reportability (Weiskrantz, 1997; Dehaene et al., 2006), namely, the fact that it can be described or commented on using words or gestures.

c. *Long-term memory circuits* provide the workspace with an access to stored past percepts and events.

These long-term memory stores are likely distributed throughout the cortex according to their original content and modality; hippocampal and parahippocampal areas through reciprocal links with workspace neurons may play a special role in mediating the storage in and retrieval from these long-term stores.

d. *Evaluation circuits* (Dehaene and Changeux, 1989, 1991; Friston et al., 1994; Schultz et al., 1997) allow representations in the workspace to be selected according to a positive or negative value.

Empirically, the main anatomical systems in this respect include mesocortical noradrenergic, dopaminergic, serotoninergic, and cholinergic pathways together with the orbitofrontal cortex, anterior cingulate, hypothalamus, amygdala, and ventral striatum (see Everitt and Robbins, 2005). Autoevaluation systems develop from reciprocal projections allowing evaluation circuits to be internally activated by the current workspace content (Dehaene and Changeux, 1991) and, conversely, to selectively maintain or change workspace activity according to whether its value is predicted to be positive or negative (Dehaene and Changeux, 1991, 1995, 1997). These evaluation systems are the targets of drugs as instrumental reinforcers eventually resulting in drug self-administration or drug taking and mobilizing in particular medial prefrontal cortex and nucleus accumbens core (Everitt and Robbins, 2005; Christakou et al., 2004).

e. *Attention circuits* allow the workspace to mobilize its own circuits independently from the external world. Changes in workspace contents need not necessarily lead to changes in overt behavior, but may result in covert attention switches to selectively amplify or attenuate the signals from a subset of processor neurons.

Although all descending projections from workspace neurons to peripheral modular processors are important in this selective amplification process, a particular role is played by areas of the parietal lobe in visuospatial attention (Posner, 1994; Posner and Dehaene, 1994).

1.38.2.4.3 Global modulation of workspace activation

The state of activation of workspace neurons is assumed to be under the control of global vigilance signals from the ascending reticular activating system. Empirically they may include cholinergic nuclei in the upper brainstem and basal forebrain, noradrenergic nuclei (e.g., from the locus coeruleus), a histaminergic projection from the posterior hypothalamus, and dopaminergic and serotoninergic pathways arising from the brainstem (McCarley, 1999) together with recently identified orexin neurons from lateral hypothalamus (de Lecea et al., 1998; Harris et al., 2005). Much if not all of the influence exerted by these pathways is mediated by the thalamus and characterized by an increase in the excitability of the corticothalamic neurons.

Slow-wave sleep, on the other hand, coincides with a reduction of activity in the cholinergic, noradrenergic, and histaminergic nuclei, the anterior hypothalamus and basal forebrain being candidates for a critical role in sleep induction (Zeman, 2001). These signals are powerful enough to control major transitions between the awake state (workspace active) and slow-wave sleep (workspace inactive) states. Others provide graded inputs that modulate the amplitude of workspace activation, which is enhanced whenever novel, unpredicted, or emotionally relevant signals occur and, conversely, drops when the organism is involved in routine activity.

In the waking state the corticothalamic neurons are tonically depolarized by a blocking of hyperpolarizing potassium conductance (Steriade, 1999) (e.g., by acetylcholine acting on muscarinic receptors and norepinephrine on α_1-adrenergic receptors) switching them out of the slow-bursting mode and into fast gamma-band oscillations (Steriade et al., 1993; Llinas and Steriade, 2006). Similar effects can be obtained by electrical stimulation of the brainstem or by direct application of acetylcholine (McCormick and Bal, 1997). Moreover, mutations in the $\alpha4$ and $\beta2$-subunit genes of the nicotinic acetylcholine receptor cause autosomal dominant frontal lobe epilepsy (Steinlein, 2004), and deletion of the $\beta2$-subunit is accompanied by a decrease of micro-arousals, which take place during slow-wave sleep (Léna et al., 2004).

As a consequence, the corticothalamic neurons show increased excitability: their signal-to-noise ratio is increased, and the response to sensory stimuli is facilitated. Their spontaneous activity is high and characterized by stochastic independence of time intervals between successive action potentials (Llinas and Paré, 1991; Steriade et al., 1993; Llinas and Steriade, 2006). By contrast, during slow-wave sleep, where consciousness is absent, signal-to-noise ratios to sensory responses are decreased, and most neurons tend to discharge in bursts synchronized over large populations, thus introducing distortions or blocking information transmission (Livingstone and Hubel, 1981).

In the resting awake state, the brain is the seat of an important baseline (Gusnard and Raichle, 2001; Raichle and Gusnard, 2005) or ongoing metabolic activity; a very large fraction of it (about 80%) being correlated with glutamate cycling and, hence, active synaptic signaling processes (Shulman and Rothman, 1998; Hyder et al., 2002; Raichle and Gusnard, 2002; Shulman et al., 2004). During slow-wave sleep, anesthesia, or coma, global cerebral glucose metabolism falls by about 20% (Heiss et al., 1985; Buchsbaum et al., 1989; Shulman et al., 2004), particularly in frontal and parietal cortices (Laureys, 2005; Laureys et al., 2006). Interestingly, optical imaging of visual cortex in anesthetized animals revealed structural states of activity which have a similar global organization as activity patterns evoked by external stimuli (Tsodyks et al., 1999; Kenet et al., 2003).

1.38.2.4.4 Spatiotemporal dynamics of workspace activity

From a theoretical point of view, the global workspace is considered the seat of a particular kind of brain-scale activity state characterized by the spontaneous activation, in a sudden, coherent, and exclusive manner, referred to as ignition (Dehaene and Changeux, 2005), of a subset of workspace neurons, the rest of workspace neurons being inhibited. The transition to this state of highly correlated activity is fast and characterized by an amplification of local neural activation and the subsequent activation of multiple distant areas. The entire workspace is globally interconnected in such a way that only one such workspace representation can be active at any given time (see Sigman and Dehaene, 2005, 2006). This all-or-none invasive property distinguishes it from peripheral processors in which, due to local patterns of connections, several representations with different formats may coexist.

A representation which has invaded the workspace may remain active in an autonomous manner and resist changes in peripheral activity (see Dehaene and Changeux, 1989, 1991). If it is negatively evaluated, or if attention fails, it may, however, be spontaneously and randomly replaced by another discrete combination of workspace neurons. Functionally, this neural property implements an active generator of diversity which constantly projects and tests hypotheses (or prerepresentations) on the outside world (Dehaene and Changeux, 1989, 1991, 1997). The dynamics of workspace neuron activity is thus characterized be a constant flow of individual coherent episodes of variable duration and their selection.

Although a variety of processor areas project to the interconnected set of neurons composing the global workspace, at any given time only a subset of inputs effectively accesses it. We postulate that this gating is implemented by descending modulatory projections from workspace neurons to more peripheral processor neurons. These projections may selectively amplify or extinguish the ascending inputs from processing neurons, thus mobilizing, at a given time, a specific set of processors in the workspace while suppressing the contribution of others. In other words, the pattern of mobilized processor neurons defines the actual subjective content of conscious perception.

1.38.3 Formal Representation of the Neuronal Workspace Model

Since the initial formulation of Dehaene et al. (1998), the general architecture and dynamics of the neural network representing the global workspace and the relevant processors have been further specified in Dehaene et al. (2003a) and Dehaene and Changeux (2005). It is well understood that in any instance these computer simulations are partial and incomplete. Yet they are expected to point to the importance of particular components or features of these minimal architectures, thus leading to critical experimental tests. In our work, we found it useful to develop two quite distinct types of computer simulations. Some of them, referred to here as 'Type 1' models, were intended to describe an entire task-related cognitive architecture and thus focused more on global connectivity than on fine physiological details (e.g., Dehaene et al., 1998). Others, referred to as 'Type 2' models, were intended to capture some fine-grained physiological characteristics of neuronal firing trains and event-related potentials during conscious and subliminal perception. These simulations therefore necessarily incorporated considerably more physiological details of receptor types and cortical layers, but were not extended in a brain-scale architecture solving a precise task (e.g., Dehaene et al., 2003a; Dehaene and Changeux, 2005). Here, we describe their principles in turn.

1.38.3.1 Detailed Physiological Simulations of Access to the Conscious Workspace

In those Type 2 simulations, we intended to describe only part of the workspace (Dehaene and Changeux, 2005), but to do so with physiological details. The goal was to simulate the bottom-up/top-down interactions occurring between four hierarchically organized areas, the lowest of which was in contact with the external world while the highest was assumed to contact other workspace areas (not simulated).

1.38.3.1.1 Single-neuron model
The model (**Figure 3(a)**), adapted from Lumer et al. (1997a,b), was simulated at the level of single-

compartment integrate-and-fire neurons whose membrane potential evolved according to semirealistic differential equations taking into account realistic temporal delays and AMPA, NMDA, and gamma-aminobutyric acid (GABA) currents. Neurons also received a diffuse neuromodulator input summarizing the known depolarizing effects of ascending activating systems, such as those from cholinergic, noradrenergic, and serotoninergic nuclei in the brainstem, basal forebrain, and hypothalamus (Steriade et al., 1993; Llinas and Steriade, 2006). This parameter was used to control the level of wakefulness (see following discussion).

1.38.3.1.2 Columnar structure
The neurons were organized into simulated thalamocortical columns comprising 80 excitatory and 40 inhibitory neurons and organized in a three-layered structure, schematizing supragranular, infragranular, and layer IV cortical neurons and a corresponding thalamic sector (**Figure 3(b)**). A fairly realistic scheme of connections was implemented, whereby thalamic excitatory neurons projected to layer IV (AMPA, 3 ms delay) and, with lesser strength, to infragranular neurons (AMPA, 3 ms). Layer IV excitatory neurons projected to supragranular neurons (AMPA, 2 ms). Supragranular excitatory neurons projected to infragranular neurons (AMPA, 2 ms). Finally, infragranular excitatory neurons projected to layer 4 (AMPA, 7 ms), to supragranular neurons (AMPA, 7 ms), and to the thalamus (AMPA, 8 ms). Those principles and parameter values capture the major properties of trans-laminar connections (Lumer et al., 1997a,b; Douglas and Martin, 2004), though they do not attempt to capture the possible functional roles of the different layers (see, e.g., Raizada and Grossberg, 2003).

1.38.3.1.3 Long-range connections
For corticocortical projections, supragranular excitatory neurons of each area projected to layer IV of the next area (AMPA, 3 ms). In agreement with physiological observations (Felleman and Van Essen, 1991; Salin and Bullier, 1995), top-down connections were slower, more numerous, and more diffuse. They connected the supra- and infragranular excitatory neurons of a given column to the supra- and infragranular layers of all areas of a lower hierarchical level. Strong top-down connections linked columns coding for the same stimulus, whereas weaker top-down connections projected to all columns of a lower area. Both were NMDA mediated, and transmission delays increased with cortical distance (delay $= 5 + 3\delta$ ms,

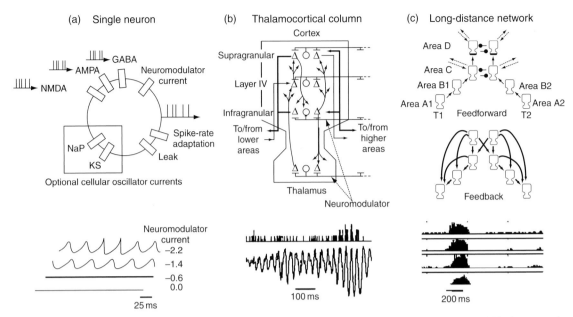

Figure 3   Detailed implementation, at the cellular and molecular levels, of the neuronal workspace model in the case of access to consciousness as in Dehaene et al. (2003b) and Dehaene and Changeux (2005). Single neurons may generate sustained oscillations of membrane potential at high enough level neuromodulator current (a) but only the thalamocortical column (b), and global network levels do generate complex waxing and waning EEG-like oscillations (b) and metastable global states of sustained firing (or 'ignition') (c). From Dehaene S, Sergent C, and Changeux JP (2003b) A neuronal network model linking subjective reports and objective physiological data during conscious perception. *Proc. Natl. Acad. Sci. USA* 100: 8520–8525, with permission from the National Academy of Sciences; and Dehaene S and Changeux JP (2005) Ongoing spontaneous activity controls access to consciousness: A neuronal model for inattentional blindness. *PLoS Biol.* 3: 910–927, with permission from the Public Library of Science.

with $\delta = 1$ for consecutive areas, 2 for areas two levels apart in the hierarchy, etc.).

1.38.3.1.4   Spontaneous activity
Although we studied stimulus-evoked activity (see later discussion), a most important goal of these stimulations was to also capture spontaneous corticothalamic activity and its modulation with states of vigilance. We studied two possible sources for spontaneous activity, both of which were meant as theoretical idealizations on a continuum of possibilities. The first case, hereafter the 'cellular oscillator model,' was a purely deterministic model in which neurons follow simple differential equations incorporating persistent sodium and slowly inactivating potassium currents whose interplay generates intrinsic gamma-band oscillations of membrane potential (Wang, 1993), comparable to those recorded experimentally (Llinas et al., 1998). We also described another simulation, hereafter called the 'random spikes' model, in which stochastic spontaneous activity arose from fast random fluctuations in membrane potential, capturing the joint effects of synaptic and postsynaptic noise on spike initiation. Both cellular

sources turned out to have a similar effect on global spontaneous corticothalamic states (for details, see Dehaene and Changeux, 2005).

1.38.3.2   Minimal Models of Cognitive Architectures for Effortful Tasks

Another line of models, Type 1 simulations, attempted to capture behavioral and neuroimaging observations on higher-level 'executive' tasks that depend on prefrontal cortex (Dehaene et al., 1998), such as the Delayed-Response, Stroop, Wisconsin, or Tower of London tests (Dehaene and Changeux, 1989, 1991, 1997). We have not found it possible to design a pertinent model of such tasks while working at the level of detailed spiking neurons and columns. Thus, those models were of a more abstract nature and incorporated neural 'units' formally similar to single neurons or clusters whose average firing rate was simulated by McCulloch-Pitts units. No attempt was made to capture intracolumnar or thalamic dynamics, but the network incorporated a series of assemblies assumed to represent relevant cortical activity at several hierarchical levels.

1.38.3.2.1 Learning by reward

An interesting advantage of these coarser cognitive models is that they allowed for the simulation of longer periods of time and, therefore, of selective learning by reward, which empirically can be accompanied by drastic changes in vigilance and conscious access to task-relevant features. The network received a reward signal (R) provided after each network response (R = +1, correct; R = −1, incorrect). This reward led to two types of internal changes: classical synaptic weight changes of the Hebbian type, and a more original hypothesis of direct workspace activity modulation.

1.38.3.2.2 Synaptic weight changes

In the initial formulation of the theory (Dehaene et al., 1998) and for simplicity, only the synaptic weights between two excitatory units were assumed to be modifiable according to a reward-modulated Hebbian rule $\Delta w^{post,pre} = \varepsilon \, R \, S^{pre} \, (2 \, S^{post} - 1)$, where R is the reward signal, pre is the presynaptic unit, and post is the postsynaptic unit (Dehaene and Changeux, 1989).

1.38.3.2.3 Workspace activity changes

Starting with our earliest modeling approaches (Dehaene and Changeux, 1989), we have assumed that reward entry can have either a stabilizing or destabilizing effect on prefrontal neuron activity. In Dehaene et al. (1998), we assumed that workspace neuron activity is under the influence of both vigilance and reward signals. The vigilance signal V is treated as having a modulatory influence on all workspace neurons. It is updated after each response: if R > 0, then $\Delta V = -0.1 \, V$, otherwise $\Delta V = 0.5 \, (1 - V)$. This has the effect of a slowly decreasing vigilance with sharp increases on error trials. The reward signal R influences the stability of workspace activity through a short-term depression or potentiation of synaptic weights (Dehaene and Changeux, 1989, 1991, 1997). A plausible molecular implementation of this rule has been proposed in terms of allosteric receptors (Dehaene and Changeux, 1989, 1991). It postulates that the time coincidence of a diffuse reward signal and of a postsynaptic marker of recent neuronal activity transiently shifts the allosteric equilibrium either toward, or from, a desensitized refractory conformation (Heidmann and Changeux, 1982, see also Changeux and Edelstein, 2005). Through this chemical Hebb rule, negative reward destabilizes the self-sustaining excitatory connections between currently active workspace neurons, thus initiating a change in workspace activity.

1.38.4 States of Vigilance as Spontaneous Thalamocortical Rhythms and Their Brain Imaging

The simulations of the vigilance states by Dehaene and Changeux (2005) type 2 modeling incorporate only minimal physiological mechanisms such as changes in a single current $I_{neuromodul}$, the depolarizing influence of ascending neuromodulation systems onto thalamic and cortical neurons (**Figure 3(a)**). They nevertheless suffice to generate a dynamical phase transition whose properties bear interesting similarity with actual empirical observations. We observed a robust threshold value of ascending neuromodulatory signaling beyond which structured neuronal activity emerged in the form of spontaneous thalamocortical oscillations in the gamma band (20–100 Hz, with a peak of the power spectrum around 40 Hz) (see also Bush and Sejnowski, 1996; Fuentes et al., 1996). The simulated waxing and waning synchronous bursts of oscillations bear similarity with empirical observations of transient periods of thalamocortical resonance, detected as bouts of gamma-band oscillations using electrophysiological recordings, for instance in the cat thalamus and cortex (Steriade et al., 1993; Steriade et al., 1996), or in humans using electro- and magneto-encephalography (Llinas and Ribary, 1993) (**Figure 3(b)**). They are proposed to represent the state of consciousness referred to as vigilance.

An original feature of the simulations is to characterize precisely the change in state in terms of a dynamical phase transition, referred to as a Hopf bifurcation. The Hopf bifurcation is continuous in the amplitude of spontaneous activity, which increases steadily from zero as vigilance increases. Thus it implements a true continuum of consciousness states, from high vigilance to drowsiness, and the various states of sleep anesthesia, or coma (Gajraj et al., 1999; Bonhomme et al., 2000; Sleigh et al., 2001). However, the Hopf bifurcation is also discontinuous in frequency space as the ascending neuromodulation increases. This may capture the observation that, during awakening or returning from anesthesia, there is a definite threshold for regaining of consciousness, which coincides with the threshold for emergence of high-frequency spontaneous thalamocortical oscillations.

Anatomically, the model predicts that in the awake state, spontaneous activity is present in all areas, but exhibits a higher degree of organization in higher cortical association areas, whose neurons are tightly interconnected by long distance into a global neuronal workspace and mobilize other low-level areas in a top-down manner. Thus, the model predicts that brain territories particularly rich in 'workspace neurons' with long-distance connections (i.e., prefrontal, parietal, superior temporal, and cingulate cortices) show the most intense and consistent spontaneous activity in the awake state. This prediction fits with the observation that the 'baseline' activity of the awake human brain at rest points to a network linking dorsal and ventral medial prefrontal, lateral parietotemporal, and posterior cingulate cortices (Gusnard and Raichle, 2001; Mazoyer et al., 2001; Raichle et al., 2001) which constantly fluctuates in synchrony with changes in electroencephalographic spectral content (Laufs et al., 2003) and shows the greatest drop in metabolism during anesthesia, sleep, coma, or the vegetative state (Maquet and Phillips, 1998; Fiset et al., 1999; Laureys et al., 2000; Paus, 2000; Balkin et al., 2002; Heinke and Schwarzbauer, 2002; Shulman et al., 2003). In striking agreement with the workspace model, volatile anesthetics have been recently shown to disrupt frontoparietal recurrent information transfer at gamma frequencies in the rat (Imas et al., 2005).

1.38.5 Interactions between External Stimuli and Ongoing Spontaneous Activity: Facilitation versus Competition

A most original aspect of Dehaene and Changeux's (2005) type 2 simulations on ongoing spontaneous activity concerns its interactions with external stimuli. These interactions can be facilitatory (higher spontaneous activity facilitates the detection of weak stimuli) or inhibitory (very high spontaneous activity preventing access to other external stimuli).

First, spontaneous activity may affect activation caused by external stimuli. The model predicts that ascending neuromodulatory current and the external input current combine in a smooth and largely additive fashion. The threshold for conscious access (ignition) is not fixed, but decreases as vigilance increases. At one extreme, very low levels of vigilance completely prevent the possibility of ignition, even by long and intense stimuli. Such stimuli only lead to a short pulse of activation through the thalamus and the early sensory areas of the model. Thus, we expect that early sensory signal can be processed, while higher cortical ones are attenuated, during altered states of consciousness. This prediction is consistent with empirical observations of auditory processing during sleep (Portas et al., 2000) or the vegetative state (Laureys et al., 2000), where stimuli activate the thalamus and auditory cortex, but fail to generate the distributed state of correlated prefrontal, parietal, and cingulate activity observed in awake normal subjects. Similar observations have been made with tactile or pain stimuli, suggesting that the lack of prefrontal–parietal–cingulate ignition is quite characteristic of those states (Laureys et al., 2002; Laureys et al., 2004).

Pharmacological agents such as nicotine, which can mimic and potentiate ascending cholinergic systems, might also have an influence on the perceptual threshold in visual masking or other psychophysical tests, which should be measurable both psychophysically and with brain imaging measures of ignition (e.g., prefrontal–cingulate activity in fMRI, P300 in event-related potentials). In schizophrenic patients, subliminal processing is intact, but the threshold for conscious perception of masked visual stimuli is increased, possibly relating to an impairment of top-down prefrontal–cingulate connectivity (Dehaene et al., 2003b; Del Cul et al., 2006). In such patients, we predict that nicotine might partially bring the conscious access threshold back toward its normal value.

Second, the model predicts that very high levels of spontaneous activity can prevent ignition by external stimuli (**Figure 4**). As mentioned, optical imaging of visual cortex in anesthetized animals has revealed structured states of spontaneous ongoing activity, which have the same global organization as activity patterns evoked by external stimulation (Tsodyks et al., 1999; Kenet et al., 2003). Moreover, high levels of spontaneous activity inhibit the sensory responses evoked by external stimuli, for instance, by whisker deflection in somatosensory cortex (Petersen et al., 2003). Such interactions with ongoing activity can provide an explanation for the large variability in spike trains evoked by repeated identical sensory stimuli (Arieli et al., 1996; Petersen et al., 2003).

The complete blocking of some incoming stimuli that occurs in the simulations of the model offers a plausible explanation for the psychological phenomenon of inattentional blindness (Newby and Rock, 1998). In this phenomenon, human observers engaged into an intense mental activity (such as

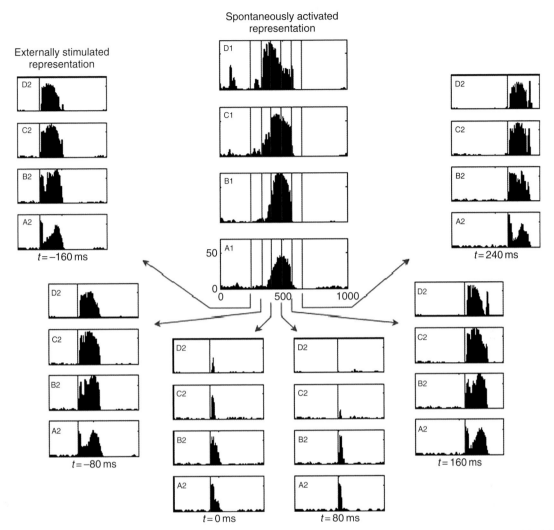

Figure 4 Competition between spontaneous workspace activity and external sensory simulation—a plausible model of the inattentional blindness state (Dehaene and Changeux (2005)). In the state of inattentional blindness, the subject fails to consciously detect external stimuli during periods of spontaneous thought. This can be reproduced by the simulations. In the boxes on the left of the figure, *before* the period of ongoing spontaneous activity, the external stimulus propagates in a bottom-up manner from the lowest (A) to the highest (B) areas of the sensory system yielding activation of the workspace (see **Figure 3(c)**). In the right boxes the same occurs *after* the period of spontaneous activity. On the other hand, when the external stimulus coincides with the period of spontaneous activity (center), its access to the workspace is inhibited. From Dehaene S and Changeux JP (2005) Ongoing spontaneous activity controls access to consciousness: A neuronal model for inattentional blindness. *PLoS Biol.* 3: 910–927; used with permission from the Public Library of Science.

detecting or counting stimuli of a certain type) become totally oblivious to other irrelevant stimuli, even when they occur within the fovea for a long duration (Simons and Chabris, 1999; Chun and Marois, 2002). Although inattentional blindness is typically studied in the laboratory by placing subjects in a predefined task, the simulations suggest that spontaneous trains of thought, unrelated to external stimuli and instructions, may also exert a temporary blocking. The model predicts that this state should be

characterized by (1) an intense prefrontal–parietal–cingulate activation by the distracting thought or object prior to the presentation of the target stimulus; and (2) a proportional reduction of the target-induced activation to a brief bottom-up activation in specialized processors. fMRI studies provide direct support for those predictions (Rees et al., 1999; Weismann et al., 2005). Future research should extend those paradigms using time-resolved neuroimaging methods such as event-related potentials to test the prediction that early bottom-up activation is preserved, but top-down recurrent reverberations are suppressed in an all-or-none manner.

1.38.6 Competition between Sensory Stimuli for Access to Consciousness: Looking for Objective Records of Subjective Perception

The model was also studied under conditions simulating a classical perceptual phenomenon referred to as the attentional blink where two sensory stimuli compete for access to reportable conscious perception (Raymond et al., 1992). In a typical experiment, participants are asked to process two successive targets, T1 and T2. When T2 is presented between 100 and 500 s after T1, the ability to report it drops, as if the participants' attention had 'blinked.' In other words, rather paradoxically, perception of a first visual stimulus may prevent the subjective perception of a second one. The paradigm is sufficiently simple and explicit to study why some patterns of brain activity have access to subjective experience and thus to establish, in a causal, mechanistic manner, a link between subjective reports and objective physiological recordings.

The minimal network proposed (Dehaene et al., 2003a; **Figure 3**) is composed of four hierarchical stages of processing where stimuli T1 and T2 evoke neuronal assemblies. At the lower level, A and B correspond to primary and secondary visual areas and C and D to higher association areas, including temporal and frontal cortex. At the lower level, the assemblies do not inhibit each other (see Arnell and Jolicoeur, 1997), but further on, T1 and T2 reach higher association areas C and D, where they compete for global access via reciprocal inhibitory interactions.

With the network placed in a regime of spontaneous thalamocortical oscillations, corresponding to a state of wakefulness (see earlier discussion), one distinguishes two principal modes of signal processing by the network. First, let us consider the simple case where T1, in the absence of competing stimuli, is consciously perceived. T1 evokes a short burst of phasic physiological activity that propagates across the A to D corticothalamic hierarchy. Reaching the highest cortical levels, the sensory input generates top-down amplification signals which, about 80 ms later, cause sustained firing in areas A and B. In a larger-scale simulation, such a long-lasting dynamic state would generate brain-scale propagation of stimulus information into the entire workspace network. It is proposed that this global broadcasting constitutes the physiological basis of conscious reportability.

The network also simulates the conditions of the 'blink' when T1 and T2 are presented in close succession. Experimentally it is known that when T2 is either presented simultaneously with T1, or long after, it is, in both cases, subjectively perceived. The network simulation indeed shows that in both conditions, sustained firing supported by joint bottom-up activation and top-down amplification takes place. Yet, under conditions of close temporal succession, a T2 stimulus presented during T1-elicited global firing elicits bottom-up activation restricted to levels A and B, but fails to propagate to higher cortical levels. As a result, the second phase of top-down amplification does not occur. The T2 stimulus is blinked from conscious perception (**Figure 5**).

The simulation predicts that a temporary drop in firing rate of pyramidal cells coding for T2 in areas C or D is associated with a loss in performance typical of the attentional blink. The model also shows a global drop of power emitted in the gamma band and of cross-correlations between distant T2-coding neurons. Thus, several indexes of firing and synchrony all point to a drop in global activity during the blink, particularly evident in the higher areas C and D.

An original property of the model is the distinction of two modes of signal processing – a nearest-neighbor bottom-up propagation of sensory stimulation across the hierarchy of areas and a long-distance top-down network that sends amplification signals back to all levels below it. In particular, it predicts a dynamic all-or-none bifurcation between the two modes associated with different subjective perception of the stimulus. Indeed, objective physiological data indicate that during this blink, T2 fails to evoke a P300 potential, but still elicits event-related potentials associated with visual and semantic processing (P1, N1, and N400) (Vogel et al., 1998).

The prediction of an all-or-none loss of conscious perception and of T2-induced higher-level brain-scale activation during the attentional blink was tested experimentally (Sergent and Dehaene, 2004; Sergent et al., 2005). We used a modified attentional blink paradigm in which human subjects merely had to report to what extent they had seen a word (T2) within a rapid letter stream that contained another target letter string (T1). To obtain a continuous measure of subjective perception, subjects were asked to move a

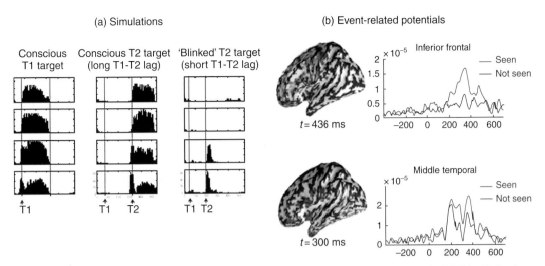

Figure 5 Comparison of the predictions of the neuronal workspace model (from Dehaene et al., 2003b) with the temporal dynamics of cortical electrical activity evoked by seen and unseen stimuli (from Sergent et al., 2005) during the attentional blink task. (a) Simulation of three trials of the attentional blink task. In each column with eight boxes (reproducing the superposed areas of **Figure 3(c)**) is shown the evolution of the computed firing rate in excitatory neurons. *Left column:* the sensory stimulus T1 accesses the workspace; *central column:* the lag between T1 and the second stimulus T2 is such that the sustained activity elicited by T1 has decayed in such a way that T2 accesses the conscious workspace; *right column:* the short lag between T2 and T1 is such that the sustained activity in T1 interferes with the access of T2 to the workspace. (b) Event-related potentials recorded during the attentional blink task at the level of the inferior frontal cortex where differences are noted between subjectively seen and not seen stimuli. Such difference is not observed in the initial bottom-up activation of the temporal cortex (200 ms) but converges later on during a global reverberation phase (300–400 ms). From Dehaene S, Sergent C, and Changeux JP (2003b) A neuronal network model linking subjective reports and objective physiological data during conscious perception. *Proc. Natl. Acad. Sci. USA* 100: 8520–8525, with permission from the National Academy of Sciences; and Sergent C, Baillet S, and Dehaene S (2005) Timing of the brain events underlying access to consciousness during the attentional blink. *Nat. Neurosci.* 8: 1391–1400, with permission from Nature Publishing Group.

cursor on a continuous scale, from 'not seen' on the left to 'maximal visibility' on the right. The results indicate that the reported subjective perception during the blink is indeed all-or-none (Sergent and Dehaene, 2004; Sergent et al., 2005) and relates to the loss of activation in a distributed, synchronous network prominently involving inferior and lateral prefrontal cortices as well as anterior cingulate (Marois et al., 2004; Gross et al., 2004; Sergent et al., 2005; Hommel et al., 2006).

The model in its simple formulation is coherent with previous proposals of a role of top-down recurrent (Lamme and Roelfsema, 2000), reentrant (Edelman, 1993), or resonant (Llinas et al., 1998) connections in the integrative processing of consciously perceived signals. It is also supported by recent experimental data. Because the blink is attributed to competition for workspace access, the proportion of T2 targets that are blinked, as a function of time, roughly traces the inverse shape of the neural activity evoked by T1 in higher-level areas C and D. In actual experiments, similarly, there is an inverse relation between the P300 waveform evoked

by T1 and the size of the blink (Sergent et al., 2005). Furthermore, the fMRI activation elicited by T1 in parietal, frontal, and cingulate areas predicts the size of the blink (Marois et al., 2000). Last, the timing of the brain events during the attentional blink using letter strings was recently resolved by event-related potentials. The data show that early potentials (P1 and N1) were equally evoked by seen and not seen words, indicating that these early brain events do not fit with conscious perception. However, a rapid divergence was observed around 270 ms, with late brain events solely evoked by seen words (Sergent et al., 2005) (**Figure 5**). The data are thus fully consistent with the proposal of the model (Dehaene et al., 2003a) that top-down amplification signals and sustained firing into the workspace network constitutes the physiological basis of conscious reportability.

Although there have been no single-neuron recordings during the attentional blink, the simulated profiles of single-neuron activity to seen and blinked T2 targets can be compared to electrophysiological recordings obtained in other paradigms of conscious and unconscious processing. In perceptual areas A and B of the model, neurons fire phasically in tight synchrony with the stimulus, then show a broader period of late amplification only in seen trials, not in blinked trials. This parallels experimental recordings in areas V1 and IT under conditions of inattention, reduced contrast, masking, or anesthesia, where late amplification occurs only for reportable stimuli (Lamme and Roelfsema, 2000; Super et al., 2001; Lamme et al., 2002). The presently available physiological data are thus consistent with the proposal of the neuronal workspace model that conscious access of reportable signals is a sudden self-amplifying bifurcation leading to a global brain-scale pattern of activity in the workspace network.

1.38.7   Preconscious States of Activity

Despite considerable progress in the empirical research on the brain imaging of conscious perception, debates have arisen about the coherence of these data. For instance, some researchers emphasize a correlation of conscious visual perception with early occipital events (Zéki, 2003), others with late parietofrontal activity (Sergent et al., 2005). Also, following Weiskrantz (1997), we insisted on the notion that subjective reports are the basic criterion that can establish whether a percept is conscious or not. Yet, the philosopher Ned Block (2005) has suggested that in reality, we may experience conscious experiences that are richer in content than what we can report. For instance, when

an array of letters is flashed, viewers claim to see the whole array, although they can later report only one subsequently cued row or column. The initial processing of the array might already be considered as 'phenomenally' conscious though not 'seen' in a fully conscious manner (Lamme, 2003; Block, 2005).

We have expressed our disagreement with the phenomenal/access distinction, whose empirical testability is debatable, and have argued instead that within nonconscious processing, one must introduce a transient preconscious state of activity in which information is potentially accessible, yet not accessed (Dehaene et al., 2006). This led to the formal distinction (Dehaene et al., 2006) (**Figure 6**) within nonconscious information processing of:

(1) *Subliminal processing* of input signals that may occur when bottom-up activation is insufficient to trigger a large-scale reverberating state. The described simulations of a minimal thalamocortical network (Dehaene and Changeux, 2005) show that in a global network of neurons with long-range axons exhibiting nonlinear self-amplifying properties, a well-defined dynamic threshold exists beyond which activity quickly grows until a full-scale ignition is seen, while a slightly weaker activation quickly dies out.

(2) *Preconscious processing*, a term coined to design a neural process that potentially carries enough activation for conscious access, but is temporarily buffered in a nonconscious store. Such a buffering might result

Subliminal	**Preconscious**	**Conscious**
- Feedforward activation - Activation decreases with depth - Depth of processing depends on attention and task set - Activation can reach semantic level - Short-lived priming - No durable frontoparietal activity - No reportability	- Intense activation, yet confined to sensorimotor processors - Occipitotemporal loops and local synchrony - Priming at multiple levels - No reportability while attention is occupied elsewhere	- Orientation of top-down attention - Amplification of sensorimotor activity - Intense activation spreading to parietofrontal network - Long-distance loops and global synchrony - Durable activation, maintained at will - Reportability

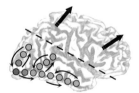

Figure 6   Schematic representation of the subliminal, preconscious, and conscious states of processing of visual stimuli. From Dehaene S, Changeux JP, Naccache L, Sackur J, and Sergent C. (2006) Conscious, preconscious, and subliminal processing: A testable taxonomy. *Trends Cogn. Sci.* 10: 204–211; used with permission from Elsevier.

from a lack of top-down attentional amplification, for example, owing to transient occupancy of the central workspace system (see preceding discussion and Dehaene and Changeux, 2005). The formal analysis of the attentional blink and inattentional blindness paradigms, indeed, has shown that even strong visual stimuli may remain temporarily preconscious. They are potentially accessible (they could quickly gain access to conscious report if they were attended), but they are not consciously accessed at the moment. At the neurocomputational level, preconscious processing is proposed to involve resonant loops within medium-range connections which maintain the representation of the stimulus temporarily active in a sensory buffer for a few hundred milliseconds.

In a fair attempt to establish objective recordings of subjectively reported conscious perception, these various conditions have to be experimentally and theoretically examined. In particular, other independent methods for decoding conscious states based, for instance, on trained pattern classifiers of fMRI or alternative physiological signals might be used to 'objectively' track signal processing in the course of conscious perception (Haynes and Rees, 2005, 2006), thus offering closer tests of the theoretical models.

1.38.8 Performance of an Effortful Deduction Task: The Stroop Task

Our modeling approach was developed along two distinct lines: *type 2* models were intended to capture some fine-grained physiological characteristics of neuronal firing trains and event-related potentials during conscious and subliminal perception. These simulations therefore necessarily incorporated considerably more physiological details of receptor types and cortical layers, but were not extended in a brain-scale architecture solving a precise task (e.g., Dehaene et al., 2003a; Dehaene and Changeux, 2005). On the other hand, the *type 1* models were intended to describe an entire task-related cognitive architecture and thus focused more on global connectivity than on fine physiological details (e.g., Dehaene et al., 1998). The Stroop task (McLeod, 1991) was selected as a simple experimental paradigm where a subject has to make a decision about the meaning of a written word under conditions where interference may occur. For instance, the subject is asked to give the color of the ink with which a color word is printed, and the meaning of the word

may differ from the actual color of the printed word. Under this last condition, the subject has to make a conscious effort to give the correct response. The task was originally simulated with the standard neuronal workspace model (Dehaene et al., 1998), in which four input units were dedicated to encoding four color words, four other input units encoded the color of the ink used to print the word, and four internal units corresponded to the four naming responses. Routine color naming and word naming are implemented by direct one-to-one connections between these units and the corresponding output naming units. Workspace activation is not needed for any of these tasks. However, the effortful task (color naming with word interference) consists of providing conflicting word and color inputs and rewarding the network for turning on the naming unit appropriate to the ink color. When the naive network is switched to the effortful condition, an initial series of errors takes place as the network steadily applies the routine naming response. Yet, the delivery of negative reward leads to an increase in vigilance and to the sudden activation of variable patterns among workspace units resulting in a search phase for the next ~30 trials. Workspace activation varies in a partly random manner as various response rules are explored, but the workspace activation patterns that lead to activating the incorrect response unit are negatively rewarded and tend to be eliminated in subsequent trials (**Figure 7**). Eventually, the network settles into a stable activation pattern, with a fringe of variability that slowly disappears in subsequent trials. This stable pattern, which leads to correct performance, is characterized by the differential amplification of the relevant word units relative to color units and by strong excitatory connections among active workspace units maintaining the pattern active in the intertrial interval.

Following the search phase, the network goes through a phase of effortful task execution in which workspace activation remains indispensable to correct performance. During this phase, workspace activity remains high, even on occasional trials in which the word and ink color information do not conflict. When performance is correct for a series of consecutive trials, vigilance tends to drop. However, any lapse in workspace activation is immediately sanctioned by an error. Each error is immediately followed by an intense reactivation of the workspace. Progressively, though, the task becomes routinized as the Hebbian rule applied to processor units tends to increase the color-to-name connections and to decrease the

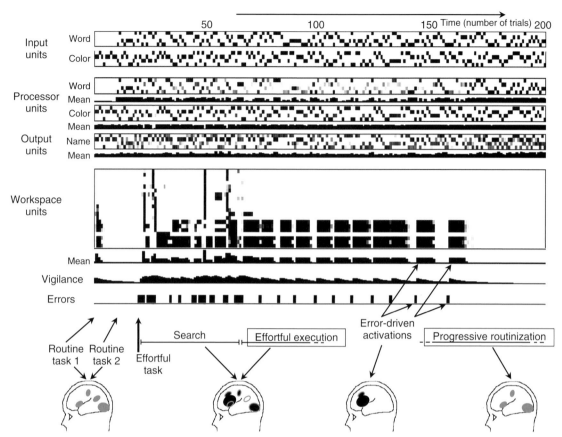

Figure 7 Simulation of the temporal dynamics of the Stroop task based on the original simulation of the neuronal workspace model of Dehaeneet al. (1998). The Stroop task was introduced without warning after routine trial no. 20. Note the selective activation of workspace units with a simultaneous amplification of color processors and a suppression of word processors. Workspace unit activation is seen in the initial phase of searching the appropriate response rule during the effortful execution of the task and following each erroneous response. Lower line: putative brain imaging correlates of workspace activation and routine are shown. From Dehaene S, Kerszberg M, and Changeux JP (1998) A neuronal model of a global workspace in effortful cognitive tasks. *Proc. Natl. Acad. Sci. USA* 95: 14529–14534; used with permission from the National Academy of Sciences.

word-to-name connections. Routinization is characterized by increasingly longer periods of correct performance in the absence of workspace activation.

The key empirical prediction of our hypothesis in the domain of brain imaging is the existence of a strong correlation between cortical areas that are found active in conscious effortful tasks and areas that possess a strong long-distance corticocortical connectivity (**Figure 7**). The global activation of neurons dispersed in multiple cortical areas is expected to be visualized as a temporary increase in the long-distance coherence of brain activity in electro- and magnetoencephalography or in studies of functional connectivity with fMRI.

The model also predicts that areas rich in workspace neurons will appear as suddenly activated when a novel, nonroutine task is introduced while being absent during routine tasks and will vary semi-randomly during the initial learning of a novel task. The level of activation should be high and stable during execution of a known but not yet routinized effortful task and should decrease during routinization, but should resume sharply following an error.

Brain-imaging experiments indicate that the workspace network which includes dorsolateral prefrontal cortex (dlPFC) and anterior cingulate (AC) is active in effortful cognitive tasks, including the Stroop test, with a graded level of activation as a function of task difficulty (Pardo et al., 1990; Cohen et al., 1997; Paus et al., 1998). With automatization, activation decreases in dlPFC and AC, but it immediately recovers if a novel, nonroutine situation occurs (Raichle, 1994). AC activates in tight synchrony with subjects' errors (Dehaene and

Cohen, 1994; Carter et al., 1998). Data consistent with the model have been recently obtained with a rather elaborate reward-based logical deduction task referred to as 'master-brain' task (Landmann et al., 2006). In the course of this trial-and-error learning process, the subjects have to infer the identity of an unknown four-key code on the basis of successive feedback signals but also through internal autoevaluation deductions. This search period is followed by a routine period during which subjects merely repeatedly execute the identified sequence. fMRI measurements reveal a sudden activation during search of the expected workspace circuits which include bilateral frontoparietal (particularly the lateral orbitofrontal and dorsolateral prefrontal cortex) and anterior cingulated cortex, striatum, and midbrain together with the cerebellum (**Figure 8**). This activation collapses during ensuing periods of routine sequence repetition. Furthermore, examination of brain activation during logical and chance discovery showed an early collapse when the correct logical sequence could be deduced without waiting to receive an actual external reward. In agreement with the simulations of the neuronal workspace model in the case of the Stroop task (Dehaene et al., 1998), the data reveal large-scale changes in interconnected distant cortical areas, which may take place tacitly according to an autoevaluation process. They add an important aspect, the differential activation of the striatum: The activation of the putamen and a part of the right caudate body indexes the sign of the reward prediction error (referred to as a ventral 'critic'), and the head of the right caudate indexes the available information that can be extracted from it (referred to as a dorsal 'actor') (see Sutton and Barto, 1981; Schultz et al., 1997; O'Doherty, 2004). This relationship between the workspace network and the underlying subcortical reward networks,

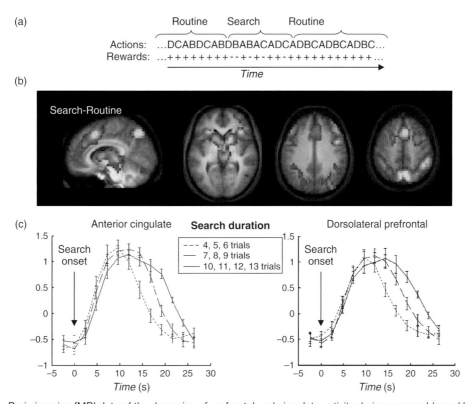

Figure 8 Brain imaging fMRI data of the dynamics of prefrontal and cingulate activity during a reward-based logical deduction task (Landmann et al., 2006). (a) Subjects were engaged in a motor trial-and-error learning task, in which they had to infer the identity of a hidden four-key press by trial-and-error (here ADBC). The design of the task allowed subjects to base their inferences not only on the feedback they received but also on internal deductions and evaluations. (b) fMRI imaging revealed, in agreement with the neuronal workspace model (**Figure 7**), a large bilateral activation of parietal, prefrontal, cingulate, and striatal networks during the search period that collapsed during ensuing routine execution. From Landmann C, Dehaene S, Pappata S, et al. (2006) Dynamics of prefrontal and cingulate activity during a reward-based logical deduction task. *Cereb. Cortex* 17: 749–759; used with permission from Oxford University Press.

which was not taken into consideration in the detailed model of access to consciousness, becomes accessible on both theoretical and experimental grounds.

1.38.9 The Evolution of Consciousness

1.38.9.1 Animal and Human Consciousness

Since the provocative statements of Thomas Huxley that "we are conscious automata," that "brutes" share consciousness with humans (1874) and that "all states of consciousness in us, as in them, are immediately caused by molecular changes of brain substance," nonhuman species and especially laboratory animals have served as experimental models for the scientific investigation of behavior but also of animal consciousness (Thorndike, 1898; Yerkes, 1916; Barresi and Moore, 1996; Jasper, 1998; Koch, 2004; Changeux, 2006). In the framework of the present discussions about neurocomputational models of consciousness, a first challenging issue is thus to what extent the neuronal workspace model may be usefully exploited to define and evaluate consciousness in animals. A second related question is whether or not functionally homologous (rather than analogous) neural structures might be at work in these nonhuman species. Answers to both questions are of importance, in particular if one wishes to use laboratory animals like the mouse as experimental models to investigate the neural bases of consciousness (see Changeux, 2006).

As early as 1921, the Italian neurologist Luigi Bianchi stated that "among the phenomenal factors of the activities of living organisms" arises a "bond of coherence" which "progresses with the development and complexity of living organisms and of their nervous system" that he referred to as consciousness. He further specified that "the dawn of higher consciousness coincides with the apparition of the frontal lobes in the evolution of the brain" and also noted their "inhibitory power" and their capacity for "intellectual syntheses." Bianchi in many respects anticipated several of the presently suggested ideas and theories about consciousness (Changeux, 1983; Shallice, 1988; Edelman, 1989; Crick, 1994; Crick and Koch, 2003; Dehaene and Changeux, 2004; Changeux and Edelstein, 2005; Naccache, 2005; and Naccache et al., 2005, among many others). Following these views, one may then argue that lower species like mice, or even birds, which have a reduced or even

absent prefrontal cortex – a critical component of the neuronal workspace circuits – have little if any consciousness. Would experimental and theoretical investigations with the laboratory mouse be simply irrelevant to a scientific investigation of consciousness (see Block, 2005)?

It is of interest to reevaluate these issues in the framework of the neuronal workspace model with nonhumans as well as with humans in the course of both ontogenetic and phylogenetic evolutions. A first point to note is that looking at the developing human infants, Preyer already stated in 1894, "There is not the least reason for assuming in advance that every human being comes into the world endowed with complete consciousness of self" and "there are several grades of consciousness." Developmental studies with humans from the newborn to the adult (Zelazo, 1996; Lagercrantz et al., 2002; Zelazo, 2004; Johnson, 2005; Lagercrantz, 2005; Bartocci et al., 2006) reveal without ambiguity that, beyond its diverse definitions, consciousness cannot be viewed as an irreducible and unique global entity. A similar conclusion emerges from ethological and experimental studies with evolutionarily distant species, such as mice, monkeys, and apes (see Boakes, 1984; Trivers, 1985; Barresi and Moore, 1996; Changeux, 2002). Comparative analysis of these systems suggests a breakdown of consciousness into multiple nested hierarchical levels. Here, we tentatively propose a first classification into four levels, all the while realizing that it remains necessarily arbitrary and simplistic (see Changeux, 2006). Note that these represent landmark points on a continuum rather than sharp distinctions, because our goal is to emphasize a continuity of phylogenetic and ontogenetic stages to full-blown adult human consciousness. The proposed levels comprise:

a. A lower level of minimal consciousness for simple organisms, like rats or mice, which undergo cycles of sleep and wakefulness, possess the capacity to display spontaneous motor activity and to create representations, for instance from visual and auditory experience, to store them into long-term memory and use them for approach and avoidance behavior; these organisms exhibit what is referred to as exploratory behavior (see Thinus-Blanc et al., 1996; Granon et al., 2003); they are amenable, as humans, to trace conditioning (which in humans requires awareness) and to delay conditioning (which does not) (Han et al., 2003). These organisms do not make reference to an *explicit* sense of self and display minimal social interactions.

In humans, the 25- to 30-week preterm fetus processes tactile and painful stimuli in the sensory cortex (see brain imaging studies by Bartocci et al., 2006) and might thus perceive pain when awake; he/she might have reached a stage of brain maturation analogous (though not identical) to that of a newborn rat/mouse (see Lagercrantz, 2005).

b. Basic consciousness, present, for instance, in vervet monkeys (possibly also in some birds), manifests itself by functional use of objects, protodeclarative pointing, and searching for hidden objects; organisms at this level may display elaborate social interactions, imitations, social referencing, and joint attention; they possess the capacity to hold several mental representations in memory simultaneously and are able to evaluate relations of others to self.

In humans, newborn infants exhibit, in addition to sensory awareness, the ability to process memorized mental representations (e.g., of a pacifier), to express emotions, and to show signs of shared feelings or empathy (Singer, 2006). Even newborns differentiate between self and nonself touch (Rochat, 2003) and imitate the tongue protrusion of an adult (Meltzoff, 1990). At a few months of age, responses to novelty are present and include a late negativity wave which has been tentatively assigned to prefrontal cortex (Dehaene-Lambertz and Dehaene, 1994; Reynolds and Richards, 2005). Prefrontal cortex is active in response to speech, but only in awake infants, not when asleep (Dehaene-Lambertz et al., 2002). Thus access of sensory information to consciousness may already be present, though capacities for internal manipulations in working memory are reduced if not absent.

c. Explicit self-consciousness develops in infants at the end of the second year, together with working and episodic memory and language; it is characterized by self-recognition in mirror tests and by the use of single arbitrary rules with knowledge of one's own behavioral potential and self–other distinction; to some extent chimpanzees might reach this level (see Boakes, 1984).

d. Reflective consciousness with theory of mind and full conscious experience, first-person ontology, and explicit report, is unique to humans and develops after 3–5 years in children.

Examination of this first preliminary classification leads to a simple and unambiguous conclusion. First, adult human consciousness develops progressively, starting from rather rudimentary dispositions in the newborn. Second, mice and rats do not go far beyond the level of minimal consciousness.

1.38.9.2 Minimal Consciousness in Mice and Rats

Careful examination of mouse and rat behavior (see Brown and Bowman, 2002; Granon et al., 2003; Han et al., 2003) in the context of the neuronal workspace and as possible models of human psychiatric disorders (see Granon and Changeux, 2006) leads to the following conclusions.

a. Multiple states of consciousness (such as wakefulness, sleep, coma, general anesthesia, epileptic seizures) and the regulation of their reversible transitions occur in the mouse, as in all mammals, including humans. The circadian sleep–waking cycle mobilizes rather universal mechanisms (Llinas and Steriade, 2006) and is controlled throughout vertebrate species by brainstem reticular formation and intralaminar nuclei of the thalamus (Bogen, 1995; Jones, 1998) with complex patterned releases of neuromodulatory substances. For instance, in the framework of the current studies on nicotinic acetylcholine receptors (nAChR) (Changeux and Edelstein 2005), gene inactivation studies demonstrate the positive contribution of the $\beta2$ subunit of the nAChR to the phasic expression of arousal promoting mechanisms by endogenous acetylcholine (Cohen et al., 2002; Léna et al., 2004), and similar phenotypes as those noticed in the knockout mice are observed after chronic in utero exposure of the fetus to nicotine (Cohen et al., 2005). These mice thus offer a plausible animal model of sudden infant death syndrome, whose prevalence is known to increase in smoking pregnant women (Cohen et al., 2005).

The use of the neuronal workspace formalism (see Dehaene and Changeux, 2005) might, in this respect, be of some help. One may, for example, view the various graded states of consciousness (from deep anesthesia and coma to full awareness) as directly related to the spontaneous activity of recurrent thalamocortical loops and reticular thalamic nuclei (see Llinas and Paré, 1991; Steriade et al., 1993) as described in the model. Conclusively, the description of the neural mechanisms involved in the transition to wakefulness appears relevant to the case of the mouse as well as its application to models of human pathologies.

b. Delayed-response tasks, exploratory behavior, and flexible goal-directed behaviors. Since the early 1990s (Kolb, 1990), a rich body of behavioral and pharmacological observations has revealed that rats display working memory, attentional processes, and flexible goal-directed behavior which rely on the contribution of the prefrontal cortex (Kolb, 1990). For example, rats may perform an effortful, counterinstinctive, delayed-response task referred to as delayed matching-to-sample that lesions of the prefrontal cortex selectively impair, at variance with a spontaneous delayed nonmatching-to-sample task (Granon et al., 1994). Moreover, in these pioneering studies, it was already shown that cholinergic pathways (Nordberg and Winblad, 1986; Levin, 1992) and specifically their nicotinic component selectively control these cognitive processes (injection of neuronal bungarotoxin into the prelimbic area of the prefrontal cortex selectively impairs the task) (Granon et al., 1995).

In the mouse, exploratory activity is a spontaneous behavior (Thinus-Blanc et al., 1996; Poucet and Herrmann, 2001) that serves to gather and store spatial information which allows allocentric coding of space, itself necessary for flexible navigational processes. Quantitative analyses (Faure et al., 2003) with mice lacking the high-affinity nAChR further reveal that the balance between navigation and exploration shifts in favor of navigation to the detriment of more precise exploration of the environment. Additional comparative studies including several objects presentations in an open-field arena and elementary social behavior (between a test resident mouse and a social intruder) revealed that mice deleted for the nAChR $\beta2$ subunit are more rigid and exhibited less behavioral flexibility than wild-type mice (Granon et al., 2003; Maskos et al., 2005). The prefrontal cortex is particularly reduced in size in the mouse, yet its lesions (Granon, unpublished) cause evident deficit in the aforementioned conflict-resolution situations and, moreover, create a behavioral phenotype which displays several features in common with the loss of $\beta2$-nAChR.

These studies unambiguously demonstrate: (1) the specialization of neural circuits engaged in such executive functions which most often (though not always) mobilize the prefrontal cortex; (2) the gating of these functions by nAChRs activated through endogenously released acetylcholine; and last, (3) the intimate relationships between reward and cognition evidenced by the joint recovery of exploratory behavior and reward functions by the targeted reexpression of the $\beta2$ subunit in the ventral tegmental area dopaminergic nucleus (Maskos et al., 2005).

In conclusion, mice under these experimental conditions do far more than to simply react to sensory information. They engage in complex extended behaviors geared toward far-removed goals and sensitive to rewards. Using the word of Denton (2005), they would display some kind of curiosity being able to orchestrate locomotor behaviors according to what might tentatively be named – at our own risks – conscious intentions. Moreover most, if not all, of all these behaviors need the integrity of the prefrontal cortex. Even if in the case of rats and mice the exact homologies with primates and humans prefrontal cortex areas are still debated (Brown and Bowman, 2005), one may – still hypothetically – propose that the flexible goal-directed behaviors examined with the mouse fall into the category of conscious processes described by the neuronal workspace model.

The model was primarily designed to account for access to consciousness and reportability (see Dehaene et al., 1998). Reporting responses have been demonstrated with some animal species, for instance, using a commentary key (Weiskrantz, 1991; Cowey and Stoerig, 1995) in the case of macaque blind-sight. Yet, a still unanswered question is whether or not reportability can be demonstrated in a species like the mouse. In any case, the invention of a reliable assay with this species is urgently needed. In conclusion, the neuronal workspace model obviously deals with important features of *minimal consciousness*. It accounts, for instance, for the active maintenance of abstract rules through top-down amplification and the flexible control of tasks that require a novel interconnection of existing processors as it typically occurs in the Stroop task (see earlier discussion) as well as with the aforementioned mice behaviors. It deals, *a fortiori*, with the active maintenance of information during a delay period (see Han et al., 2003; Koch, 2004). Even though the relevant simulations have not been carried out, the neuronal workspace architecture should adequately fit exploratory behavior and offer an appropriate mechanism for the ultimate stage of spatial processing introduced by Poucet's model (1993) where, in a workspace homologue, unified location-independent representations with one unique reference direction are being built.

1.38.9.3 Social Relationships and Consciousness

The hierarchical scale of levels of consciousness mentioned at the beginning of this section underlines the importance of social interactions to the extent that empathy was viewed as a characteristic feature of newborn consciousness. Social organisms, including humans, represent intentional relations of themselves and other agents, yet at different levels. They unambiguously distinguish their own intentional relations (or first-person information) from the qualitatively different information available about other agents' intentional relations (or third-person information). In this respect, one should remember that the analysis of the exploratory behavior leads to the distinction between allocentric and egocentric motor behavior in the mouse (Rondi-Reig et al., 2006), pointing to the still highly speculative occurrence of a self. In the mouse, such self is primarily oriented toward the outer physical world, though empathy to pain has been recently reported in the mouse (Langford et al., 2006). No evidence was found at this stage with the mouse for comparability between the actions of self and others, as is found in higher species, and no sign of imitating goal-directed activity or of understanding the viewpoints of others was observed (Barresi and Moore, 1996). In other words, the presently available evidence does not support the occurrence of authentic social relationships in the adult mouse.

The human infant at birth is already at a stage more advanced than the adult mouse; in this respect, as mentioned earlier, he or she may already distinguish between his own and others' movements, in particular by touch, and the newborn displays rudiments of imitations (Meltzoff and Gopnik, 1993; Barresi and Moore, 1996; Lagercrantz, 2005). Moreover, human neonates display emotional contagion by responding more with crying when hearing another newborn crying than when hearing white noise or their own cry (see Decety and Jackson, 2004). Thus, the mouse cannot be a good animal model to investigate intentional relations and social understanding whose highest level is reached exclusively in humans. On the other hand, it may serve as *baseline* to define the elementary neural circuits mobilized by these social relationships in higher mammals and humans.

Extension of the neuronal workspace model to these issues may help in the definition of the minimal components of neural networks able to simulate what may be referred to as social consciousness. One has first to realize that several successive hierarchical levels have to nest the basic states of consciousness of the newborn to reach the full reflective consciousness of the human adult. They include imitation, social referencing, and joint attention, but also what is referred to as the standard theory of mind (see Premack and Woodruff, 1978; Baron-Cohen et al., 2000; Frith and Frith, 2003; Gusnard, 2005). This disposition to represent other people's intentions and beliefs, commonly referred to as propositional attitudes, mobilizes circuits distinct from empathy (Singer, 2006). It develops relatively late in the child (4–5 years), long after empathy. Moreover, both empathy and mentalizing are the objects of a severe maturation before the child reaches the stage of reflective consciousness; it includes in particular the general use of symbols (linguistic or not). Interestingly, this evolution through childhood and adolescence is accompanied by a nonlinear loss of gray matter in the cerebral cortex linked to the selective stabilization (pruning) of synapses (Giedd et al., 1999a,b; Singer, 2006), which takes place during postnatal development (see Changeux, 1983, 2004).

Considerable work has to be developed to establish a useful match between an extended neuronal workspace model and reflective consciousness.

1.38.9.4 The Neuronal Workspace and Human Pathologies

On the clinical side, the neuronal workspace model offers simple interpretations of a variety of human pathologies which cannot be reviewed here. For instance, the neuronal workspace model may account for characteristic deficits caused by frontal lobe lesions in performing delayed-response tasks like the Wisconsin card sorting task (Dehaene and Changeux, 1991) or the Stroop task (see the first simulations of the model; Dehaene et al., 1998) and/or in working memory or declarative memory tasks (Squire, 1987–1988; Ungerleider, 1995; Naccache, 2005; Zeman, 2005).

Frontal lobe pathology is also associated with senescence and dementia (Parkin and Walter, 1992). Particularly relevant to the theory is the case of frontal lobe dementia. This degenerative disease is characterized by apathy, unconcern, disinhibition, distractibility, loss of social awareness, and loss of emotional empathy (Brun, 1987; Neary et al., 1988; Baker et al., 2006). Interestingly, it can be caused by either a mutation in the microtubule-associated protein tau at Chr17q21 (characterized by cytoplasmic neurofibrillary inclusions) or a null mutation in the gene of a growth factor, progranulin, at the Chr17q21

31 locus (characterized by ubiquitin–immunoreactive neuronal inclusions) (Baker et al., 2006; Mackenzie et al., 2006). It manifests itself by a selective loss of layers 2 and 3 pyramidal cells of the prefrontal cortex, the long axon neurons which were postulated as the basic anatomical components of the workspace circuits (Dehaene et al., 1998). In other words, this disease offers a striking example of a genetic dissection of the neuronal workspace in the adult human brain.

Impairments at the level of workspace neurons might also shed some light on the cognitive deficits underlying psychiatric diseases such as schizophrenia. Indeed, cognitive deficits in schizophrenia often affect a broad variety of cognitive tests, and thus may fit better within the present perspective than within the classical neuropsychological perspective, whereby an individual patient's deficits are explained by a local impairment within a modular architecture of specialized subsystems. Many neuroimaging studies suggest decreased frontal and anterior cingulate activation in schizophrenia, as well as decreased long-distance connectivity (Andreasen et al., 1997; Friston, 1998). Furthermore, a dissociation between preserved subliminal processing and impaired conscious access has been reported: the threshold for masking is systematically elevated in schizophrenia, and preserved visual, semantic, and even motor priming suggest that this deficit is due to a central integration impairment, not a basic sensory impairment (Dehaene et al., 2003; Del Cul et al., 2006). Interestingly, similar deficits of access to consciousness are also seen in patients with early multiple sclerosis (MS) and diffuse white matter damage (Reuter et al., 2007). The parallels between MS and schizophrenia, and the conceptualization of at least part of their cognitive deficits as affecting a global workspace for flexible conscious processing, offer interesting avenues for future research.

Another consequence of the workspace theory is that it leads to a plausible interpretation of drug (e.g., nicotine) addiction. Addiction may indeed be viewed as an escape from the voluntary control of drug taking behavior, for instance, as a consequence of the disconnection of a reciprocal-loop linking the neuronal workspace circuits, including prefrontal cortex, dopaminergic neurons, and striatum, thus uncovering the compulsive nonconscious aspect of drug addiction (for discussion see Gutkin et al., 2006).

Moreover, as noted earlier, the nicotinic receptor knockout mice which are compulsively navigating without pausing for exploration may offer an animal model for human attention-deficit/hyperactivity disorder behavior, for which hyperactivity symptoms are known to improve with nicotine treatment (Shytle et al., 2002; Granon and Changeux, 2006).

Last, the differential role of the ventral tegmental area in the recovery of some aspects of cognitive functions in the mouse by local reexpression of nicotinic receptors (Maskos et al., 2005) points to an analogy with the human disease called auto-activation deficit described by Laplane and Dubois (2001). Human patients display a characteristic inertia—they stay at the same place all day long without signs of spontaneous activity but may perform complex activities when stimulated. They show an empty mind for hours yet without cognitive impairment but with stereotyped activities and flattened affects. Their deficit is caused by striatopallidal lesions accompanied by frontal hypometabolism, suggesting, as in the case of the mouse model, a close link between reward and, here, the content of consciousness.

These are a few examples of human pathologies in which the Neuronal Workspace model offers simple and productive interpretations.

References

Andreasen NC, O'Leary DS, Flaum M, et al. (1997) Hypofrontality in schizophrenia: Distributed dysfunctional circuits in neuroleptic-naive patients. *Lancet* 349(9067): 1730–1734.

Amati D and Shallice T (2007) On the emergence of modern humans. *Cognition* 103(3): 358–385.

Arieli A, Sterkin A, Grinvald A, and Aertsen A (1996) Dynamics of ongoing activity: Explanation of the large variability in evoked cortical responses. *Science* 273: 1868–1871.

Arnell KM and Jolicoeur P (1997) Repetition blindness for pseudoobject pictures. *J. Exp. Psychol. Hum. Percept. Perform.* 23: 999–1013.

Baars B (1989) *A Cognitive Theory of Consciousness*. Cambridge, UK: Cambridge University Press.

Baker M, Mackenzie IR, Pickering-Brown SM, et al. (2006) Mutations in progranulin cause tau-negative frontotemporal dementia linked to chromosome 17. *Nature* 442: 916–919.

Barresi J and Moore C (1996) Intentional relation and social understanding. *Behav. Brain Sci.* 19: 107–154.

Balkin TJ, Braun AR, Wesensten NJ, et al. (2002) The process of awakening: A PET study of regional brain activity patterns mediating the re-establishment of alertness and consciousness. *Brain* 125: 2308–2319.

Baron-Cohen S, Wheelwright S, Cox A, et al. (2000) Early identification of autism by the Checklist for Autism in Toddlers (CHAT). *J. R. Soc. Med.* 93: 521–525.

Bartocci M, Bergqvist LL, Lagercrantz H, and Anand KJ (2006) Pain activates cortical areas in the preterm newborn brain. *Pain* 22: 109–117.

Bianchi L (1921) *La mécanique du cerveau et la fonction des lobes frontaux*. Paris: Louis Arnette.

Block N (2005) Two neural correlates of consciousness. *Trends Cogn. Sci.* 9: 46–52.

Boakes R (1984) From Darwin to behaviourism. In: *Psychology and the Minds of Animals*. Cambridge, UK: Cambridge University Press.

Bogen JE (1995) On the neurophysiology of consciousness: I. An overview. *Conscious Cogn.* 4: 52–62.

Bonhomme V, Plourde G, Meuret P, and Fiset P (2000) Auditory steady-state response and bispectral index for assessing level of consciousness during propofol sedation and hypnosis. *Anesth. Analg.* 91: 1398–403.

Brecht M, Roth A, and Sakmann B (2003) Dynamic receptive fields of reconstructed pyramidal cells in layers 3 and 2 of rat somatosensory barrel cortex. *J Physiol.* 553: 243–265.

Brown VJ and Bowman EM (2002) Rodent models of prefrontal cortical function. *Trends Neurosci.* 25: 340–343.

Brun A (1987) Frontal lobe degeneration of non-Alzheimer type I. Neuropathology. *Arch. Gerontol. Geriatr.* 6: 193–208.

Bush P and Sejnowski T (1996) Inhibition synchronizes sparsely connected cortical neurons within and between columns in realistic network models. *J. Comput. Neurosci.* 3: 91–110.

Buchsbaum MS, Gillin JC, Wu J, et al. (1989) Regional cerebral glucose metabolic rate in human sleep assessed by positron emission tomography. *Life Sci.* 45: 1349–1356.

Cajal S (1892) El nuevo concepto de la histologia de los centros nerviosos. *Rev. Ciencias Med.* 18: 457–476.

Carter JA, McNair LD, Corbin WR, and Black DH (1998) Effects of priming positive and negative outcomes on drinking responses. *Exp. Clin. Psychopharmacol.* 6: 399–405.

Changeux JP (1983) *L'homme neuronal*. Paris: Fayard.

Changeux JP (2002) Reflections on the origins of the human brain. In: Lagerkrantz H, Hanson M, Evrard P, and Rodeck C (eds.) *The Newborn Brain*, pp. 1–28. Cambridge, UK: Cambridge University Press.

Changeux JP (2004) *The Physiology of Truth*. Cambridge, MA: Harvard University Press.

Changeux JP (2006) The Ferrier Lecture 1998. The molecular biology of consciousness investigated with genetically modified mice. *Philos. Trans. R. Soc. Lond. B. Biol. Sci.* 361: 2239–2259.

Changeux JP, Courrege P, and Danchin A (1973) A theory of the epigenesis of neuronal networks by selective stabilization of synapses. *Proc. Natl. Acad. Sci. USA* 70: 2974–2978.

Changeux JP and Dehaene S (1989) Neuronal models of cognitive functions. *Cognition* 33: 63–109.

Changeux JP and Edelstein SJ (2005) Allosteric mechanisms of signal transduction. *Science* 308: 1424–1428.

Christakou A, Robbins TW, and Everitt BJ (2004) Prefrontal cortical-ventral striatal interactions involved in affective modulation of attentional performance: Implications for corticostriatal circuit function. *J. Neurosci.* 28: 773–780.

Chun MM and Marois R (2002) The dark side of visual attention. *Curr. Opin. Neurobiol.* 12(2): 184–189.

Cohen G, Han ZY, Grailhe R, et al. (2002) Beta-2 nicotinic acetylcholine receptor subunit modulates protective responses to stress: A receptor basis for sleep-disordered breathing after nicotine exposure. *Proc. Natl. Acad. Sci. USA* 99: 13272–13277.

Cohen G, Malcolm G, and Henderson-Smart D (1997) A comparison of the ventilatory response of sleeping newborn lambs to step and progressive hypoxaemia. *J. Physiol.* 503: 203–213.

Cohen G, Roux JC, Grailhe R, Malcolm G, Changeux JP, and Lagercrantz H (2005) Perinatal exposure to nicotine causes deficits associated with a loss of nicotinic receptor function. *Proc. Natl. Acad. Sci. USA* 102: 3817–3821.

Cowey A and Stoerig P (1995) Blindsight in monkeys. *Nature* 373: 247–249.

Crick F (1994) On consciousness. *Nature* 369: 86.

Crick FC and Koch C (1995) Are we aware of neural activity in primary visual cortex? *Nature* 375: 121–123.

Crick FC and Koch C (2003) A framework for consciousness. *Nat. Neurosci.* 6: 119–126.

Crick FC and Koch C (2005) What is the function of the claustrum? *Philos. Trans. R. Soc. Lond. B Biol. Sci.* 360: 1271–1279.

Decety J and Jackson PL (2004) The functional architecture of human empathy. *Behav. Cogn. Neurosci. Rev.* 3: 71–100.

Dehaene S, Artiges E, Naccache L, et al. (2003a) Conscious and subliminal conflicts in normal subjects and patients with schizophrenia: The role of the anterior cingulate. *Proc. Natl. Acad. Sci. USA* 100: 13722–13727.

Dehaene S and Changeux JP (1989) A simple model of prefrontal cortex function in delayed-response tasks. *J. Cogn. Neurosci.* 1: 244–261.

Dehaene S and Changeux JP (1991) The Wisconsin Card Sorting Test: Theoretical analysis and modeling in a neuronal network. *Cereb. Cortex* 1: 62–79.

Dehaene S and Changeux JP (1995) Neuronal models of prefrontal cortical functions. *Ann. N.Y. Acad. Sci.* 769: 305–319.

Dehaene S and Changeux JP (1997) A hierarchical neuronal network for planning behavior. *Proc. Natl. Acad. Sci. USA* 94: 13293–13298.

Dehaene S and Changeux JP (2000) Reward-dependent learning in neuronal networks for planning and decision making. *Prog. Brain Res.* 126: 217–229.

Dehaene S and Changeux JP (2004) Neural mechanisms for access to consciousness. In: Gazzaniga MS (ed.) *The Cognitive Neuroscience of Consciousness*, pp. 1145–1158. Cambridge, MA: MIT Press.

Dehaene S and Changeux JP (2005) Ongoing spontaneous activity controls access to consciousness: A neuronal model for inattentional blindness. *PLoS Biol.* 3: 910–927.

Dehaene S, Changeux JP, Naccache L, Sackur J, and Sergent C (2006) Conscious, preconscious, and subliminal processing: A testable taxonomy. *Trends Cogn. Sci.* 10: 204–211.

Dehaene S and Cohen L (1994) Dissociable mechanisms of subitizing and counting: Neuropsychological evidence from simultanagnosic patients. *J. Exp. Psychol. Hum. Percept. Perform.* 20: 958–975.

Dehaene S, Kerszberg M, and Changeux JP (1998) A neuronal model of a global workspace in effortful cognitive tasks. *Proc. Natl. Acad. Sci. USA* 95: 14529–14534.

Dehaene S and Naccache L (2001) Towards a cognitive neuroscience of consciousness: Basic evidence and a workspace framework. *Cognition* 792: 1–37.

Dehaene S, Sergent C, and Changeux JP (2003b) A neuronal network model linking subjective reports and objective physiological data during conscious perception. *Proc. Natl. Acad. Sci. USA* 100: 8520–8525.

Dehaene-Lambertz G and Dehaene S (1994) Speed and cerebral correlates of syllable discrimination in infants. *Nature* 370: 292–295.

Dehaene-Lambertz G, Dehaene S, and Hertz-Pannier L (2002) Functional neuroimaging of speech perception in infants. *Science* 298: 2013–2015.

DeFelipe J and Farinas I (1992) The pyramidal neuron of the cerebral cortex: Morphological and chemical characteristics of the synaptic inputs. *Prog. Neurobiol.* 39: 563–607.

DeFelipe J and Jones EG (1988) *Cajal on the Cerebral Cortex*. New York: Oxford University Press.

Delacour J (1997) Neurobiology of consciousness: An overview. *Behav. Brain Res.* 85: 127–141.

Del Cul A, Dehaene S, and Leboyer M (2006) Preserved subliminal processing and impaired conscious access in schizophrenia. *Arch. Gen. Psychiatry* 63(12): 1313–1323.

de Lecea L, Kilduff TS, Peyron C, et al. (1998) The hypocretins: Hypothalamus-specific peptides with neuroexcitatory activity. *Proc. Natl. Acad. Sci. USA* 6: 322–327.

Denton D (2005) *Les Emotion primordiales et l'éveil de la conscience*. Paris, France: Flammarion. [Translated 2005, *The Primordial Emotions: The Dawning of Consciousness*, Oxford, UK: Oxford University Press.]

Dosenbach NU, Visscher KM, Palmer ED, et al. (2006) A core system for the implementation of task sets. *Neuron* 50: 799–812.

Douglas RJ and Martin KA (2004) Neuronal circuits of the neocortex. *Annu. Rev. Neurosci.* 27: 419–451.

Edelman GM (1989) *The Remembered Present: A Biological Theory of Consciousness*. New York: Basic Books.

Edelman GM (1993) Neural Darwinism: Selection and reentrant signaling in higher brain function. *Neuron* 10: 115–125.

Edelman GM and Tononi G (2000) *A Universe of Consciousness: How Matter Becomes Imagination*. New York: Basic Books.

Elston GN (2003) Cortex, cognition and the cell: New insights into the pyramidal neuron and prefrontal function. *Cereb. Cortex* 13: 1124–1138.

Elston GN and Rosa MG (1997) The occipitoparietal pathway of the macaque monkey: Comparison of pyramidal cell morphology in layer III of functionally related cortical visual areas. *Cereb. Cortex* 7: 432–52.

Elston GN and Rosa MG (1998) Morphological variation of layer III pyramidal neurones in the occipitotemporal pathway of the macaque monkey visual cortex. *Cereb. Cortex* 8: 278–294.

Everitt BJ and Robbins TW (2005) Neural systems of reinforcement for drug addiction: From actions to habits to compulsion. *Nat. Neurosci.* 8: 1481–1489.

Fang F and He S (2005) Cortical responses to invisible objects in the human dorsal and ventral pathways. *Nat. Neurosci.* 8(10): 1380–1385.

Faure PH, Neumeister H, Faber DS, and Korn H (2003) Symbolic analysis of swimming trajectories reveals scale invariance and provides a model for fish locomotion. *Fractals* 11: 233–243.

Felleman DJ and Van Essen DC (1991) Distributed hierarchical processing in the primate cerebral cortex. *Cereb. Cortex* 1–47.

Fessard A (1954) *Nervous Integration and Conscious Experience, Symposium Sainte-Marguerite*. London: Blackwell.

Fiset P, Paus T, Daloze T, et al. (1999) Brain mechanisms of propofol-induced loss of consciousness in humans: A positron emission tomographic study. *J. Neurosci.* 19: 5506–5513.

Friston KJ (1998) The disconnection hypothesis. *Schizophr. Res.* 30: 115–125.

Friston KJ, Tononi G, Reeke GN Jr, Sporns O, and Edelman GM (1994) Value-dependent selection in the brain: Simulation in a synthetic neural model. *Neuroscience* 59: 229–243.

Frith C, Perry R, and Lumer E (1999) The neural correlates of conscious experience: An experimental framework. *Trends Cogn. Sci.* 3: 105–114.

Frith U and Frith CD (2003) Development and neurophysiology of mentalizing. *Philos. Trans. R. Soc. Lond. B Biol. Sci.* 358 (1431): 459–473.

Fuentes U, Ritz R, Gerstner W, and Van Hemmen JL (1996) Vertical signal flow and oscillations in a three-layer model of the cortex. *J. Comput. Neurosci.* 3: 125–136.

Gajraj RJ, Doi M, Mantzaridis H, and Kenny GN (1999) Comparison of bispectral EEG analysis and auditory evoked potentials for monitoring depth of anaesthesia during propofol anaesthesia. *Br. J. Anaesth.* 82: 672–678.

Giedd JN, Blumenthal J, Jeffries NO, et al. (1999a) Brain development during childhood and adolescence: A longitudinal MRI study. *Nat. Neurosci.* 2(10): 861–863.

Giedd JN, Blumenthal J, Jeffries NO, et al. (1999b) Development of the human corpus callosum during childhood and adolescence: A longitudinal MRI study. *Prog. Neuropsychopharmacol. Biol. Psychiatry* 23(4): 571–588.

Goldman-Rakic PS (1988) Topography of cognition: Parallel distributed networks in primate association cortex. *Annu. Rev. Neurosci.* 11: 137–156.

Goldman-Rakic PS (1994) Working memory dysfunction in schizophrenia. *J. Neuropsychiatry Clin. Neurosci.* 6: 348–57.

Goodale MA, Milner AD, Jakobson LS, and Carey DP (1991) Object awareness. *Nature* 352: 202.

Granon S and Changeux JP (2006) Attention-deficit/ hyperactivity disorder: A plausible mouse model? *Acta Paediatr.* 95: 645–649.

Granon S, Faure P, and Changeux JP (2003) Executive and social behaviors under nicotinic receptor regulation. *Proc. Natl. Acad. Sci. USA* 100: 9596–9601.

Granon S, Poucet B, Thinus-Blanc C, Changeux JP, and Vidal C (1995) Nicotinic and muscarinic receptors in the rat pefrontal cortex: Differential roles in working memory response selection and effortful processing. *Psychopharmacology (Berlin)* 119: 139–144.

Granon S, Vidal C, Thinus-Blanc C, Changeux JP, and Poucet B (1994) Working memory, response selection, and effortful processing in rats with medial prefrontal lesions. *Behav. Neurosci.* 108: 883–891.

Grillner S and Graybiel AM (2006) *Microcircuits: The Interface Between Neurons and Global Brain Function (Dahlem Workshop Reports)*. Cambridge, MA: MIT Press.

Gross J, Schmitz F, Schnitzler I, et al. (2004) Modulation of long-range neural synchrony reflects temporal limitations of visual attention in humans. *Proc. Natl. Acad. Sci. USA* Aug 31; 101(35): 13050–13055.

Gusnard DA (2005) Being a self: Considerations from functional imaging. *Conscious Cogn.* 14: 679–697.

Gusnard DA and Raichle ME (2001) Searching for a baseline: Functional imaging and the resting human brain. *Nat. Rev. Neurosci.* 2: 685–694.

Gutkin BS, Dehaene S, and Changeux JP (2006) A neurocomputational hypothesis for nicotine addiction. *Proc. Natl. Acad. Sci. USA* 24: 103: 1106–1111.

Han CJ, O'Tuathaigh CM, Van Trigt L, et al. (2003) Trace but not delay fear conditioning requires attention and the anterior cingulate cortex. *Proc. Natl. Acad. Sci. USA* 100: 13087–13092.

Harris G.C, Wimmer M, and Aston-Jones G (2005) A role for lateral hypothalamic orexin neurons in reward seeking. *Nature* 437: 556–559.

Haynes JD and Rees G (2005) Predicting the stream of consciousness from activity in human visual cortex. *Curr. Biol.* 15: 1301–1307.

Haynes JD and Rees G (2006) Decoding mental states from brain activity in humans. *Nat. Rev. Neurosci.* 7: 523–534.

Heidmann T and Changeux JP (1982) Molecular model of the regulation of chemical synapse efficiency at the postsynaptic level. *C. R Seances Acad. Sci.* III. 295: 665–670.

Heinke W and Schwarzbauer C (2002) In vivo imaging of anaesthetic action in humans: Approaches with positron emission tomography (PET) and functional magnetic resonance imaging (fMRI). *Br. J. Anaesth.* 89: 112–122.

Heiss WD, Pawlik G, Herholz K, Wagner R, and Wienhard K (1985) Regional cerebral glucose metabolism in man during wakefulness, sleep, and dreaming. *Brain Res.* 327: 362–326.

Hommel B, Kessler K, Schmitz F, et al. (2006) How the brain blinks: Towards a neurocognitive model of the attentional blink [review]. *Psychol. Res.* 70(6): 425–435.

Huxley TH (1874) On the hypothesis that animals are automata and its history. In: *Collected Essays of T. H. Huxley*, vol. 1, p. 199. New York: Appleton.

Hyder F, Rothman DL, and Shulman RG (2002) Total neuroenergetics support localized brain activity: Implications for the interpretation of fMRI. *Proc. Natl. Acad. Sci. USA* 99: 10771–10776.

Imas OA, Ropella KM, Ward BD, Wood JD, and Hudetz AG (2005) Volatile anesthetics disrupt frontal-posterior recurrent information transfer at gamma frequencies in rat. *Neurosci. Lett.* 387: 145–150.

Jasper HH (1998) Sensory information and conscious experience. *Adv. Neurol.* 77: 33–48.

Jeannerod M and Jacob P (2005) Visual cognition: A new look at the two-visual systems model. *Neuropsychologia* 43: 301–312.

Johnson MH (2005) Subcortical face processing. *Nat. Rev. Neurosci.* 6: 766–774.

Jones EG (1984) Laminar distribution of output cells. In: Peters A and Jones EG (eds.) *Cerebral Cortex, Vol. 1: Cellular Components of the Cerebral Cortex*, pp. 521–553. New York: Plenum.

Jones BE (1998) The neural basis of consciousness across the sleep-waking cycle. *Adv. Neurol.* 77: 75–94.

Kenet T, Bibitchkov D, Tsodyks M, Grinvald A, and Arieli A (2003) Spontaneously emerging cortical representations of visual attributes. *Nature* 425: 954–956.

Kolb B (1990) Animal models for human PFC-related disorders. *Prog. Brain Res.* 85: 501–519.

Koch C (2004) *The Quest for Consciousness: A Neurobiological Approach*. Englewood, CO: Roberts and Company Publishers.

Kunde W (2004) Response priming by supraliminal and subliminal action effects. *Psychol. Res.* 68: 91–96.

Lagercrantz H (2005) *I Barnets Hjärna*. Stockholm: Bonnier fakta.

Lagercrantz H, Hanson M, Evrard P, and Rodeck C (eds.) (2002) *The Newborn Brain: Neuroscience and Clinical Applications.* Cambridge, UK: Cambridge University Press.

Lamme VA (2003) Recurrent corticocortical interactions in neural disease. *Arch. Neurol.* 60: 178–184.

Lamme VA and Roelfsema PR (2000) The distinct modes of vision offered by feedforward and recurrent processing. *Trends Neurosci.* 23: 571–579.

Lamme VA, Zipser K, and Spekreijse H (2002) Masking interrupts figure-ground signals in V1. *J. Cogn. Neurosci.* 14: 1044–1053.

Landmann C, Dehaene S, Pappata S, et al. (2006) Dynamics of prefrontal and cingulate activity during a reward-based logical deduction task. *Cereb. Cortex* 17: 749–759.

Langford DJ, Crager SE, Shehzad Z, et al. (2006) Social modulation of pain as evidence for empathy in mice. *Science* 312: 1967–1970.

Laplane D and Dubois B (2001) Auto-activation deficit: A basal ganglia related syndrome. *Mov. Disord.* 16: 810–814.

Laufs H, Krakow K, Sterzer P, et al. (2003) Electroencephalographic signatures of attentional and cognitive default modes in spontaneous brain activity fluctuations at rest. *Proc. Natl. Acad. Sci. USA* 100: 11053–11058.

Laureys S (2005) The neural correlate of (un)awareness: Lessons from the vegetative state. *Trends Cogn. Sci.* 9: 556–559.

Laureys S, Boly M, and Maquet P (2006) Tracking the recovery of consciousness from coma. *J. Clin. Invest.* 116: 1823–1825.

Laureys S, Faymonville ME, Degueldre C, et al. (2000) Auditory processing in the vegetative state. *Brain* 123: 1589–1601.

Laureys S, Faymonville ME, Peigneux P, et al. (2002) Cortical processing of noxious somatosensory stimuli in the persistent vegetative state. *Neuroimage* 17: 732–741.

Laureys S, Owen AM, and Schiff ND (2004) Brain function in coma, vegetative state, and related disorders. *Lancet Neurol.* 3: 537–546.

Léna C, Popa D, Grailhe R, Escourrou P, Changeux J-P, and Adrien J (2004) Beta2-containing nicotinic receptors contribute to the organization of sleep and regulate putative micro-arousals in mice. *J. Neurosci.* 24: 5711–5718.

Levin ED (1992) Nicotinic systems and cognitive function. *J. Neurobiol.* 53: 633–640.

Livingstone MS and Hubel DH (1981) Effects of sleep and arousal on the processing of visual information in the cat. *Nature* 291: 554–561.

Llinas RR and Paré D (1991) Of dreaming and wakefulness. *Neuroscience* 44: 521–535.

Llinas R and Ribary U (1993) Coherent 40-Hz oscillation characterizes dream state in humans. *Proc. Natl. Acad. Sci. USA* 90(5): 2078–2081.

Llinas R, Ribary U, Contreras D, and Pedroarena C (1998) The neuronal basis for consciousness. *Philos. Trans. R. Soc. Lond. B. Biol. Sci.* 353: 1841–1849.

Llinas RR and Steriade M (2006) Bursting of thalamic neurons and states of vigilance. *J. Neurophysiol.* 95: 3297–3308.

Lumer ED, Edelman GM, and Tononi G (1997a) Neural dynamics in a model of the thalamocortical system. I. Layers, loops and the emergence of fast synchronous rhythms.

Lumer ED, Edelman GM, and Tononi G (1997b) Neural dynamics in a model of the thalamocortical system. II. The role of neural synchrony tested through perturbations of spike timing. *Cereb. Cortex* 7: 228–236.

Mackenzie IR, Baker M, Pickering-Brown S, et al. (2006) The neuropathology of frontotemporal lobe degeneration caused by mutations in the progranulin gene. *Brain* 129(Pt. 11): 3081–3090.

Maquet P and Phillips C (1998) Functional brain imaging of human sleep. *J. Sleep Res.* 7(supplement 1): 42–47.

Marois R, Chun MM, and Gore JC (2000) Neural correlates of the attentional blink. *Neuron* 28: 299–308.

Marois R, Yi DJ, and Chun MM (2004) The neural fate of consciously perceived and missed events in the attentional blink. *Neuron* 41: 465–472.

Maskos U, Molles BE, Pons S, et al. (2005) Nicotine reinforcement and cognition restored by targeted expression of nicotinic receptors. *Nature* 436: 103–107.

Mazoyer B, Zago L, Mellet E, et al. (2001) Cortical networks for working memory and executive functions sustain the conscious resting state in man. *Brain Res. Bull.* 54: 287–298.

McCarley C (1999) A model of chronic dyspnea. *Image J. Nurs. Sch.* 31: 231–236.

McCormick DA and Bal T (1997) Sleep and arousal: Thalamocortical mechanisms. *Annu. Rev. Neurosci.* 20: 185–215.

McLeod JD (1991) Childhood parental loss and adult depression. *J. Health Soc. Behav.* 32: 205–220.

Meltzoff AN (1990) Towards a developmental cognitive science. The implications of cross-modal matching and imitation for the development of representation and memory in infancy. *Ann. N.Y. Acad. Sci.* 608: 1–31.

Meltzoff AN and Gopnik A (1993) The role of imitation in understanding persons and developing a theory of mind. In: Baron-Cohen S, Tager-Flusberg H, and Cohen DJ (eds.) *Understanding Other Minds: Perspectives from Autism*, pp. 335–366. Oxford, UK: Oxford University Press.

Mesulam MM (1998) From sensation to cognition. *Brain* 121: 1013–1052.

Mishkin M and Ungerleider LG (1982) Contribution of striate inputs to the visuospatial functions of parieto-preoccipital cortex in monkeys. *Behav. Brain Res.* 6: 57–77.

Miyashita Y and Hayashi T (2000) Neural representation of visual objects: Encoding and top-down activation. *Curr. Opin. Neurobiol.* 10: 187–194.

Naccache L (2005) Visual phenomenal consciousness: A neurological guided tour. *Prog. Brain Res.* 150: 185–195.

Naccache L and Dehaene S (2001) The priming method: Imaging unconscious repetition priming reveals an abstract representation of number in the parietal lobes. *Cereb. Cortex* 11: 966–974.

Naccache L, Dehaene S, Cohen L, et al. (2005) Effortless control: Executive attention and conscious feeling of mental effort are dissociable. *Neuropsychologia* 43: 1318–1328.

Naccache L, Gaillard R, Adam C, et al. (2005) A direct intracranial record of emotions evoked by subliminal words. *Proc. Natl. Acad. Sci. USA* 102: 7713–7717.

Neary D, Snowden JS, Northen B, and Goulding P (1988) Dementia of frontal lobe type. *J. Neurol. Neurosurg. Psychiatry* 51: 353–361.

Newby EA and Rock I (1998) Inattentional blindness as a function of proximity to the focus of attention. *Perception* 27(9): 1025–1040.

Nordberg A and Winblad B (1986) Reduced number of [³H]nicotine and [³H]acetylcholine binding sites in the frontal cortex of Alzheimer brains. *Neurosci. Lett.* 72: 115–119.

Norman DA and Shallice T (1986) Attention to action: Willed and automatic control of behaviour. In: Davidson RJ, Schwartz GE, Shapiro D (eds.) *Consciousness and Self-Regulation*, vol. 4. New York: Plenum.

O'Doherty JP (2004) Reward representations and reward-related learning in the human brain: Insights from neuroimaging. *Curr. Opin. Neurobiol.* 14: 769–776.

Pardo JV, Pardo PJ, Janer KW, and Raichle ME (1990) The anterior cingulate cortex mediates processing selection in the Stroop attentional conflict paradigm. *Proc. Natl. Acad. Sci. USA* 87: 256–259.

Parkin AJ and Walter BM (1992) Recollective experience, normal aging, and frontal dysfunction. *Psychol. Aging* 7: 290–298.

Paus T (2000) Functional anatomy of arousal and attention systems in the human brain. *Prog. Brain Res.* 126: 65–77.

Paus T, Koski L, Caramanos Z, and Westbury C (1998) Regional differences in the effects of task difficulty and motor output on blood flow response in the human anterior cingulate cortex: A review of 107 PET activation studies. *Neuroreport* 9: 37–47.

Petersen CC, Hahn TT, Mehta M, Grinvald A, and Sakmann B (2003) Interaction of sensory responses with spontaneous depolarization in layer 2/3 barrel cortex. *Proc. Natl. Acad. Sci. USA* 100: 13638–13643.

Portas CM, Krakow K, Allen P, Josephs O, Armony JL, and Frith CD (2000) Auditory processing across the sleep-wake cycle: Simultaneous EEG and fMRI monitoring in humans. *Neuron* 28: 991–999.

Posner MI (1994) Attention: The mechanisms of consciousness. *Proc. Natl. Acad. Sci. USA* 91: 7398–7403.

Posner MI and Dehaene S (1994) Attentional networks. *Trends Neurosci.* 17: 75–79.

Poucet B (1993) Spatial cognitive maps in animals: New hypotheses on their structure and neural mechanisms. *Psychol. Rev.* 100: 163–182.

Poucet B and Herrmann T (2001) Exploratory patterns of rats on a complex maze provide evidence for topological coding. *Behav. Processes* 53: 155–162.

Premack D and Woodruff G (1978) Chimpanzee problem-solving: A test for comprehension. *Science* 202: 532–535.

Preyer W (1894) *Mental Development in the Child*. New York: Appleton.

Raichle ME (1994) Images of the mind: Studies with modern imaging techniques. *Annu. Rev. Psychol.* 45: 333–356.

Raichle ME and Gusnard DA (2002) Appraising the brain's energy budget. *Proc. Natl. Acad. Sci. USA* 99: 10237–10239.

Raichle ME and Gusnard DA (2005) Intrinsic brain activity sets the stage for expression of motivated behavior. *J. Comp. Neurol.* 493: 167–176.

Raichle ME, MacLeod AM, Snyder AZ, Powers WJ, Gusnard DA, and Shulman GL (2001) A default mode of brain function. *Proc. Natl. Acad. Sci. USA* 98: 676–682.

Raizada RD and Grossberg S (2003) Towards a theory of the laminar architecture of cerebral cortex: Computational clues from the visual system. *Cereb. Cortex* 13: 100–113.

Rauschecker JP and Tian B (2000) Mechanisms and streams for processing of "what" and "where" in auditory cortex. *Proc. Natl. Acad. Sci. USA* 97: 11800–11806.

Raymond CK, Howald-Stevenson I, Vater CA, and Stevens TH (1992) Morphological classification of the yeast vacuolar protein sorting mutants: Evidence for a prevacuolar compartment in class E vps mutants. *Mol. Biol. Cell* 3: 1389–1402.

Rees G, Russell C, Frith CD, and Driver J (1999) Inattentional blindness versus inattentional amnesia for fixated but ignored words. *Science* 286: 2504–2507.

Reuter F, Del Cul A, and Audoin B (2007) Intact subliminal processing and delayed conscious access in multiple sclerosis. *Neuropsychologia* Apr 19 [epub ahead of print].

Reynolds GD and Richards JE (2005) Familiarization, attention, and recognition memory in infancy: An event-related potential and cortical source localization study. *Dev. Psychol.* 41(4): 598–615.

Rochat P (2003) Five levels of self-awareness as they unfold early in life. *Conscious Cogn.* 12: 717–731.

Rondi-Reig L, Petit GH, Tobin C, Tonegawa S, Mariani J, and Berthoz A (2006) Impaired sequential egocentric and allocentric memories in forebrain-specific-NMDA receptor knock-out mice during a new task dissociating strategies of navigation. *J. Neurosci.* 26: 4071–4081.

Rose S (ed.) (1999) *From Brains to Consciousness? Essays on the New Sciences of the Mind*. Princeton, NJ: Princeton University Press.

Salin PA and Bullier J (1995) Corticocortical connections in the visual system: Structure and function. *Physiol. Rev.* 75: 107–154.

Schultz W, Dayan P, and Montague PR (1997) A neural substrate of prediction and reward. *Science* 275(5306): 1593–1599.

Sergent C, Baillet S, and Dehaene S (2005) Timing of the brain events underlying access to consciousness during the attentional blink. *Nat. Neurosci.* 8: 1391–1400.

Shallice T (1988) *From Neuropsychology to Mental Structure*. New York: Cambridge University Press.

Sergent C and Dehaene S (2004) Neural processes underlying conscious perception: Experimental findings and a global neuronal workspace framework. *J. Physiol. Paris* 98: 374–384.

Shulman GL, Hyder F, and Rothman DL (2003) Cerebral metabolism and consciousness. *C. R. Biol.* 326: 253–273.

Shulman RG and Rothman DL (1998) Interpreting functional imaging studies in terms of neurotransmitter cycling. *Proc. Natl. Acad. Sci. USA* 95: 11993–11998.

Shulman RG, Rothman DL, Behar KL, and Hyder F (2004) Energetic basis of brain activity: Implications for neuroimaging. *Trends Neurosci.* 27: 489–495.

Shytle RD, Silver AA, Sheehan KH, Sheehan DV, and Sanberg PR (2002) Neuronal nicotinic receptor inhibition for treating mood disorders: Preliminary controlled evidence with mecamylamine. *Depress. Anxiety* 16: 89–92.

Sigman M and Dehaene S (2005) Parsing a cognitive task: A characterization of the mind's bottleneck. *PLoS Biol.* 3: e37.

Sigman M and Dehaene S (2006) Dynamics of the central bottleneck: Dual-task and task uncertainty. *PLoS Biol.* 4: e220.

Simons DJ and Chabris CF (1999) Gorillas in our midst: Sustained inattentional blindness for dynamic events. *Perception* 28: 1059–1074.

Singer T (2006) The neuronal basis and ontogeny of empathy and mind reading: Review of literature and implications for future research. *Neurosci. Biobehav. Rev.* 30: 855–863.

Sleigh JW, Steyn-Ross DA, Steyn-Ross ML, Williams ML, and Smith P (2001) Comparison of changes in electroencephalographic measures during induction of general anaesthesia: Influence of the gamma frequency band and electromyogram signal. *Br. J. Anaesth.* 86: 50–8.

Squire LR (1987–1988) The organization and neural substrates of human memory. *Int. J. Neurol.* 21–22: 218–222.

Steinlein OK (2004) Genetic mechanisms that underlie epilepsy. *Nat. Rev. Neurosci.* 5: 400–408.

Steriade M (1999) Coherent oscillations and short-term plasticity in corticothalamic networks. *Trends Neurosci.* 22: 337–345.

Steriade M, Contreras D, Amzica F, and Timofeev I (1996) Synchronization of fast (30–40 Hz) spontaneous oscillations in intrathalamic and thalamocortical networks. *J. Neurosci.* 16: 2788–2808.

Steriade M, McCormick DA, and Sejnowski TJ (1993) Thalamocortical oscillations in the sleeping and aroused brain. *Science* 262: 679–685.

Strawson PF (1974) *Freedom and Resentment, and Other Essays.* London: Methuen.

Super H, Spekreijse H, and Lamme VA (2001) Two distinct modes of sensory processing observed in monkey primary visual cortex (V1). *Nat. Neurosci.* 4: 304–310.

Sutton RS and Barto AG (1981) Toward a modern theory of adaptive networks: Expectation and prediction. *Psychol. Rev.* 88: 135–170.

Thinus-Blanc C, Save E, Poucet B, and Foreman N (1996) Effects of parietal cortex lesions on spatial problem solving in the rat. *Behav. Brain Res.* 81: 115–121.

Thorndike EL (1898) *Animal Intelligence: An Experimental Study of the Association Processes in Animals.* New York: Macmillan (Psychological Review, Monograph Supplements, No. 8).

Tononi G and Edelman GM (1998) Consciousness and complexity. *Science* 282: 1846–1851.

Trivers R (1985) *Social Evolution.* Menlo Park, CA: Benjamin.

Tsodyks M, Kenet T, Grinvald A, and Arieli A (1999) Linking spontaneous activity of single cortical neurons and the underlying functional architecture. *Science* 286: 1943–1946.

Ungerleider LG (1995) Functional brain imaging studies of cortical mechanisms for memory. *Science* 270: 769–775.

Vogel EK, Luck SJ, and Shapiro KL (1998) Electrophysiological evidence for a postperceptual locus of suppression during the attentional blink. *J. Exp. Psychol. Hum. Percept. Perform.* 24: 1656–1674.

von Economo C (1929) *The Cytoarchitectonics of the Human Cerebral Cortex.* London: Oxford University Press.

Wang XJ (1993) Ionic basis for intrinsic 40 Hz neuronal oscillations. *Neuroreport* 5: 221–224 [erratum in: *Neuroreport* (1994): 5: 531].

Weiskrantz L (1991) Disconnected awareness for detecting, processing, and remembering in neurological patients. *J. R. Soc. Med.* 84: 466–470.

Weiskrantz L (1997) Fragments of memory. *Neuropsychologia* 35: 1051–1057.

Weissman DH, Roberts KC, Visscher KM, and Woldorff MG (2006) The neural bases of momentary lapses in attention. *Nat. Neurosci.* 9: 971–978.

Yerkes RM (1916) *The Mental Life of Monkeys and Apes.* New York: Holt.

Zéki S (2003) The disunity of consciousness. *Trends Cogn. Sci.* 7: 214–218.

Zelazo PD (1996) Towards a characterization of minimal consciousness. *New Ideas Psychol.* 14: 63–80.

Zelazo PD (2004) The development of conscious control in childhood. *Trends Cogn. Sci.* 8: 12–17.

Zeman A (2001) Consciousness. *Brain* 124: 1263–89.

Zeman A (2005) What in the world is consciousness? *Prog. Brain Res.* 150: 1–10.